Culture's Consequences

SECOND EDITION

CULTURE'S CONSEQUENCES

SECOND EDITION

Comparing
Values,
Behaviors,
Institutions,
and
Organizations
Across
Nations

Geert Hofstede

Sage Publications
International Educational and Professional Publisher
Thousand Oaks ▪ London ▪ New Delhi

For information:

Sage Publications, Inc.
2455 Teller Road
Thousand Oaks, California 91320
E-mail: order@sagepub.com

Sage Publications Ltd.
6 Bonhill Street
London EC2A 4PU
United Kingdom

Sage Publications India Pvt. Ltd.
B-42
Panchsheel Enclave
New Delhi 110 017 India

Printed in the United States of America

Library of Congress Cataloging-in-Publication Data

Hofstede, Geert H.
    Culture's consequences: Comparing values, behaviors,
    institutions, and organizations across nations/by Geert Hofstede.—2nd ed.
        p. cm.
    ISBN 0-8039-7323-3 (cloth: alk. paper)—ISBN 0-8039-7324-1 (pbk.: acid-free paper)
    1. Ethnopsychology. 2. National characteristics. 3. Values—
Cross-cultural studies. I. Title.
    GN502.H628 2000
    155.8′9—dc21   00-010498

06   07   08   09   12   11   10   9

Acquiring Editor:	Jim Brace-Thompson
Editorial Assistant:	Anna Howland
Production Editor:	Claudia A. Hoffman
Copy Editor:	Judy Selhorst
Typesetter:	Marion Warren
Indexer:	Marja Hennemann-Kloet
Cover Designer:	Ravi Balasuriya

Vérité en-deçà des Pyrénées, erreur au-delà. *
—Blaise Pascal, 1623-62

*From *Pensées,* 60 (294): "There are truths on this side of the Pyrenees
that are falsehoods on the other" (translation G.H.).

Contents

From the Preface to the First Edition (1980)

The survival of mankind will depend to a large extent on the ability of people who think differently to act together. International collaboration presupposes some understanding of where others' thinking differs from ours. Exploring the way in which nationality predisposes our thinking is therefore not an intellectual luxury. A better understanding of invisible cultural differences is one of the main contributions the social sciences can make to practical policy makers in governments, organizations, and institutions—and to ordinary citizens.

Highlighting culture-dependent differences in thinking and acting is not always a welcome intervention. My general experience in discussing the topics of this book with various audiences is that the amount of international exposure within the group strongly affects the way the subject is received. Internationally experienced audiences have little trouble seeing its importance and tolerating a certain amount of introspection into their own cultural constraints. Internationally naive audiences have difficulty seeing the points, and some members even feel insulted when their own culture is discussed.

Readers of the book may go through the same kind of experiences. Multicultural readers and those who have earlier gone through one or more culture shocks in their lives may find that the book expresses in formal terms much that they already intuitively knew. For readers whose activities have so far been confined within a single national culture, the book itself may have a certain culture-shock effect: They will find question marks attached to the universal validity of much that they have taken for granted so far and of much that has become dear to them.

Nevertheless, I hope the book will find both multicultural and monocultural readers in many of the countries described and in others as well. . . . The book aims at a readership of policy makers in public and private organizations and scholars and students from various disciplines: comparative management, anthropology, economics, political science, psychology, sociology, comparative law, history, and social geography.

The research project which forms the basis of this book has a long history, going back to the preparation of the first international (IBM) survey in 1966. I could not foresee then that my involvement with this survey should eventually lead to my spending five years, from late 1973 to the end of 1978, on in-depth research on *Culture's Consequences*. Some of us in IBM suspected the scientific importance of the data as early as 1968. My colleagues of those days went on to other tasks; I alone remained to follow the intellectual track offered by this unique data base. It led me from psychology into sociology and then into political science and anthropology; it also led us to living as a family in three countries, while surviving on money from five. To a large extent it has determined our lives over the past eight years.

A preface is the place for paying tribute to one's supporters. My primary tribute goes to the [IBM] Corporation and its unnamed management, who believed us when we claimed that these were useful data to collect and who afterwards made the data available to general research; while from 1975 to 1978 they also supplied a research grant to support my work. Then there is a long list of persons who at some time contributed to the progress of the project. Among the pioneers of the IBM study I must mention David Sirota, who created many of the questions that afterwards proved so important as indicators of culture, and somewhat later Paul de Koning and Allen Kraut. There are the data processors who managed my requests for handling the unwieldy data bank for the world's largest survey; in particular, Frits Claus and Jack Zandstra. There are the statistics experts who helped with some phases of the analysis: Peter

Van Hoesel at Leiden University, Klaus Brockhoff at Kiel University, and Zvi Maimon at Tel Aviv University. There are my colleagues at the European Institute for Advanced Studies in Management at Brussels who stimulated me and acted as critical discussion partners; in particular, Alan Dale, Claude Faucheux, André Laurent, and Bengt Stymne. There are those who critically read through the manuscript and commented upon it: Torbjörn Stjernberg, Steven Velds (who read everything), Harry Triandis, Alberto Marradi, Robert Marsh, Seenu Srinivasan, and Wilfrid Dixon (who read parts). There is the competent staff of the European Institute—in particular Gerry Van Dijck, who supplied library assistance, and my most essential supporter, Christiane Merckaert, who first turned 18 almost unreadable manuscripts into working papers and then typed the book.

Finally, there is a team of interested discussion partners and critics, experienced in multicultural living, sharing their observations, the younger among them even willing (if properly compensated) to act as research associate or administrative assistant. I mean Maaike Hofstede-Van den Hoek, Gert-Jan Hofstede, Rokus Hofstede, Bart Hofstede, and Gideon Hofstede. This is more their book than they will believe.

Preface to the Second Edition

Looking back on 20 years of consequences of *Culture's Consequences,* I feel like a sorcerer's apprentice; after a slow start the book has become a classic and one of the most cited sources in the entire *Social Science Citation Index.* I never expected this; I wrote down findings that seemed obvious to me, but they proved to contain news value for others, practitioners and theorists alike, across almost any discipline that compares data from different countries. The book's potential was first recognized by Walter J. Lonner and John W. Berry, who adopted it for their Cross-Cultural Research and Methodology Series. The series's publisher, Sage Publications, also played a major role in the book's success. Sage's President Sara Miller McCune recognized the potential of this oversized manuscript when she first saw it in 1978, and through excellent direct marketing, Sage contributed to the wide dispersion of the book's message. The series in which the first edition appeared expired in 1995, but this second edition has come of age and should be able to stand on its own feet, while still feeling the moral support of the Lonner-Berry team.

Culture's Consequences is a scholarly book, written for social scientists, using scientific language. For practitioners and students I recommend my short and popular text, *Cultures and Organizations: Software of the Mind* (1991), which so far has appeared in 16 languages and is more reader-friendly. However, anyone who wants to know the justification and validation of my message in empirical material, or plans to use it in research, needs the scholarly book. Sage Publications urged me to undertake a second, revised edition of *Culture's Consequences,* and I committed myself to this task in 1994, shortly after my retirement from Maastricht University. Realizing the size of the task, I promised to go for a 2000 publication date; I missed it by a year.

The book has been completely rewritten, as testified to by a new subtitle that stresses its cross-disciplinary aspirations. Chapters 1 through 6 more or less retain their original structure, but dated material has been removed, the number of countries has increased from 40 to 50 (plus three regions), arguments have been reformulated, and a large amount of new literature has been included. Nearly all calculations have been redone. I had collected relevant references since the previous edition went to press. Marja Hennemann and I reviewed all references to my work on culture in the *Social Sciences Citation Index* through the end of 1996. After that, I limited myself to a selected set of the most relevant journals and to books and papers that were brought to my attention by friends as well as through brochures and reviews.

The remaining chapters of the 1980 book disappeared as such. The contents of the old Chapters 7, 8, and 9 have been spread over other chapters or appendixes. For this new edition I have more or less followed the logic of my 1991 popular book, from which I have also borrowed some of the materials and arguments. The new Chapter 7 deals with the fifth dimension of long-term versus short-term orientation. The new Chapter 8 assembles all information about the cultural factor in organizations, both comparing countries and—based on a separate research project from the 1980s—comparing organizations within countries. The new Chapter 9 discusses the meeting of cultures in different spheres of life, and the final chapter addresses the academic users of my dimensional model with advice and warnings.

This new version of *Culture's Consequences* has its new heroes. I have already mentioned Marja Hennemann, who acted as my helper during the past 40 months, managing the reference database, producing exhibits and indexes, checking text, and keeping both of us cheerful. In an earlier stage, Ingrid Regout and Mieke Vunderink helped collect hundreds of potentially interesting books and articles. Michael Harris Bond, Marieke de Mooij, Gert-Jan Hofstede, and Louise

Pannenborg-Stutterheim read and commented on part of the draft text. Loes Ledeboer convinced me of the need for a new subtitle. My expanding family, Maaike, our four sons and their partners, and now five grandchildren have remained a source of moral support and inspiration.

Geert Hofstede
Velp, the Netherlands

Summary of the Book

This book explores the differences in thinking and social action that exist among members of more than 50 modern nations. It argues that people carry "mental programs" that are developed in the family in early childhood and reinforced in schools and organizations, and that these mental programs contain a component of national culture. They are most clearly expressed in the different values that predominate among people from different countries.

Chapter 1 describes the major theoretical issues in the study of cultures, in particular at the country level. Cross-cultural studies proliferate in all the social sciences, but they usually lack a theory of the key variable, culture itself. Names of countries are usually treated as residues of undefined variance in the phenomena found. This volume aims at being specific about the elements of which culture is composed. It identifies five main dimensions along which dominant value systems in the more than 50 countries can be ordered and that affect human thinking, feeling, and acting, as well as organizations and institutions, in predictable ways.

Chapter 2 provides a methodological justification, showing how the initial data used for the empirical part of the research were extracted from an existing database. This database compiled paper-and-pencil survey results collected within subsidiaries of one large multinational business organization (IBM) in 72 countries and covering, among others, many questions about values. The survey was conducted twice, around 1968 and around 1972, producing a total of more than 116,000 questionnaires; respondents could be matched by occupation, age, and gender. Later on, additional data were collected from other populations, unrelated to IBM but matched across countries. At first four and later five main dimensions on which country cultures differ were revealed through theoretical reasoning and statistical analysis; they reflect basic problems that any society has to cope with but for which solutions differ.

Chapters 3 through 7 describe the five dimensions:

- *Power distance* (Chapter 3) is the extent to which the less powerful members of organizations and institutions accept and expect that power is distributed unequally. The basic problem involved is the degree of human inequality that underlies the functioning of each particular society.

- *Uncertainty avoidance* (Chapter 4) is the extent to which a culture programs its members to feel either uncomfortable or comfortable in unstructured situations. Unstructured situations are novel, unknown, surprising, different from usual. The basic problem involved is the degree to which a society tries to control the uncontrollable.

- *Individualism* on the one side versus its opposite, *collectivism* (Chapter 5), is the degree to which individuals are supposed to look after themselves or remain integrated into groups, usually around the family. Positioning itself between these poles is a very basic problem all societies face.

- *Masculinity* versus its opposite, *femininity* (Chapter 6), refers to the distribution of emotional roles between the genders, which is another fundamental problem for any society to which a range of solutions are found; it opposes "tough" masculine to "tender" feminine societies.

- *Long-term* versus *short-term orientation* (Chapter 7) refers to the extent to which a culture programs its members to accept delayed gratification of their material, social, and emotional needs.

These five dimensions were empirically verifiable, and each country could be positioned somewhere between their poles. Moreover, the dimensions were statistically independent and occurred in all possible combinations, although some combinations were more frequent than others.

This volume shows that the same dimensions were validated by data from completely different sources, both survey studies of various kinds and nonsurvey comparative studies such as McClelland's achievement motivation analysis based on a content analysis of children's books. Altogether, data from 140 other studies comparing from 5 to 39 countries were found to be significantly correlated with one or more of the five dimensions. With few exceptions, these other studies so far had not been related to each other by their authors or by anyone else. In addition, the five dimensions showed significant and meaningful correlations with geographic, economic, demographic, and political national indicators.

The book divides countries on the basis of their scores on the five dimensions into culture areas and in some cases finds historical reasons for the cultural differentiation between the areas. Time-series data show no convergence between countries but some worldwide or almost worldwide value shifts.

Chapter 8 focuses on the consequences of the cultural differentiation among countries for the functioning of and theorizing about organizations. It also analyzes the phenomenon of *organizational cultures,* specific to organizations within and across countries. This part is based on a separate research project across 20 Danish and Dutch organizational units that my associates and I carried out in the 1980s.

Chapter 9 deals with the consequences of cultural differences for various types of encounters between cultures: through migration; in international politics, including development cooperation; in multinational business, including international mergers and alliances; in education; in tourism; and on the Internet. It deals with the influence of language, culture shock, intercultural training, and intercultural negotiation.

Chapter 10 collects experiences with the use of the culture dimensions for research and theory building. It provides advice and warns of pitfalls for future users.

The various appendixes contain the instruments used, country scores per survey item, original and additional country scores per dimension, and a summary of the external studies validating the dimensions. They also contain two case studies from the "organizational cultures" project and a statement (taken from the first edition) of my own values.

1

■

Values and Culture

Summary of This Chapter

This introductory chapter deals with the definition and measurement of *mental programs* in people in general, and *values* and *culture* in particular. Mental programs can be found at the universal, collective, and individual levels. In this chapter, I discuss four different strategies by which they can be measured. Values can refer to *the desired* or to *the desirable,* and the two are not equivalent. Culture is defined as collective programming of the mind; it manifests itself not only in values, but in more superficial ways: in symbols, heroes, and rituals. In most of this book, I use the word *culture* to refer to national culture; only in Chapter 8 do I consider the cultures of other collectives—organizations and occupations. A diagram suggests how national culture patterns are rooted in value systems of major groups of the population and how they are stabilized over long periods in history. An earlier term for national culture is *national character,* but studies of national character often reflected observer biases and unfounded stereotypes. The comparative study of national cultures calls for a certain amount of cultural relativism.

The chapter then goes into specific methodological problems of the study of culture: The level of analysis shifts from the individual to society as a whole. Pitfalls are the "ecological fallacy" and, even more, a "reverse ecological fallacy." The dangers of ethnocentrism and disciplinary parochialism are shown. A multitude of disciplines contribute to the comparative study of national cultures. Language and translation of research instruments are crucial, as is the matching of samples from the different cultures for functional equivalence. Marginal phenomena in societies can be as meaningful for comparison as modal phenomena.

The concept of *dimensions of culture* is introduced through an inquiry into the philosophical opposition between the specific and the general, the different and the similar. On the basis of this, four strategies for comparative multisociety studies are distinguished, of which the search for dimensions of culture represents one particular choice. Such dimensions should represent fundamental problems of societies, and the present study identified empirically five independent problems, each related to a dimension of culture: power distance, uncertainty avoidance, individualism, masculinity, and long-term orientation. The existing literature about dimensions of culture, both theory based and empirically derived, contains predictions and validations of these dimensions. In a 1954 review article, Inkeles and Levinson (1954/1969) predicted the first four of these dimensions long before I identified them empirically.

The final section of this chapter discusses when, why, and how national cultures change. The country dimension scores from the present study represent extremely persistent aspects of culture.

Definitions and Distinctions

Mental Programs

Social systems can exist only because human behavior is not random, but to some extent predictable. I predict that Mrs. X will be in the office at 8:25 A.M. tomorrow; that the taxi driver will take me to the station and not somewhere else if I ask him; that all members of the family will come if I ring the dinner bell. We make such predictions continuously, and the vast majority of them are so banal that they pass completely unnoticed. But for each prediction of behavior, we try to take both the *person* and the *situation* into account.[1] We assume that each person carries a certain amount of mental programming that is stable over time and leads to the same person's showing more or less the same behavior in similar situations. Our predictions may sometimes not prove true: Mrs. X may not turn up, the taxi driver may take me to the wrong destination, family member Y may refuse to come for dinner. But the more accurately we know a person's mental programming and the situation, the more sure our prediction will be.

It is possible that our mental programming, our "software of the mind" (the subtitle of my 1991 book), is physically determined by states of our brain cells. Nevertheless, we cannot directly observe mental programs. All we can observe is behavior: words and deeds. When we observe behavior, we infer from it the presence of stable mental software. This type of inference is not unique to the social sciences; it exists, for example, in physics, where the intangible concept of "forces" is inferred from its manifestations in the movement of objects.[2] Like forces in physics, mental programs are intangibles, and the terms we use to describe them are *constructs*. A construct is a product of our imagination, supposed to help our understanding.[3] Constructs do not "exist" in an absolute sense—we define them into existence.

One unfortunate consequence of our dealing with constructs is that their definition contains of necessity an element of subjectivity on the part of the definer. Much more than the physical sciences, the social sciences deal with systems of which the scientists themselves are a part. Social scientists approach the social reality as the blind men from the Indian fable approached the elephant; the one who gets hold of a leg thinks it is a tree, the one who gets the tail thinks it is a rope, but none of them understands what the whole animal is like. We will never be more than blind men in front of the social elephant, but by joining forces with other blind men and women and approaching the animal from as many different angles as possible, we may find out more about it than we could ever do alone. In other words, there is no such thing as objectivity in the study of social reality: We will always be subjective, but we may at least try to be "intersubjective," pooling and integrating a variety of subjective points of view of different observers.

What we do, in fact, when we try to understand social systems is this: We use *models*. A model is a simplified design for visualizing something too complex for us to grasp. In this simplification, our subjectivity enters the process. Constructs in the social sciences not only describe the object but also reflect the specific mental programming of the scholars who make or borrow them. Therefore no single definition of a social science construct is likely to do justice to its complexity.[4]

Every person's mental programming is partly unique, partly shared with others. We can broadly distinguish three levels in mental programs, as pictured in Exhibit 1.1. The least unique but most basic is the *universal* level of mental programming that is shared by all, or almost all, humankind. This is the biological "operating system" of the human body, but it includes a range of expressive behaviors, such as laughing and weeping, associative and aggressive behaviors that are also found in higher animals. This level of our programming has been popularized by ethologists (biologists who specialize in animal behavior) such as Konrad Lorenz (1967), Desmond Morris (1968), and Irenaeus Eibl-Eibesfeldt (1976). The *collective* level of mental programming is shared with some but not all other people; it is common to people belonging to a certain group or category, but different from people belonging to other groups or categories. The whole area of subjective human culture belongs to this level. (Triandis, 1972, p. 4, introduced the label "subjective" in order to distinguish culture as mental programs from "objective" human artifacts—see below.) It includes the language in which we express ourselves, the deference we show to our elders, the physical distance from other people we maintain in order to feel comfortable, and the way we perceive general human activities such as eating, making love, and defecating and the ceremonials surrounding them.

The *individual* level of human programming is the truly unique part: No two people are programmed exactly alike, not even identical twins reared together. This is the level of individual personality, and it provides for a wide range of alternative behaviors within the same collective culture. The borderlines in Exhibit 1.1 are a matter of debate; it is difficult to draw a sharp dividing line between individual personality and collective culture or to distinguish exceptional individuals from their cultural system. Nor is there consensus about which phenomena are culture specific (that is, collective) and which are human universals.[5]

Mental programs can be inherited (transferred in our genes), or they can be learned after birth. Of the three levels in Exhibit 1.1, the bottom, universal level is most likely entirely inherited: It is that part of our genetic information that is common to the entire human species. Eibl-Eibesfeldt (1976, 1988) calls this our *Vorprogrammierung* (preprogramming) and argues that parts of it are still derived from our far ancestors, who survived by

Exhibit 1.1. Three Levels of Human Mental Programming

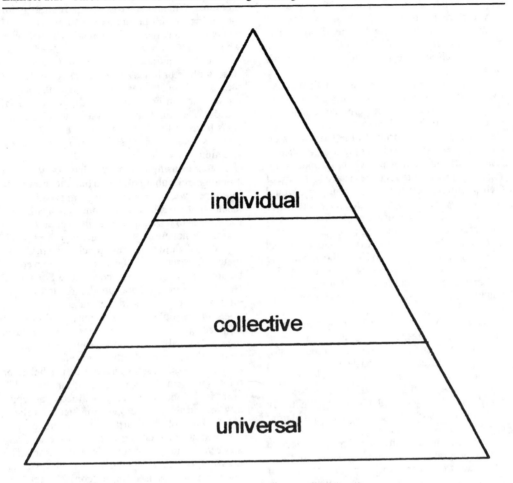

hunting and gathering. On the top, individual level, at least part of our programming must be inherited; it is difficult to explain otherwise the differences in capabilities and temperament between children of the same parents raised in very similar environments. It is at the middle, collective level that most or all of our mental programming is learned, which is shown by the fact that we share it with people who have gone through the same learning processes but who do not have the same genetic makeup. The existence of the American people as a phenomenon is one of the clearest illustrations of the force of learning: With a multitude of genetic variations, it shows a collective mental programming that is striking to the non-American. The transfer of collective mental software is a social phenomenon that, following Durkheim (1895/1937, p. 107), we should try to explain socially.[6] Societies, organizations, and groups have ways of conserving and passing on mental programs from generation to generation with an obstinacy that is often underestimated.

Since the beginning of *Homo sapiens* some 500,000 years ago (the estimates keep changing), the world population has diversified in three ways: in genes, in languages, and in cultures. Genetic diversification can now be traced using DNA research; it has operated over periods of somewhere between 10,000 and 100,000 years.[7] Linguistic diversification has operated over periods of between 1,000 and 10,000 years. Cultural diversification operates the fastest, but it still takes periods of maybe 500 to 5,000 years. The three diversifications are causally unrelated: Genes do not determine languages, and neither genes nor languages determine cultures. There are statistical relationships between gene pools, linguistic areas, and cultural areas, but these only point to common historical origins: "The flow of genes and the flow of culture take place through the same paths, and are speeded by the same routes or retarded by the same barriers. It is always people who travel, and they can spread genes or information, and frequently both"

(Cavalli-Sforza, 1987, p. 32). But there are examples of genetically close populations speaking very different languages, such as Swedes and Finns, and of linguistically nearly identical groups showing markedly different cultures, such as the Dutch and the Flemish (Dutch-speaking Belgians).

Those with a vested interest in societal inequality are fond of theories trying to prove that collective differences in behavior are due to heredity, ignoring environmental factors. The German Nazis had their race theories. In the United States, books arguing that black people are *genetically* less intelligent than white people appear with some regularity,[8] although these have lost some of their popularity, given that the same logic would show that Asians are genetically *more* intelligent than Caucasians (see also Chapter 7). A classic comparative study of the cognitive development of children in the United States and in Africa (Cole, Gay, Glick, & Sharp, 1971) showed that the abilities developed depended on the tasks. Children became good at things that were important in their society and that they had occasion to do often.[9]

The concept of a "collective programming of the mind" resembles the concept of "habitus" proposed by the French sociologist Bourdieu (1980): "Certain conditions of existence produce a *habitus,* a system of permanent and transferable tendencies. A habitus . . . functions as the basis for practices and images . . . which can be collectively orchestrated without an actual conductor" (pp. 88-89; my translation).

Learning through the transfer of collective mental programs goes on during our entire lives, but as most of it deals with fundamental facts of life, we learn most when we are very young. Humans, like other higher animals, are born very incompletely preprogrammed. To be equipped for life, humans need a period of intensive programming by their social environment. During the first 10 years of our lives we possess an uncanny ability to absorb basic learning; this ability later disappears. A Japanese proverb runs, "The soul of a 3-year-old stays with him until he is 100." This is why children who are disadvantaged in their early years will suffer the consequences for life.[10]

Describing Mental Programs in Measurable Terms

In empirical research, we look for measures of the constructs that describe mental programs; that is, we have to *operationalize* them. We need to find observable phenomena from which constructs can be inferred. In some types of research our operationalization leads to quantitative measures; in other types, to descriptive, qualitative measures. Whichever we aim for, any strategy for measuring mental programs has to use forms of behavior or outcomes of behavior. The behavior we use can be either *provoked* (stimulated by the researcher for purposes of the research) or *natural* (taking place or having taken place regardless of the research and the researcher). Also, the behavior we use can be *verbal* (words) or *nonverbal* (deeds). The combination of these two classifications leads to the diagram in Exhibit 1.2, which pictures four types of strategies for operationalization.

Strategies using provoked behavior inevitably contain a Heisenberg effect, in that the researcher interferes with the behavior observed.[11] This means that such behavior cannot always be extrapolated to circumstances in which the researcher is not present. The general problem of all operationalizations is how to achieve *validity*— that is, correspondence between the observed behavior and the underlying constructs. Some constructs are directly conceptually related to specific behavior; this is in particular the case for *intentions,* people's subjective probabilities that they will perform some behavior.[12] In this case, the operationalization can be subjected to *pragmatic validation:* establishing the relationship between expressed intentions and actual behavior following them. Other constructs, among which are attitudes and values, are not directly conceptually related to specific behavior, but are related only through other constructs, according to some assumed set of relationships. In this case pragmatic validation is not possible, and we should be satisfied with *construct validation,* which means that the measures used for our construct relate to the measures used for other, related constructs in the way predicted by our theory. To achieve good construct validity, therefore, we need *both* good measurements *and* good theory.

From the strategies pictured in Exhibit 1.2, those in cell 1 are the easiest and therefore the most frequently used, especially paper-and-pencil "instruments." These produce provoked verbal behavior, which is used to predict other behavior, both verbal in other situations and nonverbal. Frequently, the validity of these predictions is assumed without further proof, as *face validity,* whereas a rigid test has to measure the *predictive validity,* that is, compare predicted with observed behavior. Deutscher (1973) has collected an impressive set of materials to show the risk in relying on "words" to predict "deeds"; in fact, verbal and other behavior may be consistent in some situations, unrelated in others, or even inversely related. Argyris and Schön (1974) have demonstrated the difference between people's "espoused theories" and their "theories in use."

Exhibit 1.2. Four Available Strategies for Operationalizing Constructs About Human Mental Programs

	Provoked	Natural
Words	1 Interviews Questionnaires Projective tests	2 Content analysis of speeches Discussions Documents
Deeds	3 Laboratory experiments Field experiments	4 Direct observation Use of available descriptive statistics

Face validity is therefore not sufficient. On the other hand, rigid predictive solutions are often not available. The next-best solution is to avoid putting all one's eggs into one basket—that is, to use more than one approach simultaneously and look for convergence between these approaches. Webb, Campbell, Schwartz, and Sechrest (1966, p. 3) have called this process "triangulation," a term used in celestial navigation and land surveying. If we want to determine our distance from a point to which we cannot go, we choose two base points to which we can go and measure the position of the third point from there. The more different our base points, the more accurate our measurement. Thus in social science, where we cannot measure constructs directly, we should use at least two measurement approaches as different as possible (with different error sources) and go ahead only if we find convergence in their results. In practice this means that it is undesirable to use cell 1 measurements such as paper-and-pencil instruments only (see Exhibit 1.2); where possible, these should be supported by, for example, direct observation or available descriptive statistics (cell 4). If we have to rely on cell 1 measurements only, we should try to triangulate within them—for example, by approaching the same issue through cell 1 measurements from different informants.

It is, of course, equally undesirable to use cell 2, 3, or 4 measurements only. We must interpret measures based on deeds (actions, nonverbal behavior) to find the underlying constructs—to be expressed in words. Measures based on content analysis also have to be interpreted. If we collect nothing else but data about deeds, we should question whether we gain any insight by postulating mental programs at all—whether we cannot keep our analysis entirely at the level of behavior.[13] Cell 1 measurements, once they are collected, speak more for themselves and take less subjective interpretation from the researcher than cell 2, 3, or 4 measurements. The best strategy, therefore, is to use cell 1 measurement plus at least one other type.

In this book I make extensive use of cell 1 measurements. For validation purposes, I use data collected by others—mainly cell 1 measurements from different informants (various survey data) and cell 4 measurements (available descriptive statistics).

Values

The key constructs used in this book for describing mental software are *values* and *culture*. Values are held by individuals as well as by collectivities; culture presupposes a collectivity. A value is "a broad tendency to prefer certain states of affairs over others." This is a simplified version of the more precise anthropological definition by Kluckhohn (1951/1967): "A value is a conception, explicit or implicit, distinctive of an individual or characteristic of a group, of the desirable which influences the selection from available modes, means and ends of actions" (p. 395). It is also in line with Rokeach's (1972) definition: "To say that a person 'has a value' is to say that he has an enduring belief that a specific mode of conduct or end-state of existence is personally and socially preferable to alternative modes of conduct or end-states of existence" (pp. 159-160). These definitions reserve the word *value* for mental programs that are relatively unspecific: The same value can be activated in a variety of situations.[14] For more specific mental software, Rokeach and others use the terms *attitudes* and *beliefs*.

Values are feelings with arrows to them: Each has a plus and a minus pole. Values deal with such things as the following:

- Evil versus good
- Dirty versus clean
- Dangerous versus safe
- Decent versus indecent
- Ugly versus beautiful
- Unnatural versus natural
- Abnormal versus normal
- Paradoxical versus logical
- Irrational versus rational
- Moral versus immoral

Because our values are programmed early in our lives, they are nonrational (although we may subjectively feel our own to be perfectly rational!). In fact, values determine our subjective definition of rationality. "Values are ends, not means, and their desirability is either non-consciously taken for granted . . . or seen as a direct derivation from one's experience or from some external authority" (Bem, 1970, p. 16).[15] Our values are mutually related and form value systems or hierarchies, but these systems need not be in a state of harmony: Most people simultaneously hold several conflicting values, such as "freedom" and "equality." Our internal value conflicts are one of the sources of uncertainty in social systems: Events in one sphere of life may activate latent values that suddenly affect our behavior in other spheres of life. A change in our perception of a situation may swing the balance in an internal value conflict—in particular, the extent to which we perceive a situation as "favorable" or "critical." [16]

The term *value* or *values* is used in all social sciences (anthropology, economics, political science, psychology, and sociology) with different although not completely unrelated meanings; *value* is nearly as much an interdisciplinary term as *system* and therefore a natural choice as a central construct for a book like this, which borrows from several disciplines. Nearly all our other mental programs (such as attitudes and beliefs) carry a value component. Man is an evaluating animal (Kluckhohn, 1951/1967, p. 403). Christian, Judaic, and Muslim biblical mythology puts the choice between good and evil right at the beginning of humankind's history (with Adam and Eve), thus indicating the fundamental impossibility of humans' escape from choices based on value judgments.

As feelings with arrows to them, values have both *intensity* and *direction*.[17] Mathematically, they have a size and a sign; they can be represented by arrows along a line. If we "hold" a value, this means that the issue involved has some relevance for us (intensity) and that we identify some outcomes as "good" and others as "bad" (direction). For example, "having money" may be highly relevant to us (intensity), and we may consider "more" as good and "less" as bad (direction). Someone else may differ from us as to the intensity, the direction, or both. A person who takes the Christian Bible (St. Mark 10:21-25) seriously could consider having money equally relevant, but with a reversed direction sign: "More" is bad and "less" is good. For still another person, the entire issue of having money may be less relevant. In some primitive societies, "witchcraft" is both relevant and good; in medieval Europe, it was relevant and bad; to most of us today, it is simply irrelevant.

A very important distinction to be made is that between values as the *desired* and the *desirable:* what people actually desire versus what they think they ought to desire. Whereas the two are of course not independent, they should not be equated;[18] equating them is a "positivistic fallacy" (Levitin, 1973, p. 497), a confusion between reality and social desirability. In most of the psychological and sociological research literature, *social desirability* is treated as something undesirable to the researcher. The term is used in two ways: as a quality of certain measurement items and as a personality construct of the respondents.[19] In both senses, it usually represents "noise" in the measurement. In the study of values, however, asking for the desirable is perfectly respectable; it is part and parcel of the phenomenon studied. So in this case, social desirability in our measurements is not undesirable; we should only realize that we deal with values of two different kinds.[20]

Avoiding the positivistic fallacy is especially important if we try to relate values to behavior. Responding to questionnaires or interviews is also a form of behavior, but, as argued above, we should distinguish "words" (questionnaires, interviews, remarks, speeches) from "deeds" (nonverbal behavior). Values should never be equated with deeds, for the simple reason that behavior depends on both the person and the situation. However, values as the desired are at least closer to deeds than are values as the desirable. The desired/desirable distinction relates to several other distinctions, as listed in Exhibit 1.3.

Exhibit 1.3 refers to *norms* of value. We can speak of norms as soon as we deal with a collectivity. In the case of the desired, the norm is statistical: It indicates the values actually held by the majority. In the case of the desirable, the norm is absolute or deontological (pertaining to what is ethically right). The desired relates more to pragmatic issues; the desirable, to ideology.

Exhibit 1.3 Distinction Between the Desired and the Desirable and Associated Distinctions

Nature of a Value	The Desired	The Desirable
Dimension of a value	Intensity	Direction
Nature of corresponding norm of value	Statistical, phenomenological, pragmatic	Absolute, deontological, ideological
Corresponding behavior	Choice and differential effort allocation	Approval or disapproval[a]
Dominant outcome	Deeds and/or words	Words
Terms used in measuring instrument	Important, successful, attractive, preferred	Good, right, agree, ought, should
Affective meaning of this term	Activity plus evaluation	Evaluation only
Person referred to in measuring instrument	Me, you	People in general

a. The distinction between approval and choice, and so on, is based on Kluckhohn (1951/1967, pp. 404-405).

The associations among the various lines in Exhibit 1.3 should be seen as probabilistic, not rigid. For example, we may approve with deeds rather than words, or what is desired may never become expressed in deeds. There remains a discrepancy between actual behavior (deeds) and the desired, but there is another discrepancy between the desired and the desirable. Norms for the desirable can be completely detached from behavior. The tolerable size of the discrepancies may differ from person to person and from group to group, based on both personality and culture. In Catholicism, the practice of confessing can be seen as a device for coping with both discrepancies and thus making them tolerable. Ideological indoctrination will more easily affect the desirable than the desired; it is possible that it widens the gap between the two without changing the desired. Discourse, the forms of text and talk that social actors use for different occasions, reflects the desirable much more than it does the desired.[21]

Measuring Values

Questionnaires designed to measure values abound in the U.S. social science literature, as a logical consequence of U.S. empiricism.[22] In addition, we can use other questionnaires designed not for measuring values but for measuring such constructs as beliefs, attitudes, and personality to *infer* values.

In order to investigate the convergence of various value-measuring instruments, I administered eight of them to groups of managers from about 20 different countries attending executive development programs at IMEDE, Lausanne, Switzer-land.[23] The highest correlation found between conceptually related scores on different instruments was $r = .49***$ (across 64 respondents; see also Chapter 2).[24] This, although statistically significantly different from zero, is not high, which means that measures of values depend strongly on the instrument used—a proof of the subjectivity referred to earlier. Also, where I could compare the patterns of correlations between scores of an instrument for my international respondent sample with the correlations reported for American samples, I found that these correlation patterns were usually quite different. This shows that the scores did not carry the same meaning for the two samples, and that it is a questionable practice to use instruments developed in one country (usually the United States) in another cultural environment, assuming they carry the same meaning there.

Inspection of a number of instruments designed to measure human values makes it clear that the universe of all human values is not defined, and that each author has made his or her own subjective selection from this unknown universe, with little consensus among authors. This means that the *content validity* of measurements of values (their representativeness for the universe of values) is necessarily low.

Various authors have tried to classify values. Rokeach (1972, p. 160) in the United States has distinguished terminal values (end states) from instrumental values (ways to get there). Levitin (1973, p. 494) in the United States has distinguished telic (ultimate means and ends), ethical (good or evil), aesthetic (beautiful or ugly), intellectual (true or false), and economic values. Reviewing value-measuring instruments in the U.S. literature, I found three types of values: those dealing with our relationships with (1) other people, (2) things (our nonhuman environment), and (3) our own inner selves and God.

Eysenck (1953, 1954) in Britain found that political attitudes (I would also call them *values*) of British, U.S., Swedish, and German respondents reflected two main principles: radicalism/conservatism (dealing, among other things, with egalitarianism) and tough-mindedness/tender-mindedness (dealing with aggression and intolerance of ambiguity). Eysenck related these to voting behavior: Communists were tough-minded radicals, fascists were tough-minded conservatives, (British) conservatives were tender-minded conservatives, and socialists were tender-minded radicals.[25] Later, Rokeach (1973, pp. 165 ff.) presented a somewhat similar two-dimensional classification system of political values based on a content analysis of the writings of four types of politicians. He distinguished two dimensions in their ideas: *equality* and *freedom*. The writings of Lenin (communist) were high on equality, low on freedom; of Hitler (fascist), low on both; of Goldwater (conservative), low on equality, high on freedom; and of various socialist writers (who are rare in the United States), high on both.

Bales and Couch (1969) in the United States collected nearly 900 different formulations of values used in different instruments, in theoretical literature, and in group discussions they had organized. Using 500 U.S. students as a test population, they reduced the statements statistically to four clusters: authority, self-restraint, equality, and individuality. Musek (1993) in Slovenia administered a list of 54 values to 200 students and found these values to cluster into four categories: hedonistic (pleasure), potency (achievement), moral (duties), and fulfillment (self-actualization). Musek classified the first two as "Dionysian" and the second two as "Apollonian"; the importance of the Dionysian values decreased and that of the Apollonian values increased with the students' age.

The most extensive research project on values so far was carried out by the Israeli psychologist Shalom Schwartz. He composed a survey instrument of 56 values from the literature and administered the survey to samples of schoolteachers and of university students in 44 countries altogether, on all inhabited continents. By 1994, he had collected answers from more than 25,000 respondents. Using the statistical technique of "smallest-space analysis" to classify differences at the individual respondent level, Schwartz (1992) found these values to cluster into 10 categories: power, achievement, hedonism, stimulation, self-direction, universalism (like "unity with nature"), benevolence, tradition, confor-

mity, and security. These categories could be subsumed into two dimensions: openness to change versus conservation and self-transcendence versus self-enhancement (Schwartz & Sagiv, 1995). Schwartz also performed an analysis at the level of national cultures, which I will discuss later in this chapter.

In the previous section, I argued that values (by their very nature) have both intensity and direction. However, we rarely find value-measuring instruments that ask for both. Some focus on intensity and take direction for granted, some focus on direction and take intensity for granted, and some even confuse the two.[26] The focus is determined by the words used to express the values. The work of Osgood and his associates with the "semantic differential" has shown that across a large variety of languages, three basic dimensions appear regularly in the affective meaning of words: *evaluation* (good-bad), *potency* (strong-weak), and *activity* (active-passive) (Osgood, May, & Miron, 1975; Osgood, Suci, & Tannenbaum, 1957). Osgood, Ware, and Morris (1961) applied the semantic differential to a set of 13 terminal values (Morris's "ways to live"; see Morris, 1956) and found that in this case, the three dimensions collapsed into one: The preferred "ways to live" were felt to be good, strong, and active. However, the words used in questionnaire scales rarely tap all these meanings. They are often of the type good/ bad, right/wrong, agree/disagree, which is purely evaluation and deals with the *direction* of the value, or they are of the type important/unimportant, successful/unsuccessful, meaningful/meaningless, which, according to Osgood et al. (1957, pp. 62-63), represents activity as well as evaluation. In this case, they deal with the *intensity* of the value with an implicit direction.

The intensity/direction distinction is associated in Exhibit 1.3 with the distinction between "values as the desired" and "values as the desirable." In the lower part of Exhibit 1.3, I indicate what this means for the design of measuring instruments. Values as the desired are measured by such words as *important/unimportant,* expressing activity as well as evaluation, and usually refer to the respondent in the first or second person. Values as the desirable are measured by such words as *agree/disagree,* expressing evaluation only, and usually refer to people in general.

Value measurements are quantified either through ratings on a scale or through ranking. Various instruments use ratings of individual items on scales of between 2 and 11 points. Others use ranking of items relative to one another, with a minimum number of 2 and a maximum of 18 (Rokeach's Value Survey). Rating and ranking can produce different results.[27]

When the intensity of values is measured (that is, for values as the desired), the interpretation of the scores always implies some kind of ranking of one value versus other values. A rating of one value is as meaningful as the sound of one hand clapping. Most of us will value both "freedom" and "equality," but differences among people will appear only when we look at the relative value attached to freedom over equality, or vice versa, in case of conflict.

All measures of values discussed so far are cell 1 measurements (provoked words). Moreover, all are based on self-descriptions (values as the desired) or ideological statements (values as the desirable). There is another technique that is still cell 1 but avoids the distorting effects of self-descriptions and ideological statements. This technique (which is too seldom used) involves inferring values from the way respondents describe specific third people, recognizing that our perceptions are colored by our values. An instrument using this technique is Fred E. Fiedler's (1967) Least Preferred Co-Worker (LPC) questionnaire, in which a respondent describes the other person with whom he or she can work *least* well. Some respondents describe their least-preferred coworker in relatively favorable terms (high LPC score), others in extremely unfavorable terms (low LPC score). Fiedler interprets high LPC scorers as interpersonally oriented and low LPC scorers as task oriented. However, it appears that if the LPC questionnaire is administered together with self-descriptions of values, high LPC scorers tend to describe themselves as task oriented and low LPC scorers as interpersonally oriented—the reverse of what could be expected at face value (Hofstede, 1974b, p. 14).

Fiedler and Chemers (1974, p. 103) have interpreted this paradox by referring to the influence of the situation. They showed that the behavioral consequences of a high or low LPC score depend on the degree of criticalness of the situation, and that people who behave one way in a safe situation may show quite different behavior when the situation is critical. Self-descriptions of values are typically collected assuming "normal"—that is, noncritical—circumstances. LPC, however, refers to an individual's perception of someone else under dramatically critical circumstances: the impossibility of getting a job done. It should be no surprise, then, that LPC and self-descriptions of values are not, even negatively, related. Deutscher (1973, p. 45) has concluded that, in general, laboratory experimental studies show a positive correlation between attitudes and behavior, whereas field observational studies do not show such a correlation. This suggests the same phenomenon: Self-description attitude measurements provide valid predictions only for behavior under favorable (laboratory) circumstances.

In paper-and-pencil questionnaires, people rarely describe themselves under crisis circumstances. They will, however, easily describe *others* under crisis circumstances. On top of this, we are all better observers of others than of ourselves; but, as the experience with the LPC questionnaire shows, in observing others we reveal something about ourselves, too. Therefore, paper-and-pencil measures of values through perceptions of third persons can be expected to have greater behavioral validity than those based on self-descriptions—this is what Fiedler proves extensively in the case of LPC. In this book, the measure used for the value complex "power distance" will be partly based on the perception of the behavior of others: one's boss and one's colleagues (Chapter 3).

Cell 2, 3, and 4 measures of values are rarer in the literature. Nevertheless, almost any behavior that is systematically observable—verbal and nonverbal—can be used to infer mental software in general and values in particular. Examples on the cross-cultural level are McClelland's (1961) content analysis of children's stories from 41 countries (cell 2), Schachter et al.'s (1954) laboratory experiments with group discussions by schoolboys in 7 European countries (cell 3), and Adelman and Morris's (1967) factor analysis of national statistical data from 74 developing countries (cell 4).

Culture

Culture has been defined in many ways. One well-known anthropological consensus definition runs as follows:

Culture consists in patterned ways of thinking, feeling and reacting, acquired and transmitted mainly by symbols, constituting the distinctive achievements of human groups, including their embodiments in artifacts; the essential core of culture consists of traditional (i.e. historically derived and selected) ideas and especially their attached values. (Kluckhohn, 1951, p. 86, n. 5)

Kroeber and Parsons (1958) arrived at a cross-disciplinary definition of culture as "transmitted and created content and patterns of values, ideas, and other symbolic-meaningful systems as factors in the shaping of human behavior and the artifacts produced through behavior" (p. 583). Triandis (1972) distinguishes "subjective" culture from its expression in "objective" artifacts and defines the former as "a cultural group's characteristic way of perceiving the man-made part of its environment" (p. 4). In this book I treat culture as *the collective programming of the mind that distinguishes the members of one group or category of people from another*. This is a shorthand definition; it implies everything in Kluckhohn's more extensive definition above. The "mind" stands for the head, heart, and hands—that is, for thinking, feeling, and acting, with consequences for beliefs, attitudes, and skills. And as Kluckhohn has affirmed, culture in this sense includes values; systems of values are a core element of culture.

Values are invisible until they become evident in behavior, but culture manifests itself in visible elements too. From the many terms used to describe visible manifestations of culture, the following three, together with *values,* cover the total concept rather neatly: *symbols, heroes,* and *rituals.* In Exhibit 1.4, these are pictured as the layers of an onion around a core that consists of values.

Symbols are words, gestures, pictures, and objects that carry often complex meanings recognized as such only by those who share the culture.[28] The words in a language or jargon belong to this category, as do dress, hairstyle, Coca-Cola, flags, and status symbols. New symbols are easily developed and old ones disappear; symbols from one cultural group are regularly copied by others. This is why symbols appear in the outer, most superficial layer of Exhibit 1.4.

Heroes are persons, alive or dead, real or imaginary, who possess characteristics that are highly prized in a culture and thus serve as models for behavior. Even fantasy or cartoon figures such as Batman, or, as a contrast, Charlie Brown in the United States, Asterix in France, or Ollie B. Bommel (Mr. Bumble) in the Netherlands, can serve as cultural heroes. In this age of television, outward appearances have become more important in the choices of heroes than they were before.

Rituals are collective activities that are technically unnecessary to the achievement of desired ends, but that within a culture are considered socially essential, keeping the individual bound within the norms of the collectivity. Rituals are therefore carried out for their own sake.[29] Ways of greeting and paying respect to others are examples, as are social and religious ceremonies. Business and political meetings organized for seemingly rational reasons often serve mainly ritual purposes, such as allowing the leaders to assert themselves.

In Exhibit 1.4 symbols, heroes and rituals are subsumed under the term *practices.* As such, they are visible to an outside observer; their cultural meanings, however, are invisible and lie precisely and only in the ways these practices are interpreted by insiders.

Culture is to a human collectivity what personality is to an individual. Guilford (1959) has defined personality as "the interactive aggregate of personal characteristics that influence the individual's response to the environment" (p. 13). Culture could be defined as the interactive aggregate of common characteristics that influence a human group's response to its environment. Culture determines the uniqueness of a human group in the same way personality determines the uniqueness of an individual. Moreover, the two interact: "Culture and personality" is a classic name for psychological anthropology.[30] Cultural traits can sometimes be measured through personality tests.

In the English language, *culture* has a number of other meanings, all deriving from its original Latin meaning: the cultivation of soil (the same applies in French and German). Another meaning that leads to some confusion, especially in communicating with the French, is "the training and refining of the mind, manners, taste etc. or the result of this."[31] In order to avoid confusion in discussing culture with my students, I usually label this Culture 1 and the anthropological term Culture 2. Unlike Culture 1, Culture 2 is carried by even the humblest people and through the most menial acts.

The word *culture* is usually reserved for societies (operationalized as nations or as ethnic or regional groups within or across nations). Basically, the word can be applied to any human collectivity or category: an organization, a profession, an age group, an entire gender, or a family. Societies merit special consideration in the study of cultures because they are the most "complete" human groups that exist; a society is a social system "characterized by the highest level of self-sufficiency in relation to its environments" (Parsons, 1977, p. 6). Categories within societies are interdependent with other categories. The degree of national cultural homogeneity varies from one society to another, and may be especially low for some of the newer nations;[32] few of these, however, are in the sample of nations studied in this book. Even if a society contains different cultural groups (such as blacks, Hispanics, Asians, and Caucasians in the United States), these usually share certain cultural traits with one another that make their members recognizable to foreigners as belonging to that society.

Culture is not the same as *identity.* Identities consist of people's answers to the question: Where do I belong? They are based on mutual images and stereotypes and on emotions linked to the outer layers of the onion in Exhibit 1.4—symbols, heroes, and rituals—but not to values.[33] Populations that fight each other on the basis of their different "felt" identities may very well share the same values. Examples are the linguistic regions in Belgium, the religions in Northern Ireland, and tribal groups in Africa. A shared identity needs a shared Other: At home, I feel Dutch and very different from other Europeans, such as Belgians and Germans; in Asia or the United States, we all feel like Europeans.

Exhibit 1.4.   The "Onion Diagram": Manifestations of Culture at Different Levels of Depth

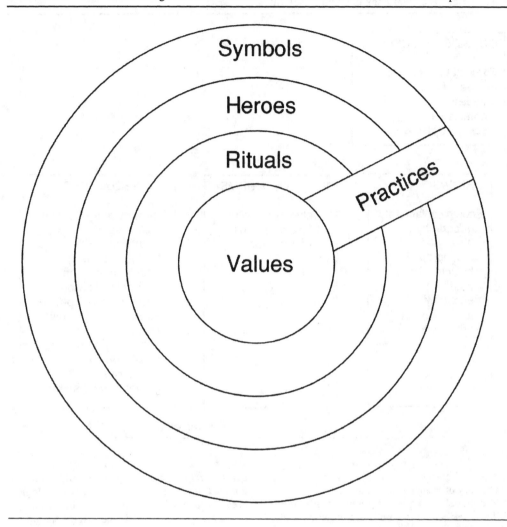

National Cultures and
Their Stability

This book is about differences in national culture among more than 50 modern nations. It will show evidence of differences and similarities among the culture patterns of countries—differences and similarities that have very old historical roots (some, for example, going back as far as the Roman Empire). There must be mechanisms in societies that permit the maintenance of stability in culture patterns across many generations. I suggest that such mechanisms operate as illustrated in Exhibit 1.5.[34]

In the center is a system of societal norms consisting of the value systems (the mental software) shared by major groups in the population. Their origins are in a variety of ecological factors (in the sense of factors affecting the physical and social environment). The societal norms have led to the development and pattern maintenance of institutions in society with particular structures and ways of functioning. These include the family, education systems, political systems, and legislation. These institutions, once established, reinforce the societal norms and the ecological conditions that led to their establishment. In a relatively closed society, such a system will hardly change at all. Institutions may be changed, but this does not necessarily affect the societal norms; and when these remain unchanged, the persistent influence of a majority value system patiently smoothes the new institutions until their structures and ways of functioning are again adapted to

Exhibit 1.5. The Stabilizing of Culture Patterns

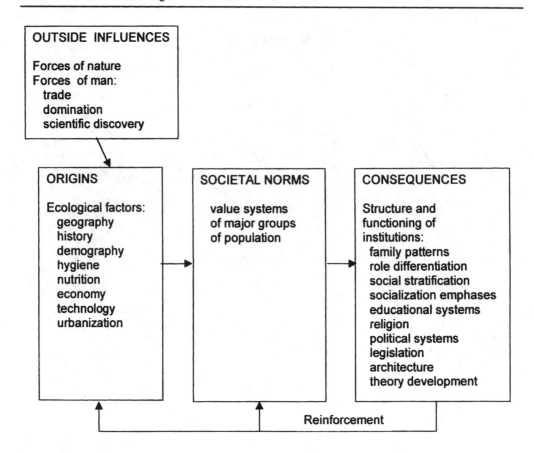

the societal norms. An example of this process is the history of France since Louis XIV.[35]

The model in Exhibit 1.5 implies that cultural differences cannot be understood without the study of history. Culture as mental programming is also the crystallization of history in the minds, hearts, and hands of the present generation. The origins of cultural differences, if explainable at all, presume a comparative study of history. Skocpol and Somers (1980) have divided comparative historical studies into three groups that form a sort of evolutionary sequence: (1) demonstration of one theory through the parallel between otherwise different cases, (2) demonstration of variety through the contrast of otherwise similar cases and their contexts, and (3) macrocausal analysis, which resembles multivariate hypothesis testing. Explanations of cultural differences rest on the second and especially the third types of comparative historical approaches.

Changes, as Exhibit 1.5 shows, are supposed to come mainly from the outside, through forces of nature (changes of climate, silting up of harbors, spreading of diseases) or forces of human

beings (trade, conquest, political and economic domination, scientific discoveries, technological breakthroughs).[36] The arrow of outside influences is deliberately directed at the origins, not at the societal norms themselves. I believe that norms change rarely through direct adoption of outside values; rather, changes occur through shifts in ecological conditions—technological, economic, and hygienic. In general, norm shifts will be gradual unless the outside influences are particularly violent (such as in the case of military conquest or deportation).

One of the most effective ways of changing mental programs of individuals is to change behavior first.[37] That value change has to precede behavior change is an idealistic assumption that neglects the contribution of the *situation* to actual behavior. This applies on the level of societies as well. Kunkel (1970), dealing with the economic development of societies, concludes that "the major problem of economic development is not the alteration of character, values or attitudes, but the change of those selected aspects of man's social environment which are relevant to the learning of new behavior patterns" (p. 76). In this case, I would omit the word "social."

The system of Exhibit 1.5 is in a homeostatic (self-regulating) quasi-equilibrium. History has shown cases of peoples that through such systems have maintained identities over hundreds and thousands of years, even in the face of such sweeping changes as loss of independence, deportation, and loss of language; examples are Jews, Gypsies, and Basques.[38] Other peoples in similar conditions have disappeared, however, when their self-regulating cycles were too much disturbed by outside influences. Obviously, both the strength of the existing self-regulation and the strength of the outside forces have played roles in these cases.

National Character
and National Stereotypes

The study of national culture was preceded by a centuries-old interest in "national character." The notion that a population or a part thereof—one's own or another—possesses collective characteristics is probably as old as the populations themselves. Every Belgian student knows a famous citation from Julius Caesar in his book on the Gallic War (written 50 B.C.) that states that of the three Gallic tribes, the Belgians were the bravest. In the 14th century A.D. the great Muslim scholar Ibn Khaldûn—considered by some to be the founder of sociology[39]—in his book *Al-Muqaddima* dwelled at length on the different characteristics of nomads and sedentary peoples, including their mentality, education, social and political behavior, and architecture. He recognized the phenomenon of "mental programming": "Indeed, the mind in its original state is ready to absorb any influence, good or bad. As Mohammed has said: 'Every child is born in a natural state. It is his parents who make him into a Jew, Christian or Zoroastrian' " (Ibn Khaldûn, 1377/1968, p. 246; my translation).

In the 18th century, philosophers such as Hume in England, Montesquieu in France, and Kant in Germany dealt with questions of national character. Popular wisdom about comparative national characteristics was codified, as in an anonymous Austrian painting in the form of a table that classifies 10 European nations according to each of 17 qualifiers, such as "manners," "personality," "worship," and "pastimes." The artist has not hidden his sym- and antipathies.[40]

In the early 20th century, the German Wilhelm Wundt (1832-1920), the father of experimental psychology, in his old age also founded cross-cultural psychology with a 10-volume book series on *Völkerpsychologie* (psychology of peoples), presenting a comparative analysis across countries of language, myths, morals, religion, art, and law, put into a psychological context (Wundt, 1911-20).[41]

"National character" was a popular research subject in anthropology in the 1930s to 1950s. One definition was as follows: "relatively enduring personality characteristics and patterns that are modal among the adult members of the society" (Inkeles & Levinson, 1954/1997, p. 17). An alternative term was *modal personality,* which fit the anthropological research current at the time called *culture and personality.* An influential publication was U.S. anthropologist Ruth Benedict's book *Patterns of Culture* (1934/1959). During and after World War II, the U.S. government called upon Benedict and her colleague anthropologists to help understand the psyche of enemy nations such as Germany, Japan, and Russia.[42]

Already in those days the use of the concept of national character was also disputed. In an article first published in 1942, British anthropologist Gregory Bateson described what he saw as the two main criticisms of the concept, which he subsequently set out to refute. The first criticism was that the concept of national character is redundant, because historical or current conditions of a nation suffice to explain differences in behavior. To this argument Bateson retorted that it ignores the known facts about learning: The concept of character could be seen as representing the present accumulation of learning from the past, and as such it makes an essential contribution. The second criticism was a "doubt whether any uniformity or regularity is likely to obtain within such a sample of humans as constitutes a nation." Bateson refuted this argument at length, the gist of his refutation being that however heterogeneously a nation may be composed, its parts interact and thus affect each other, and even a negative adaptation represents an adaptation (see Bateson 1942/1973, pp. 62-68).

Nonetheless, the national character concept lost popularity in mainstream Anglophone cultural anthropology in the mid-1950s. Its lasting legacy was the introduction of psychological concepts into anthropological studies. A further advance in the field would have required a move from the study of national characters to the study of national cultures in complex societies, an expansion from the study of personality in culture to the study of culture as a whole, and for this task, anthropology at that time lacked the tools. I believe that the crisis of the national character concept in anthropology in the mid-1950s was due to oversimplified theories that could not be improved for lack of adequate research methods. Traditional anthropological methods were unable to tackle the complexity of whole nations.[43] "National character" remained a simplistic stereotype and could not acquire the status of an empirically derived common component in the thinking and acting of the various members of a nation. Stereotypes were falsified by the obvious variety of members within complex societies.

Where anthropologists lost interest in the issue of national character, psychologists took it up. In Europe, a French-language international journal, *Revue de Psychologie des Peuples,* existed from 1946 to 1970. In the United States, psychologist David McClelland in 1961 published a study titled *The Achieving Society,* based on content analysis of children's readers from 41 nations, in which the anthropological influence is clearly present. McClelland considered children's stories in modern nations as the equivalent of folk myths in preliterate societies. However, he limited himself to the study of one main motive (achievement) and two subsidiary motives (affiliation and power) that are highly specific and, as I will argue in Chapters 4 and 6, reflect McClelland's own U.S. cultural background. The national character inheritance has also been evident in studies on the influence of society in the shaping of personality, to which I will come back later in this chapter.[44] It survives more broadly in the field that is now known as cross-cultural psychology.

The scientific status of the term *national character* as it was and still is often used has remained debatable. When a person X makes a statement about the character of a population or population group Y—his or her own or another—this statement always contains information about X, but whether it also contains valid information about Y remains to be proven. Good examples are the following quotes from the English 18th-century philosopher David Hume (1742/1964): "The Chinese have the greatest uniformity of character imaginable"; "The English, of any people in the universe, have the least of a national character; unless this very singularity may pass for such" (pp. 249, 252). Hume illustrates to what extent a statement about national character is "in the eye of the beholder"—he was able to see others' collective peculiarities (and the more so, the less he knew about them) but not those of his own countrymen. The Spaniard de Madariaga (1928) and the Dutchman Renier (1931), to name two, had no problems in writing extensively about the national character of the English.

Information about a population can be considered scientifically valid only when it meets the following four criteria:

1. It is descriptive and not evaluative (judgmental).
2. It is verifiable from more than one independent source.
3. It applies, if not to all members of the population, at least to a statistical majority.

4. It discriminates; that is, it indicates those characteristics for which this population differs from others.

If these four criteria cannot be met—which has often been the case for statements about national character—the statements are unsupported stereotypes.

A *stereotype* (the word derives from the printing industry) is a fixed notion about persons in a certain category, with no distinctions made among individuals. People hold *heterostereotypes* about others ("All Dutch are tactless") and *autostereotypes* about their own groups ("We Dutch are honest").

Stereotypes are easy to study. For example, British social psychologist Dean Peabody (1985) collected attributions by students from nine countries of adjectives applicable to people from different nations: their own and a choice of others. Respondents scored their answers on semantic differential scales—that is, scales on which choices are located between pairs of opposites. In Peabody's case, the opposites were either descriptive (such as thrifty/extravagant) or evaluative (such as stingy/generous). He found more agreement across respondents from different nationalities for descriptive than for evaluative adjectives: Evaluation depends more strongly on culturally determined standards.[45]

Stereotypes, as argued above, always reflect the mind-sets of those judging and sometimes also something real about those being judged. How much truth they contain should be validated with scientifically respectable information from less subjective sources. What is unfounded in any case is the application of stereotype information about a group to any individual member of that group. The valid part of a stereotype is a statistical statement about a group, not a prediction of the properties of particular individuals. Stereotypes are at best half-truths.

Duijker and Frijda (1960), who reviewed some 1,000 publications on "national character and national stereotypes" in 1960, reported that "no comparative studies based on representative samples of national populations are known to us" (p. 21). They suggested simplifying the task by studying cultural *elites:* "It might be that these elites represent most clearly, or even exclusively, those psychological features which distinguish one nation from another" (p. 29). Duijker and Frijda remained on the psychological level; a good sociological reason for the study of elites that they did not mention is that elites are more likely than nonelites to shape the institutions that perpetuate a culture.

Since the 1970s, interest in "national character" has been increasing again (e.g., in Lynn, 1971—

see Chapter 4), but the term is now mostly replaced by the more neutral *national cultures*. The study of national cultures is stimulated by a need for better international understanding and cooperation and is made possible by the availability of more systematic and more objective information, including the kind of comparative studies that Duijker and Frijda earlier found lacking.

Cultural Relativism

The impossibility of escaping value judgments applies to the student of values as much as to anyone else. First, we have to distinguish between a phenomenological study of values (which is the area of social science) and a deontological approach (which belongs to ethics, ideology, or theology). But even in purely phenomenological research the values of the researcher determine to a large extent the way he or she observes, describes, classifies, understands, and predicts reality. There is no way out of this dilemma but to (1) expose oneself and one's work to the work of others with different value systems and (2) try to be as explicit as possible about one's own value system. Both, to a certain extent, go against our nature. For the interested reader I have composed a picture of my own value system and its origins in Appendix 8. More about it, however, probably will be readable "between the lines" of this book.

A related issue is whether there are any absolute values at all or only relative ones. Anthropologists have tried to identify absolute values in the form of cultural universals from the phenomenological side.[46] Philosopher Erwin Laszlo (1973) assumed that such cultural universals exist, "good" being what contributes to the survival of the world system; he argued that error tolerance for the world has become so small that relativism is obsolete. However, this position in itself reflects a value choice. The problem is that human beings are at the same time the source of values and their instrument; this is a problem for which, as far as I know, systems theory has no solution. Therefore, studying differences in culture among human groups and categories that think, feel, and act differently does presuppose a position of cultural relativism. Lévi-Strauss, the Grand Old Man of French anthropology, has expressed it as follows:

> Cultural relativism affirms that one culture has no absolute criteria for judging the activities of another culture as "low" or "noble." However, every culture can and should apply such judgment to its own activities, because its members are actors as well as observers. (Lévi-Strauss & Éribon, 1988, p. 229; my translation)

Cultural relativism does not imply normlessness for oneself or for one's own society. It does call for one to suspend judgment when dealing with groups or societies different from one's own. One should think twice before applying the norms of a given person, group, or society to another. Information about the nature of the cultural differences between societies, their roots and their consequences, should precede judgment and action.

After having been informed, the foreign observer is still likely to deplore certain ways of the other society. If he or she is professionally involved in the other society—for example, as an expatriate manager or development assistance expert—the foreigner may very well want to induce changes. In colonial days, foreigners often wielded absolute power in other societies and imposed their rules on those societies. In these postcolonial days, foreigners who want to change something in another society will have to negotiate their interventions. Negotiation again is more likely to succeed when the parties concerned understand the reasons for the differences in viewpoints.

Studying Culture

Comparing Cultures:
Changing the Level of Analysis

In studying "values" we compare individuals; in studying "culture" we compare societies. When we base our study of culture on quantified data that have to be statistically treated, we meet a problem that the study of values of individuals did not present: the simultaneous analysis of data at both individual and societal levels. Some data are collected at the level of the society, such as population density or per capita gross national product. Parker (1997) defends studying cultures entirely at this level; his "physioeconomics" framework focuses primarily on soil and climate, but publishes extensive additional statistics of economic, technological, demographic, political, and social country indicators.[47] Most studies comparing cultures also use data collected from individuals within cultures, such as responses on questionnaires.

Let us suppose we want to study the relationship between two variables that belong to the latter category: stemming from individuals within societies. We want to measure this relationship using a mathematical method, the correlation coefficient. In this case we can choose among the following:

- A global correlation across all individuals regardless of the society they are in
- A number of within-society correlations, one for each society, across those individuals belonging to that society
- A between-society correlation, based on the mean scores of the variables for each society

For data collected at the level of the society, we obviously have only a between-society correlation.[48]

The problem with data from individuals within societies is that the various types of correlations referred to above most likely are not equal. First, the within-society correlations may be significantly different from one society to the other. For example, Kagitçibasi (1970) found that questionnaire item scores that correlated in the United States and together formed the F scale (used to determine the "authoritarian personality") were not correlated in Turkey. In societies where the culture imposes strong behavioral norms, certain attitudes and behaviors show such small variance that they do not correlate with other attitudes and behaviors; this is the case for some of the F-scale items in Turkey. It is precisely these differences in within-society correlations that are of interest from a culture point of view; when these occur, the use of global correlations is misleading.

Even if the within-society correlations are not significantly different from each other, they are not the same as the between-society correlations. I shall call the latter *ecological correlations:* They are calculated either from mean values of variables for each society or (in the case of yes/no variables) from percentages. It is easy to see why ecological correlations are not the same as within-society correlations if we consider some extreme cases. One extreme is that for one of the variables the mean value is the same for any single society; in this case we find only within-society correlations, and the ecological correlation is zero. The other extreme is that one of the variables is a constant for all members within a society, but differs from one society to another. In this case the within-society correlations are all zero, and we find only an ecological correlation. Usually, of course, neither variable is a constant for the societies or the individuals within them, so we find both types of correlations. However, they are rarely of equal magnitude; they may even have opposite signs.

Confusion between within-system and between-system (ecological) correlations is known as the *ecological fallacy*. It was signaled by Thorndike as early as 1939, but the classic example is found in the work of Robinson (1950, p. 352). This example deals with the relationship between skin color and illiteracy in the United States. Between percentages of blacks in the population and percentages of illiterates across nine geographic divisions of the country (1930 data), the *ecological* correlation was $r = .95$. Across 48 states, the ecological correlation was $r = .77$. Across 97 million individuals, the *individual* correlation was $r = .20$. The ecological fallacy is committed when the ecological correlations ($r = .95$ or $.77$: strong association between skin color and illiteracy) are interpreted as if they apply to individuals. Doing so is attractive because ecological correlations are often stronger than individual correlations.

The ecological fallacy is a special temptation for political scientists. In cross-cultural studies by social psychologists, however, I find another type of confusion between the individual and the ecological level that I label the *reverse ecological fallacy*. This fallacy is committed in the construction of *ecological indexes* from variables correlated at the *individual* level. Indexes are, for example, constructed through addition of the scores on two or more questionnaire items. In constructing indexes for the individual level, we make sure (or ought to make sure) that the items correlate across individuals; in constructing indexes for the national level, we ought to make sure that the country mean scores correlate across countries. The reverse ecological fallacy in cross-cultural studies occurs when researchers compare cultures on indexes created for the individual level.

An example of the reverse ecological fallacy is a questionnaire study by Bass and Franke (1972) among more than 1,000 students from six countries about approaches to success in organizations. In a pretest with Americans, the 12 items of the questionnaire could be split into 6 expressing "social" and 6 expressing "political" approaches to success—at the level of individual American students. The researchers did not test their internal consistency at the individual level for each of the other five national groups. In the international study, Bass and Franke only calculated mean scores for each of the 12 items for each of the six countries and averaged the social items into a country social index score and the political items into a political index score. Country social and political index scores were subsequently correlated with country-level indexes such as GNP/capita and population density, but no clear conclusions emerged. The authors did not look at the ecological correlations of their items—that is, the correlations of country means for each item (across six countries). On the basis of their published data, the ecological correlations could be calculated as follows: The 15 intercorrelations of the 6 "social" items varied from $r = -.48$ to $+.72$ with a median of $+.28$; the 15 intercorrelations of the 6 "political" items varied from $r = -.86$ to $+.78$ with a median of

+.14. This means that the ecological scores for "social" and "political" had no internal consistency at all. Nevertheless, Bass and Franke computed country indexes by adding country item scores that were negatively correlated (the two items correlated −.86 were *added* in calculating the country "political" index). Their purpose was not to compare individuals; rather, it was to compare nations, as is evident from their correlating their indexes with GNP/capita and other such indexes. For this purpose, individually based indexes simply make no sense. The data can be used for purposes of ecological comparison, but then the items should be divided into ecological clusters. If we do this, *three* clusters emerge, each composed of both "social" and "political" variables. They can be meaningfully interpreted, but not in terms of social and political. I shall refer to them in Chapter 5.[49]

The reverse ecological fallacy is not only a matter of inadequate data treatment. At the root of it is an inadequate research paradigm in which cultures are treated and categorized as if they were individuals.[50] Cultures are not king-size individuals: They are wholes, and their internal logic cannot be understood in the terms used for the personality dynamics of individuals. Eco-logic differs from individual logic. "One point that anthropologists have always made is that aspects of social life which do not seem to be related to each other, actually are related" (Harris, 1981, p. 8). Industrial social psychologists performing studies sometimes try to classify cultures according to Herzberg, Mausner, and Snyderman's (1959) distinction between intrinsic and extrinsic motivation, or according to Maslow's (1970) hierarchy of human needs. For example, an early and pioneering study of managers' values in 14 countries used the Maslow framework (Haire, Ghiselli, & Porter, 1966). Country scores on 11 questionnaire items dealing with needs and satisfactions were condensed into five indexes based on levels in Maslow's hierarchy. In their condensation, the authors did not test whether the items they lumped together were correlated at the ecological level. Had they done this, they would have found that, cross-culturally, the 11 items do *not* group themselves according to Maslow's theory. Within the imposed Maslow framework, their results do not make much sense. Had the authors not been caught in the Maslow paradigm, they might have been able to discover the truly *cultural* dimensions in their data that would have made sense. I will show this in Chapter 5.

Ecological and individual correlations each have their own function. Multilevel analysis, studying the same database simultaneously at two or more levels, can provide crucial insights into the working of social systems.[51] A classic example of multilevel research was published by Meltzer (1963), who, using data from more than 500 U.S. individuals divided over 79 groups, showed that social attitudes of individuals could be better predicted from their group's mean scores on group-related issues than from their own individual scores on these issues. Another example is a study by Lincoln and Zeitz (1980) among 500 employees divided over 20 U.S. social service agencies; they found that the relationship between professional qualification and supervisory duties was positive across individuals but negative across agencies. The latter was due to the fact that the more professional agencies needed less supervision.[52]

One reason the reverse ecological fallacy occurs easily is that studies with data from more than a few societies have been rare. It is not obvious to compute ecological correlations if we have only two or three cases (societies), although even in this case the reverse ecological fallacy can occur or be avoided. For example, when we compare within a population the (sub)cultures of men and women (an ecological $n = 2$), we should mistrust theories that force us to add characteristics or items for which the men/women difference does not carry the same sign. Caught in the Herzberg dichotomy between intrinsic and extrinsic motivation, U.S. researchers have tried to determine whether men are more "intrinsically" interested than women. Such studies have not shown consistent gender differences in intrinsic motivation,[53] but have indicated that some "intrinsic" factors appeal more to women whereas others appeal more to men (see Chapter 6). In such a case, we need a set of concepts other than intrinsic/extrinsic to explain why these female and male subcultures differ.

Ecological dimensions can be detected more clearly when we have data from more (e.g., 10 or 15) societies. This is one reason such multicultural studies are highly desirable.[54]

Avoiding Ethnocentrism

Ethnocentrism has been defined as an "exaggerated tendency to think the characteristics of one's own group or race superior to those of other groups or races" (Drever, 1952, p. 86). Faucheux (1976, p. 309) has compared ethnocentrism with egocentrism. Egocentrism is a phase in the development of a child before it can take the viewpoint of an Other; so Faucheux sees ethnocentrism as a phase in the development of a social science—in the case he refers to, of social psychology. In the history of anthropology there was an ethnocentric phase that was subsequently overcome. Other social science disciplines in which cross-cultural contacts play a less central role than in anthropology are less conscious of their ethnocentrism.

The cultural component in all kinds of behavior is difficult to grasp for people who have always remained embedded in the same cultural environment; it takes a prolonged stay abroad and mixing with other nationals there for us to recognize the numerous and often subtle differences in the ways they and we behave, because that is how our society has programmed us. If I take the train from Rotterdam, Holland, to Brussels, Belgium, I can usually tell the Belgian passengers from the Dutch; most Dutch people greet strangers when entering a small, enclosed space like a train compartment, elevator, or doctor's waiting room, but most Belgians do not.

Ethnocentrism can be very subtle, and it is certainly easier to recognize it in contributions from other cultures than in those from one's own. Let us take an example. In the preceding subsection of this chapter, I referred to Haire et al.'s (1966) study of managers' values in 14 countries, deploring that the authors forced their data into a classification according to Maslow's hierarchy of human needs. Maslow's hierarchy implies that needs appear in an order. Some, like "security," are lower, more basic; when a lower-level need is satisfied, the next higher need takes its place, and so on. Haire et al. ordered their five need categories as follows: security, social, esteem, autonomy, self-actualization. The last of these is Maslow's supreme category, and in Haire et al.'s order it includes three items: personal growth, self-fulfillment, and accomplishment.

Haire et al. (1966) showed the mean scores for 14 countries on the five need categories for need satisfaction (p. 89) and need importance (p. 100). The rank orders of these mean scores are extremely interesting. For three countries (Italy, England, and the United States) the *satisfaction* mean scores appeared exactly in the Maslow order: security most satisfied, self-actualization least. From these, the United States was the one for which the spread between the need category scores was widest. For need *importance* no country followed exactly the Maslow order, but the United States came closest: The rated importance of the five need categories rank correlated with Maslow with rho = .90*.[55] The next highest rank correlations were rho = .80 for Italy and rho = .70 for England and Norway. The direction of the correlation in these countries shows that self-actualization was most important, security least.

Haire et al. never looked at their data in this way, but the data show that if we follow the categorization of Maslow (who was an American), the scores from U.S. managers follow the hierarchy of Maslow's theory more closely than do those from other countries' managers. My interpretation is that this tells us more about Maslow than it

does about the other countries' managers. Maslow categorized and ordered human needs according to the U.S. middle-class culture pattern in which he himself was embedded—he could not have done otherwise. American theories fit American value patterns, and French theories fit French value patterns. If we recognize culture as an all-encompassing influence on our mental programming, this should be no surprise. In taking Maslow's theory and applying it to other cultures, however, Haire et al. were unconsciously and unintentionally ethnocentric, aside from their committing the reverse ecological fallacy, as described earlier.[56]

Ethnocentrism is often present in the instruments used for the collection of data. The literature abounds with "comparative" research by industrial social psychologists and business Ph.D. candidates who took questionnaires designed and pretested on U.S. students or business managers, sometimes translated them, and administered them in other countries. In this case the ethnocentrism starts at the data collection: The questions are only about issues raised by the U.S. designers of the instrument, issues that proved relevant to their test population and for which the American language has words.

To avoid ethnocentrism in data collection, instruments for cross-cultural use should be developed cross-culturally. A good example of how an instrument for cross-cultural use can be developed nonethnocentrically is given by Triandis, Kilty, Shanmugam, Tanaka, and Vassiliou (1972). The purpose of their study was to map cognitive structures in Greece, India, Japan, and the United States. The researchers selected 20 concepts from a list of culturally unspecific words developed empirically around the world by Osgood et al. (1975); these included *freedom, power, respect,* and *wealth.* The 20 concepts were translated into the four languages and back-translated by others for a check. Then the researchers had 100 male students in each country write down three "antecedents" and three "consequents" for each word (antecedents: "If you have . . . then you have FREEDOM"; consequents: "If you have FREEDOM then you have . . . ."). Thus 6,000 antecedents and 6,000 consequents were collected and double-translated into English. The researchers then used the total material to select 30 antecedents and 30 consequents for each of the 20 words, which formed the basis for a series of predetermined choice questionnaires suitable for use in all four countries.

The ethnocentrism still present in this case lies in the decision that such research is worthwhile—in the project design and its coordination and funding. The very idea of cross-cultural research probably reflects a Western universalist value position. This, I'm afraid, we have to live with (it ap-

Exhibit 1.6   The Division of Labor Among the Social Sciences

Level	Total Systems	Aspect Systems		
Society	Anthropology		POLITICAL SCIENCE ↕	ECONOMICS ↕
Category	Sociology	MANAGEMENT ↕		
Group	Social psychology			
Individual	Psychology			

plies to anthropology as well). Taft (1976) puts it as follows:

By the very act of engaging in cross-cultural research, the Western scholar has automatically imposed his own values into his transaction with his subjects, and if he wishes to go through with the exercise, they must accept the element of ethnocentrism that is inherent in this. (p. 327)

Ethnocentrism in sociology and political science is frequent because

most of sociology and political science have been developed by scholars studying their own societies. This means that these scholars are themselves personally caught up in the same symbols which they try to decode. . . . The very concepts and categories of thought which sociologists and political scientists employ in their analysis are themselves part of the very political ideology which they try to understand. (Cohen, 1974, p. 8)

Ethnocentrism is found not only in research design, data collection, and data analysis, but in the dissemination of research results. Articles published in languages other than their own are completely out of most researchers' conceptual worlds; in this respect multilingual Asians and Europeans are better off than most Americans. English-language professional journals usually publish articles following their own implicit research paradigm and style of communication. I have noticed that the comments of American journal reviewers on innocently submitted European manuscripts show embarrassment similar to that found in the comments of French management students on translated American textbooks.

The primitive ethnocentrism of many cross-cultural studies of organizational behavior has been, I believe, one of the main reasons for the lack of advance of the art. We cannot avoid ethnocentrism completely, but we can do a lot better than we do now. Data collection methods can be culturally decentered; even ethnocentrically collected older data can be reanalyzed avoiding ethnocentric or reverse ecological fallacies. Research teams can be expanded to include bi- or multicultural researchers—that is, people who were brought up, lived, and/or worked in more than one cultural environment. I believe the latter is more fruitful than composing teams of monocultural researchers from different cultures, who may get stuck in misunderstandings or passively submit to the chief researcher and his or her paradigms.

The Need for a Multidisciplinary Approach

Cross-cultural studies presuppose a systems approach, by which I mean that any element of the total system called *culture* should be eligible for analysis, regardless of the discipline that usually deals with such elements.

The social sciences have established a division of labor among disciplines more or less as pictured in Exhibit 1.6. There are two ways of cutting the social cake: by level and by aspect. Anthropology, sociology, social psychology, and psychology look at all aspects of social systems, but each only at a given level (at the level of societies, categories of persons, groups, or individuals, respectively). Within the social landscape, anthropology studies the gardens, sociology and social psychology study different kinds of bouquets, and (individual) psychology studies the flowers (see Chapter 8 and G. Hofstede, 1995). Management, political science, and economics look at one particular aspect each (the purposeful organization, the polity, the exchange of goods and services), but they cross levels. The same holds for other application-oriented disciplines. Often a level science and an aspect science need to cooperate in order to resolve a particular problem.

The division of labor among the social sciences has been a practical necessity, but it has had the unfortunate side effect of overspecialization. Adherents of one science communicate with colleagues only; they build a parochial loyalty to their field, even to certain paradigms within their field.[57] Consciousness that the social world exceeds the field of any one science is lost. This situation is perpetuated by the review criteria of journals and by the promotion systems in academic establishments, which seldom reward the free crossing of disciplinary boundaries.

Unwanted effects of overspecialization include compartmentalization, restriction of inputs, restriction of methods, and triviality of outputs. Compartmentalization means that adherents of given fields work in their own departments, read and cite their own journals, attend their own congresses, and follow their own career paths. Restriction of inputs means that inmates of a discipline reject certain types of information. For example, economists trying to help poor countries develop will not consider anthropological information. Restriction of methods means that methods developed within one field will not be used by researchers in others even when those methods would evidently be useful. For example, most anthropologists scorn the use of survey information even where available.[58] Triviality of outputs means that problems are abstracted to such an extent that any practical usefulness of conclusions is excluded. Entire fields survive on solving only the problems generated by the inmates themselves, without demonstrable transfer of ideas to the larger social reality.

At the level of (national) cultures, phenomena on all levels (individuals, groups, organizations, society as a whole) and phenomena related to different aspects (organization, polity, exchange) are potentially relevant. Crossing disciplines is essential for real advances,[59] as I try to demonstrate in this book (Chapter 8 provides a striking example). Those wanting to go multidisciplinary do not need to remain cornered by their initial training. Multidisciplinary bibliographic resources are available: There exist multidisciplinary bibliographies of comparative multisociety studies, and the *Social Science Citation Index* on CD-ROM or on the Internet allows users to search by keywords and combinations of keywords across all social science disciplines.[60]

In writing this book, I have consciously crossed academic borderlines. I will refer in the pages that follow to cross-cultural and cross-national studies from the disciplines of psychology (in particular, cross-cultural psychology), sociology (particularly organization sociology), anthropology, political science, economics, geography, history, comparative law, comparative medicine, international marketing, and "comparative management."[61]

Among students of national societies, a frequent dispute arises between those locating differences primarily in *institutions* and those locating them primarily in culture—that is, in *people's minds*.[62] The former, obviously, is more common among sociologists; the latter is more common among psychologists and anthropologists. The institutions-versus-culture dilemma is, I believe, a nonissue; earlier in this chapter, in explaining Exhibit 1.5, I argued that societal norms shape institutions (family, education systems, politics, legislation), which in their turn reinforce the societal norms. They are the chicken and the egg. Institutions reflect minds and vice versa:

What forms cultures take depends on what individual humans can think, imagine, and learn, as well as on what collective behaviors shape and sustain viable patterns of life in ecosystems. Cultures must be thinkable and learnable as well as livable. (Keesing, 1974, p. 86)

The interdependence of institutions and what is in people's minds has been stressed by social scientists of different disciplines. Sociologists Peter Berger (United States) and Thomas Luckmann (Germany), in *The Social Construction of Reality* (1966) describe a continuous cycle of externalization (creating a social environment), objectivation (attributing to this environment objective status), and internalization (socializing of people's consciousness by this objective social environment). They state: "Man (not, of course, in isolation but in his collectivities) and his social world interact with each other. The product acts back upon the producer" (p. 78).

British anthropologist Mary Douglas writes in *How Institutions Think* (1986) that "institutions cannot have minds of their own." Yet they constrain and mold human cognition: They classify, they confer identity, they remember and forget, they even make life-and-death decisions—as in a hospital. Douglas refers to a "thought collective" or "thought world" behind the institutions that explains how this is possible.

U.S. economists Arthur Denzau and Douglass North, in an article titled "Shared Mental Models: Ideologies and Institutions" (1994), note:

In order to understand decision-making under . . . conditions of uncertainty we must understand the relationships of the mental models that individuals construct to make sense out of the world around them, the ideologies that evolve from such constructions, and the institutions that develop in a society to order interpersonal relationships. (p. 4)

In spite of the striking similarities among the arguments of Berger and Luckmann, Douglas, and Denzau and North—all very prominent in their own disciplines—the amazing fact is that none of these three fundamental treatises refers to the author(s) of the others. The "thought collectives" to which these authors belong are too far apart.[63]

Language and Translation

Language is both the vehicle of most of cross-cultural research and part of its object. Culture, as I use the word in this book, includes language. Language is the most clearly recognizable part of culture and the part that has lent itself most readily to systematic study and theory building. Language is very evidently a learned characteristic (not an inherited one), and people are able to acquire additional languages beyond their first. The first foreign language is most difficult to master; once people have learned to switch their minds between two languages, they can absorb additional ones more easily.[64] Some people have demonstrated that the human mind can master 10 or more languages.

Language is not a neutral vehicle. Our thinking is affected by the categories and words available in our language. This has been recognized at least since Von Humboldt (in mid-19th-century Germany); Sapir and Whorf in the United States in the 1920s and 1930s stated in various ways what has become known as the "Whorfian hypothesis" (Whorf, 1956). One of its formulations is that "observers are not led by the same picture of the universe, unless their linguistic backgrounds are similar or can in some way be calibrated" (Fishman, 1974, p. 65). Differences in categories for thinking about the universe can be found in many fields and are larger for languages that are structurally further apart. Some examples are the way in which the color spectrum is divided (several languages have no separate words for *blue* and *green*), the way various aspects of "time" are distinguished (with consequences for behavior), and the way relatives are classified.[65] Translators of American literature have noted that French and many other modern languages have no adequate equivalent for the English word *achievement*; Japanese has no equivalent for *decision making*.[66]

If equivalents of a concept in another language are missing, one can usually still transfer the desired meaning through circumlocution. People whose language does not distinguish between blue and green are able to discern the two shades, but need additional words to describe this difference.[67] "Languages differ not so much as to what *can* be said in them, but rather as to what is *relatively easily* said in them" (Hockett, 1954, p. 106; quoted in Fishman, 1974, p. 81). Modern languages borrow extensively from each other to avoid the need for circumlocution to express useful concepts for which a given language has no equivalent. Words are borrowed for concrete objects (*sauna* from Finnish, *computer* from English) but also for concepts with a flavor related to the cultural context of the country of origin: *laissez-faire* and *savoir vivre* from French, *verboten* and *Weltanschauung* from German, *business* and *manager* from English.

The problems with the use of language in research about culture start before the actual translation of questions. The researchers and their informants may hold different normative expectations about the use of language. In some cultures and subcultures, being polite to the other person is more important than supplying objectively correct information; in some, respondents will never use *no*. In a comparative experiment conducted in Iran and England, one out of five passersby in Iran pointed a foreigner the way to a place even if that place did not exist; in England nobody did this (Collett & O'Shea, 1976, p. 453).

Few cross-cultural studies can escape the need for the translation of research instruments such as questionnaires and the back-translation of non-precoded responses and analytic conclusions. Such translations are rarely simple, and the wider apart the structures of the two languages, the less simple the task. Where exact equivalents do not exist, "contextual transpositions" (Gasse, 1973) must be found; apparent equivalents sometimes do not express the meaning intended by the researcher. Translators should be familiar not only with both languages but with the context of the material to be translated.[68]

Translators, obviously, must be bilinguals, if not multilinguals. Most bilinguals still have one dominant or preferred language in which they express themselves more easily; this depends, among other things, on the order in which the languages were learned. If at all possible, translators should be chosen such that they translate *into* their preferred language, as it takes greater familiarity with a language to express shades of meaning than to understand them. As soon as we have a preferred language, however, we are culturally not neutral: The translator is the first exponent of the foreign culture in the research process, and the impact of culture on our findings starts in the translator's mind. In translating questions about values for the project this book is about, I found, for the languages that I can read, at least two cases in which translators left out words of the English original in their translations, apparently because they considered them redundant. Subsequent research results showed in both cases, through the answers to other questions, that the values associated with the omitted words were particularly controversial in the translators' countries. In other words, the translators filtered meanings according to their countries' dominant value systems.

The recommended remedy against nonequivalence in translation is back-translation by a second bilingual, comparison of the back-translated text with the original, and resolution of differences through discussion. These steps are certainly a wise safeguard against translation errors, but they are costly and time-consuming and do not detract from the fact that the quality of the translation still depends on the insight and skill of the translators. I prefer a one-shot translation by a gifted translator familiar with the content matter of the document to the result of a back-translation exercise using two or more mediocre bilinguals. A translation may have passed a back-translation filter and still look clumsy in the other language (as questionnaire designers are not necessarily selected for their stylistic abilities, even untranslated questionnaires look clumsy at times).

Research has been done on the equivalence of different language versions of the same questionnaire using bilingual respondents as a test population. Katerberg, Smith, and Hoy (1977) compared answers on questions about the work situation from U.S. residents of Puerto Rican and Cuban origin in English and in Spanish. Differences in scores between the two language versions were small and, for practical purposes, negligible. Several other researchers, however, have found that language did influence answers. Bennett (1977a) administered another questionnaire about the work situation to Filipino managers in both English and Tagalog and to Hong Kong Chinese managers in both English and Chinese. For some questions the scores were independent of language, but for questions on communication and interaction processes, the native-language answers were significantly more favorable than the English-language answers. Bennett concluded that the language evokes a reference group and that, because these people communicate and interact more easily with colleagues speaking their native language than with superiors speaking only English, they give more favorable responses about these issues in their own languages.

In various studies, Michael Bond compared answers on values questionnaires administered to Hong Kong Chinese bilingual students in Chinese versus English. In some cases when using English the students gave more traditionally "Chinese" answers ("ethnic affirmation"; see Yang & Bond, 1980). In some cases the reverse occurred, with answers in English reflecting less

traditional "Chineseness" ("cross-cultural accommodation"). The more important the value was for the respondent, the more strongly the individual would show ethnic affirmation rather than cross-cultural accommodation (Bond & Yang, 1982). When asked to answer "like a typical Hong Kong Chinese" or "like a typical Westerner," the respondents differentiated more between the two when answering in Chinese than when answering in English (Bond, 1983). Bond confirmed that the language evokes a reference group: In Chinese, bilinguals answer more as if communicating with other Chinese.[69]

Marin, Triandis, Betancourt, and Kashima (1983) found many significant differences in the answers of bilingual Spanish/English college students in California, dependent on the questionnaire language, but they explain these by "social desirability" rather than by ethnic affirmation. Hofstede and Vunderink (1994) administered questionnaires on the importance of 22 work goals to bilingual Dutch students, at random either in an English or in a Dutch version. Respondents differentiated much more among the goals when answering in their native Dutch than when answering in English. Also, there were considerable differences in the rank orders of some goals (10 places for "living area"—more important when in Dutch). The words chosen in Dutch, although formally correctly translated, had evoked emotional meanings in the respondents that were different from those evoked by the English words.

The contradictory results of the studies by Katerberg et al. (1977) versus the others can be attributed to the fact that Katerberg et al.'s subjects lived in an English-speaking environment, had to use English all day, and were probably more intimately familiar with it than were the subjects of the other studies, who lived in their native countries. The fact that Marin et al. (1983) in a similar case found more differences suggests that the questionnaire content and possibly the quality of the translations may also have played a role.

For the practice of cross-cultural research, the preceding paragraphs imply that translation is a source of error. The error can be reduced through the careful selection of translators and the use of a back-translation procedure, but the latter is no guarantee of a perfect translation. I might add that it helps considerably if the researcher is multilingual. For a deeper understanding of a foreign culture and for the avoidance of ethnocentric blunders, some familiarity with the language is indispensable. Anthropologists nowadays would hardly dare to study a tribe without some mastery of its language. Something can also be done in the composition of the questionnaire. Questions destined for translation should be plain and unimaginative, free of home-country local color. The questionnaire should contain a certain amount of redundancy, so that key issues are approached from several angles and a weak translation of one question does not spoil all information on the issue.

Questionnaire translations can be tested in ways other than through back-translations. A careful check by a panel of bilingual readers familiar with the content matter is less time-consuming and may be as effective. More time-consuming but revealing is a separate correlation and/or factor analysis of individual answers on pretest (or even of final) data for each language version and a comparison of the patterns of correlations found. Convergences and divergences between factor structures not only show where meanings have been similar or different but often suggest what other meanings were attributed. However, samples of respondents in the different languages should be matched on nonlinguistic criteria (occupation, age, gender) because these, too, affect the meanings of answers.[70]

Finally, translation errors are randomized when the number of languages used is increased. One bad translation may invalidate a 2-country study, but it is unlikely that systematic translation errors will affect the conclusions of a 53-country, 20-language study such as the one described in this book. Language, in this case, becomes a variable in the analysis and not just a source of bias.

Matching Samples: Functional Equivalence

Anthropologists have studied nonliterate cultures on the basis of small samples of informants studied in great depth. In this case,

the validity of the sample depends not so much on the number of cases as upon the proper specification of the informant, so that he or she can be accurately placed, in terms of a very large number of variables: Age, gender, order of birth, family background, life-experience, temperamental tendencies (such as optimism, habit of exaggeration, etc.), political and religious position, exact situation relationship to the investigator, configurational relationship to every other informant, and so forth. Within this very extensive degree of specification, each informant is studied as a perfect example, an organic representation of his complete cultural experience. (Mead, 1962b, pp. 408-409)

From such in-depth sample studies, anthropologists draw conclusions about a culture as a whole—a process that inevitably contains a large dose of subjectivity. Anthropologists' comparisons between cultures are based on aspects of these inferred wholes.

Modern nations are too complex and subculturally heterogeneous for their cultures to be determined in this way. In the present book I therefore use the results of survey studies of values and of measurable data on the society level to infer and compare dominant national culture traits of a large number of modern nations. Within these nations, certain components of the mental software of people are specific to groups or categories—shared by people of, for example, the same educational level, socioeconomic status, occupation, gender, or age group. When we compare cultural aspects of nations, we should try to match for such categories; it is obviously not very meaningful to compare Spanish nurses with Swedish policemen. Then there may be linguistic, regional, tribal, ethnic, religious, or caste cleavages within nations; some nations are less homogeneous than others in this respect.[71] Obviously, students of culture should be aware of such cleavages, which can make data nonrepresentative for the nation as a whole.

Depending on the nature of the characteristics we want to compare, we can compose matched samples of individuals, situations, institutions (such as families), or organizations. An example of the last of these is a study about hierarchy conducted by Tannenbaum, Kavcic, Rosner, Vianello, and Wieser (1974) that covered 10 industrial companies, matched for size and product, in each of five countries.

One strategy for matching is to make the samples very broad, so that subcultural differences are randomized out. We find this in comparisons of the results of public opinion polls using representative samples of national populations. The opposite strategy is to make the samples very narrow, so that we draw from similar subcultures, but in different countries. We can compare Spanish nurses with Swedish nurses, or Spanish policemen with Swedish policemen. In the case of such narrow samples, we have to be careful about generalizing to a nation as a whole: Are police corps and hospitals functionally equivalent in both nations? That is, do they fulfill the same functions in society? A more solid research strategy, if we have to use narrow samples, is to take several from different parts of society. With a fourfold sample of Spanish and Swedish nurses and Spanish and Swedish policemen, we can test not only the nationality effect but also the occupation effect (nurses versus policemen) and the possible interaction between the two, which can give clues as to functional equivalence. The quality of the matching of narrow samples often can be proven only ex post facto: If the differences we find between cultures in one sample set are confirmed by those found by others in other matched samples, our matching was adequate.

The practical problems involved in getting access to matched samples in different cultures can be enormous, and researchers have to accept compromises in order to obtain data at all. However, the problems of both matching and access are reduced for organizations that are by their very nature multisocietal; the number of such organizations is increasing in the modern world. Possibilities are available in international professional associations, international schools and training centers, and national organizations employing personnel of different nationalities,[72] or, as in the present book, multinational business corporations. The fact that these organizations have similarly structured subsidiaries in many countries provides matched settings in which many factors are equal except the nationality of the actors. A common objection against the study of subsidiaries of multinational corporations is that these are atypical for their countries. This is true; they are just as atypical as samples of policemen or samples of nurses. Studying subsidiaries of multinational corporations represents a *narrow-sample* strategy, but with the advantage that the functional equivalence of the samples is clear. That these samples are atypical does not matter as long as they are atypical in the same way from one country to another. Multinational corporations have organizational cultures of their own; to the extent that these reduce the variability in the data from one country to another, the remaining variability will be a conservative estimate of the true variability among countries, which only speaks in favor of this setting for cross-cultural research.

Modal and Marginal Phenomena

Differences among societies cannot be studied only in what is modal in each society; we can also learn from comparisons of marginal phenomena. Focusing on what is modal has been the concern of social psychologists and sociologists. Anthropologists are more naturally attracted to what is marginal or unique. Some anthropologists have shed their discipline's predilection for nonliterate societies and include modern industrial societies in their field of research. Bovenkerk and Brunt (1976) have claimed that the special vocation of the anthropologist in modern society is to highlight society's marginal phenomena. Some of these can characterize a society more clearly than modal phenomena. Ever since Durkheim (1897/1930), suicide statistics have been used to draw conclusions about societies as a whole, even though only a marginal fraction of people actually take their own lives.

There is a good statistical reason that extreme phenomena differentiate more between cultures than do modal ones; this is pictured schematically in Exhibit 1.7. Let us assume a characteristic "x" (of individuals, institutions, or organizations) that is normally distributed across the nation, but

with a cultural difference between society a and society b, so that the two normal distributions do not quite overlap. The shift in Exhibit 1.7 is chosen of the size σ, or equal to the within-country standard deviations. For an example, let us assume that we have measured at the individual level the characteristic "aggressiveness." The percentage of individuals with an aggressiveness level beyond the common average p in this case would be 30.9 in society a and 69.1 in society b, a ratio between the two societies of 2.2. However, the percentage with an aggressiveness level beyond an extreme value q, representing a distance of 2σ from the mode of b and 3σ from the mode of a, would occur in .14% of individuals in society a but in 2.27% in society b, a ratio between the two societies of 16.8, or eight times as large as the ratio of those beyond level p. If an aggressiveness level beyond q is likely to lead to individually committed criminal offenses, such offenses are 16.8 times as likely to occur in society b. For collective phenomena, the difference becomes even larger. Suppose that a criminal gang is likely to be created where two persons with an aggressiveness level beyond q meet. This is $16.8^2 = 282$ times more likely to occur in society b than in society a.

This example is, of course, grossly oversimplified, but it shows how small modal differences between societies can become manifest in large differences in marginal phenomena. The study of the marginal and unique in society is therefore justified by more than curiosity alone.

Dimensions of Culture

The Specific and the General

The comparison of cultures presupposes that there is something to be compared—that each culture is not so unique that any parallel with another culture is meaningless. Throughout the history of the study of culture there has been a dispute between those stressing the unique aspects and those stressing the comparable aspects. The first hold that "you cannot compare apples and oranges," whereas the second argue that apples and oranges are both fruits and can be compared on a multitude of aspects, such as price, weight, color, nutritive value, and durability. The selection of these aspects obviously requires an a priori theory about what is important in fruits.

The distinction between the unique and the comparable, the specific and the general, was made by Wilhelm Windelband in late-19th-century Germany when he contrasted "idiographic" with "nomothetic" styles of scientific inquiry. The idiographic style was mainly found in "historical" disciplines looking for wholes or *Ges-*

Exhibit 1.7. Ratios Between the Frequencies in Two Societies of Those Exceeding an Average and an Extreme Value of a Normally Distributed, Culturally Influenced Characteristic

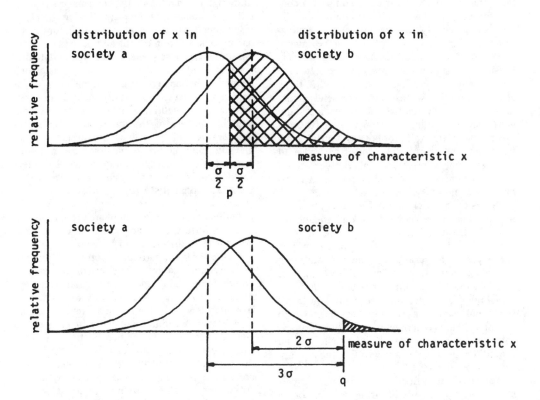

talten, unique configurations of events, conditions, or developments; the nomothetic style, mainly in natural sciences looking for general laws or *Gesetze* (Lammers, 1976, p. 31). In their subsequent development, the social sciences have moved between both styles. The choice between the two styles has been called the "Malinovskian dilemma" (Berry, 1969, p. 120) after Bronislaw Malinovski, who introduced functionalism in anthropology in the 1920s. Functionalism stresses the purposive nature of institutions in society, but the purpose is derived from the particular culture of that society, which is a unique whole. Therefore, institutions can be understood only in terms of their own cultures; functional equivalence with institutions in other societies cannot be proven, and, according to Malinovski, "cross-cultural comparison of institutions is essentially a false enterprise, for we are comparing incomparables" (Goldschmidt, 1966, p. 8; quoted in Berry, 1969, p. 120).

Similar points of view, stressing the need for understanding of social systems from the inside and through the definitions of their members, have been labeled by others *ethnoscience* and *ethnomethodology.*[73] Although few authors take the extreme position attributed to Malinowski, there is a wide range of points of view as to the importance of understanding from within versus measuring from outside.

Although the terms *idiographic* and *nomothetic* are probably better known among sociologists, cross-cultural psychologists have adopted another couple of words that cover more or less the same distinction: *emic* and *etic*. These terms were introduced into anthropology in the 1960s by the linguist Kenneth Pike.[74] In linguistics, a distinction is made between phonemic and phonetic classification. The phonetic classification is universal and allows the characterization of any sound in any language. In a particular language, only certain sound units are actually used; these are called phonemes, and in combination with other phonemes they are the carriers of meaning. Thus the phonemic is the specific and the phonetic is the general. The suffixes *-emic* and *-etic* have been promoted to independent terms in anthropology for distinguishing the study of unique and specific wholes from the application of general, polycultural classification schemes.

The fact of engaging in a comparative study of culture at all presupposes at least an etic point of departure. Berry (1990, p. 93) has suggested a three-step approach that tries to combine a concern for the general with a concern for the specific and that can be applied where functional equivalence of behaviors in two cultures can be demonstrated (or, I would add, reasonably assumed): (1) Existing descriptive categories and concepts are applied tentatively, as an imposed etic; (2) these are then modified so that they represent an adequate emic description from within each system; and (3) shared categories can then be used to build up new categories valid for both systems as a derived etic, and can be expanded if desired until they constitute a universal. This derived etic or universal is used as the basis for new measurement instruments and techniques.

Lammers and Hickson (1979c, p. 11) have remarked that in the (nomothetic-etic) search for general classification schemes, some authors search for "lawlike theories" whereas others search for "configurations." The first approach aims at determining variables that relate to other variables in a lawlike way; the second aims at establishing ideal types that are wholes in themselves and that the cases studied can be shown to resemble. "Pure" nomothetes will follow the variables approach, whereas those with an inclination toward the idiographic side will find the type approach more useful.

One's position or flexibility in the specific-versus-general spectrum will strongly affect one's choice of data treatment. Pure idiographers will probably shy away from quantitative data and the use of statistics. Those collecting comparative data that lend themselves to statistical analysis will be attracted to different statistical methods according to their degree of nomotheticity. A greater idiographic concern will express itself in a focus on relations between variables *within* cultures, followed by a comparison of the patterns found from one culture to another; this can be used for a type approach. Looking at the variances and covariances of variables *between* cultures is a step more toward the nomothetic side: It presupposes data on a greater number of cultures and means a study of ecological correlations as described earlier in this chapter.[75] Matrices of ecological correlations between variables can be used again for a type approach through some form of Q-factor or cluster analysis that shows which cultures have similar ecological correlations. Probably the most nomothetic data treatment is to use matrices of ecological correlations for a factor analysis or similar multivariate technique subsuming the original variables into dimensions that can enter laws of the greatest generality and that are at the same time least sensitive to the unique-

ness of each culture. This is the approach I take in this book.

The ideal study of culture would combine idiographic and nomothetic, emic and etic, qualitative and quantitative elements. Unfortunately, a researcher has to make choices, if only for practical reasons. The nomothetic approach in the present study is a consequence of the type of data that became available. My world-scale dimensions cannot do justice to the profound meanings of local practices in the countries;[76] on the other hand, they have the potential of making students of local situations aware of the universality of certain problems to which the local situation represents one solution. The idiographic element in my research is that I had frequently visited and interacted intensively with a fair number of the participating national IBM subsidiaries during the organization of the first survey cycle. My interpretations of the scores found are often based on personal observations and profound discussions with locals of different ranks.

A choice for one particular approach should not mean a condemnation of the alternatives. I admire other, more idiographic and qualitative approaches, such as d'Iribarne's (1989) comparative interview study in three manufacturing plants of a French aluminum company in France, the Netherlands, and the United States.[77] Studies like his contribute greatly to our understanding of the rationale behind the scores I found. In the cross-organizational study conducted by the Institute for Research on Intercultural Cooperation (IRIC) described in Chapter 8, we deliberately balanced idiographic and nomothetic elements; but unlike in the cross-national IBM study, this was a project we could shape to suit our purposes right from the start. The idiographic and nomothetic represent two sides of the same coin, two ways of finding out about the same reality: They are both equally necessary and complementary. The only thing I condemn is the absolutist claim, not uncommon among anthropologists, that a particular idiographic approach is the only true one.

Searching for Dimensions of Culture

In the process of comparing phenomena, similarity and differences are two sides of the same coin; one presupposes the other. Nevertheless, research designs usually favor either the search for similarities or the search for differences. The publication of Lammers and Hickson's (1979b) edited volume signaled a bias either way in comparative studies of organizations. Some studies want to show that different organizations are in reality "brothers under the skin"; other studies want to

Exhibit 1.8.   Four Available Research Strategies for Comparative Multisociety Studies

	Focus on Similarities Between Societies	Focus on Differences Between Societies
Concerned With Micro-Level Variables Within Societies— Culture as Black Box	1 Prove universality of micro-level laws	2 Illustrate uniqueness of each society
Concerned With Ecological Variables Between Societies— Culture Specific	3 Determine types or subsets of societies	4 Determine dimensions of societies and macro-level laws

show that superficially similar organizations are really "birds of a *different* feather." The predilection for one or the other is ideologically related to the previously described choice between the general and the specific: Who looks for brothers under the skin looks for the general; who is convinced of specificity finds birds of a different feather.

The distinction between a focus on similarities and a focus on differences can be fruitfully combined with the distinction between levels of analysis, as discussed earlier in this chapter, into a fourfold classification of research strategies. Although this classification can be extended to other types of comparative studies as well, I will apply it only to the comparison of phenomena in different societies. These phenomena can be behaviors of individuals or situations, institutions, or organizations. The classification is drawn in Exhibit 1.8.[78]

In cells 1 and 2 of Exhibit 1.8 we find those studies that focus on either similarities or differences among societies but that are concerned with micro-level variables and their relationships, measured *within* societies. In cell 1 we find studies with a nomothetic-etic orientation, which try to prove the universality of micro-level laws. Examples are the study of "managerial thinking" in 14 countries by Haire et al. (1966) and the extensions to other countries of the "Aston" studies about the relationship between organization structure and context that tried to confirm the "culture-free thesis" (Hickson, Hinings, McMillan, & Schwitter, 1974; see Chapter 3). In cell 2 we find studies with a more idiographic-emic orientation, which, through showing differences among societies, illustrate the uniqueness of each. This includes field studies by anthropologists that are only implicitly comparative, but also explicitly comparative studies such as those of Osgood et al. (1975) about the different affective meanings of words in different cultures and studies of organi-

zations in the "Aston" tradition aimed at refuting the "culture-free" thesis (Child & Kieser, 1979). Lammers and Hickson's "brothers under the skin" and "birds of a different feather" approaches correspond to cells 1 and 2, respectively.

Studies in cells 1 and 2 go across cultures, but without necessarily specifying what "culture" stands for. Culture is often treated in these studies as a "black box"; we know the box is there, but not what it contains. In cell 1 we hope it can be proven to make no difference, and then it does not matter what is in the black box; in cell 2 we hope it does matter, but we argue that our black box is a Pandora's box containing so much that it is impossible to be more specific. In cells 1 and 2 we deal with societies as names, not as variables; and as "names" they are "residua of variables that influence the phenomenon being explained but have not yet been considered" (Przeworski & Teune, 1970, p. 29)—or, I would add, are too complex to be considered.

In cells 3 and 4 we find studies that focus on either similarities or differences among societies on the basis of ecological variables and their relationships—that is, variables measured at the level of societies. In cell 3 we find studies that use ecological variables to determine types or subsets of cultures that are similar among themselves but differ from other types or subsets. For example, Adelman and Morris (1967) used factor analysis of a matrix of 41 ecological variables for 74 developing nations, but they created subsets of nations of lowest, intermediate, and high development levels. Russett (1968) used data from the *World Handbook of Political and Social Indicators,* the first edition of which he edited, to cluster countries through a Q-analysis. He arrived at an Afro-Asian, Western, Latin American, and Eastern European cluster. In cell 4, finally, we find studies concerned with determining dimensions of societies and laws at the level of societal variables, identifying the variables that can replace the names of societies in our analysis. Lammers (1976) has called cell 4 strategies "intercultural," as opposed to cell 1 strategies, which are "cross-cultural."

Przeworski and Teune (1970, pp. 31 ff.), writing from a political science background, were mainly concerned with the distinction between cell 1 and cell 4 studies. They normatively suggested for cell 1 studies a "most different systems design": If we want to prove universality of micro-level laws, it is more meaningful to test them in Sweden, Japan, and Zambia than in Sweden, Denmark, and Norway. For cell 4 studies they suggested a "most similar systems design": Taking societies that are similar in many respects except a few, which enables us to see more clearly the differences to which those few societal aspects are related. If we are interested in which societal influences affect suicide rates, it is meaningful to study Denmark, Sweden, and Norway, which are similar in many respects but of which the last has a suicide rate strikingly lower than the other two (Rotterstøl, 1975).

Cell 1 studies are most vulnerable to ethnocentricity. This is less the case for other cells; cells 2 and 3 studies are by their nature "polycentric," and cell 4 studies are "geocentric." [79] In order to avoid the inherent danger of ethnocentricity in cell 1 studies, we have to expand our strategy with cell 2 and cell 4 methods to focus on differences even if what we want to prove is similarities—that is, play the devil's advocate.[80] Lammers (1976, p. 37) recommends "loading the dice" as much as possible against the thesis that our relevant propositions are culture-free. Przeworski and Teune's "most different systems design" for cell 1 is also a way of playing devil's advocate.

The present book deals with dimensions of national culture and therefore clearly represents a cell 4 approach. The number of societies covered—more than 50—is large enough to include similar as well as different ones and to earn for the research the label *geocentric*.

Dimensions Versus Typologies

The scores for each country on one dimension can be pictured as points along a line. For two dimensions at a time, they become points in a plot. For three dimensions, they can be imagined as points in space. For four or five dimensions, they become difficult to imagine. This is a disadvantage of a dimensional model. Another way of picturing differences among countries (or other social systems) is through *typologies*. A typology describes a number of ideal types, each of them

easy to imagine.[81] The division of countries into the First, Second, and Third Worlds is such a typology. A more sophisticated example is found in the work of Todd (1983), who divides the cultures of the world into eight types according to the family structures traditionally prevailing in them. Four of these types, according to Todd, occur in Europe. Todd's thesis is that these historically preserved family structures explain the success of particular types of political ideologies in different nations (see Chapter 5).

Whereas typologies are easier to grasp than dimensions, they are problematic in empirical research. Real cases seldom fully correspond to one single ideal type. Most cases are hybrids, and arbitrary rules have to be made for classifying them as belonging to one of the types. With a dimensions model, in contrast, cases can always be scored unambiguously. On the basis of their dimension scores, cases can be empirically sorted *afterward* into clusters with similar scores. These clusters then form an empirical typology. The more than 50 countries in the IBM study could on the basis of their four dimension scores be sorted into 12 such clusters (see Exhibit 2.8).

In practice, typologies and dimensional models are complementary. Dimensional models are preferable for research and typologies for teaching purposes. In this book I use a kind of typology approach for explaining each of the five dimensions. For every separate dimension, I describe the two opposite extremes, which can be seen as ideal types. Some of the dimensions are subsequently taken two by two, which creates four ideal types. However, the country scores on the dimensions locate most real cases somewhere in between the extremes.

Five Basic Problems
of National Societies

In an article first published in 1952, U.S. anthropologist Clyde Kluckhohn (1952/1962) argued that there should be universal categories of culture:

> In principle . . . there is a generalized framework that underlies the more apparent and striking facts of cultural relativity. All cultures constitute so many somewhat distinct answers to essentially the same questions posed by human biology and by the generalities of the human situation. . . . Every society's patterns for living must provide approved and sanctioned ways for dealing with such universal circumstances as the existence of two sexes; the helplessness of infants; the need for satisfaction of the elementary biological require-

ments such as food, warmth, and sex; the presence of individuals of different ages and of differing physical and other capacities. (pp. 317-318)

The kind of framework Kluckhohn described must consist of empirically verifiable, more or less independent dimensions on which cultures can be meaningfully ordered.

This book is based on a large research project into differences in national culture among matched samples of business employees—the IBM study—across more than 50 countries, as well as a series of follow-up studies on other samples. These studies together identified five independent dimensions of national culture differences, each rooted in a basic problem with which all societies have to cope, but on which their answers vary. The dimensions, which I describe extensively in Chapters 3 through 7, are as follows:

1. *Power distance,* which is related to the different solutions to the basic problem of human inequality

2. *Uncertainty avoidance,* which is related to the level of stress in a society in the face of an unknown future

3. *Individualism* versus *collectivism,* which is related to the integration of individuals into primary groups

4. *Masculinity* versus *femininity,* which is related to the division of emotional roles between men and women

5. *Long-term* versus *short-term orientation,* which is related to the choice of focus for people's efforts: the future or the present

These five dimensions were empirically found and validated, and each country could be positioned on the scale represented by each dimension. Moreover, the dimensions were statistically distinct and occurred in all possible combinations, although some combinations were more frequent than others.

Other Dimensions of Culture
in the Literature: Theory Based

Many authors in the second half of the 20th century speculated about the nature of the basic problems of societies that present distinct dimensions of culture. For example, Aberle, Cohen, Davis, Levy, and Sutton (1950) listed nine "functional prerequisites of a society" that extend Kluckhohn's list: (1) adequate physical and social relationships with the environment; (2) role differentiation according to age, gender, and hierarchy; (3) communication; (4) shared knowledge, be-

liefs, and rules of logical thinking; (5) shared goals; (6) normative regulation of means toward these goals; (7) regulation of affective expression; (8) socialization of new members; and (9) effective control of disruptive forms of behavior.[82] These are conceptual categories, not supported by empirical research, but some relate conceptually to some of my empirical dimensions: Category 2 relates to power distance and masculinity, categories 7 and 9 relate to uncertainty avoidance, and category 8 relates to individualism.

The most common dimension used for ordering societies is their degree of economic evolution or modernity. A one-dimensional ordering of societies from traditional to modern fit well with 19th- and 20th-century "evolutionism" and belief in progress. U.S. anthropologist Naroll (1970, pp. 1242 ff.) reviewed more than 150 comparative anthropological studies of primitive societies and, quoting archaeological as well as current evidence, identified a number of characteristics in the ecology and the institutions of societies that evolve together:

- The command of the environment from weak to strong
- Occupational specialization from generalists to specialists
- Organizations from simple to complex
- Population patterns from rural to urban
- Distribution of goods from wealth sharing to wealth hoarding
- Leadership from consensual to authoritative
- Behavior of elites from responsible to exploitative
- The function of war from vengeance to political[83]

U.S. anthropologist Driver (1973, pp. 356 ff.) added to this list increases in population density, gross national or tribal product, knowledge, and the number of words in the language (since the advent of writing). U.S. anthropologists Lomax and Berkowitz (1972), combining data from Murdock's World Ethnographic Sample out of the Human Relations Area Files for 148 cultures with an analysis of song patterns in these cultures ("cantometrics"), built a taxonomy for the evolution of traditional cultures in which the main factor increasing monotonically with evolution was differentiation. Differentiation meant control of the environment through an increased complexity of society. U.S. sociologist Marsh (1967, pp. 329 ff.) constructed a single "Index of Differentiation" that ordered societies from primitive to differentiated, which order he computed for 467 primitive societies (with data from Murdock's World Ethnographic Sample) and for 114 contemporary nations.[84]

Edward Hall (1976) divided cultures according to their ways of communicating, into high and low context:

A high-context (HC) communication or message is one in which most of the information is either in the physical context or internalized in the person, while very little is in the coded, explicit, transmitted part of the message. A low-context (LC) communication is just the opposite: i.e., the mass of the information is vested in the implicit code. (p. 91)

In practice, HC communication is more often found in traditional cultures and LC communication in modern cultures, so that the HC/LC distinction overlaps at least partly with the traditional/modern distinction. In Chapter 5 we will see that it also overlaps with collectivism versus individualism.

There can be little doubt that economic evolution (modernity, differentiation) is an important dimension that is bound to be reflected in the evolution of societal norms, along the lines pictured in Exhibit 1.5. On the other hand, there is no reason economic and technological evolution should suppress cultural variety. In fact, we have seen in the second half of the 20th century an increasing tendency among former colonies to affirm their unique cultural identities against the inroads made by Western-type modernization. After political independence and a largely unsuccessful struggle for economic independence, the focus is now on cultural independence; the new nations want to be both modern *and* culturally themselves.[85] This implies that there are dimensions of culture not related to economic evolution.

One *multidimensional* classification has been offered by U.S. sociologists Parsons and Shils (1951, p. 77) in their "general theory of action." They claimed that all human action is determined by five "pattern variables," which they saw as choices between pairs of alternatives (the explanations in parentheses below are mine):

1. Affectivity (need gratification) versus affective neutrality (restraint of impulses)
2. Self-orientation versus collectivity-orientation[86]
3. Universalism (applying general standards) versus particularism (taking particular relationships into account)
4. Ascription (judging others by who they are) versus achievement (judging others by what they do)
5. Specificity (limiting relations to others to specific spheres) versus diffuseness (no prior limitations to nature of relations)

Parsons and Shils asserted that these choices are present at the individual (personality) level, at the social system (group or organization) level, and at the cultural (normative) level. They did not take into account that different variables could operate at different levels.

Parsons (1951, pp. 182 ff.) used variables 3 and 4 above (universalism/particularism and ascription/achievement) to create a fourfold taxonomy of countries in which he placed China, Germany, Latin America, and the United States. In a later publication, Parsons (1977, p. 14) suggested that the evolution of societies replaces particularism with universalism and ascription with achievement. This would mean that evolution will eventually push all societies to join the United States in the universalist/achievement corner of Parsons's taxonomy. However, Parsons was less outspoken about the relationship between evolution and the other pattern variables, and acknowledged that throughout evolution, cultural systems might continue to differ (pp. 235, 237).

Another multidimensional classification of cultures was proposed by U.S. anthropologists Florence Kluckhohn and Fred Strodtbeck (1961, p. 12) on the basis of a field study in five geographically close, small communities in the southwestern United States: Mormons, Spanish Americans, Texans, Navaho Indians, and Zuni Indians. They distinguished the communities on the following value orientations:

1. An evaluation of human nature (evil/mixed/good)
2. The relationship of man to the surrounding natural environment (subjugation/harmony/mastery)
3. The orientation in time (toward past/present/future)
4. The orientation toward activity (being/being in becoming/doing)
5. Relationships among people (lineality [i.e., hierarchically ordered positions]/collaterality [i.e., group relationships]/individualism)

To take the relationship orientation as an example, Kluckhohn and Strodtbeck found Texans and Mormons to value individualism over collaterality over lineality, but with greater stress on individualism for the Texans; Spanish Americans stressed individualism over lineality over collaterality; both groups of Indians stressed collaterality over lineality over individualism. The difference between Kluckhohn and Strodtbeck's value orientations and Parsons and Shils's pattern variables is that the former formulated their orientations around basic human problems that allow different solutions; these solutions then direct the actions. The latter merely described the dominant modes of action.

British anthropologist Mary Douglas (1973a) proposed a two-dimensional ordering of "cosmologies" (ways of looking at the world): (1) "group" or inclusion (the claim of groups over members) and (2) "grid" or classification (the degree to which interaction is subject to rules). Douglas saw these as relating to a wide variety of beliefs and social actions: views of nature, traveling, spatial arrangements, gardening, cookery, medicine, the meaning of time, age, history, sickness, and justice. Douglas herself applied the "grid" and "group" dimensions on the level of subcultures of groups and categories of people rather than on the level of national cultures, but she seemed to imply that the same dimensions are applicable to any level of aggregation.[87]

Some U.S. psychologists have looked for structure in culture-specific aspects of individuals' cognition. Foa and Foa (1974) explored different ways of structuring "the mind" in response to anthropological studies, including the ones cited above. Fiske (1992) went a step further in proposing four "elementary forms of sociability" that occur within and across cultures: (1) communal sharing, (2) authority ranking, (3) equality matching, and (4) market pricing. Each has its own set of implications for a variety of domains, such as reciprocal exchange, distributive justice, work, meaning of time, decision making, constitution of groups, motivation, aggression, and conflict. With a little fantasy, one could relate forms 2 and 3 to, respectively, large and small power distance (see Chapter 3), and forms 1 and 4 to, respectively, collectivism and individualism (see Chapter 5). Fiske's theory criticized an implicit assumption in Western psychology that all humans deep inside are asocial individualists. This is still a psychologist's approach in that it explains society from what is in the individual's mind; it does not deal with other levels of analysis. I did not find out whether Fiske meant his "elementary forms" to be dimensions or mutually exclusive ideal types.[88]

The two- or more-dimensional classifications above represent subjective reflective attempts to order a complex reality. Each is strongly colored by the subjective choices of its author(s). The classifications show some overlap, but their lack of clarity about and mixing of levels of analysis (individual-group-culture) is a severe methodological weakness (see the subsection above on changing the level of analysis). More helpful than these subjective classifications, I find, is the "intersubjective" approach taken by Inkeles and Levinson. In an extensive 1954 review article

about national character and modal personality, these authors summarized a large number of studies. What I have labeled *dimensions* they called "standard analytic issues." They proposed

> to concentrate, for purposes of comparative analysis, on a limited number of psychological issues . . . that meet at least the following criteria. First, they should be found in adults universally, as a function both of maturational potentials common to man and of socio-cultural characteristics common to human societies. Second, the manner in which they are handled should have functional significance for the individual personality as well as for the social system. (Inkeles & Levinson, 1954/1997, p. 44)

From the literature Inkeles and Levinson distilled three standard analytic issues that meet these criteria:

1. Relation to authority
2. Conception of self, including the individual's concepts of masculinity and femininity
3. Primary dilemmas or conflicts and ways of dealing with them, including the control of aggression and the expression versus inhibition of affect

Inkeles and Levinson's standard analytic issues are amazingly similar to my first four empirical dimensions. Power distance relates to the first, uncertainty avoidance to the third, and both individualism and masculinity relate to the second standard analytic issue.

Other Dimensions of Culture in the Literature: Empirical

Studies using statistical methods for determining the relationship among quantified variables across a number of cultures have been called *hologeistic*.[89] Hologeistic data matrices, showing the values of a number of variables for a number of cultures, are eminently suitable for the statistical determination of underlying dimensions. The most common method used for this purpose is factor analysis; more modern methods, which sometimes need fewer assumptions about the characteristics of the data, are cluster analysis, multidimensional scaling, and smallest-space analysis. All of these are methods of data reduction: They replace a number of original variables with a smaller number of new variables (called *factors* in the case of factor analysis) that explain as much of the total variance in the original matrix as possible in as few factors as possible.

Apart from the interpretation of the factors, which is subjective, there are three more arbitrary decisions that the user of factor analysis and similar techniques has to make. The first involves which variables and cases to include in the analysis and which to leave out. This is vital; the "garbage in, garbage out" rule applies entirely. If we include strongly intercorrelated trivial variables in our analysis, we will find strong but trivial factors. From the point of view of interpretation, the strength of a factor (its percentage of variance explained) tells nothing about its importance unless we are sure that the variables put in were important and representative of the phenomenon we wanted to study. The other two arbitrary decisions concern the choice of the number of factors to be retained and, in the case of classic factor analysis, whether to look for mutually independent factors ("orthogonal rotation") or for mutually correlated factors ("oblique rotation"). Often users will run an analysis trying several numbers of factors in succession in order to find the one for which factors are most clearly interpretable.[90]

In hologeistic studies one analyzes data at the level of cultures or societies; if one uses factor analysis, this is an *ecological* factor analysis. Earlier in this chapter we saw that correlations among variables across individuals usually differ from correlations of the mean scores of the same variables across countries. A factor analysis starts from a correlation matrix; therefore, ecological (country-level) factors are different from individual factors. For factor analysis of scores produced by individuals, statistical textbooks caution that the number of cases should be considerably larger than the numbers of variables (although different authors differ about how much larger; see Gorsuch, 1983, p. 332). If the number of cases is too small, factor structures become unstable: One single case can unduly affect the structure. However, this caution against small numbers of cases does not apply in ecological factor analysis, where the stability of the results is not determined by the number of aggregate cases, but by the number of individuals whose scores were aggregated into these cases (Hofstede, Neuijen, Ohayv, & Sanders, 1990). In ecological factor analysis one may even start from a matrix with fewer cases than variables. Of course, the number of *factors* can never exceed the number of cases.

From the extensive and mostly American literature of studies using factor analysis on ecological data, I shall limit myself to those using modern nations as units of analysis (cases) and that have been published in easily accessible sources. Such studies can be divided into two types: catchall studies and those dealing with variables selected according to a specific theoretical criterion. By *catchall*, I mean that these studies used all kinds

of variables that happened to be available, without a recognizable theoretical framework guiding their choice. I shall first discuss these studies.

A number of catchall factor-analytic studies of ecological variables have been carried out in the United States. The foundation for this type of analysis was laid by psychologist Cattell, who used factor analysis extensively in the development of self-report tests of personality (see Cattell, 1949; Cattell, Breul, & Hartman, 1952; Cattell & Gorsuch, 1965).[91] Cattell analyzed 48 and more country-level variables for 40 and more countries, dealing with geographic and demographic aspects and the supposed races of inhabitants; historical and political aspects; social, legal, and religious aspects; and economical, medical, and "elite" aspects, such as the number of Nobel Prizes. He looked for dimensions among nations of what he labeled "syntality," a parallel concept to "personality" on the level of individuals. Cattell's factors are difficult to interpret, however; the only obvious element that some of them reflect is economic development. This difficulty is due to the unsystematic selection of variables of great diversity and to the large number of factors that Cattell retained—no less than 12. Sawyer and Levine (1966) published a factor-analytic study of data from traditional societies taken from Murdock's World Ethnographic Sample from the Human Relations Area Files (Murdock, 1949), with 30 variables and 565 societies. They found nine factors dealing mainly with means of existence (agriculture, animal husbandry, fishing) and family structure (nuclear family household, patrilineality, matrilineality). Sawyer (1967) subsequently published factor analysis results for a matrix of 236 variables for 82 modern nations. Sawyer found that 40% of the total variance in his immense matrix could be explained by three factors: economic development, size, and political orientation. Russett (1968) factor analyzed 54 variables for 82 countries (not the same set). He found five factors: economic development (by far the strongest factor), communism, size, Catholic culture, and intensive agriculture. Rummel (1972, pp. 217 ff.) published four additional factors obtained from the Sawyer analysis: Catholic culture, population density, foreign conflict behavior, and domestic conflict behavior.

The factors found by Sawyer, Russett, and Rummel are easier to interpret than those of Cattell, but the unavoidable question is: So what? That a country's level of economic development, its size, and its political allegiance are meaningful criteria that affect many other aspects of life in that country are conclusions so trivial that we hardly need a factor analysis to find them. The lack of an a priori theory that has guided the selection of input variables has condemned the output to triviality. These studies have provided little insight into *why* some countries are more developed than others or *why* some became communist and others did not.

Among the second group of studies, those in which variables were selected according to specific theoretical criteria, we find Gregg and Banks (1965), U.S. political scientists who looked for dimensions of political systems. They factor analyzed 68 political and historical variables for 115 nations and found seven factors, of which the three first together explain 51% of the variance in the data. These three factors were "access," opposing countries with multiparty systems to countries with one-party systems; "differentiation," opposing old and Westernized to young and ex-colonial nations; and "consensus," opposing stable to unstable regimes.

Adelman and Morris (1967), U.S. economists, looked for social, political, and economic factors that accompany economic development of less developed countries. They collected data for 12 sociocultural, 12 political, and 17 economic indicators for 74 developing nations. They did various factor analyses of national wealth (per capita GNP in 1961) and economic growth (rate of growth of real per capita GNP from 1950-51 to 1963-64) with different combinations of sociocultural, political, and economic indicators; they did this for all countries and for subsections of their set of countries. Adelman and Morris showed that there are two clusters of social and political conditions associated with wealth: One is differentiation in society, implying, for example, the decrease of the traditional agricultural sector (also measured by Marsh's index, described above); the other is the existence of pluralistic political systems. As we go from very poor to less poor countries, the latter factor becomes more closely associated with wealth. Economic growth (increase in wealth) is associated more with economic conditions than with social and political conditions, except for the very poorest countries, where economic growth (or rather the lack of it) is associated with both economic and social conditions.

Lynn and Hampson (1975), British psychologists, elaborated on earlier work by Lynn (1971) looking for psychological dimensions of national character in data from 18 modern nations on 12 medical and related indicators, such as the frequency of chronic psychosis, average calorie intake, suicide rates, and cigarette consumption. They found two main factors explaining, respectively, 34% and 24% of total variance, which they identified as dimensions of "neuroticism" and "extraversion." [92] In Chapters 3 and 4, I relate one of Gregg and Banks's dimensions and Adelman and Morris's clusters of social and political conditions to power distance and Lynn and Hampson's neuroticism to uncertainty avoidance.

Israeli psychologist Shalom Schwartz, whose empirical classification of individual values I discussed earlier in this chapter, also classified the same values at the level of national cultures, using the mean scores of his teacher values and separately of his student values per country, for 38 national or subnational cultures. This time he found seven categories: conservatism, hierarchy, mastery, affective autonomy, intellectual autonomy, egalitarian commitment, and harmony (Schwartz, 1994). There were significant correlations between Schwartz's culture-level value types and some of the dimensions empirically found in the study described in this book; I refer to them in Chapters 4, 5, and 6.

An important ongoing study program of values via public opinion surveys was started in the early 1980s by the European Values Systems Study Group, a consortium of social scientists including Jean Stoetzel in France, Jan Kerkhofs in Belgium, and Ruud De Moor in the Netherlands. The study's first round in 1981-82 covered nine countries (Belgium, Denmark, France, Germany, Great Britain, Ireland, Italy, Netherlands, and Spain); in subsequent years, data from 15 more countries were added. In 1990, U.S. political scientist Ronald Inglehart took the lead and a second round was started, renamed the World Values Survey (WVS). It eventually covered some 60,000 respondents across 43 societies, representing about 70% of the world's population with a questionnaire including more than 360 forced-choice questions. Areas covered were ecology, economy, education, emotions, family, gender and sexuality, government and politics, health, happiness, leisure and friends, morality, religion, society and nation, and work. A summary of the data has been published in Inglehart, Basañez, and Moreno (1998). In a macroanalysis of the results, Inglehart (1997, pp. 81-98) factor analyzed country mean scores on 47 variables summarizing some 100 key questions from all areas covered. Two factors accounted for 51% of the variance; Inglehart called these factors "key cultural dimensions" and labeled them "well-being versus survival" (explaining 30% of the variance) and "secular-rational versus traditional authority" (21% of the variance). Inglehart related a shift from traditional to secular-rational authority to modernization and a shift from survival to well-being to what throughout his writings he has called "postmodernization," a substitution of material goals by expressive (psychological) goals. As Exhibit 5.18 in Chapter 5 shows, Inglehart's key cultural dimensions were significantly correlated with the IBM dimensions. Well-being versus survival correlated strongly with individualism and masculinity; secular-rational versus traditional authority correlated negatively with power distance. I refer to Inglehart's work extensively in Chapters 3 through 6.

Culture Change

The Process of Culture Change

Cultures, especially national cultures, are extremely stable over time. Exhibit 1.5 suggests how this stability can be explained from the reinforcement of culture patterns by the institutions that themselves are products of the dominant cultural value systems. The system is in a self-regulating quasi-equilibrium. Change comes from the outside, in the form of forces of nature or forces of human beings: trade, conquest, economical or political dominance, and technological breakthroughs.

Technological breakthroughs, of course, may also take place within the system. Culture itself within a system affects both the inquisitiveness of the members of society and their tolerance for new ideas, and therefore the rate of discovery and innovation.[93] Until 100 to 200 years ago, this rate nearly everywhere was low. Today the products of scientific discovery (including the mass media) represent the major force of culture change, and for most countries in the world they arrive mainly or exclusively from outside; that is why Exhibit 1.5 lists "technological breakthroughs" as an outside influence (in a strict sense, it could also be put in the "origins" box).

As all countries are gradually exposed to the products of the same scientific discoveries in the form of modern technology, and as these play an important role in culture change, some authors have concluded that all societies will become more and more similar. In the "comparative management" literature of the 1960s we find the "convergence hypothesis," which implies that management philosophies and practices around the world should become more and more alike. "The logic of industrialism will eventually lead us all to a common society where ideology will cease to matter" (Kerr, Dunlop, Harbison, & Myers, 1960, p. 101). Such a statement strikes us now as both naive and wishful thinking; a more realistic evaluation of the situation was made by Feldman and Moore (1965), who pointed out that "the inconsistent elements of pre-industrial systems do not simply disappear, lost without trace" (p. 262). They are evident in the political field: "The political order, almost by operational definition, is the residuary legatee of unsolved social problems" (p. 262). Inkeles (1981), as a result of his studies of "modernity" and its reflection in values, found

"movement toward a common pattern only with regard to certain specific qualities identified as part of the syndrome of individual modernity. There are clearly many realms of attitude and value that are independent of the industrial organizational complex common to advanced nations" (p. 11).[94]

So technological modernization is an important force toward culture change that leads to somewhat similar developments in different societies,[95] but does not wipe out variety. It may even increase differences, as on the basis of preexisting value systems societies cope with technological modernization in different ways.[96] Feldman and Moore (1965) concluded that "surely most of the changes in industrial societies, and certainly the major ones by any crude scale, are disequilibrating rather than equilibrating" (p. 265). In cybernetic terms, society shows not only negative feedback processes that stabilize but also positive feedback processes: deviation-amplifying mutual causal processes.[97] In fact, much of the cultural variety in the present world can be explained only by such processes in history.

Studies of the evolution of the cultures of modern nations are rarely neutral in their focus; they stress either similarity or uniqueness, and either stability or change, at the expense of the opposite. The convergence theorists stressed similarity and change. Students of the developments within specific countries stress uniqueness and stability. Peyrefitte (1976) has traced most of the problems of present-day France back to Louis XIV (17th century); I have shown that quotes from 18th-century visitors to the Netherlands still apply to the modern Dutch (Hofstede, 1976c); Béteille (1977, p. 25) has referred to the remarkable stability over time of the basic structure of ideas and values in India and China; Inkeles (1977) found continuity in the American national character ever since the descriptions by de Crèvecoeur dating from 1782. The last of these is particularly interesting because the United States is a country of immigrants; it shows with amazing clarity that culture is learned, not inborn.[98]

Culture Change and the IBM Data

The measures in the present study allowed me to quantify both the similarities and the uniqueness of national cultures; in a modest way they also provided a quantification of their stability and change,[99] at least between the IBM survey cycles of 1967-69 and 1971-73, through a comparison of the answers of respondents in different age brackets.

Differences in values among respondents of the same national culture but of different ages and/or at different points in time may be due to three dif-

Exhibit 1.9. Age, Generation, Zeitgeist, and Combined Effects in Values Change

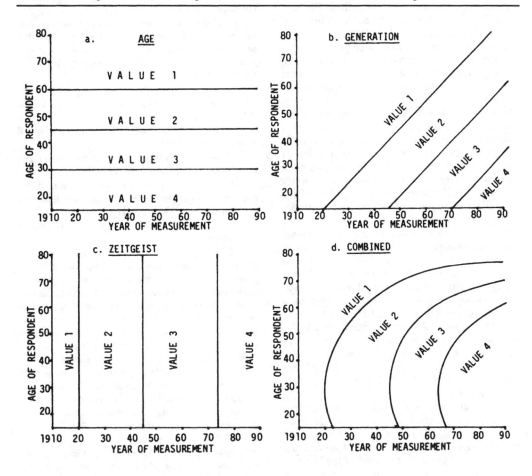

ferent causes: age (maturation), generation, and zeitgeist. Exhibit 1.9 illustrates the differences among these three causes. *Age* effects simply mean that respondents' values shift as they grow older. This is pictured in Exhibit 1.9a. Shifts over time are due only to the aging of the respondents; if at every moment we recruit respondents of the same age, no changes are found.[100] Generation effects occur for values that were absorbed by the young people of a certain period and accompanied their age cohort over its lifetime. If conditions of life have changed, subsequent generations may carry forward different values that they absorbed in their youth (Exhibit 1.9b). Zeitgeist effects occur when drastic systemwide changes in conditions cause *everyone's* values to shift, regardless of age (Exhibit 1.9c). In practice, these three effects will occur in different degrees and combinations; this could lead to a distribution of values like the one drawn in Exhibit 1.9d, in which the zeitgeist affects only the younger people and older people's values tend to be determined more by their age and/or generation.

Age and generation effects are often confused. Complaints of older people about "young people today" have been found on an Egyptian papyrus manuscript that is 3,000 years old. One of the oldest Greek texts preserved, Hesiod's *Works and Days,* which dates toward the end of the eighth century B.C., contains a pessimistic paragraph on the new generation in which "father will have no common bond with son" and "men will dishonor parents . . . and will blame and criticize with cruel words" (Hesiod, 1973, p. 64).

In data collected at one moment in time, age and generation effects cannot be separated. In longitudinal data (from at least two points in time) but without age differentiation of respondents, generation and zeitgeist effects cannot be separated (this will be immediately clear from Exhibits 1.9a, b, and c). Only in longitudinal data with age differentiation can we separate the three effects. In Chapters 3 through 6, I do this for each of the first four cultural dimensions.

The changes found within the IBM data are small, which is not surprising, as the two surveys were only 4 years apart; the dimension showing the clearest changes was individualism. The relationship of the dimensions to basic problems of societies and the historical evidence of the continuity of national solutions to such problems suggest that even over much longer periods the measures obtained will retain their validity. This is the more so because the country scores on the five dimensions do not provide *absolute* country positions, but only their positions *relative* to the other countries in the set. Influences like those of new technologies tend to affect all countries without necessarily changing their relative position or ranking; if their cultures change, they change in formation. Only if on a dimension one country leapfrogs over another will the validity of the original scores be reduced. This is a relatively rare occurrence.

Studies in the 1990s correlating the national culture index data, collected in IBM around 1970, with related variables available on a year-by-year basis find no weakening of the correlations.[101] For example, Chapter 4 shows for developed countries a strong negative correlation between their populations' total life satisfaction and their scores on the Uncertainty Avoidance Index. For life satisfaction data from 10 European countries collected in each of the years 1982-98, the correlations with the 1970 Uncertainty Avoidance Index fluctuated between −.70*** and −.87*** without any trend effect whatsoever.[102]

Culture change basic enough to invalidate the country dimension index scores will need either a much longer period—say, 50 to 100 years—or extremely dramatic outside events. Differences between national cultures at the end of the last century were already recognizable in the years 1900, 1800, and 1700, if not earlier. There is no reason they should not remain recognizable until at least 2100.

Notes

1. In mathematical notation, our predictions can be expressed (following Lewin, 1952, p. 25) by $B = f(P,S)$, in which B = predicted behavior, P = a contribution of the person, S = a contribution of the situation or environment, and f = some probabilistic interactive function, most likely not specifiable in more exact mathematical terms. The function f is probabilistic because our prediction is not perfect and interactive because the relationship between B and P may be a different one for any new situation S_i. If we know how Peter behaves when he meets Mary, how John behaves when he meets Mary, and how Peter behaves when he meets Mary's father, we still can not predict how John will react to Mary's father.

2. This analogy is borrowed from Kluckhohn (1951/1967, p. 405).

3. A construct is "not directly accessible to observation but inferable from verbal statements and other behaviors and useful in predicting still other observable and measurable verbal and nonverbal behavior" (Levitin, 1973, p. 492).

4. See Williams (1968, p. 283).

5. See Redfield (1962, pp. 439 ff.) and Albert (1968, p. 291).

6. See Lévi-Strauss (1961), Kuper (1975), and Montagu (1942/1997).

7. See Cavalli-Sforza and Piazza (1993) and Cavalli-Sforza and Cavalli-Sforza (1995).

8. For a fairly objective review, see Lynn (1978); not much has changed since that time. The most eloquent refutation is Montagu's (1942/1997).

9. See Ember (1977) for a review of cross-cultural cognitive studies.

10. It is likely that the development of values in children goes along with the development of intelligence and personality traits. Intelligence-versus-age curves usually show a very rapid development of intelligence in the early years, from 2 to about 7, with a slowing down after age 9 (Bloom, 1964, p. 64). For personality development, adequate measures are harder to get at, but such characteristics as intellectual interest, dependency, and aggression seem to a considerable extent to be developed before age 5 (Bloom, 1964, p. 177). Thence my assumption that by age 10, maximally 12, a young person's mental programs, especially his or her values, are firmly in place and unlikely to change even if that person migrates to another culture later.

11. The concept of the Heisenberg effect derives from nuclear physics; it refers to Heisenberg's "principle of indeterminacy": One cannot observe a particle without disturbing it.

12. See Fishbein and Ajzen (1975, p. 288).

13. This is an application of the epistemological principle of parsimony, also known as "Occam's razor" after William of Occam (1300-1350).

14. Rokeach (1972) has suggested that an adult possesses "only several dozens of instrumental values and perhaps only a few handfuls of terminal values" (p. 162).

15. Bem (1970) calls the first type of values (nonconsciously taken for granted) *zero-order beliefs* and the second type (direct derivations) *first-order beliefs.*

16. In some theories of leadership, the relative criticalness of the situation is therefore a key determining variable (Fiedler, 1967; Mulder, Ritsema van Eck, & De Jong, 1971).

17. Kluckhohn (1951/1967, pp. 413-414) used "intensity" and "modality."

18. See Meddin (1975, p. 898).

19. See Phillips and Clancy (1972, p. 923).

20. The distinction between the desired and the desirable plays an important role in De Mooij's (1998a,

pp. 179 ff.) explanations of paradoxical results from international market research.

21. On the relationship between discourse and ideology, see Van Dijk (1995).

22. For example, see Robinson, Athanasiou, and Head (1969, pp. 223 ff.) and Levitin (1973, pp. 489 ff.).

23. I have published the detailed results of the comparisons in four working papers (Hofstede, 1972, 1974a, 1974b, 1974c); see also Hofstede (1976d) and Chapter 2.

24. Throughout this book, r stands for the Pearson product-moment correlation coefficient, rho for the Spearman rank correlation coefficient, and R for the multiple correlation coefficient. Significance limits are indicated as follows: * = .05, ** = .01, and *** = .001.

25. Eysenck's (1953, 1954) statistical proof for this elegant model was rather weak, for which he has been criticized.

26. For a critique of an instrument that confuses intensity and direction, see Hofstede (1974a).

27. I have reported how 22 different "work goals" (work values as the desired) were scored by 1,196 respondents in five European IBM laboratories (Hofstede, 1976b, pp. 13-15). Respondents were asked to rate every single value on a 5-point scale and also to select the first, second, and third most important item from the entire list. The order of the 22 work goals based on ratings was rank correlated (Spearman) .58 with the order of the same 22 goals based on selecting ranks 1, 2, and 3.

28. "Symbols are objects, acts, relationships or linguistic formations that stand *ambiguously* for a multiplicity of meanings, evoke emotions, and impel men to action" (Cohen, 1974, p. 23). "Rather than standing for a simple referent, symbols evoke a variety of meanings, some of which may be ambiguous. Symbols do not denote: They connote, suggest, imply" (Griswold, 1994, p. 19).

29. "Collective ritual is not the product of recurring spontaneous individual creativity resulting from recurring psychic states. On the contrary, for most people it is the ritual that recreates certain psychic states in the minds of the participants, not the other way round. . . . [The rituals] become objective, in the sense that they confront the members of the group as things that exist outside their psyches and that will constrain them in their behaviour. They also become public, the collective representations of a group" (Cohen, 1974, p. 4).

30. Descriptions of the "culture and personality" school are found, for example, in Bohannan (1969) and Barnouw (1973). Lonner and Adamopoulos (1997) describe the development of the relationship between culture and psychology.

31. This definition comes from the unabridged 1979 edition of *Webster's New Twentieth Century Dictionary*.

32. See Geertz (1973, pp. 255 ff.).

33. Mass media play an important role in establishing and confirming identities. An example for the unique case of Singapore has been elaborated by Heidt (1987).

34. The terminology in Exhibit 1.5 is party taken from Berry (1975). The diagram contains elements from Parsons's (1977, p. 10) cybernetic hierarchy; the system of societal norms in the center is Parsons's "cultural system." The idea of a central value system that feeds into different types of institutions is also found in the work of Shils (1975), who argues that it is shared by at least the majority of the *elites*, not necessarily the rest of the population.

35. See Peyrefitte (1976) and d'Iribarne (1989, 1994).

36. See Rescher (1969, p. 75), who proposed a cost-benefit approach to the analysis of value changes.

37. See Bem (1970, p. 60).

38. See Spicer (1971).

39. See Dhaouadi (1990) and Habib (1995).

40. The painting described appears in Goody (1977, pp. 154-155). This is called a *Völkertafel* (peoples table). I also have a picture of three pieces from an English ABC (?) jigsaw puzzle from the late 1700s picturing a "Dutchman," an "Englishman," and a "Frenchman" and describing the presumed character of each. Unfortunately, I don't know where the rest of the puzzle is or what the other pieces represent.

41. See Boring (1968).

42. See Gorer (1943), Benedict (1946/1974), Mead (1951), and Lowie (1954). For overviews, see Duijker and Frijda (1960) and Barnouw (1973).

43. The French historian Fernand Braudel (1958, pp. 747-748) has recognized the need to promote the use of mathematical statistics in the historical and anthropological study of modern societies.

44. See, for example, Inkeles (1968), Inkeles and Levinson (1954/1969), and Wallace (1970).

45. The two main dimensions in Peabody's (1985) descriptive scores were (1) tight versus loose control over the expression of impulses and (2) assertiveness versus nonassertiveness, but they bear no relationship to the dimensions found in values studies, including mine. Peabody's student stereotypes were largely based on ignorance; for example, Finns were described as "stingy"! Other cross-national stereotype studies have been conducted by Marin and Salazar (1985), who asked students in and about seven American countries, and Wilterdink (1992), who asked staff members of the European University Institute in Florence, Italy, about five European countries. A remarkable conclusion from Marin and Salazar's study is that proximity and high levels of contact were associated with negative stereotyping.

46. See Bidney (1962, p. 450), Naroll (1983), and Boulding (1985).

47. "The basic premise of this framework is the assumption that all behaviors are inherently constrained to time-invariant laws of physiology, among other physical laws, which prevail irrespective of racial, religious, ethnic, cultural, sociological or economic origins and institutions. Two classes of effects encompass most physioeconomic factors: (1) Soil (land, terrain, mineral resources) and (2) climate" (Parker, 1997, p. 32).

48. For more extensive analysis of this problem, see Leung (1989) and Leung and Bond (1989). See also Chapter 8.

49. Correcting a reverse ecological fallacy led to the identification of a fifth dimension of national cultures: long-term versus short-term orientation (see Chapters 2 and 7). The reverse ecological fallacy is still quite frequent even in articles published by respectable journals. An example is the analysis of answers to the Rokeach Value Survey by 567 managers from 12 countries by Bigoness and Blakely (1996) in the *Journal of International Business Studies*. The authors used the results of a factor analysis across all individuals in making statements about value differences between countries.

50. A paradigm is a set of concepts used to build a theory. It is not a theory itself, but a basic way of ordering reality that inevitably has to precede any theory formation. The inadequate paradigm signaled is part of a "person-centered preoccupation and causal attribution bias" in U.S. psychological research (Caplan & Nelson, 1973).

51. On the theory of multilevel analysis, see Menzel (1950), Blau (1960), Tannenbaum and Bachman (1964), Przeworski and Teune (1970, chap. 3), Rousseau (1985), and G. Hofstede (1995).

52. Since the late 1970s, the mathematics for multilevel analysis has been elaborated, and advanced computer calculation programs have been developed (Goldstein, 1987; Hox & Kreft, 1994; Langbein & Lichtman, 1978). Most current applications take place in the field of educational research, for separating individual student effects from school or teacher effects on student performance. The disadvantage of the new methods is that owing to the complexity of its mathematics, multilevel research is becoming another specialty rather than a general paradigm for the social sciences. The crucial step is not the choice of the right computer program but the awareness that a data set can also be analyzed at another aggregation level (Klein, Dansereau, & Hall, 1994). Often no special mathematics is needed for this purpose; classical methods will do, as in the two projects described.

53. See, for example, Crowley, Levitin, and Quinn (1973, p. 446).

54. See Frijda and Jahoda (1969, p. 45).

55. Rho = Spearman rank correlation coefficient; see note 24, above.

56. In another cross-national study, Tannenbaum, Kavcic, Rosner, Vianello, and Wieser (1974, chap. 7) have shown how members of a research team from different countries interpreted the same findings differently.

57. Thoenig (1982), after conducting more than 70 interviews at five American business schools, described the management research he encountered as "hypernormal science," paraphrasing Kuhn (1970).

58. U.S. anthropologist Clifford Geertz (1973) has written: "The problem of how to get from a collection of ethnographic miniatures . . . to wall-sized culturescapes of the nation, the epoch, the continent, or the civilization is not so easily passed over with vague allusions to the virtues of concreteness and the down-to-earth mind. For a science born in Indian tribes, Pacific islands, and African lineages and subsequently seized with greater ambitions, this has come to be a major methodological problem, and for the most part a badly handled one" (p. 21).

59. This point is made for psychology by Pepitone (1976), for sociology by Smelser (1989), and for cross-cultural studies by Dinges (1977).

60. Older bibliographies are cited in the 1980 edition of *Culture's Consequences* (see Hofstede, 1980a, p. 52, n. 25).

61. Comparative management is an object-oriented field of research and teaching, rather than a discipline. It borrows from comparative organization psychology, comparative organization sociology, and microeconomics. The field was developed with travel impressions and interviews by U.S. business school professors (e.g., Harbison & Burgess, 1954; Webber, 1969) and personal memoirs of practitioners in different countries or multicultural settings (e.g., Farmer & Richman, 1965). Later, questionnaire surveys of individual managers across a number of countries became popular, starting with Haire et al.'s (1966) survey of "managerial thinking" in 14 countries. Still later, studies were published based on interviews with managers in their organizational context, such as Negandhi and Prasad's (1971) study of U.S. subsidiaries versus local firms and Tannenbaum et al.'s (1974) study of hierarchy, both covering five countries.

62. Examples are found in Whitley (1990) and Mueller (1994), and in France in a dispute between d'Iribarne (1991) and Maurice, Sellier, and Silvestre (1992) in the *Revue Française de Sociologie*.

63. A discussion in the journal *Organization Studies* between Wilkinson (1996) and Lowe (1998), about the role of institutions, culture, and "human agency" in the East Asian economies, and in Hong Kong in particular, reveals one more unconnected "thought collective"—or even two more?

64. Sarawathi and Dutta (1987, pp. 150-151) have summarized Indian studies, arguing that bi- and even multilingualism have a positive effect on psychological adjustment. They criticize the "Western" (meaning American) implicit assumption that monolingualism is the normal condition for a well-adjusted human being.

65. For example, in some tribes where individuals live in extended families, the same word is used for "mother" and "aunt." The Dutch language has only one word (*neef*) for "cousin" and "nephew." The Scandinavian languages have different words for grandparents on the mother's side and on the father's side.

66. Lewis (1996) shows many examples of the role of language in intercultural misunderstandings—even between cultural neighbors like Britain and the United States.

67. See Hoijer (1962, pp. 263-264).

68. See Brislin (1970, 1993).

69. Ralston, Cunniff, and Gustafson (1995) compared answers to the Schwartz Values Survey by Hong Kong Chinese managers, half of whom answered in Chinese and half of whom answered in English, with answers by American managers in the United States. Hong Kong Chinese managers answered more like the Americans when using English: They showed cross-cultural accommodation.

70. See Hofstede, Kraut, and Simonetti (1976, pp. 21 ff.).

71. Le Bras and Todd (1981), in an atlas of regional differences in France, seem to suggest that such regional differences are a French specialty. Of course, similar or even larger regional differences exist in all countries; even in tiny Luxembourg people distinguish two different cultural regions.

72. Examples are Rubenowitz (1968), Hofstede (1976d), and Hofstede and Kranenburg (1974).

73. See, for example, Garfinkel (1984).

74. See Headland (1990).

75. The study of correlations across primitive ethnic units was undertaken as early as the late 19th century by anthropologist Edward Tylor in Britain. His publication evoked a reaction from Sir Francis Galton, which became famous as "Galton's problem": How should such correlations be explained? Are they based on functional association of variables rooted in general laws of human society, or more simply on diffusion of patterns from one culture to another? See Driver (1973, pp. 338 ff.) and Naroll (1970, p. 1229).

76. See d'Iribarne (1997).

77. For descriptions in English, see d'Iribarne (1994, 1997) and Chapter 3 of this book.

78. Scheuch (1990, p. 31) presents a very similar table, without seemingly knowing my 1980 book, in which it appeared.

79. Perlmutter (1965) used these terms to describe the structures of multinational enterprises (see Chapter 11 of this volume). Adler (1984) has distinguished six styles of "cross-cultural management methodology." Her "parochial" and "ethnocentric" styles belong to cell 1 in Exhibit 1.8, her "polycentric" style belongs to cell 2, her "geocentric" style not to cell 4 but to cell 3, and her "comparative" style to cell 4. She also describes a "synergistic" style that deals with intercultural cooperation and is outside the scope of Exhibit 1.8.

80. Kluckhohn (1952/1962) has stated that "biological, psychological and sociosituational universals afford the possibility of comparing cultures in terms which are not ethnocentric, which depart from 'givens,' begging no needless questions" (p. 314).

81. The distinction between dimensions and typologies resembles Lammers and Hickson's (1979c) "lawlike theories" versus "configurations" mentioned earlier.

82. U.S. anthropologist and popular author Edward Hall (1959/1965, pp. 45-46), in the same vein, has listed 10 "primary message systems": interaction, association with others, subsistence, bisexuality, territoriality, temporality, learning, play, defense, and exploitation of resources.

83. Inkeles (1966) carried out a large research project on the modernity of *individuals* in 1962-64; about 1,000 young men in each of six countries (Argentina, Chile, India, Israel, Nigeria, and East Pakistan [later Bangladesh]) were interviewed. More or less the same cluster of attitudes and behaviors related to "modernity" was found in all six countries, characterized by openness to new experience, independence of parental and traditional authority, interest in planning ahead, and interest in community affairs and news from the outside world.

84. For the latter, Marsh's Index of Differentiation is computed from the summed *t* scores of the percentage of males in nonagricultural occupations and of the gross energy consumption per capita; data around 1960.

85. See Poirier (1978).

86. In his later work, Parsons dropped "self-orientation versus collectivity orientation" as a pattern variable; it did not fit into the tight paradigm he developed (see Rocher, 1974, p. 52, n. 5).

87. There is a conceptual similarity between Douglas's classification and the IBM dimensions of uncertainty avoidance and individualism; see Chapter 5, Exhibit 5.7.

88. Another attempt at classifying cultures according to what was in people's minds was "left brain versus right brain" (Israël, 1995; Trompenaars, 1985). Hines (1987) has convincingly shown that functional differences between the halves of the brain and differences in culture are of an entirely different order; their relationship is a myth, a modern form of *phrenology* (the pseudoscience that tried to measure human character from the shape of and lumps on the skull).

89. The term *hologeistic* comes from the Greek words *holos* (whole) and *gè* (earth). The term seems to have been coined by Gonggrijp in the Netherlands at the beginning of the 20th century (see Köbben, 1952, p. 131), but it was proposed anew by Schaefer (1977). For an overview of hologeistic research methods, see Naroll, Michik, and Naroll (1980).

90. "Studying a factor analysis of a set of data with a step-by-step increasing of the number of factors rotated is like focussing a microscope on an object. At first, when the number of factors is small, the picture is blurred and not understandable. Then, gradually, factors start to dissolve themselves into interpretable components. After passing the optimal number of factors, components dissolve themselves still further, but now the interpretable relationships begin to disappear and the picture disintegrates and becomes unclear again" (Hofstede, 1967, p. 121).

91. See Cattell (1949), Cattell, Breul, and Hartman (1952), and Cattell and Gorsuch (1965) for reports on factor-analytic studies of ecological variables (first 72, later 48) for large numbers of nations (first 69, then 40, then again 52).

92. Among others, Eysenck (1954, p. 177) used these two as a framework.

93. See Wallace (1970, pp. 170 ff.).

94. Other critiques of the convergence hypothesis were published in organizational sociology by Maurice (1976) and Form (1979) and in social psychology by Smith and Bond (1993).

95. Reviews of anthropological literature by Naroll (1970) and Driver (1973) and the theory of cultural evolution by Lomax and Berkowitz (1972) indicated common elements in the evolutionary patterns of traditional societies.

96. See Herbig and Palumbo (1994).

97. See Maruyama (1963).

98. Hines (1973, 1974) studied the phenomenon of the socialization of immigrants on the particular issue of achievement motivation (measured by the Lynn test). The persistence of values from the country of origin seems to depend on several factors (countries of origin and of immigration, occupation); in the case of Greeks having immigrated to the United States and New Zealand, Greek values persisted to the second generation.

99. Cattell (1953) earlier tried a quantitative approach to the assessment of "culture" change. He factor analyzed time-series data on 48 variables for Great Britain from 1837 to 1937. Earlier in this chapter, I criticized Cattell's analyses for being atheoretical and his set of variables for being "catchall." The same criticism applies to his time-series data. He did find 4 factors (out of 10) that he could interpret. Even if they did not necessarily refer to cultural evolution, they illustrated that over time different dimensions of national indexes shift in different ways, which is relevant to the present study. Cattell's interpretable dimensions were as follows: (1) "cultural pressure" (basically a modernization factor, the strength of which increased more or less monotonically over the total time span), (2) "war stress" (basically the effect of wars on the national economy and so on, peaking during war periods), (3) "emancipation" (mainly related to universal suffrage; low until about 1920, stepping up after that), and (4) "slum morale" (a poverty factor that peaked between 1860 and 1880). Cattell later tried a similar analysis for the United States and found partly the same factors, but with a different timing.

100. Age differences found in research in organizations can be based not on maturation but on seniority—not on people having physically aged but on their having spent more time in the organization. Seniority and age are of course correlated; for 12 subgroups in IBM the correlations across individuals of age and seniority varied from $r = .52^{***}$ to $r = .76^{***}$, with a median of $r = .61^{***}$.

101. See Wildeman et al. (1999).

102. These figures are based on De Mooij (2001), data provided by the Eurobarometer, percentages of representative samples of the population claiming to be "very satisfied with the life they lead." From 1996 onward, the number of countries included increased to 13, but this did not visibly affect the correlations.

2

■

Data Collection, Treatment, and Validation

Summary of This Chapter

The base data for the study discussed in this book were collected in a large multinational corporation: IBM. The company's international employee attitude survey program between 1967 and 1973 in two survey rounds produced answers to more than 116,000 questionnaires from 72 countries in 20 languages. The analysis focused on country differences in answers on questions about employee values. Similar differences between countries were obtained in a business school unrelated to IBM. In addition to statistical analyses across individuals, an analysis of variance was performed using country, occupation, gender, and age as criteria, but most crucial were correlation and factor analyses based on matched employee samples across countries. The initial analysis was limited to 40 countries with more than 50 respondents each. Only those questions were retained for which the country ranking remained stable over time. In a later stage, data from 10 more countries and three multicountry regions were added.

The country culture dimensions of power distance and uncertainty avoidance were found through an eclectic analysis of data, based on theoretical reasoning and correlation analysis. The dimensions of individualism and masculinity were derived from a country-level factor analysis of scores on work goal importance, standardized for eliminating acquiescence. A country-level factor analysis of all data combined integrates the picture of the four dimensions. A comparison between the two survey rounds shows the value shifts in IBM over this period. The statistical independence of the four dimensions is checked for

different sets of countries. Together, the dimensions allow the formation of culture clusters. Special attention is paid to multilingual countries.

The reliability of the country scores cannot be tested across individuals, only through replications on other multicountry populations. Reliability can also be inferred from validity. Validation means correlating the country scores with data from other surveys and with indexes measured at the country level. Nine economic, geographic, and demographic indicators were used throughout, including national wealth and past and future economic growth.

In the 1980s a new cross-national study, Bond's Chinese Value Survey, led to the addition of a fifth dimension: long-term versus short-term orientation. The cross-national research experience in IBM also played a vital role in a large complementary research project on differences in *organizational cultures* within countries; the methodology of this project is described. The chapter closes with a summary of and reactions to the most common criticisms of the approach used in the 1980 edition of *Culture's Consequences*.

The Research Settings

The IBM Corporation

At the time of the surveys, the International Business Machines (IBM) Corporation, headquartered in Armonk, New York, was one of the world's largest multinationals.[1] Its organization chart showed a division into IBM Domestic (United States) and IBM World Trade Corporation, representing the way the late founder,

Thomas J. Watson, Sr., had divided responsibilities between his two sons. IBM had subsidiaries in all countries around the world that admitted such subsidiaries. It manufactured and sold a range of high-technology products, in particular computers (Data Processing Division) and typewriters (Office Products Division). In the period in which the data were collected, 1967 through 1973, IBM had basic research laboratories in 2 countries, developed its products in 7 countries, manufactured in 13 countries, and marketed and serviced in about 100 countries.

The smaller national marketing-plus-service subsidiaries of IBM and the marketing-plus-service divisions of the larger subsidiaries that also had product development and/or manufacturing were organized along similar lines except for size. If the size of the operations justified it, there were branch offices in a country's main cities and a country head office in (usually) the capital. Branch offices employed managers and supervisors, salespersons, systems engineers to advise customers on applications, customer engineers to provide maintenance of the products after sales, and administrative staff. Head offices employed managers and supervisors and a professional and administrative head office staff.

Country organizations in IBM employed almost exclusively nationals of the country, except in the first years of the creation of new subsidiaries. This applied all the way up to the level of country general managers, with few exceptions. Coordination of the subsidiaries of IBM was not carried out through the delegation of nationals of the corporation's home country within the subsidiaries, but through a tight system of rules and controls and frequent personal contacts between higher managers in the country subsidiaries and personnel of the different international head offices.

International head office operations were concentrated regionally at a few points on the globe, and their managerial and professional personnel were recruited from different countries. These persons usually served in the head office for a restricted number of years, after which they returned to their countries of origin. The top management of the corporation in the United States was almost entirely American.

Promotion in IBM was usually from within; managers came from the ranks, rarely from outside. The company hired young people with good qualifications and encouraged them to continue developing themselves. The technical nature of the product made frequent retraining and updating of personnel necessary. Labor turnover varied strongly from country to country and from job to job; it was higher among young, college-trained professionals than among most other groups.

The people employed in the company's marketing, service, and product development were essentially middle-class rather than working-class. A sizable working-class population existed only in the manufacturing plants, which represented a different subculture within the corporate culture, with more traditional industrial values than were found in the marketing and product development divisions. The latter could be classified as belonging to the service industry sector as much as to the manufacturing industry sector. The degree of union membership among employees varied according to the industrial relations patterns of the countries, but was generally not high. In countries where sizable shares of employees were represented by unions, relations between the company and the unions were usually good.

IBM had a distinct corporate identity—a strong corporate culture—and it successfully encouraged in its employees a sense of pride. In the period of the surveys in two cases a national subsidiary of IBM participated in a countrywide comparative cross-company attitude survey, which allowed comparison of IBM employees' satisfaction pattern with that found within other, mostly local national, companies. In both cases, IBM-ers scored above average in their satisfaction with their job content and earnings and below average in their satisfaction with their bosses. The latter can be attributed to a combination of three factors: (1) relatively young and inexperienced managers due to fast company growth in the 1960s, (2) a generally highly qualified workforce that was handling difficult technical problems with a lot of de facto autonomy, and (3) the company's tight system of controls and rules. The relatively inexperienced managers acted as the friction point between employee autonomy and company controls.

All in all, the corporation employed more people in marketing and customer service than in manufacturing. A consequence of this was that about one out of every two IBM employees had direct face-to-face or voice-to-voice contact with customers. This contributed to the employees' identification with the corporation they represented.

A curious difference in employee attitudes was found between employees and managers in the branch offices, who regularly faced the customers, and employees and managers in the country and international head offices, who did not. Branch office personnel at all levels were more satisfied with the content of their jobs and with their own personal contributions to the company's success. Country head office personnel were less satisfied in these respects, and international head office personnel least of all. However, a question on the image of the company as such, independent of the employee's contribution to it, showed the opposite result: In this case, people in international head offices were most positive and those in the branch offices least. It is unlikely that this should be a specific IBM phenomenon; it may well exist in many large, decentralized organizations. I interpreted it as a stronger intrinsic job motivation at the periphery of the organization and signs of alienation in the center ("alienation at the top"; see Hofstede, 1976a).

Wherever in this book a comparison among *countries* has to be made, I use data from IBM's marketing-plus-service organization only, as this is the sole part of the company that operated in all countries where the company existed. Wherever the purpose is comparison *among occupations,* I use data from product development, manufacturing plants, and marketing-plus-service organizations, but limited to those few large countries in which all these three functional areas of the corporation were represented.

The Use of
Attitude Surveys in IBM

A concern of managers with employee morale was a characteristic feature of the IBM corporate culture. This could be justified partly by the intensity of IBM employees' contacts with customers: How could the company maintain good relationships with customers if its people facing these customers were disgruntled? This argument is sound, yet other organizations that depend as much on customer contact have not shown the same concern with employee morale. The deeper roots of IBM's concern with employee morale were historical; the concern grew out of the convictions of IBM's founder many decades earlier and was made one of the pillars of the IBM way of life, into which newcomers were automatically socialized.[2]

In this concern with employee morale, employee attitude surveys fit as something natural. Parts of the organization within specific countries had been incidentally surveyed by consultants since the 1950s. Each of these surveys used its own method and survey questions; results were not comparable across surveys. For comparison purposes, some mutually agreed-upon standardization of research methods and instruments would be necessary.

Obtaining standardization through mutual agreement between researchers is not an easy task. Researchers tend to see themselves as independent, creative professionals, and the adoption of tools "not invented here" for the sake of standardization does not come naturally to them. Also, when an item has been used within a particular population, there will be a sacrifice in historical information when for the next survey it is

changed in the interest of standardization with other populations. Only after IBM had appointed its own personnel research professionals at two international head office locations and in some of the main country subsidiaries did standardization become feasible. I had been hired by IBM in 1965 as the first personnel researcher for the European head office.[3] In 1966 and 1967, I headed up an international team of six researchers (three internal, three consultants) who prepared the first internationally standardized questionnaire for a simultaneous survey of the corporation's product development personnel in six countries. This first international questionnaire consisted of 180 standardized items that were chosen on the basis of open-ended pilot interviews with a random selection of personnel in the six product development laboratories and on a selection from the questionnaires used in earlier incidental surveys. The questionnaire was issued in five languages (English, Dutch, French, German, and Swedish) and administered in June 1967.

In the meantime, my functional boss in IBM World Trade's New York office was preparing another international survey, which took place in November 1967.[4] It covered the company's total personnel in 26 Asian, Latin American, and Pacific countries, most of which had never been surveyed before and did not have their own personnel research professionals. That survey's questionnaire counted 183 standardized items, including many from the previous laboratories survey; it was a condensation of a longer pilot version that had been pretested on both U.S. and Latin American test populations. The November 1967 questionnaire was issued in four language versions: English, Japanese, Portuguese, and Spanish, with small differences between the Spanish versions used in the Caribbean and southern Latin America.

These two pioneer international survey projects were followed by surveys of all European and Middle Eastern marketing and administrative operations in 1968 and 1969 and of all manufacturing plants in 1970. By the end of that year, most parts of the organization had been covered once by an international survey: a total of about 60,000 respondents from 53 countries around the world. The number of common questionnaire items was gradually reduced to 160, but in some cases supplements for certain countries and certain categories of personnel were added. The number of language versions increased to 18.

IBM's home country, the United States, was not included in the surveys. The different divisions of IBM Domestic had survey histories of their own and employed their own independent survey staffs. Through personal negotiation between my functional U.S. boss and his colleague in one of the Domestic divisions, the standardized

Exhibit 2.1   The Countries Surveyed With the IBM Questionnaire and the Languages Used

Code	Country	Cat	Language	Code	Country	Cat	Language
ARG	Argentina	1	Spanish	MAL	Malaysia	2	English
AUL	Australia	1	English	MEX	Mexico	1	Spanish
AUT	Austria	1	German	NAT	Netherlands Antilles	4	English
BAH	Bahamas	4	English				
BEL	Belgium	1	Dutch/French	NET	Netherlands	1	Dutch
BOL	Bolivia	4	Spanish	NIC	Nicaragua	4	Spanish
BRA	Brazil	1	Portuguese	NIG	Nigeria	3c	English
CAN	Canada	1	English	NOR	Norway	1	Norwegian
CHL	Chile	1	Spanish	NZL	New Zealand	1	English
COL	Colombia	1	Spanish	PAK	Pakistan	1	English
COS	Costa Rica	2	Spanish	PAN	Panama	2	Spanish
DEN	Denmark	1	Danish	PER	Peru	1	Spanish
DOM	Dominican Republic	4	Spanish	PHI	Philippines	1	English
				POR	Portugal	1	Portuguese
ECA	Ecuador	2	Spanish	SAF	South Africa	1	English
EGY	Egypt	3a	Arabic	SAL	Salvador	2	Spanish
ETH	Ethiopia	3b	English	SAU	Saudi Arabia	3a	Arabic
FIN	Finland	1	Finnish	SIL	Sierra Leone	3c	English
FRA	France	1	French	SIN	Singapore	1	English
GBR	Great Britain	1	English	SPA	Spain	1	Spanish
GER	Germany (West)	1	German	SWE	Sweden	1	Swedish
GHA	Ghana	3c	English	SWI	Switzerland	1	French/ German
GRE	Greece	1	Greek				
GUA	Guatemala	2	Spanish	TAI	Taiwan	1	English
HOK	Hong Kong	1	English	TAN	Tanzania	3b	English
HOD	Honduras	4	Spanish	THA	Thailand	1	Thai
IDO	Indonesia	2	English	TRI	Trinidad	4	English
IND	India	1	English	TUR	Turkey	1	Turkish
IRA	Iran	1	Farsi	UAE	United Arab Republic	3a	Arabic
IRE	Ireland	1	English				
IRQ	Iraq	3a	Arabic	URU	Uruguay	2	Spanish
ISR	Israel	1	Hebrew	USA	United States	1	English
ITA	Italy	1	Italian	VEN	Venezuela	1	Spanish
JAM	Jamaica	2	English	VIE	Vietnam (South)	4	English
JPN	Japan	1	Japanese				
KEN	Kenya	3b	English	ZAM	Zambia	3b	English
KOR	Korea (South)	2	English				
KUW	Kuwait	3a	Arabic	**Non-IBM**			
LEB	Lebanon	3a	Arabic	YUG	Yugoslavia	1	Serbo-Croat/ Slovene
LYA	Libya	3a	Arabic				
				Later divided into			
				CRO	Croatia	2	Serbo-Croat
				SER	Serbia	2	Serbo-Croat
				SLO	Slovenia	2	Slovene

NOTE: Categories are as follows:

Category 1 = 40 countries included in first analysis; Category 2 = countries added in later analyses; Category 3a = countries combined into Arabic-speaking region (ARA); Category 3b = countries combined into East African region (EAF); Category 3c = countries combined into West African region (WAF); Category 4 = countries not included in analysis.

See Appendix 2, Exhibit A2.4, for numbers of respondents per country. There were small differences in the various Arabic, Dutch, English, French, German, Portuguese, and Spanish versions due to local idiom.

international questions were included in one of the U.S. surveys, so that comparisons could be made between the United States and other countries.

The simple statement that so many people were surveyed in so many countries hides a complex process of decision making, negotiation, and persuasion of a "political" nature. It did not happen because a top manager decided one day that "from now on we shall survey." The initiative was not taken at the top of the organization at all: It came from two committed psychologists employed in two different international head offices who at the right time conceived of an idea that fit the corporate culture, and who were politically smart enough to mobilize their superiors and colleagues to carry it out. Country subsidiaries could not be told to participate; top managers in the countries had to be "sold" on the project. Some were known to have a spontaneous interest in applications of social science, and they were approached first; some usually went along with projects that seemed to have the approval of their superiors in the head office, and they were approached second; some were expected to be difficult, and they were approached last with the strong argument that all the other countries had already decided to join. In a few cases this did not work, and the first survey round showed some blank spots for parts of country organizations that had not been surveyed. By the time of the second survey round, the idea had become so well accepted that almost everyone agreed to participate.

The international attitude surveys were sold to IBM not as a research project but as a management tool for organization development. Considerable effort was spent in providing data feedback to managers of different levels and to rank-and-file employees. Feedback was handled carefully in order to avoid defensive reactions by managers whose departments showed unfavorable results. The reactions of nonmanagerial employees, after some initial suspicion, were invariably positive, although sometimes skeptical as to the likelihood of the results leading to corrective action by their managers.[5]

In 1970, the international surveys had become an established fact in IBM. Personnel departments of all major parts of the organization had appointed personnel research officers. The new personnel research fraternity got together to design a survey approach for the next 4 years. It was agreed that on the basis of the results obtained in the first survey round, a core set of 60 question items would be selected that would remain compulsory for all surveys. The figure 60 was estimated as the minimum acceptable based on the number of factors found in factor analyses and on the desire for reliability of measurement by covering key factors with more than one question. The

selection of the core items is described in detail in Hofstede, Kraut, and Simonetti (1976); it was based on an extensive study of the available literature and on a number of factor analyses of the first round's survey results.[6] Next to the 60 core questions, 66 other questions used previously were recommended for further use on an optional basis. Beyond those, local managers and researchers could add their own questions.

The 1970 selection of core and recommended questions was based on a factor analysis *within (sub)cultures* only. A *between*-cultures (ecological) analysis had not been done at that time, for two reason: first, because the main purpose of the survey operation was organization development— that is, use within parts of the organization— which made the within-(sub)culture analysis obvious; and second, I must confess that the difference between within-culture and between-cultures analysis had not occurred to us at that time.

As it was, a resurvey of the product development laboratories of IBM took place in 1971 with a transition questionnaire (partly old, partly new), and a resurvey of the marketing and administrative departments using the new questionnaire was spread over 1971, 1972, and 1973. In 1974, IBM took a new approach to its surveys and considerably reduced the number of questions, eliminating those concerning personal goals and beliefs, which later proved essential for the cross-cultural analysis in this book, because they were judged insufficiently practical. Attempts to use these questions again in IBM since that time have never been successful.

The second survey round—which did not include the manufacturing plants—numbered, again, about 60,000 respondents, of whom about 30,000 had also participated in the first survey round; 20,000 had joined the company since the first survey, and 10,000 were in groups and countries that had not been included the first time. The number of countries covered in either or both survey rounds had grown to 71; the number of languages stayed at 18. Exhibit 2.1 lists the countries and the languages.

In 1971, an opportunity arose to include data from Yugoslavia, a country in which IBM had had a subsidiary prior to World War II. I was asked to act as a consultant to Intertrade, a Yugoslav worker-self-managed import-export organization that among other things had inherited the marketing and servicing of IBM products from IBM Yugoslavia. The Yugoslav company was interested in measuring its employees' attitudes, and we surveyed these employees using basically the IBM questionnaire. It was thus possible to add Yugoslavia to the list of countries covered, although it was not in the IBM database. The survey was held in the Serbo-Croat and Slovene languages, bringing the total language count to 20. When Yugoslavia disintegrated in 1991, I reanalyzed the Yugoslav data on file and was able to split them into Croatia (Zagreb branch office), Serbia (Beograd branch office), and Slovenia (Ljubljana head office). The index scores per republic are shown in Appendix 5.

Questionnaire Translation and Survey Administration

The master versions of the international questionnaires were always formulated in English. It had been noticed early on that some words (for example, *achievement*) were difficult to translate into many of the other languages; such words were henceforth avoided. In general, the master versions sought plain formulations without culturally loaded idiom.

The translations were made and checked by in-company personnel. It is a definite advantage that in an international organization capable bi- and multilingual persons are numerous. As the surveys were meant to be not scientific instruments but practical management tools, and as their preparation was subject to a tight business time schedule, back-translation was used only exceptionally. In most cases it was considered sufficient to have a draft translation made by the person who was going to act as the local survey coordinator or by another person selected by him or her for linguistic skills. The translators translated into their native languages. Their translations were then checked by some of the company's bilingual managers. In some cases, pilot runs of the translated versions were made with small panels of employees who were asked to signal any difficulties or ambiguities they met in answering.

In later stages of the analysis, I did several back-translation checks on items that in some countries had produced unexpected results. In all these cases the translations proved to be right. Comparative correlation and factor analysis between items in various language versions revealed some differences, but again translation errors were ruled out as causes. In spite of the pragmatic, unscientific approach to the translation process followed, I feel reasonably confident about the quality of the translations. Only in two cases were translations recognized as weak and containing definite errors; in both they had been made by persons qualified as psychologists who had decided their work did not need any checking by others.

The administration of a survey in 71 countries is a heroic adventure that could never have succeeded without the help of the existing corporate infrastructure. After the initial approval of the countries' general managers had been obtained, the most suitable way of administering the sur-

veys was determined separately for each country and each department, with advice from international head office researchers, who issued a "Survey Administration Manual" for each survey phase. In the larger subsidiaries that had their own personnel research persons or staffs, the latter handled the entire survey administration. In the medium-sized subsidiaries that lacked personnel research persons, lay survey coordinators were nominated, trained by the international head office research staff, and entrusted with the handling of the survey. In the smallest subsidiaries, either a traveling regional head office person distributed the questionnaires and took the completed questionnaires away, or the whole process was handled by mail.

The task of the local survey coordinators included providing advance information to managers and employees; some designed extensive and imaginative internal publicity campaigns to prepare employees for the survey. The actual filling out of the questionnaires was preferably done during working hours: for employees who had desks, usually at their desks, individually, and for employees who did not have desks, usually in the cafeteria, in groups.

The questionnaires were always anonymous and contained reassurances that no attempt to identify respondents would be made and that respondents were free not to answer any questions they did not want to answer. Respondents dropped their completed questionnaires in boxes that were supervised by persons who could be assumed to have the employees' confidence. The contents of the boxes were later bundled and sent to data processing. Employees in remote locations received and returned questionnaires by mail.

Initially, data processing was done centrally in two places, but later more and more subsidiaries handled their own data processing and sent in copies of their data on card or tape for the international database. Data were transferred to punched cards by manual key punching from the questionnaires, or from answer sheets attached to the questionnaires, or by the use of machine-readable answer sheets. Results were printed out in data books with various degrees of specificity (by division in a country, by country, international) using special-purpose computer programs that allowed comparisons among groups and with previous surveys of the same group. A page from such a data book is depicted in Exhibit 2.2.

The analysis of the data for organization development purposes was coordinated by the personnel research staff but entrusted as much as possible to line managers, sometimes assisted by analysis task forces of employee delegates. In most cases employees were informed about their country or division results through a written brochure and in one or more group meetings with

Exhibit 2.2. An Example of Information Output for IBM Survey Feedback

PERSONNEL RESEARCH   -   PREFER PROGRAM
OPINION SURVEY 1972-73
NON MANAGERS

QUESTION LABEL A5
HOW IMPORTANT IS IT TO YOU TO HAVE CHALLENGING WORK TO DO   1-OF UTMOST IMP   2-VERY IMP   3-MODERATE IMP
4-LITTLE IMP   5-VERY LITTLE/NO IMP
ALLOWABLE RESPONSES 1 THROUGH 5   VALID RESPONSES 1 THROUGH 5

CATEGORY		MEAN	STD. DEV.	VALID RESP.	TOTAL RESP.	DISTRIBUTION OF RESPONSES - PER CENT					OTHER
						1	2	3	4	5	
(HEAD QUARTERS)											
BELGIUM	1973	1.82	0.66	415	423	31	50	12	1	0	2
BELGIUM	1969	1.95	0.75	285	297	28	52	19	1	1	4
DENMARK	1973	1.66	0.69	270	270	45	46	9	1	0	0
DENMARK	1969	1.88	0.79	171	174	34	47	16	2	1	2
FINLAND	1973	1.77	0.63	115	115	34	55	11	2	0	0
FINLAND	1969	1.98	0.77	107	110	29	46	23	2	0	3
IRELAND	1973	1.56	0.63	41	42	51	41	7	0	0	2
IRELAND	1969	1.65	0.68	26	28	46	42	12	0	0	2
NETHERLANDS	1973	1.85	0.72	263	268	32	53	13	2	0	7
NETHERLANDS	1969	1.73	0.64	215	218	37	53	9	0	0	1
NORWAY	1973	2.01	0.68	138	142	20	62	17	1	1	3
NORWAY	1969	2.02	0.74	96	99	23	55	19	3	0	3
SWEDEN	1973	1.77	0.66	350	351	34	57	8	1	1	0
SWEDEN	1969	1.61	0.62	343	358	45	51	3	1	0	4
AUSTRIA	1973	1.65	0.65	207	208	44	46	10	0	0	0
AUSTRIA	1969	1.59	0.71	213	213	53	36	10	1	0	0
ITALY	1973	NO VALID DATA FOR THIS UNIT									
ITALY	1969	1.51	0.65	487	493	56	39	4	1	0	1
PORTUGAL	1973	1.51	0.63	55	55	56	36	7	0	0	0
PORTUGAL	1969	1.79	0.82	24	25	42	42	13	4	0	4

their colleagues and superiors. Managers were expected to develop strategies for corrective actions that the survey showed to be necessary. The effectiveness of this procedure varied widely.

Even with the help of the existing company infrastructure, the purely administrative aspects of such a survey remain delicate. Working through so many different persons in so many different cultures means a large number of sources of error, misunderstanding, and accidents. Questions were mysteriously missing in some countries, answer categories were inadvertently left out, packages of questionnaires got lost in the mail. Once, a box containing the answer sheets of a thousand respondents was stolen from an airplane and never returned. Questions were coded on the wrong number, so that, for example, the answers on the preferred type of manager (question A54; see Appendix 1) of country X showed up among the answers on the actually perceived manager (A55) of the other countries. Some groups were found coded on the wrong occupations. In international survey administration, as in any large human undertaking, Murphy's Law applies: If anything can go wrong, it will. A painful process of correcting, recoding, and discounting suspect information was necessary in order to arrive at results that made sense.

The IBM Survey Database

The computerized survey database contained the scores on all questions for all surveys held between November 1967 and 1973. The June 1967 product development survey was not part of the database because it had too many different questions. Some data, such as those from the United States, were not integrated into the database and were analyzed separately. With 70 countries (71 including the United States) and about 88,000 different respondents on about 117,000 questionnaires, the IBM database represented probably the largest body of survey data ever collected with one instrument up to that time.

The entries into the database were coded by country (65 countries were retained) and by occupation (50 different occupations). This produced a matrix of $65 \times 50 = 3,250$ cells, but many of these were empty; only about 1,150 really occurred, and then often with very small numbers of respondents. The part of the matrix that was full is L-shaped: Only a few large countries had all occupations, and only a few general occupations (such as sales representatives, customer engineers, and office clerks) occurred in all countries.

As stated earlier, 60 "core" questions and 66 "recommended" questions were standardized in 1971. According to their content, they could be divided into four types:

1. *Satisfactions* supplied a personal evaluation of an aspect of the work situation (for example: "How satisfied are you with . . ." but also "How do you like your job—the kind of work you do?" with answers from *it is very good* to *very poor*).

2. *Perceptions* were subjective descriptions of an aspect or problem of the work situation; about half of the "perception" questions dealt with the behavior of various managers (for example: "How often does your manager expect a large amount of work from you?"). Included in this category is a question about job stress (A37 in Appendix 1).

3. *Personal goals and beliefs* were statements not about the job or the company as such but related to an ideal job or to general issues in industry. Personal goals (for example: "How important is it to you to have an opportunity for high earnings?") dealt with the *desired* and beliefs (for example, "Competition between employees usually does more harm than good") with the *desirable*; there need not always be consistency between the two (see Chapter 1). This category included the preferred manager (A54).

4. *Demographics* dealt with age, gender, years of education, years with the company, and so on.

The present study is concerned with questions that can be assumed to represent values—that is, people's more permanent mental programming—reflecting the contribution of the *person* more than of the *situation*. For all questions except perhaps those dealing with demographics, the answers reflect both the person and the situation, but the situational component can be expected to be stronger for satisfactions than for personal goals and beliefs, with perceptions in between. The choice of the questions for further analysis reflects this: For the present study, 1 satisfaction question, 14 perception questions, and 44 personal goals and beliefs questions have been used; the latter include 19 questions that had actually been dropped from the questionnaire in 1971 or before but for which the results available on file still proved interesting.

Four demographic questions served as controls; thus the cross-cultural analysis of IBM survey data was based on $1 + 14 + 44 + 4 = 63$ questions. The text of these questions can be found in Appendix 1.[7]

The use of the personal goals and beliefs questions represents a feature of the IBM questionnaires without which this book would not have been written.[8] The content of the personal goals questions derived from the U.S. literature and survey experience and from open interviews with laboratory personnel in six European countries.

The various versions used in IBM counted between 26 and 14 goals. The beliefs questions were produced through brainstorming among international head office personnel experienced in dealing with IBM people in different countries. Various versions of their list contained between 19 and 10 items.

A Second Research Setting: IMEDE Business School

IMEDE Management Development Institute in Lausanne, Switzerland (later rebaptized IMD), is a postgraduate and postexperience international business school. It was founded by the Nestlé Corporation in 1958 and in the 1970s provided training to managers from all over the world through courses whose length could vary from a few days to a full year.

I taught courses in organizational behavior at IMEDE from 1971 to 1973, on leave from IBM. By that time it had become clear that certain questions in the IBM questionnaire that could be expected to express values produced stable and predictable differences in answer patterns among countries. In my IMEDE courses I administered a 17-item "Questionnaire on Work Goals and Preferences" derived from the IBM material;[9] I used the results as teaching material in the course. Answers on this questionnaire were obtained from 362 managers from about 30 different countries and from a variety of private and public organizations unrelated to IBM. As I will show in Chapters 3 and 5, the major country differences found among IBM employees were reproduced in the IMEDE managers sample. This supplied the first hard proof that the differences among countries found inside IBM were not company specific, but had to be due to the respondents' socialization *before* they joined the corporation. At IMEDE all respondents used an English version of the questionnaire, whereas in IBM different language versions had been used. The similarity between IBM and IMEDE data therefore also ruled out a hypothesis that the differences among countries could be due to translation of the questionnaire.

In addition to the IBM questions, I administered to some IMEDE classes other tests of values and personality in order to explore convergence between different instruments and the IBM questionnaire. I tried seven other instruments.[10] The highest correlation found between scores on the IBM questionnaire and on another instrument was $r = .49***$ (across 64 respondents).[11] This was as good as any other correlation between different test scores; the highest correlation found between any two other tests was $r = .48$.

All in all, the IMEDE experience showed that the differences among countries found in IBM could be at least partly reproduced with non-IBM respondents, that the IBM questions on personal goals were acceptable as a test of values, and that it was therefore worthwhile to continue the analysis of the IBM data. I conducted this analysis in the period 1973-79, after I had left IBM and was based at the European Institute for Advanced Studies in Management (EIASM) in Brussels, Belgium.[12] IBM allowed me to use its database for further study.

Data Treatment

Frequency Distributions and Central Tendency Within Groups

The first information obtained from the IBM survey database consisted typically of frequency distributions for the different answer categories of each question, as reproduced in Exhibit 2.2. The question analyzed in the exhibit is A5 from Appendix 1: "How important is it to you to have challenging work to do—work from which you can get a personal sense of accomplishment?" Five valid answer categories follow. The page shown displays the frequency distribution in full percentages for nonmanagers in country head offices for a number of countries. For each country, the 1973 data are followed by the results of the same group in the previous survey round (1969) for a historical comparison.

Any paper-and-pencil instrument produces some invalid responses: items left blank, double answers (more than one answer checked for a question for which only one is allowed), and sometimes data entry errors that produce, for example, some answer codes of 6 for a case where only 5 choices exist. In the IBM surveys invalid answers rarely exceeded 5% of the total (see the last column in Exhibit 2.2, labeled "other"), and they were excluded from further analysis; this means that the percentages in the frequency distribution are based on valid responses only.

Most questions in the IBM questionnaire used 5-point answer scales, and most frequency distributions were skewed; nearly all were unimodal. The vast majority used *ordinal* scales, which means that the answer categories showed a natural and unambiguous rank order from less to more important, satisfied to dissatisfied, or vice versa. They were not *interval* scales in the strict sense of the word, which would imply that the distance between, for example, answers 1 and 2 (such as from *very good* to *good*) is equal to the distance between answers 3 and 4 (such as from *average* to *poor*). A few questions (for example, A55) did not use ordinal scales but only *nominal* scales (no unambiguous rank order for the answers).

The measure of central tendency used is the mean. The mean formally presupposes interval scales; for ordinal scales the median would have been the theoretically more correct measure, but for short scales with many cases per answer category it approaches the mean closely.[13] The mean loses less information, is easier to compute, and plays a role in all parametric statistical calculations, such as product-moment correlations. In the analysis of the IBM data scales of the type *very good* to *very poor, of utmost* . . . to *no importance,* and *strongly agree* to *strongly disagree* were considered *quasi-interval scales* for which the mean could be validly used. For the few questions with nominal scales (A43, A54, A55), the frequency distributions were dichotomized at the most meaningful point and the answers summarized in percentages.

In addition to the means, Exhibit 2.2 shows standard deviations, which, however, were rarely used in the analysis; large standard deviations are a warning that a respondent group was heterogeneously composed.

The data were analyzed extensively within groups, "groups" being any sets of respondents considered homogeneous for the purposes of the analysis. Usually a group for analysis represented one occupation (or set of similar occupations) in one country; sometimes it represented one or more occupations across a set of countries. The major analysis tools were cross-tabulations, correlations, and factor analysis. *Within*-group characteristics (correlation coefficients, factor loadings) were then compared *between* groups.

ANOVA: Country, Occupation, Gender, and Age

The main criteria responsible for group differences in the survey data and that apply to all data were country, occupation, gender, and age of the respondents. From these, occupation and gender were closely related: Only a few occupations had sizable numbers of both men and women. Other possible criteria were length of service with the company and education level. Length of service with the company was obviously correlated with age and was not used as a separate criterion.[14] Educational level was closely related to occupation. For our international survey population, however, data about education levels were less accurate than data about occupations, as education systems vary from one country to another, but the occupation classification was standardized throughout the corporation. Occupation was used as the main criterion, but where it was necessary to order the various occupations on a one-dimensional scale, this was done according to the mean number of years of formal education of the incumbents.[15]

The relative contribution to the variance in the data of the four criterion variables country, occupation, gender, and age was tested through an analysis of variance (ANOVA) on a subsample of the data covering a wide range of respondents on all four criteria. The subsample was taken from the 1970 survey in the manufacturing plants. It included 10 countries (Argentina, Brazil, Canada, France, Great Britain, Germany, India, Japan, the Netherlands, and Sweden) and five occupational groups (managers, professionals, technicians plus skilled workers, clerks, and unskilled workers). The number of cases per cell of one country, one occupation, was randomly reduced for the larger plants so that it varied between 12 (professionals in India) and 181 (unskilled in Netherlands); the average number per cell was 64 (a total of 3,220 cases for 50 cells). Gender and age group were taken as covariants. The variance analysis was done separately for the six questions A37, A43, A54, A55, B46, and B61 that will be used in Chapters 3 and 4 to form the Power Distance Index and the Uncertainty Avoidance Index. In addition, separate variance analyses were done on two composite scores computed for each respondent as the differences between the scores on two questions each: an individualism score (A18-A9; see Chapter 5) and a masculinity score (A7-A8; see Chapter 6). The reason for analyzing the difference between two questions in this case, rather than single questions, was that this eliminated acquiescence (see below); otherwise the ANOVA would have mainly shown variance in acquiescence.

Exhibit 2.3 presents the outcome of the analysis. The country effect is highly significant (beyond the .001 level) in all eight cases. This is not surprising given that the eight questions were selected because of their ability to discriminate between countries. The occupation effect is also significant in all eight cases, although not always at the .001 level. Gender and age effects are each significant in five out of eight cases.

The fact that the nationality of the respondents, and sometimes the other criterion variables occupation, gender, and age, affected the scores of these questions highly significantly does not mean, of course, that a respondent's answer was fully predictable from his or her nationality or any other identification. In fact, of the total variance in the answers of the 3,220 respondents in the variance analyses, only 4.2% was accounted for by their belonging to one of the 10 nationalities in the sample. This, however, was 16 times as much as could be expected on the basis of pure chance. The distribution of answer scores within and between countries resembles Exhibit 1.7: a broad dispersion across individuals and relatively small shifts of group means with, nevertheless, considerable consequences for group behavior and the functioning of institutions.

Exhibit 2.3 Summary of Results of ANOVA on Data from 3,220 Respondents from the 1970 Manufacturing Survey

Question	F Value and Significance of Effects for				
	Country 9 df	Occupation 4 df	Country × Occupation 36 df	Gender 1 df	Age 1 df
B46: Employees afraid to disagree	7.1***	24.9***	2.3***	.4	.4
A54: Preferred manager number 3	3.2***	19.8***	1.0	7.3**	.1
A55: Perceived manager number 1 or 2	5.9***	5.8***	.7	1.6	2.0
A37: Stress	46.7***	3.8**	1.5*	3.2	5.8*
A43: Continue less than 5 years	8.8***	6.7***	1.8**	120.8***	92.7***
B60: Company rules should not be broken	6.0***	19.8***	1.6*	3.9*	56.9***
A18-A9: Importance personal time but not training (individualism)	12.9***	2.8*	1.6*	39.3***	21.5***
A7-A8: Importance earnings but not cooperation (masculinity)	25.8***	6.0***	1.5*	11.7***	13.2***
Significance limits for F					
.001	3.1	4.6	2.1	10.8	10.8
.01	2.4	3.3	1.7	6.6	6.6
.05	1.9	2.4	1.3	3.8	3.8

NOTE: The survey involved 10 countries and five occupations for six questions plus two composite scores; df equals degrees of freedom.
$*p = .05$; $**p = .01$; $***p = .001$.

The main purpose of this book is comparison by country. This will be supplemented with comparisons by occupation, gender, and age groups where such comparisons seem meaningful (for effects of gender and age, see especially Chapter 6).

Comparing 40 Countries: Matching Occupations

In computing scores on survey questions by country, I had to control for occupation. The composition of occupational groups by gender and age varied only marginally among subsidiaries of IBM, which made it unnecessary to control for gender and age after controlling for occupation.

The scores to be composed by country were either mean scores on 5-point quasi-interval scales or percentages of answers on nominal scales. The country comparison used only data from the marketing and service departments of the corporation, not from product development or manufacturing. The marketing and service departments were surveyed twice, once in 1967-69 and once in 1971-73. For each of these two survey rounds a

country score was computed as the arithmetic mean of the scores for seven occupational categories:

1. Managers (all levels), country head office
2. Managers (all levels), branch offices, including sales, systems engineering, and customer engineering managers[16]
3. Systems engineers
4. Data processing sales representatives
5. Data processing customer engineers
6. Office products customer engineers
7. Administrative personnel, country head office, including clerks and professionals[17]

All of these categories carried equal weight in the computation of the country score, regardless of the actual numbers of respondents.

The computer program used for database information output (Exhibit 2.2) did not print results for groups smaller than eight respondents. The use of smaller groups was seen as a threat to the anonymity of respondents, but it is also statistically undesirable. Many of the smaller subsidiaries, however, had fewer than eight respondents in one or more of the seven occupational categories. For the analysis described in the first edition of *Culture's Consequences,* I set a conservative minimal criterion for including a country: At least four out of the seven categories should have eight or more respondents and therefore have their data printed out.[18] Data for missing occupational categories were extrapolated from the available data.[19] In this way, scores for 39 out of the 71 countries in the IBM database could be used, from which 30 had been surveyed twice. These countries are marked as Category 1 in Exhibit 2.1. Yugoslavia was the 40th country. The total number of respondents involved was 72,215 (31,218 for 1967-69 and 40,997 for 1971-73); the minimum for a country was 58 (Singapore, surveyed in 1971-73 only) and the maximum 11,384 (Germany, with 3,477 respondents in 1967-69 and 7,907 in 1971-73). For the complete list of numbers of respondents, see Appendix 2, Exhibit A2.1.

Extension to 50 Countries
Plus Three Regions

Including in the analysis only countries for which at least four out of the seven occupational categories were represented with eight or more respondents was a very conservative, safe criterion.[20] It meant that initially 32 countries for which at least some data were available in the IBM database had been left out. In 1982, after the first edition of *Culture's Consequences* had appeared, I was asked to do a small study comparing the national cultures of Indonesia and the Netherlands (Hofstede, 1983a). Indonesia had been one of the countries that just fell short of the conservative criterion, with 91 respondents (43 [three groups] in 1969 and 48 [four groups] in 1972). Going back to the database, I found another 9 countries with between 132 and 56 respondents per country that with a slightly less conservative selection could be added to the existing list of 40. They are marked as Category 2 in Exhibit 2.1 and are listed with their numbers of respondents in Appendix 2, Exhibit A2.4.

A particular problem arose for seven Arabic-speaking countries that within the IBM organization had formed the "Middle East region": Egypt, Lebanon, Libya, Kuwait, Iraq, Saudi Arabia, and United Arab Republic. They had been surveyed both in 1969 and in 1972, but when I tried to extend the country list in 1982, it turned out that IBM had not only inadvertently wiped the tape with the raw survey data, it had destroyed the data printouts as well. The only data printouts that were saved pertained to the total region, so I was

forced to treat these countries as one region, whereas I might have wanted to keep Egypt and Lebanon separate: Now the region is culturally less homogeneous than would be desirable. The total Arabic-speaking region had 141 respondents, 79 in 1969 and 62 in 1972. The countries are marked as Category 3a in Exhibit 2.1.

English-speaking countries in sub-Saharan Africa had very small IBM offices in those days; they were surveyed in 1972 only.[21] Ghana had two occupational categories with more than eight respondents, and Nigeria, Zambia, and Kenya had one such occupational category each. There were IBM offices in Ethiopia, Tanzania, and Sierra Leone in which no occupational category met the eight-respondent criterion, and which therefore did not appear in the data printouts at all. Already in the analysis of the 1972 survey data the African data had therefore been pooled into an East African region (Kenya, Ethiopia, Tanzania, and Zambia) with 46 respondents from four occupations and a West African region (Ghana, Nigeria, and Sierra Leone) with 43 respondents from three occupations. These regions were added as such to the extended country list; the countries are marked as Categories 3b and 3c, respectively, in Exhibit 2.1. Cultural differences in sub-Saharan Africa do not necessary follow the divisions into countries inherited from colonial days, so the East Africa/West Africa distinction may be as good as any.

Thus what was added to the list of countries in 1982 were 10 single countries and three regions, bringing the total count to 50 countries plus three regions representing another 14 countries. Eight countries represented in the IBM database with very small numbers of respondents stayed definitively out of the analysis. They are marked as Category 4 in Exhibit 2.1. For the full list of numbers of respondents per country, see Appendix 2, Exhibit A2.4.

In spite of the fact that the country scores added were based on fewer respondents than those in the initial set of 40, there was no evidence that they were less reliable.[22] They fit smoothly into the four-dimensional framework developed from the 40-country set, demonstrating the robustness of the framework. In this and the following chapters I refer to the 40-country set when describing the development of the framework, and to the 50+3 unit set when comparing with data added since the publication of the first edition of *Culture's Consequences.*

Selecting Stable Questions

The fact that most countries were surveyed twice within a 4-year interval allowed a test of the stability of the between-country differences. I wanted to retain only questions for which the differences in score level from country to country were relatively stable from the first to the second survey round (from about 1968 to about 1972), for the following reasons:

1. The purpose of the analysis was to find value differences among countries and to relate these to characteristics of the countries; one could not expect to find meaningful relationships for measures that were not more or less stable over time.

2. Country score levels reflect both the collective state of mind of the respondents and the collective situation in which these respondents find themselves. I was interested in the first more than in the second. Collective states of mind of the type that interests us change slowly; the situation, however, may change much faster, such as through a change in market conditions, company policy, or management practice. Weeding out questions for which score levels were unstable over time allowed me to avoid such situationally determined issues.

The stability data for 44 questions selected for further analysis (the A and B questions from Appendix 1, but not the C questions, none of which were used twice) are shown in Exhibit 2.4. The stability coefficients were computed as (Spearman) rank correlations of mean country scores (based on seven occupations) between the first and the second survey rounds. They varied from $rho = .12$ to $rho = .95$.[23] Arbitrarily, I considered scores as reasonably stable if the coefficient exceeded .50.[24] I found .39 for overall satisfaction; the questions dealing with perceptions had stabilities ranging from $rho = .12$ to .94, with a median of .53; the coefficients for "personal goals and beliefs" ranged from .40 to .95, with a median of .77; the stabilities of the demographics ranged from $rho = .56$ to .78, with a median of .65. Thus the country scores for personal goals and beliefs were the most stable over time, in accordance with the above-mentioned assumption that these are least affected by situational factors. The satisfaction measure was fairly unstable; the stabilities for the perceptions varied strongly. It should be stressed that these stability coefficients were based on country mean scores—that is, *aggregate data*. For comparison purposes, the last column of Exhibit 2.4 shows, for those questions for which they are available, stability (test-retest reliability) data for *individual* answers. These were determined in a test-retest experiment with 62 managers in IMEDE and retest after 2 weeks (Hofstede, 1975b). There is no visible relationship between the two types of stability.[25]

Based on the stability coefficients displayed in Exhibit 2.4, five questions from the perceptions group were excluded from further analysis: A48, B39, B47, B49, and B51, with stabilities between .35 and .12. For the last four, the stability coefficients were not even significantly different from zero. For the remaining questions the stability coefficients ranged from .39 to .94, with a median of .76. Five questions with stability coefficients between .39 and .49 were provisionally retained (two of them were dropped later; see below). For the questions that were retained, country scores were computed as means between the values found in the two survey rounds. From a comparison between the two survey rounds, it became clear that there had been worldwide shifts on some questions (see below, Exhibit 2.6). For the countries surveyed only once, either in the first or in the second round, it was necessary to correct for these shifts. Scores for countries surveyed only once were therefore corrected with half the worldwide shifts between 1968 and 1972 based on the countries surveyed twice. In this way for all countries the country scores can be assumed to approximate as well as possible the situation around 1970.

Eclectic Analysis: Power Distance and Uncertainty Avoidance

From the earliest surveys onward, it had been clear that answers to questions dealing with hierarchical relationships differed systematically across countries. An early publication explored the differences in preferred and perceived leadership styles (questions A54 and A55) in six countries (Sadler & Hofstede, 1972). Later, for conceptual reasons related to Mulder's (1976, 1977) power distance reduction theory, the question "How frequently are employees afraid to express disagreement with their managers?" (B46) was chosen as a central question measuring power distance. Country scores on this question were correlated with those on six other conceptually related questions (A48, A52, A54, A55, B55, B56). Based on these ecological correlations, the three questions A54, A55, and B46 were selected to form a Power Distance Index (PDI; the exact computation of the index is described in Chapter 3).

The Uncertainty Avoidance Index was developed in an analogous way. I had an early theoretical interest in the phenomenon of work stress, which was measured by the question "How often do you feel nervous or tense at work?" (A37), but my interest had been in stress differences by occupation rather than by country (Hofstede, 1994a). However, stress scores varied much more by country than by occupation (see Exhibit 2.3). A subsequent analysis of stress differences among countries showed these to be highly significantly correlated with anxiety factor scores based on na-

Exhibit 2.4 Stability Coefficients of Country Mean Scores on 44 Questions, From 1967-69 to 1971-73

Question Number	Question	Number of Countries Surveyed Twice	Stability Coefficient of Country Mean Scores	Stability of Individual Scores[a]
Satisfaction				
A58	Overall satisfaction	28	.39	
Perceptions				
A37	Stress	29	.94	
A43	Answer 1 + 2: Continue less than 5 years	28	.70	
	Answer 4: Continue until retirement	28	.91	
A48	Would complainer suffer?	28	.35[d]	
A52	Manager helps ahead	29	.65	
A55	Perceived manager 1 or 2	29	.82	
B9	Prefer specialist career	13	.53	
B24	Prefer foreign company	22	.77	
B25	Other job available?	25	.48	
B39	Manager insists on rules	23	.34[d]	
B44	Prefer manager own nationality	21	.47	.66
B46	Employees afraid to disagree	26	.70	
B47	Unclear on duties	13	.12[d]	
B49	Superiors involved in details	21	.18[d]	
B51	Groups looking down on others	10	.28[d]	
Personal goals and beliefs				
A5	Importance challenge	19	.57	.46
A6	Importance desirable area	19	.81	.66
A7	Importance earnings	19	.74	.73
A8	Importance cooperation	19	.66	.37
A9	Importance training	19	.77	.51
A10	Importance benefits	19	.90	.54
A11	Importance recognition	19	.77	.53
A12	Importance physical conditions	19	.76	.67
A13	Importance freedom	19	.95	.31
A14	Importance employment security	19	.69	.64

tional statistics from 18 countries, calculated by Lynn (1971). The ecological correlation of stress scores with the Power Distance Index was weak ($r = .30*$), so it seemed that stress scores might reflect another and separate ecological dimension. There was a good theoretical reason for this assumption. The "Aston group" in Great Britain (Pugh, 1976; Pugh & Hickson, 1976) had empirically demonstrated that organizational structures reflected two main dimensions: "concentration of authority" and "structuring of activities." The first was clearly conceptually related to power distance; I guessed that the second could relate to stress. A search in the IBM questionnaire revealed three questions expressing structuring of activities, of which, however, only one showed stable country differences over time: the belief that "company rules should not be broken—even when the employee thinks it is in the company's best interests" (B60).[26] Country scores on this question were indeed significantly correlated with country stress scores. A search for questions ecologically correlated with both "stress" and "company rules should not be broken" produced a third stable item: "How long do you think you will continue working for this company?" (A43). The combination of stress, a need for fixed company rules, and the intent to continue with the company

Exhibit 2.4 Continued

Question Number	Question	Number of Countries Surveyed Twice	Stability Coefficient of Country Mean Scores	Stability of Individual Scores[a]
A15	Importance advancement	19	.49	.33
A16	Importance manager	19	.49	.33
A17	Importance use of skills	19	.76	.36
A18	Importance personal time	19	.89	.53
A54	Preferred manager 1 or 2	29	.94	.53
B52	Corporation responsible for employees	22	.79	.72
B53	Interesting work as important as earnings	23	.90	.25
B54	Competition harmful	21	.84	.76
B55	Employees lose respect for consultative manager	20	.74	.09
B56	Employees should participate more	0	b	.51
B57	Individual decisions better	17	.79	.61
B58	Corporation responsible for society	0	b	.58
B59	Staying with one company desirable	21	.79	.56
B60	Company rules should not be broken	20	.75	.57
B61	Most employees avoid responsibility	20	.40	.55
Demographics				
A1	Percentage female respondents	26	.65	
A2	Seniority in company	29	.56	
A56	Educational		c	
A57	Age	29	.78	

a. Determined on IMEDE data.
b. Question newly created in 1971.
c. Data from 1967-69 not reliable.
d. Excluded from further analysis.

was interpreted as expressing a level of "uncertainty avoidance" in the country, among other things conceptually related to the Aston "structuring of activities." Country scores on the three questions A37, A43, and B60 were then used to form an Uncertainty Avoidance Index (UAI; for further explanation of the concept of uncertainty avoidance, as well as for the exact calculation of the index, see Chapter 4).

The phase of the analysis in which the Power Distance Index and Uncertainty Avoidance Index were developed can be called "eclectic" because questions were selected on the basis of theoretical reasoning (with the exception of A43), and statistics (ecological correlation analysis) was used only *after* theoretical reasoning had singled out certain questions as potentially relevant. That is, theory preceded the use of statistics—as opposed to an alternative approach that simply would have taken all available questions regardless of their

theoretical relevance and subjected their country scores to an ecological factor analysis right away. As I shall relate below, I did use an ecological factor analysis, but only at the very end of the analysis process, in order to put the total picture together.

The difference between using heavy statistical treatment (factor analysis) at the beginning or at the end of the analysis may look trivial, but this is not so: The atheoretical, statistics-first approach carries three substantial risks that the theory-first approach avoids. The first risk is that potentially important nuances in data may be overlooked. For example, it is doubtful whether I would have discovered in a wholesale factor analysis the difference in cultural meaning of the 1967-69 and 1970-73 versions of manager 4 in question A54, the "preferred manager" (see Chapter 3). The second risk is the operation of a kind of Gresham's law, according to which "bad data drive out good data": Many trivial variables in a factor analysis cloud the meaning of a few crucial ones. Finding a "strong factor" just means that many variables are intercorrelated, not that they mean anything important (the correlation may be due to response set); a weak factor may hide an essential variable for which the questionnaire had no correlates due to the cultural bias of the people who composed it. For example, as authors of the IBM questionnaire, we were strongly concerned with employee-manager relationships, which led to many questions related to power distance. We were, however, naive with regard to issues of formal organization, which led to a lack of questions related to uncertainty avoidance. The third risk of a statistics-first approach is that the theoretical meaning of the results may remain hidden: Once the results of the analysis are there, the researcher is seriously constrained in his or her search for theoretical clarification by the "findings" and tempted to be quickly satisfied with a few superficial interpretations. Studies of this kind often show remarkably little synergy with other studies.

Work Goal Importance Data:
Eliminating Acquiescence

A potentially rich source of information was available in the "work goal importance" questions, which form a self-contained block. The 1968-71 surveys contained 22 such questions;[27] after that the list was reduced to 14 (A5 through A18). A fundamental problem with these questions is that respondents' answers to them are strongly affected by *acquiescence*. Acquiescence is the tendency to give a positive answer to any question, regardless of its content ("yes-manship"; Schuman & Presser, 1981, pp. 203 ff.). In general, we find that the lower the status and educational level of a category of respondents, the stronger their acquiescence. This is clearly demonstrated in Exhibit 2.5.

For 38 occupations, gross mean work goal importance scores were computed taking 15 European countries and all 22 work goals together (1968-71 data).[28] A low gross mean indicates that people in this occupation tend to score *all* goals more frequently as *of utmost importance* or *very important*. Exhibit 2.5 shows that gross means for the 38 occupations vary from 1.82 to 2.28, and that the rank correlation of the gross mean with the occupation's mean years of formal education is as high as $r = .83***$. That is, the tendency to rate everything more important is for $.83^2 = 69\%$ a matter of the occupation's educational level.[29] Greater acquiescence by less-educated, lower-status employee categories is probably due to both a desire to please the (higher-status) author of the questionnaire and less differentiated "cog-

nitive maps" in the respondents: They distinguish less clearly between the different goals.

Acquiescence varies not only among occupations but among countries as well. The gross mean work goal importance score across 14 goals has been taken as the measure of acquiescence for each of the 40 countries. It is abbreviated IMP; its values are displayed in Appendix 3, Exhibit A3.1.

Acquiescence is an interesting phenomenon per se, but it is irrelevant for determining the importance of a particular work goal for a certain category of respondents. It tends to distort the answers. In general we can say that the *absolute* importance score of a single goal is irrelevant: It is as meaningful as the sound of one hand clapping. Importance becomes meaningful only when we can compare at least two goals.[30] Earnings and cooperation are both important for almost anyone; only the relative importance of one over the other tells us something about the values of a person or group. This means that work goal importance scores for single goals should not be shown in their raw state—they should be shown relative to other goals. This can be done through ranking or standardizing across the *n* goals. In ranking, the information about the relative distances between the goals is lost; in standardizing it is preserved. Standardizing replaces the scores with the distance from their common overall mean, divided by their common standard deviation. The overall mean of the standardized scores for the *n* goals for each group is always zero.[31]

The necessity of ranking or standardizing work goal importance scores before comparing them has unfortunately not always been recognized in the literature; quite a few studies have produced meaningless results by comparing nonstandardized group means of work goal importance scores (see Chapter 5).

In this book, I always give work goal importance scores in their standardized form (Appendix 3). In order to avoid negative scores and decimal points, I have given the standardized scores a mean of 500 and a standard deviation of 100; also, their sign has been reversed, so that a very important goal (raw score $2 \times SD$ below mean) now scores around 700 and the least important goals now score below 300.[32]

The work goals questions are the only items for which acquiescence was eliminated by standardizing. For most other questions the answers show a clear midpoint (such as *undecided* between *agree* and *disagree*) that provides an objective anchoring of responses. Standardizing for the other questions was also difficult to carry out because they used varying answer formats that might have been differentially affected by acquiescence. Only the "general beliefs" (B52 through B61 and C9 through C19) all used the same format. The problem in this case was that because B and C

Exhibit 2.5   Comparison Between Educational Level and Mean "Importance" Scores Across 22 Work Goals for 38 Occupations, Europe or Worldwide, 1968-71 Data ($n = 48,895$)

Identification Number	Occupation	Mean Formal Educational Level (Years)	Mean Work Goal Importance Score Over All 22 Goals
21	Unskilled card plant personnel	10.4	1.86
46	Unskilled machine plant direct personnel	10.5	1.82
49	Unskilled machine plant indirect personnel	10.9	1.86
47	Skilled machine plant direct personnel	11.0	1.87
11	Office products customer engineering managers	11.2	2.02
12	Office products customer engineers	11.3	1.98
50	Skilled machine plant indirect personnel	11.5	1.97
51	Machine plant clerks	11.5	2.01
19	Card plant managers	11.6	1.96
64	Product development laboratory clerks	11.6	2,04
31	Office secretaries and typists	11.7	2.04
14	Branch office clerks	11.8	1.98
07	Data processing customer engineering managers	11.9	2.14
63	Product development laboratory technicians	12.1	2.09
08	Data processing customer engineers	12.2	2.13
09	Office products sales managers	12.3	1.90
74	Product test laboratory clerks	12.3	2.13
10	Office products sales representatives	12.4	1.90
18	Data processing service bureau operators	12.4	1.98
73	Product test laboratory technicians	12.7	2.15
26	Head office clerks	12.9	2.00
41	Machine plant managers, first line	13.3	2.09
13	Branch office administration managers	13.3	2.10
24	Head office managers	14.1	2.08
43	Machine plant professionals	14.3	2.13
15	Data processing service bureau managers	14.4	2.09
42	Machine plant managers, second level and up	14.4	2.10
25	Head office professionals	14.8	2.09
17	Data processing service bureau professionals	14.9	2.13
02	Data processing sales representatives	15.6	2.11
01	Data processing sales managers	15.6	2.16
62	Product development laboratory professionals	15.6	2.22
61	Product development laboratory managers	15.6	2.22
05	Branch office systems engineers	15.8	2.15
06	Branch office sales and systems engineering trainees	15.9	2.19
71	Product test laboratory managers	15.9	2.27
72	Product test laboratory professionals	15.9	2.28
82	Research laboratory professionals	16.5	2.27
	Mean of 38 occupations	13.2	2.07

Spearman rank correlation Education Level × Mean Work Goal Importance Score   Rho = .83*** questions were optional, there were many missing country data, and one cannot standardize an incomplete set of data. I have therefore left these other question scores in their raw state, but afterward corrected them for acquiescence tendencies where these were visible. I did this assuming that acquiescence in these questions would be a linear function of acquiescence in the "importance" questions. The latter was measured by IMP (Appendix 3, Exhibit A3.1). By computing partial correlation coefficients controlling for IMP, I corrected for the acquiescence tendency (bottom lines in Appendix 2, Exhibits A2.2 and A2.3).

Work Goal Importance:
Ecological Factor Analysis

In Chapter 1, I dealt at length with the problem of changing the level of analysis when comparing cultures rather than individuals. In the study of the IBM data, the need for changing the level of analysis became particularly clear for the block of first 22, then 14 work goal importance questions. The issue was how to reduce meaningfully the amount of information contained in 22 (14) questions to a smaller number of underlying variables. In the earlier phases of the research we had factor analyzed unstandardized individual within-country, within-occupation work goal importance scores. We usually found six factors, related to job content, reward, interpersonal relations, security, comfort, and company. Sometimes, especially for lower-educated occupational categories, two or more of these factors collapsed into one. The selection of 14 goals made in 1972 aimed at achieving adequate representation of five dimensions of individual goals: job content, reward, interpersonal relations, security, and comfort.[33] These more or less fit the categorization of Maslow's (1970) hierarchy: self-actualization, esteem, belongingness, safety, and physiological needs. The "company" goals C3, C4, and C5 were not selected in 1971, although they did form a factor of their own, because they did not fit our individualistic paradigm of human needs, which had been strongly influenced by Maslow.

At that time, I had not yet grasped the implications of changing the level of analysis from individuals to countries. I tried to use the five dimensions—job content, reward, interpersonal relations, security, and comfort—for comparing occupations and for comparing countries, drawing occupation and country profiles according to the relative importance of the five. The resulting picture was confusing.

A methodological breakthrough occurred when a friendly statistician offered his help in analyzing the work goals data. He suggested that we try analyzing at two levels.[34] We both learned from this

exercise that within-group factors were different from between-group (ecological) factors. The exercise also showed that ecological categories should not be mixed: A cross-country analysis should be kept separate from a cross-occupation analysis. So I factor analyzed the work goals data across occupations (controlling for country) and also across countries (controlling for occupation). Data were available for 22 work goals in 38 occupations, for 22 work goals in 19 countries surveyed in 1968 and 1969, and for 14 work goals in all 40 countries. All data were standardized (Appendix 3). The factor analyses are described in the statistical section of Chapter 5, confirming that a Maslowian framework made some sense for comparing occupations but not at all for comparing countries. Countries did not group themselves according to Maslow's categories. Instead, national goal patterns could be classified according to two dimensions, an individual/collective dimension and an ego/social dimension. Based on the 14-goals, 40-countries ecological factor analysis, I used the factor scores of the 40 countries on the axes corresponding to these two dimensions to construct the Individualism Index (IDV) and the Masculinity Index (MAS; for details, see Chapters 5 and 6).

Putting the Four Dimensions Together

So now four dimensions of national culture differences had been identified: power distance, uncertainty avoidance, individualism, and masculinity. Other dimensions did not readily appear, nor could they be inferred from theory. As a final check on whether the four dimensions adequately explained the ecological variations, I ran a cross-national factor analysis of all relevant data combined. In various phases of the research I also tried other methods of multivariate analysis, such as cluster analysis and smallest-space analysis. As these led to results very similar to those from factor analysis, I continued to use the latter, with which I am most familiar.

A first factor analysis included 48 variables and, of course, 40 countries.[35] The full data used in this factor analysis are displayed in Appendixes 2 and 3. The first four factors together explained 37% of the variance. Factor 1 combined individualism with the reverse of power distance. Factor 2 was uncertainty avoidance; Factor 3, masculinity. Factor 4 was a weak and unclear second power distance factor (see Chapter 3). I trimmed the 48-variable matrix down to 32 variables by weeding out redundant and unclear items.[36] This time three distinct factors together explained 49% of the variance. After orthogonal varimax rotation, the factors were as follows (all loadings of .35 and over are shown):

Factor 1 (factor variance 24%)

.82	A18	Importance personal time
.82	B53	Interesting work not as important as earnings
.78	B52	Corporation not responsible for employees
−.76	A55	Low percentage perceived manager 1 or 2
.75	B46	Employees not afraid to disagree
.74	A54	High percentage preferred manager 3 (1967-69)
.69	B59	Staying with one company not desirable
.63	B56	Employees should not participate more
−.62	A12	Low importance physical conditions
−.61	A9	Low importance training
.59	A13	Importance freedom
.59	B55	Employees don't lose respect for consultative manager
.59	B24	Does not prefer foreign company
−.58	A17	Low importance use of skills
.41	A5	Importance challenge (second loading)
.37	B58	Corporation not responsible for society
−.35	A15	Low importance advancement (third loading)

Factor 2 (factor variance 13%)

−.71	A16	Low importance manager
.68	A7	Importance earnings
−.67	A8	Low importance cooperation
.60	A11	Importance recognition
.54	A5	Importance challenge
−.53	A6	Low importance desirable area
−.51	A14	Low importance employment security
−.46	A37	High stress (second loading)
−.45	B57	Individual decisions better (second loading)
.43	A17	Importance use of skills (second loading)
.39	A15	Importance advancement (second loading)
−.35	B52	Corporation responsible for employees (second loading)
−.35	B58	Corporation responsible for society (second loading)

Factor 3 (factor variance 12%)

.76	B60	Company rules may be broken
.62	A37	Low stress
.59	A43	Continue less than 5 years
.56	B9	Prefers manager rather than specialist career
−.50	B57	Individual decisions better
.49	B44	Does not prefer manager of own nationality
.49	A58	Low overall satisfaction
.46	A15	Importance advancement
−.46	B55	Employees lose respect for consultative manager (second loading)
.45	B54	Competition not harmful
−.43	A9	Low importance training (second loading)
−.35	A10	Low importance benefits

All variables show a loading of at least .35 on one of these three factors.

Again, Factor 1 represents an individualism/ low power distance factor: It includes the individual/collective dimension of work goals (questions A18, A12, A9, A13, A17, and A5) and power distance with a negative sign (questions A55, A46, and A54). In addition, it shows loadings for six "beliefs" (B53, B52, B59, B56, B55, and B58, all with a positive sign) and with two other questions (B24 and A15).

Factor 2 is a masculinity factor (with questions A16, A7, A8, A11, A5, A6, A14, A17, and A15). It has collected only four second loadings from other questions. This factor is further explored in Chapter 6.

Factor 3 corresponds to uncertainty avoidance with reversed sign. The three highest-loading items are the ones that together form the Uncertainty Avoidance Index. This factor is further explored in Chapter 4.

Power distance and individualism load on the same factor, but as I will show later in this chapter (Exhibit 2.7), this is the effect of both being correlated with a third, external variable, national wealth. If wealth is controlled for, by separating poorer from wealthier countries, the correlation between the two indexes disappears. Moreover, they are conceptually distinct, power distance being related to inequality and individualism/collectivism with the relationship between the individual and the primary group.

The ecological factor analysis did not include the C questions, which were dropped after the 1968, 1969, or 1970 survey rounds and for which the available data were therefore based on one survey only. They nevertheless provide interesting additional information. For the "general beliefs" C9 through C19, country scores are listed in Appendix 2, Exhibit A2.3,[37] together with their ecological correlations with the four dimensions.

The ecological factor analysis, as explained, was based on the data for the 40 Category 1 countries listed in Appendix 2 (Exhibits A2.1, A2.2, and A2.3) and Appendix 3 (Exhibit A3.1). For the 10 countries and three regions added later (Categories 2 and 3), Exhibit A2.4 in Appendix 2 lists the scores for the six questions on which the Power Distance and Uncertainty Avoidance Indexes were based. The bottom part of Exhibit A3.1 lists their scores on the 14 work goal questions, which formed the basis for their Individualism and Masculinity Index scores.[38] The scores on the other questions for these countries were not retrieved from the files, as they played no role in the calculations.

Value Shifts in IBM
Between 1967-69 and 1971-73

For the 36 questions in the IBM questionnaire used in both 1967-69 and 1971-73 and for which country differences were reasonably stable (Exhibit 2.4), the score shifts between the two survey rounds (for Category 1 countries) can be read from Exhibit 2.6.[39] The questions have been classified into four groups according to the dimension indexes (PDI, UAI, IDV, MAS) with which they showed the strongest ecological correlation across the 40 Category 1 countries. Also shown (under IDV) is the shift in the mean raw work goal importance score across 14 goals (IMP). A plus or minus sign indicates the direction in which the total index (PDI, UAI, IDV, or MAS) would have shifted due to the shift of answers on each question. The significance of the shifts (that is, whether they can be considered worldwide shifts) has been determined by the sign test across all countries surveyed twice; for example, scores on question A18 shifted positively in *all* 19 countries surveyed twice and question A9 shifted negatively in 18 out of 19 countries (all except Pakistan).

The shifts in the answers of IBM respondents may, of course, be due to situation (IBM)-specific causes as well as to shifts in values in the societies outside IBM. From 1968 to 1972, IBM's growth rate was considerably reduced. This meant fewer opportunities for advancement and more competition for resources within the company. The overall satisfaction of employees with the company (question A58) decreased in virtually all countries. The company climate became less benevolent.

Exhibit 2.6 shows shifts on individual questions; however, we should not, without further analysis, summarize these into shifts "in power

distance," "in uncertainty avoidance," and so on. This would represent a reverse ecological fallacy as described in Chapter 1. Let us take the case of power distance. From the three questions that have been used to compose PDI (B46, A55, and B54), one shifted significantly in the direction of a larger power distance and two in the direction of a smaller power distance. This means that, as far as the shift over time is concerned, the Power Distance Index was not homogeneous, and it is not suitable for describing changes over time. We can read from Exhibit 2.6 that only individualism and masculinity showed more or less homogeneous shifts, so that we can, as a whole, speak of "shifts in IDV" and "shifts in MAS."

I discuss the implications of the shifts for each of the dimensions in Chapters 3 to 6; in these chapters the shift data are split according to the respondents' age groups.

Correlations Between Index Scores

The four IBM indexes are supposed to represent independent dimensions, so their country scores should not be systematically correlated. Exceptions are PDI and IDV, which loaded on the same factor in the overall factor analysis across 40 countries. Exhibit 2.7 shows that this was still the case for the extended set of 53 countries and regions, but also that if one controls for GNP/capita (by separating wealthy from poor countries) the correlation between PDI and IDV becomes insignificant.

An important conclusion from Exhibit 2.7 is that across the 22 wealthier countries (but not at all across the poorer countries), UAI was significantly correlated with IDV, PDI, and MAS, in spite of the fact that these three other indexes did not show significant intercorrelations. Across these wealthier countries UAI functioned as a kind of summary index. Comparative studies that are limited to wealthy countries will easily distinguish only one dimension, uncertainty avoidance, which subsumes low individualism and strong power distance and masculinity.

Across all countries there was still a weak correlation between UAI and low IDV, but it is unlikely to lead to a confusion of these two dimensions.[40] The direction of the correlation of UAI and MAS reverses between the poor and the wealthy countries, which explains why across all countries the correlation is about zero. The correlation between IDV and MAS across the 40 countries must be .00 because these indexes were based on orthogonal factors (Chapter 5).

Exhibit 2.7 illustrates clearly that the correlation pattern among the dimensions depends on the set (or subset) of countries included. Validation studies in which external data are correlated with

Exhibit 2.6   Shifts in Mean Scores of Survey Questions From 1967-69 to 1971-73

Question Number	Question	Mean Score[a] 1967-69	Mean Score[a] 1971-73	Corresponding Shift in Index[b]	Total Surveyed Twice	Shifting in Same Direction[c]	Countries Shifting in Opposite Direction
Primarily correlated with PDI							
B46	Employees afraid to disagree	3.09	2.93	+	26	18*	AUT, BRA, GER, ISR, NET, PAK, TUR
A55	Perceived manager, % 1 + 2	47.9	45.4	−	29	22**	ARG, BRA, ISR, GRE, PER, PHI
A54	Preferred manager, % 1 + 2	27.1	22.9	−	29	22**	AUT, FIN, SPA
B55	Employees lose respect	4.02	4.10	−	20	15**	FIN, GER, GRE, SPA
A52	Manager helps ahead	2.34	2.52	+	29	23***	ARG, AUT, BRA, PAK, PER
A13	Importance freedom	529	544	−	19	16***	GBR, ISR, NOR
B52	Corporation responsible	1.74	1.72	0	22	11	Many
B53	Interesting work important	1.78	1.84	−	23	16*	FIN, GER, MEX, PAK, SAF, TUR, VEN
Primarily correlated with UAI							
B60	Rules shouldn't be broken	2.80	2.87	0 (−)	20	12	Many
A43	Continue with company, % 1 + 2	20.0	20.7	0 (−)	28	12	Many
A37	Stress	3.19	3.10	+	29	24***	ARG, NET, PAK, PHI, VEN
B9	Prefer specialist career	3.09	3.23	−	13	11*	FRA, ISR
B44	Prefer manager own nationality	1.73	1.68	+	21	14*	IRE, ISR, NET, PHI, VEN
B54	Competition harmful	3.02	2.84	+	21	17**	AUT, GER, PAK, PHI
B57	Individual decisions better	3.53	3.64	+	17	13*	ARG, COL, FRA, PER
B61	Most employees avoid responsibility	3.36	3.38	0	20	11	Many
A10	Importance benefits	376	392	+	19	14*	FRA, GER, IRA, NET, SAF
A15	Importance advancement	546	510	+	19	17***	IRA, ISR
A58	Overall satisfaction	2.79	3.14	−	28	27***	PAK
A2	Seniority in company	3.10	3.27	+	29	22**	ARG, BRA, COL, ISR, JPN, PAK, SWI
A57	Age	3.87	4.03	+	29	24***	ARG, BRA, IRE, ISR, JPN
Primarily correlated with IDV							
A18	Importance personal time	438	484	+	19	19***	None
A9	Importance training	578	526	+	19	18***	PAK
A12	Importance physical conditions	363	348	0 (+)	19	13	Many
A17	Importance use of skills	555	530	+	19	17***	NET, SWE
B24	Prefer foreign company	1.79	1.88	+	22	15*	ISR, MEX
B25	Other job available?	1.85	1.87	0	25	15	Many
B59	Staying one company desirable	3.19	3.06	−	21	16**	AUT, FRA, ISR, JPN
IMP	Mean raw goal importance	197.2	199.7	0	19	13	Many

(Continued)

Exhibit 2.6   Continued

		Mean Score[a]		Corre-sponding Shift in Index[b]	Number of Countries		
					Total Surveyed Twice	Shifting in Same Direction[c]	Countries Shifting in Opposite Direction
Question Number	Question	1967-69	1971-73				
Primarily correlated with MAS							
A7	Importance earnings	501	525	+	19	14*	FIN, SWE, PAK, SAF, SPA
A16	Importance manager	566	531	+	19	16***	GER, IRE, ISR
A8	Importance cooperation	554	542	0 (+)	19	11	Many
A11	Importance recognition	480	486	+	19	14*	BEL, GRE, ISR, PAK, TUR
A6	Importance desirable area	433	468	–	19	14*	GRE, IRA, PAK, SPA, TUR
A5	Importance challenge	587	619	+	19	17***	NET, SWE
A14	Importance employment security	496	495	0	19	11	Many
A1	Gender (% female)	7.0	7.3	0	26	16	Many

a. Expressed in percentages (Appendix 2) for A1, A43, A54, and A55; in standardized scores (Appendix 3) for A5 through A18; in points on the scale used (3, 4, 5, or 7) for all other questions.
b. Sign of shift multiplied by sign of correlation between this question and the index (PDI, UAI, IDV, or MAS).
c. Tested with the sign test, one-tailed.
*$p = .05$; **$p = .01$; ***$p = .001$.

the four dimensions should always take possible intercorrelations between the dimensions into account; these can be eliminated through multiple regression, as I will show throughout Chapters 3 through 7.

Country Clusters

In principle, a data matrix of variables (questions) × cases (countries) can be simplified in two ways. One is to summarize the variables into a smaller number of compound dimensions. This was done by the factor analysis described above. The second way is to summarize the cases into a smaller number of clusters—in our case, clusters of countries. On the basis of their scores on the four IBM indexes PDI, UAI, IDV and MAS, the 53 countries and regions in IBM were clustered using a hierarchical cluster analysis (available in the statistical program SPSS). This analysis produced the *dendrogram* shown in Exhibit 2.8, in which the configuration of countries appears as a family tree.

The dendrogram in Exhibit 2.8 should be read from right to left. A split into two large clusters separates Korea through Jamaica from Denmark through Japan. The next split separates Korea through Costa Rica from Malaysia through Jamaica, and so on.

Somewhat arbitrarily, I have split the dendrogram into the following 12 branches:

1. Korea, Peru, Salvador, Chile, Portugal, and Uruguay (in which Korea is historically/linguistically the odd one out)
2. (former) Yugoslavia, Turkey, Arabic-speaking countries and Greece, plus Argentina, Spain, and Brazil (two different historical subclusters intermingled)
3. Ecuador, Venezuela, Colombia, and Mexico
4. Pakistan and Iran, Indonesia, Thailand and Taiwan, East and West Africa (three or four subclusters intermingled)
5. Guatemala, Panama, and Costa Rica
6. Malaysia, Philippines, India, Hong Kong, Singapore, and Jamaica (all former British or American colonies)
7. Denmark, Sweden, Netherlands, Norway, and Finland
8. Australia, United States, Canada, Great Britain, Ireland, and New Zealand
9. Germany, Switzerland, South Africa, Italy (two or three subclusters intermingled)[41]
10. Austria and Israel (the state of Israel was founded by Austrian intellectuals)
11. Belgium and France
12. Japan (all by itself!)

Exhibit 2.7   Correlations Among the Four IBM Indexes Across Different Groups of Countries

Indexes	53 Countries and Regions	Product-Moment Correlations Across		
		40 Countries	31 Poorer Countries and Regions[a]	22 Wealthier Countries
PDI × UAI	.23	.28*	−.04	.63**
PDI × IDV	−.68***	−.67***	−.24	−.19
PDI × MAS	.06	.10	.23	.14
UAI × IDV	−.33**	−.35*	−.30	−.69***
UAI × MAS	−.03	.12	−.47**	.37*
IDV × MAS	.08	.00	.21	−.15

a. 1970 GNP/capita < $1,000.

*p = .05; **p = .01; ***p = .001.

Some of these clusters represent clear historical and/or linguistic culture areas (3, 5, 7, 8, 10, 11, and 12), but the others are combinations of culture areas, probably brought together in the same cluster by other factors, such as comparable economic development and/or political systems.[42]

Multilingual Countries:
Belgium, Switzerland, and Yugoslavia

In three countries the surveys were administered in two languages each: Belgium, Switzerland, and former Yugoslavia (see Appendix 5, Exhibit A5.2). Both Belgium and Switzerland combined Germanic and Latin languages. In Belgium about 54% of the population spoke Dutch, 45% spoke French, and 1% spoke German. In Switzerland, the figures were about 75% German, 20% French, 4% Italian, and 1% Rhaeto-Romanic. In former Yugoslavia the survey was administered in Serbo-Croat and Slovene; the scores could be split to fit the present independent republics of Croatia, Serbia, and Slovenia.

The index values for respondents from the main language areas in Belgium show that they shared basically the same culture, which closely resembled the French culture. The culture gap between the Netherlands and Dutch-speaking Belgium was somewhat smaller than that between the Netherlands and French-speaking Belgium, but it was still very wide. In fact, no two countries in the IBM data with a common border and a common language were so far apart culturally, according to the IBM indexes, as Belgium and the Netherlands. The gap occurred in power distance, uncertainty avoidance, and masculinity; only in individualism did Belgium and the Netherlands come together.

The common French culture of the two language areas of Belgium can be explained by their common history. For centuries Belgium was a distant dependent province of foreign powers (successively of Spain, Austria, France, and the Netherlands); it did not gain its independence until 1831. After independence, French was the language of government, the upper classes, and secondary and higher education for more than 100 years. The emancipation movement of the Dutch-speaking majority in Belgium, which led to regionalization, gained momentum only in the 1950s. Language is still a hot political issue in Belgium, in spite (or because) of the shared cultural traits.

A completely different picture was found for Switzerland. In this case, respondents from German-speaking Switzerland were clearly culturally associated with Germany and those from French-speaking Switzerland with France; there was a wide culture gap between the two language areas, in particular on the dimension of power distance. In scores on Gordon's Values Surveys among course participants at IMEDE, I had also found German-speaking Swiss to be part of the Germanic cluster and French-speaking Swiss to be part of the Latin cluster (Hofstede, 1976d). In that case, all responses were collected with an English-language questionnaire, which proves that the split was not an artifact of translation.

Switzerland was created in 1291 as a voluntary federation of three cantons (provinces) and grew gradually by the more or less voluntary addition of 19 other cantons, reaching its present size in 1815. Its political structure has always been federal, with more than 20 generally monolingual cantons with a large amount of internal independence. In one case where a Swiss canton was bilingual (Bern), this led in the 1960s to political con-

Exhibit 2.8. Hierarchical Cluster Analysis for 53 Countries and Regions Based on the Four IBM Indexes: Dendrogram Using Average Linkage (Between Groups)

```
                     Rescaled Distance Cluster Combine
                 0         5         10        15        20        25
         Label  +---------+---------+---------+---------+---------+

         KOR    -+
         PER    -+
    1    SAL    -+-+
         CHL    -+ +-+
         POR    -+-+ +---+
         URU    -+   I   I
         YUG    -----+   +-+
         ARG    ---+-+   I I
         SPA    ---+ +---+ I
    2    BRA    -+-+ I       +---+
         TUR    -+ +-+     I   I
         ARA    ---+       I   I
         GRE    -----------+   I
         ECA    -+-+           +-+
         VEN    -+ +-+         I I
    3    COL    ---+ +-----+   I I
         MEX    -----+     I   I I
         IDO    -+---+     +---+ I
         WAF    -+   I     I       +---+
         PAK    -+-+ +-----+   I   I
    4    TAI    -+ +-+         I   I
         EAF    -+-+ I         I   I
         THA    -+   I         I   +-----------------+
         IRA    -----+         I   I                 I
         GUA    ---+-----------+   I                 I
    5    PAN    ---+           I       +-----------+ I
         COS    -----------------+     I           I I
         MAL    ---+---+             I           I I
         PHI    ---+   +---------+   I           I I
         IND    --------+         +-------------------+           I
    6    HOK    -----+-----+   I                         I
         SIN    -----+     +-----+                       I
         JAM    -----------+                             I
         DEN    ---+-----+                               I
         SWE    ---+     +-------------------------+     I
    7    NET    -+-+     I                         I     I
         NOR    -+ +-----+                         I     I
         FIN    ---+                               I     I
         AUL    -+                                 I     I
         USA    -+-+                               I     I
    8    CAN    -+ +-+                             I     I
         GBR    ---+ +---+                         +-------------+
         IRE    ---+-+ I                           I
         NZL    ---+ +---------+                   I
         GER    -+-+ I         I                   I
    9    SWI    -+ +-+ I       +---------+         I
         SAF    ---+ +---+     I         I         I
         ITA    -----+         I         I         I
         AUT    ---------+---------+     +-------+
   10    ISR    ---------+         I
         BEL    -+-------------------------+ I
   11    FRA    -+                         +-+
   12    JPN    ---------------------------+
```

flicts not unlike those in Belgium, but these were resolved through the splitting of the canton (creating the new canton Jura). Unlike Belgium, Switzerland never underwent a process of forced cultural unification.

The data for former Yugoslavia were collected in 1971 but were split in a reanalysis in 1993 (the country fell apart in 1991).[43] The scores of respondents from the three republics were by and large quite similar; all showed high PDI and UAI, low IDV, and medium to low MAS. Comparatively, however, Serbia had by far the highest PDI and the most extreme scores on the other three dimensions as well (highest UAI, lowest IDV, highest MAS). Slovenia scored remarkably feminine.[44]

Validation

The Reliability of Country Dimension Scores

The scores for the more than 50 countries on the four dimensions were based on the answers on three questions each for power distance and uncertainty avoidance, and on factor scores derived from the answers on the same 14 work goals for both individualism and masculinity.[45] As described above, for each question and in each country, mean scores were calculated for the respondents (IBM employees) in each of seven different occupations, at each of two points in time. The average of those 7×2 occupation means became the country score for the question. The country scores therefore were based on the central tendencies in the answers by the individuals in each country.

In order for three or four questions to form a scale suitable for locating a country on a dimension, it is methodologically necessary that the country scores on these questions are strongly correlated across the full set of countries. Only in that case will the scales be methodologically reliable instruments for measuring the cultures of the countries.

The answers of individual respondents within countries on these same questions do not show the same correlations. For example, the country scores for uncertainty avoidance are based on three questions: stress, rule orientation, and intent to stay with the company. At the country level, these three are strongly correlated. In countries with high stress we also find strong rule orientation and the intent to stay longer with the company, and in countries with lower stress we find less rule orientation and greater willingness to leave. But for individuals these three questions are not correlated in the same way. In most employee groups there is a positive correlation between rule orientation and intent to stay, but there is no correlation whatsoever between stress and

rule orientation, and the correlation between stress and intent to stay across individuals in most groups is even negative: More stressed individuals are somewhat less likely to want to stay with the company (see Chapter 4).

If this seems paradoxical, remember that a positive correlation at the country level does not need to be based on answers from the same individuals. If stress and intent to stay are positively correlated across countries (as is the case), this just means that if in a country there are more stressed people, there will also be more people who want to stay with the company—but these are evidently not the same persons. Feeling stress and deciding to want to stay are two alternative ways of coping psychologically with the anxiety (strong uncertainty avoidance) in a society. A culture does not produce one single type of psychological reaction; it can produce many alternative, complementary, and even conflicting types of reaction in individuals.

It is tempting to take an individual's scores on the three to four questions associated with a dimension and interpret these as a test of this individual's personality, indicating in what kind of culture she or he would fit. The problem is that the questions chosen to form a culture dimension scale do not satisfy the criteria for being used as a personality dimension scale. For the latter purpose, they would have to be correlated across individuals in the same way they are correlated across cultures, and, as we have seen, this is not the case. The national culture questionnaire is not a reliable personality test.[46] Statements about someone's personality and predictions of a person's functioning based on answers on these questions have such a large error margin as to be worthless, as well as unethical.

This also means that the reliability of the scales for the four dimensions cannot be calculated with the usual formulas for the reliability of tests, which are based on individual answers. They could only be based on country means across a number of countries—but few people have access to such data. I discuss the available cases in the next subsection of this chapter.

Something can be said about the confidence intervals for the country scores, based on the standard deviations of the individual answers for each question. We should count with the error reduction through taking the means for a number of individuals, the means of these means for seven occupations and for two survey rounds, and the weighted means of three or four questions. The confidence intervals depend, obviously, on the number of individuals per country. In the worst case (El Salvador, a Category 2 country with 70 respondents, all from one occupation but divided over two survey rounds), the 99% confidence interval is approximately ±6 points on the 100-point scales of the four dimensions. In the best case (Germany, with 11,384 respondents from all seven occupations and also divided over two survey rounds), the 99% confidence interval is smaller than ±1 point. For overall use, a 99% confidence interval of ±3 points is a safe estimate. This assumes, of course, that only *random* variance occurred. Systematic influences are excluded.

Replicating the IBM Research

As mentioned before, IBM in 1973 changed its survey approach and removed the values and beliefs questions from its questionnaires. The company never replicated the cross-national values research. Two small replications were done by interested individuals. Fred L. Hall, a retired managing director of IBM Australia Ltd., replicated the study in IBM Australia in 1984-85 for a master's thesis (Hall, 1989). Using the same questions and occupational groups, he found only small shifts in index scores,[47] but he did not have data from other IBM subsidiaries at the same time to compare with his data. Lowe (1996b) received support from the local managements of IBM Hong Kong and IBM United Kingdom for a replication in 1993. The samples were matched between the two countries but not necessarily equivalent to those in the original study, so that only a comparison of the *differences* between Hong Kong and the United Kingdom makes sense. The gap in the Power Distance Index from 1970 to 1993 had increased from 33 to 40 points (with United Kingdom lower). The gap in the Uncertainty Avoidance Index had shifted from −6 points (Hong Kong lower) to +13 points (United Kingdom lower). The gap in the Individualism Index had shrunk from −64 to −50 points (United Kingdom always much more individualist). The gap in the Masculinity Index had almost disappeared (from −9 points to −1 point, United Kingdom more masculine). In view of the fast development of the Hong Kong economy and the aging of the Hong Kong employee population (which in particular should have increased the respondents' UAI scores), these shifts are very credible and supportive of the reliability of the instrument used.

The publication of the first edition of *Culture's Consequences* in 1980 led others to attempt replications using the IBM set of questions elsewhere. The quality of these replications has varied tremendously. Some readers assumed naively that any group of respondents in a country would score the questions exactly as the IBM respondents had done around 1970, regardless of their occupations, employers, or the point in time.[48] There were even those who believed that any *single* respondent in a country would score that way! Of course, what can be measured are only differences in the statistical distributions of scores for groups of sufficient size. Absolute scores do not mean anything at all; only differences between the scores from at least two countries can be interpreted and compared to the IBM database, and this only if the samples are sufficiently large (at least 20-50 per country) and sufficiently matched from country to country (that is, similar in all relevant respects except nationality). Chapter 10 gives a few examples.

Mikael Søndergaard (1994) from Denmark reviewed 61 published and unpublished replications, mostly on a few countries at a time, often just 2. As the four IBM dimensions represent statistical trends in a "population" of 40 countries, a replication across just 2 of these countries is statistically likely to reflect the same trends, but a certain percentage of cases disconfirming the trend can occur even for samples that are perfectly matched and of sufficient size. A trend found in a cloud of 40 dots cannot be falsified by just 2 of the dots (letting alone those studies that tried to [in]validate the research on a single sample). Søndergaard looked at the macro trend across these small replications. Taken together, they were more likely to confirm than to disconfirm the dimensions; confirmation was almost universal in the case of Individualism and partial for the other three dimensions, with the cases of nonconfirmation spread more or less randomly over the studies. In the following chapters, I will refer to some of the small replications that did meet minimum methodological criteria and produced insights complementary to earlier studies.

The most professional replication so far was done by Michael H. Hoppe (1990) for his Ph.D. dissertation. With a questionnaire containing the IBM questions plus a section on organizational learning, Hoppe approached alumni of the Salzburg Seminar, a U.S.-sponsored conference center in Austria that received in its courses elites (leaders in politics, business, labor, art, and education) from mainly European countries. The country differences found within this elite population replicated significantly those earlier found among IBM employees. For three of the four dimensions, the IBM formulas could be used as they were; only the masculinity dimension called for a somewhat different selection of questions and computation formula (Hoppe, 1998).

Hoppe's research was the first clear indication that no single set of questions can be expected to work in all cases. The ideal questions for a cross-cultural survey instrument are those for which answers depend as much as possible on nationality and as little as possible on anything else, and that carry the same meaning for widely different respondents, from academics to semiliterates, from politicians to artists, from children to senior citizens. Replications using questions from the IBM surveys on populations other than IBM subsidiary employees assume that these questions mean the same things to these other populations as they did to IBM-ers around 1970. Experience has shown that this assumption is not universally warranted. There very likely is no single set of questions that can be used to measure national cultural differences for all kinds of respondents in all types of organizations at any point in time. Questionnaires have to be adapted to their intended respondent population, situation, and period.

As an example, the Masculinity Index computed from the IBM data and from the Values Survey Module 1982 (VSM 82; see Appendix 4) was based on the combined importance of "advancement" and "earnings," because across IBM subsidiaries higher scores for the importance of promotions went hand in hand with higher scores for the importance of earnings. For Hoppe's (1998) elites, but also for students in Eastern European countries studied later by Hofstede, Kolman, Nicolescu, and Pajumaa (1996), the importance of "earnings" in a country was negatively correlated with the importance of "advancement." In these cases the importance of "advancement" expresses what the masculinity dimension stands for; "earnings" contradicts it. In the Values Survey Module 1994 (VSM 94; see Appendix 4), the "earnings" item has disappeared from the masculinity formula. But there is still no guarantee that the new formula will work with all new populations and for all times.

In the period 1993-97, a research team from the University of Texas at Austin included a number of the IBM questions in a survey study among commercial airline pilots. This Aerospace Crew Research Project, carried out by Ashleigh Merritt with the support of principal investigator Robert L. Helmreich, covered more than 15,000 respondents from 23 countries and thus surpassed Hoppe's project in size. Using VSM 82 formulas, Helmreich and Merritt (1998, p. 249) found that the pilots replicated the IBM country score differences for power distance and individualism, but only marginally for uncertainty avoidance and not at all for masculinity. IBM questions used for computing the Uncertainty Avoidance and Masculinity Indexes (such as "How often do you feel nervous or tense at work?") seemed to carry different connotations in the pilots' professional subculture. As in Hoppe's case, a somewhat different selection of questions and computation formulas was needed to measure what these dimensions stand for in this population. The underlying syndrome can still be universal and permanent, but the measuring instruments have to be adapted

to the population and probably also to the zeitgeist—that is, the spirit of the times, or the fashion of the day.

Another large-scale replication has been undertaken by the Dutch advertising expert Marieke de Mooij, who collaborated with the Amsterdam-based international market research agency Inter/View International. In this case, the Values Survey Module 1994 was included in a consumer panel survey across 15 European countries. Results to be shown in Chapters 4 to 6 strongly confirm country differences on uncertainty avoidance, individualism, and masculinity, but this time, surprisingly, power distance scores were not well replicated. This may have something to do with the fact that the new VSM version had been rewritten to be relevant to respondents without bosses or employers, such as entrepreneurs, students, and housewives. Under these circumstances, power distance differences are more difficult to measure.

Comparing With
Data From Other Sources

Whereas the reliability of the indexes computed from national culture differences in IBM could only in a few cases be tested directly through replications, it could in many more cases be inferred from their validity. Validity of a test means that its scores relate to outside measures of the same or related phenomena in ways predicted by the test's theory. Validity implies reliability: An unreliable test cannot produce scores that meaningfully relate to outside data. Validation in this case meant correlating the IBM country scores on the four dimensions with country scores derived from other studies in different disciplines and conceptually related to the same issues. These other studies were of three different kinds: (1) survey studies of other narrow but matched samples of populations, such as university students; (2) representative sample polls of entire national populations; and (3) characteristics of countries measured directly at the country level, such as government spending on development aid. All in all, by the time the first edition of *Culture's Consequences* went to press, I had found 38 other studies comparing between 5 and 39 countries for which the results were significantly correlated with one or more of the four dimensions. Since then, the number of validations has grown considerably. Those validations that have come to my attention are described in detail in Chapters 3 through 7 and summarized in Appendix 6.

When correlating the country scores from these other studies with the IBM index scores, I always included GNP/capita as an additional variable.

The epistemological principle of parsimony, also known as "Occam's razor" (see Chapter 1), states that simpler explanations should have priority over more complex ones. To me this means that if "hard" variables (economic, biological, technological) predict a country variable better, cultural indexes are redundant.[49] GNP/capita plays a role so often that I included it in all correlations as a matter of routine.

For correlating I had the choice between the Spearman rank correlation coefficient or the (Pearson) product-moment correlation coefficient. If scores are based on scales of unknown properties, the Spearman rank correlation coefficient (rho) gives the safer estimate of a relationship, because individual observations cannot play an overpowering role in the result. The product-moment correlation coefficient (r), on the other hand, offers the possibility of multiple regression on more than one index simultaneously. I handled cases in which Spearman rank and product-moment correlation led to considerably different results by first transforming variables into rank numbers and then using multiple regression.[50]

The importance of multiple regression is that often data from other sources are significantly correlated with more than one culture index. Depending on which countries were involved in the comparison, the IBM indexes may be intercorrelated, and a significant correlation of outside data with one of the IBM indexes can indirectly lead to correlations of the same data with other IBM indexes. This problem can be resolved through a stepwise regression of these outside data on all four indexes together, plus GNP/capita as argued above, showing which of the indexes contributed significantly to the relationship with the outside data *by their own merit*—that is, independent of the influence of the other indexes.

Comparison of IBM scores with results of other studies across fewer than five countries will not easily show statistically significant correlations, but some of these still yielded qualitative insight into the meaning of a dimension, so I refer to a selected set of such studies in Chapters 3 through 7 as well.

Economic, Geographic,
and Demographic Indicators

Chapters 3 through 7 also explore the relationships of the dimensions with a number of geographic, demographic, and economic indicators of the countries. On the basis of a literature search, I selected in the first instance the nine indicators listed in Exhibit 2.9. The first seven are country specific; the last two, company specific.

Wealth (GNP/capita, abbreviated as GNP) is the usual measure of a country's economic development. GNP/capita takes a special position among the indicators because, as mentioned earlier, it also serves for correlating with external variables along with the five culture indexes, as an alternative to cultural explanations. It is a debatable measure (see Morgenstern, 1975), but it is used for lack of a better one.[51] Unless otherwise mentioned, GNP data refer to 1970—that is, the mean year of the surveying period. Correlations with external data collected in later years sometimes use GNP data for 1980 or 1990.[52] The same proviso applies for *economic growth* as an indicator. In this edition I have included two measures of economic growth: not only past growth (1960-70 average growth in GNP/capita, EGP) but also growth in the period following the survey (EGF). The best available figures are for the period 1965-90, which somewhat overlaps with the survey period, but I have considered this acceptable. *Latitude* (LAT; determined for the country's capital city) is an unambiguous measure of the country's geographic position and a crude measure of climate (tropical/moderate/cold). *Population size* (POP) is an obvious demographic measure that various factor-analytic studies have associated with social and political variables (see Chapter 1). In view of its skewed distribution among the countries studied, it has been measured on a logarithmic scale. *Population growth* (PGR) is an obvious complement to population size. *Population density* (PDN) appears as an explanatory variable in various theories of cultural behavior. Its distribution is fairly normally shaped except for the two city-states of Hong Kong and Singapore. In order to prevent these countries' data from dominating all correlations, I have divided the values for Hong Kong and Singapore by eight, which puts them at the top of the list but within the range of values for the other countries. The variables *organization size* (ORS) and *relative organization size* (ROS) have been added because we should check the possibility that attitudes in an IBM subsidiary could be determined by the demographics of that subsidiary rather than by nationwide indicators.

The values for the nine indicators for 50 countries are listed in Exhibit 2.10. Their intercorrelations are shown in Exhibit 2.11, both across the 40 countries of the first analysis (Category 1) and across the full set of 50 (Categories 1 + 2). Exhibit 2.11 shows that adding the 10 countries of Category 2 hardly changes the correlation patterns.

The organizational variables ORS and ROS were included only for the 40 Category 1 countries. The analysis shows a correlation of r =

Exhibit 2.9   Indicators Considered for Relating to Value Dimensions

Code	Indicator	Definition	Source of Data
GNP	Wealth	1970 GNP/capita in $/10	*World Bank Atlas*, 1972
EGP	Economic growth, past period	1960-70 average annual growth rate of GNP/capita in % × 10	*World Bank Atlas*, 1972
EGF	Economic growth, following period	1965-90 average annual growth rate of GNP/capita in % × 10	*World Development Report*, 1992
LAT	Latitude	Geographic latitude in degrees N or S of country's capital city	Regular geographic atlas
POP	Population size	Decimal logarithm of 1970 number of inhabitants in millions × 100	*World Bank Atlas*, 1972
PGR	Population growth	1960-70 average annual growth rate of population × 10	*World Bank Atlas*, 1972
PDN	Population density	Population divided by area in square km (values for Hong Kong and Singapore divided by 8)	POP and *Oxford Economic Atlas*, 1972
ORS	Organization size	Decimal logarithm of number of IBM employees per 1/1/1970 × 100 (excluding manufacturing and product development)	Company statistics
ROS	Relative organization size	Number of IBM employees divided by number of inhabitants in millions	POP and ORS

.96*** between GNP and ROS. As IBM marketed advanced technological products, the size of its subsidiary in a country reflected almost perfectly the country's economic development. The correlation is so high that ROS as an indicator could be dropped, as it merely duplicates the GNP variable.

The eight remaining variables show one cluster of three variables (wealth, latitude, and slow population growth). Another, completely separate, cluster combines past and following economic growth and population density. Across the 50 countries the correlations between population growth and economic growth are $r = -.20$ for 1960-70 and $r = -.09$ for 1965-90. The economist Kuznets (1973, p. 43) found $r = -.31$ for all noncommunist countries in the 1950-60s. It seems that the negative relationship between the two is weakening, possibly an effect of population control programs.

The correlation of economic growth with population density reflects the influence of the fast-growing economies of densely populated East Asia. It suggests that the population density played a role in the East Asian economic miracle in this period—for example, through low internal transport costs, easy exchange of goods and services, and/or a historically grown ability to coordinate a complex society.[53] IBM organization size, unsurprisingly, correlated with both wealth and country population size.

The correlations of these indicators with the culture indexes are interpreted in Chapters 3 through 7; a summary and a test of multiple and stepwise correlations of the indicators on the four indexes are found in Appendix 6.

Adding a Fifth Dimension

A productive research partnership developed in the 1980s between Michael Harris Bond of the Chinese University of Hong Kong and myself. We had met in December 1980 at a cross-cultural psychology conference, where I served as a discussant for a joint paper Bond presented (Ng et al., 1982). I had argued that the paper contained a "reverse ecological fallacy" (see Chapter 1), and to my surprise Bond afterward came to me and agreed. When he then reanalyzed his data at the country level, he found them to reflect all of my

Exhibit 2.10 Country Scores on Nine Economic, Geographic, and Demographic Indicators

Country	Code	GNP	EGP	EGF	LAT	POP	PGR	PDN	ORS	ROS
Argentina	ARG	116	25	−3	35	137	15	8	298	41
Australia	AUL	282	31	19	36	110	20	2	324	139
Austria	AUT	201	39	29	48	87	5	88	298	128
Belgium	BEL	272	40	26	51	99	6	318	323	160
Brazil	BRA	42	24	33	23	197	29	11	320	17
Canada	CAN	370	36	27	46	133	18	2	380	288
Chile	CHL	72	16	4	33	99	23	13	254	35
Colombia	COL	34	17	23	5	133	32	19	250	15
Costa Rica	COS	56	32	14	10	24	33	34		
Denmark	DEN	319	37	21	56	69	7	114	301	224
Ecuador	ECA	29	17	28	0	78	34	13		
Finland	FIN	239	39	32	60	67	6	14	274	116
France	FRA	310	46	24	49	171	10	92	398	195
Great Britain	GBR	227	22	20	52	175	6	243	385	127
Germany (West)	GER	293	35	24	51	179	10	248	409	199
Greece	GRE	109	66	28	38	95	7	67	230	22
Guatemala	GUA	36	20	7	15	72	31	48		
Hong Kong	HOK	97	84	62	22	60	25	500	216	36
Indonesia	IDO	8	10	45	6	206	20	61		
India	IND	11	12	19	29	273	23	164	277	1
Iran	IRA	38	54	1	36	146	29	18	219	5
Ireland	IRE	136	36	30	53	46	4	42	229	67
Israel	ISR	196	47	26	32	46	32	140	260	138
Italy	ITA	176	46	30	42	173	8	178	360	75
Jamaica	JAM	67	35	−13	18	28	16	164		
Japan	JPN	192	96	41	36	201	10	282	365	44
Korea (s)	KOR	25	68	71	38	150	26	324		
Malaysia	MAL	38	31	40	3	104	31	33		
Mexico	MEX	67	37	28	19	171	35	26	295	17
Netherlands	NET	243	39	18	52	111	13	387	340	194
Norway	NOR	286	41	34	60	59	8	12	281	167
New Zealand	NZL	270	21	11	41	45	17	10	259	139
Pakistan	PAK	10	24	25	25	211	27	138	189	1
Panama	PAN	73	42	14	9	17	33	19		
Peru	PER	45	14	−2	12	113	31	11	237	17
Philippines	PHI	21	29	13	15	157	30	124	251	9
Portugal	POR	66	53	30	39	98	9	105	260	41
South Africa	SAF	76	30	13	26	135	30	18	292	38
Salvador	SAL	30	17	−4	14	55	37	168		
Singapore	SIN	92	52	65	1	32	24	438	205	53
Spain	SPA	102	61	24	40	153	11	67	316	44
Sweden	SWE	404	38	19	59	90	7	18	327	232
Switzerland	SWI	332	25	14	47	80	15	152	326	288
Taiwan	TAI	39	71	70	25	115	29	388	215	10
Thailand	THA	20	49	44	14	156	31	70	221	5
Turkey	TUR	31	39	26	40	155	25	45	214	4
Uruguay	URU	82	−4	8	35	46	13	16		
United States	USA	476	32	17	41	231	12	22	478	280
Venezuela	VEN	98	23	-10	10	102	35	11	274	53
Yugoslavia	YUG	65	43	29	45	131	11	80	248	15

NOTE: Countries with codes in *italics* belong to Category 2 (see Exhibit 2.1); others belong to Category 1. For explanation of column headings, see Exhibit 2.9.

Exhibit 2.11 Product-Moment Correlation Coefficients of Nine Geographic, Economic, and Demographic Indicators Across 40 and 50 Countries

	GNP	EGP	EGF	LAT	POP	PGR	PDN	ORS	ROS
GNP		-.03	-.09	.68***	-.17	-.60***	-.03	.74***	.96***
EGP	.08		.65***	.06	-.14	-.19	.50***	-.08	-.13
EGF	-.06	.59***		-.09	-.15	-.07	.62***	-.20	-.12
LAT	.71***	.20	.01		-.14	-.84***	-.09	.47***	.63***
POP	-.03	-.00	.12	.07		.15	-.08	.39**	-.19
PGR	-.63***	-.20	-.09	-.83***	-.03		-.08	-.46***	-.51***
PDN	-.00	.53***	.55***	.05	.01	-.11		-.04	-.00

NOTE: For explanation of indicator abbreviations, see Exhibit 2.9. Correlation coefficients above the diagonal are based on 40 countries (Category 1 only); those below the diagonal are based on 50 countries (Categories 1 + 2). ORS and ROS are included for Category 1 only; their mutual correlation is .70***.
$*p = .05; **p = .01; ***p = .001$.

four dimensions. We later reported this supportive result in a joint article (Hofstede & Bond, 1984).

In 1981, Bond and I met again, and as we talked about cultural relativity, we wondered to what extent our own minds were preprogrammed by our cultures. Bond then conceived the Chinese Value Survey project: Recognizing that the results of surveys designed by Westerners are biased by their designers' Western minds, he asked his Chinese colleagues to compose a questionnaire with a deliberate Chinese mental bias and then administered this survey around the world in Asian and non-Asian countries (Chinese Culture Connection, 1987).

Bond's Chinese Value Survey again produced four country-level dimensions. Three were significantly correlated with three of the IBM dimensions, but no counterpart of uncertainty avoidance was found using the Chinese questions; instead, there was a new dimension, which Bond called "Confucian work dynamism" and which I later rebaptized "long-term orientation" and adopted as a fifth dimension (I discuss this dimension further in Chapter 7). Country scores for long-term orientation correlated with national economic growth in the past 25 years; as far as we knew, this was the first values measure ever that did so (Hofstede & Bond, 1988).

People sometimes wonder how many more dimensions there are. One should realize that dimensions do not "exist." Like "culture" itself, they are constructs, products of our imagination, that have been introduced because they subsume complex sets of mental programs into easily remembered packages. In a classic essay, Miller (1956) has argued that "the magical number seven, plus or minus two," represents a limit to the human capacity for processing information. Models of culture with more categories will no

longer be felt as useful; they do not make reality simpler. And in empirical research a new dimension can be recognized only if it is statistically independent from the established ones. If this condition is not satisfied, we are just dealing with another aspect of an existing dimension.

Studying Organizational Cultures

In the early 1980s, the topic of "organizational," or "corporate," cultures suddenly became extremely popular in the management literature (e.g., Deal & Kennedy, 1982; Peters & Waterman, 1982). If national cultures describe the collective mental programming of otherwise similar persons from different nations, organizational cultures should describe the collective mental programming of otherwise similar persons from different organizations. "Otherwise similar" also means from within the same nation(s). Paradoxically, the cross-national IBM study, in spite of its huge database, did not supply any systematic information on IBM's organizational culture, as there had been no comparison with organizations outside of IBM in the countries studied. Comparative research across organizations up until that time had been very rare, and with the cross-national project completed with the publication of the first edition of *Culture's Consequences,* I set out to move into the cross-organizational field and contribute to filling the research gap. That project was carried out under the label of the Institute for Research on Intercultural Cooperation (IRIC); I describe its results in the second half of Chapter 8.

Acquiring access to a sufficient number of suitable organizations that, moreover, were prepared to share the costs of the project took several years. The project finally ran in 1985 and 1986 within 20 organizational units in Denmark and in IRIC's home country, the Netherlands. On the national culture dimensions from the IBM study, these two countries belonged to the same Nordic-Dutch culture cluster. We attempted to cover a wide range of different work organizations, to get a feel for the size of culture differences that can be found in practice, which would, then, enable us to assess the relative weight of similarities and differences. The units studied belonged to 10 different organizations, 5 in Denmark and 5 in the Netherlands. These 20 units were from three broad kinds of organizations: private manufacturing companies, private service companies, and public agencies. Unit sizes varied from 60 to 2,500 persons. The sample of 20 units was a small enough number to allow us to examine each unit in depth, qualitatively, as a separate case study. At the same time, it was large enough to permit statistical analysis of comparative quantitative data across all cases.

Unlike in the IBM study, where the data had been collected for other purposes and for the research I had to make do with whatever there was, in the IRIC organizational cultures study we could design the project from scratch and try to be methodologically perfect and orthodox. So we designed an approach in three phases: interviews, a survey, and the collection of contextual data.

In the first phase, we conducted in-depth interviews of 2 to 3 hours' duration each with 9 informants per unit, a total of 180 interviews. These interviews allowed us to get a qualitative feel for the gestalt of the unit's culture and to collect issues to be included in the questionnaire for the subsequent survey. Informants were chosen nonrandomly in discussion with our contact person(s) in the unit. They included, in all cases, the unit top manager (all top managers were male) and his secretary, and then a selection of men and women in different jobs from all levels, sometimes a gatekeeper or doorman, an old-timer, a newcomer, an employee representative (equivalent to a shop steward). A criterion in their selection was that they were assumed to be sufficiently reflective and communicative to be valuable discussion partners.

The checklist used for the in-depth interviews was based on a survey of the literature on the ways in which organizational cultures are supposed to manifest themselves and on our own ideas. We classified manifestations of culture into the four categories mentioned in Chapter 1: symbols, heroes, rituals, and values. The interview team consisted of 18 members (Danish or Dutch), most of them with social science training but deliberately naive about the type of activity going on in the unit studied. Each unit's interviews were divided among 2 interviewers, a woman and a man, so that the gender of the interviewer would not affect the observations obtained. All interviewers received the same project training beforehand, and all used the same broad checklist of open-ended questions. Interviews were taped, and reports were written in a prescribed sequence, using respondents' actual words.

In the second phase, we administered a standardized survey questionnaire consisting of 135 precoded questions to a random sample from the unit, consisting of about 25 managers, 25 college-level nonmanagers ("professionals"), and 25 non-college-level nonmanagers ("others"). Altogether 1,295 usable questionnaires were collected, an average of 65 per unit. About 60 of the questions in the survey were taken from the earlier cross-national study and its later extensions; the remaining items, with a few exceptions, were developed on the basis of the interviews and were directed at the issues that the interviewers found to differ substantially between units. These included, in particular, many perceptions of daily practices, which had been almost entirely missing in the cross-national studies. The survey scores were factor analyzed at the level of organizational units—that is, ecologically—and revealed six independent dimensions of organizational culture. These were entirely different from the five dimensions of national cultures found in the cross-national study; I will describe them in Chapter 8. Each unit could be positioned on each of the six dimensions. The results of the interviews and of the surveys were discussed with the management of the units and were sometimes fed back to larger groups of unit members, if the management allowed us to do so.

In the third phase, we used questionnaires, followed by personal interviews, to collect "structural" data at the level of the unit as a whole on such factors as its total employee strength, budget composition, key historical facts, and the demographics of its key managers. I conducted the interviews personally in all 20 cases, because finding out what comparable data *could* meaningfully be collected from such a varied set of organizations was a heuristic process difficult to share across researchers. The informants for the unit-level data were the top manager, the chief personnel officer, and the chief budget officer. The purpose of this phase was to find out to what extent measurable differences among the cultures of different organizations could be attributed to unique features of the organization in question, such as its history or the personality of its founder. To what extent did these differences reflect other characteristics of the organization, such as its structure and control systems, which in themselves might have been affected by culture? To what extent were they predetermined by given factors like nationality, industry, and task? This phase represented for the cross-organizational study what the correlations with data from other sources had done for the cross-national study: validation of our internal measurements against external, independent numbers.

Following the 20-unit study, IRIC got involved in the study of employee attitudes and organizational subcultures within a Danish insurance company with some 3,000 employees, all of whom were surveyed. This study allowed us to relate culture to attitudes and also to develop a method for mapping the different subcultures within one large organization. That project is also described in Chapter 8.

Some years later, at the initiative of Michael Bond and with the expert help of his then student assistant Chung-Leung Luk, I reanalyzed the 1,295 organizational culture questionnaires at the *individual respondent* level (Hofstede, Bond, & Luk, 1993). For this purpose the between-organizations variance was separated from the within-organization variance, after which the within-organization data could be lumped together and factor analyzed across the 1,295 individuals. The resulting six factors, again entirely different from the cross-national and cross-organizational factors, reflected personality differences; I discuss these in Chapter 8 as well.

Support and Criticisms
of the Approach Followed

The disrespect I showed for academic borderlines in the first edition of *Culture's Consequences* paid off in a multidisciplinary readership. It also caused very mixed reviews—some enthusiastic (e.g., Eysenck, 1981; Sorge, 1983; Triandis, 1982), some irritated, some condescending, and some taking a tone of ridicule (e.g., Cooper, 1982; Roberts & Boyacigiller, 1984). I had made a paradigm shift in cross-cultural studies, and, as Kuhn (1970) has shown, paradigm shifts in any science meet with strong initial resistance.

Five standard criticisms of my approach were as follows:[54]

1. Surveys are not a suitable way of measuring cultural differences. (My answer: They should not be the only way.)
2. Nations are not the best units for studying cultures. (My answer: True, but they are usually the only kinds of units available for comparison, and they are better than nothing.)
3. A study of the subsidiaries of one company cannot provide information about entire national cultures. (My answer: What were measured were *differences between* national cultures. Any set of functionally equivalent samples from national populations can sup-

ply information about such differences. The IBM set consisted of unusually well-matched samples for an unusually large number of countries. The extensive validation in the following chapters will show that the country scores obtained correlated highly with all kinds of other data, including results obtained from representative samples of entire national populations.)
4. The IBM data are old and therefore obsolete. (My answer: The dimensions found are assumed to have centuries-old roots; only data that remained stable across two subsequent surveys were maintained, and they have since been validated against all kinds of external measurements; and recent replications show no loss of validity.)[55]
5. Four or five dimensions are not enough. (My answer: Additional dimensions should be both conceptually and statistically independent from the five dimensions already defined and should be validated by significant correlations with conceptually related external measures; candidates are welcome to apply.)

Since the late 1980s, the idea of dimensions of national cultures has become part of what Kuhn calls "normal science." The message of the first edition of *Culture's Consequences* has been integrated into the state of the art in various disciplines dealing with culture. The four or five dimensions I introduced have become part of intercultural training programs and of textbooks and readers in cross-cultural psychology, organizational psychology and sociology, management, and communication.[56] They have also been used in a number of other areas and disciplines; these will emerge in the following chapters, and in Chapter 10, I summarize some of the more surprising applications.

In fact, this extensive use has its disadvantages. Some people have tried to imitate my approach cheaply for commercial purposes. Some carry the concepts further than I consider wise. At times, my supporters worry me more than my critics. But fortunately the message has also reached serious academics and practitioners who carry on with research and experimentation in intercultural cooperation to meet the crying need for integration of human efforts in a shrinking world.

Notes

1. In the first edition of *Culture's Consequences*, I used the pseudonym Hermes for the corporation, after the Greek god of commerce. McClelland (1961,

pp. 301 ff.) saw in Hermes the personification of achievement motivation.

2. A number of books have been written about IBM, including those by Belden and Belden (1962), Rodgers (1969), Foy (1974), and Carroll (1993). Pagès, Bonetti, de Gaulejac, and Descendre (1979) deal with IBM France, for which they use the pseudonym TLTX.

3. I have described my personal adventures in IBM in previous works (see Hofstede, 1996c, 1997a).

4. At the time, my boss was Dr. David Sirota. In 1970 he was succeeded by Dr. Allen Kraut; I was succeeded in 1971 by Dr. John Hinrichs.

5. Various studies were devoted to factors that helped and hindered the use of survey data by managers (Hofstede, 1975a; Klein, Kraut, & Wolfson, 1971; Sirota, 1970). A list of practical aspects of the use of attitude surveys, based on the IBM experience, is found in the first edition of *Culture's Consequences* (Hofstede, 1980a, fig. 2.1).

6. Factor analyses were done separately on three sets of questions: 54 "satisfaction" questions, 50 "management" questions, and 42 "culture" questions (dealing with preferences, values, and beliefs). For each set of questions a separate within-subculture factor analysis was carried out for each of five very diverse subpopulations: systems engineers in France, systems engineers in Great Britain, clerks in Great Britain, unskilled manufacturing operators in Great Britain, and unskilled manufacturing operators in Japan. Among these five subpopulations, both similarities and differences in factor structure were found. In about 80% of cases, questions showed a first or a significant second loading on a common factor; the remaining 20% of cases represented relationships between a question and a factor that were specific to one or two subpopulations only (Hofstede, Kraut, & Simonetti, 1976, p. 10).

7. In Appendix 1, "core" questions are numbered A1-A60, as in the official IBM questionnaire, but only those used in this book are reproduced. For the other questions, see Hofstede et al. (1976). Appendix 1, however, does include the core "satisfaction" questions A19-A32, which were not analyzed cross-culturally but are still referred to in Chapter 6. Also included are the "recommended" questions (numbered B1-B66 but also only reproduced insofar as they are used in this book) and the 19 "other" personal goals and beliefs questions (numbered C1-C19).

8. These types of questions are not part of most standard attitude survey instruments. Personal goals questions were used in many research studies in the United States in the 1950s and 1960s, mostly for testing theoretical models of job satisfaction. The researchers in IBM felt that these questions would help in the understanding of differences in mentality among countries.

9. These items are A5 through A18, A54, B46, and C1 in Appendix 1.

10. These instruments were as follows: the Allport-Vernon-Lindzey Study of Values (AVL), L. V. Gordon's Survey of Interpersonal Values (SIV), L. V. Gordon's Survey of Personal Values (SPV), L. V.

Gordon's Personal Profile (GPP), G. W. England's Personal Values Questionnaire (PVQ), F. E. Fiedler's Least Preferred Co-Worker (LPC), and W. C. Schutz's FIRO-B. Detailed results of the comparisons have been published in a series of working papers (Hofstede, 1972, 1974a, 1974b, 1974c). The Gordon SIV and SPV scores from 372 IMEDE participants were also compared for 14 countries (Hofstede, 1976d). See Chapters 3 and 5.

11. The correlation noted here was found between the "recognition" score of Gordon's SIV and a score computed from the items "importance of recognition" (A11) and "importance of advancement" (A15) of the IBM questionnaire. Throughout this book, r stands for the Pearson product-moment correlation coefficient. Significance limits are indicated with * = .05, ** = .01, and *** = .001.

12. During the same period I was also a professor at INSEAD, Fontainebleau, France.

13. In a random sample of 100 5-point frequency distributions from the IBM data, the median never differed more than .10 points from the mean; the mean difference between the two was .02 points (the median lower).

14. For a random sample of 12 subpopulations from the database, age group and length of service correlated across individuals with coefficients between .52 and .76, with a median of .61.

15. In the 1967-69 survey round, education data were not reliable due to coding differences among countries and between subsequent versions of the questionnaire. For the occupations surveyed twice, educational levels have therefore been determined on the basis of 1971-73 data only.

16. This category is actually a combination of five occupation codes: data processing sales managers, office products sales managers, systems engineering managers, data processing customer engineering managers, and office products customer engineering managers.

17. This category represents a combination of two occupation codes: head office professionals and head office clerks. The ratio between these two varied only slightly between countries.

18. Two exceptions were made: (1) for Pakistan 1969, which had data for three occupational categories only, because Pakistan in 1972 met the minimum criterion easily with 70 respondents; and (2) for the United States, because the international questions had been used only in a survey of the data processing customer engineering division, which meant we had data for only one occupational group, plus its managers. However, the number of participants in this survey was very large: 3,967. We computed approximate seven-occupation scores from the U.S. DPCE scores by correcting for the worldwide occupation effect for DPCEs.

19. If data for this category were available in 1971-73 but not in 1967-69, we derived the earlier data from the later data by correcting for the mean shift that occurred in the country's other occupational categories between the two surveys, and vice versa if data were available in 1967-69 but not in 1971-73. If data for this

category were missing in both surveys, they were derived from the other categories' data correcting for the occupational differences found in the total world data. For the "work goals" and "general beliefs" we simplified this by substituting the data of occupational category 1 for 2 or 2 for 1 if either was missing, 3 for 4 or 4 for 3, and 5 for 6 or 6 for 5.

20. I have described the part of the research discussed in this subsection in detail elsewhere (see Hofstede, 1983c).

21. All French-speaking former colonies were still handled by IBM France; IBM France's management successfully resisted the inclusion of these countries in the surveys.

22. I have shown this in previous work by comparing the intercorrelation patterns among the four indexes across 40 countries and across 53 units, by comparing their correlations with GNP per capita, and by showing side by side a cluster analysis for 40 countries and for 53 units (Hofstede, 1983c).

23. Throughout this book, rho stands for the Spearman rank correlation coefficient. As for the Pearson product-moment correlation coefficient, significance limits are indicated with $*$ = .05, $**$ = .01, and $***$ = .001.

24. In this case the reliability of the measurement of country differences based on the mean of *both* surveys, according to the Spearman-Brown formula, will be .67.

25. Across 24 questions for which both types of stability were available, the median stability for country mean scores over 4 years was .77; for individual scores over 2 weeks it was .55. The rank correlation between the two sets of stability coefficients was rho = .03.

26. I called agreement with this belief *rule orientation*. Lammers and Hickson (1979a) used a classification of countries according to my power distance and rule orientation scores. At the time their chapter was written, I had not yet chosen the label *uncertainty avoidance*.

27. The 1967 laboratories survey used 26 goals; the 1967 Asia-Pacific-Latin America survey, 16 goals. The questions eliminated after 1971 are C1 through C8.

28. For manufacturing and product development the available occupation totals were worldwide (excluding the United States). In these, however, European countries dominated strongly numerically.

29. Data reported from the United States by Friedlander (1965, p. 10) also showed that lower-status employees attached higher average importance to work goals than did higher-status employees.

30. This argument applies to values in general. It even applies to the concept of "value" in economics. Pareto pointed out that for economic value only ordinal utility, not cardinal utility, is relevant (see Bannock, Baxter, & Rees, 1972, p. 310).

31. The standardization across the n goals can be carried out on the scores of individuals or on the mean scores of groups. The result is not necessarily the same: Standardizing individual scores before calculating a group mean in general will lead to a somewhat different rank order of goals than calculating a group mean first, before standardizing. Ritti (1964, pp. 317-318) has recommended "double" standardization of individual scores as a preparation for factor analysis: first across goals, then across individuals. (The reverse makes no sense, because the subsequent factor analysis starts with a correlation matrix that is invariant to standardization across goals.) Ritti notes, however, that single standardization across individuals has largely the same effect as double standardization (p. 307). In my analysis I have single-standardized group means across goals (first calculating group means, then standardizing) because this is much simpler to carry out; also, I am interested in eliminating acquiescence as a *group* phenomenon, before comparing groups, not as an individual phenomenon.

32. In the composition of the data in Exhibit A3.1, a problem existed for two countries (Chile and India) surveyed only in 1967. In the 1967 surveys a partly different list of goals was used, so that data on "desirable area," "cooperation," "manager," and "use of skills" were missing. In order not to lose Chile and India completely from the data, I have substituted the values of Argentina for the missing data from Chile and those of Pakistan for India, after correcting for differences in overall score level (acquiescence) between each pair of countries, visible in the scores for the remaining 10 goals.

33. See Hofstede et al. (1976, p. 48).

34. This statistician was Peter Van Hoesel at the University of Leiden in the Netherlands. The results were published in a working paper (Hofstede & Van Hoesel, 1976).

35. From the 44 items listed in Exhibit 2.4, 39 were retained. For question A43 (intent to continue with company), two variables were created (see Exhibit 2.4): percentage answering 1 or 2 (continue less than 5 years) and percentage answering 4 (continue until retirement). For question A54 (preferred manager), four variables were created: percentage answering 1 or 2, percentage answering 3 (1967-69 version only), percentage answering 3 (1972-73 version only), and percentage answering 4 (1972-73 version only). I explain the rationale for this distinction in Chapter 3. For question A55 (perceived manager), the scores used are percentage answering 1 or 2, autocratic or persuasive boss (see Appendix 2). For questions A5 through A18 (the work goals), the standardized scores were used that are listed in Appendix 3, Exhibit A3.1. Finally, the four indexes for power distance, uncertainty avoidance, individualism, and masculinity were added to the matrix, plus the mean raw work goal importance (IMP). Some data in the matrix were missing: B56 and B58 were used in only 28 countries, and for the other questions the number of countries varied between 33 and 40. Altogether, 65 cells in the matrix, or 3%, were empty.

Several times in this book I refer to factor analyses in which the number of observations (countries) is smaller than the number of variables. As explained in Chapter 1, this is allowable when we use ecological data, because the stability of the results depends not on the number of ecological categories but on the number of individuals whose scores were integrated into the ecological data.

36. Weeded out were the five indexes; the four demographics that are, strictly speaking, not "values"; three of the four variables for question A54, the preferred manager (only the percentage preferring manager 3, style 1967-69, was maintained; this is the variable used in composing the Power Distance Index); and one of the two variables for question A43, the intent to continue with the company (only the percentage intending to continue less than 5 years was retained). Finally, three more questions were eliminated: B61, which did not load on any factor and showed marginal stability in Exhibit 2.5; B25, with a .49 loading on Factor 1 and marginal stability in Exhibit 2.5, and which does not seem to relate conceptually to the other items on the factor (there is no real indication that it reflects much of a value); and A52, which only loaded .51 on Factor 4.

37. The scores for C9 through C14 are means across the usual seven occupations. For C15 through C19 (dropped after 1968) they are means across five occupations; they do not include head office managers and head office clerks, as in the European countries these were first surveyed in 1969.

38. The calculation of Individualism and Masculinity Index scores for Category 2 countries and Category 3 regions implied that the factor scores INV and SOC had to be computed for these 13 new cases that were not part of the original 40. This was done on the basis of the factor score coefficients; the method is described in Appendix 4. A simplified approximation formula for the Individualism and Masculinity Index scores for replications of the survey was developed later (Values Survey Module 1982, see also Appendix 4), but this was *not* used for the Category 2 countries and Category 3 regions.

39. Exhibit 2.7 is a summary of Exhibits 8.2 and 8.3 in the first edition of *Culture's Consequences* (Hofstede, 1980a).

40. It accounts for $.33^2 = 11\%$ of shared variance.

41. The clustering of Italy and South Africa with Germany and Switzerland in cluster 12 rather than in the Latin and Anglo clusters, respectively, was a surprise. The clusters found depend partly on the statistical method used. Thanks to the kind help of Dr. Zvi Maimon of Tel Aviv University, I also tried a smallest-space analysis (Guttman, 1968) using the country scores on 12 IBM questions (the three strongest correlated questions for each of the four dimensions). This technique is not intended for cluster analysis, but rather for the identification of dimensions in the data (as for factor analysis); however, it produces two-dimensional plots. One of these largely reproduced a UAI × PDI plot with Latin, Asian, and Germanic-Anglo-Nordic superclusters, but it put Italy (and also Japan) closer to the Germanic countries than my UAI × PDI plot in Exhibit 4.2.

42. I reviewed several older studies that produced country clusters in the first edition of *Culture's Consequences* (Hofstede, 1980a, pp. 331-332). A review of

eight clustering studies has been published by Ronen and Shenkar (1985). On the basis of World Values Survey data from 43 countries, Inglehart (1997, p. 93) produced a cluster diagram with some overlap with my results.

43. See Hofstede (1993).

44. The company's head office was in Ljubljana, Slovenia, which explains the large number of Slovene respondents, producing also a low MAS score for the former Yugoslavia as a whole.

45. In the 1982 and 1994 versions of the Values Survey Module made available for replications of the IBM-style survey, the country scores for individualism and masculinity were based on four questions each.

46. See Bosland (1985a) and Appendix 4 in this volume.

47. These shifts were as follows: PDI, +5 points; UAI, +7 points; IDV, +6 points; MAS, −2 points. Hall's calculation of IDV and MAS was not quite equivalent to the calculation in the original study, but this does not seem to have mattered much.

48. Singh (1990) has presented an unfortunate cumulation of unfounded conclusions, followed by my own "Reply and Comment." Unfounded conclusions also appear in an article by Fernandez, Carlson, Stepina, and Nicholson (1997). In 1989-90, they administered a questionnaire developed for the individual level of analysis but inspired by my four IBM dimensions (Dorfman & Howell, 1988) to unmatched convenience samples of "employed business professionals and advanced business students" in Chile, China, Germany, Japan, Mexico, Russia, the United States, Venezuela, and Yugoslavia (between 111 and 1,819 per country) and used the relative country mean scores on the Dorfman and Howell (1988) dimensions as proof of a culture shift in the seven overlapping countries since the IBM data were collected around 1970. As neither the instrument used nor the respondents were equivalent, such a conclusion could not be drawn. Fernandez et al. made no attempt at validating their scores, not even face validating; they found, for example, Yugoslavs to score low on power distance and high on individualism, which, for an article published in 1997, would beg at least an explanation.

49. Students of culture risk becoming so enthused about their subject that they forget other parts of the social system (Chirot, 1994, p. 119).

50. Unless a distribution is quite skewed, the correlation coefficients based on true data and on ranked data are strongly correlated (O'Brien, 1979).

51. In fact, most quantitative data about countries should be taken critically (Dogan, 1994). If significant correlations between such data and cultural indexes are found, these validate the external as much as the internal data.

52. Country GNP per capita values for successive years are strongly correlated, so the choice of the year does not immediately affect the correlation patterns with external data.

53. Jacobs (1985) has stressed the role of cities in the creation of wealth; the correlations provide support for her arguments.

54. See Harzing and Hofstede (1996).

55. This was, for example, explicitly demonstrated by Barkema and Vermeulen (1997).

56. For examples in cross-cultural psychology, see Segall, Dasen, Berry, and Poortinga (1990); Berry, Poortinga, Segall, and Dasen (1992); Smith and Bond (1993); M. H. Bond and Smith (1996); and Berry, Segall, and Kagitçibasi (1997; in particular, within Berry et al.'s edited volume, see Smith & Schwartz, 1997). For examples in organizational psychology and sociology, see Lammers and Hickson (1979b); Lammers (1981); Osigweh (1989b); Bhagat, Kedia, Crawford, and Kaplan (1990); Pugh and Hickson (1993); and Hickson and Pugh (1995). For examples in management, see Weinshall (1993), Redding (1994), Lowe and Oswick (1996), Smith (1996), Warner (1997), and Usunier (1998), as well as numerous textbooks on international management and even on management in general. For examples in communication, see Gudykunst (1987) and Gudykunst and Ting-Toomey (1988).

3

■

Power Distance

Summary of This Chapter

The first of the four dimensions of national culture revealed by the IBM data is called *power distance*. The basic issue involved, which different societies handle differently, is human inequality. Inequality can occur in areas such as prestige, wealth, and power; different societies put different weights on status consistency among these areas. Inside organizations, inequality in power is inevitable and functional. This inequality is usually formalized in boss-subordinate relationships. The term *power distance* is borrowed from the Dutch social psychologist Mulder, who in the 1960s conducted experiments to investigate interpersonal power dynamics. The present study suggests that power distances are to a considerable extent societally determined.

The countries covered in the IBM study could each be given a score on the Power Distance Index (PDI). This index was derived from country mean scores or percentages on three survey questions. These questions dealt with perceptions of subordinates' fear of disagreeing with superiors and of superiors' actual decision-making styles, and with the decision-making style that subordinates preferred in their bosses. PDI scores differed strongly across occupations as well, especially in countries where the country PDI was low. Differences on PDI between the genders were inconsistent.

The major part of this chapter is devoted to a validation of PDI scores against other data. First, PDI scores were correlated with other questions in the IBM survey and with PDI scores computed in straight replications of the IBM research on other populations; these show the stability of the index over the past decades. Next, PDI scores were correlated with country scores on a number of other cross-national surveys of values, both general values and work-related values, on a large variety of survey populations. The correlation pattern found has been integrated into a picture of the "power distance norm" as a value system held by the majority of a country's middle class.

Connotations are shown of power distance differences for various institutions: in the family, for schools and educational systems, in work and organization, in political systems, and in religion and ideas. These relate to power distance norm differences in a process of mutual feedback between the norm and the institutions that support it.

Correlations of PDI with geographic, economic, and demographic country indicators and consideration of historical factors lead to a suggested causal chain for the origins of national differences. Trend data do not suggest that such differences will disappear in the foreseeable future.

Inequality and Power Distance

On Animal and Human Inequality

A pet food manufacturer keeps 30 cats as a consumer panel. At the time of feeding, the cats queue up in a definite order, always the same. Only when a new cat enters is there some disorder: It tries to take a place in the queue and is bitten by every neighbor until it has found a place where henceforth it is tolerated.

Similar orders of inequality expressed in "dominance behavior" have been found among chickens (hence the term *pecking order*) and among

79

many other animals, in species of apes, birds, and fish. On the other hand, there are species that do not show consistent dominance behavior, such as ducks and carp.

From a biological point of view, the human species belongs to the category that shows dominance behavior. Human pecking orders are part of the "universal" level of human mental programming (Exhibit 1.1). How the basic fact of dominance is worked out in human social existence, however, varies from one society to another and from one group to another; it belongs to the "collective," cultural level. Some societies have elaborate formal systems of dominance; others go to great lengths to de-emphasize dominance. The great diversity of forms in which human societies deal with inequality and stratification has been described by historians, anthropologists, and sociologists.[1] The general conclusion to be drawn from these descriptions is that stratification systems are extremely culturally dependent and so extrapolating experiences from one culture to another is not necessarily justified.

Inequality is one of the oldest concerns of human thinking. In Homer's *Odyssey,* written some 2,700 years ago, Odysseus's faithful swineherd Eumaeus complained:

Servants, when their masters are no longer there to order them about, have little will to do their duties as they should. All-seeing Zeus takes half the good out of a man on the day when he becomes a slave. (Homer, 1980, p. 267)

This was in a society where slavery was the lot of those captured in war. And in Plato's *Laws,* written some 350 years later, the Master declares:

Even if you proclaim that a master and his slave shall have equal status, friendship between them is inherently impossible. The same applies to the relations between an honest man and a scoundrel. Indiscriminate equality for all amounts to *in*equality, and both fill a state with quarrels between its citizens. How correct the old saying is that "equality leads to friendship"! It's right enough and it rings true, but what kind of equality has this potential is a problem which produces ripe confusion. This is because we use the same term for two concepts of "equality" which in most respects are virtual opposites. The first sort of equality (of measures, weights and numbers) is within the competence of any state and any legislator; that is, one can simply distribute equal awards by lot. But the most genuine equality, and the best, is not so obvious.... The general method I mean is to grant much to the great and less to the less great, adjusting what you give to take account of the real nature of each. (Plato, 1970, pp. 229-230)

The ambiguity of "the real nature of each" is precisely the reason equality, before and after Plato, has always remained problematic. It is striking that Plato plays on two meanings of the word *equality;* this points to a semantic confusion that has forever existed and has sometimes been exploited, as immortalized by George Orwell in *Animal Farm* (1945): "All animals are equal but some are more equal than others." (In)equality is a multifaceted phenomenon.

Inequality in Society

Inequality can occur in a variety of areas:

- Physical and mental characteristics (This is a basic fact of human existence.)
- Social status and prestige
- Wealth
- Power
- Laws, rights, and rules ("Privileges" are private laws.)

Inequality in these areas need not go together; social inequality is multidimensional.[2] Successful athletes, artists, and scientists who show unique physical and/or mental characteristics usually enjoy status, but only in some societies do they enjoy wealth as well, and rarely do they have power. Politicians in some countries can enjoy status and power without wealth; businessmen, wealth and power without status. In general, in every society we can distinguish two opposing forces. One force tries to eliminate status inconsistencies between the various areas.[3] Sports figures become professionals to gain access to wealth; politicians exploit their power to achieve the same. In some traditional societies, whoever is strong and smart gains prestige, wealth, power, and privileges. The counterforce tries to maintain equality by offsetting rank in one area against another. The stress in the Christian Bible and in Buddhism on the merits of poverty is a manifestation of this force, as is Marx's plea for a "dictatorship of the proletariat."[4] Universalistic legal systems deny privileges on the basis of status, wealth, and power, but the ways in which such systems operate often reintroduce such privileges.

The battle between the two forces—status consistency versus overall equality—is one of the basic issues in any human society. We find it in the quote from Plato above, in which he clearly defends status consistency. Jean-Jacques Rousseau (1762/1972) takes the opposite point of view in his *Contrat Social*:

The fundamental treaty substitutes moral and legal equality for any physical inequality between men which nature may have caused; and while they may be unequal in force or intelligence, they become all equal by agreement and by law. (pp. 122-123; my translation)[5]

Rousseau proposes a distinction between "moral" and "natural" inequality, and he rejects the first while accepting the second as a fact of human existence.[6]

Living in a country in which people were not equal before the law (18th-century France), Rousseau expected too much from the establishment of this formal legal equality. For a 20th-century discussion of the same topic, consider the following quote from a U.S. newspaper:

President Carter took issue yesterday with former President Richard Nixon's claim that the chief executive has an inherent power to order burglaries and other illegal actions against dissidents. President Carter does not feel any president has a right to break the law, said White House Deputy Press Secretary Rex Granum. He feels very strongly that it is a tragic mistake to follow that philosophy, as past events have shown so dramatically. He does feel there are adequate judicial means to prevent danger to the country. Mr. Nixon, defending some of the illegal acts that took place in his administration, made the assertion during the third of his televised interviews with David Frost, broadcast last night. (*International Herald Tribune*, May 21-22, 1977, p. 3)

Carter in this case defended equality before the law against Nixon, who wanted to let the law yield to power.

In the manifestation of the dilemma of status consistency versus equality, we should distinguish sharply between the ideological and the pragmatic level, the level of the desirable versus the desired, as described in Chapter 1 (Exhibit 1.3). Plato, Rousseau, and Carter all operated at the ideological level. Nixon was trying to justify his acts and therefore was operating exceptionally at the pragmatic level; it is extremely unlikely that he would have made the same statement in other circumstances. The reactions of the public to the Watergate affair, to which the Carter and Nixon quotes refer, can be seen as an attempt in American society to close the gap between the desired and the desirable. Other societies at other moments in history have shown even larger gaps in this respect. The *liberté, égalité, fraternité* (freedom, equality, brotherhood) of the French Revolution of 1789 was an ideological statement that did not cover the behavior of the revolutionaries at all.[7]

In practice, no society has ever obtained equality in the form of complete consistency among different areas of rank. To paraphrase Orwell: All so-cieties are unequal but some are more unequal than others.[8] What has been obtained in some societies is what Galtung (1966) has called "criss-cross" in social structure: the existence of individuals who belong to disparate groups in the structure and can thus serve as bridges in case of conflict. These individuals form a middle layer in society between the "top dogs" and the "under-dogs." The stabilizing role in society of a middle stratum is an age-old truth:

It is clear then both that the political partnership which operates through the middle class is best, and also that those cities have every chance of being well-governed in which the middle class is large, stronger if possible than the other two together, or at any rate stronger than one of them. For the addition of its weight to either side will turn the balance and prevent the extravagances of the opposition. (Aristotle, 1962, p. 173, written 330 B.C.)

Societies with crisscross structures can be called *pluralist*; societies without crisscross but with status consistency, *elitist*. Pluralist societies are less unequal than elitist societies but still maintain large inequalities.[9] In all modern societies, probably without exception, there are disadvantaged groups that are behind in physical and mental abilities, having been undernourished and undereducated, who earn less and enjoy life less and who die younger.[10]

Related to the pluralist/elitist distinction is the aspect of social mobility. Other factors being equal, in pluralist societies new members will be more easily admitted into the ranks of elites than in elitist societies, because the middle groups in the pluralist society are stepping stones to the top-dog ranks.

Societies differ in the implications of rank inequalities for social functioning. Bohannan (1969, pp. 198 ff.) distinguishes among caste, estate, and class. *Castes* as they existed formally in preindependence India are organized associations of extended families, membership in which determined a person's rank in all areas of life. In modern India, castes have formally been abolished, but they continue to affect daily life very deeply.[11] Estates as they existed in feudal Europe (nobility, yeomanry, and serfs) were legal categories of people with specific rights and obligations but without organizations uniting members of the same category. *Classes* in modern sociology are categories of people who are not necessarily organized as such (Marx wanted them to organize) or legally identified but who share characteristics on which they can be ranked: prestige, wealth, power. Class members are usually identified by their economic activity and/or educational background, and they can be shown to share the same values, forming subcultures. Aron (1969) distinguishes between a "nominalist" definition of class, which he sees as typical for U.S. sociology, and a "realist" definition, which he found in French sociology. In the nominalist definition the central concept is the "deference" present in the mind of the individual member of the lower classes. In the realist definition, there is a collective consciousness of the members of a class of belonging together. Behind this difference in definitions is a difference in societies; in France, "class" is much more a reality than it is in the United States.

Inkeles (1960) reviewed data on attitudes and values from a large number of studies, each comparing different classes within one society from a variety of societies; he concludes, "The average proportion of persons holding a particular view may be distinctive of a given country, but within all modern societies the order or structure of response is the same, following the typical status ladders of occupation, income, and education" (p. 1). Dominant value systems among elites are complemented by subordinate value systems, accommodating to the dominant system, held by nonelites. Both together support the status quo.[12]

Castes, estates, and classes represent more or less integrated systems; the existence of one class presupposes other classes. However, societies may also contain unintegrated groups. Bohannan (1969) calls these the "pariahs," after the untouchables of India. Racial minorities or even majorities may be such pariahs; the millions of migrant workers from poor countries in wealthier countries are another case. "Pariahs are, by definition, kept outside the recognized major institutions of the social structure, although they usually have an economic link with them" (pp. 183-184). In the case of pariahs, the inequality is total.

Inequality in Organizations

Within organizations as units of society, we inevitably find inequality of members' abilities and inequality of power.[13] An unequal distribution of power over members is the essence of organization. Without it, we get something like "a flock of birds, in which the only rule of behaviour for each bird is to change the direction of its flight so that, relatively, it always sees its fellows in the same position and thus never leaves the group" (Cotta, 1976, p. 178). Inequality of power in organizations is essential for control and for temporarily overcoming the law of entropy, which states that disorder will increase (Cotta, 1976, p. 176). Even organizations designed to be egalitarian, such as political parties, develop their power elites; this is Michels's (1915/1962, pp. 342 ff.) "iron law of oligarchy."[14]

In most utilitarian organizations the distribution of power is formalized in hierarchies.[15] The basic element from which hierarchical pyramids are built is the relationship between a boss B and a subordinate S. If we know that S "reports to B," we know certain formal aspects of their relationship; it is likely that B can set priorities for S's work and possible that B has some influence on S's rewards and career. Luhmann (1975, p. 104) argues that power in organizations is mainly exercised through influence on people's careers, but this may be more true in societies and groups in which careers are more important (as in Germany; see Chapter 6). Beyond the few formal aspects, the existence of a hierarchical relationship tells little about the actual power relationship between B and S. A boss and a subordinate can fill in their formal hierarchical relationship in very different ways.[16] Objective factors play a role, such as the expertise of both parties, the history of their relationship, the task at hand, and the relative criticalness of the situation. Then there are the subjective factors of the way in which B and S choose to play their hierarchical roles, which depends on their mental programming and their psychological impact on each other. Their mental programming contains their personalities and their values, affected by the societal norms that control their behavior.

The boss-subordinate relationship is a basic human relationship that bears resemblance to even more fundamental relationships earlier in life: those of parent and child and of teacher and pupil.[17] Both as bosses and as subordinates, people can be expected to carry over values and norms from their early life experiences as children and school pupils. As family and school environments differ strongly among cultures, we can expect to find the traces of these differences in the exercise of power in hierarchies.

Differences in the exercise of power in a hierarchy relate to the value systems of both bosses *and* subordinates and not to the values of the bosses only, even though they are the more powerful partners. The popular management literature on "leadership" often forgets that leadership can exist only as a complement to "subordinateship."[18] In the same way that patterns of inequality between groups in society are supported by both dominant and subordinate value systems, patterns of power inequality within organizations reflect the values of both parties. Subordinates as a group are accessory to the exercise of power in a hierarchical system: The way the system functions reflects their collective complicity and the role relationship to which both parties contribute. Authority exists only where it is matched by obedience. In 1548, a teenage French nobleman named Étienne de La Boétie published an essay titled *Le Discours de la servitude volontaire* in which he argued that a tyrant has no other power than that which is given to him, and that the problem is less the tyrant than the "voluntary servitude" of his subjects (La Boétie, 1548/1976).[19] On the psychological level, the need for independence in people is matched by a need for dependence, and the need for power by a need for security. Dependence and security needs stem from early childhood and are common to all human beings; independence and power are developed only later in our lives, if they are developed at all. "Submission to power is thus the earliest and most formative experience in human life" (Wrong, 1980, p. 3). "We have to think of the individual . . . as trained in dominance-submission, not in either dominance *or* submission" (Bateson, 1942/1973, p. 65).

The Concept of Power Distance

The relationship between a boss B and a subordinate S in a hierarchy, including its values component, is better understood if we introduce the concept of power distance. Power distance is a measure of the interpersonal power or influence between B and S as perceived by the less powerful of the two, S. The term *power distance* is taken from the work of the Dutch social psychologist Mauk Mulder (1976, 1977; Mulder et al., 1971), who based his power distance theory on laboratory and field experiments with simple social structures. Mulder (1977) defines *power* as "the potential to determine or direct (to a certain extent) the behavior of another person or other persons more so than the other way round," and *power distance* as "the degree of inequality in power between a less powerful Individual (I) and a more powerful Other (O), in which I and O belong to the same (loosely or tightly knit) social system" (p. 90). He proved about 20 hypotheses, of which the most relevant to this study are the following:

1. The mere exercise of power will give satisfaction.
2. The more powerful individual will strive to maintain or to increase the power distance to the less powerful person.
3. The greater this distance from the less powerful person, the stronger the striving to increase it.
4. Individuals will strive to reduce the power distance between themselves and more powerful persons.
5. The smaller this distance from the more powerful person, the stronger the tendency to reduce it.

3/5. The "downward" tendencies of the powerful to maintain the power distance and the "upward" power distance reduction of the less powerful reinforce each other. (Mulder, 1977, p. 92)

The implication of Hypothesis 5 is that the strongest power distance reduction tendency "will not be found in the powerless, but in people whose power striving is partly satisfied. *The power striving is not fed by dissatisfaction* but by satisfaction. Having power feeds the need, making it comparable to the need for hard drugs. An individual can become addicted to 'power distance reduction' " (p. 46).

Mulder's work made it plausible that the hypotheses proven in his laboratory setting are valid for (Dutch) societal settings in general, such as labor-management relationships. In the United States, Kipnis (1972) independently carried out laboratory experiments similar to Mulder's and arrived at similar conclusions. Kipnis showed that more powerful persons tended to devalue the worth of the performance of less powerful ones and to attribute the cause of the less powerful's efforts to themselves. Kipnis, Castell, Gergen, and Mauch (1976) showed that this applied even between partners in marriage and among U.S. housewives employing maids. The conclusions from Mulder's and Kipnis's psychological experiments converge with those from sociological studies on the forming of power elites, such as Michels's iron law of oligarchy, to which I referred earlier; Michels's "law" is based on an analysis of the German Social Democratic Party before World War I and of other European socialist parties. There is therefore evidence from a number of Western countries that supports the validity of Mulder's hypotheses. This evidence shows how inequality confirms and perpetuates itself. Boulding (1978, pp. 282-283) refers to the "Matthew principle" (from the Christian New Testament, Matthew 13:12: "For he who has, to him shall more be given"); he found the Matthew principle to be present in both the concentration of power and the concentration of wealth.

Borrowing from Mulder, I will use the following definition of power distance:

The power distance between a boss B and a subordinate S in a hierarchy is the difference between the extent to which B can determine the behavior of S and the extent to which S can determine the behavior of B.[20]

What I shall try to show in this chapter is that *the power distance, thus defined, that is accepted by both B and S and supported by their social environment is to a considerable extent determined by their national culture.* Culture sets the level of power distance at which the tendency of the powerful to maintain or increase power distances and the tendency of the less powerful to reduce them will find their equilibrium.

Power Distance and Human Inequality

If different cultures can be shown to maintain consistently different power distances in hierarchies, the power distance norm can be used as a criterion for characterizing cultures (without excluding other criteria). In fact, the literature contains many references to the existence of such a criterion. In Chapter 1, I mentioned ways of dealing with hierarchy and authority as a proposed criterion for ordering cultures in reference to the work of Kluckhohn and Strodtbeck (1961) and of Inkeles and Levinson (1954/1997). Gasse (1976) argues that "each culture justifies authority using its major values" and has proposed a continuum from "monolithism" to "pluralism" (p. 6). At the monolithic pole, power is held by few people; at the pluralistic pole, competition between groups and leaders is encouraged, control by leaders is limited because members can join several organizations, democratic politics are fostered, and information sources are independent of a single organization.

So far, the term *power distance* has been rather indiscriminately applied regardless of the level of aggregation: from the small group (Mulder's experiments) to society as a whole. However, different norms may apply *within groups* and *between groups* in society. Sik-hung Ng (1980) from Hong Kong (later in New Zealand) has criticized Mulder's "model of power change as inherently conservative and individualistic" (p. 228). In Mulder's experimental settings, all actors were individuals. Ng distinguishes "situations in which an individual acts in terms of self, and others in which he does so in terms of his membership and/ or reference group" (p. 229). Also, it is crucial whether the actor "is acting towards an ingroup or an outgroup member. The former overlaps partly with intragroup behavior, while the latter is identical to intergroup behavior" (p. 230).

The in-group/out-group distinction will be connected in Chapter 5 with the individualism versus collectivism dimension. Within certain groups, small power distances between "bosses" and "subordinates" can be maintained, whereas from one group to another power and other inequalities are large (Béteille, 1977, p. 44). Class distinctions in low-PDI Britain provide an example. In Britain's history, the democratic power of a wealthy class meant the power of a wealthy class; it passed the laws that legally chased the peasants off their land, condemning them to abject poverty (Moore, 1966). Power in relationships between groups and organizations is not just a replication of power between people within groups and organizations (Crozier, 1973, p. 225). Whether norms for power distances between groups covary with norms for power distance within groups is a matter for empirical research.

Measuring National Differences in Power Distance in IBM

Organization of Chapters 3 Through 7

Chapters 3 through 6, and partly also Chapter 7, are organized in the following way: Each chapter deals with a separate dimension of national cultures, which is introduced through reference to the general problem area for human societies with which it deals—as for the dimension of power distance above. Next, the computation of a country index for this dimension is described and differences according to occupation and gender are analyzed, as well as the various questions in the IBM surveys that correlated with this dimension. The chapter then looks at replications of the IBM surveys on other populations and validations of the index against other broad cross-national studies of values and related phenomena. Then follows the core part of the chapter: a description of the two poles between which the dimension's societal norm is positioned and the origins and implications of that norm for various spheres of life, including the family, the school, the workplace, politics, religion, and theories, as much as possible supported by empirical data. The comparisons between studies use a fair amount of statistical argumentation, applying factor analysis, product-moment correlations (Pearson, coefficients labeled *r*), rank correlations (Spearman, coefficients labeled rho), multiple and stepwise regression, and significance tests. In the interest of readability, the purely statistical parts of Chapters 3 through 6 appear in separate sections at the ends of these chapters. In the main body of each chapter only the results of the statistical analysis are discussed; readers are referred to the statistical section for details. As noted previously, statistical significance is shown by * for the .05 level, ** for the .01 level, and *** for the .001 level, one-tailed unless otherwise mentioned.

As mentioned in Chapter 2, I always checked to what extent a correlation with one of the four IBM indexes might be a by-product of correlations with one or more of the other indexes, as well as with national wealth (GNP/capita). In the present chapter I basically report only comparisons with outside studies in which PDI makes an *independent* significant contribution (or is expected to do so but does not).

A Power Distance Index
for IBM Countries

As the central questionnaire item for exploring power distance differences between countries, I chose: "How frequently, in your experience, does the following problem occur: Employees being afraid to express disagreement with their managers?" (B46 in Appendix 1, with a 5-point answer scale from *very frequently* to *very seldom*). Of all the questions in the questionnaire, this one most clearly expresses power distance. It is a projective question: Respondents are not asked how frequently they *themselves* are afraid to disagree, but their answers can be expected to reflect a projection of their own feelings. However, the question works well only for *nonmanagers*. Answers from managers had to be excluded, as managers' perceptions of employees' fear to disagree (with them!) are not equivalent to employees' perceptions: They may be distorted by low sensitivity or wishful thinking precisely in those cases where employees are most afraid.

Other researchers have also used fear of disagreement as a measure. In a series of surveys conducted in the United States, Patchen (1965) used an index of "willingness to disagree with supervisors" (pp. 48-54). Across individual respondents it correlated with employee control over work goals, interest in work innovation, and (in most cases) the supervisor's ranking of employees in order of readiness to disagree. A reference to fear of disagreement as part of a country's culture is found in Whyte (1969), who deals with an example from Venezuela:

In a highly stratified society where all powers are concentrated in the hands of the superior, the subordinate learns that it can be dangerous to question a decision of the superior. In this type of situation, people learn to behave submissively—at least in the presence of the boss. They do not learn to thrash things out with him, face-to-face. Then, when there is no reason to fear, they still do not feel that it is natural to speak up. (p. 37)

This attitude occurs not only among lower-level employees. Negandhi and Prasad (1971) quote a senior Indian executive with a Ph.D. from a prestigious American university:

What is most important for me and my department is not what I do or achieve for the company, but whether the Master's (i.e., an owner of the firm) favor is bestowed on me. . . . This I have achieved by saying "yes" to everything the Master says or does. . . . to contradict him is to look for another job. . . . I left my freedom of thought in Boston. (p. 128)

In the IBM data on the "employees afraid" question (Column B46 in Appendix 2, Exhibit A2.2), Venezuela and India (from which the two quotes above originate) are among the most "afraid" countries.

Two other questions in the IBM questionnaire, A54 and A55 (see Appendix 1), provided unique information about power distances in boss-subordinate relationships. They used a description of four types of decision-making behavior by managers and asked subordinates to indicate (1) their preferred type and (2) their perception of their bosses' actual type. The descriptions of the four types were originally taken from Tannenbaum and Schmidt (1958). In the version of the questionnaire used from 1967 to 1969, the four decision-making styles were as follows: (1) autocratic ("tells"), (2) persuasive/paternalistic ("sells"), (3) consultative ("consults"), and (4) democratic (majority vote, "joins"). Since 1970, the description of the fourth type was changed to a participative (consensus) style, more or less conforming to Likert's (1967) "System 4." This was done because the actual occurrence of the old type 4 was perceived as very rare, and offering respondents a possibility to choose the "participative" style was seen as desirable for organization development purposes. This change obviously affected the response distribution; it could be expected to affect especially the distribution of responses between managers 3 and 4, less the choices for 1 and 2.[21]

Whereas the "employees afraid" question asked for a perception of the behavior of fellow employees, the "perceived manager" question asked for a perception of the behavior of the boss. It is a subjective description of the boss's decision-making behavior, but in order to understand the boss's impact on subordinate behavior, a subjective description by the subordinate is probably more relevant than would be any objective description (assuming we would be able to obtain such a description). There was a significant correlation across the 40 (Category 1) countries of the mean "employees afraid" scores and the mean percentage of employees perceiving a manager 1 or 2 (autocratic or persuasive/paternalistic): If bosses were more often seen as autocratic, employees were more likely seen as afraid to disagree with them, and vice versa (see Exhibit 3.11 in the statistical section of this chapter).

As opposed to the "employees afraid" and "perceived manager" questions, which dealt with perceptions rather than values, the "preferred manager" question directly expressed a value; in the terminology of Chapter 1, I call this a "value as the desired." The statistical analysis shows that across the 40 Category 1 IBM countries the percentages of employees preferring a certain type of manager were correlated with the perceptions both of employees being afraid and of managers being seen as autocratic or persuasive/paternalistic. The correlations, however, were much higher for the 1967-69 data (using a manager 4 = democratic, majority vote) than for the 1971-73 data (manager 4 = participative, consensus). This is why for the IBM Power Distance Index I have used only the 1967-69 data for the "preferred manager" question. Interestingly, the pattern of correlations (Exhibit 3.11) opposed the preference for manager 3 (consultative) to all others (1, 2, or 4: autocratic, persuasive, *or democratic*). In countries where few employees were perceived as afraid, many preferred a "consultative" manager. In countries where many employees were perceived as afraid, employees tended *not* to prefer the consultative manager but to vote for the autocratic, the persuasive, *or* the democratic, majority-vote manager.

The correlation between a preference for a consultative manager and "employees not afraid" shows that a particular power relationship is established through the values of *both* partners, the superiors as well as the subordinates. In systems in which superiors maintain large power distances, subordinates *prefer* such superiors (*dependent reaction*) or go to the other extreme—that is, they prefer a superior who does not decide at all but who governs by a majority vote of subordinates. This latter type of decision making is unlikely to be effective in work organizations; it would be feasible only if departments were completely autonomous and independent of other departments, whereas in fact most work organizations are complex interdependent systems. Therefore the preference for a majority-vote decision type is unrealistic; I interpret it as a *counterdependent reaction* to a situation of large power distance. So we see that where superiors maintain a large power distance, subordinates tend to polarize into dependence and counterdependence.[22] On the other hand, where superiors maintain a smaller power distance, subordinates tend to prefer the consultative decision style; this can be interpreted as *interdependence* between superior and subordinate. This interdependent relationship is more in line with the requirements of work organizations as complex systems.

The participative manager (manager 4, 1971-73) did not collect counterdependence votes. The preference for this type was unrelated to the country's power distance level. An unpublished study of IBM's manufacturing employees showed that a preference for a participative manager related to the respondents' age: In an international population, 37% of those between 25 and 30 years old

chose a participative manager, but only 25% of those between 40 and 50 did so.

A Power Distance Index for each of the 40 countries was computed on the basis of the country mean scores for the three items:

a. Nonmanagerial employees' perception that employees are afraid to disagree with their managers (B46)

b. Subordinates' perception that their boss tends to take decisions in an autocratic (1) or persuasive/paternalistic way (2, A55)

c. Subordinates' preference for anything but a consultative (3) style of decision making in their boss; that is, for an autocratic (1), a persuasive/paternalistic (2), *or* a democratic style (4, A54).

The actual computation of the country PDI uses mean percentage values for questions b and c: In the case of b, with 1967-69 plus 1971-73 data; in the case of c, with 1967-69 data only. It uses mean scores on a 5-point scale (1 = *very frequently*, 5 = *very seldom*) for question a; these mean scores have been multiplied by 25 to make their range, and therefore their contribution to the PDI, roughly equal to the range in percentage values of questions b and c. The actual formula used is as follows:

$$PDI = 135 - 25 \text{ (mean score employees afraid)}$$
$$+ \text{ (percentage perceived manager } 1 + 2)$$
$$- \text{ (percentage preferred manager 3, 1967-69).}$$

The constant 135 has been added to give the country index values a range between about zero (small power distance) and 100 (large power distance). The theoretical range of the index is from −90 (no one afraid, no manager 1 + 2, everyone prefers 3) to +210 (everyone afraid, all managers 1 + 2, no one prefers 3).

The computation of the PDI values listed in the "actual" column of Exhibit 3.1 can be checked from the values in Appendix 2, Exhibits A2.1, A2.2, and A2.4 (for the handling of missing data, see the statistical section).

Country index values range from 104 for Malaysia (large power distance) to 11 for Austria (small power distance), with an overall mean for the 50 countries and 3 regions of 57 and a standard deviation of 22. Compare also the country clusters in Chapter 2, Exhibit 2.8.

The Power Distance Index is a measure of *values* found in the IBM subsidiaries, but it differs from classical values tests in several respects. First, it applies to entire subsidiaries, not to indi-

Exhibit 3.1 Power Distance Index Values for 50 Countries and Three Regions

Rank	Country	PDI Actual	PDI Predicted[a]	Rank	Country	PDI Actual	PDI Predicted[a]
1	Malaysia	104	78	27/28	South Korea	60	61
2/3	Guatemala	95	68	29/30	Iran	58	61
2/3	Panama	95	65	29/30	Taiwan	58	65
4	Philippines	94	76	31	Spain	57	56
5/6	Mexico	81	72	32	Pakistan	55	75
5/6	Venezuela	81	70	33	Japan	54	57
7	Arab countries	80		34	Italy	50	52
8/9	Ecuador	78	78	35/36	Argentina	49	57
8/9	Indonesia	78	86	35/36	South Africa	49	64
10/11	India	77	77	37	Jamaica	45	61
10/11	West Africa	77		38	United States	40	41
12	Yugoslavia	76	53	39	Canada	39	36
13	Singapore	74	70	40	Netherlands	38	37
14	Brazil	69	73	41	Australia	36	45
15/16	France	68	40	42/44	Costa Rica	35	66
15/16	Hong Kong	68	59	42/44	Germany (F.R.)	35	41
17	Colombia	67	79	42/44	Great Britain	35	44
18/19	Salvador	66	68	45	Switzerland	34	33
18/19	Turkey	66	60	46	Finland	33	29
20	Belgium	65	36	47/48	Norway	31	26
21/23	East Africa	64		47/48	Sweden	31	23
21/23	Peru	64	73	49	Ireland	28	37
21/23	Thailand	64	76	50	New Zealand	22	37
24/25	Chile	63	57	51	Denmark	18	28
24/25	Portugal	63	54	52	Israel	13	47
26	Uruguay	61	51	53	Austria	11	40
27/28	Greece	60	52				
				Mean of 53		57	
				Standard deviation of 53		22	

a. Predicted values are based on multiple regression on latitude, population size, and wealth. See Exhibit 3.20.

viduals: It is an *ecological* index (for the difference between individual and ecological measures, see Chapter 1). Second, all three questions were answered by the subordinates rather than the superiors—that is, by the least powerful partners in the relationship, who are better judges of power distance than their more powerful superiors. Third, only question c asks for a value in the strict sense: a preference for one state of affairs over others. Question b deals with a characteristic of the organizational "regime" (the superior's style of decision making) and question a with an aspect of the organizational "climate" (the extent to which employees are afraid to disagree). Obviously the scores on questions a and b represent perceptions that are in the beholder as well as in the objective situation, but this is true for any measure of regime or climate. People are more accurate in describing others than in describing themselves.[23]

As the statistical analysis shows (Exhibit 3.12), the correlations among the country scores on the three questions are well over .50, so that in this case value, regime, and climate go together, forming a coherent pattern that differentiates between

Exhibit 3.2   Power Distance Index Values for Six Categories of Occupations

Categories of Occupations	Number of Occupations in This Category	PDI Range From	To	Mean
Unskilled and semiskilled workers	3	85	97	90
Clerical workers and nonprofessional salesmen	8	57	84	71
Skilled workers and technicians	6	33	90	65
Managers of the previous categories	8	22	62	42
Professional workers	8	–22	36	22
Managers of professional workers	5	-19	21	8
Total	38	-22	97	47

SOURCE: This is a summary of Table 2 in Hofstede (1977b).
NOTE: Data are based on a stratified sample from France, Germany, and Great Britain.

one country and another. Across 38 occupations, the mean scores on the three questions are also highly correlated (see below). However, the correlations among the three questions across *individuals* are virtually zero. It is not necessarily the individual who sees his or her boss as autocratic who will also describe colleagues as afraid and who will prefer an autocratic boss. The lack of individual correlations should remind us that power distance as measured here can be used only as a characteristic of *social systems,* not of *individuals.* It cannot be used to measure, for example, the authoritarianism of individuals; however, it can be used to measure the "authoritarianism" of whole societies and their dominant supervision styles.[24]

Power Distance Index
Scores by Occupation

The strong correlations among the *occupation* scores for the three PDI questions shown in Exhibit 3.12 mean that a Power Distance Index can also be meaningfully computed by occupation. This has been done elsewhere (Hofstede, 1977b); a summary of the scores found (using the same formula as for countries) is listed in Exhibit 3.2.

In the same way as country scores had to be computed for a stratified sample of occupations, occupation scores had to be computed for a stratified sample of countries. The data in Exhibit 3.2 are based on responses from the three large countries France, Germany, and Great Britain, giving equal weight to each. The lower-education,

lower-status occupations tended to produce high PDI values, and the higher-education, higher-status occupations tended to produce low-PDI values. Education was by far the dominant factor: The correlation of the occupation's PDI with the average years of formal education was an amazing $r = -.90***$. Every additional year of formal school education needed for an occupation reduced the occupation's PDI score by about 18 points.[25]

Paradoxically, the correlation between PDI and educational level that was so strongly negative across occupations was positive across countries (see question A56, Exhibit A2.1, $r = .44***$). In higher-PDI countries, IBM employees in the particular set of occupations used for comparison (managerial, professional, technical, and clerical) tended to have *more* years of formal education than those in lower-PDI countries. This is a consequence of both the labor market situation and the educational system in many poorer countries: a large offer of candidates with extensive but impractical formal schooling.

Across occupations there was also a tendency for managers to produce lower PDI values than nonmanagers.[26] The multiple correlation of PDI with education and hierarchical level was $R = .94$, showing that the occupation's PDI was highly predictable from these two factors ($R^2 = 88\%$ of the variance in occupational PDI was explained).

The conclusions of the occupational data analysis so far are as follows:

1. Power distances between less educated and nonmanagerial employees and their superi-

Exhibit 3.3 Power Distance Index Values for Four Occupations in Each of 11 Countries

Country	Occupation					Δ Occupa-tions (Highest-Lowest)	Spearman Correlation With Occupation PDI
	All Occupations	BO Systems Engineers	HO Clerks	DP Customer Engineers	Unskilled Plant Workers		
	PDI	29	61	63	97		
Mexico	81	83	97	99	99	16	.95
India	77	80	81	87	88	8	1.00*
Brazil	69	64	90	96	115	51	1.00*
France	68	58	84	86	108	50	1.00*
Colombia	67	48	94	95	106	58	1.00*
Japan	54	58	57	84	92	35	.80
Argentina	49	57	96	77	106	49	.80
Canada	39	24	42	55	80	56	1.00*
Netherlands	38	17	59	41	83	66	.80
Germany (F.R.)	35	14	53	62	90	76	1.00*
Great Britain	35	15	50	42	102	87	.80
Δ countries (highest-lowest)	46	69	55	58	.35		.80
Spearman rank correlation with country PDI		.96***	.70**	.90***	.35	−.82***	

NOTE: Each cell (one country, one occupation) counts at least 20 respondents. BO = branch office; HO = home office; DP = data processing.
*p = .05; **p = .01; ***p = .001.

ors tended to be larger than between more educated and managerial employees and their superiors.

2. The range of PDI scores among different countries (Exhibit 3.1), holding occupation and thereby education constant, was still nearly as large as among different occupations (Exhibit 3.2). The differences in hierarchical power distance found between equally educated employees in different countries were therefore of the same magnitude as those between unskilled workers and college-trained professionals within one country.

The country and the occupation effect on power distance interact. Exhibit 3.3 shows PDI scores for 44 one-country, one-occupation subpopulations. Four nonmanagerial occupations are covered:

1. Branch office systems engineers, average educational level 15.8 years

2. Head office clerks, average educational level 12.9 years

3. Data processing customer engineers, average educational level 12.2 years

4. Unskilled machine plant direct personnel, average educational level 10.5 years

Occupation 1 is college level and can be rated upper-middle-class; occupations 2 and 3 are high school level and lower-middle-class; 4 is less than high school and working-class. Data on occupation 4 were available only for 11 countries from the 13 in which IBM had manufacturing plants. The PDI scores for the other three occupations are shown only for these same 11 countries. These three are included in the seven occupational categories that were used to compute country PDI scores; occupation 4, evidently, was not.

We see in Exhibit 3.3 that the ranking of the four occupations in order of power distance was largely retained for each country and that the ranking of the 11 countries was similar across the first three occupations (which contributed to the country scores) but less between these and the un-skilled workers. The exhibit shows an interaction effect between country and occupation: The coun-try differences were much larger for the more highly educated than for the less-educated occu-pations, and the occupation differences were much larger on the low-PDI than on the high-PDI side. The theoretical maximum PDI score is 210, but it looks as if there is a practical maximum of around 100, and all respondents in high-PDI countries (regardless of educational level) and all respondents in unskilled jobs (regardless of coun-try) are pushed against this ceiling. Low PDI val-ues occurred only for highly educated occupa-tions in small power distance countries. Class differences in power distance scores were particu-larly large in Great Britain and Germany. Such differences were low in India and Mexico, where power distances were large for everyone regard-less of class. Japan took a middle position with middle-range PDI scores for all four occupations.

The fact that less-educated, lower-status em-ployees hold more "authoritarian" values has been signaled before—for example, for employ-ees in banking, insurance, and government ad-ministration in France by Crozier (1964b); for au-tomobile workers in Detroit by Kornhauser (1965, p. 267); and for parents of 10- to 11-year-old children in the United States and Italy by Kohn (1969).[27]

Kohn (1969) combined educational and occu-pational level into a social class index. U.S. par-ents higher on this index were "more likely to em-phasize children's self-direction, and working-class parents to emphasize their conformity to ex-ternal authority" (p. 34). Some quotes:

The class relationships are built on the cumulative effects of educational training and occupational experience. The former is present insofar as it pro-vides or fails to provide the capacity for self-direc-tion, the latter insofar as it provides or fails to pro-vide the experience of exercising self-direction in so consequential a realm of life as work. (p. 188)

The essence of higher class position is the expec-tation that one's decisions and actions can be con-sequential; the essence of lower class position is the belief that one is at the mercy of forces and people beyond one's control, often beyond one's understanding. (p. 189)

Kohn also found that social class and national environment interacted in the maintenance of au-thoritarian values. Working-class fathers put high value on their children's obedience in both Italy and the United States, but middle-class fathers stressed this point much more in (higher-PDI) Italy (p. 42).[28]

Gender Differences in Power Distance

In addition to country and occupation, the two other universal criteria by which the IBM survey data can be differentiated are the gender and the age group of the respondents. I discuss age group differences later in this chapter. Gender and occu-pation are highly interdependent, so analysis by gender makes sense only for occupations that have sizable shares of both men and women doing the same work. In Exhibit 3.4, the computation of PDI by gender is shown for one professional and one clerical occupation that more or less fulfill this criterion. As the relative numbers of men and women in these occupations vary only modestly among the larger country subsidiaries, I have, for simplicity, used total world data in Exhibit 3.4 (all respondents together, regardless of country); I have also taken the mean of the two survey rounds, at least for questions a and b.

We should first check whether comparing the genders on a power distance *index* makes sense. That is, do the three questions that make up the PDI differentiate in the same direction between the genders? The table shows that questions a and c differentiate and that question b does not differ-entiate at all. Only one difference is statistically significant: Female clerks have less preference for a consultative manager than do their male col-leagues. In the ANOVA of Exhibit 2.3, too, only the preference for a consultative manager showed a significant gender effect, and inspection of the data (not visible in the exhibit) confirmed that this effect was in the same direction: Female manufac-turing employees had lower preference for a con-sultative manager. In Exhibit 3.4, I have com-puted PDI values, which are higher for women than for men, especially in the case of the less-ed-ucated group, the clerks. It is, however, question-able whether one statistically significant differ-ence out of six justifies the use of PDI for comparing between the genders. PDI is not the proper index for this—using it would represent a "reverse ecological fallacy" (see Chapter 1).

Country Power Distance Index Scores and Other IBM Survey Questions

Aside from the three questions making up the PDI, several other items in the IBM questionnaire were significantly correlated with PDI across countries (Appendix 2, Exhibits A2.1, A2.2 and A2.3). For the following items related to em-ployee-manager relations, the highest significant zero-order correlation was with PDI: "My man-ager is not concerned with helping me get ahead" (A52, $r = .42***$); "Employees lose respect for a consultative manager" (B55, $r = -.49***$); "A good manager gives detailed instructions"

Exhibit 3.4   Power Distance Index Computation for Men and Women in the Same Occupations

Occupations (2 surveys, total world data)	(A) Not Perceiving Employees Afraid Mean Score	(B) % Perceiving Superior as Autocratic or Paternalistic	(C) % Preferring Consultative Manager (1967-69)	Power Distance Index = 135 − 25a + b − c
Branch office systems engineers				
Men (*n* = 9,917)	3.32	43	67	28
Women (*n* = 591)	3.26	43	64	33
Head office clerks				
Men (*n* = 7,665)	2.98	48	52	57
Women (*n* = 5,496)	2.96	48	41***	68

NOTE: The differences between men and women on question a, tested by the *t* test for differences of means, do not reach statistical significance. The differences between men and women on question c, tested by the Kolmogorov-Smirnov test, are not significant for branch office systems engineers but are significant at the .001 level for head office clerks.
*p = .05; **p = .01; ***p = .001.

(C9, $r = -.47$**); and "Even if an employee may feel he deserves a salary increase, he should *not* ask his manager for it" (C18, $r = -.51$***). The manager in a high-PDI environment is more of an initiator. Factor-analytic studies of leadership behavior, such as the classic Ohio State studies (Stogdill & Coons, 1957), typically show two dimensions: a "people" and a "task" dimension (in the Ohio State studies these were labeled "consideration" and "initiating structure"). In IBM, the question "manager helps ahead" was the most central "consideration" question (Hofstede, Kraut, & Simonetti, 1976, p. 25). A high-PDI environment stands for more initiating structure and less consideration.

Another item correlated with PDI stressed the relationship between the employee and the company: "There are few qualities in a man more admirable than dedication and loyalty to his company" (C12, $r = -.78$***). The dependence relationship in higher-PDI countries is not only with the boss, but also with the company.

Respondents in high-PDI countries agreed more than those in low-PDI countries with the statement "The average human being has an inherent dislike of work and will avoid it if he can" (C13, $r = -.75$***). This item was taken directly from McGregor's (1960, p. 33) "Theory X"; it shows that McGregor's famous Theory X/Theory Y distinction is rooted in culture and is not just a matter of the manager's personal choice.[29]

A seemingly paradoxical result is that agreement with the statement "Employees in industry should participate more in the decisions made by management" (B56) was positively correlated with PDI ($r = -.65$***). The images of the ideal manager and of the ideal control structure (participation/nonparticipation in the decisions made by management) are contradictory. This is a conflict between "values as the desirable" (employee participation as an ideology) and "values as the desired" (my own interaction with my boss in day-to-day matters). The ideological statement acts to some extent as compensation for what happens on the pragmatic level. In low-PDI countries, where there is not only a more delegating manager ideal but also more de facto delegation, people are less emphatic about a need for more employee participation. In high-PDI countries there can be a strong ideological push toward some model of formal participation (for example, through party or union representatives, workers' councils, or collective ownership) while at the same time there is little de facto participation of subordinates in daily issues.

Validating PDI Against Data From Other Sources

Straight Replications of the IBM Survey

Course participants at IMEDE. A total of 362 practicing managers, none of them from IBM, answered the PDI question about their "preferred manager." Percentages of those with a preference for the autocratic or persuasive/paternalistic manager were rank correlated between IMEDE and IBM, across 15 countries or country groups, with rho = .71***.[30] This is amazingly high if we also take into account that IMEDE managers answered the question in English and IBM employees in a multitude of local languages.[31]

Elite alumni from the Salzburg Seminar. Hoppe (1990, 1993) administered the Values Survey

Module 1982, which contained the three PDI questions, as part of a survey study of alumni from the Salzburg Seminar, a high-level international conference center in Salzburg, Austria. The Salzburg participants belonged to the elites of their respective societies. They worked in high-level positions in academia, government, business and industry, the arts and professions, the media, not-for-profit and international organizations, and multinational businesses. They included CEOs of large corporations, chancellors of universities, judges, professors, journalists, high-level civil servants, administrators of international organizations, and independent lawyers. Responses to Hoppe's Salzburg Seminar Alumni Study were collected from 1,590 former participants from 17 European countries plus Turkey and the United States who had attended one or more of the seminar's sessions between 1964 and 1983. They were surveyed between late 1983 and mid-1984; all, obviously, answered to the same English-language version of the questionnaire. For comparison of their scores with the IBM scores, see the statistical analysis at the end of this chapter (Exhibit 3.13). The Salzburg alumni scored lower on PDI than the IBM employees, in line with their higher education level (see Exhibit 3.2). The PDI scores of the 18 overlapping countries in the two studies were nevertheless significantly correlated, $r = .67**$. In view of the very different nature of the two survey populations, this similarity is striking. Differences in values between countries found among IBM employees were also present among their countries' elites. Hoppe's study, together with other replications of the IBM survey, has been used as a basis for the 1994 revision of the IBM Values Survey Module (VSM 94; see Appendix 4). PDI values computed from Hoppe's Salzburg study using the VSM 94 questions and formulas correlate even higher with the IBM scores, $r = .80***$.[32]

Commercial airline pilots. Helmreich and Merritt (1998) included items from the Values Survey Module 1982, among which were the three PDI questions, in a survey of more than 15,000 commercial airline pilots from 36 companies in 23 countries; the survey was conducted between 1993 and 1997. Translations of the questionnaire were used in seven countries; the others used the English version.[33] Company scores were the average of the mean scores for captains and for first/second officers. In countries with more than one company participating, country scores were the means of the scores for those companies. For comparison with the IBM scores, see the statistical analysis at the end of this chapter (Exhibit 3.13). In spite of their higher education level, which would lead to prediction of lower PDI values, the pilots scored somewhat higher on PDI than did the

IBM employees. This reflects the pilots' occupational culture: Giving and receiving clear orders is a normal part of their work. In an earlier study that used a different questionnaire, Merritt and Helmreich (1996) included both pilots and flight attendants; the flight attendants' answers reflected even higher power distances than those of the pilots. The PDI scores of the 21 overlapping countries in Exhibit 3.13 are strongly correlated between IBM and pilots, $r = .76***$, rho $= .81***$. Again, the two survey populations were very different; also, the surveys were conducted 25 years apart, so the similarity in results is even more remarkable. The sample sizes are much larger than for Hoppe's elites, but the results are affected by the corporate cultures of the companies, which differ for more reasons than nationality only, such as corporate histories and management idiosyncrasies.

Other replications. Shane and Venkataraman (1996, p. 761) included the original PDI questions in a survey of more than 6,000 employees of six organizations in 28 countries in 1991-92. They reported a correlation with the IBM scores of $r = .59***$. Given that their respondent samples were not particularly well matched across countries, this is remarkably strong. A review article by Søndergaard (1994) listed 19 smaller replications that allowed testing dimension score differences between countries; 15 of these confirmed the PDI differences found in IBM.

PDI Versus Studies of
General Values in Society

The IBM survey took place in a work context, and the values it reflects are therefore all more or less work related. People do not carry separate mental programs for work and nonwork situations, however. Dominant work values in a society have their roots in the family and at school, and they are also reflected in political systems and in dominant ideas, philosophies, and theories. A multitude of cross-national comparative studies of general, nonwork values and related phenomena show differences along the power distance continuum. Some refer explicitly to power distance differences whereas others illustrate them implicitly.

In this subsection I will describe results of studies of general values in society for which the results were significantly correlated with PDI, more than with any of the other IBM indexes or with GNP/capita. Studies referring specifically to the family, the school, the work situation, politics, or ideologies will be collected in the next part of this chapter.

An obvious association can be made between PDI and the famous F-scale (authoritarianism scale) developed in the United States by Adorno, Frenkel-Brunswik, Levinson, and Sanford (1950). Meade and Whittaker (1967) compared F-scale scores of students in Brazil, Hong Kong, India, Lebanon, Rhodesia, and the United States. Across the four countries for which comparison with IBM is possible, their F-scale scores were rank correlated with PDI with rho = .80 (which was not significant but encouraging; the correlations with the other IBM indexes were lower). However, the use of a ready-made U.S. scale in this way meant both an ethnocentric and a reverse ecological fallacy, as Kagitçibasi (1970) demonstrated. She administered the F-scale to male and female high school students in the United States (lower PDI) and Turkey (higher PDI). The various components of "authoritarianism" were much more strongly intercorrelated for Americans than for Turks: The relatively coherent "authoritarian personality" syndrome found in the United States was missing in Turkey, although Turks tended to score higher on most authoritarian values. Kagitçibasi concluded that in international comparisons, *norm* authoritarianism should be distinguished from *personal* authoritarianism. Norm authoritarianism applies to the culture level and cannot be explained in terms of personality dynamics. PDI measures norm authoritarianism.[34]

U.S. psychologist Leonard V. Gordon published a personality test named the Survey of Interpersonal Values (SIV); mean country data on the six scales of this test (Support, Conformity, Recognition, Independence, Benevolence, and Leadership) were available for female students in 11 countries from the IBM set and for male students in 17 (Gordon, 1976, pp. 4, 55). Correlations of Gordon's country scores with the IBM indexes and with 1970 GNP/capita are shown in Exhibit 3.14 in the statistical section of this chapter. For both men and women, PDI was the strongest correlating index for Independence, negatively: In high-PDI countries students did *not* stress wanting the right to do whatever one wanted to do, *not* being free to make one's own decisions, *not* being able to do things in one's own way (women, $r = -.90***$; men, $r = -.79***$). The value of Conformity (doing what is socially correct, following regulations closely, doing what is accepted and proper, being a conformist) was positively correlated with PDI (women, $r = .82**$; men, $r = .80***$), but for men the correlation with GNP/capita per se was marginally stronger than that with PDI ($r = -.81***$), and after we controlled for GNP/capita (through a multiple regression) no independent contribution of PDI to the differences in Conformity remained. For the countries with both female and male respondents, no systematic gender effects were found for the importance of either Conformity or Independence: Women and men shared the same values in this respect.

The 1981-82 European Values Study, initially across 9 and later 24 countries,[35] and the subsequent 1990-93 World Values Survey (WVS) across 43 societies, described in Chapter 1, contained many items significantly correlated with the IBM indexes. Most of these refer to the family context, and they will be listed under the corresponding heading. A summary of the WVS data was published by Inglehart, Basañez, and Moreno (1998).[36] One WVS question (question 247) asked respondents to choose between two statements, one arguing that personal freedom is more important than equality and the other arguing the opposite. The percentages in each country choosing "freedom" were significantly correlated with PDI, across all 26 overlapping countries ($r = -.49**$) but also across the 17 rich countries ($r = -.54*$).[37] So respondents in higher-PDI—that is, more unequal—countries more often chose "equality" and those in lower-PDI, more equal countries more often chose "freedom."[38]

In Chapter 1, I referred to Inglehart's (1997, pp. 81-98) macroanalysis of the WVS (47 key variables summarizing some 100 from the more than 350 questions). The results of this factor analysis for 27 countries overlapping with the IBM set are shown in Chapter 5 (Exhibit 5.18). Inglehart found two strong factors. His second factor, "secular-rational versus traditional authority," explaining 21% of the variance in his data, was significantly correlated with PDI ($r = -.56**$), in the sense that high-PDI countries would favor traditional authority and low-PDI countries would favor secular-rational authority.[39] Like PDI, Inglehart's second factor was correlated with national wealth, $r = .76***$.

Triandis, Kilty, Shanmugam, Tanaka, and Vassiliou (1972) compared the cognitive structures of male students in Greece, India, Japan, and the United States (I mentioned this study in Chapter 1). Among 20 concepts used in their research project, four are conceptually related to the issue of power distance: "freedom," "power," "respect," and "wealth."[40] The researchers asked their students to choose three "antecedents" and three "consequents" for each concept. In Exhibit 3.5, those antecedents and consequents are listed that were chosen with a frequency that rank correlated with the PDI with rho = 1.00 (the PDI ranking of the four countries is United States, Japan, Greece, India). Such a perfect rank agreement has less than a 5% probability of occurring by chance.

Exhibit 3.5 shows a convincing picture of two types of society—a welfare society on the low-PDI side (no negative antecedents or consequents scored at all) and a class society on the high-PDI side, where money leads to freedom and freedom to a disorderly society, where power is acquired

Exhibit 3.5 Antecedents and Consequents of Four Concepts as Measured Among Male Students by Triandis et al. (1972)

Low Power Distance Index		High Power Distance Index
	Antecedents of "Freedom"	
Respect of individual Equality		Tact Servitude Money
	Consequents of "Freedom"	
		Industrial production Disorderly society Wealth
	Antecedents of "Power"	
Leadership Knowledge		Wrestling
	Consequents of "Power"	
		Cruelty
	Antecedents of "Wealth"	
Happiness Knowledge Love		Inheritance Ancestral property High interest charges Stinginess Crime Deceit Theft
	Consequents of "Wealth"	
Satisfaction Happiness		Fear of thieves Arrogance Unhappiness
	Antecedents of "Respect"	
Love		Old age
	Consequents of "Respect"	
Friendship Recognition of superiority Liking		

NOTE: Frequency across four countries is perfectly rank correlated with the Power Distance Index.

through wrestling and leads to cruelty, where wealth is inherited and threatened and leads to arrogance, and where old age leads to respect. On the low-PDI side, all associations with "power" and "wealth" were favorable; on the high-PDI side, nearly all were unfavorable. To students on the high-PDI side (which in this case means especially India), wealth and power were conflict-ridden issues; to U.S. students they were not.

The relationship between PDI and respect for old age was seemingly contradicted in comparative international market research data published by Reader's Digest (1970). This interview study of representative samples of a total of more than 17,500 persons in 16 European countries dealt with consumption patterns, but it also covered attitudes toward younger and older generations. The statistical analysis in Exhibit 3.15 shows that across 15 countries. favorable attitudes toward older people (over age 45) were *negatively* correlated with both PDI and UAI ($r = -.56**$ for both, but the correlation with PDI was marginally stronger). So in high-PDI countries, respondents reported a less favorable impression of seniors. Attitudes toward younger people were strongly negatively correlated with UAI (see Chapter 4).

This paradoxical finding of a negative relationship between attitudes toward older people and PDI should be seen in the context of a larger de facto age difference between leaders and led in high-PDI countries. This was demonstrated in research by de Bettignies and Evans (1977), who published the average ages of top leaders in the business community in 11 European countries around 1970; as Exhibit 3.15 in the statistical section shows, these were strongly positively correlated ($r = .75**$) with PDI. In countries in which power distances are larger, old leaders are less prepared to give up their power. High PDI stands for "gerontocracy" (old people's rule), a strong relationship between age and power and more respect for old age. But the power aspect of older age evidently also fostered less favorable attitudes toward older people. This is an example of the *latent conflict* between powerful and powerless in higher-PDI countries (Exhibit 3.7).

Best and Williams (1996) have reported on a survey study about "anticipation of aging" among male and female students in 19 countries (about 50 of each gender per country). One survey item was "When you hear someone described as being 'old,' what age do you think of? At least _____ years"; the next was "When you hear someone described as being 'middle aged' " (and so on). Across 18 overlapping countries, the age at which a person was described as middle-aged (across countries a mean of 40 for men and 41 for women) correlated strongly negatively with PDI (rho = $-.73***$ for men and rho = $-.69**$ for women; no significant second-order correlations).[41] So in high-PDI countries, people were earlier considered to be middle-aged. As in these countries age is a source of power, being middle-aged is desirable, so the students chose to get there earlier. The age at which a person was described as old correlated positively with GNP/capita for men and negatively with long-term orientation for women (see Chapter 7).

Furnham (1993) collected answers on a scale measuring "just world beliefs" from 1,659 students in 12 different countries.[42] This scale was developed for internal use inside the United States (Rubin & Peplau, 1973); it measured attitudes toward the notion that the world is a just place. It contained 16 items, of which 9 were worded in the "just" and 7 in the "unjust" direction. Individual "just" and "unjust" scores within countries, obviously, were negatively correlated, but Furnham, to his surprise, found the country means for the 9 "just world" items and the country means for the 7 "unjust world" items to be *positively* correlated. Across 10 countries both were positively correlated with PDI. The "unjust" scores were also, and even more strongly, negatively correlated with GNP/capita (for 1985); the "just" were not.

Furnham's interpretation of this paradoxical reversal of the correlation between "just" and "unjust" from the individual to the country level is complex: He refers to a random versus a nonrandom world. My explanation for Furnham's results is a lot simpler: The country scores reflect national response bias tendencies. Authoritative-looking statements about the world in general, whatever their content, will meet more agreement in high-PDI countries, so that in these countries both the "just" and the "unjust" opinions receive more support. I reanalyzed Furnham's country means across all 12 countries, using my Jamaica data for the British West Indies and my East Africa data for Zimbabwe. This confirmed Furnham's findings, but I went a step further.[43] I recalculated the "unjust world" correlations *while controlling for country "just world" scores*. This eliminated the common response set in the "just" and "unjust" country means. Without the response set, "unjust" feelings were still significantly correlated with national poverty ($r = -.75**$ with 1990 GNP/capita), with collectivism ($r = -.60*$ with IDV), and with power distance ($r = .54*$ with PDI). However, GNP/capita, IDV, and PDI are not independent of each other. To get the full picture, I ran a stepwise multiple regression with "unjust world" as the dependent variable and "just world," 1990 GNP/capita, PDI, UAI, IDV, and MAS as potential independent variables. The following variables turned out to contribute *independently* to explaining the country differences in "unjust world" feelings:

1. GNP/capita 1990 (negative), $R^2 = .66$
2. Same plus MAS (positive), $R^2 = .84$
3. Both plus PDI (positive), $R^2 = .94$

R^2, the squared multiple correlation coefficient, is the share of the variance in the dependent variable that was explained, so very little of the variance in "unjust world" country means remained unexplained. The picture is quite clear now. Across the 12 countries that supplied Furnham's student samples, levels of agreement with the "*just* world" statements were dominated by a response set, a reflection of the respect for authoritative statements implicit in the country PDI score. Levels of agreement with the "*unjust* world" statements reflected much more than mere response set; they were stronger where (1) the country was poor, (2) its society was tough (expressed in the country MAS index, to which we

Exhibit 3.6   Summary of Values and Attitudes Differences Found Correlated with PDI

Low PDI	High PDI
National elites hold relatively unauthoritarian values.	National elites hold relatively authoritarian values.
Commercial airline pilots hold relatively unauthoritarian values.	Commercial airline pilots hold relatively authoritarian values.
Authoritarian attitudes in students a matter of individual personality.	Authoritarian attitudes in students a social norm.
Students put value on independence.	Students put value on conformity.
Freedom more important than equality.	Equality more important than freedom.
Authority based on secular-rational arguments.	Authority based on tradition.
Students have positive associations with "power" and "wealth."	Students have negative associations with "power" and "wealth."
Positive attitudes toward older people.	Negative attitudes toward older people.
Top leaders younger.	Top leaders older.
Middle age starts after 40.	Middle age starts before 40.
Students see world as a just place.	Students see world as an unjust place.
Less acquiescence in answering survey questions.	More acquiescence in answering survey questions.

will come back in Chapter 6), and (3) its society was unequal, expressed in the country PDI.

Williams, Satterwhite, and Saiz (1998) collected data from students in 20 countries about "psychological importance," defined in their questionnaire as importance "in describing what a person is really like" (pp. 112-113).[44] Across 16 countries they found significant correlations of PDI (and to a lesser extent IDV) with 9 out of 10 condensed measures of psychological importance.[45] In fact, 18 countries overlapped with the IBM set.[46] Recalculating, I found correlations with (1990) GNP/capita in some cases even stronger than with PDI. Students from poorer, high-PDI, low-IDV countries attached more importance to eight measures of psychological importance that were formulated in a favorable sense and less to the one that was formulated in an unfavorable sense. This is evidently a form of acquiescence: more response to the authority or demand characteristics of the questionnaire in poorer, higher-PDI countries.

Summary of General
Connotations of the Power Distance
Index Found in Survey Material

The values and attitudes found, at the national level, to be related to PDI are summarized in Ex-

hibit 3.6, which opposes "low-PDI countries" to "high-PDI countries." This is a dichotomy that serves to clarify the distinctions, but it should be kept in mind that (1) PDI is a continuum, so countries are not just polarized between "high" and "low" but may be anywhere in between; (2) statements in the exhibit are based on the situation in particular countries or on statistical trends across a number of countries, but not every statement applies with equal strength to all countries; and (3) individuals in countries show a wide range of variation around the country's societal norms (compare Exhibit 1.7).

With these provisos, we find in Exhibit 3.6 a picture of two types of society; the differences were found in answers by different categories of respondents: political and cultural elites, airline pilots, students, and representative samples of total adult populations in public opinion surveys. All results point to more power inequality in high- than in low-PDI countries, a situation maintained not only by the more but also by the less powerful. The roots of power differences in the high-PDI countries are traditional; in low-PDI countries, they are more pragmatic.

Inequality is rarely considered desirable on an ideological level; in high-PDI countries where it is, in practice, expected and desired by the less powerful, it remains problematic at the same time, and students in higher PDI countries show negative associations not only with "power" but also with "wealth." Exhibit 3.3 shows that higher education reduces authoritarian values on the low-PDI side, but not on the high-PDI side.

Together with PDI, attitudes about age vary. Middle age starts earlier in high-PDI societies, and attitudes toward older people are more negative, while at the same time these older people retain their power longer.

Not surprisingly, students in high-PDI countries are less likely to see the world as a just place than are those in low-PDI countries.

In the interpretation of the various surveys, the effect of acquiescence (yes-man-ship) had to be taken into account; a practical effect of PDI differences is that the tendency to answer yes to any survey question, regardless of its content, is markedly stronger in high-PDI countries than in low-PDI countries.

Origins and Implications of Country Power Distance Differences

The Power Distance Societal Norm

It is time now to take a step back from the data and try to describe the general societal norm that is behind the "low-PDI" and "high-PDI" syndromes. This is an exercise in induction, which means that I complete the picture with elements based on intuition rather than on empirical evidence, much as an archaeologist completes ancient pottery from which shards are missing. The societal norm is meant to be a value system shared by a majority in the middle classes in a society. It contains both values as the desirable and values as the desired and is only at some distance followed by reality. All the provisos of the previous section apply: Most countries are in between, not all statements apply equally strongly in all countries, and individuals in countries vary widely around the norm.

The PDI norm deals with the need for dependence versus interdependence in society. Inequality in a low-PDI society is seen as a necessary evil that should be minimized; in a high-PDI society, inequality is seen as the basis of societal order. Both low- and high-PDI countries have hierarchies, but on the low-PDI side this is an arrangement of convenience. On the high-PDI side the hierarchy is existential: Superiors are seen as superior persons.

Values about inequality are coupled with values about the exercise of power. It may in fact be true to some extent in all societies, not just in high-PDI countries, that "power is a basic fact of society that antedates good or evil and whose legitimacy is irrelevant." [47] Even in lower-PDI Netherlands, Mulder's (1977, p. 15) laboratory experiments showed that people react to illegitimate power in the same way they react to legitimate power. However, in some societies (high PDI) power needs less legitimation than in others (low PDI). The difference is more clearly visible on the next item in Exhibit 3.7, concerning whether power holders should obey the same rules as others. Does the president of the company punch a time-clock if the workers do so? Does he have a private toilet? Should the general legitimate himself to the sentry? In low-PDI countries, power is something of which power holders are almost ashamed and that they will try to underplay. I once heard a Swedish (low PDI) university official state that in order to exercise power he tried not to look powerful. Leaders may enhance their informal status by renouncing formal symbols. In (low PDI) Austria, Prime Minister Bruno Kreisky was known to sometimes take the streetcar to work. In 1974, I actually saw the Dutch (low PDI) prime minister, Joop Den Uyl, on vacation with his motor home at a camping site in Portugal. Such behavior of the powerful would be very unlikely in high-PDI Belgium or France: It is hard to imagine the prime minister of either country in a streetcar or a motor home.

To French and Raven (1959) we owe a well-known classification of the bases of social power into five types: reward power, coercive power, legitimate power (based on rules), referent power (based on personal charisma of the powerful and identification with him or her by the less powerful), and expert (specialist) power. I surmise that, other things being equal, more coercive and referent power will be used in high-PDI societies and more reward, legitimate, and expert power in low-PDI societies.

The statement that in high-PDI countries the underdog is the first to be blamed for anything wrong in the system whereas in low-PDI countries the system is blamed is inspired by a research review about Latin America and India conducted by Negandhi and Prasad (1971, p. 105). I have noticed this tendency in some European countries as well. On the other hand, the blame may revert to the powerful, and this is the "revolution" philosophy on the high-PDI side: Change the top person, and you change the system.

On the high-PDI side there is a latent conflict between the powerful and the powerless, a basic mistrust that may never explode but is always present. On the low-PDI side the ideal model is harmony between the powerful and powerless, which in practice may also be "latent," that is, it

Exhibit 3.7   The Power Distance Societal Norm

Low PDI	High PDI
All should be interdependent.	A few should be independent; most should be dependent.
Inequality in society should be minimized.	There should be an order of inequality in this world in which everyone has his/her rightful place; high and low are protected by this order.
Hierarchy means an inequality of roles, established for convenience.	Hierarchy means existential inequality.
Subordinates are people like me.	Superiors consider subordinates as being of a different kind.
Superiors are people like me.	Subordinates consider superiors as being of a different kind.
The use of power should be legitimate and is subject to the judgment between good and evil.	Power is a basic fact of society that antedates good or evil; its legitimacy is irrelevant.
All should have equal rights.	Power holders are entitled to privileges.
Powerful people should try to look less powerful than they are.	Powerful people should try to look as powerful as possible.
Stress on reward, legitimate and expert power.	Stress on coercive and referent power.
The system is to blame.	The underdog is to blame.
The way to change a social system is by redistributing power.	The way to change a social system is by dethroning those in power.
Latent harmony between the powerful and the powerless.	Latent conflict between the powerful and the powerless.
Older people neither respected nor feared.	Older people respected and feared.

does not exclude de facto conflict, but this tends to be pragmatic rather than fundamental.

Finally, the ambiguous relationship between PDI and attitudes toward older people described above can be understood as a combination of respect and fear in high-PDI societies, whereas neither respect nor fear is normal in low-PDI societies. As a one-line definition of Power Distance as a dimension of national culture, I propose: **"The extent to which the less powerful members of institutions and organizations within a country expect and accept that power is distributed unequally."**

Power Distance in the Family

Mental programming about (in)equality is acquired very early in life. Children model their behavior after the examples set by the elders in whose presence they are growing up.

Both the European and the World Values Surveys contained blocks of questions about "qualities which children can be encouraged to learn at home." In the 1990-93 round (questions 226-

236), across the 26 overlapping countries, the importance of "hard work" and "obedience" correlated primarily with PDI (rho = .69*** and rho = .65***, respectively); "independence" correlated negatively with PDI (rho = -.66***; WVS questions 227 ff.).[48] Children in high-PDI countries are socialized to hard work and obedience, whereas in low-PDI countries they are socialized more to independence.[49]

In the first, 1981-82, round only, a question asked about "various changes in our way of life that might take place in the near future . . . whether you think it would be a good thing . . . ?" (Harding & Phillips, 1986, question 308). One of these changes was "decrease in the importance of work in our lives." The proportions of respondents judging a decrease in the importance of work to be a good thing varied from 12% in Norway to 57% in France (Halman, 1991, p. 312); these percentages correlated positively with PDI ($r = .67**$). So in high-PDI countries the hard work that children should learn was at the same time felt as a burden, and respondents said they would welcome its reduction. However, they wanted society to do this for them; they would not decide *themselves* to work less hard and teach this to their children.

The first round also contained a block of questions about "sufficient reasons for divorce" (Harding & Phillips, 1986, question 255). Across the 12 overlapping, developed countries for which results were published in Halman (1991, p. 334), "can't have children" was one of the less frequently chosen reasons for divorce (chosen by between 11% [in France] and 2% of respondents [in Ireland]), but the percentages per country were still strongly positively correlated with PDI ($r = .79***$), confirming that even across these relatively affluent societies larger power distances were associated with a stronger need to have (authority over) children.

The same survey contained a block of questions about to what extent 22 controversial behaviors and petty offenses were considered justifiable (Harding & Phillips, 1986, question 315). Answers were scored on a 10-point scale (1 = *never justified* to 10 = *always justified*). Across the 12 overlapping countries for which results were published in Halman (1991, p. 302), high-PDI societies tended to be more lenient toward the following behaviors:

- Sex under the legal age of consent (from 4.8 in the Netherlands to 1.1 in Norway, correlation with PDI $r = .59*$)
- Lying in your own interest (from 3.5 in France to 1.9 in Norway, correlation with PDI $r = .59*$)
- Claiming state benefits to which you are not entitled (from 3.4 in France to 1.4 in Denmark and Norway, correlation with PDI $r = .68**$)
- Fighting with the police (from 2.7 in France to 1.4 in Ireland, correlation with PDI $r = .71**$)
- Someone accepting a bribe in the course of his or her duties (from 2.6 in France to 1.3 in Norway, correlation with PDI $r = .80***$)
- Buying something you know was stolen (from 2.3 in France to 1.2 in Norway, correlation with PDI $r = .69**$)
- Joyriding (from 1.7 in Spain to 1.1 in Denmark, correlation with PDI $r = .85***$)

Thus large power distances in these developed societies went together with a certain degree of informal leniency toward rules of civil morality.[50]

The pattern of childhood socialization revealed in the European and World Values Surveys has been confirmed by a number of other studies. The correlation of PDI with "hard work" was confirmed by Furnham et al. (1993), who in 1986-88 administered a scale designed to measure "Protestant work ethic" (PWE) to 1,688 students in 13 different countries.[51] The PWE stood for a conservative call for hard work. Across 12 countries, PWE scores correlated with PDI with $r = .80**$.[52]

The relationship of PDI with "obedience" was visible in the study conducted by Kohn (1969, p. 42) to which I referred earlier in this chapter for the relationship between conformity and working-class status. Kohn used interviews with parents of 10- to 11-year-old children in Turin, Italy, and in Washington, D.C. For both middle and working classes, fathers and mothers in Italy (PDI 50) put higher value on their children's obeying them than did parents in the United States (PDI 40).

In the large power distance situation, children are expected to be obedient toward their parents. Sometimes there is even an order of authority among the children themselves, with younger children being expected to yield to older children. Independent behavior on the part of a child is not encouraged. *Respect* for parents and other elders is seen as a basic virtue; children see others showing such respect and soon acquire it themselves. In a novel by the Indonesian author Pramoedya Ananta Toer (1982), a mother reminds her rebellious son: "Javanese bow down in submission to those older, more powerful; this is a way to achieve nobility of character. People must have the courage to surrender" (p. 114). There is often considerable warmth and care in the way parents and older children treat younger ones, especially when these children are very small. But they are looked after—they are not expected to experiment for themselves. Physical punishment is acceptable, although in a study on childhood memories of Colombian, Venezuelan, Cuban, and Anglo-American students in the United States, Escovar and Escovar (1985) found that the Anglos (lower PDI) reported more physical punishment by their fathers than did the Latinos; one wonders whether the difference is in the actual practices or in what was remembered and reported.

Respect for parents and older relatives lasts through adulthood: Parental authority continues to play a role in people's lives as long as their parents are alive. Parents and grandparents are treated with formal deference even after their children have actually taken control of their own lives. There is a pattern of dependence on seniors that pervades all human contacts, and the mental software that people carry contains a strong *need* for such dependence. Joshi and MacLean (1997) compared the ages at which mothers in Britain, India, and Japan expected children to be competent at each of 45 tasks. On average, the ages were highest in India (PDI 77); between Japan (PDI 54) and Britain (PDI 35), ages depended on the tasks, with the Japanese children being expected to be competent earlier at self-care and the British expected to be competent earlier in social contacts.

In the small power distance situation, children are more or less treated as equals as soon as they are able to act, and this is visible even as early as in the way babies are bathed.[53] The goal of parental education is to let children take control of their own affairs as soon as they can. Children's active experimentation is encouraged, and children are allowed to contradict their parents; they learn to say no very early. Children's relationships with others are not dependent on the others' status; formal respect and deference are seldom shown. Family relations in such societies often strike people from other societies as cold, distant, and lacking in intensity. When children grow up, they replace their child-parent relationships with relationships of equals, and grown-up persons are not supposed to ask their parents' permission or even advice on important decisions. The model is one of personal independence from the family. A need for independence is supposed to be a major component of the mental software of adults.

Kagitçibasi (1982) has reported results of a "value of children" study in nine countries.[54] The more than 20,000 respondents were married women under age 40 and, where possible, their husbands. Kagitçibasi looked at the extent to which old-age security was mentioned as a reason for having children, who were expected to support their aged parents. I calculated the rank correlations between Kagitçibasi's scores for "old-age security value of children" and the four IBM indexes, plus national wealth (GNP/capita). For women the highest correlation was with GNP/capita (rho = .88***) followed by PDI (rho = .73*); for men, with PDI (rho = .74*) followed by GNP/capita (rho = .67*). Among the women, poverty as such was felt as the primary burden children can help to alleviate; for the men, the need to have authority over children was an even stronger reason than poverty alone.

In 1983-84, a Dutch market research agency administered a values survey to more than 4,000 small entrepreneurs in 11 countries around the world.[55] Pompe, Bruyn, and Koek (1986) divided the entrepreneurs on the basis of their value orientations into "family oriented" and "job content oriented." Percentages of "family" minus "job content" across 9 countries correlated with PDI with $r = .90$***. In the high-PDI countries, entrepreneurs were working primarily for their family interest; in the low-PDI countries, they were working out of job interest. Pompe et al. also detected an individualism factor in the data, which will be explained in Chapter 5.

As we saw earlier, the social class and education levels of the parents, especially in low-PDI countries, also play an important role. Families develop their own family cultures, which may be at variance with the norms of their societies, and the personalities of individual parents and children may be strong enough that they can get away with nontypical behavior.

The impact of the family on our mental programming is extremely strong, and programs set in childhood are very difficult to change. Psychoanalysts are aware of this importance of family history, but not always of its cultural context. Psychoanalysts deal with the extent to which individual personalities adapt to societal norms, the extent to which they are "adjusted." Our study describes the norms themselves as they vary from one society to another. The fact that norms change means that providing psychoanalytic help to a person from another type of society or even from a different sector of the same society is a risky affair. It demands that the helper be aware of his or her own cultural biases versus the culture of the client.

Power Distance, Schools,
and Educational Systems

In most societies today, children go to school for at least some years.[56] In the more affluent societies, the school period may cover more than 20 years of a young person's life. In school, children further develop their mental programming. Teachers and classmates inculcate additional values honored in the culture. It is an unanswered question to what extent an education system can contribute to changing a society. Can a school create values that are not already there, or can it only unwittingly reinforce what already exists in a given society? Anyway, in a comparison of schools across societies the same patterns of differences emerge that have been found within families. The role pair parent-child is replaced by the role pair teacher-student, but basic values and behaviors are carried forward from one sphere into the other. And, of course, most schoolchildren continue to spend most of their time within their families.

In the large power distance situation, the parent-child inequality is perpetuated by a teacher-student inequality that caters to the need for dependence well established in the student's mind. Teachers are treated with respect (and older teachers even more so than younger ones); students may have to stand up when a teacher enters the room. The educational process is teacher centered; teachers outline the intellectual paths to be followed. There is sometimes a need for rote learning. In the classroom there is supposed to be a strict order, with the teacher initiating all communication. Students in class speak up only when invited to; teachers are never publicly contradicted or criticized and are treated with deference even outside school. When a child misbehaves, teachers involve the child's parents and expect them to help in disciplining the child. The educational process is highly personalized; especially in more advanced subjects at universities, what is transferred is seen not as impersonal "truth," but as the personal wisdom of the teacher. The teacher is a *guru,* a term derived from the Sanskrit word meaning "weighty" or "honorable," which in India and Indonesia is, in fact, what a teacher is called. In such a system the quality of an individual's learning is virtually exclusively dependent on the excellence of his or her teachers.

In the small power distance situation, teachers are supposed to treat their students as basic equals and expect to be treated as equals by the students. Younger teachers are more equal, and therefore usually more liked, than older ones. The educational process is student centered, with a premium on student initiative; students are expected to find their own intellectual paths. Students make uninvited interventions in class and are supposed to ask questions when they do not understand something. They argue with teachers, express disagreement and criticisms in front of teachers, and show no particular respect to teachers outside school. When a child misbehaves, the parents often side with the child against the teacher. The educational process is rather impersonal; it involves the transfer from teacher to student of "truths" or "facts" that exist independent of the particular teacher. Effective learning in such a system depends very much on whether the supposed two-way communication between students and teacher is, indeed, established. The entire system is based on the students' well-developed need for independence; the quality of learning is to a considerable extent determined by the excellence of the *students.*

Corporal punishment at school, at least for children of prepuberty age, is basically more acceptable in high-PDI cultures than in low-PDI cultures. It accentuates and symbolizes the inequality between teacher and student and can be seen as good for the development of the child's character. In a low-PDI society, corporal punishment will readily be classified as child abuse. There are exceptions, however. Norms of masculinity (versus femininity, see Chapter 6) may also play a role; in Great Britain (low PDI but masculine), a tradition of corporal punishment at school has survived.

An important conditioning factor is the ability of the students: Less-gifted or handicapped children in low-PDI societies will not develop the culturally expected sense of independence and will be handled more in the high-PDI way. Able children from working-class families in low-PDI societies are at a disadvantage in educational institutions, such as universities, that assume a low-PDI

norm: As shown in Exhibit 3.3, working-class families in lower-PDI countries tend to have a higher-PDI subculture.

Lower-PDI countries generally have more literate, better-educated populations. These countries tend to be wealthier and thus have more money for education. In the comparison of occupations in IBM we saw a strong negative relationship between average years of education and PDI (Exhibits 2.5 and 3.2).[57] Lower-PDI societies use technology more but maintain a more critical attitude toward it. One question in the World Values Survey asked whether "more emphasis on the development of technology" would be a good or a bad thing (question 266). Across 26 overlapping countries, percentages responding "a good thing" were correlated with PDI with rho = .78***, showing that the public in high-PDI countries held greater expectations.

Spencer-Oatey (1997) reported on a comparative survey study of students and their tutors in Great Britain (low PDI) and China (high PDI) about their mutual relationships. Chinese respondents (students and tutors) described the relationship as both closer and more unequal than did the British respondents. Several of the Chinese respondents compared the teacher-student relationship to a father-son relationship.

One measure of the mastery of technology in a country is the number of Nobel Prize winners in the physical sciences the country has produced. Moulin (1961) once composed a "Nobel Index" that divided the number of Nobel Prize winners in physics, chemistry, medicine, and physiology between 1901 and 1960 by the average numbers of inhabitants of their countries in millions. Across 14 countries, this Nobel Index was significantly negatively correlated with PDI (rho = −.50*).[58] Peyrefitte (1976, p. 194), in a critique of French society, has cited Moulin's study to illustrate "the French disease": High-PDI France appears only ninth on the Nobel Index list.[59]

In spite of this evidence of a negative correlation of PDI with peak scientific performance, the crucial aspect of a country's educational system that is logically linked with the power distance norm is not the relative number of top-educated scholars. They could just form an isolated elite. The crucial aspect is the educational level of the rank and file, which contributes to the middle strata in society. Mulder (1976, p. 92) has argued that power distance reduction is learned at intermediary levels in between the powerful and the powerless. Gaspari and Millendorfer (1978, p. 198) used the ratio between the number of secondary school students and the number of university students as a measure of the development of middle strata. Northern and Western European countries over time showed a development toward higher ratios (more secondary school students), whereas Eastern European countries (but also Italy) had permanent low ratios (a relative predominance of higher education—that is, the maintenance of an elite).[60]

Power Distance in Work and Organization

People familiar with organizations in different countries are often struck by the variety of organizational solutions to the same task problem. That is, organizational structures and management processes, other factors being equal, vary among countries.

The relationship between national cultures and organizational structures is covered more extensively in Chapter 8. In Chapter 2, I have already referred to the work of the "Aston group," a team of researchers originally located at the University of Aston in Birmingham, England, who developed standardized measuring methods for organizational structures (Pugh, 1976; Pugh & Hickson, 1976; Pugh & Hinings, 1976). Using data from a large number of work organizations, first in Great Britain and later in other countries as well, the Aston group found that the two main dimensions along which structures varied were "concentration of authority" (which includes centralization) and "structuring of activities" (including standardization, specialization, and formalization). These two dimensions seemed to apply across all kinds of organizations in all kinds of environments. PDI is clearly conceptually related to "concentration of authority."[61] The Aston dimension of "structuring of activities" will be discussed in Chapter 4.

The Aston researchers are sometimes cited as having a "culture-free thesis" (Child & Kieser, 1979). In fact, they did not claim that culture did not affect structure, only that relationships between context and structure should be stable across societies. "Simply stated, if Indian organizations were found to be less formalized than American ones, bigger Indian units would still be more formalized than smaller Indian units" (Hickson, Hinings, McMillan, & Schwitter, 1974, p. 59). So the issue was whether the effects of culture and other factors are additive or interactive, whether culture affects the *degree* to which structural characteristics are present or (also) the *relationship* between structural characteristics and organizational context factors; the Aston researchers accepted the first but not the second.

Evidence for the relationship between "concentration of authority" and power distance is found in a study by Brossard and Maurice (1974), who compared carefully matched industrial manufacturing plants in France (PDI 68) and Germany (PDI 35). They showed marked differences be-

tween the two countries on variables related to concentration of authority, with greater concentration in France. French plants tended to have five hierarchical levels against German plants' three. French plants had an average of 26% of personnel in management and specialist roles; German plants, 16%. A similar difference in number of hierarchical levels was reported by Negandhi and Prasad (1971, p. 60) between Indian-owned and American-owned plants in India, which is in line with the PDI difference between India and the United States.

Wong and Birnbaum-More (1994) collected Aston-type data from 39 multinational banks from 14 different mother countries operating in Hong Kong in the period 1981-84. They concluded that "the acceptance of unequal power distances in the bank's home society" (home-country PDI) explained the degree of centralization of authority in the Hong Kong subsidiaries (p. 115).[62]

Danish researcher Schramm-Nielsen (1989) studied work relations in seven companies in France (PDI 68) led by a Danish general manager and in five companies in Denmark (PDI 18) led by a French general manager. Through in-depth interviews, she concluded that the French organizations were structured as steep hierarchical pyramids (one Dane described them as pyramids crowned by a mast on top of which sits the company president; a Frenchman used the image of a rake pulled by the president with all the others at its teeth). The Danish organizations presented flatter structures with flexible borderlines. The French talked about delegation of power and the Danes about delegation of responsibility—and there was much more delegation in Denmark. French bosses were highly respected and always right. In Denmark, respect relations were independent of rank, and subordinates were sometimes right. A Danish boss could do the work of a subordinate without loss of prestige; a French boss could not. There was, however, no evidence of a difference in productivity between the two countries' systems. In another comparison of French and Danish organizations, Søndergaard (1988) studied the relationships between head offices and branch units in banks. French respondents indicated that the boss had to be consulted because he was the boss; Danish respondents indicated that the boss had to be consulted only when he knew the correct answer to their problem. These findings illustrate that hierarchy in low-PDI countries is an inequality of roles established for convenience, and roles may be changed, so that someone who today is my subordinate may tomorrow be my boss; they also reflect the existential inequality between higher-ups and lower-downs in high-PDI countries.

While teaching at IMEDE (see Chapter 2), I asked 315 course participants (practicing managers) to score Gordon's (1967, 1975, 1976) Surveys of Personal Values and Interpersonal Values (SPV and SIV). The two tests together contained 12 value scales, which I clustered into three cross-national dimensions via an ecological factor analysis across 14 countries. Although the samples per country were small, I found a highly significant correlation ($r = .80$***) between PDI and an ecological dimension, "decisiveness versus practical-mindedness."[63] This meant that IMEDE participants from high-PDI countries, compared with those from low-PDI countries, tended to score themselves as more decisive (having strong and clear convictions, making decisions quickly and sticking to them) and as more benevolent (doing things for other people, sharing with others, helping the unfortunate, being generous). The self-image of the IMEDE manager from a high-PDI country was that of a benevolent decision maker. IMEDE participants from low-PDI countries scored themselves as more practical-minded (always getting one's money's worth or doing things that will pay off), out for support (valuing being treated with understanding or receiving encouragement from other people), and orderly (following a systematic approach or doing things according to a schedule). The typical self-image was that of a practical, orderly person who likes to be treated with understanding. It is by no means sure that others would also see the individual like this; this self-image actually indicates how the person would *like* to be seen.[64] The answers to the "perceived manager" question (A55) on which the Power Distance Index is partly based show that subordinates in high-PDI countries saw their managers primarily as type 2, well-meaning autocrats; subordinates in low-PDI countries saw their managers as type 3, resourceful democrats.

These managers' self-description profiles were not the same as those found in Gordon's SIV student data (see above and Exhibit 3.14). Students from high- versus low-PDI countries differed significantly on conformity and independence, whereas managers did not. Managers attending courses at IMEDE were (1) preselected on initiative and (2) imbued with espoused values about independence and nonconformity, so their cultural variance in this respect was probably reduced.

Pavett and Morris (1995) surveyed all 180 managers in five plants of a U.S. multinational corporation that produced disposable medical products, in Great Britain, Italy, Mexico, Spain, and the United States. They used Likert's (1976) classic Profile of Organizational Characteristics, which asks for perceptions of the management style along Likert's four-"systems" continuum (0-5 = exploitative authoritative, 5-10 = benevolent authoritative, 10-15 = consultative, and 15-20 = participative). The mean ratings by country for the "total management system" Pavett and Morris reported (p. 1180) varied from 7.9 in Mexico to 14.1 in Great Britain and correlated with the country's PDI with rho = -1.00**. Thus the larger the power distance, the less participative the management system. There was no significant correlation between management style and productivity, however.

Smith et al. (1994) reported on a survey study of *event management* among about 100 middle managers in each of 14 countries around the world.[65] An organizational event was defined as any occurrence impinging upon the awareness of an organization member. Event management is the way in which a manager deals with such regular occurrences. Eight hypothetical organizational events were presented to the respondents, for example, "Appointing a new subordinate in your department."[66] For each, the respondents had to rate on 5-point scales the importance of eight sources of guidance: (1) formal rules and procedures, (2) unwritten rules, (3) specialists, (4) subordinates, (5) others at my level, (6) my superior, (7) my own experience and training, and (8) beliefs that are widespread in my country. Across their 14 countries, Smith et al. correlated the mean scored importance for the eight events with my four IBM indexes. The strongest correlations were with PDI, $r = -.78$*** with "my own experience and training," $r = .70$** with "formal rules" and $r = -.55$* with "subordinates." So, using a very different research approach, these authors showed that in high-PDI countries middle managers relied less on their own experience and on subordinates and more on formal rules when solving such everyday problems.[67]

The answers to the "preferred manager" question (A54), which also contributed to the Power Distance Index, showed that subordinates in low-PDI countries preferred a type 3, consultative manager; they expected to be consulted before a decision was made that affected their work. Subordinates in high-PDI countries were polarized between types 2 and 4, with a majority preferring the paternalist type 2; they expected and accepted to be told. A sociologist from higher-PDI Italy teaching business students in lower-PDI Netherlands described what he found there as "centrifugal diffusion of decision making" according to his standards (Inzerilli, 1989, p. 27). Several other studies have supplied additional insights into these differences in appreciation.

Williams, Whyte, and Green (1966) surveyed workers in two large electrical utility companies, one in Peru (high PDI) and one in the United States (lower PDI). Among both white- and blue-collar employees, the correlations between perceived closeness of supervision and general satisfaction with the boss were significantly *positive* in Peru and *negative* in the United States.

Cascio (1974) published comparative data from the use of a role-playing exercise called "Supervise" with managers from different countries attending courses.[68] They had to play the role of subordinates with three different superiors, of whom one acted in a directive, one in a persuasive, and one in a participative way. The proportions of subordinates who afterward declared themselves to have been most satisfied with the participative superior varied from 29% in India to 65% in "Western Europe." [69] As India scored higher on PDI than any Western European country, this suggests that satisfaction with a participative superior decreased with increasing power distance.

Birnbaum and Wong (1985) collected satisfaction data among Chinese managerial employees in 20 banks in Hong Kong, as well as data on the structure of the organizations in which they worked (using "Aston" measures; see above). In this high-PDI culture they found a significant positive correlation between centralization of decision making in the bank and the managers' job satisfaction.

Redding and Richardson (1986) compared the relationship between management style and productivity in manufacturing firms in the Asian city-states of Hong Kong and Singapore. They found that in Singapore participation according to Likert's systems correlated significantly with productivity ($r = .71^*$ across seven firms), but in Hong Kong, where productivity was higher overall, participation was unrelated to it ($r = .04$ across seven firms). Redding and Richardson explain this by noting that in Singapore at that time 55% of the manufacturing workforce worked for foreign companies, whereas in Hong Kong the corresponding figure was just 9%; management in Hong Kong, they argue, was much more Asian in style, and in this case participation was not an asset for productivity.

Welsh, Luthans, and Sommer (1993) reported on experiments with the introduction of U.S. management techniques in a large Russian textile factory. Russia was not part of the IBM survey, but a study among Russian engineers in the late 1980s suggested Russian culture to be quite high in power distance.[70] In the first experiment, material rewards in the form of coveted consumer goods were given for good performance. In the second, supervisors were trained to give explicit verbal praise in the case of desired behaviors and corrections for undesired behaviors. In the third, workers were asked to participate in suggestions for improving their work situation without their supervisors present. The first and second approaches significantly improved performance, whereas the third reduced it.

In the early days of cross-cultural management studies, Harbison and Burgess (1954) compared U.S. with "European" industrial management, but their European sample consisted of France, Belgium, and Italy—three countries from the high-PDI group. Their conclusions were predictable:

> Workers in European plants seldom talk back to their bosses. Upward communication is neither expected nor encouraged. . . . In these countries, the paternalistic employer appears to develop in the working forces a feeling of gratitude and dependence mingled with resentment. Socially irresponsible management creates active opposition and outright hatred. (pp. 19-20)

Harbison and Burgess gave an insightful description of the large power distance syndrome, but their extrapolation to "Europe" was not justified. In a later study in which Harbison and Myers (1959) collected qualitative evidence on management processes in 12 countries, European countries were no longer placed in one category. In fact, these researchers introduced a dimension from paternalism to pluralism that closely resembles my power distance dimension: They put Japan, Italy, and France on the paternalist side and Sweden, England, and the United States on the pluralist side (p. 65). Pluralist relations tend to be pragmatic; paternalist relations are more emotional, with the potential for both very positive and very negative feelings on the side of the subordinate:

> The often strongly emotional character of hierarchical relationships in France is intriguing. There is an extreme diversity of feelings towards superiors: They may be either adored or despised with equal intensity. This situation is not at all universal: We found it neither in the Netherlands nor in the USA. (d'Iribarne, 1989, p. 77)

In the IBM study, France scored 68 on PDI, the United States scored 40, and the Netherlands scored 38.[71]

Schmidt and Yeh (1992) compared self-descriptions of the ways leaders claimed to influence subordinates from five countries: Australia, Great Britain, Japan, Taiwan, and United States. Respondents were mixed groups of managers (from about 100 in Great Britain to more than 2,000 in Taiwan) who scored how often they used each of 33 "influence tactics." Answers from the five countries were factor analyzed separately, and each factor found was given a name. The two strongest factors for each of the five countries were as follows:

- Great Britain (PDI 35)
  1. Bargaining
  2. Invoke higher authority

- Australia (PDI 36)
  1. Friendly reasoning
  2. Bargaining

- United States (PDI 40)
  1. Bargaining
  2. Reasoning

- Japan (PDI 54)
  1. Assertive reasoning
  2. Invoke higher authority

- Taiwan (PDI 58)
  1. Sanctions
  2. Assertive reasoning

With increasing PDI, the amount of inequality in the influence tactics increased.

Schmidt and Yeh's (1992) findings have implications for the use of management by objectives (MBO), one of the most popular U.S. management techniques—a system of periodic meetings between superior and subordinate in which the latter commits him- or herself to the achievement of specific objectives; in the next meeting the subordinate's achievement is assessed and new objectives for the coming period are agreed upon. This can only work, however, if there is room for bargaining between boss and subordinate. In high-PDI countries where such bargaining does not fit, MBO is not a feasible technique.

Being a victim of power abuse by one's boss in a high-PDI country is just seen as bad luck; there is no assumption that subordinates should have options for redress in such a situation. If it gets too bad, people may join forces to initiate a violent revolt. Bond, Wan, Leung, and Giacalone (1985) compared responses to verbal insult by a "boss" in a simulated business meeting with male psychology undergraduates in Hong Kong (high PDI) and the United States (lower PDI) and found the Hong Kong students significantly less critical of the insulter, as long as he had a higher status. Organizations in low-PDI cultures are supposed to have institutionalized grievance channels, structured ways of dealing with employee complaints about alleged abuses of power.

Shane, Venkataraman, and Macmillan (1995, p. 945) reported on survey results collected from more than 1,200 employees of four multinationals in 30 countries about their roles in championing innovations at work. Their questionnaire contained 24 questions, which, in an ecological factor analysis across the 30 countries, clustered into three factors. One factor combined three questions stressing the need for support from the hierarchy. In a regression analysis, factor scores on this factor were significantly related to PDI and not to any demographic characteristics of respondents.[72] So, in countries with a larger power dis-

tance, innovators felt a greater need to get approval from the hierarchy. The two other factors were related to uncertainty avoidance and individualism, respectively; these will be discussed in Chapters 4 and 5.

Dutch advertising expert Marieke de Mooij (1998a, 1998b, 2001) found validations of all four IBM dimensions in data from consumer surveys across European countries by market research agencies. Data were from the Reader's Digest Eurodata 1991, the European Media and Marketing Survey 1997, and the Consumer Europe Euromonitor 1997, across 16 countries.[73] Correlations with PDI were mostly in the areas of work and media relations, and less in consumption patterns. One block of questions in the European Media and Marketing Survey 1997 asked respondents, who were all in professional and managerial jobs, whether at their workplace they had "responsibility, some involvement, or no involvement" in purchasing decisions on 26 categories of products or services. Across 16 countries (those listed in Exhibit 3.15, plus Greece), significant correlations with PDI existed for 24 out of the 26 categories, all in the sense that respondents in low-PDI countries reported more involvement (answers "responsibility" or "some involvement") than did those in high-PDI countries; the strongest correlations with PDI were found for the purchasing of advertising services ($r = -.71***$); organizing conferences, exhibitions, and trade fairs ($r = -.69***$); and purchasing construction equipment ($r = -.66**$).

Privileges ("private laws") for superiors are normal in high-PDI cultures. Visible signs of status in these countries contribute to the authority of bosses; it is quite possible that a subordinate feels proud if he can tell a neighbor that *his* boss drives a bigger car than does the neighbor's boss. In low-PDI cultures, it is basically undesirable for higher-ups to enjoy privileges; all employees should use the same parking lots, rest rooms, and cafeteria. Status symbols are suspect and subordinates will most likely comment negatively to their neighbors if their boss spends company money on an excessively expensive car.

Power distances also explain inequalities in earnings between hierarchical levels in organizations. In the French and German plants studied by Brossard and Maurice (1974), wage differentials (earnings of the upper 1% divided by earnings of the lowest 10%) varied between 3.7 and 5.5 in France, and between 2.0 and 2.3 in Germany; trend data in France over an 18-year period showed no narrowing of income gaps (Centre d'Etude des Revenus et des Coûts, 1976). A more recent study of major companies in 12 countries (Den Tex, 1992) confirmed that wage ratios between chief executives and workers were significantly positively correlated with country PDI (rho = .72**; see Exhibit 3.16 in the statistical section).

In 1980, the journal *International Management* published the results of a survey among its readers, whom the journal optimistically described as "executives" (Arbose, 1980). Data were collected from 930 respondents in 10 European countries.[74] Country mean scores for the following questions were significantly correlated with PDI:

- Do you feel that you are underpaid? (from 39.8% in Spain to 7.3% in Denmark, correlation with PDI rho = .81**)
- What gives you the most satisfaction: your home life, your career, or outside interests? (choosing "career": from 42.5% in Germany to 21.7% in Italy, correlation with PDI rho = −.67*)
- Do you find your work less satisfying than you did at the start of your career? (from 23.3% in France to 10.0% in Germany, correlation with PDI rho = .63*)
- Would you resign if your boss insisted that you commit a business act that you felt was unethical? (This is a loaded question that is very unlikely to get an honest answer, but the proportions of those answering that they would *not* resign varied from 16.3% in France to 6.3% in Denmark; correlation with PDI rho = .67*)

The correlations found suggest that whatever their actual job positions, readers of *International Management* in high-PDI countries felt less in control of their careers than did those in low-PDI countries. An "executive" who felt underpaid could quit for a better-paid job elsewhere, as could one who felt forced to commit unethical acts, but this was more likely to happen in low-PDI than in high-PDI countries. Some other questions in this survey produced answers correlated (primarily) with the masculinity dimension, and we will therefore come back to it in Chapter 6.

Peterson et al. (1995) have reported on findings concerning "role conflict," "role ambiguity," and "role overload" among managers in 21 countries.[75] Measures for role ambiguity and role overload were correlated significantly with PDI (multiple correlation coefficient $R = .75***$); measures for role conflict were not, and correlations with the other IBM indexes were lower or nonsignificant. The questions used were as follows. *Role ambiguity:* "I do not have clear planned goals and objectives for my job"; "I do not know exactly what is expected of me"; "I do not know what my responsibilities are"; "I do not feel certain about how much responsibility I have"; "My responsibilities are not clearly defined." *Role overload:* "There is a need to reduce some parts of my role"; "I feel overburdened in

my role"; "I have been given too much responsibility"; "My workload is too heavy"; "The amount of work I have to do interferes with the quality I want to maintain." Once more, and this time in a truly worldwide study, a negative relationship was shown between PDI and respondents' perceived control over their work situation.[76]

Harzing (1997), in a Ph.D. study of control mechanisms in multinational companies, sent mail survey questionnaires to chief executive officers and human resource managers at the head offices of 122 multinational companies and to the managing directors of some 1,650 subsidiaries of these multinationals in 22 countries. She notes that her response rates varied considerably across countries: For an overall response rate of 20%, rates varied from 7% for subsidiaries in Hong Kong to 42% in Denmark. She found that subsidiaries in high-PDI countries and respondents with high-PDI nationalities had significantly lower response rates than did those from low-PDI countries. I calculated correlations between Harzing's response rates and PDI, and found across 22 countries a rho = −.61*** for subsidiary and rho = −.67*** for respondent nationality, both across 22 countries. Adding the country's wealth (1990 GNP/capita) and the other IBM indexes did not significantly increase the correlations. I interpret this result as an unobtrusive measure showing greater willingness in low-PDI countries to provide information to someone who is not a superior.

High-PDI countries also tend to have a strong preference for "white-collar" (office) work over "blue-collar" (manual) work. Vlassenko (1977) has shown that the high income inequality scores she found for France and Italy were mainly due to the salary gap between office and manual workers. Whyte (1969) has reported from Latin America "a sharp line of social distinction between white collar and blue collar jobs" (p. 35). This culture-related distinction is bound to affect the division of labor in organizations.

Exhibit 3.8 summarizes the key differences between low- and high-PDI societies discussed so far: in the family, the school, and the work organization. The role patterns of parent-child and teacher-student are continued in the role pattern of boss-subordinate.

Power Distance, Worker Participation, and "Industrial Democracy"

Above, in the comparison of country PDI scores and other IBM questions, we found that in countries higher in PDI, more employees agreed that "employees should participate more in the decisions taken by management" (B56). I inter-

Exhibit 3.8   Key Differences Between Low- and High-PDI Societies I: Family, School, and Work Organization

Low PDI	High PDI
In the Family	
Parents treat children as equals.	Parents teach children obedience.
Children should enjoy leisure.	Children should work hard even if this is a burden.
Infertility no reason for divorce.	Infertility may be reason for divorce.
Children should respect rules of civil morality.	Informal lenience toward rule of civil morality.
Children treat parents and older relatives as equals.	Respect for parents and older relatives is a basic virtue and lasts throughout life.
Children expected to be competent at a young age, especially socially.	Children not seen as competent until at a later age.
Children play no role in old-age security of parents.	Children a source of old-age security, especially to fathers.
Small enterprises set up for job reasons.	Small enterprises for family interest.
At School	
Teachers treat students as equals.	Students dependent on teachers.
Students treat teachers as equals.	Students treat teachers with respect, even outside class.
Student-centered education.	Teacher-centered education.
Students initiate some communication in class.	Teachers initiate all communication in class.
Teachers are experts who transfer impersonal truths.	Teachers are gurus who transfer personal wisdom.
Parents may side with students against teachers.	Parents supposed to side with teachers to keep students in order.
Quality of learning depends on two-way communication and excellence of students.	Quality of learning depends on excellence of teachers.
Lower educational levels maintain more authoritarian relations.	Authoritarian values independent of education levels.
Educational system focuses on middle levels.	Educational system focuses on top level.
More Nobel Prizes in sciences per capita.	Fewer Nobel Prizes in sciences per capita.
More modest expectations on benefits of technology.	High expectations on benefits of technology.
In the Work Organization	
Decentralized decision structures; less concentration of authority.	Centralized decision structures; more concentration of authority.
Flat organization pyramids.	Tall organization pyramids.
Small proportion of supervisory personnel.	Large proportion of supervisory personnel.
Hierarchy in organizations means an inequality of roles, established for convenience.	Hierarchy in organizations reflects the existential inequality between higher-ups and lower-downs.
The ideal boss is a resourceful democrat; sees self as practical, orderly, and relying on support.	The ideal boss is a well-meaning autocrat or good father; sees self as benevolent decision maker.
Managers rely on personal experience and on subordinates.	Managers rely on formal rules.
Subordinates expect to be consulted.	Subordinates expect to be told.
Consultative leadership leads to satisfaction, performance, and productivity.	Authoritative leadership and close supervision lead to satisfaction, performance, and productivity.

(Continued)

Exhibit 3.8   Continued

Low PDI	High PDI
Subordinate-superior relations pragmatic.	Subordinate-superior relations polarized, often emotional.
Institutionalized grievance channels in case of power abuse by superior.	No defense against power abuse by superior.
Subordinates influenced by bargaining and reasoning; MBO is feasible.	Subordinates influenced by formal authority and sanctions; MBO cannot work.
Innovations need good champions.	Innovations need good support from hierarchy.
Managers involved in relevant purchasing decisions.	Managers not involved in relevant purchasing decisions.
Privileges and status symbols for managers are frowned upon.	Privileges and status symbols for managers are expected and popular.
Narrow salary range between top and bottom of organization.	Wide salary range between top and bottom of organization.
Managers feel adequately paid.	Managers feel underpaid.
Managers (increasingly) satisfied with career.	Managers dissatisfied with career.
Possibilities to escape from role ambiguity and overload.	Frequent role ambiguity and overload.
Openness with information, also to nonsuperiors.	Information constrained by hierarchy.
Manual work same status as clerical work.	White-collar jobs valued more than blue-collar jobs.

preted this as a conflict between "values as the desirable" (employee participation as an ideology) and "values as the desired" (my own interaction with my boss in day-to-day matters). In high-PDI countries there can be a strong ideological push toward formal participation (for example, through party or union representatives, workers' councils, or collective ownership) but little de facto participation of subordinates in daily issues.

Haire, Ghiselli, and Porter (1966) found a similar paradox in the first large-scale survey study of "managerial thinking" across countries. Their original set of 14 countries was extended to 22 through replications by others.[77] The survey included a series of eight questions about "management attitudes and assumptions" that were merged two by two into subscales.[78] Across 19 overlapping countries a subscale labeled "capacity for leadership and initiative" was significantly *positively* correlated with PDI ($r = .54**$).[79] It combined the following items:

a. (Disagreement with) "The average human being prefers to be directed, wishes to avoid responsibility, and has relatively little ambition."
b. (Agreement with) "Leadership skills can be acquired by most people regardless of their particular inborn traits and abilities."

Thus in high-PDI countries respondents were optimistic about people in general's capacity for leadership and initiative.[80] But such ideological statements, "values as the desirable," should again be distinguished from pragmatic statements about actual subordinates and superiors, "values as the desired." [81]

In a study across 10 Swedish companies, Rubenowitz, Norrgren, and Tannenbaum (1983) compared three modes of employee participation: (1) personal authority to make decisions, (2) own work group's authority to make collective decisions, and (3) one's elected representatives' authority to decide. Employee commitment to and satisfaction with the decisions was highest in case 1, lower in case 2, and virtually absent in case 3. Yet formal employee participation schemes, established by laws and rules, can hardly do anything other than operate through representatives.

Tannenbaum, Kavcic, Rosner, Vianello, and Wieser (1974), in a classic study on "hierarchy in organizations," highlighted the differences between formal employee participation structures and informal consultation. They surveyed people in five small manufacturing plants (30-130 employees) in each of four countries (Austria, Italy, the United States, and former Yugoslavia), 10 small plants in Israeli kibbutzim, and five medium-sized plants (200-1,500 employees) in the first four countries, all in matched industries. The study produced a large number of indexes of hierarchy and of gradients of decision making, opportunities, and reactions across the hierarchy. Measures of productivity, however, were not reported—these are notoriously difficult to compare. The ranking of the indexes can be compared to the ranking of PDI, but as we have only five cases, significant correlations with PDI were unlikely. It appeared, however, that where Tannenbaum et al. measured *formal* elements of hierarchy, these did not show any relationship with PDI at all. An example is their summary measure of "Emphasis placed on hierarchy" (p. 118). Where they measured *informal* elements of hierarchy, these followed more or less the PDI order. Examples are their questions "What do workers communicate to their superior?" (accurate relevant information yes/no, pp. 52-53, question 33) and "Is your immediate superior inclined to take into account your opinions and suggestions?" (not at all/very much, pp. 57-58, question 42). Accurate information and suggestions taken into account were negatively correlated with PDI. As in the case of the IBM statement in favor of employee participation (B56), Tannenbaum et al.'s data showed that the formal and informal levels should be sharply distinguished. Italy scored low on both types of participation, Yugoslavia high on formal but low on informal, Israel high on both, and Austria and the United States low on formal but higher on informal participation.

The contrast between formal and informal participation emerged also in the European Values Survey. In one question (Harding & Phillips, 1986, question 143), respondents could choose between the statements "The owners should run their business and appoint the managers" and "The owners and the employees should participate in the selection of managers." Across 12 countries, the share of those who chose the first answer varied from 67% in low-PDI Norway to 19% in high-PDI France (Halman, 1991, p. 314); the correlation with PDI was $r = -.65*$. In countries with lower PDI scores, more respondents wanted to let the owners appoint the managers—but managers in these countries are more accessible to employees.

Formal worker participation was a hot issue in the management literature of the 1970s. A consortium of sociologists and psychologists from 12 mainly European countries had formed the IDE (Industrial Democracy in Europe) International Research Group.[82] Their purpose was "to assess the effects of national schemes for employee participation on a comparative basis" (IDE International Research Group, 1981a, p. v). They collected data within a total of 134 organizations, divided into services, high-skill manufacturing, and low-skill manufacturing, and into small, me-

dium, and large size. Questionnaires were filled out in group and individual sessions with a total of about 1,000 key informants (managers, workers' council members, and so on) and about 8,000 ordinary organization members. The entire project took 6 years. In the spirit of the 1970s, the research looked for general principles: The independent variable of formal (de jure) participation, either directly or through the intervening variable of informal (de facto) participation, was related to a set of dependent variables—attitudes, aspirations, and actions. "Culture" was not explicitly included, but between the lines the research report is heavy with national culture issues, if only in the different approaches and underlying values of team members from different countries and disciplines.[83] An important conclusion was that the de facto influence of top management depends mostly on structural factors such as organization size, but the de facto influence of employees and their representative bodies depends almost entirely on country, with all that "country" stands for (IDE International Research Group, 1981a, p. 167). None of the measures of industrial democracy found correlated with PDI.[84] This implies that there was also no relationship between industrial democracy and political democracy (which did correlate, negatively, with PDI). A replication study was done 10 years later. The leading team members, Heller, Pusic, Strauss, and Wilpert, in 1998 published a retrospective set of essays on the subject of "organizational participation," sticking with their tenacious attempts to find general principles and to avoid the national culture variable. It should by now be evident that one cannot write meaningfully about organizational participation without embedding it within a national cultural context, but these authors were still trying.

Using a very different approach, Franke (1997), in a macroanalysis across 14 mostly Western countries, showed that, economically, industrial democracy is a good thing: Higher levels of (formalized) worker decision-making rights in the 1970s and 1980s were associated with higher GNP/capita growth rates, but this type of study always makes one wonder about the intervening variables.

The 1981 IDE study found the former Yugoslavia to be the most successful country in establishing industrial democracy. Yugoslavia was one of the battlegrounds of World War II and came out as a communist state under the leadership of Josip Broz Tito, who managed to steer an independent course outside the influence sphere of the then Soviet Union. In 1950, he introduced "worker self-management," which was further reinforced in 1965 and meant a considerable degree of decentralization and market influence in the economy. Politically the country remained a one-party state, composed of six republics and two territories with a history of internal fighting and feuding. After Tito's death in 1980, the country slowly disintegrated and in a bloody civil war from 1991 to 1996 fell completely apart into four independent republics (Bosnia, Croatia, Macedonia, and Slovenia) and a remaining "Yugoslav Federation" with a majority of ethnic Serbs trying to suppress various remaining minorities.

It is a historical riddle how the IDE study at one time could identify this Yugoslavia as the world's model for industrial democracy. With the hindsight of history one has to conclude that really important facts in this society must have been overlooked in the research approach.[85] Adizes (1971), who studied self-management in two Serbian textile plants in 1967, drew attention to the frustration of managers in the system. In the IBM surveys the data for "Yugoslavia" were collected in 1971 within a Yugoslav trading company importing and servicing IBM products (see Chapter 2). One remarkable fact of the results obtained (not published earlier) was the extremely low job satisfaction of the managers in the Yugoslav sample, which contrasted with the generally high satisfaction of managers in IBM subsidiaries in other countries. On the basis of the employees' values, I classified Yugoslavia as high PDI. In their retrospective book on "organizational participation," the IDE authors Heller et al. (1998) deal only summarily with the Yugoslav disaster and the lessons to be drawn from it for their subject; aren't organizations and political systems products of the same national cultural context?

Some 10 years after the initial IDE research, Globokar (1989) did an in-depth study of the management of an aluminum plant in Herzegovina, part of Bosnia, which had been built up since 1978 with the assistance of a French company.[86] Globokar found the foremen (first-line managers) to be rarely present on the work floor and to exercise hardly any control over the workers, who operated autonomously in teams of three—uncontrolled, to the detriment of product quality. The foremen's role was bureaucratic; from their office they rather arbitrarily distributed sanctions and rewards to workers. The director was very powerful, not only inside the factory but also in the community, where he figured as a big hero and pursued all kinds of private interests. The chief engineer made most internal decisions. Globokar explained this situation, which surprised the French advisers greatly, by referring to the extended family structure of the local population, in which fathers wielded all the power and all other men were equal as brothers; those who wanted to escape would leave. The director and chief engineer took father roles, the workers took brother roles, and the foremen were squeezed in between. Moreover, the local population was divided into

the three ethnic groups of Croats, Serbs, and Muslims. The giving of orders by anyone other than respected fathers threatened the delicate balance between these groups and was therefore avoided. Globokar's picture of the plant's reality was entirely different from that presented by the IDE researchers but more compatible with later political developments.

Power Distance and Political Systems

The preceding subsections have looked at the implications of power distance differences among countries for the role pairs of parent-child, teacher-student, and boss-subordinate. Another role pair that is obviously equally affected is that of authority-citizen. It must be immediately evident to anyone who reads any world news at all that various countries handle power differences between authorities and citizens in very different ways and that different convictions dominate the perceptions of desirability of the various ways of handling such power differences.

In Chapter 1, I described various large factor-analytic studies of country data. The one focusing specifically on political systems was a study by Gregg and Banks (1965). Among 68 aspects of political systems across 115 countries, they found a strong first factor, "access," which combined at its positive pole having an electoral system; a constitutional regime; oppositional groups; a horizontal distribution of power; a representative, not a totalitarian regime; and press freedom. This factor represents a main dimension of political systems.[87] Date for the IBM countries on this measure around 1970 were not available; instead, I subjectively divided the 50 countries into those with and without "balanced power in government," based on events in the period 1975-98. As the statistical analysis shows (Exhibit 3.18), the "balanced versus unbalanced power" split is highly significantly associated with PDI. This is not necessarily a matter of cause and effect; political systems and PDI both vary according to historical and cultural continuities (Eisenstadt, 1974); both political systems and PDI scores are symptoms of the same underlying societal norms. As Aristotle (1962, p. 28) noted 23 centuries ago, man is by nature a political animal, and political decision making depends to a large extent on factors outside politics itself.[88]

For countries with electoral systems and representative regimes, the distribution of votes over parties also reflects the power distance norm. In the 1981-82 European Values Survey, representative samples of the population in nine European democracies were asked to indicate their political position on a 10-point scale from *left* to *right* (Stoetzel, 1983, p. 60). On the basis of their choices, a coefficient of variation of political positions was computed; this coefficient was significantly correlated with PDI (rho = .71*). High-PDI parliamentary countries such as France, Italy, and Japan presented a polarization between left and right with a weak center (just as with the preferences for managers' decision-making styles in IBM discussed earlier). Lower-PDI countries such as Sweden, Germany, and Britain produced more votes to center parties or support to center tendencies within broad left and right parties. Also, in France, Italy, and Japan the ruling parties had more often been those right of the middle; in which "right" stands for de-emphasizing and "left" for stressing equality. Most low-PDI countries have frequently had left-of-center governments. An interesting case is Germany; the German Federal Republic before the unification with East Germany was composed of 10 states (*Bundesländer*), and since the Republic's establishment the states in the traditionally Catholic south had right-wing governments (Christian Democrats); those in the traditionally Protestant north had left-wing governments (Social Democrats). The unification added six new East German states, and from these, the two to the south voted for Christian Democrat governments in the 1999 elections, and the four to the north voted for Social Democratic governments.[89] Even the 45-year-long communist interval did not change the north/south rift, which, as I will argue below, is an inheritance from the days of the Roman Empire. The empire included the German south but never the north; it also determined the prevalence of either Catholic or Protestant Christianity.

Inglehart (1990) reported percentages of national populations agreeing with the following statement: "The entire way our society is organized must be radically changed by revolutionary action" (p. 39). Across 17 developed countries, these percentages, although generally low (between 2% and 14%, with an overall mean of 6%), correlated significantly with PDI (r = .77**).[90] Larger power distances were associated with more revolutionary fervor.[91] The same source showed percentages of the public in 20 countries claiming to discuss politics frequently or occasionally (Inglehart, 1990, p. 343). Across again 17 overlapping countries, these varied from 43% in Belgium to 83% in Germany; they were significantly negatively correlated with PDI (r = −.70**).[92] Politics is more *discussable* in lower-PDI cultures.

The Eurobarometer, the periodic attitude measurement system across the countries of the European Union, in 1997 asked random samples of about 1,000 EU citizens in each member country about their satisfaction with the way democracy worked in their countries. Correlations with Eurobarometer data were mostly with uncertainty avoidance and will therefore be analyzed in Chapter 4 (Exhibit 4.15), but answers on the satisfaction-with-democracy question (4-point scale) were correlated primarily and negatively with PDI (r = −.68** across 14 countries).

Smaller power distances are associated with a certain consensus among the population that reduces the chance of disruptive conflicts.[93] In the first edition of *Culture's Consequences,* I correlated the IBM indexes with three independent measures of domestic political violence between 1948 and 1968, across 37, 37, and 10 countries; in all three cases PDI was significantly, and more than the other dimensions, correlated with violence (.39**, .71***, and .93***).[94] Van de Vliert, Schwartz, Huismans, Hofstede, and Daan (1999) calculated a domestic political violence index from data on political riots and armed attacks between 1948 and 1977 reported by Taylor and Jodice (1983). Across 50 countries our index correlated with PDI with r = .51***. In these studies especially the countries in the lower third of the PDI range had less political violence and contributed to the correlation. Since the 1970s, countries that suffered most from revolutionary changes in government—such as Argentina, Iran, Greece, Portugal, Chile, Thailand, and Peru—were mainly found in the middle part of the PDI scale. Countries higher in the PDI range tended to continue with relatively stable, authoritarian governments; those lower in PDI, with relatively stable, pluralist systems. In the middle-range countries, governments could no longer count on the dependence needs of an increasing section of the population, especially of the new middle classes. These countries swung back and forth between egalitarian and elitist regimes, and elitist rulers tried to use outright oppression and totalitarianism to maintain their position.

As we saw in the beginning of this chapter, high-PDI societies support status consistency. The powerful are entitled to privileges and are expected to use their power to increase their wealth. Their status is enhanced by symbolic behavior that makes them look as powerful as possible. Although formally everybody may be equal before the law, in practice the powerful always win their cases.[95] The main sources of power are one's family and friends, one's charisma, and one's ability to use force; the last of these explains the frequency of military dictatorships in countries on this side of the power distance scale. It is expected that persons in power will become involved in scandals, and it is expected that such scandals will be covered up. If something goes wrong, the blame is placed on people lower down the hierarchy. If it gets too bad, the system may have to be changed through replacement of those in power, via revolution. Most such revolutions fail even if they succeed, because the newly powerful after some time repeat the behaviors of their predecessors, in which they are supported by the prevailing values regarding inequality.

In the lower-PDI societies, power, wealth, and status need not go together; it is even considered a good thing if they do not. The main sources of power are one's formal position, one's assumed expertise, and one's ability to give rewards. Scandals usually mean the end of political careers. Revolutions are unpopular, and the system is changed in evolutionary ways, without necessarily deposing those in power.

In the section on work organizations, we saw that income distribution across the hierarchy is more unequal in high-PDI than in low-PDI countries. The same holds for the populations as a whole. Data from the *Human Development Report 1996* (United Nations Development Program, 1996; reproduced in Exhibit 3.16) show income ratios of households (highest versus lowest 20%) for 40 of the IBM countries, which again correlated significantly with PDI ($r = .42**$). Wage differentials were (much) larger in poor countries than in wealthier ones, but PDI explained the differences even better than did national wealth (GNP/capita).

Taxation in most countries has an equalizing effect on incomes, but in a cross-national study Bégué (1976) showed data from the Organization for Economic Cooperation and Development (OECD) to the effect that taxation in high-PDI France had an *une*qualizing effect on incomes.[96] It had no effect on income equality in Australia, and it increased equality in eight other lower-PDI countries, the most so in Norway.

The social origins of administrative elites differ among countries. In the higher-PDI countries France and Italy, administrative elites were reported to be distinctively *unrepresentative* of the total population as far as their social origins were concerned, more so than in the lower-PDI countries Great Britain, Germany, the Netherlands, and the United States (Aberbach & Putnam, 1977).

On issues of public interest, such as environmental protection, citizens of high-PDI societies tend to wait for action by the government. Citizens of low-PDI societies are more likely to cooperate with their governments. An indirect measure of cooperation of public and authorities is the degree of recycling of waste. Nearly all developed countries in the 1990s introduced some form of garbage separation, but this works, obviously, only if the public cooperates. For one type of waste, paper, percentages recycled for 15 European countries were published in the Dutch newspaper *NRC Handelsblad* (January 22, 1997). The figures varied from 19% in Greece to 68% in Germany. The percentage of total paper consumption recycled was correlated significantly with PDI ($r = -.67**$).[97] In high-PDI countries the public tends to leave issues of public interest such as this one to the authorities.

A factor possibly contributing to the negative correlation between paper recycling and PDI is that, according to the consumer data research by De Mooij mentioned earlier in this chapter, people in low-PDI countries read more newspapers ("read 7 days a week" versus PDI, rho = $-.69***$ across 16 countries; "read any yesterday," rho = $-.66**$). Newspapers are probably more easily recycled than other paper products, but the correlation also shows that people in low-PDI countries takes a more active role in information gathering than do those in high-PDI countries (the alternative to newspaper reading is TV watching). Interestingly, reading more newspapers goes together with lower confidence in the press. De Mooij found that for the same 16 countries "showing a great deal or quite a lot of confidence in the press" was *positively* correlated with PDI, rho = $.55*$. This positive relationship was confirmed in the 1990-93 World Values Survey (question 276): Across 25 common countries, PDI and confidence in the press were correlated with rho = $.66***$.

Whereas the level of confidence in the press is higher in countries with larger power distances, the level of confidence in the police is lower (rho = $-.81***$ across 25 countries). The two correlations have opposite signs. Confidence in other institutions is mainly (negatively) related to uncertainty avoidance; this entire issue is addressed in Chapter 4 (for the correlation data, see Exhibit 4.14).

A major threat to the functioning of any political and administrative system is corruption. Since 1995, Transparency International, a nongovernmental organization located in Berlin, has issued a yearly Corruption Perception Index (CPI) on the Internet.[98] The CPI, which was developed by Johann Graf Lambsdorff, an economist at the University of Göttingen, Germany, combines information from several different sources.[99] The 1998 CPI covered 85 countries. The statistical section of this chapter (Exhibit 3.19) shows that across 50 overlapping countries, CPI correlated primarily with wealth ($r = .82***$ with 1997 GNP/capita; as higher CPI values stand for "cleaner" countries, this means less corruption in wealthier countries). The next-highest zero-order correlation was with IDV ($r = .71***$), followed closely by PDI ($-.70***$, meaning more corruption in countries with larger power distances). As we have seen, wealth and PDI are negatively correlated. In Chapter 5, I will show that wealth and IDV are even more strongly positively correlated. A stepwise multiple regression showed that after the influence of wealth had been accounted for, PDI still contributed significantly to the prediction of CPI; IDV did not. If instead of my 1970 scores collected from IBM personnel we use the 1984 scores of elites from mainly wealthy countries measured by Hoppe (1990; see Exhibit 3.13), the highest zero-order correlation is with Hoppe's PDI, no less than $r = -.86***$ across 18 countries. These elite Salzburg participants' answers on the PDI questions predicted almost perfectly the amount of corruption in their countries perceived by Transparency International's sources more than 10 years later.

What is corruption and what is not is to some extent arbitrary; the giving of gifts is an important ritual in many societies, and the borderline between gift giving and bribing is diffuse.[100] To a purist, even a tip can be considered a form of bribe. Corruption is indisputable where those in power use illegal means to enrich themselves; assuming that the CPI raters used this same criterion, the CPI's correlation with wealth shows that illegal enrichment happens more frequently in countries in which the majority of the population is poor. Corruption is a way for politicians to escape from poverty, which they need less if there is no poverty. The influence of power distance points to the influence of checks and balances in a society on the use of power. Lord Acton, a 19th-century British politician turned Cambridge professor, is credited with a famous aphorism: "Power tends to corrupt and absolute power corrupts absolutely."[101] Larger power distances in a society mean fewer checks and balances on the use of power—that is, a stronger temptation for power holders to enrich themselves illegally. Enlightened rulers can impose checks where traditional culture does not provide them. Examples are high-PDI countries Singapore and Hong Kong, which the Transparency International list classifies as reasonably "clean." This reflects the iron hands of Senior Minister Lee Kuan Yew in Singapore and of the ICAC (Independent Commission Against Corruption) in Hong Kong. It remains to be seen to what extent these checks will last over time.

Labor unions in high-PDI societies are instruments of the government or of political parties; in low-PDI societies they are independent and less oriented to ideology and politics than to pragmatic issues on behalf of their members.

The reader will easily recognize that some elements of both poles can be found in many countries. A country like Spain, ruled dictatorially until the 1970s, has shifted remarkably smoothly to a pluralist government system. The government in Britain, an old democracy, tried hard to prevent the publication of unwanted revelations by a former secret agent. *Glasnost* (openness) undermined the autocratic institutions of the former Soviet Union.

Power Distance and Religion, Ideology, and Theories of Power

Parents, teachers, managers, and rulers are all children of their cultures. In a way, they are the followers of their followers, and one can understand their behavior only if one also understands the mental software of their children, students, subordinates, and subjects. However, not only the doers in this world but also the thinkers are children of their cultures. The authors of management books and those who formulate political ideologies generate their ideas based on their own backgrounds, on what they learned as they grew up. Thus differences among countries along value dimensions such as power distance help us not only to understand differences in thinking, feeling, and behaving among leaders and those they lead but to appreciate the theories produced or adopted in those countries to explain or prescribe thoughts, feelings, and behavior.

Power distance norm differences are definitely associated with aspects of religious life, but it is doubtful whether religion can "explain" PDI; power distances and religious creeds should rather be seen as growing from common roots. In Europe there is a striking similarity between the former limits of the Roman Empire and the present limits of Roman Catholicism; with few exceptions, the various Church reformations have been successful only in countries or areas not once under Roman rule. As Thomas Hobbes wrote in 1651:

If a man consider the originall of this great Ecclesiasticall Dominion, he will easily perceive, that the *Papacy,* is no other, than the *Ghost* of the deceased *Romane Empire,* sitting crowned upon the grave thereof: For so did the Papacy start up on a Sudden out of the Ruines of that Heathen Power. (Hobbes, 1651/1973, p. 381)[102]

Among the European countries with Catholic majorities, only Ireland and Poland do not have a Latin past; both used their Catholicism as a source of identity to protect them against powerful non-Catholic occupants. Present-day Germany and the Netherlands were both border areas of the Roman Empire. The southern parts of both countries that once were Roman are still in majority Catholic, the northern parts Protestant. As shown above, in Germany the former borderline of the Roman Empire is also a political dividing line: The (more conservative) Christian Democrats have a stronger base in the south, and the Social

Democrats are stronger in the north, even in the states of former East Germany.

For PDI (and other cultural dimensions), the earlier Empire appears to have been more decisive than the later Church, as can be seen in the fact that Ireland (Catholic but not Latin) scores similar to Britain (mainly Protestant but also not Latin). However, once a religion has been established in a country, it will reinforce the values that led to its adoption. Catholicism, with the supreme authority of the pope and the intermediate authority of the priest, fits better with a high PDI than does Protestantism, with its "general priesthood of the believers." Max Weber (1930/1976) quotes a 17th-century Puritan Protestant text about "the sinfulness of the belief in authority, which is only permissible in the form of an impersonal authority" (p. 224). In *The Protestant Ethic and the Spirit of Capitalism,* Weber associates Protestantism with the capitalist modernization of countries.

In Asia, religion can be seen as a factor in explaining the difference in power distance between Muslim Pakistan and Hindu India: Islam is more egalitarian. In Islam, all believers are equal before God—although they may be very unequal in society.[103] The religious split in the Indian-Pakistani subcontinent was the outcome of a historical development in which certain castes embraced Islam, so that the Muslim part of the population was already more homogeneous, castewise. In present-day India the caste system, with its power distance aspect, is a more fundamental element of society than the Hindu religion; Christians and Muslims have become absorbed in it and have acquired the status of new castes (Srinivas, 1969).

In China around 500 B.C., Kong Ze, whose name the Jesuit missionaries 2,000 years later Latinized as Confucius (from the older name Kong Fu Ze), maintained that the stability of society is based on unequal relationships between people. He distinguished the *wu lun,* the five basic relationships: master-follower, father-son, elder brother-younger brother, husband-wife, and senior friend-junior friend. These relationships contain mutual and complementary obligations: The junior partner owes the senior respect and obedience; the senior owes the junior partner protection and consideration. Confucius's ideas have survived to the present as guidelines for proper behavior for Chinese people (see Chapter 7). In the People's Republic of China, Mao Zedong tried to wipe out Confucianism, but in the meantime his own rule contained Confucian elements. Countries in the IBM study with a Chinese majority or that have undergone Chinese cultural influences are, in order of PDI: Singapore, Hong Kong, South Korea, Taiwan, and Japan. The Confucian heritage in these countries helps to explain their populations' respect for hierarchy, but one may

wonder which is older, Confucianism or the hierarchical norm (Kawasaki, 1969, p. 208).

In European ideological and philosophical thinking we find different theories about power in high-PDI and low-PDI countries. Among the classics, Niccolò Machiavelli (1517/1955) pictured the high-PDI society par excellence. Machiavelli identified with the powerful; more recent authors who have done the same are Gaetano Mosca (1848-1941) and Vilfredo Pareto (1848-1923), both Italians like Machiavelli, who explained history as determined by a constant circulation of ruthless ruling classes; and Robert Michels (1876-1936), with his iron law of oligarchy (1915), who, although German, lived and worked in Italy. I referred earlier to another classical author, Étienne de La Boétie (1548/1976), who also wrote from a high-PDI viewpoint but identified with the powerless. Not infrequently, authors from high-PDI backgrounds identify with the powerless when they are young (La Boétie was 16 when he wrote his *Discours de la servitude volontaire*) but switch to the point of view of the powerful later in life. All these authors are "elitists." To them, power is a zero-sum entity; one can obtain it only by taking it from someone else. A high-PDI philosopher who, like Michels, came from a lower-PDI country (Britain) was Thomas Hobbes, whom I have quoted above. Hobbes spent 11 years in exile in France and met, among others, Descartes and Galilei. Hobbes (1651/1973) took a pessimistic view: "I put for a generall inclination of all mankind, a perpetuall and restless desire of Power after power, that ceaseth only in Death" (p. 49). Hobbes derived the human desire for power from the laws of physics and defended a strong state and sovereign as the way to avoid chaos. The difference between Hobbes and Machiavelli is that Machiavelli addressed himself to the rulers, whereas Hobbes addressed himself to the public.

In the low-PDI countries, apart from Hobbes, we tend to find "pluralist" theories. The phenomenon of polarization between the powerful and the powerless, between wealthy and poor, is considered a fact, but an undesirable one. The pluralists usually assume that power can be shared and that power distances can be reduced. This presupposes a range of intermediate strata between the powerful and the powerless; these strata are larger in the low-PDI countries. We find in this category Thomas More (1516/1965) and, among modern social scientists, Mauk Mulder (1976, 1977) and Arnold Tannenbaum (1968). Tannenbaum explicitly defends a non-zero-sum theory of power in which all parties can gain. The group of pluralists includes those who try to reduce power distances through formal means (as in the case of the German *Mitbestimmung,* or codetermination). To this category belong Karl Marx and Friedrich Engels

(1848/1974) and Max Weber (see Gerth & Mills, 1948/1970). Marx believed that once the powerless replace the powerful, power distribution will be equal. Weber pictured a system of impersonal rules to which the use of power is tied and that protects both the more and the less powerful. Pluralists who want to reduce power distance by informal means are found in the United States ("participative management"; Likert, 1967) and in Britain (sociotechnical systems; Miller, 1976). The formal/informal distinction will reappear in Chapter 4.

In the terminology of Machiavelli, the high-PDI countries apply a "lions" approach to the exercise of power, whereas the low-PDI countries apply a "foxes" approach. Pareto (1916/1976) held that only the lions approach leads to stability, but Pareto lived in a lions country. For authors such as Mulder and Likert, only a foxes approach leads to stability; they lived in foxes countries. Where lions and foxes value systems clash within the same society it can become unstable, as we have seen in the previous section.

In high-PDI thinking the use of force is seen as the essence of power. In low-PDI thinking it is a sign of the breakdown of power (Wrong, 1980, p. 88).

Exhibit 3.9 summarizes the differences between low- and high-PDI societies with regard to political systems, religions, ideologies, and philosophical ideas as described above. The differences are "culture's consequences," but in the sense of the far right-hand box in Exhibit 1.5, with a feedback loop to the societal norm (PDI) itself and its origins, so that we should not assume a one-way causality.

Power Distance and Aviation Safety

In August 1994, an article appeared in the *Washington Post* that was reprinted in the *International Herald Tribune* (on August 23, 1994) and in several other newspapers around the world. The article, written by Don Phillips and headlined "Aviation Safety vs. National Culture? Boeing Takes a Flyer," was based on a presentation by Weener and Russell (1994) at the 22nd International Air Transport Association Technical Conference. These authors were executives in the safety section of the Boeing Commercial Airplane Group, and they looked for possible cultural reasons for the considerable differences in aviation accident rates between 1959 and 1992 by nationality of carrier. They plotted accident rates against my four IBM indexes and showed clear correlations with power distance (positive) and individualism (negative). The correlation with PDI was especially suggestive; if the relationship between pilot and copilot is hierarchical rather than colle-

gial, this may lead to a copilot's not correcting errors made by the pilot. Standard procedures in the cockpit assume two-way communication between pilot and copilot. In a discussion I had at Boeing's office with the person responsible for cockpit procedures, the latter remarked, "We construct airplanes for people like ourselves—maybe this is not always right." The suggestion of the influence of power distance and individualism on aviation safety had earlier been made by Redding and Ogilvie (1984) in a conference paper and was supported by data supplied by Ramsden (1985) in the journal *Flight International*.

Exhibit 3.17 in the statistical section of this chapter shows the correlation of the aviation accident rate data from Ramsden (1985; 18 countries, 1973-84) and Weener and Russell (1994; 33 countries, 1959-92) with the first four IBM indexes but also with 1980 GNP/capita, a precaution not taken by the earlier analysts of the correlations. The conclusion is sobering. Although in both cases the rank correlations with PDI were significant (rho = .68*** and .47**, respectively), the correlations with IDV were stronger (rho = −.69*** and −.62***) and the correlations with GNP/capita were the strongest of all (rho = −.75*** and −.85***). As both PDI (negatively) and IDV (positively) are correlated with GNP/capita, we had to check whether IDV and/or PDI contributed to the explanation of the accident rates after controlling for GNP/capita. *This was not the case.* When I split the countries into wealthier (1990 GNP/capita greater than $4,800) and poorer, GNP/capita remained the dominant variable.[104] So low GNP/capita by itself explained these accident rates, and the cultural indexes did not add to that. Poor countries have fewer resources to maintain and renew their air fleets, select and train their personnel, and manage their airports. This explanation, unfortunately, makes the power distance and individualism explanations redundant in this particular case. This does not mean that culture does not affect aviation safety. Helmreich and Merritt (1998) have made a convincing case for including the culture factor in aviation safety research. The present case shows only that this role is as complex as the subject of aviation safety itself and that other influences should be considered as well.[105]

Predictors of PDI: Latitude, Population Size, and Wealth

A stepwise regression (see Exhibit 3.20) shows that across 50 countries, 43% of the variance in PDI can be predicted from the geographic latitude (of the country's capital) alone; 51% can be predicted from a combination of latitude and population size, and 56% from latitude, population size, and wealth (1970 GNP/capita). The "predicted"

Exhibit 3.9   Key Differences Between Low- and High-PDI Societies II: Politics and Ideas

Low PDI	High PDI
In Political Systems	
Pluralist governments based on outcome of majority vote.	Military, autocratic, or oligarchic government based on co-optation.
Political parties exist and tend to be in the center with relatively weak left and right wings.	If political parties exist, there is a polarization between left and right with a weak center.
Government is frequently led by parties stressing equality, usually social democrats.	If government is based on election results, it tends to be led by right-wing parties.
Gradual changes in form of government (evolution and stability).	Sudden changes in form of government (revolution and/or instability).
Much discussion but little violence in domestic politics.	Little discussion but frequent violence in domestic politics.
Citizens satisfied with the way democracy works.	Citizens dissatisfied with the way democracy works.
Power, status, and wealth do not need to go together.	Status consistency: power brings status and wealth.
Small income differentials in society, further reduced by the tax system.	Large income differentials in society, further increased by the tax system.
Administrative elites recruited from broad range of population.	Administrative elites unrepresentative for total population.
Citizens cooperate with authorities, as in waste recycling.	Citizens wait for action by authorities, as in environmental protection.
Citizens read more newspapers.	Citizens watch more television.
Citizens distrust press but trust police.	Citizens trust press but distrust police.
Less corruption; scandals end political careers.	More corruption; scandals expected to be covered up.
Free labor unions exist and are pragmatically oriented.	If free labor unions exist, they are ideologically and politically oriented.
In Religion, Ideas, and Ideologies	
Prevailing religions and philosophical systems stress equality.	Prevailing religions and philosophies stress stratification and hierarchy.
Prevailing political ideologies stress and practice power sharing.	Prevailing political ideologies stress and practice power struggle.
Pluralist ideas about society.	Elitist ideas about society.
Non-zero-sum theories of power.	Zero-sum theories of power.
Use of force reveals the failure of power.	Use of force is the essence of power.
More, Marx, Engels, Weber, Mulder, Tannenbaum, Likert, Miller.	Machiavelli, La Boétie, Hobbes, Mosca, Pareto, Michels.

column in Exhibit 3.1 lists the values of PDI that would be predicted in this latter case. The mean absolute prediction error is 11 points; the maximum error, 34 points (for Israel).

That geographic latitude is the strongest predictor of PDI (with negative sign) may come as a surprise. However, a country's geographic position is a fundamental fact that is bound to have a strong effect on the subjective culture of its inhabitants,

as this culture is shaped over many generations. Even when people migrate, they usually prefer migrating to climatic zones not very different from those they leave, which means staying within roughly similar latitudes (north or south). The logic of the relationship between latitude (by definition an independent variable) and power distance is, of course, a matter of educated speculation. In any case, latitude is a rough global indicator of climate (tropical/moderate/cold). In my interpretation of the relationship between latitude and power distance, the key intervening variable is the need for technology as a condition for survival. Human survival in colder climates presupposes protection against the hardships of nature, which means that only those people survived who were able to master the minimal technical skills necessary for survival. In warmer climates there was less need for technology, but the primary threat to survival was aggression by others. Levinson (1977, p. 760), who reviewed anthropological cross-cultural studies, has related the frequency of aggression to warm climate; this fits with the correlation between PDI and latitude.

The difference in climates is at the beginning of a possible causal chain (see Exhibit 3.10) that suggests how two different dominant types of social structure may have developed. Some would probably attribute the effect of climate on human society primarily to its impact on physical performance: A tropical climate would make people less inclined to work.[106] I believe, rather, that over the long term with which we are dealing here, the human species is highly adaptable: If humans perform less in tropical countries, it is not because they cannot become high performers there, but because there is less need for it.

The (positive) relationship between PDI and our second predictor, population size, can be interpreted in two ways: Large population size can be classified both as a consequence and as an origin of large power distance. The question is, why have some small nations remained independent while others have been absorbed into larger states? Obviously, military accidents have played an important role, but the will to be independent is an indispensable ingredient that in the long term has often proven stronger than military violence. It is not difficult to see a link between the will to be independent as a small nation and the maintenance of small power distances in other institutions. Thus small population size can be a consequence of a small power distance norm. On the other hand, once a large nation exists, its members will have to accept a political power that is more distant and less accessible than that for a small nation.[107] This should then reinforce a norm in society of less questioning of authority in general—that is, a larger power distance. In larger countries consensus between citizens is less easily achieved, and the use of power is more readily considered.[108]

Wealth, itself highly correlated with latitude, is the third predictor of PDI, with negative sign, after the effects of latitude and population size have been eliminated. Wealth, too, can be interpreted as both a consequence and an origin of smaller power distances. National wealth is obviously associated with a whole complex of other factors.

Adelman and Morris (1967, tab. IV-1), in a factor analysis of 24 economic, social, and political indicators for 74 noncommunist developing countries, found a first factor associating GNP/capita with small size of the traditional agricultural sector, more mass communication, social mobility, literacy, urbanization, and a more important middle class. For the 25 relatively most developed countries out of their set (tab. VII-5), they could add to this list modernization of agricultural techniques, strength of the labor movement, decentralization of political power, a nonpolitical role of the military, "modern" views of society, and modernization of industry. All these indicators are conceptually related to lower power distances as well. I have fitted them into the causal chain in Exhibit 3.10.

Power Distance and Historical Factors: D'Iribarne's Contribution

The inverse relationship of the Power Distance Index with geographic latitude implies that the roots of country PDI differences must be very old. Archaeological evidence from 4,000 years ago suggests that at that time already the present Middle East region had centralized governments and kings, whereas what is now Scandinavia was run as "a primitive vigorous democracy" (Bibby, 1965, pp. 31, 41). Eisenstadt (1981) located "the origins and different modes of ideological politics . . . not in the present or in the modern era but in the distant past, in some very formative periods of human history" (p. 177). In fact, he suggested that they emerged and became institutionalized sometime during the first millennium B.C.

Latitude, population size, and wealth leave 44% of the variance in PDI unexplained. The specific history of every country has affected its population's ways of handling power differentials beyond the influences of the country's latitude, population size, or wealth.[109] Eisenstadt (1981) has referred to the dynamics between mundane and transcendental (secular and religious) authorities as one factor that varies widely between civilizations, both in theory and in practice.

A classic study of the historical roots of authority relations in *work organizations* is Reinhard Bendix's *Work and Authority in Industry* (1956/1974). Bendix compared England and Russia in the 18th and 19th centuries. He shows how in England the working classes were emancipated through reading and writing, and how in Russia, in spite of Marxist ideology, the servitude of czarism continued in Soviet industries. He also compared the United States and East Germany in the 1950s, and he shows that the Marxist ideology was received quite differently in East Germany,

Exhibit 3.10 Origins of National PDI Differences

	Origins of Power Distance Norm	
Causal Chain	Low PDI	High PDI
	Moderate to cold climates.	Tropical and subtropical climates.
	Survival and population growth more dependent on human intervention with nature.	Survival and population growth less dependent on human intervention with nature.
	More need for technology.	Less need for technology.
	Historical events: early legislation applied to rulers; one-son inheritance.	Historical events: early legislation not applied to rulers; divided inheritance.
	Less traditional agriculture, more modern industry, more urbanization.	More traditional agriculture, less modern industry, less urbanization.
	More need for education of lower strata (literacy, mass communication).	Less need for education of lower strata.
	Greater social mobility and strong development of middle class.	Less social mobility and weak development of middle class.
	Greater national wealth.	Less national wealth.
	Wealth more widely distributed.	Wealth concentrated in hands of small elite.
	Political power based on system of representation.	Political power concentrated in hands of oligarchy or military.
	Strong will to be independent: smaller size of population.	Little popular resistance to integration into a large state: large size of population.
	Historical events: independence, federalism, negotiation.	Historical events: occupation, colonialism, imperialism.
	Less centralization of political power.	Centralization of political power.
	Faster population increase in wealthy countries.	Slower population increase in wealthy countries.
	Technological momentum of change.	More static society.
	Children learn things that elders never learned: less dependent.	Children dependent on parents and elders.
	Some teaching is two-way.	Teachers are omniscient, teaching is one-way.
	More questioning of authority in general.	Less questioning of authority in general.

which had a history of organized labor, than in Russia, which had a history of serfdom.

A more recent contribution to explaining how a country's history affects subordinate-superior relations in modern industry has been made by the French anthropologist Philippe d'Iribarne (1989, 1994, 1997). His book *La Logique de l'honneur* (*The Logic of Honor*) is based on in-depth interviews in three production plants of a French-owned aluminum company, one in France, one in the United States, and one in the Netherlands.[110] The plants are technically identical, but the ways

in which they are managed differ dramatically. D'Iribarne identifies three different "logics"— philosophies—that control the interpersonal relationships: *honor* in France, the *fair contract* in the United States, and *consensus* in the Netherlands.[111] These philosophies represent patterns of thinking distinguishable in the histories of the three societies for centuries. In France, d'Iribarne refers to the *ancien régime* (the 18th-century monarchy before Napoleon) and cites Montesquieu (1689-1755), in particular his *De l'Esprit des lois* (*The Spirit of the Laws;* 1748/

1989), as a suitable authority on present-day French management. The most important feature is that France was and still is a class society— d'Iribarne even compares it to the caste society of India. Within the plant, different classes meet. There are at least three levels—the *cadres* (managers and professionals), the *maîtrise* (first-line supervisors) and the *non-cadres* (the levels below)—but within each of these there are further status distinctions, such as between higher and lower cadres and between skilled craftworkers and production personnel. The interaction between the classes is governed by a sense of respect for the honor concomitant to each class. The system is profoundly hierarchical, yet the kinds of orders a supervisor can give are constrained by a need to respect the honor of the subordinates, which implies their autonomy for certain tasks.[112]

In the United States, on the contrary, everybody is supposed to be equal; the relationship between management and workers is contractual. Within the limits of the contract, managers can give orders and subordinates will carry them out. Paradoxically, although this system is basically less hierarchical than the French situation, American managers can get away with demanding things from their workers that in France would be impossible, and the freedom of the contract may be that of "the free fox in the free chicken coop." D'Iribarne suggests that this type of relationship is based on the country's immigrant past. The United States had no traditional aristocracy as in France; the immigrants developed a middle-class society that sought a free association of equal citizens, related by a social contract; d'Iribarne calls them "pious merchants." He refers to the French author Alexis de Tocqueville (1805-59), who visited the United States in 1831-32 and wrote the famous book *Democracy in America* (1835/1956). Many of Tocqueville's observations still apply today, such as his description of American individualism. About the relationship between masters and servants in the United States, Tocqueville wrote: "The masters, from their side, only demand that their servants faithfully and rigorously execute their contract; they do not ask for their respect; they expect neither their love nor their devotion; it suffices them to find them punctual and honest" (quoted in d'Iribarne, 1989; my translation).[113]

Management in the Netherlands, as d'Iribarne describes it, is based not on orders but on consensus—on convincing the other, subordinate or superior, about what should be done. This calls for a lot of talking, either person-to-person or in meetings. D'Iribarne was struck in the Dutch plant he studied by everybody's respect for facts, which he found stronger there than in either France or the United States; in France, status and power often prevail over facts, and Americans want to make facts yield to moral principles. The Dutch also have their pious merchant ancestors, but since their revolt against their Spanish overlords in the 16th century, the former rebels have cooperated across religious and ideological dividing lines; compromise is a Dutch virtue. Relationships are not primarily contractual, and contract negotiations may be reopened the day after conclusion, if new facts emerge.

D'Iribarne's in-depth historical study is complementary to my quantitative cross-national surveys. He puts the flesh on the skeleton of the dimension profiles, showing what is behind the PDI scores for France (68), United States (40), and the Netherlands (38).[114]

Power Distance and Historical Factors: The Roman Empire and Colonialism

Going back to Exhibit 3.1, we find that the countries deviating most from the predicted values of PDI are 20 or more points above (Panama, +30; Belgium, +29; France, +27; Guatemala, +27; Malaysia, +26; and Yugoslavia, +23) or 20 or more points below (Israel, −34; Costa Rica, −31; Austria, −29; and Pakistan, −20).

The high scores for Belgium and France show them to be Latin countries. All Latin countries, in Europe as well as in the Americas, show relatively high PDI values, whereas all Germanic countries (including the English-speaking ones) show lower PDI values. Latin languages indicate the cultural inheritance of the Roman Empire. Half of Belgium speaks Dutch, a Germanic language, but until recently the French language and culture in that country have been strongly dominant. In Chapter 2, I have noted the similarities in values of the linguistic groups in Belgium.

In the Latin countries of Europe, the Roman Empire was the first large and effective state to be established. In the same way early childhood experiences have major impacts on personality, these early societal experiences must have had lasting impacts on polity, affecting all institutions that have followed. In the Roman Empire, the emperor had absolute authority and stood above the law: "By an implied contract the people confer upon the Emperor all power and authority over them so that his will has the force of the law" (Smith, 1964, p. 272). A very Latin proverb is *Quod licet Iovi, non licet bovi* (What is allowed to Jupiter is not allowed to an ox). The authority of the emperor was but an extension of the "awesome and almost absolute" power of the father in the Roman family (Berger, 1971, p. 178; Dudley, 1975, p. 45). When the Roman Empire disintegrated, this absolute authority of the ruler was adopted by the Germanic invaders of France who mixed with the Romanized population (Pirenne,

1939, p. 32). In France, the ability of judges to condemn authorities has been very limited up to the present day. In May 1999 a scandal erupted in the French island of Corsica when the *préfet,* the highest public authority, was jailed for having secretly ordered the burning of a beach restaurant. This was seen as an unheard-of rupture of the French tradition of judges yielding to *raison d'état* (national interest).[115]

In the Germanic tradition, in contrast, the power of the king was subordinate to the assembly of free men. In his *Germania,* Tacitus (55-120 A.D.) wrote about the Germanic tribes:

> The power even of the kings is not absolute or arbitrary.... On matters of minor importance only the chiefs debate; on major affairs, the whole community.... such hearing is given to the king or state-chief as his age, rank, military distinction, or eloquence can secure—more because his advice carries weight than because he has the power to command. (Tacitus, 1970, pp. 107-111)

In Britain, where the Germanic Anglo-Saxon invaders chased the Romanized Celts without mixing with them, an absolutist rule could not settle; when the Norman kings attempted to establish rule they were forced to recognize the rights of the people in the Magna Carta of 1215 (Pirenne, 1939, p. 257). The German sociologist and historian of European civilization Norbert Elias (1897-1990) has argued that during the Renaissance (14th to 16th century) at least part of the power in Germany moved to the universities, whereas in Latin Europe it stayed with the rulers (Elias, 1936/ 1980b, p. 3). In Germany up until the 19th century a central authority could never be established and the country was a quilt of small principalities.

Jordan (1973, p. 69) has pointed to the influence of the different inheritance laws in Roman and Germanic Europe. The former Roman Empire practiced divided inheritance: Land and other possessions were divided equally among all heirs so that children remained on ever-smaller farms, and birth control was a practical necessity. In Germanic and English common law, the land was usually inherited by the oldest son only, and the remaining offspring were compensated in other ways, if at all (a familiar picture from several of Grimm's German fairy tales). In a later stage of history this made younger sons move to cities— and thus contribute to the urbanization of the population—or emigrate. "The younger sons have made England great" (Sauvy, 1966, p. 26).[116] The differences in population growth among the four largest European countries between 1720 and 1970 are startling (Jordan, 1973, p. 72): France, from 19 million to 50 million, a growth factor of 2.6; Italy, from 13 to 53 million, growth factor 4.1; Germany (East and West), from 14 to 77 mil-

lion, growth factor 5.5; and Great Britain, from 7 to 55 million, growth factor 7.9.[117]

France had by far the slowest population increase; at the same time, it supplied fewer overseas migrants than the other countries. This was a matter of lower birthrates (that is, of voluntary birth prevention), given that death rates in France were not systematically different from those in other countries (Sauvy, 1966, p. 54). The French-speaking part of Belgium had an equally slow population increase. In the causal chain in Exhibit 3.10 I have linked slower population increases to a more static society (Sauvy, 1966, p. 30). Smaller family sizes also mean that parental authority weighed more heavily on the children.

A difference in inheritance laws such as that between Germanic and Latin Europe also existed between Japan and China (Hsu, 1971, p. 38). One-son inheritance in Japan supported the faster rate of modernization through the energy of the younger sons, who had to find other activities, and it helps to explain the relatively lower PDI score of Japan (54) versus other East Asian countries.

A frequently asked question about former colonial countries such as the Philippines, India, Singapore, and Hong Kong is to what extent their generally high level of PDI is inherited from their colonial past or rooted in local value systems that preceded the colonial period. After the colonial period the new local managers generally continued the existing management systems based on inequality (Kakar, 1971). However, traditional precolonial relationships also contained elements of large inequality: There is no better example than the Indian caste system.[118] As the colonial heritage fades away, it becomes more and more clear that the large power distances in these countries are innate and not just a colonial relic. The Filipino author and national hero José Rizal (1861-96) has a character in one of his novels say, "Why independence if the slaves of today will be the tyrants of tomorrow?" (quoted in Roces & Roces, 1985, p. 157).

Among the former colonies, Pakistan scored relatively low on PDI and lower than predicted. It may be that the Pakistani sample, one of the smallest in the data set, was particularly enlightened compared with its environment; also, as I have suggested above in the subsection on religion, Islamic Pakistan should stress stratification less than does Hindu India.

The Latin American countries generally score high on PDI; the Spanish and Portuguese invaders, Latins themselves, met local Indians' civilizations also based on class and status in which they could take over political control, often with surprising ease. "Exploitation of the masses was not an innovation of the colonial period" (Gibson, 1966, pp. 57-58). Among the six small Central American republics, Panama and Guatemala produced even higher PDI values than predicted, but Costa Rica lower. Panama is a somewhat artificial state, split off in 1903 from neighboring Colombia during (and for the purpose of) the construction of the Panama Canal; Guatemala is the poorest of the Central American republics in the IBM sample.[119] Costa Rica is widely recognized as an exception to the Latin American rule of dependence on powerful leaders, which in Spanish is called *personalismo*. It does not have a formal army. It is described as Latin America's most firmly rooted democracy, in spite of its relative poverty (it is poorer than Panama, which benefits from revenues from the canal).[120]

Two other countries that deviated particularly from their predicted PDI values are Israel and Austria. There are cultural links between the two: The modern state of Israel was founded by an Austrian, Theodor Herzl, and in the intellectual life in Austria before the Nazi period the Jewish part of the intelligentsia played a key role. The low PDI score for Israel makes intuitive sense for a society that developed the ultraegalitarian kibbutz system. Since 1970, when the IBM data were collected, Israel's population has more than doubled through massive immigration, mainly from cultures much higher in PDI, such as the Arab world and Russia. It is therefore likely that power distances in many sectors of Israeli society have become much higher than the 1970 data suggest.[121] The very low score for Austria is surprising, but the position of Austria becomes clearer if we also take its uncertainty avoidance score into account (that score is quite high; see Chapter 4).[122] The egalitarian ethos in Austria is recognizable in the traditionally strong position of that nation's socialist party.

The historical factors mentioned fill some missing links in the hypothesized causal chain in Exhibit 3.10.

The Future of Power Distance Differences

Impressionistically at least, it seems that dependence on the power of others in a large part of our world has been reduced over the past two generations. Most of us feel less dependent than we assume our parents and grandparents to have been. Moreover, independence is a politically attractive topic. Liberation and emancipation movements abound. Educational opportunities have been improved in many countries, and we have seen that power distance scores within countries decrease with increased education level. This does not mean, however, that the *differences* between countries described in this chapter should necessarily have changed. Countries could all have moved to lower power distance levels without changes in their mutual ranking.

The French sociologist André Béteille wrote in 1969:

> In spite of the great diversity of patterns, certain trends seem to emerge from a consideration of the events of the last hundred and fifty years. Everywhere there seems to have come about a steady erosion in the legitimacy accorded to social inequality. If social inequality continues to exist as a fact, it is no longer accepted by all as a part of the natural order but is challenged, or at least questioned, at every point. . . . The decline of the legitimacy of social inequality did not start everywhere at the same time and has not proceeded equally far in every society. But today there are few societies in the world where an ideology of inequality would be allowed to pass unchallenged. (pp. 366-367)

Béteille's analysis leads to a prediction of a worldwide reduction in PDI. In Chapter 2, Exhibit 2.6 shows what happened to the answers on the PDI questions between 1967-69 and 1971-73. From the three questions on which PDI was based, two indeed pointed to a worldwide decrease in power distance. From the correlated questions, another three pointed in the same direction. However, questions B46 ("How frequently does it occur that employees are afraid to express disagreement with their managers?") and A52 ("How often is your manager concerned about helping you get ahead?") showed significant shifts in the opposite direction—that is, toward larger power distances.

The shift on these questions could be situationally determined: It might be a result of the decrease in IBM's growth rate (fewer actual possibilities for getting ahead) and the unfavorable shift in climate described in Chapter 2. However, even in that case the way different national cultures coped with the situation differed. The phenomenon of the combination of negative and positive shifts in power distance becomes clearer if we consider the countries with large PDI values (49 and over) separately from those with smaller PDI values (40 and under). These data are displayed in Exhibit 3.21 (see the statistical section). It turns out that the increase in fear to disagree was virtually limited to the high-PDI countries; on the other hand, the decrease in the perception of autocratic or persuasive behavior on the part of the manager was virtually limited to the low-PDI countries. The only phenomenon common to both groups was the decrease of respondents' preference for an autocratic or persuasive manager. All in all, the gap between low- and high-PDI countries increased rather than decreased. This was confirmed by Lowe's (1996b) replication of the IBM survey in IBM Great Britain (low PDI) and IBM Hong Kong (high PDI) in 1993: Compared to the original scores of around 1970, the PDI scores had decreased more for Britain (–19 points) than for Hong Kong (–12 points).[123] There is no support yet for a convergence theory according to which all countries move toward a low-PDI stable state. Inequality perpetuates itself (Béteille, 1977, pp. 132 ff.; Kohn, 1969, p. 200).

Following the causal chain in Exhibit 3.10, we can understand the shift to a desire for more equality through the increase in technology, which is indispensable for the survival of an increasing world population and the corresponding increase in education and development of middle classes. However, only in the low-PDI countries did the system seem able to cope with the new middle-class values; in the high-PDI cluster the rigidity of existing structures resisted change, and the shift to less directive relationships was slight, leading to an increase of frustration on the part of the middle strata. It should be no surprise that PDI was ecologically correlated with domestic political violence.

In Chapter 2, I argued that the difference in shifts among the three questions used to compose the PDI makes it undesirable to use the index for describing shifts over time: Such descriptions would represent a summation of heterogeneous elements. The only question suitable for studying shifts from 1968 to 1972 is A54 (the percentage of respondents preferring an autocratic or persuasive manager), which, according to Exhibit 3.21, decreased as much in the high-PDI as in the low-PDI countries.

The preferences for an autocratic or persuasive boss are plotted by employee category and by age bracket in Exhibit 3.22 (see the statistical section). As would be expected (compare Exhibit 3.2), the overall level of preference for an autocratic or persuasive manager differed among employee categories: It was higher for technicians, clerks, and secretaries than for professionals and managers. The less-educated employees liked the autocratic or persuasive boss least when they were young (20-29 age bracket); the professionals and managers liked such a boss least in the middle of their careers, between ages 30 and 50.

The shifts between 1968 and 1972 could be due to an age, a generation, or a zeitgeist effect (see Chapter 1).[124] Exhibit 3.22 shows for this question a combination of an age and a zeitgeist effect, and no generation effect—something like Exhibit 1.9d. The zeitgeist effect varied by education level as well as by age bracket. For the less-educated employees it was strongest among the 20-29 age bracket and disappeared after age 40. The more highly educated employees (managers and professionals) remained in touch with the zeitgeist (trends in society) even after age 50. They reached maturity (in the sense of a low need for

dependence) later in their lives, but as they grew older they remained more flexible.

The IBM data cover only a short, 4-year time span, although that period was marked by historical events (such as the 1968 student revolt in France and the Vietnam War) that affected the zeitgeist. The fact that young people are more sensitive than their elders to the appeal for more equality can be observed in many places in the world, but equally visible are the very different reactions of their environments.[125] Since the IBM surveys in 1973, power distances have been reduced in some countries, but they have not converged across countries. I believe that the picture of national variety presented in this chapter, with its very old historical roots, is likely to survive for a long time, at least for some centuries. A worldwide homogenization of mental programs about power and dependence, independence, and interdependence under the influence of a presumed cultural melting-pot process is still very far away, if it will ever happen.

One may try to develop a prediction about longer-term changes in power distance by looking at what could happen to the underlying forces identified in this chapter. Of the factors shown to be most closely associated with power distance (latitude, size, and wealth), the first is immutable. As to the second, size of population, one could argue that small and even large countries will be less and less able to make decisions at their own level. The European Union, the creation of free trade areas elsewhere, and the activities of supranational organizations make us more and more dependent on decisions made above the country level. Fans of "globalization" often forget that it may very well increase power distances worldwide.

The third factor, wealth, will very likely remain unequally distributed. Where national wealth stagnates or decreases, no reduction in power distance is to be expected; where it increases, the move toward concentration of businesses into global actors produces an increase in income inequality between those at the bottom and those at the top. Higher managers in private and privatized public enterprises pay themselves exorbitant salaries and benefits regardless of business results, while at the same time there are political pressures for lowering or even abolishing minimum wage rates—and for increasing groups of marginal immigrants, minimum rates do not exist anyway. The inequality in incomes leads to inequality in rights because the amount of money available for defending private interests, even immoral and illegal ones, far exceeds the amount of money available for defending public interests. Modestly paid civil servants are no match for the superrich citizens they are supposed to control; short of straightforward bribing, money buys lobbying and adviserships. In maintaining the laws, top lawyers who only defend private interests and have no commitment to the truth are paid much more than publicly employed police officers, prosecutors, and judges. All of this suggests for the coming decades an increase in power distance precisely in those Western countries that currently boast equality.

Statistical Analysis of Data Used in This Chapter

Calculating the
Power Distance Index by Country

As shown earlier in the text, PDI scores were computed from three IBM survey questions:[126]

a. *The "employees afraid" question (B46):* Normally, as described in Chapter 2, country scores from IBM data are a mean across seven occupational categories: two categories of managers and five of nonmanagers. As argued earlier in this chapter, for this question exceptionally the answers from *managers* should be excluded, as managers' perceptions of employees' fear to disagree with them are not equivalent to employees' perceptions. The values thus computed are listed in Appendix 2, Exhibit A2.2. The range of means between the least "afraid" country, Austria, and the most "afraid," Guatemala, is $3.64 - 2.34 = 1.30$ points on a scale from 1 to 5, or about one-third of the total scale width; for mean scores across large numbers of responses (about 1,000 for Austria, 100 for Guatemala), such a range is considerable.

b. *The "perceived manager" question (A55):* This time, the data for all seven occupational categories, including those from managers, were used. Managers in this case have described the behavior of *their* bosses, and there is evidence that their perceptions of their bosses' behavior do not differ much from employees' perceptions of their bosses' behavior (Sadler & Hofstede, 1972). The upper part of Exhibit 3.11 lists the distribution of answers over the five categories used for this question (manager type 1, 2, 3, 4, or none of these), by survey round (1967-69 and 1971-73) for the 28 Category 1 countries surveyed in both rounds. It is clear that the change in definition of manager type 4

(democratic to participative) has not influenced the answers very much. We also see in the upper part of Exhibit 3.11 the rank correlations between the "employees afraid" question and the choices of a particular type of perceived manager. In countries where employees are more frequently seen as afraid to disagree with their bosses (lower "afraid" scores), managers are more frequently seen as autocratic and, to a lesser extent, persuasive; managers are less frequently seen as consultative. There are no significant correlations between "employees afraid" and the percentage of those perceiving a democratic, participative, or "none of these types" manager. On the basis of Exhibit 3.11 there should be no problem in averaging the "perceived manager" data for 1967-69 and 1971-73. I used the mean percentage *manager 1 + 2* of both survey rounds as a country measure of perceived manager type (correcting for trend effects in the case of countries surveyed only once, as in the case of the "employees afraid" scores). The combined percentage of the perceived manager 1 + 2 is shown in Exhibit 2.4 to be quite stable over time (stability coefficient .82). The data by country can be found in Appendix 2, Exhibits A2.1 (for Category 1 countries) and A2.4 (for Category 2 countries and Category 3 regions).

c. *The "preferred manager" question (A54):* The lower part of Exhibit 3.11 shows that whereas the perceptions (upper part) were more or less equally distributed over types 2 and 3, preferences concentrated more on type 3. There was, however, a considerable shift between the two survey rounds toward preferring the manager 4 new style (the participative, rather than democratic, manager). In this case a "none of these" category was not included in the questionnaire; everyone was asked to express a preference for one of the four types. The nonresponses (which were treated as invalid) constituted less than 5%.

As with the perceived manager, the country "preferred manager" percentages were rank correlated with country "employees afraid" scores. The preference for a 1967-69 type 3 (consultative) manager was the strongest correlate of "employees less afraid"; all three other types were weakly correlated with "employees more afraid." This effect was much less pronounced in the 1971-73 data, obviously due to the reformulation of manager 4. The correlation coefficients in Ex-

Exhibit 3.11 Spearman Rank Correlations Among Answer Frequencies for Perceived and Preferred Manager, and Employees Afraid

	Type 1	Type 2	Type 3	Type 4	None
A55: Perceived manager					
% choosing in 1967-69	18	30	32	7(d)	13
% choosing in 1971-73	17	28	31	11(p)	13
Correlation with 1967-69	−.62***	−.34*	.60***	.01	−.07
"Employees afraid" 1971-73	−.73***	−.32*	.67***	.25	.15
A54: Preferred Manager					
% choosing in 1967-69	4	23	57	16(d)	
% choosing in 1971-73	3	20	50	27(p)	
Correlation with 1967-69	−.34*	−.31*	.76***	−.28	
"Employees afraid" 1971-73	−.34*	−.31*	.44*	−.03	

NOTE: Preferred and perceived types of managers: 1 = autocratic, 2 = persuasive, 3 = consultative, 4 = (d)emocratic (1967-69) or (p)articipative (1971-73). Mean percentage distributions across seven occupations and across 28 Category 1 countries surveyed twice, and ecological correlations (Spearman rank) with question B46, employees afraid to disagree.
$*p = .05; **p = .01; ***p = .001.$

hibit 3.11 suggest that the preference or lack of preference for a consultative manager in the 1967-69 data can be used as a (negative) measure of power distance, but that 1967-69 and 1971-73 data should not be combined in this case. From a research point of view, the reformulation of type 4 in 1970 was therefore regrettable (but the new formulation was more fashionable in the management literature at that time). As things stood, I did not use the 1971-73 data. The country data can be found in Appendix 2, Exhibit A2.1, separately for manager 1 + 2 (both survey rounds combined), 3A (1967-69), 3B (1971-73), and 4B (1971-73). Only the data in column 3A have been used for computing PDI.

In computing PDI for some countries, missing data had to be filled in. These were extrapolated according to the regression line of the missing variable on the sum or difference of the two other variables. Thus, for example, the missing value for the United States on "employees afraid" is found by drawing the regression line of "employees afraid" scores against the difference (percentage perceived manager 1 + 2) − (percentage preferred manager 3, 1967-69) based on the available country data and finding the point where the U.S. value for the latter difference intersects with this regression line.

Exhibit 3.12 shows the correlations between the three PDI items across individuals, countries, and occupations. The correlations across individuals within homogeneous groups are virtually zero. These individual correlations were computed for the five subpopulations used for developing the 1971 core questionnaire (see Chapter

2). Each of these covered one occupation in one country; sizes varied from 200 to 458 respondents. For the "perceived" and "preferred" manager questions, one difference between the scores used for the individual and the aggregate correlations should be noted. In the individual correlations the scores used for these questions were their mean values on ordinal scales (1-2-3-4); for the perceived manager, the answer "none of these" was treated as invalid and missing. For the perceived manager, substituting percentage manager 1 or 2 with a scale value did not affect the correlations very much. For the preferred manager, however, substituting percentage manager 3 with a scale value *did* change the correlations. For another subpopulation (a test population of 1,075 professionals and technicians from all European countries) a dichotomous variable has been created: preferred manager 3/not manager 3. This "pure" variable correlated .03 with "employees afraid." It does not seem, therefore, that the correlations of the preferred manager would have been much higher had we used the pure variable in all cases.

The correlations of the three questions across the 40 Category 1 countries were stronger than after inclusion of the 10 Category 2 countries and the three Category 3 regions (correlation coefficients are in parentheses in Exhibit 3.12). As described in Chapter 2, these latter 13 cases were added from data that had originally been left out because of small samples. It appears that the decision to leave them out at the time the index was designed was a correct one. The additional data contained more random error, which lowered the

Exhibit 3.12 Product-Moment Correlations Among Scores on Three Questions Composing the Power Distance Index, Across Individuals, Countries, and Occupations

| Pairs of Questions | Correlation of Individual Scores in Five Homogeneous Groups (200-458 respondents) | | | Correlation of Mean Scores Across 40 (53) Countries | | Correlation of Mean Scores Across 38 Occupations |
	Minimum	Maximum	Median			
A × b: B46 × A55 Employees not afraid × perceived manager autocratic/persuasive	−.08	.05	−.05	−.67***	(.44***)	−.77***
A × c: B46 × A54 Employees not afraid × preferred manager consultative	−.11*	.08	.03	.57***	(.53***)	.68***
b × c: A55 × A54 Perceived manager autocratic/persuasive × preferred manager consultative	−.07	.12**	.07	−.54***	(−.45***)	−.69***

NOTE: Country scores are means of mean scores for seven occupational groups. Occupation scores are means of mean scores for three large country subsidiaries (France, Germany, and Great Britain).
$*p = .05; **p = .01; ***p = .001.$

correlations between the PDI questions. The product-moment correlations of the three questions with PDI across the 40 Category 1 countries were −.87, .85, and −.84, respectively; across the 53 countries + regions the coefficients were still −.80, .78 and −.84, so that the PDI values for the added cases are still quite reliable.

Power Distance Index Scores by Occupation

The occupational PDI scores were calculated averaging between the occupational means for the PDI questions for France, Germany, and Great Britain.[127] For occupations surveyed in both 1967-69 and 1971-73 the data for "employees afraid" and the "perceived manager" were obviously the mean of the two survey scores.

Two problems had to be overcome in the calculation. First, half of the occupations were surveyed only since 1970, after the text of question A54, the preferred manager 4, had been changed. The scores, however, should be based on the 1967-69 version of question A54. Fortunately, the 15 occupations surveyed twice (4 were surveyed in all three countries only in 1967-69) showed a very clear, somewhat curvilinear relationship between 1967-69 and 1971-73 scores on question

A54. The best-fitting curve has been used to transpose, for those occupations for which no 1967-69 data existed, the 1970-73 data into 1967-69-style scores.

Second, I have argued above that the answers by *managers* on question B46 (are employees afraid to disagree with their managers?) should be taken with a grain of salt—they were excluded for the cross-country comparison. This is because, given the way question B46 is formulated, it deals with employees in general, who for the nonmanagerial respondents are their colleagues, but for the managers are their subordinates. The answers to this question by managers therefore are not equivalent to the answers by nonmanagers, although they probably also reflect, to some extent, the managers' own power distance with their bosses. The difference between managers' and nonmanagers' responses on question B46 was determined through comparison of the regression lines between A55-A54 and B46 for managerial occupations with those for nonmanagerial occupations. It appears that the two regression lines ran about parallel, but that for a given score (A55-A54) managers tended to score about .16 points higher on B46 than did nonmanagers, indicating that they perceived less fear to disagree. To make managers' scores comparable with nonmanagers' scores, I have therefore reduced all scores on B46 for managers by .16 points when calculating the occupational PDI. For the final occupational PDI values, the correlations of the three questions with PDI across the 38 occupations were $-.85$, $.89$, and $-.93$, respectively; these strong correlations justified the calculation of occupational Power Distance Indexes.

Straight Replications of the IBM Survey

Elite alumni from the Salzburg Seminar surveyed by Hoppe (1990). See the three columns under "Hoppe, elites" in Exhibit 3.13. Valid returns ranged from 30 for Malta to 183 for Great Britain, for an almost 60% return rate. The respondents of SSAS averaged 5 more years of formal education than the IBM employees. More than two-thirds held doctorates or master's-level degrees. About 60% worked in public service or similar environments: municipal, national, or international governments; academia; or not-for-profit or semigovernmental organizations. The mean age of the Salzburg alumni was 43, against 32 in the IBM survey population, and 19% were women, against 8% in IBM. Across the 18 overlapping countries, the Salzburg alumni on average scored a PDI of 14.7, nearly 30 points lower than the IBM employees from the same countries. This was predictable from Exhibit 3.2: Inside IBM, the categories of professional workers scored a mean PDI of 22, and the managers of professional workers a mean of 8. The PDI scores of the countries in the two studies are correlated with $r = .67**$. However, surprisingly the IBM scores for the Uncertainty Avoidance Index were even more strongly correlated with Hoppe's PDI scores, $r = .71**$, rho $= .81***$. This has to do with the particular selection of countries covered by Hoppe's study; I will come back to it in Chapter 4.

Hoppe's data can be used to compute best estimates for the scores on the IBM scale, through regression of the IBM scores on the Salzburg scores (the fifth column in Exhibit 3.13). For 13 countries the Hoppe scores are within 10 points of the IBM scores; the outliers are Austria (+32), Portugal (−23), France (−21), Belgium (−15), and Denmark (+14). The selection and self-selection criteria for elites participating in the Salzburg seminars may have differed by country; there was also an amount of co-optation, past participants recommending (the courses to) future participants with similar values. The Hoppe study provided an estimated PDI score for Malta (MAT): 56.

Commercial airline pilots surveyed by Helmreich and Merritt (1998). See the three columns under "Merritt, pilots" in Exhibit 3.13. Valid returns ranged from 39 for Argentina to 8,654 for the United States. Across the 21 overlapping countries, the pilots scored an average PDI of 67.8, 18 points above the IBM employees from the same countries.[128] The PDI scores of the countries in the two studies were correlated with $r = .76***$; the rank correlation that reduces the influence of outlying scores was even stronger, rho $= .81***$.[129] Again the data can be used to compute best estimates for the scores on the IBM scale, through regression of the IBM scores on the pilots' scores (far right-hand column in Exhibit 3.13). For 19 countries the pilots' scores are within 15 points of the IBM scores; the outliers are Malaysia (−36), the Philippines (−25), and Germany (+24). The pilots' study provided an estimated PDI score for Morocco (MRC): 70.

Results of Other Survey Studies Significantly Correlated With PDI

Students scoring Gordon's Survey of Interpersonal Values. Exhibit 3.14 lists product-moment correlations of the mean country scores for five of the six scales of this test for male students in 17 countries and for three of the scales for women in 11 countries (Gordon, 1976, pp. 4, 55) with the four IBM indexes as well as for GNP/capita (1970 values).[130] In three cases (Conformity and Support for men, Support for women) the highest correlations are with GNP/capita: negative for Conformity, positive for Support. In a multiple regression only GNP/capita remains as an explaining factor. Three significant links with PDI are stronger than those with GNP/capita: a negative correlation with Independence for men and a negative correlation with Independence plus a positive correlation with Conformity for women. Independence for women is the only value to show a significant second-order relationship: a negative correlation with uncertainty avoidance (remarkably, the zero-order correlation with UAI was weakly positive!). For men, Benevolence and Recognition show significant relationships with Masculinity; we will come back to these findings in Chapter 6.

Reader's Digest data on attitudes of the public toward younger and older people. The questions were as follows: "Considering young people today between 16 and 25 years old, would you say that, in the main, you have a favorable or an unfavorable impression of them, or neither one nor the other?" (3-point answer scale). "And what about people over 45, would you say that, in the main, you have a favorable or unfavorable impression of them or neither one nor the other?" (same scale; Reader's Digest, 1970, p. 202, questions 22, 23). The comparison between the Reader's Digest data and the four indexes plus GNP/capita for 15 coun-

Exhibit 3.13 Power Distance Index Scores Computed From Surveys of Elites (Hoppe, 1990) and Airline Pilots (Helmreich & Merritt, 1998): Same Questions, Same Formulas as Used in IBM

Countries in Order of Original PDI	Original PDI	Hoppe, Elites			Merritt, Pilots		
		n	Raw PDI	Regressed[a]	n[b]	Raw PDI	Regressed[a]
Malaysia	104				801 (1)	99	68
Philippines	94				120 (1)	100	69
Mexico	81				167 (1)	100	69
Brazil	69				467 (2)	125	84
France	68	47	24	47			
Turkey	66	72	67	71			
Belgium	65	47	28	50			
Portugal	63	49	11	40			
Greece	60	41	48	61	65 (1)[c]	63	47
Korea (South)	60				176 (1)	105	72
Taiwan	58				499 (2)	90	63
Spain	57	75	25	48			
Malta		30	40	56			
Japan	54				51 (1)	62	46
Italy	50	183	38	55	517 (1)	72	52
Argentina	49				39 (1)	89	62
South Africa	49				238 (1)	44	35
United States	40	157	3	36	8,654 (10)	52	40
Netherlands	38	139	−1	34			
Australia	36				640 (2)	36	31
Germany	35	142	8	39	228 (1)	84	59
Great Britain	35	194	4	37	557 (1)[d]	59	44
Switzerland	34	57	14	42	211 (2)	65	48
Finland	33	59	7	38			
Norway	31	64	−22	22	216 (1)	17	19
Sweden	31	71	−7	31	443 (1)	36	31
Ireland	28	48	6	38	420 (1)	55	42
New Zealand	22				485 (1)	41	33
Denmark	18	41	−4	32	243 (1)	29	26
Austria	11	74	15	43			
Morocco					60 (1)	103	70
United Arab Emirates					145 (1)	—[e]	
Total n		1,590			15,454 (36)		
Mean (elites)	42.4		14.7[f]	42.4			
SD (elites)	17.3		21.2[f]	11.5			
Mean (pilots)	49.4					67.8[g]	49.4
SD (pilots)	22.9					29.1[g]	17.3
Correlation with IBM							
PDI							
Product-moment			.67**			.76***	
Spearman rank			.66**			.81***	
UAI							
Product-moment			.71**		.46*		
Spearman rank			.81***		.50*		

a. Predicted from regression of IBM scores on raw new scores.
b. Number of airlines participating shown in parentheses.
c. Greek Cyprus.
d. British pilots in Hong Kong.
e. No data published.
f. Without Malta.
g. Without Morocco.
*p = .05; **p = .01; ***p = .001.

Exhibit 3.14 Product-Moment Correlations of Student Scores on Gordon's Survey of Interpersonal Values With Four IBM Indexes and GNP/Capita

SIV Scale	Zero-Order Correlation With				
	PDI	UAI	IDV	MAS	GNP/Capita
Men, 17 countries					
Conformity	.80***	.34	−.76***	.44*	**−.81*****
Independence	**−.79*****	−.17	.41	−.54*	.55*
Support	−.70***	.14	.68***	−.09	**.78*****
Benevolence	.10	−.49*	−.29	**−.59****	−.13
Recognition	.28	.11	.17	**.50***	.06
Women, 11 countries					
Conformity	**.82****	−.21	−.57*	.34	−.74**
Independence	**−.90*****	.21	.60*	−.29	.81**
Support	−.77**	.28	.86**	.02	**.95*****

NOTE: The countries are as follows: men + women, HOK, IND, ITA, JPN, NET, PHI, SPA, TAI; men only, AUL, BRA, CAN, DEN, FIN, GER, SAF, SWE, USA; women only, IDO, KOR, THA. GNP/capita data are for 1970. Highest first-order correlations are printed in **boldface**. Multiple regression did not produce any significant second-order correlations except for independence for women, which shows a *negative* second-order correlation with UAI (total variance explained R^2 = .81 for PDI, .91 for PDI + UAI).
*p = .05; **p = .01; ***p = .001.

tries (all except Luxembourg, for which I have no data) is shown in Exhibit 3.15. The correlation between attitudes toward young people and UAI is highly significant, $r = -.77***$. The correlation with PDI is a by-product of this. However, the stepwise regression with the four indexes shows that the Individualism Index contributes to an explanation of the variance (in a sense *opposite to* the zero-order correlation); after we have controlled for UAI, more "individualistic" countries are more critical of younger people. The attitudes toward *older* people correlate somewhat with both PDI and UAI ($r = -.56**$ for both, but the correlation with PDI is marginally stronger): Favorable attitudes toward older people tended to be found in countries with smaller power distances and weaker uncertainty avoidance.

De Bettignies and Evans's (1977) data on the average age of top executives in 11 countries. The data are listed in the last column of Exhibit 3.15. The strongest correlation is with PDI ($r = .75**$); in the stepwise regression there is no significant second-order correlation, so the correlation with UAI is just a by-product of the correlation with PDI.[131]

Indexes at the National Level Significantly Correlated With PDI

Income inequality. In the 1980 edition of *Culture's Consequences* I showed significant correlations of PDI with three measures of income in-

equality that are now dated.[132] The *Human Development Report 1996* listed the ratio of highest to lowest 20% of incomes (1981-93) for 40 countries from the IBM set (United Nations Development Program, 1996). Some of the data are difficult to believe (such as 4.7 for India and Pakistan and 4.9 for Indonesia), but I used them as they were published. The highest/lowest 20% ratio correlated $r = .42**$ with PDI, more so than with 1993 GNP/capita ($r = -.37*$); see Exhibit 3.16. That exhibit also contains data on the average compensation ratio between the chief executive officers of major companies and their ordinary workers for 12 countries, published by the Dutch newspaper *NRC Handelsblad* (Den Tex, 1992). This ratio correlated with rho = .72** with PDI and rho = −.69* with 1991 GNP/capita.

Aviation accident rates. Exhibit 3.17 shows aviation accident rate data published by Ramsden (1985; 18 countries, 1973-84) and data read from Weener and Russell (1994; 33 countries, 1959-92), and their correlations with the first four IBM indexes and with 1980 GNP/capita. Because of the extreme accident scores for some countries, Spearman rank correlations were used. For both data sets the correlations with GNP/capita and IDV (negative) and with PDI (positive) are all highly significant. However, GNP/capita, IDV, and PDI are also strongly intercorrelated. In a multiple regression, only GNP/capita remained as an explaining variable for accident rates; neither IDV nor PDI made an independent additional contribution.

Exhibit 3.15 Attitudes of the Public Toward Younger and Older People, and Average Age of Top Business Executives, Versus Four IBM Indexes and GNP/Capita

Countries in Order of UAI	Reader's Digest Survey % Favorable Attitudes Toward		de Bettignies and Evans (1977)
	Younger People	Older People	Average Age of Top Executives
Portugal	40	55	
Belgium	42	64	58
France	40	51	59
Spain	48	58	
Italy	28	45	54
Austria	49	61	
Germany (F.R.)	48	75	57
Finland	64	78	51
Switzerland	56	63	
Netherlands	45	56	56
Norway	64	69	52
United States			55
Great Britain	55	65	55
Ireland	69	70	
Sweden	67	71	50
Denmark	64	70	52
Mean of all countries	52	63	54
Zero-order product-moment correlation with			
PDI	$-.65**$	$-.56**$	$.75**$
UAI	$-.77***$	$-.56**$	$.70**$
IDV	.16	.12	.24
MAS	$-.35$	$-.22$	$.59*$
GNP/capita 1970	.35	.38	$-.13$
R^2 with 4 indexes + GNP/capita 1970	.74	.44	.68
Order of indexes in stepwise regression, cumulative R^2 and sign of coefficient			
1	.59 – UAI	.31 – PDI	.57 + PDI
2	.72 – IDV		

SOURCES: Reader's Digest (1970, p. 191) and de Bettignies and Evans (1977, p. 286).

Balance of power in government. I dichotomized the 50 countries according to their PDI values (25 above and 25 below 59) and divided them into those with "balanced power" and those with "periods of unbalanced power." The "balanced power" countries had government systems, at least since 1975, in which the majority of the population could elect periodically the persons or parties it wanted in power, whereby history has shown that peaceful changes in the ruling coalition could indeed take place. These are 24, mostly wealthy countries. The other 26 had at least one period of unbalanced government power (auto-cratic or oligarchic) since 1975, with or without revolutions or periods of political instability. The classification is shown in Exhibit 3.18. With chi-square = 18.1*** and one degree of freedom, the association between balanced power in government and PDI is highly significant. As the "balanced power" countries in 1970 were nearly all wealthy and the others poor, 1970 GNP per capita was an even better predictor of balanced power than PDI. However, in the past decades more unbalanced power countries have become wealthy, which suggests that it was not wealth per se but small power distance that accounted for the

(Text continued on page 132)

Exhibit 3.16 Comparison of IBM Indexes With Data on Income Inequality

Countries in Order of PDI	HDR 96 Highest/ Lowest 20% of Households	NRCH 92 CEO vs. Worker Compensation
Malaysia	11.7	
Guatemala	30.0	
Panama	29.9	
Philippines	7.4	
Mexico	13.6	
Venezuela	10.3	59
Indonesia	4.9	
India	4.7	
Nigeria (WAF)	9.6	
Singapore	9.6	
Brazil	32.1	62
France	7.5	16
Hong Kong	8.7	37
Colombia	15.5	
Belgium	4.6	13
Zimbabwe (EAF)	15.6	
Peru	10.5	
Thailand	8.3	
Chile	18.3	
South Korea	5.7	
Spain	4.4	15
Pakistan	4.7	
Japan	4.3	11
Italy	6.0	
South Africa	19.2	
Jamaica	8.1	
United States	8.9	25
Canada	7.1	12
Netherlands	4.5	11
Australia	9.6	
Costa Rica	12.7	
Germany	5.8	
Great Britain	9.6	17
Switzerland	8.6	
Finland	6.0	
Norway	5.9	
Sweden	4.6	9
New Zealand	8.8	
Denmark	7.1	
Israel	6.6	
Correlation with		
PDI	.42**	.72**
UAI	.29	−.07
IDV	−.39*	−.37
MAS	−.05	.43
GNP/capita 91		−.69*
GNP/capita 93	−.37*	

NOTE: HDR 96 = *Human Development Report 1996* (United Nations Development Program, 1996)); NRCH = *NRC Handelsblad* (Den Tex, 1992). Correlations with HDR are product-moment (Pearson); with NRCH, rank (Spearman).

Exhibit 3.17 Aviation Accident Rates Versus IBM Indexes and GNP/Capita

Countries in Order of PDI	Accident Rates per Million Departures	
	1973-84	1959-92
Malaysia		3.9
Philippines		9.8
Mexico		4.1
Venezuela	4.1	2.4
Egypt (Arab countries)	13.4	
Ecuador		13.8
Indonesia		6.4
India	5.5	14.8
Brazil	4.4	7.0
France	1.2	3.5
Hong Kong		4.1
Colombia	27.5	10.4
Turkey	17.4	12.9
Belgium	1.9	
Peru		13.0
Thailand		9.8
Chile		8.9
Portugal		3.8
Greece		3.7
South Korea		12.0
Taiwan		12.9
Spain		5.1
Pakistan		11.8
Japan	0.6	2.8
Italy	1.8	2.3
Argentina	3.5	8.2
South Africa		4.6
United States	1.2	2.2
Canada	2.9	2.5
Netherlands	2.5	3.7
Australia	0.3	
Germany	1.3	1.7
Great Britain	1.3	3.6
Switzerland		3.5
Sweden	0.5	1.8
Denmark		4.0
Spearman rank correlation with		
PDI	.68***	.47**
UAI	.27	.16
IDV	−.69***	−.62***
MAS	−.15	−.27
GNP/capita 1980	−.75***	−.85***
Significant variables in multiple regression	GNP/capita 1980	GNP/capita 1980

SOURCES: For 1973-84, Ramsden (1985); for 1959-92, diagrams in Weener and Russell (1994).
*p = .05; **p = .01; ***p = .001.

Exhibit 3.18 Classification of 50 Countries According to Balance of Power in Government Systems and Power Distance Scores

	PDI	
Number of Countries With	11-58	60-104
Balanced power since 1975	20[a]	4[b]
Periods of unbalanced power since 1975	5[c]	21
Chi-square	18.1***	

a. AUL, AUT, CAN, COS, DEN, FIN, GBR, GER, IRE, ISR, ITA, JAM, JPN, NET, NOR, NZL, SPA, SWE, SWI, USA. (For country abbreviations, see Exhibit 2.1.)

b. BEL, FRA, GRE, POR.

c. ARG, IRA, PAK, SAF, TAI.

maintenance of balanced power. I shall come back to this issue in Chapter 5.

Transparency International's Corruption Perception Index. The CPI 1998 table covered 85 countries, of which 50 overlapped with the IBM set (if we use IBM East Africa index scores for Kenya, West Africa for Nigeria, and Arabic-speaking countries for Egypt). Exhibit 3.19 (lower right) shows that across these 50 countries the strongest correlation of CPI is with (1997) GNP/capita, $r = .82***$. As the CPI values are higher for cleaner countries (1 = totally corrupt, 10 = totally clean), this means that across all countries, corruption as perceived by the TI sources is primarily a matter of poverty. However, the stepwise multiple regression pattern shows that after GNP/capita, three of the IBM indexes still make independent contributions to the variance in CPI: PDI, MAS, and UAI, in this order, and all three with negative signs.[133] So the Individualism Index is the only one that does not play a role in the explanation of corruption perceptions, after the influence of wealth has been controlled for.

The correlation with wealth suggests that it should be useful to study wealthy and poor countries separately. I divided the 50 countries at the limit of $10,000 GNP/capita for 1997, which means that all five East Asian dragons (Japan, Hong Kong, South Korea, Singapore, and Taiwan) are included in the wealthy category. For 26 wealthy countries (left-hand side of Exhibit 3.19), wealth (1997 GNP/capita) no longer plays a role in the multiple regression pattern: The first contribution is by UAI, and a sizable second-order contribution is made by PDI. I will come back to the role of UAI in Chapter 4. The strongest of all correlations in Exhibit 3.19 is between CPI and Hoppe's PDI scores (see Exhibit 3.13), $r = -.86***$ across 18 countries. Hoppe's scores, as we have seen, are based on the answers on the

IBM questions by elites from developed countries in the 1980s (17 out of the 18 countries belong to the "wealthy" group; only Turkey is part of the "poor" category in Exhibit 3.19).

For 17 poor countries (top right-hand part of Exhibit 3.19) the corruption index is no longer correlated with PDI at all. The correlations are weaker here; the highest is with 1997 GNP/capita ($r = .46*$), but there is a sizable second-order contribution of the Masculinity Index, to which I will come back in Chapter 6.

PDI Versus Eight Geographic, Economic, and Demographic Indicators

In Chapter 2, I identified nine geographic, economic, and demographic indicators of countries for which it is likely that they show systematic relationships to the value systems revealed by the survey data. One (ROS) was so strongly correlated with national wealth (GNP) that it could be dropped, which left eight indicators. An analysis of the literature and commonsense reasoning allows us to hypothesize the following relationships of the seven indicators with PDI (for their definitions, see Exhibit 2.9):

- *Wealth* (GNP) should be negatively correlated with PDI because wealth goes together with the growth of middle strata in society, which can form a bridge between the powerful and the powerless (Adelman & Morris, 1967, pp. 151, 255).

- *Economic growth,* past and future (EGP and EGF), could be related to PDI in different ways. Some hold that the relationship should be positive because authoritarian coordination of the economy is necessary for growth (Tugwell, 1972). Some hold that the relationship should be negative because authoritar-

Exhibit 3.19 Transparency International Internet Corruption Perception Index 1998 Versus IBM Indexes, for 26 Wealthy and 24 Poor Countries

Wealthy Countries 1997 GNP/ Capita > $10,000			Poor Countries 1997 GNP/ Capita < $10,000		
Country	PDI	CPI98	Country	MAS	CPI98
Denmark	18	10.0	Chile	28	6.8
Finland	33	9.6	Costa Rica	21	5.6
Sweden	31	9.5	Malaysia	50	5.3
New Zealand	22	9.4	South Africa	63	5.2
Canada	39	9.2	Peru	42	4.5
Singapore	74	9.1	Uruguay	38	4.3
Netherlands	38	9.0	Brazil	49	4.0
Norway	31	9.0	Jamaica	68	3.8
Switzerland	34	8.9	Salvador	40	3.6
Australia	36	8.7	Turkey	45	3.4
Great Britain	35	8.7	Mexico	69	3.3
Ireland	28	8.2	Philippines	64	3.3
Germany	35	7.9	Guatemala	37	3.1
Hong Kong	68	7.8	Argentina	56	3.0
Austria	11	7.5	Thailand	34	3.0
United States	40	7.5	Egypt (ARA)	53	2.9
Israel	13	7.1	India	56	2.9
France	68	6.7	Pakistan	50	2.7
Portugal	63	6.5	Kenya (EAF)	41	2.5
Spain	57	6.1	Ecuador	63	2.3
Japan	54	5.8	Venezuela	73	2.3
Belgium	65	5.4	Colombia	64	2.2
Taiwan	58	5.3	Indonesia	46	2.0
Greece	60	4.9	Nigeria (WAF)	46	1.9
Italy	50	4.6			
South Korea	60	4.2			

Product-moment correlation across 26 wealthy countries with

UAI	−.78***
PDI	−.55***
IDV	.47**
GNP97	.45*
MAS	−.33*

Order of contribution in stepwise regression

1	−UAI	$R^2 = .60$
2	−PDI	$R^2 = .71$

Product-moment correlation across 18 countries (17 wealthy) with Hoppe's PDI scores   −.86***

Product-moment correlation across 24 poor countries with

GNP97	.46*
MAS	−.43*

Order of contribution in stepwise regression

1	GNP97	$R^2 = .21$
2	−MAS	$R^2 = .37$

Product-moment correlation across all 50 countries with

GNP97	.82***
IDV	.71***
PDI	−.70***
UAI	−.38**

Order of contribution in stepwise regression

1	GNP97	$R^2 = .67$
2	−PDI	$R^2 = .73$
3	−MAS	$R^2 = .77$
4	−UAI	$R^2 = .81$

Exhibit 3.20 Product-Moment Correlations and Multiple and Stepwise Regression Across Countries of PDI Scores With Eight System-Level Indicators

	Zero-Order Correlations With PDI Scores Across		
Indicator	All 50 Countries	28 Poorer Countries	22 Wealthier Countries
GNP	−.64***	−.09	−.18
EGP	−.08	−.14	.43*
EGF	.07	.07	.07
LAT	−.67***	−.34	−.21
POP	.19	.09	.54**
PGR	.54**	.21	−.24
PDN	−.00	−.13	.22
ORS	−.30*	.27	.29
Squared multiple correlation with first seven R^2	.56	.19	.48
Order of indicators in stepwise regression, cumulative R^2, and sign of coefficient			
1	.43 −LAT	None	.30 +POP
2	.51 +POP		
3	.56 −GNP		

NOTE: For definitions of the indicators, see Exhibit 2.9. The 22 countries are ARG, AUL, AUT, BEL, CAN, DEN, FIN, FRA, GBR, GER, GRE, IRE, ISR, ITA, JPN, NET, NOR, NZL, SPA, SWE, SWI, and USA.

ian systems do not innovate (Hagen, 1962, p. 79). Dick (1974) has found empirically for 59 less-developed countries a curvilinear relationship between economic development and the concentration of power in a few hands: The authoritarian states do either very well or very poorly. To the extent that the authoritarianness of the state is reflected in the PDI, the relationship between EGP/EGF and PDI should also be curvilinear.

- *Geographic latitude* (LAT) should be negatively related with PDI because, impressionistically, there is more power inequality in warm countries.

- *Population size* (POP) should be positively related with PDI because larger social systems mean by definition a larger distance between the top and the bottom.

- *Population growth* (PGR) is stronger in poor countries, so we would expect it to be positively correlated with PDI, but less strongly than wealth (GNP).

- *Population density* (PDN) may be positively related with PDI because in densely popu-

lated countries people are forced to interact more, which could mean a need for authority to settle conflicts.

- *Organization size* (ORS; size of the local IBM subsidiary) should be negatively related with PDI because wealthier countries had larger IBM subsidiaries; also, the causality could be partly reversed because greater size enforces decentralization (Pugh, 1976, p. 74; Pugh & Hickson, 1976, p. 88).

The actual correlations of PDI with the eight indexes are shown in Exhibit 3.20. I have computed these across all 50 countries, but also separately across the 28 economically less-developed countries (1970 GNP/capita less than $1,000) and the 22 more-developed ones. For all 50 countries together, we find significant correlations in the expected direction with GNP, LAT, and PGR; the remaining correlations are negligible. If we divide the countries into poorer and wealthier ones, the correlations fall, which is no wonder, as we deliberately restrict the range of one of the two strongest correlates. The poor/wealthy split does not

Exhibit 3.21 Shifts in Mean Scores of PDI Questions From 1967-69 to 1971-73, Separately for High and Low PDI Countries

		Mean Score[a]		Corre-sponding Shift in Index[b]	Number of Countries		
Question Number	Question	1967-69	1971-73		Total Surveyed Twice	Shifting in Same Direction[c]	Countries Shifting in Opposite Direction
For countries with PDI = 49-94							
B46	Employees afraid to disagree	2.92	2.69	+	17	13*	BRA, PAK, TUR
A55	Perceived manager, % 1 + 2	52.7	51.6	0(−)	15	9	Many
A54	Preferred manager, % 1 + 2	31.5	27.5	−	15	11**	SPA
For countries with PDI = 11-40							
B46	Employees afraid to disagree	3.42	3.40	0(+)	9	5	Many
A55	Perceived manager, % 1 + 2	42.9	38.8	−	14	13**	ISR
A54	Preferred manager, % 1 + 2	22.3	17.9	−	14	11*	AUT, FIN

a. Expressed in percentages for A54 and A55 and in points on a 5-point scale for B46.
b. Sign of shift multiplied by sign of correlation between this question and PDI.
c. Tested with the sign test, one-tailed.

show any clear curvilinear relationships with GNP. Other curvilinear relationships were not studied; I wonder whether the data are robust enough for such refinement.

If we compare the pattern of zero-order correlations across 50 countries for PDI with the intercorrelation pattern of the eight indicators (Exhibit 2.11), we see that PDI is associated with the cluster of wealth, latitude, and slow population growth and not with the cluster of economic growth and population density. The fact that the indicators are correlated among themselves makes the use of a stepwise multiple regression technique desirable. I limited this to the first seven indicators because ORS scores were available only for the 40 Category 1 countries. The seven indicators contribute to the prediction of PDI in the following order (see the lower part of Exhibit 3.20):

1. Latitude (LAT), $R = .64$, $R^2 = .43$
2. Population size (POP), $R = .71$, $R^2 = .51$
3. Wealth (GNP), $R = .75$, $R^2 = .56$

The squared multiple correlation coefficient R^2 indicates the fraction of the total variance ex-

plained. The other four indicators do not add substantially to the prediction of PDI.

Trends in PDI

Exhibit 3.21 splits the data for the top three questions in Exhibit 2.6 into high- and low-PDI countries. A significant shift in both groups was found only for question A54 (decrease of preference for manager 1 or 2). In actual fact, PDI was not computed from the percentage preferring manager 1 or 2 but from the percentage preferring manager 3 in the 1967-69 formulation, reversing the sign. As this measure was available only for one survey round, it could not be used to show a trend over time. The descriptions of managers 1 and 2 did not change from 1967-69 to 1971-73.

A significant decrease for question A55, the percentage perceiving their managers as 1 or 2, was found only in the low-PDI countries. The high-PDI countries showed a significantly lower mean score for question B46 ("How frequently does it occur that employees are afraid to express disagreement with their managers?"), which means that their employees had become *more* afraid.

Exhibit 3.22. Answers to Question A54 (Percentages of Respondents Preferring an Autocratic or Persuasive Manager) for Five Large Categories of IBM Employees, Worldwide Data, by Age Bracket, in Two Survey Rounds

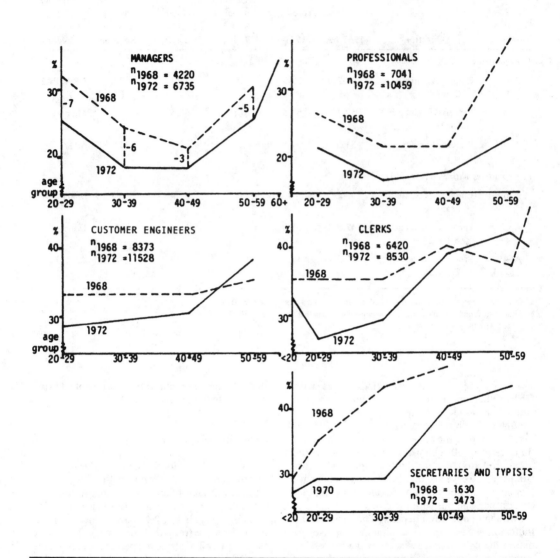

In Exhibit 3.22 the answers on question A54 (percentages preferring manager 1 or 2, world totals) have been plotted against age brackets for five large categories of employees. Percentages in the 1967-69 survey round are indicated by dotted lines; those in the 1971-73 round appear as solid lines.

In this kind of diagram an age or seniority shift would produce an overlap of the 1968 and 1972 curves: Respondents in, for example, the 30-39 age bracket in 1972 would score exactly like those who were in the 30-39 age bracket in 1968. A generation shift would produce a horizontal displacement of the curves by 4 years: The 30-39 age bracket of 1968 would have become a 34-43 age bracket in 1972, but it would have maintained its score level. A zeitgeist shift would manifest itself in a vertical shift of the curve from 1968 to 1972, affecting all age brackets equally.

Exhibit 3.22 actually shows a combination of zeitgeist and age. The zeitgeist effect (see the dotted vertical lines for the "managers" as an example) varied somewhat with age: It was smaller for the very young (clerks and secretaries under age 20). For the (relatively few) respondents over 50, the more highly educated employees (managers and professionals) still lowered their preference for manager 1 or 2 from 1968 to 1972, but the less-educated employees (technicians and clerks) showed a small *increase* rather than a reduction.

Notes

1. For the historians, see Moore (1966); for the anthropologists, see Bohannan (1969, chap. 11) and Balandier (1972, chap. 4); for the sociologists, see Bendix and Lipset (1966), Lenski (1966), Parkin (1971), and Béteille (1977).

2. Boulding (1978, pp. 240 ff.) argues that status and wealth lead to power. In fact, he distinguishes among (1) threat power, or force; (2) exchange power, or wealth; and (3) integrative power, related to legitimacy and status. Not all status and not all wealth leads to power, however; see Runciman (1969).

3. See Lenski (1966, p. 86).

4. The Christian Church, however, did not escape the force toward status consistency itself. Monks' orders have collectively become wealthy and powerful. A study by George and George (1966) has shown that of 2,489 official Roman Catholic saints and beatified living between the 1st and 20th centuries, 78% belonged to the upper classes of their time and only 5% to the lower classes.

5. "Le pacte fondamental substitue . . . une égalité morale et légitime à ce que la nature avait pu mettre d' inégalité physique entre les hommes, et . . . pouvant être inégaux en force ou en génie, ils deviennent tous égaux par convention et de droit" (Rousseau, 1762/1972, pp. 122-123). See also Bottomore (1976).

6. Béteille (1977, pp. 10, 166) has argued that this does not resolve the problem, because natural inequalities acquire meaning only by a process of evaluation that is culturally defined; it differs among societies and among epochs in history.

7. Even as an ideological statement it was weak because it did not take into account that equality imposes restrictions on freedom and vice versa.

8. After having written this, I discovered that Parkin (1971) had preceded me with the same paraphrase.

9. See Blais (1974) and Playford (1976).

10. See Sauvy (1966, pp. 80 ff.), Desplanques (1973), and Berthoud (1976).

11. See Srinivas (1969) and Béteille (1977, pp. 28 ff.).

12. This does not exclude the simultaneous existence of a complementary radical value system that opposes the existing inequalities (Parkin, 1971, pp. 81 ff.).

13. In addition to this subsection, I will treat more aspects of inequality in organizations in Chapter 8.

14. A number of my own studies on power and control in organizations have been collected in a book titled *Uncommon Sense About Organizations: Cases, Studies, and Field Observations* (Hofstede, 1994b); these show the multiple forces that compete in influencing organizational processes.

15. Evan (1977) suggested that hierarchical structure is negatively related to organizational effectiveness. However, he did not take the cultural environment into account (although he referred to the need for it).

16. See Crozier (1964, p. 160); Hofstede (1967, pp. 9 ff.); Mulder, Ritsema van Eck, and De Jong (1971); and Luhmann (1975, p. 111).

17. Regarding parent-child relationships, see Levinson, Price, Munden, Mandl, and Solley (1962) and Kakar (1971).

18. Even Stinchcombe (1965, p. 181), a prominent U.S. sociologist, related the nature of the relationship between superiors and inferiors solely to the ideology of superiors, not of inferiors.

19. La Boétie's modern compatriot Godelier (1978), without reference to his intellectual ancestor, affirms: "The power of domination consists of two indissoluble elements whose combination constitutes its strength: Violence and consent. At the risk of shocking a certain number of readers, I would go so far as to say that, of these two components of power, the stronger is not the violence of the dominant, but the consent of the dominated to their domination" (p. 767). Boulding (1978) has argued that "it is the images of roles in the minds of the human race that give them [the roles] their power and nothing else" (p. 248).

20. Mathematically, power distance could be represented by a ratio as well as by a difference, but as the "extents" involved can be measured only in very approximate terms, this distinction is not relevant. A ratio,

however, corresponds better with Blais's (1974) term *slope*, which he uses in a way similar to my use of *power distance*.

21. Results obtained with the early version in six countries have been published in Sadler and Hofstede (1972). Results obtained with the later version in eight countries have been collected by Schaupp (1973, chap. 4).

22. The dependence, counterdependence, and interdependence mechanisms are illustrated in a case study titled "Confrontation in the Cathedral" based on a school incident in Lausanne, Switzerland, in 1972 (Hofstede, 1994b, chap. 11).

23. For evidence, see Sadler and Hofstede (1972, p. 50) and Hofstede (1974b, p. 16).

24. See Glaser (1971, pp. 96-98).

25. Inkeles (1969) has constructed a "modernity scale" based on the answers of survey respondents in six developing countries and shows that across individuals in these countries, "modernity" relates to educational level. Every year longer in school leads to 2 to 3 points of gain on a modernity scale of 0 to 100. In our case the theoretical length of the PDI scale is 300 points; a gain of 18 points per year on a 300-point scale means 6 points' gain per year on a 100-point scale. Lower power distances are one aspect of Inkeles's modernity. PDI, however, is an aggregate, not an individual index.

26. This is in spite of the correction of managers' scores for B46 described in the statistical section.

27. The last two of these studies started from an interest in mental health and showed that among less-educated, lower-status people there was also a greater frequency of mental health problems (compare Chapter 4).

28. Kohn's data for mothers also show a class effect and a country effect but not an interaction between the two, as for the fathers.

29. Item B61, "Most employees in industry prefer to avoid responsibility, have little ambition, and want security above all," was also taken from Theory X. This item was not correlated with PDI but with uncertainty avoidance ($r = -.31*$). In a later book, published posthumously, McGregor (1967, p. 78) recognized the link between his "theories" and people's basic values.

30. The data per country were published in the first edition of *Culture's Consequences* (Hofstede, 1980a, fig. 3.12). Exceptionally in this case, I combined countries into groups (such as Belgium plus France) and I accepted a minimum cell size of seven respondents.

31. The only other PDI item included was "employees afraid to disagree," which correlated only weakly (rho = .27, not significant) between IMEDE and IBM. But, as argued earlier, managers' answers to this question are not equivalent to nonmanagers' answers.

32. Hoppe (1998, tab. 2.2) reports .76***, but this is the Spearman rank correlation.

33. Translations of the questionnaire were used in ARG, BRA, GER, ITA, KOR, MEX, and TAI.

34. The F scale is evidently not the proper instrument for measuring norm authoritarianism across countries. Its validity as a test for individuals within in the United States has also been disputed (Ray, 1976).

35. According to Inglehart (1997, p. 393), the data added were from ARG, AUL, CAN, FIN, JPN, KOR, MEX, NOR, SAF, SWE, USA, Hungary, Iceland, Northern Ireland, and Russia (from the town of Tambov only). I did not find, however, any comprehensive report on the results for the first (1981-82 and beyond) survey round across all these countries. Information about the questionnaire used in the European countries was found in Harding and Phillips (1986) and in Halman and Vloet (1994); information about results for these countries was found in Stoetzel (1983), Halman (1991), and Ester, Halman, and De Moor (1993).

36. The wholesale extension to so many countries raises questions about the quality of some of the data; certain published figures are hardly credible, suggesting errors of understanding, translation, and data handling and a lack of critical data cleaning. I have coped with this problem by using Spearman rank rather than Pearson product-moment correlations when the two would produce different results; this reduces the effects of outlying scores.

37. Across the nine countries from the 1981-82 round the dominant variable had become (1990) GNP/capita, $r = .76**$.

38. For the 1981-82 round the ratio "preference for freedom" divided by "preference for equality" could be read from a graph in Stoetzel (1983, p. 78). This ratio ran from about 1 in Spain (equal preference) to about 3 in Great Britain (freedom three times as popular as equality). The ranks of the freedom/equality ratio for the nine countries surprisingly did not correlate at all with PDI ($r = .02$), but correlated strongly with IDV ($r = .84**$).

39. Inglehart's (1997) first factor, "well-being versus survival," was primarily correlated with IDV. A stepwise regression showed a sizable second-order correlation with MAS and a weaker third-order correlation with PDI, in the sense that large PDI went with "survival" goals and small PDI with "well-being" goals. See Exhibit 5.18.

40. The other concepts were "anger," "courage," "fear," "laughter," "peace," "truth," "punishment," "crime," "knowledge," "progress," "success," "death," "defeat," "love," "sympathy," and "trust."

41. These countries were CAN, CHL, FIN, GER, IND, KOR, MAL, NZL, NOR, PAK, PER, POR, SAF, TUR, USA, VEN, Wales (for GBR), and Zimbabwe (for EAF).

42. These countries were AUL, GBR, GER, GRE, HOK, IND, ISR, NZL, SAF, USA, British West Indies, and Zimbabwe.

43. Furnham (1993) had rank correlated his country "just" and "unjust" scores with my four indexes across the 10 countries, but as in the case mentioned earlier in this chapter, again his results differ somewhat from what I get with the same calculation: "just" × PDI, Furnham rho = .75*, Hofstede rho = .80**; "unjust" × PDI, Furnham rho = .92**, Hofstede rho = .81**; "unjust" × IDV, Furnham rho = −.51*, Hofstede rho = −.52

(ns). For my 12-country set I used product-moment (Pearson) correlations, as the data sets do not show strong outliers. Country "just world" means correlated positively with PDI ($r = .66^*$) and also positively with country "unjust world" means ($r = .64^*$). Country "unjust world" means correlated positively with PDI ($r = .73^{**}$) but even more strongly negatively with GNP/capita ($r = -.81^{**}$ for 1990 data).

44. Williams, Satterwhite, and Saiz (1998) used the Gough and Heilbrun Adjective Checklist, a collection of 300 adjectives used for the description of persons. The psychological importance of each of the 300 adjectives was rated separately on a 5-point scale. Sample sizes were between 60 and 147 per country, equally divided between the genders; questionnaires were translated into 12 other languages from the original English.

45. The 300 adjectives were condensed into those related to the Big Five personality traits and into those related to five transactional analysis ego states. The condensation was based on the attribution of the adjectives to the traits and states by U.S. judges.

46. These countries were ARG, AUL, CHL, FIN, GBR, GER, HOK, IND, JPN, KOR, NET, NOR, PAK, POR, SIN, USA, VEN, and WAF (for Nigeria). Williams et al. (1998) had not been aware of the IBM data for Korea and Nigeria.

47. This statement about power is based on the work of Anderson (1972) and Martyn-Johns (1977, p. 350), who dealt in particular with the Javanese (Indonesian) situation.

48. Obedience correlated with both PDI ($r = .64^{***}$, rho $= .65^{***}$) and 1990 GNP/capita ($r = -.62^{***}$, rho $= -.67^{***}$). In the first round of the survey, across the 12 overlapping countries for which results were published in Halman (1991, p. 340), the rated importance of "hard work" was also positively correlated with PDI ($r = .76^{**}$) and "independence" also negatively ($r = -.75^{**}$).

49. Several other items correlated primarily with 1990 GNP/capita: "determination" (rho $= .67^{***}$), "imagination" (rho $= .42^*$), and "thrift" (rho $= .38^*$) positively; and "religious faith" (rho $= -.65^{***}$) and "good manners" (rho $= -.49^{**}$) negatively. Affluence leads to a stress on determination, imagination, and thrift (!— but see also Chapter 7) but less stress on religious faith and good manners.

50. Across the 26 countries of the 1990-93 WVS only "joyriding" showed a similar correlation with PDI ($r = .58^{**}$). The rejection of lying and buying stolen goods correlated with long-term orientation. The other behaviors were probably too specific to be comparable across these very diverse societies; they produced no significant meaningful correlations.

51. These countries were AUL, GBR, GER, GRE, HOK, IND, ISR, NZL, SAF, USA, British West Indies, Ciskei (one of the black homelands within predemocratic South Africa), and Zimbabwe.

52. Rank correlation rho $= .83^{***}$. I substituted the PDI score of Jamaica for the British West Indies, and of East Africa for Zimbabwe. Without these two countries,

the correlation PWE × PDI across 10 countries is $r = .79^{**}$, rho $= .85^{**}$. Furnham et al. (1993) surprisingly report for this case $r = .91^{***}$.

53. A classic motion picture, *Four Families*, produced by the National Film Board of Canada in 1959 with expert advice from Margaret Mead, shows the relationships between parents and small children in more or less matched farm families in India, France, Japan, and Canada. Audiences to whom I showed the film (and to whom I did not mention the power distance scores) were able to rank the four countries correctly on power distance just on the basis of the parent-child relationships pictured in the film.

54. The countries in this study were GER, IDO, KOR, PHI, SIN, TAI, THA, TUR, and USA.

55. See Huisman and De Ridder (1984) and Huisman (1985). The researchers collected data from 11 countries: BRA, Cameroon, CAN, COL, GBR, GER, IDO, JPN, KEN, NET, and USA. Surveying so many entrepreneurs in such diverse countries was impressive, but the results were not. Hardly any conclusions other than the obvious were drawn. Pompe et al. from the University of Groningen in a reanalysis did some essential data cleaning; among other things, they eliminated CAN and USA because in these countries respondents were from larger companies not matched with the others.

56. Material in this subsection is largely based on Hofstede (1986a).

57. Paradoxically, across countries in the IBM data, PDI and years of education for a given occupation are *positively* correlated (Appendix 2, Exhibit A2.1, question A56). This is because in the poorer, higher-PDI countries there is a relative oversupply of people with extensive formal schooling for these jobs.

58. The values of the Nobel Index were as follows: SWI, 2.62; DEN, 1.43; AUT, 1.19; NET, 1.15; SWE, 1.13; GER, .71; GBR, .67; USA, .41; FRA, .40; FIN, .29; BEL, .26; ITA, .10; JPN, .01; NOR, .00. The lack of prizes for Norwegian scholars granted by a Nobel Committee composed of Swedish judges is remarkable.

59. About the influence of the French educational system on the maintenance of large power distances see, for example, Schonfeld (1976); Marceau (1977); Maurice, Sellier, and Silvestre (1978); and d'Iribarne (1989). Educational levels in France determine the legal status of employees: The higher-educated become *cadres* and the lower-educated become *non-cadres*, and this remains a lifelong distinction.

60. Another indicator used by Gaspari and Millendorfer (1978, p. 199) was the average number of nurses per doctor in a country. Across 15 countries this correlated with PDI with rho $= -.52^*$, but as it correlated even more with UAI and IDV, I shall deal with it in Chapter 4 rather than here.

61. An earlier impressionistic study by Granick (1962) of French, Belgian, German, and British executives seen from an American viewpoint had found least centralization in Britain (PDI 35). French, Belgian, and German companies were more centralized, but in Germany (PDI 35) the central authority tended to be a *team*

and thus was less concentrated; in France (PDI 68) and Belgium (PDI 65), the central authority was always a *person*.

62. Across the 39 banks the correlation between mother-country PDI and the Aston measure of centralization of authority was $r = .55***$.

63. For the factor scores, see the first edition of *Culture's Consequences* (Hofstede, 1980a, fig. 3.13). I recalculated the correlations and took rs instead of rhos. From the other factors, only the first, "conformity versus variety," showed a significant correlation, $r = -.61***$ with IDV; see Chapter 5.

64. Self-descriptions always contain a lot of wishful thinking. See Table 5 in Sadler and Hofstede (1972) and its analysis.

65. The countries in this study were AUL, BRA, EAF (Uganda), FIN, GBR, HOK, IRA, JPN, KOR, NET, NIG, POR, SAF, and USA.

66. The other items were as follows: (2) "A subordinate does consistently good work"; (3) "A subordinate does consistently poor work"; (4) "Equipment or machinery in your department needs replacement"; (5) "Another department does not provide the resources or support you require"; (6) "There are differing opinions within your department"; (7) "You see the need to introduce new work procedures in your department"; (8) "Evaluating the success of new work procedures."

67. Just before I completed work on the manuscript for this book, I received a draft version of an article by Smith, Peterson, Schwartz, and the Event Management Team Project (2000) reporting results for 42 countries, newly including from the IBM set AUT, CHL, COL, FRA, GER, GRE, IND, IDO, ISR, ITA, JAM, MEX, NOR, PAK, PHI, SIN, SPA, SWE, THA, TUR, and Zimbabwe ($n = 35$, including the old set). The country means across all 64 "importance" scores (8 events × 8 sources of guidance) correlated with PDI with $r = .53***$, indicating a strong acquiescence response set. The authors subsequently partialed out this "culture mean" and found correlations with PDI for the individual sources of guidance to have become much lower; only the correlation with "my subordinates" remained significant ($r = -.33*$). This is no miracle!

68. "Supervise" is part of a set of exercises developed by Bernard M. Bass and distributed by a network, the International Research Group on Management (IRGOM).

69. Unfortunately, Cascio's (1974) results were not published by country but by country cluster. Across six clusters, the percentage most satisfied with a participative superior and the cluster's mean PDI rank correlated with rho = $-.78$ (which for this small number of cases stays below the .05 significance level).

70. See Appendix 5, Exhibit A5.2. For those who read Russian, see also Gaskov (1985).

71. Graves (1971, 1972) compared data from small samples of managers within a multinational corporation (not IBM) in Great Britain (lower PDI) and France (higher PDI). In spite of the common corporation subculture, the attitudes and communication patterns of the managers differed sharply. In Britain, the organization tended to be held together by ties of personal or general loyalty (Graves, 1971, p. 83). The French tended to have a clear conception of authority: They either accepted authority absolutely or rejected it entirely (Graves, 1972, p. 54).

72. Shane, Venkataraman, and Macmillan (1995) show not correlations but regression coefficients for various explanatory models.

73. The countries were AUT, BEL, DEN, FIN, FRA, GBR, GER, GRE, IRE, ITA, NET, NOR, POR, SPA, SWE, and SWI. European Media and Marketing Survey (EMS) data are copyright Inter/View International, Amsterdam, and are used in this book with permission.

74. The countries in this study were BEL, DEN, FRA, GBR, GER, ITA, NET, SPA, SWE, and SWI. In each country, 300 questionnaires were mailed; usable returns varied from 69 in Italy to 120 in Great Britain, an average overall response rate of 31%; the response rates per country did not follow any recognizable cultural pattern.

75. The countries were AUL, BRA, EAF (Uganda), FIN, FRA, GBR, GER, HOK (+ Macao), IND, IDO, IRA, JPN, KOR, MEX, NET, NIG, POR, SIN, SAF, SPA, and USA.

76. Van de Vliert and Van Yperen (1996) have suggested that hot climates, a factor not considered by Peterson et al. (1995), explain role overload better than PDI; Peterson and Smith (1997), in a reaction, have maintained their original explanation. As we will see later, PDI and geographic latitude (which is associated with ambient temperatures) are correlated.

77. The set was extended to Australia by Clark and McCabe (1970) and to seven Southeast Asian countries by Redding and Casey (1976).

78. In Chapter 1, I used another section of Haire, Ghiselli, and Porter's (1966) study as an illustration of the reverse ecological fallacy and of ethnocentric research. In fact, the same applies to the "management practices" section. The eight items have been combined into four subscales without proof that the items making up a subscale were correlated across countries. For countries only subscale scores, not item scores, were reported.

79. Correlation coefficients for all four subscales with the IBM indexes (but not with GNP/capita) were published in the first edition of *Culture's Consequences* (Hofstede, 1980a, fig. 3.15). The other subscales, "sharing information and objectives," "participation," and "internal control," were primarily correlated with GNP/capita (more "modern" viewpoints for wealthier countries). Two of the subscales showed a significant second-order effect for UAI; see Chapter 4.

80. Haire et al. (1966, p. 24) signaled the same paradox when looking at the country mean scores for their subscales: On "capacity for leadership and initiative" the majority in nearly all countries scored "traditional"; on sharing information and objectives, participation, and internal control, the majority scored "modern."

81. Haire et al.'s (1966) other items were formulated in terms of interaction between superiors and subordinates and are therefore more pragmatic, closer to "values as the desired" countries. The same paradox applies in the case of employee participation in decision making (ideological) versus being consulted by one's boss (pragmatic). In the present case the negative correlation can be explained as follows: When answering about "the average human being" and "most people," respondents unconsciously select a reference group. In societies more affected by caste and class differences, the managers who answered the question are more likely to have taken as a reference group their own class; others are no part of their world. The more this is the case, the more an optimistic picture of humankind's capacities will result, and vice versa. However, the opposite applies to pragmatic rules about the interaction between superiors and subordinates.

82. Members of the IDE consortium come from BEL, DEN, FIN, FRA, GBR, GER, ISR, ITA, NET, NOR, SWE, and (former) YUG.

83. See also an article by the IDE International Research Group in *Organization Studies* (1981b) and my review of the IDE International Research Group's book reporting its study (Hofstede, 1982).

84. Drenth and Groenendijk (1984, pp. 1211 ff.) criticized my power distance measure for this reason.

85. In an article written around 1980 but published in 1985, Drenth recognized the lack of validation of the IDE project results in other studies but did not offer a conclusive explanation.

86. This was the same company d'Iribarne (1989) studied—see later in this chapter. Globokar was a collaborator of d'Iribarne's institute.

87. The access factor corresponds to Aron's (1965) distinction between constitutional-pluralistic and monopolistic regimes and to Cutright's (1967) Political Representativeness Index.

88. Haniff (1976) has shown, for example, that social policy outputs, as measured by the expenditure of funds for citizen welfare, across 125 sovereign states could be predicted from wealth and literacy rather than from political variables.

89. This information is based on a map published in the Dutch newspaper *NRC Handelsblad,* September 20, 1999. The CDU-led states in the South were Baden-Württemberg, Hessen, Saarland, Bavaria (where the CDU is called CSU) and the former East German states of Thüringen and Sachsen. The SDP-led states in the North were Rheinland-Pfalz, Nordrhein-Westfalen, Niedersachsen, Schleswig-Holstein, Bremen, and Hamburg and the former East German states of Mecklenburg-Vorpommern, Sachsen-Anhalt, Berlin, and Brandenburg (the latter in fact was led by a CDU-SPD coalition).

90. The countries were AUL, BEL, CAN, DEN, FRA, GBR, GER, GRE, IRE, ITA, JPN, NET, NOR, POR, SPA, SWE, and USA.

91. Inglehart's data were partly from the 1981-82 European Values Survey, partly from later Euro-

barometer surveys, the latest from 1985. He included data for Argentina, Mexico, and South Africa. I excluded South Africa because it produced 25% of revolutionary answers (this was the apartheid period) and Argentina and Mexico because they were so much poorer than the other countries; if I include them, the highest correlation for the percentage revolutionary answers is with 1980 GNP/capita ($r = -.78**$) before PDI ($r = .72**$).

92. The countries were the same set minus AUL, NOR, and SWE but including AUT, FIN, and SWI.

93. Stinchcombe (1965, p. 171) has listed an intuitive ranking of some countries or regions according to their means of resolving political conflict: Scandinavia, Britain, United States, France, Mexico. This follows perfectly the PDI sequence.

94. See Figure 3.19 in the statistical section of Chapter 3 in the first edition of *Culture's Consequences* (Hofstede, 1980a, p. 150).

95. Louis de Bettignies (1976) has written a case study about the upheaval in (high-PDI) France when a plant manager was indicted for negligence after a fatal accident at his plant.

96. Bégué's (1976) data are shown in the first edition of *Culture's Consequences* (Hofstede, 1980a, fig. 3.17).

97. The figures published were as follows: GRE, 19%; ITA, 29%; GBR, 35%; BEL, 35%; POR, 37%; FRA, 38%; SPA, 41%; NOR, 45%; DEN, 47%; SWE, 54%; FIN, 58%; SWI, 61%; NET, 65%; AUT, 65%; and GER, 68%. Aside from the $r = -.67**$ correlation with PDI there were significant zero-order correlations with wealth (1990 GNP/capita, $r = .66**$) and with UAI ($r = -.49*$), but in a stepwise multiple regression only PDI contributed significantly to the percentage recycled paper.

98. The CPI can be found on the World Wide Web at http://www.gwdg.de/~uwvw/icr.htm.

99. Lambsdorff cites his sources as follows: *The World Competitiveness Yearbook* 1998, 1997, and 1996; Political Risk Services (in Syracuse, New York) 1998; assessments by Political & Economic Risk Consultancy (Hong Kong), 1998 and 1997; Gallup International, Global Risk Service (DRI/McGraw-Hill), 1998, 1997, and 1996; the World Bank's *World Development Report, 1997;* and EIU 1998.

100. Examples are discussed in Hofstede (1983a, pp. 16-17) and Maruyama (1996).

101. Lord Acton made this statement in a letter to Bishop Mandell Creighton dated April 5, 1887.

102. The great Belgian historian Pirenne (1939, p. 397) also saw the Roman Catholic Church as a historical continuation of the Roman Empire. Swanson (1967), across 41 countries and provinces, demonstrated a relationship between the kind of regime at the time of the Reformation and the adoption or rejection of Protestantism.

103. See Wertheim (1956, pp. 194 ff.).

104. Across the 17 wealthier countries, the Pearson (product-moment) correlation of the accident rates with

IDV was marginally stronger than with 1980 GNP/capita ($r = -.68**$ and $r = -.65**$, respectively). However, the Spearman rank correlation coefficients favored GNP/capita (rho = $-.59**$ and rho = $-.68**$, respectively), and in view of the occurrence of extreme values in the variables, this is the more reliable measure.

105. Just before this volume went into production, Soeters and Boer's (2000) study of cultural factors in military aviation accidents appeared. As in the civilian case, these researchers found IDV to be the most strongly correlated cultural dimension. Using their data, I included GNP/capita (which they had not done). Across 14 NATO countries, accident ratios in the period 1988-92 correlated with IDV with $r = -.55*$, 1990 GNP/capita $r = -.53*$. Across 11 NATO countries, accident ratios for 1991-95 correlated with IDV with $-.84**$, 1990 GNP/capita $r = -.87***$. After the percentage of technical failures was controlled for, the latter correlations became IDV $r = -.894***$, GNP/capita $r = -.890***$. So in the military case the influences of IDV and GNP/capita were of about equal strength; national wealth was a less dominant factor than in the civilian case.

106. See Myrdal (1968, p. 2136) and Bandyopadhyaya (1978).

107. See Dahl and Tufte (1974, p. 87).

108. Stavig and Barnett (1977) demonstrated across 75 nations that one of the measures of domestic conflict between 1948 and 1968, which we had found to be related to PDI, also correlated with the country's population size; the same was true for *foreign* conflict. This fits with the contribution of population size to the variance in PDI.

109. The PDI scores of course also reflect idiosyncrasies of the country's particular sample of IBM respondents (nonrepresentativeness for the differences between the populations of their countries at large), and the measurements contain their share of random error.

110. As this is written, an English translation of d'Iribarne's *La Logique de l'honneur* is forthcoming. A Dutch version appeared in 1998 and a German version in 2000.

111. Another three-country typology including France was presented in the early 20th century in an essay by the Spanish philosopher Salvador de Madariaga (1928, p. 11). From his personal experience of living and studying in these countries, de Madariaga compared the "national characters" of France, England, and Spain and suggested that the "psychological centre of gravity" for the French lay in thought and intellect (represented by *le droit,* the right); for the English, in action (represented by *fair play*); and for the Spaniards, in passion (*el honor*). Both d'Iribarne and de Madariaga attribute "honor" to their own cultures.

112. In one of my classes for French managers a participant remarked, "Les cadres ont la logique de l'efficacité, les non-cadres de la contestation" (Cadres think in terms of efficiency; non-cadres in terms of protest).

113. For William Graham Sumner (1840-1910), the founder of American sociology, employer and employee "as parties to a contract are antagonistic," and to say that they "are partners in an enterprise is only a delusive figure of speech" (quoted in Guillén, 1994, p. 33). This is a long way from the Dutch logic about employer-employee relations, and also from the Japanese.

114. Barzini (1983), in an anecdotal way, has also illustrated the historical continuity in the national cultures of a number of countries: France, Germany, Great Britain, Italy, the Netherlands, and the United States.

115. This was the response of the French newspaper *Libération* (May 7, 1999).

116. Others have made the same point. In the 19th century, the French sociologist le Play showed the effects of inheritance laws on population; see Pitts (1968, p. 86). Differences in the inheritance system also played a role in the lack of integration between Czechs and Slovaks in former Czechoslovakia that led to the split of the country in 1989. The Czechs had single heirs, whereas the Slovaks divided inheritance among children of both genders (Musil, 1993, pp. 485-486). The younger sons in Czechia went to the cities and developed Czech industry; in 1939, Czechoslovakia ranked fifth among industrial nations in the world.

117. McEvedy and Jones (1978) have published population growth curves for all parts of the world. The ratios of population 1975/1700 for various parts of Europe on the basis of their data are as follows: European Russia, 8.0; Scandinavia plus Finland, 7.3; Netherlands, 6.8; Great Britain plus Ireland, 6.4; Germany, 6.1; Greece, 6.0; Belgium plus Luxembourg, 5.7; Switzerland, 5.2; Italy, 4.3; Spain, 4.3; Portugal, 4.0; Austria, 3.0; and France, 2.4. The North clearly grew much faster than the South.

118. Heginbotham (1975) in the Indian state of Tamil Nadu identified four different and conflicting "cognitive models of organization" from which both the traditional Indian and the British colonial model stress vertical relationships.

119. Nicaragua and Honduras are even poorer, but—for that very reason—their IBM subsidiaries were too small to be included—see Exhibit 2.1.

120. On Costa Rica, see Pendle (1976, pp. 139, 161) and Harrison (1985, pp. 55-56). There are historical reasons for the exceptional values of Costa Ricans. The country is said to have been populated mainly by Spanish Jews who had been forced to embrace Catholicism; it no longer has a large native Indian population as does, for example, Guatemala.

121. The political assassination in 1995 of Prime Minister Yitzhak Rabin has broken the low power distance consensus rule that "Israelis don't shoot at Israelis." In July 1998 a prominent longtime member of the Israeli Labor Party, Ori Orr, himself of European (Ashkenazi) origin, caused a national uproar by criticizing the later immigrants, the Sephardim of North African and Middle Eastern descent, especially Israel's large community of Moroccan Jews, who, he said, lacked "the

curiosity to know what's happening around them and why it happened. . . . The problem is I can't speak with these people like I speak with others who are more Israeli in their character. . . . They interpret every legitimate criticism as driven by ethnicity" (quoted in *International Herald Tribune,* August 1-2, 1998, p. 4).

122. Austria is the only country in which IBM employees rated themselves on question B46 as *less* afraid to disagree with their bosses than these bosses rated them. In Switzerland, employees and their bosses broke even in this respect.

123. Lowe (1996b) did not publish separate results for the three PDI questions.

124. Theoretically, the age effect could also be due to seniority in IBM. For three large employee groups, I checked cross-tabulations of the preferred type of manager against age group and seniority category; in all three, the age effect was stronger than the seniority effect, so that we may assume that physical age, rather than length of service with the company, explained the differences in type of manager preferred.

125. Lederer (1982) compared studies of authoritarianism among adolescents in Western Germany and the United States between 1945 and 1978-79 and found that over this period authoritarianism in both countries had decreased, but much more in Germany than in the United States: In 1945 the Germans were more authoritarian than the Americans; in 1978-79, they were less so. Social upheaval after the lost war explains the stronger values shift in the German case. In the IBM study around 1970, PDI was 35 for West Germany and 40 for the United States. Georgas (1990) compared values about hierarchical parent-child relations in Greek families, both in urban (Athens) and in rural environments, and found that the values of the 18-year-old adolescent sons and daughters had shifted away from hierarchy in both cases, but only in the urban environment did the parents' values show some shift.

126. The detailed calculation of the PDI for the 40 Class 1 countries can be found in Hofstede (1977b).

127. For details, see Hofstede (1977b).

128. Helmreich and Merritt (1998) counted 22 overlapping countries. They compared Greek Cyprus to IBM Greece and Hong Kong (British pilots) to IBM Great Britain, which I consider reasonable; but they also compared Morocco to IBM West Africa, which is incorrect. IBM West Africa was a cluster of Nigeria, Ghana, and Sierra Leone, with a culture completely different from the North African Maghreb countries to which Morocco belongs.

129. The Hoppe and Merritt replications overlap for six countries only. Across these, their intercorrelation is $r = .36$, rho $= .58$, *ns.*

130. Israel was omitted in both cases because its samples were small (10 and 15 respondents). The other samples were all larger than 20 (some as large as 1,000). Unfortunately, scores on individual items from the scales were not published, so we are forced to commit a "reverse ecological fallacy" (see Chapter 1).

131. Due to a calculation error, in the first edition of *Culture's Consequences* I reported that the strongest correlation of de Bettignies and Evans's age data was with UAI, and both this study and the conceptually related Reader's Digest study were dealt with in the UAI chapter (Hofstede, 1980a, fig. 4.12).

132. These measures were published by Kravis (1960), Kuznets (1963), and Bégué (1976).

133. After this was written, Husted (1999) published an article in which he correlated the 1996 Transparency International Corruption Perception Index with 1994 GNP/capita and the four IBM indexes, across 44 countries. Husted's results were virtually identical to mine.

4

■

Uncertainty Avoidance

Summary of This Chapter

The second dimension of national culture found in the data has been labeled *uncertainty avoidance*. Uncertainty about the future is a basic fact of human life with which we try to cope through the domains of technology, law, and religion. In organizations these take the form of technology, rules, and rituals. Uncertainty avoidance should not be confused with risk avoidance. The term is borrowed from Cyert and March's book *A Behavioral Theory of the Firm* (1963).

The countries from the IBM study could each be given an Uncertainty Avoidance Index (UAI) score, which differs from the PDI score described in Chapter 3, although for European and Western countries PDI and UAI tend to be correlated. UAI was derived from country mean scores or percentages on three survey questions dealing, respectively, with rule orientation, employment stability, and stress. The same index cannot be used for distinguishing occupations, nor does it apply to gender differences. It was correlated, however, with the mean age of the IBM respondents in the subsidiary.

The major part of this chapter is devoted to a validation of the UAI scores against other data. First, they were correlated with other questions in the IBM survey and with UAI scores computed in straight replications of the IBM research on other populations. Important correlations were found with national anxiety levels as computed from national medical statistics by Lynn, and negative correlations were found with various measures of subjective well-being. Next, UAI scores were correlated with country scores on a number of other cross-national studies of values on a variety of survey populations. The correlation pattern found has been integrated into a picture of the "uncertainty avoidance norm" as a value system held by the majority of a country's middle class.

Origins and implications are shown of UAI differences in several areas: the family; schools and educational systems; "need for achievement," as measured in children's stories from 1925 by McClelland; work and organization; consumer behavior; political systems and legislation; religions; and games and theory development. Correlations were computed of country UAI scores against geographic, economic, and demographic indicators. Correlation patterns differ strongly between wealthy and poor countries. For wealthy countries, UAI is correlated positively with past economic growth and negatively with the age of the country's present political system. The historical roots of uncertainty avoidance differences are explored. The index has been remarkably stable over the past decades: Although uncertainty avoidance levels do fluctuate over time, the differences between countries on which the index was based are robust. UAI differences are not expected to disappear in the foreseeable future.

The Concept of Uncertainty Avoidance

Time, Future, Uncertainty, and Anxiety

A basic fact of life is that time goes only one way. We are caught in a present that is just an infinitesimal borderline between past and future. We have to live with a future that moves away as fast as we try to approach it, but onto which we project our present hopes and fears.[1] In other words, we are living with an uncertainty of which we are conscious.

Extreme uncertainty creates intolerable anxiety, and human society has developed ways to cope with the inherent uncertainty of living on the brink of an uncertain future. These ways belong to the domains of technology, law, and religion. I use these terms in their broad senses: *Technology* includes all human artifacts; *law,* all formal and informal rules that guide social behavior; *religion,* all revealed knowledge of the unknown. Technology has helped us to defend ourselves against uncertainties caused by nature; law, to defend against uncertainties in the behavior of others; religion, to accept the uncertainties we cannot defend ourselves against. The knowledge of a life after death is the ultimate certainty of believers that allows them to face uncertainties in this life.[2] The borderline between defending ourselves against uncertainties and accepting them is fluid; many of our defenses intended to create certainty do not really do so in an objective sense, but they allow us to sleep peacefully.

Different societies have adapted to uncertainty in different ways. These ways differ not only between traditional and modern societies, but also among modern societies. Ways of coping with uncertainty belong to the cultural heritages of societies, and they are transferred and reinforced through basic institutions such as the family, the school, and the state. They are reflected in collectively held values of the members of a particular society. Their roots are nonrational, and they may lead to collective behavior in one society that may seem aberrant and incomprehensible to members of other societies. I will call a behavior *rational* if it consists of activities that "are logically linked to an end, not only in respect to the person performing them but also to those other people who have more extensive knowledge," and *nonrational* if it consists of other activities (the quote is from Italian sociologist Vilfredo Pareto, 1916/1976, pp. 165 ff., 184).[3] What seems rational to an actor may be nonrational to a larger public. What is rational to people sharing the same culture may be nonrational to people not sharing that culture.[4]

Psychologists, especially since World War II and especially in Great Britain and the United States, have devoted much research to personality dispositions that affect individuals' ability to live with uncertainty. The "authoritarian personality syndrome" described in 1950 by Adorno, Frenkel-Brunswik, Levinson, and Sanford has been investigated by many others since.[5] Attitudes correlated with it (at least in the United States) include intolerance of ambiguity, rigidity, dogmatism, intolerance of different opinions, traditionalism, superstition, racism, and ethnocentrism next to pure dependence on authority.

Fromm (1965) has suggested that fascism and Nazism were a result of a need to "escape from freedom," a response to the anxiety that freedom created in societies with a low tolerance for such anxiety. Freedom implies uncertainty in the behavior of oneself and of others. Totalitarian ideologies try to avoid this uncertainty.

We have met the "authoritarian personality" (F-scale) syndrome in Chapters 1 and 3. Kagitçibasi (1970) found that attitudes associated across individuals in the United States were not so associated in Turkey. Cross-cultural studies have found a component of *norm authoritarianism* related to the Power Distance Index, but across cultures, intolerance of ambiguity, dogmatism, and the rest need not be related to PDI. Allport (1954/1979, pp. 395 ff.) described a "prejudiced personality," of which "authoritarianism" was just one of several traits; the others were as follows:

- Ambivalence toward parents (declaring love but showing hate)
- Moralism: stressing conventional virtues
- Dichotomization: dividing people and situations into good and bad, without accepting that they may be both at the same time
- A need for definiteness: simplification in cognition
- Externalization: attributing problems to external causes beyond one's influence
- Institutionalism: devotion to institutions such as clubs, churches, the nation

The present chapter will show that national cultures possess norms for (in)tolerance of ambiguity that are independent of the norms for dependence on authority. In a literature review, Furnham and Ribchester (1995) found that (in)tolerance of ambiguity had been almost exclusively studied at the individual level; they cite the first edition of *Culture's Consequences* (Hofstede, 1980a) as the only source suggesting its cultural variability.[6] Because of its serious social and political consequences, intolerance of ambiguity at the cultural level merits at least as much attention as such intolerance at the personality level. My basic proposition, supported in the present chapter with a wealth of research data, is that on the national cultural level, tendencies toward prejudice, rigidity and dogmatism, intolerance of different opinions, traditionalism, superstition, racism, and ethnocentrism all relate to a norm for intolerance of ambiguity that I have measured and expressed in a national Uncertainty Avoidance Index.

Uncertainty Avoidance in Organizations

The term *uncertainty avoidance* derives from U.S. organization theorists Richard M. Cyert and

James G. March, who use it in their book *A Behavioral Theory of the Firm* (1963). Organizations, they argue, avoid uncertainty in their environments in two major ways. First,

> they avoid the requirement that they correctly anticipate events in the distant future by using decision rules emphasizing short-run reaction to short-run feedback rather than anticipation of long-run uncertain events. They solve pressing problems rather than develop long-run strategies. Second, they avoid the requirement that they anticipate future reactions of other parts of their environment by arranging a negotiated environment. They impose plans, standard operating procedures, industry tradition, and uncertainty-absorbing contracts on that situation by avoiding planning where plans depend on prediction of uncertain future events and by emphasizing planning where the plans can be made self-confirming by some control device. (p. 119)

In the same way human societies at large use technology, law, and religion to cope with uncertainty, organizations use technology, rules, and rituals. Technology (such as replacing people with computers) obviously creates short-term predictability as to outcomes (perhaps at the cost of longer-term risks of complete breakdown, which are often overlooked). The use of technology looks extremely rational, but it hides implicit nonrational value choices.

Rules are the way in which organizations reduce the internal uncertainty caused by the unpredictability of their members' and stakeholders' behavior. As Perrow (1972) has noted: "Rules stem from past adjustments and seek to stabilize the present and future" (p. 29); "A multitude of rules and regulations appears to be the very essence of a bureaucracy" (p. 24); "Rules are the scapegoats for a variety of organizational problems" (p. 30). *Bureaucracy* has become something of a bad word, but this is because bad rules are more likely to be noticed than good ones, and rules do hold organizations together. Rules are semirational: They try to make the behavior of people predictable, and as people are both rational and nonrational, rules should take account of both aspects. Good rules lead to the desired outcome if they are obeyed (their rational side) and concur with the values of the people whose behavior they try to influence, which means they are likely to be obeyed (their nonrational side). Bad rules fail on either or both of these criteria.

Bad rules may arise out of differences in values between those who make them and those who have to follow them. In both a Dutch sample and an international sample of company employees, I found people in accounting, planning, and control roles stressing the *form* of information whereas people in operating roles stressed its *content*

(Hofstede, 1994b, chap. 9). Baker (1976) found that scores on a values test set U.S. students majoring in accounting apart from others; accounting majors attributed higher value to being "clean" and "responsible" and lower value to being "imaginative." This suggests that people in accounting, planning, and control roles have a higher need to avoid uncertainty than do others; their scores as students show that they may be self-selected on this characteristic. Therefore, the rules they set may not correspond to other people's needs and values.

Good rules can set energies free for other things; they are not necessarily constraining. Inkson, Schwitter, Pheysey, and Hickson (1970) showed that British executives in more structured organizations (those with more rules) did more innovative work than did executives in less structured ones. Kohn (1971), in a cross-national sample of more than 3,000 U.S. men, showed that employees of more bureaucratic organizations (larger, government, and nonprofit organizations) tended to be more flexible intellectually than employees of less bureaucratic organizations, counter to the public image of bureaucracies.

Rules, on the other hand, may destroy people's autonomous judgment and lead them to do things they would normally consider bad. We can think of the behavior of soldiers at war, but also, for example, of the outcome of Milgram's (1974) classic experiments with obedience to authority. Ordinary U.S. citizens were led to torture others (at least they thought they were doing so) by the mere fact of the experimenter telling them that this was part of the rules of the experiment. In this case the rules protected against the uncertainty of independent judgment. The stronger a culture's tendency to avoid uncertainty, the greater its need for rules.

The authority of rules is something different from the authority of persons. The first relates conceptually to uncertainty avoidance; the second, to power distance. The German expression *Befehl ist Befehl* (an order is an order) refers to the authority of the rule: The person who gives the order is irrelevant, as long as he or she occupies the position to which the rule assigns the giving of orders. The French *bon plaisir* (literally, "good pleasure," used to describe the arbitrary will of the ruler in the 17th century), which Crozier (1964a, p. 222) still found in contemporary French bureaucracies, puts the authority of the person above the system of rules. The first suggests strong uncertainty avoidance; the second, large power distance.

Rituals serve social as well as uncertainty avoidance purposes.[7] The former keep people together; the latter try to control the future. Religions prescribe praying or sacrificing to ensure the season's crop, the healing of disease, or the success of a venture. Unbelievers smile at such practices because they think they know at the rational level that such rituals do not change anything. But this is immaterial: The rituals are functional because they allow the members of that society to continue their lives in the face of otherwise intolerable uncertainty.

Rituals are not limited to primitive societies. They cater to human nature, and there is no evidence of a basic change of human nature in the process of modernization. With our primitive ancestors we share a need for social cohesion and a limited tolerance for uncertainty. We hold infinitely better technological means to defend ourselves against risks, but unfortunately these means themselves always bring new risks; and we still feel the future to be very uncertain indeed. Like the social systems of primitive man, ours have developed their rituals to make uncertainty tolerable.

Anybody can recognize in modern society the rituals in religious, academic, and state ceremonies, in family celebrations, in youth movements, and in countercultures. The ritual elements in business and public organizations are less easily recognized. Social rituals in organizations include business meetings, which have their own liturgy, sacred language, and taboos. Management training programs are initiation rituals for future leaders. Uncertainty-avoiding rituals include the writing and filing of memos and reports, accounting, planning and control systems, computer simulations, and the nomination of experts as persons who are beyond uncertainty.[8]

This chapter will show that the tendency to avoid uncertainty in organizations varies along with the tendency to avoid ambiguities in society at large, which is a major component of national cultures.

Uncertainty Avoidance Is
Not the Same as Risk Avoidance

Many readers of my earlier work have interpreted "uncertainty avoidance" as "risk avoidance"—for example, in business decisions. But *uncertainty avoidance does not equal risk avoidance.* Uncertainty is to risk as anxiety is to fear. Fear and risk are both focused on something specific: an object in the case of fear, an event in the case of risk. Risk is often expressed in a percentage of probability that a particular event may happen. Anxiety and uncertainty are both diffuse feelings. Anxiety has no object, and uncertainty has no probability attached to it. It is a situation in which anything can happen and one has no idea what. As soon as uncertainty is expressed as risk, it ceases to be a source of anxiety. It may become a source of fear, but it may also be accepted as routine, such as the risks involved in driving a car or practicing a dangerous sport.

More than toward an escape from risk, uncertainty avoidance leads to an escape from ambiguity. Uncertainty-avoiding cultures shun ambiguous situations. People in such cultures look for structure in their organizations, institutions, and relationships, which makes events clearly interpretable and predictable. Paradoxically, they are often prepared to engage in risky behavior in order to reduce ambiguities—such as starting a fight with a potential opponent rather than sitting back and waiting. Countries with weaker uncertainty avoidance tendencies demonstrate a lower sense of urgency, expressed, for example, in lower speed limits. In such countries not only familiar but also unfamiliar risks are accepted, such as changing jobs and starting activities for which there are no rules.

Measuring National Differences in Uncertainty Avoidance in IBM

An Uncertainty Avoidance
Index for IBM Countries

In the preceding pages I have argued that coping with the inevitable uncertainties in life is partly a nonrational process that different individuals, organizations, and societies resolve in different ways. The main underlying dimension is the tolerance for uncertainty (ambiguity), which can be found in individuals and which in identical situations leads some individuals to feel more pressed for action than others. This tolerance for uncertainty is partly a matter of individual personality and partly a matter of collective culture. Societies differ in their societal norms (Exhibit 1.5) for uncertainty avoidance, and in a given society's institutions, members are socialized toward that society's norm.

In Chapter 2, I described how three questions in the IBM database were selected to form a country Uncertainty Avoidance Index. The three questions refer to three components of uncertainty avoidance: rule orientation, employment stability, and stress. It is possible that other and perhaps better survey indicators of national levels of uncertainty avoidance can be developed, but I had to use the data available in the IBM archives, and uncertainty avoidance was not a familiar concept to us when we composed the IBM questionnaire in 1967.

The "rule orientation" item in the IBM questionnaire is as follows: "Company rules should not be broken—even when the employee thinks it is in the company's best interests" (B60 in Appendix 1, with a 5-point answer scale from *strongly agree* to *strongly disagree*). The selection of this item was guided by the findings of the Aston group in Great Britain (Pugh, 1976; Pugh & Hickson, 1976; see Chapter 3). The Aston group found, among different organizations in Britain, two strong dimensions of organizational structure: "concentration of authority" (conceptually related to power distance) and "structuring of activities." [9] The item in the IBM questionnaire most closely conceptually related to "structuring of activities" is the one just mentioned.[10]

Disagreement with the rule orientation statement indicates a tolerance for uncertainty: It is acceptable that employees break company rules if they believe this is in the company's interest. The opposite position, agreement with the rule orientation statement, avoids the uncertainty of employees' deciding for themselves whether or not to follow a rule.

The "employment stability" item in the IBM questionnaire is as follows: "How long do you think you will continue working for this company?" Answers are (1) 2 years at the most, (2) from 2 to 5 years, (3) more than 5 years (but I probably will leave before I retire), and (4) until I retire (A43). It had long been noticed that this question showed considerable and consistent differences in answer distributions among countries. What was not evident from the start is that country scores on this question would be correlated with rule orientation country scores, which, however, appeared to be the case ($r = .59***$ across 40 countries; see the statistical analysis section later in this chapter).[11] The link between the two questions is that a low percentage of employees planning to leave within 5 years and a low rule orientation score (which means a strong rule orientation) both indicate a strong uncertainty avoidance norm in a country: Employment stability and rule orientation are two ways of avoiding uncertainty.

There was evidence that the answers on the employment stability question did reflect actual behavior. An unpublished study in IBM showed that across 14 countries, country scores on this question in the 1968 survey of customer engineers correlated highly with 1967 turnover rates among customer engineers.[12]

The "stress" question in the IBM questionnaire is as follows: "How often do you feel nervous or tense at work?" Answers range from (1) I always feel this way to (5) *I never feel this way* (A37). This question was taken from earlier surveys of managers in IBM USA run by the company medical department; it correlated with self-reports on medical symptoms (see the statistical section of this chapter). Lynn and Martin (1995) report that across 22 countries it was correlated with the national normative scores for "neuroticism versus emotional stability," one of three dimensions measured with the Eysenck Personality Questionnaire ($r = .50**$).[13]

The stress question taps a fundamental phenomenon in human life. There is probably no human being who does not feel stressed at times. Stress is a state of mind and body that corresponds to the state of preparation for aggression in primitive humans, released through acts of aggression. When social norms forbid overt aggression, modern humans must cope with stress in different ways.

Stress is a subjective experience. "Stress is in the eye of the beholder. If you think you are under stress, you are under stress" (Pettigrew, 1972). One person may find a particular situation stressful whereas another finds the same situation to be relatively stress-free. However, in spite of its soft, subjective character, stress has hard, objective consequences. Medical studies have shown that stress affects the metabolism of the body.[14] This is not necessarily bad; a certain amount of stress is indispensable for activity, for physical and mental health, and for performance. Satisfying jobs combine stresses with opportunities to release them. In a separate study, I have shown the stress-satisfaction balance across 38 occupations within the IBM World Trade Corporation (Hofstede, 1994a). The occupations that posed risks of physiological and mental disorders were those combining *high* stress with *low* satisfaction.

Physiological and mental disorders related to stress include diseases of the heart and blood vessels, diseases of the stomach and intestines, nervous breakdowns, and disruption of interpersonal relations, in extreme cases leading to suicide.[15] Stress can also lead to a reduction of perceived alternatives in decision making and to the use of negative rather than positive evidence.[16]

Stress reactions are provoked by four kinds of influences:

- The individual's personality, including personal history and traits[17]
- The individual's nonwork, private-life environment[18]
- The individual's work and organizational environment
- The sociocultural, larger environment in which the individual's personality, nonwork life, and the organization in which he or she works are all embedded[19]

In the IBM data we can identify stress differences due to the sociocultural environment (in the form of differences among nationalities) and due to one organizational factor, occupation.[20] The differences in stress due to other organizational factors, to the nonwork environment, and to personality will be treated as random error.[21] This, however, does not mean they are unimportant; they have been the subject of many studies by others.

At the country level, higher mean stress turned out to be associated with stronger rule orientation and greater employment stability, and vice versa. The statistical section of this chapter shows stress, rule orientation, and employment stability forming one common societal "uncertainty avoidance" syndrome. The conceptual link between the stress question and the other two questions is the mean *level of anxiety* in a country. When this is higher, people feel more stressed, but at the same time they try to cope with their anxiety by searching for security, which is visible in both rule orientation and employment stability.[22]

An Uncertainty Avoidance Index for each of the IBM countries has therefore been computed on the basis of the country mean scores for the three questions:

a. Rule orientation: agreement with the statement "Company rules should not be broken—even when the employee thinks it is in the company's best interest" (B60).

b. Employment stability: employees' statement that they intend to continue with the company (1) for 2 years at the most, or (2) from 2 to 5 years; this, of course, taken with a negative sign (A43).

c. Stress, as expressed in the mean answer to the question "How often do you feel nervous or tense at work?" (A37).

The actual computation of the Uncertainty Avoidance Index uses mean percentage values for question b and mean scores on 5-point scales for questions a and c. These mean scores have been multiplied by 30 (for question a) and 40 (for question c) to make their range, and therefore their contribution to UAI, roughly equal to the range in percentage values of question b. The actual formula used is as follows:

UAI = 300 − 30 (mean score rule orientation) − (percentage intending to stay less than 5 years) − 40 (mean stress score).

The resulting values of UAI for 50 countries and three regions are summarized in Exhibit 4.1 (first column). The constant 300 has brought country index values in a range between 8 (lowest UAI: Singapore) and 112 (highest UAI: Greece). The mean over 50 countries and 3 regions is 65. The theoretical range of the index is from −150 (all think that rules can be broken, no one wants to stay, no one ever feels nervous) to +230 (all think that rules should not be broken, everyone wants to stay more than 5 years, everyone always feels nervous). Of the theoretical range of the UAI (380 points), 104 points, or 27%, are really used for differentiating among the countries covered. The UAI scores in Exhibit 4.1 oppose all Latin countries (from Ecuador, 67, to Portugal, 104) to all Germanic countries (from Denmark, 13, to Austria, 70). In Asia, Japan (92) and Korea (85) scored high. Singapore (8), Hong Kong (29), Ma-

laysia (36), India (40), the Philippines (44), and Indonesia (48) scored low; Taiwan (69) and Thailand (64) are in the middle. The Islamic countries scored medium high, from Iran (59) to Turkey (85); Israel scored 81.

Uncertainty Avoidance
Versus Power Distance

The ranking of the countries in Exhibit 4.1 differs from the Power Distance Index ranking in Exhibit 3.1. Exhibit 4.2 plots UAI against PDI. The combination invites clustering; impressionistic clusters are circled in Exhibit 4.2. The combinations high UAI/high PDI and low UAI/low PDI occur more often than the other two possibilities. This suggests a positive correlation between the two dimensions. Across all 53 countries and regions the correlation of UAI × PDI is $r = .23$ (Exhibit 2.7), which falls just short of the .05 level of significance. So on a worldwide level, UAI and PDI can be considered independent.

However, closer inspection of Exhibit 4.2 shows that the upper right-hand quadrant (low UAI, high PDI) contains only Asian and African countries. This means that if we limit ourselves to European or Western countries, the correlation between UAI and PDI must be stronger. There were 17 European countries in the IBM set.[23] Across these 17, the correlation between UAI and PDI is, in fact, $r = .78***$; so $.78^2 = 61\%$ of the variance of UAI and PDI across Europe is shared.[24] European countries tend to score on the diagonal (upper left to lower right) of Exhibit 4.2. The practical consequence of this is that in studies limited to European or Western countries, the effects of PDI and UAI differences are difficult to separate.

The strong correlation of UAI and PDI for European countries can be explained by the fact that the 17 European countries split into 10 Germanic/Nordic and 7 Latin/Mediterranean ones. The latter have inherited from the centralized, structured Roman Empire both a large power distance and a strong uncertainty avoidance; the former lack both. I will come back to this in the subsection of this chapter on historical factors. I discuss implications of the UAI × PDI configuration for organizations in Chapter 8.

The level of uncertainty avoidance in a country affects the way power is exercised there. Barsoux and Lawrence (1990) have reported on what they consider a paradoxical finding about France, which among European countries is one of the highest on both PDI (68) and UAI (86). They refer to previously unpublished data showing that among respondents from nine European countries, the French are the second to lowest in agreeing with the statement "Basically, I will carry out instructions from my superior," and among eight countries the French are highest in agreeing with

Exhibit 4.1   Uncertainty Avoidance Index Values for 50 Countries and Three Regions

Rank	Country	UAI Actual	UAI Controlling for Age[a]	Rank	Country	UAI Actual	UAI Controlling for Age[a]
1	Greece	112	98	28	Ecuador	67	
2	Portugal	104	102	29	Germany (F.R.)	65	53
3	Guatemala	101		30	Thailand	64	73
4	Uruguay	100		31/32	Iran	59	59
5/6	Belgium	94	80	31/32	Finland	59	54
5/6	Salvador	94		33	Switzerland	58	62
7	Japan	92	112	34	West Africa	54	
8	Yugoslavia	88	77	35	Netherlands	53	45
9	Peru	87	91	36	East Africa	52	
10/15	Spain	86	89	37	Australia	51	47
10/15	Argentina	86	74	38	Norway	50	38
10/15	Panama	86		39/40	South Africa	49	62
10/15	France	86	73	39/40	New Zealand	49	60
10/15	Chile	86	66	41/42	Indonesia	48	
10/15	Costa Rica	86		41/42	Canada	48	55
16/17	Turkey	85	61	43	United States	46	36
16/17	South Korea	85		44	Philippines	44	45
18	Mexico	82	86	45	India	40	48
19	Israel	81	73	46	Malaysia	36	
20	Colombia	80	77	47/48	Great Britain	35	43
21/22	Venezuela	76	78	47/48	Ireland	35	54
21/22	Brazil	76	74	49/50	Hong Kong	29	61
23	Italy	75	58	49/50	Sweden	29	23
24/25	Pakistan	70	82	51	Denmark	23	32
24/25	Austria	70	77	52	Jamaica	13	
26	Taiwan	69	73	53	Singapore	8	31
27	Arab countries	68					
				Mean of 53		**65**	
				Standard deviation of 53		**24**	

a. UAI values controlling for the average age of the IBM respondents in the country; computed only for Category 1 countries (see Appendix 2).

"I only follow the instructions of superiors when my reason is convinced." [25] Barsoux and Lawrence explain this as French individualism, but the percentages agreement on both questions are primarily correlated with UAI ($r = -.89**$ and $r = .83**$; no significant second-order correlations). Both statements deal with the avoidance of uncertainty. Both express a feeling; emotionally, they appeal more in some countries than in others, and it is up to respondents how they want to interpret "basically" and under what circumstances they will consider that their "reason is convinced." The statements do not necessarily correspond to what an outside observer would see these respondents doing when given orders. But the statements also remind us of what d'Iribarne (1989) has written about the French honor principle (see Chapter 3): The things a French superior can order a subordinate to do are constrained by the "honor" of both classes. In a strongly uncertainty-avoiding context like French society, power is limited by traditional and fixed patterns of thought.

Occupation and Gender Differences in the Scores on the Uncertainty Avoidance Items

The statistical section of this chapter shows that the three items contributing to the Uncertainty Avoidance Index *for countries* were

Exhibit 4.2. A UAI × PDI Plot for 50 Countries and Three Regions

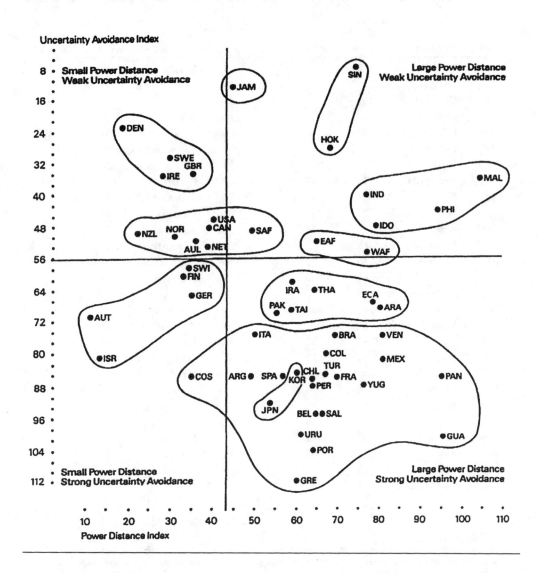

uncorrelated across *occupations*. Therefore the calculation of occupational UAI values made no sense, unlike for the Power Distance Index (Chapter 3), where the correlations of the index items across occupations were even stronger than across countries.

The statistical analysis also illustrates that an occupation's mean level of *rule orientation* depended mainly on the occupation's average formal educational level (more highly educated occupations were less rule oriented). An occupation's mean *employment stability* level was a combined function of (1) the average age of its incumbents (the older, the more stable), (2) their average educational level (the higher, the

less stable), and (3) the occupation's percentage of female incumbents (the more women, the less stable). An occupation's mean *stress level* depended somewhat on its hierarchical level (managers higher than nonmanagers).

The fact that rule orientation, employment stability, and stress related quite differently to the demographic factors of educational level, hierarchy, age, and percentage female explains why for occupations the three UAI questions were uncorrelated and could not be integrated into one index.[26]

As far as gender was concerned, there was a slight tendency for occupations with more women to show higher stress scores, after elimination of

Exhibit 4.3 Scores on UAI Questions for Women and Men in the Same Occupations

Occupations (2 surveys, total world data)	(A) Rule Orientation Mean Score	(B) Employment Stability: % Stay Less Than 5 Years	(C) Stress Mean Score
Branch office systems engineers			
Women ($n = 591$)	2.94	45	3.14
Men ($n = 9,917$)	2.94	34***	3.21
Head Office Clerks			
Women ($n = 5496$)	2.77	31	3.06
Men ($n = 7665$)	2.78	19***	3.08

NOTE: The differences between women and men on questions a and c, tested by the t test for difference of means, do not reach statistical significance. The differences between women and men on question b, tested with the Kolmogorov-Smirnov test, are significant beyond the .001 level for both occupations.

the effect of hierarchy (see Exhibit 4.9 in the statistical section). This does not mean, however, that women *within the same occupations* were necessarily under higher stress than men. For two occupations with sizable numbers of both men and women who did about the same work, Exhibit 4.3 lists the scores on the three Uncertainty Avoidance Index items separately for women and for men (compare Chapter 3, Exhibit 3.4).

For rule orientation women and men scored equally, and for stress women produced slightly lower scores—meaning higher stress—but the gender differences in stress scores were statistically insignificant, even with these very large numbers of respondents. The stress difference was therefore negligible.[27] On employment stability women scored significantly less "stable" than men, but this evidently had nothing to do with their attitude toward uncertainty; it followed from their` family role.[28] The computation of a UAI by gender therefore made as little sense as computation by occupation. As a whole, gender and uncertainty avoidance were unrelated.

Country UAI Scores
and Other IBM Survey Questions

Country means on several other questions in the IBM surveys were significantly correlated with UAI. First, there was a strong relationship of a country's UAI level and the average age of the IBM respondents in the country (see the statistical section of this chapter). To check whether the country differences in UAI might not just be due to these average age differences, see Exhibit 4.1; the second column of the exhibit lists UAI values controlling for age—the ones that would apply if all country samples had the same average age. The various country clusters remain essentially the same, but some countries shift somewhat; the separation between the Asian countries (except Japan) and the Latin-Mediterranean group becomes slightly less sharp. Nevertheless, the country differences in UAI certainly cannot be accounted for

by an average age artifact. We cannot claim, either, that the age-corrected UAI scores are more "correct" than the raw ones. The average age of IBM employees in a country was partly a *consequence* of a high UAI norm. The employment stability component in UAI implies less job change in high-UAI countries; therefore the average seniority in such a country will be higher and, with it, the average age, which reinforces the tendency to stay. I shall therefore continue to use the "raw" UAI values in order to characterize countries, not the values corrected for age.

Aside from issues of age, respondents in high-UAI countries tended to differ from those in low-UAI countries in their responses on the following questions:

1. A lower ambition for advancement (A15) and a preference for specialist over manager positions (B9)
2. A preference for large over small organizations (C17) and more approval for loyalty to those organizations (C12), whereas the more senior managers were considered to be the better ones (C11)
3. A tendency to avoid competition among employees (B54) and to prefer group decisions (B57) and consultative management (B55) over individual decisions and more authoritative management (Note that question B55 is correlated in opposite ways with PDI and UAI.)
4. A dislike of working for a foreigner as a manager (B44)
5. Resistance to change (C16)
6. A pessimistic outlook on the motives guiding companies (C10, in spite of admiration for loyalty to companies)

Finally, the level of overall employment satisfaction in IBM (A58) in a country was positively related to UAI.

If in a country there was a high level of uncertainty avoidance as evidenced by the UAI items rule orientation, employment stability, and stress, then advancement to a manager position, working for a small organization, competition among employees, individual decisions, working for a foreign manager, and a high rate of organizational change were likely to be felt as uncertain situations that fewer people were willing to face. In such countries people were more pessimistic about employers in general, but they produced higher satisfaction scores with their employment in IBM. This looks paradoxical; it suggests that the satisfaction score levels within a country's IBM subsidiary reflected partly an element of avoidance of "cognitive dissonance" (Festinger, 1957). It also reminds us of Allport's (1954/1979) finding that ambivalence toward parents (declaring love but showing hate) was part of the prejudiced personality; ambivalence toward one's employer may be another manifestation of it. If people did not consider leaving the organization a feasible alternative, they were more likely to declare themselves satisfied with it, in spite of any frustrations.

The country-level correlation of UAI with a dislike of competition among employees does not mean that there will be, in effect, less competition among employees in high-UAI countries; there may even be more. The correlation of UAI with a preference for group decisions reminds us of the Japanese *ringi* system of collective decision making; in fact, Japan scores high on UAI, although Japanese IBM employees compared to other IBM employees did *not* score high on the group decisions item (B57 in Appendix 2).[29] Group decision making can be seen as a way of avoiding risk for the individual.

Validating UAI Against Data From Other Sources

Straight Replications of the IBM Survey

Elite alumni from the Salzburg Seminar. I have already discussed Hoppe's (1990, 1993) replication with the Values Survey Module 1982 in Chapter 3 because it significantly replicated PDI differences between countries (for the data, see Exhibit 3.13). Hoppe's questionnaire also contained the three UAI questions. As in the case of PDI, the 1,590 Salzburg Seminar alumni from 17 European countries plus Turkey and the United States significantly replicated the UAI country differences found among IBM employees some 14 years earlier. Exhibit 4.10 in the statistical section of this chapter shows a correlation of $r =$

.64** between the Hoppe scores and the IBM scores; for PDI this had been $r = .67**$ (see Chapter 3). The Salzburg alumni on average scored some 33 points lower on UAI than did the IBM employees. Their much higher education level implied less rule orientation and less employment stability (see Exhibit 4.9). In Chapter 3, I explained that Hoppe's study contributed to the design of the new, 1994 version of the Values Survey Module (VSM 94, see Appendix 4). When recalculated from the VSM 94 questions and formulas, Hoppe's Salzburg UAI scores correlate with the original IBM scores with $r = .94***$.[30]

Commercial airline pilots. I have mentioned Helmreich and Merritt's (1998) study of pilots in Chapters 2 and 3. It covered more than 15,000 commercial airline pilots from 36 companies in 23 countries, surveyed between 1993 and 1997. The questionnaire included the three UAI questions. However, as mentioned in Chapter 2, for these pilots the UAI questions did not differentiate among the countries in the same way as they did in IBM. Across 21 countries there was a marginally significant correlation between UAI in IBM and the corresponding score computed for the pilots ($r = .49*$, rho $= .47*$).[31] Whereas the IBM employee respondents all shared the same employer, the pilots shared not their employer but their profession. We see that for people in this profession the three questions of rule orientation, employment stability, and stress carried different connotations from those they carried within IBM, which led to another pattern of between-country differences.

Higher-income consumers surveyed by the EMS 97. In Chapter 2, I referred to a replication of the IBM questions in the European Media and Marketing Survey 1997 by Inter/View International. This market research agency included in the EMS 97 the 20 questions of the VSM 94 (the revised experimental version of IRIC's Values Survey Module; see Appendix 4). The EMS 97 covered a sample of main income earners in the top 20% income households within each of 16 countries. Respondents were contacted by telephone and asked about their willingness to complete a postal questionnaire; about 50% of those who participated in the telephone interview also accepted the questionnaire. Completed questionnaire sample sizes varied from 100 in Ireland to more than 1,000 in Denmark, for a total of some 6,600 respondents. The initiative for this use of the VSM 94 had been taken by Dutch advertising expert Marieke de Mooij, who earlier had found correlations with all four IBM indexes in the consumer data from the 1995 round of the EMS. The EMS country scores on uncertainty avoidance are listed in Exhibit 4.10 in the statistical section of this chapter. These were not calculated in the same way as the IBM scores, but are based on the VSM 94 questions and formula. These included the rule orientation and stress questions from the IBM set, but for this public—not necessarily employed—the employment stability question was dropped. It was replaced by two other questions: "One can be a good manager without having precise answers to most questions that subordinates may raise about their work" (*strongly agree* to *strongly disagree,* agreement means low UAI) and "Competition between employees usually does more harm than good" (*strongly agree* to *strongly disagree,* agreement means high UAI).

Across the 15 overlapping European countries, the UAI scores from the IBM employees in 1970 and from the EMS consumers in 1997 were correlated with $r = .86***$—in view of the different respondent groups, the different questions, and a time lag of almost 30 years, a stunning result. As I mentioned in Chapter 2, the questions in EMS 97 meant to replicate PDI did not do so. Because, as we have seen above, for these European countries the PDI and UAI in IBM were strongly correlated, EMS UAI can be used as a proxy for EMS PDI; it was correlated with IBM PDI with $r = .75**$ (see Exhibit 4.10 and the corresponding discussion in the statistical section of this chapter). Individualism and masculinity in EMS 97 did replicate the IBM results, as will be shown in Chapters 5 and 6.

Other replications. Shane (1995, p. 56) included the original UAI questions in a survey of more than 4,400 employees of work organizations in 68 countries. Across 32 countries from the IBM set and for which he had 20 or more respondents, Shane found a correlation with the IBM scores of $r = .44**$, rho $= .41**$, somewhat lower than for PDI but still strong in view of his less-than-perfect matching across countries.[32] I have already mentioned Søndergaard's (1994) review of 61 smaller replications in Chapter 3. Of 19 replications allowing comparison of country score ranks with IBM, 14 confirmed the UAI differences.

UAI, Anxiety, and Emotions:
Studies by Lynn and Others

The analysis of national differences in anxiety-related behavior goes back to Durkheim (1895/1937). He showed systematic and stable differences in suicide rates between the countries on which he had data, next to systematic differences between other societal categories, such as men and women, married and divorced. Durkheim used his analysis of the suicide phenomenon to demonstrate how a highly individual act could be caused by social forces. He discarded purely psychological explanations: Although some people may be psychologically more predisposed to suicide than others, the force that really determines whether they will commit the act, according to Durkheim, is social.[33] At the individual level, psychologists have linked stress and anxiety. Kahn, Wolfe, Quinn, Snoek, and Rosenthal (1964, pt. 5) established a relationship between stress reactions and the personality dimensions of neurotic anxiety, extraversion/introversion, flexibility/rigidity, and achievement versus security. Popular wisdom and stereotypes attribute to people from different countries different levels of stress-related behavior, such as aggressiveness, expressiveness, talkativeness, and patience. Differences in anxiety levels among countries or subcultures in countries have been revealed by medical studies of bodily reactions.[34] Tannenbaum, Kavcic, Rosner, Vianello, and Wieser (1974, pp. 156 ff.), in a psychological survey study of five countries, found country differences in levels of "psychological adjustment," which included depression, resentment, and low self-esteem.[35]

An extensive study of country-level medical and related statistics was done by Richard Lynn and his colleagues from Northern Ireland.[36] Lynn and Hampson (1975) factor analyzed 12 variables for 18 developed countries measured in 1960 and found two factors (accounting for 57% of the variance in the data).[37] They labeled their first factor "neuroticism" or "anxiety." It combined the following variables (the figures are factor loadings):

−.79	Low chronic psychosis (patients per 1,000 population)
.78	High suicide death rate
−.69	Low caffeine consumption
.68	High alcoholism (liver cirrhosis death rate)
−.68	Low daily calorie intake
−.66	Low coronary heart disease rate
.66	High accident death rate
.51	High punished crime rate (number of prisoners per 10,000 population)

Lynn's first factor can also be seen as a "stress" factor. Its negative correlation with the coronary heart disease rate may look surprising because it has been shown in U.S. studies that stress and coronary heart disease are *positively* correlated (Friedman & Rosenman, 1975; Jenkins, 1971). But this was a correlation across *individuals*; the correlation in the Lynn data is an *ecological* one, across countries, and the two may well have opposite signs. Jenkins (1971) has cited a number of studies that have shown that the effects of stress on the cardiovascular system are conditioned by people's ability to show emotions. One study found mortality from coronary disease in Japan to be much lower than among American citizens of Japanese ancestry; this was attributed to cultural institutions in Japan that encourage free expression of emotions and provide social support for the individual (Jenkins, 1971, p. 309). This suggests that in certain countries with higher national anxiety levels, social systems have developed that allow for emotions to be expressed and therefore prevent stress from leading to coronary death. Latins are more anxious, but because the Latin environment allows them to be more talkative and expressive, Latins in Latin countries are less prone to coronary problems. This and other social systems characteristics can overcompensate for the negative effect of stress on the heart.

Exhibit 4.11 in the statistical section of this chapter shows that Lynn and Hampson's "neuroticism" (anxiety) factor scores for 18 countries were strongly correlated (rho = .73***) with the IBM Uncertainty Avoidance Index (and also with the IBM stress scores). This high correlation of UAI and "neuroticism" is encouraging for the validity of the IBM data in general and UAI in particular. There is—at least among these 18 countries—a national syndrome that relates to neuroticism, anxiety, stress, uncertainty avoidance, or whatever we want to call it, that differentiated among modern nations and affected IBM employees as much as anyone else.[38]

Two decades later, Lynn and Martin (1995) correlated medical and related indexes for 37 countries with the national normative scores for an individual-level personality test, the Eysenck Personality Questionnaire (EPQ). The EPQ distinguished three personality dimensions: "neuroticism versus emotional stability," "extraversion versus introversion," and "psychoticism versus ego control." The national norms for this test varied, and Lynn and Martin used these as a measure of national culture. In fact, across 25 overlapping countries the national norms for "neuroticism versus emotional stability" were significantly correlated with UAI (rho = .44*).[39]

Independent of Lynn's work and unaware of it, Hans Millendorfer (1976, p. 10) from Austria did a similar analysis of data on suicides, psychoses, accidents, and divorces from 15 countries and also found differences in stress levels among countries. Across the 12 countries studied by both Lynn and Millendorfer, their country rankings correlated with rho = .69**; and Millendorfer's stress ranking correlated with UAI with rho = .71***.[40] Millendorfer's study included the Eastern European countries Hungary, Czechoslovakia, and Poland, for which I had no data. The three countries did not cluster: Hungary scored high, Czechoslovakia medium, and Poland low on stress.[41]

Gudykunst, Yang, and Nishida (1987) studied self-reports of self-consciousness and anxiety among female and male students in South Korea, Japan, and the United States (more than 200 respondents per country), using an American questionnaire. They distinguished three components: public self-consciousness, private self-consciousness, and social anxiety. Social anxiety was measured by the following questions: "It takes me time to overcome my shyness in new situations"; "I have trouble working when someone is watching me"; "I get embarrassed very easily"; "I don't find it hard to talk to strangers" (reversed); "I feel anxious when I speak in front of a group"; and "Large groups make me nervous." The authors hypothesized that social anxiety in a culture should be related to its level of uncertainty avoidance, and that is, in fact, what they found. Social anxiety in the United States (UAI 46) was low; in Korea (UAI 85) it was high, and in Japan (UAI 92) it was even higher. We will meet Gudykunst et al.'s other personality dimensions in Chapters 5 and 6.

Edelmann et al. (1989) studied self-reports about the expression of embarrassment among female and male students in Germany, Great Britain, Greece, Italy, and Spain (between 96 and 200 respondents per country). Open-ended answers were coded by the local research team members. The countries' UAI scores were significantly correlated with reported duration of embarrassment ($r = .98**$) and with verbalization of emotions ($r = .85*$) and marginally with intensity of emotions ($r = .76$, significant at the .07 level). This study supports the relationship of UAI to the expression of affect, which is associated with a higher cultural anxiety level.

Scherer and Wallbott (1994) reported on a questionnaire study in 37 countries on self-reports of emotions (ISEAR, International Survey on Emotion Antecedents and Reactions). Their questions dealt with seven emotions: joy, fear, anger, sadness, disgust, shame, and guilt. Unfortunately, their article did not contain country-level data, but in 1999 data for 1,096 individuals from 16 countries were published on the Internet;[42] 14 of these could be matched with data from the IBM set. I used the variable for expressive nonverbal reactions, coded 0-6 on the basis of reported laughing/smiling, crying/sobbing, other facial expression change, screaming/yelling, other voice changes, and changes in gesturing, separately for women and men. Across the 14 overlapping countries, UAI was significantly *positively* correlated with the reported nonverbal expression of "anger" by men ($r = .54*$) and with the expression of "guilt" by women ($r = .53*$) and by men ($r = .77**$). The ISEAR database also produced significant correlations with the Individualism Index

(IDV) and Masculinity Index (MAS), which will be discussed in Chapters 5 and 6.

Matsumoto (1989) published a meta-analysis of studies of the recognition of emotions in facial expressions. He found several relationships with individualism, which will be discussed in Chapter 5. He had also hypothesized that across countries the ability to recognize fear should be negatively correlated with UAI, but this hypothesis was not supported. Schimmack (1996) redid Matsumoto's meta-analysis. The research literature provided reliable accuracy scores for the recognition by students of happiness, surprise, sadness, fear, disgust, and anger, from photos of faces, for 15 countries from the IBM set.[43] For all 15 countries, data were available concerning percentages of observers correctly identifying each of the six emotions. Schimmack noticed that all photos shown had been of Caucasian faces, with which some of the collectivist countries were less familiar. Using the races (Caucasian/non-Caucasian) of the observers and also their fields of study as control variables, he found the recognition of "fear" to show a significant negative zero-order correlation with UAI ($r = -.49*$). The recognition of "sadness" showed a significant negative second-order correlation with UAI, after field of study was controlled for (increasing R^2 from .60 to .71, $R = .84***$). The mean accuracy across the six emotions also showed a significant negative second-order correlation with UAI, after race was controlled for (increasing R^2 from .37 to .57, $R = .75***$). The negative correlations with UAI look puzzling at first, because high-UAI societies are supposed to express emotions more strongly. Schimmack explains the negative correlations using a hypothesis formulated by Matsumoto (1989), that high-UAI cultures have formed institutions to deal with emotions and therefore recognize them less well. It seems that in less emotive cultures, facial expressions are often the only visible signs of emotions, and observers have learned better to take their clues from watching faces than in cultures where emotions are expressed in more powerful ways. This seems to contradict the positive correlations reported by Edelman et al. and by ISEAR (noted above), but these were based on self-reports, whereas Schimmack measured the perceptions by others.

Put together, the various studies mentioned in this subsection show that UAI is associated with country differences on a broad range of measures of anxiety and emotions.

UAI and Subjective Well-Being

From decades of studying the modernization of societies, Inkeles (1993) has concluded that in-dustrialization and modernization have objectively improved the quality of life of populations for most people in most historical periods—this in terms of the availability of food, housing, piped water, sewage, medicine and health, education, communications and information, leisure time, physical and social security, and environmental and ecological conditions. Subjective measures of well-being across countries broadly reflect objective conditions, but "they are often contradicted by the distinctive propensities of some national populations" (p. 1). Measures comparing categories *within* countries react to changes in objective conditions, but the effects of such changes wear off quickly and country means in reported satisfaction return to their previous stable level. I found that subjective measures of well-being across countries are strongly negatively related to UAI.

The 1981-82 European Values Survey among random samples of national populations, described in Chapter 3, included a set of questions about the quality of the respondent's home life (Harding & Phillips, 1986, questions 233-242). Stoetzel (1983) conducted an analysis of these questions for the first nine countries studied and calculated two indexes: an index of satisfaction with the family (p. 288) and the balance of positive versus negative feelings (p. 265). Both were strongly negatively correlated with UAI ($r = -.87**$ for satisfaction, $r = -.88**$ for balance).[44] In societies where uncertainty avoiding was greater, people had more worries about their home life.

The replication of this study, the 1990-93 World Values Survey (WVS), retained the question "How satisfied are you with your home life?" and included or reincluded questions about happiness and satisfaction with health, life as a whole, and job (see the statistical section of this chapter, Exhibit 4.12). Percentage scores for these questions were published for 43 countries (Inglehart, Basañez, & Moreno, 1998); from these, 26 overlap with the IBM set. Across the 19 wealthier countries (including the nine earlier studied by Stoetzel) all five satisfaction questions were strongly negatively correlated with UAI (from rho = $-.69**$ for happiness to rho = $-.79***$ for health); there were no significant secondary correlations with the other indexes or with GNP/capita. Across all 26 countries, rich and poor, happiness (rho = $-.55**$) and health (rho = $-.75***$) still correlated primarily with UAI; satisfaction with life as a whole, job and home life related more to the Individualism Index (positively; see Chapter 5).

These questions all measure forms of subjective well-being.[45] Again, higher UAI tends to stand for lower subjective well-being; if we include poorer countries in the analysis, strong collectivism may also reduce feelings of well-being, at least in the areas of life as a whole, job, and home life.

Veenhoven (1993) has compiled an extensive collection of data about subjective well-being ("happiness in nations"). He derived his data from a variety of sources and years (1946-92). Happiness scores on a 3-point scale dating mainly from the 1970s or 1980s were available for 24 countries from the IBM set, both rich and poor. These scores correlated primarily with GNP/capita (1980, $r = .53**$), but if we limited ourselves to the 15 richer countries, the first correlation was with UAI ($r = -.61**$). Happiness scores on a 4-point scale dating mainly from 1990 were available for 21 IBM countries, nearly all rich. These scores also correlated primarily negatively with UAI ($r = -.64**$). If we included poor countries, unhappiness was primarily a matter of poverty (low GNP/capita); among rich countries it was a matter of higher UAI, which means cultural anxiety.[46]

Similar conclusions can be drawn from data reported by Diener, Diener, and Diener (1995) on a measure of "subjective well-being" (SWB) collected in 1984-86 by A. Michalos among college students in 55 countries (a total of more than 18,000 respondents with a minimum country sample of 91). In a stepwise regression of SWB scores against four IBM indexes plus 1980 GNP/capita, across 39 countries overlapping with the IBM set, I found as the first predictor of SWB GNP/capita ($r = .63***$, $R^2 = .40$), but there was a sizable negative second-order correlation with UAI ($R^2 = .56$). So again, unhappiness was primarily a matter of poverty, but after poverty was partialed out, it was a matter of weak uncertainty avoidance.[47] In another study, Diener and Diener (1995) looked for correlates of the same data across 31 countries. They found, and discuss extensively, a positive correlation of SWB with individualism (based upon my measure), but they included neither GNP/capita nor the other IBM indexes in their analysis. In my calculations across 39 countries I also found a significant zero-order correlation with the Individualism Index ($r = .62***$), but it disappeared in the stepwise regression after the influences of GNP/capita and UAI were controlled for.[48] The discrepancy between Diener and Diener's conclusion and mine shows the pitfalls of statistical inference in general and of cross-cultural inference in particular: By overlooking one or more key variables, one can drift toward a very different conclusion.

For a number of countries Veenhoven (1993) published a measure for the *dispersion* of happiness among individual respondents. These dispersion scores, across 20 rich and 6 poor countries, also correlated primarily negatively with UAI ($r = -.50**$).[49] In countries higher in UAI, not only did

people tend to feel less happy, there was also a wider dispersion of happiness. This means that high- and low-UAI countries both had their share of very satisfied persons, but in high-UAI countries there was a category of very dissatisfied persons as well, more so than in the low-UAI countries.

Hastings and Hastings (1981) published results from a public opinion survey of "human values" held in 13 countries across several continents.[50] This survey contained a set of 17 questions on "satisfaction of life goals." The statistical section of this chapter describes the results of an ecological factor analysis of the 17 satisfaction scores across the 13 countries. UAI was significantly correlated ($r = .59*$) with a factor combining living sincerely and seriously, living independently, being concerned about peace in the world, but having worries about one's finances and about one's health. So in more uncertainty-avoiding societies, people saw themselves as sufficiently sincere, serious, independent, and concerned about peace, but insufficiently blessed with money and health. Once more, UAI was negatively associated with subjective well-being.

The negative correlation between UAI and subjective well-being seems to contradict what was found inside IBM (see earlier in this chapter): IBM respondents in higher-UAI countries tended to score their overall employment satisfaction (A58) in the company higher than did those in lower-UAI countries. This, however, was in answer to a question on a survey run by their employer, and, as I suggested earlier, in this case people in high-UAI cultures would likely want to suppress the cognitive dissonance of confessing their frustrations.

UAI Versus Studies of
General Values in Society

Within the context of comparative international market research, the Reader's Digest (1970) survey showed attitudes toward younger and older generations across 15 European countries (see Exhibit 3.15). Favorable attitudes toward younger people were strongly negatively correlated with UAI ($r = -.77***$). Favorable attitudes toward older people were, less strongly, negatively correlated with both PDI and UAI (both $r = -.56**$, but the correlation with PDI was marginally stronger). Earlier in this chapter, I demonstrated that UAI correlated with the average age of the IBM respondent population. This is due to the greater employment stability in high-UAI countries, but it contributes to the generation gap: In more uncertainty-avoiding societies, older people are also more likely to disapprove of the behavior of young people and to wait longer before leaving responsibility in the hands of juniors. The Reader's Digest findings suggest more conservatism in high-UAI countries.

The 1990-93 World Values Survey contained the question: "Generally speaking, would you say that most people can be trusted or that you can't be too careful in dealing with people?" (question 94). The 1990-93 data (Exhibit 4.12) varied from 7% "can be trusted" in Brazil to 66% in Sweden; they showed robust correlations with UAI, both across all 26 countries (rho = $-.72$***) and across the 17 richer ones (rho = $-.81$***).[51] Another WVS question was: "Could you tell me how much you trust your family?" (question 340). Percentages scoring "completely" or "a little" generally exceeded 90%, yet they were significantly negatively rank correlated with UAI, both across all 25 countries (no data for Switzerland, rho = $-.51$**) and across the 16 rich ones (rho = $-.56$**). Trusting someone, even one's own family, implies some tolerance of ambiguity and a potential loss of control. These are more easily found in lower-UAI societies. An American resident of Brussels discussed with her Belgian neighbors the increasing number of burglaries in the area. She said that in such a case people in the United States would probably organize a neighborhood patrol. Her Belgian neighbors responded, "Well, we could never do that here, since we don't trust one another." The United States has a UAI index value of 46; Belgium's is 94.

Schwartz's (1994) massive values research project collected answers on a questionnaire with 56 value items from samples of elementary school teachers and of university students in 44 countries; by 1994, the project had covered more than 25,000 respondents. Schwartz used the statistical technique of smallest-space analysis to classify differences at the individual level but also at the national cultures level, separately for teachers and students, for 38 national and subnational cultures. The analysis produced a map of the positions of the values relative to one another in which Schwartz identifies seven categories: conservatism, hierarchy, mastery, affective autonomy, intellectual autonomy, egalitarian commitment, and harmony. Because the strongest statistical links of the Schwartz categories are with individualism, I will discuss his project in more detail in Chapter 5; the correlations are shown in Exhibit 5.17. However, the category of harmony, across 23 overlapping countries, was positively correlated ($r = .45$*) with UAI. "Harmony values . . . stand in opposition to value types that promote actively changing the world through self-assertion and exploitation of resources" (Schwartz, 1994, pp. 105-106). On Schwartz's map, harmony stands for unity with nature, protecting environment, and world of beauty. These appealed more in high- than in low-UAI countries.[52]

Summary of General Connotations of the Uncertainty Avoidance Index Found in Survey Material

Exhibit 4.4 presents a summary of the connotations of UAI found so far, analogous to the one for PDI in Exhibit 3.6. Again, it should be stressed that (1) the "low UAI" and "high UAI" columns in Exhibit 4.4 present extreme ideal types, between which country cultures are somewhere placed on a continuum; (2) not all connotations apply with equal strength to any given country; and (3) individuals in countries vary widely around their countries' norms.

The findings to which Exhibit 4.4 refers have been grouped into studies associated primarily with the stress component of UAI (anxiety, the expression of emotions, and lower subjective well-being), with the employment stability component, and with the rule orientation component (suspicion of new experiences and information and of other people). The UAI relates to a broad range of psychological characteristics that are mutually related by a societal logic that is not necessarily obvious at the individual level. In fact, the three basic UAI questions of stress, employment stability, and rule orientation are uncorrelated for individual respondents (as Exhibit 4.8 in the statistical section illustrates). They are correlated across countries because they represent alternative reactions to a similar underlying phenomenon: a stronger or weaker national norm for the avoidance of ambiguity. Eco-logic differs from individual logic, and it takes precisely the kind of quantitative international comparisons made here in Chapters 3 to 7 to reveal its secrets.

Origins and Implications of Country Uncertainty Avoidance Differences

The Uncertainty Avoidance Societal Norm

Exhibit 4.5 presents an integrated picture of the general societal norm behind the low-UAI and high-UAI syndromes. As in the case of the power distance norm (Exhibit 3.7), the uncertainty avoidance norm represents a value system shared by the majority in the middle classes in a society. The UAI norm deals fundamentally with the level of anxiety about the future in a country and the consequent need to protect society through three kinds of measures: technology, rules, and rituals. Higher anxiety leads to higher stress and a more hurried social life, but also to higher energy release, which means an inner urge to be busy. On the high-UAI side, anxiety is released more through the showing of emotions, for which soci-

Exhibit 4.4   Summary of Values and Other Psychological Characteristics Related to UAI

Low UAI	High UAI
Stress, Anxiety, and Expression of Emotions	
Lower work stress.	Higher work stress.
Lower anxiety level in population.	Higher anxiety level in population.
Emotions have to be controlled.	Expression of emotions normal.
People claim not to express embarrassment, anger, and guilt.	People claim the expression of embarrassment, anger, and guilt.
Facial expressions of sadness and fear easily readable by others.	Nature of emotions less accurately readable by others.
Subjective Well-Being (Happiness)	
More subjective well-being.	Less subjective well-being.
Feelings of happiness shared.	Feelings of happiness widely dispersed.
Employment Stability, Seniority, Generation Gap	
Less hesitation to change employers.	Tendency to stay with same employer.
Lower average seniority in jobs.	Higher average seniority in jobs.
Company loyalty is not a virtue.	Company loyalty is a virtue.
Managers should be selected on criteria other than seniority.	Managers should be selected on basis of seniority.
Preference for smaller organizations.	Preference for larger organizations.
Optimism about employers' motives.	Pessimism about employers' motives.
Admit dissatisfaction with employer.	Don't admit dissatisfaction with employer.
More ambition for advancement and management positions.	Lower ambition for advancement and preference for specialist positions.
Individual decisions, authoritative management, and competition among employees acceptable.	Ideological preference for group decisions, consultative management, against competition among employees.
Favorable attitudes toward younger people; smaller generation gap.	Critical attitudes toward younger people; larger generation gap.
Openness to New Experience and Information; Trust	
If necessary, employees may break rules.	Company rules should not be broken.
Less resistance to changes.	More resistance to changes.
Most people can be trusted.	One can't be careful enough with other people, not even with family.
Acceptance of foreigners as managers.	Suspicion of foreigners as managers.
Harmony with nature less appealing.	Ideological appeal of harmony with nature.

ety has created outlets; on the low-UAI side, anxiety is released more through passive relaxation, and emotions are supposed to be controlled. Higher anxiety levels reduce subjective well-being, including feelings about health, work, and family.

There is more openness to change and new ideas on the low-UAI side, more conservatism and a stronger desire for law and order on the

high-UAI side. Risks are taken on either side, but if UAI is high they are limited to known risks (such as driving fast, which is a way of stress release in high-UAI countries); if UAI is low, risk-taking includes unknown risks, such as changing employers. There is more tolerance of diversity in low-UAI countries, more fear of things foreign in high-UAI countries. The strong uncertainty avoidance sentiment is "What is different is dan-

Exhibit 4.5   The Uncertainty Avoidance Societal Norm

Low UAI	High UAI
The uncertainty inherent in life is relatively easily accepted and each day is taken as it comes.	The uncertainty inherent in life is felt as a continuous threat that must be fought.
Ease, lower stress, less anxiety.	Higher stress, anxiety, neuroticism.
Being busy is not a virtue per se.	Inner urge to be busy.
Suppression of emotions.	Expression of emotions.
Subjective well-being.	Less subjective well-being.
Openness to change and innovation.	Conservatism, law and order.
Willingness to take unknown risks.	Only known risks are taken.
What is different is curious.	What is different is dangerous.
Tolerance of diversity.	Xenophobia.
Younger people are respected.	Older people are respected and feared.
Comfortable with ambiguity and chaos.	Need for clarity and structure.
Appeal of novelty and convenience.	Appeal of purity.
Belief in one's own ability to influence one's life, one's superiors, and the world.	Feeling of powerlessness toward external forces.

gerous"; the weak uncertainty avoidance sentiment, in contrast, is "What is different is curious." [53] Tolerance of diversity also stretches to young people and their ideas, which are more easily accepted in low-UAI countries. Both in ideas and in rules, the high-UAI society seeks clarity, structure, and purity; the low-UAI society is comfortable with ambiguity, chaos, novelty, and convenience.

People in high-UAI societies feel relatively powerless toward external forces. The following subsections of this chapter will show that both as employees and as citizens, people in low-UAI societies feel more able than those in high-UAI societies to influence their lives, their superiors and authorities, and the world at large. Sociologists sometimes call the high-UAI syndrome *alienation*.[54]

The UAI norm contains some components of Adorno et al.'s (1950) authoritarian personality (translated to the societal level) and Eysenck's (1954) tough-mindedness. The latter stands, among other things, for intolerance of ambiguity.[55]

In the last resort, the UAI norm refers to a society's way of coping with death; this is the ultimate certainty and the ultimate source of anxiety. The duality of life and death is nature's number one law, and many fundamental values derive from the role death occupies in a society (Magli, 1984). People in high-UAI societies are more conscious of death than are those in low-UAI societies.

As a one-line definition of Uncertainty Avoidance as a dimension of national culture, I propose:

"The extent to which the members of a culture feel threatened by uncertain or unknown situations."

Uncertainty Avoidance in the Family

Family life in strong uncertainty avoidance societies is inherently more stressful than in weak ones. Parents behave more emotionally in the expression of both positive and negative feelings. As we saw earlier in this chapter, the 1981-82 European Values Survey and the 1990-93 World Values Survey both showed satisfaction with home life to be strongly negatively correlated with UAI, especially in the more affluent countries.

Among the first things a child learns are the distinctions between clean and dirty and between safe and dangerous. What is considered clean and safe, or dirty and dangerous, varies widely from one society to the next, and even among families within a society. Anthropologist Mary Douglas (1966) has related the need for purity to the sense of danger. Dirt—that which pollutes— is, Douglas argues, a relative concept, depending on a cultural interpretation. Dirt is basically matter out of place. Dangerous and polluting are things that do not fit our usual frameworks of thinking, our normal classifications. What a child has to learn is to classify clean versus dirty things and safe versus dangerous things.[56]

Dirt and danger are not limited to matter. They also refer to people. Racism is bred in families. Children learn that persons from particular categories are dirty and dangerous. Cultures with strong uncertainty avoidance probably even *need* categories of dangerous others to distinguish themselves from.

Ideas, too, can be considered dirty and dangerous. Children in families learn that some ideas are good and others taboo. Taboos are supposed to be a characteristic of traditional, primitive societies, but modern societies are also full of taboos. The family is the place where these taboos are transmitted from generation to generation. In some cultures the distinction between good and evil ideas is very sharp. There is a concern about Truth with a capital *T*. Ideas that differ from this Truth are dangerous and polluting. Little room is left for doubt or relativism.

Weak uncertainty avoidance cultures also have their classifications as to dirt and danger, but these are wider and more prepared to leave the benefit of the doubt to unknown situations, people, and ideas. Norms are expressed in basic terms, such as being honest and being polite, but allow a wide range of personal interpretation as to what this means in a given case. Deviant behavior is not so easily felt as threatening. Norms as to dress, hairstyles, and speech are looser, and children are expected to treat other people equally regardless of their looks.

Children in high-UAI societies are subject to stronger systems of rules and norms, and will more often feel guilty and sinful. In fact, the education process in high-UAI societies develops in its children stronger "superegos" (a concept developed by Freud in Austria, UAI 70). Children in high-UAI societies are more likely to learn that the world is a hostile place and to be protected from experiencing unknown situations. In low-UAI societies, rules are more flexible and superegos weaker; the world is pictured as basically benevolent, and experiencing novel situations is encouraged.

A study by Kashima and Kashima (1998), which I will describe more extensively in Chapter 5, showed that the stronger systems of rules and norms for children in higher-UAI cultures also apply to language learning. Languages in more uncertainty-avoiding cultures usually require learning to choose between different modes of address, such as *tu* and *vous* in French, but also between using the first-person pronoun *I* when referring to oneself and using a phrasing in which the *I* is dropped and remains implicit. Languages in higher-UAI cultures involve the making of more choices according to tight cultural rules. Languages in lower-UAI cultures tend to have fewer such rules.[57]

Uncertainty avoidance is also associated with conventional gender roles in the family. The World Values Survey 1991-93 contained the question, "If someone says a child needs a father and a mother to grow up happily, would you tend to agree or disagree?" (question 214). Although nearly 90% of respondents worldwide agreed, percentages agreeing in the 18 wealthier countries did correlate strongly with UAI (rho = .78***; see Exhibit 4.12). If poor countries were included, the highest correlation was with IDV (negative):[58] Collectivist countries favored the traditional family more. A related item was, "A job is alright but what most women really want is a home and children" (question 220). Agreement varied from 25% in Denmark to 91% in India. Across the wealthier countries, percentages agreeing were correlated primarily with UAI (rho = .70**).[59] In the wealthier high-UAI countries, fewer people were willing to accept the possibility of success for less traditional family compositions.[60]

Uncertainty Avoidance,
Schools, and Educational Systems

One way in which the level of uncertainty avoidance in a society affects educational systems is in determining the proper amount of structure in the teaching process.[61] When uncertainty avoidance is relatively strong (such as in France or Germany), both students and teachers favor structured learning situations with precise objectives, detailed assignments, and strict timetables. They like situations in which there is one correct answer that they can find. They expect to be rewarded for accuracy. When uncertainty avoidance is weaker (such as in Britain or Sweden), both students and teachers despise structure. They like open-ended learning situations with vague objectives, broad assignments, and no timetables at all. The suggestion that there can be only one correct answer is taboo with them. They expect to be rewarded for originality.

Students from high-UAI countries expect their teachers to be the experts who have all the answers. Teachers who use cryptic academic language are respected; some of the great gurus from these countries write such difficult prose that one needs the explanations of more ordinary creatures to understand what the gurus mean. "German students are brought up in the belief that anything which is easy enough for them to understand is dubious and probably unscientific" (Stroebe, 1976, p. 510). Some French academic books contain phrases that are half a page in length. Students in these countries will not, as a rule, voice intellectual disagreement with their teachers. A Ph.D. candidate who finds him- or herself in conflict with a thesis adviser on an important issue has the choice of changing his or her mind or finding another adviser. Intellectual disagreement in academic matters is interpreted as personal disloyalty.

Students from low-UAI countries accept a teacher who says, "I don't know." Their respect goes to teachers who use plain language and to books that explain difficult issues in ordinary terms. The educational process in high-UAI countries is guided by a sense of search for Truth with a capital *T;* in low-UAI societies there is more of a sense of empiricism and relativity, more room for unconventional ideas. Intellectual disagreement in academic matters in these cultures can be seen as a stimulating exercise, and I know of thesis advisers whose evaluations of Ph.D. candidates are positively related to how well the candidates argue their positions in disagreement with the professors' positions.[62]

Students in high-UAI countries are less likely to attribute their achievements to their own ability than are students in low-UAI countries. Chandler, Shama, Wolf, and Planchard (1981) studied attributions of causes for success and failure among female and male students from five countries.[63] They used an American scale, the Multidimensional Multiattribution Causality Scale (MMCS). Attributions could be made to ability and effort (internal locus of control) and to context (or task) and luck (external). The data Chandler et al. present show a tendency in some countries to use *all* four categories more frequently than in others, so I standardized the mean country scores across the four categories, which extracts the *relative* tendency in each country to prefer one category over another. In spite of the small number of countries, the relative tendency to attribute achievement to ability was significantly negatively correlated with UAI ($r = -.87*$).[64] Yan and Gaier (1994) used the MMCS with 358 students at a U.S. university who were classified as Chinese, Southeast Asian, Japanese, Korean, and American. After standardizing their data, I again found a significant negative correlation of attribution to ability with UAI ($r = -.91*$).[65]

The examples used so far stem from university and postacademic teaching and learning situations, but the behaviors and expectations of both students and teachers in these examples were clearly developed during earlier school experiences. Oettingen (1995) studied self-efficacy of schoolchildren in West and East Berlin and in Los Angeles. *Self-efficacy* refers to one's sense of personal ability, which is reinforced by successes and weakened by failures. East Berlin children (after the reintegration of Berlin) were most pessimistic about self-efficacy. It is likely that this pessimism was fostered by the East German communist education philosophy, in which public social comparison, an anxiety-arousing practice, played a large role. West Berlin children showed stronger self-efficacy, which Oettingen explains as both weaker uncertainty avoidance and stronger individualism. Low-UAI Los Angeles schoolchildren were most optimistic about their self-efficacy.[66]

A difference between the two types of cultures that operates specifically at the elementary and secondary school level is the expected role of parents versus teachers. In cultures with strong uncertainty avoidance, parents are supposed to watch over their children's proper motivation and behavior at school—for example, by signing children's homework assignments and/or performance records. They are sometimes invited to information meetings with teachers, but they are rarely consulted. Parents are laypersons and teachers are experts who know. I experienced the embarrassed reaction of an (eminent) Belgian teacher when the parents of her English and Dutch pupils wanted to raise an issue not on her agenda (Belgium is a high-UAI country, Britain and Holland are much lower). In countries with weak uncertainty avoidance, it is normal for teachers to try to get parents involved in school issues: Parents' ideas may be actively sought.

Another way in which uncertainty avoidance may affect the teaching process is in the amount of tolerance for the use of local dialect speech. A small comparative study by Gerritsen (1995) among women and girls on either side of the German-Dutch border shows a much greater tolerance for use of the local dialect in the Netherlands (UAI 53) than in Germany (UAI 65).[67]

In the previous subsection, UAI was shown to be associated with a preference for more traditional gender roles in the family. Chapter 3 showed that in Gordon's (1976) SIV test "independence" for female students was significantly *negatively* correlated with UAI (Exhibit 3.14, note about second-order correlation). This means that, other things being equal, independence was a stronger value for these female students in lower-UAI than in higher-UAI countries.

UAI and Achievement Motivation:
McClelland's Data

A classic source of measures of social norms—although its author would not call them that—is David McClelland's *The Achieving Society* (1961). McClelland argued that differences in social action among societies can be explained through different dominant motive patterns in their populations.[68] He distinguished three types of motives: achievement, affiliation, and power. He measured the strength of these motives for a number of nations through a content analysis of stories appearing in schoolbooks to be read by children from 7 to 9 years old. McClelland considered these stories to be the modern equivalent to folktales for primitive nations, and folktales have been widely used by anthropologists to infer the motive patterns of preliterate tribes.

McClelland's research team content analyzed 21 children's stories dating from 1925 from each of 25 countries, and 21 children's stories from 1950 from each of 41 countries. They determined scores for each country on "need for achievement," "need for affiliation," and "need for power." In his 1961 book, McClelland focused on need for achievement (n_{Ach}). He found a relationship of a country's n_{Ach} scores for 1925 with growth in per capita electric power production from 1929 to 1950, and of n_{Ach} scores for 1950 with growth of absolute electric power production from 1952 to 1958. On the basis of his theories, McClelland defended achievement motivation training for managers from developing countries; he himself actually gave such training. McClelland's later work shifted attention to the need for power as a motive (McClelland, 1975; McClelland & Burnham, 1976).[69]

McClelland's work has had considerable influence, both in the development of the psychology of motivation and on certain areas of policy making in development assistance. However, his original findings about a relationship between achievement motives in children's readers and some measures of economic growth afterward have raised questions. A reanalysis by Barrett and Franke (1971) comparing McClelland's scores with various measures of economic growth over various periods showed that the relationship on which McClelland built his economic growth theory was fortuitous; it was an artifact of the particular measures and measuring periods that were chosen. The period 1929-50, which includes a world war, is not an ideal one in which to isolate the effects of inner motives on economic performance: Outside influences during these years played an overwhelming role in what happened to nations. Another puzzling fact about McClelland's motive scores is that from 1925 to 1950 there was no consistency among country scores (the Spearman rank correlations between 1925 and 1950 scores across the 25 countries studied twice are .16 for n_{Ach}, .21 for n_{Aff}, and even negative, -.14, for n_{Pow}). Is it likely that something as fundamental as a basic motive pattern can change completely in one generation? Or has the measurement been unreliable?

Exhibit 4.13 in the statistical section of this chapter shows across 22 countries a strongly negative correlation (rho = -.64***) between IBM UAI scores and *1925* n_{Ach} scores, but none (across 31 countries) between any IBM dimension and any of McClelland's *1950* scores. The multiple correlation of McClelland's 1925 n_{Ach} with IBM UAI and MAS (see Chapter 6) was even higher (R^2=.54, R = .74***).[70] A high score for need for achievement in a country's 1925 children's

stories predicted weak uncertainty avoidance and strong masculinity among its IBM respondents around 1970.

Two questions must now be resolved: Why are IBM scores correlated with McClelland's 1925 data but not his 1950 data? And why are low UAI and high MAS associated with high 1925 n_{Ach}? As for the first question, the average IBM respondent learned to read between 1945 and 1947; if people's values reflect what was taught to them in school, we should expect the IBM data to be correlated with the 1950 rather than with the 1925 children's stories' content. However, around 1925 children's stories were certainly more traditional; they came closer to the anthropologist's folktales that McClelland tried to match, and to expressing basic themes of a country's subconscious norm pattern. In 1950 the education systems in many countries had been caught in a postwar process of modernization, and innovative schoolbook editors replaced traditional stories with modern ones, often imported. Therefore the 1925 stories must have been much more reliable as measures of a country's underlying culture pattern than those from 1950. This also explains the shocking lack of correlation between 1925 and 1950 scores. It was the 1925 stories that most purely expressed the underlying culture patterns, and in spite of the 1950 book editors, these basic patterns still showed up in people's mental programs around 1970, when the IBM surveys took place. In fact, the assumption that by changing the content of children's readers one can change basic motives of a population is naive. For one thing, the preschool conditioning of children by their families is a more powerful element in a nation's mental programming than what these children are supposed to read in school.

Low UAI implies a greater willingness to enter into unknown ventures. High MAS, as we shall see in Chapter 6, means assertiveness or ambitiousness. The two together match the picture of McClelland's achievement-motivated individual. The countries that show both low UAI and high MAS are primarily the Anglo countries, in particular Great Britain, Ireland, and the United States. Indeed, these did relatively well economically in the 1929-50 period because they suffered less from the war than did countries that were occupied. However, they definitely did *not* do as well economically as some other countries after 1950 (we shall go deeper into this later in this chapter). It is therefore unallowable to present McClelland's achievement motive as a *universal and perennial* model for economic success in the world. The American McClelland described a typical Anglo-American value complex—the one present in his own environment—as a model for the world. A Frenchman, Swede, or Japanese would have been unlikely to discover a worldwide achievement motive (even the word *achievement* is difficult to translate into most languages other than English).

Achievement motivation may have to be differentiated into "hope of success" in low-UAI countries versus "fear of failure" in high-UAI countries. This would at least explain a difference between Belgians (UAI 94) and Americans (UAI 46) found in a comparative laboratory experiment by McClintock and McNeel (1966). They used a two-player game in which either player could get a maximum payoff by cooperating but a competitive advantage by not cooperating. Belgians preferred the competitive strategy when they were behind, whereas Americans preferred it more when they were ahead. Belgians wanted to avoid losing; Americans wanted to win.[71]

Sagie, Elizur, and Yamauchi (1996) collected answers on the Achievement Motive Questionnaire, developed by Elizur, from convenience samples of managers, employees, and students in five countries.[72] Respondents were asked to score on 5-point scales whether they (1) used to undertake, (2) preferred, and (3) felt most satisfied with each of six types of tasks: (a) with uncertain or sure outcomes, (b) difficult or easy, (c) with personal or shared responsibility, (d) involving a calculated risk versus no risk or an excessive risk, (e) requiring problem solving versus following instructions, and (f) gratifying a need to succeed rather than avoidance of failure. Thus the questionnaire counted $3 \times 6 = 18$ items. In a discriminant analysis across the five countries, task types a, d, and e formed a cluster. I found scores for the five countries on this cluster rank correlated significantly with UAI (rho = .90*)[73] in the sense of respondents from less uncertainty-avoiding cultures choosing more often uncertain, calculated risk and problem-solving tasks.[74] The cluster did not include task type f, success versus failure, but in a self-scored instrument this is probably a taboo question.

Uncertainty Avoidance
in the Work Situation

The Uncertainty Avoidance Index was correlated with a number of other items in the IBM surveys that by definition were work related. These are summarized in Exhibit 2.4 ("employment stability, seniority, generation gap"). In this subsection I will describe validation from other work-related studies.

The association of UAI with employment stability was validated by a 1997 report from the Organization for Economic Cooperation and Development that listed average duration of the employment relationship in 17 OECD countries, varying from 6.4 years in Australia to 11.6 years in Italy.[75] Across the 17 countries, UAI and average duration of employment were correlated with rho = .63**; there were no significant secondary correlations with any of the other IBM indexes or with GNP/capita. So in spite of the different way of measurement, target populations, and moment in time, UAI was still associated with employment stability after nearly 30 years. Stable employer-employee relations are of course an exemplary way for both sides of avoiding uncertainty.

Wildeman et al. (1999) studied differences in *self-employment* rates across 23 industrialized countries.[76] Although one would expect that in high-UAI cultures fewer people would risk self-employment (UAI was associated with a preference for large over small companies), the opposite turned out to be the case: Self-employment levels across 21 overlapping countries, measured every second year between 1974 and 1994, were consistently positively correlated with UAI. Further examination revealed that the low subjective well-being (happiness) component of strong UAI, in particular, accounted for the correlation with self-employment. Across 12 countries for which happiness data were also available biannually, more self-employed persons were consistently found where and when people in general reported lower satisfaction with their lives and with the way democracy works: Self-employment was chosen out of dissatisfaction, not out of a desire for adventure. A study across a population cohort within one country, Britain, showed that at the *individual* level within British society, those who had become self-employed were more satisfied with their lives than those who had not (Blanchflower & Oswald, 1998). This suggests that (at least on average) the flight from dissatisfaction into self-employment for these people paid off. There is no obvious reason the same would not be true within other industrialized countries as well.[77]

In the first section of this chapter, I referred to the use of technology, rules, and rituals for the avoidance of uncertainty in organizations as parallels to technology, law, and religion in the wider society.[78] The appeal of technology in high-UAI cultures is evident from a study by Schneider and De Meyer (1991) among some 300 INSEAD participants, partly MBA students, partly executives, on perceptions of strategic issues and recommended actions for a particular test-case study. The researchers divided their subjects into five cultural clusters (North American, English, Germanic, Latin, and Nordic). Subjects from higher-UAI clusters recommended significantly more often that the problem be resolved through massive investment in computer technology.

The appeal of rules in higher-UAI cultures should be evident from the greater "structuring of activities" found in Aston-type studies (see Pugh,

1976, p. 68; see also Chapter 3). Structuring of activities includes formalization, specialization, and standardization. Hickson, McMillan, Azumi, and Horvath (1979) compared Aston measures for six countries. The IDE International Research Group (1981a, p. 110) collected formalization data in 12 countries.[79] None of the results were conclusive as to a relationship with UAI, but this could be due to a "reverse ecological fallacy" (see Chapter 1): The Aston measures were composed of structure variables that correlated within Britain, but these need not have correlated across societies.[80]

Shane and his colleagues have obtained more convincing results about the relationship between UAI and rules in organizations. Shane, Venkataraman, and Macmillan (1995, p. 944) have reported on the results of surveys conducted with more than 1,200 employees of four multinationals in 30 countries about the employees' roles in championing innovations at work. In an ecological factor analysis of 24 questions across 30 countries, they found three factors, of which one (need for support from the hierarchy) correlated with PDI (which is why I have mentioned this study already in Chapter 3). Another factor combined eight questions expressing independence from existing rules and regulations in case of innovations. In a regression analysis, factor scores on this factor were negatively related to UAI; there were weaker relationships with two demographic characteristics, average years of work experience (also negative) and percentage women (positive). So in higher-UAI countries innovators felt more constrained by rules and regulations, the more so if they were more experienced and male. The third factor found was related to individualism; it will be discussed in Chapter 5.

Shane and Venkataraman (1996, p. 762) also conducted an analysis of a somewhat different database (6,000 respondents, six organizations, 28 countries) in which preferences for two types of championing behavior were opposed: promoting innovation inside existing organizational norms, rules, and procedures ("rational championing") versus promoting innovation outside these constraints ("renegade championing"). In a multiple regression against the four IBM indexes, the preference for renegade championing was primarily negatively related with UAI, and secondarily, positively, with IDV.[81] Innovating outside existing organizational norms, rules, and procedures appealed more in low-UAI, high-IDV cultures.

The appeal of rituals should, among other things, be visible in a need for detailed planning. Horovitz (1980), in a comparison of 175 British, French, and German top managers, found that the (higher-UAI) French and Germans focused much more on details and short-term feedback than did their (lower-UAI) British counterparts. Hoffman (1987) collected views about decision power from some 300 top managers in 78 manufacturing business units and divided them into Anglo (British and American), Germanic (German and Swiss), and Nordic (Danish, Norwegian, and Swedish). The Germanic cluster (higher UAI) more often mentioned rational forecasting as a source of decision power. On the other hand, strategic planning, which avoids details, appeals less in high-UAI countries. Faucheux (1977) has argued that U.S. (low-UAI) approaches to strategic management do not apply to (high-UAI) Latin countries in general and to France in particular.

The UAI norm in a country affects the way power in organizations is exercised. Power in an organization is not just an interpersonal process, affected by the country's PDI norm. Power in organizations is also exercised among groups and organizational subsystems and, as such, is strongly affected by the control of uncertainty.[82] "Coping with uncertainty is the variable most critical to power, and is the best single predictor of it" (but not the only one; Hinings et al., 1974, p. 40). If the societal norm tolerates less uncertainty, those who control uncertainty will be more powerful than if uncertainty is more easily tolerated. This explains the differences among Indian, French, and German "authoritarianism" (see the UAI-PDI plot in Exhibit 4.2). Authority in India is pure personal power ("a basic fact of society that antedates good or evil"; see Exhibit 3.7). In France it is the same, *plus* the fact that power holders control uncertainties, which many people find too threatening to face. In Germany "the use of power should be legitimate" (Exhibit 3.7), but the impact of formal role power is strong because it controls uncertainties, which corresponds to many people's profound needs.

Competencies should be more clearly defined in high-UAI societies than in low-UAI societies. Laurent (1978, 1983) designed a questionnaire on organizational issues and administered it to managers from 10 different countries in courses at INSEAD, Fontainebleau. Five items (see the statistical section), all expressing a low tolerance for ambiguity in hierarchical structures, were strongly intercorrelated at the country level. Exhibit 4.14 shows that the average percentages agreement for these five questions were significantly correlated with UAI (rho = .78**). Laurent linked this to the acceptability of a "matrix organization" philosophy in a country. A successful application of matrix organization presupposes a tolerance for ambiguity in the hierarchy, as a subordinate may have two (or three) bosses. Therefore matrix-organization structures are less acceptable in high-UAI countries.[83] A later analysis that I conducted on more extensive data provided by Laurent (un-published) showed UAI to be strongly correlated (rho = .77**) with an ecological factor that at its positive pole stands for a highly formalized conception of management.

Shane et al.'s (1995) questionnaire described above measured respondents' correspondence to four different championing roles, identified on the basis of the literature. Using a more extensive database (more than 4,400 employees from 43 organizations in 68 countries), Shane (1995) performed a factor analysis *at the individual level* and found support for the independence of the four roles in the form of four separate factors. Subsequently, he gave each individual the IBM scores of his or her country and did regression analyses for each of the four roles across the 4,400 cases, on the four indexes plus a number of demographics.[84] UAI was the only variable appearing with the same negative sign in all four regressions. In order of strength of their negative relationship with UAI, the four roles were as follows:

1. *Transformational leader:* The champion persuades other members of the organization to provide support for the innovation. Other variables correlated with this role were power distance (positive), individualism, and masculinity (both negative), being female, and working in finance.

2. *Organizational buffer:* The champion creates a loose monitoring system to ensure that the innovators make proper use of organizational resources, while at the same time allowing the innovators to act creatively. Other variables correlated with this role were individualism (negative), masculinity (positive), being an expatriate, and not working in marketing.

3. *Network facilitator:* The champion defends the innovators against interference by the organizational hierarchy through the development of cross-functional coalitions between managers in different functional areas of the organization who support the innovation. Other variables correlated with this role were individualism (positive), level of education, championing experience, and being male.

4. *Organizational maverick:* The champion provides the innovators with autonomy from the rules, procedures, and systems from the organization so that innovators can establish creative solutions to existing problems. Other variables correlated with this role were individualism (positive), level of education, work experience (negative), championing experience (positive), and not working in a support function.[85]

Shane's analysis pointed to the country's uncertainty avoidance level as the one common denominator that affected his respondents' perceptions of their various roles in championing innovations, always opposing a loose, unstructured approach to innovation.

D'Iribarne (1998) has described a case study illustrating the social and technical processes involved in innovation. He studied the interactions in a mixed design team of French (PDI 68, UAI 86) and Swedish (PDI 31, UAI 29) engineers in an automotive joint venture. The French operated in a strictly controlled way, having to check frequently with their superiors. The Swedes were much more autonomous and arranged things among themselves. However, this did not mean that the Swedes necessarily came up with more innovative designs. Autonomy does not guarantee creativity.

Shane (1993) had earlier studied national rates of innovation, defined as the per capita number of trademarks granted to nationals of 33 countries from the IBM set. He used four sets of data, for the United States and for the world market, and for 1975 as well as for 1980. He regressed these against GNP/capita plus percentages of GNP acquired by value added in a number of innovating industries, as well as against my four IBM indexes, one by one. The only variable making a consistent significant contribution across all four regressions was UAI, with a negative sign.[86] Less uncertainty-avoiding cultures showed higher rates of innovation in terms of trademarks granted.

In summary, it seems that in higher-UAI countries innovations are more difficult to bring about. At the same time, the example of Japan, a high-UAI country, suggests that once innovations are accepted, they are taken more seriously than in low-UAI countries. In the latter, people may welcome innovations a bit too easily but may not put enough energy into their application. Also, the precision and punctuality needed to make an innovation work is likely to come more naturally in high-UAI societies; in low-UAI societies these have to be learned and managed. An international organization could benefit by collecting innovations from low-UAI subsidiaries and developing them in high-UAI subsidiaries!

A tolerance for ambiguity in subordinate-manager relationships is also found in the data I collected at IMEDE among managers from 16 countries using Fiedler's (1967) Least Preferred Co-Worker questionnaire (Hofstede, 1974b). In Chapter 1, I referred to the LPC as an original test of values: The values of a respondent are inferred from the way in which he or she describes a third person—that is, the one other person with whom the respondent could work least well.

High LPC scorers described their least preferred coworkers in relatively favorable terms, and Fiedler interpreted this as interpersonal orientation; low LPC scorers described their least preferred coworkers in very unfavorable terms, and this was interpreted as task orientation. High LPC scores show a large tolerance for ambiguity and low LPC scores the reverse. Therefore, in high-UAI countries LPC score levels should be lower. The statistics in Exhibit 4.14 show that in spite of the small samples of respondents used, there was in fact a marginally significant negative correlation between UAI and LPC,[87] confirming the link between UAI and low tolerance for ambiguity in describing one's least preferred coworker.

Lower LPC scores in higher-UAI countries also imply that managers in these countries are more task oriented. An illustrative incident is that in one phase of the IBM survey, two questions about whether managers were seen as task oriented were suppressed in the two higher-UAI countries Japan and Germany, although they belonged to the accepted core of the questionnaire. Local management considered these questions redundant and/or unacceptable. When in Germany these questions were reintroduced in the next survey phase, they proved to be unrelated to employees' perceptions of these managers' leadership styles, contrary to what was found in other countries. Task orientation among German managers was an imperative rather than a variable.

Paradoxically, however, flexible working hours—systems in which workers determine their own starting and finishing hours within certain constraints—had greater appeal in high-UAI than in low-UAI countries, especially in combination with low PDI. Such flexible scheduling was invented in Germany and was introduced in, for example, Switzerland and Japan, but the idea has never become as popular in France, Britain, the United States, or Hong Kong. In a high-UAI environment, time rules are a source of considerable subjective stress, as they are difficult to *always* live up to; therefore, a system that allows people relief from strict time rules is attractive. And if at the same time PDI is low, people have the *superego* that enables them to make the flextime system a success. In high-PDI countries, flextime implies a loss of hierarchical control, which is resisted. In low-UAI countries, resistance is directed mainly against the reintroduction of time registration (clocking in and out), which the flextime system usually demands; also, the relief value of a less restrictive time rule system is lower, as the rules are probably already interpreted less strictly.

High-UAI societies foster a belief in experts; low-UAI societies look to the intelligent layperson. In Chapter 3, I referred to the very classic study of Haire, Ghiselli, and Porter (1966) and

its later additions, about management attitudes and assumptions across 19 countries.[88] A significant negative second-order correlation with UAI, after PDI, was found for "capacity for leadership and initiative." Managers in high-UAI countries, after elimination of PDI differences, were less optimistic about the leadership capacities of ordinary people.

Studies comparing work behavior in Germany and the United States are particularly relevant for the present chapter because the two countries differed considerably on uncertainty avoidance (UAI for Germany 65, for United States 46) while scoring very similarly on PDI and MAS; on IDV both were high scorers, but the United States more so. Fridrich (1965) found that German middle managers, more than their U.S. colleagues, stressed economic performance and expertise, were more concerned with security and showed greater status anxiety, and placed more value on stability in their society and its institutions. Preiss (1971) found German engineers oriented toward anxiety avoidance and a professional career, earnings, cooperation, and security, whereas U.S. engineers were oriented toward the company, wanting management careers, and valuing their private lives. Friday (1989) interviewed U.S. and expatriate German managers at a German subsidiary in Pittsburgh, Pennsylvania. The Germans had a higher general education level and a belief in formal instruction in case of learning needs on the job. They believed more in individual expertise than did the Americans, who favored solving problems through teamwork. On the other hand, the Americans' relationships with the company were impersonal; they were ready to move on when the business no longer served their needs. For the Germans, their identity was more closely associated with their position, and they expected the company to meet their security needs. Discussion behavior was informal for the Americans, who needed to be liked; for the Germans, it was highly formal and based on their positions. Both groups acted assertively, but the Americans' assertiveness was tempered by a need for fair play. Friday (1989) describes the common social intercourse in the following terms. For the Americans: "Discussion about sports, weather, occupation; what you do, what you feel about someone. Logical, historical analysis rarely ventured." For the Germans: "*Besprechung*—rigorous local examination of the history and elements of an issue. Politics favorite topic. Forceful debate expected" (p. 437). These various studies provide a nice overview of differences in work behavior associated with uncertainty avoidance.

Exhibit 4.6 summarizes the differences discussed so far between low-UAI and high-UAI societies for family, school, motivation, and the work situation.

Exhibit 4.6   Key Differences Between Low- and High-UAI Societies I: Family, School, Motivation, and Work Situation

Low UAI	High UAI
In the Family	
Parents control their emotions.	Parents behave emotionally.
Higher satisfaction with home life.	Lower satisfaction with home life.
Lenient rules on what is dirty and taboo.	Tight rules on what is dirty and taboo.
Truth is relative.	Concern for Truth with a capital T.
Few rules; if children cannot obey the rules, the rules should be changed.	Many rules; if children cannot obey the rules, they are sinners who should repent.
Mild superegos developed.	Strong superegos developed.
Children learn that the world is benevolent.	Children learn that the world is hostile.
Children exposed to unknown situations.	Children protected from the unknown.
Undifferentiated, informal ways of address.	Strictly differentiated forms of address.
Nontraditional gender roles accepted.	Traditional gender roles preferred.
At School	
Students expect open-ended learning situations and good discussions.	Students expect structured learning situations and seek right answers.
Teachers may say, "I don't know."	Teachers supposed to have all answers.
Students learn that truth may be relative.	Students learn that Truth is absolute.
Students attribute achievements to own ability.	Students attribute achievements to effort, context, and luck.
Children rate self-efficacy high.	Children rate self-efficacy low.
Parents' ideas sought by teachers.	Parents seen as extension of teachers.
Dialect speech positively valued.	Dialect speech negatively valued.
Independence for female students important.	Traditional role models for female students.
In Motivation	
Traditional children's stories stress strong achievement motivation.	Traditional children's stories stress strong security motivation.
Hope of success.	Fear of failure.
Preference for tasks with uncertain outcomes, calculated risks, and requiring problem solving.	Preference for tasks with sure outcomes, no risks, and following instructions.
In the Work Situation[a]	
Weak loyalty to employer; short average duration of employment.	Strong loyalty to employer, long average duration of employment.
Preference for smaller organizations but little self-employment.	Preference for larger organizations but at the same time much self-employment.
Skepticism toward technological solutions.	Strong appeal of technological solutions.
Innovators feel independent of rules.	Innovators feel constrained by rules.
Renegade championing.	Rational championing.
Top managers involved in strategy.	Top managers involved in operations.
Power of superiors depends on position and relationships.	Power of superiors depends on control of uncertainties.

(Continued)

Exhibit 4.6   Continued

Low UAI	High UAI
Tolerance for ambiguity in structures and procedures.	Highly formalized conception of management.
Appeal of transformational leader role.	Appeal of hierarchical control role.
Many new trademarks granted.	Few new trademarks granted.
Innovations welcomed but not necessarily taken seriously.	Innovations resisted but, if accepted, applied consistently.
Precision and punctuality have to be learned and managed.	Precision and punctuality come naturally.
Relationship orientation.	Task orientation.
Flexible working hours not appealing.	Flexible working hours popular.
Belief in generalists and common sense.	Belief in specialists and expertise.
Superiors optimistic about employees' ambition and leadership capacities.	Superiors pessimistic about employees' ambition and leadership capacities.

a. See also Exhibit 4.4.

Uncertainty Avoidance and Consumer Behavior

As mentioned in Chapter 3, De Mooij (1998a, 1998b, 2001) found validations of all four IBM dimensions in data from consumer surveys across European countries by market research agencies.[89] Country consumption data showed many meaningful correlations with UAI—that is, cases where the correlation with UAI was not only statistically significant but stronger than the correlations with the other three IBM indexes and with GNP/capita or purchasing power parity (PPP), a theoretically more attractive alternative to GNP/capita.

In the consumption of beverages and food, UAI correlated positively with the use of mineral water (Eurodata 91, "drinking almost every day," $r = .57**$; EMS 97, "consume regularly," $r = .47*$; Euromonitor 97, liters/capita sold in 1996, $r = .78***$). It correlated positively with the sales of fresh fruits (Euromonitor 97, kg/capita sold in 1996, $r = .66**$) and of sugar (same source and measure, $r = .46*$). UAI correlated negatively with the consumption of ice cream ($r = -.76***$), frozen foods ($r = -.69***$), confectionery ($r = -.59**$), savory snacks ($-.57**$), cereals ($-.55*$), tea ($r = -54*$), milk ($r = -.51*$), and fruit juices ($r = -.48*$). These figures suggest a link between UAI and a search for purity and simplicity in beverage and food purchases.

The same search for purity was found in a positive correlation of UAI with the consumption of textile washing powders (Euromonitor 97, kg/capita, $r = .63**$) and negative correlations with

women's claims to use cosmetics (Eurodata 91, lipstick, $r = -.90***$; body lotions, $r = -.84***$; deodorants, $r = -.84***$; hair conditioner, $r = -.83***$; facial moisturizing cream, $r = -.75***$; face cleanser, $r = -.73***$; mascara, $r = -.64**$).

UAI correlated negatively with the adoption of new media, use of Internet (EMS 97, heavy and medium use, $r = -.72***$) and of teletext (same source, $r = -.74***$). However, it also correlated negatively with the use of conventional media, newspaper reading (Eurodata 91, read yesterday, $r = -.84***$), daily newspaper sales (Euromonitor 97, $r = -.66**$), and book reading (Eurodata 91, at least one book in past year, $r = -.74***$). This suggests for *low-UAI* countries a more open-minded mentality, in searching for information and in accessibility to innovation.

In financial matters, people from higher-UAI countries invested less in stocks (EMS 97, $r = -.64**$) and more in precious metals and gems ($r = .55*$), which shows a link between UAI and a search for safety. De Mooij also cites a newspaper source about terms of payment in 15 of the 16 countries that correlated positively with UAI, $r = .62**$ for agreed terms and $r = .68**$ for actually observed terms.[90] High-UAI countries are slower in paying.

UAI also correlated with main car bought new (EMS 97, $r = .80***$) and not secondhand ($r = -.79***$) and with no "do-it-yourself" in wallpapering (Eurodata 91, $r = -.48*$) or in home painting (walls or woodwork, $r = -.44*$). These answers also suggest more playing it safe in high-UAI countries and leaving tricky jobs to experts.

Uncertainty Avoidance
and Political Systems

In a classic study on the "civic culture" in five countries, based on a survey of representative samples of the populations, Almond and Verba (1963) developed an index of "subjective competence" of citizens in dealing with their local government. Subjective competence is the extent to which respondents believed they could participate in political decisions at the local level or whether, on the contrary, they should leave such decisions to specialists. Across the five countries, Almond and Verba's measure of subjective competence was significantly negatively correlated with UAI ($r = -.96**$; see Exhibit 4.15 in the statistical section of this chapter). In the higher-UAI countries in this study, citizens felt less able to participate in local political decisions.[91] Within IBM, UAI was correlated with pessimism about the interest of companies in employees' welfare (question C10). In higher-UAI countries individuals more often feel alienated from the systems that affect their lives.

Anecdotal confirmation of the difference in influence that people assume to have over government decisions is found in the following story, told to me by an American resident of Belgium.[92] (The United States has a UAI value of 46; Belgium's is 94.) The American lived in a neighborhood in suburban Brussels that suffered more and more from noise pollution caused by the nearby airport. The American went around the neighborhood with a petition for the authorities to take noise-limiting measures. Other expatriates in the neighborhood, mainly from Britain and the Netherlands, all signed. The Belgians reacted to the request either with a denial of the problem ("What noise?") and refusal to sign or with resignation ("We are willing to sign but it won't help").[93]

The 1981-82 European Values Survey and the 1990-93 World Values Survey both included a set of 14 questions about "how much confidence you have in" a number of institutions (WVS questions 272-285). Exhibit 4.12 in the statistical section includes the correlations of the WVS data for five institutions that I assumed to be functionally equivalent across countries: the legal system, the press, trade (or labor) unions, the police, and civil service. Confidence in the civil service correlated significantly negatively with UAI, both across all 25 countries and across the 18 wealthier ones. Confidence in the legal system only correlated negatively with UAI across all countries; across the wealthier countries it correlated positively with GNP/capita. Confidence in the police was negatively correlated with PDI across all countries and with UAI across the wealthier countries. The possibilities for power abuses by police in poor countries are larger than in rich countries.

The negative correlations with UAI confirm the sense of alienation toward the government system in more uncertainty-avoiding national cultures.

Confidence in the two other institutions included in the analysis, the press and the trade unions, did not relate to UAI. Confidence in the press was *positively* correlated with PDI (see Chapter 3); confidence in the unions was correlated negatively with the Masculinity Index (see Chapter 6). Press and unions are not so much sources of authority (although in totalitarian states they could be used as such) as they are ways to counterbalance authority.

The 1990-93 WVS asked also about participation in "voluntary associations and activities." A summary score of participation in 16 different types of activities (such as trade unions, sports clubs, and environmental conservation groups; WVS questions 19-34) was strongly negatively correlated across 23 countries with UAI (rho = $-.70***$; see Exhibit 4.16). This illustrates another aspect of citizen competence: In lower-UAI countries citizens are more likely to organize themselves voluntarily for their benefit or their society's.

The Eurobarometer, the periodic attitude survey of representative samples of European Union country citizens conducted twice yearly since 1974, has intermittently included the question "To what extent would you say you are interested in politics?" Exhibit 4.17 in the statistical section shows that mean scores on this question (on a 4-point scale) for 11 EU countries surveyed in 1994 (the 12 countries before the addition of Austria, Finland, and Sweden, minus Luxembourg, for which no IBM data exist) correlated with both UAI and PDI with $r = -.76**$, but the correlation with UAI was marginally stronger; there was no significant second-order effect. Interest in politics was larger in low-UAI countries, which confirms of course the greater citizen competence in these countries. This greater competence went along with a more critical attitude toward European unification. The same survey asked, "Are you for or against the formation of a European Union, with a European Government responsible to the European Parliament?" The "for" answers varied from 24% in Denmark to 72% in Italy and correlated (Exhibit 4.17) with UAI with $r = .68*$ and with PDI with $r = .67*$; in a multiple regression only UAI remained. In the high-UAI countries, where authorities are remote, the public tended to be more prepared to accept a Europewide authority.

For the Power Distance Index it made sense to divide countries into those with political systems with "balanced power" (since 1975) and those with systems with "unbalanced power" (Exhibit 3.18): The "balanced power" countries tended to show much lower PDI values. For the Uncertainty

Avoidance Index, the statistical analysis (Exhibit 4.18) shows that it made sense to divide the "balanced power" countries into "old" and "young" democracies. The young democracies (which developed their present form of government since World War I: Austria, Finland, France, Germany, Ireland, Israel, Italy, Japan, and Turkey) tend to show higher UAI scores than do the old democracies (Australia, Belgium, Canada, Denmark, Great Britain, the Netherlands, New Zealand, Norway, Sweden, Switzerland, and the United States).[94] Each of the young democracies acquired its present form of government after losing or winning a war in which the country played a more or less aggressive role. Lynn and Hampson (1977) have proven the continuity of their anxiety factor from 1935 to 1978 (see below). This means that the stress levels were not caused by the war, but rather contributed to the fact that countries took part in it.

Political systems cannot survive for long if they are not in harmony with the mental programming of the citizens. Almond and Verba's (1963) study included data showing how "citizen competence" was fostered in family, school, and job relationships. For example, the percentages who "remembered freedom to protest decisions" in Almond and Verba's five countries followed exactly the (reverse) ranking of their UAI scores; the same was true for the percentages who claimed they actually did protest about decisions on the job (p. 343).

Kaase and Marsh (1976) studied representative samples of the populations of Austria, Germany, Great Britain, the Netherlands, and the United States. They measured "protest potential" (the acceptability of unorthodox political behavior, such as boycotts and occupations) and "repression potential" (the desirability of repression of such behavior by the authorities). On both dimensions, the higher-UAI countries Austria and Germany contrasted with the lower-UAI countries Great Britain, the Netherlands, and the United States. In Austria and Germany, fewer respondents declared themselves prepared to go beyond the more classical forms of protest, such as petitions, demonstrations, and boycotts, and more respondents favored repression of political demonstrations by the government. This fits with the lower citizen competence in higher-UAI countries found by Almond and Verba: Citizens are not only more dependent on government, but they want it that way; citizen attitudes and behaviors of officials in both high- and low-UAI countries reinforce and confirm the societal norm.

In the subsection of this chapter on schools, I referred to findings by Chandler et al. and by Yan and Gaier that students in higher-UAI countries are less likely to attribute their achievements to their own abilities. This also discourages political participation. It is a reasonable assumption, supported by history, that (1) political systems in countries in which citizens feel they cannot participate will be less stable, and (2) younger balanced-power political systems following periods in which citizens were deliberately kept incompetent will not show the same level of subjective citizen competence as older and established political systems.

One aspect of citizen competence on which modern nations differ and that, for example, divides Western Europe is whether citizens are obliged to carry identity cards or documents that they must produce at the request of the police or other authorities. In the lower-UAI countries (Denmark, Sweden, Ireland, Great Britain, Norway, the Netherlands, and Finland) this obligation does not exist (although many people do carry credit cards and other identifying material for convenience); not being able to identify oneself to a police officer is not an offense. In the higher-UAI countries (Belgium, France, Spain, Italy, Austria, Germany, and Switzerland) this obligation exists and is usually maintained very strictly.[95] The identity card obligation splits the countries almost perfectly according to UAI level (rho = .85***). The relationship of the citizen to the authorities and vice versa is different in the two kinds of countries: In lower-UAI countries the citizen feels more competent, and if the authorities want to identify him or her, the burden of proof is on the authorities; in countries where the societal norm is one of stronger uncertainty avoidance, the citizen feels more at the mercy of the authorities and his or her dependence is accentuated by the continuous need to be able to justify his or her existence by carrying a document.

Citizen competence reduces the ability of authorities to make fast and autonomous decisions on issues that influence citizens' interests. Reitsma (1995) compared the duration of decision making about major public works (such as the construction of a new motorway) in six European countries. For similar projects, the decision-making process lasted 17 months in Belgium, 20 months in France, 52 months in the Netherlands, 53 months in Germany and Switzerland, and 67 months in Great Britain. These durations are correlated with UAI with $r = -.97**$ and with PDI with $r = -.96**$; in a multiple regression both UAI and PDI contributed significantly. In the high-UAI, high-PDI countries Belgium and France, there are no avenues of appeal through which citizens or public bodies whose interests are involved can try to delay authorities' decisions; the four other countries do have procedures for appeal that considerably retard the decision process—they force the authorities to take a variety of interests into account when preparing to make their decisions. It is not surprising that the Eurolink rail connection between London on the one side and Brussels and Paris on the other, through the Channel Tunnel, had its fast own tracks in Belgium and France right from the beginning, but the construction of a special track on the British side has been waiting for many years.

Putnam (1973) surveyed political attitudes among high civil servants in Germany, Great Britain, and Italy. He distinguished between "classical bureaucrats," who showed negative attitudes toward the political process, and "political bureaucrats," who were positive. On an "Index for Tolerance of Politics" (ITP), 94% of the Italian civil servants ranked below the mean, as did 38% of the Germans and 7% of the British. This follows, of course, the three countries' UAI ranks and shows that alienation about the political process exists not only among citizens, but among those who are supposed to represent the system.[96] In a later publication using some of the same material, Aberbach and Putnam (1977) compared the backgrounds of civil servants in five countries: the three previous ones plus the Netherlands and the United States. Of special relevance here are the proportions of higher civil servants with law degrees: 3% in Britain, 18% in the United States, 39% in the Netherlands, 53% in Italy, and 65% in Germany. This sequence is almost identical to the sequence of UAI scores (rho = .90*). Choosing law graduates for the civil service can be seen as a form of avoiding uncertainty.

Another sign of the norms prevalent in a country is the relative priority given to the training of experts versus lay personnel for particular tasks. Countries higher in UAI will be more likely to train experts. The Austrian researchers Gaspari and Millendorfer (1978) drew attention to *the number of nurses per doctor* as an index for the involvement of laypersons; it has the attractive feature of being independent of national wealth. They showed data from 1971 for 15 of the IBM countries. Their numbers of nurses per doctor varied from .4 in Greece to 5.5 in Ireland, with a mean of 2.6. Exhibit 4.19 in the statistical section of this chapter shows that these numbers correlated strongly with UAI (rho = −.78***). Inspired by Gaspari and Millendorfer's work, I looked for more recent data for more countries and found information on population per doctor and population per nurse for 50 countries from the IBM set in the 1990 *World Development Report* (World Bank, 1990), complemented by the 1984 *World Development Report* (World Bank, 1984). Dividing the population per doctor by the population per nurse produced again the number of nurses per doctor. The correlation pattern of these data is also shown in Exhibit 4.19. The relative numbers of doctors and of nurses in a country are obviously both strongly dependent on national wealth.

Wealth put aside, there were relatively more doctors in countries with high UAI and high IDV, and more nurses in countries with lower PDI, where doctors seem to delegate more. Nurses per doctor varied from .4 in Argentina to 10.5 in Kenya, with a mean of 3.5; across 50 countries these numbers were again strongly correlated with UAI (rho = −.52***). There are many activities in hospitals that can be done by either doctors or nurses. In more uncertainty-avoiding countries, there is a greater tendency to have doctors carry out these activities. This can be interpreted as a consequence of a stronger belief in expert knowledge. Wealth per se is hardly a predictor of nurses per doctor; the zero-order correlation with wealth is weakly positive (rho = .27*). Investing national income in doctors rather than nurses is societally inefficient, because a poor country should be better able to pay for nurses than for doctors.

Exhibit 3.19 shows the correlation pattern of the 1998 Transparency International Internet Corruption Perception Index across 50 countries. In Chapter 3, I related the perception of corruption to higher PDI values, but it is also linked to higher UAI values. Across all 50 countries, a stepwise regression showed that (1) higher GNP/capita, (2) lower PDI, (3) lower MAS, and (4) lower UAI all reduced perceptions of corruption significantly. Across the 26 wealthy countries, only UAI and PDI contributed to explaining corruption perception, and UAI had the strongest influence (r = −.78***). Only across the 17 poor countries did UAI not play a role. The relation between UAI and corruption perception is easy to explain. If citizens are incompetent toward the authorities and the dominant feeling is that decisions should be left to experts, there will be a greater temptation for authorities to accept bribes, fewer opportunities for lay citizens to check up on them, and higher levels of both actual corruption and suspicion of corruption.

In the United States, the Heritage Foundation (an organization inspired by the economic free market theories of Milton Friedman) has since 1994 published annually a volume titled *Index of Economic Freedom*. The 1998 edition contains data for 156 countries that were scored on 10 economic factors: trade policy, taxation, government intervention in the economy, monetary policy, capital flows and foreign investment, banking, wage and price controls, property rights, labor market regulation, and black market (Johnson, Holmes, & Kirkpatrick, 1998). Across 53 countries from the IBM set, the Index of Economic Freedom was primarily correlated with 1997 GNP/capita (r = −.59***; high values of the index stand for low economic freedom).[97] In a stepwise regression with GNP/capita and the IBM indexes, none of the latter played a role. Across 45 overlapping countries the Index of Economic Freedom was also correlated, even more strongly than with GNP/capita, with the Transparency International CPI (see the preceding paragraph), $r = -.71***$. This shows that in the type of estimates made for both indexes similar judgments played a role. Across 26 wealthy countries, however, the Index of Economic Freedom was not correlated with GNP/capita ($r = -.08$) but was correlated highly significantly with UAI ($r = .66***$). Wealthy countries with strongly uncertainty-avoiding cultures allow less freedom to economic markets. In a stepwise multiple regression across these wealthy countries, 44% of the variance of the index was explained by high UAI, 61% by high UAI and low MAS, and 76% by high UAI, low MAS, and low PDI. So in addition to uncertainty avoidance, femininity and a concern for equality reduced the freedom left to economic markets. Countries in which there is a concern for protecting the weak (low MAS) and a tendency to maintain equality (low PDI) will be quicker to set limits on the freedom of market mechanisms.[98] Across just the 27 poorer countries, the Economic Freedom Index showed no significant correlations at all, not even with GNP/capita.

Uncertainty Avoidance and Legislation

Laws and bylaws are the form par excellence in which societal norms are expressed: "Legislation" is one of the consequences of societal norms in the diagram displayed in Exhibit 1.5; it serves, in its turn, to reinforce the norm. The cultural heritage of the Roman Empire is partly transferred by Roman law. Uncertainty-avoiding countries will have a greater need for legislation than will less uncertainty-avoiding countries. For example, Germany (UAI 65) has an extensive set of laws even for emergencies that *might* occur (*Notstandsgesetz*); Great Britain (UAI 35) does not even have a written constitution. Attempts at codifying labor-management relations in Britain (the Industrial Relations Act) failed because they were too much against societal norms.

Curiously, the need for legislation in uncertainty-avoiding societies does not imply a greater trust in the legal system. In fact, the proliferation of laws seems to diminish the extent to which the system is trusted. As mentioned above, the World Values Survey question about "confidence in the legal system" (question 275; see Exhibit 4.12) was significantly negatively correlated with UAI (rho = $-.45*$).

Gibson and Caldeira (1996) studied the differences in "legal cultures" among European Union countries, basing their work on the 1992 Eurobarometer survey across 12 countries and on their own telephone resurvey of samples of respondents. They distinguished two dimensions of legal values: (1) legal alienation (feeling that law is usually against me) and (2) (no) rule of law (okay to break a law I consider unjust). Across 11 overlapping countries, I found both the "legal alienation" and the "no rule of law" scores strongly correlated with UAI ($r = .88***$ and $r = .78**$, respectively).[99] Thus in high-UAI countries people more often felt the law was against them and said it was okay to break an unjust law. This contradicts the UAI item "Company rules should not be broken" (B60 in Appendix 1); I interpret it as another contrast between the desirable and the desired. A third dimension referred to valuation of liberty (people should not be allowed to express extreme ideas).[100] This was not correlated with UAI at all ($r = .09$), but was correlated negatively with national wealth (1990 GNP/capita, $r = -.69**$).[101] Valuation of liberty was a luxury that came with national wealth.

An interesting example of how "positive law" (actual regulations) reflects "living law" (unwritten societal norms; these terms are taken from Northrop, 1962, p. 427) is the following. After the 1973 oil crisis, the governments of all Western European countries felt a need—or had an excuse in the face of public opinion—to establish or at least consider maximum allowed speeds on motorways. Whether these speeds were actually respected is irrelevant here—the concern is with formal law, not with practice (although practice will at least to some extent be affected by formal law). The statistical analysis in Exhibit 4.20 shows across 14 Western European countries a significant correlation (rho = $.58*$) between the maximum speeds adopted and the countries' UAI scores. Maximum speeds are also a means of reducing fatal accidents on motorways. We could assume, naively, that the countries with the highest traffic death rates before the oil crisis would have chosen the lowest maximum speeds. In the statistical section of this chapter the relationships among maximum speeds, IBM indexes, and traffic deaths is explored. The naive logic about maximum speeds does not hold; countries with higher accident mortality did not adopt lower maximum speeds. Governments do not legislate just on the basis of facts, but at least as much on the basis of prerational values. The emotionality in high-UAI cultures produces a sense of stress, of urgency, which in turn leads the people in those cultures to want to drive faster. I have also observed that in countries that allow high speeds, experts regularly prove that speed reduction will not make traffic safer; in countries that have established lower maximum speeds, experts prove the opposite. Expertise is not value-free either. The higher allowed speeds in higher-UAI countries show, in fact, a priority of saving time over saving lives.

Uncertainty Avoidance,
Nationalism, and Xenophobia

Exhibit 4.4 suggests that UAI is associated with more resistance to changes. The Reader's Digest (1970) findings mentioned earlier in this chapter suggested more conservatism in high-UAI countries. At the level of individuals (among some 5,000 male university students from 18 countries all around the world), Eckhardt (1971) found that respondents who described their political position as "to the right" shared the following values: personal conformity, no personal benevolence, resistance to social change, lack of political interest, never writing to a newspaper to express a point of view, interest in national rather than international affairs, national loyalty, and a call for national leadership. Several of these values emerged in the previous sections as being associated with high UAI, suggesting a link between UAI and politically conservative ideas.

A relationship between UAI and nationalism was suggested by the suspicion of foreigners as managers found in the higher-UAI countries in the IBM surveys (see also Exhibit 4.4). The 1990-93 World Values Survey contained two questions that might be relevant in this respect: "Of course, we all hope that there will not be another war, but if it were to come to that, would you be willing to fight for your country?" (question 263, answers *yes/no/don't know*) and "How proud are you to be [your nationality]?" (question 322, 4-point scale). For the correlations, see Exhibit 4.12. Both across all 26 countries and across the 19 wealthier ones, these questions produced substantial zero-order or second-order correlations with UAI. However, surprisingly all correlations with UAI were *negative*, so in higher-UAI countries people were *less* willing to fight for their country and *less* proud of their nationality. Dogan (1998), who looked at the same questions, has suggested that the unwillingness to fight for one's country represented the hangover from World War II; the correlations mean that this hangover was worse in the higher-UAI societies, which is not unlikely. See also Chapter 6.

Gudykunst (1989) collected answers on a survey of "ethnolinguistic identity" from 158 female and male foreign students at a U.S. university. Their answers were correlated with the IBM index values of the places they came from, a total of 32 different countries and regions in the IBM set. Gudykunst found significant correlations with UAI for two of the five subscales in his survey. One was "intergroup comparisons"; it consisted of the items "In relation to the U.S., my culture is [inferior/superior]" and "In the U.S., my status is [low/high]." Students from low-UAI cultures saw their own culture and status more positively; Gudykunst interprets this as a sign that they feel

less anxiety in intergroup encounters. The second subscale significantly correlated with UAI was "ethnolinguistic vitality"; it consisted of the items "How highly regarded is your native language in the city in which you live in the U.S.?" (very low/ very high) and "How highly regarded is your native language internationally?" (very low/very high). Students from high-UAI cultures saw their language as more highly regarded. This looks paradoxical if they felt their status to be lower; I interpret it as a compensation for anxiety through chauvinism. The study also produced correlations with individualism and masculinity, which will be discussed in Chapters 5 and 6.[102]

Several questions in the 1981-82 European Values Survey and the 1990-93 World Values Survey suggest a relationship between UAI and levels of trust and tolerance in countries. The WVS contained a list of 14 groups of deviant people and asked the respondents, "Could you please sort out any that you would not like to have as neighbors?" (Inglehart et al., 1998, questions 69-82). For the 26 countries in the WVS set overlapping with the IBM set, I correlated the percentages of those who included "people of a different race" (question 70) in their selection. These varied from 2% in Switzerland to 58% in South Korea. The answers obviously reflected specific local circumstances (the Swiss may have thought of diplomats, whereas the Koreans may have thought of Japanese). Exhibit 4.12 shows that across all 26 countries the percentages correlated mainly with PDI. Across the 17 richer countries (which are more comparable), however, the main correlation was with UAI (rho = .63**): High UAI stood for a stronger tendency to reject people from a different race as neighbors.

The European Commission, during the "European Year Against Racism," published a special Eurobarometer report titled *Racism and Xenophobia in Europe* (1997). The correlations in Exhibit 4.17 show that UAI was the first predictor of the opinion in a country that immigrants (from outside the European Union) should be sent back, especially if they are unemployed or illegal. Uncertainty avoidance is a major component of xenophobia and racism (however, the correlations show that another component is cultural masculinity, to which we will come back in Chapter 6). In the IBM questionnaire the acceptance of foreigners as managers was also negatively correlated with UAI (see Exhibit 4.4).

Ornauer, Wiberg, Sicinski, and Galtung (1976) published the results of a survey about "images of the world in the year 2000" conducted among more or less representative samples of the populations in nine countries. The relevance of their study in the context of UAI is that uncertainty avoidance is likely to be reflected in views of the future. Out of 20 items conceptually related to uncertainty avoidance, 4 were significantly correlated with UAI (Exhibit 4.15). These items expressed that in countries lower in UAI more people believed they themselves could do something to contribute to peace (which resembles Almond and Verba's subjective competence); more people believed that compromising with opponents was not dangerous;[103] more people were prepared to live from day to day; and a somewhat larger fraction of the respondents were prepared to live abroad. Lower-UAI countries thus showed less alienation from what happened in the world, greater tolerance of other opinions, less fear for tomorrow, and less fear of the unknown.

There is a certain resemblance between the uncertainty avoidance dimension of societies and the distinction made by anthropologists between "tight" and "loose" societies, although authors differ on the definitions of these polar concepts. Pelto's (1968) well-known definition of loose societies states that in such societies norms are expressed with a wide range of alternative channels, deviant behavior is easily tolerated, and values of group organization, formality, permanence, durability, and solidarity are undeveloped. The opposite characteristics are found in tight societies. These discrepancies fit well with some of the connotations of "low-UAI countries" in Exhibit 4.5.[104] UAI can thus be seen as a measure of tightness for modern societies. Many modern societies are even looser than those Pelto considered.

Chan, Gelfand, Triandis, and Tzeng (1996) tried to operationalize the tight/loose dichotomy. They compared the answers of high school boys in Japan and the United States (1,200 in each country, aged 13-18) on the affective meanings of concepts from the *Atlas of Affective Meaning* (Osgood, May, & Miron, 1975). Japan was assumed to be tight and the United States loose. Chan et al. found that Japanese boys gave a narrower range of answers than did American boys on nearly all concepts. Examples of concepts on which the Japanese boys agreed more are guilt, sin, tragedy, truth, and duty. The exceptional concepts on which the Japanese boys agreed less were aggression, problem, conflict, questioning things, contemplation, and tradition; at least the first four of these refer to uncontrolled situations for which the tight society has no standard coping strategy. In an attempt to explain these tightness/ looseness differences, Chan et al. suggest possible links to individualism/collectivism as well as to uncertainty avoidance.[105] Their study is based on two cultures from which dimensions cannot be disentangled, but the cultural gap between Japan and the United States in my data is much larger for uncertainty avoidance (36 places among 53 countries) than that for individualism (21 places). Also, Pelto earlier gave examples of

collectivist societies that were quite loose, such as Thailand.[106]

Uncertainty Avoidance and Religions

In Chapter 3, I argued that differences in religion by themselves do not explain differences in power distance; rather, the adoption of a certain religion and a national power distance norm should both be seen as results of a common cause. However, once a religion has been established in a country, it will reinforce the values that led to its adoption. Power distance deals with the relationships between people and their fellow humans, in which the supernatural is only indirectly involved. In the opening section of this chapter I mentioned religion as one of the three fundamental ways for human society to cope with uncertainty. In countries with stronger uncertainty avoidance norms, religions can be expected to stress absolute certainties and manifest intolerance toward other religions.

In the statistical section of this chapter, Exhibit 4.21 shows that for the 36 countries in the IBM set that were predominantly Christian, there was a strong association of Catholicism (Roman or Orthodox) with UAI. Catholicism stresses life after death and the believer's ability to ensure participation in it more than do most Protestant groups; also, Catholicism stresses certainties, such as the infallibility of the pope and the uniqueness of the Church. Protestantism, and especially Calvinism, encourages the use of worldly ways to cope with uncertainty (technology and law) as willed by God rather than ritual ways (see Weber, 1930/ 1976, p. 224). Swanson (1967) found a main difference between Catholicism and Protestantism in the former's belief in "immanence," that is, God being incorporated in persons, organizations, or objects in the natural world. Protestantism denies such immanence, which demands a greater tolerance for anxiety in believers. In Exhibit 4.1, all Christian countries on the left-hand side (high UAI) are Catholic, and all but three of the Christian countries on the right-hand side (low UAI) are Protestant or mixed.[107]

Within one church, different kinds of religiosity may coexist. This became evident in a unique study conducted by British sociologist Robert Towler (1984). In 1963, John A. T. Robinson, then Anglican bishop of Woolwich, England, published a little book titled *Honest to God,* containing critical ideas about traditional elements in Christian religion. As a result, he received about 4,000 spontaneous letters, some supportive, some critical, from mainly British readers (or nonreaders). Robinson donated this letter collection to Towler, who with his collaborators did an extensive content analysis. Towler found evidence of five different "varieties of religion" among the correspondents:

1. Exemplarism, Jesus Christ as an example to follow
2. Conversionism, based on a personal experience of having been saved from sin
3. Theism, a sense of wonder and awe in the face of God's works in nature and the world
4. Gnosticism, focusing on possession of secret knowledge about the spiritual world
5. Traditionalism, uncritical acceptance of the teachings of the church, whatever their content

Had Towler's material covered more people from Asian cultures, at least one more variety would have been added:

6. Mysticism, focusing on a personal experience of unity with God

The five British varieties of religiosity occurred within the same church. The strong individualism in British culture (see Chapter 5) may encourage different individual beliefs and feelings, but a similar variety could very well exist within religious denominations elsewhere as well. The different varieties accommodate different and contrasting personal value systems, and cultural influences will make some of these varieties more or less popular among certain groups. Towler, whose book is titled *The Need for Certainty,* recognized groups with stronger and weaker tolerance of uncertainty. He characterized the beliefs of the first as "certitude" and those of the second as "faith." Among his five varieties of religion, he associated conversionism and gnosticism with certitude and exemplarism and theism with faith (p. 105).

The non-Christian high-UAI countries include Japan (UAI 92), which from a religious point of view may seem surprising, although a Chinese writer has argued that "it is not generally realized how much more important religion and religious affiliation are to the Japanese than to the Chinese" (Hsu, 1971, p. 40). Japanese Zen Buddhism is stricter than other forms of Buddhism. Korea (UAI 85) is unique as an East Asian country in being half Buddhist and half Christian, although only one-third of Korean Christians are Catholics. Religion is very much an issue in Korea. The high-UAI side also contains the Muslim countries of Turkey and Pakistan, and the Arab speakers, but not those from East Asia; Iran is in the middle, but Israel is again high (UAI 81). Islam and Judaism together with Christianity are the world's revelation religions; they have common roots, and both Islam and orthodox Judaism claim absolute truths as much as Catholic Christianity does.

On the low-UAI side, aside from the mixed Catholic-Protestant and the Protestant countries, appear Buddhist countries (Singapore and Hong Kong; Thailand and Taiwan are in the middle) and Hindu India. The Eastern religions are less concerned with the absolute and generally more tolerant; certainties are not imposed from the outside but may arrive through meditation. The Chinese have been described as showing an "exceedingly relativistic sense of morality" (Inkeles & Levinson, 1954/1969, pp. 481-482). The low-UAI side also includes the East Asian Muslim countries Malaysia and Indonesia; Islam in Java, the dominant heart of Indonesia, is strongly imprinted by a tolerant form of mysticism (Geertz, 1968; Mulder, 1978), and Malaysian Islam varies by state but is generally fairly tolerant too. Finally, on the low-UAI side we find both East and West African countries, with their broad mixture of traditional and modern religious practices.

In summary, religion and uncertainty avoidance appear to be meaningfully related. Religion is not the root cause of UAI differences, as is evident from the low UAI scores for Catholic Ireland and the Philippines and Muslim Indonesia and Malaysia. As I argued at the beginning of this subsection, both the adoption of a certain religion and the national norm for uncertainty avoidance should rather be seen as results of a common cause; an established religion reinforces the values that led to its adoption, however, confirming either strong or weak uncertainty avoidance.

What applies to religions also applies to ideologies, which are secular religions. Dogmatic, intolerant ideological positions are more likely in countries with higher UAI norms. Problems will more often be interpreted ideologically in higher-UAI countries and pragmatically in lower-UAI countries. Ever since the adoption of the Universal Declaration of Human Rights (in 1948), the conflicts among religious, political and/or ideological fundamentalisms and respect for human rights have been on the world's political agenda. Although other dimensions (power distance, individualism) also play a role, a culture's level of uncertainty avoidance indicates the strength of fundamentalist forces that threaten human rights—value systems that consider their Truth more important than the rights, freedoms, and sometimes lives of people.

Uncertainty Avoidance, Theories, and Games

In Chapter 3, I argued that a country's PDI norm affects the types of theories about power that will be developed in that country: elitist theories in high-PDI countries, pluralist theories in low-PDI countries. A country's UAI norm affects the type of intellectual activity in the country in an even more fundamental way. In high-UAI countries, scholars look for certainties, for Theory with a capital *T,* for Truth. In low-UAI countries they take a more relativistic and pragmatic stand and look for usable knowledge.

The difference between the high-UAI and low-UAI approach is most pronounced in the social sciences.[108] In low-UAI countries the scientific logic favors *induction*—that is, the development of general principles from empirical facts. In high-UAI countries *deduction*—that is, reasoning from general principles to specific situations—is more popular. The great theoreticians and philosophers of the West tend to come from higher-UAI countries, especially Germany and Austria: Kant, Marx, Freud, Weber, and Popper, to mention but a few. Theories based on nonfalsifiable hypotheses, such as those developed by Freud and Marx, appeal most to scholars in high-UAI countries (see Magee, 1975, p. 44, on Karl Popper). Up to the present day, empirical studies in the social sciences in such high-UAI countries as Germany and France are rare; in a society with a strong uncertainty avoidance norm scholars fear the risk of exposing their truths to experiments with unpredictable outcomes. On the other hand, in lower-UAI countries like the United States and Great Britain empirical studies dominate. The orthodox methodological justification of such studies is that the progress of scientific knowledge passes through the falsification of hypotheses in testing them on reality; actually attempting to falsify one's hypotheses requires that one have a large tolerance for uncertainty.

Of course, good hypotheses presuppose good theory. Social science research in the Anglo-American tradition often suffers from a lack of such theory. Empirical studies degenerate into fishing expeditions equipped with powerful computing tools that are doomed to find only trivialities because they do not know what to look for (see also my critique of "catchall" ecological factor analysis in Chapter 1 and my description of my own search for a theory-first approach in Chapter 2).[109] A marriage between a high-UAI concern for theory and a low-UAI tolerance for empiricism represents the best of both worlds. This explains the influence of Austrian and German social scientists such as Kurt Lewin and Theodor Adorno, who emigrated to the United States. More in general, collaboration and exchange among scholars of different national backgrounds, and therefore different scientific approaches, can only benefit all.

Scholars from high-UAI cultures who adhere to opposing scientific points of view are unlikely to be personal friends (a case in point is the rupture between Sigmund Freud and Carl Jung). In low-UAI cultures there is more chance that the scientific and the personal can be kept separate.[110]

The country's uncertainty avoidance norm also affects its native theories of organization, especially their assumptions about rationality. High-UAI countries like Germany have produced rational organization theories (for example, Kieser & Kubicek, 1983). Cyert and March's (1963) "behavioral theory of the firm," from which I have borrowed the term *uncertainty avoidance,* was part of a stream of nonrational theories in the United States started by Simon's (1945/1976) concept of "bounded rationality." March and Simon (1958) argued that "in the case of uncertainty, the definition of rationality becomes problematic" (p. 138). March and Olsen (1976; the latter was from Norway) studied educational institutions (universities and schools), which they found to be "organized anarchies." In these, "choices" are made rather than "decisions" in a "garbage can" process in which collections of choices look for problems, issues and feelings look for decision situations in which they might be aired, solutions look for issues to which they might be an answer, and decision makers look for work. Choices are made by oversight or flight as well as by resolution. Elements of this can be found in earlier work by political scientists who always were more accustomed to dealing with uncertain situations; in a classical paper, the American Lindblom (1959) described the activities of the public administrator as "the science of muddling through." Concepts such as "garbage can," "muddling through," and "chaos" have subsequently also been used for business organizations. Czarniawska and Wolff (1986, p. 23) have called this the "Scandinavization" of organization theory, stressing the popularity of such theories in low-UAI Scandinavian cultures.[111]

Another form in which uncertainty avoidance can be manifested is in the kinds of games played in a certain culture. In a classic anthropological study of games in traditional cultures, Roberts, Arth, and Bush (1959) distinguished three kinds of games: games of physical skill, which aim at mastery of the self and the environment; games of strategy, which aim at mastery of the social system; and games of chance, which aim at mastery of the supernatural. These resemble the three categories to which I referred in the opening of this chapter: technology, law, and religion. Roberts et al. suggested that games of chance are more often played where gods are seen as benevolent and are played less where the gods are believed to be aggressive (p. 602). As societies tend to project their cultural norms on their gods, the aggressiveness of the gods reflects the aggressiveness of the particular society, and games of chance should be played more often in low-UAI countries. In comparing Great Britain and Germany, but also in comparing Hong Kong and Japan, the relationship between low UAI and the popularity of chance games seems to hold.[112]

Thiriez (1995) has linked dominant business strategies in Western countries, East Asian countries, and Middle Eastern countries to the three different games of strategy most popular in these regions (chess in the West, go in the Far East, and backgammon in the Middle East) without making a direct link with uncertainty avoiding behavior.

Exhibit 4.7 summarizes the differences between low- and high-UAI societies for consumer behavior, political systems, legislation, nationalism and xenophobia, religion, and theories and games, as discussed above.

Predictors of UAI

The statistical analysis in Exhibit 4.22 shows the correlations of UAI with eight economic, geographic, and demographic indicators that were identified in Chapter 2 and correlated with the Power Distance Index in Chapter 3. Across all 50 countries, the correlations with UAI are much weaker than those with PDI (Exhibit 3.20). Only the zero-order correlation of UAI with wealth (GNP, negative) is weakly significant. When we divide the countries into poor and wealthy, most correlations become stronger, and the signs for the two groups tend to be opposite. Looking at the contrasting correlations with GNP/capita, latitude, and population density, we find that UAI tends to be lower in poor countries when they are tropical and densely populated, and in wealthy countries when they are cold and sparsely populated.[113] However, these correlations are strongly influenced by extreme scores such as the low UAI values for Singapore (on the equator and very densely populated) and Sweden (high latitude and sparsely populated). The real factors explaining UAI differences are not necessarily latitude and population density at all, but implicit other dimensions differentiating Asia, Latin America, and parts of Europe, such as history and religion, as discussed elsewhere in this chapter.

The $r = .59***$ correlation between UAI in wealthy countries and past economic growth (EGP) confirms a finding of Lynn (1971, pp. 92 ff.), who for 18 developed countries found a $rho = .67***$ correlation between anxiety level (measured from data collected between 1960 and 1965) and economic growth in the period 1950-65. There is no correlation, however, with future economic growth (EGF), which covers the 1965-90 period. This suggests that the causality went

from economic growth to UAI and not vice versa. Fast economic growth in a society is an anxiety-producing condition.

Historically, country economic growth rates have been far from stable. Exhibit 4.23 in the statistical section shows that for a subset of 13 out of the 22 wealthy countries in the IBM set UAI, measured around 1970, was positively correlated with economic growth around that time, but as strongly *negatively* with economic growth for the 1925-50 period, which included the 1929 depression and World War II. There is no correlation with economic growth over a 100-year period. UAI therefore only relates positively to economic growth in wealthy countries under post-World War II conditions. UAI also correlates with aggressive belligerence in World War II, a condition that over the 1925-50 period led to *low* economic growth because of the damages of the war. The same cultural syndrome, uncertainty avoidance, that was associated with warfare and economic disaster during the first half of the 20th century was associated with economic success during the century's second half.

The sign reversal between correlations with 1925-50 and 1960-70 economic growth explains how UAI can be negatively correlated with McClelland's 1925 n_{Ach}, whereas McClelland found his n_{Ach} to be positively correlated with (1929-50) economic growth, and UAI is also positively correlated with economic growth (but over 1960-70). The ranking of countries on economic growth has changed drastically from 1925-50 to 1960-70. McClelland's n_{Ach} scores have also changed, but not in the same way. I tested the correlation of McClelland's 1950 n_{Ach} with 1960-70 economic growth (EGP) and found it to be rho = $-.07$ (across 35 countries for which data for both n_{Ach} and EGP existed). Again, the data do not support McClelland's claim that n_{Ach} has been measured reliably for 1925 *and* 1950 and that both measurements relate to subsequent economic growth.

Uncertainty Avoidance and Historical Factors

The origins of the UAI syndrome are less clear than those of the PDI syndrome; I see no "causal chain" leading to a high- or low-UAI norm, like the one drawn for PDI in Exhibit 3.10. Stronger uncertainty avoidance is negatively related to geographic latitude, like PDI, but only for the wealthier countries; the poorer countries show a positive relationship (Exhibit 4.22). As wealth is not an immutable characteristic, latitude cannot be considered a fundamental cause. The association of uncertainty avoidance with past economic

Exhibit 4.7   Key Differences Between Low- and High-UAI Societies II: Consumer Behavior, Politics, Legislation, Nationalism and Xenophobia, Religion, and Theories and Games

Low UAI	High *UAI*
In Consumer Behavior	
Consumption of convenience products.	Consumption of "purity" products: mineral water, fresh fruits, sugar, textile washing powders.
Reading books and newspapers.	Less reading books and newspapers.
Use Internet and teletext.	Less use of Internet and teletext.
Main car bought secondhand.	Main car bought new.
"Do it yourself" in home.	Use specialists in home.
Investment in stocks.	Investment in precious metals and gems.
Short payment terms for bills.	Long payment terms for bills.
In Political Systems	
Citizens competent toward authorities.	Citizens incompetent toward authorities.
Citizens have confidence in civil service.	Citizens lack confidence in civil service.
Much participation in voluntary associations and activities.	Little participation in voluntary associations and activities.
Strong interest in politics.	Weak interest in politics.
EU members less in favor of European government.	EU members more in favor of European government.
Old democracies.	Young democracies.
Citizens may protest government decisions.	Citizen protest should be repressed.
No identity card obligation.	Carrying of identity card obligatory.
Decisions about infrastructure slow.	Decisions about infrastructure fast.
Civil servants positive toward politics.	Civil servants dislike politics.
Few law graduates in civil service.	Many law graduates in civil service.
Laypersons in key positions; high ratio of nurses to doctors.	Experts in key positions; low ratio of nurses to doctors.
In wealthy countries, less corruption.	In wealthy countries, more corruption.
In wealthy countries, less government intervention in the economy.	In wealthy countries, more government intervention in the economy.
In Legislation	
Few and general laws and regulations.	Many and precise laws and regulations.
Citizens positive toward legal system.	Citizens negative toward legal system.
Laws usually on my side.	Laws usually against me.
Rule of law should prevail.	Laws should be broken if unjust.
Lower speed limits on motorways.	Higher speed limits on motorways.
Nationalism and Xenophobia	
Weak appeal of right-wing politics.	Strong appeal of right-wing politics.
Proud of own nation, willing to fight for it.	Not proud of own nation, unwilling to fight for it.
Expatriate students in United States consider own culture as superior but own language as undervalued.	Expatriate students in United States consider own culture as inferior but own language as highly respected.
Other races acceptable as neighbors.	Other race rejected as neighbors.
Immigrants tolerated.	Immigrants should be sent back.
Citizens can contribute to peace.	Citizens powerless to contribute to peace.
Compromising with opponents is safe.	Compromising with opponents is dangerous.

Exhibit 4.7   Continued

Low UAI	High UAI
Willing to live day to day.	Worried about the future.
More prepared to live abroad.	Less prepared to live abroad.
Loose societies.	Tight societies.

In Religion

Low UAI	High UAI
If Christian, predominantly Protestant.	If Christian, predominantly Catholic or Orthodox.
Faith: exemplarism and theism.	Certitude: conversionism and gnosticism.
Buddhism, Taoism, Hinduism, mysticisms.	Islam, Judaism, Shintoism.
Own truth should not be imposed on others.	There is only one Truth, and we have it.
Human rights: no persecution for beliefs.	Aggressive fundamentalisms.

In Theories and Games

Low UAI	High UAI
In philosophy and science, tendency toward relativism and empiricism.	In philosophy and science, belief in ultimate values and grand theories.
Induction: from the specific to the general.	Deduction: from the general to the specific.
Scientific opponents can be personal friends.	Scientific opponents must be personal enemies.
Games of chance popular.	Games of skill and strategy popular.

growth in Exhibit 4.22 can be interpreted as a short-term effect of beginning modernization—that is, a high rate of change in a society.

We have seen that uncertainty avoidance varies with the dominant religion, but all great religions have their strongly and weakly uncertainty-avoiding versions, so we still need culture to explain why a particular version was adopted in a particular country or part of it.

With no convincing systematic causes, only historical events can explain why different societies have developed such different ways of coping with uncertainty. Historical influences on power distance differences were explored in Chapter 3. The grouping of countries suggested that the roots of the differences go back as far as the Roman Empire, 2,000 years ago. In East Asia it assumed roots in the even older Chinese Empire. Both empires left legacies of large power distances.

On uncertainty avoidance we again find the countries with Romance languages together. These heirs of the Roman Empire all scored on the high-UAI side. However, unlike in the case of PDI the countries with Roman and those with Chinese heritage were not together on UAI. The Chinese-speaking countries Taiwan, Hong Kong, and Singapore scored much lower on UAI than the Latin countries, as did countries with important minorities of Chinese origin: Thailand, Indonesia, the Philippines, and Malaysia.

The Roman and Chinese Empires were both powerful centralized states, conditioning their populations to take orders from the center. But the two differed in an important respect. The Roman Empire developed a unique system of codified laws that in principle applied to all people with citizen status regardless of origin. The Chinese Empire never knew this concept of law. The main continuous principle of Chinese administration has been described as "government by man," in contrast to the Roman idea of "government by law." Chinese judges were supposed to be guided by broad general principles such as those formulated by Confucius around 500 B.C. (see Chapter 7). As Michael Harris Bond has noted, "In Chinese cultures, rule is by the rulers; in Western cultures, rule is by the rules, created by the ruled to protect them from the rulers" (personal communication).

The contrast between the two intellectual traditions explains the fact that IBM employees from countries with a Roman inheritance scored much higher on UAI than their colleagues from countries with a Chinese inheritance. It is another powerful illustration of the profound historical roots of national culture differences.

The Future of Uncertainty
Avoidance Differences

The questions composing UAI did not shift together over time (Exhibit 2.6), so UAI should not be used as an index for longitudinal culture change (the same applied to PDI, see Chapter 3).[114]

What did change significantly and worldwide between the two IBM survey rounds of 1967-69 and 1971-73) was the "stress" component of UAI (A37, "How often do you feel nervous or tense at work?"). A separate analysis of the stress scores for five large categories of employees (world totals) by age groups and by survey round (1967-69 and 1971-73; see Exhibit 4.24 in the statistical section) showed both age and zeitgeist effects. The relationship of stress with age was mostly inverted U-shaped, stress being highest for those in a middle age range. The zeitgeist effect was that between 1968 and 1972 stress increased for virtually all occupational categories and all age brackets. For those over 50 there was a decrease of stress for managers and professionals, but an increase for technicians and clerks. Older people in jobs requiring higher qualifications seem to have had more opportunities to adapt their work situations to themselves than did older people in jobs requiring lower qualifications. In Chapter 3 we found that in this age bracket those in more highly educated employee categories also remained better in touch with developments in society than did those with less education.

The shift toward higher stress occurred in both high- and low-UAI countries. The countries with the highest stress in 1967-69 manifested the largest increases, so the gap between countries became wider (no convergence). The two other UAI questions (B60, rule orientation, and A43, employment stability) did not show significant worldwide shifts, for all countries or for either high- or low-UAI countries.[115] However, most other questions listed in Exhibit 2.6 as correlated with UAI showed shifts in the direction of higher UAI.[116]

Earlier in this chapter, I noted strong relationships among stress, uncertainty avoidance, and anxiety. Exhibit 4.11 shows a rho = .72*** correlation with stress and a rho = .73*** correlation with UAI for a "neuroticism" or "anxiety" factor found by Lynn and Hampson in medical and related statistics for 18 countries. In a later phase of their research, these authors did an analysis over time using data from 1935, 1950, 1955, 1960, 1965, and 1970 (see Lynn, 1975; Lynn & Hampson, 1977).[117] The five countries with the highest anxiety scores in 1935 were Austria, Finland, Germany, Italy, and Japan—the World War II Axis powers and two countries that became involved in the war on their side. From 1935 to 1950, all countries defeated or occupied during World War II increased in anxiety level, whereas six out of the nine countries not defeated or occupied decreased in anxiety level. The mean anxiety scores across all 18 countries developed as follows: 1935, 50.6; 1950, 51.3; 1955, 50.6; 1960, 49.0; 1965, 48.6; 1970, 50.4 (Lynn & Hampson, 1977, tab. 5).

The postwar increase of 1950 had disappeared in 1955, and 1960 and 1965 were years of relatively low anxiety; this applies also to individual countries.[118] From 1965 to 1970 there was a sharp increase in anxiety in 14 out of the 18 countries— all except Finland, France, Japan, and Norway.[119] The 1965-70 period overlaps partly with the 1968-72 period for which we found a worldwide increase in stress in IBM, which confirms that this was not just a phenomenon within this corporation.

Lynn and Hampson's longitudinal data suggest that at least the anxiety (stress) component in UAI is subject to long-term oscillations. The wavelength of such oscillations may be somewhere between 25 and 40 years. High anxiety levels are associated with wars and economic crises. The process could be as follows: When anxiety levels in a country increase, uncertainty avoidance increases. This is noticeable in intolerance, xenophobia, religious and political fanaticism, and all the other manifestations of uncertainty avoidance discussed in this chapter. Leadership passes into the hands of fanatics, and these may drive the country toward war. War, of course, pulls in other countries that did not show the same fanaticism, but that then develop increasing anxiety because of the war threat. In countries experiencing war within their territory, the anxiety mounts further as the war rages on. After the war, the stress is released, first for the countries not directly touched and some years later for the others that start reconstructing. Anxiety decreases and tolerance increases, but after a number of years the trend is reversed and a new wave of anxiety sets in that could be a prelude to a new war. The challenge to world order is to break this vicious circle.

In Chapter 3, I did away with the assumption of a convergence of countries on power distance norms. The inheritance of 4,000 years or more of history will not be eradicated in a matter of decades, or even centuries. The same applies to uncertainty avoidance norms, which have equally old roots. Their long history should make us modest about expectations of fundamental changes in these value differences within our lifetime.

At the same time, global levels of power distance and uncertainty avoidance may shift while differences between countries remain. Impressionistically, dependence on the power of others in many countries over the past two generations has been shrinking. The same is not true for dependence on rules; if anything, this has been increasing worldwide. In the foreseeable future, global integration of governing bodies, an increase in the number of supranational organizations, and the mergers and takeover processes of multinational corporations will lead to an increase in the amount of formal structure to which people will be exposed.[120]

Statistical Analysis of Data Used in This Chapter

Calculating the Uncertainty
Avoidance Index by Country

Country scores for the three questions A37, A43, and B60 can be found in Appendix 2.[121] The "stress" question, A37, as mentioned earlier in this chapter, was taken from earlier surveys of managers in IBM USA, run by the company's medical department. Across divisions in the company, mean stress scores were significantly correlated with complaints about an upset stomach (rho = .49*) but not with headaches or sleep disturbance.[122] Interestingly, mean scores on the stress question were negatively correlated with "Do you have any particular physical or health problems now?" (rho = −.48*), suggesting that denial of health problems could be part of the stress syndrome.

For question A43 (employment stability) the combined percentage of answers 1 + 2 has been used, because these correlated more strongly with the two other UAI questions than the combined answers 1 + 2 + 3 (= 100 − answer 4). The answers for question A43 for the United States and Yugoslavia, although available, have been treated as missing. The reason is that the question serves as a measure of *values*; we should therefore exclude answers differentially affected by situational influences. The data for the 38 countries that have been used were obtained from people working for a subsidiary of a foreign company that in their own country was not a major employer. As the United States was the home country of IBM, U.S. respondents referred to a major and famous domestic company. It is likely that the attraction of a long-term career with a large domestic employer is of a different order than the attraction of a foreign company, one of many foreign employers in the host country. For Yugoslavia the different societal context and relationship to the company of the Yugoslav respondents should be taken into account. Contrary to respondents in the 39 other countries, they did not refer to a large, worldwide employer but to a small, self-managed trade firm under Yugoslav law. This is likely to have affected considerably the attraction of the company as a long-term employer; thus the Yugoslav data should not be compared with IBM subsidiary data. Consequently, for both the United States and

Yugoslavia the values to be used in the computation of UAI have been extrapolated from the 38 other countries, based on the regression line of "employment stability" scores with the sum of the two other UAI question scores. The extrapolated data are United States 30 and Yugoslavia 11; the actual data (not used) were United States 15 and Yugoslavia 35.

Exhibit 4.8 lists the correlations among the three UAI questions across individuals, countries, and occupations. For country scores the three intercorrelations were between .40** and .59***, somewhat lower than for PDI (Exhibit 3.12); nevertheless, the correlations of the three items with UAI across countries were −.80***, −.81***, and −.80***, respectively.

The correlations of the three items across individuals present an interesting picture. As in the case of PDI (Exhibit 3.12), these individual correlations were computed for five one-country, one-occupation subpopulations used for developing the 1971 core questionnaire. It turned out that across individuals, the following was true:

1. Rule orientation and employment stability tended to be significantly positively correlated (just as across countries).
2. Rule orientation and stress were uncorrelated.
3. Employment stability and stress tended to be *negatively* correlated—that is, within the subpopulations those people who perceived more stress were more likely to think of leaving the company early.

The negative relationship between employment stability and stress is an example of how individual and ecological correlations of the same variables can have opposite signs (as argued in Chapter 1). The reason for the sign reversal is that at the country (ecological) level, a societal norm (Exhibit 1.5) intervenes that pushes everyone toward a higher overall level of employment stability in higher-stress countries, even if within each country the higher-stressed individuals may more often leave the company.

Calculating Differences in
Item Scores by Occupation

Exhibit 4.8 also shows that the three UAI items were *not* correlated across occupations. This means that one cannot use them to measure the "uncertainty avoidance level" of an occupation. One should consider occupational differences in the scores of the three items separately.

Exhibit 4.8　Product-Moment Correlations Among Scores on Three Questions Composing the Uncertainty Avoidance Index, Across Individuals, Countries, and Occupations

Pairs of Questions	Correlation of Individual Scores in Five Homogeneous Groups (200-458 respondents)			Correlation of Mean Scores Across 40 (53) Countries	Correlation of Mean Scores Across 38 Occupations
	Minimum	Maximum	Median		
a × b: B60 × A43 Rule orientation × employment stability	.02	.26***	.14**	.59*** (.58***)	−.11
a × c: B60 × A 37 Rule orientation × stress	−.03	.05	.00	.40** (.46***)	.23
b × c: A43 × A37 Employment stability × stress	−.18**	.04	−.11*	.44** (.44**)	−.09

NOTE: Correlations with question A43 for *individuals* are with score values (1-2-3-4). In order to make them comparable to the country and occupation correlations, which are based on percentages 1 + 2, the sign of the correlation coefficient has been reversed. Country scores are means of mean scores for seven occupational groups. Occupation scores are means of mean scores for three large country subsidiaries (France, Germany, and Great Britain).
*p = .05; **p = .01; ***p = .001.

Across 38 occupations rule orientation was strongly correlated with the occupation's *PDI* (r = −.72***, not in the table; as a low score on the question means *more* rule orientation, this indicates a higher occupational rule orientation for a higher occupational PDI, which is plausible). Employment stability was uncorrelated and stress only weakly correlated with the occupation's PDI.

The correlations of occupational rule orientation, employment stability, and stress with the four demographic indicators—average educational level of the occupation, hierarchy level (1 = nonmanagers, 2 = managers), average age, and percentage female—are listed in Exhibit 4.9. This exhibit shows that the amount of rule orientation for an occupation depended mainly on its education level (negatively); the amount of employment stability, on its average age; and the amount of stress, somewhat on its hierarchical level. In the interpretation of the zero-order correlations we should, however, take into account that an occupation's average age was strongly correlated with its hierarchy level (r = .83***) and negatively correlated with its percentage female (r = .55***). It is therefore more meaningful to look at the lower part of Exhibit 4.9, which shows the results of a stepwise regression on all four demographic items. Aside from education, other demographics contributed little to occupational differences in rule orientation. An occupation's level of employment stability depended on the combination of three different factors—age (posi-

tively), education (negatively), and percentage female (negatively)—but not on hierarchical level per se. Aside from relating to its hierarchical level (managers higher stress), an occupation's stress level related somewhat to its percentage female incumbents (more women higher stress).

Country UAI, Average Age of Respondents, and Other IBM Survey Questions

Returning to our analysis at the country level, in addition to the three items used to calculate the UAI, several other IBM questions were associated with UAI. In a country-level factor analysis with 40 countries and 48 variables (not reproduced in Chapter 2), the highest factor loadings on the UAI factor were for two demographic items, .74 for the average age of the sample (A57) and .68 for its average seniority in IBM (A2). Age and seniority were, of course, highly intercorrelated across the 40 countries (r = .72***). Age and UAI correlated with r = .52*** across these countries. Age correlated separately with rule orientation (−.45***), with employment stability (−.46***), and with stress (−.36*). I checked to see whether the differences among countries in UAI level were not just an artifact of the age differences among IBM subsidiaries. For the 40 Category 1 countries, the average ages varied from 27.1 in Hong Kong (a score of 3.01 on A57; see Appendix 2) to 35.2 in Turkey (a score of 4.63). In order to show how strong the effect of age differences on

Exhibit 4.9 Zero-Order Correlations and Stepwise Regressions of UAI Questions for 38 Occupations, With Four Demographic Items

	UAI Questions		
	A. Rule Orientation	B. Employment Stability	C. Stress
Zero-order product-moment correlation across 38 occupations with			
Hierarchy level	−.17	.56***	.40**
Average formal education in years	−.73***	−.21	−.19
Average age in years	−.01	.70***	.34*
Gender (% women)	.26	−.62***	.13
Squared multiple correlation with all four R^2	.60	.80	.32
Order in stepwise regression, cumulative R^2, and sign of coefficient			
1	.53 −Educ	.49 + Age	.16 + Hierarch
2		.61 − Educ	.25 + Gender
3		.79 − Gender	

NOTE: The signs of all correlations have been reversed so that a positive coefficient stands for a positive association between the two concepts. For gender, + is female.
*$p = .05$; **$p = .01$; ***$p = .001$.

the UAI country scores really was, I have included in Exhibit 4.1 the UAI values that resulted when age differences were controlled for. The regression formula was UAI = 7 ×(average age in years) − 157, which means that 1 year of increase in the average age of a country sample corresponded to a UAI increase of 7 points. As the Category 1 countries supplied sufficient proof that average age did not explain UAI differences, I did not repeat the calculation for Category 2 countries and Category 3 regions.

Across *individuals* (rather than across countries), age related to two of the three UAI questions. If we take the median correlation across individuals for the five subpopulations (one country, one occupation) on which the 1971 questionnaire was developed, we find $r = .00$ for age versus stress, $r = −.13*$ for age versus rule orientation (older people more rule oriented), and, not surprisingly, $r = −.32***$ for age versus employment stability (older people more stable).

The subsequent factor analysis with 40 countries and 32 variables, reproduced in Chapter 2, excluded the demographics. In addition to the three questions used to compute UAI, the factor analysis found the following A and B questions loading on the UAI factor (I reversed the sign of the factor so that high loadings stand for strong UAI):

B9 Prefer managerial or specialist position (1 = specialist, 5 = manager). Loading −.56, so high UAI prefers specialist.

B57 Decisions made by individuals are usually of higher quality than decisions made by groups (1 = agree). Loading .50, so high UAI disagrees.

A58 Overall satisfaction (1 = satisfied). Loading −.49, so high UAI more satisfied.

B44 Feelings about working for a foreign manager (1 = prefer own nationality). Loading −.49, so high UAI prefers own nationality.

A15 Importance of opportunity for advancement (standardized score, low = less important). Loading −.46, so high UAI considers less important.

B55   Employees lose respect for a manager who asks them for their advice before he makes a final decision (1 = agree). Loading .46, so high UAI disagrees.

B54   Competition between employees usually does more harm than good (1 = agree). Loading –.45, so high UAI agrees.

In addition, several C questions, which were used only in the first survey round and not included in the factor analysis, produced country scores that were significantly correlated with UAI:

C17   A large corporation is generally a more desirable place to work than a small company (1 = agree). Correlation r = –.72***, so high UAI agrees.

C16   By and large, companies change their policies and practices much too often (1 = agree). Correlation r = –.52**, so high UAI agrees.

C10   Most companies have a genuine interest in the welfare of their employees (1 = agree). Correlation r = .45**, so high UAI disagrees.

C11   In general, the better managers in a company are those who have been with the company the longest time (1 = agree). Correlation r = –.44**, so high UAI agrees.

C12   There are few qualities in a man more admirable than dedication and loyalty to his company (1 = agree). Correlation r = –.40**, so high UAI agrees.

Straight Replications of the IBM Survey

Elite alumni from the Salzburg Seminar. Exhibit 4.10 shows Hoppe's Salzburg alumni scores for UAI, just as Exhibit 3.13 lists the scores for PDI. There is a highly significant correlation of $r = .64**$ (rho = $.63**$) between Hoppe's UAI scores and the IBM UAI scores. The Salzburg alumni on average scored $64.7 - 31.8 = 32.9$ points lower on UAI than did the IBM employees.

Comparing Exhibits 3.13 and 4.10, we find that Hoppe's *PDI* correlated with $r = .71**$, rho = $.81***$ with IBM UAI; even higher than with IBM PDI. Across the 18 IBM countries also represented in the Salzburg set, PDI and UAI in IBM correlated with $r = .78***$, rho = $.75***$; Hoppe's PDI and UAI correlated with $r = .65**$, rho = $.81***$. This means that the two dimensions are difficult to separate, and their correlation pattern leads to multicollinearity in statistical operations. With the newly developed VSM 94 formulas,

Hoppe's PDI still correlates more strongly with IBM UAI than with IBM PDI ($r = .87***$ versus $r = .80***$), but at least Hoppe's UAI has become a better predictor of IBM UAI than Hoppe's PDI is ($r = .94***$ versus $r = .87***$).

As in the case of PDI, I used Hoppe's data for computing best estimates for the scores on the IBM scale, by regressing the IBM scores on the Salzburg scores (third column under "Hoppe, elites" in Exhibit 4.10). This time the Hoppe scores are within 13 points of the IBM scores for 12 countries; the outliers are Portugal (–47), Ireland (+33), Greece (–32), Great Britain (+31), Spain (–26), and Switzerland (+19). As suggested in Chapter 3, this may have something to do with the selection and self-selection criteria for elites participating in the Salzburg seminars in these countries. The Hoppe study provided an estimated UAI score of 96 for Malta.

Higher-income consumers surveyed by the EMS 97. Exhibit 4.10 also shows the UAI scores found in the European Media and Marketing Survey 1997 by the market research agency Inter/View International. This survey included the 20 questions of the VSM 94 (Appendix 4). The EMS UAI scores are based on the VSM 94 questions and formula, which differ from those used in IBM. Across the 15 overlapping countries the UAI scores from the IBM employees in 1970 and the EMS consumers in 1997 are correlated with $r = .86***$ (rho = $.87***$). These data could also be used to compute best estimates for the scores on the IBM scale through regression of the IBM scores on the EMS scores (third column under "EMS, consumers" in Exhibit 4.10). For 12 countries the EMS scores are within 15 points of the IBM scores; the outliers are Great Britain (+25), Portugal (–22), and Ireland (+21). These three countries were also among the outliers in Hoppe's Salzburg study. Again they are based on some kind of elite respondents with a degree of self-selection; it seems that elites in Portugal in the 1980s and 1990s, in comparison to those in other countries, were less uncertainty avoiding than IBM employees in the 1960s and 1970s, and that the reverse was the case in Britain and Ireland.

The share of women among the respondents varied from 15% in Denmark and the Netherlands to 31% in France and 35% in Portugal; the European average was 22%. These percentages were also strongly correlated with IBM UAI ($r = .82***$, rho = $.86***$). This is rather surprising, and I have no ready explanation.

In Chapter 2, I mentioned that for these respondents the IBM power distance dimension could not be replicated. People approached in their role as consumers did not produce reliable data about their power relations (the correlations of EMS PDI with IBM PDI were $r = .07$, rho = $.10$). De

Exhibit 4.10 Uncertainty Avoidance Index Scores Computed From Surveys of Elites (Hoppe, 1990) and Consumer Market Research (EMS 97)

Countries in Order of Original UAI	Original UAI	Hoppe, Elites			EMS, Consumers		
		Raw UAI			Raw UAI		
		n		Regressed[a]	n		Regressed[a]
Greece	112	41	47	80			
Portugal	104	49	24	57	192	81	82
Belgium	94	47	67	100	270	78	80
France	86	47	54	87	661	90	89
Spain	86	75	27	60	599	90	89
Turkey	85	72	39	72			
Malta		30	63	96			
Italy	75	183	44	77	293	79	80
Austria	70	74	33	66	343	50	64
Germany	65	142	37	70	228	62	67
Finland	59	59	31	64	486	34	44
Switzerland	58	57	44	77	153	62	67
Netherlands	53	139	14	47	337	45	53
Norway	50	64	22	55	447	33	44
United States	46	157	16	49			
Great Britain	35	194	33	66	544	54	60
Ireland	35	48	35	68	100	49	56
Sweden	29	71	8	41	534	9	24
Denmark	23	41	–2	31	1,111	7	23
Total n		1,590			6,680		
Mean (elites)	64.7		31.8[b]	64.7			
SD (elites)	26.2		16.8[b]	16.8			
Mean (consumers)	61.5					55.4	61.5
SD (consumers)	24.6					26.5	21.1
Correlation with IBM							
UAI:							
Product-moment			.64**			.86***	
Spearman rank			.63**			.87***	
PDI:							
Product-moment			.56**			.75**	
Spearman rank			.52*			.78***	

NOTE: For Hoppe, same questions and formulas as used in IBM. For EMS 97, questions and formulas according to VSM 94 (see text). Data copyright Inter/View International, Amsterdam; used with permission. See also De Mooij (2001).

a. Predicted from regression of IBM scores on raw new scores.

b. Without Malta.

$*p = .05; **p = .01; ***p = .001$.

Mooij (1998a), using EMS 95 consumption data, found that consumption patterns correlated with IBM UAI rather than with IBM PDI; but as Chapter 3 showed, she did find significant correlations with IBM PDI rather than with IBM UAI in the areas of work and media relations. Exhibit 4.10 shows that EMS UAI correlated nearly as strongly with IBM PDI ($r = .75**$, rho = $.78***$) as it did with IBM UAI. This is no doubt due to the multicollinearity among the IBM scores for these

Exhibit 4.11 Factor Scores for 18 Countries on Two Factors Found by Lynn and Hampson in Medical and Related Statistics Versus Four IBM Indexes and GNP/Capita

| | Factor Score on | |
Country	Neuroticism	Extraversion
Austria	3.73	1.61
Japan	2.95	−2.37
France	2.37	−.94
Germany (F.R.)	2.11	−.19
Italy	1.05	−1.61
Finland	.61	1.73
Switzerland	.28	.47
United States	.18	4.56
Belgium	.15	−1.29
Canada	−.29	.15
Denmark	−.55	.41
Australia	−.75	.36
Norway	−.86	−2.03
Sweden	−.86	.99
Netherlands	−1.52	−2.30
New Zealand	−1.61	.29
Great Britain	−2.41	.30
Ireland	−4.58	−.17
Spearman rank correlation with		
Stress score (A37)[a]	.72***	.39
UAI	.73***	−.44*
PDI	.35	−.47*
IDV	−.53*	.08
MAS	.41*	−.02
GNP/capita 1970	.01	.38
Squared multiple correlation with 4 indexes + GNP/cap (based on ranks) R^2	.77	.49

SOURCE: Data from Lynn and Hampson (1975).

NOTE: A stepwise multiple regression of ranks showed no significant second-order correlations.

a. Sign reversed so that high score = high stress.

*$p = .05$; **$p = .01$; ***$p = .001$.

15 countries, but it means that for lack of anything better, EMS UAI can be used as a proxy for EMS PDI.

Studies of Stress and Well-Being

Country neuroticism and extraversion factor scores according to Lynn and Hampson (1975). Exhibit 4.11 shows that Lynn's "neuroticism" factor was significantly correlated with UAI (rho = .73***) and also with the "stress" scores separately (rho = .72***); so stronger neuroticism goes with higher stress and higher UAI. Lynn's "extraversion" factor combined the following:

.73   High divorce rate

.65   High murder rate

.61   High cigarette consumption

.61   High punished crime rate (also loading on Factor 1)

.60   High coronary heart disease rate (loading on Factor 1 with opposite sign)

.53   High "illegitimacy" (percentage of extra-marital births)

This factor correlated moderately (rho = −.47*) with PDI, in the sense that "introvert" countries tended to score high on PDI and extravert countries low. The correlation of "extraversion" with UAI was a by-product of the correlation with PDI.

Attitude questions in the 1990-93 World Values Survey. Results from this survey operation across

43 countries were published by Inglehart et al. (1998). Of these 43 countries, 26 were also part of the IBM set. Data for South Africa were not used because in IBM these were only collected from whites, and in the World Values Survey they were collected from a sample of the total population. Nigeria was taken as equal to IBM's West Africa region, in which Nigeria was the major country.

The data in Inglehart et al.'s volume contain extreme scores for certain countries that could unduly dominate the correlation pattern. Therefore only Spearman rank correlations were used for data from this source. Exhibit 4.12 contains the correlations with 17 attitude scores conceptually related to UAI. The correlations are shown for all overlapping countries (26, sometimes 25 or 24, as Switzerland and/or South Korea did not use some of the questions) and for the 19 (sometimes 18) wealthier countries only (1990 GNP/capita > U.S.$480), which included South Korea and Portugal with the wealthier countries but excluded four Latin American countries, India, Nigeria, and Turkey.

Among the zero-order correlations only the highest suggests a direct relationship; the other significant correlations can be by-products of the intercorrelations among the indexes. The stepwise multiple regression sorts out which significant second- and third-order correlations survive when these intercorrelations are controlled for. For the same reason I chose Spearman rank correlations for the zero-order correlations, the stepwise multiple regressions are based on the ranks of the question scores and of GNP/capita.

Satisfaction with life goals. Hastings and Hastings (1981) published the *Index to International Public Opinion 1980-1981,* which contains the results of a 13-nation public opinion survey conducted in 1979 concerning "human values." [123] Of interest to us are the answers to the following block of items:

Here is a list of life goals people may have. Please name all items you are satisfied with already:

1. To improve my character (to become sensible and maintain efforts for improvement)
2. To be considerate of others (to be tolerant to and cooperative with others)
3. To live without financial worries (to have pleasant and convenient conditions in clothing, food, and housing)
4. To live mentally fulfilled (to value the meaning of life)
5. To live in a beautiful environment (to live in an attractively planned neighborhood, house interior decoration and furniture, or to live in the richness of nature)
6. To live religiously (to respect others and live with deference to others)
7. To live independently (to live on my own without counting on others as much as possible)
8. To make efforts to correct social inequality and injustice (to bring about fair and equal life for everybody)
9. To make efforts to create a pleasant community (to have a friendly and pleasant neighborhood)
10. As a citizen of my country, to be concerned seriously about the nature of my country
11. As one human being, to be concerned seriously about peace in the world
12. To be healthy physically as well as mentally
13. To have an intellectual life (to acquire culture and knowledge)
14. To live sincerely and seriously (to be liked by everybody and do right things)
15. To be socially successful and famous
16. To be attentive to daily human relations (to deepen human bonds in family, neighborhood, and friends/acquaintances)
17. To have human beings understand each other and live with friendship beyond ethnic origins and countries

This is a curious list, and the explanations in parentheses sometimes confuse more than they clarify. I tried to extract the broad picture of country differences without getting caught in details of individual questions. The data were published as percentages of respondents in each country answering "satisfied" with each question. I decided to ignore absolute levels of satisfaction and instead look at the relative satisfaction in each country with each goal compared to other goals. I therefore standardized for each country the percentages "satisfied" across the 17 goals. Then I factor analyzed the resulting matrix of 17 standardized goals (variables) for 13 countries (cases). A scree analysis showed three substantial factors in the data that together explained 63% of the variance. I rotated (varimax) with these three factors and found the following rotated components:

- Factor 1

Loading	Question	Content
.87	13	Have intellectual life
.79	8	Correct social injustice
.68	16	Daily human relations
.67	9	Create pleasant community
−.75	4	*Not* live mentally fulfilled
−.75	17	*Not* have interethnic friends
−.60	11	*Not* concerned about world peace

- Factor 2 (reversed)

Loading	Question	Content
.77	14	Live sincerely and seriously
.72	7	Live independently
.56	11	Concerned about world peace (2)
−.87	3	*Not* without financial worries
−.66	12	*Not* physical and mental health

- Factor 3

Loading	Question	Content
.82	1	Improve my character
.75	2	Considerate of others
.70	6	Live religiously
.60	10	Concerned about country
−.75	5	*Not* beautiful environment

Goal 15 (successful and famous) loaded on none of these factors. I computed factor scores for each country on each factor, and correlated these with the four IBM indexes and with 1980 GNP/capita. Factor 1 correlated with $r = .56*$ with long-term orientation (LTO), and we will come back to it in Chapter 7. Factor 2 correlated with $r = .59*$ with UAI. Factor 3 showed a multiple correlation ($R = .76**$), negatively with 1980 GNP/capita ($R^2 = .35$) and positively with the Individualism Index ($R^2 = .57$). It does not make sense to me.

McClelland's Study of Motivation

McClelland (1961) developed scores for dominant motives found in children's stories from different countries from 1925 and from 1950. The IBM data set included 22 of McClelland's 1925 countries and 31 of his 1950 countries. The correlations between McClelland's data and the IBM data are presented in Exhibit 4.13. The most obvious hypothesis is a correlation between IBM PDI scores and McClelland's 1950 "need for power." However, this correlation was not significant ($r = .20$). In addition, the correlation of PDI with $n_{Pow} - n_{Aff}$ (which, according to McClelland [1961, p. 168], might be an important measure) was not significant ($r = .25$; not shown in Exhibit 4.13). Instead, however, we find an unexpected and highly significant correlation of (1970) IBM indexes with McClelland's *1925* scores for n_{Ach}. The highest correlation is with UAI ($r = -.64***$). The correlations with PDI and IDV can be shown to be by-products of the correlation with UAI, but the stepwise regression shows that there is a siz-

able contribution to the variance in 1925 n_{Ach} by MAS, the Masculinity Index score (which in the zero-order correlation pattern was suppressed by the correlation with UAI). In fact, the best predictor of McClelland's 1925 n_{Ach} is low UAI plus high MAS (see Chapter 6). There is, in addition, a weaker correlation of 1925 n_{Aff} with IDV, to which I shall come back in Chapter 5.

Results of Other Surveys Correlated With UAI

Fiedler's (1967) Least Preferred Co-Worker questionnaire. Although there is a body of literature about the use of LPC, I found no studies comparing LPC score levels between countries beyond my small exercise at IMEDE in 1971-73 (Hofstede, 1974b). I administered the LPC questionnaire to 154 managers during training courses. Exhibit 4.14 lists the mean scores for those countries from which I had at least three participants (a very small sample, but if I do not use small samples in this case, hardly any data are left). It appears that in spite of the extremely small sample sizes, UAI does correlate significantly negatively with the country LPC level. Moreover the stepwise regression shows that the correlation with UAI suppresses a second-order correlation with PDI in the sense that if we control for UAI, countries with higher power distance levels tend to score *higher* on LPC. This would mean that in high-PDI countries relationships between people play a more important role and in low-PDI countries tasks play a more important role.

Laurent's (1978) survey data of attitudes of managers in management courses. Laurent's questionnaire contained 56 value statements about organizational issues. The first published results show answers from 635 managers in 10 countries on the following five statements:

1. Most organizations would be better off if conflict would be eliminated forever.
2. It is important for a manager to have at hand precise answers to most of the questions that his subordinates may raise about their work.
3. If a manager gives his subordinates more freedom of initiative, he must at the same time reinforce the extent to which he controls their activities.
4. In order to have efficient work relationships, it is often necessary to bypass the hierarchical line (disagree).
5. An organizational structure in which certain subordinates have two direct bosses should be avoided at all costs.

Exhibit 4.12 Spearman Rank Correlations and Stepwise Multiple Regressions of Questions From the 1990-93 World Values Survey With Four IBM Indexes and GNP/Capita, Across 26 Countries and Across 19 Wealthier Countries (1990 GNP/capita > U.S.$480)

Question Number	Question	Countries[a]	Zero-Order Correlation With				GNP/ Capita	Cumulative R^2 in Stepwise Regression[b]
			PDI	UAI	IDV	MAS		
About subjective well-being								
18	Your happiness, % very happy	All	−.35*	−.55**	.48**	−.12	.13	.30 −UAI
		Rich	−.47	−.69**	.66**	−.16	−.12	.50 −UAI
83	Your health, % (very) good	All	−.42*	−.75***	.49**	−.14	.38*	.56 −UAI
		Rich	−.53*	−.79***	.45*	−.21	.28	.62 −UAI
96	Your life, % satisfied[c]	All	−.63***	−.56**	.68***	−.16	.58**	.46 +IDV, .56 −PDI
		Rich	−.52*	−.73***	.58**	−.29	.34	.56 −UAI
116	Your job, % satisfied[c]	All	−.56**	−.53**	.59**	−.10	.55**	.35 +IDV
		Rich	−.53*	−.70***	.53*	−.24	.55**	.51 −UAI
180	Your home life, % satisfied[c]	All	−.49**	−.52**	.67***	−.27	.35*	.44 +IDV, .53 −MAS
		Rich	−.36	−.71***	.67**	−.34*	.12	.50 −UAI
About trust and tolerance								
70	Not as neighbors, % different race[d]	All	.51**	.30	−.46	−.13	−.37*	.26 +PDI
		Rich	.50*	.63**	−.44*	−.13	−.29	.40 +UAI
94	% "Most people can be trusted"	All	−.69***	−.72***	.62***	−.18	.71***	.55 −UAI, .80 +GNP
		Rich	−.63*	−.81***	.40*	−.46*	.57**	.66 −UAI, .73 −MAS
340	Trust your family, % trusting[e]	All	−.37*	−.51**	.16	.17	.17	.26 −UAI
		Rich	−.52*	−.56**	.05	.16	.16	.32 −UAI
About views on the family								
214	Child needs father and mother, % yes	All	.53**	.54**	−.59**	.33	−.45*	.35 −IDV, .47 +MAS
		Rich	.38	.78***	−.59**	.46*	−.02	.58 +UAI
220	Women really want home and children	All	.68***	.47*	−.66***	.29	−.67***	.45 +PDI, .56 −IDV[g]
		Rich	.55*	.70**	−.46*	.55*	−.34	.51 +UAI, .74 +MAS
About nationalism								
263	Fight for country, % willing	All	−.08	−.45*	−.12	−.55**	−.05	.30 −MAS. .45 −UAI[h]
		Rich	−.43	−.58**	.10	−.70***	.32*	.51 −MAS, .65 −UAI
322	Proud to be . . . , % very proud	All	.23	−.30	−.21	.16	−.60**	.36 −GNP, .57 −UAI
		Rich	−.28	−.43*	.16	.07	−.35	.18 −UAI
Confidence in institutions								
275	The legal system, % confident[f]	All	−.28	−.45*	.11	−.28	.42*	.20 −UAI
		Rich	−.45	−.33	−.06	−.33	.72***	.52 +GNP
276	The press, % confident[f]	All	.66***	.20	−.38*	.09	−.30	.44 +PDI
		Rich	.60**	.43*	−.18	.10	−.05	.35 +PDI
277	Trade unions, % confident[f]	All	.15	−.28	−.29	−.44*	−.32	.21 −MAS, .36 −GNP
		Rich	−.29	−.29	−.07	−.49*	−.14	.27 −MAS
278	The police, % confident[f]	All	−.81***	−.66***	.68***	−.22	.70***	.66 −PDI, .75 +IDV
		Rich	−.78***	−.90***	.47*	−.22	.46*	.84 −UAI
280	The civil service, % confident[f]	All	.11	−.47**	.00	−.20	−.24	.23 −UAI, .41 +PDI
		Rich	−.16	−.53*	.34	−.18	−.11	.25 −UAI

SOURCE: Data from Inglehart, Basañez, and Moreno (1998).

a. Rich countries are AUT, BEL, CAN, DEN, FIN, FRA, GBR, GER, IRE, ITA, JPN, KOR, NET, NOR, POR, SPA, SWE, SWI, and USA. Other countries are ARG, BRA, CHL, IND, MEX, NIG (= WAF), and TUR. Questions 83, 134, 197, and 214 were not used in KOR; 220 was not used in SWE; 101, 102, 134, 214, 220, 233, 275-280, and 340 were not used in SWI.

b. Regressions of ranks of GNP/capita and of question scores.

c. Scores 7 to 10 on a 10-point scale where 10 = *satisfied*.

d. Percentage mentioning this category as unwanted neighbor.

e. Percentage answering "trust them completely" or "a little."

f. Percentage answering "a great deal" or "quite a lot."

g. Third-order .67 +MAS

h. Third-order .58 −IDV.

*p = .05; **p = .01; ***p = .001.

Exhibit 4.13 Zero-Order Correlations and Stepwise Regressions of McClelland's Motivation Scores Across 23 and 32 Countries Versus Four IBM Indexes and GNP/Capita

	1925 Readers, Need for			1950 Readers, Need for		
	Achievement	Affiliation	Power	Achievement	Affiliation	Power
Spearman rank correlation with						
PDI	−.56**	−.09	−.06	.07	−.05	.17
UAI	−.60**	−.36*	.09	.03	.12	−.07
IDV	.42*	.48**	−.21	−.06	.12	−.02
MAS	.30	.22	.06	.07	−.10	.15
GNP/capita 1970	.41*	.23	−.00	−.17	.20	−.12
R^2 with 4 indexes + GNP/capita 1970	.49	.22	.10	.07	.15	.16
Order of indexes in stepwise regression, cumulative R^2, and sign of coefficient						
1	.31 − UAI	.18 + IDV				
2	.44 + MAS					

NOTE: The countries in both years are ARG, AUL, AUT, BEL, BRA, CAN, CHL, DEN, FIN, FRA, GBR, GER, GRE, IRE, JPN, NET, NOR, NZL, SAF, SPA, SWE, URU, and USA. The countries in 1950 only are IND, IRA, ISR, ITA, MEX, PAK, POR, SWI, and TUR.
*$p = .05$; **$p = .01$; ***$p = .001$.

Answers were scored on the usual 5-point scale from *agree* to *disagree*. The five statements form an ecological dimension; that is, differences in percentages of agreement among countries are in the same direction for all five. Average agreement (*strongly agree* and *agree*) across the five questions varied from 24% in the United States to 63% in Italy (Exhibit 4.14). All statements express a low tolerance for ambiguity in hierarchical structures. The level of agreement with Laurent's statements in the 10 countries correlates significantly with UAI ($r = .78**$).

In a later stage, I did an ecological factor analysis of Laurent's scores on 56 value statements for 11 countries (those in Exhibit 4.14 plus Japan, which had been added). I found three factors; the first and strongest, after rotation, correlated with UAI with rho = .77**. This factor showed loadings over .60 for 17 statements, among which were four of the five statements in Laurent's earlier analysis (1, 2, 4, and 5). Below are some of the other statements loading on the factor:

1. A good manager is able to express his feelings and emotions in the majority of situations (disagree).

2. It is desirable that management authority can be questioned (disagree).

3. If you want a competent person to do a job properly, it is often best to provide him with very precise instructions on how to do it.

4. When the respective roles of the members of a department become complex, detailed job descriptions are a useful way of clarifying.

These items represent a highly formalized conception of management.

Almond and Verba's (1963) study of political attitudes of representative samples of the population in five countries (Great Britain, Germany, Italy, Mexico, and the United States; about 1,000 respondents in each country). One of Almond and Verba's key concepts was "subjective political competence": the extent to which respondents believed they could participate in political decisions. Almond and Verba designed a 5-point Guttman scale of subjective competence in dealing with *local* government. On this scale they found the United States and Great Britain highest in subjective competence and Germany, Italy, and

Exhibit 4.14 Scores of Managers on Fiedler's LPC and Laurent's Acceptability of Matrix Organization, Versus Four Indexes and GNP/Capita

Countries in Order of UAI	Fiedler's LPC Score Collected at IMEDE		Laurent's Need for Clarity of Hierarchy	
	Respondents	Score	Respondents	% Agree
Belgium			35	57
Japan	4	2.70		
France	5	3.42	179	54
Spain	4	3.00		
Brazil	7	3.69		
Italy	6	2.95	24	63
Germany (F.R.)	15	3.53	47	47
Iran	7	3.60		
Switzerland	34	3.85	48	45
Netherlands	3	3.78	29	36
Australia	4	4.10		
Norway	7	3.50		
United States	7	3.78	44	24
India	3	5.30		
Great Britain	14	3.49	150	38
Sweden	10	2.92	43	30
Denmark	6	3.79	36	40
Total and mean	136	3.59	635	43
Spearman rank correlation with				
PDI		−.02		.49
UAI		−.42[a]		.78**
IDV		.14		−.36
MAS		−.01		.46
GNP/capita 1970		.03		.55*
Squared multiple (rank) correlation with 4 indexes + GNP/capita, R^2		.30		.80
Order of indexes in stepwise regression, cumulative R^2, and sign of coefficient				
1		.19 − UAI		.61 + UAI
2		.53 + PDI		

SOURCES: For Fiedler's LPC scores, Hofstede, (1974b, p. 10); for Laurent's need for clarity of hierarchy, Laurent (1978, p. 11).
a. Significance level .051; product-moment correlation $r = -.44*$.

Mexico lower, in that order. As we see in Exhibit 4.15, their scores correlated with UAI with $r = -.96,***$ (and not appreciably with the other indexes after UAI was controlled for).

Ornauer et al.'s (1976) 11-country survey study of "images of the world in the year 2000." In total, nearly 10,000 persons were interviewed or reached by mail questionnaires in more or less representative samples of the populations. The data were collected in 1967. Nine of the countries also appear in the IBM sample. The book lists mean answer percentages for the 11 countries for 187 questions; I have tested ecological correlations with UAI for 20 of these questions for which such correlations made conceptual sense to me. Significant correlations with UAI (Exhibit 4.15) emerged for the following:

1. (II/49; Ornauer et al., 1976, p. 674): Do you think that there is anything you yourself can do to contribute to the realization of this proposal [that is, a proposal that is likely to lead to peace]? Answer: No.

Exhibit 4.15 Percentage Answers on Public Opinion Studies by Almond and Verba and by Ornauer et al. Versus Four IBM Indexes and GNP/Capita

Countries in Order of UAI	Almond and Verba Citizen Competence % Score	Ornauer et al. % Agreement			
		Can You Yourself Contribute?	Compromise Not Dangerous	Take One Day After Another	Like to Live Abroad
Japan		18	28	15	6
Yugoslavia		6	21	24	9
Spain		19	21	36	5
Mexico	38				
Italy	40				
Germany (F.R.)	46	18	31	22	10
Finland		13	41	41	10
Netherlands		27	44	21	13
Norway		28	38	49	7
United States	65				
India		28	39	52	16
Great Britain	63	21	48	49	15
Mean	50	20	35	34	10
Product-moment correlation with					
PDI	−.66	−.25	−.43	−.10	.06
UAI	−.96**	−.64*	−.90***	−.73*	−.80**
IDV	.79	.55	.79**	.32	.41
MAS	−.86*	−.05	−.15	−.20	.04
GNP/capita 1970	.75	.17	−.58	−.12	−.15
Squared multiple correlation with 4 indexes + GNP/ capita, R^2	1.00	.47	.86	.87	.84

SOURCES: For Almond and Verba citizen competence score, Almond and Verba (1963, p. 233); for Ornauer et al. percentages of agreement, Ornauer, Wiberg, Sicinski, and Galtung (1976, pp. 674, 682, 685, 695).
NOTE: There were no significant second-order correlations.
$*p = .05$; $**p = .01$; $***p = .001$.

2. (III/13; p. 682): To compromise with our opponents is dangerous because it usually leads to the betrayal of our own side. Answer: Agree.

3. (III/27; p. 685): The future is so uncertain that the best thing one can do is to take one day after the other. Answer: *Disagree.*

4. (III/61; p. 695): Would you like to live the *main part* of your life in a foreign country or would you prefer to live most of your life in your native country? Answer: Most in native country.

Among 20 items, 1 could correlate at the .05 level by pure chance, but not 4. All are in the direction that fits with the meaning of UAI as described in this chapter.

Descriptive questions in the 1990-93 World Values Survey. Besides attitude questions, this survey operation also collected various other information from samples of the public. Included were 16 questions about voluntary associations and activities, asking whether the respondent (1) belonged to it and (2) did unpaid work for it (Inglehart et al., 1998, WVS questions 19-34). The 16 types of voluntary agencies were as follows: (1) social welfare services for elderly, handicapped, or deprived people; (2) religious or church organizations; (3) education, arts, music,

Exhibit 4.16 Spearman Rank Correlations and Stepwise Multiple Regressions of 1990-93 World Values Survey Data With Four IBM Indexes and GNP/Capita, Across 23 Countries

| Question Number | Question | Zero-Order Correlation With | | | | | Cumulative R^2 in Stepwise Regression |
		PDI	UAI	IDV	MAS	GNP/Capita	
19-34	Participation in 16 voluntary associations[a]	−.52**	−.70***	.51**	−.47*	.48**	.50 −UAI, .61 −MAS

a. Summary score read from Inglehart (1997, fig. 6.5).

or cultural activities; (4) trade unions; (5) political parties or groups; (6) local community action on issues such as poverty, employment, housing, racial equality; (7) Third World development or human rights; (8) conservation, the environment, ecology; (9) professional associations; (10) youth work (e.g., Scouts, Guides, youth clubs); (11) sports or recreation; (12) women's groups; (13) peace movement; (14) animal rights; (15) voluntary organizations concerned with health; and (16) other groups. In some of the poorer countries these questions were not asked. Inglehart (1997, p. 190) has summarized the answers of the 16 types of voluntary associations, and Exhibit 4.16 shows correlations of his summary scores with the IBM indexes across the 23 countries for which both types of scores are available. The highest correlation was with UAI (rho = −.70***); there was a significant negative second-order correlation with MAS (see Chapter 6).

Survey data from European Union member states collected by the Eurobarometer. Exhibit 4.17 shows correlations with four IBM indexes and GNP/capita for a number of Eurobarometer questions. The 1994 data (Eurobarometer, 1994, pp. 161, 153) refer to the following questions:

- "To what extent would you say you are interested in politics?" (mean scores on 4-point scale from *not at all* to *a great deal*)
- "Are you for or against the formation of a European Union, with a European Government responsible to the European Parliament?" (2-point scale; percentages "for")

The 1997 data (Eurobarometer, 1997) refer to the following questions and indicators:

- "Would you say that you are very satisfied, fairly satisfied, not very satisfied, or not at all satisfied with the way democracy works in your country?" (percentages "very satisfied")
- An "indicator of opinions about the institutions and political establishment" was com-

posed by the Eurobarometer from the answers on seven items: (1) "The people who run this country are more concerned with themselves than with the good of the country"; (2) "Corruption amongst politicians is increasing"; (3) The way government and public bodies work is getting worse"; (4) I have little control over what is happening in the world around me"; (5) Public services look less and less after the interests of people like me"; (6) The rich get richer and the poor get poorer"; and (7) "There is nothing one can do to change things in our society." The index is the percentage of respondents who gave negative scores to no more than five of these seven items.

- Self-scores on how racist the respondent feels he or she is (percentages scoring 7-10 on a 10-point scale).
- "All immigrants, whether legal or illegal from outside the European Union and their children, even those who were born in our country, should be sent back to their country of origin." (percentages "tend to agree")
- "Legally established immigrants from outside the European Union should be sent back to their country of origin if they are unemployed." (percentages "tend to agree")
- "All illegal immigrants should be sent back to their country of origin without exception." (percentages "tend to agree")
- Percentages agreeing with "integration" of minorities and not with "assimilation." The "integration" statement ran: "In order to be fully accepted members of society, people belonging to these minority groups must give up such parts of their religion or culture which may be in conflict with the law." The "assimilation" statement ran: "In order to be fully accepted members of society, people belonging to these minority groups must give up their own culture."

The first three questions in Exhibit 4.17 relate about equally strongly to both PDI and UAI

Exhibit 4.17 Product-Moment Correlations and Stepwise Multiple Regressions of Questions From the Eurobarometer With Four IBM Indexes and GNP/Capita

| Question | Zero-Order Correlation With | | | | GNP/ Capita[a] | Cumulative R^2 in Stepwise Regression |
	PDI	UAI	IDV	MAS		
1994 data across 11 countries[b]						
Interest in politics	−.76**	−.76**	.55*	−.24	.64*	.58 −UAI
Pro a European government	.67*	.68*	−.19	.21	−.29	.46 +UAI
1997 data across 14 countries[c]						
Satisfied with democracy	−.68**	−.66**	.10	−.39	.13	.46 −PDI
Opinion about institutions	−.51*	−.58*	.17	−.72**	.43	.50 −MAS, .77 −PDI
Call yourself a racist	.13	.20	.30	.27	.32	None
Should be sent back						
All immigrants	.31	.58*	−.24	.54*	−.09	.34 +UAI
Unemployed immigrants	.47*	.75**	−.35	.61**	−.38	.57 +UAI, .75 +MAS
Illegal immigrants	.44	.71**	−.31	.67**	−.48*	.51 +UAI, .75 +MAS
Pro integration, not assimilation	−.37	−.64**	.48*	−.72**	.69**	.51 −MAS, .78 +GNP

SOURCES: For 1994, Eurobarometer (1994, pp. 161, 153); for 1997, Eurobarometer (1997, pp. 9, 10, 6, 25, 24, 26, and 20). See text of chapter for ways of scoring.
a. 1990 data.
b. BEL, DEN, FRA, GBR, GER, GRE,IRE, ITA, NET, POR, SPA.
c. Same countries plus AUT, FIN, SWE.
*p = .05; **p = .01; ***p = .001.

(which for these European countries are intercorrelated, with r = .77** across 11 countries and with r = .78** across 14 countries). The item "Call yourself a racist" (self-scores on how racist the respondent feels he or she is) is atypically clumsy and unprofessional for the Eurobarometer; it assumes that the term *racist* is functionally equivalent and equally understood across the countries and languages of the European Union, which is evidently false. The scores obtained correlate with none of the IBM indexes and with none of the other questions in Exhibit 4.17, except for a marginal r = .48* correlation with "All immigrants should be sent back." The other 1997 questions show that aside from uncertainty avoidance, masculinity also plays a role in racism and xenophobia.

Preiss's (1971) mail survey of 345 U.S. and 227 German engineers working in five more or less matched companies in either country. Forty-seven of Preiss's questions were in the format of "work goal importance" items (such as A5-A18 in the IBM questionnaire; see Appendix 1). As the scores for the German and the U.S. samples had almost identical overall means across all goals (2.39 for Germany and 2.42 for the United States) and identical ranges (2.42 points in both cases), the data could be compared without standardization. Preiss found several significant differences: U.S. engineers scored as more important (1) six goals dealing with contributing to the interest of the company, (2) working for a successful company, (3) five goals dealing with becoming an administrator or manager, (4) personal time, and (5) living in a desirable area. German engineers scored as more important (1) three goals dealing with anxiety avoidance, (2) challenge, (3) freedom, (4) earnings, (5) advancement in general, (6) training, (7) up-to-dateness and professional learning, (8) employment security, (9) cooperation (but not friendly atmosphere), and (10) physical conditions. The text of the three anxiety avoidance goals that Germans scored as significantly more important than Americans runs as follows:

Exhibit 4.18 Classification of 24 "Balanced Power" Countries According to the Age of Their Present Political System Versus Their UA Scores

Number of Balanced Power Countries in Which Present Political System Has Existed	UAI	
	13-53	58-112
Uninterruptedly since 1915[a]	9	1
Since a date later than 1915[b]	2	12
Chi-square	10.5** (1 df)	

NOTE: Compare Exhibit 3.21.

a. AUL, CAN, DEN, GBR, NET, NZL, NOR, SWE, SWI, USA.

b. AUT, BEL, COS, FIN, FRA, GER, GRE, IRE, ISR, ITA, JAM, JPN, POR, TUR.

1. Work in a well-defined job situation where the requirements are clear. (Mean score United States 3.06, Germany 2.03, on a scale from 1 = *of utmost importance* to 5 = *of very little or no importance*. This is the largest difference found among all 47 questions.)

2. Be given clear, detailed instructions as to how to proceed with the job. (Mean score United States 3.81, Germany 3.58.)

3. Have little tension and stress on the job. (Mean score United States 3.46, Germany 3.31.)

In IBM, Germany scored considerably higher on UAI (65) than did the United States (46). Preiss's findings on differences in anxiety avoidance confirm this difference. Preiss's first and third anxiety avoidance item were included in later versions of the Values Survey Module (Appendix 4).

Indexes at the National Level
Correlated With UAI

Age of the political system. PDI appeared to be strongly related to a country's political system (balanced power since 1975 versus periods of unbalanced power since 1975; see Exhibit 3.18). UAI does not discriminate between balanced-power and unbalanced-power countries.[124] However, if we divide the balanced-power countries according to the age of their present political system (uninterrupted/not uninterrupted since 1915), we get the picture of Exhibit 4.18. The relationship between age of political system and UAI for these countries is highly significant; there is no relationship with PDI.[125]

Nurses per doctor. Statistics comparing the numbers of nurses to the numbers of doctors in 22 countries in 1971 were published by Gaspari and Millendorfer (1978, p. 199). The rank correlations for the 15 countries overlapping with the

IBM set are presented in Exhibit 4.19. The strongest correlation, and the only significant one in the multiple regression, was with UAI (rho = −.78***). More recent data about "population per physician" and "population per nursing person" were published in certain annual *World Development Reports,* but the numbers of missing data increased over the years. I got nearly complete coverage of the IBM countries from 1984 data published in the *World Development Report, 1990* (World Bank, 1990), complemented by some 1980 data published in the *World Development Report, 1980* (World Bank, 1980). The correlations for these data are also shown in Exhibit 4.19. The populations per physician and per nursing person are correlated primarily with GNP/capita. There are significant second- and third-order correlations of population per physician with UAI and with IDV, both negative. There is also a significant second-order correlation of population per nursing person with PDI (positive). The number of nurses per doctor is again highly significantly correlated with UAI, and in this case UAI is once more the only index showing up in the multiple regression.

Maximum speeds on motorways and traffic deaths. The maximum speeds allowed on the motorways of 14 European countries in 1975 are listed in Exhibit 4.20. We see that these correlated with Lynn's neuroticism scores with rho = .67**, with the IBM country scores on the "stress" question with rho = .62**, and with UAI with rho = .58*. In the higher-stressed, more uncertainty-avoiding countries, cars were allowed to drive faster.

Speed on motorways affects accident rates; did countries with higher accident rates before the oil crisis establish lower maximum speeds? Exhibit 4.20 also lists 1971 accident death rates; these were uncorrelated with maximum speeds, but positively correlated with UAI, stress, neuroticism, and MAS. Their strongest correlation, however, was a negative one with the Individualism

Exhibit 4.19 Spearman Rank Correlations and Stepwise Multiple Regressions of Data About Number of Nurses per Doctor, Versus Four IBM Indexes and GNP/Capita

Source	Zero-Order Correlation With					Cumulative R^2 in Stepwise Regression
	PDI	UAI	IDV	MAS	GNP/ Capita	
Gaspari and Millendorfer (1978), 1971 data, 15 countries[a]						
Nurses per doctor	−.54**	−.78***	.62**	−.30	.44*	.68 −UAI
1990 World Development Report, 1984 data, 50 countries[b]						
Population per physician	.56***	−.16	−.65***	.01	−.84***	.70 −GNP, .76 −UAI[c]
Population per nursing person	.65***	.17	−.67***	.05	−.88***	.77 −GNP, .80 +PDI
Nurses per doctor	−.32*	−.52***	.31*	−.09	.27*	.27 −UAI

a. Gaspari and Millendorfer (1978, p. 199). Countries were AUT, DEN, FIN, FRA, GBR, GER, GRE, IRE, NET, NOR, POR, SPA, SWE, SWI, and USA. GNP/capita data are for 1970.

b. All IBM countries except ITA, SAF, TAI; ARA = EGY; EAF = KEN; WAF = NIG. Data for FRA, GBR, PER, POR, SIN, URU, and VEN were 1980 values taken from World Bank (1984). GNP/capita data are for 1980.

c. Third order .80 −IDV.

Index, and in a stepwise multiple regression (based on rank correlations) with the four IBM indexes and 1970 GNP/capita only IDV made a significant contribution. We shall come back to this in Chapter 5.

The Catholic/Protestant ratio in Christian countries. For the Christian countries in the IBM set Exhibit 4.21 correlates the Catholic/Protestant ratio with the four IBM indexes and with GNP/capita. As the Catholic side included many poor countries, which could lead to the confusion of Catholicism with poverty, correlations were also computed separately across wealthy countries (1970 GNP/capita more than $1,000) only. In both cases, however, the strongest correlate of the Catholic/Protestant ratio was UAI. The stepwise regression showed that Catholic countries tended to score more uncertainty avoiding and more masculine; Protestant countries scored less uncertainty avoiding and more feminine.

UAI Versus Eight Geographic, Economic, and Demographic Indicators

Exhibit 4.22 lists the correlations and regressions of UAI with the eight indicators identified in Chapter 2 (Exhibits 2.9, 2.10, and 2.11) and correlated with PDI in Chapter 3 (Exhibit 3.20). As in the case of PDI, these were computed for all 50 countries, for the 22 wealthier countries (1970 GNP/capita more than $1,000), and for the 28 poorer ones.

The eight indicators predicted only a small part of the variance in UAI; unlike in the case of PDI, they did not explain how country UAI levels became so different. Other and less measurable factors must have played a major role in the genesis of country uncertainty avoidance differences.

For 13 Western countries, Kuznets (1971, p. 38) supplied data on economic growth in different historical periods since about 1865; I extended these with World Bank data to 1990. In Exhibit 4.23 these have been correlated with these countries' UAI scores. The correlations with UAI depend greatly on the historical period.

Trends in UAI

In Exhibit 4.24, in analogy to Exhibit 3.22, the answers on question A37 (mean stress scores, world totals) have been plotted against age brackets for five large categories of employees. Lower scores mean higher stress. Scores in the 1967-69 survey round are indicated by dotted lines, and those in the 1971-73 round by solid lines. An age or seniority shift would again produce an overlap of the 1968 and 1972 curves. A generation shift would produce a horizontal displacement of the

Exhibit 4.20 Maximum Speeds on Motorways in 1975 and Traffic Death Rates in 1971 in 14 European Countries, Versus Four Indexes Plus GNP/Capita

Countries in Order of UAI	1975 Maximum Speeds on Motorways (km/hour)	1971 Traffic Death Rate per 1,000 Vehicles
Belgium	120	1.21
France	140	.72
Spain	130	1.28
Italy	120	1.02
Austria	130	1.66
Germany (F.R.)	None	1.21
Finland	80	1.38
Switzerland	130	1.13
Netherlands	100	.99
Norway	90	.55
Great Britain	112	.56
Ireland	96	1.18
Sweden	110	.51
Denmark	110	.89
Spearman rank correlation with 1971 traffic deaths	.26	
Stress score (–A37)	.62**	.54*
Lynn's neuroticism[a]	.67**	.48*
PDI	.43	–.00
UAI	.58*	.56*
IDV	–.22	–.62*
MAS	.52*	.51*
GNP/capita 1970	.10	–.51*
Squared multiple correlation with 4 indexes + GNP/capita, R^2	.62	.75

SOURCES: For 1975 maximum speeds, ANWB (1975); for 1971 traffic death rates, United Nations (1973).
NOTE: A stepwise multiple regression of ranks showed no significant second-order correlations.
a. See Exhibit 4.12. Not available for Spain.

curves by 4 years. A zeitgeist shift would cause a vertical shift of the curve from 1968 to 1972.

As I have reported in an earlier study, there were considerable differences in stress levels between the occupation categories: The highest stress was found among unskilled workers and managers, the lowest among technicians (Hofstede, 1994a). As in Exhibit 3.22, the age curves showed a combination of zeitgeist and age. Eight out of 12 curves of stress against age were inverted U-shaped, which means that stress was highest for those in the 30-39 age bracket. The zeitgeist effect implied that with few exceptions 1972 stress was higher for all occupational categories and all age brackets. The stress increase tended to be largest for the 20-29 and 40-49 groups. In the case of those over 50, we find a decrease of stress for managers and professionals, but an increase for technicians and clerks. For managers over 60 there was again an increase in stress.

Notes

1. These remarks are inspired by and partly paraphrased from Luhmann (1976, p. 143).

2. "Above all we want release from fear.... And in the end most fears . . . are forms of fear of the unknown. So we are all the time pressing for assurances that the unknown is known really, and that what it contains is something we are going to want anyway. We embrace religions which assure us that we shall not die, and

Exhibit 4.21 Catholic/Protestant Ratio in Christian Countries Versus Four IBM Indexes and GNP/ Capita[a]

Countries	% Catholic – % Protestant / % Catholic + % Protestant		Countries	% Catholic – % Protestant / % Catholic + % Protestant	
	36 Christian Countries	20 Wealthy Christian Countries Only[b]		36 Christian Countries	20 Wealthy Christian Countries Only[b]
Argentina	.96	.96	Italy	.99	.99
Australia	−.45	−.45	Jamaica	−.84	
Austria	.85	.85	Mexico	.95	
Belgium	.98	.98	Netherlands	.03	.03
Brazil	.80		Norway	−.99	−.99
Canada	.16	.16	New Zealand	−.65	−.65
Chile	.76		Panama	.88	
Colombia	.98		Peru	.98	
Costa Rica	.99		Phillippines	.74	
Denmark	−.98	−.98	Portugal	.99	
Ecuador	.94	.94	Salvador	.50	
Finland	−.96	−.96	Spain	.99	.99
France	.95	.95	Sweden	−.99	−.99
Great Britain	−.75	−.75	Switzerland	−.01	−.01
Germany	−.06	−.06	Uruguay	.94	
Greece	.99	.99	United States	−.09	−.09
Guatemala	.75		Venezuela	.98	
Ireland	.90	.90	Yugoslavia	.98	

	36 Christian Countries	20 Wealthy Christian Countries Only[b]
Product-moment correlation with		
PDI	.63***	.59**
UAI	.77***	.75***
IDV	−.59***	−.47*
MAS	.26	.53**
GNP/capita 1970	−.62***	−.55**
Squared multiple correlation with 4 indexes + GNP/capita, R^2	.75	.73
Order of indexes in stepwise regression, cumulative R^2, and sign of coefficient		
1	UAI +.59	UAI +.56
2	MAS +.69	MAS +.66
3	GNP −.74	

SOURCES: Data from Taylor and Hudson (1972, tab. 4.16). For countries added since the 1980 edition of *Culture's Consequences,* Frémy and Frémy (1998).
NOTE: South Africa is omitted, as IBM indexes refer to whites only.
a. "Christian countries" are those in which Christians are the largest religious group. Catholics include Eastern Orthodox. Protestants include Anglicans and all Protestant sects.
b. GNP/capita 1970 more than U.S.$1,000.

Exhibit 4.22 Product-Moment Correlations and Multiple and Stepwise Regression Across Countries of UAI Scores With Eight System-Level Indicators

Indicator	Zero-Order Correlations With UAI Scores Across		
	All 50 Countries	28 Poorer Countries	22 Wealthier Countries
GNP	−.28*	−.07	−.55**
EGP	.04	−.24	.59**
EGF	−.15	−.25	.17
LAT	−.05	.34*	−.56**
POP	.06	−.04	.22
PGR	.12	.04	.10
PDN	−.21	−.47**	.22
ORS	−.05	−.18	−.11
Squared multiple correlation with first 7 R^2	.23	.62	.59
Order of indicators in step-wise regression, cumulative R^2, and sign of coefficient			
1	.08	.44	.34 + EGP
2	− GNP	− PDN	.51 − LAT

NOTE: The 22 countries are ARG, AUL, AUT, BEL, CAN, DEN, FIN, GBR, GER, GRE, IRE, ISR, ITA, JPN, NET, NOR, NZL, SPA, SWE, SWI, USA. For definitions of indicators, see Exhibit 2.9.

Exhibit 4.23 Spearman Rank Correlations Between UAI and Economic Growth in Different Historical Periods

Average Economic Growth Rate Over Period	Correlation With UAI Scores (1970)	Correlation With 1865-1965 Growth Rate
1965-90	.50*	.55*
1960-70	.61*	.48*
1950-67	.43	.48*
1925-50	−.63*	.52*
Ca. 1890-1950	−.08	.79**
Ca. 1865-1965	−.14	1.00

SOURCES: For average growth rates 1965-90, World Bank (1992); 1960-70, World Bank (1972); 1950-67, 1925-50, ca. 1890-1950, and ca. 1865-1965, Kuznets (1971).
NOTE: The countries are AUL, BEL, CAN, DEN, FRA, GBR, GER, ITA, JPN, NET, NOR, SWE, USA.

political philosophies which assure us that society will become perfect in the future" (Magee, 1975, p. 88, based on Karl Popper).

3. Pareto (1916/1976), however, uses the terms *logical* and *nonlogical*.

4. *Nonrational* and *nonlogical* are not the same as *irrational* and *illogical*. The former are meant to be value-free terms describing the origins of behavior; the latter have negative value connotations implying that a behavior is wrong.

5. For a review of 27 paper-and-pencil instruments measuring attitudes related to the "authoritarian personality syndrome," see Shaver (1973).

6. Roney and Sorrentino (1995) describe "uncertainty orientation" as a personality variable and suggest that it may vary with culture along my uncertainty avoidance and individualism dimensions. They misquote my data to support their argument, however (p. 1327), claiming that uncertainty avoidance is weak in Western and strong in Eastern cultures, which is obviously incorrect.

Exhibit 4.24. Answers to Question A37 (Mean Stress Scores) for Five Large Categories of IBM Employees, Worldwide Data, by Age Bracket, in Two Survey Rounds

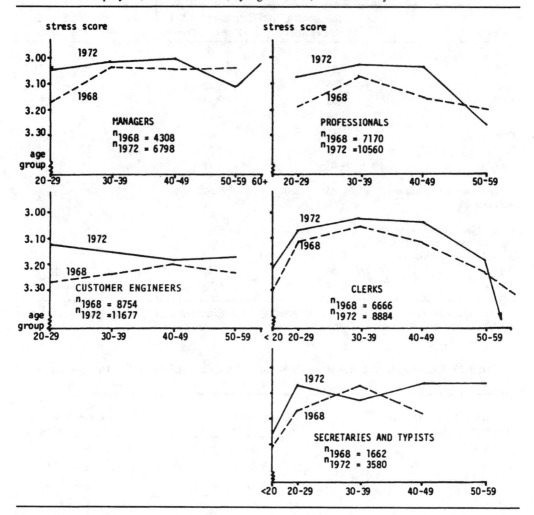

7. "Ritual is a stereotyped, symbolically concentrated expression of beliefs and sentiments regarding ultimate things. It is a way of renewing contact with ultimate things, of bringing more vividly to the mind through symbolic performances certain centrally important processes and norms" (Shils, 1975, p. 154)—this is part of a clarifying article on ritual in modern society. For a study of rituals in 20th-century Britain, see Bocock (1974).

8. March and Simon (1958, p. 165) have noted that accounting is an "uncertainty-absorbing" process, and in an amusing series of comparisons between business and primitive society, Cleverley (1971, p. 67) has called planning the "fertility rites" of business. Our cave-dwelling ancestors drew in advance pictures of the animals they *planned* to kill. Weick (1969, p. 102) suggests that having a planning system allows managers to sleep in peace, even if the system does not really work.

Most control systems use a cybernetic philosophy that presupposes some kind of a standard, measurability of accomplishment, and the opportunity to use feedback. If one or more of these conditions is not fulfilled, cybernetic control becomes solely ritual (Hofstede, 1981b, 1994b, chap. 9; Van Gunsteren, 1976).

Regarding computer simulations, an in-depth study in the Netherlands showed the nonuse by managers of the computer-based interactive planning models made for them (G. J. Hofstede, 1992). Faucheux, Laurent, and Makridakis (1976) have criticized the use of computer models for the national and international levels. In both cases the model by definition missed the unforeseen events that were the most crucial to the users.

In discussing reliance on experts as persons who are beyond uncertainty, Cleverley (1971, p. 53) has compared consultants to the "sorcerers" of primitive societies.

9. They did find a third dimension, but it was relatively weak.

10. Two other questions in the IBM questionnaire were also tried: B39 ("Manager insists on rules and procedures") and B47 ("Unclear on what duties and responsibilities are"). As Exhibit 2.5 shows, both had to be dropped due to low stability of country scores from 1968 to 1972.

11. As in the other chapters in this volume, statistical significance is indicated as follows: * = the .05 level, ** = the .01 level, and *** = the .001 level.

12. Rho = .73*** for "stay less than 2 years" and rho = .77*** for "stay less than 5 years." The survey answers were thus correlated with *past* turnover levels in countries. Their correlation with *future* turnover levels unfortunately has not been tested in IBM, but turnover-level differences for this occupation tended to be fairly stable, and studies in other organizations have shown that for individuals within countries, answers on similar survey questions did predict their actual turnover in the period following the survey (Kraut, 1975; Mangione, 1973; Price & Bluedorn, 1977).

13. I found 25 overlapping countries and an *r* = .53**.

14. For example, see Selye (1974) and Friedman and Rosenman (1976). A popular summary of such studies can be found in Toffler (1971, chap. 15).

15. On diseases of the heart and blood vessels, see Jenkins (1971) and Friedman and Rosenman (1975). On diseases of the stomach and intestines, see Vertin (1954) and Dunn and Cobb (1962). On disruption of personal relations, see Levinson (1964, 1965).

16. See Kalsbeek (1976) on the reduction of perceived alternatives and Wright (1974) on the use of negative evidence.

17. Friedman and Rosenman (1975) created the distinction between persons showing "Type A" and "Type B" behavior. The typical Type A person tries to do more and more things in less and less time, whereas the Type B person is unhurried and patient. Type A persons are more likely to suppress fatigue (Carver, Coleman, & Glass, 1976). Friedman and Rosenman found that for U.S. men between the ages of 35 and 60, those who were Type A were seven times more likely to develop coronary heart disease than were those who were Type B.

18. Holmes and Rahe (1967) developed the Social Readjustment Rating Scale, allocating point values to stressful life events such as the death of a spouse, getting married, and losing a job. In the United States, Japan (Masuda & Holmes, 1967), Sweden, and Denmark, these authors and their associates have shown that if the sum of the point values of crucial life events within a period exceeds a certain level, the subject is highly likely to suffer physical and/or mental disorders.

19. See Zaleznik, Kets de Vries, and Howard (1977) and Beehr and Bhagat (1985).

20. A variance analysis of the scores on the "stress" question can be found in Chapter 2, Exhibit 2.3. The variance in stress scores due to country and due to occupation are both significant, but the country effect is much stronger than the occupational effect. The same was found by Kraut and Ronen (1975).

21. The variance in stress scores due to other organizational factors may be considerable. For example, in one large office with about 350 persons divided into 23 working groups, group mean scores on the "nervous or tense" question varied between 2.69 and 3.56. The differences between the extreme groups are statistically significant in spite of the small size of the groups (9 and 13 persons, difference of means, tested by *t* test, two-tailed, significant at .05 level). In fact, one of the main reasons IBM conducted the surveys was to discover such differences on this and other questions and feed the information back to the manager and members of the groups. However, departmental pressures leading to such stress differences are diverse and do not lend themselves to macroanalysis.

22. Van Gunsteren (1976) had postulated the association between anxiety and rule orientation independent of my work; the IBM data provided statistical evidence for it.

23. These countries were AUT, BEL, DEN, FIN, FRA, GBR, GER, GRE, IRE, ITA, NET, NOR, POR, SPA, SWE, SWI, and YUG.

24. In Exhibit 2.7, the correlation between PDI and UAI across the 22 wealthier countries was .63**. These included 15 of the 17 European countries (all but POR and YUG).

25. Their data are from a 1988 conference paper by Ackermann; they are based on a comparative public opinion survey by the German Allensbach Institute.

26. Two more reasons a UAI by occupation makes no sense are that (1) occupational differences in rule orientation can be shown not to be stable from 1968 to 1972, and (2) the range of scores for stress across occupations is much smaller than the range across countries. Kraut and Ronen (1975, p. 675) also found that stress scores depend more on country than on occupation; employment stability scores depend more on occupation than on country.

27. In the analysis of variance data for the manufacturing personnel analyzed in Chapter 2 (Exhibit 2.3) we found also no gender effect on stress and only a weak gender effect in rule orientation. Jick and Mitz (1985) reviewed 19 studies of gender differences in stress, mostly from the United States; they suggest that women report stress earlier, and that men suppress it and therefore are more likely to suffer serious effects, but even this difference was not found in our data.

28. See also the strong gender effect for this question in the analysis of variance of Exhibit 2.3.

29. Interestingly, employees' employment stability answers for IBM's subsidiary in Japan were not very different from those in other industrial countries: Only about 40% of respondents stated that they wanted to stay until retirement. Abroad, the myth is widespread that all Japanese work under a system of permanent employment (*nenko*). It is likely that in purely Japanese companies the percentage of employees wanting to stay until

retirement was and still is higher; but even there, the *nenko* system was used less often than non-Japanese believe, and actual labor turnover in Japan was not so low (Azumi, 1974; Marshall, 1977; Oh, 1976).

30. Hoppe (1998) reported .90***, but this was the Spearman rank correlation.

31. The pilots' *PDI* correlated almost as strongly with the IBM UAI scores (see Exhibit 3.13), $r = .46*$, rho = .50*.

32. Shane and Venkataraman (1996, p. 761) reported a correlation of $r = .47**$ across 28 countries.

33. See also Aron (1967, pp. 33-45). For a confirmation of the validity of Durkheim's analysis, see Besnard (1976). Comparative studies of suicide in different cultures are reviewed in Hippler (1969), and Farberow (1975) has collected 16 papers in an edited volume.

34. See Dunn and Cobb (1962), Levinson (1964), Jenkins (1971), Zaleznik et al. (1977), and Hofstede (1994a). A major source of information on country differences in such reactions is the death rate statistics published by the Statistical Office of the United Nations, and several authors have built theories on the basis of these (e.g., Barrett & Franke, 1970; Rudin, 1968).

35. The countries in this study were AUT, ISR, ITA, USA, and YUG.

36. See Lynn (1971, 1973, 1975), Lynn and Hampson (1975, 1977), and Lynn and Martin (1995).

37. The countries in the study were AUL, AUT, BEL, CAN, DEN, FIN, FRA, GBR, GER, IRE, ITA, JPN, NET, NZL, NOR, SWE, SWI, and USA. A study such as Lynn's makes sense only for developed countries, where a certain level of medical care and a certain accuracy of statistics exist. Haas (1969) has factor analyzed medical variables for 72 countries (including less-developed ones) together with political variables. In this case, all death causes converged on a "medical development" factor associated with economic development.

38. Lynn (1981, pp. 266-269) commented extensively on the findings I published in a 1976 working paper. He showed that one could further reinforce correlations by leaving some countries out, but I saw neither the rationale nor the need for this. Lynn and Martin (1995) have reported alcoholism data for 1985; I calculated their correlation with IBM UAI across 22 overlapping countries and found a rho = .65***.

39. There was a second-order correlation with MAS. Extraversion did not correlate with any of the indexes; psychoticism also correlated with MAS. See Chapter 6.

40. The 12 countries were AUT, BEL, DEN, FIN, FRA, GBR, GER, ITA, NET, NOR, SWE, and SWI.

41. A cross-national public opinion sample study provided anxiety data for Denmark, Finland, Norway, and Sweden (Kata, 1975; about 1,000 respondents per country). Kata and Lynn found the same rank order of anxiety scores: Sweden (lowest), Norway, Denmark, Finland (highest; for Lynn, Sweden and Norway break even). The IBM stress and UAI data also put Finland highest, but Denmark lowest.

42. These data were published on the World Wide Web at http://www.psy.uva.nl/dce. The countries were from the IBM set: AUT, AUL, BRA, FIN, IND, NET, NOR, NZL, SPA, SWE, and USA. For China, I used HOK data except for MAS (66, see Chapter 6) and LTO; for Honduras, GUA; and for Zambia, EAF. I did not use the emotion data for Bulgaria and Malawi. The designers of the database request that the following information be included in any work published by its users: "The development of the data bank has been supported by the Maison des Sciences de l'Homme (Paris, France), the Thyssen Foundation (Germany) and the Société Académique de l'Université de Genève (Switzerland). The data bank consortium consists of Agneta Fischer (University of Amsterdam), Pierre Philippot (University of Louvain at Louvain-la-Neuve) and Harald Wallbott (University of Salzburg)."

43. These countries were ARG, BRA, CAN, CHL, FRA, GBR, GER, GRE, HOK, ITA, JPN, SWE, SWI, TUR, and USA.

44. The "balance" scores show a significant negative second-order correlation with the Masculinity Index, producing a multiple $R = .97***$. See Chapter 6.

45. See Diener (1996).

46. In 1999, Veenhoven's World Database on Happiness data were made accessible in a renewed Internet site at http://www.eur.nl/fsw/research/happiness.

47. Gallup (1976) had earlier related levels of happiness within nations to national wealth; he also noticed appreciable differences among the countries of Western Europe (which, I conclude, could not be explained by differences in wealth).

48. Arrindell et al. (1997) came to a similar conclusion. They also found a complex relationship with the Masculinity Index, to which I will come back in Chapter 6.

49. There was a significant second-order correlation with (1990) GNP/capita; the multiple correlation with UAI and GNP/capita was $R = .63**$, $R^2 = .40$.

50. These countries were AUL, BRA, CAN, FRA, GBR, GER, IND, ITA, JPN, KOR, PHI, SIN, and USA.

51. Across all 26 countries there was a significant second-order positive correlation with GNP/capita; and across the 19 wealthier countries, a negative second-order correlation with MAS (more trust in feminine countries; see Chapter 6).

52. The category of "conservatism" in a stepwise regression showed a substantial negative second-order relationship with UAI, after a negative first-order correlation with individualism. Conservatism on Schwartz's (1994) map is adjacent to harmony, but, surprisingly, across the 23 countries also in the IBM set conservatism scores were negatively correlated with harmony scores. Conservatism values on Schwartz's map close to the harmony area are wisdom, forgiving, respect tradition, clean, and family security. As we will see in Chapter 5, these are collectivist values all right, but one would expect them to be positively rather than negatively associated with UAI. The negative second-order correlation

may be a statistical artifact caused by combining smallest-space analysis with factor analysis scores.

53. My own country, the Netherlands (UAI 53), takes a middle position, with a prevailing sentiment that I would define as "What is different is ridiculous."

54. In a classic American sociological article, Dean (1961) defines alienation as being composed of three major components: powerlessness, normlessness, and social isolation.

55. Eysenck (1954, p. 178) followed Guilford in a distinction between two personality factors: neuroticism and extraversion. For individuals, he related tough-mindedness to extraversion. Eysenck's student, Lynn, operationalized the factors of neuroticism and extraversion at the societal level. As I have shown (Exhibit 4.10), UAI in this case is correlated with neuroticism, not with extraversion.

56. Douglas and Wildavsky (1982) have extended the message of Douglas's "purity and danger" to the issues of technological and environmental risks, taking a relativistic point of view toward such risks, which they see as being mainly in the eye of the beholder.

57. Across 52 countries, the correlation between having more than one second-person pronoun and UAI was $r = .43**$.

58. There was also a significant positive second-order correlation with MAS (see Chapter 6).

59. If poor countries were included, agreement correlated with PDI and negatively with IDV. In both cases there was also a significant correlation with MAS (see Chapter 6).

60. In Chapter 5, correlations will be shown with WVS questions on "things that some people think make for a successful marriage." The item "faithfulness" (WVS question 198, after standardization) was negatively correlated with UAI (rho = −.39*). In high-UAI countries faithfulness was considered somewhat less important for judging a marriage as successful, showing a more formal concept of a successful marriage.

61. This section makes extensive use of an article of mine that was inspired by my experiences in 5 years of teaching at the International Teachers Program (ITP) around 1980 (Hofstede, 1986a). The ITP was a summer refresher course for management teachers. In a class of 50, there might be 20 or more different nationalities. The ITP offered excellent opportunities to watch the different learning habits of the students (who were teachers themselves at other times) and the different expectations they had regarding the behavior of those who taught them.

62. For example, see David Hickson's (1998, p. 109) autobiographical essay.

63. The countries and numbers of subjects in them were as follows: IND, 78; JPN, 250; SAF, 131; USA, 126; and YUG, 99.

64. Chandler, Shama, and Wolf (1983) reported on a split of the same data by gender. Across the five countries, females attributed success to internal causes more often than did males, but the male/female differences did not correlate with either UAI or MAS.

65. The other categories, after standardization, showed different significant correlations for Chandler, Shama, Wolf, and Planchard's (1981) and Yan and Gaier's (1994) studies, although the signs were mostly in the same direction. Effort correlated −.83* with IDV for Chandler et al. and .88* with UAI for Yan and Gaier; context (task) correlated .82* with IDV for Chandler et al. and .97** with MAS for Yan and Gaier; luck correlated −.80 ($p = .052$) with IDV for Chandler et al. and −.91* with MAS for Yan and Gaier. I attribute the differences to idiosyncrasies of the two populations.

66. Oettingen (1995) also compared East Berlin children with children in Moscow, Russia. The latter showed more self-efficacy, which the author explains as counterdependence against authoritarian teachers.

67. Gerritsen (1995) attributed the difference in tolerance for dialect use to the large difference in Masculinity Index scores between the two countries. Conceptually, however, this issue relates to UAI, not to MAS.

68. Le Vine (1973, p. 51) calls this a "psychological reductionist" theory of society.

69. McClelland's later work compared with his earlier publications shows a shift in the connotations of the power motive. In his original study, he suggested that "a combination of high n_{Pow} and low n_{Aff} is very closely associated with the tendency of a nation to resort to totalitarian methods in governing its people" (McClelland, 1961, p. 168). Later, he applied measures of need strength to more and less successful business managers in the United States and concluded that the "better managers we studied are high in power motivation, low in affiliation motivation" (McClelland & Burnham, 1976, p. 103). McClelland could have used this conclusion to explain the evident sympathy of some business managers for totalitarian regimes.

70. There was a weaker correlation of 1925 n_{Ach} with PDI, but this disappeared after UAI was controlled for. A cross-cultural review of achievement motivation studies by Schludermann and Schludermann (1977, p. 155) described a possible curvilinear relation between PDI and n_{Ach}, but my country data did not support this.

71. All in all, the U.S. players cooperated more frequently, so the authors called the Belgians more competitive. In a comment, Faucheux (1976, p. 286) called the U.S. players more competitive; he saw the Belgian behavior as "legalistic," valuing equity more than efficiency, and the U.S. behavior as more "realistic." Legalism, of course, fits with a high UAI score.

72. The countries were Hungary, ISR, JPN, NET, and USA; there were between 100 and 560 respondents per country.

73. For Hungary I used the estimated country scores from Exhibit A5.2.

74. The authors of the study only noticed a relationship with individualism. In fact, the cluster scores rank correlated equally strongly with IDV (rho = −.90*), but I find the correlation with UAI easier to interpret.

75. The data were reported by Arlen Poort in the Dutch newspaper *NRC Handelsblad* on October 4, 1997 (p. 17). The values are AUL, 6.4 years; USA, 7.4; GBR, 78; CAN, 7.9; DEN, 7.9; KOR, 8.7; NET, 8.7; SPA, 8.9; SWI, 9.0; GER, 9.7; GRE, 9.9; FIN, 10.5; SWE, 10.5; FRA, 10.7; BEL, 11.2; JPN, 11.3; and ITA, 11.6.

76. I have summarized this study in my Schuman Lecture *Entrepreneurship in Europe* (Hofstede, 1998b).

77. McGrath, Macmillan, and Scheinberg (1992) compared survey data about values and beliefs about entrepreneurship, collected from entrepreneurs and career professionals in eight countries, but they reported only on significant differences between the two categories, not between countries. They tried to associate these differences with my four IBM dimensions, but the purpose and success of this association are unclear to me. In another paper, McGrath, Macmillan, Yang, and Tsai (1992) compared entrepreneurs from China, Taiwan, and the United States and found that the two Chinese cultures contrasted most with the United States on questions opposing the collective to the individual—which is not surprising given that I found that IDV is the dimension on which the United States differed by far the most from the others.

78. The need for avoiding uncertainty in an organization is not only a matter of culture; personality variables of top managers also play a role. "Some individuals may have a very high tolerance for ambiguity and uncertainty so they may perceive situations as less uncertain than others with lower tolerances" (Duncan, 1972, p. 325). Downey, Hellriegel, and Slocum (1977) showed for a sample of 51 U.S. business division managers that their perceptions of uncertainty related more to personality variables (their cognitive processes) than to environmental conditions.

79. The countries in the Hickson, McMillan, Azumi, and Horvath (1979) study were CAN, GBR, GER, JPN, SWE, and USA; in the IDE International Research Group (1981a) study, they were BEL, DEN, FIN, FRA, GBR, GER, ISR, ITA, NET, NOR, SWE, and YUG.

80. Already in comparing Britain and the United States, Inkson, Schwitter, Pheysey, and Hickson (1970) could not use "structuring of activities" as a homogeneous dimension for international comparison because, although no differences were found in specialization and standardization, Britain was systematically lower on one aspect of formalization: reliance on written rules. Child and Kieser (1979) found more managerial job descriptions in Britain than in Germany, but in other respects German organizations were more formalized than British ones. Drenth and Groenendijk (1984, pp. 1214-1216) distinguished among formalization, bureaucratic control, and routine work and suggested that my UAI dimension is related to the last two rather than the first.

81. Using index scores from Shane's own replication rather than from IBM, I found that the first regression variable was still UAI but there was also a *positive*

contribution of PDI to renegade championing: more rule-breaking innovations in high-PDI societies.

82. See Crozier (1964a, pp. 107 ff.); Hickson, Hinings, Lee, Schneck, and Pennings (1971); and Hinings, Hickson, Pennings, and Schneck (1974). Lack of attention to structural aspects of the exercise of power is one of the points of critique regarding Mulder's (1977) power distance reduction theory. Ng (1977) has reported on an extension of Mulder's experiments in which structural properties of organizations are shown to affect power distance reduction tendencies.

83. Even in the United States the matrix structure did not meet the general acceptance predicted by its protagonists in the 1970s (Pitts & Daniels, 1984).

84. This research approach looks like a level-of-analysis fallacy, but it is not. Using country-level indexes for individuals implies using country samples as small as one individual, but the resulting unreliability is partly compensated for by the large number of countries/regions; also, countries represented by more individuals automatically carry more weight in the correlations.

85. Shane (1994a) has reported on a comparison, based on the same data, between champions and nonchampions. Across cultures, champions showed stronger preferences for building cross-functional ties, establishing autonomy from organizational norms and rules, enabling innovators to circumvent organizational hierarchy, using informal means to persuade others to support the innovation effort, and building a decision-making mechanism that includes all organization members.

86. GNP/capita, PDI, and IDV each made a significant contribution in 1975 only.

87. Fiedler (1967; Fiedler & Chemers, 1974) explained leadership effectiveness as a combination of the leader's LPC score and the difficulty of the situation. Differences in LPC levels among countries would mean that a person can be an effective leader in one country and not in another, which of course is an entirely reasonable proposition. Bennett (1977b) has shown that among managers working for U.S. banks, a low LPC was functional in the Philippines but not in Hong Kong.

88. Correlation coefficients for all four subscales with the IBM indexes (but not with GNP/capita) appear in the first edition of *Culture's Consequences* (Hofstede, 1980a, fig. 3.15).

89. Data were from the Reader's Digest Eurodata 1991, the European Media and Marketing Survey 1997 (EMS 97), and the Consumer Europe Euromonitor 1997, across 16 countries: AUT, BEL, DEN, FIN, FRA, GBR, GER, GRE, IRE, ITA, NET, NOR, POR, SPA, SWE, and SWI.

90. De Mooij cites an article in *NRC Handelsblad* (August 5, 1998) by Marco Van Baardwijk titled "Wanbetalers"; the article includes a graph by Rik Van Schagen with Intrum Justitia noted as the source.

91. Seeman (1977, p. 775), comparing 450 French with 450 U.S. workers, found the former much more frequently believing that "experts" should make political

decisions; this fits with the UAI score differences between these countries.

92. Barbara Sumner, a cross-cultural consultant and trainer, told me this story.

93. In early 2000, a political crisis broke out in Belgium when a "Green" minister of the environment wanted to limit night flights from Brussels Airport.

94. Inglehart (1997), whose work I cited in the 1980 version of this book but who never acknowledged the synergy between his studies and mine, has used the "age of political system" for various comparisons of 1990-93 World Values Survey data: percentage saying most people can be trusted (p. 174), subjective well-being index (p. 177), percentage of respondents belonging to voluntary organizations (p. 190), and percentage high minus low on Inglehart's Postmaterialist Index (p. 214). The first was most strongly correlated with PDI (see Chapter 3), but it does correlate with UAI as well; the second is typically UAI related (see Exhibit 4.12); the third could be seen as a form of citizen competence and is shown to be UAI related in Exhibit 4.16; and the fourth subsumes too many issues to be simply linked to any dimension. Anyway, Inglehart also noticed the importance of the age of the political system for related issues.

95. During World War II, the German occupants introduced identity cards in the Netherlands. Laws requiring individuals to carry them were immediately abolished when the Germans left.

96. In Putnam's study the attitudes of German civil servants were the most polarized. Civil servants sympathizing with the SPD (Socialists), who mostly had arrived on the scene later, tended to be more "politically" oriented; those sympathizing with the CDU (Christian Democrats) more frequently took a "classical" stand. Putnam's study contained questions conceptually related to PDI and others more related to UAI; on the former, Germany and Great Britain produced more similar answers.

97. In the sample, Egypt was taken for the Arabic-speaking countries, Kenya for East Africa, and Nigeria for West Africa. Johnson and Lenartowicz (1998) correlated reversed 1995 Index of Economic Freedom data (high values, high freedom) with 1985 GDP/capita and 1985-94 economic growth across 38 countries and found correlations of $r = .70***$ with both; a multiple regression showed that countries with a low initial GDP/capita and a high index value showed the largest economic growth. This is not surprising in view of the economic variables that were part of the index.

98. Johnson and Lenartowicz (1998) also correlated the 1995 Index of Economic Freedom values with UAI and MAS (across 26 countries) and with Schwartz's conservatism, hierarchy, and mastery (across 33 countries). They looked only at zero-order correlations and found significant correlations of the reversed index (high values, high freedom) with UAI ($r = -.46*$ for the 1975 index—in fact it should be $r = -.46**$—and $r = -.40*$ for the 1995 index) and with Schwartz's conservatism ($r = -.42**$).

99. Gibson and Caldeira (1996) evidently had not discovered the uncertainty avoidance concept; they only correlated their scores with my Individualism Index and found marginally significant coefficients, but in fact these were by-products of the correlation pattern that disappeared when I controlled for UAI and wealth.

100. Gibson and Caldeira's (1996) dimensions were based on a factor analysis across all individuals regardless of country. In their paper they show country mean scores on these dimensions. They therefore commit a reverse ecological fallacy, comparing countries on dimensions developed for the individual level. The correlation pattern at the country level showed "rule of law" and "alienation," in fact, to be so strongly intercorrelated ($r = -.87***$) as to form one single ecological dimension; "liberty," however, was uncorrelated with it.

101. Gibson and Caldeira (1996) also computed a summary score of "legal values"; it was primarily correlated with UAI ($R = .78$, $R^2 = .61$) but with a significant negative second-order correlation with GNP/capita ($R = .88***$, $R^2 = .78$).

102. As in the study by Shane (1995), the research approach used in this study looks like a level-of-analysis fallacy, but it is not. Gudykunst (1989) used country-level indexes for his individuals. This implied using country samples as small as one individual, but the resulting unreliability was partly compensated for by the large number of countries/regions (32); also, countries represented by more individuals automatically carried more weight in the correlations. The most debatable aspect of this study was the selection of two items per subscale at face value, as Gudykunst himself signals in his discussion section.

103. Inkeles and Levinson (1954/1969) have written about Germany (which is above average in UAI) that a "major contributing power in the fall of the Weimar republic was the inability of large numbers of Germans to tolerate the necessity for political compromise" (p. 476).

104. Pelto (1968) measured the tightness of a number of traditional societies with a (Guttman) scale that used characteristics of the society's political system, in which "theocracy" (government by priests claiming to rule with divine authority) was at the "tight" end and political control without legitimate use of power was at the "loose" end. This scale is not applicable to modern nations; however, Pelto also described Japan and Israeli kibbutzim as "tight" and Thailand as "loose." In the IBM data the Thai UAI score is not low (64), but it is considerably lower than the UAI scores for Japan (92) and Israel (81). (Whereas kibbutzim will be "tighter" than Israeli society as a whole, I assume they reflect partly the same norms.)

105. About uncertainty avoidance, Chan, Gelfand, Triandis, and Tzeng (1996) have written: "Hofstede [1980a] used an inductive approach to identify this dimension, and only used three items as justification of its existence. It is unknown whether or not this dimension would be replicated in future work" (p. 10). This was written in 1994, when replications and validations were

plenty, but already on the evidence of the first edition of *Culture's Consequences,* the statement is clearly false.

106. Peabody (1985, 1999) identified a tight/loose dimension in his international study of stereotypes among students, but it bears no relationship to Pelto's (1968) categories: Peabody described as loose those societies in which people were perceived as generous, extravagant, spontaneous, and impulsive—including French, Greeks, Italians, and Spanish—precisely the ones that Pelto would classify as tight.

107. The three Christian countries that are exceptions were ECA, IRE, and PHI.

108. The Nobel Index for the physical sciences described in Chapter 3 correlated nearly as highly (negatively) with UAI as with PDI (rho = −.46*), which means more Nobel Prizes in the applied physical sciences for lower-UAI countries, but in a multiple regression PDI explained all the differences.

109. For analyses of different national interests in the area of organization theory, see Hofstede and Kassem (1976:22) and Hofstede (1996a).

110. This is analogous to what I found concerning the relationship between UAI and the Least Preferred Co-Worker index earlier in this chapter.

111. For examples, see Westerlund and Sjöstrand (1979) and Brunsson (1985).

112. Sutton-Smith and Roberts (1981) offer suggestions for the role of culture in play and games. Among other things, they distinguish between the integrative and the innovative role of play; we might expect that the first will be more frequent in uncertainty-avoiding societies and the second more frequent in uncertainty-accepting societies.

113. The $r = -.47**$ correlation between UAI and PDN in poor countries conflicts with a prediction by Levi and Andersson (1974, pp. 80-88) of a positive relationship between population density and stress. Their claim was based on extrapolations from animal life (deer, monkeys, fish, birds, rats). The biological need for space leads to aggression when others come too near. In the case of humans, this does not seem to be the case.

114. Lowe's (1996b) replication of the IBM survey in IBM Great Britain and IBM Hong Kong (both weak uncertainty avoidance cultures) in 1993, compared to the original scores of around 1970, produced a minimal shift for Britain (−4 points) and a sizable increase for Hong Kong (+15 points), but the Hong Kong employee population in 1970 had been the youngest in the world (Appendix 2, Exhibit A2.1, question A57), and an aging population implies higher UAI (Exhibit 4.1). Lowe's data do not show a split by question.

115. In both cases developments inside the company may have suppressed such shifts. Rule orientation across 38 occupations was strongly negatively correlated with educational level (Exhibit 4.9). From 1968 to 1972 the mean educational level of IBM employees increased because of higher education requirements for new employees. The increase in educational level is not visible from the survey data because of an incompatibility in the educational level scales used in the 1967-69 and 1971-73 questionnaires, but it is shown by unpublished company data. It probably offset the increase in rule orientation that we would expect with an increase in stress. The answers to the employment stability question were also affected by developments inside the company and on the labor market; the actual labor turnover in IBM decreased over this period, and so did the career opportunities. Figure 8.6 in the first edition of *Culture's Consequences* (Hofstede, 1980a) shows the shifts in each answer category of the employment stability question, as well as in actual labor turnover across 13 countries.

116. The exceptions were B9, more people preferring a manager career over a specialist career, and A58, lower overall satisfaction. Both can be explained by developments within IBM.

117. Due to World War II, data for 1940 and 1945 were not available for several countries in Lynn and Hampson's sample.

118. The year of highest anxiety per country was as follows: 1935, FIN, SWI, USA; 1950, AUT, DEN, FRA, GER, ITA, JPN, NET, NOR; 1955, BEL, SWE; 1960, none; 1965, none; 1970, AUL, CAN, GBR, IRE, NZL.

119. According to the sign test, this is a significant overall shift at the .05 level.

120. The economic, geographic, and demographic indicators correlated with UAI do not facilitate predictions, contrary to what was the case for PDI (compare Exhibits 3.20 and 4.22).

121. A detailed calculation of UAI for the Category 1 countries can be found in Hofstede (1977a). The extension with Category 2 countries and Category 3 regions is described in Hofstede (1983c).

122. Unfortunately, the results of the earlier medical surveys were never fully published. The data on file did not contain the correlations justifying the inclusion of the question in the later attitude surveys. What I refer to here is a report comparing managers from 13 organizational divisions (total $n = 1,500$). Among these divisions, mean stress scores differed significantly (chi-square = 41.3*** with 12 degrees of freedom).

123. In AUL, CAN, FRA, GBR, GER, ITA, JPN, PHI, SIN, and USA, nationwide samples of about 1,000 respondents were drawn; in BRA, IND, and KOR, samples of the same size were drawn in urban areas only.

124. Chi-square = 2.5 with 1 degree of freedom (*ns*).

125. Chi-square = 0.1 with 1 degree of freedom (*ns*).

5

■

Individualism and Collectivism

Summary of This Chapter

The third dimension of national culture is called *individualism,* as opposed to *collectivism.* It describes the relationship between the individual and the collectivity that prevails in a given society. It is reflected in the way people live together—for example, in nuclear families, extended families, or tribes—and it has many implications for values and behavior. In some cultures, individualism is seen as a blessing and a source of well-being; in others, it is seen as alienating. Sociology offers a variety of distinctions associated with the individualism dimension, of which the best known is probably Tönnies's distinction between gemeinschaft (low individualism) and gesellschaft (high individualism).

The IBM database allowed the computation for each of 53 countries and regions of an Individualism Index (IDV). The same index is not suitable for distinguishing among occupations, the genders, age groups, or individuals, however. The Individualism Index is negatively correlated with the Power Distance Index, but the correlation all but disappears when national wealth is controlled for. Within Europe, IDV is negatively correlated with uncertainty avoidance.

In this chapter, the country Individualism Index is validated against a large number of country data from other sources. These include straight replications of the IBM survey on other populations as well as large cross-national studies of values by Schwartz, by Smith, Dugan, and Trompenaars, and by Inglehart (the World Values Survey). These and other correlates of IDV are integrated into a coherent list of connotations of individualism or collectivism as a country characteristic.

From this, a picture of the individualism/collectivism dimension of societal norms is drawn. In separate sections, its implications are elaborated for the family (including its relationships with the results of Buss's survey of preferred marriage partners), for personality and behavior (including the meta-analysis of conformity studies by R. Bond and Smith, the ISEAR and Matsumoto studies of the expression of emotions, and the study of the pace of life by Levine and Norenzayan), for language (Kashima and Kashima's comparative analysis of pronoun use), for school education, for the work situation, the applicability of management methods, consumer behavior, issues of health and disability, political systems and legislation, religions, and theories. National wealth and geographic latitude together predicted 78% of the variance in IDV, but they left room for specific historical influences. Some speculations are made about these historical influences, and about the future of country differences in individualism and collectivism, which may become smaller with increasing affluence but are very unlikely to disappear altogether.

The Individual and the Collectivity

Individualism in Society

Some animals, such as wolves, are gregarious; others, such as tigers, are solitary. The human species should no doubt be classified with the gregarious animals, but different human societies show gregariousness to different degrees. Here again, then, we have a fundamental dimension on which societies differ: the relationship between the individual and the collectivity.

If we look across a broad range of human societies, traditional as well as modern, we recognize differences in gregariousness through, for example, differences in the complexity of the family units in which people live and that affect their day-to-day behavior. Some people live in nuclear families (husband, wife, and children); others live in (patrilineal or matrilineal) extended families, or clans, with grandparents, uncles, aunts, and cousins; still others live in tribal units based on kinship ties of an even more distant nature.[1] Blumberg and Winch (1972) supported a "curvilinear hypothesis" for the relationship between family complexity and the complexity of societies as they develop from traditional to modern. Very traditional hunting-gathering tribes tend to live in nuclear families. In more complex agricultural societies, people aggregate into extended families, clans, or tribal units. As agricultural societies develop toward still more complex urban-industrial societies, family complexity decreases again and extended families disintegrate into nuclear families; grandparents are sent to homes for the aged, and single relatives lead solitary lives. Thus modern industrial societies in this respect reapproach the state of the hunter-gatherer societies. In several cases in modern society even the nuclear family is threatened with disintegration, but attempts to replace it with some other institution that takes account of the fundamental gregariousness of human nature have so far not been very successful.

The relationship between the individual and the collectivity in human society is not only a matter of ways of living together, it is intimately linked with societal norms (in the sense of value systems of major groups of the population; see Exhibit 1.5). It therefore affects both people's mental programming and the structure and functioning of many institutions aside from the family: educational, religious, political, and utilitarian. The central element in our mental programming involved in this case is the self-concept. "The tradition-directed person . . . hardly thinks of himself as an individual" (Riesman, Glazer, & Denney, 1953, p. 33). Hsu (1971) has argued that the Chinese tradition has no equivalent for the Western concept of "personality": a separate entity distinct from society and culture. The Chinese word for "man" (ren) includes the person's intimate societal and cultural environment, which makes that person's existence meaningful. Chinese tend to adapt their views relatively easily to this environment. Later in this chapter, I will show that Chinese culture countries score considerably lower on individualism than do those of the Western world. Markus and Kitayama (1991), in a broad

review of psychological and anthropological literature, have argued that our cognition, emotion, and motivation all differ depending on whether our culture has provided us with an independent or an interdependent "self-construal."

An example of the consequence of a more individualist or more collectivist self-concept is the case of religious or ideological conversion. In Western individualist society, converting oneself is a highly individual act; if I would choose to convert myself to, for example, Catholicism or Islam, it is unlikely that even my closest relatives would follow me. However, the history of all great religions has been one of collective rather than individual conversions. "Then he . . . got baptized instantly, *he and all his family* . . . overjoyed *like all his household* at having believed in God" (New Testament, Acts 16:33-34; translation J. Moffatt). Similarly, in 20th-century China ideological conversions tended to take place collectively. This is not just a matter of deference to more powerful persons; rather, people have a sense of collective identity that makes it only natural that they should change their views together. In Western Europe this was still the case at the time of the Reformation (16th century). Lower classes followed the conversion of their lord: *Cuius regio, eius religio* (In whose region one lived determined one's religion).

Because they are tied to value systems shared by the majority, issues of collectivism versus individualism carry strong moral overtones. Many Americans see the individualism in their culture as a major reason for the greatness of the United States. In a classic study reported in a volume titled *The Lonely Crowd,* Riesman et al. (1953) distinguished between "tradition-directed types," who are typical for traditional societies with high birthrates and high death rates, and "inner-directed types," who are typical for societies in periods of transitional growth, such as the United States in the 18th through 20th centuries. Inner-directed types have no stable traditions to go by; rather, they are guided by a "psychological gyroscope" (p. 31) that is set during their early education and keeps them on a steady track in a turbulent environment. Riesman et al. quoted the gravestone inscription of an 18th-century American, Thomas Darling: "A gentleman of strong mental powers . . . habituated to contemplation and reading . . . in moral reasoning . . . of deep penetration and sound judgement . . . with a rational and firm faith in his God and Saviour: He knew no other master" (p. 133). Riesman et al. did not restrict their concept of inner-directedness to people brought up in the "Protestant ethic"; they found it equally present in, for example, descendants of Catholic cultures. In fact, Riesman et al.'s concern was that the inner-directed type was disappearing in the United States and that an incipient decline of population stimulated a new stabilization around another dominant type, the "other-directed" American: a new kind of collectivist who took his bearings from his peer group and from the mass media. The data in this chapter will show, however, that at least within the IBM Corporation a comparison of U.S. employees with their counterparts from other nations showed the former around 1970 still scoring higher on individualism than all others.

A very different moral stance is found in China. For Mao Zedong, individualism was evil. In his opinion, individualism and liberalism were manifest in the selfishness and aversion to discipline characteristic of the petty bourgeoisie. The selfish behavior that Mao condemned was not necessarily at the expense of others. It was sufficient to place personal interests above those of the group or simply to devote too much attention to one's own things (Ho, 1978, pp. 395-396). Mao's anti-individualist, pro-collectivist ethos is deeply rooted in the Chinese tradition. Collectivism does not mean a negation of the individual's well-being or interest; it is implicitly assumed that maintaining the group's well-being is the best guarantee for the individual (Ho, 1979, p. 144).

Not all Western thinkers are happy with individualism, of course, and not all Eastern thinkers are satisfied with collectivism. There is a certain symmetry between the criticism of Western society by Brittan (1977) and the criticism of Japanese society by Kawasaki (1969). The first stressed the alienation of the "privatized" individual; the second, the tyranny of the collectivity. They represent the devil and the deep blue sea, between which societies and the people within them try to steer their course.

The different forms of society that go with more collectivist and more individualist self-concepts were recognized early by sociologists. Tönnies (1887/1963) introduced the distinction between gemeinschaft and gesellschaft (the German terms were translated in the English version of his book as *community* and *society*). These concepts describe two types of social entities. Gemeinschaft entities result from mutual sympathy, habit, or common beliefs and are "willed" for their intrinsic value to their members; gesellschaft entities are intended by their constituents to be means to specific ends (Heberle, 1968, p. 100). Tönnies further noted in history a transition from a predominantly gemeinschaft-like to a predominantly gesellschaft-like social order, which he attributed to increasing commercialization, the rise of the modern state, and the progress of science (p. 101).

An association between the degree of collectivism or individualism in a society and its degree of modernity was suggested by at least three of the sources quoted above: by Blumberg and Winch, who associated modernity with lower familial complexity; by Riesman et al., who associated transitional growth with inner-directedness; and by Tönnies, who associated the modern state with gesellschaft. Chapter 1 referred to other studies that suggest that a society's degree of economic evolution or modernity is a major determinant of societal norms. The present chapter will show that among the four dimensions of national culture found empirically in the IBM data, the individualism/collectivism (ind/col) dimension is the most closely linked to a country's level of economic development.

Triandis (1971) has summarized psychological studies on the effect of modernization on attitudes as follows:

> Modern man . . . is open to new experiences; relatively independent of parental authority; concerned with time, planning, willing to defer gratification; he feels that man can be the master over nature, and that he controls the reinforcements he receives from his environment; he believes in determinism and science; he has a wide, cosmopolitan perspective, he uses broad in-groups; he competes with standards of excellence, and he is optimistic about controlling his environment. Traditional man has narrow in-groups, looks at the world with suspicion, believes that good is limited and one obtains a share of it by chance or pleasing the gods; he identifies with his parents and receives direction from them; he considers planning a waste of time, and does not defer gratification; he feels at the mercy of obscure environmental factors, and is prone to mysticism; he sees interpersonal relations as an end, rarely as means to an end; he does not believe that he can control his environment but rather sees himself under the influence of external, mystical powers. (p. 8)

In Chapter 1, I also referred to Parsons and Shils's (1951, p. 77) "pattern variables," which are part of their "general theory of action." From the five pattern variables suggested, especially variable 2, "self-orientation versus collectivity orientation," calls for association with the ind/col dimension. Parsons and Shils wrote:

> The high frequency of situations in which there is a disharmony of interests creates the problem of choosing between action for private goals or on behalf of collective goals. This dilemma may be resolved by the actor either by giving primacy to interests, goals and values shared with other members of a given collective unit of which he is a member, or by giving primacy to his personal or private interests without considering their bearing on collective interest. (pp. 80-81)

In his later work, Parsons dropped "self-orientation versus collectivity orientation" as a pattern variable: It did not fit into the tight paradigm he had developed (see Rocher, 1974, pp. 52, 43). In his theory of the evolution of societies, Parsons (1977) did not use the self-versus-collectivity orientation distinction. Parsons's other pattern variables are less clearly conceptually related to individualism/collectivism. However, as will appear later in this chapter, pattern variable 3, "universalism versus particularism," is statistically related to individualism. This variable refers to whether or not value systems should take particular relationship systems of the actor into account (such as family or friendship ties). The individualist society tends to be universalist (particular relationships should not be counted).

U.S. anthropologist Ruth Benedict (1946/1974) stressed the distinction between cultures that "rely heavily on shame and those that rely heavily on guilt. . . . True shame cultures rely on external sanctions for good behavior, not, as true guilt cultures do, on an internalized conviction of sin." Shame "requires an audience or at least a man's fantasy of an audience. Guilt does not. In a nation where honor means living up to one's own picture of oneself, a man may suffer from guilt though no man knows of his misdeed" (pp. 222-223). Benedict applied this distinction to the case of Japan versus the United States, but it fits the description of collectivist versus individualist societies in general. The classic British novel *A Passage to India* contains the following reference to the motives of the chief character, an Indian doctor:

> Aziz upheld the proprieties, though he did not invest them with any moral halo, and it was here that he chiefly differed from an Englishman. His conventions were social. There is no harm in deceiving society as long as she does not find you out, because it is only when she finds you out that you have harmed her; she is not like a friend or God, who are injured by the mere existence of unfaithfulness. (Forster, 1924/1936, p. 116)

In Chapter 1, I referred to Edward Hall's (1976) distinction of cultures on the basis of their ways of communicating. Hall introduced a distinction between high- and low-context communication. High-context communication implies that little has to be said or written because most of the information is either in the physical environment or internalized in the person; only a small part is in the coded, explicit part of the message. Low-context communication implies that the mass of information is made explicit. Gudykunst and Ting-Toomey (1988) have argued, and I agree with them, that Hall's distinction can be considered as an aspect of collectivism versus individualism: High-context communication fits the collectivist society, and low-context communication is typi-

cal for individualist cultures. Many things that in collectivist cultures are self-evident must be said explicitly in individualist cultures. American business contracts are much longer than Japanese business contracts. Unwritten rules represented bones of contention in the negotiations between Western countries and Japan about the opening of the Japanese markets for Western products. The Japanese rightly argued that there were no formal rules preventing the import of foreign products, but the Western would-be importers collided with the implicit rules of the Japanese distribution system, which they did not understand.[2]

Individualism in Organizations
and Organization Theories

The norm prevalent in a given society as to the degree of individualism or collectivism expected from its members will strongly affect the nature of the relationship between a person and the organization to which he or she belongs. More collectivist societies call for greater emotional dependence of members on their organizations; in a society in equilibrium, the organizations should in return assume a broad responsibility for their members. Whenever organizations cease to do that—as in the incipient capitalism in 19th-century Europe, and today in many less-developed countries—there is disharmony between people's values and the social order; this will lead to a shift in values toward more individualism, to pressure toward a different, more collectivist social order (such as state socialism), or both.

The level of individualism or collectivism in society will affect the organization's members' reasons for complying with organizational requirements. Following a terminology introduced by Etzioni (1975), we can assume more "moral" involvement with the organization where collectivist values prevail and more "calculative" involvement where individualist values prevail. Etzioni distinguished between "pure" and "social" moral involvement. He argued that the first occurs in vertical relationships, such as between teachers and students, priests and parishioners, leaders and followers. The second, social involvement, develops in horizontal relationships, such as in various types of primary groups. Pure and social moral involvement may occur together, but, as a rule, one orientation predominates (Etzioni, 1975, p. 11). Pure moral involvement corresponds to the values of the subordinate in a large power distance society, and social involvement to the values of the organization member in a collectivist society. As will be shown later in this chapter, large power distance and collectivism go together in most, but not all, societies.

The level of individualism or collectivism in society will also affect the types of persons who will be admitted into positions of special influence in organizations. A useful distinction in this case is Merton's (1949/1968, p. 447) "locals" versus "cosmopolitans" (the terms are derived from a translation of Tönnies's work). The local type is largely preoccupied with problems inside the organization and is most influential in a collectivist culture. The cosmopolitan type must maintain a minimum set of relations within the organization but considers him- or herself an integral part of the world outside it. Cosmopolitans are more influential in organizations within an individualist culture. Evidence for this is found in the IBM data.

The degree of individualism in organizations depends, obviously, on other factors in addition to a societal norm, such as employees' educational level and the organization's history and organizational culture. Also predictable is a relationship with organization size. In a study among workers of large and small production firms in Bradford, England, Ingham (1970, pp. 117 ff.) found more moral involvement in the smaller firms and more calculative involvement in the larger. This suggests a positive correlation between organization size and individualism, which, as we shall see later in this chapter, is supported by the IBM data.

There is an obvious relationship between the organization's technology and the position of its members along the continuum from individualism to collectivism. Technologies developed in Western individualist settings more or less presuppose an individualist mentality in entrepreneurs, managers, and workers, which is part of "modernity" (Stinchcombe, 1965, pp. 145 ff.; Triandis, 1973b, p. 166).

Introducing such technologies in more collectivist countries represents one of the main forces toward a shift of societal norms in those countries (see Exhibit 1.5). On the other hand, the collectivist value pattern in more traditional societies sets a limit on possibilities for transferring technologies; this is one of the dilemmas of the economic development of poor countries. One solution is sought in the transfer of "intermediate" or "appropriate" technologies that are better adapted to what already exists in the traditional collectivist societies. Another solution is the local design of political and organizational structures that allow collectivism and modern technology to coexist. Examples of the latter are Japan and China; attempts at combining collectivism and modernity failed in the former Soviet Union and the former Yugoslavia. In spite of the successful integration of modern technology with more traditional Japanese and Chinese values, there are definite signs of increasing individualism in these countries as well (see below).

The ind/col dimension is also visible in the normative organization theories coming from different countries. The United States is the major exporter of modern organization theories, but its position of extreme individualism in comparison to most other countries makes the relevance of some of these theories for other cultural environments doubtful. As we have seen, in the United States there has been and still is a strong feeling that individualism is good and collectivism bad. Riesman et al. were concerned about their inner-directed type being replaced by an other-directed one. In his once-classic bestseller *The Organization Man,* William H. Whyte, Jr. (1956) accused large organizations in the United States of destroying individualism and exhorted individuals to defend themselves against collectivist organizational pressures.[3] In the ensuing dispute, Sayles (1963) defended U.S. big business against Whyte's attacks; being as much in favor of individualism as Whyte, Sayles claimed that big business fostered individualism rather than the opposite. The strong feelings about the desirability of individualism in the United States make it difficult for Americans to understand that people in less individualistically oriented societies may want to resolve societal and organizational problems in other ways.[4]

One of the rare non-American collections of organization theory literature is a volume of European contributions for which I served as coeditor (Hofstede & Kassem, 1976). In it, Hjelholt (1976), who was from Denmark, argued for the importance of the organization and its external and internal boundaries as sources of collective identity for the members:

I think the identity of groups and systems is important. Without identity the system or the group is neither productive nor satisfying as a place to live. And if we have to get our identity from other systems and just be a prisoner in the working organization, we create a society which is clearly asking for trouble.

From this outburst you can guess my attitude toward the predominantly American organization theories advocating the organization structure as matrix-organizations or temporary systems. I think that the theories which try to get away with or loosen boundaries are attacking the group identities, and in this way, while temporarily ensuring flexibility inside the organization, they export problems to the outside, where we get a society of alienated, rootless individuals. I feel much more in accordance with the moves of groups to extend or redefine their boundaries, trying to let their values influence the organization as a whole. I refer to the unions' demand for a better work environment, their demand to be included in decision-making for the whole organization, and the like. (pp. 241-242)

Of course, American unions did not as a rule demand to be included in this type of decision making; unions in some European countries did so. This is no accident; union-management relationships, too, reflect dominant value systems. The quote from Hjelholt shows that a normative stance in favor of individualism is not the only possibility for the organization theorist and that a different value position leads to a different theory.

Measuring National Differences in Individualism in IBM

An Individualism Index for Countries in the IBM Sample

In the statistical analysis section of this chapter, I describe the calculation of a country Individualism Index. This index and the Masculinity Index (MAS), which is the subject of Chapter 6, use country mean answer scores on 14 "work goals" questions, questions of the format "How important is it to you to . . ."—for example, "How important is it to you to have an opportunity for high earnings?" or "How important is it to you to fully use your skills and abilities on the job?" For the exact text of the 14 questions, see A5 through A18 in Appendix 1. The questions are also listed in Exhibit 5.11 in the statistical analysis section, together with the short names that I shall use to refer to them.

The Individualism Index and the Masculinity Index were derived from the two main factors that explained the country differences in IBM employees' answers to the 14 work goals questions, after standardization of the raw country mean scores as described in Chapter 2. In the factor analysis, nearly half of the variance in country mean scores on the two questions could be accounted for by these two factors. The Individualism Index was based on the first of these factors, which accounted for 24% of the variance in the country mean work goals scores. It was mainly affected by the scores for the following six work goals:

Loading	Work Goal
.86	Personal time
.49	Freedom
.46	Challenge
−.63	Use of skills
−.69	Physical conditions
−.82	Training

The "loading" represents the correlation coefficient (across 40 countries) between the factor score and the country mean score for each work goal. Thus the Individualism Index is strongly related to the mean importance attached in a country to personal time ("have a job which leaves you sufficient time for your personal or family life") and sharply *negatively* related to the importance of training ("have training opportunities [to improve your skills or learn new skills]").

Psychologists, especially American psychologists, have done a considerable amount of research using work goals questions (Hofstede, 1976b). After the publication of a seminal book by Herzberg, Mausner, and Snyderman (1959), it became customary to divide such goals into "intrinsic" (work related) and "extrinsic" (non-work related). The factor loadings shown above do not oppose intrinsic to extrinsic goals; Herzberg et al. probably would have classified freedom, challenge, use of skills, and training as intrinsic job aspects, and personal time and physical conditions as extrinsic. What the three goals with positive loadings have in common is that they stress the actor's independence from the organization. Even challenge ("have challenging work to do—work from which you can get a personal sense of accomplishment"), although it takes place within the organization, stresses the individual's *personal* involvement. The three goals with negative loadings, in contrast, stress what the organization does for the individual: provide him or her with training, with working conditions, allow the individual to use his or her skills. The latter goals reflect a more "local" mentality, whereas the former are more "cosmopolitan."

The distinction between challenge and use of skills may appear trivial to a Western-educated reader. In fact, across individuals within each country and each occupational group the importance scores for challenge and for use of skills are always positively correlated (Hofstede, Kraut, & Simonetti, 1976, p. 29). And yet this distinction discriminates sharply between national cultures; challenge (with its stress on a "personal sense of accomplishment") appeals more in one group of cultures, and use of skills (with no mention of accomplishment) appeals more in others.

The contrast between goals stressing independence from the organization and goals assuming dependence has been the argument for calling this factor *individual/collective* and using the country factor scores as the basis for a country Individualism Index. The index, by a simple mathematical transformation, has been brought into a range between 0 and 100: Its values for 50 countries and three regions are listed in the first column of Exhibit 5.1.[5] The highest IDV values were found for the United States (91), Australia (90), and Great Britain (89); the lowest, for Guatemala (6), Ecuador (8), and Panama (11).

Exhibit 5.1   Individualism Index Values for 50 Countries and Three Regions

Rank	Country	IDV Actual	IDV Predicted[a]	Rank	Country	IDV Actual	IDV Predicted
1	United States	91	90				
2	Australia	90	64	28	Turkey	37	36
3	Great Britain	89	66	29	Uruguay	36	39
4/5	Canada	80	80	30	Greece	35	44
4/5	Netherlands	80	68	31	Philippines	32	20
6	New Zealand	79	65	32	Mexico	30	28
7	Italy	76	54	33/35	Yugoslavia	27	43
8	Belgium	75	71	33/35	Portugal	27	39
9	Denmark	74	80	33/35	East Africa	27	
10/11	Sweden	71	92	36	Malaysia	26	15
10/11	France	71	75	37	Hong Kong	25	33
12	Ireland	70	56	38	Chile	23	37
13	Norway	69	78	39/41	Singapore	20	21
14	Switzerland	68	76	39/41	Thailand	20	19
15	Germany (F.R.)	67	74	39/41	West Africa	20	
16	South Africa	65	33	42	Salvador	19	21
17	Finland	63	72	43	South Korea	18	34
18	Austria	55	61	44	Taiwan	17	28
19	Israel	54	51	45	Peru	16	21
20	Spain	51	44	46	Costa Rica	15	21
21	India	48	27	47/48	Pakistan	14	24
22/23	Japan	46	53	47/48	Indonesia	14	13
22/23	Argentina	46	43	49	Colombia	13	16
24	Iran	41	34	50	Venezuela	12	26
25	Jamaica	39	27	51	Panama	11	23
26/27	Brazil	38	27	52	Ecuador	8	12
26/27	Arab countries	38		53	Guatemala	6	22
				Mean of 53			43
				Standard deviation of 53			25

a. Predicted values are based on multiple regression on wealth and latitude; see Exhibit 5.22.

Societal Versus Individual
Individualism and Collectivism, and Whether
Ind and Col Are One or Two Dimensions

Since the first edition of *Culture's Conse-quences* appeared in 1980, the individualism/collectivism dimension has gained great popularity among cross-cultural psychologists, especially those from the economically emerging Asian nations. Two books have been devoted entirely to this dimension (Kim, Triandis, Kagitçibasi, Choi, & Yoon, 1994; Triandis, 1995).[6] Smith and Bond (1993) have written a very readable social psychology textbook paying a lot of attention to the dimension, and Kagitçibasi (1997) has written a handbook chapter about the dimension. Literally

hundreds of journal articles refer to it. The dimension provides psychologists with a paradigm implying that traditional psychology is not a universal science: It is a product of Western thinking, caught in individualist assumptions. When these are replaced by more collectivist assumptions, another psychology emerges that differs in important respects. For example, individualist psychology is universalist, opposing the "ego" to any "other." In collectivist psychology the ego is inseparable from its social context; I earlier cited Hsu's (1971) argument that the Western concept of a "personality" separate from its environment does not exist in the Chinese tradition. Collectivist society is particularist: The crucial distinction is between the in-group (which includes the ego) and the out-group. In psychology this means, for example, that the results of laboratory experiments in a collectivist society depend on whether participants belong to the same in-group or not. A good example is a study by Noesjirwan (1977) involving patients in doctors' waiting rooms in Jakarta, Indonesia, and Sydney, Australia. The waiting patients' behavior was observed, and a number of them were afterward interviewed and asked whether they would initiate a conversation with a stranger in the waiting room. In the interview, 62% of the Indonesians and 43% of the Australians said they would probably not address a stranger. However, the previous observations had shown that of the Indonesians, 56% had been silent; of the Australians, 76%.[7] The explanation is that the interview did not distinguish between addressing in-group and out-group members; for the collectivist Indonesians this was an important distinction, and it is likely that at least some of the people in their doctor's waiting room would be known to them or belong to the same neighborhood or ethnic group, so they would be seen as in-group members, not as "strangers."

Nevertheless, the paradigm shift in psychology from ego to ego-in-context is not without its problems. The individualism/collectivism antithesis as I use it is not a psychological but an anthropological distinction; it refers to societies, not to individuals within those societies. Most psychologists have been mentally programmed to focus at the individual level, not the societal level. The empirical fact, basic to the present book, that relationships between the same variables may be different at different levels is still not commonly recognized by psychologists. Articles in psychological journals still often measure individualism and collectivism at the level of individuals and then try to draw conclusions about societies.

Triandis (1995, p. 5) has proposed to avoid confusion between levels by using different terms: for individuals, *idiocentric* (self-oriented) versus *allocentric* (social context-oriented); for societies, *individualist* versus *collectivist*. So a person can be an allocentric within an individualist society, and vice versa. This would indeed be a useful way to establish clarity between levels, but the new terms have not been widely accepted, and even Triandis himself has not used them consistently.[8]

A related question has been whether individualism and collectivism can be treated as opposites. Are they indeed two poles of one dimension, or should they be treated as two separate dimensions?[9] The answer to this question lies in an understanding of the level issue. At the individual level there is no reason a person cannot show idiocentric and allocentric personality traits at the same time, so the two should be treated as separate dimensions. At the societal level, however, col-

lective mental programs and institutions that are individualistically inspired exclude those that are collectivistically inspired. This is an empirically, statistically verified matter of fact. So at the societal level, individualism and collectivism should be treated as opposite poles of one dimension, based on alternative solutions for the same basic dilemma of societies: the level of gregariousness of the human species on which society should be built. We will return to this issue in Chapter 6, where the question arises concerning whether masculinity and femininity are one or two dimensions.

Individualism Versus Power
Distance and Uncertainty Avoidance

The clustering of countries on the Individualism Index suggests a correlation with the Power Distance Index. The relationship between PDI and IDV is shown graphically in Exhibit 5.2. The PDI × IDV plot shows that there is a broad overall correlation between the two dimensions. Across 53 countries and regions the correlation coefficient is $r = -.68***$. In Chapter 2, in the factor analysis of all IBM value questions, PDI and IDV showed up (with opposite signs) on the same factor. I will nevertheless deal with them as separate dimensions for the following reasons:

1. They are conceptually different. Power distance refers to emotional dependence on more powerful people; individualism to emotional (in)dependence on groups, organizations, or other collectivities.

2. Although most high-PDI countries are also low-IDV countries, and vice versa, this is not always the case. The Latin European countries (in particular France and Belgium) combine large power distances with strong individualism; Costa Rica is collectivist with a relatively small power distance; Austria and Israel combine small power distances with only medium individualism. Collapsing PDI and IDV into one dimension would obscure the unique value patterns of these countries.

3. Most important, PDI and IDV are both correlated—the first negatively, the second positively—with a third variable, national wealth. If we control for (eliminate the influence of) wealth (1970 GNP/capita), the correlation coefficient between PDI and IDV across 50 countries is reduced to an only marginally significant $r = -.32*$.

People in IBM subsidiaries in the Latin European cluster (to which also South African whites marginally belong) have a need for strict authority

Exhibit 5.2. An IDV × PDI Plot for 50 Countries and Three Regions

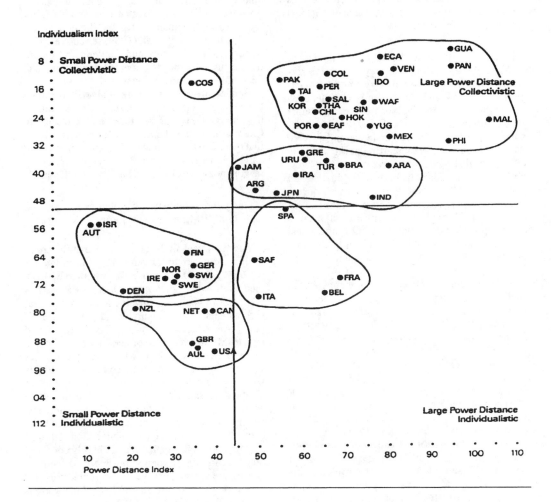

of hierarchical superiors, but at the same time they stress their personal independence from any collectivity: They are dependent individualists. This culture pattern of dependent individualism has been recognized in the case of France by, for example, Michel Crozier, who has written in *The Bureaucratic Phenomenon* (1964a):

> Face-to-face dependence relationships are . . . perceived as difficult to bear in the French cultural setting. Yet the prevailing view of authority is still that of universalism and absolutism. . . . The two attitudes are contradictory. However, they can be reconciled within a bureaucratic system since impersonal rules and centralization make it possible to reconcile an absolutist conception of authority and the elimination of most direct dependence relationships. (p. 222)

The opposite pattern (no strict authority but relative personal dependence on the collectivity, as found in Costa Rica, Austria, and Israel, could be called independent collectivism. The unique case of Costa Rica as Latin America's "most firmly rooted democracy" has been discussed in Chapter 3. An Austrian psychologist interpreted his country's cultural pattern as follows:

> The political structure of this country is based on a more primitive organization of society, in which the family model is more clearly present than, for example, in France, where political superstructures prevail. . . . At the same time, our society is sufficiently advanced not to be threatened by this family model in personal relationships. The easygoing relationship between superiors and individuals in private and public organizations is inter-

preted by the Germans as "Austrian charm." Yet I believe that this friendly relationship pattern applies only to face-to-face relationships, such as personally known superiors. (T. Lindner, personal communication; my translation)

In Chapter 3, I referred to Ng's critique of Mulder; Ng argued that the way power is exercised differs between *within-group* and *between-group* situations, and consequently also depends on whether the actors involved belong to the same or to different in-groups. Ng's (1980, p. 229) argument means that power distance and ind/col interact. From a different starting point, Triandis (1995) has distinguished "horizontal" from "vertical" individualism: "In both individualist and collectivist cultures, the vertical dimension accepts inequality, and rank has its privileges. . . . In contrast, the horizontal dimension emphasizes that people should be similar on most attributes, especially status" (pp. 44-45). Evidently, this vertical/horizontal distinction is the same thing as power distance. Triandis (1995, pp. 46-47) recognizes the similarity between the concepts. At the society level, recognizing the interaction between ind/col and power distance renders a horizontal/vertical distinction within individualism/collectivism redundant. At the individual level the distinction may still be useful (power distance is by definition only a societal characteristic, not an individual one). Singelis, Triandis, Bhawuk, and Gelfand (1995) have described the development of a test for dividing U.S. students into horizontal individualists, vertical individualists, horizontal collectivists, and vertical collectivists.

Exhibit 2.7 in Chapter 2 shows the correlation pattern among the four IBM indexes. Across all 53 countries and regions, IDV is correlated primarily with PDI; across the 22 wealthier countries, it is correlated primarily with UAI ($r = -.69***$). For these (mainly European) countries, PDI and UAI are strongly correlated ($r = .63***$, for Europe even $r = .78***$; see Chapter 4), and the UAI differences are much larger than the PDI differences. So across the wealthy countries, stronger individualism tends to go together with weaker uncertainty avoidance. An IDV × UAI plot will be presented later in this chapter (Exhibit 5.7).

Individualism and
Occupation, Gender, and Age

The IDV values are based on the results of a factor analysis of work goals *across countries*. The statistical section of this chapter supplies the details on this factor analysis and also shows the results of a factor analysis of mean work goals scores *across 38 occupations* with country held constant. In this occupational factor analysis there is no trace of an individual/collective dimension: We cannot label one occupation as more "individualist" than another. Instead, for occupations we do find a factor that corresponds fairly well to the "intrinsic/extrinsic" dichotomy according to Herzberg et al. (1959; see above). This factor opposes freedom and challenge on the intrinsic side to benefits, physical conditions, and personal time on the extrinsic side.[10]

Gender differences in work goals will be shown to be closely related to the issue of "masculinity" in value systems and will therefore be treated in Chapter 6. In that chapter it will become evident that there are no systematic differences in individualism between women and men. Age differences in work goals are discussed later in this chapter.[11]

Country Individualism Index Scores
and Other IBM Survey Questions

The statistical analysis indicates that the country Individualism Index was strongly correlated ($r = .66***$ across 53 countries and regions) with the mean raw work goal importance (IMP) scores across all 14 goals. A low value of IMP means that respondents in the country tended to score all goals—regardless of content—as more important.[12] IMP is a measure of acquiescence, that is, the tendency to say yes to whichever question. In Chapter 3, acquiescence in some other studies was also found to be correlated with PDI.[13] In Chapter 2, Exhibit 2.5 shows that within countries acquiescence in answering work goals questions depended strongly on occupation: Respondents in occupations requiring less education showed more acquiescence than did more highly educated respondents. Respondents in a more collectivist culture are more sensitive to the social pressure they perceive to be emanating from the questionnaire, and those in a high-PDI culture are more sensitive to the authority of the persons who have created and are administering the survey instrument, the more so if the respondents have lower education levels.[14]

Paradoxically, across countries (holding occupation constant) IDV and the mean number of years of formal education of employees were negatively correlated. In less individualist (poorer) countries, IBM employees on the average went to school *longer* to reach particular occupations. This suggests that in collectivist countries, the qualification for jobs was based more on years of schooling; in individualist countries it was based on more practical criteria, such as performance at previous tasks.

In addition, respondents in more individualist countries, compared with those in more collectivist countries, tended to endorse significantly more frequently the following items in the questionnaire:

1. Staying with one company is *not* desirable (B59), and the better managers in a company are *not* those that have been in the company the longest time (C11).

2. A larger corporation is generally *not* a more desirable place to work than a small company (C17), and respondents are also less happy about the fact that IBM is a foreign company (B24).

3. A corporation is *not* responsible for its employees (B52).

4. Interesting work is *not* as important as earnings (B53).[15]

5. For getting ahead in industry, knowing influential people is usually more important than ability (C15).

6. Decisions made by individuals are usually of higher quality than decisions made by groups (B57).

7. In the first survey round (1967-70) the IBM questionnaire included 22 rather than 14 work goals. Two of the goals eliminated in 1971 were particularly characteristic of the collectivist side of the individual/collective dimension: the importance of working in a successful company (C4) and the importance of working in a modern company (C5).

Points 1, 2, 3, and 7 confirm the lesser dependency of the individual on the company in more individualist cultures. They suggest that on the more individualist side, respondents defended more a calculative involvement with the organization, according to Etzioni's (1975) terminology; point 4 shows that this also implies a stress on earnings. The skeptical attitude about careers in point 5 confirms this calculative, rather than moral, involvement. Point 6, finally, is not surprising: Individual decisions are more ideologically appealing than collective decisions in more individualist cultures.

Validating IDV Against Data From Other Sources

Distinguishing IDV
From PDI and GNP/Capita

This chapter will validate the Individualism Index against comparative cross-national data from many other studies, by other researchers from a variety of disciplines, as Chapters 3 and 4 have done for PDI and UAI. A study will be considered to make a valid contribution to the explanation of the IDV syndrome if its results show a stronger zero-order correlation with IDV than with any of the other IBM indexes, or with national wealth

(GNP/capita).[16] It will also be accepted as valid proof if IDV emerges as a significant explaining variable in a stepwise multiple regression. The comparison of the correlations of IDV with those of PDI and GNP/capita is crucial in this case, as we have seen that (depending on the mix of countries included) IDV, PDI, and GNP/capita can be strongly mutually correlated. Other authors have sometimes reported seemingly impressive zero-order correlations with IDV without being aware that these were by-products of even higher correlations with PDI or GNP/capita. So not all validations of IDV reported in the literature have been accepted for inclusion in the present chapter.

Straight Replications
of the IBM Survey

Managers attending courses at IMEDE. In Chapters 2 and 3, I have referred to the answers of non-IBM managers participating in IMEDE courses answering IBM questions. A sample of 362 participants scored the 14 work goals questions in their English version. Across 15 countries, in spite of (1) the small and poorly matched IMEDE samples, (2) the fact that the respondents at IMEDE were all managers and those in IBM were mostly rank-and-file workers, and (3) the fact that at IMEDE all people answered in English and in IBM they answered in their native tongues, there was significant agreement between the two surveys on the following points:

1. The acquiescence pattern (the tendency to rate all goals as more important, rho = .62**).

2. The presence of the same two factors in the IMEDE data as found in the IBM data, an individual/collective and an ego/social factor.

3. The scores of the 15 countries on the IMEDE individual/collective factor agreed with those on the IBM individualism dimension (rho = .64**).

4. For 5 out of the 14 goals separately, countries in the IMEDE sample ranked significantly like countries at IBM; for 12 out of the 14 goals, the rank orders of countries at IMEDE were positively correlated with those at IBM.[17]

Elite alumni from the Salzburg Seminar. I have discussed Hoppe's (1990, 1993) research using the Values Survey Module 1982 in Chapters 2, 3, and 4; it was shown to significantly replicate PDI and UAI differences between countries. Hoppe's questionnaire also contained 18 work goals questions, including the set of 14 used as the basis for the computation of IDV and MAS. As in the cases of PDI and UAI, the 1,590 Salzburg Seminar alumni from 17 European countries plus Turkey and the United States significantly replicated the IDV country differences found among IBM employees some 14 years earlier. Exhibit 5.15 in the statistical section of this chapter shows a correlation of $r = .69^{**}$ between the Hoppe scores and the IBM scores; for PDI and UAI this had been $r = .67^{**}$ and $r = .64^{**}$, respectively. The Salzburg alumni on average scored at about the same levels of IDV as the IBM employees. In Chapter 3, I explained that Hoppe's study contributed to the design of the new, 1994 version of the Values Survey Module (VSM 94; see Appendix 4). When recalculated from the VSM 94 questions and formulas, Hoppe's Salzburg UAI scores correlated with the original IBM scores with $r = .72^{***}$.

Commercial airline pilots. Helmreich and Merritt's (1998) study of pilots has also been mentioned in Chapters 2, 3, and 4. It covered more than 15,000 commercial airline pilots from 36 companies in 23 countries, surveyed between 1993 and 1997. The researchers' questionnaire contained 15 work goals items, including 9 from the 14 used as the basis for the computation of IDV and MAS.[18] Exhibit 5.16 shows a significant correlation, across 21 countries, between the IDV scores from IBM employees and pilots ($r = .70^{***}$). The overall level of individualism for the pilots was much higher than for IBM employees (a mean of 142 instead of 57 for the same countries in IBM), and the range of IDV scores for the 14 countries was smaller for the pilots (44 points) than it had been for the same countries in IBM (74 points). Pilots seem to be individualists, and pilots from collectivist countries are more different from their home-country cultures in this respect than are pilots from individualist countries.[19]

Higher-income consumers surveyed by the EMS 97. In Chapters 2 and 4, I referred to a replication of the IBM questions in the European Media and Marketing Survey 1997 by Inter/View International, inspired by Marieke de Mooij, which used the 20 questions of the VSM 94 (Appendix 4). The EMS 97 sampled 6,680 main income earners in the top 20% of households by household income within each of 15 countries, from 100 in Ireland to more than 1,000 in Denmark.[20] The EMS country scores on IDV based on the VSM 94 questions and formula are included in Exhibit 5.15. Across the 15 countries, the IDV scores from the IBM employees in 1970 and from the EMS consumers in 1997 were correlated with $r = .60^{**}$; this is a weaker correlation than in the cases of PDI ($r = .74^{***}$) and UAI ($r = .89^{***}$), but the EMS survey was limited to industrialized European countries with a restricted range of IDV scores.[21]

Replications using only the work goals questions. Between 1989 and 1994, work goals questions were used in a number of studies with student populations, referring to their ideal job after graduation. Hofstede, Kolman, Nicolescu, and Pajumaa (1996) analyzed the scores for 10 student samples, 4 from Eastern European countries not in the IBM set (Estonia, Russia, Czechia, and Romania), the others from Belgium (two language groups), West Germany, the Netherlands (surveyed either in English or in Dutch), and the United States. In spite of the fact that these were poorly matched convenience samples, a factor analysis of the country/sample means produced again an individual/collective and an ego/social factor. However, the association of some items with these factors differed between the students and the IBM population. From the items loading on the individual/collective factor, "physical conditions," which stood for collectivism in the IBM samples, was found at the individualist pole in the student samples. This led to the paradoxical result that when IDV scores for the students were computed according to the formulas in the Values Survey Module 1982, in which "physical conditions" were heavily weighted, the students' IDV scores across five overlapping country/language groups correlated strongly *negatively* with the IBM scores ($r = -.98^{**}$!). The experience with the student samples contributed to the revision of the VSM 82 into a VSM 94, in an attempt to make the formulas robust across a wider range of respondents.

Other replications. Shane and Venkataraman (1996, p. 761) included the VSM-IDV questions in a survey of more than 6,000 employees of six organizations in 28 countries in 1991-92. They reported a correlation with the IBM scores of $r = .63^{***}$, quite strong in view of the imperfect matching of their respondent samples.[22] I have mentioned Søndergaard's (1994) review of 61 smaller replications in Chapters 3 and 4. Of 19 replications allowing comparison of country score ranks with IBM, 18 confirmed the IDV differences. This dimension seems to be exceptionally robust, probably because it relates so closely to GNP/capita, which in the not-too-long run is also a robust measure.

IDV Versus Schwartz's Values Surveys of Teachers and Students

In Chapters 1 and 4, I have referred to the massive study of values by the Israeli psychologist Shalom Schwartz (1992, 1994). Respondents were elementary school teachers and university students. The questionnaire consisted of 56 items; by 1994, data had been collected for 44 countries, or subcultures in countries, from more than 25,000 respondents. Analyzing his data at the culture level for 38 national or subnational cultures, Schwartz (1994, p. 102) clustered his 56 values into seven categories: conservatism, hierarchy, mastery, affective autonomy, intellectual autonomy, egalitarian commitment. and harmony. He published the mean importance scores for these categories in 38 teacher samples. These scores for the 23 countries overlapping with the IBM set and their correlations with the IBM indexes are listed in Exhibit 5.17 in the statistical section of this chapter.

Schwartz's categories were based on a multivariate statistical technique, smallest-space analysis, which produced a two-dimensional map on which his 56 values were located. The seven categories represent sectors of a circle. On this circle, conservatism is adjacent to hierarchy, hierarchy is adjacent to mastery, and so on, leading to harmony again adjacent to conservatism. We find conservatism and hierarchy to be significantly negatively correlated with IDV; mastery correlated positively with MAS; affective autonomy, intellectual autonomy, and egalitarian commitment correlated positively with IDV; and harmony correlated positively with UAI. Schwartz (1994, p. 109) himself has also published correlations with the IBM indexes, not only for the teacher samples but also for the student samples. These show basically the same pattern, except that they also indicate significant correlations with PDI for conservatism and affective autonomy (teachers) and for conservatism, affective autonomy, intellectual autonomy, and egalitarian commitment (students)—always with the opposite sign from IDV.

The Schwartz value categories positively correlated with IDV comprise the following values (remember that the work goals in IBM at the positive pole of IDV were personal time, freedom, and challenge):

- *Affective autonomy* (teachers $r = .45*$, students $r = .85***$):[23] enjoying life, pleasure, exciting life, varied life
- *Intellectual autonomy* (teachers $r = .53**$, students $r = .48*$): broad-minded, curious, creativity
- *Egalitarian commitment* (teachers $r = .49**$, students $r = .45*$): loyal, equality, accepting my portion, freedom, responsible, honest, social justice, world at peace, helpful

Schwartz's list of correlated values suggests that the IBM items are really exponents of a broader syndrome of optimistic, responsible enjoyment.

Within the Schwartz categories negatively correlated with IDV, he put the following:

- *Conservatism* (teachers $r = -.55**$, students $r = -.66***$): forgiving, wisdom, respect tradition, family security, clean, politeness, obedient, moderate, honoring elders, social order, preserving public image, national security, self-discipline, devout, reciprocation of favors
- *Hierarchy* (teachers $r = -.53**$, students $r = -.22$): humble, authority, health, social power, influential

The items at the negative pole of IDV in IBM were training, physical conditions, and use of skills. In the replication of the IBM questions with students, we have seen that "physical conditions" to them had a different connotation—on the Schwartz map we would rather put it with affective autonomy. Training and use of skills fit the conservatism and hierarchy categories better; both seem to be exponents of a broader syndrome of fulfilling one's duty within the existing social order. It is interesting that Schwartz's "hierarchy" was associated with collectivism for teachers (who work in a hierarchical relationship between their superiors and their pupils) but not for students (who do not work in a hierarchy yet).

Schwartz (1994) refers to the seven clusters of values as "dimensions." I use the word *categories*—dimensions to me should be statistically independent. For the IBM indexes this is the case, except that IDV and PDI were negatively correlated; but as we have seen above, this correlation all but disappeared when wealth was controlled for (GNP/capita). The data in Exhibit 5.17 show Schwartz's categories of conservatism and hierarchy (negatively) and affective autonomy, intellectual autonomy, and egalitarian commitment (positively) all to be strongly intercorrelated ($r = .31$ to $.85$; 9 out of 10 significant). But if we control for 1990 GNP/capita, the categories split into two groups: conservatism versus autonomy (affective plus intellectual) and hierarchy versus egalitarian commitment.[24] Conceptually, the first is closer to the reverse of IDV and the second to PDI, but the correlation data are ambiguous in this respect.

Only two of Schwartz's seven categories did not correlate with IDV: harmony, which correlated with UAI (see Chapter 4), and mastery, which correlated with MAS and to which we will come back in Chapter 6.

IDV Versus Smith and Dugan's
Analysis of Trompenaars's Data

Smith, Trompenaars, and Dugan (1995; see also Smith, Dugan, & Trompenaars, 1996) analyzed a database collected by Trompenaars between 1982 and 1993. As part of his Ph.D.

research, Trompenaars had composed a 79-item questionnaire from items addressing seven hypothesized dimensions of cultural valuing. The first five were derived directly from Parsons and Shils's (1951) "general theory of action" (see Chapter 1): Trompenaars labeled them universalism-particularism, individualism-collectivism (corresponding to Parsons's "self-orientation versus collectivity orientation"), affectivity-neutrality, specificity-diffuseness, and achievement-ascription. The remaining two, time orientation and relation to nature, were inspired by Kluckhohn and Strodtbeck (1961; see Chapter 1). The items intended to measure these dimensions were borrowed from a variety of sources in the U.S. social science literature of the 1950s and 1960s.

In his Ph.D. dissertation, Trompenaars (1985) reported on the answers on his questionnaire from 653 respondents, divided over nine countries, two industries (oil and hosiery), and seven job categories (from unskilled labor to managers of managers). He concluded that the nine countries studied could be divided into two types, "left brain" (United States, Netherlands, Sweden, Austria, and Greece) and "right brain" (Venezuela, Spain, Italy, and Singapore).[25] Country scores on all subscales were correlated with this distinction, so that left-brain cultures were at the same time universalist, individualist, neutral, specific, attributing status by achievement, future oriented, and dominating nature; right-brain cultures were the opposite. In fact, therefore, Trompenaars found evidence for one bipolar dimension of culture, not seven.

In subsequent years Trompenaars continued to administer the same questionnaire, or a revised version, to much larger groups of respondents, either participants in management training courses or employees of companies. In his 1993 book, he showed country scores for 39 countries on 17 questionnaire items; in a review article, I did some statistical analyses on these data and showed that they did not support Trompenaars's hypothesized dimensions (Hofstede, 1996d).[26] At that time, I had not yet seen the two articles by Smith et al. (1995, 1996) that were based on the full Trompenaars database (almost 9,000 respondents from 43 countries) and that largely agreed with my analysis.[27]

Smith et al. (1995) looked at the answers to the "Relation to Nature" subscale. These were measured with the 23-item Rotter Locus of Control Scale, originally developed in 1966 for comparing individuals within the United States. The Rotter scale measures the extent to which success and failure are attributed to internal or external causes. The multivariate technique Smith et al. used for analyzing the matrix of scores for the 43 countries on the 23 items was multidimensional scaling (MDS). They identified three cross-national dimensions in the matrix. One of these was labeled *individual-social;* across 35 overlapping countries, Smith et al. found it to correlate with my IDV with $r = .70***$ and with PDI with $r = -.47**$. The individual pole stressed the making of plans and having them work out well as reasons for success; the social pole stressed the role of personal relationships in success and failure. Another MDS dimension dealt with the role of personal effort versus political conditions. The "political" pole was represented by seven Eastern European countries (Bulgaria, Czechoslovakia, East Germany, Hungary, Romania, Russia, Yugoslavia) that, except for Yugoslavia, were not in the IBM set; not surprisingly, its correlations with the IBM indexes did not reach statistical significance ($r = -.28$ with PDI, $r = .23$ with IDV).[28] A third, weaker MDS dimension dealt with the role of luck, which was rated especially important in Japan, Korea, Pakistan, and Thailand; it correlated negatively with Christianity but not with any of the IBM or Schwartz indexes.

Smith et al. (1996) dealt with the remaining subscales. The researchers considered relevant for analysis 39 other questions in the questionnaire derived from a number of sources and in a variety of formats. The matrix of scores for the 43 countries on the 39 items was again subjected to multidimensional scaling. Smith et al. identified three cross-national dimensions in the matrix:

1. A large dimension (21 questions) combining achievement-ascription (5 out of the 6 questions), universalism-particularism (5 out of the 8 questions), and 11 other items from various parts of the questionnaire.

2. Another dimension made up of 11 items, most of which Trompenaars (1985) used to measure his concept of collectivism versus individualism. They contrasted involvement in a group or organization on the basis of loyalty with involvement out of utilitarian considerations.

3. A weak third dimension composing only two items.

Smith et al. (1996, p. 257) found a strong association, across 33 countries, between my IDV scores and both of their first two MDS dimensions, $r = .70***$ with the first and $r = -.74***$ with the second. PDI related to the same two dimensions but somewhat less and, of course, with the reverse sign.[29] If the communist and former communist nations that were not in the IBM set were deleted from the MDS analysis, the correlations for the first dimension increased to $r = .80***$ with IDV and $r = -.68***$ with PDI. Correlations with either UAI or MAS were insignificant, but there were signs of a relationship of the third dimension with LTO, which will be discussed in Chapter 7.

When discussing the Schwartz research above, I suggested that his distinctions referred to *categories,* not *dimensions.* As I argued, dimensions should be statistically independent. Trompenaars's seven distinctions also represented categories, not dimensions; as the Smith et al. studies have shown, Trompenaars's extensive questionnaire measured only various intercorrelated flavors of individualism. In my own work I had drawn the same conclusion by doing a factor analysis of the 17 questions for which Trompenaars (1993) had published country scores (see Hofstede, 1996d). I interpreted the intercorrelation among Trompenaars's categories as indicating a lack of content validity. Content validity is the extent to which an instrument covers the universe of relevant aspects of the phenomenon studied, in our case national culture. Trompenaars did not start his research with an open-ended inventory of issues that were on the minds of his future respondents around the world; he took his concepts, as well as most of his questions, from the American literature of the middle of the 20th century, a time when the discussion about individualism and threats to it was at its fiercest (see the references to the discussion between Whyte and Sayles earlier in this chapter).

The fact that both Schwartz and Smith et al. found *two* factors, both significantly correlated with IDV—but not separating IDV from PDI—indicates that the dimension can be subdivided. On the other hand, this is true for *any* dimension if one increases the number of items measuring it. I have argued that Trompenaars used an excessive number of individualism items and overlooked other aspects of culture; this criticism applies less to Schwartz, but the sources of his value items may still have favored ind/col-related value areas over others. The outcome of a multivariate analysis depends on what one puts into it. At the present time, the nuances separating the flavors of individualism do not seem to me to be clear and fundamental enough to split the dimension.

IDV Versus Inglehart's
Analysis of the World Values Survey

In the preceding chapters I have referred extensively to the 1981-82 European Values Survey and its replication, the 1990-93 World Values Survey. The replication (Inglehart, 1997; Inglehart, Basañez, & Moreno, 1998) covered 43 countries around the world, of which 26 overlap with the IBM set. In a macroanalysis of country scores from all parts of the WVS, Inglehart found two "key cultural dimensions," which he labeled "well-being versus survival" and "secular-rational versus traditional authority." Exhibit 5.18 in the statistical section correlates country scores on these dimensions with the four IBM indexes, and

separately with GNP/capita. Both of Inglehart's dimensions were strongly correlated with GNP/capita, but "well-being versus survival" was almost as strongly correlated with high IDV. In a stepwise multiple regression, well-being was particularly associated with the combination of strong IDV and weak MAS ($R^2 = .74, R = .86***$). The second dimension related (negatively) only to PDI; this has been discussed in Chapter 3.

To Inglehart, a shift from survival to well-being is the essence of "postmodernization." A variable at the extreme "well-being" pole of the dimension was "postmaterialist values." Postmaterialists would give high priority to the following (Inglehart, 1997, p. 355):

a. Seeing that people have more to say about how things are done at their jobs and in their communities

b. Giving people more say in important government decisions

c. Protecting freedom of speech

d. Progress toward a less impersonal and more humane society

e. Progress toward a society in which ideas count more than money

Postmaterialists would give lower priority to the following:

f. Maintaining a high level of economic growth

g. Maintaining order in the nation

h. Fighting rising prices

i. A stable economy

j. The fight against crime

In terms of my dimensions, this list contains power distance-related items (–a), uncertainty avoidance-related items (–b, +g, +i, +j), individualism-related items (+c), and masculinity-related items (–d, –e, +f, +h). In fact, in Exhibit 5.18 Inglehart's well-being dimension does show significant zero-order correlations with all these four dimensions.

In Chapter 4, Exhibit 4.12 shows correlations of IBM indexes with items in the World Values Survey related to subjective well-being, trust and tolerance, nationalism, and confidence in institutions. Although usually UAI was the strongest correlate, IDV emerged in four cases, *but only if we included the poorer countries.* The four items associated with IDV were life satisfaction, job satisfaction, home life satisfaction, and the feeling that a child does *not* necessarily need a father and a mother.[30] These poor countries represent strongly collectivist (low-IDV) values, which is why adding them made IDV the strongest correlate.[31]

IDV Scores and
Other Studies of General Values

Samples of managers in 14 countries provided scores on Haire, Ghiselli, and Porter's (1966) "managerial motivations and satisfactions" questions. Another part of the same survey has been discussed in Chapters 3 and 4. Like the rest of the survey, the "managerial motivations and satisfactions" can be criticized for a reverse ecological fallacy (see Chapter 1) and for ethnocentrism. Haire et al. combined the country scores on 11 "need importance" items (work goals) into five categories based on Maslow's (1970) theory without statistical proof (through ecological correlations) that this combining was justified.[32] As it was, a direct comparison was possible only between the *acquiescence* levels in the Haire et al. and IBM scores.[33] The correlation of the acquiescence levels in both studies was $r = -.71**$. The Haire et al. acquiescence level also correlated with IDV ($r = -.75**$), more than with 1970 GNP/capita ($r = -.74**$). We see again that the acquiescence phenomenon is stable across different populations and questionnaire items, and that it is an indirect measure of (low) individualism.[34]

Morris (1956) designed a questionnaire about "ways to live" that was administered between 1945 and 1952 to samples of students from six countries: Canada, Hong Kong, India, Japan, Norway, and the United States. Morris's 13 "ways" are terminal values, fundamental attitudes toward life, each of which is described in a fairly lengthy paragraph. The respondents were required to score on a 7-point scale how much they would like or dislike living according to each of the 13 ways. In an ecological reanalysis of Morris's published data, I found two main dimensions that I labeled "enjoyment versus duty" and "engagement versus withdrawal" (for details, see Hofstede, 1980a, fig. 5.18).[35] The first factor was significantly ($r = .73*$) correlated with IDV, more than with 1970 GNP/capita ($r = .70$). In more individualist countries, students preferred the "enjoyment" ways to live: "Experience festivity and solitude in alteration"; "Integrate action, enjoyment and contemplation"; "Live with wholesome, carefree enjoyment"; and "Chance adventuresome deeds." In less individualist countries, students tended toward the "duty" side: "Cultivate independence of persons and things"; "Show sympathetic concern for others"; "Constantly master changing situations"; and "Control the self stoically." The second dimension did not correlate with any of the indexes.

In the 1960s, U.S. professor Bernard M. Bass created a network organization called IRGOM (International Research Group on Management), which distributed a number of classroom exercises meant to serve simultaneously as cross-cultural research tools. One exercise was called "Life Goals" (Bass & Burger, 1979); it asked respondents to rank 11 goals in order of importance: self-realization, leadership, expertness, wealth, independence, prestige, affection, service, duty, security, and pleasure. So these goals covered a broader area than the work goals in IBM. Using scores from 3,082 managers in 12 countries or country groups, I performed an ecological factor analysis (see the statistical section and Exhibit 5.19). There were two factors, of which one (which I labeled "hedonism-skill") was strongly correlated with IDV (rho = .76**); the other ("assertiveness-service") was strongly correlated with the Masculinity Index (rho = .84***). This means that the two main factors found in the IRGOM Life Goals were virtually identical to the two main factors found in IBM work goals. This occurred in spite of the differences in samples (managers from a variety of organizations versus employees of one company), the different data collection periods (the IRGOM data were collected between 1968 and 1976), the different data collection setting (training versus employee survey), the different questions used, and the different methods of scoring (ranking versus rating). The convergence between the factors in the two studies means that individualism (personal time, freedom, challenge) was also associated with hedonism (pleasure, security, affection); collectivism (training, physical conditions, use of skills) was also associated with skill (expertness, prestige, duty). The assertiveness-service factor will be discussed in Chapter 6.

A creative approach to collecting nonverbal value data has been described by Rorer and Ziller (1982). They gave disposable cameras to 40 U.S. students in Florida and 36 Polish students in Warsaw (both groups 50% female) and asked each student to make three photos of "the good life from your point of view" during a weekend. The photos were developed by the experimenters and coded by two independent raters. The Americans shot significantly more "privatistic" and hedonistic themes, such as stereos, single persons of the opposite gender, and male-female couples. The Poles shot more "institutional" themes, such as children, schools, homes, and religious themes. There are no IBM data for Poland, but the level of individualism in Polish culture at that time was certainly much lower than in the United States (see also Appendix 5, Table A5.3). The difference in the themes chosen reflects the contrast between individualist and moderately collectivist life goals.

Chiasson, Dubé, and Blondin (1996) reported on a study of "what can make a person happy" across students in Canada (English speakers and French speakers, separately), El Salvador, and the United States; sample sizes were about 50 per country, with more female than male respondents. Students were randomly given one of three open questions: (1) "What makes you happy?" (2) "What does a person need to be happy?" (3) "What is a happy person?" The researchers content analyzed the results and found family relationships, having meaning in life, and a positive self-concept mentioned as the most important facets of happiness across all four groups. The three North American, individualist, groups mentioned more intrapersonal, hedonistic factors; the Salvadoran, collectivist (IDV 19), group emphasized more *inter*personal factors. The Salvadorans also were the only ones to mention religion; in addition, the Salvadoran men mentioned good sociopolitical conditions (no miracle in a country involved in civil war) and the women mentioned family. The three North American groups hardly showed any gender differences. They much more frequently referred to *friendship* than did the Salvadorans. In a collectivist country with strong traditional social ties (such as with extended family), people have less need to make specific friendships. One's friends are predetermined by the social relationships into which one is born. In individualist societies, affective relationships are not socially predetermined; they must be acquired by each individual personally. Thus making friendships becomes more of an issue.

The same conclusion could be drawn from McClelland's (1961) scores for "need for affiliation" (n_{Aff}) based on a content analysis of 1925 children's readers, which are shown in Exhibit 4.13 to be significantly correlated with IDV (rho = .48** across 23 countries).[36] McClelland defined affiliation as "establishing, maintaining, or restoring a positive affective relationship with another person. This relationship is most adequately described by the word friendship" (p. 160).

Summary of Value
Connotations of the Individualism
Index Found in Surveys and Related Material

Exhibit 5.3 summarizes the value connotations of low and high IDV found so far (compare Exhibit 3.6 for PDI and Exhibit 4.4 for UAI). Readers should recall the warnings given in Chapter 3 in reviewing this exhibit: Countries may be anywhere in between the two extremes pictured, not all connotations apply in all countries, and individuals within countries can deviate from societal norms. The data on which Exhibit 5.3 is based are derived from a very broad range of studies, including narrow-sample surveys (students, employees, teachers), broad public opinion surveys, and nonsurvey country comparisons.

Origins and Implications
of Country Individualism Differences

The Individualism Societal Norm

Exhibit 5.4 presents an integrated picture of the general societal norm behind the low-IDV and high-IDV syndromes. It shows the main conceptual differences between the two poles of the dimension, supported by the findings summarized in Exhibit 5.3. The individualism norm should also be seen as a value system shared especially by the majority in the middle classes in a society, according to the diagram in Exhibit 1.5. Its implications for various domains of life will be elaborated in the following subsections.

One-line definitions of Individualism and Collectivism as the two poles of a dimension of national culture are: **"Individualism stands for a society in which the ties between individuals are loose: Everyone is expected to look after him/herself and her/his immediate family only. Collectivism stands for a society in which people from birth onwards are integrated into strong, cohesive in-groups, which throughout people's lifetime continue to protect them in exchange for unquestioning loyalty."**

The psychological and management literature of the late 1980s and especially the 1990s contains many two-country comparative studies which attribute differences found to individualism versus collectivism although the cultures studied often also differed on other dimensions like masculinity versus femininity. The following sections rarely cite such studies but mostly use studies across at least three cultures which allow separating the effect of individualism from other dimensions.

Individualism and
Collectivism in the Family

The first group in our lives is always the family into which we are born. Culture learning starts in the family; families are minimodels of society to which children learn to adapt. The society is thus a product of its families, but families are also the products of their society (see Exhibit 1.5). Most people grow up in collectivist societies, among a number of people living closely together, not just their parents and other children, but members of an extended family—grandparents, uncles, aunts, and cousins, and sometimes also neighbors, housemates, co-villagers, and lords or servants. In this situation children learn to think of themselves as part of a "we"-group or in-group, a relationship that is not voluntary but predetermined by birth.

As Baker (1979) has put it in referring to traditional China, "It was not the family which existed

Exhibit 5.3   Summary of Value Connotations of IDV Differences Found in Surveys and Other Comparative Studies

Low IDV	High IDV
Importance of provisions by company, such as physical conditions.	Importance of employees' personal lives (time).
More importance attached to training and use of skills in jobs.	More importance attached to freedom and challenge in jobs.
More acquiescence in response to "importance" questions.	More differentiation in response to "importance" questions.
Qualification for jobs in terms of years of schooling.	Qualification for jobs in terms of performance at previous tasks.
Staying with one company desirable, old-timers make better managers.	Staying with company undesirable, old-timer managers not better.
Large, foreign, successful, modern company attractive.	Smaller, local company attractive.
Company responsible for employees.	Employees responsible for themselves.
Moral involvement with company.	Calculative involvement.
Interesting work as important as earnings.	Earnings more important than interesting work.
Knowing the right people most important for career.	Ability most important for career.
Group decisions are better.	Individual decisions are better.
Collectivism among non-IBM managers and elites.	Individualism among non-IBM managers and elites.
Collectivism among airline pilots and consumers.	Individualism among airline pilots and consumers.
Collectivism among employees of other multinational companies.	Individualism among employees of other multinational companies.
In Schwartz's values surveys among teachers and students, conservatism; among teachers also hierarchy.	In Schwartz's values surveys: affective autonomy, intellectual autonomy, and egalitarian commitment.
In Trompenaars's data from company personnel: personal relationships, ascription, particularism, and collectivism.	In Trompenaars's data: planning, achievement, universalism, and individualism.
In Inglehart's WVS analysis: survival values (materialist).	In Inglehart's analysis: well-being values (postmaterialist).
Duty in life appealed to students.	Enjoyment in life appealed to students.
Managers chose duty, expertness, and prestige as life goals.	Managers chose pleasure, affection, and security as life goals.
Interpersonal relations important for students' happiness.	Intrapersonal hedonism important for students' happiness.
Friendships predetermined by social network.	Importance of making specific friendships.

in order to support the individual, but rather the individual who existed in order to continue the family" (p. 26). Members of the we-group are distinct from other people in society who belong to they-groups or out-groups, and there are many such people and such out-groups. The in-group is the major source of one's identity, and the only secure protection one has against the hardships of life. Therefore one owes lifelong loyalty to one's in-group, and breaking this loyalty is one of the worst things a person can do. Between the person and the in-group a dependence relationship develops that is both practical and psychological.

A minority of people live in individualist societies, in which the interests of the individual pre-

Exhibit 5.4   The Individualism Societal Norm

Low IDV	High IDV
In society, people are born into extended families or clans, which protect them in exchange for loyalty.	In society, everyone is supposed to take care of him- or herself and his or her immediate family only.
"We" consciousness.	"I" consciousness.
Gemeinschaft (community).[a]	Gesellschaft (society).[a]
Collectivity orientation.[b]	Self-orientation.[b]
Value standards differ for in-groups and out-groups: particularism.[b]	Value standards should apply to all: universalism.[b]
Identity is based in the social system.	Identity is based in the individual.
"Shame" cultures.[c]	"Guilt" cultures.[c]
High-context communication.[d]	Low-context communication.[d]
Emotional dependence of individual on institutions and organizations.	Emotional independence of individual from institutions or organizations.
Emphasis on belonging: membership ideal.	Emphasis on individual initiative and achievement: leadership ideal.
Private life is invaded by institutions and organizations to which one belongs.	Everyone has a right to a private life.
Survival.	Hedonism.
Activities imposed by context.	Self-started activities.
Expertise, order, duty, security provided by organization or clan.	Autonomy, variety, pleasure, individual financial security.
Traditional society.	"Modern" or "postmodern" society.[e]

a. Tönnies (1887/1963).
b. Parsons and Shils (1951).
c. Benedict (1946/1974).
d. Hall (1976).
e. Inglehart (1997).

vail over the interests of the group. Whereas in the collectivist society the family is the smallest unit, in the individualist society the individual is the smallest unit. Most children in such societies are born into nuclear families—that is, families consisting of just their parents and, possibly, other children.[37] Other relatives usually live elsewhere and are rarely seen. An increasing share of children grow up in one-parent families. Lester (1995) has shown that divorce rates in 1980, across 26 countries, correlated strongly with IDV ($r = .76***$; after GNP/capita was controlled for, the correlation was still significant, $pr_{GNP} = .40*$). Marriages in individualist societies tend to be less stable.

Children in this situation, as they grow up, learn to think of themselves as "I." This I, an individual's personal identity, is distinct from other people's I's, and these others are classified not according to their group membership but according to individual characteristics. Playmates are cho-

sen mostly on the basis of personal preferences. The purpose of education is to enable the child to stand on his or her own two feet. The child is expected to leave the parental home as soon as he or she has achieved this ability. Neither practically nor psychologically is the healthy person in this type of society supposed to be dependent on a group.

In between the extended family and the nuclear family structures is the "stem" or lineal family structure found in traditional Japan. The stem family consisted of all those who commonly resided together and shared social and economic life, both relatives and nonrelatives (Befu, 1971, p. 38). Usually only one of the sons of the stem family head stayed with the stem group after marriage and maintained the family line; if there was no son, a son-in-law took this role, or a son was adopted for the purpose. The stem family made no sharp distinction between kin and nonkin. The tradition of the stem family as a functional economic unit helps to explain why Japanese can transfer their family loyalty relatively easily to other groups, such as the companies they work for. Exhibit 3.1 shows that Japan scored halfway on the Individualism Index (rank 22/23 out of 53, IDV 46).

Collectivist societies usually have ways of creating familylike ties with persons who are not biological relatives but who are socially integrated into one's in-group. In Latin America, for example, this can be done via the institution of *compadres* and *comadres,* who are treated as relatives even if they are not. In Japan, younger sons in past times became apprentices to crafts masters through a form of adoption. Similar customs existed in medieval central Europe.

People in collectivist societies are integrated not only horizontally but also vertically. They stay in close contact with their parents, grandparents, and other elders as long as these are alive, and they can expect their own offspring and other juniors to maintain close contact with them. But vertical integration extends beyond the grave; the collectivist family honors the memories of deceased ancestors and cares for their graves. Members are often able to recite their genealogy over many generations from memory. In the Chinese tradition this vertical integration is called *filial piety,* but comparable traditions exist among other peoples. Behind the honoring of elders and ancestors is a static or circular concept of time, in which things of the past retain full relevance for the present and the present exists for the future. "Descent is a unity, a rope which began somewhere back in the remote past and which stretches to the infinite future. . . . That is, the individual alive is the personification of all his forbears and of all his descendants yet unknown" (Baker, 1979, pp. 26-27).

People in individualist societies lack not only horizontal but also vertical integration. Adolescent children leave the homes of their parents and do not necessarily maintain much contact after that. Grandparents live apart and are supposed to lead lives of their own, the "third age." If they become infirm, they move, or are moved, to homes for the aged, where they are taken care of by special personnel, not by their children or grandchildren. The memories of deceased ancestors quickly fade away; their names fall into oblivion unless registered by hobby genealogists. Their experience is not considered relevant for "modern" life. Among the findings of De Mooij (2001), who correlated the IBM indexes with data from consumer surveys across 16 European countries by market research agencies (see Chapters 3 and 4), is an attitude question in Eurodata 91, in which respondents from high-IDV countries tended to *disagree* with the statement "A marriage without children is not complete" (rho = $-.72***$).

Hastings and Hastings (1980), in their *Index to International Public Opinion 1979-1980,* reported on a five-nation survey of the values of 10- to 15-year-old children (about 1,500 per country) and of their mothers. Among other things, the mothers were asked, "In your old age, what sort of relationship would you like to have with your children?" The answer "To live together and have my daily needs looked after" was endorsed by 2% of mothers in France and Great Britain, 21% in Japan, 34% in South Korea, and 73% in Thailand. These percentages were, of course, strongly (negatively) correlated with IDV, $r = -.84*$.[38]

In 1996, the *Far Eastern Economic Review* published data from a survey among businesspersons in 9 Southeast Asian countries plus Australia about living with parents.[39] Proportions of the respondents currently living with their parents varied from 6% in Australia to 47% in Thailand, and across the 10 countries these percentages were significantly negatively correlated with IDV ($r = -.67*$), not with national wealth. On a question concerning whether their parents would eventually live with them in the future, the proportions of respondents answering yes varied from 13% in Australia and Hong Kong to 57% in Thailand. This time the highest correlation, and the only one surviving in a multiple regression, was with 1990 GNP/capita ($r = -.78**$). This is an interesting finding: It suggests that the current situation of family cohabitation in Southeast Asia was still culture driven, but that these businesspersons' ambitions for the future were shaped primarily by their countries' level of material wealth; it supports the assumption that an increase in wealth leads to an increase in individualism.

The child in a collectivist society is seldom alone, either during the day or at night. An African student who came to Belgium for a university study told us that this was the first time in her life she had ever been alone in a room for any sizable length of time. In an individualist society, such a lack of "privacy" would be highly abnormal. In a situation of intense and continuous social contact, the maintenance of *harmony* with one's social environment becomes a key virtue that extends to other spheres beyond the family. In most collectivist cultures, direct confrontation of another person is considered rude and undesirable. The word *no* is seldom used because saying no *is* a confrontation; "You may be right" and "We will think about it" are examples of polite ways of turning down a request. In the same vein, the word *yes* should not necessarily be seen as approval; rather, it may be used to maintain the communication line: *Hai* in Japanese stands not for yes but for "Yes, I heard you."

In individualist cultures, on the other hand, speaking one's mind is a virtue. Telling the truth about how one feels is seen as a characteristic of a sincere and honest person. Confrontation can be salutary; a clash of opinions is believed to lead to a higher truth. One should take into account the effects of one's communications on other people, but this does not, as a rule, justify changing the facts. Adult individuals are expected to have learned to take direct feedback constructively. In the family, children are told that one should always tell the truth, even if it hurts. Coping with conflict is a normal part of living together as a family.[40]

In the collectivist family, children learn to take their bearings from others when it comes to opinions. Personal opinions do not exist—they are predetermined by the group. If a new issue comes up on which there is no established group opinion, some kind of in-group conference is necessary before an opinion can be given. A child who repeatedly voices opinions that deviate from what is collectively felt is considered to have a bad character. In the individualist family, in contrast, children are expected and encouraged to develop opinions of their own, and a child who always only reflects the opinions of others is considered to have a *weak* character. The behavior corresponding with a desirable character depends on the cultural environment.

The loyalty to the group that is an essential element of the collectivist family also means that resources are shared. If a member of an extended family of 20 persons has a paid job and the others have not, the earning member is supposed to share his or her income in order to help feed the entire family. On the basis of this principle, a family may collectively cover the expenses of sending a single member to get a higher education, expecting that when this member subsequently gets a well-paid job, the income will also be shared. In individualist cultures, parents are proud if their children at an early age take small jobs in order to earn pocket money of their own, which the children spend according to their own decisions. Students who do not have wealthy parents or do not get scholarships have to earn their own education money.

Obligations to the family in a collectivist society are not only financial but also ritual. Family celebrations such as baptisms, marriages, and, especially, funerals are extremely important and should not be missed. Expatriate managers from individualist societies are often surprised by the family reasons that employees from a collectivist host society give when applying for special leave; the expatriates often think they are being fooled, but most likely these reasons are authentic.

In an individualist culture, when people meet they feel a need to communicate verbally. Silence is considered abnormal. Social conversations can be depressingly banal, but they are compulsory. In a collectivist culture, the fact of being together

can be emotionally sufficient; there is no compulsion to talk unless there are emotions or information to be transferred. Elsewhere, I have described a family visit in a Javanese noble family, as remembered by an Indonesian businessman (Hofstede, 1991, p. 60). Relatives would show up unannounced and would be welcomed warmly, after which the family members would sit silently together, enjoying each other's presence.

Earlier in this chapter I referred to two studies that showed *friendship* to be more of an issue in the individualist society than in the collectivist society. In a collectivist culture, who one's friends are is predetermined by existing group ties; in an individualist society, friendships have to be specifically cultivated.

Both individualist and collectivist cultures have their costs in terms of family life. In *The Culture of Narcissism,* a best-selling criticism of U.S. society, Christopher Lasch (1980) has written, "Our society, far from fostering private life at the expense of public life, has made deep and lasting friendships, love affairs, and marriages increasingly difficult to achieve" (p. 30). Similar criticisms could be directed at other Western or Eastern European societies where divorce rates approach or exceed 50%. On the other hand, family life in collectivist societies can be oppressive and stultifying, with no escape for those suffering abuse, especially girls. Turkish psychologist Çigdem Kagitçibasi (1996) has described an original action research approach, the Turkish Early Enrichment Project in the shantytowns of Istanbul, to help especially mothers to find a middle way between the horns of the individualism/collectivism dilemma. Between an independence family model (individualist) and an interdependence model (collectivist), she worked toward an emotional interdependence family model that allowed families in a collectivist society setting to cope with change through the development of children's cognitive and emotional capabilities.

Members of the collectivist family are partially kept in order by the threat of shame. Earlier in this chapter I referred to Benedict's (1946/1974) distinction between *shame* and *guilt* cultures. A child in an individualist society who infringes upon a rule learns to feel guilty, ridden by an individually developed conscience that functions as a private inner pilot. Collectivist societies, in contrast, are shame cultures: Not only the culprit him- or herself but also his or her in-group mates are made to feel ashamed when a misdeed has been committed. Shame is social in nature, whereas guilt is individual; whether a person feels shame or not depends on whether the infringement has become known by others. This becoming known is the source of the shame, more so than the infringement itself. Such is not the case with guilt, which a person feels whether or not his or her misdeed is known by others.

Another concept bred in the collectivist family is *face*. Losing face, in the sense of being humiliated, is an expression that penetrated into the English language from the Chinese; English had no equivalent for it. "Face is lost when the individual, either through his action or that of people closely related to him, fails to meet essential requirements placed upon him by virtue of the social position he occupies" (Ho, 1976, p. 867). The Chinese also speak of "giving someone face," in the sense of honor or prestige. Basically, face describes the proper relationship with one's social environment, which is as essential to a person (and that person's family) as the front part of his or her head. The importance of face is the consequence of living in a society that is very conscious of social contexts. The languages of other collectivist cultures have words with more or less similar meanings. In Greece, for example, there is the word *philotimo*:

> A person is *philotimos* to the extent in which he conforms to the norms and values of his in-group. These include a variety of sacrifices that are appropriate for members of one's family, friends, and others who are "concerned with one's welfare"; for example, for a man to delay marriage until his sisters have married and have been provided with a proper dowry is part of the normative expectations of traditional rural Greeks as well as rural Indians (and many of the people in between). (Triandis, 1972, p. 38)

In the individualist society the counterpart characteristic is *self-respect,* but this again is defined from the point of view of the individual, whereas face and *philotimo* are defined from the point of view of the social environment.

Because families are so important in collectivist societies, selection of marriage partners is a crucial event, not only for the partners but for both their families. Buss (1989; see also Buss et al., 1990) reported on a study of criteria for selecting a potential marriage partner as scored by samples of young women and men (average age 23), almost 10,000 respondents from 37 countries. Buss found some characteristics to be universally desired: mutual love, kindness, emotional stability, intelligence, and health. Some others varied strongly across countries. Preferences of bridegrooms referring to their brides across 28 overlapping countries showed strong correlations with IDV for age difference (rho = −.75***), wealth (rho = −.70***), industriousness (rho = −.70***), and chastity (rho = −.57**).[41] However, unlike the three other criteria, chastity in brides was even more strongly correlated, negatively (rho = −.72***), with (1987) GNP/capita. In collectivist countries, bridegrooms preferred age differences at marriage to be larger and put more stress on the bride's being wealthy, industrious, and chaste; the desire for chastity was stronger in poorer countries than in wealthier ones.

The preferences of *brides* referring to their *bridegrooms* that correlated significantly with IDV were age difference (rho = −.75***), wealth (rho = −.73***), and industriousness (rho = −.50**), but not chastity (rho = −.36; *ns*). However, desired chastity of the bridegroom still correlated negatively with GNP/capita (rho = −.53**). So brides in collectivist countries also wanted their husbands to be the right age and wealthy, but their industriousness played a smaller role and their chastity none at all.

The stress on industriousness, wealth, and chastity in collectivist societies can be explained by the fact that marriage in such a society is a contract between families rather than between individuals. These will be the aspects that families can observe. Marriages in collectivist societies are often arranged by marriage brokers, and brides and grooms may have little say in the choice of their partners; they may even be prevented from meeting or seeing each other. This does not mean that such marriages are less happy than other kinds of marriages. Research in India has shown more marital satisfaction in arranged than in love marriages, and more in Indian love marriages than in American marriages (Yelsma & Athappilly, 1988). Dion and Dion (1993) have concluded that although cultural individualism fosters the valuing of romantic love, certain aspects of individualism at the psychological level make developing intimacy problematic. Levine, Sato, Hashimoto, and Verma (1995) administered three questions about the role of love in marriage to female and male undergraduate students in 11 countries.[42] One question was, "If a man (woman) had all the other qualities you desired, would you marry this person if you were not in love with him (her)?" The answers varied from 4% yes and 86% no in the United States to 50% yes and 39% no in Pakistan. The ranking of the 11 countries according to the percentage of no answers minus the percentage of yes answers correlated with IDV with r = .64*, more than with 1990 GNP/capita (r = .57*). In collectivist societies, considerations other than love weigh heavily in marriage.[43]

The negative relationship between a stress on chastity of the partner and 1987 GNP/capita revealed another mechanism as well. GNP/capita and IDV were closely related (rho = .68***), but it was less increased individualism in a society that led young people to put less weight on chastity than it was increasing affluence. The mechanism, which has operated in all industrialized societies over the past one or two generations (Hofstede & Associates, 1998, p. 160), is probably as follows:

Increasing affluence provides women with more educational opportunities (in any society, when education becomes available, parents give priority to boys, who are not needed around the house). Girls start to move around more freely and so get more opportunities to meet boys. Increasing affluence also gives people more living space and more privacy. Medical care and information improve, including information on contraception. Young people get more opportunities for sexual exploration, and sexual norms adapt to this situation. The assumption that behavior follows values is often naive; more often, values and norms follow modal behavior. "What people want and what they do, in any society, is to a large extent what they are made to want, and allowed to do" (Caplan, 1987, p. 25).

In Chapter 6, I will come back to the Buss study to show that whereas all correlations of partner preferences in general were with IDV, *differences between men's and women's preferences* were correlated with the Masculinity Index.

The 1990-93 World Values Survey contained a block of 13 questions about the importance of "things which some people think make for a successful marriage" (questions 198-210). After standardization, 3 items were significantly correlated with IDV across the 26 overlapping countries: "living apart from in-laws" positively (rho = .36*) and "shared religious beliefs" (rho = −.37*) plus "an adequate income" (rho = −.35*) negatively.[44] In the collectivist society, living with in-laws is normal, and marriage partners are more dependent in religious and income matters.

Individualism and Collectivism
Versus Personality and Behavior

The differences in childhood socialization between individualist and collectivist societies lead to differences in modal personality characteristics and in behavior patterns. Chapter 3 referred to a study by Williams, Satterwhite, and Saiz (1998) of the importance of psychological traits using the 300-item Gough and Heilbrun Adjective Checklist. Respondents were both male and female students in 20 countries, 13 languages, between 60 and 147 students per country. Psychological importance was defined in the questionnaire as importance "in describing what a person is really like." The importance of each of the 300 adjectives was scored on a 5-point scale. One adjective was *individualistic,* and I was curious to see how important this term would be across the 18 overlapping countries.[45] In fact, the importance attached to *individualistic* in describing a person correlated with $r = .41*$ with the countries' IDV scores.[46]

Chapter 4 described a study by Gudykunst, Yang, and Nishida (1987) about "self-consciousness" among students; countries covered were South Korea (IDV 18), Japan (IDV 46), and the United States (IDV 91). Gudykunst and his colleagues divided self-consciousness into public self-consciousness, private self-consciousness, and social anxiety; the last was shown in Chapter 4 to be related to UAI. They hypothesized a relationship between public self-consciousness and the IBM individualism dimension. Public self-consciousness was measured by six questions; a typical item was "I'm concerned about what other people think of me." U.S. respondents scored highest (most self-conscious) on this subscale, but Japanese respondents did not score higher than South Koreans; in fact, the Japanese scored somewhat lower. Still, a relationship between cultural individualism and public self-consciousness (presenting oneself as an individual) makes conceptual sense. Private self-consciousness might be related to MAS; we will return to it in Chapter 6.

In the same study, Gudykunst, Yang, and Nishida measured the related concept of "self-monitoring," the degree to which a person takes his or her cues for behavior from the behavior of others. They divided self-monitoring into other-directedness, acting, and extraversion. An example of an other-directedness item was "Even if I am not enjoying myself, I often pretend to be having a good time." Acting was measured by items such as "I can make impromptu speeches even on topics about which I have almost no information." A typical extraversion item was "In a group of people I am rarely the center of attention" (reversed). U.S. respondents scored lowest and Koreans highest on other-directedness; Americans highest and Koreans lowest on acting; and U.S. respondents much higher than those in other countries on extraversion, although in this case Japan scored lowest. So in an individualist culture people take fewer behavioral cues from others, but they are more likely to take an acting role and on average they are more extraverted.

Gudykunst et al. (1992) reported on a manipulated survey among some 200 students in each of four countries: Australia and the United States (high IDV), and Hong Kong and Japan (lower IDV). Half of the respondents were asked to imagine a person from an in-group; the others were asked to imagine a person from an out-group. They were then asked to indicate to what extent they would do the following: talk with the person they imagined about themselves, ask about the other, expect shared attitudes and networks, and have confidence in the other. The differences between the in-group answers and the out-group answers were largest in Hong Kong and Japan and much lower in Australia and the United States— in this order, which is also the order of the countries' IDV scores.

Leung, Au, Fernández-Dols, and Iwawaki (1992) extended a study by Leung, Bond, Carment, Krishnan, and Liebrand (1990) about preferred ways of handling conflicts. Both studies produced data from some 500 college students from Canada, Japan, the Netherlands, and Spain, 50% female, who had been presented with a script about a conflict between two student neighbors in a dormitory and asked for their preferred ways of resolving it. The researchers presented the scores for the four countries for eight preferred "procedures." I correlated these with the IBM indexes and found the preferences for "threatening," "accusing," "falsely promising," and "ignoring" all significantly correlated with IDV (rho = .95* in all four cases). All of these are confrontational. The less individualist cultures demonstrated a need for formal harmony by avoiding confrontation. Three procedural alternatives—"negotiation," "mediation," and "arbitration"—were not correlated with any of the IBM indexes or with (1990) GNP/capita. The last alternative, "complying," however, was correlated with PDI (rho = 1.00**): There is more complying in large power distance cultures.

An important chapter in Western psychology is devoted to the study of conformity, following Asch's (1956) famous experiment. The subject is one member of a group of people who are asked to judge which of two lines is longer. Unknown to the subject, all the other group members are confederates of the experimenter, and they deliberately give false answers. A sizable proportion of subjects tend to conform with the group. R. Bond and Smith (1996) cross-analyzed 97 Asch-type studies in the United States and 36 studies in 16 other countries. Across 14 countries overlapping with the IBM set, they found a highly significant relationship with IDV, in the sense of greater conformity in collectivist cultures. They also found highly significant relationships with Schwartz's affective autonomy and Trompenaars's individualism-collectivism. Bond and Smith used the U.S. data for a longitudinal analysis, showing that conformity has declined since the 1950s. Below (in the subsection headed "The Future of Individualism Differences"), we will see that individualism can be assumed to have increased over this period, which provides an explanation for the decline in conformity.

Chapter 3 described how mean scores of IMEDE participants (managers) from 14 countries on L. V. Gordon's Surveys of Personal and Interpersonal Values were subjected to an ecological factor analysis. Three factors were found, of which one, "decisiveness versus practical-mindedness," was strongly correlated with PDI. Another factor, "conformity versus variety," correlated significantly negatively with IDV ($r = -.61$**): IMEDE managers from more individualist countries tended to stress leadership and variety, whereas those from less individualist countries tended to stress conformity and orderliness.

Chapter 4 described Scherer and Wallbott's (1994) ISEAR questionnaire study of self-reports of *emotions* in 37 countries. The researchers asked about seven emotions: joy, fear, anger, sadness, disgust, shame, and guilt. As explained in Chapter 4, I correlated their data for expressive nonverbal reactions with the IBM indexes across 14 overlapping countries. IDV was significantly correlated with the differences in reported nonverbal expression between women and men, for guilt ($r = .70$**), joy ($r = .63$**), shame ($r = .55$*), anger ($r = .53$*), and disgust ($r = .50$*). All correlations were in the sense that in individualist cultures, women expressed these emotions more strongly than did men; in collectivist cultures, women expressed them less strongly than did men. In collectivist societies, women live with, and are dependent on, relatives and in-laws, and men spend a larger share of their time outdoors; social harmony being a prime value in these cultures, women learn to (or at least claim to) suppress their emotions. In individualist cultures there is no need for such suppression.

Matsumoto (1989) published a meta-analysis of studies of the recognition of emotions in facial expressions. The research literature provided reliable accuracy scores for the recognition by students of happiness, surprise, sadness, fear, disgust, and anger, from photos of faces, for 15 countries from the IBM set.[47] For all 15 countries data were available on the percentages of observers correctly identifying each of the six emotions. Percentages of observers correctly perceiving happiness were correlated positively ($r = .51$*) and those perceiving sadness were correlated negatively ($r = -.50$*) with IDV. For seven countries, means and standard deviations of ratings of the intensity of the six emotions were also available. The intensities of the expressions of anger and fear were positively correlated with IDV ($r = .67$* and $r = .79$*), and the standard deviation of the recognition of fear was negatively correlated with IDV ($r = -.78$*). My interpretation of Matsumoto's results is that individualist cultures encourage the showing of happiness but discourage the showing of sadness; collectivist cultures do the opposite. Furthermore, individualist cultures tolerate the expression of individual anger more easily than do collectivist cultures. The same holds for the expression of fear, which is easily recognized in individualist cultures but which only some observers in collectivist cultures are able to identify.

Schimmack (1996) reanalyzed the studies used by Matsumoto and explained some of the relationships with IDV from the fact that all the photos shown had been of Caucasian faces, with which some of the respondents in collectivist countries were less familiar. Using the race (Caucasian/non-Caucasian) of the observers as a control variable, he still found that IDV predicted the accurate perception of happiness. He also found some correlations with UAI that Matsumoto had hypothesized but not confirmed. Schimmack's correlations with UAI have been discussed in Chapter 4.

Levine and Norenzayan (1999) have recently reported on a study of the pace of life in 31 countries around the world. Building on an earlier body of research in this area, they collected three types of data from the major cities (almost all with more than a million inhabitants) in these countries: walking speed, working speed, and clock accuracy. Walking speed was measured as the time it took 70 healthy adults (of both genders, 50/50) to cover a distance of 60 feet in one of two uncrowded locations in each city, when walking alone on a clear summer day during main business hours. The researchers measured working speed by timing at least eight postal clerks in each city as each complied with a request to sell a stamp and change a bill. Clock accuracy was measured for 15 clocks inside randomly selected bank offices in each city. The three measures were correlated across cities, and they were combined into an overall Pace of Life Index (via z scores for each measure). From the 31 countries, 23 overlapped with the IBM set.[48]

Reversing their index and its components, so that a higher score means a faster pace, and correlating it with the four IBM indexes plus 1990 GNP/capita, I found clock accuracy and the overall index to be primarily correlated with GNP/capita (more accurate clocks and a faster pace of life in more affluent countries, $r = .55**$ and $r = .70***$). Walking speed, however, was primarily correlated with IDV (faster walking in individualist cultures, $r = .62**$) and working speed with PDI (slower working in large PDI countries, $r = -.57**$). There were no significant secondary correlations for the three component measures.[49] So, in the context of the study of individualism, the conclusion is that people in individualist cultures tend to walk faster. I see this as a physical expression of their self-concept. People in more individualist cultures focus more on themselves, and they are more active in trying to get somewhere. The slower working in high-PDI countries has a different reason: Postal clerks in these cultures tend to put in less effort when working for clients who are not their superiors.

Earlier, Converse (1972) studied the self-recorded time use of citizens from 12 countries. He found that the major differences in overall time use among these countries could be clustered into two dimensions, North-South and East-West. Because Converse's study included six Eastern European countries not in the IBM set, I could compare it with IBM data only across six countries.[50] Across these, Converse's North-South dimension correlated with IDV (rho = 1.00**). People studied in the North countries (high IDV) spent more time watching TV, shopping, as members of voluntary organizations, in personal care, in religious activities, and reading papers. People studied in the South countries (lower IDV) spent more time resting, cooking, tending animals, gardening, being outdoors, sleeping, and eating. So people in high-IDV countries reported more self-started activities, which confirms their being guided by a more active self-concept as suggested by the outcome of the Levine and Norenzayan study.[51]

Individualism and Collectivism in Language Use and Group Identity

Kashima and Kashima (1998) have published an extremely interesting analysis of the relationship between culture and language. For each of 39 languages used in 71 different countries, they recorded three linguistic features: (1) pronoun drop—that is, the practice of omitting the first-person singular pronoun (*I*) from a sentence; (2) single or multiple second-person pronouns, such as *you* in English versus *tu* or *vous* in French; and (3) single or multiple first-person pronouns, such as *I* in English versus *watasi, boku, ore,* and others in Japanese. They measured culture using the IBM dimensions (except masculinity) and dimensions derived from Bond (see Chapter 7), Schwartz, and Smith et al.—a total of 15 variables.

As linguistic feature 1 could be partly dependent on features 2 and 3, Kashima and Kashima controlled for features 2 and 3 when computing the correlations with feature 1, pronoun drop. The zero-order correlations of pronoun drop with 14 out of the 15 dimension variables included were all significant, but the strongest zero-order correlation was with IDV ($r = -.75**$ across 60 countries, $r = -.64**$ across 30 languages). Controlling for IDV made all the other dimension variables disappear from the correlation picture; only UAI made an independent second-order contribution to pronoun drop (partial correlation $pr_{IDV} = .38*$). So the languages spoken in individualist cultures tend to require speakers to use the *I* pronoun when referring to themselves; languages spoken in collectivist cultures allow the dropping of this pronoun. It is also remarkable that the language spoken in the most individualist countries, English, is the only one I know of that writes *I* with a capital letter.[52] An Arab, collectivist, saying is, "The satanic term 'I' be damned!" (Habib, 1995, p. 102).

Single or multiple second- and first-person pronouns were not related to IDV, but multiple second-person pronouns were significantly related to UAI. Languages in more uncertainty-avoiding cultures tended to require that speakers choose between different modes of address. This may help to explain the positive second-order correlation of UAI with pronoun drop, which also requires choosing: To drop or not to drop? I referred to this conclusion in Chapter 4 when discussing language learning in the family in higher-UAI cultures: Children in such cultures face more choices according to tight cultural rules.

Chapter 4 also referred to Gudykunst's (1989) survey about the "ethnolinguistic identity" of 158 female and male foreign students at a U.S. university. Across 32 countries and regions, IDV was significantly correlated with two out of five subscales. One was "ethnolinguistic vitality," which I mentioned in Chapter 4 because it also correlated with UAI.[53] It consisted of the items "How highly regarded is your native language in the city in which you live in the U.S.?" (very low/very high) and "How highly regarded is your native language internationally?" (very low/very high). Students from high-IDV cultures saw their language as more highly regarded. The other was "multiple group memberships"; it consisted of the items "How important is being a male/female to you?" (unimportant/important) and "How important is being a member of your religion to you?" (unimportant/important). Students from low-IDV cultures (collectivist) rated their gender and religion as more important. Significant correlations from this study with masculinity will appear in Chapter 6.

Bochner (1994) tested individualism/collectivism differences in people's self-concepts by asking respondents to complete 10 statements beginning with "I am."[54] Respondents were 26 adults in Malaysia, 32 in Australia, and 20 in Britain. Two judges blindly divided the statements into three categories:

1. Statements that do not imply other people, such as "I am honest" or "I am happy." This is the "idiocentric" category.

2. Statements about group or category membership, such as "I am a daughter," "I am a plumber," or "I am a Catholic." This is the "group" category.

3. Statements implying relationships with other people, such as "I am considered a kind person" or "I am a person who wants to help others." This is the "allocentric" category.

Seven statements per respondent were classified and weighted according to their rank on the answer sheet (7-1). The results showed that the allocentric category was the least used and did not show significant differences among the three national groups. The idiocentric category was used in 48% of cases in Malaysia, 68% in Australia, and 61% in Britain. The group category was used in 41% of cases in Malaysia, 19% in Australia, and 18% in Britain. The difference between the collectivist Malaysian culture and the individualist Australian and British cultures is, of course, highly significant. Although respondents in all three cultures used a majority of idiocentric statements, group or category statements were much more frequent in the collectivist society. Collectivist identity is to a large extent derived from group membership.

Individualism and Collectivism, Schools, and Educational Systems

The relationship between the individual and the group that has been established in a child's consciousness during his or her early years in the family is further developed and reinforced at school.[55] This is very visible in classroom behavior. Tobin, Wu, and Davidson (1989) produced both a book and a video about a day in the life of a preschool for 3- to 4-year-olds, one each in China, Japan, and Hawaii (United States). Teachers in Hawaii (individualist) dealt mainly with individual children; teachers in Japan (moderately collectivist) and China (strongly collectivist) dealt with the children as a group, but in Japan more individual initiatives from children were tolerated and even expected.[56]

Lambert and Klineberg (1967) reported on a UNESCO-sponsored study of "children's views of foreign peoples." Respondents, in a sample of 100 6-year-olds, 100 10-year-olds, and 100 14-year-olds, were interviewed in 11 countries or parts of countries.[57] Only the 14-year-olds were also asked to complete an "ethnocentrism questionnaire" (Frenkel-Brunswik, 1948). In the statistical part of this chapter, the 13 questions in this questionnaire are shown. In fact, only 3 questions dealt with ethnocentrism; the others dealt with traditional versus modern views in a number of areas, such as the necessity of wars, the role of women, caring for the weak, and participative teaching methods. The country scores, in spite of a grave reverse ecological fallacy, correlated strongly negatively with both IDV and GNP/capita (both rho = $-.89$***).

In the collectivist society, in-group versus out-group distinctions learned in the family sphere continue at school, so that students from different ethnic or clan backgrounds often form subgroups in class. In the individualist society, the assignment of joint tasks leads more easily to the formation of new groups than in the collectivist society.

In the latter, students from the same ethnic or family background as the teacher or other school officials expect preferential treatment on this basis. In an individualist society this would be considered nepotism and intensely immoral, but in a collectivist environment it is immoral *not* to treat one's in-group members better than others.

In the collectivist classroom the virtues of harmony and the maintenance of face reign supreme. Confrontations and conflicts should be avoided, or at least formulated so as not to hurt anyone; neither teachers nor students should lose face. Shaming—that is, invoking the group's honor—is an effective way of correcting offenders: They will be put in order by their in-group members. At all times the teacher deals with the student as part of an in-group, never as an isolated individual. In the individualist classroom, of course, students expect to be treated as individuals and impartially, regardless of their background. Group formation among students is much more ad hoc, according to the task or to particular friendships and skills. Confrontations and open discussions of conflict are sometimes considered salutary, and face consciousness is weak or nonexistent. Good educators are supposed to reinforce the students' self-esteem.

In the context of development assistance, it often happens that teachers from more individualist cultures are sent to more collectivist environments. A typical complaint from such teachers is that students do not speak up in class, even when the teacher puts a question to the class. For the student who conceives of him- or herself as part of a group, it is illogical to speak up without being sanctioned by the group to do so. If the teacher wants students to speak up, he or she should address particular students personally. But the desirability of having students speak up in class is more strongly felt in individualist than in collectivist cultures. Because most collectivist cultures also maintain large power distances, their education tends to be teacher centered, with little two-way communication (see Chapter 3).

Boehnke, Scott, and Scott (1996, p. 135) compared factors affecting students' academic performance, collecting opinions from students, parents, and teachers in three Asian countries (Hong Kong, Japan, and Taiwan) and four Western ones (Australia, Canada, Germany, and the United States). They found that aggressive behavior by students was negatively correlated with academic performance in East Asia but hardly in the Western countries. Students' self-esteem was positively correlated with academic performance in the West, but hardly in the East.

The purpose of education is perceived differently by individualist and collectivist societies. In the former, education is seen as aimed at preparing the individual for a place in a society of other individuals. This means learning to cope with new, unknown, unforeseen situations. There is a basically positive attitude toward what is new. The purpose of learning is not so much to know *how to do* as it is to know *how to learn*. The assumption is that learning in life never ends; even after school and university it will continue, for example, through refresher courses. In its schools, the individualist society tries to provide the skills necessary for students to get along in the "modern world." In the collectivist society, education stresses adaptation to the skills and virtues necessary to be an acceptable group member. This leads to a premium on the products of tradition. Learning is more often seen as a one-time process, reserved for the young only, who have to learn *how to do* things in order to participate in society.

The role of a diploma or certificate as a result of the successful completion of study is also different between the two poles of the individualism/collectivism dimension. In the individualist society, the diploma improves the holder's economic worth but also his or her self-esteem: It provides a sense of achievement. In the collectivist society, a diploma is an honor to the holder and his or her in-group that entitles the holder to associate with members of higher-status groups—for example, to find a more attractive marriage partner. The social acceptance that comes with the diploma is more important than the individual self-esteem that comes with mastering a subject, so that in collectivist societies the temptation is stronger to obtain diplomas in some irregular way, such as on the black market.

Exhibit 5.5 summarizes the key differences between collectivist and individualist societies in family life, personality and behavior, language and group identity, and schools and educational systems.

Individualism and Collectivism in the Work Situation

Employed persons in an individualist culture are expected to act rationally according to their own interest, and work should be organized in such a way that this self-interest and the employer's interest coincide. Workers are supposed to act as "economic men," or as people with a combination of economic and psychological needs, but anyway as individuals with their own needs. In a collectivist culture, an employer never hires just an individual, but a person who belongs to an in-group. The employee will act according to the interest of this in-group, which may not always coincide with his or her individual interest. Self-effacement in the interest of the in-group belongs to the normal expectations in such a society. Often, earnings have to be shared with relatives.

Exhibit 5.5 Key Differences Between Collectivist and Individualist Societies I: Family, Personality, Language, and School Issues

Low IDV	High IDV
In the Family	
Horizontal integration: People live with or close to relatives or clan members.	People live in nuclear or one-parent families.
Others classified as in-group or out-group.	Others classified as individuals.
Family provides protection in exchange for lifelong loyalty.	Children are supposed to take care of themselves as soon as possible.
Strong family ties, frequent contacts.	Weak family ties, rare contacts.
Fewer divorces.	More divorces.
Children learn to think in terms of "we."	Child learns to think in terms of "I."
Nonfamily, unrelated persons can be adopted into family.	Family versus nonfamily distinction irrelevant.
Vertical integration: care for aged relatives and worship of ancestors.	Aged relatives should care for themselves; ancestors unknown, irrelevant.
A marriage without children is not complete.	Choosing to have no children in a marriage is a socially acceptable option.
Mothers expect to live with children in their old age.	Mothers expect to live apart in their old age.
Businesspersons live with parents.	Businesspersons live separately.
Nobody is ever alone.	Privacy is normal.
Harmony should always be maintained and direct confrontation avoided.	Speaking one's mind is a characteristic of an honest person.
Opinions predetermined by in-group.	Personal opinions expected.
Financial and ritual obligations to relatives.	Financial independence of relatives; few family rituals.
Togetherness does not demand speaking.	Visits are filled with talking.
Friendships predetermined by in-groups.	Need for specific friendships.
Family relationships can be oppressive.	Lasting relationships difficult to achieve.
Trespassing leads to shame and loss of face for self and in-group.	Trespassing leads to guilt and loss of self-respect.
Criteria for marriage partner: right age, wealth, industriousness, and chastity of bride.	Criteria for marriage partner not predetermined.
Marriages often arranged.	Marriages supposed to be love based.
Living with in-laws and shared income and religion normal.	Living with in-laws undesirable; independence in income and religion.
In Personality and Behavior	
"Individualistic" not important as a personality characteristic.	"Individualistic" important as a personality characteristic.
Low public self-consciousness.	High public self-consciousness.
Other-directed behavior.	Extravert and acting behavior.
Attitudes toward others depend on their group membership.	Attitudes toward others independent of group membership.
Harmony: confrontations to be avoided.	Confrontations are normal.
More conformity behavior (Asch).	Less conformity behavior.
Managers stress conformity and orderliness.	Managers stress leadership and variety.
Women express emotions less strongly than men.	Women express emotions more strongly than men.
Emotional expression of sadness encouraged, happiness discouraged.	Emotional expression of happiness encouraged, sadness discouraged.
Activities dictated by role and context, slower walking.	More self-started activities, faster walking.

Exhibit 5.5   Continued

Low IDV	High IDV
In Language and Group Identity	
Languages in which the word I is not pronounced.	Languages in which the word I is indispensable for understanding.
Students abroad consider their language as not respected.	Students abroad consider their language as highly respected.
Students' gender and religion important for their identity.	Students' gender and religion less important for their identity.
Self-concept in terms of group.	Self-concept idiocentric.
At School	
Teachers deal with pupils as a group.	Teachers deal with individual pupils.
Pupils' individual initiatives discouraged.	Pupils' individual initiatives encouraged.
Schoolchildren report ethnocentric, traditional views.	Schoolchildren report "modern" views.
Students associate according to preexisting in-group ties.	Students associate according to tasks and current needs.
Students expect preferential treatment by teachers from their in-group.	In-group membership no reason to expect preferential treatment.
Harmony, face, and shaming in class.	Students' selves to be respected.
Students will not speak up in class or large groups.	Students expected to speak up in class or large groups.
Students' aggressive behavior bad for academic performance.	Students' self-esteem good for academic performance.
Purpose of education is learning how to do.	Purpose of education is learning how to learn.
Diplomas provide entry to higher-status groups.	Diplomas increase economic worth and/or self-respect.

The hiring process in a collectivist society always takes the in-group into account. Usually preference in hiring is given to relatives, first of all of the employer, but also of other persons already employed by the company. Hiring persons from a family one already knows reduces risks. Also, relatives will be concerned about the reputation of the family and help to correct misbehavior of any family members. In the individualist society, family relationships at work are often considered undesirable, as they may lead to nepotism and to a conflict of interest. Some companies have a rule that if an employee marries another employee, one of them has to leave.

In a collectivist society, the workplace itself may become an in-group in the emotional sense of the word. In some countries this is more the case than in others, but the feeling that it should be this way is nearly always present. The relationship between employer and employee is seen in moral terms. It resembles a family relationship, with mutual obligations of protection in exchange for loyalty. Poor performance of an employee in this relationship is no reason for dismissal: One does not dismiss one's child. Performance and skills, however, do determine what tasks an employee is assigned. This pattern of relationships is best known from Japanese organizations; however, in Japan it applies in a strict sense only to the group of permanent employees, which may be less than half of the total workforce. Japan is perceived as collectivist by Westerners only; Asians tend to see Japan as individualist. In the IBM data, Japan scored halfway on the IDV scale.

In the individualist society, the relationship between employer and employee is primarily conceived as a business transaction, a calculative relationship between actors on a "labor market." Poor performance on the part of the employee or a better pay offer from another employer are legitimate and socially accepted reasons for terminating a work relationship. Yet Randall (1993, p. 104), who reviewed 27 studies of organizational commitment in different countries, concluded that levels of commitment as measured by questionnaires might be *lower* in more collectivist countries. We see the same process as in the case of friendships: In a collectivist society, one's friends and one's employer are predetermined by the social context. In an individualist society, both are a matter of personal choice and a source of greater affect.

In practice there is a wide range of types of employer-employee relationships *within* collectivist and individualist societies. There are employers in collectivist countries who do not respect the societal norm to treat their employees as in-group members, but then the employees in turn do not repay them in terms of loyalty. Labor unions in such cases may replace the work organization as an emotional in-group, and there can be violent union-management conflicts, as there have been in parts of India. There are employers in individualist societies who have established strong group cohesion with their employees, with the same protection-versus-loyalty balance that is the norm in collectivist societies. Organization cultures can to some extent deviate from majority norms and derive a competitive advantage from their originality (see Chapter 8).

In a simulated in-basket experiment with 48 Chinese and 48 U.S. management trainees, Earley (1989) found that the Chinese, coming from a collectivist culture, performed best when told that their performance would be measured for groups of 10 and when their names were not marked on the documents they handled.[58] They performed worst when operating individually and with their names marked on the products of their work. The American, individualist, participants performed best when told that their performance would be measured individually and with their names marked, and abysmally low when operating for a group target and anonymously. In a follow-up experiment with 60 Chinese, 45 Israeli, and 60 U.S. managers, Earley (1993) introduced a refinement consisting of describing the members of the group with whom their performance would be pooled either as complete strangers from different parts of the country, selected on this criterion (out-group condition), or as close colleagues and persons sharing as much as possible the same background (in-group condition). Again the Americans performed best in the individual condition; they performed equally poorly in both group conditions. The Chinese produced very well in the in-group condition but low in both the individual and out-group conditions. The Israelis (medium individualism) produced best in the in-group condition, next best in the individual condition, and worst in the out-group condition.

In a third article, Earley (1994) reported on experiments with approaches to management training, either individual focused or group focused. Data were collected in a laboratory experiment in China, Hong Kong, and the United States and in a 6-month field experiment in China and the United States. Earley argued that training affects a person's "self-efficacy" (Bandura, 1986), the level

of target setting by the person that affects his or her effort and persistence for a task, and that this process is culturally dependent. Earley concluded "that individualists performed best when exposed to training focused at an individual level, whereas collectivists performed best when exposed to training at a group level" (p. 112). This applied both at the cultural level and at the level of individuals within cultures. So there is no one best way of training regardless of culture.

Chapter 3 referred to an older study by Williams, Whyte, and Green (1966) among workers in Peru and the United States. They established a relationship between a high Power Distance Index value and low "faith in people" or interpersonal trust; the difference between the two countries on individualism, however, is even larger (Peru scores 16 on IDV, U.S. scores 91). So collectivism in this case is associated with low interpersonal trust, which looks paradoxical. The paradox can be eliminated if we distinguish between in-groups and out-groups. In collectivist cultures the contrast between the two is particularly strong. Interpersonal trust did not develop in this case because the Peruvian work groups that Williams et al. studied remained out-groups to the workers. In collectivist cultures one does not trust just anybody—one trusts only "one of us." [59] Relationships between colleagues in more collectivist cultures depend on whether these colleagues see each other as belonging to the same in-groups. Veiga and Yanouzas (1991), comparing U.S. and Greek managers, described Greeks (IDV 35) in out-group situations as "extremely competitive, hostile and suspicious" but in in-group situations as "cooperative, self-sacrificing or warmly accepting" (p. 102).

The distinction between in-group and out-groups that is so essential in the collectivist culture pattern has far-reaching consequences for business relationships, beyond those between employers and employees. In individualist societies the norm is universalist, treating everybody alike. Preferential treatment of one customer over others is considered bad business practice and unethical. In collectivist societies the norm is particularist. As the distinction between "our group" and "other groups" is at the very root of people's consciousness, treating one's friends better than others is natural and ethical, and sound business practice.

Zurcher, Meadow, and Zurcher (1965) surveyed 38 Mexican American and 149 Anglo-American bank employees near the Mexico-U.S. border about their endorsement of values of universalism versus particularism on the job. Mexican Americans (IDV 30) gave more particularist answers; Anglo-Americans (IDV 91) were more universalist. Zurcher et al. explain the Mexican

American particularism in terms of the maintenance of an extended kinship system (p. 541).
They quote Oscar Lewis (1961): "Without his
family, the Mexican individual stands prey to
every form of aggression, exploitation and humil-
iation" (p. 54). This family becomes extended
through a large number of *compadres,* or godpar-
ents. Therefore individuals in this type of society
perceive social situations in terms of close personal bonds, where Americans would perceive
them impersonally.

A consequence of particularist thinking is that
in a collectivist society a relationship of trust
should be established between two parties before
they can do any business. Through this relationship, both parties adopt the other into their in-
groups, and from that moment onward both are entitled to preferential treatment. This process of
adoption takes time—depending on the situation,
from several hours to several years. A relationship
is established with a person rather than with a
company. To the collectivist mind, only natural
persons are worthy of trust, and via these persons
their friends and colleagues, but not impersonal
legal entities like companies. So in the collectivist
society *the personal relationship prevails over
the task and over the company* and should be established first; in the individualist society, in contrast, *the task and the company are supposed to
prevail over any personal relationships.* Naive
Western businesspersons who try to force quick
business in a collectivist culture condemn themselves to negative discrimination as out-group
members.

Leung and Bond (1984) reported on two laboratory experiments with psychology students in
Hong Kong and the United States (about 100 students per country for either experiment) about
sharing a reward with an imaginary working partner. In the first experiment, subjects were told that
they had either done twice as much or half as much
as this partner, who was not an in-group member.
The allocation of the reward could be based on *equity* (according to performance) or *equality* (equal
sharing) and had to be done either publicly or privately. The individualist U.S. students chose equity more often than equality. The collectivist
Hong Kong Chinese chose equality when their
choices were public, but equity when they were
kept private. In the second experiment, other students were asked to choose a way of reward allocation for a similar situation, in which the partners
were either from the same in-group or not. For the
Americans this made no difference. The Chinese
chose equality for allocating the reward between
in-group members, and even more so when their
own performance had been high. They chose equity between out-group members, and even more
so when their own performance had been low. In

both cases the Chinese behavior was much more
context dependent than the American behavior;
the Chinese demonstrated particularism, the
Americans universalism.

Chapter 1 referred to Bass and Franke's (1972)
use of the Organizational Success Questionnaire
among samples of students from six countries.
The original analysis suffered from a reverse ecological fallacy, but through ecological correlations I reshuffled the 12 items into three dimensions. One of these, which I labeled "openness
versus secrecy," was significantly negatively correlated with IDV ($r = -.91**$).[60] In more collectivist countries, respondents were less inclined to
link the road to success to "withholding information" and more inclined to relate it to "sharing in
decision making," "openly committing themselves," and "making political alliances." Earlier
in this chapter it was shown that the statement in
the IBM surveys "Decisions made by individuals
are usually of higher quality than decisions made
by groups" (B57 in Appendix 1) also appealed
less in collectivist than in individualist countries.

Chapters 3 and 4 both referred to a survey by
Shane, Venkataraman, and Macmillan (1995,
p. 946) among more than 1,200 employees of four
multinationals in 30 countries about their roles in
championing innovations at work. Shane et al.'s
24 questions split into three ecological factors, of
which one was found related to PDI and one to
UAI. The remaining factor, "cross-functional appeal," combined four questions stressing the importance of involving all persons who can contribute, even if they are from other departments.
In a regression analysis, factor scores on this factor were significantly negatively related to IDV,
although demographic characteristics of respondents, the influence of the particular firm, and
GNP/capita also contributed. So, in less individualist countries, innovators were more inclined to
get other organization members involved and less
to venture out on their own. The organization and
not just their own department acted as their collectivist in-group.

Chapter 4 also mentioned the study by Shane
and Venkataraman (1996, p. 762) across 28 countries in which preferences for two types of championing behavior were opposed. In a multiple regression against the four IBM indexes, a preference for innovating outside existing organizational norms, rules, and procedures was primarily
negatively related with UAI, and secondarily,
positively, with IDV. In individualist countries,
such innovations outside the existing networks
were more acceptable.

In a study of inventiveness, Shane (1992b) correlated invention patents granted to nationals of
33 countries in 1967, 1971, 1976, and 1980, as a
measure of national inventiveness, to these coun-

tries' PDI and IDV scores. Shane's inventiveness measure was significantly positively correlated with IDV and negatively with PDI, but on average slightly more with the first.

Chapter 3 referred to a 1983-84 survey of entrepreneurs reanalyzed across nine countries by Pompe, Bruyn, and Koek (1986).[61] For an overview, they reduced the questionnaire to 21 items, which they subjected to a discriminant analysis. Three discriminant functions explained 77% of the variance in the data. The first stood for self-confidence, in the sense of entrepreneurs attributing to themselves a large amount of influence on their results and not depending on others. Pompe et al. called this function "individualism," and in fact across the nine countries the country scores correlated (rho = .70*) with IDV. The second function correlated with PDI; it included an orientation to family versus job interest (Chapter 3).[62]

Bochner and Hesketh (1994) tested power distance and individualism/collectivism differences among 263 computer programmers and programming managers in a major Australian bank. The population, which had been hired from all over the world, contained people from 28 different ethnic backgrounds. Bochner and Hesketh divided the respondents into two groups: 136 from low-PDI, high-IDV cultures (including 76 native Australians) and 127 from higher-PDI, lower-IDV cultures. The two groups were well matched except that the latter had considerably more years of education; this confirms a finding inside the IBM population (see earlier) that employees in the same occupations tended to have more years of formal education in low- than in high-IDV countries. Bochner and Hesketh's respondents completed a specially developed questionnaire about work issues related to power distance, individualism, and working in a multicultural workforce. The questionnaire included 27 bipolar statements that were carefully written to avoid social desirability. Scoring was done on mostly 7-point scales. Those in the low-IDV group claimed significantly more than those in the high-IDV group to work in a team, to know other people on the job, and to have informal contacts with fellow workers. The two groups also, but to a somewhat lesser extent, differed on power distance items such as high-PDI-ers describing their boss's supervisory style as more close and direct, and declaring themselves less inclined to argue against a management decision. Those in the low-IDV, high-PDI group also perceived much more discrimination and had a much more positive view on the benefits of a multicultural workforce.

In 1991, a survey of the work environment was conducted by the European Union in its then 12 member states, with about 1,000 respondents per country. Smulders, Kompier, and Paoli (1996, p. 1301) divided the 19 questions asked into six

(individual-level) factors, which I have renamed as follows: physical working conditions, job stress, control over job, job support, length of working week, and amount of night work. The authors published country means for these six factors. Across 11 countries (Luxembourg excluded), I found three factors to be significantly correlated with IDV: control over job (rho = .81**), length of working week (rho = .80**), and good physical working conditions (rho = .65*). The working population in more individualist EU member states was more positive about control over the job and about working conditions, but they put in more hours.[63]

Individualism/collectivism differences operate also within countries. Orpen (1982) reported on a comparison of 90 black and 93 white clerks in South Africa. Peer and leader support were much more important for the blacks than for the whites; for the blacks this support moderated the relationship of job stress with performance and satisfaction, but not for the whites. In countries with a dominant individualist middle-class culture, regional rural subcultures have sometimes retained strongly collectivist elements. The same applies to the migrant worker minorities that form majorities among the workforce in some industries in some individualist countries. Such cases risk a culture mismatch between mainstream managers and regional or minority workers.

The first edition of Culture's Consequences contained two measures of social mobility (Cutright, 1968; Miller, 1960): to what extent sons of fathers in manual occupations entered nonmanual occupations and vice versa.[64] Across 12 countries, Cutright's measure was significantly correlated with IDV (rho = −.71**), more than with GNP/capita. In more individualist countries children could more easily enter occupational groups that were different from those of their fathers. See also later in this chapter.

Collectivism and the Applicability of Management Methods

Cultural patterns at work reflect cultural patterns in the wider society. Trying to study "management culture" without insight into societal culture is a trivial pursuit. Managers share the cultures of their society and of their organization with their subordinates—a category to which, often, they once belonged themselves. Managers are culturally the followers of their followers, and both act according to the values they learned as children. "The child is 'father' to the manager." [65]

Management in individualist societies is management of individuals, and this is reflected in mainstream management theories written in such societies. Subordinates can be moved around individually; if incentives or bonuses are given, these should be linked to the individuals' performance. Management in a collectivist society is management of groups. The extent to which people actually feel emotionally integrated into a work group may differ from one situation to another. Ethnic and other in-group differences within the work group play a role in the integration process, and managers within a collectivist culture will be extremely attentive to such factors. It often makes good sense to put persons from the same ethnic background into one crew, although individualistically programmed managers usually consider this dangerous and want to do the opposite. If the work group functions as an emotional in-group, incentives and bonuses should be given to the group, not to individuals.

Leadership is a different process in collectivist and individualist societies. Earlier in this chapter, I referred to Ng's criticism of Mulder, arguing that in a collectivist setting the way power is exercised depends on whether the actors involved belong to the same or to a different in-group. Smith and Peterson (1988) published a book illustrating how different societal cultures produce different kinds of leadership. Although Kurt Lewin (1952) inspired both Western and Japanese leadership research programs, they generated very different results. The United States produced the Ohio State studies (Stogdill & Coons, 1957), the managerial grid (Blake & Mouton, 1964), and the contingency theorists (Fiedler, 1967; Vroom & Yetton, 1973). All of these treat leadership as a property of the leader. The context is a separate and independent issue; in the contingency theories, distinct leader behaviors are matched with distinct contexts. The Japanese psychologist Misumi (1985) devoted more than three decades to the elaboration of "performance-maintenance" (PM) leadership theory. PM theory argues that any leader is concerned with two broad problems, task performance and group maintenance, but the social context determines which behaviors represent P and M. In fact, leadership is a property of leader and context inextricably intertwined. In a series of questionnaire research studies inspired by Misumi, it turned out, for example, that a supervisor who shows disapproval of latecomers at work was seen as P+ in Britain and Hong Kong, as M– in the United States, and as neither of these in Japan (Smith & Peterson, 1988, p. 110).[66]

Management techniques and training packages have been developed almost exclusively in individualist countries, and they are based on cultural assumptions that may not hold in collectivist cultures. A standard element in the training of first-line managers is how to conduct "appraisal interviews": periodic discussions in which the subordinate's performance is reviewed. These can form part of management by objectives, but even where MBO does not exist, the ability to conduct performance appraisals well and the ability to communicate "bad news" are considered key skills for a successful manager. In a collectivist society, discussing a person's performance openly with him or her is likely to clash head-on with the society's harmony norm and may be felt by the subordinate as an unacceptable loss of face. Such societies have more subtle, indirect ways of communicating feedback, such as through the withdrawal of a normal favor or verbally via a mutually trusted intermediary.

The sensitivity training (T-group) fashion from the 1960s, the encounter group fashion from the 1970s, and the transactional analysis fashion from the 1980s were all developed in the United States, the country with the highest Individualism Index score (see Exhibit 5.1). Each of these defends direct sharing of feelings about other people. Such training methods are unfit for use in collectivist cultures. Sensitivity training in these cultures is training in *in*sensitivity. Daily life is filled with encounters, so that no special groups have to be formed for this purpose, and relationships between people are never seen as "transactions" between individuals—they are moral in nature, not calculative.

Individualism and Consumer Behavior

Chapters 3 and 4 referred extensively to the validations of PDI and UAI by De Mooij (1998a, 1998b, 2001), who correlated the IBM indexes with data from consumer surveys across European countries by market research agencies.[67] Country consumer survey data also showed many meaningful correlations with IDV.

Persons in high-IDV countries, De Mooij found, were more likely than those in low-IDV countries to live in detached houses (Eurodata 91, rho = .45*) and less likely to live in apartments or flats ($r = -.56*$). They were more likely to have a private garden ($r = .74***$) and to own a motor home for leisure ($r = .51*$). They more frequently had dogs (Euromonitor 97, rho = .62**) and especially cats (rho = .73***) who consumed pet food ($r = .72***$). (Cats are more individualistic animals than dogs!) They were more likely to possess insurance, such as home insurance (Eurodata 91, rho = .64**) and life insurance (rho = .63**). They would more often engage in do-it-yourself activities: painting walls and woodwork ($r = .65**$), wallpapering ($r = .63**$), home carpentry ($r = .50*$), electric innovations and repairs ($r = .50*$), and plumbing ($r = .50*$). All of these suggest a lifestyle in which the person tries to be self-sufficient and not dependent on others.

Persons in high-IDV countries read more books (Eurodata 91: 12 or more a year, $r = .72***$) and were more likely to own a home computer (rho = $.63**$) and a telephone answering machine (rho = $.50*$). In all these cases, the IDV index explained the country differences better than did differences in national wealth. High-IDV country residents claimed to enjoy TV about as much as they had 5 years before (EMS 97, $r = .72***$), but not more ($r = -.83***$). They tended to see advertising on TV as a useful source of new product information (EMS 95, rho = $.47*$). All in all, persons in high-IDV countries seemed to rely more on media and less on, for example, their social networks for information.

Health and Disability in
Individualist and Collectivist Societies

What is considered abnormal and unhealthy in a society is the mirror image of what is considered normal and healthy, so it contains an evident cultural component. For example, obesity in many African societies is considered beautiful; in U.S. society it is considered a fact of life that should not lead to discrimination; in many European societies it is considered pathological and a reason for medical treatment.

The way normally healthy people cope with stressful situations varies with culture. Olah (1995) has reported on a questionnaire study about coping with stressful situations among some 700 17- to 18-year-old boys and girls in Hungary, India, Italy, Sweden, and Yemen. In the individualist Swedish and Italian populations, the adolescents predominantly reported trying to change the environment to their own benefit. In the collectivist Indian and Yemenite populations, the adolescents predominantly reported emotionally adapting themselves to the situation; they also reported acceptance, passivity, and seeking social support. Hungarian adolescents were in between. Essau and Trommsdorff (1996) obtained similar results in a study among 365 university students (average age 22) in Canada, Germany, Malaysia, and the United States. The questionnaire used referred to university-related problems. Again students from the collectivist culture (Malaysia) reported more emotion-focused coping, as opposed to more problem-focused coping by students from the three individualist cultures. The survey also asked for physical symptoms. Interestingly, in the individualist cultures more emotional adaptation was associated with fewer symptoms, whereas in the collectivist culture more problem-focused adaptation was associated with fewer symptoms. It seems that an atypical, culturally flexible way of coping helped individuals to avoid physical symptoms.

Draguns (1990, 1997) and Tanaka-Matsumi and Draguns (1997) have written on cross-cultural variations in psychopathological symptoms, in particular depression and schizophrenia, and ways of dealing with them. These manifestations of abnormal behavior are universal across the world, but their frequencies, intensities, and treatments vary. The authors assume that all four IBM dimensions may relate to differences in psychopathological symptoms, but research so far has suggested links only with the ind/col dimension. Depressed patients in individualist cultures suffer more from guilt and are often unable to overcome the stress of personal decisions. Depressed patients in collectivist cultures can more often continue functioning because their social networks make the necessary decisions for them anyway. Schizophrenic patients in individualist cultures will usually be hospitalized and isolated from their families. In collectivist cultures, their illness may be seen as a family affair and "the subjective experience of an individual's distress is apparently minimized" (Tanaka-Matsumi & Draguns, 1997, p. 475). Dwairy and Van Sickle (1996) have discussed the use of psychotherapy in traditional Arabic societies:

The generic goal of psychotherapy has often been described as "self-integration" or "self-actualization." Such goals would be condemned in Arabic society, where collective identity is given precedence over the self. Although Western psychotherapy can help to alleviate internal conflicts within the Arabic client, it will often result in greater conflict between the individual and society. In fact, many of the basic techniques of psychotherapy are at odds with core beliefs of the Arabic culture. (p. 231)

Saner (1989) showed a cultural clash in the opposite direction in the way Gestalt therapy as developed by the German Fritz Perls (1893-1970) was adapted in the United States, neglecting people's dependence on social or institutional contexts: "I believe that most American Gestalt therapy theorists and practitioners are unaware of being influenced by culture values or fixed Gestalten best described as individualism or individualistic neurosis" (p. 59).[68]

Health care practices vary considerable among countries, as any traveler who has consulted a doctor abroad can testify. Payer (1989) has written a delightful book, based largely on her personal experiences, about notions of health and sickness in Britain, France, Germany, and the United States. All of these are individualist countries, but even among these there are remarkable differences. Theories and practices of medicine are tightly interwoven with cultural traditions, and this goes beyond the general classifications offered by cultural dimensions. For example, low blood pressure is seen as a reason for living longer (and maybe getting a lower life insurance premium) in Britain and the United States, but it is treated as a disorder in Germany, and on the German market several drugs are available to cure it.

People in individualist cultures invest more in their individual health than do people in collectivist cultures. Among the higher-income countries, those with more individualist cultures spend a greater share of their public and private budgets on health care (Humana, 1992; Organization for Economic Cooperation and Development (OECD), 1992; see later in this chapter). Lueschen et al. (1994) have reported on a telephone interview survey of population samples in Belgium, France, Germany, the Netherlands, and Spain about experiences with the health care system and with doctors. I correlated their published results with the IBM indexes and 1990 GNP/capita. Satisfaction with the health care system was positively associated with IDV ($r = .93*$ across four countries—no data for Spain). Waiting times of patients correlated negatively with IDV ($r = -.86*$ across all five countries): Doctors in more individualist cultures showed more respect for the value of their patients' time. Preference for cure rather than care from the doctor, however, correlated with PDI ($r = .85*$). In low-PDI cultures, doctors treated patients more as equals.

Individualist and collectivist cultures deal differently with disability as well. Westbrook, Legge, and Pennay (1993) surveyed 665 Australian health practitioners about men's reactions to becoming disabled. The practitioners worked with patients from the Anglo, Arabic-speaking, Chinese, German-speaking, Greek, and Italian ethnic communities. In the individualist communities (Anglo and German) the disabled tended to remain cheerful and optimistic, to resent dependency and being helped, and to plan for a future life as normal as possible. In the collectivist communities (Greek, Chinese, Arabic) there was more expression of grief, shame, and pessimism; family members would be asked for advice and assistance, and they would be expected to make the main decisions about the disabled's future. The Italians were often in between; many Italian immigrants in Australia are from collectivist southern Italy. In another article, Westbrook and Legge (1993) described the answers of the same panel of health professionals about the way the different groups dealt with disabled children. Again in the individualist communities the dominant philosophy was to treat the disabled children as much as possible like other children, letting them participate in all activities where this was feasible. In the collectivist communities the disability was seen as a shame on the family and a stigma on its members—especially if the child was a son—and the child would more often be kept out of sight.

Traffic deaths were shown in Exhibit 4.20 to be significantly negatively correlated with IDV (rho $= -.62*$ across 14 European countries). In the more individualist countries, traffic was safer. These countries tended to be wealthier, which is likely to increase the numbers of vehicles available and to decrease the number of kilometers per vehicle; also, roads are probably better adapted to heavier traffic in the wealthier countries. Nevertheless, the correlation of traffic deaths with GNP/capita was only rho $= -.51*$, so there was more to the correlation between IDV and traffic safety than just greater wealth. If we expand Etzioni's distinction between a "calculative" and a "moral" involvement to the traffic situation, it is likely that drivers in more individualist countries show a more calculative involvement in traffic, and that this leads to safer driving.

Exhibit 5.6 summarizes the key differences between collectivist and individualist societies in the work situation, in the applicability of management methods, in consumer behavior, and in issues of health and disability.

Individualism or Collectivism, Political Systems, and Legislation

It is indispensable for a government system "to base itself on political norms that are accepted by the masses, which will then subject themselves to its laws" (Ibn Khaldûn, 1377/1968, p. 368; my translation). The great Muslim philosopher Ibn Khaldûn realized that politics reflects the mindset of the masses as much as that of the kings. A key concept in his work was the clan spirit (*al açabiyyah*), which he saw as the cement that keeps individuals together, but also as a danger because it leads to fanaticism and sets one clan against another. In fact, he referred to collectivism, and he compared the collectivist Bedouin tribes to the individualist urban populations of his time. He even recognized the cultural constraints of theories about human behavior: He criticized the writings of his famous predecessor, the Muslim philosopher Averroes (1126-98), for their implicit individualism. He claimed that Averroes as an urban dweller had no notion of what moved the people in the desert (Habib, 1995, pp. 106-109).

Especially in the United States, the term *collectivist* was and sometimes still is used to describe political systems, almost as a synonym of *communist*. In fact, communist political systems presuppose a certain level of cultural collectivism, but not all collectivist cultures have been touched by communism. The IBM data did not include countries with communist regimes, except Yugoslavia when it was still one country; it did score quite collectivist (IDV 27). Among the countries identified in the IBM study as culturally moderately or

Figure 5.6   Key Differences Between Collectivist and Individualist Societies II: Work Situation, Management Methods, Consumer Behavior, and Health

Low IDV	High IDV
In the Work Situation	
Employees act in the interest of their in-group, not necessarily of themselves.	Employees supposed to act as "economic men."
Hiring and promotion decisions take employees' in-group into account.	Hiring and promotion decisions should be based on skills and rules only.
Relatives of employer and employees preferred in hiring.	Family relationships seen as a disadvantage in hiring.
Employer-employee relationship is basically moral, like a family link.	Employer-employee relationship is a business deal in a "labor market."
Poor performance reason for other tasks.	Poor performance reason for dismissal.
Employee commitment to organization low.	Employee commitment to organization high.
Potential emotional commitment to union.	Relationship with union calculative.
Employees perform best in in-groups.	Employees perform best as individuals.
Training most effective when focused at group level.	Training most effective when focused at individual level.
Preferred reward allocation based on equality for in-group, equity for out-group.	Preferred reward allocation based on equity for all.
Relationships with colleagues cooperative for in-group members, hostile for out-group.	Relationships with colleagues do not depend on their group identity.
Treating friends better than others is normal and ethical: particularism.	Treating friends better than others is nepotism and unethical: universalism.
In business, personal relationships prevail over task and company.	In business, task and company prevail over personal relationships.
Organizational success attributed to sharing information, openly committing oneself, and political alliances.	Organizational success attributed to withholding information, not openly committing, and avoiding alliances.
Belief in collective decisions.	Belief in individual decisions.
Innovation champions in organizations want to involve others.	Innovation champions in organizations want to venture out on their own.
Innovations within existing networks.	Innovations outside existing networks.
Fewer invention patents granted.	More invention patents granted.
Entrepreneurs claim contribution of others to their results.	Entrepreneurs claim own results without depending on others.
Employees and managers report teamwork, personal contacts, and discrimination at work.	Employees and managers report working individually.
Less control over job and working conditions; fewer hours worked.	More control over job and working conditions, longer hours worked.
Less social mobility across occupations.	Greater social mobility across occupations.
In the Applicability of Management Methods	
Management is management of groups.	Management is management of individuals.
Theories based on individual psychology of limited use.	Some theories based on individual psychology useful.
Employee has to be seen in family and social context.	Employee can be seen as individual.

Figure 5.6   Continued

Low IDV	High IDV
Keeping ethnic or other in-groups together supports productivity.	Composition of work groups based on individual criteria; in-groups unwanted.
Incentives to be given to in-groups.	Incentives to be given to individuals.
Leadership is inseparable from the context (PM leadership theory).	Leadership is a property of the leader (various U.S. theories).
Direct appraisal of performance is a threat to harmony.	Direct appraisal of performance improves productivity.
Openly sharing with a person one's feelings about him or her spoils cooperation.	Openly sharing with a person one's feelings about him or her may be productive.

In Consumer Behavior

Low IDV	High IDV
Live in apartments or flats.	Live in detached houses with private gardens; own motor homes.
Live with human companions.	Live with cats and/or dogs.
Security by social network.	Security by home and life insurance.
Ask friends for jobs around the house.	Do-it-yourself for jobs around the house.
Other-dependent lifestyles.	Self-supporting lifestyles.
Read fewer books, use fewer home computers, enjoy TV more.	More books, use computer, use answering machine.
Social network main source of information.	Media main source of information.

In Matters of Health and Disability

Low IDV	High IDV
Ways of coping with stress mainly emotional.	Ways of coping with stress mainly problem focused.
Depressed and schizophrenic patients remain integrated into social network.	Depressed and schizophrenic patients isolated from social network.
Smaller share of public and private money spent on health care.	Larger share of public and private money spent on health care.
Less satisfaction with health care.	More satisfaction with health care.
Disability is a shame for the family.	Disability is a handicap to be overcome.
Disability is a source of grief and pessimism.	Disability is a challenge to be handled with optimism.
Proportionally more traffic deaths.	Proportionally fewer traffic deaths.

strongly collectivist, many (from Asia, Africa, the Middle East, and Latin America; see Exhibit 5.1) had a form of state capitalism. The weaker the individualism in the citizens' mental software, the greater the likelihood of a dominating role of the state in the economic system. The stronger the individualism, the greater the appeal of market capitalism. Both historically and geographically, individualism is linked with market capitalism, competition, and political democracy (Béteille, 1977, pp. 162 ff.).

In discussing power distance in Chapter 3, I argued that the relationship between authority and citizen in a country is modeled after the relationships between boss and subordinate, teacher and student, and parent and child. An author who developed a grand theory about the link between what happens at the level of the family and what happens at the level of the state is the French social historian Emmanuel Todd (1983). Todd tried to explain the ideological system adopted in a country's government through the family structure historically prevailing in that country. In doing so, he trod in the footsteps of his compatriot Frédéric Le Play (1806-82), a pioneering field researcher of family economics in Europe and a controversial political philosopher.

Todd classified family structures around the world by three criteria: (1) whether married sons continue to live with their parents or set up an independent home (community versus nuclear family), (2) whether inheritances are shared among all brothers or exclude all but one (divided inheritance versus primogeniture), and (3) whether marriage between first cousins is accepted or not (weak versus strong incest taboo). With these three criteria, Todd arrived at $2^3 = 8$ possibilities, of which two could be combined because they always occur together. To the seven remaining he added "African systems" as a new eighth category; in this category marriages are supposed to be unstable, and partners change frequently.

Todd has drawn maps of Europe and the world with the supposed distribution of these eight family types. He has related each type to a particular ideological/political system or set of systems, arguing that the real reason a country adopted a particular way of government was because it fit the way of thinking of the people, based upon the family structure in which they or their ancestors grew up. For example, in Russia, traditionally, the "exogamous community family structure" prevailed, characterized by cohabitation of married sons with their parents, equality between brothers defined by rules of inheritance, and a taboo on marriage between the children of two brothers. Todd claimed a similar traditional structure for Yugoslavia, Slovakia, Bulgaria, Hungary, Finland, Albania, central Italy, China, Vietnam, Cuba, and northern India; these countries, Todd (1983, p. 42) argued, were attracted to communism because communism is a transference to the party state of the moral traits and regulatory mechanisms of the exogamous community family. Todd took a shortcut from the family to the ideology, ignoring all other factors, such as economic development, and he did not support the relationships he postulated with any type of statistical significance tests. So his statements are impossible to verify or falsify. But he did make an eloquent plea for relating influences of culture in these different areas of societal life.

Schmitter (1981, p. 294) compared political systems among 15 wealthier countries in Europe and North America on their degree of "societal corporatism." Societal corporatism stands for a political system in which interest groups, especially of labor and employers, are represented by formal associations, historically grown rather than established by the state itself, which are given monopoly power by the state to represent those interests. The Swedish national labor union

(LO) and the corresponding employers' confederation (SAF) are examples. Schmitter's index was significantly correlated with IDV (see Exhibit 5.20). At closer scrutiny, Schmitter found it composed of two separate components: "organizational centralization" and "associational monopoly." Only organizational centralization correlated with IDV: It measured the degree of institutionalization of the interest associations (large own staff, own strike funds, and so on). Associational monopoly measured to what extent interests were represented by one single organization rather than several different ones, and it was correlated with PDI, not with IDV. What Schmitter showed is that the less individualist, somewhat collectivist Western countries gave more power to well-organized private associations formally representing interest groups, and that in countries with lower power distances, governments were more likely to allow such associations a monopoly.

If differences in the political systems found in countries are rooted in their citizens' mental software, the possibilities of influencing these systems through propaganda, money, or arms from other countries are limited. If the minds are not receptive to the message, propaganda and money are probably spoiled. The ineffectiveness of the millions of dollars spent in the 1970s by the U.S. government in helping the Nicaraguan "Contras" is a case in point. It also explains why peacekeeping actions by international armed brigades rarely succeed.

Chapter 3 related the Power Distance Index to the difference between balanced power and unbalanced power in political systems. Exhibit 3.18 shows that 20 countries in the PDI range showed balanced power and 21 in the upper-PDI range showed unbalanced power since 1975. There were 9 exceptions: France, Belgium, Portugal, and Greece, with higher PDI and balanced power; and Argentina, Iran, Pakistan, South Africa, and Taiwan, with lower PDI and unbalanced power. IDV is even more closely associated with balanced power than PDI: From the top 19 countries in Exhibit 5.1, 18 had balanced power since 1975 (all but South Africa); from the remaining 31 countries only 5 had balanced power (Japan, Turkey, Greece, Portugal, and Costa Rica), and some of these went through political upheaval shortly before 1975.

I included the "balanced versus unbalanced political power" distinction in Chapter 3 because it made conceptual sense to relate political power to power distance. Why did individualism predict balanced political power even more accurately? For the answer to this question, we should look at two exceptional countries, Belgium and France, which produced both high PDI *and* high IDV (Exhibit 5.2) as well as balanced political power. In spite of traditions of power inequality, these countries have continued to maintain political pluralism because of their populations' individualism: No would-be dictator in either country would obtain sufficient passive compliance to survive. The universalist norm that we found associated with individualism resists regimes based entirely on particularism (which does not rule out a lot of de facto particularism).

In 1970, GNP/capita per se was an almost perfect predictor of balanced political power, but, as I argued in Chapter 3, in the ensuing decades more unbalanced-power countries have joined the wealthy group (Singapore, Hong Kong, Taiwan, South Korea), which showed that, at least for a time, wealth could coexist with unbalanced power. In Chapter 3, I drew a suggested causal path for PDI (Exhibit 3.10) in which social mobility and the development of a middle class were central factors. Individualism, too, is associated with the development of a middle class: Individualist values tend to be middle-class values. The development of a middle class presupposes social mobility, and earlier in this chapter I showed IDV to be correlated with two different measures of social mobility (Cutright, 1968; Miller, 1960). The stronger correlation was with Cutright's index, which eliminated the influence of the numerical strength of the middle class (coinciding mostly with the nonmanual occupations, and associated with lower PDI). Cutright's data showed the *ease of access* to middle-class positions for people regardless of their fathers' professions: Individual careers are not constrained by family background.

Individualism and balanced political power—that is, political stability—can be related in still another way: through sectoral equality, that is, the distribution of the national wealth across sectors of the economy (such as between farming and manufacturing workers). Sectoral equality or inequality differs from equality or inequality of individual incomes; the latter was associated with PDI (Exhibit 3.16). In the first edition of *Culture's Consequences,* I showed significant correlations between IDV and two measures of sectoral inequality, from Cutright (1967) and from Taylor and Hudson (1972), across 33 (32) countries ($r = -.60***$ and $r = -.71***$); they indicated greater sectoral equality in more individualist countries (see Hofstede, 1980a, fig. 5.22). I interpret this as the outcome of a universalist attitude among both decision makers and population, but it will definitely increase political stability, as underprivileged economic sectors are a threat to the stability of any regime. In his article, Cutright showed for 44 countries a relationship between equality of sectors of the economy and "political representativeness"; the latter resembles my "balanced power" criterion. Cutright (1967, p. 565) argued that political representativeness decreases sec-

toral inequality because it forces the political elites to respond to the needs of the nonelite classes for a greater share of the national product.

Bierbrauer (1994) has related individualism and collectivism to "legal cultures." He based this on extensive in-depth interviews with recent Kurdish-Turkish and Lebanese immigrants in Germany (collectivist) versus an educationally matched group of Germans (individualist).[69] His main conclusion was that interviewees from the two collectivist groups "had a greater preference for abiding by the norms of tradition and religion and were less willing to let state law regulate ingroup disputes." German, more individualist, interviewees "showed a clear preference for formal procedures and guidelines" (p. 243). So legal norms are not universal, which means that appeals to legality in international or intercultural disputes are of limited value.

The same section in the first edition of *Culture's Consequences* showed that an (intersubjective) measure of press freedom (Taylor & Hudson, 1972) was also significantly correlated with IDV (rho = $.51***$ across 39 countries). However, 1970 GNP/capita was an even better predictor of the Press Freedom Index (rho = $.67***$), and IDV made no independent additional contribution to predicting press freedom. So beyond values there are more compelling reasons that push toward more press freedom in wealthier countries, such as more newspapers and more interest groups wanting their opinions to be known and having the means to disseminate those opinions.

A former researcher for Amnesty International, Charles Humana, has published periodically a volume titled *World Human Rights Guide*; its third edition appeared in 1992. On the basis of 40 questions derived from United Nations criteria (including the Universal Declaration of Human Rights), Humana calculated human rights (HR) ratings for a large number of countries. As Exhibit 5.21 in the statistical section of this chapter shows, across 52 countries in the IBM set, the HR ratings correlated positively with 1990 GNP/capita ($r = .71***$) and IDV ($r = .61***$) and negatively with PDI ($r = -.56***$), but in a stepwise multiple regression only GNP/capita made an independent contribution.[70] However, within the group of the 25 wealthier countries (1990 GNP/capita > \$4,800) the single explaining variable for the HR ratings was IDV, $r = .73***$, no other variables contributing significantly in the stepwise regression. Across the remaining 27 poorer countries there was only a weak ($r = .38*$) correlation between the HR rating and 1990 GNP/capita. My conclusion from these relationships is that respect for human rights as formulated by the United Nations is a luxury that wealthy countries can afford much more easily than poor ones; to what extent these wealthy countries do conform to U.N. criteria, however, depends on the degree of individualism in their cultures. The United Nations' 1948 Universal Declaration of Human Rights and other U.N. covenants were inspired by the values of the dominant powers at the time of their adoption, which were highly individualist (see also Chapter 9).

Humana's *World Human Rights Guide* (1992) also contains, for a large number of countries, the proportion of government budgets spent on health, education, and the military. Exhibit 5.22 in the statistical section proves that the explaining variables for government *health* expenditures were the same as those for human rights ratings: Across all countries health budgets depended solely on national wealth ($r = .77***$), but across the 25 wealthy countries they depended not on wealth but on individualism as measured by IDV ($r = .56**$). Government health care in the most individualist wealthy countries is more expensive than in the less individualist ones. The same applies for private spending on health. The Organization for Economic Cooperation and Development (1992) has published for 22 countries from the IBM set figures for total health expenditure in 1990 as a share of total domestic expenditure, including private spending. The countries included are virtually identical with the wealthy countries in Exhibit 5.22.[71] Again, expenditures for health are a function of IDV ($r = .66***$). In another statistic, the OECD shows for the same countries health expenditures as a share of "purchasing power parity," a measure of national wealth that takes the cost of living into account. In this case, health expenditures are first correlated with 1990 GNP/capita ($r = .74***$), but there is a significant secondary correlation with IDV ($R^2 = .67$, $R = .82***$). What this shows is that in wealthier countries the cost of health rises faster than the average cost of other products and services, and that this tendency is still reinforced by cultural individualism.

Humana's data for education budgets correlated with IDV even across all 52 countries (see again Exhibit 5.22, $r = .56***$). Education and individualism are evidently closely linked in a process of two-way causation. Across the wealthy countries only, education budgets did not depend on individualism, but they increased with lower PDI and lower MAS (Chapter 6): The egalitarian, nurturing cultures reserved the largest part of their resources for education.

Humana's figures for military budgets across the 25 wealthy countries were significantly *negatively* correlated with their GNP/capita (Exhibit 5.22, $r = -49**$). The causality in this case also probably goes two ways: Money spent on arms, especially foreign arms, is a drain on national wealth; and inversely, wealthier countries need a smaller share of their income for a minimum of defense. Across all countries, and across the poor countries only, no clear correlation patterns for military budgets were visible. I imagine, however, that official figures for military spending, especially from a number of the poorer countries, should be taken with more than a grain of salt. Both the sellers and the buyers of armaments have a vested interest in keeping such figures secret. So the numbers in the exhibit should be considered as almost random, and random numbers don't produce significant correlations.

In analyzing the political situation in a country, it also makes sense to look at the combination of IDV with UAI; the position of the countries in the IBM set on these two dimensions is plotted in Exhibit 5.7. The combination of collectivism with strong uncertainty avoidance in a society tends to aggravate intergroup conflicts. The presence within the borders of a country of different ethnic, linguistic, or religious groups is a historical fact; some countries are more homogeneous than others. The relative size and social class composition of the groups affect their potential for conflict. How a population and a government deal with such conflict, however, is a cultural phenomenon. In countries in the upper right-hand corner of Exhibit 5.7, strong uncertainty avoidance ("What is different is dangerous") is combined with collectivist particularism (strong identification with ingroups). Such countries often tend to eliminate intergroup conflict by denying it and by trying either to assimilate or to repress minorities; in extreme cases, they practice "ethnic cleansing," that is, expulsion of the minorities or even genocide. The chances of violent intergroup strife within these countries are considerable, as the minorities often hold the same strong uncertainty avoidance, collectivist values. Several countries with severe intergroup conflicts are found inside or near the upper right-hand corner of Exhibit 5.7: African countries, Arabic-speaking countries, Guatemala, Iran, Israel, Mexico, Turkey, and the former Yugoslavia.[72]

Countries in the upper left-hand corner of Exhibit 5.7 may contain different groups with strong group identities but are more likely to find a modus vivendi in which groups tolerate and complement each other. Countries in the lower right-hand corner often harbor considerable antagonism against minorities and ethnic, religious, or linguistic opponent groups, but the universalism of the individualist state usually at least formally tries to guarantee that everybody's rights are respected; extremism versus others is restricted to the political margin. Soeters (1996) has pointed to individualism in explaining the difference in ethnic violence between Belgium and the former Yugoslavia. Finally, countries in the lower left-hand corner are likely to try actively to integrate minorities and to guarantee equal rights.[73]

Exhibit 5.7.   An IDV × UAI Plot for 50 Countries and Three Regions

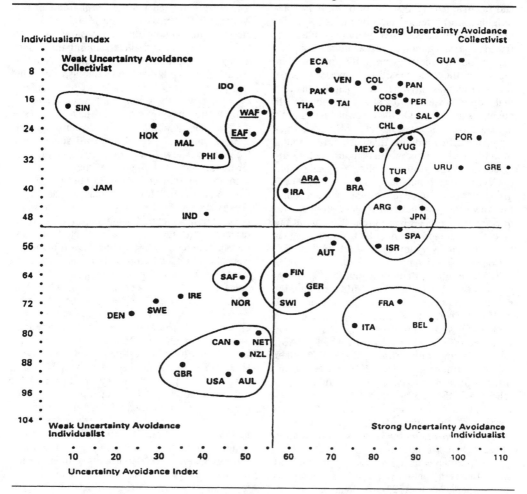

The IDV-UAI plot in Exhibit 5.7 also reminds us of Douglas's (1973a, chap. 4) taxonomy of "grid and group" (see Chapter 1). *Group* clearly corresponds to collectivism, in the sense that high group ("ego increasingly controlled by other people's pressure") represents the collectivist end of the scale. *Grid* resembles uncertainty avoidance: High grid stands for a "system of shared classifications." However, as argued earlier, Douglas did not specify the level of aggregation at which her taxonomy should apply; she used it mainly for small units in societies, not for entire societies.

Individualism and Collectivism, Religions, and Ideas

Individualist societies support individualist religions, in which the stress is on the individual's relationship with the supernatural. Earlier in this chapter I mentioned religious or ideological conversion as a case in which the difference between individualist and collectivist self-concept becomes evident: whether converting oneself is an individual act or a collective change of identity undertaken by entire families or even communities together. In individualist societies, schisms within religious communities happen easily and frequently; a dominant person will consider his or her new ideas or religious revelations sufficient reason to leave a given community with a number of followers. In collectivist societies such aberrant ideas are first of all not encouraged, but if they occur they are absorbed within the context of the larger religious community—for example, through the establishment of a new school or monastic order.

Human beings' images of God or the gods reflect the values of human society. All traditionally individualist societies developed in countries with monotheist religions, especially Christianity and Judaism (the reverse is not true). Polytheist religions are professed in collectivist societies; their gods are constrained by family relations, friendships, and enmities, just as humans are.

Individualist societies not only practice individualism, they also consider it superior to other forms of mental software. Most Americans feel that individualism is *good,* and at the root of their country's greatness. On the other hand, as I have argued above, the late Chairman Mao Zedong of China identified individualism as evil. He found individualism and liberalism responsible for selfishness and aversion to discipline; they led people to place their personal interests above those of the group, or simply to devote too much attention to their own things. The IBM project produced no data for the People's Republic of China, but the countries with predominantly Chinese populations all scored very low on IDV (Hong Kong 25, Singapore 20, Taiwan 17).

The religious-ideological-political consequences of individualism merit further study. Individualism reminds us of the "Protestant ethic" of Max Weber, but as Exhibit 4.21 shows, the Catholic/Protestant ratio in wealthy countries was unrelated to IDV (but related to UAI and MAS); we are dealing with a "modernist ethic" rather than a "traditionalist ethic." The Chinese *ren* philosophy of man described earlier in this chapter (Hsu, 1971) is the best formulation of the low-IDV sentiment I have found so far; the American worship of the independent actor in Whyte's (1956) *Organization Man* is the best formulation of the high-IDV sentiment.

Economics as a discipline was founded in Britain in the 18th century; among its founding fathers, Adam Smith (1723-90) stands out. Smith assumed that the pursuit of self-interest by individuals through an "invisible hand" would lead to the maximal wealth of nations. This is a highly individualist idea from a country that still today ranks near the top on individualism. Economics has remained an individualist science, and most of its leading contributors have come from strongly individualist nations, such as Britain and the United States. However, because of the individualist assumptions on which they are based, economic theories as developed in the West are unlikely to apply in societies in which not individual interests but group interests prevail. Unfortunately, few alternative economic theories have yet been formulated to explain collectivist economies. A Dutch sociologist writing on Indonesia contrasted the Western orientation toward "return on investment" with an Indonesian "return on favors" (Vroom, 1981).

In 1992, the European Commission (the central authority of the European Union) contracted a consulting firm for a study of public understanding of and attitudes toward science and technology in the member countries (INRA, 1993). The data were collected via the Eurobarometer network in 1992. Across 11 countries IDV was associated, more than the other dimensions and more than GNP/capita, with understanding the experimental method (i.e., the need to try things out systematically; $r = .80***$), rejecting astrology and lucky numbers ($r = -.66*$ and $r = -.75**$), and *disagreement* with the statement "Science and technology are making our lives healthier" ($r = -.55*$).[74] The combination of these items suggests a more "magical" attitude toward science and technology in low-IDV countries and a more matter-of-fact attitude in high-IDV countries.

In another project for the European Commission, Van Baren, Hofstede, and Van de Vijver (1995) studied public acceptance of *biotechnology* as a new societal phenomenon. We based our research on survey data collected by the Eurobarometer network in 1993. Levels of knowledge about biotechnology in the countries studied were tested with 12 "quiz" statements (true/false/don't know) about the genetic facts on which biotechnology is based. The mean number of correct answers varied from 7.4 in Denmark to 4.6 in Greece and Portugal.[75] Across the 12 countries overlapping with the IBM set, these scores correlated with 1990 GNP/capita (rho = .76**), with IDV (rho = .72**), and negatively with UAI (rho = -.70**). In a multiple regression based on the rank correlations, GNP/capita explained 58% of the variance and GNP/capita plus IDV together 81% (UAI did not add significantly to the explanation). So the public in wealthier countries was better informed, which should come as no surprise given the better opportunities for education and information in these countries. However, on top of this there was a sizable effect of individualism measured by IDV: Wealth being equal, people in more individualist cultures scored additionally better. This confirms the conclusions of the preceding paragraphs that persons in high-IDV countries tend to be better informed.

Exhibit 5.8 can be considered a continuation of Exhibits 5.5 and 5.6: It summarizes the key differences between collectivist and individualist societies from the past two sections. On the low-IDV side this exhibit calls for some caution: Some statements apply to all societies studied, which means that "low IDV" coincides with "non-Western." Others are derived from a comparison of Western countries, so that "low IDV" stands for "medium IDV" on a world scale. I have nevertheless maintained the two types of statements in one column because they show a certain coherence.

Predictors of IDV: Wealth and Latitude

The statistical analysis in Exhibit 5.23 explores the relationship of the Individualism Index with

Figure 5.8   Key Differences Between Collectivist and Individualist Societies III: Politics and Ideas

Low IDV	High IDV
In Political Systems	
Collective interests supposed to prevail over individual interests.	Individual interests supposed to prevail over collective interests.
Economy based on collective interests.	Economy based on individual interests.
State capitalism or state socialism.	Market capitalism or market socialism.
Economic monopolies.	Competition stimulated.
Private life is invaded by public interests.	Everyone has a right to privacy.
Opinions and votes predetermined by in-group memberships.	Everyone is expected to have a private opinion: one person, one vote.
Political power exercised by interest groups.	Political power exercised by voters.
Political power unbalanced.	Political power balanced.
Rigid social and occupational class system.	Social and occupational mobility.
Large differences in wealth between sectors of the economy.	Wealth distributed fairly equally across sectors of the economy.
Laws and rights differ by group according to tradition and religion.	Laws and rights supposed to be the same for all.
In wealthy countries, low human rights ratings.	In wealthy countries, high human rights ratings.
Small share of national budget spent on education.	Large share of national budget spent on education.
High risk of domestic intergroup conflict.	Low risk of domestic intergroup conflict.
In Religions and Ideas	
Religions stress collective devotional practices.	Religions stress individual's relationship with the supernatural.
Collective conversions.	Individual conversions.
Polytheist religions.	Monotheist religions.
Placing individual over collective interests is evil.	Individualism is good.
Traditionalist ethic.	Modernist ethic.
Imported economic theories largely irrelevant because unable to deal with collective and particularist interests.	Native economic theories based on pursuit of individual self-interest.
Science and technology treated as magic.	Science and technology treated as matter-of-fact.
Public uninformed about technological facts.	Public knowledgeable about technological facts.

eight economic, geographic, and demographic indicators that were identified in Chapter 2 and used in Chapters 3 and 4. We have seen that IDV was strongly correlated with wealth (1970 GNP/capita). Across 50 countries the correlation coefficient was a striking $r = .84***$. In view of the large error margins of IDV (composed from answers of IBM employees to translated paper-and-pencil questionnaires) and of GNP (World Bank data based on imprecise statistics and shaky exchange rates), this level of correlation is really remarkable. The strong correlation between IDV and GNP per capita is illustrated by the graph in Exhibit 5.9.

Respondents in countries to the right-hand side of the regression line scored less individualist than their countries' 1970 wealth would predict;

those in countries to the left scored more individualist. We notice that the three Chinese countries of Singapore, Hong Kong, and Taiwan are located well to the right side of the regression line: Their respondents scored less individualist than the countries' wealth would warrant, which is in agreement with the *ren* philosophy referred to earlier.

The statistical analysis shows that, in addition to wealth, geographic latitude (positively), population growth (negatively), and the size of the IBM subsidiary (positively) were strongly correlated with IDV.[76] In a stepwise regression with the first seven indicators, only wealth and latitude remained as significant predictors (slow population growth being preempted by these two). Wealth plus latitude explained 78% of the variance in

Exhibit 5.9.   An IDV × 1970 GNP/Capita Plot for 50 Countries

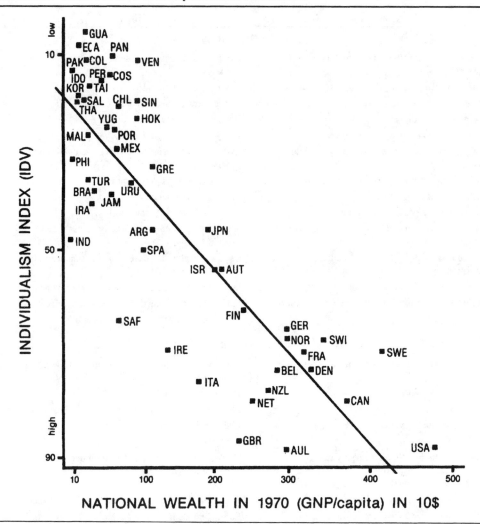

IDV. The values of IDV predicted on the basis of wealth plus latitude are listed next to the actual values in Exhibit 5.1. Differences of 14 or more points between actual and predicted value of IDV occurred for the following countries: *more individualist,* South Africa (+32 points), Australia, Great Britain, Italy, India, Ireland, New Zealand; *less individualist,* Sweden, Guatemala, South Korea, Yugoslavia, Chile, Venezuela. These differences represent the variance in IDV scores related not to wealth or latitude but, for example, to historical or traditional factors.

The deviant score for South Africa is due to the fact that the IDV score was based on the answers of white respondents only, whereas the GNP/capita referred to the total population, in majority black. More in general we find at the more individualist side an Anglo cluster in which only Can-

ada and the United States are missing. One particularity of these countries is an atomized trade union system (especially in Great Britain, which has been the model for the other British-culture countries), with craft unions that compete with each other; we can see this as an outcome of an individualist value system. The less individualist side presents fewer extreme scores and no clear cluster.

Across the 28 poorer countries only latitude was weakly significantly related to IDV. Across the 22 wealthier countries wealth was still positively related to IDV, but negatively related to past (1960-70) economic growth (EGP): Less individualist wealthy societies during this period developed faster. However, this trend did not continue after 1970; future economic growth (EGF) was not related to IDV.[77]

This leads us to the issue of whether there is a cause-and-effect relationship between individualism and wealth. Exhibit 5.9 does not show which of the two related phenomena is cause and which is effect, or whether both could be caused by a third factor, not shown in the graph. If individualism were the cause of wealth, one should find that IDV scores relate not only to national wealth per se but also to ensuing economic growth (EGF), but we have just seen that this was not the case.[78] Across all countries the relationship between IDV and subsequent economic growth was, if anything, negative. The reverse causality, national wealth causing individualism, is more plausible. As I will show below (in the subsection headed "The Future of Individualism Differences"), it was statistically supported in the IBM case for the period from 1968 to 1972.

The explanation of the causal relationship from wealth toward individualism is that poverty makes people depend on the support of their in-groups, but when a country's wealth increases, its citizens get access to resources that allow them to "do their own thing." The storyteller in the village market is replaced by television sets, first one per village, but soon more. In wealthy Western family homes every family member may have his or her own TV set. The caravan through the desert is replaced by a number of buses, and these by a larger number of motor cars, until each adult family member drives a different car. The village hut in which the entire family lives and sleeps together is replaced by a house with a number of private rooms. Collective life is replaced by individual life.

Individualism and Historical Factors

At the beginning of this chapter, I referred to Blumberg and Winch's (1972) "curvilinear hypothesis," suggesting that as human societies developed since prehistory, family complexity first increased and then decreased again. Hunter-gatherers and nomads lived (and still live) in nuclear families or small bands. Sedentary agricultural societies mostly showed and still show more complex extended families or village community in-groups. Protosociologist Ibn Khaldûn (1377/ 1968, p. 301) described in 1377 the different family and clan structures of nomads versus sedentary people, and why the latter were able to dominate the former.

When farmers migrate to cities, extended families become smaller and the typical urban family is again nuclear. In most countries today one finds only agricultural and urban subcultures. For these two types, modernization corresponds to individualization.[79]

Following the logic of this hypothesis, *differences* in individualism among countries should be primarily a matter of differences in modernization due to different degrees of economic development. Exhibit 5.10 lists those differences discussed in the preceding pages as being statistically associated with IDV, with some inferences that make the pattern more coherent.

There are similarities between the origins of IDV and the origins of PDI as pictured in the proposed causal chain of Exhibit 3.10. However, in the case of IDV, economic development must be a first cause, as it correlates so highly. Climate in this case is a secondary factor that either supports or discourages individual initiative. Slower population growth (Exhibit 5.23) means that parents have fewer children; the child from a smaller family, other factors being equal, is more often treated as an individual than the child from a large family. The longer education for a given job, which seems to go together with lower IDV (as mentioned earlier in this chapter), suggests a more traditional educational system with more rote learning of revealed truths; also, this educational system will cover a smaller part of the population than the more pragmatic education likely on the high-IDV side.

Apart from all these systematic characteristics, we should take idiosyncratic historical factors into account. Le Play, whom I mentioned above, actually did field research in 19th-century France on the differences in family life across Europe. He focused on the economic factors that also appear prominently in my cross-national analysis. Todd (1983) drew a causal arrow from these family differences to political systems, but there is also a case for the reverse causality, or, even better, a two-way interdependence between family and state. Ariès (1973, p. 238) cited research by Georges Duby in one of the French regions between the 9th and 13th centuries A.D. This shows family ties to tighten in periods of political upheaval, as a refuge for the individual, and to slacken in periods of political stability.

A nuclear rather than extended family structure is also both a cause and an effect of individualism. Shorter (1975, p. 30) compared old family statistics and found that around 1700, the nuclear family was already the norm in Britain and among North American colonists, and to a lesser extent in parts of Europe such as the Netherlands—countries that in the IBM data showed the highest IDV scores some 300 years later. The extended family dominated elsewhere. Economic or political factors do not suffice to explain such differences. The growth of European individualism was also linked to the development of manners (Elias, 1936/1980a) and of art and science; the Italian Renaissance in the 15th century is considered to have been a major milestone for both manners and

Exhibit 5.10 Origins of National Individualism Index Differences

Low IDV	High IDV
Less economic development.	More economic development.
Less social mobility and weak development of middle class.	Greater social mobility and stronger development of middle class.
Tropical and subtropical climates.	Moderate to cold climates.
Survival less dependent on individual initiative.	Survival more dependent on individual initiative.
More traditional agriculture, less modern industry, less urbanization.	Less traditional agriculture, more modern industry, more urbanization.
Extended family or tribal structures.	Nuclear family structure.
More children per parent couple.	Fewer children per nuclear family.
Traditional education systems, for minority of population.	Pragmatic educational systems, for majority of population.
Historical factors: tradition of collectivist thinking and action.	Historical factors: tradition of individualist thinking and action.
Smaller, particularist organization.	Larger, universalist organizations.

art. Yet the Russian historian Gurevich (1995) has found roots of European individualism several centuries earlier; and anyway the Renaissance was a rebirth of individualistic tendencies in Greek and Roman art, between 2,000 and 1,000 years past. Where and when do historical roots begin? There are many ways to develop a society, and for complex reasons, buried in a distant past, every society has chosen its own particular one.

The Future of
Individualism Differences

From 1967-69 to 1971-73, the IBM data showed a clear increase in individualism. Across 19 countries surveyed twice with the same goals questions, the six goals associated with IDV (personal time, freedom, challenge, use of skills, training, and physical conditions) all shifted toward a larger IDV score, the first five significantly (see Exhibit 2.6).[80] This is explained by the strong association between IDV and national wealth (Exhibit 5.23): From 1967 to 1973, 18 of the 19 countries became wealthier. Separate calculations of IDV from the 1967-69 and the 1971-73 data showed the mean IDV score across the 19 countries to have shifted from 50 to 70, by +20 points. The country with the highest IDV, Great Britain, had gone from 75 to 101, +26 points. Yet the only country among the 19 that had become poorer, Pakistan, which already had the lowest IDV score in 1969, went from 15 to 12, −3 points.[81] So the extremes did not converge over these four years: The gap between Pakistan and Great Britain increased from 60 to 89.

The strong increase in individualism in Britain between the two IBM survey rounds did not con-

tinue after 1973. Lowe's (1996b) replication of the IBM survey in IBM Great Britain (high IDV) and IBM Hong Kong (low IDV) in 1993 showed an IDV score for Britain in 1993 at the same level as the average for 1967-73 (−2 points, or +3 points when corrected for age). Lowe found a clear shift toward increased individualism in Hong Kong (+12 points, or +8 points when corrected for age). In 1993 the GNPs/capita of Britain and Hong Kong were exactly the same ($18,060), but the IDV scores were still widely different, in spite of the shift in Hong Kong: a gap of 50 points against 64 points in 1970. There was some convergence in IDV, but the increase of wealth in no way wiped out societal differences.

The trends in IDV over the 4-year period have also been analyzed by age group for five large groups of IBM employees (see Exhibit 5.24 in the statistical section). All five groups produced a relatively flat age curve, in most cases inverted U-shaped: The youngest and oldest age categories were less individualist, but this was due to different goals. On the basis of the importance attached to personal time and physical conditions, the older employees were less individualist, but on the basis of use of skills and training the young were less individualist (see Exhibit 6.6). There was a strong zeitgeist effect for all age brackets for the managers and professionals (they all became much more individualist from 1967-69 to 1971-73) and for the younger age brackets of technicians, clerks, and secretaries; as in Exhibit 3.22, we see that the older, less-educated employees did not follow the trends in society so much any more, whereas the older, more highly educated employees did keep up with them.

For the longer term, we can assume that as long as the wealth of nations grows, the individualism of those nations' citizens will increase. If there is to be any convergence between national cultures it should be on this dimension. The strong relationship between national wealth and individualism is undeniable, with the arrow of causality directed, as argued above, from wealth to individualism. Countries that have achieved fast economic development have experienced shifts toward individualism. Economic development affects the lives of families, where collectivist and individualist values are transferred. With increasing wealth, family patterns shift from the extended to the nuclear family. Japan is an example: The Japanese press regularly publishes stories of breaches of traditional family solidarity. Care for the aged in the past was considered a task for the Japanese family, but provisions by the state have become necessary in cases where families have stopped fulfilling their traditional duties.[82]

Nevertheless, even at a level of per capita income equal to or larger than Western countries, Japanese society will very likely conserve distinctive collectivist elements in its family, school, and work spheres. The same holds for other Asian and European countries.[83] Yang (1988) divided shared psychological characteristics in a society into functional and nonfunctional ones. Only the characteristics functional for economic development will converge with such development; others are "purely stylistic, expressive, or terminal in nature" (p. 83). Moreover, some functional characteristics are still specific to developments taking place in the particular society only. Next to a noticeable convergence toward individualism under the influence of common economic and technological influences, relationships between the individual and the group continue and will continue to differ among, say, Britain, Germany, Spain, and Taiwan.[84] Cultures shift, but they shift in formation, so that the differences between them remain intact.

If economies were to level off into zero growth, individualism should stabilize. Threats to the common physical environment may also bring the increase in individualism to a halt; it is unlikely that it will increase forever. There may even be forces we don't know about yet that will reestablish collectivist ties between people. And as far as the poor countries of the world are concerned, there is no reason they should become more individualist as long as they remain poor.

So differences in values associated with the individualism/collectivism dimension will continue to exist and to play a big role in international affairs, such as in negotiations between rich and poor countries. The ind/col dimension accounts for many misunderstandings in intercultural encounters; some of these will be discussed in Chapter 9.

Statistical Analysis of Data Used in This Chapter

Calculating the Individualism Index by Country

The Power Distance Index and Uncertainty Avoidance Index described in Chapters 3 and 4, respectively, were each based on the country means for three questions in the IBM questionnaire. As I explained in Chapter 2, the two remaining indexes, for individualism and masculinity, were found in a different way. Both are based on the scores among IBM subsidiary employees in 40 countries on the same 14 "work goals" questions. Earlier, I had studied the validity of these questions: what it actually is that the scores measure (see Hofstede, 1976b). The 14 questions are listed in Exhibit 5.11, together with the short names used throughout this and the next chapter to refer to them. Eight additional work goals, also in Exhibit 5.11, were used only in the first (1968-71) survey round.

Scores for all goals were standardized for each one-country, one-occupation subset of the data in order to eliminate acquiescence (see Chapter 2). They were subsequently averaged across seven occupational groups. Two matrixes were composed: one for the 14 goals used throughout 1968-73 for all 40 Category 1 countries (in this case the scores, after standardization, were averaged over the two survey rounds) and another matrix for all 22 goals used in 1968-71, limited to the 19 countries included at that time. The two matrices are reproduced in Appendix 3, Exhibits A3.1 and A3.3.

Factor analysis of the 14-goal, 40-country matrix produced two factors that together explained 46% of the variance. The two factors were of virtually equal strength even before rotation; the orthogonal rotation hardly affected the loadings. The results were as follows:

Factor 1 (variance 24%) Individual/collective	Factor 2 (variance 22%) Social/ego
Positive	Positive
.86 Personal time	.69 Manager
.49 Freedom	.69 Cooperation
.46 Challenge (2nd loading)	.59 Desirable area
.35 Desirable area (2)	.48 Employment security
Negative	Negative
−.82 Training	−.70 Earnings
−.69 Physical conditions	−.59 Recognition
−.63 Use of skills	−.56 Advancement
−.40 Benefits	−.54 Challenge
−.37 Cooperation (2)	−.40 Use of skills (2)

Exhibit 5.11 Work Goals Used in IBM Studies and Replications

Number[a]		Short Name	Full Questionnaire Wording
Fourteen Work Goals Used in All Questionnaires 1968-73			
A5	(15)	Challenge	Have challenging work to do—work from which you can get a personal sense of accomplishment
A6	(18)	Desirable area	Live in an area desirable to you and your family
A7	(1)	Earnings	Have an opportunity for high earnings
A8	(6)	Cooperation	Work with people who cooperate well with one another
A9	(9)	Training	Have training opportunities (to improve your skills or learn new skills)
A10	(4)	Benefits	Have good fringe benefits
A11	(12)	Recognition	Get the recognition you deserve when you do a good job
A12	(11)	Physical conditions	Have good physical working conditions (good ventilation and lighting, adequate work space, etc.)
A13	(7)	Freedom	Have considerable freedom to adapt your own approach to the job
A14	(2)	Employment security	Have the security that you will be able to work for your company as long as you want to
A15	(17)	Advancement	Have an opportunity for advancement to higher-level jobs
A16	(19)	Manager	Have a good working relationship with your manager
A17	(21)	Use of skills	Fully use your skills and abilities on the job
A18	(5)	Personal time	Have a job which leaves you sufficient time for your personal or family life
Eight Work Goals Used in 1968-71 Questionnaires Only			
C1	(3)	Position security	Have the security that you will not be transferred to a less desirable job
C2	(8)	Efficient department	Work in a department which is run efficiently
C3	(10)	Contribute to company	Have a job which allows you to make a real contribution to the success of your company
C4	(13)	Successful company	Work in a company which is regarded in your country as successful
C5	(14)	Modern company	Work in a company which stands in the forefront of modern technology
C6	(16)	Friendly atmosphere	Work in a congenial and friendly atmosphere
C7	(20)	Up-to-dateness	Keep up to date with the technical developments relating to your work
C8	(22)	Day-to-day learning	Have a job on which there is a great deal of day-to-day learning
Eight Work Goals Added in the 1989-94 Student Surveys			
3		Stress-free	Have little tension and stress on the job
4		Consulted	Be consulted by your direct superior in his/her decisions
10		Contribute[b]	Make a real contribution to the success of your company or organization
12		Country	Serve your country
15		Variety	Have an element of variety and adventure in the job
16		Prestige[c]	Work in a prestigious, successful company or organization
17		Helping	Have an opportunity for helping other people
18		Clear job	Work in a well-defined job situation where the requirements are clear

a. See Appendix 1. Numbers in parentheses indicate the order of the questions in the 1968-71 questionnaire.
b. Compare C3.
c. Compare C4.

All goals loaded .35 or more on one of the two factors. High scorers on Factor 1 were the United States, Australia, and Great Britain; low scorers were Venezuela, Colombia, and Pakistan. High scorers on Factor 2 were Sweden, Norway, Netherlands, and Denmark; low scorers were Japan, Austria, and Venezuela.

Factor analysis of the 22-goal, 19-country matrix produced also two interpretable factors that together explained 43% of the variance. After orthogonal rotation the loadings over .35 were as follows:

Factor 1 (variance 23%) Ego/social	Factor 2 (variance 20%) Individual/company
Positive	*Positive*
.90 Advancement	.79 Freedom
.68 Earnings	.69 Personal time
.61 Challenge	.65 Up-to-dateness
.50 Recognition (2nd)	.48 Training
.45 Use of skills	.43 Cooperation (2nd)
.44 Modern company	.40 Physical conditions
Negative	*Negative*
−.79 Friendly atmosphere	−.88 Successful company
−.78 Desirable area	−.83 Contribute to company
−.70 Manager	−.53 Recognition
−.66 Cooperation	−.43 Modern company (2nd)

No loading of at least .35 on any factor:
  Benefits (−.32 on Factor 2)
  Efficient department (−.31 on Factor 1)
  Employment security (−.22 on Factor 1)
  Position security (.21 on Factor 2)
  Day-to-day learning (.20 on Factor 2)

Factor 1 opposed Austria, Germany, and Ireland to Sweden, Yugoslavia, and Norway; Factor 2 opposed Finland, Spain, and Denmark to Greece, Turkey, and Sweden.

Factor 2 in the 14-goal, 40-country matrix and Factor 1 in the 22-goal, 19-country matrix were virtually identical, except for a reversal of the sign. The factor scores for the 19 countries appearing in both matrices (columns SOC in Exhibit A3.1 and EGO in Exhibit A3.3) correlate with rho = .92***. In Chapter 6 this factor will be related to masculinity (ego pole) and femininity (social pole); the factor scores for the 14-goal, 40-country matrix became the basis for computing the Masculinity Index.

Factor 1 in the 14-goal, 40-country matrix differed from Factor 2 in the 22-goal, 19-country matrix because in the former the three "company" goals that form one pole of the 22-goal factor were missing. The two factors share one pole but not the other, and their factor scores are uncorrelated (rho = .19 across the 19 overlapping countries). In the 14-goal solutions, personal time and freedom now oppose training plus some other goals that have a somewhat passive, being-looked-after flavor (see the opposition between "challenge" and "use of skills"). Rather than individual/company, I have labeled the 14-goal, 40-country Factor 1 *individual/collective*. Factor scores on this axis have been used as a basis for computing the Individualism Index. These factor scores are listed in Exhibit A3.1 in the column INV.

In order to bring the values for the Individualism Index in a range between 0 and 100, I used the formula IDV = 50 + 25 × INV, in which INV is the factor score. The values found for IDV are listed in Exhibit 5.1.

Nine work goals had loadings of .35 and over on the individual/collective factor: on the positive side, personal time, freedom, challenge, and desirable area; on the negative side, training, physical conditions, use of skills, benefits, and cooperation. As the zero-order contribution of each work goal to the variance in the factor is determined by the square of the loading, the goals with the lower loadings hardly affected the dimension. In the analysis earlier in this chapter only the six goals with loadings over .45 were considered.

IDV scores for the Category 2 countries (those added after the appearance of the 1980 edition of *Culture's Consequences*) had to be computed in a different way, as these countries were not part of the 14-goal, 40-country factor analysis. Computing factor scores for cases that were not part of the original factor analysis is possible via the *factor score coefficients* for each factor on each variable. For the base data and the resulting INV values, see Appendix 3, Exhibit A3.2; for the calculation procedure and the factor score coefficients, see Appendix 4.

Work Goal Dimensions by Occupation

In the IBM surveys between 1968 and 1971, the 22 work goals were scored by more than 50,000 employees in virtually all occupations in the company.[85] The matrix of standardized mean scores on the 22 goals for 38 major occupational groups is shown in Appendix 3, Exhibit A3.4. The data in this exhibit are based on totals for 15 European countries (the non-European countries were surveyed in 1967 with a slightly different list of work goals).[86]

In a factor analysis of the occupational goal data two factors explained 54% of the variance.

After orthogonal rotation, the following loadings over .35 were found:

Factor 1 (variance 27%) Intrinsic/extrinsic	Factor 2 (variance 27%) Social/ego
Positive	*Positive*
.80 Freedom	.88 Manager
.73 Challenge	.86 Cooperation
.68 Contribute to company	.84 Friendly atmosphere
.55 Successful company	.74 Efficient department
.54 Use of skills	.58 Physical conditions (2)
.40 Day-to-day learning	.41 Position security
Negative	*Negative*
−.79 Benefits	−.76 Up-to-dateness
−.72 Physical conditions	−.68 Modern company
−.65 Personal time	−.67 Advancement
−.62 Employment security	−.59 Training
−.59 Desirable area	−.50 Earnings (2)
−.50 Earnings	−.40 Day-to-day learning (2)
−.37 Recognition	

All goals loaded over .35 on one of the two factors. Factor 1 does not resemble the individual/collective factor across countries, but it opposes "intrinsic" to "extrinsic" goals, with job content on the positive pole, job context on the negative. High-scoring occupations on this factor were data processing sales managers and head office managers; low-scoring occupations were unskilled card plant personnel and skilled machine plant direct personnel. The factor is evidently related to education level.

Factor 2 closely resembles the social/ego factor across countries. High-scoring occupations were product development laboratory clerks and office secretaries and typists; low scorers were office products customer engineers and branch office systems engineers.

Exhibit 5.12 plots the 38 occupations according to their factor scores on the two occupational dimensions. Similar occupations cluster together:

- *Sales representatives* are both intrinsic and ego oriented.
- *Managers* tend to be intrinsic and vary between social (clerical managers) and ego oriented (sales managers).
- *Professionals* vary between intrinsic and extrinsic but are always ego oriented.
- *Technicians* are extrinsic and tend to be ego oriented.
- *Clerks* vary between intrinsic and extrinsic but are always social oriented.

- *Unskilled workers* are extrinsic and tend to be social oriented.

This two-dimensional picture of the work goal orientations of the various occupations is richer than the one-dimensional distinction common in the U.S. literature of the 1960s and 1970s.[87] This ranks occupations from upper right to lower left in Exhibit 5.12, mixing the extrinsic and social dimensions.

Country IDV Scores and Other IBM Survey Questions

The other IBM survey questions correlated with IDV could be identified in the overall factor analysis shown in Chapter 2. However, as PDI and IDV loaded on the same factor, it is necessary to separate the questions into those more related to PDI and those more related to IDV.

More related to IDV ($r = .64***$) than to PDI was the mean raw work goal importance score across 14 goals (IMP; see Appendix 3, Exhibit A3.1). I consider it a measure of the respondents' acquiescence, a yes-man-ship in answering the work goal questions, and I have treated it as another variable in the analysis.

All other survey questions loading on the IDV-PDI factor are listed in Exhibit 5.13, divided into those related primarily to IDV, those related primarily to PDI, and those related to both. The split has been made on the basis of partial correlations, holding either IDV or PDI constant. The questions related primarily to PDI were referred to in Chapter 3.

The correlations of IDV with the work goals A18, A9, A12, A17, A5, and A13 are obvious because these are the goals the IDV score was based on. This leaves only the questions B24, B59, B52, and B53 as additional correlates of IDV. In addition, we can read in Appendix 2 that question B57 (which in the factor analyses loaded on other factors) was in fact more strongly correlated with IDV ($r = -.44**$) than with any other of the four indexes. As for the C questions (discontinued in 1971 or before), the following had their highest correlations with IDV (Appendix 2): C11 ($r = .70***$), C15 ($r = .63***$), and C17 ($r = .70***$).

Earlier Studies of Work Goals in IBM

The earliest publication about IBM work goal data was a *Harvard Business Review* article by Sirota and Greenwood (1971). They covered 25 countries, three occupations, and 14 goals, ranked for eliminating acquiescence. Their main conclusion was that there *were* national differences, but

Exhibit 5.12. Factor Scores for 38 Occupations on Two Factor Axes: Intrinsic-Extrinsic and Social-Ego

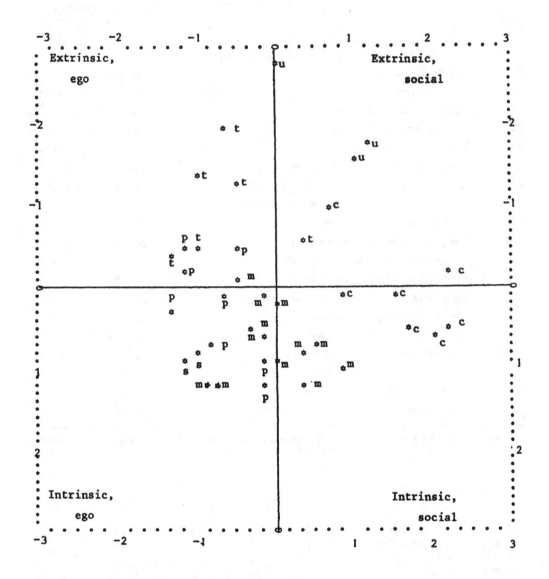

NOTE: m = managers, s = sales representatives, p = professionals, t = technicians and skilled workers, c = clerks, and u = unskilled workers.

the author did not have a framework to analyze these. They divided the 25 countries into five clusters with more or less similar goal rankings, and some leftover countries that did not fit into any cluster. Their countries were mainly wealthy, except for those from Latin America; they observed that the latter stressed individual achievement less and benefits more, but this was their only implicit reference to the individualism dimension. Sirota and Greenwood's data reflect more

clearly the masculinity/femininity distinction (see Chapter 6).[88]

In one study, I used work goal data to show the profile of one particular country, the Netherlands, in comparison to a European mean (Hofstede, 1976c). The comparison was done separately for each of the 21 occupations for which data were available. The sign test on the 21 occupational score differences between the Netherlands and Europe showed that for 18 out of the 22 work

Exhibit 5.13 Correlations Across 40 Countries of Country Scores for Questions Loading on Factor 1

Question Number	Question	Correlation With	
		IDV	PDI
	Correlated With Individualism, Not With Power Distance		
A18	Importance personal time	.86 (.75)	−.64 (−.16)
A9	Low importance training	−.83 (−.75)	.50 (−.15)
A12	Low importance physical conditions	−.69 (−.60)	.43 (−.06)
B24	Does not prefer foreign company	.68 (.55)	−.48 (−.04)
A17	Low importance use of skills	−.63 (−.49)	.47 (.09)
B59	Staying with one company not desirable	.61 (.45)	−.48 (−.12)
A5	Importance challenge	.46 (.38)	−.28 (.05)
	Correlated With Power Distance, Not With Individualism		
B46	Employees not afraid to disagree	.58 (.00)	−.87 (−.80)
A55	Low percentage perceived manager 1 or 2	−.50 (.18)	.85 (.80)
A54	High percentage preferred manager 3 (1967-69)	.66 (.25)	−.84 (−.72)
B56	Employees should not participate more	.41 (−.05)	−.65 (−.57)
B55	Employees do not lose respect for consultative manager	.35 (.03)	−.49 (−.38)
B58	Corporation not responsible for society	.16 (−.10)	−.34 (−.32)
	Equally Correlated With Individualism and Power Distance		
B52	Corporation not responsible for employees	.62 (.35)	−.63 (−.37)
B53	Interesting work not as important as earnings	.60 (.31)	−.63 (−.38)
A13	Importance freedom	.49 (.24)	−.50 (−.27)
A15	(Low importance advancement)	−.19 (−.07)	.21 (.11)

NOTE: For 40 cases, the .05 significance level for *r* is at .27. Figures outside parentheses are zero-order correlations; figures in parentheses are partial correlations: for IDV, while controlling for PDI; for PDI, while controlling for IDV.

goals the Dutch scored consistently different from the European mean, regardless of their occupations. Later, I followed the same procedure for two other countries, Norway and Sweden. The results for the three countries are compared in Exhibit 5.14.

Exhibit 5.14 uses the data for all available occupations, not only for the matched sample of seven occupations on which the other country comparisons in this book were based. It confirms that compared with respondents in other European countries, respondents in the Netherlands scored relatively individualist and those in Sweden relatively collectivist, with Norway in between (on IDV Norway scored marginally lower than Sweden, but in 1970 Sweden was still much wealthier; see Exhibit 5.9). On the masculinity dimension all three countries scored definitely to the low, feminine side (see Chapter 6).

Straight Replications of the IBM Survey

Elite alumni from the Salzburg Seminar. Exhibit 5.15 shows Hoppe's Salzburg alumni scores for IDV, just as Exhibits 3.13 and 4.10 list the scores for PDI and UAI. There is a highly significant correlation of $r = .69**$ between Hoppe's IDV scores and those computed for IBM. The Salzburg alumni on average scored at about the same level of IDV as the IBM employees.

As in the cases of PDI and UAI, I used Hoppe's data for computing best estimates for the scores on the IBM scale, by regressing the IBM scores on the Salzburg scores. The regressed IDV scores were within 16 points of the IBM scores for 15 countries; the outliers were Spain (+23), Portugal (+20), and Turkey (+18). As suggested in Chapter 3, this may have something to do with the selection and self-selection criteria for Salzburg partic-

Exhibit 5.14 Comparison of Standardized Importance Scores for 22 Work Goals, Between Each of Three Countries and the 15-Country European Average

Individualism Goals	Sign of Difference With European Average			Masculinity Goals	Sign of Difference With European Average		
	NET	NOR	SWE		NET	NOR	SWE
Positive pole				*Positive pole*			
Freedom	+		–	Advancement	–	–	–
Personal time	+		–	Earnings	–	–	–
Up-to-dateness	–		–	Challenge	–		–
Training				Recognition	–	–	–
Cooperation	+	+	+	Use of skills	–		–
Physical conditions	+	+		Modern company	–	–	
Position security		+	+	Employment security	–		
Day-to-day learning			+	Efficient department	–	+	
Benefits	+		+	Cooperation	+	+	+
Modern company	–	–		Manager	+	+	+
Recognition	–	–	–	Desirable area	+	+	+
Contribute to company	–	–	+	Friendly atmosphere			+
Successful company	–	–	+				
Negative pole				*Negative pole*			

SOURCE: For the Netherlands data, Hofstede (1973, p. 345); the Norway and Sweden data have not been published previously.

NOTE: Significance has been determined through comparison of all available occupations separately and application of the sign test for consistency across occupations. Numbers of occupations compared are as follows: Netherlands, 21; Norway, 15; Sweden, 26. The classification of goals into "individualism" and "masculinity" follows the result of the ecological factor analysis for 22 goals and 19 (mostly European) countries.

ipants from these countries; they seem to have been an exceptionally individualist selection from the local population. The Hoppe study provided an estimated IDV score of 59 for Malta.

Higher-income consumers surveyed by the EMS 97. Exhibit 5.15 also shows the IDV scores found in the European Media and Marketing Survey 1997 by the market research agency Inter/View International. This survey included the 20 questions of the VSM 94 (Appendix 4). The VSM 94 questions and formula differ from those used in IBM. Across the 15 overlapping countries the IDV scores from the IBM employees in 1970 and the EMS consumers in 1997 were correlated with $r = .60**$. These data could also be used to compute best estimates for the scores on the IBM scale, by regressing the IBM IDV scores on the EMS scores. For 13 countries the EMS scores

were within 11 points of the IBM scores; the outliers were Portugal (+33) and Germany (–18).

Commercial airline pilots surveyed by Helmreich and Merritt (1998). This survey was described in Chapter 3. For the IDV scores, see Exhibit 5.16. Valid returns ranged from 39 for Argentina to 8,654 for the United States. Across the 21 overlapping countries, the pilots scored an average IDV of 141, 86 points above the IBM employees from the same countries. The IDV scores of the countries in the two studies were correlated with $r = .70**$; the IDV scores from the airline pilots and from Hoppe's elites were correlated across the 10 overlapping countries with $r = .83**$. Again the data could be used to compute best estimates for the scores on the IBM scale, through regression of the IBM IDV scores on the pilots' scores. For 14 countries the pilots' scores

Exhibit 5.15 Individualism Index Scores Computed from Surveys of Elites (Hoppe, 1990) and Consumer Market Research (EMS 97)

Countries in Order of Original IDV	Original IDV	n	Hoppe, Elites		n	EMS, Consumers	
			Raw IDV	Regressed[a]		Raw IDV	Regressed[a]
United States	91	157	90	80			
Great Britain	89	194	91	81	544	106	78
Netherlands	80	139	78	71	337	91	69
Italy	76	183	63	60	293	90	69
Belgium	75	47	72	67	270	90	69
Denmark	74	41	64	61	1,111	107	78
Sweden	71	71	90	80	534	102	75
France	71	47	63	60	661	93	89
Ireland	70	48	54	54	100	97	73
Norway	69	64	84	76	447	97	73
Switzerland	68	57	76	70	153	92	70
Germany	67	142	62	60	228	55	49
Finland	63	59	84	76	486	73	59
Austria	55	74	66	63	343	66	55
Spain	51	75	82	74	599	71	58
Turkey	37	72	55	44			
Greece	35	41	28	35			
Portugal	27	49	45	47	192	74	60
Malta		30	61	59			
Total n		1,590			6,680		
Mean (elites)	64.9		69.3[b]	64.9			
SD (elites)	17.7		17.1[b]	12.3			
Mean (consumers)	67.1					86.9	67.1
SD (consumers)	14.4					15.5	8.7
Correlation with IBM IDV							
Product-moment			.69**			.60**	
Spearman rank			.54*			.62**	

SOURCES: For Hoppe, same questions and formulas as used in IBM. For EMS 97, questions and formulas according to VSM 94 (see text). Data copyright Inter/View International, Amsterdam, used with permission. See also De Mooij (2001).

a. Predicted from regression of IBM scores on raw new scores.
b. Without Malta.
*p = .05; **p = .01; ***p = .001.

were within 16 points of the IBM scores; this time the outliers were Taiwan (+34), Argentina (+26), Japan (+24), and Mexico (+24), and Italy (−32), Germany (−23), and the United States (−21). The pilots' study provided an estimated IDV score for Morocco (MRC): 46.

Students surveyed with a work goals questionnaire. Hofstede et al. (1996) analyzed scores on 22 work goals obtained between 1989 and 1994 from about 1,000 students divided into 10 samples. The introductory question had been changed to: "Imagine the job you would like to get after graduation. In choosing an ideal job, how important would it be to you to . . . ?" The goals included the 14 used in all IBM surveys (Exhibit 5.11), with small adaptations of wording, plus 8 new goals listed at the bottom of Exhibit 5.11. Four

Exhibit 5.16 Individualism Index Scores Based on Survey of Airline Pilots (Helmreich & Merritt, 1998, p. 249)

Countries in Order of Original IDV	Original IDV	n^a	Raw IDV	Regressed[b]
United States	91	8,654 (10)	152	70
Australia	90	640 (2)	158	78
Great Britain	89	557 (1)[c]	154	73
New Zealand	79	485 (1)	155	74
Italy	76	517 (1)	131	44
Denmark	74	243 (1)	143	59
Sweden	71	443 (1)	157	77
Ireland	70	420 (1)	147	64
Norway	69	216 (1)	149	66
Switzerland	68	211 (2)	145	61
Germany	67	228 (1)	131	44
South Africa	65	238 (1)	152	70
Japan	46	51 (1)	152	70
Argentina	46	39 (1)	153	72
Brazil	38	467 (2)	126	37
Greece	35	65 (1)[d]	127	38
Philippines	32	120 (1)	133	46
Mexico	30	167 (1)	139	54
Malaysia	26	801 (1)	118	27
Korea (South)	18	176 (1)	114	22
Taiwan	17	499 (2)	137	51
Morocco		60 (1)	133	46
United Arab Emirates		145 (1)	—[e]	
Total n		15,454 (36)		
Mean	57.0		141.6[f]	57.0
SD	24.2		13.2[f]	16.9
Correlation with IBM				
IDV				
Product-moment			.70***	
Spearman rank			.67***	

a. Figures in parentheses are the numbers of airlines participating.
b. Predicted from regression of IBM scores on raw new scores.
c. British pilots in Hong Kong.
d. Greek Cyprus.
e. No data published.
f. Without Morocco.
*p = .05; **p = .01; ***p = .001.

samples were from Eastern European countries not in the IBM set. Students in Estonia and Russia had been surveyed just before the fall of communism, students in Czechia and Romania just after. The other samples were from Belgium, West Germany, the Netherlands, and the United States. The Belgians were divided into French and Dutch speakers; the Dutch into two subsamples, having been surveyed with either an English-language or a Dutch-language questionnaire; the Americans were surveyed during a study semester in the Netherlands. The students' field of study was mostly, but not in all cases, business administration. The samples were thus poorly matched. Scores for IDV and MAS were computed using the simplified method from the VSM 82. Across the countries also covered in IBM (five, as for the IBM sample separate scores for the Dutch- and French-speaking Belgians were available; see Chapter 2), the IDV scores for the students were correlated with IDV in IBM with $r = -.98**$ and the MAS scores with MAS in IBM with $r = .72$ ($p = .086$). Beware, the correlation of IDV with the student scores was *negative*! A comparison of the factor structures for the items in IBM and in the student study showed that this was due to the goal "physical conditions" carrying a connotation for the students that was opposite to the one it had for the IBM population.

Results of Other
Surveys Correlated With IDV

Samples of elementary school teachers and of university students in 23 countries scoring the Schwartz Values Survey. The questionnaire consists of 56 items. Schwartz used the multivariate technique of smallest-space analysis, an alternative to factor analysis developed by the Israeli statistician Louis Guttman (1968) that is very popular in Israel.[89] This analysis produces two-dimensional maps of the positions of the values relative to each other. Schwartz found one two-dimensional map for the individual respondent level on which he clustered the 56 values into 10 categories (see Chapter 1). Schwartz also performed an analysis at the level of national cultures, using the mean scores from 86 samples for 38 national or subnational cultures. This time he found a somewhat different two-dimensional map on which he clustered the same 56 values into 7 categories: conservatism, hierarchy, mastery, affective autonomy, intellectual autonomy, egalitarian commitment, and harmony (Schwartz, 1994, p. 102). He published the mean importance scores for these categories in 38 teacher samples. These scores for the 23 countries overlapping with the IBM set and their correlations with the IBM indexes are listed in Exhibit 5.17. Five of the seven categories were significantly correlated with IDV, one with MAS (see Chapter 6) and one with UAI (already mentioned in Chapter 4). The categories correlated with IDV were also, and sometimes more strongly, correlated with 1990

GNP/capita. Across 14 countries for which long-term orientation scores were available, hierarchy was positively and affective autonomy negatively correlated with LTO; see Chapter 7. The correlations with PDI did not reach significance, but in a table of correlations published by Schwartz (1994, p. 109) himself, marginally significant correlations are shown with PDI for conservatism ($r = -.45*$) and for affective autonomy ($r = .46*$).[90] Schwartz also showed correlations for the student samples, across 22 overlapping countries. The values were as follows: conservatism, $r_{IDV} = -.66***$, $r_{PDI} = .70***$; hierarchy, not significant; affective autonomy, $r_{IDV} = .85***$, $r_{PDI} = -.83***$; intellectual autonomy, $r_{IDV} = .48*$, $r_{PDI} = -.49**$; egalitarian commitment, $r_{IDV} = .45*$, $r_{PDI} = -.47*$.

Inglehart's (1997) factor analysis of country scores from the 1990-93 World Values Survey. The WVS public opinion survey program covered 43 countries with mostly 1,000 or more respondents per country, 60,000 in total. Of the 43, 27 countries overlapped with the IBM set. Inglehart factor analyzed country mean scores for 47 variables, summarizing some 100 from the more than 350 questions in the WVS. Two strong factors explained 51% of the variance in the country scores. Inglehart did not publish factor loadings or country scores on the two dimensions, but these can be read from 2×2 plots in his book.[91] Countries excluded in Exhibit 5.18 because they were missing in the IBM set are mainly those from Eastern Europe: Belarus, Bulgaria, Czechoslovakia, East Germany, Estonia, Hungary, Latvia, Lithuania, Poland, Romania, and Russia (for Russia, Inglehart et al. showed two scores, one for Moscow and one for the rest of the country). Also excluded were China, Iceland, Northern Ireland, and South Africa. The South African data were not used because the IBM scores refer to the white minority only and the WVS scores to the total, mainly black, population.

Inglehart's first dimension, "well-being versus survival," produced significant zero-order correlations with all five of my indexes, but the correlation with 1990 GNP/capita was still marginally stronger. In a stepwise regression with only the four IBM indexes both strong IDV and weak MAS made sizable independent contributions toward explaining this dimension; small PDI made a modest third-order contribution. Inglehart's second dimension, "secular-rational versus traditional authority," was even more strongly correlated with GNP/capita; in a stepwise regression with only the IBM indexes small PDI was the only remaining correlate. Using ranks of country

Exhibit 5.17 Product-Moment Correlations of Schwartz's Culture-Level Scores on Seven Value Dimensions for Teachers from 23 (14) Countries With IBM Indexes

Countries in Order of 1990 GNP/ Capita	Country Scores on Schwartz's Dimensions						
	Conservatism	Hierarchy	Mastery	Affective Autonomy	Intellectual Autonomy	Egalitarian Commitment	Harmony
Switzerland (F)	3.25	2.20	4.18	4.24	5.33	5.19	4.50
Finland	3.84	2.03	3.63	3.51	4.62	5.26	4.54
Japan	3.87	2.86	4.27	3.54	4.68	4.69	4.07
Germany	3.42	2.27	4.07	4.03	4.75	5.37	4.42
Denmark	3.64	1.86	3.97	4.01	4.58	5.52	4.16
United States	3.90	2.39	4.34	3.65	4.20	5.03	3.70
France	3.35	2.16	3.89	4.41	5.15	5.45	4.31
Netherlands	3.68	2.26	3.98	3.51	4.44	5.39	3.98
Australia	4.06	2.36	4.09	3.50	4.12	4.98	4.05
Italy	3.82	1.69	4.08	2.95	4.60	5.57	4.80
New Zealand	3.73	2.38	4.23	3.98	4.36	5.15	3.99
Hong Kong	4.04	2.83	4.18	3.11	4.08	4.85	3.34
Singapore	4.38	2.75	3.93	3.04	3.68	4.79	3.72
Spain	3.42	2.03	4.11	3.97	4.90	5.55	4.53
Israel	4.08	2.69	4.06	3.62	4.31	4.78	3.01
Greece	3.68	2.01	4.53	3.96	4.09	5.35	4.39
Taiwan	4.31	2.85	4.11	3.21	3.93	4.68	4.17
Portugal	3.76	2.08	4.25	3.54	4.12	5.62	4.29
Brazil	3.97	2.64	4.16	3.30	4.13	4.92	4.02
Mexico	4.03	2.35	4.34	3.23	4.20	4.99	4.67
Malaysia	4.46	2.43	4.34	3.16	4.07	4.66	3.50
Poland[a]	4.31	2.53	4.00	3.13	4.09	4.82	4.10
Turkey	4.27	3.30	3.90	3.25	4.12	5.12	4.26
Thailand	4.22	3.32	3.99	3.62	4.08	4.34	3.93
Zimbabwe[a]	4.21	3.14	4.62	3.85	3.82	4.48	3.42
China[a]	3.97	3.70	4.73	3.32	4.27	4.49	3.71
Product-moment correlation with							
IDV	−.55**	−.53**	−.17	.45*	.53**	.49**	.17
MAS	.03	.13	.53**	−.13	.06	−.26	.06
UAI	−.33	−.09	.27	.25	.27	.27	.45*
PDI	.31	.25	.30	−.34	−.19	−.29	.08
Order of contribution in stepwise regression on 4 IBM indexes							
1	−IDV $R^2 = .31$	−IDV $R^2 = .28$	MAS $R^2 = .28$	IDV $R^2 = .20$	IDV $R^2 = .28$	IDV $R^2 = .24$	UAI $R^2 = .20$
2	−UAI $R^2 = .46$						
Product-moment correlation with							
LTO (14 countries)	.23	.56*	.23	−.53*	.29	−.32	−.30
1990 GNP/capita	−.65***	−.52**	−.39*	.46**	.72***	.46**	.29

SOURCE: Data from Schwartz (1994, pp. 112-115).
a. Only for correlation with LTO.
$*p = .05; **p = .01; ***p = .001.$

Exhibit 5.18 Product-Moment Correlations of Inglehart's Two Key Cultural Dimensions With IBM Indexes

Countries in Order of 1990 GNP/Capita	Score on Factor 1 (30% of variance): Well-Being vs. Survival	Score on Factor 2 (21% of variance): Secular-Rational vs. Traditional Authority
Switzerland	.16	.02
Finland	.27	.12
Japan	−.05	.18
Sweden	.31	.16
Norway	.21	.09
Germany	.09	.19
Denmark	.28	.09
United States	.17	−.11
Canada	.18	−.01
France	.04	.01
Austria	.05	.00
Netherlands	.30	.13
Italy	.08	−.04
Great Britain	.13	.01
Belgium	.11	.02
Spain	.04	−.07
Ireland	.10	−.20
South Korea	−.09	.05
Portugal	−.05	−.05
Slovenia	−.13	.06
Brazil	−.06	−.26
Mexico	.01	−.11
Argentina	.01	−.12
Chile	−.06	−.23
Turkey	−.11	−.12
India	−.19	−.19
Nigeria (WAF)	−.08	−.42
Product-moment correlation with		
PDI	−.72***	−.56**
IDV	.74***	.49**
MAS	−.39*	−.11
UAI	−.55**	−.11
Order of contribution in stepwise regression on 4 IBM indexes		
1	IDV $R^2 = .54$	−PDI $R^2 = .31$
2	—MAS $R^2 = .74$	
3	—PDI $R^2 = .82$	
Product-moment correlation with		
LTO (11 countries)	−.53*	.19
1990 GNP/capita	.74***	.76***

SOURCE: Data from diagram in Inglehart (1997, p. 93).
*$p = .05$; **$p = .01$; ***$p = .001$.

Exhibit 5.19 Factor Scores in Ecological Analysis of IRGOM Life Goals Data Versus IBM Indexes

Country or Area	Bass IRGOM Data: Factor Scores on	
	Hedonism-Skill	Assertiveness-Service
United States	.32	.58
Great Britain	1.42	−.17
Netherlands	.02	−1.14
Belgium	−.31	−.18
Germany, Austria	−.27	1.71
Scandinavia	1.35	−.54
France	.10	−.30
Italy	1.40	.49
Spain, Portugal	−.42	−1.02
Latin America	−.92	−.44
India	−1.72	−.92
Japan	−.97	1.92
Spearman rank correlation with		
PDI	−.66**	−.24
UAI	−.49	.15
IDV	.76**	.18
MAS	−.03	.84***
1970 GNP/capita	.55*	.27

SOURCE: The matrix of base data is taken from Hofstede (1978, tab. 4). Since then, the base data were published also in Bass and Burger (1979).
NOTE: Signs of factor scores for IRGOM data have been reversed so that positive scores mean high importance of goals with positive loading on the factor.
*p = .05; **p = .01; ***p = .001.

scores rather than the scores themselves (to eliminate the effect of extremes, such as Nigeria) did not change the conclusions at all.

Samples of managers in 12 countries doing the IRGOM Life Goals exercise. Scores were available for 3,082 managers from 12 countries or country groups (Bass & Burger, 1979). There was no problem of acquiescence, as the respondents answered by ranking; the data were therefore ipsative (that is, they added up to a constant for each country). My ecological factor analysis of the country data matrix produced two strong factors that together explained 54% of the variance. After orthogonal rotation, the following loadings resulted:

Factor 1 (variance 28%) Hedonism-skill	**Factor 2** (variance 26%) Assertiveness-service
Positive	*Positive*
.87 Pleasure	.86 Leadership
.77 Security	.85 Independence
.72 Affection	.57 Self-realization
Negative	*Negative*
−.74 Expertness	−.92 Service
−.58 Prestige	−.56 Duty

No loading of .40 or over on either factor: wealth (−.20 on Factor 1).

The labels *hedonism-skill* and *assertiveness-service* are, of course, mine. "Security" in the Life Goals exercise was formulated as "to achieve a secure and stable position in work and financial situation," so it pertained to individual financial security.

Exhibit 5.19 lists the factor scores for the 12 countries or areas and their correlations with the IBM indexes and 1970 GNP/capita (where Bass combined countries into areas, I have weighted the IBM indexes and GNP/capita scores according to the population sizes of the countries). Hedonism-skill correlated strongly with IDV (rho = .76**) and assertiveness-service with MAS (rho = .84***).

Samples of 14-year-old school pupils in 11 countries or parts of countries scoring on Frenkel-Brunswik's (1948) "ethnocentrism" test. The test was originally designed for the individual level within the United States. Lambert and Klineberg (1967) used it for comparing countries in their study of "children's views of foreign peoples." They therefore committed a reverse ecological fallacy (see Chapter 1). The 13 items in the test were administered as part of interviews with 100 pupils per country. All questions were in the format: "Do you think . . . ?" (yes/no).

Five questions were scored negatively (no = ethnocentric):

1. People of different races and religions would get along better if they visited each other and shared things?
2. Our country is a lot better off because of the foreign races that live here?
5. It is interesting to be friends with someone who thinks or feels differently from the way you do?
7. Weak people deserve as much consideration from others as do strong people?
9. Teachers should try to find out what children want to do and not just tell them what to do?

Eight questions were scored positively (yes = ethnocentric):

3. That most of the other countries of the world are really against us, but are afraid to show it?
4. There will always be war, that it is part of human nature?
6. Girls should only learn things that are useful around the house?
8. That a person must watch out or else somebody will make a fool out of him?
10. There is only one right way to do anything?
11. That someday a flood or earthquake will destroy everybody in the whole world?
12. There are more contagious diseases now than ever before?
13. You can protect yourself from bad luck by carrying a charm or good luck piece?

So in fact only questions 1, 2, and 5 really dealt with ethnocentrism; the others are a hodgepodge of traditional versus modern views. It could as well be called a "modernity" questionnaire. The scores per respondent group were as follows: Bantus in South Africa, 47; Brazil, 41; Lebanon, 37; Turkey, 34; Israel, 33; West Germany, 30; France, 28; Japan, 23; French Canadians, 22; English Canadians, 20; United States, 18. Across 10 countries these scores rank correlated with rho = −.89*** with both IDV and 1970 GNP/capita, using IBM scores for Canada for the English Canadians, for East Africa for the Bantus, and for Arabic-speaking countries for Lebanon. The Bantu 1970 GNP/capita was estimated at U.S.$200. The "ethnocentrism" score for the French Canadians was not used; through regres-

sion the IDV score for the French Canadians could be estimated at 73.

Indexes at the
National Level Correlated With IDV

Schmitter's (1981) rankings on societal corporatism. Rankings for 15 European and North American countries on societal corporatism and its components, organizational centralization and associational monopoly, in Exhibit 5.20 were derived from a table in Schmitter (1981, p. 294). Organizational centralization was exclusively correlated with IDV (lower IDV, more centralization within interest organizations). Associational monopoly, on the other hand, was correlated with PDI and secondarily with MAS (stronger PDI and stronger MAS imply less monopoly for interest associations). The summary index of societal corporatism, which is the sum of the two components, is correlated primarily with IDV, secondarily with MAS, and tertiarily with PDI, in the same sense as its components.

Humana's (1992) world human rights ratings data. Exhibit 5.21 shows for 52 countries in the IBM set Humana's human rights ratings, and Exhibit 5.22 shows from the same source the per thousands of the national budget spent on health, education, and the military. Correlations with the four IBM indexes and with 1990 GNP/capita have been calculated across all countries, across the 25 wealthier countries (1990 GNP/capita > $4,800), and across the 27 poorer countries. In each case a stepwise multiple regression was run on the five variables. Across all countries the dominant explaining variable for the HR ratings was national wealth (GNP/capita), but across the wealthier countries the dominant variable was IDV. The same applied for health budgets. For education budgets, IDV was the dominant explaining variable even across all 52 countries. For the group of wealthy countries, however, IDV played no dominant role; in this case the country differences were explained by PDI and MAS—both were negatively related to education spending. For military budgets the (product-moment) correlations were calculated from the ranks of the figures in the column in order to limit the impact of some extreme cases (Israel, Iran). Nevertheless, only the group of wealthier countries produced significant correlations, GNP/capita being the dominant variable, but negatively (wealthier countries tended to spend less on their militaries)!

Exhibit 5.20 Country Index Rankings on Societal Corporatism Versus IBM Indexes and GNP/Capita

Countries in Order of IDV Scores	Organizational Centralization	Associational Monopoly	Societal Corporatism[a]
United States	11-15	7-11	10-12
Great Britain	11-15	12	14
Canada	11-15	7-11	10-12
Netherlands	2	7-11	6
Italy	11-15	13-15	15
Belgium	3	7-11	7
Denmark	8	1-2	3-5
Sweden	4-6	4-5	3-5
France	10	13-15	13
Ireland	11-15	7-11	11
Norway	4-6	1-2	2
Switzerland	7	13-15	9
Germany (F.R.)	9	6	8
Finland	4-6	4-5	3-5
Austria	1	3	1
Product moment correlation with			
PDI	.20	.65**	.56*
UAI	−.25	.37	.14
IDV	.57*	.41	.60**
MAS	.41	.52*	.53*
1980 GNP/capita	−.47*	−.20	−.43
Order of indexes in stepwise regression, cumulative R2, and sign of coefficient			
1	.32 +IDV	.42 +PDI	.36 +IDV
2		.65 +MAS	.63 +MAS
3			.75 +PDI

SOURCE: Schmitter (1981, p. 294).
NOTE: 1 = most corporatism, 15 = least corporatism.
a. Sum of organizational centralization and associational monopoly.
*$p = .05$; **$p = .01$; ***$p = .001$.

IDV Versus Eight Geographic, Economic, and Demographic Indicators

Exhibit 5.23 shows correlations and multiple and stepwise regressions of IDV with the indicators GNP, EGP, EGF, LAT, POP, PGR, PDN, and ORS (Exhibit 2.9) for all 50 countries, for the 28 poorer ones (1970 GNP/capita < $1,000), and for the 22 wealthier ones. IDV is mostly correlated, with opposite sign, with the same indicators as

PDI (Exhibit 3.20), only more so. The $r = .84***$ correlation between IDV and GNP is the strongest between any of the IBM indexes and any of the eight indicators; GNP/capita differences alone predicted 71% of the variance in IDV.

Geographic latitude (LAT) in the stepwise regression for 50 countries added another 7% to the prediction of IDV. Colder countries tend to be more individualist, even after wealth has been controlled for. As I have argued regarding PDI

Exhibit 5.21 Country Human Rights Ratings Versus IBM Indexes and GNP/Capita

Wealthy Countries 1990 GNP/Capita > $4,800			Poor Countries 1990 GNP/Capita < $4,800		
Country	IDV	HR Rating	Country	IDV	HR Rating
United States	91	90	South Africa	65	50
Australia	90	91	India	48	54
Great Britain	89	93	Argentina	46	84
Canada	80	94	Iran	41	22
Netherlands	80	98	Jamaica	39	72
New Zealand	79	98	Brazil	38	69
Italy	76	90	Egypt (ARA)	38	50
Belgium	75	96	Turkey	37	44
Denmark	74	98	Uruguay	36	90
Sweden	71	98	Philippines	32	72
France	71	94	Mexico	30	64
Ireland	70	94	Yugoslavia	27	55
Norway	69	97	Kenya (EAF)	27	46
Switzerland	68	96	Malaysia	26	61
Germany F.R.	67	98	Chile	23	80
Finland	63	99	Thailand	20	62
Austria	55	95	Nigeria (WAF)	20	49
Israel	54	76	Salvador	19	53
Spain	51	87	Peru	16	54
Japan	46	82	Costa Rica	15	90
Greece	35	87	Pakistan	14	42
Portugal	27	92	Indonesia	14	34
Hong Kong	25	79	Colombia	13	60
Singapore	20	60	Venezuela	12	75
South Korea	18	59	Panama	11	81
			Ecuador	8	83
			Guatemala	6	62

Significant zero-order product-moment correlations across 25 rich countries with

IDV	.73***
GNP90	.52**
PDI	−.48**
LTO (12 countries)	−.52*

Order in stepwise regression

1 IDV R^2 = .53

Significant zero-order product-moment correlations across 27 poor countries with

GNP90	.38*

Order in stepwise regression

None

Significant zero-order product-moment correlations across all 52 countries with

GNP90	.71***
IDV	.61***
PDI	−.56***

Order in stepwise regression

1   GNP90 R^2 = .50

SOURCE: Human rights ratings from Humana (1992, pp. xxvii-xix).
*p = .05; **p = .01; ***p = .001.

Exhibit 5.22 Shares of Budget Spent on Health, Education, and the Military Versus IBM Indexes and GNP/Capita

Wealthy Countries in Order of IDV 1990 GNP/Capita > $4,800				Poor Countries in Order of IDV 1990 GNP/Capita < $4,800			
	Per 1,000 of Budget for				Per 1,000 of Budget for		
Country	Health	Education	Military	Country	Health	Education	Military
United States	45	53	67	South Africa	6	46	39
Australia	51	51	27	India	9	34	35
Great Britain	53	53	50	Argentina	16	33	15
Canada	66	56	22	Iran	14	46	200
Netherlands	75	66	31	Jamaica	28	56	15
New Zealand	56	48	22	Brazil	24	34	9
Italy	45	40	23	Egypt (ARA)	11	55	89
Belgium	56	56	31	Turkey	5	28	49
Denmark	53	75	21	Uruguay	27	66	16
Sweden	80	76	29	Philippines	7	24	17
France	66	59	39	Mexico	22	28	6
Ireland	78	69	19	Yugoslavia	43	38	40
Norway	55	68	32	Kenya (EAF)	17	61	12
Switzerland	68	48	19	Malaysia	18	79	61
Germany F.R.	63	45	31	Chile	21	40	36
Finland	60	59	17	Thailand	10	32	40
Austria	84	60	13	Nigeria (WAF)	2	14	10
Israel	21	73	192	Salvador	8	19	37
Spain	43	32	23	Peru	8	22	16
Japan	49	50	10	Costa Rica	54	45	0
Greece	35	25	57	Pakistan	2	22	67
Portugal	57	43	33	Indonesia	7	23	25
Hong Kong		28		Colombia	8	28	10
Singapore	13	50	55	Venezuela	22	43	16
South Korea	4	30	52	Panama	57	54	14
				Ecuador	12	42	16
				Guatemala	7	18	13

Zero-order product-moment[a] correlations across 25 (24) rich countries with

IDV	.56**	.52**	−.22
GNP90	.50**	.44*	−.49**
PDI	−.41*	−.63**	.37*
UAI	−.17	−.41*	.12
MAS	−.03	−.39*	−.24
LTO (11 countries)	−.58*	−.61*	.53*

Order in stepwise regressions

1	IDV R^2 .32	−PDI R^2 .40	−GNP90 R^2 .24
2		−MAS R^2 .52	

Significant product-moment[a] correlations across 27 poor countries with

GNP90	.50*	.44*	−.02
MAS	−.35*	.00	−.12

Order in stepwise regressions: None

Significant product-moment[a] correlations across 52 (51) countries with

GNP90	.77***	.53***	.03
IDV	.68***	.56***	.19
PDI	−.61***	−.48***	−.03
UAI	−.12	−.37**	−.11

Order in stepwise regressions

1	GNP90 R^2 .60	IDV R^2 .31	None

SOURCE: Human rights ratings from Humana (1992).
a. Correlations with "military" are with the rank of the numbers in the column.
*$p = .05$; **$p = .01$; ***$p = .001$.

Exhibit 5.23 Product-Moment Correlations and Multiple and Stepwise Regression Across Countries of IDV Scores With Eight System-Level Indicators

	Zero-Order Correlations With IDV Scores Across		
Indicator	All 50 Countries	28 Poorer Countries	22 Wealthier Countries
GNP	.84***	.12	.66***
EGP	.03	.00	−.61**
EGF	−.11	−.16	−.18
LAT	.79***	.49**	.32
POP	.12	.31	.14
PGR	−.69***	−.29	.03
PDN	.00	−.07	−.03
ORS	.72***	.25	−.19
Squared multiple correlation with first seven R^2	.81	.40	.72
Order of indicators in stepwise regression, cumulative R^2, and sign of coefficient			
1	.71 + GNP	.24 + LAT	.44 + GNP
2	.78 + LAT		.59 − EGP

NOTE: The 22 wealthier countries are ARG, AUL, AUT, BEL, CAN, DEN, FIN, GBR, GER, GRE, IRE, ISR, ITA, JPN, NET, NOR, NZL, SPA, SWE, SWI, and USA. For definitions of indicators, see Exhibit 2.9.
*$p = .05$; **$p = .01$; ***$p = .001$.

(Exhibit 3.10), colder climates may force people to show more individual initiative in order to survive.

Ingham (1970) suggested a positive relationship between the individualism in an organization and its size. Organization size (ORS) and IDV were indeed correlated with $r = .72***$, but this was a consequence of both being related to GNP/capita. As ORS data were available only for the 40 Category 1 countries, ORS could not be included in the multiple regression of IDV on the indicators. In a multiple regression of ORS on the seven other indicators, 82% of the variance in ORS was, not surprisingly, explained by GNP/capita plus country population size.

Across the 22 wealthier countries IDV was strongly negatively related to economic growth in the 1960-70 period (EGP). This was not predicted. Exhibit 4.23 shows that economic growth rates of countries have varied dramatically over time. The strong negative relationship between IDV and economic growth was short-term; it did not extend to the 1965-90 period (EGF). The rela-

tionship between *wealth* (GNP) and IDV, on the other hand, is probably long-term and universal. The minus signs of the correlations between IDV and EGP plus EGF prove that over the 1960-90 period individualism followed wealth, and not the other way around.

Trends in IDV

In Exhibit 5.24, IDV values are plotted by age group, both for 1967-69 (dotted lines) and for 1971-73 (solid lines), for five large categories of IBM employees. This diagram is analogous to Exhibits 3.22 and 4.24, except that the vertical axes show index scores rather than scores for a single question. All five groups produced relatively flat age curves, in most cases inverted U-shaped. There was a strong zeitgeist effect for all age brackets for the managers and professionals and for the younger age brackets of technicians, clerks, and secretaries.

Exhibit 5.24. IDV Scores for Five Large Categories of Employees, Worldwide Data, by Age Bracket, in Two Survey Rounds

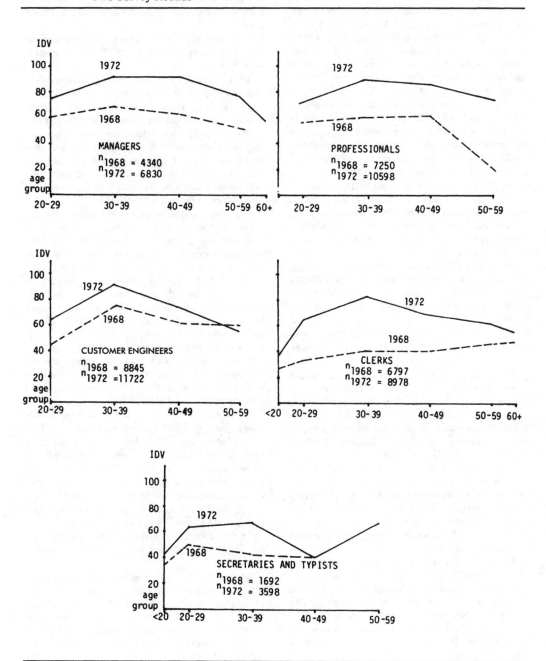

Notes

1. Differences in family structures are reflected in the words available in a language to describe kinship ties. See Chapter 1.

2. Uncertainty avoidance also plays a role, as it affects the need for having rules at all. Compare, for example, France versus Sweden in Exhibit 5.7.

3. Among other things, Whyte (1956) supplied a practical guide in a section titled "How to Cheat on Personality Tests" (p. 449).

4. The results of a survey of more than 1,800 readers of *Harvard Business Review* by Martin and Lodge (1975) showed a fear of collectivism as an alien but inescapable force. The researchers asked which ideology the readers expected to prevail in the United States in 1985: traditional individualism or a new "communitarianism." Some 70% of the respondents said that they preferred individualism, but 73% expected communitarianism to prevail in 1985.

5. Unlike in the cases of PDI and UAI, theoretical maximum and minimum scores for IDV cannot be given. IDV is based not on scores for separate questions but on factor scores; the factor analysis computation produces factor scores that rarely exceed ± 2.00; this corresponds to an index value range of 0-100.

6. For a thoughtful review, see Segall (1996).

7. In the first edition of *Culture's Consequences,* I cited this study as an example of the difference between "words" and "deeds" (Hofstede, 1980a, p. 18), which of course it is, but the explanation lies in neglecting the ingroup/out-group distinction.

8. A scale for measuring individualism and collectivism at the individual level was called the INDCOL scale, not the IDIALLO scale (e.g., Hui & Yee, 1994).

9. See, for example, Gelfand, Triandis, and Chan (1996).

10. For a goal-by-goal analysis of work goal differences among occupations, see Hofstede (1994b, chaps. 2-3).

11. In Chapter 2, Exhibit 2.4 shows the results of a number of ANOVAs (analyses of variance) carried out on the scores of individuals in IBM manufacturing plants. The seventh line concerns the difference between the importance of personal time and the importance of training (taking the difference eliminates acquiescence). In addition to the strong country effect there is a weak occupation effect, but strong gender and age effects. This, however, does not allow us to draw conclusions as to the relevance of the individualism concept for gender and age differences, as it uses only two of the goals, and these combined.

12. Slocum, Topichak, and Kuhn (1971) compared importance scores of Mexican versus U.S. glassworkers and found that the Mexicans scored everything much more important, which is in line with my data.

13. Across 53 countries and regions, IMP correlated not only with IDV ($r = .66***$, as mentioned) but also with 1970 GNP/capita ($r = .60***$), with PDI ($r = -.56***$), and with UAI ($r = -.33**$). However, in a stepwise multiple regression only IDV made a significant contribution.

14. The highest IMP scores (first column in Appendix 3, Exhibit A3.1), and so the least acquiescence, are found for Finland (IMP 2.33). To Professor Osmo Wiio from Finland, who did extensive survey research, I owe the remark that Finns seem to be a nation of flip-flops; they readily choose extreme answers on survey questions.

15. There is no correlation between the country mean scores for this belief (which is formulated as an

ideological statement) and the importance of "earnings" as a personal work goal (A7). We see again the difference between a value "as the desirable" and "as the desired."

16. I refer here to Pearson product-moment correlation, or Spearman rank if the results from the other study show extreme scores.

17. For details, see the first edition of *Culture's Consequences* (Hofstede, 1980a, figs. 5.13-5.14).

18. "Have good physical conditions" was omitted, as physical conditions were supposed to be standard across planes. This was a debatable decision, as goals may still differ even if actual conditions are the same (and are they really?). This item was one of the four from which IDV was calculated; Merritt replaced it with $.69 \times$ the combined scores for the other 3 items, the best approximation on the basis of the IBM scores.

19. Merritt and Helmreich (1996) reported on the use of a 20-item "Cockpit Management Attitudes Questionnaire" with a population of some 600 pilots from three countries and 1,200 flight attendants from seven countries. Using an analysis technique called INDSCAL, they found three clusters in the answers: (1) Asian pilots and flight attendants, low IDV and high PDI; (2) U.S. flight attendants, high IDV and moderate PDI; and (3) U.S. pilots, high IDV and low PDI. Merritt and Helmreich think that their questionnaire had a U.S. monocultural bias. My comment is that mixing countries and occupations in one analysis is undesirable anyway (see Chapter 2), but the PDI difference between pilots and attendants is in line with the occupational PDI differences shown in Exhibit 3.2.

20. In fact, there were 16 countries if we include Luxembourg, for which I did not have data.

21. The range of IDV scores for these countries in IBM was 55-89, except for Portugal, which in 1970 was an outlier with an IDV of 27. Portugal went through a fast modernization process since; in the 1997 EMS data it scored at the same level as Spain and Finland.

22. Shane and Venkataraman (1996) did not include the VSM MAS questions in their instrument.

23. The correlation coefficient for teachers is based on my calculation; the one for students, on Schwartz's calculation.

24. The partial correlations controlling for GNP/capita are as follows: autonomy (affective, intellectual) versus conservatism, $.49**, -.69***, -.73***$; egalitarian commitment versus hierarchy, $-.78***$. The partial correlations controlling for GNP/capita between the variables from the two clusters are $-.08, -.16, .21, .37*,$ and $-.63***$.

25. See note 88 in Chapter 1.

26. In Trompenaars's (1993) book, methodological aspects are briefly handled in an appendix written by Smith (pp. 179-181); it shows several significant correlations among six of the seven scales (all except time orientation). My article reinterpreting Trompenaars's published data (Hofstede, 1996d) led to a reaction by Hampden-Turner and Trompenaars (1997) and a rejoinder by me (Hofstede, 1997b). Surprisingly, in their reac-

tion, Hampden-Turner and Trompenaars did not refer to the two articles by Smith, Trompenaars, and Dugan (1995) and Smith, Dugan, and Trompenaars (1996) that in fact confirmed my reinterpretation.

27. Trompenaars (1993, p. 2) claimed 15,000 responses. In the appendix to his book, which was written by Smith but "edited" by Trompenaars, the number was specified as 14,993. However, in the Smith et al. (1995, 1996) articles the number of questionnaires in the database was counted as 10,993, from which 8,841 could be used after data cleaning. Trompenaars (1993) also claimed that "75% of the participants belong to management" (p. 2), but Smith et al. (1996, p. 240) specified that 54.2% of the respondents were categorized as managerial or professional workers, 24.2% had lower socioeconomic status, and 21.6% could not be categorized because their questionnaire version had not requested this information.

28. The personal/political dimension did correlate with the Schwartz (1994) categories of hierarchy ($r = .56*$), mastery ($r = -.62*$), and harmony ($r = .67**$); of course, Schwartz's country set did include Eastern European countries.

29. The article gave only a few correlation coefficients (and no data to compute them from). Associations with the IBM indexes (across 33 countries) and the Schwartz categories (across 16 countries) could be read from the beta weights: Beta $= -.51$ for IDV on the second dimension and .36 on the first; .44 for PDI on the second dimension and $-.30$ on the first. The first dimension was also associated with Schwartz's conservatism (beta $= -.58$) versus egalitarian commitment (.48).

30. In Inglehart's (1997, fig. 3.2) factor analysis, life satisfaction was one of the key "well-being" variables, and "child needs both parents" was one of the key "survival" variables.

31. For the first round, Stoetzel (1983, p. 78) published a graph of the ratio *preference for freedom* divided by *preference for equality* for the nine countries. This ratio ran from about 1 in Spain (equal preference) to about 3 in Great Britain (freedom three times as popular as equality). The ranks of the freedom/equality ratio for the nine countries correlated strongly with IDV ($r = .84**$) and not at all with PDI ($r = .02$); the more individualist a country, the stronger was its citizens' preference for freedom over equality. However, in the replication the percentage choosing "freedom" (Inglehart, Basañez, & Moreno, 1998, question 247) across these nine countries correlated primarily with (1990) GNP/capita. Across all 26 overlapping countries, the dominant variable was PDI: more preference for equality in high-PDI (less equal) countries.

32. When I asked the authors for their base data so that I could reanalyze them at the proper level, it turned out that the data had been destroyed. Of course, raw data for this type of study should always remain accessible for secondary analyses by others if we take our contribution to scientific discovery seriously. Maybe someone will want to do a trend study over a 20-, 50-, or 100-year period.

33. This was also about the only aspect of the country differences in "need category" scores for which Haire, Ghiselli, and Porter (1966, p. 105) offered an interpretation: the tendency in the developing countries Argentina, Chile, and India to rate *everything* as more important. Haire et al. attributed it to an acquiescence response set. In their data table, the "security" column was based on one questionnaire item, "social" and "autonomy" were each based on two items, and "esteem" and "self-actualization" were each based on three (p. 100). The acquiescence score is the mean raw score across all 11 items; it could be reconstructed by taking the published values for security 1 $\times$, social and autonomy 2 $\times$, esteem and self-actualization 3 $\times$, and dividing by 11. The results were as follows: DEN, 5.30; GER, 5.61; NOR, 5.29; SWE, 5.53; BEL, 5.60; FRA, 5.51; ITA, 5.74; SPA, 5.88; GBR, 5.53; USA, 5.62; ARG, 6.34; CHL, 6.16; IND, 6.06; and JPN, 5.82. Higher scores meant stronger acquiescence.

34. In the 1980 edition of *Culture's Consequences,* I showed significant correlations between Haire et al.'s (1966) "security" and "autonomy" needs and IDV (the first negative, the second positive). However, I did not check for the correlations with 1970 GNP/capita, which turned out to be stronger than those with IDV; in a stepwise regression, the influence of IDV disappeared.

35. A fair amount of statistical research has been done on Morris's data. For example, Morris and Jones (1955) have shown that factor analyses of the scores of Americans showed the same factors as those of Indians. Morris (1956, p. 194) related these factors to Parsons and Shils's (1951) five pattern variables (see Chapter 1). In Chapter 1, we also saw that Osgood, Ware, and Morris (1961) analyzed the 13 "Ways" with the semantic differential. Finally, Dempsey and Dukes (1966) studied the coherence of Morris's lengthy formulations of the "Ways" and proposed more coherent, shorter formulations.

36. Again, McClelland's 1925 data, not his 1950 data, correlated with an IBM index; this confirms their greater reliability.

37. As applied to the family, the word *nuclear* is taken from the Latin *nucleus,* which means core; it has no relation to atomic energy.

38. Rho $= -.87*$. The correlations with 1980 GNP/capita were marginally weaker, $r = -.836*$, rho $= -.82*$. The correlations with the other IBM indexes were nonsignificant.

39. See "Father Figures" (1996). The countries were AUL (current 6%, future 13%), HOK (22%, 13%), IDO (18%, 46%), JPN (20%, 24%), KOR (27%, 55%), MAL (22%, 49%), PHI (28%, 55%), SIN (31%, 43%), TAI (37%, 46%), and THA (47%, 57%).

40. In Chapter 3, I referred to the World Values Survey data on "qualities which a child can be encouraged to learn at home." From the list of 11 "qualities," "unselfishness" (rho $= .53**$) and "tolerance/respect" (rho $= .46**$) were primarily correlated with IDV.

41. For chastity a similar association was obtained by Bond, who surveyed male and female students in 23

countries using the Chinese Value Survey (Chinese Culture Connection, 1987). The value of "chastity in women" was at the collectivist pole of a dimension correlated with IDV.

42. The countries were AUL, BRA, GBR, HOK, IND, JPN, MEX, PAK, PHI, THA, and USA.

43. Levine, Sato, Hashimoto, and Verma's (1995) two other questions dealt with whether the disappearance of love from a marriage should be a reason for ending it; one correlated with long-term orientation (see Chapter 7).

44. In the same way the work goal importance scores in IBM were subject to acquiescence, the unstandardized answer percentages for these WVS questions showed a strong tendency by country to score all six topics as more or less important. The mean percentage "very important" across the 13 topics varied from 34% in Portugal to 73% in Nigeria. This should be seen as a response set, which makes the raw scores unsuitable for drawing other conclusions. What I was interested in was the *relative* importance attached to each topic related to the others, which is what became visible after the standardization.

45. The countries were ARG, AUL, CHL, FIN, GBR, GER, HOK, IND, JPN, KOR, NET, NOR, PAK, POR, SIN, USA, VEN, and WAF (for Nigeria).

46. Someone with sufficient persistence could correlate the importance scores for all 300 objectives, which Williams, Satterwhite, and Saiz (1998) have published in their book, with the IBM indexes. I just selected this one at face value. Chapter 7 will show that the same item was also correlated with long-term orientation. Williams et al.'s book also contains favorability scores for the same 300 adjectives, collected in 10 countries, 9 of them overlapping with the IBM set. These could also be compared to the IBM indexes.

47. The countries were ARG, BRA, CAN, CHL, FRA, GBR, GER, GRE, HOK, ITA, JPN, SWE, SWI, TUR, and USA.

48. The 23 countries that overlapped with the IBM set were AUT, BRA, CAN, COS, FRA, GBR, GER, GRE, HOK, IDO, IRE, ITA, JPN, KEN (for EAF), KOR, MEX, NET, SAL, SIN, SWE, SWI, TAI, and USA. Levine and Norenzayan (1999) were not aware of my publications after 1980, and they mention that "Hofstede's ratings were not available for many of the countries in the present study" (p. 188). They collected individualism estimates from Triandis and found these to correlate with their index.

49. For the overall index a stepwise multiple regression showed a significant secondary correlation on PDI ($R^2 = .54$ for GNP/capita, $R^2 = .63$ for GNP/capita plus PDI), which is not surprising in view of the different correlates of the three components.

50. These countries were BEL, FRA, GER, PER, USA, and YUG.

51. Converse's East-West dimension rank correlated .89* with PDI. This is not as easy to interpret; it opposes more book reading, movies, and radio and more time at work and traveling to it in higher-PDI countries;

more magazine reading, TV watching, social activities, home chores, conversation, and sleep in lower-PDI countries. Converse (1972, p. 155) sees in it a work-versus-free-time dimension.

52. This is an observation I owe to Marieke de Mooij.

53. In Gudykunst's set of 32 countries and regions, IDV and UAI were not correlated ($r = -.03$), so the relationships with the two variables were independent of each other.

54. This approach derives from the Twenty Statements Test (TST), which was developed in the United States in the 1950s for comparing individuals. Bond and Cheung (1983) started to use it cross-culturally, comparing students in Hong Kong, Japan, and the United States. They developed their own classification scheme, which was quite complex and showed many differences between the countries that were, however, difficult to summarize. Later cross-cultural studies with the TST by Dhawan, Roseman, Naidu, Thapa, and Rettek (1995) with Indian versus U.S. college students, and by Stiles, Gibbons, and Desilva (1996) with Sri Lankan versus U.S. schoolgirls, were equally inconclusive. Bochner (1994) judged 20 statements too many for use "in collective cultures, where the western preoccupation with the self in whatever complexion is not as prevalent" (p. 276).

55. This subsection is derived in part from an award-winning article: Hofstede (1986a).

56. Hamilton, Blumenfeld, Akoh, and Miura (1991) conducted an observation study in 10 Japanese and 9 U.S. classrooms for approximately 11-year-old children (fifth grade) and again found that Japanese teachers attended significantly more to groups than to individual children.

57. These were BRA, CAN (English and French speakers separately), FRA, GER, ISR, JPN, LEB, SAF (Bantu speakers), TUR, and USA.

58. A simulated in-basket experiment is a popular management training device in which the trainee receives a pile of documents from a supposed in-basket and is asked to handle as many of them as he or she can as efficiently as possible.

59. Williams, Whyte, and Green (1966, p. 117) have tried to explain the paradox by distinguishing individualism as the taking of individual initiative from individualism as the nonidentification with a group. I find their explanation unconvincing; they do not seem to recognize the importance of the in-group versus out-group distinction.

60. For details, see the first edition of *Culture's Consequences* (Hofstede, 1980a, fig. 5.17).

61. These countries were BRA, CAM(eroun), COL, GBR, GER, IDO, JPN, KEN, and NET.

62. The third function combined a motley mix of items, probably clustering because they were all associated with GNP/capita.

63. GNP/capita for 1990 was correlated only with the amount of night work (rho = .54*). Lower job stress and less job support were both only correlated with PDI

(rho = .53* and rho = −.52*, respectively). It seems that where PDI was higher, these people felt less driven by the job itself.

64. See Hofstede (1980a, fig. 5.21).

65. This is the title of an article deriving management themes of technical rationality from 29 stories for U.S. children up to 6 years old (Ingersoll & Adams, 1992).

66. Smith, Peterson, Misumi, and Bond (1992) published results of a PM theory-based study of more than 1,000 assembly-line workers in Japanese-owned plants in Britain, Hong Kong, Japan, and the United States. Significant differences among countries were found; for example, workers in Hong Kong and Japan experienced less pressure from their supervisors than did workers in Britain and the United States. Smith et al. assumed differences in individualism/collectivism to play a role, but their study is unclear as to how.

67. Data were from the Reader's Digest Eurodata 1991 and 1995, the European Media and Marketing Surveys (EMS) 1995 and 1997, and the Consumer Europe Euromonitor 1997, across 16 countries (AUT, BEL, DEN, FIN, FRA, GBR, GER, GRE, IRE, ITA, NET, NOR, POR, SPA, SWE, and SWI).

68. Yiu and Saner (1985) earlier showed cultural influences on mental health counseling, comparing Taiwan with the United States. They found both affective disorders and cognitive coping mechanisms to be strongly influenced by cultural norms and values.

69. The three cultures differ on the other three IBM dimensions as well; the PDI differences between Germany and the two others (taking Turkish data for the Kurds) are even larger than the IDV differences. Differences on UAI and MAS are smaller. However, conceptually the results found belong clearly to the domain of individualism/collectivism.

70. The 52 countries included all but Taiwan, taking Egypt for the Arabic-speaking IBM region, Kenya for the East African region, and Nigeria for the West African region.

71. They are all the wealthy countries in Exhibit 5.22 minus ISR, HOK, SIN, and KOR, but including TUR.

72. For a division of the former Yugoslavia into Croatia, Serbia, and Slovenia, see Appendix 5.

73. The conflict between Protestants and Catholics in Northern Ireland does not seem to fit the diagram; the IBM data, however, are from the Irish Republic.

74. These countries were BEL, DEN, FRA, GBR, GER, GRE, IRE, ITA, NET, POR, and SPA.

75. The complete scores are as follows: DEN, 7.4; NET, 7.1; GBR, 7.0; FRA, 6.7; NOR, 6.5; Luxembourg, 6.3; GER (West), 6.1; GER (East), 6.0; BEL, 5.9; ITA, 5.5; Northern Ireland, 5.4; IRE, 5.4; SPA, 5.3; GRE, 4.6; POR, 4.6; overall mean 6.0. As there were 12 statements, this overall mean just corresponds to the result that would be attained by random guessing.

76. Data were available only for the 40 Category 1 countries.

77. "Future" GNP/capita was still strongly correlated with IDV. Although the correlation between IDV and 1970 GNP/capita across 50 countries, as shown, was r = .84***, the correlations of (1970) IDV with 1980 and 1990 GNP/capita were still r = .79*** and r = .76***, respectively. This does not imply a causal relationship; rather, it simply reflects the inertia in GNP/capita. Shifts from one year to the next are always incremental.

78. Craig, Douglas, and Grein (1992) studied "hard" societal development variables for 17 European countries plus the United States for 1960, 1970, 1980, and 1988. Most of their variables clustered into one dimension, standard of living. Changes in standard of living between the years were correlated with IDV with r = .52*. Craig et al. interpret this as IDV having been a causal factor in the changes, but as IDV was measured only once, in 1970, this conclusion cannot be drawn. If anything, their 1960-70 period *preceded* the measurement of IDV.

79. Across 74 less-developed nations, Adelman and Morris (1967, p. 151) showed a close relationship between level of economic development and "basic social organization": from strong tribal allegiances to extended family to nuclear family.

80. The 19 countries were AUT, BEL, DEN, FIN, FRA, GBR, GER, GRE, IRA, IRE, ISR, NET, NOR, PAK, SAF, SPA, SWE, SWI, and TUR.

81. For the method of calculation of these scores, see Appendix 4.

82. See Takezawa (1975). Increased individualism in Japan has been described by both Trommsdorff (1983) and Schooler (1998).

83. Inkeles (1980), in an article reviewing trends in family patterns around the world, distinguished both elements that change in parallel fashion or even converge from elements that differ and continue to do so. Heuer, Cummings, and Hutabarat (1999) compared VSM94 scores of Coca-Cola managers and MBA students in Indonesia (n = 46) and the United States (n = 104). The only dimension showing significant differences between the countries was IDV (IDO 81, USA 97). Their Indonesian sample may have been unusually acculturated to giving U.S.-style answers.

84. Differences in individualism remain within countries as well. Georgas (1989) found significant differences between urban and rural Greek students; the rural students maintained extended rather than nuclear family values, even after 4 years spent studying in Athens.

85. For a more extensive description, see Hofstede and Spangenberg (1987).

86. In the chapters on power distance and uncertainty avoidance, data for comparing occupations were taken from the three large countries France, Germany, and Great Britain only. For work goals, German data for several of the occupations were missing. Therefore, in this case I preferred using European totals, which differed only slightly from weighted means of the large countries. For card plants and laboratories, worldwide work goal averages were used, including some from outside Europe (15% and 8% of respondents, respectively);

their influence was too small to warrant the additional effort of eliminating them.

87. Examples are Inkeles (1960, p. 10), Friedlander (1965), Centers and Bugenthal (1966), Shepard (1971, pp. 101-102), and Quinn (1973, p. 244).

88. Schaupp (1973), in work for his master's thesis in the United States, used 1971 IBM data from manufacturing plants in eight countries. His data treatment shows several weaknesses (reverse ecological fallacy, neglect of occupational differences, sign errors in the analysis), but he did recognize an inverted relationship between a country's degree of economic development and the importance of "training" and "company" goals—that is, the negative pole of the individualism axis (p. 168).

89. In the first edition of *Culture's Consequences*, I reported on having tried out smallest-space analysis for clustering the countries based on the IBM country data for 12 items (Hofstede, 1980a, p. 333); the results were only marginally different from those obtained using other techniques.

90. Schwartz's (1994) other correlation coefficients for the teachers are also slightly different from mine. He may not have been aware of the separate scores for French-speaking Switzerland in the IBM study, which differ considerably from those for total Switzerland, especially for PDI. Schwartz's Swiss data are from French speakers.

91. In Inglehart (1997), loadings can be read from Figure 3.2 (p. 82) and country scores from Figure 3.5 (p. 93). The country scores are technically not factor scores but loadings for dummy variables in which one country was coded "1" and the other 42 were coded "0." The effect should be the same as if factor scores were used.

6

■

Masculinity and Femininity

Summary of This Chapter

The fourth dimension along which national cultures differ systematically has been called *masculinity,* with its opposite pole *femininity.* The duality of the sexes is a fundamental fact with which different societies cope in different ways; the issue is what implications the biological differences between the sexes should have for the emotional and social roles of the genders. Surveys on the importance of work goals, both inside IBM and elsewhere, show that almost universally women attach more importance to social goals such as relationships, helping others, and the physical environment, and men attach more importance to ego goals such as careers and money. However, the IBM database revealed that the importance respondents attached to such "feminine" versus "masculine" work goals varied across countries as well as across occupations.

A factor analysis of mean country work goal scores from the IBM data produced a strong factor opposing social to ego goals. Factor scores on this factor for each of 53 countries and regions were converted into a country Masculinity Index (MAS). In higher-MAS countries, values of men and women in the same jobs differed more than in lower-MAS countries. MAS values also varied among occupations. MAS was correlated across countries with other IBM questions and with an indirect measure of work centrality in IBM. MAS is entirely different from, and should not be confused with, individualism.

The country Masculinity Index is validated against many country data from other sources. These include straight replications of the IBM survey on other populations but also large cross-national studies of values, including Schwartz's Values Surveys, the European and World Values Surveys analyzed by Stoetzel and by Inglehart, and McClelland's content analysis of children's books. These correlates of MAS are integrated into a coherent list of connotations of masculinity as a country characteristic.

From this a picture of the masculinity/femininity dimension of societal norms is drawn. In separate subsections of this chapter, its origins and implications are elaborated for family life, school education, gender roles (including Best and Williams's cross-national comparisons of gender stereotypes), consumer behavior (De Mooij's analyses of market research data), the workplace, politics, sexual behavior, and religion, including the relationship between the last two of these. One study suggests a curvilinear relationship between MAS and geographic latitude, but most of the variance in MAS among countries should be due to specific historical influences within regions. There is no indication whatsoever of convergence on this dimension over time.

Sexes, Genders, and Gender Roles

Absolute, Statistical, and Social Sex Differences

If the duality of life and death is nature's number one law, the duality of female and male, which governs procreation in all higher vegetable and animal species, is the number two law and follows very closely. In human societies of all ages and levels of complexity, this nature-given fact has been one of the very first issues with which each society has had to cope in its own specific way, and has profoundly affected a multitude of societal institutions: "The sex-role system is at the core of our cultural norms" (Chetwynd & Hartnett, 1978, p. 3).

The only difference between women and men that is absolute is that women bear children and men beget them. The biological differences between the sexes not immediately related to their roles in procreation are statistical rather than absolute: Men are *on average* taller and stronger (but many women are taller and/or stronger than many men), women have *on average* greater finger dexterity and, for example, faster metabolism, which makes them recover faster from fatigue.[1] These absolute and statistical biological differences are the same for all human societies, but these differences leave a wide margin for the actual division of roles between women and men. In a strict sense, only behaviors directly connected with procreation (childbearing and child begetting) are "feminine" or "masculine." Yet every society recognizes many other behaviors as more suitable to females or more suitable to males; these represent relatively arbitrary choices, mediated by cultural norms and traditions.

In the following pages I will follow the modern, politically correct trend in the English language of distinguishing between *sex* and *gender*. I will use *sex* when referring to biological functions and *gender* when referring to social functions. This distinction has become popular only in the past decade or so, so where I cite older literature we still find *sex* used for both cases—and I did not want to start rewriting history on this point. In the first edition of *Culture's Consequences*, I also used *sex* universally.

There is a common trend among the vast majority of societies, both traditional and modern, as to the distribution of gender roles apart from procreation: Men must be more concerned with economic and other achievements and women must be more concerned with taking care of people in general and children in particular. It is not difficult to see how this role pattern fits the biological sex roles: Women first bear children and then breast-feed them, so they must stay with them. Anthropologist Margaret Mead suggested that the dominant concern for achievement in men is related to the fact that men cannot bear children. She argued that women in every society attain a "sense of irreversible achievement" in giving birth to their children.[2] Men lack this achievement, and "the recurrent problem of civilization is to define the male role satisfactorily enough—whether it be to build gardens or raise cattle, kill game or kill enemies, build bridges or handle bank-shares—so that the male may in the course of his life reach a solid sense of irreversible achievement" (Mead,

1950/1962a, p. 158). Men, in short, are supposed to be assertive, competitive, and *tough*. Women are supposed to be more concerned with taking care of the home, the children, and people in general—to take the *tender* roles.

The common pattern of male assertiveness and female nurturance leads to male dominance at least in matters of politics and, usually, of economic life; within households, whether nuclear or extended family groups, different societies show different distributions of power between the genders.

Anthropology, psychology, and political science confirm the male assertiveness versus female nurturance pattern. For example, Barry, Bacon, and Child (1957), in a secondary analysis of anthropological reports of 110 mostly nonliterate societies, found that in the vast majority of cases girls were socialized toward nurturance and responsibility and sometimes obedience; boys were socialized toward achievement and self-reliance. The pervasiveness of the common gender role pattern is shown in cases where deliberate attempts have been made to abolish it, as in Israeli kibbutzim; even here, quite a bit survived—kibbutz women preferred maternal activities to participating as fully as men in the general assembly and kibbutz committees.[3]

On the other hand, there is evidence of variations on the common gender role pattern. Mead (1950/1962a, pp. 102-107) gave the example of the Iatmul and the Tchambuli, two New Guinea tribes living close to one another, of which the first showed the usual pattern of male aggressiveness and female nurturance but the second presented a reverse pattern: The females showed initiative in practical matters and the nonaggressive males concentrated on art and theater.

Gender role socialization starts in the family; it continues in peer groups and in school. It is furthered through the media, starting with children's literature (which usually pictures children and adults in traditional gender roles) and reinforced by motion pictures, television, and the press. Women's magazines, in particular, are obvious gender role socializers. Gender role-confirming behavior has been considered healthy by mental health professionals.[4]

Discussion of gender differences in values has been popularized by Deborah Tannen (1992), who has shown the difference between female and male discourse in the United States: more "report talk" for the men (transferring information) versus more "rapport talk" for the women (using conversation to exchange feelings and establish relationships). Tannen's work illustrates that each gender has its own way of thinking, feeling, and acting. Some of this is probably present in all human societies.

Gender Differences in Work Goals

An important role will be played in this chapter by measurements of work goal importance. When the answers of men and women on work goal importance scores are compared, significant differences tend to appear. A review of the literature of the 1950s to 1970s in the first edition of *Culture's Consequences* (Hofstede, 1980a, pp. 269-271) led to the following conclusions:

1. Gender differences in work goal importance may easily be confounded with educational and/or occupational differences. Goals differed by gender and by occupation, but occupation differences outweighed gender differences.
2. In samples from the United States, the Netherlands, and France (not from IBM), women compared with men tended to score interpersonal aspects, rendering service, and sometimes the physical environment as more important, and advancement, sometimes independence, responsibility, and earnings as less important. As far as job content was concerned, women scored no different from men, although they might value different detail aspects. There was no indication that it made sense to translate the gender differences in work goal importance in Herzbergian terms (one gender was not more intrinsically oriented than the other) or in Maslowian terms (one gender is not higher on a hierarchy of human needs, although there may be differences at the intermediate levels of social and esteem needs).[5]

In IBM, work goal importance was measured in all surveys, first with 22 and later with 14 questions (see Exhibit 5.11). As gender differences should not be confused with occupational differences, only men and women in the same occupations should be compared. Among the 38 occupations in IBM for which data were available, only a few satisfied the conditions of (1) being performed by both men and women in sufficient numbers to allow statistical treatment of data and (2) not being subject to an internal division of labor in which the women still performed tasks different from those performed by men. Seven occupations surveyed with the 22-goal set and two with the 14-goal set more or less satisfied these conditions. Work goal importance scores for men and women in these occupations (taking a number of countries together) were standardized as usual, and the differences between standardized scores for women and men are summarized in Exhibit 6.1.[6]

Across the nine occupations, the following significant gender difference trends appeared:

- More important for men
  Advancement
  Earnings
  Training
  Up-to-dateness
- More important for women
  Friendly atmosphere
  Position security
  Physical conditions
  Manager
  Cooperation[7]

No significant gender differences were found for job content goals (challenge, use of skills) or for private life goals (personal time, desirable area).[8]

These IBM data confirmed the results of a literature review of national studies outside IBM. Gender differences in the importance of advancement, earnings, atmosphere plus cooperation, physical conditions, and manager had been reported in a 1957 U.S. review by Herzberg, Mausner, Peterson, and Capwell. The differences in reference groups on which these women and men based their goal importance scores seemed to have been pervasive both over time and across countries.

In IBM, head office managers went against the general trend in that among them "cooperation" was scored marginally *less* important by women than by men. Herrick (1973) compared samples of male and female U.S. government executives on 13 work goals. Reanalyzing his rather primitively reported data, I found his women executives to score self-actualization goals as more important and social goals as less important than did their male colleagues. Powell, Posner, and Schmidt (1984) compared values of matched samples of 130 male and 130 female members of the American Management Association and found that the women placed greater emphasis on careers as opposed to family and home life than did the men. All three studies suggest that at least within IBM and in U.S. samples, the women who had been promoted to management jobs were those holding more "masculine" goals than the average male executive—those who beat the men at their own game. This tells us something about the selection mechanisms involved.

Exhibit 6.1 shows how work goals clustered by gender. Clusters depend on the level of analysis; how does this gender clustering compare to what we got across individuals, occupations, and countries?

Clustering on the basis of differences between *individuals* within groups (one occupation, one country) generally produced six factors (see Chapter 2). These are the ones used for categoriz-

Exhibit 6.1 Differences of Standardized Mean Scores for the Importance of 22 (14) Work Goals Between Men and Women in the Same 9 (7) Occupations

Work Goal	Mean of 9 (7) Occupations (+ more important for men)	Number of Occupations		
		With +	With −	Sign Test
Job content and learning				
Challenge	+22	5	4	
Use of skills	+22	5	3	
Training	+73	8	1	m*
Up-to-dateness	+60	7	0	m*
Learning	+10	5	2	
Reward				
Recognition	−13	2	7	
Advancement	+152	9	0	m*
Earnings	+101	9	0	m*
Interpersonal relations				
Manager	−57	0	9	w*
Cooperation	−52	1	8	w*
Freedom	0	4	5	
Friendly atmosphere	−101	0	7	w*
Efficient department	−22	2	5	
Security				
Employment security	−11	4	5	
Benefits	−47	2	7	
Position security	−84	0	7	w*
Comfort				
Personal time	−2	5	4	
Desirable area	+13	7	2	
Physical conditions	−77	0	7	w*
Company				
Contribution to company	+39	6	1	
Modern company	−1	4	3	
Successful company	−59	1	6	

NOTE: Total number of respondents = 18,970 men, 4,871 women. Occupations were as follows: 1968-69 data for selected countries, head office managers, head office professionals, branch office systems engineers, data processing service bureau professionals, head office clerks, branch office clerks; 1970-73 data for total world, unskilled card plant personnel, branch office systems engineers, head office professionals and clerks. For details, see Hofstede (1980a, fig. 6.1).

ing goals in Exhibit 6.1. The trend in Exhibit 6.1 is for the "job content and learning" and the "reward" factors to be scored more important by men, and for the "interpersonal relations" and "security" factors to be scored more important by women.

Clustering goals on the basis of differences between *occupations* (taking total Europe data) pro-

duced two bipolar factors: "intrinsic/extrinsic" and "social/ego" (Exhibit 5.12). The goals related to the intrinsic/extrinsic factor did not differ significantly in importance for the genders.[9] However, the social/ego factor contained four goals significantly more important to women on the "social" side (manager, cooperation, friendly atmosphere, physical conditions) and four goals

Exhibit 6.2   Factor Scores on Occupational Work Goal Factors for Two Occupations by Gender

Occupation	Factor 1 Intrinsic/Extrinsic	Factor 2 Social/Ego
Head office clerks, 5 countries		
Both genders	.52	1.10
Men only (n = 1,467)	.48	.45
Women only (n = 710)	.61	2.43
Branch office systems engineers, total world		
Both genders	.27	−1.42
Men only (n = 2,015)	.23	−1.49
Women only (n = 92)	1.10	.12

NOTE: Factors were based on 1968-69 data for 22 work goals. For a description, see the statistical section in Chapter 5.

significantly more important to men on the "ego" side (up-to-dateness, advancement, training, earnings). The social/ego factor is virtually identical to a female preference versus male preference factor.

One reason for a female versus male factor to appear across occupations could be that some occupations are mainly engaged in by women, others mainly by men. It is true that in Exhibit 5.12 the occupations on the "social" side were mainly clerks and unskilled workers, with sizable percentages of women (from 18% for unskilled machine plant direct personnel to 99% for office secretaries and typists). The occupations on the "ego" side generally employed fewer than 10% women, or no women at all. However, this does not mean that the women in the "social" occupations were responsible for those occupations' high social scores. Exhibit 6.2 allows us to test this. It compares the intrinsic/extrinsic and social/ego factor scores for two occupations separately for the genders.[10] Head office clerks were a typical social occupation; branch office systems engineers a typical ego occupation, as the mean scores for both genders on the social/ego factor show. Within both occupations women scored considerably more to the social side than men, and the gender difference in scores was larger for the less educated group (clerks) than for the more educated (systems engineers). Still, between male clerks and male systems engineers and between female clerks and female systems engineers there were also large differences. Female systems engineers had lower social scores than male clerks. This confirms the conclusion of my literature survey that goals differed by gender and occupation, but that occupation differences outweighed gender differences.

The scores on the intrinsic/extrinsic factor in Exhibit 6.2 illustrate that male and female clerks differed little in this respect, but the (college-educated) female systems engineers tended to be more intrinsically oriented than males. It may be that women chose a systems engineering job only if they were really interested in it, whereas at least some of the men chose such a job arbitrarily.

Clustering goals on the basis of differences between *countries* (taking the standard sample of seven occupational groups) again produced two factors. On the basis of the data for 40 countries and 14 goals, the two factors could be labeled *individual/collective* and *social/ego* (see Chapter 5). The goals related to the individual/collective factor did not differ systematically in importance for the genders.[11] However, the social/ego factor contained two goals significantly more important to women on the social side (manager, cooperation) and two goals significantly more important to men on the ego side (earnings, advancement). In the factor analysis across countries for 22 goals (which, however, was available for only 19 countries; see the statistical section of Chapter 5), "friendly atmosphere" also was found at the social pole of the social/ego factor. Again, the social/ego factor closely resembled a female preference versus male preference factor.[12]

In the same way the social/ego factor across occupations had something to do with the percentages of women in these occupations, the social/ego factor across countries was related to the percentages of women in the seven standard occupational groups in each country. In fact, the social factor score and the percentage of women per country (across the 40 countries) were significantly correlated ($r = .43**$). However, the percentages of women in the country samples did not *account for* the social factor score; in all countries women formed only a minor fraction of the respondents in the seven occupational groups (varying from 4% in Pakistan to 16% in Finland; see Appendix 2, question A1). Rather, the social factor score of a country expressed a value complex that made it more likely that women would be hired for some occupations. This will be explained below.

Measuring National Differences in Masculinity in IBM

A Masculinity Index for Countries in the IBM Sample

In Chapter 5, I explained how the factor scores of countries on the first of two rotated factors (individual/collective) in a 14-goal, 40-country factor analysis were converted into an Individualism Index (IDV). The second rotated factor in this case, mentioned above, was labeled *social/ego*. It accounted for 22% of the variance in the country mean work goals scores (against 24% for individual/collective). The work goals that together composed this factor were the following (see the statistical section of Chapter 5 for the factor loadings and Exhibit 5.11 for the full wording; I excluded the second loading for "use of skills"):

Loading	Work Goal
.69	Manager
.69	Cooperation
.59	Desirable area
.48	Employment security
−.54	Challenge
−.56	Advancement
−.59	Recognition
−.70	Earnings

As the (zero-order) contribution of each work goal to the variance in the factor is determined by the square of the loading, the social/ego factor is characterized mainly by high importance of "manager" and "cooperation" and low importance of "earnings." Essentially the same factor was found in the factor analysis of the 22-goal, 19-country matrix (the two factors were correlated with rho = .92; see Chapter 5); the 22-goal analysis added "friendly atmosphere" on the positive side. The previous section showed that for these goals there was a significant difference in the preferences of men and women in the same oc-

cupations, in the sense of women scoring more "social" and men more "ego."

In the same way as the index of country individualism versus collectivism was measured with an index derived from individual/collective factor scores (IDV), the new dimension will be measured with an index based on social/ego factor scores. Reversing the sign of the scores, I have called this dimension *masculinity versus femininity* (mas/fem).

The label chosen needs some explanation. The English language (unlike, for example, Dutch) distinguishes between *male/female* and *masculine/feminine*. The first pair of words usually refer to what is biologically determined, and I shall use these words in that sense. The latter pair of words usually refer to what, in a given environment, is deemed socially suitable for members of one gender rather than the other:

> The words *masculine* and *feminine* do not refer in any simple way to fundamental traits of personality, but to the learned styles of interpersonal interactions which are deemed to be socially appropriate to specific social contexts, and which are imposed upon, and sustain and extend, the sexual dichotomy. (Newson, Newson, Richardson, & Scaife, 1978, p. 28)

Masculinity and *femininity,* in the sense in which I shall use these terms, refer to the dominant gender role patterns in the vast majority of both traditional and modern societies as described in the early part of this chapter: the patterns of male assertiveness and female nurturance. These words should not be taken to imply that men always actually behave in a more masculine manner than do women or that women behave in more feminine ways than do men; rather, statistically, men as a rule will show more "masculine" and women more "feminine" behavior.

As described above, I found both occupations and countries in the IBM data to differ along a social/ego dimension of work goals, opposing interpersonal relations goals (relationship with manager, cooperation, and friendly atmosphere) to ego-directed goals (earnings and advancement). This dimension is related to the percentage of women within the occupation or country sample, but is not accounted for by the varying shares of women only; we find it also in the responses by men in these occupations or countries. The fact that the social/ego difference appears on a worldwide ecological level means that it must be associated with a fundamental dilemma of humankind. This dilemma is the relative strength of nurturance interests (relation with manager, cooperation, atmosphere) versus assertiveness interests (earnings, advancement)—of interests that in nearly all traditional and modern societies are traditionally more feminine versus those that are traditionally more masculine. This ecological dimension measures to what extent the IBM respondents in a country (mainly men) showed a traditionally masculine interest pattern. The fundamental dilemma behind this dimension, then, can be no other than the distribution of roles over the genders, and this gender role distribution differed among the 40 nations. I have therefore interpreted it as a femininity/masculinity dimension (using the words in the sense described earlier, of learned styles of interpersonal interaction). Because the respondents were mainly men, I have called the dimension *masculinity,* thereby reversing its sign.

Like the Individualism Index, the Masculinity Index has been brought in a range between 0 and 100. The values of the Masculinity Index found for 50 countries and three regions are listed in Exhibit 6.3.

The list of countries in order of MAS shows Japan at the top. German-speaking countries (Austria, Switzerland, and Germany) scored high; so did the Caribbean Latin American countries Venezuela, Mexico, and Colombia, and Italy. The Anglo countries (Ireland, Great Britain, South Africa, the United States, Australia, New Zealand, and Canada) all scored above average. Asian countries, other than Japan, were rather in the middle. The feminine side harbors other Latin countries (France, Spain, Peru, El Salvador, Uruguay, Guatemala, Portugal, Chile, Costa Rica) and former Yugoslavia; at the extreme feminine pole were the four Nordic countries Finland, Denmark, Norway, and Sweden, and the Netherlands.

The columns in Exhibit 6.3 headed "Controlling for % Women" show MAS scores after the percentage of women in the IBM sample was controlled for—the scores that would have been obtained if all country samples included the same percentage of female respondents. The basic ordering of the countries is hardly affected; the largest differences occurred for Finland (+25 points) and former Yugoslavia (+21 points), because these had the highest percentages of women. High percentages of women, however, were not only a cause but also partly an *effect* of the country's relatively low MAS norm, so I have continued using the original MAS values.

Masculinity and Occupation, Gender, and Age

The Individualism Index could be used only to compare countries, not occupations, because in the factor analysis of work goals by occupations (Chapter 5) there was no such thing as an individual/collective factor. However, across occupations there was a social/ego factor largely similar to the social/ego factor across countries. Thus oc-

cupations can be labeled as more "masculine" (ego) or more "feminine" (social); the MAS index can be used to describe occupations.

As for other demographic criteria, the MAS index can, of course, be used for discriminating between the genders; this is why it was given its name. But even more interesting is the combined effect of country and gender. Most IBM respondents were men, so the MAS scores listed in Exhibit 6.3 reflect mainly the values of men in these countries. In order to contrast the values of women within a country with those of men, we again need data from occupational categories with sufficient numbers of women and men doing the same work. This condition was fulfilled for three categories. Two of them, head office clerks and branch office systems engineers, we have seen already in Exhibit 6.2. The clerks are of secondary school education level, the systems engineers of college education level. The third category was unskilled card plant personnel, the least-educated employee category in the IBM database (see Exhibit 2.5); these scores were available for six countries.

Exhibit 6.4 shows separate MAS scores for men and women in these three occupations for those countries in which there were at least 20 female respondents in either occupation.[13] Several conclusions can be drawn from Exhibit 6.4. If we look first to the rank correlations with country MAS scores, we see that country differences in MAS were present in the scores of men and women separately and in all three occupations. The men's scores followed the MAS ranking somewhat more closely than the women's scores, not surprisingly, as the MAS scores were based mainly on men's answers. However, we also see from the bottom line of Exhibit 6.4 that the score differences Δ between men and women (a measure of gender role differentiation) were themselves positively correlated with MAS. For systems engineers and clerks, the correlations of Δ(men − women) with MAS were significant. For unskilled workers the data for Japan were out of line, but the sample of women in Japan was just 20, the lowest limit of what I considered acceptable. Without Japan the correlation of Δ(men − women) with MAS for the unskilled became rho = .83, almost significant.

This pattern means that in the high-MAS countries the values of men and women in the same occupations tended to be more different than in the low-MAS ones. Our measure of masculinity in a country is therefore also a measure of gender role differentiation. The two most feminine countries, Sweden and Norway, even showed a reversal of gender role values: In these countries, the women scored more masculine than did the men in the same occupations.

The general pattern of country × gender differences in MAS is pictured in the diagram in Exhibit

Exhibit 6.3   Masculinity Index Values for 50 Countries and Three Regions

Rank	Country	Actual	MAS Controlling for % Women[a]	Rank	Country	Actual	MAS Controlling for % Women[a]
1	Japan	95	87	28	Singapore	48	52
2	Austria	79	75	29	Israel	47	41
3	Venezuela	73	70	30/31	Indonesia	46	
4/5	Italy	70	72	30/31	West Africa	46	
4/5	Switzerland	70	67	32/33	Turkey	45	53
6	Mexico	69	64	32/33	Taiwan	45	38
7/8	Ireland	68	74	34	Panama	44	
7/8	Jamaica	68		35/36	Iran	43	52
9/10	Great Britain	66	66	35/36	France	43	41
9/10	Germany	66	59	37/38	Spain	42	35
11/12	Philippines	64	58	37/38	Peru	42	32
11/12	Colombia	64	56	39	East Africa	41	
13/14	South Africa	66	60	40	Salvador	40	
13/14	Ecuador	63		41	South Korea	39	
15	United States	62	—[b]	42	Uruguay	38	
16	Australia	61	59	43	Guatemala	37	
17	New Zealand	58	55	44	Thailand	34	45
18/19	Greece	57	73	45	Portugal	31	32
18/19	Hong Kong	57	61	46	Chile	28	26
20/21	Argentina	56	50	47	Finland	26	51
20/21	India	56	47	48/49	Yugoslavia	21	42
22	Belgium	54	53	48/49	Costa Rica	21	
23	Arab countries	53		50	Denmark	16	22
24	Canada	52	53	51	Netherlands	14	—[c]
25/26	Malaysia	50		52	Norway	8	10
25/26	Pakistan	50	40	53	Sweden	5	6
27	Brazil	49	44				
					Mean of 53	**49**	
					Standard deviation 53	**18**	

a. MAS values controlling for the percentage of women among the IBM respondents in the country; computed only for Category 1 countries (see Appendix 2).

b. Only data for occupations filled by men available.

c. Gender identification not asked in surveys.

6.5. From the most "feminine" to the most "masculine" countries the values of both men and women became more masculine, but the country effect was larger for men than for women. From the lowest- to the highest-MAS countries, the range of MAS scores for men was about 50% larger than for women. There was less difference in women's values in this respect than in men's.

Exhibit 6.5 illustrates gender cultures. In Chapter 1, I argued that the word *culture* can also be ap-plied to the genders. Part of our mental programming depends on whether we were born as girls or boys. Like nationality, gender is an involuntary characteristic. Because of this, the effects of both nationality and gender on our mental programming are largely unconscious. Although both nationality and gender cultures are learned, not in-born, we learn their consequences so early that we never know anything else, and we are usually un-aware of other possibilities. Exhibit 6.5 shows

Exhibit 6.4 Masculinity Index Scores for Women and Men Separately, in Three Occupations and 15 Countries

Country	Country MAS Score	Unskilled Card Plant Personnel			Head Office Clerks			Branch Office Systems Engineers			Δ Scores Between Occupations (M and W)		
		M	W	Δ (M − W)	M	W	Δ (M − W)	M	W	Δ (M − W)	Clerks − Unskilled	Engineers − Clerks	Engineers − Unskilled
		(n = 3,211)	(n = 1,169)		(n = 3,388)	(n = 1,807)		(n = 4,123)	(n = 260)				
Japan	95	89	92a	(−3)	99	77	22	102	73	29	(−3)	−1	(−3)
Austria	79				69	34	35						
Great Britain	66	63	13	50	80	28	52	80	69	11	16	21	37
Germany (F.R.)	66	45	18	27	47	16	31	83	79	4	0	50	50
South Africa	63				52	19	33						
Australia	61				35	19	16	74	52	22		36	
Argentina	56				75	37	38						
Belgium	54				61	33	28						
Brazil	49				35	18	17	59	39	20		23	
France	43	28	0	28	71	−6	77	55	51	4	19	21	39
Spain	42				43	38	5						
Denmark	16				4	−10	14						
Netherlands	14	−8	21	13	−12	−9	−3						
Norway	8												
Sweden	5	−14	3	−17	−30	−28	−2	7	19	−12	−24	42	19
Mean of 5 countries (JPN, GBR, GER, FRA, SWE)		42	25	17	53	17	36	65	58	7	2	27	28
Mean of all available country scores	48	34	18	16	45	19	26	66	55	11	2	27	28
Spearman rank correlation with MAS		.99**	81	.33	.73***	.63**	.61**	.99***	.90**	.71*	.11	−.29	−.13

NOTE: M = men, W = women. Number of respondents = 10,722 men, 3,326 women (13,958 total).
a. Based on answers of 20 women only.

Exhibit 6.5.   Country MAS Scores by Gender

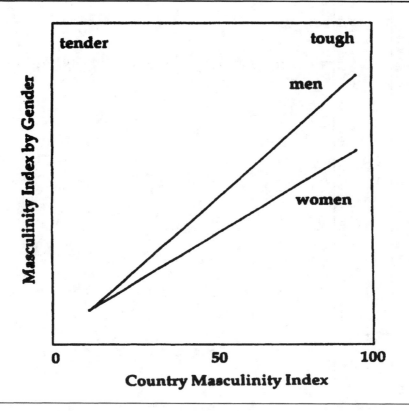

that, on average, men have been programmed with tougher values and women with more tender values, but that the gap between the genders varies by country. Even in countries at the feminine extreme of the Masculinity Index scale, like Sweden and Norway, men's values and women's values need not be identical, only they do not differ along a tough/tender dimension. Cultural differences according to gender are statistical rather than absolute: There is an overlap between the values of men and those of women so that any given value may be found among both men and women, only with different frequency.

The last three columns in Exhibit 6.4 show occupational differences in MAS taking men and women together. Systems engineers distinguished themselves considerably from the two other groups: They scored more masculine (compare Exhibit 6.2). The average female systems engineer scored more masculine than the average male clerk or unskilled worker. Occupation stands also for education plus social class; in all countries for which data were available, except Japan, the more highly educated, upper-middle-class systems engineers scored more masculine, assertive values than the others. In Japan there

was no systematic occupation/education difference (or at least it went one way for men, the other way for women). The largest occupation/education differences were visible for Germany, Sweden, and Australia.

Occupation/education and gender difference interacted also, as we can see by comparing the Δ scores between women and men for unskilled, clerks, and engineers. In France, Britain, and Germany female systems engineers scored almost as masculine as their male colleagues. Swedish female systems engineers and female unskilled scored even more masculine than their male colleagues. The women engineers pursued a career in an essentially male world. However, not in all countries did their values approach those of their male colleagues: In Japan, Australia, and Brazil the female engineers differed even more from their male colleagues than the female clerks. Most likely, in these countries they did not consider themselves as seriously competing with the men. The French pattern was extreme in that gender value differences were virtually zero for the engineers: Both men and women *cadres* scored average on MAS. For the *non-cadre* clerks, however, the men and women scored wide apart; among the

14 countries they showed the widest gap between male assertiveness and female nurturance. The German female engineers scored the most masculine of any of the samples of women except the Japanese unskilled. These German college-graduate women showed an assertiveness that bypassed many groups of men in other countries.

Work goals obviously also differed by age category. In the first edition of *Culture's Consequences,* I reviewed seven studies (six U.S., one German), published between 1957 and 1976, about the relationship between work goal importance and age (Hofstede, 1980a, pp. 361-362). The following trends were suggested by one or more of them:

- More important with age
  Security
  Social relationships
  Comfort
  Service
- Less important with age
  Intrinsic work
  Developing abilities
  Advancement
  Pleasure

Exhibit 6.6 shows the relationship between work goal importance and age for the international IBM population. Goal importance scores for four age brackets (20-29, 30-39, 40-49, and 50-59) were computed as the means across five large categories of employees covering the full range of status and educational levels: managers, professionals, customer engineers, clerks, and unskilled workers (a total of about 40,000, all 1971-73 data). For each goal and age bracket, the deviation from the mean of all four age brackets (expressed in standardized score points) was calculated. The trends in Exhibit 6.6 are very similar to those found in the literature review:

- More important with age
  Employment security
  Benefits
  Physical conditions
  Desirable area
  Manager
  Cooperation
- Less important with age
  Advancement
  Training
  Earnings
  Challenge
  Use of skills
  Personal time

Virtually no age effect at all was visible for recognition and freedom.

The IBM findings (based on an international respondent population) thus largely confirm the trends found in the (mainly U.S.) literature. The importance of "comfort" goals (desirable area and physical conditions) did not increase monotonically with age, but it did increase. For "service" and "pleasure" the IBM questionnaire had no items. A separate analysis by employee category (not in the exhibit) showed that employees with less education started worrying about employment security at an earlier age and also lost their interest in challenge and training earlier. Professionals and clerks showed a stronger interest in cooperation that was much less dependent on age than for the other three employee categories. Living in a desirable area was particularly important for those in the 40-49 age bracket regardless of education and job level.

The last column of Exhibit 6.6 shows whether each of the 14 work facets was primarily related to IDV or to MAS, and in what sense. The age effects for the facets related to IDV were mixed, as was mentioned in Chapter 5. However, the age effects for *all* facets related to MAS indicated decreasing masculinity with increasing age. So the link between age and MAS was quite strong and unequivocal.

Gradually, from age 25 to age 50, men and women at work reorient themselves with respect to the values associated with the masculinity/femininity dimension. Self-assertion (advancement, earnings, challenging work) becomes less important; security, environment (desirable area), and social relationships (manager, cooperation) become more important. Moreover, differences in these values between men and women disappear. Taking two employee categories with roughly equal educational levels, customer engineers (all male) and secretaries/typists (all female) and comparing their 1971-73 MAS scores for the 20-29 and the 50-59 age brackets, we find the following:

- Engineers, 20-29: MAS = 76
- Secretaries, 20-29: MAS = 29
- Engineers, 50-59: MAS = –19
- Secretaries, 50-59: MAS = –17

The gap of almost 50 points on the MAS scale between the male customer engineers and the female secretaries in the 20-29 age bracket completely disappeared for those 50-59.

Exhibit 6.7 shows schematically the age effects on MAS. When people grow older they tend to become more social and less ego oriented (lower MAS). At the same time, the gap between women and men's MAS values becomes smaller, and around age 50 it has closed completely. This is the age at which a woman's role as a potential

Exhibit 6.6   Differences of Standardized Mean Scores for the Importance of 14 Work Goals Among Each of Four Age Groups and Their Common Mean, Averaged Across Five Large Employee Categories

Work Goals	Standardized Goal Importance Score Differences – Mean of Five Employee Categories				Most Closely Associated Dimension and Sign of Corresponding Age Effect
	Ages 20-29	Ages 30-39	Ages 40-49	Ages 50-59	
Job content and learning					
Challenge	+42	+28	–20	–51	–MAS
Use of skills	+28	–8	0	–21	+IDV
Training	+103	+4	–36	–72	+IDV
Reward					
Recognition	+4	+7	–5	–5	±MAS
Advancement	+149	+50	–60	–140	–MAS
Earnings	+50	+45	–31	–64	–MAS
Interpersonal relations					
Manager	–47	–19	+16	+50	–MAS
Cooperation	–27	–14	+13	+27	–MAS
Freedom	–5	+5	–1	+2	±IDV
Security					
Employment security	–114	–22	+61	+74	–MAS
Benefits	–63	–29	+3	+88	–IDV
Comfort					
Personal time	+25	+13	–1	–37	–IDV
Desirable area	–60	–5	+46	+19	–MAS
Physical conditions	–31	–43	–7	+80	–IDV

NOTE: The categories are as follows: managers, professionals, clerks, customer engineers, and unskilled workers. Total number of respondents = 39,973; worldwide data, 1971-73.

childbearer has ended; there is no more reason for her values to differ from those of men.

This development fits the observation that young men and women foster more technical interests (which could be considered masculine), and older men and women foster more social interests. In terms of values (but not necessarily in terms of energy and vitality), older persons are more suitable as people managers and younger persons as technical managers.

Country MAS Scores and
Other IBM Survey Questions

IBM respondents in more masculine countries, compared with those in more feminine countries,

tended to endorse significantly more frequently the following items in the questionnaire (see the statistical section at the end of this chapter):

1. High stress (A37).
2. Decisions made by individuals are usually of higher quality than decisions made by groups (B57).
3. A large corporation is generally a more desirable place to work than a small company (C17), a corporation is responsible for its employees (B52) and for society (B58), and the private life of an employee is properly a matter of direct concern to the company (C19).
4. Most employees have an inherent dislike of work and will avoid it if they can (C13), and

Exhibit 6.7. MAS Scores by Gender and Age

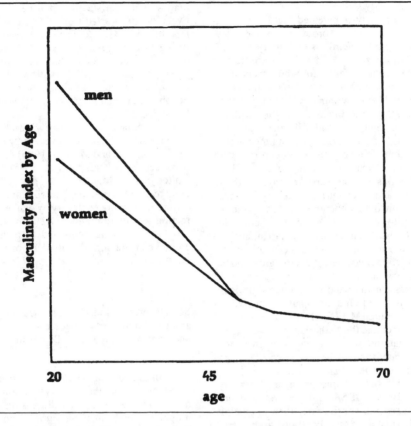

for getting ahead in industry, knowing influential people is usually more important than ability (C15).

The association of masculinity with higher stress is interesting because in Chapter 4 we saw that there is no evidence of systematic differences in stress between men and women in the same jobs. The conclusion is that stress is not in the gender but in the *gender role*. The association of masculinity with individual decisions being preferred over group decisions confirms the picture of the masculine decision maker who is not socially oriented. The "company" questions show that masculinity in a country is also (somewhat) associated with support for the large, responsible corporation that has a right to interfere in its employees' lives, whereas the feminine pattern is more to prefer the smaller company ("Small is beautiful"), to leave social responsibility to other institutions, and to reject company interference with people's private lives. The corporation belongs to the masculine world.

Finally, people in more masculine countries tend to hold more skeptical views of others, which

is demonstrated by their lesser rejection of McGregor's (1960) Theory X (employees dislike work) and their agreement that knowing influential people counts more than ability.

MAS and Work Centrality in IBM

An earlier analysis of the IBM survey data (reprinted in Hofstede, 1994b, chap. 3) compared two measures of the importance of work goals, also called work facets. One was the set of direct questions ("How important is it to you to . . .") used for computing the country Individual and Masculinity Indexes. This can be called a "sociological" measure because the answers reflect the respondents' social frames of reference and feelings of social desirability. The other measure is the strength of the correlation (for a group or category of respondents) between the respondents' satisfaction with each work facet and their overall satisfaction in the company: Those facets for which facet satisfaction correlates most strongly with overall satisfaction can be considered the most central ones. This is a "psychological" measure because it is unconscious and unaffected by social desirability.[14]

The earlier analysis revealed that the psychological measure tended to produce the same ordering of work facets regardless of country or occupation: *Challenge* and *earnings* were nearly always the two work facets for which facet satisfaction was most strongly correlated with overall satisfaction. That is, within any category of IBM employees, those scoring more satisfied with the challenge in their jobs and with their earnings were normally also the ones scoring more satisfied with their jobs in general. In contrast with this, the sociological measure, as we saw in Chapter 5 and in this chapter, varied strongly with the occupations and the countries of the respondents.

For 18 more or less homogeneous categories of IBM employees, representing five countries (France, Great Britain, Germany, Japan, and the Netherlands) and four groups of occupations, the rank correlations between the sociological and the psychological measure were computed across 22 work facets. Positive and sometimes significant correlations were found for Japan, Germany, and Great Britain (high MAS) and correlations around zero for France and the Netherlands (low MAS).[15] The correlations were stronger for the more highly educated than for the less educated occupations in all countries.

In the high-MAS countries Japan, Germany, and Great Britain, IBM employees rated as personally and socially desirable in their job mainly those facets that were associated with high overall job satisfaction. In the lower-MAS countries (France and the Netherlands), employees rated other job facets as personally and socially desirable (important). In rating work goal *importance* respondents chose their own frames of reference. They were not told in the questionnaire that their ultimate criterion should be maximal *job* satisfaction. It is obvious that in the lower-MAS countries, the ultimate criterion was *not* maximal job satisfaction. If we accept the hedonistic principle that people always try to maximize some kind of satisfaction, this leads to the conclusion that respondents in the lower-MAS countries tried to maximize a *life* satisfaction that was felt as socially desirable but did not overlap with job satisfaction. That is, in the higher-MAS countries the job took a more central position in the respondents' total life space than it did in the lower-MAS countries.

This is confirmed by data supplied by Near and Rechner (1993), who used 1976 Eurobarometer data for 10 countries to compute (product-moment) correlations between total life satisfaction on the one hand and both job satisfaction and nonwork satisfaction on the other. For all countries the correlation coefficient of life satisfaction

with nonwork satisfaction was slightly stronger than with job satisfaction, but the difference between the two varied from $.57 - .54 = .03$ in Ireland to $.65 - .41 = .24$ in France. Across 8 countries overlapping with the IBM set, the correlation of the difference in correlation coefficients with MAS was rho = $.73*$.[16] This shows that the more masculine a culture, the higher the relative weight of job rather than nonwork in determining total life satisfaction.[17]

The conclusion is a positive relationship between MAS and national levels of "work centrality."[18] England and Misumi (1986) found greater work centrality in Japan (MAS 95) than in the United States (MAS 62). Vroom (1964, p. 43) cited research within the United States showing a difference in work centrality by gender: Job satisfaction was more highly correlated with general satisfaction among employed men than among employed women, which also supports the association between work centrality and MAS.[19]

Societal Versus Individual Masculinity and Femininity, and Whether Mas and Fem Are One or Two Dimensions

As in the case of IDV, the objection is sometimes made that masculinity/femininity should not be seen as one bipolar dimension but as two unipolar dimensions, *masculine* and *feminine*. Bem (1974) developed the Sex Role Inventory, which consists of adjectives that a sample of male and female U.S. students judged to be more socially desirable in American society for one gender than for the other. Bem's inventory contains both "feminine" and "masculine" scales. On the basis of their self-descriptions, students were divided into four types: masculine, feminine, androgynous (scoring both types of characteristics), and undifferentiated (scoring neither). From 444 male students, 55% scored masculine only and 11% feminine only; from 279 female students, 54% scored feminine only and 20% masculine only; the others were androgynous or undifferentiated. Thus only just over half of these respondents corresponded in their own eyes to gender trait stereotypes (Bem, 1975, p. 636). Typical items from Bem's masculine scale are "aggressive," "ambitious," and "competitive"; typical items from the feminine scale are "affectionate," "compassionate," and "understanding." Masculine and androgynous persons yielded less to pressure to conform than did feminines; feminine and androgynous persons showed more supportive behavior toward a lonely fellow student than did masculines. Bem's studies showed that actual behavior need not correspond to the national stereotype; differences were statistical rather than absolute.

Bem compared individuals; I compared countries. An individual can be both masculine and feminine at the same time, but what I found is that at the country level a culture is predominantly either one or the other. When one moves to a higher level of analysis, the number of factors found normally gets smaller: At the level of country means, "more people with masculine values" was statistically so strongly correlated with "fewer people with feminine values" that together they formed one single dimension.[20] In Chapter 5, I used the same argumentation for the individualism/collectivism dimension: A person can be both individualist and collectivist, but a country culture is predominantly either one or the other.

Masculinity Versus Individualism

In the psychological literature, the masculinity/femininity distinction is sometimes confused with the distinction between individualism and collectivism. American authors have considered feminine goals as an expression of collectivism; on the other hand, a Korean student sent me a master's thesis in which she associated collectivist goals with *masculinity*.

The ind/col and mas/fem dimensions are statistically wholly independent, as is immediately visible from Exhibit 6.8, in which the country scores on mas/fem (from Exhibit 6.3) and ind/col (from Exhibit 5.1) are plotted against each other. The dimensions have to be statistically independent because they were based on orthogonal factors. The difference between them is that individualism/collectivism is about "I" versus "we," independence from versus dependence on in-groups. Relationships in collectivist cultures are basically predetermined by group ties: "Groupiness" is collectivist, not feminine. Masculinity/femininity is about ego enhancement versus relationship enhancement, regardless of group ties. The biblical story of the Good Samaritan who helps a Jew in need—someone from an enemy ethnic group—is an illustration of feminine and not of collectivist values.

The difference between the two dimensions has been clearly demonstrated in a series of laboratory experiments by Bond, Leung, and Wan (1982), Nauta (1983), and Kim, Park, and Suzuki (1990). These researchers studied reward allocation by students in different countries. Bond et al.'s subjects were about 100 students each in Hong Kong and in the United States; Nauta extended this with more than 100 students in the Netherlands. Kim et al. did a slightly modified replication of the study with more than 100 stu-

dents each in South Korea, Japan, and again the United States. Participants read a scenario describing a student group member who made high, medium, or low task contributions toward a group project for a university course and also high, medium, or low "maintenance" (of interpersonal relationships) contributions. They then scored their intentions as to how to reward this person; both what grade to give her or him (a competence reward) and whether they would choose this person as a friend (a maintenance reward). Students in Hong Kong and South Korea (low IDV) favored a more egalitarian distribution of rewards, whereas those in Japan, the Netherlands, and the United States (medium to high IDV) favored a more equitable distribution (rewards according to performance). However, other country differences suggested an interaction between cultural individualism and cultural masculinity. Students in the United States (high IDV, high MAS) were more equitable in distributing competence rewards, and those in the Netherlands (high IDV, low MAS) were more equitable in distributing maintenance rewards. Students in Hong Kong and the United States (high MAS) chose the high task performer as a preferred future study group partner, whereas students in the Netherlands (low MAS) chose the person with a high maintenance contribution both as a preferred future study group partner and as a friend.[21]

Another illustration of the difference between IDV and MAS is found in a research project by Kashima et al. (1995), who used a questionnaire to study the self-concepts of female and male students in introductory psychology courses in Australia, Japan, South Korea, Hawaii, and the mainland United States, a total of more than 1,000 respondents. They subjected 40 questionnaire items to a discriminant analysis across 10 groups: the men and the women in each of the five locations. Two main discriminant functions emerged. The first separated women and men in Australia and the United States from those in Korea and Japan, with Hawaii in between. It was associated with "agency," meaning independence of action and opinion, and "assertiveness," that is, expressing opinions, on the positive pole, and "cohesiveness" on the opposite pole. Across four countries—I have no data for Hawaii—it rank correlated perfectly with IDV (rho = 1.00**). Kashima et al.'s second discriminant function separated men and women from Korea from those in Japan, with the others in between. It was associated with "relatedness"; a typical item was "I feel like doing something for people in trouble because I can almost feel their pains." From the five culture indexes it was most strongly correlated with MAS (rho = −.80 across four countries). Gender differences within the locations were mainly

Exhibit 6.8. An IDV × MAS Plot for 50 Countries and Three Regions

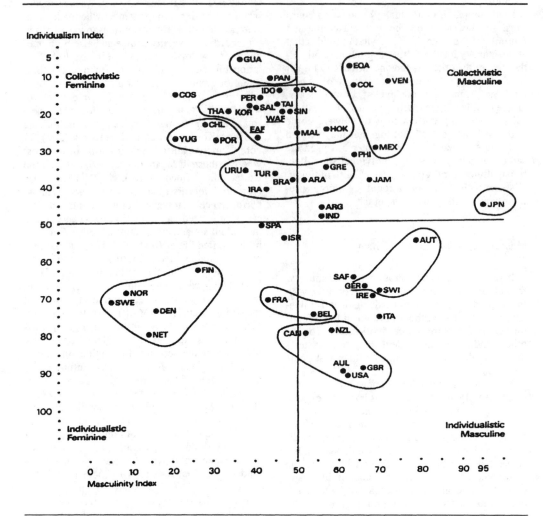

associated with this latter discriminant function, but they were smaller than the country differences. A plot of the scores showed that gender differences were largest for Japan, followed by United States and Australia, and very small for Korea (Kashima et al., 1995, fig. 1). These differences rank correlated perfectly with MAS (rho = 1.00** across the four countries).

Kashima et al. (1995), in their discussion, recognize the distinction between "the individualist dimension of the self" and "the relational dimension of the self"; they also recognize that "gender differences emerged most clearly on the relational difference of the self, the extent to which people regard themselves as emotionally related to others" (p. 932). However, they overlook the obvious link between this second dimension and national masculinity versus femininity.

Validating MAS Against Data From Other Sources

The Need to Control for Wealth Differences

Since the first edition of *Culture's Consequences* appeared in 1980, mas/fem has been the most disputed and overlooked of the four dimensions of national cultures found. At the same time, the number and scope of validations of the dimension have increased dramatically. A volume titled *Masculinity and Femininity: The Taboo Dimension of National Cultures,* which is partly monograph, partly reader (Hofstede & Associates, 1998), has been devoted to this dimension alone. The remainder of this chapter draws partly on the content of that book. It will show the wide range of issues in societies related to the mas/fem dimension. "One important point that anthropologists have always made is that aspects of social life which do not seem to be related to each other, actually are related" (Harris, 1981, p. 9). The measures correlated with masculinity/femininity are perfect examples.

Masculinity/femininity is the only one of the four IBM dimensions that is entirely unrelated to national wealth: There are just as many poor as there are wealthy masculine, or feminine, countries. Many data that can be used for validating the culture dimensions are at least partly dependent on wealth: This is even more the case for country-level indicators than for country means on survey data. Therefore it is often necessary to control for wealth (for example, by separating wealthy from poor countries) before one can determine relationships with MAS. In the validation studies listed in the first edition of *Culture's Consequences,* each of the four indexes appeared with about equal frequency, but in regressions MAS came significantly more often in second or even in third place after one or two of the other dimensions that were associated with wealth (see Hofstede & Associates, 1998, p. 22). This means that it may take a somewhat more sophisticated research approach to find the full implications of MAS differences than it takes to validate the other three indexes.

Straight Replications of the IBM Survey

Chapter 2 referred to the general problem of measuring cultural differences across varying populations. This problem applies particularly strongly in the measurement of mas/fem. Different respondent groups may require different ways of measuring. Although the underlying cultural syndrome is universal, the measurable issues that relate to it are not always the same across categories of respondents.

Managers attending courses at IMEDE. Chapter 5 showed that in the work goals of 362 IMEDE participants from 15 countries, both factors individual/collective and ego/social were replicated. The ranks of seven out of the eight goals associated with MAS were positively correlated across the IMEDE and IBM studies, and for "advancement" and "desirable area" the correlations were significant (rho = .59** and rho = .52*, respectively).[22]

Elite alumni from the Salzburg Seminar. As described in Chapters 2 to 5, Hoppe (1990, 1993, 1998) replicated the IBM research on elites from 19 countries. Using VSM 82 formulas, Hoppe found significant correlations between his elite country scores and IBM country scores for IDV, PDI, and UAI, but not for MAS (a nonsignificant *r* = .36). MAS scores in IBM combined the importance of "advancement" and "earnings," because in the IBM system promotions and earnings went hand in hand. For Hoppe's elite respondents, country mean scores for the importance of advancement and of earnings were negatively correlated: In countries where respondents stressed advancement they focused less on earnings, and vice versa. It turns out that for non-IBM respondents "advancement" more than "earnings" expressed what the mas/fem syndrome stands for. On the basis of data from a number of replications of which the Hoppe results formed an important part, a new version of the VSM was developed (the VSM 94; see Appendix 4). It kept only the work goals "advancement" and "cooperation" and replaced "earnings" and "security" in the MAS formula with new items based on beliefs, not on work goals. Hoppe (1998) recalculated his MAS scores with the new formulas. They are found in Exhibit 6.18 in the statistical section of this chapter, and they correlated with MAS in IBM with *r* = .83***.

Higher-income consumers surveyed by the EMS 97. Chapters 2, 4, and 5 referred to a replication of the IBM questions in the 15-country European Media and Marketing Survey 1997 by Inter/View International; it used the 20 questions of the VSM 94 (Appendix 4). The EMS country scores on MAS based on the VSM 94 questions and formula are included in Exhibit 6.18; they represent an independent validation of the new formula. Across the 15 countries, the MAS scores from the IBM employees in 1970 and from the EMS consumers in 1997 surveyed with the VSM 94 were correlated with *r* = .72**, rho = .78***.

Commercial airline pilots. The study of more than 15,000 commercial airline pilots from 23 countries by Helmreich and Merritt (1998) was also mentioned in Chapters 2 through 5. Across 21 overlapping countries, Helmreich and Merritt found an insignificant correlation between MAS in IBM and the MAS scores for pilots, computed with the VSM 82 formula (*r* = .17). For the pilot population "advancement" and "earnings" country scores did correlate positively, as in IBM, but the mean importance of both other MAS items "job security" and "cooperation" hardly varied across countries at all; for both items it was high anywhere. Whereas the IBM employee respondents all shared the same employer, the pilots shared not their employer but their profession. As in the case of UAI (Chapter 4), the MAS questions from IBM proved unsuitable for differentiating countries within the pilots' professional culture. The pilots' scores could not be recalculated with the VSM 94 because the necessary items had not been included in their survey.

Replications using only the work goals questions. Hofstede, Kolman, Nicolescu, and Pajumaa (1996) surveyed student samples from 10 countries and language groups about the work goals in the students' ideal job after graduation. The results for IDV were discussed in Chapter 5. Scores for MAS, computed with the VSM 82 formulas, across five overlapping groups correlated with MAS in IBM with $r = .72$ ($p = .086$).[23] Again the scores could not be recalculated with the VSM 94 because the new belief questions had not been included in the surveys.

Other replications. Søndergaard's (1994) review of 61 smaller replications was mentioned in Chapters 3 through 5. Of 19 replications allowing comparison of country score ranks with IBM, 14 confirmed the MAS differences; according to the sign test, this provides significant support for the dimension at the .05 level (one-tailed).

MAS Scores Versus Other Values Surveys

I have referred in Chapters 1, 4, and 5 to the massive study of values by the Israeli psychologist Shalom Schwartz (1992, 1994) among elementary school teachers and university students in 44 countries or subcultural groups, covering more than 25,000 respondents. Exhibit 5.17 shows that in the teachers' data one of Schwartz's value dimensions, "mastery," across 23 overlapping countries correlated significantly with MAS ($r = .53**$). This dimension comprises the values ambitious, capable, choosing own goals, daring, independent, and successful, all on the positive pole. These values clearly confirm a masculine ethos. In the responses to the same survey by students, mastery correlated with MAS with $r = .39*$ across 22 overlapping countries. None of the other IBM indexes correlated with mastery.

In a handbook chapter on "values," Smith and Schwartz (1997) have reinterpreted Schwartz's culture-level map of values as representing three dimensions: conservatism versus autonomy, hierarchy versus egalitarianism, and mastery versus harmony. My correlations with Schwartz's data confirmed the first two (see Chapter 5), but they do not support treating mastery and harmony as opposite poles of one dimension.[24] A dimension "dealing with the environment," of which mastery and harmony would be the opposite poles, appeals to New Age and postmodern fashions, but the correlations of mastery with MAS and harmony with UAI suggest underlying psychological mechanisms of a different nature. What I read in the Schwartz culture-level values database is a strong IDV-PDI dimension and additional independent dimensions associated with MAS and with UAI; so the basic three factors found in the factor analy-

sis of the IBM data (Chapter 2) reappear in the much broader values set used by Schwartz, which strongly supports the construct validity of the dimensions.

Chapters 3, 4, and 5 all used data from the 1990-93 World Values Survey (WVS; Inglehart, 1997; Inglehart, Basañez, & Moreno, 1998) across 43 countries around the world, of which 26 or 27 overlapped with the IBM set. In Chapter 5, I referred to the macroanalysis of country scores from all parts of the WVS, in which Inglehart found two "key cultural dimensions" labeled "well-being versus survival" and "secular-rational versus traditional authority." Exhibit 5.18 showed that the dimension "well-being versus survival" in a stepwise multiple regression was associated with the combination of high IDV and low MAS ($R^2 = .75$, $R = .86***$). This links femininity to well-being.

A similar link has been made by Arrindell et al. (1997) and Arrindell (1998), who used data on subjective well-being from 36 countries in the IBM set compiled by Veenhoven (1993) plus one additional source; the Veenhoven data were partly derived from the WVS. Arrindell found (as I did; see Chapter 4) that UAI was the only significant independent predictor of well-being, but that the interaction between national wealth and MAS also played a significant role ($R^2 = .47$, $R = .69***$): MAS was positively correlated with well-being across the 17 poorer countries, but negatively across the 17 wealthier countries.[25] Wealthy feminine countries reported the highest levels of well-being. People in poor countries are more involved in the struggle for survival, and it seems that under these conditions feminine values would tend to make them more vulnerable.

Chapter 4 introduced McClelland's (1961) country scores for "need for achievement" (n_{Ach}) based on a content analysis of children's readers. Exhibit 4.13 shows across 22 countries a significant negative correlation between UAI and 1925 n_{Ach} (rho = $-.60**$). It also identifies a substantial second-order positive correlation of 1925 n_{Ach} with MAS (multiple regression R^2 with UAI .31, with UAI + MAS .44). High n_{Ach} as a national characteristic stands for a willingness to take risks (low UAI) combined with masculine assertiveness (high MAS). Five of the seven highest n_{Ach} countries were from the Anglo group (Ireland, Australia, Canada, Great Britain, and United States). The lowest n_{Ach} country was the Netherlands, which did not score high on UAI but scored very low on MAS.[26]

McClelland's "need for achievement" defines human accomplishment in a way specific to a certain cultural and economic environment—in particular, to the economic environment of early capitalism. In a wider sense, in the spirit of the quote from Margaret Mead at the beginning of this chapter, achievement can apply to anything a human being can accomplish. In low-UAI, high-MAS cultures, achievement tends to be defined in terms of ego boosting, wealth, and recognition. In no country does wealth have so strong a symbolic value as in the United States, which also happens to be McClelland's home culture.[27] In high-UAI cultures, in contrast, achievements are defined in terms of the security they offer; in low-MAS cultures, they are defined in terms of the quality of human contacts and of the living environment.

In Exhibit 3.14, the answers from samples of students from 17 countries answering L. V. Gordon's Survey of Interpersonal Values are correlated with the four IBM indexes and GNP/capita. For the male students higher MAS was associated with less benevolence (importance of doing things for other people, sharing with others, helping the unfortunate, being generous; $r = -.59**$) and with more need for recognition (importance of being looked up to and admired, being considered important, attracting favorable notice, achieving recognition; $r = .50*$). This shows the positive association of masculinity among men with assertiveness and the negative association with nurturance. Interestingly, among the women student samples (from 11 countries) these associations were *not* found, which confirms the finding in the IBM data that women's values along this dimension differ less among countries than do men's values.

In Exhibit 5.19, the results are reported of Bass's IRGOM Life Goals exercise among samples of managers in 12 countries. My ecological factor analysis of the Life Goals scores showed the existence of two factors. The first, labeled *hedonism-skill*, was correlated with IDV (rho = .76**). The second factor, labeled *assertiveness-service*, was strongly correlated with MAS (rho = .84***). This factor contrasts leadership, independence, and self-realization with service. These goals are defined in the exercise as follows. Leadership means "to become an influential leader; to organize and control others; to achieve community or organizational goals." Independence means "to have the opportunity for freedom of thought and action; to be one's own boss." Self-realization means "to optimize personal development; to realize one's full creative and innovative potential." These were all found at the masculine end of the scale. Service means "to contribute to the satisfaction of others; to be helpful to others who need it." This was located at the feminine end of the scale. So on a very different sample the assertive goals were again associated with masculinity and the service, or nurturing, goal was associated with femininity.

Lynn and Martin (1995) correlated medical and related indexes for 37 countries with the national normative scores for three dimensions of an individual-level personality test, the Eysenck Personality Questionnaire (EPQ). In Chapter 4, it was shown that across 25 overlapping countries the national norms for "neuroticism versus emotional stability" were significantly correlated with UAI (rho = .44*). There was a second-order positive correlation with MAS ($R^2 = .19$ for UAI, .36 for UAI + MAS, based on ranks). Uncertainty-avoiding and masculine cultures had lower national norms for emotional stability. National norms for "psychoticism versus ego control" also correlated with MAS (rho = .36*); masculine cultures also had lower norms for ego control. In masculine cultures the norms for minding others seem to be lower.

Summary of Connotations
of the Masculinity Index Found
in Surveys and Related Material

In analogy with Exhibits 3.6, 4.4, and 5.3, Exhibit 6.9 integrates the connotations of low and high MAS scores found so far. Again, the polarized picture does not mean that all cultures have to be placed either left or right; actual values will often be somewhere between the extremes. The data on which Exhibit 6.9 is based were once more derived from a very broad range of studies, including narrow-sample surveys, public opinion surveys, and nonsurvey country comparisons. The variety of phenomena correlated with the mas/fem dimension is as large as the variety related to ind/col; both dimensions describe extremely fundamental collective mental programs affecting oth individuals and societies.

Origins and Implications of Country Masculinity Differences

The Masculinity Societal Norm

Exhibit 6.10 condenses and complements the summary of Exhibit 6.9 into an integrated picture of the general societal norm behind the low- and high-MAS syndromes, in analogy with the previous chapters. Again this is a value system shared by the majority in the middle classes in a society.

One-line definitions of Masculinity and Femininity as the two poles of a dimension of national culture are: **"Masculinity stands for a society in which social gender roles are clearly distinct: Men are supposed to be assertive, tough, and focused on material success; women are supposed to be more modest, tender, and concerned with the quality of life. Femininity stands for a society in which social gender roles overlap: Both men and women are supposed to be modest, tender, and concerned with the quality of life."**

Exhibit 6.9 Summary of Value Connotations of MAS Differences Found in Surveys and Other Comparative Studies

Low MAS	High MAS
Cooperation at work and relationship with boss important.	Challenge and recognition in jobs important.
Living area and employment security important.	Advancement and earnings important.
Values of women and men hardly different.	Values of women and men very different.
Lower job stress.	Higher job stress.
Belief in group decisions.	Belief in individual decisions.
Preference for smaller companies.	Preference for large corporations.
Private life protected from employer.	Employer may invade employees' private lives.
Belief in Theory Y.	Belief in Theory X.
Promotion by merit.	Promotion by protection.
Work not central in a person's life space.	Work very central in a person's life space.
Relational self: empathy with others regardless of their group.	Self is ego: not my brother's keeper.
Among elites and consumers, stress on cooperation.	Among elites and consumers, stress on advancement.
Schwartz's values surveys among teachers and students: low mastery.	Schwartz's surveys: high mastery: ambitious, daring, independent.
Inglehart's World Values Survey analysis: well-being values.	Inglehart's WVS analysis: survival values.
Higher well-being in rich countries.	Higher well-being in poor countries.
Achievement in terms of quality of contacts and environment.	Achievement in terms of ego boosting, wealth, and recognition.
Gordon's male students: more benevolence.	Gordon's male students: greater need for recognition.
IRGOM managers' life goals: service.	IRGOM managers' life goals: leadership and self-realization.
Higher norms for emotional stability and ego control.	Lower norms for emotional stability and ego control.

Masculinity and Femininity in the Family

As only a small part of gender role differentiation is biologically determined, the stability of gender role patterns is almost entirely a matter of socialization (Exhibit 1.5). Socialization means that both girls and boys learn their place in society and, once they have learned it, the majority of them *want it that way*. We find the same process here as we found in Chapter 3 for the relationship between superiors and subordinates (La Boétie's "voluntary servitude"): In male-dominated societies, most women want the male dominance.

A very important part of gender role socialization takes place in the family, whether this be the nuclear family of the modern industrial society, the extended family of more traditional societies, the one-parent family more and more common in "postindustrial" societies, the commune, or even the day nursery, which partly replaces the family. In all these institutions children see adults of different genders (but mostly females) fulfilling certain roles; they more or less quickly become

aware of their own gender category and look for adults to identify with.

In the family the gender role pattern is transferred together with other values. Power distance, for example, is also transferred in the family; I assume it to reflect the degree of absoluteness of the authority of adults over the children.[28] Masculinity or femininity reflects the difference in roles between the parents and between other male and female adults.

Exhibit 6.11 plots PDI scores (from Exhibit 3.1) against MAS scores (from Exhibit 6.3). In the right half of the diagram, where PDI is high, inequality between parents and children is a societal norm. Children are supposed to be controlled by obedience. In the left half, where PDI is low, children are controlled by the examples set by parents. In the lower half of the diagram, where MAS is high, inequality between fathers' and mothers' roles (father tough, mother less tough) is also a societal norm. Men are supposed to deal with facts, women with feelings, which means that children are socialized toward a strong differentiation be-

Exhibit 6.10 The Masculinity Societal Norm

Low MAS	High MAS
Relationship orientation.	Ego orientation.
Quality of life and people are important.	Money and things are important.
Stress on who you are.	Stress on what you do.
Work in order to live.	Live in order to work.
Minimum emotional and social role differentiation between the genders.	Maximum emotional and social role differentiation between the genders.
Men should be tender and take care of both performance and relationships; women should be the same.	Men should be tough and take care of performance; women should be tender and take care of relationships.
Men and women should be modest.	Men should be and women may be assertive and ambitious.
Sympathy for the weak.	Sympathy for the strong.
Small and slow are beautiful.	Big and fast are beautiful.

Exhibit 6.11. A MAS × PDI Plot for 50 Countries and Three Regions

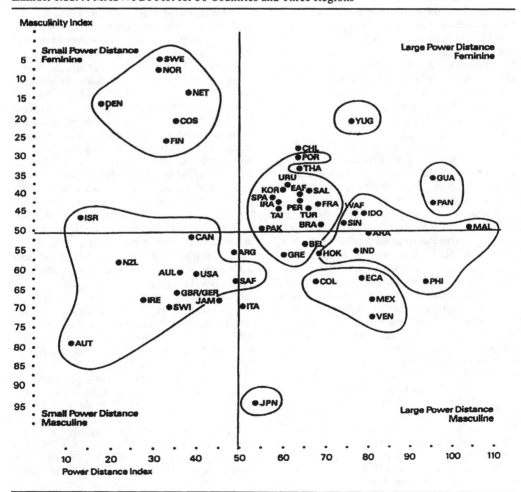

tween the genders. This differentiation is extreme in Japan, the most masculine country.[29] In the upper half of the diagram, where MAS is low, roles of mothers and fathers overlap: Both deal with the facts and with the soft things in life, socializing children toward weak gender differentiation.

Thus the lower right-hand quadrant of Exhibit 6.11 (unequal and tough) stands for a norm of a dominant, tough father and a submissive mother who, although also fairly tough, is at the same time the refuge for consolation and tender feelings. The extreme example is Japan, where the division of labor between the parents is almost complete.[30] The upper right-hand quadrant (unequal and tender) represents a societal norm of two dominant parents, sharing the same concern for the quality of life and for relationships, both providing at times authority *and* tenderness. In the countries in the lower left-hand quadrant (equal and tough) the norm is for nondominant parents to set an example in which father is tough and deals with facts and mother is somewhat less tough and deals with feelings. The resulting role model is that boys should assert themselves and girls should please and be pleased. Boys don't cry and should fight back when attacked; girls may cry and don't fight. Finally, in the upper left-hand quadrant (equal and tender) the norm is for fathers and mothers not to dominate and for both to be concerned with relationships, with the quality of life, with facts *and* feelings, setting an example of a relative equality of gender roles in the family context.

The above typology has the weakness of all typologies in that no real-life situation entirely fits its descriptions. Also, the family context depends strongly on the country's position on the individualism/collectivism dimension. In a collectivist society the "family" is the extended family, and the center of dominant authority could very well be the grandfather as long as he is still alive, with the father as a model of obedience. Ultraindividualist societies contain many one-parent families in which role models are incomplete, or in which outsiders provide the missing roles. The typology serves to stress the importance of a society's role distributions in the family with regard to the values that are transferred from one generation to the next.

Gender-related values and behaviors are programmed into us in subtle ways and from a very early age. A comparative study of the behaviors of mothers and 3- to 4-month-old babies in Japan and the United States showed among other things that the Japanese baby boys were significantly noisier than the Japanese girls, whereas the reverse was true for the U.S. babies (Otaki, Durrett, Richards, Nyquist, & Pennebaker, 1986). This difference cannot be inborn. It is a result of the mother's con-

ditioning of her child, which differs according to the child's gender and the nationality of the mother. The mother encourages or soothes the child according to the expectations in her society about the behavior of boys and girls. Parents' expectations become self-fulfilling prophecies.[31]

Best and Williams (1993) reported on a study of gender trait stereotypes of children 5-6 and 8-9 years old in 25 countries. They used a set of 32 very short stories for which each child respondent had to choose whether the actor was female or male. The scoring system was based on stereotypes found in the United States and characterized answers as gender-stereotypical or counter-stereotypical. The proportion of gender-stereotypical answers increased from 61% at age 5 to 71% at age 8, and the country differences at both ages were about equally large. Children in Muslim countries tended to learn gender stereotypes earlier than did those in Christian countries. In an earlier study in the United States, these researchers had found that in that country at age 15, 89% of answers were stereotypical.

Van Rossum (1998) reported survey data on the goals that 11-year-old children claimed to pursue in the games they played. Across more than 500 children in the United States (MAS 62), playing goals of boys and girls differed significantly in the sense that boys went after performance and girls went after relationships and avoiding being left out. Across 129 children in the Netherlands (MAS 14) no significant differences in playing goals between boys and girls were found. Van Rossum's study confirms that gender differentiation in child socialization is strong in the masculine culture and weak in the feminine culture.

The mas/fem dimension does not affect only how families develop role differences between boys and girls. According to Exhibit 6.5, both men *and* women hold tougher values in masculine countries and more tender values in feminine ones. In masculine countries both boys and girls learn to be ambitious and competitive, although the ambition of the girls may be directed toward the achievements of their brothers and later of their husbands and sons. In feminine countries both boys and girls learn to be nonambitious and modest. Assertive behavior and attempts at excelling, which are appreciated in masculine cultures, are easily ridiculed in feminine ones, where excellence is something one keeps to oneself. In masculine cultures children learn to admire the strong; popular fiction heroes made in the United States include Batman and Rambo.[32] In feminine cultures children learn sympathy for the underdog and the antihero. "Rasmus Klump" (called Petzi in translations), small and friendly, is a Danish comic hero; "Ollie B. Bommel" (Mr. Bumble), a clumsy and naive antihero, has become a national cartoon personality among Dutch intellectuals.

Gibbons, Richter, Wiley, and Stiles (1996) did a classroom exercise with 11- to 16-year-old adolescents in Guatemala, Iceland, Mexico, and the United States. The task was to rank individually 10 characteristics of the ideal person of the opposite sex. The smallest sample size was 49 in Iceland. Seven characteristics showed significant differences between countries: "likes children," "is very intelligent," "has a lot of money," "is kind and honest," "is fun," "has good looks," and "is sexy." I correlated the reported country mean scores on these seven characteristics with the four IBM indexes and with 1990 GNP/capita across the four countries, substituting Norway for Iceland.[33] Primarily correlated with IDV were the importance of "is fun" ($r = .98**$), "is sexy" ($r = .86$), and "has good looks" ($r = .73$). Primarily (negatively) correlated with MAS was the importance of "likes children" ($r = -.84$, $p = .08$). The importance of "has a lot of money" correlated highest with GNP/capita ($r = .84$) and so did, negatively, "is very intelligent" ($r = -.98**$) and "is kind and honest" ($r = -.70$). So adolescents in individualist societies showed hedonistic values, whereas those in feminine societies looked for opposite-sex partners who liked children. High-MAS societies tend to treat children as adults; some German authors (MAS 66) have characterized their own society as *kindfeindlich* (hostile to children).

In an earlier study, Gibbons, Stiles, Schnellmann, and Morales-Hidalgo (1990) compared pictures drawn of the ideal man or woman by the same adolescents in Guatemala, Mexico, and the United States. Compared to Mexico (MAS 69) and the United States (MAS 62), Guatemalan (MAS 37) adolescents showed fewer gender differences in their ideal pictures. Stiles, Gibbons, and Peters (1993) compared pictures by adolescents from the United States and the Netherlands (MAS 14). In the United States, in 45% of cases the ideal person was drawn as being at work; in the Netherlands, this was true in only 20% of cases. U.S. drawings linked work with success, achievement, and wealth. Dutch drawings focused on the quality of life: sports, relaxation, attractiveness, and humor.

Chapter 4 referred to Stoetzel's (1983, p. 265) analysis of the 1981-82 European Values Survey, in which he showed the balance of positive versus negative feelings about the family. Across nine European countries the "balance" scores were negatively correlated with UAI ($r = -.88**$) with a strong second-order negative correlation with MAS ($R = .97***$). In the 1990-93 World Values Survey across 26 countries, satisfaction with home life (Exhibit 4.12; WVS question 180) was correlated with IDV (rho = .67***) with again a significant second-order negative correlation with MAS ($R = .73***$). Family life, other factors being equal, was more rewarding in feminine countries.

Ryback, Sanders, Lorentz, and Koestenblatt (1980) asked students in six countries to answer, on the basis of their general ideas about child-rearing practices in their countries as well as their own home experience, whether children in their countries were allowed to express aggression. The proportions of yes answers varied from 61% in the United States to 5% in Thailand; these answers were correlated with MAS ($r = .90**$).[34]

The WVS questionnaire started with a block of questions of the type "Please say, from each of the following, how important it is in your life," followed by the topics of work, family, friends, leisure, politics, and religion (questions 4-9). Inglehart et al. (1998) published the percentages answering "very important," which I standardized across the six topics.[35] Across the 26 overlapping countries the standardized importance of three topics correlated significantly with national wealth (1990 GNP/capita) only: work (negatively, rho = $-.65***$)[36] and leisure and politics (positively, rho = .56** and rho = .42*). In affluent societies work was rated less important in people's lives and leisure and politics more important, independent of culture as measured by the IBM dimensions. The other three topics showed multiple correlation patterns as follows:

- *Family* (question 5) was correlated with MAS (rho = .50**) followed by IDV ($R = .65***$).[37] The family was rated relatively more important in masculine, individualist societies.

- *Friends, acquaintances* (question 6) were correlated with PDI (rho = $-.55**$) followed by MAS (with negative sign, $R = .67***$) and by IDV ($R = .74***$). Friends were rated more important in low power distance, feminine, individualist societies.

- *Religion* (question 9) was correlated with national wealth (rho = .78***) followed by MAS ($R = .83$); see the discussion of religion later in this chapter.

The three topics share their correlation with MAS. The masculine values syndrome rated the family and religion as more important and friends as less important.

The difference in importance of the family versus importance of friends can be understood from the answers to another WVS question (question 224), which asked for a choice between two statements:

A. Regardless of what the qualities and faults of one's parents are, one must always love and respect them.

B. One does not have the duty to respect and love parents who have not earned it by their behavior and attitudes.

Across the 26 overlapping countries percentages choosing answer A correlated with PDI ($r = .65***$) plus MAS ($R = .80***$).[38] In countries in the upper left-hand corner of Exhibit 6.11 (low PDI and feminine) the feeling was strongest that parents have to *earn* the love and respect of their children. This shows that there is something absolute, even religious, about the family as an institution in masculine societies. In feminine societies the quality of relationships, including those with friends and acquaintances, occupies a more important place.

The European and World Values Surveys included data about demographics and values related to marriage and cohabitation. In the 1981-82 round of these surveys, percentages of respondents cohabiting (living together unmarried, whether or not with children) across 12 countries correlated with MAS with rho = $-.52*$.[39] The institution of marriage was holier in masculine than in feminine countries.[40] Exhibit 4.12 shows the correlations with two statements from the 1990-93 round. The first was "A child needs a home with both a father and a mother to grow up happily" (WVS question 214). The second: "A job is alright but what most women really want is a home and children" (WVS question 220). Both items correlated with IDV across all countries and with UAI across the wealthier countries, but both also showed significant positive higher-order correlations with MAS, the first across 24 countries (second-order, $R = .68***$), the second both across 24 countries (third-order, increasing R from .75*** to .82***) and across 17 wealthier countries (second-order, $R = .86***$). Masculine cultures prefer women to stay home.

Chapter 5 mentioned a block of 13 WVS questions about "things which some people think make for a successful marriage" (questions 198-210). After standardization, the importance of "tastes and interests in common" correlated significantly with MAS (rho = .37*). In feminine cultures marriage partners—and especially the wife—are less dependent on each other in these matters.

Chapter 5 also discussed the 37-country study by Buss (1989, 1994) of criteria for selecting a potential marriage partner. Across 28 overlapping countries, grooms' and brides' preferences were strongly correlated with IDV. In collectivist countries bridegrooms preferred age differences at marriage to be larger and wanted their brides to be industrious, wealthy, and chaste; brides also wanted their husbands to be the right age and wealthy, but grooms' industriousness played a smaller role and their chastity none at all. There were no relationships between either grooms' or brides' preferences and MAS. However, the *differences between grooms' and brides' desires* produced two significant correlations with MAS, for "chastity" and for "industriousness." For chastity, the grooms/brides difference correlated significantly with both UAI (rho = .49**) and MAS (rho = .39*); the multiple correlation coefficient with UAI and MAS was $R = .61***$.[41] In masculine societies women are supposed to be chaste before marriage, men are not. The difference between industriousness of the partner as desired by grooms versus brides was only significantly correlated with MAS (rho = $-.50***$). The negative correlation means that in masculine countries industriousness is deemed more important for women than for men; in feminine countries, it is equally important or unimportant for both.

The Japanese market research agency Wacoal Corporation (1993) collected data about preferred partners among young women in eight Asian capital cities. I later did a secondary analysis on these data (Hofstede, 1996b). A unique aspect of this project was that the comparison with the IBM data was made exclusively across Asian countries, showing that mas/fem can also be validated without the inclusion of European countries. The study asked for preferred characteristics of husbands and of steady boyfriends. There was an almost perfect rank correlation with MAS for the extent to which "personality" was looked for in a boyfriend rather than in a husband (rho = .94*** across seven countries). In more masculine cultures husbands should be more "healthy," "wealthy," and "understanding"; boyfriends should not only have more personality but also more "affection," "intelligence," and "sense of humor." In the more feminine cultures there were hardly any differences between the preferred characteristics of husbands and of boyfriends. If we see the boyfriend as the symbol of love and the husband as the symbol of family life, this means that in the masculine countries love and family life were more often seen as separated, whereas in the feminine countries they were expected to coincide. In the feminine countries, the husband was the boyfriend.

Demographic data to be shown later in this chapter suggest that the mas/fem dimension also affects the number of children a couple will have. In masculine cultures the father's choice prevails, leading to more children in poor countries and fewer children in wealthy countries; in feminine countries the mother's choice prevails, with the reverse effect.

Masculinity, Schools, and Educational Systems

Criteria for evaluating both teachers and pupils or students differ between masculine and feminine cultures.[42] On the masculine side teachers' brilliance and academic reputation and students' academic performance are the dominant factors. On the feminine side teachers' friendliness and social skills and students' social adaptation play a bigger role.

Failing in school is a disaster in a masculine culture. In strongly masculine countries such as Japan (MAS 95) and Germany (MAS 66), the newspapers report each year about students who have killed themselves after failing examinations. In the United States (MAS 62), a Harvard MBA graduate counted four suicides—one teacher, three students—during his time at this elite American institution (Cohen, 1973). Failure in school in a feminine culture is a relatively minor incident. Some young people in feminine cultures take their lives too, but for reasons unrelated to performance, such as depression.

In feminine cultures teachers will not openly praise good students, although they may praise weaker students to encourage them. Awards for excellence are not popular; in fact, *excellence* is a masculine term. In masculine cultures awards and public praise are popular for students and even for teachers.[43]

Competitive sports play an important role in the curriculum in countries such as Britain and the United States. To U.S. sports coach George Allen the dictum is attributed, "Winning isn't the most important thing—it's the only thing" (Lasch, 1980, p. 117)—an attitude that doesn't encourage friendly encounters in sports. In most European countries sports are extracurricular and not a part of the school's task.

The United States and the Netherlands in the IBM research produced quite similar scores on three dimensions, but they differed greatly on mas/fem. U.S. students (MAS 62) in a semester program in the Netherlands (MAS 14) were struck by the lack of concern for grades among the Dutch (Vunderink & Hofstede, 1998). The Dutch students considered passing to be enough; excelling was not an openly pronounced goal. In the Netherlands, competing in class is not done. In masculine cultures students try to make themselves visible in class and compete openly with each other (if the culture is also collectivist, the competition is among groups rather than among individuals).[44] In more feminine cultures the *average* student is considered the norm; in more masculine countries like the United States the *best* student is the norm. Parents in masculine countries expect their children to try to match the best. In the Netherlands,

the "best boy in class" is a somewhat ridiculous figure.

Curriculum choices in masculine countries are strongly guided by perceived career opportunities, whereas in feminine countries students' intrinsic interest in particular subjects plays a bigger role. A U.S. professor who interviewed Dutch students for a place at a U.S. university was surprised that the Dutch did not present clear pictures of their future careers. At that age (around 22), Dutch students tend still to be working out what their personal skills and abilities are, who they are, and where they will fit in society. They like to do well, but they do not aspire to be the best. U.S. students at that age tend to have planned their careers in detail (Vunderink & Hofstede, 1998, p. 147).

Above, I noted a relationship between MAS and the expression of aggression in the family. Chapter 5 cited a five-nation survey of the values of 10- to 15-year-old children (about 1,500 per country; Hastings & Hastings, 1980). The children were shown a picture of one person sitting on the ground with another standing over him; the person who was standing was saying, "Go ahead and fight back if you can!"[45] They were asked to choose one of eight responses from a card. I divided these answers into the categories of "aggressive" and "appeasing." Aggressive answers listed were as follows: "You've hit me. Now I'm going to teach you a lesson" (chosen on average by 15.4% of respondents); "I'll tell the teacher" (4.4%); "We are not friends anymore" (4.0%); and "You'll get caught by the police" (.4%). Appeasing answers were "We don't have to fight. Let's talk it over" (28.8%); "Let's not fight. Let's be friends" (28.8%); "I'm sorry. I was wrong" (11.4%); and "What if somebody gets hurt by fighting?" (5.6%). The total proportions of children choosing aggressive answers were 38% in Japan, 26% in Britain, 22% in Korea, 18% in France, and 17% in Thailand.[46] These proportions were almost perfectly correlated with the countries' MAS scores ($r = .97**$). In spite of the small number and wide geographic range of countries, this question provides a convincing picture of the different socialization of children with regard to responding to aggression.

Corporal punishment in school for children of prepuberty age has been associated in Chapter 3 with the power distance between the teacher and the students, but in some schools in masculine cultures with small power distances—such as Great Britain—corporal punishment is considered beneficial for the character development of boys, less of girls. Corporal punishment, of course, is also a form of aggression.

Verhulst, Achenbach, Ferdinand, and Kasius (1993) reported on a surprising difference between matched groups of U.S. (MAS 62) and

Dutch (MAS 14) adolescents (aged 11-18, more than 800 per country) who completed "Youth Self-Reports" (YSRs) about their personal problems and competencies. The Americans reported many more problems *and* competencies than did the Dutch, although earlier studies had shown no difference in the frequencies of adolescents' problem behavior as perceived by parents and teachers; but U.S. parents did rate their children's competencies higher than Dutch parents did. Some of the YSR items on which Americans scored higher were as follows: "argues a lot," "can do things better than most kids," "stores up unneeded things," and "acts without thinking." The only item on which the Dutch scored higher was "takes life easy." The differences can be attributed to the ego-boosting norm in U.S. society, which socializes young people to take both their problems and their competencies more seriously, in contrast with the ego-effacing norm in the Netherlands. A Dutch comment I sometimes overhear is "Americans always talk about themselves." Lasch (1980) has written about "the culture of narcissism" in the United States. However, Verhulst et al. mentioned that an earlier comparison of YSRs between the United States and *Germany* (MAS 66) had shown considerable similarity.

A confirmation of differences in ego-boosting behavior related to MAS was visible in a seven-country study on literacy (Organization for Economic Cooperation and Development & Ministry of Industry of Canada, 1995). In 1994, representative samples of between 2,000 and more than 4,000 younger and older adults (ages 16 to 65) in each of seven countries were given equivalent tests to measure their literacy for three skills: reading, writing, and numeracy. I looked at the subset in each country with the highest ratings: literacy levels 4 and 5 out of 5. Respondents also *subjectively* rated their daily life reading, writing, and numeracy skills. The proportions of those objectively highly literate respondents who subjectively rated their skills "excellent" (rather than good, moderate, or poor) varied from 31% in the Netherlands to 79% in the United States (Hofstede & Associates, 1998, tab. 5.2). Across seven overlapping countries and language groups these percentages were significantly correlated with MAS (rho = .71*). Respondents in masculine countries rated themselves as excellent more often than did equally skilled respondents in feminine countries.[47]

Chapters 4 and 5 referred to Gudykunst's (1989) survey about the "ethnolinguistic identity" of 158 female and male foreign students at a U.S. university. Across 32 countries and regions, MAS was significantly correlated with three out of five subscales. One was "ethnolinguistic vitality"; it consisted of two items indicating how highly regarded the respondent's native language was in the United States and internationally. Students from high-MAS cultures saw their language as more highly regarded. The same was found for students from high-UAI and high-IDV countries. The second subscale significantly correlated with MAS was "group boundaries" (to what extent an outsider tried to bridge the cultural gap with the respondent, and whether this indicated a positive intention), and the third was "in-group identification" (to what extent the respondent identified with his or her native culture). Boundaries and in-group identification were also stronger in masculine cultures. So sojourners from masculine cultures boosted their national ego more.[48]

Mas/fem differences are also related to gender differentiation in educational systems. One aspect of this is whether teachers are women or men. In masculine societies women mainly teach younger children and men teach at universities. In feminine societies roles are more mixed and men also teach younger children. Paradoxically, therefore, in masculine societies children are longer exposed to female teachers. These teachers' status, however, is often low, so that they are anti-heroines rather than role models.

Hamilton, Blumenfeld, Akoh, and Miura (1991) reported on an observation study in 10 Japanese and 9 U.S. classrooms for children approximately 11 years old. In both countries teachers paid more individual attention to boys than to girls, but the gender difference was larger in Japan (2.6 times as much attention to boys as to girls) than in the United States (2.0 times as much attention to boys).[49] Both countries have masculine cultures, but MAS is higher for Japan.

Mas/fem cultural differences also affect the subjects chosen by male versus female students at universities. Weinreich (1979) studied stereotypes of academic disciplines in the United Kingdom and found science to be seen as masculine (except for biology)[50] and arts as feminine (except for philosophy). Kelly (1978, p. 41) compared the performance of 14-year-old girls and boys in schools across 14 countries and found boys to be doing significantly better on science subjects in all countries; gender differences were smallest in biology. In the United States, biology (along with biochemistry) was also the science discipline with the highest proportion of women scientists (McClelland, 1965, p. 179). The association of science with masculinity seems to be universal. In the first edition of *Culture's Consequences,* an Index of Gender Segregation in Higher Education was shown to be significantly correlated with MAS across 38 countries ($r = .28*$) and more strongly across the 18 wealthier countries ($r = .56**$) (Hofstede, 1980a, p. 307).[51] In feminine countries men and women more often followed the same academic curricula.

Gender differences in curriculum choice and school performance between feminine and masculine societies are not only social in nature. There are strong indications that mas/fem is related to the actual distribution of perceptual abilities between the genders. U.S. psychologist Herman A. Witkin (1977, p. 85) pioneered the study of "psychological differentiation," which is the distinction between *field-dependent* and *field-independent* persons. Field-dependent persons are influenced in their perception by characteristics of their physical and social environment. Field-independent persons will perceive an object separately from its and their environment. Field-dependent persons tend to rely on external frames of reference as guides to behavior; field-independent persons rely more on internal frames of reference. Field-dependent people generally have better social skills; field-independent people have better analytic skills (Witkin & Goodenough, 1977, p. 682). Psychological differentiation is measured by various tests of perceptual ability, such as the Embedded Figures Test, the Rod and Frame Test, and the Body Adjustment Test (Cronbach, 1970, pp. 240 ff., 627 ff.). The abilities measured by these tests are part of the testee's mental programming.

Canadian cross-cultural psychologist John Berry (1976) carried the study of psychological differentiation to the ecological level. Between 1964 and 1974 he tested more than 1,000 members of 21 different communities in Africa, Australia, Europe, and North America using a battery of psychological differentiation tests. He found systematic differences in levels of field dependence that he related to factors in the ecological and cultural situations of these communities. His research did not compare modern societies, but a number of arguments speak in favor of a link between societal masculinity and field independence:

1. If field-dependence levels were culturally determined in the largely traditional communities Berry studied, there is no reason the same would not be true for modern societies.

2. Psychological differentiation is related to gender. Many studies in Western settings have shown that, starting around early adolescence, women tend to be more field dependent than men (McClelland, 1965, p. 179). The difference between the genders is slight but persistent: The range within each gender is vastly larger than the mean difference between the genders (Witkin, 1977, p. 88). The gender difference varies from one society to another (Berry & Annis, 1974b).

3. Dutch (low-MAS) undergraduates showed smaller gender differences in psychological differentiation than did U.S. (high-MAS) undergraduates (Van Leeuwen, 1978, p. 110, based on a 1955 master's thesis by O. C. Wit). Exhibit 6.5 illustrates that gender differences in MAS were also smaller in low-MAS countries.[52]

4. Psychological differentiation is also related to age; data from both nonliterate and Western settings seem to indicate a U-shaped relationship, with maximum field independence between the ages of 21 and 40 (Witkin & Berry, 1975, pp. 37 ff.). Exhibit 6.7 shows that MAS, too, decreases after age 40.

5. Conceptually, valuing social relationships (cultural femininity) converges with relying on external frames of reference as guides to behavior (field dependence); valuing ego gratification (cultural masculinity) converges with relying more on internal frames of reference (field independence).[53]

Exhibit 6.12 summarizes the key differences between feminine and masculine societies in the family and at school.

Masculinity and Femininity in Gender Roles

Different traditional societies present very different gender role division patterns (Hendrix, 1994), but men, being on average taller and stronger and free to get out, have historically dominated in professional and social life outside the home in virtually all societies. Only exceptional women, usually belonging to the upper classes, had the means to delegate their child-rearing activities to others and to step into a public role. If women entered dominant positions in society at all this was mostly after age 45, when their mother status changed to grandmother status (compare Exhibit 6.7). Unmarried women were (and are still) rare in traditional societies and were (are) often ostracized.

"Gender" literature usually focuses on women. Italian sociologist Silvia Gherardi (1995) has written: "I too have inherited a tradition which only recently has become aware that half of the history of gender is missing if the social construction of masculinity is not considered" (p. 187). Giving equal attention to the social roles of both is my explicit purpose in this subsection.

A frequent assumption is that women's emancipation presupposes their having their own careers. U.S. psychologist David McClelland (1975) refutes this assumption in the following

Exhibit 6.12 Key Differences Between Feminine and Masculine Societies I: Family and School

Low MAS	High MAS
In the Family	
Weak gender differentiation in the socialization of children.	Strong gender differentiation in the socialization of children.
Similar role models: Both fathers and mothers deal with facts and feelings.	Different role models: Fathers deal with facts, mothers with feelings.
Both boys and girls are allowed to cry but neither should fight.	Girls cry, boys don't; boys should fight back, girls shouldn't fight.
No gender difference in children's playing goals.	Boys prevail in performance games, girls in relationship games.
Both boys and girls learn to be modest.	Both boys and girls learn to be ambitious.
Ideal opposite-sex partner likes children and quality of life.	Ideal opposite-sex partner has success at work.
Positive feelings about home and family.	Less satisfied with home life.
Children don't express aggression.	Children may express aggression.
Friends and acquaintances important.	Family important.
Parents should earn children's love and respect.	Children should love and respect parents regardless of behavior.
More unmarried cohabitation.	More quick marriages.
Flexible family concepts.	Traditional family concepts.
Each partner has own interests.	Partners should share interests.
Same standards for brides and grooms.	Chastity and industriousness for brides, not for grooms.
In Asia, same criteria for husbands and boyfriends.	In Asia, husbands to be wealthy, boyfriends to have personality.
Mothers decide on number of children.	Fathers decide on family size.
At School	
Friendliness in teachers appreciated.	Brilliance in teachers appreciated.
Students' social adaptation important.	Students' performance important.
Failing in school is a minor accident.	Failing in school is a disaster.
Public praise to encourage weak students.	Public praise to reward good students.
No special awards.	Awards for good students, teachers.
Competitive sports extracurricular.	Competitive sports part of curriculum.
Average student is the norm.	Best student is the norm.
Curriculum choices guided by intrinsic interest.	Curriculum choices guided by career expectations.
Children socialized to avoid aggression.	Children socialized to fight back.
Students take own problems less seriously.	Own problems taken very seriously.
Ego effacing: own performance underrated.	Ego boosting: performance overrated.
Foreign students in U.S. efface national ego.	Foreign students in U.S. boost national ego.
Young children taught by men and women.	Young children taught by women only.
Teachers give equal attention to girls and boys.	Teachers pay more attention to boys.
Boys and girls study same subjects.	Boys and girls study different subjects.
Small gender difference in perceptual abilities.	Large differences in perceptual ability: boys analytic, girls contextual.

description of the American Quaker subculture into which he was introduced as a young man:

The women seemed to be so much more self-assured and important in the community than even

the career-oriented feminists I had known at Illinois Woman's College. They were vigorous, self-confident, and obviously influential. They were wives and mothers, for the most part, and not career women, but many had strong intellectual and artistic interests, even though few of them had gone to college. I realized that my feminist upbringing had led me to take it for granted that the "housewife" role would be weak or passive, a second best that many women had to choose. But here were women who gloried in their role, regarding it in no way as a hindrance: Yet I could not dismiss them as simple homebodies. As I wondered how this could be, I realized that Quakerism as a religion gives strong support to the sharing rather than the assertive life style. . . . I found the emphasis on career muted among both men and women. . . . The life goal was to develop a certain character and to live in a simple, harmonious way rather than to achieve a career of great significance. It is the only society I have ever entered in America in which the first question asked of a man is not "What do you do?" but "Who are you?" In fact I discovered that many of the women seemed to have only a very vague idea of what their men did. Though they realized of course that it was necessary to have an occupation and to earn money, that was not the most salient or valued feature of a person's life, as it is nearly everywhere else in contemporary America. (pp. 108-109)

In this case the entire subculture, women and men alike, endorsed values that elsewhere in the United States would be seen as feminine. Greater gender role equality can be attained not only when women are more assertive or instrumentally oriented, but also when men are more nurturing or expressively oriented.

The relationship between cultural masculinity and the gender gap is pictured in Exhibit 6.5, but this refers to values, not necessarily to jobs. Women's participation in the paid workforce per se is not a matter of masculinity/femininity.[54] Women being allowed, or forced, to work for money is not necessarily a sign of a more equal division of gender roles. It can just as well be another form of slavery. Lower-class women have nearly everywhere entered work organizations in low-status, low-paid jobs—not for self-fulfillment, but out of necessity. Only recently in history have women in any numbers been sufficiently freed from other constraints to enter the worlds of work and politics as men's equals. This has happened only where economic possibilities and necessities have allowed it. The effects of cultural differences along the mas/fem dimension on women's roles in society have therefore been visible only for countries that have reached a certain level of economic development.

Sullivan (1991, p. 290) computed a (reversed) Gender Gap Index (GGI) based on 20 indicators of male/female inequality in the areas of political and economic discrimination, marriage status, level of education, and employment. Across 51 countries from the IBM set, GGI depended only on 1990 GNP/capita (rho = .77***).[55] Across the 20 wealthier countries (1990 GNP/capita > $10,000) GGI depended on GNP/capita, IDV plus MAS, in this order ($R = .82***$).[56] Wealthy, individualist, feminine countries showed the smallest gender gaps.[57]

Burkholder, Moore, and Saad (1996) published results of a Gallup public opinion survey on gender issues based on representative samples (at least 1,000 per country) of the adult population (aged 18 and over) of 22 countries around the world. The survey contained the following two questions about equal job opportunities:

1. Do you think that women in this country have equal job opportunities with men, or not?
2. Do you think that women in this country should have equal job opportunities with men, or not?

Across 15 overlapping countries the yes answers on question 1, the actual situation, depended only on 1994 GNP/capita (rho = –.78***).[58] The negative sign meant that in poorer countries job opportunities for women were rated more equal. It is evident that in these countries, "job opportunities" was taken to refer to simple manual jobs. Economic development limits the demand for women as low-paid labor, limits women's home tasks, and opens their educational possibilities so they can consider better jobs.[59] Across the seven wealthier countries in Burkholder et al.'s study (1990 GNP/capita > $10,000) the only index correlated with question 1 was MAS (rho = –.69*, masculine countries less gender equality), in spite of the fact that countries with very feminine scores, such as the Nordic countries and the Netherlands, were not included. On question 2, whether job opportunities *should* be equal, answers were universally positive, and there was no significant relationship with wealth, MAS, or the actual situation (question 1).[60] In the case of gender, job opportunities practices differed more than ideologies.

More than whether women do paid work, the gender role division depends on what jobs they hold and how they are paid for those jobs. In the first edition of *Culture's Consequences,* I compared two measures of the position of women in society in different nations: women in professional and technical work as a percentage of all working women and as a percentage of all professional and technical workers (Hofstede, 1980a, p. 306).[61] The correlations with all indexes were considerably higher for the percentage of working women than for the percentage of professional and technical workers. The former figures are more meaningful: They implicitly control for differences in participation of women in the job market in general. Also, it again made a considerable difference whether we took all countries, wealthy and poor alike, or only the wealthy ones, where more professional and technical jobs were available. In wealthier and more feminine countries a greater share of working women were found in the more qualified jobs. Across 16 wealthy countries professional and technical women as a percentage of all working women correlated with MAS with $r = -.64**$. The more masculine the culture, the lower the share of working women in professional and technical positions.

More recent data about women as a percentage of all professionals and technicians across 47 countries (United Nations Development Program, 1996) produced a multiple correlation with PDI ($r = -.60***$) plus MAS ($R = .71***$),[62] even without excluding the poor countries. In high-PDI countries men held more strongly to these jobs, but more so if the culture was also masculine. Power distance concerns the sharing of power in society in general.[63] In high-PDI countries the relationship between men and women is likely to be seen as hierarchical—men are higher.

Denmark and Waters (1977) content analyzed children's readers in five countries (France, Romania, Spain, Sweden, and the former Soviet Union) for gender role models. Only the Swedish stories had more female than male leading characters, and some of both in nontraditional gender roles, such as a boy as a baby-sitter. Sweden has a long history of educational policies for training girls and boys in the same roles; it scored very feminine in the IBM data (MAS 5), but also low in power distance.

Lynn (1991), in a massive survey among university students (at least 150 males and 150 females in each of 42 countries), included a measurement of "competitiveness." He used a questionnaire consisting of the following five items: "I enjoy working in situations involving competition with others"; "It is important to me to perform better than others on a task"; "I feel that winning is important in both work and games"; "It annoys me when other people perform better than I do"; and "I try harder when I'm in competition with other people." [64] Furnham, Kirkcaldy, and Lynn (1996) found country competitiveness scores to be significantly negatively correlated with national wealth.

Van de Vliert (1998, tab. 7.1) transformed Lynn's country mean competitiveness scores of male and female students into two aggregate scores: an Overall Competitiveness Index and a Gender Ratio of Competitiveness Index.[65] The Overall Competitiveness Index was indeed significantly negatively correlated with national wealth ($r = -.51**$ with 1990 GNP/capita) and also with IDV ($-.41*$), and positively with PDI ($r = .44**$), across 31 overlapping countries.[66]

Furnham et al. attributed the lower competitiveness scores for wealthy countries to a lower work ethic once wealth has been achieved. I prefer a more mundane explanation: All five items of the competitiveness scale were formulated in the same, competitive direction (the scale was developed for use across individuals in the United States, not for cross-cultural comparisons), so the scale is very sensitive to acquiescence. Respondents in poorer countries with larger power distances and lower individualism yielded more to the demand characteristics of the authoritative questionnaire.[67] Van de Vliert's Gender Ratio of Competitiveness Index was lowest in Norway and highest in Germany; across 32 overlapping countries, both wealthy and poor, it was significantly correlated with MAS ($r = .44**$; across 23 wealthy countries $r = .43*$; across 9 poor countries $r = .70*$). This ratio was, of course, entirely free from response set. So "competitiveness" *as measured by Lynn's questionnaire* as such was not correlated with MAS, but the competitiveness ratio between men and women was. This meant a larger gap between the genders in masculine cultures (compare Exhibit 6.5).

U.S. psychologists Deborah Best and John Williams devoted two decades of research effort to the study of gender stereotypes around the world. In their first cross-national study, they collected gender stereotypes from university students in 25 countries (50 men and 50 women per country) using a list of 300 adjectives, the Gough and Heilbrun Adjective Check List (ACL; see Williams & Best, 1982). Later, they added five more countries (Williams & Best, 1990a). Best and Williams (1998) found no convergent validity between what respondents in their studies considered masculine or feminine and my mas/fem dimension of national cultures, but their studies and mine dealt with different phenomena and used different measures. The relationships between their results and mine are more complex.

Across 21 overlapping countries, Williams and Best found two variables correlated with MAS beyond the .01 level.[68] One was the *typicality of the gender stereotypes,* the extent to which the stereotypes in a country differed from the average across all countries. Stereotypes were significantly more different in masculine than in feminine countries ($r = .52**$). The stereotypes recognized in the feminine countries were those associated with male and female roles worldwide—that is, those rooted in the basic human facts of life dictated by nature, such as women bearing children and men begetting them. The stereotypes recognized in the masculine countries were more country specific; that is, they were more arbitrary from a universal point of view.

The other variable correlated with MAS was the *extent to which characteristics were associ-*

ated with women only or with men only within each country, which was significantly larger in feminine than in masculine countries ($r = -.56**$). In feminine countries respondents associated ACL adjectives more freely with one gender only than in countries scoring masculine. I interpret this as follows: In feminine countries respondents did not feel inhibited about classifying an adjective as associated with men or with women, because for them either choice did not imply a positive or negative value judgment. Respondents in these countries saw women as just as good or bad as men (Hofstede & Vunderink, 1994, p. 331).

The stronger differentiation in gender-associated characteristics within feminine countries was confirmed by Williams and Best (1990b; see also Best & Williams, 1994). In a new study, they collected actual and ideal *self-descriptions* of female and male students in 14 countries, again using the 300-item ACL. They then gave each of these actual and ideal self-descriptions a country "M%" score by referring to the gender stereotypes for that country found in the earlier study. Thus self-descriptions in each country were measured against that country's own stereotypes. Across 12 overlapping countries, *the differences between the actual self-concepts of men and women* (expressed in M%) were negatively correlated with MAS ($r = -.67**$; Best & Williams, 1998, p. 113). This means that in countries with higher MAS scores, women respondents scored their self-concepts more like men. In masculine societies, women used masculine terms to describe themselves. In feminine societies, women again differentiated their terms more than did men. Interestingly, there was no significant correlation with MAS for the differences in *ideal* self-concepts of men and women. These differences were smaller in all countries than the differences in actual self-concept.[69]

From a culturally masculine point of view, the fact that men and women use the same terms for their self-concepts is positive: It creates equality between the genders. From a culturally feminine point of view, the imposition of masculine terms for female self-concepts represents a violation of the freedom of women to be themselves. If the fact of life is that women and men experience their selves differently, then this should be acknowledged.

Fioravanti, Gough, and Frere (1981) reported on a small study in which they gave the 300-item ACL in translation to 18 French, 51 Italian, and 28 U.S. male and female raters and asked them to judge the desirability of the items for men and for women. Elsewhere I showed the scores by country for 4 adjectives (out of 45) that presented significant gender differences (Hofstede & Associates, 1998, p. 98). In France (MAS 43), "feminine" and "weak" for a man were less undesirable and "gen-

tle" for a man was more desirable than in the other two countries. In the United States (MAS 62) it was more desirable for a woman to be "feminine" and "gentle" than in the other countries, but less desirable for her to be "weak."

The Wacoal Corporation (1993) study about partner preferences mentioned above in the subsection on family also contained data about gender stereotypes among the same young women in eight Asian capital cities. In my secondary analysis of these data I found their stereotypes very similar to those identified by Williams and Best, but differing between masculine and feminine cultures (Hofstede, 1996b). The extent to which "sense of responsibility" was seen as a characteristic of men only (and not of women) correlated almost perfectly with MAS (rho = .96*** across seven overlapping countries). In the more masculine countries, "decisiveness," "liveliness," and "ambitiousness" were also more often seen as characteristics of men, whereas "caring" and "gentleness" were more often seen as characteristics of women. In the more feminine cultures, in contrast, all these characteristics were seen as applying to both genders.

A term obviously associated with masculinity is *machismo* (from the Spanish, used to describe a need for ostentatious manliness), which is usually attributed to Latin American countries, especially Mexico (De Vos & Hippler, 1969, p. 365; Lewis, 1961, pp. xxvii). In the IBM data some Latin American countries scored far to the masculine side (Venezuela, Mexico, and Colombia), which fits with their macho image. Argentina and Brazil, however, scored in the middle, whereas Peru and Chile scored more feminine. Private discussions I have had with Latin Americans confirm that machismo is more present in the countries around the Caribbean than in the remainder of South America. The term has gained international acceptance, even, for example, in reference to British working-class youngsters. In more feminine cultures, macho behavior is easily ridiculed. In Latin America the female complement to machismo is *marianismo,* a combination of near saintliness, submissiveness, and frigidity (Stevens, 1973). Gonzalez (1982), discussing Mexican attitudes, has used the word *hembrismo,* from *hembra,* a female animal. It stands for extreme femininity, passivity, and self-abnegation.

Chapters 4 and 5 referred to Scherer and Wallbott's (1994) ISEAR questionnaire study on self-reports of emotions in 37 countries, from which 14 could be matched with the IBM set. Across these, MAS was significantly positively correlated with the claimed expression of sadness ($r = .51*$) and joy ($r = .50*$) by men. In masculine cultures men claim to show their joy and sadness.

Femininity is sometimes confused with feminism, or women's liberation. Feminism is not a cultural trait at all but an ideology, and it takes different forms in masculine and feminine cultures: There is masculine feminism and there is feminine feminism. The first is about access of women to jobs hitherto taken only by men; it is about competition between the genders. A typical representative of masculine feminism from the United States is Sandra Scarr (1996), who has spoken up against pregnancy leave because it is believed to damage a woman's career. This kind of feminism also leads to a stress on politically correct language use with regard to gender. In terms of Exhibit 6.5, it wants to move the female line up toward the male line. The second, feminine form of feminism is about a redistribution of roles inside and outside the home; it is about complementarity and interdependence between the genders, and it implies men's lib as much as women's lib. It stresses the contributions to society that women can make precisely because they are different from men.[70] In Exhibit 6.5 this could be achieved by moving the male line downward toward the female line, or moving the entire society toward a more feminine value position (more toward the left).

Psychological theories about gender (and sex) are often based on U.S. models, simply because most internationally read books and journals in psychology appear in the United States, where psychology—focusing on the individual—is immensely popular. Psychologists in other parts of the world often naively apply such theories to their countries' situations where they do not apply.[71]

There is no "one best way" of dividing gender roles. Women and/or men in one type of society do not necessarily feel "better off" than in another. Women from one culture may consider those from another to be oppressed or immoral, but many of those others consider themselves the moral ones, and usually, "the oppressed women like the oppressing men" (Bártová, 1976, p. 257). Japan, which has probably the most absolute gender role division of any country in the world, has produced women writers who applaud their situation as well as others who deplore it.[72]

Individualism also affects the role distribution between women and men. Williams and Best (1990b, p. 91) studied the degree of "modernity" in the gender role conceptions of about 100 students from each of 14 countries. The test they used (the Kalin Sex Role Ideology measure) focused on the legal position of women and their access to jobs. Modernity scores correlated with 1987 GNP/capita (rho = .52*) but even more with IDV (rho = .54*).

Imamoglu, Küller, Imamoglu, and Küller (1993) interviewed 502 elderly Swedes (ages 60 to 71) and 448 Turks (55 to 71) about their social networks, self-images, life satisfaction, attitudes toward aging, and feelings of loneliness. Turks (IDV 37) had larger social networks and interacted more than Swedes (IDV 71), Swedes (UAI 27) felt greater life satisfaction than Turks (UAI 85), and differences between the genders were larger in Turkey (MAS 45) than in Sweden (MAS 5). Turkish men had the most positive self-images and Turkish women the least positive; Swedish men and women were in between and did not differ from each other in this respect.

Religious traditions of course affect gender roles as well, especially in Muslim countries, but this does not mean that Muslim countries have necessarily masculine cultures. Iran, for example, in the IBM study presented a relatively feminine score (MAS 43). An anthropologist wrote (before Khomeini's 1979 restoration of orthodox Islamic rules):

> In Iran . . . men are expected to show their emotions. Iranian men read poetry; they are sensitive and have well-developed intuition and in many cases are not expected to be too logical. They are often seen embracing and holding hands. Women, on the other hand, are considered to be coldly practical. They exhibit many of the characteristics we associate with men in the United States. A very perceptive Foreign Service Officer . . . once observed "If you will think of the emotional and intellectual gender roles as reversed from ours, you will do much better out here." (Hall, 1959/1965, p. 50)

And this in a country where the formal place of women, under the influence of Islam, is limited to the family. Muslim countries vary considerably regarding the roles of mothers within their homes (Bank & Vinnicombe, 1995).

Masculinity and Consumer Behavior

Chapters 3 to 5 discussed the validations of PDI, UAI, and IDV by De Mooij. She correlated the IBM indexes with data from consumer surveys across 16 affluent European countries by market research agencies.[73] Country consumer survey data also showed meaningful correlations with MAS.[74]

The position of a country on the mas/fem dimension is reflected in the sharing of buying decisions between family partners. Data from EMS 95 showed that the involvement of the partner in the choice of the main car correlated with MAS with rho = -.63**. But also ordinary food shopping was more shared in feminine cultures (Eurodata 91, "women are main food shoppers" and MAS correlated with rho = .68**; without the more traditional, less affluent Southern countries Greece, Portugal, and Spain, rho = .91***). "It seems that cultural values influencing role behavior which are latent in the more traditional countries become manifest when countries modernize" (De Mooij, 1998b, p. 67).

Coffee serves a social purpose in many cultures. Electric filter coffeemakers were used more in feminine European cultures, where coffee should be permanently available in the home as a symbol of togetherness; ownership of such coffeemakers correlated negatively with MAS (Eurodata 91, rho = -.46*). In feminine cultures more people made their own dresses (Eurodata 91 showed that the share of households in which a member makes dresses or knits correlated with MAS across 16 countries with rho = -.73***). Among smokers, those in feminine cultures more often rolled their own cigarettes (Euromonitor 97 showed a correlation with MAS of rho = -.69***). Homemade products seem to have more appeal in feminine cultures. Percentages of homes with household members doing carpentry themselves was also negatively correlated with MAS (Eurodata 91, rho = -.56**).

Status purchases are more frequent in masculine cultures. In feminine cultures more people wore cheap watches (EMS 95, owning a main watch costing less than £100 correlated with MAS with rho = -.51*); watches in feminine countries served less as a symbol of success. In feminine cultures people also bought less jewelry (Euromonitor 1997, value per capita of [real] jewelry sold correlated with MAS with rho = .66**); this points again to a lower need to show off. Purchasing power according to World Bank 1994 data was unrelated to the sales of real jewelry (rho = .23). In feminine cultures consumers disagreed with the statement "Foreign goods are more attractive than our own" (EMS 95, correlation with MAS rho = -.52*). Owning foreign goods is a way to show off.

The car has often been described as a sex symbol, or at least as a status symbol. Cars are extensions of the self, and the type of car one owns plays a strong role in showing what kind of person one is or wants to be. The engine power of a car is more important in masculine cultures. In feminine cultures people may not even know their car engine's power. Knowledge of engine power was negatively correlated with MAS (Eurodata 91, percentage "no answer" rho = -.60**). In EMS 95, with higher-educated respondents and a larger percentage of males, the percentage of "don't know" answers still correlated negatively with MAS (rho = -.52*). Preferences for the body types of cars also varied with the mas/fem dimension, but also over time. The Eurodata 91 showed that the feminine cultures in Europe then preferred the coupé type (correlation with MAS rho = -.67**). The EMS 95 showed the masculine cultures then preferred the hatchback type (correla-

tion with MAS rho = .57**), at least as a second family car. In the EMS data the second car is a better measure, as a large number of first cars in certain countries are company cars, to which other selection criteria apply.

In feminine cultures more people took a "home" with them on vacation (Eurodata 91, ownership of caravans [trailers or motor homes] correlated with MAS with rho = -.57**). When flying on pleasure trips, respondents from masculine cultures more often paid for business class (EMS 95, correlation with MAS rho = .59** within Europe, rho = .61** outside Europe)— again a matter of status.

Earlier in this chapter, I mentioned Tannen's (1992) distinction between female and male discourse: more "report talk" for men (transferring information) versus more "rapport talk" for women (using conversation to exchange feelings and establish relationships). Interestingly, across countries it appears that feminine cultures read more fiction and masculine cultures more nonfiction (Eurodata 91, percentage "bought mostly fiction" of all adults who in the past year bought at least one book, correlation with MAS rho = -.53*; same, of all adults who in the past year bought 10 or more books, rho = -.49*; percentage of fiction bought by men rho = -.53*). Members of masculine cultures seem to be more concerned with data and facts; members of feminine cultures are more interested in the stories behind the facts.

Masculine cultures showed more confidence in the advertising industry (Eurodata 91, correlation with MAS rho = .53*). In EMS 95, percentages of "strongly agree" answers to the statement "I often enjoy advertising on TV" were correlated with MAS with rho = .55*. De Mooij (1998b) thinks that the skepticism of feminine cultures toward advertising is based on their markets having been "relatively swamped by advertising reflecting US masculine values, thus advertising not made for the local culture and not liked. This masculine orientation of import advertising from the US is a lesser problem for other masculine markets such as the UK and Germany which also happen to have more indigenous advertising" (p. 71).

Exhibit 6.13 summarizes the key differences between feminine and masculine societies in gender roles and in consumer behavior.

Masculinity and Femininity in the Workplace

As I have suggested above, national cultural differences along the mas/fem dimension affect the meaning of work in people's lives. Whyte (1969) quotes a successful early-20th-century U.S. inventor and businessman, Charles F.

Exhibit 6.13 Key Differences Between Feminine and Masculine Societies II: Gender Roles and Consumer Behavior

Low MAS	High MAS
In Gender Roles	
Small gender culture gap.	Large gender culture gap.
More equal job and education opportunity, but only in affluent countries.	Less equal opportunity in affluent countries.
Larger share of women in professional and technical jobs.	Smaller share of women in professional and technical jobs.
Socialization toward nontraditional gender roles.	Socialization toward traditional gender roles.
Women describe themselves as more competitive than men do.	Men describe themselves as more competitive than women do.
Gender stereotypes rooted in universal biological differences.	Gender stereotypes country specific.
Characteristics freely attributed to one or the other gender.	Attribution of characteristics less easily differentiated.
Women describe themselves in their own terms.	Women describe themselves in same terms as men.
Men allowed to be gentle, feminine, and weak.	Women should be gentle and feminine; nobody should be weak.
To Asian women, characteristics differ little by gender.	To Asian women, responsibility, decisiveness, ambition are for men, caring and gentleness are for women.
Macho behavior ridiculed.	Machismo in men, marianismo or hembrismo in women.
Men claim suppressing joy and sadness.	Men claim showing joy and sadness.
Women's liberation means that men and women should take equal shares both at home and at work.	Women's liberation means that women should be admitted to positions hitherto occupied only by men.
In Consumer Behavior	
Buying decisions and shopping shared between partners.	Men make main buying decisions, women shop for food.
Coffeemakers for coziness.	Fewer filter coffeemakers.
Homemade products popular.	Fewer products homemade.
Purchases for use.	Purchases for showing off.
Less appeal of foreign goods.	More appeal of foreign goods.
Engine power of cars irrelevant.	Engine power of cars important.
Motor homes: vacations in home on wheels.	Vacations include business-class flights.
Reading: more fiction.	Reading: more nonfiction.
Less confidence in advertising.	More confidence in advertising.

Kettering, to illustrate a culturally masculine view of the meaning of work:

> I often tell my people that I don't want any fellow who has a job working for me: What I want is a fellow whom a job has. I want the job to get the fellow and not the fellow to get the job. And I want that job to get hold of this young man so hard that no matter where he is the job has got him for keeps. I want that job to have him in its clutches when he goes to bed at night, and in the morning I want that same job to be sitting on the foot of his bed telling

him it's time to get up and go to work. And when a job gets a fellow that way, he's sure to amount to something. (p. 31)

It is no accident that Kettering referred to a "young man"—his was a masculine ideal from a masculine society. Between the two poles of *living in order to work* and *working in order to live,* masculine cultures are closer to the first and feminine cultures closer to the second.

In the 1980s, an international consortium ran a "meaning of work" (MOW) study (Harpaz, 1990).

Representative samples of the working population in seven industrial countries were asked to rank 11 work aspects in order of importance.[75] In a reanalysis of the data, I factor analyzed the mean ranks for the 11 goals across the seven countries (see the statistical section of this chapter). The first factor opposed the goals of security, pay, and interesting work to the goals of good physical working conditions and interpersonal relations. The factor scores correlated significantly with MAS ($r = .69*$). Masculine countries stressed pay, security, and job content; feminine countries stressed relationships and physical conditions.

The concerns for relationships and life quality in feminine cultures and for material rewards, performance, and competition in masculine cultures are carried over from the family and school to the work environment. In distributing the rewards of work, feminine cultures favor equality and mutual solidarity, whereas masculine cultures favor equity—that is, pay according to merit and performance.

The division of jobs over the genders is a matter of cultural convention. Jobs are stereotyped as being "masculine" or "feminine," but these designations differ from one country or even organization to another and over time; examples are police officer, soldier, doctor, dentist, pharmacist, secretary, and nurse. Jobs considered feminine often enjoy lower status and pay. In the previous discussion of gender roles, we saw that in feminine cultures there is a tendency toward more equal opportunities for women, at least in affluent societies.

Of particular cultural significance is the gender division of management roles.[76] Etymologically, the root of the word *manage* is linked with two French words: *manège* (a place where horses are drilled) and *ménage* (household). *Manège* is the masculine element and *ménage* the feminine element in the management process.[77] Classical American studies distinguished two dimensions in individual leadership: "initiating structure" and "consideration" (Fleishman, Harris, & Burtt, 1955; Stogdill & Coons, 1957), or concern for work and concern for people (Blake & Mouton, 1964)—again, a masculine and a feminine element. Both are equally necessary for the success of an enterprise. Koprowski (1983) has referred to "the manager's dual nature, which is both masculine and feminine" (p. 51).

Women may be better able than men to balance the two sides of the manager's nature. Statham (1987), in an in-depth interview study of 22 female and 18 matched male U.S. managers *and their secretaries,* found that the women predominantly treated job and people aspects as interdependent, whereas the men saw these aspects as being in opposition. Gibson (1995), in a survey study about leadership conceptions among male and female managers in Australia, Norway, Swe-den, and the United States, found that on average the men stressed goal setting more and the women stressed interaction facilitation more. However, unlike Statham, Gibson did not ask these managers' subordinates about how *they* perceived the behavior of their female and male bosses.[78]

Admitting more women to management jobs may also make the organization more responsive. Kanter (1983) has put it as follows: "Clearly, decision-makers, via their patterns of attention and inattention, intervene between a company and its environment. And this, of course, means that a company with a diverse group in the 'dominant coalition' at the top . . . is more likely to pick up more external cues" (p. 281). In Chapter 8, I will show that in a cross-organizational research project in Denmark and the Netherlands, organizations with more women in management were found to have more open communication climates. Yet even in these feminine national cultures, shifts in this direction, in organizations traditionally led by men, are part of an uphill fight. In Western countries, organization development stressing openness and dealing with feelings has defended a feminine counterculture in a masculine business world for at least 30 years; it has rarely had lasting success.

Historically, management is an Anglo-Saxon concept, developed in masculine British and American cultures. The manager in these countries is the culture hero par excellence. Kanter (1977) interviewed a U.S. manager's wife who "said she got the impression from her husband's conversation that everyone at . . . was a manager; there seemed to be no one underneath" (p. 114). I once gave a series of guest lectures to a U.S. evening MBA class that, according to the regular professor, consisted entirely of managers. When I asked each of the 24 students what he or she did, it turned out that only 2 were actually managing something! Academic research on management in these countries almost universally collects data from managers, rarely from their subordinates, which to me is as reliable as basing product research on statements by producers, never by consumers. In feminine cultures there is less tendency to consider the manager role as particularly heroic; the manager is an employee like any other.

Masculine and feminine cultures create different management hero types. The masculine manager is, of course, assertive, decisive, and "aggressive" (only in masculine societies does this word carry a positive connotation).[79] Masculine business is the survival of the fittest (Bendix, 1956/1974, p. 256). The manager in a feminine culture is less visible, intuitive rather than decisive, and accustomed to seeking consensus; feminine business can be a cooperative venture.[80] What the two types of cultures have in common is that both believe managers should be resourceful—managers are believed to be endowed with above-average intelligence and drive.

Japan is a unique case; Hamada (1996) has criticized the high MAS score for Japan in my work on the basis of her finding that "Japanese prefer non-masculine managers" (p. 168). Of course, they may not get what they prefer, but such statements are based on an "emic" definition of what is masculine or feminine (see Chapter 1), which is different from the "etic" measures used in my international comparison. A much-studied emic concept in Japan is *amae*, or need for dependence, a carryover from

the feelings that all normal infants at the breast harbor towards the mother—dependence, the desire to be passionately loved, the unwillingness to be separated from the warm mother-child circle and cast into a world of objective "reality." . . . In a Japanese [man] these feelings are somehow prolonged into and diffused throughout his adult life, so that they come to shape, to a far greater extent than in adults in the West, his whole attitude to other people and to "reality." (Doi, 1971, pp. 7-8)

The *amae* phenomenon can be understood from the extreme gender role split in the Japanese family (discussed earlier in this chapter).

Female and male business students in five countries (China, Germany, Great Britain, Japan, and the United States) were given the Schein Descriptive Index, a list of 92 terms for describing people (Schein, Mueller, Lituchy, & Liu, 1996). A random one-third of the class answered for "men in general," one-third answered for "women in general," and one-third answered for "successful middle managers." The researchers calculated for each country the correlations between "successful managers" and "men in general" and between "successful managers" and "women in general." They did this separately for female and male respondents. In all five countries the correlations between the descriptions of successful managers and of men were strong in the answers of both male and female students. The correlations between the descriptions of the successful manager and of women were nil in the answers of the male students and mostly positive but weak in the case of the female students. Across the five countries, the degree to which female students' descriptions of the successful manager and of the typical woman were correlated was significantly negatively correlated with MAS ($r = -.92*$). The less masculine a country's culture, the more some characteristics of women were recognized in managers.[81]

Maurice, Sellier, and Silvestre (1978, p. 5) compared wage differentials across organizations in France and Germany. Although wage differentials between hierarchical levels were smaller in (lower-PDI) Germany, wage differentials between men and women were smaller in (lower-MAS) France.[82] This is just one example of an almost universal inequality of opportunity and reward for women versus men in the workforce, with men considered breadwinners and women cakewinners. This inequality extends into the management ranks. In the United States, a longitudinal survey study conducted for the *Harvard Business Review* showed that between 1965 and 1985 executive women had become an accepted phenomenon, but that the women who entered management still saw resistance to their progress and were, in fact, paid less than men in similar positions (Sutton & Moore, 1985). Jacobs (1992), on the basis of U.S. Census data for 1969 and 1987, concluded that over this period the gender gap in earnings among managers had narrowed, but that it still exceeded the gender gap in earnings of the labor force as a whole. And as far as authority went, the gender gap had remained constant. Kanter (1977) in the United States and Mant (1979) and Roper (1994) in Britain have explicitly described the masculine bias in business management that women have to overcome and that rewards those who most behave like men. As was shown earlier in this chapter, in the IBM study female managers in comparison with a matched group of male managers held more masculine values than did the men.[83]

In more feminine cultures, resistance against women entering higher jobs tends to be weaker. Data published by the Dutch-British multinational Unilever showed percentage female managers across its 15 European subsidiaries to be correlated significantly negatively with MAS ($rho = -.45*$; see Ford, 1985; Hofstede & Associates, 1998, p. 90) and not, for example, with GNP/ capita; so the more feminine countries did tend to promote more women into management positions.[84]

Bruins et al. (1993) asked 40 male and 40 female Dutch students each to nominate a successor to a position in a hierarchy of which the respondent was supposed to be a subordinate member. Dutch males strongly overnominated themselves; Dutch females in majority nominated either themselves or another female. In a replication in Poland with about 50 male and 50 female students, both nominated mostly males.[85] Poland, in a student survey using the Values Survey Module, scored 30 points higher on PDI, 40 points higher on UAI, and 50 points higher on MAS than the Netherlands (Kolman, Hofstede, Noorderhaven, & Dienes, 1999; see Appendix 5).

Differences in career advancement of men and women are also affected by the fact that levels of career ambition vary according to national cultures. The family in a masculine society socializes especially male children toward assertiveness, ambition, and competition. The family within a feminine society socializes both male and female children toward modesty and solidarity. Men in masculine societies are expected to aspire to career advancement.[86] For women in such societies career aspirations are optional; if they want careers, they acculturate to the men's culture. In feminine societies, career aspirations are optional for both genders.

The contrast between "live" and "work" becomes operational in the priority given to families versus careers. Exhibit 6.19 in the statistical section shows answer percentages in a survey of (male) business executives in 10 Western and Southern European countries (Arbose, 1980) about relationships between career and family. The percentages of both those indicating that they aspired to become chief executive and those indicating they were prepared to uproot their families on behalf of their careers were significantly correlated with MAS. Respondents in masculine countries were more ambitious and more prepared to uproot their families. In both cases there was a significant negative second-order correlation with 1980 GNP/capita, indicating less ambition and willingness to uproot the family in more affluent countries, where the additional benefit of promotion may be relatively smaller.

The conflict between career and family exists equally strongly for married women in career jobs. Etzion and Bailyn (1994) reported on a survey of 176 Israeli and 269 U.S. women pursuing technical and scientific careers in their countries. Of the Israelis (MAS 47), 16% were single without children and 77% were mothers. The typical pattern was a dual-career family with both husband and wife in middle-level careers. Of the Americans (MAS 62), 30% were single without children and 31% were mothers. On average, the Americans had somewhat higher jobs, but they complained more about energy depletion. Etzion and Bailyn conclude that for the Israeli women raising a family was a point of departure, and they accommodated their careers according to family condition and life stage. For the American women in the study, pursuing a career was a point of departure, and whether and when they would have a family depended on their career condition and stage.

What is missing in Etzion and Bailyn's article is information on the family involvement and energy depletion of the partners. I have shown results from a broad employee survey in an insurance company in Denmark ($n = 2,590$, 50% female; Hofstede, 1998c). Denmark, like the Netherlands, scored very feminine in the IBM study (MAS 16). On a question regarding whether employees experienced conflicts between their work and their family lives, 21% of the women answered yes and so did 30% of the men, although their family situations were equal. In the feedback phase, the women commented that when they had taken their jobs they had first resolved their family problems, whereas many men never consciously addressed their problems.

In previous work I have described my personal experience with the different behavior expected from job applicants in the United States (MAS 62) versus the Netherlands (MAS 14):

> American applicants, to Dutch eyes, oversell themselves. Their CVs are worded in superlatives, mentioning every degree, grade, award and membership to demonstrate their outstanding qualities. During the interview they try to behave assertively, promising things they are very unlikely to realize—like learning the local language in a few months. Dutch applicants in American eyes undersell themselves. They write modest and usually short CVs, counting on the interviewer to find out by asking how good they really are. They expect an interest in their social and extra-curricular activities during their studies. They are very careful not to be seen as braggarts and not to make promises they are not absolutely sure they can fulfill. American interviewers know how to interpret American CVs and interviews and they tend to discount the information provided. Dutch interviewers, accustomed to Dutch applicants, tend to upgrade the information. The scenario for cross-cultural misunderstanding is quite clear. To an uninitiated American interviewer an uninitiated Dutch applicant comes across as a sucker. To an uninitiated Dutch interviewer an uninitiated American applicant comes across as a braggart. (Hofstede, 1991, p. 79)

Many jobs in business demand few skills and cause a qualitative underemployment of people. This has been recognized as a problem in industrialized masculine as well as feminine countries. The recommended solutions have varied according to the type of culture. They have been labeled "humanization of work," "job restructuring," and "empowerment," but what constitutes a humanized job depends on one's definition of what is human. In a masculine culture a humanized job should give opportunities for recognition, advancement, and challenge. In a feminine culture the stress will lie on cooperation and the working atmosphere. This is illustrated by a most fascinating case study (Gohl, 1977, pp. 267 ff.). In 1974, six U.S. automobile workers (two women and four men) spent 3 weeks working in the Saab-Scania plant in Södertälje, Sweden, where a new "humanized" system of group assembly had been installed. Journalist Robert B. Goldmann went with them, and at the end of the third week he asked them whether they preferred the Detroit (U.S.) or the Södertälje (Swedish) system. The only American who reported preferring the Swedish system was a woman. The other five chose the U.S. system, although two said they would accept the Swedish system under certain conditions. About the woman who chose the United States, Goldmann (1975) wrote: "Lynette Stewart chose Detroit. In the Cadillac plant where she works, she is on her own and can make her own challenge, while at Saab-Scania she has to consider people in front and behind her" (p. 48). Goldmann also noticed that this very feature had been mentioned by a Swedish woman he interviewed as a point of attraction. This is clearly a value issue. Humanization of work is a matter of values, of the masculinity or femininity of one's point of departure.

A Dutchman who had worked with a prestigious consulting firm in the United States before he joined the top management team of a company in the Netherlands once commented to me on the different functions of *meetings* in his subsequent jobs. In the Dutch situation, meetings were places where issues were addressed and common solutions sought. In the U.S. situation as he had known it, meetings were opportunities for participants to tell success stories—not to address issues, as one was not supposed to raise problems without also suggesting their solutions. Issues were discussed between individuals, at other times.

Polley (1989) developed a method of mapping group dynamics in small working groups and used it to compare descriptions of group behavior by members of working groups in Norway, Sweden, and the United States (around 100 per country). U.S. groups were in majority reported to be of one mind (58%), but if they were seen as polarized, their conflicts were seen as severe. Scandinavian groups were much more rarely described as of one mind (26%) and more often as involved in moderate conflict, which the Scandinavians seemed better able to tolerate than the Americans.[87]

Ways of handling conflicts in organizations also differ according to the mas/fem dimension. In the United States as well as in other masculine cultures, such as Britain and Ireland, there is a feeling that conflicts should be resolved by a good fight: "Let the best man win." The industrial relations scene in these countries is marked by such fights. If possible, management tries to avoid having to deal with labor unions at all, and labor unions' behavior justifies their aversion. In feminine cultures such as Denmark, the Netherlands, and Sweden there is a preference for resolving conflicts through compromise and negotiation.[88]

Van Oudenhoven, Mechelse, and de Dreu (1998) asked 100 middle managers from five different national subsidiaries of a multinational corporation (in Belgium, Denmark, Great Britain, the Netherlands, and Spain) to describe their most recent conflicts with a superior and with a colleague, and how these were handled. Whether a problem-solving approach toward the superior was used related negatively to PDI and UAI (more in Denmark, Britain, and the Netherlands than in Spain and Belgium), but whether a problem-solving approach toward the colleague was used related negatively to MAS (more in the Netherlands and Denmark than in the three other countries).

Each country has its own institutional context for conflict resolution. In France, which scored moderately feminine in the IBM studies (MAS 43), there is occasionally a lot of verbal insult, both between employers and labor and between bosses and subordinates, but there is also a practical sense of moderation that enables parties to continue working together while agreeing to disagree (d'Iribarne, 1989, pp. 31, 60-61).

Prins and De Graaf (1986; see also Prins, 1990) studied sickness absence from work in Belgium, Germany, and the Netherlands. Controlling for incompatibilities in the available statistics, they found time lost from work in Belgium to be 3%, in Germany 5%, and in the Netherlands 8%, two and a half times as much as in Belgium. Prins and De Graaf make only a superficial reference to cultural factors, but as there is no evidence at all of different states of either health or wealth among the three populations, the explanation must be in the institutions and in the cultures. I think the decisive cause is the attitude of the medical officers who have to certify these absences. There is an aspect here of power distance (higher in Belgium) but also of masculinity (lower in the Netherlands). Dutch doctors have less authority over patients and give more weight to their opinions, but they also treat patients more kindly. We see the same patient-oriented attitude in the Dutch position toward euthanasia, and in the treatment of drug addiction.

Schaufeli and Van Dierendonck (1995) reported on results obtained with an American test of "burnout" of employees, the Maslach Burnout Inventory, in the Netherlands. The 22-item test produced three components labeled "emotional exhaustion," "depersonalization," and (reduced) "personal accomplishment"; this structure applied reasonably well in both countries. However, the mean scores for large normative samples of healthy employees showed significantly higher emotional exhaustion and depersonalization, but less admitted reduction of personal accomplishment, in the United States compared to the Netherlands.[89] Schaufeli and Van Dierendonck attribute this to the masculine versus feminine culture difference. They also administered the test in the Netherlands to 142 outpatients who were under medical treatment for work-related mental problems, most of them on sick leave but without major mental illness. These persons obviously scored higher on the three burnout components, but on depersonalization the Dutch *patients* scored at the same level as the U.S. *healthy employees*. Depersonalization stands for a stress on objectivity, distance, and instrumentality, elements of a masculine gender role socialization, and what is normal in this respect in the United States was considered pathological in the Netherlands.

McGee (1977) reported on a public opinion survey conducted with about 7,000 respondents in six European Union countries.[90] The purpose of the survey was to find out about the public's preferences for free versus nationalized enterprises. One question asked respondents in what size enterprise they would prefer to work. The mean preferred size scores for the six countries were significantly correlated with MAS (rho = .84*).[91] Higher MAS thus stood for "Big is beautiful," lower MAS for "Small is beautiful."

The European Commission in 1977 sponsored a public opinion survey with about 9,000 respondents in the then nine European Union countries about issues related to retirement (Commission des Communautés Européennes, 1978). One question asked: "If the economic situation were to improve so that the standard of living could be raised, which of the following two measures would you consider to be better: Increasing the salaries (for the same number of hours worked) or reduce the number of hours worked (for the same salary)?" Preferences varied from 62% in favor of salary in Ireland to 64% in favor of fewer hours worked in the Netherlands. Across the eight overlapping countries (all except Luxembourg), the differences (salary minus fewer hours) were significantly correlated with MAS (rho = .86**), more than with 1977 GNP/capita (rho = .78*).[92] Although respondents in the poorer countries stressed the need for increasing salaries more, values (MAS) played a stronger role than national wealth.

Based on their cultural characteristics, masculine versus feminine countries excel in different types of industries. Industrially developed masculine cultures have a competitive advantage in manufacturing, especially in large volume—doing things efficiently, well, and fast. They are good at the production of big and heavy equipment and in bulk chemistry. Feminine cultures have a relative advantage in service industries such as consulting and transportation, in manufacturing according to customer specifications, and in handling live matter, such as in high-yield agriculture and biochemistry. There is an international division of labor in which countries are relatively more successful in activities that fit their populations' cultural preferences than in activities that go against these (see also Exhibit 9.4). Japan is the world leader in high-quality consumer electronics; Denmark and the Netherlands excel in services, agricultural exports, and biochemistry (enzymes and penicillin).

Exhibit 6.14 summarizes the key differences between feminine and masculine societies in the workplace.

Masculinity, Femininity, and Political Priorities

National value patterns are present not only in the minds of ordinary citizens, of course, but also in the minds of political leaders, who grew up as children of their societies. As a matter of fact, people are usually elected, co-opted, or tolerated for political leadership *because* they are supposed to stand for certain values dear to citizens.

Politicians translate the values dominant in their countries into political priorities. The latter are most clearly visible in the spending of national government budgets. The mas/fem dimension affects priorities in the following areas: (1) solidarity with the weak in one's society versus reward for the strong; (2) international relations, including levels of aid to poor countries and the resolution of conflicts; and (3) protection of the environment versus economic growth.

Masculine culture countries strive for a tough, performance society; feminine countries, for a tender, welfare society. They get what they pay for: Across 17 developed industrial countries, the proportion of the population living in poverty varied from 6.8% in feminine Sweden to 16.5% in masculine United States (United Nations Development Program, 1998);[93] its only significant correlation was with MAS (r = .57**). The proportion of persons earning less that half the average income varied from 5.5% in Belgium to 19.1% in the United States; across the same 17 countries this again correlated only with MAS (r = .48*). The proportion of functional illiterates (people who completed school but in actual fact cannot read or write) across the 10 developed countries for which data were available varied from 7.5% in Sweden to 22.6% in Ireland; once more this correlated only with MAS (r = .88***).[94]

In criticisms in the press from masculine countries such as the United States and Great Britain (MAS 62 and 66, respectively) about the politics of feminine countries such as Sweden and the Netherlands (MAS 5 and 14, respectively), and vice versa, strong and very different value positions appear. There is a common belief, for example, in the United States that if there are economic problems in Sweden and the Netherlands, these are likely due to the high taxes in those countries, which are used to subsidize the poor; conversely, there is a belief in feminine European countries that if there are economic problems in the United States or Great Britain, these are likely due to too

Exhibit 6.14 Key Differences Between Feminine and Masculine Societies III: The Work Situation

Low MAS	High MAS
In the Workplace	
Work in order to live.	Live in order to work.
Meaning of work for workers: relations and working conditions.	Meaning of work for workers: security, pay, and interesting work.
Stress on equality, solidarity, and quality of work life.	Stress on equity, mutual competition, and performance.
Management as ménage.	Management as manège.
Managers are employees like others.	Managers are culture heroes.
Managers expected to use intuition, deal with feelings, and seek consensus.	Managers expected to be decisive, firm, assertive, aggressive, competitive, just.
Successful managers seen as having both male and female characteristics.	Successful managers seen as having solely male characteristics.
More women in management.	Fewer women in management.
Smaller wage gap between genders.	Larger wage gap between genders.
Women choose female boss.	Women choose male boss.
Career ambitions are optional for both men and women.	Career ambitions are compulsory for men, optional for women.
Managers hold modest career aspirations.	Managers hold ambitious career aspirations.
Managers less prepared to uproot their families for career reasons.	Managers more prepared to uproot their families for career reasons.
Women in management take having families for granted and adapt their careers.	Women in management take having careers for granted and adapt their families.
Job applicants undersell themselves.	Job applicants oversell themselves.
Humanization of work through creation of work groups.	Humanization of work through provision of task challenge.
Resolution of conflicts through problem solving, compromise, and negotiation.	Resolution of conflicts through denying them or fighting until the best "man" wins.
More sickness absence.	Less sickness absence.
Lower job stress: fewer burnout symptoms among healthy employees.	Higher job stress: more burnout symptoms among healthy employees.
Preference for smaller companies.	Preference for larger companies.
Preference for fewer hours worked.	Preference for higher pay.
Competitive advantage in service industries, consulting, live products, and biochemistry.	Competitive advantage in manufacturing industries, price competition, heavy products, and bulk chemistry.

much tax relief for the rich. Taxation systems, however, do not just happen: They develop as a consequence of preexisting value judgments. In Sweden and the Netherlands it is considered important to establish a minimum quality of life for everybody, and the financial means to that end are collected from those who have them. This is not a recent invention: The French philosopher Denis Diderot, who visited the Netherlands in 1773-74, described both the high taxes and the absence of poverty as a consequence of welfare payments, good medical care for all, and high standards of public education. "The poor in hospitals are well cared for: They are each put in a separate bed" (Diderot, 1780/1982, pp. 124-125; my transla-

tion). Even right-wing politicians in Northwestern European countries do not basically disagree with these policies, only with the extent to which they can be realized.

This is reflected in views about the causes of poverty. The Eurobarometer (1990) included the following question: "Why, in your opinion, are there people who live in need? Here are four opinions, which is the closest to yours? (1) Because they have been unlucky; (2) Because of laziness and lack of willpower; (3) Because there is much injustice in our society; (4) It is an inevitable part of modern progress." Across 11 of the then 12 European Union member states (all except Luxembourg), the proportions attributing poverty to having been unlucky varied from 14% in Germany to 33% in the Netherlands; they were significantly negatively correlated with MAS ($r = -.63*$). The proportions attributing poverty to laziness varied from 10% in the Netherlands to 25% in Greece and Luxembourg; these were marginally positively correlated with MAS ($r = .52, p = .053$). In masculine countries more people believe that the fate of the poor is the poor's own fault, that if they would work harder they would not be poor, and that the rich certainly should not pay to support them.

Attitudes toward the poor are replicated in attitudes toward lawbreakers. Stoetzel's (1983) analysis of the 1981-82 European Values Survey across nine European countries contained an Index of Permissiveness according to whether certain debatable acts—including joyriding, using soft drugs, accepting bribes, prostitution, divorce, and suicide—were justifiable. The national Permissiveness Index was strongly negatively correlated with MAS (rho = $-.83**$, see Hofstede, 1991, p. 98): Feminine cultures were more permissive; mother is less strict than father. Permissiveness also means that the stress in dealing with lawbreakers is on correction, not on punishment. In feminine societies, at least among the wealthier ones, sentences tend to be relatively lenient, prisons relatively comfortable, and rehabilitation programs relatively developed. These practices are supported by a public belief that "most people can be trusted" (World Values Survey question 94); across the 17 wealthier countries this belief showed a significant negative second-order correlation with MAS ($R = .86***$; see Exhibit 4.12).

A comparable difference is found in opinions about the right way of handling immigrants. In general, two opposing views are found: One defends *assimilation* (immigrants should give up their old culture), the other emphasizes *integration* (immigrants should adapt only those aspects of their culture and religion that conflict with their new country's laws; see also Chapter 9). Data from a Eurobarometer (1997) report on "racism and xenophobia in Europe" showed that across 14 European Union countries the public preference for integration over assimilation was strongly negatively correlated with MAS ($r = -.72**$, see Exhibit 4.17); there was a second-order correlation with GNP/capita. Respondents in more masculine and poorer countries required assimilation, whereas those in feminine and wealthier countries favored integration. Data from the same Eurobarometer survey showed also significant second-order correlations for MAS (after UAI) with percentages of respondents wanting to send illegal immigrants back to their countries of origin and with percentages wanting to send all unemployed immigrants back, even legal ones (see also Exhibit 4.17). In masculine cultures the opinion was more in favor of sending these people back. The correlations with MAS are less a matter of pure xenophobia (this is the domain of uncertainty avoidance) than an outcome of lower levels of compassion and benevolence toward the weak in society.

In the wealthier countries, the value choice between reward for the strong and solidarity with the weak also becomes operational in the share of the national budget spent on development assistance to poor countries. Since the late 1950s, large amounts of development assistance money have been disbursed by countries in the lower half of Exhibit 6.8 to countries in the upper half, but the percentages of the countries' GNP spent have varied widely among donors. Feminine culture countries, those in the lower left-hand corner of Exhibit 6.8, have showed considerably greater benevolence than have masculine countries, those in the lower right-hand corner. Across 20 donor countries the correlation between percentage of the 1994 government budget spent on development assistance and MAS was $r = -.78***$ (see Exhibit 6.20 in the statistical section).[95] The range was from .15% for the United States to 1.05% for Norway. National wealth (GNP/capita of the year) appeared only as a second-order correlate. Exhibit 6.20 also includes data for 1983-84. The mean percentage disbursed across the 20 countries was stable from 1983 to 1993, but individualist and uncertainty-avoiding countries tended to reduce their development assistance spending over this period, whereas collectivist and uncertainty-tolerant countries increased it.

The data in Exhibit 6.20 show no evidence that former colonial powers gave more (or less) than countries that had no colonies. The prime explanation of a high aid quote is a feminine national value system. Paradoxically, the amount of money transferred is therefore determined not by the needs of the recipients but by the (psychological) needs of the donors. Also with regard to development aid many people in masculine countries feel that the fate of the poor is their own fault, that if they worked harder they would not be poor, and that the rich countries certainly should not pay to support them.[96]

Countries that spend little money on helping the poor in the world may spend more on armaments. However, data on defense spending collected by Humana (1992) and presented in Exhibit 5.22 show no significant correlations for the official figures, except across 24 wealthy countries a negative correlation between percentage spent on defense and GNP/capita. In Chapter 5, I expressed my skepticism on the reliability of these data, as both the suppliers and the purchasers of arms have a vested interest in secrecy.

In the preceding subsection, I argued that ways of handling conflicts in organizations differ according to the mas/fem dimension: a preference for a good fight versus a preference for compromise. The same distinction can be made with regard to ways of resolving international conflicts. Historically, masculine countries have more often tried to resolve such conflicts by fighting; feminine countries have more often employed compromise and negotiation. A striking example is a comparison between two rather similar incidents of the 20th century, the Åland crisis and the Falkland crisis.

The Åland Islands are a small archipelago halfway between Sweden and Finland; they were part of Finland before 1917, when Finland itself belonged to the czarist Russian empire. When Finland gained independence in 1917, the majority of the 30,000 inhabitants of the islands wanted to join Sweden, which had ruled their lands before 1809. The Finns then arrested the leaders of the pro-Swedish movement. After emotional negotiations in which the newly created League of Nations played a major role, all parties in 1921 agreed to a solution in which the islands remained Finnish but with a large amount of regional autonomy.

The Falkland Islands are also a small archipelago disputed by two nations: Great Britain, which occupied the islands in 1833, and nearby Argentina, which claimed rights on them dating from 1767 and tried to get the United Nations to support its claim. The Falklands are about eight times as large as the Ålands, but they hold far fewer inhabitants, about 1,800 poor sheep farmers. The Argentine military occupied the islands in April 1982, whereupon the British sent an expeditionary force that chased the occupants off, at the cost of (officially) 725 Argentine and 225 British lives as well as enormous monetary expense. In addition, the economy of the islands was further damaged because it economically needed trade relations with the Argentine hinterland.

The differences in approach and in results between these two remarkably similar international disputes can be understood from cultural factors: Finland and Sweden are both feminine cultures; Argentina and Great Britain are both masculine. The masculine symbolism in the Falkland crisis was evident in the language used on both sides.

On the issue of protection of the environment versus economic growth, the report of the Club of Rome on the "limits to growth" in 1972 was the first warning signal that continued economic growth and conservation of our living environment are fundamentally conflicting objectives (Meadows, Meadows, Randers, & Behrens, 1972). The report has been attacked on details, and for a time the issues it raised did not seem particularly urgent. Its basic thesis, however, has never been refuted; at least in my view, it is irrefutable.[97] Governments will have to make painful

choices, and, apart from local geographic and ecological constraints, these choices will be made according to the values dominant in each country. The essential choices are not rational. Douglas (1970) has argued that we are far from being the first civilization to realize that our environment is at risk, although the dangers differ. Every society has its ideas about things that pollute and argues about measures against pollution in terms of "time, money, God, and nature." The dangers of pollution today are certainly very real, but their evaluation is still not a rational process.[98] The main nonrational value issue that opposes growth economists and environmentalists in this discussion is based on cultural differences along the mas/fem dimension.[99]

The most eloquent defender of the need to limit growth has been the German-British economist E. F. Schumacher, in his 1973 book *Small Is Beautiful: A Study of Economics as if People Mattered.* "Things or people" is of course the key choice that distinguishes a masculine from a feminine value system. Governments in masculine cultures are more likely to give priority to growth and to be prepared to sacrifice the living environment for this purpose. Governments in feminine cultures are more likely to choose the reverse priority. Among the (in 1999) 15 countries of the European Union, MAS scores range from 79 (Austria) to 5 (Sweden). Resolving common issues of growth versus conservation is a major challenge for EU policy making.

Public opinion about environmental issues is not only a matter of mas/fem values. This became evident in the results of a 24-country survey of representative samples of those countries' populations about environmental issues (Dunlap, Gallup, & Gallup, 1993). In the context of this chapter, two questions from that survey are of particular interest. The first asked whether priority should be given to protecting the environment or to economic growth. A majority of respondents in 21 out of 24 countries chose the environment. The second question asked whether the respondent would be willing to pay higher prices to protect the environment. In this case a majority in 16 out of the 24 countries said that they would be willing to pay, but the country means on the two questions were not significantly intercorrelated ($r = .34$). Exhibit 6.21 in the statistical section shows that across 20 overlapping countries the answers on the first question correlated weakly significantly with PDI only: Respondents in lower-PDI countries were more in favor of giving priority to the environment. On the second question the percentages saying that they were willing to pay for the environment were correlated significantly negatively with PDI *and* MAS. The questions illustrate the difference between a *value as the desirable* and a *value as the desired* (see Chapter 1).

The first question is a typical statement of the desirable: choosing between virtue and sin but without consequences for the respondent's personal behavior. The question is noncommittal and answers are only weakly related to PDI, showing that in high-PDI countries more people are accustomed to leaving decisions about the environment to the authorities. The second question touches the desired: what people are prepared to do themselves. In this case the answer levels in the countries are much more significantly linked to the culture indexes. The first relationship is still with PDI: Where power distances are smaller, more people were prepared to get personally involved. But there was also a significant additional correlation with MAS: In feminine cultures more people said they were prepared to pay for the environment.[100]

In Chapter 5, I referred to the study of public acceptance of biotechnology conducted on behalf of the European Commission by Van Baren, Hofstede, and Van de Vijver (1995), based on 1993 Eurobarometer data. Biotechnology is a subject that raises severe environmental concerns in many people. The answers to the Eurobarometer questions could be empirically summarized into three clusters: knowledge of biotechnology, biotechnology as a promise, and biotechnology as a threat. Chapter 5 showed a positive correlation between knowledge and IDV. "Threat" questions referred to the degree to which research into different applications of biotechnology should be controlled by governments, because of their risk to human health or to the environment or because of their ethical implications. Across 12 overlapping countries the factor scores for threat were correlated with MAS ($r = -.55^*$) and PDI ($r = -.52^*$); the multiple correlation with MAS and PDI was $R = .69^{**}$. Respondents in masculine, large power distance cultures perceived less threat. The explanation of this is the same as in the preceding paragraph: The stronger the masculinity, the less people are concerned about environmental issues; the larger the power distance, the more people refer such issues to the judgment of the authorities.

Masculinity, Femininity,
and Political Mores

Masculinity and femininity in politics are not only a matter of policy priorities; they are also reflected in informal rules of the political game. In masculine cultures such as Britain, Germany, and the United States, the style of political discourse is strongly adversarial. This is not a recent phenomenon. In 1876 the Dutch-language newspaper *De Standaard* reported that "the American political parties eschewed no means to sling mud at

their adversaries, in a way which foreigners find disgusting" (Lammers, 1989, p. 43)—a statement that could have been repeated in 1999. In feminine cultures such as the Nordic countries and the Netherlands, governments are nearly always coalitions made up of different parties who treat each other gently.

The 1990-93 World Values Survey contained a question (question 248) asking the respondents to place their political views on a 10-point scale from *left* to *right*. Across 26 countries, the percentages *center* (point 5 or 6) were significantly positively correlated with MAS (rho = $.59^{**}$) and the percentages *left* (points 1-4) were correlated negatively (rho = $-.36^*$). The percentages *right* (points 7-10) were not correlated with any index. So in feminine countries there was more support for the political left, and in masculine countries there was greater support for the "no-nonsense," tougher attitudes of people who see themselves at the political center.

Chapter 3 contained an extensive reanalysis of Furnham's (1993) findings about "just world beliefs" among 1,659 students from 12 different countries.[101] Furnham computed mean scores for nine items stating that the world is a just place and for seven items stating the opposite. The "just world" and the "unjust world" country scores were both positively correlated with PDI; I concluded that they were affected by the same response set, the tendency to agree with authoritative statements. The "just world" scores did not show any other significant correlations, but for the "unjust world" scores the correlation pattern was much more complex. I did a multiple regression of the country "unjust world" scores on the four IBM indexes, 1990 GNP/capita, *and the country "just world" scores*—which eliminated the common response set. Without the response set, the following variables in the multiple regression contributed to explaining the country differences in "unjust world" feelings: (1) GNP/capita 1990, negative, $R^2 = .66$; (2) MAS, positive, $R^2 = .84$; and (3) PDI, positive, $R^2 = .94$. So feelings that the world is an unjust place were stronger where (1) the country was poor, (2) its culture was masculine (so its society was tough), and (3) its society was unequal (high PDI).

Exhibit 4.17 presents correlations of IBM indexes with Eurobarometer (1997) data across 14 countries. For each country an "indicator of opinions about the institutions and political establishment" was composed from the answers on seven items (see the statistical section of Chapter 4; they referred to the national institutions and establishment, not to the European Union). The indicator was negatively correlated with MAS ($r = -.72^{**}$); there was a significant second-order correlation with PDI. Across these wealthy countries, respondents in more masculine and higher PDI—that is, tough and unequal—cultures held lower opinions about their countries' institutions and political establishment.

In Exhibit 3.19, Transparency International's 1998 Corruption Perception Index data across 24 poorer countries are shown to be significantly correlated with MAS ($r = -.43*$) after 1997 GNP/ capita ($r = .46*$); in a stepwise regression MAS made a substantial contribution ($R^2 = .21$ for GNP/capita, .37 for GNP/capita plus MAS). A high CPI value stands for low corruption; thus the more masculine among the poorer countries were perceived to be more corrupt. A masculine culture leads to a desire to show off; among power holders in poor countries this desire easily fosters corrupt practices. Across the 26 wealthier countries the CPI was not related to MAS.

In Exhibit 4.12, 1990-93 World Values Survey data illustrate that confidence in the legal system and the civil service were negatively correlated with UAI, but that confidence in *labor unions* (WVS question 277) was negatively correlated with MAS, both across all 25 overlapping countries (rho = $-.44*$) and across the 16 wealthier countries (rho = $-.49*$). Unions generated more confidence in feminine cultures than in masculine ones; they seem to act more as support of the weak member toward the strong employer.

Exhibit 4.16 shows WVS data about participation in voluntary associations and activities. Across 23 countries a summary score of participation in 16 different types of activities (such as trade unions, sports clubs, and environmental conservation groups) was strongly negatively correlated with UAI, which was interpreted as an aspect of citizen competence: In lower-UAI countries, citizens were more likely to organize voluntarily for the benefit of themselves or their society. However, there was a significant second-order correlation with MAS, in the sense of more participation in voluntary associations and activities in feminine countries. This indicates that in feminine, tender cultures people can more easily be mobilized for "issues" (such as the environment); in masculine, tough countries people are more ego oriented and skeptical about issues.

The influence of mas/fem cultural norms on the involvement of women is much clearer in politics than in business management. For one thing, women in feminine countries are more interested in politics than are their sisters in masculine countries. Data from Inglehart (1990) has shown that the extent to which citizens discuss politics is inversely related to PDI (see Chapter 3). For 20 countries Inglehart also published separate percentages of women and of men claiming to discuss politics (p. 348). Across 17 overlapping countries, the gender gap varied from 5% in the Netherlands to 27% in Italy; it correlated primarily negatively with (1980) GNP/capita

($r = -.66**$) but with a significant second-order contribution of MAS ($R = .79***$, smaller gender gap in feminine cultures).[102]

In line with this, feminine democracies have more women in their parliaments or other governing bodies and as government ministers. Exhibit 6.22 in the statistical section shows that across 22 countries the percentages of both in 1995 were highly significantly negatively correlated with MAS. Women in parliament and women in government are obviously related phenomena, but the percentages of women in parliament showed a secondary negative correlation with power distance, and women in government with uncertainty avoidance. The first means an equality norm within political parties; the second, a break with convention. The combination of low UAI and low MAS also differentiates Protestant from Catholic Christian countries (see Exhibit 4.21). Catholic and Orthodox Christianity maintain a strong gender segregation in church leadership, the data in Exhibit 6.22 imply that these forms of Christianity also eschew the admission of women into secular politics.

Exhibit 6.15 summarizes the key differences between feminine and masculine societies in political priorities and political mores.

Masculinity and Sexual Behavior

Sexual norms differ from one country to another.[103] More generally, the ways in which sex is practiced and experienced are not human universals. Yet the cultural component in sexuality has attracted relatively few studies. In fact, such studies often meet with strong resistance, especially in masculine cultures. In the United States, for example, after a sexual revolution in the 1950s, there has been a considerable moralistic, conservative backlash, and the taboo on discussing sex in public has been lifted much less than in some European countries in which the sexual revolution came later but with a more lasting impact. Even the universal threat of AIDS has not broken existing taboos on discussing sexual behavior. For example, Goldman (1994) tried to study children's sexual cognition in Australia, Great Britain, Sweden, and the United States, but after strong resistance in the last of these she had to replace the U.S. sample with a "North American" sample, half U.S. and half Canadian.

Broad survey studies of sexual behavior have so far been conducted only at national, not intercultural, levels. Hatfield and Rapson (1995) collected the results of such national studies and compared them side by side. This type of undertaking is often frustrating; national survey studies are rarely cross-nationally compatible, and differences may be due as much to the method of data

Exhibit 6.15 Key Differences Between Feminine and Masculine Societies IV: Politics

Low MAS	High MAS
In Political Priorities	
Welfare society ideal.	Performance society ideal.
Low percentage poor and illiterate.	High percentage poor and illiterate.
The needy should be helped.	The strong should be supported.
The wealthy pay taxes to help the poor.	The fate of the poor is the poor's problem.
Permissive and corrective society.	Punitive society.
Immigrants should be integrated.	Immigrants should assimilate or be sent back.
Larger development cooperation budget.	Small development cooperation budget.
International conflicts should be resolved through negotiation and compromise.	International conflicts should be resolved through show of force or fighting.
Preservation of the environment should have the highest priority.	Economic growth should have the highest priority.
Greater public concern about risks of biotechnology.	Less public concern about risks of biotechnology.
In Political Mores	
Political discourse moderate.	Political discourse adversarial.
More voters place themselves at the political left, fewer at the center.	More voters place themselves at the political center, fewer at the left.
More people see the world as a just place.	More people see the world as an unjust place.
Positive attitudes toward institutions and political establishment.	Negative attitudes toward institutions and political establishment.
In poor countries, less corruption.	In poor countries, more corruption.
More confidence in labor unions.	Less confidence in labor unions.
More participation in voluntary activities and associations.	Less participation in voluntary activities and associations.
Men and women discuss politics equally frequently.	Men discuss politics more often than do women.
More women in elected political positions and government.	Fewer women in elected political positions and government.

collection as to real properties of the respondent populations. Internationally designed comparative studies of sexual values and behavior (like the one by Goldman mentioned above) are rare, although the German Italian sociologist Robert Michels (1911, p. 33) at the beginning of the 20th century expressed the need for a "comparative love science" (*vergleichende Liebeswissenschaft*). Michels's material at that time remained limited to personal impressions. In this subsection I will try to provide more objective comparative information.

Differences in sexual behavior can sometimes be inferred from cross-cultural studies covering other topics. Comparative studies explicitly addressing sexual issues so far have at best covered two, three, or four countries. When these were countries that in the IBM studies differed considerably on the mas/fem dimension but not on the other three, a relationship to mas/fem could be inferred. This was the case when an English-speaking country (Australia, Britain, Ireland, United States—MAS between 61 and 68) was compared to one of the Nordic countries or the Netherlands (MAS between 5 and 26).

I referred in the subsection on family above to the research of Buss (1989, 1994) about criteria for selecting a marriage partner, showing that the differences between men's and women's desires for their partner's chastity were correlated with UAI and MAS: larger differences in uncertainty-avoiding, masculine cultures. Differences between men's and women's criteria for a partner point to a double moral standard (women should be chaste, men need not be), and the gap in the moral standard is correlated with the culture's masculinity.

In the subsection on gender roles, I referred to the terms *machismo* for men and *marianismo* or *hembrismo* for women. *Marianismo* implies sexual frigidity (Stevens, 1973). Women in strongly masculine cultures are not expected to be sexually active. Even from the United States it has been reported that men feel threatened when they really meet sexually unreserved women (rather than fantasize about them; Komarovsky, 1976; Lasch, 1980). In March 1993, Janet L. Wolfe, American sexologist and author of the book *What to Do When He Has a Headache* (1992), visited the Netherlands during a promotional tour. In an interview with a Dutch columnist, Wolfe described how the men who consulted her in the United States said they felt turned off when their partners took the initiative. When her interviewer cited Dutch research showing exactly the opposite—that Dutch men want their women to initiate sex—Wolfe muttered, "Bullshit." [104] The idea that norms for sexual interaction might differ between countries had obviously never occurred to her.

A reserve among men about women whose careers are more successful than their own is more likely in masculine than in feminine cultures. Mead (1950/1962a, pp. 271 ff.) observed that in the United States, boys became less attractive sex partners when they experienced career failure; girls, when they had career success. In Japan at the end of the 20th century a career still diminished a woman's marriage chances.

Jones et al. (1986) conducted a 37-country study of *teenage pregnancies*, and their work provides implicit comparative data on sexual behavior. The researchers found that country rates of pregnancy among girls under 18 years old covaried positively with the frequency of abortions among women ages 15-44, with maternal mortality, with the percentage of the labor force in agriculture, and with religiosity (the statement that God is important in the respondent's life). Pregnancy rates for girls under 18 covaried negatively with policies favoring provision of contraceptives to young and unmarried women, with the actual use of condoms by married people, with open attitudes in society about sex, with income equality (percentage of national income going to those in the lowest 20%), and with per capita government expenditure on education. So early pregnancies were part of a broader cultural syndrome.

Surprisingly, across 22 overlapping countries early pregnancies were correlated (negatively) only with national wealth, not with any of the IBM indexes. See Exhibit 6.23 in the statistical section of this chapter. Looking for cultural influences unrelated to economic development, I had a closer look at the relationships with UAI and MAS. Zero-order and multiple correlations of UAI and MAS with pregnancies among girls under 18 were virtually nil, but as Exhibit 6.23 shows, the relationship was curvilinear: Pregnancy rates were high in the case of high UAI plus low MAS, but also for low UAI plus high MAS. Five out of the six low-UAI, high-MAS countries (Great Britain, United States, Australia, New Zealand, and Can-

ada) had pregnancy rates in the under-18 age group of more than 40 per 1,000 women; but rates were also high in high-UAI, low-MAS Portugal. Pregnancy rates were low in the case of high UAI plus high MAS (Japan), but also for low UAI plus low MAS (Denmark, Finland, Netherlands, Norway, Sweden). My interpretation of this unique configuration is that in the strong uncertainty avoidance countries the behavior of young girls is subjected to a rigid social code, the more so if the culture is also more masculine (the combination that Buss's data showed to produce a double moral standard; see above). Japan had the world's lowest teenage pregnancy rate but a very high abortion rate (Jones et al., 1986, p. 10). In the weak uncertainty avoidance countries, social codes are more tolerant. In this case, if the culture is masculine, the boys have things their way, leaving the girls with teenage pregnancies. If the culture is feminine, the girls have things their way, and they are more careful. These countries are also the ones with the most open attitudes about sex and easy availability of contraceptives.

Earlier in this chapter, the combination of weak uncertainty avoidance and strong masculinity was shown to be associated with a strong "need for achievement" as identified in 1925 children's readers by McClelland. Sexual performance can be experienced as achievement, especially for the male partner. Thus the achievement motive in sexual activity will play a more important role in weak uncertainty avoidance, masculine countries than in others.

This is supported by a study by Gibbons, Helweg-Larsen, and Gerrard (1995), who surveyed female and male adolescents, ages 13-15, in rural areas of the United States (*n* = 500) and Denmark (*n* = 224), about influences that led young people to engage in risky behaviors. The Americans showed themselves more sensitive to social comparison, which is an essential component of achievement motivation. They reported comparing themselves to and being influenced by their peers more than did the Danes. The Danes reported being influenced by their parents more than did the Americans. This survey covered four risky behaviors: smoking, drinking alcohol, sex, and use of drugs. Danes reported drinking alcohol much more than Americans (79% versus 28%), smoking more (16% versus 6%), and using more drugs (10% versus 1%). There was no difference between the two countries in the proportions claiming to have had sex (12% for both), but Danish boys and in particular Danish girls reported more intention to have sex in the next year than did their American counterparts. Both country samples overestimated the percentages of their peers who engaged in risky behaviors, but the Americans overestimated much more than did the Danes. If young people in a masculine culture overestimate risky behaviors more, they develop a stronger support for such behaviors.

Strong achievement motivation in teenage sexual relations leads to a need for "scoring"—and anecdotal impressions from especially U.S. articles, books, and films confirm that boys, and sometimes girls too, often think about sex in terms of scoring. Scoring is ego oriented—it is a lonely adventure in which the partner remains an object. Cultural masculinity contains an element of ego boosting, more so than cultural femininity, which is oriented primarily toward establishing relationships. We can expect that girls in masculine cultures more often feel exploited than do girls in feminine ones—that they feel their feelings do not count. This is confirmed by the answers on an item in the 1990-93 World Values Survey (question 197): "If someone said that individuals should have the chance to enjoy complete sexual freedom without being restricted, would you tend to agree or disagree?" Across 25 overlapping countries, the proportions agreeing varied from 7% (India) to 55% (Spain—could this be an error?), and they correlated primarily with MAS (rho = .38*): more agreement in masculine countries. Respondents in a feminine country confronted with this question are more likely to wonder what "complete sexual freedom" would mean for the partners of these "individuals."

Less frequent feelings of being exploited among women in a feminine culture were confirmed in a survey study by I. M. Schwartz (1993) about sexual experiences among U.S. and Swedish unmarried female students ages 18-25. In this sample, 79% of the Americans ($n = 217$) and 90% of the Swedes ($n = 186$) claimed to be sexually experienced. The survey asked about their affective reactions to their first coitus. The mean age for first sex did not differ; it was 17 in both countries, with a 19-year-old partner. Swedes, however, reported a lower age of social acceptance for girls having sex (16) than Americans (19), and in general a greater acceptance of premarital sex, regardless of the existence of a love relationship. Americans significantly more than Swedes reported the following feelings: guilty, fearful, anxious, sorry, exploited, confused, and embarrassed. More Swedes than Americans reported that they used contraceptives (76% versus 57%). Swedes had sex earlier in the relationship (31% within one month versus 15% for the Americans) and reported more sex partners in their lifetimes (69% more than two versus 57% for the Americans). From the period before their first sex, Swedes reported more experience with masturbation and Americans more experience with various other erotic activities, from kissing to fellatio.[105] Feelings about sex are culturally influenced. As Caplan (1987) has noted, "Our heads are our most erogenous zones" (p. 2).

These studies help us to understand why *sexual harassment* is more an issue in the United States than in the Netherlands and the Nordic countries. Sex in a masculine culture is more likely to be experienced as exploitative; in a feminine culture, sex is more likely to be experienced as part of a relationship. In the Dutch language *sexual harassment* is translated as *unwanted intimacies,* implying that there are wanted intimacies as well. In a survey feedback session in Denmark (Hofstede, Neuijen, Ohayv, & Sanders, 1990), a female research partner and I asked respondents why nobody in their company had considered "a married man having sexual relationships with a subordinate" a valid reason for the man's dismissal. One female respondent explained this as follows: "Either she likes it, and then there is no problem. Or she doesn't like it, and then she will tell him to go to hell." There are two assumptions in this answer: (Most) Danish subordinates will not hesitate to speak up to the boss (small power distance), and (most) Danish bosses will "go to hell" if told so. In such a society, sexual harassment is unlikely to become a big issue. However, power distance is not the decisive dimension. Pryor et al. (1997) studied to what extent certain interactions between a professor and a student were interpreted as sexually harassing by college students in Germany (MAS 66), the United States (MAS 62), Australia (MAS 61), and Brazil (MAS 49, PDI 69). Brazilian students "demonstrated a substantially different understanding of the concept of sexual harassment than participants from any of the other cultural milieus. Both Brazilian men and women generally defined sexual harassment as less of an abuse of power, less related to gender discrimination, and more likely to be a relatively harmless sexual behavior than did US students" (Pryor et al., 1997, p. 526).[106]

Attitudes toward *homosexuality* are also affected by the masculinity in the culture. Ross (1989) surveyed 600 homosexual men in Australia, Ireland, Finland, and Sweden. Young homosexuals had more problems accepting their sexual orientation in Ireland and Australia, less in Finland, least in Sweden. Ross considers the societies in question as homophobic in this order; it is also the order of the countries on MAS. Homosexuality tends to be felt as a threat to masculine norms and so is rejected in masculine cultures (Bolton, 1994); this goes together with an overestimation of its frequency (Diamond, 1993). In feminine cultures, homosexuality is more often considered a fact of life.[107]

In an earlier study, Ross (1983) had administered the Bem Sex Role Inventory (BSRI; Bem, 1974) to 163 Australian and 176 Swedish homosexual men, and to control groups of 98 Australian and 57 Swedish heterosexual men. The BSRI is a U.S. questionnaire that allows the placement of individuals on two scales, one of masculine and one of feminine gender role acceptance. Australian heterosexuals, Swedish heterosexuals, and Swedish homosexuals did not differ in their positions on the masculine and feminine BSRI scales. Only the Australian homosexuals differed: They scored as masculine as the other three samples, but with a significantly higher feminine role acceptance. Ross concluded that "gender role in homosexuals has a strong societal component" (p. 287): It is the antihomosexual Australian context that leads these homosexual men to identify more than other men with a feminine role. In the more accepting Swedish context, this identification process was not found.

Ross (1983) also used a questionnaire on "Sex Role Conservatism" that showed the two groups of Australians scoring much more conservative than the two groups of Swedes, but with a wider gap for homosexuals than for heterosexuals: Swedish homosexuals were less conservative than heterosexuals, but Australian homosexuals were considerably more conservative than Australian heterosexuals. A set of questions on "attitudes toward parents" showed that the two national groups did not differ in their attitudes toward their fathers, but that the Swedes rated their mothers as significantly more "active" than did the Australians. Finally, demographic questions showed the Swedes had become homosexually active earlier (age 19) than the Australians (age 21), suggesting the latter had more resistance to overcome.

Foa et al. (1987) studied to what extent the attitudes of young female and male hetero- and homosexuals in the United States ($n = 390$) and Sweden ($n = 179$) differentiated between *sex* and *love*. They used an ingenious method of asking their subjects to sort cards into two piles; no labels for the piles were imposed, but some cards implicitly referred more to sex and others to love. Within each country, men saw sex and love as more different than did women. Among the men, homosexuals saw sex and love as most different, married heterosexuals saw the least difference, and single heterosexuals were in between. Among women the order was reversed: Married heterosexuals saw sex and love as most different, single heterosexuals saw them as less different, and lesbians saw the least difference. The perception gap between the sexes was smallest for married couples (who have to accommodate to their partners), larger for singles, and largest for homosexuals (who do not have to accommodate to the other sex at all). However, much larger than the differences between these categories within the countries were the differences between the two countries as a whole: All Swedish groups distinguished much less between sex and love than did the corresponding U.S. groups; there was no overlap between the

answers from the two countries in this respect. All groups in the feminine culture, Sweden, came much closer to equating sex with love.

This may explain why in the feminine European countries there is less sex, either implicit or explicit, in the media, especially on television. TV programs and advertising in the United States, for example, are often strongly eroticized. The weaker taboo on discussing sex in more feminine countries seems to reduce the attraction of sexual themes in publicity. The same applies to an even larger extent to violence (and the combination of sex and violence): Programs showing explicit violence, common in more masculine countries, are unattractive to the public in more feminine countries.

Van Yperen and Buunk (1991) studied factors that contributed either positively or negatively to a love relationship. Respondents were about 40 male and about 100 female students majoring in psychology in the Netherlands (MAS 14) and equal numbers in the United States (MAS 62). All were currently involved in a dating or more serious relationship. Americans attached greater value to their partners' being successful, ambitious, healthy, mentally stable, and attractive; the Dutch attached more value to their partners' being all-around educated and social, having many friends, and taking care of children. American attitudes differed more between the genders than did Dutch attitudes and were more gender stereotyped. Americans were most satisfied when they felt the relationship partners treated each other equitably; the Dutch, when they felt they overbenefited from the relationship (received more than they gave).

Gudykunst and Nishida (1986) reported on two studies comparing perceptions of communication behavior between Japanese and U.S. university students, which they related to the IBM dimensions of uncertainty avoidance, individualism, and masculinity. Because they compared only two countries, their attributions to the dimensions are conceptual, not statistical. They predicted and found that for the Japanese, opposite-sex relationship terms (*lover, fiancé, mate, spouse, boy-/girlfriend,* and *steady*) were perceived as less intimate than for the Americans; only *date* was more intimate for the Japanese. They attributed these differences to the stronger masculinity in Japan, which leads to clearly differentiated gender roles in which interaction is superficial.

Of course, sexual norms and behaviors also vary among subcultures inside countries. Nevertheless, the various studies described above show beyond doubt that there is a significant national component, and that this component is related to the position of the country's culture on the mas/fem dimension. The difference can be summarized in the following terms: In masculine cultures, sex is more often experienced by the partners as *performance*; in feminine cultures, it is experienced as *a way of relating*.

Culture is heavy with values, and values imply judgment. The issues discussed in this subsection are strongly value laden. They are about moral and immoral, decent and indecent behavior. The comparisons offered should remind us that morality is in the eye of the beholder, not in the act itself. There is no one best way, in social or in sexual relationships; any solution is best according to the norms that come with it.

Masculinity, Femininity, and Religion

A religion, according to U.S. anthropologist Clifford Geertz (1973), is

(1) a system of symbols which acts to (2) establish powerful, pervasive, and long-lasting moods and motivations in men by (3) formulating conceptions of a general order of existence and (4) clothing these conceptions with such an aura of factuality that (5) the moods and motivations seem uniquely realistic. (p. 90)

The issues related to the mas/fem dimension are central to any religion. Masculine cultures worship a tough God or gods who justify tough behavior toward fellow humans; feminine cultures worship a tender God or gods who demand caring behavior toward fellow humans.

Christianity has always maintained a dialectic between tough, masculine elements and tender, feminine ones. In the Christian Bible as a whole, the Old Testament reflects tougher values (an eye for an eye, a tooth for a tooth) and the New Testament more tender values (turn the other cheek). God in the Old Testament is majestic. Jesus in the New Testament can hardly be called a macho hero.[108] Catholicism has produced some very masculine, tough currents (Templars, Jesuits) but also some feminine, tender ones (Franciscans); outside Catholicism we also find groups with strongly masculine values (such as the Mormons) and groups with very feminine values (such as the Quakers and the Salvation Army). However, on average, countries with Catholic traditions tend to maintain more masculine and those with Protestant traditions more feminine values (see Exhibit 4.21).

Outside the Christian world there are also tough and tender religions. Buddhism in masculine Japan is very different from Buddhism in feminine Thailand. Some young men in Japan follow Zen Buddhist training aiming at self-development through meditation under a tough master. More than half of all young men in Thailand spend some time as Buddhist monks, serving and begging.[109]

In Islam, Sunni is a more triumphant version of the faith than Shia, which stresses the importance of suffering, following the founder Ali, who was persecuted. In the IBM studies, Iran, which is predominantly Shia, scored more feminine than the predominantly Sunni Arabic-speaking countries.

Verweij (1998a, 1998b; see also Verweij, Ester, & Nauta, 1997) has convincingly made the link between religion and the mas/fem dimension. He analyzed data on secularization collected by the 1990-93 World Values Survey across 16 Christian countries and found that MAS was the best available predictor of a country's degree of secularization: Countries with feminine values had secularized faster than those with masculine ones. In masculine Christian countries people rated their religiosity higher and attached more importance in their lives to God, Christian rites, orthodoxy, and Christian worldviews. Earlier theories of secularization had sought the reason in the modernization of society, but these theories had to make an exception for the United States, a modern country relatively untouched by secularization. Verweij's results apply across the board, including the United States.[110] Verweij's study supports the conclusion in Chapters 3 and 4 that the direction of causality is from preexisting values to religion, not, as popular wisdom wants it, vice versa. However, once a particular current of a religion has been established in a country, it reinforces the values that led to its being adopted in the first place.

Earlier in this chapter, in the subsection on the family, I reported on the answers to a block of items in the World Values Survey questionnaire: "Please say, from each of the following, how important it is in your life," followed by the topics of work, family, friends, leisure, politics, and religion (questions 4-9). After standardization, the importance of religion (question 9) was correlated with national wealth (rho = .78***) followed by MAS (R = .83***). Religion was rated relatively more important in poor, masculine societies.

The earlier version of the WVS, the 1981-82 European Values Survey, contained a large number of questions about religion, including claimed observance of the Ten Commandments in the Christian Bible, one by one. French sociologist Jean Stoetzel published an insightful analysis of the survey's results across nine countries as early as 1983, in which he divided the commandments into three categories: moral commandments ([4] honoring parents, [5] no killing, [7] no stealing, [8] no false witness, [9] do not covet thy neighbor's goods), sexual commandments ([6] no adultery, [10] do not covet thy neighbor's wife), and purely religious commandments ([1] no other gods, [2] not using God's name in vain, and [3] keeping the Sabbath holy).[111] Overall, the claimed observance was highest for the moral commandments and lowest for the religious commandments. For all three categories, observance was correlated with the rated "importance of God in my life," both at the level of individual respondents and at the level of country means. However, the correlations were strongest for the religious commandments and weakest for the moral commandments (Stoetzel, 1983, pp. 98-101). As Verweij has shown for the 1990-93 survey round, the importance of God was significantly correlated with MAS.

One could argue that it is obvious that among Christian countries the tough, masculine societies endorse more strongly the importance of God—and other values derived from it. The Christian God is the Father: He is masculine. Such a God appeals more to the population of a masculine society—including the women who were socialized to inequality of gender values. In a feminine society, the stress is more on the importance of relationships with fellow humans than on a relationship with God.

The moral and sexual commandments define relationships with fellow humans; the religious commandments define relationships with God. In masculine countries, God is more important; and if God is more important, the commandments that define a relationship with God are stressed at least as much as those that define relationships with fellow humans. If God is less important, which is the case in feminine countries, the moral commandments remain important, but the sexual and in particular the religious commandments carry less weight.

The Christian Gospel offers a choice of values for different positions on the mas/fem scale. The New Testament carefully balances the importance of relationships with God and with one's fellow humans. In one story, Jesus is approached by a Pharisee with the question, "What is the greatest command in the Law?" He replies:

> You must love the Lord your God with your whole heart, with your whole soul, and with your whole mind. This is the greatest and chief command. There is a second like it: you must love your neighbor as yourself. The whole Law and the prophets hang upon these two commands. (St. Matthew 22:37-40; translation J. Moffatt).

The comparison between Christian religiosity in more masculine and more feminine countries implies that the balance between these two commands is difficult to find. There are cultural imperatives that lead Christians in some countries to stress the first and those in other countries to stress the second.

In a comparison of European/World Values Survey data for 1981-82 and 1990 for Ireland, the Netherlands, and Switzerland, Halman and Petterson (1996) found no evidence that secularization is related to a loss of morality. Another hypothesis, that shifts in morality would be related to the transition from materialism to postmaterialism, according to Inglehart's classification, was also disconfirmed. Simplistic recipes that immoral behavior should be countered by a return to religion are thus empirically falsified.

The 1981-82 European/World Values Survey across 12 countries also asked for qualities that children should learn at home (Hofstede & Associates, 1998, tab. 12.1). "Religious faith" was positively correlated with MAS, whereas "politeness and neatness" and "feeling of responsibility" were negatively correlated with MAS. It seems that masculine cultures—which, as Verweij has shown, have remained more religious—put less stress on civil education. Feelings of responsibility may contrast with the religious value of relying on God.

In Chapter 4, I referred to six varieties of religiosity based on Towler's (1984) study in Britain: exemplarism, conversionism, theism, gnosticism, traditionalism, and mysticism. Whereas all of these might be represented to some extent in all Christian societies, conversionism (being "born again"), theism, and traditionalism fit the values of, and therefore are likely to be more frequent in, more masculine societies. Exemplarism (Jesus Christ as an example to follow) and mysticism are likely to be more frequent in more feminine societies. Gnosticism is probably unrelated to mas/fem.

One issue conceptually linked to religious convictions is euthanasia, "the act or method of causing death painlessly, so as to end suffering." [112] The public opinion survey of "human values" across 13 countries published by Hastings and Hastings (1981) and referred to in Chapter 4 contained a question about this subject.[113] Respondents were asked to choose between two statements:

1. When a patient has a fatal disease such as cancer and maintaining his/her life only serves to increase his/her pain, mercy killing should be allowed if the patient wants it.

2. Whatever the circumstances, every effort should be made to maintain the patient's life.

Proportions of respondents choosing euthanasia varied from 17% in the Philippines to 71% in France and Germany (48% in the United States). However, contrary to what might be hypothesized, these percentages did not relate to MAS, or to UAI. The single dominant correlation was with (1980) GNP/capita, $r = .82***$, rho = .77**. In wealthier countries people live longer and more comfortably, so the dissonance of painful fatal disease is more strongly felt. On a global level, religion is not the decisive influence on people's opinions in this respect.

All religions specify different religious roles for men and for women. In Christianity, many Protestant churches now practice equality between men and women in their leadership and clergy, whereas the Roman Catholic Church strongly maintains the male prerogative to the priesthood. Ambiguity about the roles of the sexes is present even in Genesis, the first book of the Judeo-Christian Old Testament, which contains the myths of creation (and which was codified in the fifth century B.C.). This book contains two conflicting versions of the creation of the sexes. The first states:

> So God created man in his own image, in the image of God created he him; male and female created he them. And God blessed them, and God said to them, Be fruitful, and multiply, and replenish the earth, and subdue it. (Genesis 1:27-28)

This text suggests equal partnership between the sexes. In the second version (Genesis 2:8 ff., which is supposed to have derived from a different source document), we find the story of the Garden of Eden, in which God first put "the man" alone. Then Genesis 2:18 states: "And the Lord God said, It is not good that the man should be alone: I will make him a help meet for him." [114] Then follows the story of the woman being made from one of Adam's ribs. This text gives clear priority to the male partner and defines the woman as "a help meet" (that is, appropriate) for him; it justifies a society in which there is male dominance.

Paradoxically, in most religions women participate more than men. The 1981-82 European Values Study confirmed this for all nine countries included. So at least within Christianity in countries with a masculine culture religious values are more strongly endorsed, but these same values are more practiced by the women than by the men. "God is apparently not an equal opportunity employer: He has a bias to the women" (Walter, 1990, p. 87).

It should be no surprise that the same dimension, masculinity/femininity, relates to both sexual and religious behavior. Religion is a way for human beings to influence the supernatural—to provide certainties beyond the unpredictable risks of human existence. Birth, marital fertility, and death figure foremost among these unpredictables. All religions accentuate and celebrate the events of procreation: births, weddings, and deaths. Fertility rites are known from virtually all human civilizations since prehistory; they survive to the present day in such forms as wedding ceremonies and sanctuaries devoted to prayers for

pregnancy.[115] In Judaism and most of Islam, circumcision of the male organ is a condition for being admitted to the religious community. In Hinduism, the architecture of temples models the *lingam* and *yoni* (phallus and vulva). Chinese philosophy and religious practices give strong importance to the complementarity of *yang* and *yin,* the male and female elements.

Most or all religions contain dos and don'ts about love and sex. U.S. sociologist Peter Berger (1967/1990) has written:

> Every society is faced with the problem of providing for its physical procreation. This has meant, empirically, that every society has worked out more or less restrictive "programs" for the sexual activity of its members. . . . The problem of legitimation is to explain why the particular arrangement that has developed in a particular society . . . should be faithfully adhered to, even if it is at times annoying or downright painful. One efficient way of solving the problem is to mystify the institution in religious terms. (p. 90)

Human sexuality has always had the two facets of procreation and of recreation, or pleasure. In fact, the latter, at least in the modern era, plays a more important role than the former—which is fortunate in a world threatened by overpopulation (Abramson & Pinkerton, 1995, pp. 17-18). Different religions, and currents within religions, have taken different positions toward the pleasure side of sex; the general trend is for religions in masculine cultures to stress procreation and for those in more feminine cultures to value pleasure. Masculine Roman Catholicism has from its beginnings been uneasy about sex and rejected its use for pleasure, institutionalizing celibacy for priests, the cult of the *Virgin* Mary, and marriage as a sacrament with the purpose of procreation, and prohibiting divorce, contraception, and abortion.[116] Less masculine Protestant Christian churches when they split from Rome did away with celibacy, did not consider marriage a sacrament, and accepted divorce.[117] "If sex is considered healthy, there is more autonomy for women" (Caplan, 1987, p. 24). Orthodox Islam accepts sexual pleasure for men but considers sexual pleasure in women a danger. Currents in Hinduism have taken a very positive attitude toward sexual pleasure, as manifested by the *Kama Sutra* and the erotic temples of Khajuraho and Konarak in India. In feminine Buddhist Thailand the profession of prostitute carries less of a stigma than it does in the West.[118]

In the domain of scientific theories, it is remarkable that the work of Sigmund Freud (1856-1939) originated in Austria, the country with the second-highest MAS score in the IBM list (MAS 79). Freud, of course, defended the primordial

Exhibit 6.16 Key Differences Between Feminine and Masculine Societies V: Sexuality and Religion

Low MAS	High MAS
In Sexual Behavior	
Matter-of-fact attitudes about sex.	Moralistic attitudes about sex.
AIDS prevention campaigns very outspoken.	AIDS prevention campaigns restricted by taboos.
Single standard for women and men.	Double standard: Women should be chaste at marriage, men needn't.
Norm of active role of woman.	Norm of passive role of woman: machismo vs. marianismo.
Sexual attraction unrelated to career success.	Men become more attractive by career success, women less.
In uncertainty-accepting cultures, few teenage pregnancies.	In uncertainty-accepting cultures, frequent teenage pregnancies.
Young people more influenced by parents.	Young people more influenced by peers.
Other-oriented sex.	Ego-oriented sex.
Women enjoy first sex.	Women feel exploited by first sex.
Unwanted intimacies not major issue.	Sexual harassment major issue.
Homosexuality is a fact of life.	Homosexuality is a taboo and a threat.
Weak distinction between sex and love.	Sharp distinction between sex and love.
Sex and violence in media taboo.	Sex and violence in media frequent.
Lovers should be educated, social.	Lovers should be successful, attractive.
Happy lovers overbenefit from the other.	Happy lovers get equitable mutual deal.
Interaction with other sex more intimate.	Interaction with other sex less intimate.
Sex is a way of relating to someone.	**Sex is a way of performing.**
In Religion	
"Tender" religions and religious currents.	"Tough" religions and religious currents.
Secularization in Christian countries.	Maintenance of traditional Christianity.
Religion not so important in life.	Religion most important in life.
Religion focuses on fellow human beings.	**Religion focuses on God or gods.**
Children socialized toward responsibility and politeness.	Children socialized toward religious faith.
Exemplarism and mysticism.	Traditionalism, theism, and conversionism.
Dominant religions stress complementarity of the sexes.	Dominant religions stress male prerogative.
Men and women can be priests.	Only men can be priests.
Sex is for procreation and recreation.	Sex is primarily for procreation.
Positive or neutral attitude toward sexual pleasure.	Negative attitude toward sexual pleasure.
Sexuality as one area of human motivation.	Sexuality as primordial area of human motivation.

importance of sexuality in the development of the human personality; he attributed many psychopathological problems to the repression of sexuality. I find it doubtful that an author from a less masculine society would have attributed "penis envy" to all women (Freud, 1938/1963, p. 202). Every author is a child of his or her society; Freud wrote about what he felt and was able to perceive.

Exhibit 6.16 summarizes the key differences between feminine and masculine societies in the areas of sexuality and religion. Of course the themes of Exhibits 6.12 (the family and the school), 6.13 (gender roles and consumer behavior), 6.14 (work), 6.15 (political issues), and 6.16 (sex and religion) are linked in many ways. In masculine United States, a preacher has been quoted as saying: "Business is religion, and religion is business. . . . If God gives us the possibilities and power to get wealth, to acquire influence, to be forces in the world, what is the true conception of life but divine ownership and human administration?" [119] And the following statement is ascribed to a leading economist and consumer psychologist: "Business is like sex. When it's good, it's very, very good; when it's not so good, it's still good." [120]

Masculinity and Geographic, Economic, and Demographic Factors

In analogy with the preceding chapters, I studied the relationship of MAS with eight economic, geographic, and demographic indicators (see Exhibit 6.24 in the statistical section). The correlations across all 50 countries were weak; they became somewhat stronger when poor and wealthier countries were separated. For both poor and wealthy countries, significant zero-order correlations were found between MAS and geographic latitude (lower latitude more masculine). Chapter 3 showed a negative relationship between latitude and power distance, which I interpreted as the result of a greater need for technology for survival in colder climates, imposing a certain level of education and equality upon people. We can extend this argument to equality between the genders. In colder climates survival presupposes the mastery of complex skills by both men and women, which makes extreme inequality between the genders untenable.

Van de Vliert, Schwartz, Huismans, Hofstede, and Daan (1999) established relationships between MAS and temperature plus domestic political violence across 53 countries. This work suggests that the relationship between temperature (related to latitude) and MAS is actually curvilinear. Van de Vliert et al. found masculinity, and also violence, to be higher in moderately warm countries than in cold and very warm ones.

It makes sense that men in countries with warm climates, compared to men in colder and hotter countries, expect and accept more violence. Women in these societies are socialized toward more submissive and docile behavior. Men try to bend not only women but also other men to their will. Violent actions also serve to impress women and win their sexual favors. (Van de Vliert, 1998, p. 129)

Van de Vliert et al. refer to a "paternal investment theory," which suggests that fathers in colder and in very hot climates are obliged to invest more care in their families as a matter of survival.

Exhibit 6.24 also shows two significant zero-order correlations between MAS and population size (larger countries more masculine); this is in line with the "Small is beautiful" ethos in feminine cultures noted earlier in this chapter.

The relationship between MAS and population growth was complex. Across the 28 poorer countries MAS showed a positive zero-order correlation with population growth; across the 22 wealthier countries, a significant second-order *negative* correlation. Population growth depends strongly on the average family size (and, of course, on the level of medical care); thus femininity means smaller families in poorer countries and larger families in wealthier countries. This is precisely what we would expect in those cultures in which the woman has a say in the number of children she bears: She will adapt the family size to the available wealth. Where male choice prevails in matters of family size, we find (too) large families in poor countries and small families in wealthy countries. Levinson (1977, p. 763), after reviewing anthropological studies of traditional cultures, concluded that population increases where females are subservient to males. Family planning programs falter on the attitudes of men (Adebayo, 1988). The United Nations Fund for Children has published a graph showing that if in all countries women could choose the number of children they would have, they would have an average of 1.41 fewer children, which amounts to 1.3 billion fewer people in the world in 35 years' time (UNICEF, 1995, p. 29).[121]

Mas/fem differences undoubtedly play a role in what is becoming a dramatic problem for mainly Asian countries: the prevention or suppression of female births. It has been estimated that in all of Asia there are 100 million fewer females than would have been produced by normal birthrates (Emerson, 1995). The reasons include the desire of parents to have sons rather than daughters, the availability of ultrasound scanning of the sex of a fetus followed by selective abortion, and the old practice of female infanticide. The female/male ratio in the population is higher in feminine cultures such as Thailand and Indonesia than in masculine cultures such as India, Hong Kong, and China. However, it is also high in masculine Japan (which has a low birthrate for girls *and* boys) and low in Taiwan and South Korea, which scored below the mean on MAS. Specific historical factors that play a role are the Confucian obligation of carrying on the (male) family line, which is mitigated in Japan by the possibility of passing through a son-in-law, and the Indian dowry system, which makes daughters costly.

Masculinity and (Pre)Historical Factors

The correlations of the Masculinity Index with the various ecological indicators are not very conclusive and explain at best only a small part of the variance in MAS. One reason could be, as suggested by Van de Vliert et al. (1999; see above), that relationships are actually curvilinear. Their research suggests that MAS should be higher in moderately warm countries than in cold and very warm ones. "Male supremacy is no more natural than warfare" (Harris, 1977, p. 65); the occurrence of both would depend on climatic conditions, on whether the people had to compete for scarce resources or collaborate for common survival.

Mary Catherine Bateson (1994), viewing modern societies from an anthropological perspective, distinguishes between zero-sum and non-zero-sum patterns of thinking, associated with competition and with collaboration, respectively. Hunter-gatherer societies (the oldest form of human society, currently surviving only in very cold and very warm areas) tend to be collaborative and peaceful.[122] Zero-sum thinking entered human history, Bateson believes, with the development of agriculture, in which "one man's loss came to be another man's gain" (p. 182). Within societies, competition has been mainly men's business, whereas women have been reared to collaborate. This would explain the strengthening of masculine values where there is competition for land and other resources and the strengthening of feminine values where cooperation for survival is necessary. Such value systems, once rooted in a society, will tend to perpetuate themselves. The mechanisms for their conservation are solid (Exhibit 1.5); as will be shown below, there is no sign of convergence in the direction of either masculinity or femininity among modern nations.

Elias (1987) has argued that the development of the balance of power between the genders can be understood only as part of the overall development of a society. In the Roman Republic and early Roman Empire (400 B.C. to 100 A.D.) the influence and rights of patrician women improved gradually along with the development of the city-state into a world empire and of the senatorial class from peasant warriors into aristocrats. With the disintegration of the Roman Empire in the third century A.D., the status of women deteriorated. In an earlier book Elias (1936/1980b, pp. 105 ff.) described how in Europe, and particularly in France, around the 11th century A.D. the gradual reestablishment of an orderly society and reduction of fighting reinforced the social and civilizing role of women in the nobility. This was the time of *troubadours* and of courtly love—according to Tuchman (1978, p. 67) a literary fantasy, like modern pornography. In the history of European civilization the French nobility and court have been a major model, being followed at a distance by other countries and classes. This process of gradual change has evidently had different speeds and outcomes in different countries, leading up to the present differentiation on the mas/fem dimension of national cultures. For example, I found France, Spain, and Portugal to be less masculine than Britain, Germany, and Italy.

One possible explanation of the strongly feminine scores of the Nordic countries Denmark, Finland, Norway, and Sweden is that these are an inheritance from the Viking society of the 8th to 11th centuries A.D., where the women managed the villages while the men were away on their long trips (cooperating, not competing with each other). But this begs the question why these men traveled so far and so long; it could be seen as a survival strategy of people with a cold and not-too-fertile home country.

The Viking period was followed by the Hanseatic League period (1200 to 1500 A.D.); the Hansa was active in the Nordic countries but also in the Netherlands, in the free German cities of Hamburg, Bremen, and Lübeck and in the Baltic states. It was a free association of trading towns and, for the maintenance of such a system, values associated with femininity were functional. Women played an important role in the Hansa:

> Although the wife did not share her husband's legal status, they usually formed a business team. Even in merchant circles, the family was the smallest functional cell of society, where the women and the children had a role to play. This meant that women had a certain degree of emancipation, and their independence and business skills increased. Indeed, some women managed to win the "battle for the trousers" even while their husbands were still alive. (Schildhauer, 1985, p. 107)[123]

Comparing Britain (MAS 66) and the Netherlands (MAS 14), the English statesman Sir Francis Walsingham in a political pamphlet in 1585 wrote that England and the Low Countries "have been by common language resembled and termed as man and wife" (quoted in Haley, 1988, p. 39). Half a century later, "some Englishmen connected Dutch commercial success with the fact that they 'generally breed their youth *of both sexes* more in the study of Geometry and Numbers than the English do.' " And elsewhere it was remarked that Dutch merchants *and their wives* were more conversant in trade than the English (Haley, 1988, pp. 110-111). Although women in 17th-century Netherlands were excluded from public office, "within these limits they managed to assert themselves, both individually and collectively, in public life" (Schama, 1987, p. 404). And in paintings from this period, "fathers are occasionally shown participating in the work of caring for small children" (Schama, 1987, p. 541). Also: "Military glory . . . was liable to be regarded with more circumspection than enthusiasm in the Netherlands. . . . Even though professional soldiers . . . played a crucial role in the defense of the [Dutch] Republic in the seventeenth century, they went conspicuously without honor in the patriotic culture of the time" (Schama, 1987, p. 240). Military heroes belong to the histories of masculine countries such as Britain and the United States.

Symbolic personalities representing Western countries in the 19th and 20th centuries were remarkably gendered according to their cultures' masculinity or femininity: John Bull for Britain and Uncle Sam for the United States, but Marianne for France and the Dutch maiden (called Frau Antje in Germany) for the Netherlands.[124]

Latin American countries in the IBM set differed considerably on MAS. The small Central American countries of Costa Rica, Guatemala, Panama, and El Salvador scored feminine; Mexico, Venezuela, Colombia, and Ecuador scored very masculine; and Peru and Chile scored again more feminine. One speculative explanation is that these differences reflect the heritages of the different Indian civilizations dominant prior to the Spanish conquest. Most of Mexico would have inherited the tough Aztec culture, but the southern Mexican peninsula of Yucatán and the adjacent Central American republics would have inherited from the much more sensitive Maya culture. Peru and Northern Chile would reflect the Inca inheritance, resembling the Maya.

Exhibit 6.17 plots MAS against UAI. The lower right-hand corner, which combines masculinity with strong uncertainty avoidance, contains the Axis powers from World War II: Germany, Italy, and Japan. This combination of cultural values was instrumental in their aggressive role, but also in their remarkable recovery afterward. Their main adversaries, Great Britain and the United States, are found in the upper right-hand corner, where masculinity is combined with weak uncertainty avoidance. So the main belligerents (except France) are all found on the high-MAS side.

In this respect the correlations of one of the 1990-93 World Values Survey questions in Exhibit 4.14 are revealing: "Would you be willing to fight for your country?" (question 263). Across 26 countries the answers to this question were negatively correlated (1) with MAS and (2) with UAI. So, paradoxically, in masculine, higher-UAI countries people were *less* willing to fight. In the 1980-81 survey round across 16 countries similar correlations had been found (rho = −.64** with MAS, rho = −.70** with UAI).[125] The average proportion "willing to fight" for these 16 countries increased from 52% in 1980-81 to 65% in 1990-93, but the shift in the percentages per country was again negatively correlated with MAS, rho = −.45*, so that the masculine countries shifted less. Dogan (1998) has interpreted the low

overall percentages in 1980 as a hangover from World War II; the increase in 1990 with the progress of time is in line with his conclusion. It seems that the memory of World War II was more painful in masculine and uncertainty-avoiding cultures than in feminine ones, so that resistance to fighting for one's country was stronger and lasted longer.[126]

The Future of Masculinity/
Femininity Differences

Between the 1967-69 and 1971-73 survey rounds in IBM, six out of the eight goals associated with MAS shifted toward a larger MAS score (manager, challenge, earnings, recognition, cooperation, and security), the first four significantly, and two (advancement and desirable area) shifted significantly in the opposite direction (see Exhibit 2.6). A separate calculation of MAS from 1967-69 and 1971-73 data showed an average shift among the 19 countries using the same questions in both survey rounds from MAS = 43 to MAS = 48, +5 points (against +20 points for IDV; see Chapter 5). The country lowest in 1967-69 (Sweden) shifted from 7 to 5 (−2 points) and the highest country (Austria) from 76 to 81 (+5). All these shifts are almost negligible. The gap between the highest and lowest countries increased by 7 points; so once more there was no sign of convergence.

As I did for the other dimensions, I analyzed the trends in MAS over this 4-year period by age group for five categories of IBM employees (see Exhibit 6.25 in the statistical section). The curves for MAS contrasted with those for IDV (Exhibit 5.24). The strong decrease of MAS with age (Exhibit 6.7) was clearly visible in both periods. MAS reached a peak for the 20-29 age bracket and then monotonically decreased, even for the secretaries and typists who were almost 100% female. However, the zeitgeist effect was much weaker than in the case of IDV, and it was negative for the older managers, technicians, and secretaries. Especially those in the 20-29 and 30-39 age brackets increased in masculinity between 1967-69 and 1971-73. Those over 40 were already less masculine in 1967-69, and they remained so or decreased further in 1971-73.

These results supply no evidence whatsoever that we should expect *convergence* on the mas/fem dimension over time. What might be possible is that global developments in population age structure, technology, and the state of the environment will cause *all* countries to shifts along this dimension while maintaining their divergence.

The demographic development in the industrialized world is toward lower birthrates—that is,

Exhibit 6.17. A UAI × MAS Plot for 50 Countries and Three Regions

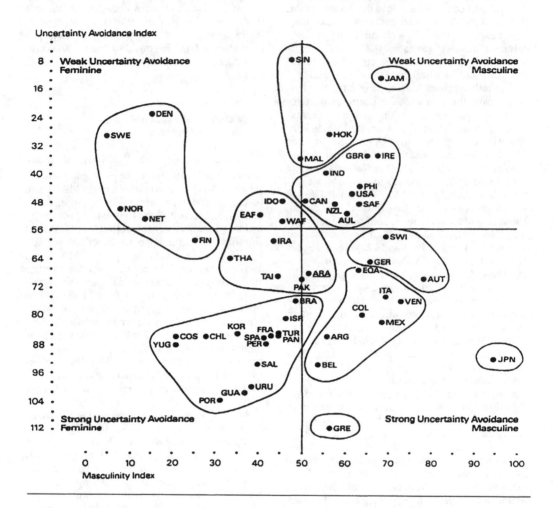

relatively fewer young people. An aging population will shift toward more feminine values (Exhibit 6.7). When birthrates fall this also implies that more women will be both available for and needed in the workforce (as there will be fewer young men). In many poor countries birthrates are still very high, but in the long term even these countries are likely to follow the above pattern.

Technological and social developments enable even women with young children to participate in society outside the home, along with men. This is nowhere a fast and undisputed process, but it looks irreversible. In virtually all industrialized countries the number of women in higher-level jobs will increase. As their numbers increase, these women will be more able to maintain their own feminine values. They will no longer have to acculturate themselves to the male majority. This increase in the numbers of women in positions in

society hitherto held by men should therefore also shift societies as a whole toward more feminine values.

Technology imposes changes on work itself. The ongoing information revolution eliminates many old jobs and creates new ones. The future is bound to show a further automation of jobs previously done by humans. What will remain are jobs that by their very nature cannot be automated. These are in the first place jobs dealing with the setting of human and social goals, with defining the purpose of life for individuals and societies. These include all political and organizational top leadership functions. In the second place they are the creative jobs, those concerned with inventing new things and subjecting them to criteria of usefulness, beauty, and ethics. A third and very large category of jobs that cannot be automated are those that deal with the unforeseeable: safety, security, defense, maintenance. Finally, there are many jobs whose essence is human contact: supervision, entertainment, keeping people company, listening to them, helping them materially and spiritually, motivating them to learn. In some of these nonautomated jobs computers can be introduced as resources, but they can never take over the jobs themselves.

What strikes one about these nonautomated jobs is that feminine values are as necessary as masculine ones in performing them (regardless of whether the job incumbents themselves are women or men). For the last category in which human contact is the core of the task, feminine values are even superior. Tasks associated with achievement can be automated more easily than can nurturing tasks. In balance, technological developments are more likely to support a need for feminine than for masculine values in society.

Finally, the environment poses very serious threats to the survival of humankind. If one species after another of fungi, plants, and animals becomes extinct, we should start to worry when it is the turn of *Homo sapiens*. Whether we like it or not, we will all be forced to become more conservation-conscious. This development also will encourage more feminine values and will reinforce the other shifts mentioned.

Statistical Analysis of Data Used in This Chapter

Computing MAS for Old and New Cases

For the Category 1 countries, MAS, like IDV, was based on a factor score for each country in the 40-country, 14-work-goal factor analysis. In Appendix 3, Exhibit A3.1, the factor score has been labeled SOC (social/ego). SOC scores have been transposed into Masculinity Index scores through a linear transformation: MAS = 50 − 20 × SOC, which brings MAS into a range between 0 and 100 and reverses its sign.

MAS scores for the Category 2 countries (those added after the appearance of the 1980 edition of *Culture's Consequences*) had to be computed via a more complex procedure, using factor score coefficients, in the same way IDV scores for these countries were arrived at. For the procedure and the coefficients, see Appendix 4. The MAS scores for men and women in Exhibit 6.4 were computed in a similar way, also using the same factor score coefficients.

The occupational factor scores for men and women in Exhibit 6.2 were based on the work goals factor analysis across 38 occupations (see Chapter 5) and computed in an analogous way us-

ing the factor score coefficients for that particular factor analysis.

Country MAS Scores and Other IBM Survey Questions

Chapter 2 showed an ecological factor analysis of all IBM survey items included in the cross-national comparisons. Factor 2 in this analysis was identified as a masculinity factor. The work goals on which the MAS index was based all loaded on this factor (A5, A6, A7, A8, A11, A14, A15, A16, and A17). Four other questions loaded both on Factor 2 and on another factor: A37 and B57 (reversed) also on uncertainty avoidance, and B52 and B58 (reversed) also on individualism.

For the C questions (discontinued in 1971 or before), significant correlations with MAS were found (Appendix 2, Exhibit A2.3) for C13 ($r = -.45*$), C17 ($r = -.41*$), and C19 ($r = -.48*$), as well as for C15 after acquiescence was controlled for ($r = -.40*$).

MAS was finally correlated with A58, the overall satisfaction score ($r = .40*$), although in the factor analysis of all items A58 loaded highest on UAI. In more masculine countries, respondents tended to score less satisfied.

The 1971 study of IBM data by Sirota and Greenwood for 14 goals, 25 countries, and three occupations, was mentioned in Chapter 5. These authors noticed in the goal profiles for their clusters of countries an opposition between getting-ahead goals and concern with the immediate environment, which is the same distinction that I, on more extensive data, labeled *masculinity/femininity*.

Chapter 5 also referred to my earlier study of IBM work goals in 21 occupations in the Netherlands, compared with Europe (Hofstede, 1976c), a study that was later extended to Norway and Sweden. The results showed that the three countries were similar in their relatively low scores on advancement and earnings and their high scores on cooperation, manager, and desirable area. This is why all three show up on the low end of the MAS scale (Exhibit 6.3). The 1976 study was based on all available occupations and not just on the seven occupations on which the MAS index has been founded; it illustrates that the MAS dimension was present in the other occupations as well.

Straight Replications of the IBM Survey

Elite alumni from the Salzburg Seminar. Exhibit 6.18 shows Hoppe's Salzburg alumni scores for MAS. Contrary to the Hoppe elite scores in Exhibits 3.13, 4.10, and 5.14, which were based

Exhibit 6.18 Masculinity Index Scores Computed from Surveys of Elites (Hoppe, 1998) and Consumer Market Research (EMS 97)

Countries in Order of Original MAS	Original MAS	Hoppe, Elites			EMS, Consumers		
		n	Raw MAS	Regressed[a]	n[b]	Raw MAS	Regressed[a]
Austria	79	74	18	60	343	60	59
Switzerland	70	57	43	82	153	46	47
Italy	70	183	32	80	293	80	77
Ireland	68	48	5	49	100	54	54
Germany	66	142	14	57	228	51	51
Great Britain	66	194	7	51	544	44	45
United States	62	157	21	63			
Greece	57	41	17	60			
Belgium	54	47	−1	44	270	41	42
Turkey	45	72	2	46			
France	43	47	19	61	661	75	72
Malta		30	3	47			
Spain	42	75	−19	28	599	44	45
Portugal	31	49	−24	24	192	48	48
Finland	26	59	−6	39	486	11	16
Denmark	16	41	−38	11	1,111	33	35
Netherlands	14	139	−25	23	337	12	17
Norway	8	64	−29	19	447	32	34
Sweden	5	71	−15	31	534	12	17
Total n		1,590			6,680		
Mean (elites)	45.7		1.2[b]	45.8			
SD (elites)	23.8		22.6[b]	19.3			
Mean (consumers)	43.9					42.9	43.9
SD (consumers)	25.7					20.8	18.4
Correlation with IBM MAS							
Product-moment			.83***			.72**	
Spearman rank			.82***			.78***	

NOTE: For both Hoppe and EMS, MAS questions and formulas were based on VSM 94 (see text). EMS data copyright © Inter/View International, Amsterdam; used with permission. See also De Mooij (2001).

a. Predicted from regression of IBM scores on raw new scores.

b. Without Malta.

*p = .05; **p = .01; ***p = .001.

on the VSM 82 questions and formulas, the scores in Exhibit 6.18 were recomputed using the VSM 94 questions and formulas (see Hoppe, 1998). The VSM 82 elite scores for MAS only showed a r = .36 correlation with IBM MAS. The new, VSM 94 questions were partly chosen and the formulas partly developed on the basis of the Hoppe database, so it is not surprising that the VSM 94 elite scores correlate quite strongly with IBM MAS, r = .83***. The Salzburg alumni were on average much older than the IBM employees (43 years, compared to 32 in IBM), and in accordance with

Exhibit 6.7 they scored much lower on MAS, a mean of 1.2 instead of 45.7 across the same countries in IBM. The "regressed" column shows the predictions of IBM MAS made on the basis of the elite scores. The largest deviations from the IBM data are for Sweden (+26 points) and Austria (−19 points). The Hoppe study provided an estimated MAS score of 47 for Malta.

Higher-income consumers surveyed by the EMS 97. Exhibit 6.18 also shows the MAS scores found in the European Media and Marketing Survey 1997 by the market research agency Inter/ View International, which included the 20 VSM 94 questions. Like Hoppe's elite scores in the same table, the EMS MAS scores are based on the VSM 94 questions and formula, but unlike in the case of Hoppe's elites the formula had not been influenced by the data; so the EMS study provides an independent validation of the new formula. Across the 15 overlapping countries the MAS scores from the IBM employees in 1970 and the EMS consumers in 1997 were correlated with r = .72**, and if we use rank correlations even with rho = .78***. Again the data were used to compute best estimates for the scores on the IBM scale by regression. The outliers were Norway (+26 points) and Switzerland (−23 points).

Results of Other Studies Correlated With MAS

Harpaz (1990) reported results of a "meaning of work" study among representative samples of the working population in Belgium, Germany, Great Britain, Israel, Japan, the Netherlands, and the United States—a total of 8,192 respondents. Respondents had to rank 11 work aspects in order of importance to them: (1) a lot of opportunity to learn new things, (2) good interpersonal relations (supervisors, coworkers), (3) good opportunity for upgrading or promotion, (4) convenient work hours, (5) a lot of variety, (6) interesting work (work that you really like), (7) good job security, (8) a good match between your job requirements and your abilities and experience, (9) good pay, (10) good physical working conditions (such as light, temperature, cleanliness, low noise level), and (11) a lot of autonomy (you decide how to do your work).

Using Harpaz's published data, I factor analyzed the mean ranks for the 11 goals across the seven countries. The two first factors together explained 57% of the variance in the data. After orthogonal varimax rotation, the loadings were as follows:

Factor 1 (variance 29%)	Factor 2 (variance 28%)
.94 Security	.86 Autonomy
.73 Pay	.75 Good match
.59 Interesting work	.40 Learning opportunity
−.72 Interpersonal relations	−.49 Convenient hours
−.81 Physical conditions	−.72 Promotion opportunity

Factor scores on Factor 1 correlated significantly with MAS (r = .69*). In analogy to the IBM work

goals, one would expect factor scores on Factor 2 to correlate with IDV, but this was not the case; instead, they correlated significantly with PDI (r = .68*). For this subset of countries PDI and IDV were not related (r = .07), and the range of scores on IDV was rather restricted. I find the correlation with PDI difficult to interpret.

Arbose (1980) published results from a survey by the magazine *International Management* that asked questions about relationships between career and family of more than 900 male business executives in 10 Western and Southern European countries.[127] Exhibit 6.19 shows answer percentages for the following two questions: (1) Do you aspire to be the chief executive of a company? (base: respondents who were not yet chief executives; n = 571); (2) To further your career, would you uproot your family now to move to a new location for a higher-paying and more responsible job? (base: all respondents; n = 930). Both percentages were significantly correlated with MAS, before a second-order correlation with 1990 GNP/capita.

The amounts of money spent by wealthier countries in development assistance to Third World countries, from both official (government) and private funds, are published by the United Nations. Exhibit 6.20 shows data from the *Human Development Report 1996* on 1983-84 and 1994 official development assistance in percentage of GNP for 20 donor countries (United Nations Development Program, 1996, tab. 37). We find r = −.67** and −.78*** between official development assistance and MAS. A significant correlation with GNP/capita (r = .51*) existed in 1983-84 when the moderately affluent countries Finland, Ireland, New Zealand, Portugal, and Spain had newly joined the donor group, starting with relatively small contributions; it had almost disappeared in 1994 (r = .32). The mean percentage spent was .45% in both years; the shift from 1983-84 to 1994 was correlated not with MAS but with IDV (contributions lowered in more individualist cultures) and in the multiple regression also with UAI (contributions lowered in uncertainty-avoiding cultures).

Exhibit 6.21 shows for 20 overlapping countries mean scores from Dunlap et al.'s (1993) public opinion survey about environmental issues on the following two questions:

1. With which of these statements about the environment and the economy do you most agree?
   a. Protecting the environment should be given priority, even at the risk of slowing down economic growth.
   b. Economic growth should be given priority, even if the environment suffers to some extent.

Exhibit 6.19 Answers by Business Executives From 10 European Countries on Two Questions About Career and Family Life

Countries in Order of MAS	% Want to Be CEO (n = 571)	% Would Uproot Family (n = 930)
Italy	72.1	55.4
Switzerland	43.4	49.0
Great Britain	66.2	56.0
Germany	44.2	53.2
Belgium	64.0	48.4
France	56.1	51.8
Spain	54.1	50.0
Denmark	44.1	28.0
Netherlands	36.9	43.8
Sweden	42.0	38.0
Spearman rank correlation with		
PDI	.53	.41
UAI	.51	.38
IDV	.27	.10
MAS	.60*	.73*
1980 GNP/capita	−.53	−.39
Order of indexes in stepwise regression[a], cumulative R^2, and sign of coefficient		
1	.36 +MAS	.53 +MAS
2	.66 −GNP80	.71 −GNP80

SOURCE: Data from Arbose (1980).
a. Based on ranks of variables.
*p = .05; **p = .01; ***p = .001.

2. Increased efforts by business and industry to improve environmental quality might lead to higher prices for the things you buy. Would you be willing to pay higher prices so that industry could better protect the environment, or not?

Agreement with "protection" in question 1 was only weakly negatively correlated with PDI (r = −.42*). For question 2 the percentages willing to pay were correlated significantly negatively with PDI (r = −.60**) and MAS (−.48*). In a stepwise regression, MAS made a sizable second-order contribution (for PDI and MAS combined: R^2 = .48, R = .69***). For neither of the two questions did the answers relate to per capita national income.

Exhibit 6.22 shows 1995 percentages of women in parliaments and as government ministers across 22 parliamentary democracies. The two columns are obviously intercorrelated (r = .89***). The dominant variable in the correlation is MAS (negatively), but there is a rich multiple regression pattern with, as a secondary correlate, PDI (negatively) for women in parliament and UAI (negatively) for women in government; both show a third-order positive correlation with national wealth.

Jones et al. (1986) published figures for teenage pregnancies per year between 1971 and 1980 for 30 countries, 22 of which overlapped with the IBM set. Pregnancy rates per 1,000 women were given for the age ranges below 20 and below 18. These were uncorrelated with the four IBM indexes but significantly correlated with national wealth (1980 GNP/capita): National wealth correlated with 1979-80 pregnancies below 20 with rho = −.57*** and below 18 with rho = −.49**.

Exhibit 6.20 Net Official Development Assistance Disbursed as % of GNP in 20 Countries

Countries in Order of MAS	1983-84	1994	Shift
Japan	.33	.29	−.04
Austria	.26	.33	.07
Italy	.24	.27	.03
Switzerland	.31	.36	.05
Ireland	.21	.25	.04
Great Britain	.34	.31	−.03
Germany	.47	.34	−.13
United States	.24	.15	−.09
Australia	.47	.35	−.12
New Zealand	.26	.24	−.02
Canada	.48	.43	−.05
Belgium	.58	.32	−.26
France	.59	.64	.05
Spain	.06	.28	.22
Portugal	.15	.35	.20
Finland	.34	.31	−.03
Denmark	.79	1.03	.24
Netherlands	.96	.76	−.20
Norway	1.06	1.05	−.01
Sweden	.82	.96	.14
Product-moment correlation with			
PDI	−.17	−.22	−.10
UAI	−.37	−.39*	−.05
IDV	.31	.07	−.51*
MAS	−.67**	−.78***	−.25
1983 GNP/capita	.51*		
1993 GNP/capita		.32	−.12
Order of indexes in stepwise regression, cumulative R^2, and sign of coefficient			
1	.45 −MAS	.61 −MAS	.26 −IDV
2	.65 + GNP83	.78 + GNP93	.50 −UAI

SOURCE: Data from United Nations Development Program (1996, tab. 37).
$*p = .05; **p = .01; ***p = .001$.

The stronger correlation with the "below 20" rate shows that the retarding effect of economic development on marriage age is more universal than is its effect on very early pregnancies. The "below 18" rates therefore are better implicit indicators of sexual habits. They are listed in Exhibit 6.23.

Significant correlations of 1979-80 pregnancy rates for girls younger than 18 with MAS were found only after the 22 countries were split into those with strong and weak uncertainty avoidance.[128] Across the 11 high-UAI countries, pregnancies among girls under 18 were significantly negatively correlated (rho = −.49*) with MAS.

Across the 11 low-UAI countries, the reverse was the case (rho = .59**). This unique configuration suppressed the zero-order and multiple correlations with UAI and MAS.

MAS Versus Eight Geographic, Economic, and Demographic Indicators

Like the other indexes—PDI, UAI, and IDV—MAS has been correlated with the eight standard ecological indicators listed in Exhibit 2.9; see Exhibit 6.24. Across all 50 countries, the multiple

Exhibit 6.21 Answers by Representative Samples of the Public in 20 Countries on Two Questions About Protection of the Environment

Countries in Order of MAS	% Protect Rather Than Grow	% Willing to Pay for Protection
Japan	57	31
Switzerland	62	70
Mexico	71	59
Ireland	65	60
Great Britain	56	70
Germany (F.R.)	73	59
Philippines	59	30
United States	58	65
India	43	56
Canada	67	61
Brazil	71	53
Turkey	43	44
Korea (South)	63	71
Uruguay	64	54
Portugal	53	61
Chile	64	64
Finland	72	53
Denmark	77	78
Netherlands	58	65
Norway	72	72
Product-moment correlation with		
PDI	−.42*	−.60**
UAI	−.15	−.32
IDV	.17	.40*
MAS	−.24	−.48*
1990 GNP/capita	.37	.29
Order of indexes in stepwise regression, cumulative R^2, and sign of coefficient		
1	.18 − PDI	.36 − PDI
2		.48 − MAS

SOURCE: Data from Dunlap, Gallup, and Gallup (1993, tab. 14).
*$p = .05$; **$p = .01$; ***$p = .001$.

correlation of MAS with the first seven ecological indicators was low: $R^2 = .27$. Only population size produced a significant zero-order correlation (larger countries more masculine). The multiple correlation became higher if we split the countries, as we did in the previous chapters, into poorer and wealthier ones. Across the poorer countries MAS was significantly negatively correlated with latitude (countries near the equator more masculine) and positively correlated with population growth (faster-growing countries more masculine), but only the correlation with latitude appeared in the stepwise multiple regression. For the wealthier countries MAS was again significantly negatively correlated with latitude and positively correlated with population size. In the stepwise regression a *negative* correlation with population growth appeared after latitude was controlled for; latitude for these countries correlated negatively with population growth ($r = −.63**$), which suppressed its zero-order correlation with MAS.

Trends in MAS

In Exhibit 6.25, MAS values are plotted by age group, for both 1967-69 (dotted lines) and 1971-

Exhibit 6.22 Percentages of Women in Parliaments and Governments of Parliamentary Democracies, 1995

Countries in Order of MAS	% Women in Parliament/Government	% Women Ministers
Japan	6.7	6.7
Austria	23.2	21.1
Italy	13.0	3.4
Switzerland	16.7	16.7
Ireland	12.8	18.2
Great Britain	7.8	9.1
Germany	25.5	16.0
United States	10.4	21.1
Australia	13.5	13.3
New Zealand	21.2	7.4
Greece	6.0	0.0
Canada	18.0	19.2
Belgium	15.4	10.5
Israel	9.2	13.0
France	5.9	6.5
Spain	14.6	15.0
Portugal	8.7	9.1
Finland	33.5	35.0
Denmark	33.0	30.4
Netherlands	28.4	26.3
Norway	39.4	40.9
Sweden	40.4	47.8
Product-moment correlation with		
PDI	−.49*	−.47*
UAI	−.56**	−.62**
IDV	.21	.22
MAS	−.67***	−.70***
1995 GNP/capita	.29	.34
Order of indexes in stepwise regression, cumulative R^2, and sign of coefficient		
1	.45 − MAS	.49 − MAS
2	.65 − PDI	.69 − UAI
3	.73 + GNP95	.78 + GNP95

SOURCE: Data from United Nations Development Program (1996, tabs. 3, 35).
*p = .05; **p = .01; ***p = .001.

73 (solid lines), for five large categories of IBM employees. This diagram is analogous to Exhibit 5.24. All five groups produced negative age slopes after age 20. The zeitgeist effect was weak; it was positive for the professionals and for the younger employees of all categories, but negative for the older managers, customer engineers, and secretaries.

Notes

1. In fourth-century B.C. Greece, Plato already recognized the statistical nature of gender differences: "In general the one sex is much better at everything than the other. A good many women . . . are better than a good many men at a good many things" (Plato, 1974, p. 234).

Exhibit 6.23 Teenage Fertility Below Age 18 (1979/80; per 1,000 women)

Weak Uncertainty Avoidance		Strong Uncertainty Avoidance	
Countries in Order of MAS	Fertility	Countries in Order of MAS	Fertility
Ireland	23	Japan	2
Great Britain	41	Austria	41
United States	101	Italy	28
Australia	45	Switzerland	8
New Zealand	64	Germany (F.R.)	21
Canada	46	Greece	80
Finland	18	Belgium	26
Denmark	16	Israel	32
Netherlands	10	France	25
Norway	29	Spain	37
Sweden	15	Portugal	59
Spearman rank correlation with MAS	.59**		−.49*

SOURCE: Data from Jones et al. (1986, pp. 243-244; based on Westoff, Calot, & Foster, 1983, p. 105).
*p = .05; **p = .01; ***p = .001.

In the Roman Empire, the dominant philosophical trends considered males to be superior (*sexus melior*), but, for example, the philosopher C. Musonius Rufus (first century A.D.) defended the equality of the sexes and, in particular, the study of philosophy by women and men alike (Eyben, 1976).

2. A French duchess at the court of Louis XIV is supposed to have said to her husband: "I can produce peers of France without you—you cannot without me." In the same vein is the following quote from a story by Isak Dinesen (1942), set in 18th-century Denmark: "The ladies . . . carried the future of the name in their laps. . . . They were . . . conscious of their value. . . . For how free they were, how powerful! Their lords might rule the country, and allow themselves many liberties, but when it came to that supreme matter of legitimacy which was the vital principle of their world, the centre of gravity lay with them" (p. 32).

3. See Quinn (1977, pp. 191-192) and Bateson (1994, p. 147).

4. See Broverman, Vogel, Broverman, Clarkson, and Rosenkrantz (1972).

5. The references here are to Herzberg, Mausner, and Snyderman (1959) and to Maslow (1970).

6. Exhibit 6.1 is a summary of the corresponding exhibit in the first edition of *Culture's Consequences* (Hofstede, 1980a, fig. 6.1).

7. "Cooperation" comes close to "friendly atmosphere" (the latter was dropped after 1971), but "friendly atmosphere" led to greater score differences between the genders than did "cooperation." It seems that "atmosphere" has more a nurturing and "cooperation" more an assertive flavor. "Friendly atmosphere"

also discriminated more between occupations than did "cooperation" (Appendix 3, Exhibit A3.3). On the other hand, the two terms showed hardly any difference in discriminating between countries, and "cooperation" discriminated better between age groups. The fact that different formulations of apparently almost the same concept discriminate differently among genders, occupations, countries, and age groups is one of the reasons ecological factors differ according to the criterion of aggregation.

8. There may have been an interaction between gender and education, in that in the higher-educated occupations the women would be relatively more job content oriented than the men, whereas in the lower-educated occupations the opposite was the case. Women professionals were at least as educated as men, but women clerks and unskilled tended to be less educated and might therefore still not do exactly the same work. The data on education level by gender by occupation can be found in Figure 6.1 in the first edition of *Culture's Consequences* (Hofstede, 1980a).

9. A comparison of Exhibit 6.1 with the statistical section of Chapter 5 shows that on the positive side of the intrinsic/extrinsic factor there are no goals significantly discriminating between men and women, and on the negative side "earnings" was more important for men and "physical conditions" was more important for women.

10. For the method of calculation of these scores, see Appendix 4.

11. Goals belonging to this factor with significant gender differences were "training" and "physical conditions," but both appeared on the "collective" side; the

Exhibit 6.24 Product-Moment Correlations and Multiple and Stepwise Regression Across Countries of MAS Scores With Eight System-Level Indicators

Indicator	Zero-Order Correlations With IDV Scores Across		
	All 50 Countries	28 Poorer Countries	22 Wealthier Countries
GNP	−.04	.08	−.27
EGP	.07	−.09	.19
EGF	−.04	−.12	.10
LAT	−.21	−.39*	−.58**
POP	.28*	.17	.40*
PGR	.05	.34*	.05
PDN	.10	.04	.17
ORS	.20	.17	.19

Squared multiple correlation with first seven R^2

	.27	.52	.75

Order of indicators in stepwise regression, cumulative R^2, and sign of coefficient

1	.08 + POP	.15 − LAT	.34 − LAT
2			.50 − PGR

NOTE: For definitions of the indicators, see Exhibit 2.9. The 22 countries are ARG, AUL, AUT, BEL, CAN, DEN, FIN, GBR, GER, GRE, IRE, ISR, ITA, JPN, NET, NOR, NZL, SPA, SWE, SWI, and USA.

first was more important to men, the second more important to women.

12. The fact that I associated the social/ego factor (and not the individual/collective factor) with female-male preference seems to contradict the results of the variance analysis in Exhibit 2.4. There I found a strong gender effect for earnings minus cooperation (= ego/social) but an even stronger gender effect for personal time minus training (= individual/collective). But the variance analysis was based on different data, five other occupations (all from manufacturing plants) in only 10 countries, and only two of these occupations (clerks and unskilled workers) had sizable numbers of female incumbents.

13. The figure of 20 is a practical minimum for data reliability. I used 1971-73 survey data, which generally showed larger numbers of respondents than the earlier survey round.

14. For "how important" questions, see Appendix 1, A5-A18; for facet satisfaction, Appendix 1, A19-A32; for overall satisfaction, Appendix 1, A58.

15. See Figure 6.10 in the first edition of *Culture's Consequences* (Hofstede, 1980a).

16. The eight countries were BEL, DEN, FRA, GBR, GER, IRE, ITA, and NET; there were no IBM data for Luxembourg and Northern Ireland.

17. The 1990-93 World Values Survey contained a block of questions of the type "Please say, from each of the following, how important it is in your life," followed by the topics of work, family, friends, leisure, politics, and religion (questions 4-9). Across 26 overlapping countries the standardized importance of work was neg-

atively correlated only with national wealth (rho = −.65), not with any of the culture dimensions; but this was again a sociological (conscious) measurement of importance. I will come back to these questions in the subsection on family.

18. The concept of work centrality has been used in sociology since Dubin's study of "central life interests" of U.S. workers (Dubin, 1956; Dubin & Champoux, 1977; Dubin, Champoux, & Porter, 1975). A related concept in the literature is job involvement (Lodahl, 1964; Lodahl & Kejner, 1965).

19. This same reasoning can be applied to occupational differences: Only the higher-educated occupations (managers and professionals) rated as personally and socially desirable those facets that went together with high overall job satisfaction; and the job *does* occupy a more central position in the life space of managers and professionals than in that of lower-status employees.

20. Maloney, Wilkof, and Dambrot (1981) administered the Bem Sex Role Inventory to more than 600 Israeli and U.S. undergraduate college students. The mean score on Bem's individual masculinity dimension was significantly higher for U.S. males than for Israeli males. This is in line with my cultural MAS score of 62 for the United States against 47 for Israel.

21. Törnblom, Jonsson, and Foa (1985) compared the way students from Sweden (low MAS, high IDV, *n* = 41) and from the United States (high MAS, high IDV, *n* = 50) allocated resources in a set of hypothetical cases. For *status* and *money,* Swedes chose allocation on the basis of equality and Americans again on the basis of eq-

Exhibit 6.25. MAS Scores for Five Large Categories of Employees, Worldwide Data, by Age Bracket, in Two Survey Rounds

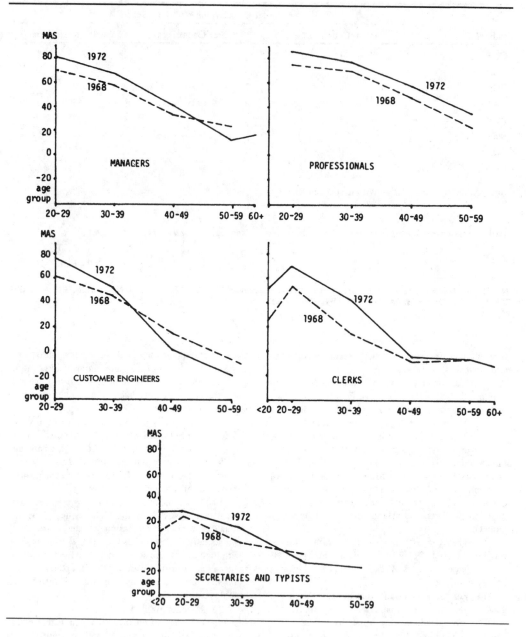

uity. For allocating *love, information, goods,* and *services,* however, both nationalities agreed that equality was the best principle.

22. Individual/collective in IMEDE mainly opposed "personal time" to "use of skills," and the scores of the 15 countries on this factor for IMEDE and IBM were significantly correlated (rho = .64**). Ego/social in IMEDE mainly opposed "advancement" to "benefits"

and "manager." In IBM benefits were not related to this factor; the term carried a very special company meaning and the item was only weakly related to the "collective" pole of the first factor. Consequently, the second factor in IMEDE hardly correlated with MAS (rho = .12); instead it correlated with PDI (rho = .63**). IMEDE executive trainees from high-PDI countries stressed advancement and training more; those from lower-PDI countries stressed benefits and manager. For details, see Figures 5.13 and 5.14 in the first edition of *Culture's Consequences* (Hofstede, 1980a).

23. As in the Hoppe replication, for the student samples "advancement" and "earnings" did not go hand in hand, as they did in IBM. "Earnings" in some countries was interpreted more as the means for physical survival than as a measure of success.

24. The scores for mastery and harmony in Exhibit 5.16 are only weakly negatively correlated ($r = -.28$), whereas, as shown, mastery correlated significantly with MAS ($r = .53$**) and harmony with UAI ($r = .45$*).

25. Arrindell's wealth data were based on purchasing power parity and were available for only 34 out of the 36 countries.

26. For the n_{Ach} scores, see Figure 6.13 in the first edition of *Culture's Consequences* (Hofstede, 1980a).

27. Regarding the symbolic value of wealth in the United States, see, for example, Kluckhohn (1950, p. 392) and Béteille (1977, p. 85).

28. Ariès (1973, p. 202) has mentioned that in France between the 16th and 18th centuries the feeling existed that children, even among the nobility, should be humiliated in their own interest. They were treated just like the lowest social classes.

29. Nakane (1973) compared marital roles between her native Japan and India; both countries scored masculine in the IBM studies, but Japan much more so (Japan, MAS 95; India, MAS 56). On IDV there was hardly any difference (Japan, IDV 46; India, IDV 48). She wrote: "Moral ideas like 'the husband leads and the wife obeys' or 'man and wife are one flesh' embody the Japanese emphasis on integration. Among Indians, however, I have often observed husband and wife expressing quite contradictory opinions without the slightest hesitation. This is indeed rare in front of others in Japan" (p. 11).

30. See Benedict (1946/1974, p. 263).

31. In the Netherlands, Meyer (1994) followed 40 first children and their parents from the seventh month of pregnancy through the children's fourth year. She found that the acquisition of gender-specific characteristics largely followed parents' expectations.

32. In Australia, the term *tall poppy* is used for a very successful person, and seeing such persons fall at times is supposed to give satisfaction. Feather and McKee (1996) compared answers of samples of Australian and Japanese students on a "Tall Poppy Scale." In both countries the dominant feeling was that high achievers should be rewarded, rather than that they should fall. The Japanese showed more satisfaction when high achievers fell than did the Australians; among the Australians it was especially those with lower self-esteem who showed "tall poppy" feelings. A Japanese saying is "The nail that sticks out will be hammered down." This, however, is an expression of collectivism, not of femininity. Neither Japan nor Australia has a feminine culture.

33. Iceland was colonized by Norwegian Vikings; the two countries are currently at about the same level of economic development (1990 GNP/capita $21,400 for Iceland, $23,120 for Norway).

34. The other countries were ISR (46%), IND (38%), EAF for Ethiopia (22%), and TAI (19%). The percentages responding yes also correlated with IDV ($r = .95$**); for these six countries IDV and MAS, exceptionally, are strongly correlated ($r = .86$*).

35. In the same way the work goal importance scores in IBM were subject to acquiescence (see Chapters 2 and 5), the unstandardized answer percentages for these WVS questions showed a strong tendency by country to score all six topics as more or less important. The mean percentages "very important" across the six topics varied from 29% in Portugal to 72% in Nigeria. This should be seen as a response set, which makes the raw scores unsuitable for drawing other conclusions. What I was interested in was the *relative* importance attached to each topic related to the others, which is what becomes visible after the standardization.

36. See note 17, above.

37. I used Spearman rank correlations because of outlying values in the standardized scores and in GNP/capita. The multiple regression was also based on ranks.

38. There was a negative third-order correlation with GNP/capita ($R = .86$***). Affluence increased the need for parents to earn the love and respect of their children.

39. These figures are from Hofstede and Associates (1998, tab. 10.1), based on Halman (1991, p. 331). The countries were BEL, CAN, DEN, FRA, GBR, GER, IRE, ITA, NET, NOR, SPA, and USA.

40. Inglehart, Basañez, and Moreno (1998, question 181) do not present the percentages "living as married" separately, so I cannot compute the correlations for the 1990-93 data.

41. The following observation from Buss (1994) helps to explain the influence of uncertainty avoidance: "We expected that men worldwide would value chastity, and would value it more than women. This is because of the differences between men and women in the certainty of their parenthood. Women are 100 percent certain that they are the mothers of their children. But men can never be exactly sure that they are the fathers. . . . Valuing chastity might have been one way that men could be 'confident' that they were the fathers. We found that not all men feel that way" (p. 198). Our data showed that whether men feel that way is a matter of their culture's level of uncertainty avoidance.

42. On the general topic of masculinity, schools, and educational systems, see also Hofstede (1986a).

43. I have suggested that in masculine cultures "teachers openly praise good students" (Hofstede, 1986a). In 1987, Dr. M. Karen O'Kain from Canada wrote to me and related that in her experience in masculine cultures such as Canada and Jamaica, openly praising students was difficult to sell to teachers; as positive reinforcement it was seen as a nurturing activity that conflicted with their masculine value system. I guess the difference is whether praise is given in a way that im-

plies competition (you are better than . . .) or as individual reinforcement.

44. Bateson (1994) has commented on the U.S. practice of grading on a curve: "There are only so many good grades, and every gain for someone else is a loss for you" (p. 180). As far as I know, this system does not exist in the Netherlands. Henry (1963) has argued that the U.S. school teaches children how to hate, "for what has greater potential for creating hostility than competition?" (p. 295). However, feminine cultures foster jealousy toward achievers, which is another form of hostility.

45. Hastings and Hastings (1980) provided no information about the gender composition of the samples of children, but the question text showed that both girls and boys were included. I assume that the gender composition of the sample was 50/50 for all five countries. In this picture the actors were clearly boys. The majority of appeasing answers fits with a sample in which 50% of the respondents were girls.

46. "The Thai learns how to *avoid* aggression rather than how to *defend* himself against it. If children fight, even in defence, they are usually punished. The only way to stay out of trouble is to flee the scene" (Cooper & Cooper, 1982, p. 80).

47. The high self-ratings in the United States cannot be only a matter of masculinity; individualism must also play a role. Little, Oettingen, Stetsenko, and Baltes (1995) studied more than 2,000 boys and girls, ages 8 to 12, in schools in Germany (East and West Berlin), Russia (Moscow), and the United States (Los Angeles). Data collected concerned (1) the children's school performance and (2) their beliefs about what explained this performance. U.S. children rated the influence of their own effort on their performance higher than did the others, but in fact the correlation between their self-ratings and their actual performance was lowest. In East Berlin, 47% of the variance in performance could be predicted from self-rated effort; in Los Angeles, only 15%. Germany and the United States do not differ on MAS, but the United States is considerably more individualist.

48. Chapters 4 and 5 also described a study in which Gudykunst, Yang, and Nishida (1987) measured self-consciousness among students in South Korea, United States, and Japan. They associated two components of self-consciousness with UAI and IDV, respectively. The third, "private self-consciousness" (example: "I'm constantly examining my motives") followed the order of MAS, suggesting more private self-consciousness in more masculine cultures.

49. Japanese teachers also attended significantly more to groups than to individual children, which fits the lower IDV in the Japanese culture.

50. As Murphy (1979, p. 160) has remarked, biology is, genderwise, the "odd one out" of the sciences.

51. The Index of Gender Segregation in Higher Education is a measure of the proportion of males or females that would have to change their fields of study for there to be equality in the distribution of the genders in

the fields of education, law, social sciences, engineering, and agriculture (Boulding, Nuss, Carson, & Greenstein, 1976, p. 346).

52. Huth (1980) applied psychological differentiation tests to schoolchildren in southern Germany and in Yucatán, southern Mexico. I assume the first group to represent a masculine culture and the second (which, like neighboring Guatemala, has a Maya past) a feminine culture. For 18-year-olds, Huth found girls to be more field dependent than boys in Germany but less field dependent than boys in Yucatán (p. 99).

53. An additional indication of a link between field independence and masculinity is found in a study by Kohn (1971) of a cross-national sample of more than 3,000 American men. Kohn found a significant positive correlation between field independence and the size of the organization in which the men worked. We found an association of masculinity with a preference for larger organizations.

54. In the first edition of *Culture's Consequences* (Hofstede, 1980a), I computed a crude labor force participation rate for women from the 1976 *Yearbook of Labour Statistics* (International Labour Office, 1976, tab. 1). Across 38 countries, this index was uncorrelated with MAS (rho = −.01).

55. Zero-order correlation with IDV rho = .66***, with PDI rho = −.60***, and with MAS rho = −.02; in a stepwise regression only GNP/capita remained.

56. The zero-order correlation between GGI and MAS was rho = −.38*. A stepwise regression on ranks of GGI produced $R^2 = .32$ with 1990 GNP/capita, $R^2 = .52$ for GNP/capita plus IDV, $R^2 = .67$ for GNP/capita plus IDV plus MAS.

57. For four components of the GGI (health gap, family status gap, education gap, and employment gap; listed in Population Crisis Committee, 1988) I checked the correlation patterns separately, but all four were primarily correlated with GNP/capita. Only the employment gap showed a second-order correlation with UAI (more gender equality in employment in low-UAI countries: for 1990 GNP/capita $R^2 = .51$, for GNP/capita plus UAI .58, regression based on ranks).

58. Zero-order correlations with PDI rho = .74** and with IDV rho = − .60**. The countries were CAN, CHL, COL, FRA, GBR, GER, IND, JPN, MEX, PAN, SAL, SPA, TAI, THA, and USA.

59. Burkholder et al.'s survey also included questions about gender stereotypes. There was more consensus across countries about the female than about the male stereotypes, but with a much shorter list than used by Williams and Best (1990b). Exceptional stereotypes were mostly from women in low-MAS countries, supporting Williams and Best's finding of more differentiation in feminine countries (Hofstede & Associates, 1998, p. 99).

60. There was a weak correlation with PDI (rho = .50*), which suggests the answers were subject to acquiescence (sensitivity to the authority of the interviewer).

61. The data were from Boulding et al. (1976, tabs. 28, 37).

62. Zero-order correlation with GNP/capita $r = .52***$, and with MAS $r = -.44***$.

63. Kanter (1977) has argued that "the problem of equality for women cannot be solved without structures that potentially benefit all organization members more broadly" (p. 266).

64. These items were taken from Spence and Helmreich (1983).

65. The Overall Competitiveness Index was computed as the square root of the sum of the squared male and squared female scores. The Gender Ratio of Competitiveness Index was computed as the arctan of the male score divided by the female score.

66. This was my computation on the basis of Van de Vliert's (1998) index scores. Van de Vliert reported across 32 countries significant correlations of total competitiveness with PDI ($r = .49**$) and with IDV ($r = -.41*$). I did a stepwise regression in which only the correlation with GNP/capita survived.

67. The correlation between the Overall Competitiveness Index and 1990 GNP/capita sinks to $r = -.32*$ if PDI and IDV differences are controlled for.

68. From my 40 Category 1 countries 25 overlapped with Williams and Best's 30 (1982, pp. 341-345). Williams and Best's correlation calculations overlooked my scores for CHL, SAF, TAI, and THA.

69. Best and Williams (1998) also dealt with gender differences in the affective meanings of the ACL adjectives (see earlier in this chapter) on three dimensions of Osgood's semantic differential (Osgood, Suci, & Tannenbaum, 1957). In poorer and less literate countries, and in those where fewer women attended university, affective meanings of gender stereotypes presented a wider gender gap than in more developed ones; the gap between the affective meanings of men's and women's self-concepts across the 12 countries was strongly correlated with PDI ($r = .78***$; Best & Williams, 1998, p. 115).

70. In the 1960s, McClelland pleaded for a new self-image for American women that came close to what I call feminine feminism: avoiding thinking in categories defined by men (McClelland, 1965, p. 174). But he reflected a minority opinion. See also McClelland's analysis of the Quaker culture with which he had come into contact as a young man earlier in this chapter.

71. "But what's 'masculine' and what's 'feminine'? Modern psychoanalytic books are full of absurd statements based on the assumption that sex roles in our society embody biological universals. We know by now that there are few characteristics defined in every culture as masculine or feminine" (Slater, 1976, p. 74).

72. This information comes from a contribution by Yayori Matsui to a newsletter for foreigners in Japan titled *Peace, Happiness and Prosperity* (December 1981). See also Nakamaru (1985).

73. Data were from the Reader's Digest Eurodata 1991 and 1995, the European Media and Marketing Survey 1995 and 1997, and the Consumer Europe Euromonitor 1997, across 16 countries (AUT, BEL, DEN, FIN, FRA, GBR, GER, GRE, IRE, ITA, NET, NOR, POR, SPA, SWE, and SWI).

74. See De Mooij (1998b).

75. The seven countries were BEL, GBR, GER, ISR, JPN, NET, and USA.

76. Authors who write about gender-related issues are often strongly ideologically and polemically motivated and assume their and their countries' problems and solutions to be the world norm. An example is a contribution to a reader by Mills (1989) in which Mills quotes part of a sentence from the 1984 abridged edition of *Culture's Consequences* (Hofstede, 1984b) and, by truncating it, reverses its meaning. On the basis of this misquotation, he classifies me as one of those who "excludes gender from the dynamics of organizational experience and from the construction of organizational culture and human identities" (p. 42). He evidently did not read the chapter from which he quotes.

77. Søndergaard (1996) has applied the two terms in a comparison between Danish and French banks in which *manège* stands for the French higher PDI and UAI, and *ménage* for the more flexible Scandinavian (Danish) approach.

78. Gibson's (1995) findings about country differences are ambiguous, but I doubt whether leadership characteristics can be measured through statements by leaders (except when they are asked about *their* bosses). Also, Gibson's samples were small ($n = 209$ divided over four countries and two genders) and not very well matched.

79. Richins and Verhage (1987) showed that behaviors seen as "assertive" in the United States (MAS 62) were interpreted as "aggressive" in the Netherlands (MAS 14).

80. Powell and Johnson (1995) have reviewed English-language literature about the role of gender in decision making. They argue that formal decision support systems for managers may have to take the manager's gender into account.

81. All five countries had high MAS scores in the IBM data; in this case the United States was the *least* masculine country in the set. The overall mean correlation between manager and men was $r = .71***$ in the answers of male students and $r = .67***$ in the answers of female students. The overall mean correlation between manager and women was $r = -.00$ in the answers of male students. For female students the correlation coefficients r between manager and women were as follows: Japan, $-.04$; Germany, $.19*$; China, $.28**$; Great Britain, $.31**$; and United States, $.43***$.

82. Rees and Brewster (1995) have tried to explain differences in women's employment, gender pay ratio, part-time versus full-time employment ratio, and public child-care provisions among Britain, France, and the Netherlands using my IBM scores for these countries on MAS and PDI. They conclude that "the indices proposed by Hofstede are too broad for this type of analy-

sis" (p. 37), a conclusion with which I agree. For one thing, in any country's specific institutional arrangements, historical developments and the particular moment in time within these developments play important roles. I have explained in previous work the exceptional historical reasons in the Netherlands for the late start of women's move into management positions—reasons that have little to do with emancipation (Hofstede & Associates, 1998, p. 91).

83. A classic study in the Netherlands by Philipsen and Cassee (1965) compared scores of leadership styles as rated by subordinates for matrons in hospitals, middle managers in industrial companies, and section heads in government offices. Hospital matrons received the highest scores on "initiating structure" and the lowest on "consideration" from their subordinates—and this in a nurturing type of organization in a feminine national cultural environment (MAS 14).

84. The data showed the Netherlands, the location of one of Unilever's two head offices, to be an outlier with extremely few female managers in Unilever, whereas the country's culture scored very feminine in the IBM data (MAS 14). Without the Netherlands, the correlation between percentage female managers and MAS became rho = −.74***.

85. In an older experiment Bartol and Butterfield (1976) gave two versions of descriptions of manager behavior to 255 male and 57 female U.S. students. The managers' names indicated whether they were males or females, but no other differences were present. Students, regardless of their gender, evaluated managers with men's names more positively on "initiating structure" and managers with women's names more positively on "consideration."

86. The gender gap is not necessarily a women's problem. Men's compulsory ambition in some cultures can be equally problematic (Cheng, 1996; Collinson & Hearn, 1996).

87. Polley (1989) also analyzed the nature of conflict in Scandinavia versus the United States along three dimensions: dominance versus submissiveness, group-centeredness versus self-centeredness, and conventional versus nonconventional. Scandinavians were much more group centered than Americans, which fits with their lower individualism.

88. The German Swiss sociologist Ernest Zahn (1984, p. 67), who taught at the University of Amsterdam for 20 years, has remarked that (unlike in Germany) conceding to an opponent is not perceived in the Netherlands as a lack of firmness, nor is confrontation perceived as a sign of courage.

89. The U.S. sample was made up of 11,067 healthy employees; the Netherlands sample, 3,892.

90. The countries were BEL, FRA, GBR, GER, ITA, and NET.

91. For details of the calculation, see Figure 6.11 in the first edition of Culture's Consequences (Hofstede, 1980a).

92. For details, see Figure 6.12 in Hofstede (1980a).

93. The other scores were as follows: NET, 8.2%; GER, 10.5%; NOR, 11.3%; ITA, 11.6%; FIN, 11.8%; FRA, 11.8%; CAN, 12.0%; DEN, 12.0%; JPN, 12.0%; BEL, 12.4%; AUL, 12.5%; NZL, 12.6%; SPA, 13.1%; GBR, 15.0%; and IRE, 15.2%.

94. Morris (1979) designed the Physical Quality of Life Index (PQLI), which consists of (1) infant mortality before age 1, (2) life expectancy at age 1, and (3) official percentage literacy. Across the 53 countries/regions in the IBM set his PQLI scores for the 1970s were highly correlated with 1970 GNP/capita (rho = .92***) without significant contributions of the culture indexes. The same was true across the 22 wealthier countries (rho = .69***) and across the 31 poorer countries (rho = .71***). It would be interesting to redo the calculation for the 1990s, but I could not find any later lists of PQLI scores.

95. I have shown the relationship of development assistance with MAS in the first edition of Culture's Consequences (Hofstede, 1980a), using average percentages between 1967 and 1976, for 15 countries (rho = −.81***).

96. Taormina, Messick, Iwawaki, and Wilke (1988) asked about 40 students from each of three nationalities to rate the extent to which each of 96 recipient countries deserved foreign aid. Students from the Netherlands (MAS 14) were more responsive to information about the needs of the recipients; students from the United States (MAS 62) and from Japan (MAS 95) were more responsive to potential benefits to their own nation. The authors commented that they preferred the term *pragmatism* to *masculinity*!

97. "It was perhaps useful, but hardly essential, for the MIT group to make so many elaborate and hypothetical calculations. In the end, the group's conclusions derive from its assumptions, and it does not require more than a simple act of insight to realise that infinite growth of material consumption in a finite world is an impossibility" (Schumacher, 1973, pp. 118-119).

98. In a discussion between Wildavsky (1976) and Coppock (1977), the former argued that the search for environmental quality contains many ritual, rather than rational, elements; the latter answered that the nonrationality was as much on the side of the economists who oppose the environmentalists as of the environmentalists themselves. As mentioned in note 56 in Chapter 4, Douglas and Wildavsky (1982) have used Douglas's anthropological views to propagate a relativistic point of view toward issues of technological and environmental risks, which they see as being mainly in the eye of the beholder. I think they have thrown the baby out with the bathwater.

99. Gray (1973) has linked the impossibility in the United States of imagining a future without growth to the "masculine consciousness" in that country.

100. Schultz and Zelezny (1998) reported on a questionnaire survey of students in Mexico, Nicaragua, Peru, Spain, and the United States about "pro-environmental behaviors": recycling, using public transporta-

tion, conserving water, conserving energy, and purchasing safe products. They found some significant correlations between claimed behaviors and values across individuals within countries. Their mean country scores for "recycling" correlated with rho = 1.00** with both 1990 GNP/capita and IDV (estimating Nicaragua scores as the mean between Guatemala and Panama); the other behaviors did not show any significant correlations at the country level.

101. The countries were AUL, EAF (for Zimbabwe), GBR, GER, GRE, HOK, IND, ISR, JAM (for British West Indies), NZL, SAF, and USA.

102. The 17 countries were AUT, BEL, CAN, DEN, FIN, FRA, GBR, GER, GRE, IRE, ITA, JPN, NET, POR, SPA, SWE, and USA.

103. Discussion in this subsection draws heavily on Hofstede and Associates (1998, chap. 10).

104. The interview with Wolfe appeared in *NRC Handelsblad* on March 31, 1993. Shortly thereafter, I commented in a letter to the editor (*NRC Handelsblad,* April 8, 1993).

105. Masturbation is less of a taboo in Northwestern Europe than in the United States, where President Clinton fired Surgeon General Joycelyn Elders "for suggesting at an international AIDS conference that children be taught how to masturbate as an integral component of safe sex education" (Abramson & Pinkerton, 1995, p. 149). A survey study on "sex in America" asked whether U.S. respondents felt guilty after masturbation; 54% of men and 47% of women said that they did (Laumann, Gagnon, Michael, & Michaels, 1994, p. 82). In a Dutch study asking about feelings after masturbation (relaxed, comfortable, satisfied, energetic, active, sexually aroused, lonely, guilty, sad, tense, or awful; Van Zessen & Sandfort, 1991), 6% of men and 7% of women answered that they felt guilty (see Hofstede & Associates, 1998, p. 165).

106. Pryor et al. (1997) were looking for gender differences across countries in what behaviors were seen as sexually harassing, but only in the United States did women consider certain behaviors as more harassing than did men. This seems to be a specific outcome of the U.S. context with regard to litigation and political correctness.

107. In previous work I have shown, using data from the 1981-82 European/World Values Survey, that rejection of homosexuality and abortion were positively rank correlated with MAS, but at that time I did not control for affluence (GNP/capita) (see Hofstede & Associates, 1998, p. 166). It turned out that in both cases the (negative) correlation with GNP/capita was stronger (rho = −.71** for homosexuality and rho = −.68** for abortion) and did not leave any significant contribution to MAS. The public in wealthier countries was simply more tolerant. In the 1990-93 round of the same survey across 26 countries, the rejection of homosexuality was also negatively related to GNP/capita (rho = −.67***) but even more to IDV (rho = −.74***; the extended set of 26 countries showed a wider range of IDV scores). The re-

jection of abortion did not show any significant correlation with cultural indexes or GNP/capita at all.

108. Of course, there have been attempts to change that. The title of the musical *Jesus Christ Superstar* is a case in point (although the show's content refutes the title). The Dutch newspaper *De Volkskrant* reported on June 26, 1997, that the Vatican had commissioned the Brazilian designer Claudio Pastro to make a new portrait of Jesus in which the face would not only be less European but also would convey not suffering but silent triumph. This looks like the masculinizing of Christ.

109. See Cooper and Cooper (1982, p. 97).

110. Tobacyk and Pirttilä-Backman (1992) compared students from Finland and from the southern United States on traditional religious beliefs but also on paranormal beliefs, such as concerning witchcraft. Americans scored higher not only on traditional religion but also on paranormal beliefs. Across both countries men scored higher on paranormal beliefs than did women.

111. The nine countries were BEL, DEN, FRA, GBR, GER, IRE, ITA, NET, and SPA.

112. This definition comes from the second edition of the unabridged *Webster's Dictionary* (1979).

113. The 13 countries were AUL, BRA, CAN, FRA, GBR, GER, IND, ITA, JPN, KOR, PHI, SIN, and USA.

114. The quotations are from the authorized version of the Bible published by the British and Foreign Bible Society (1954).

115. For an extensive study of fertility rites, see Schubart (1941).

116. A link between femininity and the acceptance of abortion is suggested by the results of a study about attitudes toward abortion by Wall et al. (1999). They compared college students of both genders in Croatia, Czechia, Slovenia, and United States. The proportion of prochoice answers (in 1994) was considerably higher in Slovenia (83%) than in the three other countries (CRO, 64%; CZE, 74%; USA, 64%). In my reanalysis of 1970 IBM data I had found Slovenia to have a pronouncedly feminine culture (MAS 19; see Appendix 5).

117. See Ravesloot (1995, p. 71).

118. See Kirsch (1985, p. 312).

119. This statement was made by the Reverend M. D. Babcock in 1900, according to Bendix (1956/1974, p. 257).

120. This statement has been attributed to George Katona (1901-81).

121. The UNICEF graph is based on a study by Ken Hill of Johns Hopkins University.

122. See Leakey and Lewin (1981, p. 222).

123. This quote is a translation by Schildhauer (1985) of a quote from Samsonowicz (1970).

124. A French reader on collective identities edited by Michaud (1978) referred to the "feminine image of France" (p. 75).

125. See Dogan (1998). The 16 countries were AUL, BEL, CAN, DEN, FIN, FRA, GBR, GER, IRE, ITA, JPN, NET, NOR, SPA, SWE, and USA. Across these

countries the correlations in the 1990-93 WVS were rho = −.79*** with MAS, rho = −.70** with UAI.

126. See Buruma (1994) for discussion of the ways Germany and Japan were dealing with the memories of World War II.

127. The survey report does not mention the gender distribution of the respondents; gender was not asked in the survey questionnaire. I assume the questionnaire was sent only to male executives (given that this was 1980).

128. In assigning countries to the two groups, I put Finland (UAI 59) with the weak and Switzerland (UAI 58) with the strong uncertainty avoidance countries to keep the clusters (Nordic versus Central European) intact.

7

■

Long- Versus Short-Term Orientation

Summary of This Chapter

This chapter adds a fifth dimension of national cultures that is independent of the four identified in the IBM studies and covered in the preceding chapters.[1] The new dimension, *long- versus short-term orientation,* was found in the answers of student samples from 23 countries around 1985 to the Chinese Value Survey (CVS), an instrument developed by Michael Harris Bond in Hong Kong from values suggested by Chinese scholars. The fact that this dimension was not found in the IBM data can be attributed to the Western minds of the designers of the IBM questionnaire and other values lists used in international research so far. The CVS was composed from a values inventory suggested by Eastern minds, which only partly covered the themes judged important in the West. In fact, the long-/short-term orientation dimension appears to be based on items reminiscent of the teachings of Confucius, on both of its poles. It opposes long-term to short-term aspects of Confucian thinking: persistence and thrift to personal stability and respect for tradition.

This chapter shows country scores on a Long-Term Orientation Index (LTO) for the 23 countries originally included; East Asian countries scored highest, Western countries on the low side, and some Third World countries lowest. Results are given of the replications and extensions available so far, which include LTO scores for 11 more European countries. Like the preceding chapters, the present one then describes various validations of the country scores, provided by the 1990-93 World Values Survey and other surveys of values. Another type of validation is found in national savings rates ("marginal propensity to save") according to a study by Read.

Implications of LTO differences are divided into two sections, one dealing with family, work, and social life and one dealing with ways of thinking. The latter includes religious and philosophical themes; the dimension expresses to what extent virtuous living is a goal, independent of any religious justification. The dimension is also related to the ability to solve well-defined problems, as evidenced by secondary school performance levels in basic mathematics.

LTO scores are strongly correlated with national economic growth in the period 1965-85, preceding the CVS study, and even more in the period 1985-95 following it. Long-term orientation is thus identified as a major explanation of the explosive growth of the East Asian economies in the latter part of the 20th century; this confirms the "neo-Confucian hypothesis" so far considered speculative. The chapter ends with discussion of the positions of Hindu and Muslim countries, specific values found in African countries, and the future of long-term orientation in the world.

East Versus West

Cultural Biases in the
Researchers' Minds

The IBM studies, the results of which I have described in the preceding chapters, used a questionnaire composed by Western minds. The team that first designed it contained British, Dutch, French, Norwegian, and U.S. members. If the arguments within the preceding chapters about the cultural relativity of practices *and* theories are taken seriously, then this restrictive Western input into the research instrument should be a matter of concern. When the surveys were administered, not only Western but also non-Western respondents were confronted with Western questions. They dutifully answered them, but could the results really be supposed to express their values fully? As a consequence of our own research findings, we—the researchers—have worried about this limitation of our instruments.[2] The traditional solution for avoiding cultural bias in research suggested up to that moment was "decentering," a process in which researchers from different cultures all develop research questions out of their different cultural environments. This approach had to some extent been used in the development of the IBM questionnaire by a five-nationality team and in its pretest in 10 countries. The problem of decentered research, however, lies in the dynamics of the research team. All members are equal, but usually some are more equal than others. There is often a senior researcher, the one who has taken the initiative to begin the research, and he (rarely she) is usually from a Western background. Researchers from countries in which values such as respect for the senior guru and harmony within the team prevail will often be almost too eager to follow the magic of the prestigious team leader. This social dynamic means that the project team will maintain its Western bias even with a predominantly non-Western membership. When the chief researcher comes from a non-Western country, he or she has often studied in the West and sometimes overadopts Western value positions, becoming "more Catholic than the pope." Doing research without culture bias is impossible; there will always be a researcher effect.

I have described in Chapter 2 how Michael Harris Bond of the Chinese University of Hong Kong, inspired by discussions he and I had about a joint article (Hofstede & Bond, 1984), conceived the Chinese Value Survey. Our joint article described the reanalysis of data from a nine-country values study with the U.S.-designed Rokeach Value Survey (see Chapter 1), which had reproduced the four IBM dimensions. Recognizing that the results of surveys designed by Westerners are necessarily biased by the designers' Western minds, Bond decided to introduce a deliberate Eastern bias. He asked four Chinese colleagues from Hong Kong and Taiwan to prepare in Chinese a list of at least 10 "fundamental and basic values for Chinese people." Through the elimination of overlap and, on the other side, by adding some values that from his reading of Chinese philosophers and social scientists seemed to be similarly important, Bond arrived at a questionnaire of 40 items—the same number as in the Rokeach Value Survey.

The Chinese Value Survey

The Chinese Value Survey was translated from Chinese into English, and, through a series of checks by different bilingual persons, two versions (one in Chinese, one in English) were prepared that were as closely as possible equivalent. Colleagues from the International Association for Cross-Cultural Psychology helped to administer the questionnaire to 100 students—50 men, 50 women—in each of 22 countries around the world, Asian and non-Asian. After the initial publication of the results (see Chinese Culture Connection, 1987), data for mainland China were added, increasing the number of countries to 23. Eight other language versions were translated, where possible, directly from the Chinese. Respondents were taken from any class year, and from as wide a range of undergraduate majors as possible, within institutions of higher learning with relatively high admission standards according to local ratings.

For each of the 40 CVS items, the respondents scored how important this concept was to them on a 9-point scale, where 9 = *of supreme importance* and 1 = *of no importance at all*. A factor analysis of the standardized mean scores for 22 countries yielded again four dimensions. Factor scores for 20 overlapping countries showed that one CVS dimension labeled *moral discipline* correlated with power distance, $r = .55**$, and with individualism, $r = -.54**$.[3] A second CVS factor labeled *integration* correlated with individualism, $r = .65***$, and with power distance, $r = -.58**$. A third CVS factor labeled *human-heartedness* correlated with masculinity, $r = .67***$.

To a Western mind some of the CVS items seem strange, such as "filial piety" (explained as "honoring of ancestors and obedience to, respect for, and financial support of parents"). Of course, to the Chinese mind some of the items on the Rokeach or IBM questionnaire may have seemed equally unusual. Few of the items in the CVS have direct equivalents in the IBM questionnaire. Also, the way the CVS questions are formulated is very different from the way items are worded in the IBM questionnaire. The CVS asks for conscious endorsement of "values as the desirable," or abstract virtues; most IBM questions refer to "values as the desired," or personal objectives. As I argued in Chapter 1, the desirable and the desired do not always overlap; they may even lead to opposite answers.[4] If we put the values that compose a CVS dimension next to those within the correlated IBM dimension, we are in for some surprises. We should assume that the IBM dimensions represent a Western and the CVS dimensions an Eastern interpretation of common basic value complexes. Within each of these value complexes there is more than either the Western or the Eastern mind will detect by itself.

The CVS factor moral discipline, which correlated with power distance on the pole corresponding with high PDI, stood for the following values:[5]

Having few desires
Moderation, following the middle way
Keeping oneself disinterested and pure

On the pole corresponding with low PDI this factor stood for these values:

Adaptability
Prudence (carefulness)

It seems that the questions composed by Western minds have tapped in particular the power aspect of this dimension. The Eastern questions show that the inequalities in power go together with different virtues in an individual's personal life. The ideal person in a high-PDI culture should balance status with restraint; the ideal person in a low-PDI culture should move around with care.

The CVS factor integration, which correlated with individualism/collectivism on the pole corresponding with high IDV, stood for the following:

Tolerance of others
Harmony with others
Noncompetitiveness
A close, intimate friend
Trustworthiness
Contentedness with one's position in life
Solidarity with others
Being conservative

The pole corresponding with collectivism stood for these values:

Filial piety (obedience to parents, respect for parents, honoring of ancestors, financial support of parents)
Chastity in women
Patriotism

These associations are more in line with what was already found in the IBM studies. In the individualist society, relationships with others are not obvious and prearranged, they are voluntary and have to be carefully fostered. In the collectivist society there is no need to make specific friendships: One's friends are predetermined by one's group membership. This group membership is maintained through filial piety and chastity in women, and is associated with patriotism. In the 1982 version of the Values Survey Module (Appendix 4), the work goal "serve your country" was

added. This, too, was found to be strongly associated with collectivism.

The CVS factor human-heartedness, which correlated with masculinity/femininity on the pole corresponding with high MAS, stood for the following values:

Patience
Courtesy
Kindness (forgiveness, compassion)

The opposite pole, corresponding with femininity, stood for these:

Patriotism (also associated with collectivism)
A sense of righteousness

The IBM dimension at the masculine pole stresses the assertive, materialistic, performance-oriented side of this value complex. The CVS again shows that there are other virtues associated with masculinity. Courtesy reminds us of the chivalrous ideals of the Western medieval knights. Patience and kindness we would rather expect at the feminine pole, but we are dealing with "values as the desirable," or abstract virtues; the IBM work goals questions on which the mas/fem dimension is based asks for "values as the desired," or personal objectives.[6] The desirable and the desired in this case seem to compensate for each other. Chinese philosophers have always stressed that the masculine (*yang*) and the feminine (*yin*) elements in life are intertwined; the CVS dimension human-heartedness seems to support this postulate of Taoism. The feminine pole in the CVS stresses subordination to higher purpose: patriotism and righteousness.

The three dimensions common to the Chinese Value Survey and the IBM studies are the ones that refer to three types of expected social behavior: toward seniors or juniors, toward the group, and as a function of one's gender. These represent cultural choices so fundamental to any human society that they are found regardless of whether the questions asked were designed by Eastern or by Western minds. They are truly universal human issues in the sense that all societies share the same problems, but different societies have found different answers to these problems.

Long-Term Orientation as a Fifth Dimension

One IBM dimension was missing in the CVS results. None of the CVS factors correlated with uncertainty avoidance. In Chapter 4, this dimension was associated with, among other things, humankind's search for Truth. It seems that for the Chinese minds that composed the Chinese Value Survey, the need to define Truth was not strong. The Chinese tradition does not hold laws and abstract principles in high regard.

The analysis of the CVS data revealed a fourth dimension in the worldwide answers to the Chinese questions unrelated to anything found with Western questions. Michael Bond calls it *Confucian work dynamism*—Confucian because the items on both poles of the dimension remind him of some of the teachings of Confucius, and dynamism because the positive pole groups future-oriented items and the negative pole groups past- and present-oriented items. In practical terms, the dimension refers to a long-term versus a short-term orientation in life. It deals with values that the Western mind will clearly recognize, but that did not enter the inventory of key issues of the designers of Western questionnaires.

Kong Ze (Confucius), whose ideas about inequality I have mentioned in Chapter 3, was an intellectual of humble origins in China around 500 B.C. He rather unsuccessfully sought to serve various local rulers in the divided China of his day. He did, however, gain a reputation for wit and wisdom, and in his later life was surrounded by a host of disciples who recorded what we know about his teachings.[7] Confucius thus held a position rather similar to that held in ancient Greece by Socrates, who was his virtual contemporary (Socrates lived 80 years later).

Confucius's teachings are lessons in practical ethics without any religious content. "The early Chinese sages . . . were men of extraordinary insight. Realizing that religion was an alienation of the individual from his essence, they began the process of replacing it with pure ethics. People had to rely upon themselves, not some external force, to maintain their humanity" (Liang Shuming, 1893-1988, quoted in Alitto, 1986, p. 179). Confucianism is not a religion but a set of pragmatic rules for daily life derived from what Confucius saw as the lessons of Chinese history; it is "a secular social theory, the foremost principle of which is to achieve a harmonious society" (King & Bond, 1985, p. 30). The following are key principles of Confucian teaching:

1. *The stability of society is based on unequal relationships between people.* The *wu lun,* or five basic relationships, already discussed in Chapter 3, are master-follower, father-son, elder brother-younger brother, husband-wife, and senior friend-junior friend. These relationships are based on mutual and complementary obligations. For example, the junior partner owes the senior respect and obedience; the senior owes the junior partner protection and consideration.

2. *The family is the prototype of all social organizations.* A person is not primarily an individual; rather, he or she is a member of a family. Children should learn to restrain themselves, to overcome their individuality so as to maintain harmony in the family (if only on the surface; one's thoughts remain free). Harmony is found in the maintenance of everybody's *face,* in the sense of dignity, self-respect, and prestige. The importance of face in the collectivist family and society has been described in Chapter 5. Losing one's dignity in the Chinese tradition is equivalent to losing one's eyes, nose, and mouth. Social relations should be conducted in such a way that everybody's face is maintained. Demonstrating respect to someone is called "giving face."

3. *Virtuous behavior toward others consists of not treating others as one would not like to be treated oneself* (the Chinese Golden Rule is negatively phrased!). There is a basic human benevolence toward others, but it does not go as far as the Christian injunction to love one's enemies. Confucius is reputed to have said that if one should love one's enemies, what would remain for one's friends?

4. *Virtue with regard to one's tasks in life consists of trying to acquire skills and education, working hard, not spending more than necessary, being patient, and persevering.* Conspicuous consumption is taboo, as is losing one's temper. Moderation is prescribed in all things.

The new dimension, discriminating among the answers of students from 23 countries who completed the Chinese Value Survey, was composed of the following values. On the long-term orientation pole:

Loading	Value
.76	Persistence (perseverance)
.64	Ordering relationships by status and observing this order
.63	Thrift
.61	Having a sense of shame

On the short-term orientation pole:

Loading	Value
−.76	Personal steadiness and stability
−.72	Protecting your "face"
−.62	Respect for tradition
−.58	Reciprocation of greetings, favors, and gifts

The values that together form the new dimension will probably puzzle many Western readers. Their perplexity should not be surprising, because the dimension is composed precisely of elements that Western questionnaires had not registered. A Westerner would not normally find them important.

I have not maintained Bond's label of *Confucian* for the dimension, as it was found across 22 countries, most of them unfamiliar with Confucius's teachings, and anyway, *both* opposing poles of the dimension contain Confucian values. Some non-Confucian countries, such as Brazil and India, also score fairly high on the index. To the Western observer, East Asian countries seem to be more oriented toward traditions and face than do Western countries, but the index measures the *relative* value given to one side over the other.[8] If the students in the East value tradition, they value thrift even more. Paying attention to face is seen as both a weakness and a strength; in the first case it is motivated by pride, in the second case by love.[9] The responding students from Eastern countries evidently had mostly the weakness in mind. Finally, the argument can be made that a number of very Confucian values are *not* related to the dimension, such as filial piety, which appeared to be associated with collectivism.

Measuring and Validating National Differences in Long-Term Orientation

A Long-Term Orientation
Index for 23 Countries

Bond published factor scores on this dimension for his first 22 countries; these varied from −1.00 for Pakistan to .91 for Hong Kong (see Chinese Culture Connection, 1987, tab. 3). These factor scores were brought into a 0-100 range by a linear transformation.[10] The data for China came in after the scale had been fixed, and they put China outside the range, at LTO = 118, which is not unreasonable for Confucius's home country. The figures, of course, represent *relative* positions of countries, not absolutes. The LTO scores are listed in Exhibit 7.1.

The top five positions in Exhibit 7.1 are taken by East Asian countries: China, Hong Kong, Taiwan, Japan, and South Korea. Singapore is in ninth position. European and other Western countries are mainly found in the lower half of the scale, but other non-Western countries in Africa and Asia (Zimbabwe, Philippines, Nigeria, and Pakistan) occupy the bottom end. So this dimension does not oppose East to West; it splits the world along new lines.

Exhibit 7.2 shows the correlations between LTO and the four IBM indexes across all 20 overlapping countries, across the 9 poorer and the 11 wealthier countries. Across all countries and across the poorer countries, LTO is quite independent from the other indexes. Across the wealthier countries, LTO is negatively correlated with IDV and positively correlated with PDI. This can be seen at a glance from Exhibit 7.1: If the poor countries Zimbabwe, Philippines, Nigeria, and Pakistan are eliminated, the high-IDV, low-PDI Anglo countries remain to oppose the lower-IDV, higher-PDI countries Singapore, Japan, and Hong Kong.[11]

Replications of the
Measurement of Long-Term Orientation

A U.S.-Hong Kong team of researchers led by Ralston collected answers to the CVS from about 300 middle-level managers in different organizations in China, Hong Kong, and the United States.[12] Their LTO scores again placed China on top, Hong Kong in the middle, and the United States last.

Chapter 2 referred to a replication of the IBM questions in the European Media and Marketing Survey 1997 by Inter/View International. This market research agency incorporated in its EMS 97 the 20 questions of the VSM 94 (Appendix 4), including 4 questions intended to measure LTO. The EMS 97 covered a sample of main income earners in the top 20% of households in 16 European countries, of which 15 were part of the IBM set, but only 4 of the CVS set. The EMS 97 represented the first larger-scale use of the LTO questions on new respondents. The results showed that only the country scores for the importance of "thrift" and of "respect for tradition" were mutually correlated in the expected (negative) direction and suitable for developing a scale.[13] I therefore revised the original formula based on 4 questions into a formula based on 2 questions (see Appendix 4). The results are listed in Exhibit 7.3.

The EMS LTO scores are positively but weakly correlated with the four available CVS LTO scores, but this means little for so few cases. More important is that the new scores are significantly correlated with Read's "marginal propensity to save" (MPS), which across all 23 CVS countries serves as an external validator for LTO; we will come back to it below.

Validating LTO Against
Other Studies of Values

The preceding chapters all used data from the World Values Survey (WVS; Inglehart, Basañez,

Exhibit 7.1   Long-Term Orientation Index Values
for 23 Countries

Score Rank	Country or Region	LTO Score
1	China	118
2	Hong Kong	96
3	Taiwan	87
4	Japan	80
5	South Korea	75
6	Brazil	65
7	India	61
8	Thailand	56
9	Singapore	48
10	Netherlands	44
11	Bangladesh	40
12	Sweden	33
13	Poland	32
14	Germany (F.R.)	31
15	Australia	31
16	New Zealand	30
17	United States	29
18	Great Britain	25
19	Zimbabwe	25
20	Canada	23
21	Philippines	19
22	Nigeria	16
23	Pakistan	00

& Moreno, 1998). The 43 countries for which the WVS data have been published included 13 for which LTO scores were available and 11 for which both LTO and the other four indexes were available.[14] These countries varied widely on wealth, from a 1990 GNP/capita of U.S.$290 in Nigeria to U.S.$25,430 in Japan.

Exhibit 7.4 lists seven WVS questions that across these 11 countries were more strongly correlated with LTO than with the other indexes, taking national wealth into account. One block of 11 questions dealt with "qualities which children can be encouraged to learn at home" (questions 226-236); respondents were asked to choose up to five qualities that they considered to be especially important. The proportions choosing "thrift" (question 232) varied from 8% in Nigeria to 56% in China, with a worldwide mean of 36%. Exhibit 7.4 shows that these percentages correlated strongly with LTO ($r = .70**$), which validates both measures in view of the different respondent populations, different ways of asking, and different time periods.[15] In the same block the proportions choosing "tolerance and respect for other

people" (question 231) varied from 55% in South Korea to 91% in Sweden, with a worldwide mean of 70%. These percentages were *negatively* correlated with LTO ($r = -.58*$). Tolerance and respect for other people have lower priority in long-term orientation cultures.

A strong work ethic in high-LTO countries was evident from the answers to a block of six questions asking, "How important are the following in your life?" Worldwide, the order of importance produced was as follows: family (83% very important), work, friends, leisure, religion, and, finally, politics (12% very important). For the item "leisure time" the relative importance across the overlapping countries was most strongly, negatively, correlated with LTO ($r = -.51*$); it was rated very important by 68% in Nigeria and by 14% in China.[16] The other questions in Exhibit 7.4 will be discussed later in this chapter.

In Smith and Dugan's multidimensional scaling analysis of the Trompenaars database (see Chapter 5), the (weak) third dimension contained an item dealing with the respondents' time perspective. It asked whether their 10 most important life experiences had occurred in the past or present or would occur in the near future or distant future. Long-term-oriented countries tended to choose the future (Smith, Dugan, & Trompenaars, 1996, p. 259).

Wirthlin Worldwide (1996), a commercial opinion research institute based in the United States, Britain, and Hong Kong, reported on a ranking of 17 values by 60 "senior Asian business leaders" compared to their U.S. database.[17] The top 7 espoused values for the Asians were hard work, respect for learning, honesty, openness to new ideas, accountability, self-discipline, and self-reliance. For the Americans, the top 7 were freedom of expression, personal freedom, self-reliance, individual rights, hard work, personal achievement, and thinking for oneself. Even recognizing that this was a values inventory made by Western minds, we can see that it shows both the LTO differences (hard work, learning, openness, accountability, self-discipline) and the IDV differences (freedoms, rights, thinking for self) between East and West.

Chapters 3 and 5 referred to a study by Williams, Satterwhite, and Saiz (1998) in which students in 20 countries rated the importance of a large number of psychological traits "in describing what a person is really like." Among the traits Williams et al. used were "individualistic" (number 124), "persistent" (number 174), and "thrifty" (number 267). Twelve of the countries in their study overlapped with the LTO set.[18] Across these, the students' scores for the importance of "individualistic" were primarily correlated with LTO ($r = -.61*$), but Chapter 5 showed that across 18 countries they were also correlated with IDV.

Exhibit 7.2   Correlations of LTO With Four IBM Indexes Across Different Groups of Countries

Indexes	Product-Moment Correlations Across		
	20 Countries	9 Poorer Countries[a]	11 Wealthier Countries
LTO × PDI	.23	−.27	.72**
LTO × UAI	.23	.40	.12
LTO × IDV	−.33	.16	−.77**
LTO × MAS	.08	−.32	.26
PDI × UAI	−.02	−.71*	−.32
PDI × IDV	−.77***	.58	−.88***
PDI × MAS	.09	.72*	.20

a. 1990 GNP/capita < $10,000.
*p = .05; **p = .01; ***p = .001.

Exhibit 7.3   LTO Scores for 15 Countries Computed From Consumer Survey (EMS 97) and Marginal Propensity to Save in Percentages (Read)

Countries	CVS LTO	EMS LTO[a]	Read MPS[b]
Austria		31	27
Belgium		38	22
Denmark		46	36
Finland		41	32
France		39	16
Germany	31	30	31
Great Britain	25	35	12
Ireland		43	55
Italy		34	18
Netherlands	44	38	31
Norway		44	38
Portugal		30	28
Spain		19	21
Sweden	33	22	23
Switzerland		40	34
Mean of 4 countries	33.7	31.3	24.3
Mean of 15 countries		35.4	28.3
SD of 15 countries		7.8	10.6
Product-moment correlations			
CVS LTO × EMS LTO	.29		
CVS LTO × MPS	.73		
EMS LTO × MPS		.49*	

NOTE: In Appendix 5, Table A5.1, LTO scores are listed for 34 countries, 23 based on the CVS and 11 additional European countries based on the EMS.

a. EMS 97, higher-income consumers in 16 European countries. Questions and revised formula according to VSM 94 (see Appendix 4). Data copyright © Inter/View International, Amsterdam; used with permission. See also De Mooij (2001).

b. Marginal propensity to save according to Read (1993): Change in saving in percentage of (change in consumption plus change in saving), 1970-90.

Exhibit 7.4   Correlations With LTO of Questions From the 1990-93 World Values Survey Across 13
Countries, and Contributions to Stepwise Regression Across 11 Countries

Question Number	Question	Countries	Zero-Order Correlation With LTO	Order in Stepwise Regression and Cumulative R^2
7	Importance of leisure time.[a]	13	−.51*	.32 −LTO
142	There are clear guidelines about good and evil.	13	−.25	.30 −GNP, .51 −LTO
206	Important for marriage: living away from in-laws.[b]	12[c]	−.60*	.28 −LTO
210	Important for marriage: interests in common.[b]	12[c]	−.51*	.47 −LTO
219	Child will suffer if mother works.	12[c]	.52*	.29 +LTO
231	Children should learn at home: tolerance and respect for others[d]	12[c]	−.62*	.58 −LTO
232	Children should learn at home: thrift.[d]	12[c]	.70**	.28 +GNP, .55 +LTO

a. Standardized across 6 items.
b. Standardized across 13 items.
c. No data for Poland.
d. Unstandardized; after standardization across 11 items, $r = -.70$** for 231, $r = -.69$** for 232.
*$p = .05$; **$p = .01$; ***$p = .001$.

The scores for "persistent" were only correlated with LTO ($r = .61$*), but the scores for "thrifty" were primarily correlated with IDV ($r = -.53$*, individualist countries attaching less importance to someone being thrifty) and not with LTO ($r = .11$). But at least the relationship between LTO and persistence was validated.

LTO and Savings
Rates: Read's Study

In a Ph.D. dissertation written at the Stanford University Department of Political Science, Read (1993) has tried to explain the wide differences in economic growth between countries; he used the five indexes described in this book among his variables. He found LTO to be significantly correlated with various measures of saving, from which he chose the "marginal propensity to save" as the best proxy for LTO.[19] MPS is defined as the change in real per capita gross domestic saving from 1970 to 1990, in percentages of the sum of the changes in private consumption plus domestic saving over the same period. MPS ranged from 3% in the United States to 64% in Singapore. The correlation between LTO and MPS across the 23 countries is $r = .58$**. Exhibit 7.3 shows MPS scores for the 15 European countries in the 1997 EMS consumer survey next to the LTO scores computed from two EMS survey items. The MPS

and EMS scores were significantly correlated ($r = .49$*).

Chapters 3 through 6 all referred to validations of the IBM dimensions by De Mooij (1998a, 1998b, 2001) against consumer survey data. Some data about personal finance in the EMS 97 correlated significantly with the LTO scores produced by the same EMS 97 (Exhibit 7.3). Investing in mutual funds correlated negatively with LTO (rho = −.66**) and investing in real estate correlated marginally positively (rho = .43, $p = .054$); the latter is more of a long-term commitment. Daily use of a credit card correlated positively with LTO (rho = .54*), primarily because it correlated negatively with the question on "respect for tradition." Credit cards represent a nontraditional way of payment. Their use does not necessarily imply buying on credit; in many European countries, credit cards are used mainly as debit cards.

In Read's MPS table the low savings rate in the United States is striking. "Thrift" was missing from the Rokeach Value Survey, which was supposedly based on a complete inventory of American values in the 1960s ("perseverance" was also not included). Spending, not thrift, seems to have been a value in the United States, at both the individual and the government levels.[20] Herbert Stein, former chairman of the Council of Economic Advisers of two Republican U.S. presidents, said when asked why Americans do not save more: "Economists have been unable to answer this question. Our savings quote . . . has always been lower than elsewhere. . . . It is most likely a reflection of the American life style, although this is no explanation." [21]

In a selection from Confucius's *Analects,* we read: "The second time Duke Ching called Confucius to an audience, he again asked him 'What is the secret of good government?' Confucius replied 'Good government consists in being sparing with resources' " (in Kelen, 1971/1983, p. 44). Among Western societies, the Netherlands scored relatively highest on LTO; the Dutch have been teased by other Europeans for their stinginess and have been called "the Chinese of Europe."

Summary of Validations and Connotations of the Long-Term Orientation Index Found in Surveys and Related Material

Exhibit 7.5 summarizes the validations and connotations of LTO found so far. The material is more limited than in the previous chapters; LTO data were available for fewer countries, the dimension has been introduced more recently, and the concepts related to it are less obvious to Western authors. Yet a fairly coherent picture emerges. Its implications will be elaborated in the next section.

A short definition of Long Term Orientation is: **"Long Term Orientation stands for the fostering of virtues oriented towards future rewards, in particular, perseverance and thrift. Its opposite pole, Short Term Orientation, stands for the fostering of virtues related to the past and present, in particular, respect for tradition, preservation of 'face' and fulfilling social obligations."**

Implications of Country Long-Term Orientation Differences

LTO and Family, Social Relationships, and Work

Individuals learn their values and norms in the family environment in which they grow up. The connotations of long-term orientation in Exhibit 7.5 evoke a close link between family and work, or even family entrepreneurship.

Earlier in this chapter, I cited the 1990-93 World Values Survey results in Exhibit 7.4, which shows that among 11 qualities that children can be encouraged to learn at home, the importance of "thrift" was positively correlated and that of "tolerance and respect for other people" negatively correlated with LTO. Thrift had a high priority in the high-LTO family; tolerance and respect for other people were less frequently chosen than in

low-LTO countries. High-LTO families tend to keep to themselves.

McClelland's (1961) scores for "need for affiliation" (n_{Aff}), based on a content analysis of 1925 children's readers, were shown in Chapter 4 to be significantly correlated with IDV.[22] However, across the 10 countries for which LTO scores were also available, the highest correlation of 1925 n_{Aff} was with LTO, rho = -.85** (against rho = -.79** for IDV, no significant second-order correlations).[23] McClelland defined affiliation as "establishing, maintaining, or restoring a positive affective relationship with another person. This relationship is most adequately described by the word friendship" (p. 160). McClelland's "affiliation" refers to outsiders, not to relationships within the family. The strong negative correlation between LTO and n_{Aff} confirms the prevalence of pragmatic, nonaffective social relationships outside the family in high-LTO countries.

Hill and Romm (1996) interviewed 20 white Australian, 20 Israeli, and 20 Sino-Vietnamese Australian mothers about their motivations in giving gifts to their children, the selection and presentation of the gifts, and the child's reactions. The white Australian mothers justified the gift giving "to gain short-term benefits for their children, i.e., enhanced self-concept, and for themselves, i.e., their children's love" (p. 23). The Sino-Vietnamese mothers justified it "to gain long-term benefits for their children, i.e., enhanced education and finances. There was no mention of gifts being given to benefit the Sino-Vietnamese mothers themselves" (p. 23). The Israeli mothers justified it "to gain long-term benefits for their children, i.e., enhanced education, and short-term benefits for themselves, i.e., their children's love" (p. 23). The Sino-Vietnamese represented a long-term-oriented motivation and the white Australians a short-term-oriented one; I have assumed that the Israelis (for whom Exhibit 7.1 shows no data) should be located somewhere in between.[24]

Argyle, Henderson, Bond, Iizuka, and Contarello (1986) conducted an ingenious study about "relationship rules" in Great Britain, Hong Kong, Italy, and Japan. A total of nearly 1,000 respondents divided over the four countries, females and males, from two age groups (18-25 and 30-60), completed one of three questionnaires asking to what extent each of 33 possible rules applied—or whether the rule's opposite applied—for each of 22 relationships. Examples of the rules are "Should appear neatly or smartly dressed when with the other person" and "Should not criticize the other person publicly." Examples of the relationships are "sibling" and "work subordinate." Results showed consistent differences between the Eastern (Hong Kong and Japan) and the Western cultures for rules avoiding loss of face and rules about maintaining harmony in groups. Both

Exhibit 7.5   Summary of Connotations of LTO Differences Found in Surveys and Other Comparative Studies of Values

Low LTO	High LTO
Quick results expected.	Persistence, perseverance.
Status not major issue in relationships.	Relationships ordered by status and this order observed.
Nice people know how to spend.	Nice people are thrifty, sparing with resources.
Shame is not a common feeling.	A sense of shame common.
Personal steadiness and stability.	Personal adaptability.
Protection of one's "face."	Face considerations common but considered a weakness.
Respect for traditions.	Adaptation of traditions to new circumstances.
Reciprocation of greetings, favors, and gifts.	Reciprocation considerations are problematic, risk of overspending.
Children should learn tolerance and respect for other people.	Children should learn thrift.
Leisure time important.	Leisure time not so important.
Most important events in life occurred in past or occur in present.	Most important events in life will occur in future.
Students consider "persistent" not an important personality trait.	Students consider "persistent" an important personality trait.
Small share of additional income saved.	Large share of additional income saved.
Investment in mutual funds.	Investment in real estate.

Eastern cultures stressed obedience relationships among siblings, indicating differentiation between elder and younger brothers and sisters. As only four cultures were covered, these differences could be attributed to individualism/collectivism (ind/col) as well as to long-/short-term orientation, but I have chosen to refer to them here because of their clear link with Confucian ethics: the ordering of relationships by status and the observation of this order.

Three other questions in the World Values Survey (Exhibit 7.4, questions 206, 210, and 219) dealt with marriage and family life. The first two were part of a block of 13 questions about "things that make a marriage successful." Respondents in high-LTO countries scored lower on the importance of "living away from in-laws" ($r = -.60*$, answers varied from 59% very important in the Netherlands to 5% in South Korea, worldwide mean 42%); they also scored lower on the importance of "tastes and interests in common" ($r = -.51*$, from 78% very important in Nigeria to 20% in South Korea, worldwide mean 41%). These two questions suggest that marriage in high-LTO countries is a pragmatic arrangement. The third item was "A pre-school child is likely to suffer if his or her mother works." Respondents in higher-LTO countries tended to agree ($r = .52*$); agreement varied from 92% in India to 52% in the

United States, worldwide mean 69%. The high-LTO division of family tasks sees taking care of preschool children clearly as the mother's role.

Chapter 5 referred to an 11-country study by Levine, Sato, Hashimoto, and Verma (1995) about the role of love in marriage.[25] Their questionnaire contained the item "If love has completely disappeared from a marriage, I think it is probably best for the couple to make a clean break and start new lives." The respondents were undergraduates of both genders. Answers varied from 29% yes and 31% no in Australia to 78% yes and 13% no in Brazil. Across 10 overlapping countries, percentage yes minus percentage no correlated with LTO with rho = .76** and not at all with any of the other indexes or GNP/capita.[26] This again suggests a pragmatic attitude, not a moralistic one, toward marriage issues in high-LTO countries.

Chapter 6 described my secondary analysis of data about gender stereotypes and partner preferences among young women in eight Asian capital cities (from the Japanese market research agency Wacoal, in Hofstede, 1996b). Among the gender stereotypes, the trait "humility" correlated strongly with LTO (rho = .87***).[27] In the high-LTO cultures humility was considered a general human virtue; it recalls the "sense of shame" in the CVS.[28] In low-LTO countries humility was seen as feminine. In the same study, among the traits preferred in husbands versus steady boyfriends, "affection" was correlated with LTO (rho = .71*). In high-LTO cultures affection was more often associated with the husband, not only with the boyfriend.

Chapter 4 referred to results from a public opinion survey of "human values" in 13 countries published by Hastings and Hastings (1981); for 11 of the countries LTO scores were available.[29] The survey contained a set of 17 questions on "satisfaction of life goals" (see the statistical section of Chapter 4). Mean percentages "satisfied" per country were standardized across the 17 goals. LTO was significantly correlated ($r = .83**$) with the satisfaction of goal 16, "To be attentive to daily human relations (to deepen human bonds in family, neighborhood and friends or acquaintances)," and with goal 8 ($r = .64**$), "To make efforts to correct social inequality and injustice (to bring about fair and equal life for everybody)." [30] Respondents in long-term-oriented cultures felt satisfied with their daily human relations and their contribution toward correcting injustice (and therefore were less likely to be mobilized for social issues).

Chapter 3 referred to Best and Williams's (1996) survey study about "anticipation of aging" among male and female students in 19 countries. The age at which a person was described as "middle-aged" correlated negatively with PDI. The age at which a person was described as "old" (a mean of 60 for men and 62 for women) correlated positively with GNP/capita (rho = .57** for men; rho = .38, $p = .057$, for women) and (across 10 overlapping countries)[31] negatively with LTO (rho = −.63* for men; rho = −.62* for women). In wealthier countries, but also in low-LTO cultures, old age was seen as starting later. But the survey also showed that a nine-question index on how satisfied respondents expected to be with their life when they were old correlated positively with LTO ($r = .59*$ for men; $r = .54$, $p = .052$, for women). So in high-LTO cultures people saw old age coming earlier, but they had positive feelings about it.

In summary, family life in the high-LTO culture is a pragmatic arrangement, but it is supposed to be based on real affection and with attention paid to small children. The children learn thrift, not to expect immediate gratification of their desires, tenacity in the pursuit of whatever goals, humility,[32] and adaptation to circumstances. They learn these things by implication: Confucian values cannot be transferred through preaching.[33] If possible, the children are groomed toward succeeding as entrepreneurs. Thrift leads to savings and to availability of capital for investment by oneself or one's relatives. A sense of shame supports decency in business and social contacts and a stress on keeping one's commitments. The overall picture is one of an industrious and satisfying family. Reality, of course, may fall short of this picture.[34]

Children growing up in a low-LTO culture experience two opposing forces. One is toward immediate need gratification, spending, sensitivity to social trends in consumption ("keeping up with the Joneses"), and enjoying leisure time. The other is toward respecting "musts": traditions, face-saving, being seen as a stable individual, respecting the social codes of marriage even if love has gone, tolerance and respect for others as a matter of principle, and reciprocation of greetings, favors, and gifts as a social ritual. There is potential tension between these two forces that may lead to feelings of guilt, and that lowers satisfaction with daily human relations and makes conflicts with in-laws standard. Fewer families in such cultures will muster the initiative, risk seeking, and adaptability required of entrepreneurs in quickly changing markets. Strong respect for tradition impedes innovation.

Businesses in long-term-oriented cultures are accustomed to working toward building up strong positions in their markets; they do not expect immediate results. Managers (often family members) are allowed time and resources to make their own contributions. In short-term-oriented cultures the "bottom line" (the results of the past month, quarter, or year) is a major concern; control systems are focused on it and managers are constantly judged by it. This state of affairs is supported by arguments that are assumed to be rational, but the cultural distinction reminds one of the fact that this entire rationality rests on cultural— that is, prerational—choices. The cost of short-term decisions in terms of "pecuniary considerations, myopic decisions, work process control, hasty adoption and quick abandonment of novel ideas" (Mamman & Saffu, 1998) is evident; managers are rewarded or victimized by today's bottom line even where it is clearly the outcome of decisions made by their predecessors or pre-predecessors years ago; yet the force of cultural belief perpetuates the system.

The Hastings and Hastings (1981) "human values" survey mentioned earlier also contained this question:

Here are two opinions about conditions existing in our country. Which one do you happen to agree with? (a) There is too much emphasis upon the principle of equality. People should be given the opportunity to choose their own economic and social life according to their individual abilities. (b) Too much liberalism has been producing increasingly wide differences in people's economic and social life. People should live more equally.

The proportions of respondents choosing response b varied from 30% in France to 71% in Japan; these were correlated with LTO with $r = .69**$. Long-term orientation stands for a society in which wide differences in economic and social conditions are considered undesirable. Short-term orientation stands for "meritocracy," differentiation according to abilities.

Redding (1990) divided the sources of efficiency *and* failure of overseas Chinese businesses into vertical cooperation, horizontal cooperation, control, and adaptiveness. About vertical cooperation, Redding states:

> [The] atmosphere is not . . . one in which workers and owner/managers naturally divide into two camps psychologically. They tend to be similar socially, in terms of their values, their behavior, their needs, and their aspirations. . . . One of the outcomes of this vertical cooperativeness is willing compliance. This tendency is also reinforced by early conditioning of people during childhood and education, and the respect for authority figures, deeply ingrained in the Confucian tradition, tends to be maintained throughout life. . . . An extension of this willingness to comply is willingness to engage diligently in routine and possibly dull tasks, something one might term perseverance. This nebulous but nonetheless important component of Overseas Chinese work behavior, a kind of micro form of the work ethic, pervades their factories and offices. . . . It was noticed earlier that the huge diligence required to master the Chinese language has played a part here, as has also the strict order of a Confucian household. (p. 209)

We recognize the LTO components of ordering relationships by status and maintaining this order and perseverance; the latter functions not only in the sustained efforts of the entrepreneur in building a business, but in those of his or her workers in carrying out their daily tasks.

Horizontal coordination refers to networks. The key concept of *guanxi* in Asian business is by now known worldwide. It refers to personal connections; it links the family sphere to the business sphere. Having a personal network of acquaintances is extremely important in these societies. This is an evident consequence of collectivism (relationships before task), but it also contributes to a long-term orientation. One's capital of *guanxi* lasts a lifetime, and one would not want to destroy it for short-term, bottom-line reasons (Yeung & Tung, 1996).

Long-term-oriented entrepreneurship is evidently not only based on the values of the entrepreneurs. The way the CVS scores were found, by surveying student samples, suggests that the decisive values are held broadly within societies; among entrepreneurs and future entrepreneurs, among their employees and their families, and among other members of the society.

LTO and Ways of Thinking

The feeling that there are basic differences in thinking between "East" and "West" has been expressed ever since these parts of the world first came into contact. Definitions of *East* and *West* have not always been very clear, and our present findings imply that one should be prepared to distinguish among Asian countries and among Western countries as well. In Western eyes, the Chinese in particular were deemed inscrutable; in Chinese eyes, Europeans were foreign devils. Before Michael Bond orchestrated his CVS, Gordon Redding (1980a), also in Hong Kong, had stressed the importance of differences in cognition: "That there are fairly large-scale differences in cognitive processes is often a matter of surprise to Westerners viewing Oriental people and vice versa" (p. 131). Redding went on to divide forms of cognition into causation, probability, time, self, and morality. All of these are in some way related to differences on the LTO scale.

The assumption of such differences was the key argument for Bond's Chinese Value Survey research project, and the results confirmed this assumption. The comparison of the results of the (Western) IBM and Rokeach Value Survey studies versus the (Eastern) Chinese Value Survey showed that three dimensions dealing with basic human relationships were so universal that they showed up in all cases, albeit with partly different emphases. These were the equivalents of the power distance, individualism/collectivism, and masculinity/femininity dimensions in the IBM study. Both the Western studies and the Eastern study produced also a fourth dimension, but its nature depended on the culture of the designers of the questionnaire. With the Western-made questionnaires (IBM and RVS), the dimension of uncertainty avoidance was found; with the Chinese Value Survey, another dimension was found, long-/short-term orientation.

The Chinese social scientists who supplied the items for Bond's CVS questionnaire did not produce anything supporting an uncertainty avoidance concept. Elsewhere, studies comparing native Chinese and native English speakers have shown repeatedly that English speakers are more likely to use probabilistic thinking—that is, to view the world in terms of uncertainty, to ascribe degrees of uncertainty to events, and to express these either in words or in percentages of probability. Chinese speakers are more likely to express full confidence (yes or no), and they use fewer probability terms such as *possibly* and *maybe*

(Lau & Ranyard, 1999).[35] This confirms that the notion of uncertainty and the need to avoid it are more present in a Western cognitive frame than in an Eastern one. Such a notion will reward short-term thinking, as the long term is very uncertain anyway; this supports the finding of lower LTO scores in non-Chinese countries.

Chapter 4, which described the uncertainty avoidance dimension, showed it to reflect a society's search for Truth. Uncertainty-avoiding cultures foster a belief in an absolute Truth, whereas uncertainty-accepting cultures take a more relativistic stance. Long-term orientation, on the other hand, with its roots in the ethical imperatives of Confucius, can be interpreted as dealing with a society's search for Virtue. Long-term-oriented cultures teach virtues directed at the future, such as education, frugality, and persistence. Short-term-oriented cultures teach virtues directed at the past and present, such as respecting traditions, social spending, and maintaining face. The choice of items that led to the identification of either UAI or LTO was a choice between a focus on Truth and a focus on Virtue.

The 1990-93 World Values Survey (Exhibit 7.4, question 142) asked respondents to choose between two statements: "(a) There are absolutely clear guidelines about what is good and evil. These always apply to everyone, whatever the circumstances; (b) There can never be absolutely clear guidelines about what is good and evil. What is good and evil depends entirely upon the circumstances at the time." The agreement with statement a varied from 60% in Nigeria and 50% in the United States to 19% in Sweden and 15% in Japan. The first zero-order correlation was with GNP/capita (poorer countries showed more belief in absolute guidelines), but it was accompanied by a significant second-order correlation with LTO. Respondents in high-LTO countries believed less in universal guidelines about what is good and evil, and more in considering the circumstances.

Eastern religions (Hinduism, Buddhism, Shintoism, Taoism) are separated from Western religions (Judaism, Christianity, Islam) by a deep philosophical dividing line. The three Western religions belong to the same thought family; historically, they have grown from the same roots. As argued in Chapter 4, all three are based on the existence of a Truth that is accessible to true believers. Each of the three has a sacred book. In the East, Confucianism and Taoism, which are nonreligious ethical systems as well as major religions, are not based on the assumption that there is a Truth that a human community can embrace.[36] Buddhism stresses the limits of truth: "Every being, human or non-human, is in relativity. Therefore, it is foolish to hold a certain idea or concept or ideology as the only absolute" (Bukkyo Dendo Kyokai, 1980, p. 592). Eastern religions offer var-

ious ways in which a person can improve him- or herself, but these do not consist in believing; rather, they involve ritual, meditation, or ways of living. Some of these may lead to a higher spiritual state, eventually to unification with God or gods. U.S. mythologist Joseph Campbell (1972/1988, pp. 71-75), comparing Eastern and Western religious myths, has concluded that Judaism, Christianity, and Islam have dissociated matter and spirit, whereas Eastern religions and philosophers have kept matter and spirit integrated.[37] This is why a questionnaire invented by Western minds led to the identification of a fourth dimension dealing with Truth and a questionnaire invented by Eastern minds found a fourth dimension dealing with Virtue.

Dissociation of matter and spirit explains the opposing forces in short-term orientation cultures: need gratification versus respecting "musts," which frequently clash. Above, I referred to the correlation between LTO and the satisfaction with making "efforts to correct social inequality and injustice" (Hastings & Hastings, 1981). Respondents in short-term-oriented cultures felt less satisfied with their contributions toward correcting injustice. Although these cultures are more likely to believe in absolute criteria for good and evil, at the same time they are less satisfied with their efforts at doing good. In long-term-oriented cultures a strong concern for Virtue allows a pragmatic integration of morals and practice. Virtue is not based on absolute standards for good and evil; what is virtuous depends on the circumstances. Further, when one is behaving virtuously, one does not feel a strong need to do more to correct social injustice.

The Western concern with Truth is supported by an axiom in Western logic that a statement excludes its opposite: If "A" is true, "non-A," which is the opposite of A, must be false. Eastern logic does not have such an axiom. If A is true, non-A may also be true, and together they produce a wisdom that is superior to either A or non-A. This is sometimes called the complementarity of *yang* and *yin,* using two Chinese characters that express the male and the female elements present in all aspects of reality (see also Chapter 6). Human truth in this philosophical approach is always partial. Worm (1997) cites a 1936 book titled *My Country and My People,* by the Chinese author Lin Yutang:

[Lin] emphasizes that rather than cultivating logic, the Chinese have always cultivated intuition and "common sense." In continuation of this, he claims the Chinese prioritize sensibility over rationality. Rationality is abstract, analytical, and idealistic with a tendency to logical extremes, whereas the spirit of common sense is more realistic, human, in closer contact with reality, and yields a much more genuine understanding of the actual situation. (p. 52)

People in East and Southeast Asian countries place less value on "cognitive consistency." [38] Also, it has been shown that in comparison with North Americans, Chinese view "disagreement" as less face-threatening to personal relationships than "injury" or "disappointment" (Gao, Ting-Toomey, & Gudykunst, 1996, p. 293). A different opinion does not affect their egos so much.

Cultures that tolerate cognitive *inconsistency* can adopt elements from different religions or adhere to more than one religion at the same time. In countries with such a philosophical background a practical nonreligious ethical system like Confucianism could become a cornerstone of society. In the West, ethical rules tend to be derived from religion: Virtue from Truth. Maruyama (1974) contrasted three paradigms: a "unidirectional causal paradigm," a "random process paradigm," and a "mutual causal paradigm." Redding (1980b, p. 198) associated the unidirectional causal paradigm with Western and the mutual causal paradigm with Eastern thinking. For "knowledge" the unidirectional paradigm lists "Belief in one truth. If people are informed they will agree," and the mutual causal paradigm lists "Polyocular. Must learn different views and take them into consideration." For "analysis," the former has "Pre-set categories used for all situations" and the latter, "Changeable categories depending on the situation" (Maruyama, 1974, p. 143).

Through their different logics East and West followed different paths in developing government and in developing science and technology. Whereas the Romans spread the principle of "government by law," the main continuous principle of Chinese administration has been "government by man" (see also Chapter 4). "Throughout history, Westerners have been ruled by one external alien force or another—by God through priests or by the state through law. . . . As a consequence bonds do not exist among people except in legal form" (Liang Shu-ming, 1934, quoted in Alitto, 1986, p. 179).

Kim (1995) has written about the need for Western psychological science to examine its implicit assumptions about East Asia:

Psychology . . . is deeply enmeshed with Euro-American cultural values that champion rational, liberal and individualistic ideals. . . . This belief affects how conferences are organized, research collaborations are developed, research is funded, and publications are accepted. In East Asia, human relationships that can be characterized as being "virtue-based" rather than "rights-based" occupy the center stage. Individuals are considered to be linked in a web of inter-relatedness and ideas

are exchanged through established social networks. (p. 663)

In science and technology, Western Truth stimulated analytic thinking, whereas Eastern Virtue led to synthetic thinking.[39] During the Industrial Revolution in the West the search for Truth led to the discovery of the laws of nature, which could then be exploited for the sake of human progress. It is not surprising that Chinese scholars, despite their high level of civilization, never discovered Newton's laws: They were simply not looking for laws. The Chinese script betrays this lack of interest in generalizing: It needs 5,000 or more different characters, one for each syllable, whereas by splitting the syllables into separate letters, Western languages need only about 30 signs. "Chinese epistemology is event-oriented, not substance-oriented" (Maruyama, 1978, p. 464). Western analytic thinking focused on elements; Eastern synthetic thinking focused on wholes. Dr. Yukawa Hideki, a Japanese Nobel Prize winner in physics, has been quoted as saying that "the Japanese mentality is unfit for abstract thinking" (in Moore, 1967, p. 290).

By the middle of the 20th century, the Western concern for Truth gradually ceased to be an asset and turned instead into a liability. Science may benefit from analytic thinking, but management and government are based on the art of synthesis. With the results of Western, analytically derived technologies freely available, Eastern cultures could start putting these technologies into practice using their own superior synthetic abilities. What is true or who is right is less important than what works and how the efforts of individuals with different thinking patterns can be coordinated toward a common goal. This is most clearly demonstrated by the functioning of Japanese business companies. "The superior man goes through his life without any one preconceived action or any taboo. He merely decides for the moment what is the right thing to do" (from the *Li Chi,* a collection of writings of the disciples of Confucius codified around 100 B.C.; in Watts, 1979, p. 83).

This synthetic way of thinking surprisingly goes together with proficiency in basic mathematics, in spite of the fact that at first sight mathematics seems to call for analytic rather than synthetic skills. Basic mathematics poses well-defined problems in which goals are explicitly stated. High-LTO cultures prove to be well equipped for solving such well-defined problems; low-LTO cultures seem to try more heuristic approaches, even where problems can be basically structured. Redding (1980b) notes: "It is a common question why an active tradition of scientific investigation failed to develop in China in the way it did in the West? The most appealing explanations for it centre upon differences in cognitive structures of a fundamental kind" (p. 196). He goes on:

> The Chinese student, if he has been initially educated in his own culture, and in his own language, will have begun to use a set of cognitive processes which give him a "fix" on the world of a very distinctive kind. . . . It is possible to see some rationale for the noticeable tendency of Chinese to excel in certain subjects, particularly the applied sciences, where "the individual and the concrete" is paramount, and for their tendency not to move naturally into the abstract realms of philosophy and sociology; operations research yes, organization theory no. (p. 197)

Under the sponsorship of the Organization for Economic Cooperation and Development, an international comparative test of mathematics and science performance by secondary school students was conducted in 1997. This TIMSS (Third International Mathematics and Science Study; see National Center for Educational Statistics, 1999) produced mean country performance scores on mathematics and science for fourth-grade students (age about 10) in 26 countries and for eighth-grade students (age about 14) in 41 countries. For the older students Singapore obtained the highest scores in both subjects; South Africa's scores were the lowest. U.S. students scored 28th on math and 17th on science. Across 11 overlapping countries for the younger and 13 for the older students, math scores correlated with LTO with $r = .58*$ for fourth grade, $r = .72**$ for eighth grade. Science scores and math scores were correlated for the two age groups with $r = .81***$ and $r = .87***$, respectively, *but science scores were not correlated with LTO* ($r = .06$ for fourth grade, $r = .18$ for eighth grade). Performance correlated weakly with GNP/capita (wealthier countries, obviously, better results; $r = .38*$ for both math and science, eighth grade) but not with any of the IBM indexes.

The good performance of high-LTO culture students in basic mathematics refutes the traditional argument that these cultures focus on rote learning instead of comprehension. The good academic performance in beta subjects by Asian expatriate students in other countries is well-known, but a satisfactory explanation has been lacking. Biggs (1996) has suggested that Western assumptions about the relationships among student characteristics, the teaching context, students' learning processes, and learning outcomes do not apply to the Asian case. Apparently similar behaviors may have different deep meanings. For example, what is interpreted as rote learning appears to be memorizing to understand. Students' silence in class may be followed by one-to-one contact with the teacher after class, or by discussions about the subject matter with fellow students. Biggs also refers to studies reporting that Asian more than Western cultures attribute success to effort and failure to lack of effort, rather than to ability. Chapter 4 reported on a study of attributions by Yan and Gaier (1994) with 358 students at a U.S. university, classified as Chinese, Southeast Asian, Japanese, Korean, and American. After standardizing their data, I found that indeed the Asian students attributed success more to effort, and failure to lack of it, than the U.S. students did. So the Asians were likely to put in more effort.[40]

Yet the argument that Asian students simply work harder is insufficient, because then they should do as well in science as in math, which as we have seen is not the case.[41] The strong correlations between math performance and LTO suggest that aside from motivation and commitment, cognitive processes play a role: There is something common in the mental programming dominant in the high-LTO cultures and in the mental requirement for performing well in basic mathematics. Chinese children in the United States also performed well in space conceptualization and reasoning tests; more in general, they were good at solving well-defined problems in which goals were explicitly stated—that is, formal rather than open problems.[42] Basic mathematics belongs to this same category, more than basic science.[43]

Exhibit 7.6 lists the key implications of short- versus long-term orientation for family, social relations, work, and ways of thinking. It is less extensive than the corresponding tables for the four IBM dimensions, which are supported by much longer lists of correlated phenomena. However, as we will see in the next subsection, the new dimension covers issues extremely relevant for economic development and not related to the other dimensions.

In Exhibit 7.7 the essence of the long- versus short-term orientation societal norm is summarized, in analogy with what was done for the four IBM dimensions in Exhibits 3.7, 4.5, 5.4, and 6.10.

LTO and Economic Growth

Exhibit 7.8 shows the correlations of LTO with the same geographic, economic, and demographic indicators that were used for correlating with the IBM indexes.[44] As the CVS data were collected around 1985, for GNP/capita this time 1980 data were used. For past and future economic growth (EGP and EGF), data for 1965-85 and 1985-95 were used. The correlations are again shown across all (23) countries and separately across the 12 economically less-developed countries (1980 GNP/capita < $4,000) and the 11 more-developed ones.

Exhibit 7.6   Key Differences Between Short- and Long-Term-Oriented Societies

Low LTO	High LTO
In Family, Social Relations, and Work	
Children should learn tolerance and respect for other people.	Children should learn thrift.
Strong need for affiliation in traditional children's stories.	Weak need for affiliation in traditional children's stories.
Gifts to children for their self-concept and love.	Gifts to children for their education and finances.
All siblings are equal.	Differentiation between elder and younger brothers and sisters.
Living with in-laws is a problem.	Living with in-laws is no problem.
Couple should share tastes and interests.	Shared tastes and interests not a requirement for marriage.
Preschool child need not suffer if mother works.	Preschool child will suffer if mother works.
Marriage should last even if love has disappeared.	If love has disappeared from marriage it is best to make a new start.
"Humility" is a feminine virtue.	"Humility" is a general human virtue.
Young women expect affection from boyfriend, not husband.	Young women expect affection from husband.
Less satisfied with daily human relations.	Daily human relations (family, neighborhood, friends) satisfying.
Less satisfied with own attempts at correcting social injustice.	No need to contribute more to correcting social injustice.
Old age seen as coming later.	Old age seen as coming sooner but as a satisfying life period.
In business, short-term results: the bottom line.	In business, building of relationships and market position.
Family and business sphere separated.	Vertical coordination, horizontal coordination, control, and adaptiveness.
Meritocracy: economic and social life to be ordered by abilities.	People should live more equally.
In Ways of Thinking	
Probabilistic thinking.	Either full or no confidence.
Belief in absolute guidelines about good and evil.	What is good and evil depends on the circumstances.
Short-term virtues taught.	Long-term virtues taught.
Need for cognitive consistency.	Opposites complement each other.
Government by law.	Government by men.
Analytic thinking.	Synthetic thinking.
Lower performance in basic mathematics tasks.	Higher performance in basic mathematics tasks.

The dominant correlation is with economic growth, which is not surprising given that the top five countries in Exhibit 7.1 are known for their fast economic growth in the period 1965-95. The strongest correlation across all countries and across the poorer countries was with future economic growth, but across the wealthy countries with past economic growth. There was also a significant correlation with population density (PDN) across the wealthy countries and weakly across all countries, but in a stepwise regression this did not survive after the correlation with economic growth had been taken into account: As Exhibit 2.11 shows, economic growth and population density were strongly correlated.

A comparison with the parallel tables for the four IBM indexes (Exhibits 3.20, 4.22, 5.23, and 6.24) shows that none of the four was consistently correlated with either past or future economic growth. The only significant correlations were for past economic growth (EGP 1960-70) among the 22 wealthier countries; it correlated $r = -.61**$

Exhibit 7.7   The Long-Term Orientation Societal Norm

Low LTO	High LTO
Immediate gratification of needs expected.	Deferred gratification of needs accepted.
Traditions are sacrosanct.	Traditions adaptable to changed circumstances.
Family life guided by imperatives.	Family life guided by shared tasks.
Short-term virtues taught: social consumption.	Long-term virtues taught: frugality, perseverance.
Spending.	Saving, investing.
The bottom line.	Building a strong market position.
Analytic thinking.	Synthetic thinking.
Fuzzy problem solving.	Structured problem solving.

Exhibit 7.8   Product-Moment Correlations and Multiple Regression of LTO Scores With Seven Country-Level Indicators

Indicator	Zero-Order Correlations With LTO Scores Across		
	All 23 Countries	12 Poorer Countries	11 Wealthier countries[a]
GNP 1980[b]	−.22	−.00	−.47
EGP 65-85[c]	.64**	.59*	.71**
EGF 85-95[d]	.70***	.72**	.66*
LAT	−.05	.41	−.49
POP	.17	.13	−.17
PGR	.11	.28	.38
PDN	.39*	.26	.70**
Squared multiple correlation with all seven R^2			
	.62	.74	.68

NOTE: A stepwise regression did not produce any significant higher-order correlations. For definitions of the indicators, see Exhibit 2.9.
a. GNP/capita > $4,000. Countries: AUL, CAN, GBR, GER, HOK, JPN, NET, NZL, SIN, SWE, USA.
b. From World Bank (1982).
c. From World Bank (1987). Data for Poland were for 1965-80, from World Bank (1982).
d. From World Bank (1997).
*$p = .05$; **$p = .01$; ***$p = .001$.

with IDV, $r = .59$ with UAI, and $r = .43*$ with PDI, but in a stepwise regression only IDV made a significant contribution. In wealthy countries with faster growth between 1960 and 1970, IBM employees between 1967 and 1973 scored less individualistic. Future economic growth (EGF 1965-90) correlated with none of the indexes—not for all countries or for the poorer ones or for the wealthier ones. LTO, on the other hand, correlated significantly positively with economic growth over the period 1965-85 preceding the CVS survey and over the period 1985-95 following it, for all countries, for the poorer ones, and for the wealthier ones. Stepwise regressions for both economic growth measures with LTO plus the four IBM indexes showed no significant second-order correlations.[45]

A correlation does not prove a causal link. In Chapter 4, for the relationship between GNP/ca-

pita and IDV, the arrow of causality was shown to point from wealth to individualist values. In the case of LTO, however, the fact that the correlation (across all 23 countries) with *future* economic growth (EGF 85-95) was stronger than with past economic growth (EGP 65-85) speaks in favor of an arrow of causation *from* LTO values *to* growth. Across the 11 wealthier countries only, the correlation with EGP was stronger, but it can be argued that these countries were hitting a ceiling. The nature of the values involved supports their being a cause rather than an effect. The Chinese and Japanese were known to value thrift and perseverance before their boom started; their adherence to tradition was weakened by the historical events of World War II and the period thereafter.

The relationship between certain Confucian values—as opposed to other equally Confucian values—and economic growth over these decades is a surprising, even sensational, finding. "It indicates to me, as a student of Confucian culture, not the passing of a traditional society, but a marvelous demonstration of *tradition within modernity*" (Tu, 1991, p. 5; emphasis added). The economic miracle of the East Asian Dragons has taken economists by surprise.[46] By economic criteria, Colombia, for example, should have outperformed South Korea, whereas the reverse was true.[47] The existence of a relationship between Confucius's teachings and economic growth in the latter part of the 20th century had been suggested before, but it had never been proven. One of its defendants was the American futurologist Herman Kahn (1922-83), who formulated a "neo-Confucian hypothesis" (1979). Kahn suggested that the economic success of the countries of East Asia could be attributed to their common cultural roots going back far into history, and that this cultural inheritance under the world market conditions of the post-World War II period became a competitive advantage for successful business activity. The data collected with the Chinese Value Survey proved Kahn right, and they also specify *which* Confucian values are associated with economic growth. It is remarkable that it took an East Asian instrument—the CVS—to prove the role of culture in the development of East Asia.

In a Ph.D. dissertation at the University of Hong Kong School of Business, Chew-Lim Fee Yee (1997) wrote an ethnography of a Singapore department store from its founding in 1932 to 1996. She presented a fascinating illustration of long-term orientation in action. She interpreted the history of the company in a framework of Chinese (Confucian) values, with the role of thrift and persistence in its earlier years, and the negative role of the owners' face consciousness in the later years, when they did not want to give up loss-causing activities. These value contexts stand at opposite ends of the LTO dimension.

Culture in the form of certain dominant values among the population is a necessary but not a sufficient condition for economic growth. Two other conditions are the existence of a market and the existence of a political context that allows development; the latter, of course, is also strongly affected by culture.[48] The need for a market explains why the growth of the East Asian economies started only after 1955, when for the first time in history the conditions for a truly global market were fulfilled. The need for a supportive political context was met in all five "Dragons"—Hong Kong, Japan, Korea, Singapore, and Taiwan—but in very different ways, with the role of government varying from active support to laissez-faire. "In all Asiatic nations, under whatever regime, authority from above always reaches down and meets in some middle ground local self-management rising from be-

low" (Benedict, 1946/1974, p. 82). Labor unions were weak and company oriented in all five countries (a Chinese explained to me that a combative labor union would never be successful, because it would violate the norm of harmony in society), and a relatively egalitarian income distribution meant that support for revolutionary social changes was weak.[49] The Confucian norm of moderation affected political life as well, in spite of occasional outbreaks of unrest and violence.

The influence of the political context was more ambiguous in China, Confucianism's cradle and the top scorer on LTO. The economic growth of China was hampered by the violence of the 1966-76 Cultural Revolution. This period, which represents a traumatic memory for almost all Chinese, was among other things an attempt by Mao Zedong to escape the Confucian tradition. Mao preached the positive value of contradiction and conflict, as opposed to the Confucian value of harmony.[50] Eventually, Confucius has won again. In spite of the Cultural Revolution, China's average economic growth rate for 1965-85 is reported as 4.8%, equal to the 4.7% of Japan (World Bank, 1987). Of course, China started at a very low national income level. Politics has played a major role in its economic development and will continue to do so. It is obviously immensely more difficult to turn around a nation of more than a billion people than one of 3 million, like Singapore. The question is whether China's rulers can cope with the domestic political consequences of the country's economic opening toward the rest of the world.

As this is written (1999), the constant growth of the East Asian economies has been interrupted, or at least slowed down. It is possible that the strong relationship between LTO and economic growth will eventually prove to have been a temporary phenomenon, brought about by the interaction of LTO values with the global economic and political conditions of the second half of the 20th century. A curious fact is that in the first half of the 20th century the Confucianist legacy of the East Asian countries was cited as a reason for their *backwardness*. Certain values are functional in certain periods. It could also be, of course, that East Asian growth will resume and that the party is not over.

Long- and Short-Term Orientation in the Hindu and Muslim Worlds

References to "the East" in the preceding pages have been mainly about China, the overseas Chinese, Korea, and Japan; but Hindu India also scored fairly high on LTO (61). What has been written above about the relativity of truth applies to Hinduism as well. In previous work, I have described some of the experiences of a Nepalese anthropologist who in the period 1987-88 did a 10-month field research project in a Calvinist Dutch village (Hofstede, 1991, chap. 7). Dr. Pradhan became a regular churchgoer and, invited to people's homes for coffee after church, was asked about his religion. He used to explain that his parents respected Hindu rituals, but then he stopped doing this because it took him too much time. His Dutch hosts always wanted to know what he *believed*—an exotic question to which he did not have a direct answer. "Everybody over here talks about believing, believing, believing," he said, bewildered. "Where I come from, what counts is the ritual, in which only the priest and the head of the family participate. The others watch and make their offerings. Over here so much is *mandatory*. Hindus will never ask 'Do you believe in God?' Of course one should believe, but the important thing is what one *does*." [51] One recognizes the dilemma of Truth versus Virtue. Indian philosophy also stresses the priority of ethical principles (Sinha, 1992).

The difference between the Hindu and the Chinese culture countries is that Hinduism is more spiritual: Its aim is to attain a detached attitude toward life. "The archetypal Westerner resolves the contradiction between the Will's demand for shelter and the environmental obstacle of a dilapidated house by completely demolishing the house and building a new one. The Chinese will repair the old house, and the Indian will attempt to extinguish the desire for housing" (Alitto, 1986, p. 83, after Liang Shu-ming's *Eastern and Western Cultures,* 1922). But like other people of the East, most Indians have kept matter and spirit integrated. Even more than the Chinese, however, the Indians have been better able to show their pragmatic side when living overseas than at home.[52]

From the Muslim countries covered by the CVS study, Bangladesh scored 40 and Pakistan 0 on LTO. Contrary to East Asia, many countries with dominant Muslim traditions are still caught in a definition of Truth that hinders their coping with modernity. Muslim countries that have temporarily collected enormous riches from their oil resources have hardly adapted better to the modern world than those that have remained poor. The oil benefits may have been a liability rather than an asset. None of the Asian Dragons had any natural resources worth mentioning aside from the mental software of their populations.

There was a period in history from about the 9th to the 14th century A.D. when the Muslim world was not only militarily but also scientifically advanced while Christian Europe was backward. With the Renaissance and the Reformation, Christian countries entered the road toward modernization, whereas the world of Islam withdrew into traditionalism. Contrary to what happened in East

Asia, many opinion leaders in the Muslim world seem to experience modern technology and Western ideas as threats rather than as opportunities. The concern for Truth that Muslim cultures share with the Christians can be seen as a competitive disadvantage versus the Dragons, which search primarily for Virtue.

African Values: A New Dimension?

Africa, and particularly Africa south of the Sahara, is a development economist's headache. In the 1997 *World Development Report,* 9 out of the 10 poorest countries were African (World Bank, 1997).[53] The example of Bond's Chinese Value Survey led me to suggest a similar exercise for Africa: Ask Africans to develop a values questionnaire, administer this in both African and non-African countries, and see whether any new dimension emerges that might explain why Western recipes for development don't seem to work in Africa. The execution of this project started after my retirement from the university, under the leadership of Niels Noorderhaven, my successor as director of IRIC. The results of the first, pilot phase were published in Noorderhaven and Tidjani (1998). African scientists in Africa and African students abroad were asked to suggest value survey items. Through a "Delphi" approach the first results were anonymously fed back to the contributors, and their comments were incorporated. More than 100 draft items were collected; these were reduced to 82 by the elimination of overlaps. The draft questionnaire, in an English or a French version, was then administered to samples of male and female students in Cameroon, Ghana, Senegal, Tanzania, and Zimbabwe; to white students in South Africa; and to students outside Africa in Belgium, Germany, Great Britain, Guyana, Hong Kong, Malaysia, the Netherlands, and the United States—a total of 1,100 respondents in 14 countries.

An ecological factor analysis produced six factors. I correlated the country scores on these factors with the four IBM dimensions, 1997 GNP/capita, and LTO, the latter across 10 countries for which data were available. The first factor had its most significant correlation with IDV,[54] the second with LTO, the fourth with PDI, the fifth with MAS, and the sixth with UAI. This perfect replication of the existing model did not mean that the interpretation of the relationship of the new items to the existing dimensions was always obvious; we met a similar situation for the Chinese Value Survey. The fourth factor correlated with none of the existing indexes; it opposed French-speaking to English-speaking African countries, at least partly because of translation errors between the two versions of the questionnaire. It was no serious candidate for a new, African-inspired, cultural dimension.

The second factor, which correlated with LTO ($r = -.95$*** across 10 cases), was called "wisdom," and the country scores were composed from the following items: "It is important to show hospitality to strangers"; "Wisdom is more important than knowledge"; "Wisdom comes from experience and time, not from education"; and "It is better to discuss a decision than to impose a decision." These statements proved fiercely contrary to the high-LTO mind-set.[55] This factor opposed the African to the Asian countries and thus did provide a possible explanation for their differences in development rate. Attributed wisdom that is not based on knowledge and education is a dubious foundation for the development of a country.[56]

The Future of Long-Term Orientation

The future of short- and long-term orientation is difficult to predict. Will Asian cultures with increasing affluence become more short-term oriented? Will the necessity for an increasing world population to survive in a world with limited resources foster more long-term orientation? Confucius's answer to Duke Ching, "Good government consists in being sparing with resources," will become even more relevant in the future than it was 2,500 years ago.

Notes

1. My warmest thanks to Michael Harris Bond, who commented on an earlier version of this chapter.

2. We were not the only ones to worry. Adler, Campbell, and Laurent (1989) expressed similar doubts after having administered Laurent's management questionnaire to more than 100 Chinese managers: "Whereas this research study was originally designed to advance our understanding of Chinese managerial behavior, it in fact led us to new understandings of the ways in which we must question the research process itself" (p. 72).

3. The 20 countries were those listed in Exhibit 7.1. Nigeria (NIG) has been matched with IBM West Africa (WAF) and Zimbabwe (ZIM) with IBM East Africa (EAF).

4. An example is the negative ecological correlation between the answers on questions A54 and B56; see Chapter 3.

5. For the factor loadings, see Chinese Culture Connection (1987, tab. 2).

6. A similar conclusion can be drawn from a study by Boski, Van de Vijver, Hurme, and Miluska (1999). To female and male students in four countries, they showed video clips showing various examples of cour-

teous behavior by Polish men toward Polish women and asked for the students' approval of such behavior. Approval rates were higher in Poland (estimated MAS 64; see Appendix A5.3) and the United States (MAS 62) than in Finland (MAS 26) and the Netherlands (MAS 14).

7. See Kelen (1971/1983).

8. In all of Asia a form of "face" is a central concept, but its precise nature and implications vary from country to country (Redding & Ng, 1982; Tsai, 1996).

9. This observation comes from a personal communication that I had with a Chinese student.

10. LTO = 50 × F + 50, in which F is the factor score.

11. Yeh and Lawrence (1995) tried to prove that long-term orientation and individualism are one and the same thing by arbitrarily excluding the data from Zimbabwe, Nigeria, and Pakistan. By eliminating cases that don't suit the argument, one can, of course, prove almost anything.

12. See Ralston, Gustafson, Elsass, Cheung, and Terpstra (1992) and Ralston, Gustafson, Cheung, and Terpstra (1993).

13. Product-moment correlation $r = -.64$**; after standardization across the 4 questions, $r = -.86$***.

14. All five indexes are available for BRA, CAN, GBR, GER, IND, JPN, KOR, NET, NIG (for WAF), SWE, and USA. Only LTO scores are available for CHI and POL.

15. Across the 11 countries for which IBM indexes were also available—that is, excluding China—the first correlation of question 232 was with 1990 GNP/capita (positively, so wealthier countries more thrifty!), but as Exhibit 7.2 shows, even without the extreme score of China there was still a strong second-order contribution of LTO. I have also tested the effect of standardizing the scores across the 11 items in the block, but this did not noticeably affect the correlations.

16. In this case the correlations are based on scores after standardization across the six items, questions 4 to 9. Each item was separately scored on a 4-point "importance" scale, and, as we have seen in Chapter 2, such scales are very sensitive to acquiescence.

17. The business leaders were from HOK, JPN, KOR, SIN, TAI, and THA.

18. These countries were AUL, CHI, GER, HOK, IND, JPN, KOR, NET, NIG, PAK, SIN, and USA.

19. Read used data from world tables published by Johns Hopkins University Press in 1992. In an article written in 1989, Leff and Sato (1993) did not find any correlations between any of my five dimensions and savings data on a tape from the International Monetary Fund.

20. In the early 1990s, U.S. President Bush sent a mission to Japan to try to convince the Japanese to spend more, in order to redress the skewed balance of payments between the two countries.

21. This quote comes from an article by Dutch journalist Ben Knapen in *NRC Handelsblad* (February 9, 1989). I have back-translated it from the Dutch.

22. Rho = .48** across 23 countries; see Exhibit 4.12.

23. These 10 countries were AUL, BRA, CAN, GBR, GER, JPN, NET, NZL, SWE, and USA.

24. Read's (1993) MPS values are 6 for Australia, 25 for Israel, and 47 for Thailand, which is the closest proxy for the Sino-Vietnamese I can find. Hill and Romm (1996, pp. 25 ff.) themselves relate the differences they found to power distance and individualism/collectivism, but I believe the link with long-term orientation is more revealing.

25. The 11 countries were AUL, BRA, GBR, HOK, IND, JPN, MEX, PAK, PHI, THA, and USA.

26. Surprisingly, Levine, Sato, Hashimoto, and Verma (1995) report a rho = −.74* correlation across eight countries between agreement with this item and actual divorce rates, showing that those agreeing refer to a relatively rare occurrence.

27. LTO scores were available for seven of the eight countries; I assumed a low LTO value for the eighth country, Indonesia.

28. A Chinese student spontaneously interpreted "having a sense of shame" as humility: "Without a sense of humility we become worse than an animal" (personal communication).

29. The countries for which LTO scores were available were AUL, BRA, CAN, GBR, GER, IND, JPN, KOR, PHI, SIN, and USA.

30. The statistical section of Chapter 4 showed the results of a factor analysis of the matrix of 17 standardized goals (variables) for 13 countries (cases). Three factors explained 63% of the variance. After varimax rotation the first factor correlated primarily with LTO ($r =$ .56*, no significant second-order correlations). Another factor correlated with UAI. The LTO factor opposed the satisfaction of the four goals of intellectual life, correcting social injustice, daily human relations, and pleasant community (numbers 13, 8, 16, and 9) to three others: live mentally fulfilled, have interethnic friends, and be concerned about world peace (numbers 4, 17, and 11). I find the correlations of LTO with the separate goals easier to explain than the correlation with the LTO factor.

31. The 10 countries were CAN, GER, IND, KOR, NZL, PAK, POL, USA, Wales (for GBR), and Zimbabwe (for EAF).

32. Chinese parents do not tolerate self-assertion (Bond & Wang, 1983, p. 60).

33. "I have a feeling that if I have to tell my son about all the virtues and so on it becomes hypocritical. So a lot of these are implied, and a matter of leading by example" (from an interview with an overseas Chinese entrepreneur by Redding, 1990, p. 187).

34. "Do not tell me that Mr. Liang has not heard of those many kinds of hostility and enmity [that exist], such as brothers fighting over property inheritance or friends breaking up [because of] calculating [self-interest]. Do not tell me that Mr. Liang does not know about the jealousy, the secret plots, and the many kinds of misery almost universally present in family life?" (Yen Chi-

Cheng, in a review of Liang Shu-ming's *Eastern and Western Cultures*, 1922; quoted in Alitto, 1986, p. 131).

35. Yates and Lee (1996, p. 344) found that Taiwanese Chinese had more trouble than Americans in generating counterarguments against the correctness of their own answers. However, Japanese produced more counterarguments than Americans in this case. This may be related to the strong uncertainty avoidance I found in the Japanese culture (Chapter 4).

36. On Taoism, see Worm (1997, p. 52).

37. Ruth Benedict (1946/1974) has remarked that in Japan the flesh and the spirit can be combined: "It is a part of wisdom to enjoy the pleasures of the senses. The one condition is that they be sacrificed to the serious duties of life" (p. 238).

38. This observation has been made by Carr, Munro, and Bishop (1996), who conclude that in attitude assessment, the use of "Likert scales," which are based on the assumption that respondents want to create consistency among their cognitions, may be invalid in non-Western cultures. A lower need for cognitive consistency means that "cognitive dissonance" (Festinger, 1957) is less of a problem in these cultures.

39. In a personal communication, a Chinese student told me: "The biggest difference between the Chinese and the Western society is that the Western society worships the hero and the Chinese worship the saint. If one is good in doing one thing, one can be a hero. To be a saint, you have to be good in everything."

40. Stevenson and Lee (1996, p. 136) drew the same conclusion from other research.

41. The "hard work" argument may apply in the case of Singapore eighth graders, who were at the top in both math and science. According to Wu (1980), Singapore Chinese children were (are?) taught that industriousness is good and play is bad. Caplan, Choy, and Whitmore (1992) reviewed the academic achievement of Vietnamese "boat people" refugees in the U.S. school system. They were found to work very hard, and they did well overall, but again exceptionally well in mathematics.

42. See Liu (1986, p. 85). For the distinction between formal problems and open problems, see G. J. Hofstede (1995).

43. In view of the high correlation between LTO and math performance, I have checked whether math performance would be a better predictor of economic growth than LTO (see later in this chapter). This, however, was not the case. Across the 13 countries involved, LTO correlated with economic growth over 1985-95 with $r =$ .65**, math ranking with $r = -.56*$.

44. The discussion in this subsection is based on Hofstede and Bond (1988).

45. In a research note, Franke, Hofstede, and Bond (1991) published results of stepwise regressions for 1965-80 and 1980-87 economic growth, both for 18 countries (excluding Africa) and for 20 countries (including Africa). We found for these periods and country groupings a positive contribution of LTO in all cases and a negative contribution of IDV in most cases. In all

cases, the cultural variables explained more than 50% of the variance in economic growth.

46. Hicks and Redding (1983a, 1983b) made this point; they also showed that in 1966 the World Bank economists Chenery and Strout did not even mention Hong Kong and Singapore in their statistics because these places were considered insignificant.

47. Colombia's GNP/capita was U.S.$280 in 1965 and $1,240 in 1987. In South Korea, the figures were $150 in 1965 and $2,690 in 1987 (World Bank, 1989).

48. Gray (1996) has argued for policy as the intervening variable between culture and economic performance.

49. See also Bond (1988, pp. 204-207) and Dunphy and Shi (1989, p. 194)

50. Liang Shu-ming defended the Confucian values against Mao (see Alitto, 1986, p. 217).

51. These quotes are from an article by Dutch journalist Herman Vuijsje in *NRC Handelsblad* (April 16, 1988). The translations are mine.

52. Tayeb (1996) has suggested that the backlog of India versus the East Asian Tigers may be explained by India's ineffective educational system and protectionist industrial and economic policies. Blaming the institutions begs the question why other scions of the same colonial stem were more successful. A cultural explanation could be that India, if we take its poverty into account, has a much more individualist culture (IDV 48) than do the Tigers (from IDV 18 in South Korea to 25 in Hong Kong), which, in addition to its size, has made it less manageable.

53. These countries were Mozambique, Ethiopia, Tanzania, Burundi, Malawi, Chad, Rwanda, Sierra Leone, and Niger, in this order from below. Non-African Nepal came in ninth position.

54. Noorderhaven and Tidjani (1998) split the first factor further through a secondary factor analysis; it divided into three components, of which two had their strongest correlation with IDV and one with 1997 GNP/capita.

55. In the negative correlation the low score from Hong Kong was crucial. However, Malaysia, for which no LTO score was available, scored even lower on this factor. With estimated LTO values for the missing countries Belgium (38), Guyana (10), Malaysia (40), and South African whites (30), the correlation remained highly significant, $r = -.62**$.

56. The Western countries also scored fairly high on this factor, some as high as African countries, but they were already developed and may have had different associations with the word *wisdom*.

8

■

Cultures in Organizations

Summary of This Chapter

This chapter is divided into two main parts. The first integrates conclusions from Chapters 3-7 about cross-national differences in the functioning of organizations and of the people in them. It shows strong evidence that global solutions to organization and management problems do not exist. Not only organizations are bound by national cultures, so are the theories that have been developed to explain and direct their functioning; theories betray the nationalities of their authors, and their validity may stop at national borders (if not before). The first part of the chapter also summarizes the cultural side of various aspects of management: planning, control, and accounting; corporate governance; motivation and compensation; leadership and the empowerment of subordinates; management development as well as organization development; and performance appraisal plus management by objectives.

The second part of the chapter deals not with *national* but with *organizational* cultures—that is, the differences in collective mental programming found among people from different organizations, or parts thereof, within the same national context. Organizational cultures were the object of a separate study, the 1985-86 IRIC project, covering 20 organizational units in Denmark and the Netherlands. Whereas national cultures differed primarily in their values, organizational cultures turned out to differ mainly in their practices. A major part of the differences among the 20 units could be explained by six factors representing six independent dimensions of perceived practices. These related to established concepts from organizational sociology and management theory.

Scores of the units on the six dimensions were validated against a variety of task, structural, and control system characteristics, but they also showed unique features based on the organizations' histories and leadership. In a subsequent study in one large insurance company, the same measures allowed identification of the major subcultures within the organization. These research experiences led to a critical analysis of the usefulness of the "organizational culture" construct for management. The research approach developed for the IRIC project can be generalized to organizations elsewhere; the conclusions and the six dimensions can only partly be generalized. An extension of the IRIC project explored why individuals within organizations differed in their perceptions of the same organizational reality. Demographic characteristics such as age, education, and gender played roles, but so did personality: Surprisingly, the individual variance within the IRIC data reproduced the "Big Five" model of personality structure. This is used as a strong argument for matching one's research purposes with the appropriate level of analysis of one's data. The chapter closes with speculations about possible dimensions of *occupational* cultures.

Organizations and National Cultures

There Are No Universal Solutions to Organization and Management Problems

In 1980, I published an article in the U.S. journal *Organizational Dynamics* titled "Motivation,

Leadership and Organization: Do American Theories Apply Abroad?" (Hofstede, 1980b). It had a stormy history; after the untimely demise of the editor who had invited and accepted it, the article was at first refused and then published with hesitation by his successor. The new editor invited a U.S. and an Australian colleague to write assuaging comments, which were published in a later issue along with my reply.[1] The article raised an upheaval far beyond what I had expected; in it I argued, with empirical support, that generally accepted U.S. theories such as those of Maslow, Herzberg, McClelland, Vroom, McGregor, Likert, Blake and Mouton, might not apply, or only very partially apply, outside the borders of their country of origin—assuming they did apply within those borders. Among the requests for reprints of the article, by the way, a larger number were from Canada than from the United States itself.

After the discoveries that employees are human (the U.S. human relations school and Mayo, 1933) and that managers are human (Simon's [1945/1976] "bounded rationality" and Cyert & March's [1963] "behavioral theory of the firm"), the time had come to see that management scientists, theorists, and writers are human, too: They grew up in particular societies in particular periods, and their ideas cannot but reflect the constraints of the environments they have known. The success of businesses in East Asian countries that very evidently did not follow most of the generally accepted U.S. theories made this conclusion inevitable.[2]

My doubts about the exportability of American theories have since become respectable; my article in *Organizational Dynamics* has been included in many readers for American management students. Others have shown the limits of theories developed in one country in their own excellent ways. U.S. ethnopsychologist Edward C. Stewart (1985) has demythologized theories of rational decision making: "North American decision-makers do not observe rational decision-making in their own work and lives, as a general rule, but they restructure past events according to a decision-making model. . . . Thus, in the United States rational decision-making is a myth" (p. 209). Indian/U.S. business professor Uma Sekaran has shown that a universally applicable definition of organizational effectiveness and a universal prescription for its attainment do not exist (Sekaran & Snodgrass, 1989). U.S. business historian Robert Locke (1996) has described how the successful industrialization of the United States took place in a very distinct historical context and how it owes much more to external circumstances than to the quality of the management principles used.

The idea that the validity of a theory is constrained by nationality was more obvious in Eu-rope, with all its borders, than in a huge, borderless country like the United States. In Europe the cultural relativity of the laws that govern human behavior had been recognized as early as the 16th century in the skepticism of Michel de Montaigne (1533-92). The quote from Pascal (1623-62) at the beginning of this book, "There are truths on this side of the Pyrenees that are falsehoods on the other" (the Pyrenees being the border mountains between France and Spain), was in fact based on a statement made by Montaigne.[3]

The preceding chapters have demonstrated five ways in which national cultures can be distinguished; all of these have implications for organization and management processes. Theories, models, and practices are basically culture specific; they may apply across borders, but this should always be proven. The naive assumption that management ideas are universal is not only found in popular literature: In scholarly journals—even in those explicitly addressing an international readership—the silent assumption of universal validity of culturally restricted findings is frequent. Articles in such journals often do not even mention the country in which the data were collected (which usually is the United States, as can be concluded from the affiliations of the authors). As a matter of scientific etiquette, I suggest that articles written for an international public should always mention the countries—and the time periods—in which the data were collected.

Ideas and theories about management and organization are often exported to other countries without regard for the values context in which these ideas were developed. Fad-conscious publishers and gullible readers in those other countries encourage such exports. The economic success of the United States in the decades before and after World War II led some people in other parts of the world to believe that U.S. ideas about management must be superior and therefore should be copied. They forgot to ask about the kind of society in which these ideas were developed and applied—*if* they were really applied as the books and articles claimed. G. B. Shaw is credited with the aphorism "He who can, does. He who cannot, teaches";[4] this criticism fits the management profession, where the world of the practitioners and the world of those who write the books are often quite separate.

A similar naïveté with regard to foreign solutions is often found among journalists and political writers, whether they want to export German-type *Mitbestimmung* to Britain, Swedish job reform to Italy, or U.S. private enterprise to Russia. There exists a widespread tendency to underestimate the force of deeply rooted societal norms for arriving at political or organizational solutions that will work and be stable. But, to rephrase a famous dictum, there is nothing as impractical as a bad theory.[5]

U.S. business professor and consultant Michael Porter (1990) analyzed why some nations succeeded much better than others in the international competition of the latter part of the 20th century. His "diamond" of the determinants of national advantage recognized four attributes: (1) factor conditions, (2) demand conditions, (3) related and supporting industries, and (4) firm strategy, structure, and rivalry. Porter's extensive documentation of these attributes for a number of industrial and industrializing countries stops short of the issue of *why* some countries got better diamonds than others. Porter still assumes universal applicability of the ethnocentric laws of competitive markets.[6] Fukuyama (1995) recognizes the role played by "social capital" in the differential development of countries, but about the sources of differences in social capital he is as vague as Porter.[7] The analysis of mental programming starts explaining national differences at the point where these popular authors leave off.

The lack of universal solutions to management and organization problems does not mean that countries cannot learn from one another: On the contrary, looking across the border is one of the most effective ways of getting new ideas for management, organization, or politics. But transfer of these ideas across borders calls for prudence and judgment.

The Functioning of Organizations

Organizations are symbolic entities; they function according to implicit models in the minds of their members, and these models are culturally determined.[8] The crucial dimensions are power distance and uncertainty avoidance; power distance is involved in answering the question of who decides what, and uncertainty avoidance is involved in answering the question how one can assure that what should be done will be done. So the UAI × PDI plot in Exhibit 4.2 can serve as a map for the way organizations function. Exhibit 8.1 describes the differences in the functioning of organizations among the quadrants of Exhibit 4.2.

Chapters 2, 3, and 4 associated power distance and uncertainty avoidance with the two main dimensions of organization structure revealed by the Aston studies in Great Britain: power distance with "concentration of authority" (centralization) and uncertainty avoidance with "structuring of activities" (formalization). Pugh (1976, p. 70) used a fourfold typology for describing organizations with high and low concentrations of authority and high and low structuring of activities. In Exhibit 8.1, Pugh's types are put in their corresponding quadrants. The distinctions apply *cet-*

eris paribus (task and size of organization, for example, being equal). In the full bureaucracy, the relationships both among people and between people and the work processes tend to be rigidly prescribed, either in formal rules and laws or in traditions. In the personnel bureaucracy, relationships among people are prescribed but not the work processes; in the work-flow bureaucracy, the opposite is the case. Finally, in the implicitly structured organizations, neither the relationships among people nor those between people and the work processes are strictly prescribed.

The "implicit models" in Exhibit 8.1 are based on discussions I had at INSEAD business school, Fontainebleau, France, with my then colleague Owen J. Stevens. The largest national groups of MBA students at INSEAD were French, German, and British. Stevens, himself an American, asked students of the three nationalities to analyze individually the same case study of an organizational conflict. The majority of the French tended to resolve the problem by referring to the hierarchy; the British, through horizontal negotiation; and the Germans, through the establishment of procedures. Stevens identified the implicit model of a well-functioning organization for the French as a pyramid, that for the British as a (village) market, and that for the Germans as a well-oiled machine. This fits the types of full bureaucracy, implicitly structured organizations, and work-flow bureaucracy.[9] Stevens did not have Asian students available, but, based on the work of Kumar and Singh (1976) on Indian managers, I chose the "family" as the implicit model for an Indian organization. The "personnel bureaucracy" means that relationships among people are strictly determined by the hierarchical framework, but that the work flow is much less codified.[10] In China, which I located in the same first quadrant, the main continuous principle of administration has been described as "government of man," in contrast to the Western idea of "government by law" (Chang, 1976; see also Chapter 7).[11]

A classic joke puts it that in Britain everything is permitted except that which is forbidden; in Germany everything is forbidden except that which is permitted; and in France everything is permitted, even that which is forbidden. The German word *verboten* has even found its way into the American language.

The surreptitious way in which societal norms affect organizational functioning is shown by the following small case: IBM's policies prescribed that salary increase proposals should be initiated by the employee's direct superior. In IBM France this policy was interpreted in such a way that the superior's superior's superior—three levels above the employee—was the one who initiated salary proposals. This way of working was seen as natural by both superiors and subordinates in France.

The industrial relations structures (labor-management relations) of France, Germany, and Great Britain support the typology of Exhibit 8.1. The German labor unions are the most orderly and united; they do not like to strike (uncertainty avoidance), but they have achieved considerable formal codetermination (small power distance). The British unions are disorderly and resist codifying industrial relations rules (low uncertainty avoidance). The French unions are politically oriented, reasonably orderly (predictable strike behavior), and in majority not very interested in formal codetermination.

Maurice, Sorge, and Warner (1980), in a comparison of France, Germany, and Great Britain, analyzed the mechanisms through which national cultures affected technologically similar organizations. Each of the three countries showed its own specific pattern on the following three blocks of variables:

1. *The configuration of the organization:* The kind of categories the labor force is broken into varied from one country to the next, as well as the relative size of the categories when these were made comparable.

2. *Work structuring and coordination:* The joining of individual tasks into work positions and the way in which work is coordinated.

3. *The qualification and career system:* Schooling, on-the-job training, and the way individuals progress in typical careers.

The three blocks are interrelated; they form integrated systems of which the elements reinforce one another. It becomes evident that we cannot take just one element out of the whole and change it.

The UAI × PDI matrix in Exhibit 8.1 can also be used for a cultural refinement of Henry Mintzberg's (1983) fivefold classification of organization structures. Mintzberg sees organizations in general as containing up to five distinct parts: (1) the operating core (the people who do the work), (2) the strategic apex (the top management), (3) the middle line (the hierarchy in between), (4) the technostructure (people in staff roles supplying ideas), and (5) the support staff (people in staff roles supplying services). Organizations in general use one or more of five mechanisms for coordinating activities: (1) mutual adjustment (of people through informal communication), (2) direct supervision (by a hierarchical superior), (3) standardizing of work processes (specifying the contents of work), (4) standardizing of outputs (specifying the desired results), and (5) standardizing of skills (specifying the training

required to perform the work). Finally, most organizations show one of five typical configurations: (1) the simple structure (in this case, the key part is the strategic apex, and the coordinating mechanism is direct supervision), (2) the machine bureaucracy (key part, the technostructure; coordinating mechanism, standardizing of work processes), (3) the professional bureaucracy (key part, the operating core; coordinating mechanism, standardizing of skills), (4) the divisionalized form (key part, the middle line; coordinating mechanism, standardizing of outputs), and (5) the adhocracy (key part, the support staff, sometimes with the operating core; coordinating mechanism, mutual adjustment).

A link between Mintzberg's five configurations and the quadrants of the UAI × PDI matrix is shown in Exhibit 8.2.[12] Mintzberg's machine bureaucracy corresponds not with Stevens's "machine" but with his "pyramid." [13] In order to avoid confusion, I have in Exhibit 8.2 renamed it *full bureaucracy*. This is the term used for the same configuration in the Aston studies. The adhocracy corresponds with the "village market" implicit organization model; the professional bureaucracy corresponds with the "well-oiled machine" model; the full (machine) bureaucracy, with the "pyramid" model; the simple structure, with the "family" model; and the divisionalized form takes a middle position on both culture dimensions, containing elements of all four models. A typical country near the center of the diagram in Exhibit 8.2 is the United States, where the divisionalized form has been developed and enjoys great popularity.

Exhibit 8.2 explains a number of national characteristics known from the professional and anecdotal literature about organizations; these are especially clear in the "preferred coordination mechanisms." *Mutual adjustment* fits the market model of organizations and the stress on ad hoc negotiation in the Anglo countries. *Standardization of skills* explains the traditional emphasis in countries like Germany and Switzerland on the professional qualification of workers and the high status in these countries of apprentice systems. *Standardization of work processes* fits the French concept of bureaucracy as it is pictured, for example, by Michel Crozier in his classic *The Bureaucratic Phenomenon* (1964a). *Direct supervision* corresponds to what we know about Chinese organizations, also outside mainland China, which emphasize coordination through personal intervention of the owner and his relatives. *Standardization of outputs* is very much the preferred philosophy in the United States; it is even tried in cases where outputs are difficult to assess.[14]

Stressing the cultural element in organizational structure and functioning does not represent an attempt to reduce all differences among organiza-

Exhibit 8.1. Connotations of the UAI × PDI Matrix for the Functioning of Organizations

4	1
Small power distance	Large power distance
Weak uncertainty avoidance	Weak uncertainty avoidance
Countries: Anglo, Scandinavian, Netherlands	Countries: China, India
Organization type: implicitly structured	Organization type: personnel bureaucracy
Implicit model of organization: *market*	Implicit model of organization: *family*
3	2
Small power distance	Large power distance
Strong uncertainty avoidance	Strong uncertainty avoidance
Countries: German-speaking, Finland, Israel	Countries: Latin, Mediterranean, Islamic, Japan, some other Asian
Organization type: work-flow bureaucracy	Organization type: full bureaucracy
Implicit model of organization: *well-oiled machine*	Implicit model of organization: *pyramid*

NOTE: For the Aston types of organizations, see Pugh (1976, p. 70).

Exhibit 8.2. Mintzberg's Preferred Configurations of Organizations Projected on the UAI × PDI Matrix, With a Typical Country for Each Configuration

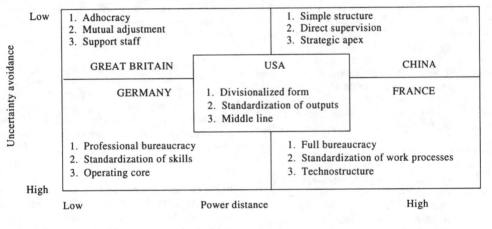

NOTE: 1 = preferred configuration; 2 = preferred coordination mechanism; 3 = key part of organization.

tions to culture. It is only—and I believe this is necessary—a warning that the structure and functioning of organizations are not determined by a universal rationality. Making shoes, producing electricity, or treating the sick in Germany as opposed to France calls for organizational structures and processes that differ in several respects. As d'Iribarne (1989) demonstrated in his comparison of aluminum production plants in France, the Netherlands, and the United States (see Chapter 3), technology contributes to the shaping of organizations, but it is insufficient for explaining

how they work. There is no "one best way" that can be deduced from technical-economical logic.[15]

A somewhat different fivefold typology has been proposed by Dutch consultant Huib Wursten. Maintaining the pyramid, machine, and family models, he split the market model into "competition" and "network" in order to accommodate the mas/fem difference between the Anglo world and the Nordic countries plus the Netherlands. This distinction is particularly relevant in the latter countries, which have been much exposed to

Anglo models at conflict with the central feminine values in the Nordic/Dutch cultures.

Chapters 3 and 4 gave several examples of studies comparing perceptions of the functioning of organizations that supported the power distance and uncertainty avoidance distinctions (e.g., Peterson et al., 1995, for PDI; Shane, Venkataraman, & Macmillan, 1995, for UAI). The results of an elegant little study that did both at the same time have been published by Offermann and Hellmann (1997). These researchers analyzed data from 425 mid-level managers from 39 different nationalities who worked for the same multinational organization. In the context of a management training program, four subordinates from each of these managers had completed questionnaires describing their perceptions of their bosses' behavior. The results, scored on five scales, were fed back to the managers as input to their training. Across the 19 countries with at least four respondents each, PDI was significantly and negatively correlated with the managers' scores on four of the scales: approachability ($r = -.54$**), team building ($r = -.52$*), delegation ($r = -.44$*), and communication ($r = -.41$*).[16] UAI was significantly and positively correlated with the managers' score for control ($r = .61$**). Control included time emphasis, attention to details, and goal pressure. Although these results validated the two dimensions, they should of course not be used for judging the leadership effectiveness of the persons involved. The questionnaire used was ethnocentric: It was made in the United States according to dominant U.S. criteria concerning what is important in a leader; both its content and its meaning for leadership effectiveness are culture-bound.[17]

Another study attempting to validate several dimensions at the same time was conducted by Van Oudenhoven (2001). Respondents were approximately 70 advanced business administration students from each of 10 countries.[18] They were asked to describe one particular local company using a number of freely chosen adjectives. A content analysis identified three bipolar themes in the adjectives that correlated with the countries' IBM indexes: bureaucracy (from weak to strong) with PDI ($r = .66$*) and UAI ($r = .63$*), teamwork to individual work with IDV ($r = .47, p < .10$), and work ambiance (friendly to hostile) with MAS ($r = .49, p < .10$).[19]

Culture and Organization Theories: Nationality Constrains Rationality

The founding parents of the theory of modern organizations, such as Tolstoy (1828-1910), Fayol (1841-1925), Taylor (1856-1915), Weber (1864-1920), and Follett (1868-1933), and most of their successors up to the present day have not followed Montaigne's relativism; they were typically looking for universal principles.[20] The paradox is that in their theories the influence of their own cultural environment is clearly recognizable. Not only organizations are culture-bound; theories about organizations are equally culture-bound. The authors of these theories are themselves children of their cultures; they grew up in families, went to schools, worked for employers. Their experiences represent the material on which their thinking and writing is based. Scholars are as perfectly human and as culturally biased as other mortals.

For each of the four corners of Exhibit 8.1, I selected a classical author who described organizations in terms of the model belonging to his corner of the diagram: the pyramid, the machine, the market, or the family. The four are approximate contemporaries; all were born in the mid-19th century.

Henri Fayol (1841-1925) was a French engineer whose management career culminated in the position of *président-directeur-général* of a mining company. After his retirement, he formulated his experiences into a pioneering text on organization: *Administration industrielle et générale*. On the issue of the exercise of authority, Fayol (1915/1970) wrote:

> We distinguish in a manager his *statutory* authority which is in the office, and his *personal* authority which consists of his intelligence, his knowledge, his experience, his moral value, his leadership, his service record, etc. For a good manager, personal authority is the indispensable complement to statutory authority. (p. 21; my translation)

In Fayol's conception the authority is both in the person *and* in the rules (the statute). We recognize the model of the organization as a pyramid of people with both personal power *and* formal rules as principles of coordination.

Max Weber (1864-1920) was a German academic with university training in law and some years' experience as a civil servant. He became a professor of economics and a founder of German sociology. Weber (1930/1976) quoted a 17th-century Puritan Protestant Christian textbook about "the sinfulness of the belief in authority, which is only permissible in the form of an impersonal authority" (p. 224). In his own design for an organization, Weber described the *bureaucracy*. The word was originally a joke, a classic Greek ending grafted onto a modern French stem. Nowadays it has a distinctly negative connotation, but to Weber it represented the ideal type for any large organization. About the authority in a bureaucracy, Weber wrote:

The authority to give the commands required for the discharge of (the assigned) duties should be exercised in a stable way. It is strictly delimited by rules concerning the coercive means . . . which may be placed at the disposal of officials. (in Gerth & Mills, 1948/1970, p. 196)

In Weber's conception, the real authority is in the rules. The power of the "officials" is strictly delimited by these rules. We recognize the model of the organization as a well-oiled machine that runs according to the rules.

Frederick Winslow Taylor (1856-1915) was an American engineer who, contrary to Fayol, had started his career in industry as a worker. He attained his academic qualifications through evening studies. From chief engineer in a steel company he became one of the first management consultants. Taylor was not really concerned with the issue of authority at all; his focus was on efficiency. He proposed to split the task of the first-line boss into eight specializations, each exercised by a different person. Thus a worker would have eight bosses, each with a different competence. This part of Taylor's ideas was never completely implemented, although we find elements of it in the matrix organization model. Taylor's book *Shop Management* (1903) appeared in a French translation in 1913, and Fayol read it and devoted six full pages in his own 1915 book to Taylor's ideas. Fayol showed himself generally impressed but shocked by Taylor's "denial of the principle of the Unity of Command" in the case of the eight-boss system. "For my part," Fayol (1915/1970) wrote, "I do not believe that a department could operate in flagrant violation of the Unity of Command principle. Still, Taylor has been a successful manager of large organizations. How can we explain this contradiction?" (p. 85; my translation). Fayol's rhetorical question had been answered by his compatriot Blaise Pascal two and a half centuries before: There are truths in one country that are falsehoods in another.

André Laurent (1978), another of Fayol's compatriots, found French managers in a survey reacting strongly against a suggestion that one employee could report to two different bosses, whereas, for example, Swedish and U.S. managers in the same survey showed fewer misgivings. Matrix organization has never become popular in France as it has in the United States. It is amusing to read Laurent's suggestion that in order to make matrix organizations acceptable in France they should be translated into hierarchical terms—that is, one real boss plus one or more staff experts. Fayol put forward exactly the same solution in his 1915 discussion of the Taylor system; in fact, Fayol wrote that he supposed this was how the Taylor system really worked in Taylor's companies.

Whereas Taylor dealt only implicitly with the exercise of authority in organizations, another American pioneer of organization theory, Mary Parker Follett (1868-1933), did address the issue squarely. She wrote:

How can we avoid the two extremes: Too great bossism in giving orders, and practically no orders given. . . . My solution is to depersonalize the giving of orders, to unite all concerned in a study of the situation, to discover the law of the situation and to obey that. . . . One *person* should not give orders to another *person,* but both should agree to take their orders from the situation.[21]

In the conception of Taylor and Follett, the authority is neither in the person nor in the rules but, as Follett puts it, in the situation. We recognize the model of the organization as a market, in which market conditions dictate what will happen.

Sun Yat-sen (1866-1925) was a scholar from the first quadrant of the UAI × PDI diagram, from China. He received a Western education in Hawaii and Hong Kong and became a political revolutionary. As China started industrialization much later than the West, it has no indigenous theorist of industrial organization contemporary with Fayol, Weber, and Taylor. However, Sun was concerned with organization, albeit political. He wanted to replace the ailing government of the Manchu emperors with a modern Chinese state. He eventually became for a short period the first president of the Chinese Republic. Sun's design for a Chinese form of government represents an integration of Western and traditional Chinese elements. From the West, he introduced the *trias politica:* the executive, legislative, and judicial branches. However, unlike in the West, all three were placed under the authority of the president. He added two more branches, both derived from Chinese tradition and bringing the total up to five: the examination branch (determining access to the civil service) and the control branch, supposed to audit the government.

This remarkable mix of two systems is formally the basis of the government structure of China's dissident province of Taiwan, which has inherited Sun's ideas through the Kuomintang party. It stresses the authority of the president (large power distance): The legislative and judicial powers that in the West are meant to guarantee government by law are made dependent on the ruler and are paralleled by the examination and control powers, which are based on government of man (weak uncertainty avoidance). It is the family model, with the ruler as the country's father; whatever structure there is in this model is based on personal relationships.

Paradoxically, in the other China that expelled the Kuomintang, the People's Republic, the Cultural Revolution experiment can also be interpreted as an attempt to maintain the authority of the ruler (in this case Chairman Mao) while rejecting the authority of the rules, which were felt to suffocate the modernization of the people's minds. The Cultural Revolution in hindsight was a disaster. What passed for modernization may in fact have been a revival of centuries-old unconscious fears.

In the preceding paragraphs I have related the models of organization in different cultures to the theories of the 19th-century founding fathers (including one founding mother) of organization theory. The different models can also be recognized in the dominant theories of the late 20th century.

In the United States in the 1970s and 1980s it became fashionable to look at organizations from a point of view of "transaction costs." Economist Oliver Williamson (1975) opposed "hierarchies" to "markets." The reasoning is that human social life consists of economic transactions between individuals. These individuals will form hierarchical organizations when the cost of the economic transactions (getting information, finding out whom to trust, and the like) is lower in a hierarchy than when all transactions would take place on a free market. What is interesting about this theory from a cultural point of view is that *the market is the point of departure or base model,* and the organization is explained from market failure. A culture that produces such a theory is likely to prefer organizations that internally resemble markets to organizations that internally resemble more structured models, such as pyramids. The ideal principle of control in organizations in the market philosophy is *competition* between individuals.

Williamson's compatriot and colleague William Ouchi (1980) suggested *two* alternatives to markets: "bureaucracies" and "clans." These come close to what I have referred to above as the machine and family models, respectively. Combining Williamson's and Ouchi's ideas, we find all four organizational models described. The market, however, takes a special position as the theory's starting point, and this can be explained by the nationality of the authors.

In the work of both German and French organization theorists markets play a very modest role. German books (e.g., Kieser & Kubicek, 1983) tend to focus on formal systems—on the running of the machine. The ideal principle of control in organizations is a system of *rules* on which everybody can rely. French books stress the exercise of power and sometimes the defenses of the individual against being crushed by the pyramid (Crozier & Friedberg, 1977; Pagès, Bonetti, de Gaulejac, & Descendre, 1979). The principle of control is *hierarchical authority;* there is a system of rules

but, contrary to the German case, the personal authority of the superiors prevails over the rules.[22]

In China in the days of Mao and the Cultural Revolution, neither markets nor rules nor hierarchy but *indoctrination* was the attempted principle of control in organizations, in line with a national tradition that for centuries used comparative examinations as a test of adequate indoctrination. Political developments since 1989 have shown this principle still to be popular with Chinese leaders.

The activity of theorizing is only semirational. "There are large sections of culture that act as a bar to the free exercise of rationality" (Kluckhohn, 1951, p. 91, after E. Sapir). Or, as I would rather put it, there is no such thing as absolute rationality; there are different rationalities colored by different culturally influenced values, and your rationality differs from mine. There is no standard to determine which of the two is more rational. Our culture affects in particular those ideas that are taken for granted without further proof because no one in our environment ever challenges them. Only comparisons among cultures can show that other ideas are possible. It has been said that the last thing the fish will discover is water; it finds out about water only when it has landed on the fishmonger's cart.

Douglas (1973b) collected documentary evidence on the relevance of an "anthropology of everyday knowledge": Our reality is human-made. We also have a natural tendency to choose our environments such that certain of our basic ideas are not challenged. Ideas are entangled with values and interests—a fact that we recognize more easily in others than in ourselves.[23] Ideas and theories become popular or unpopular at certain times not because they are more or less true but because the value systems that support them are activated or suppressed by ecological and institutional developments (more or less in the way pictured by the diagram in Exhibit 1.5). For example, the human relations ideology was developed in the United States in the 1930s as a combined product of traditional American values, labor union expansion, the economic depression, the New Deal, and the bureaucratization of industrial organizations (Bartell, 1976).

Since Montaigne and Pascal, the link between nationality and ways of thinking has been recognized and forgotten again and again.[24] Galtung (1981) distinguished Saxonic, Teutonic, Gallic, and Nipponic "intellectual styles." [25] Fisher (1988), in the context of international relations, spoke of "mindsets," Douglas (1996) of "thought styles." In the same way as certain nations excel in certain sports, nations are associated with disciplines. Psychology, including social psychology, is predominantly a U.S. discipline: rationalist, individualist, masculine.[26] Sociology is predominantly European.[27] Yet a great European sociologist like Pierre Bourdieu, in his insightful analyses of why art, science, and television maintain the norms they do, never explicitly addressed the influence of nationality. In fact, he defended himself fiercely against those who pointed to the Frenchness in his own *habitus* (Bourdieu & Wacquant, 1992, pp. 45, 115). And yet, as Douglas (1996, pp. 30, 112) has noted, Bourdieu's models are very French. Far from invalidating them, in my eyes, recognizing this fact makes them more useful—just as we can use U.S. models better if we realize their Americanness.

In organization theories, I propose, the nationalities of the authors point to implicit paradigms as to what organizations came from, are, and try to achieve.[28] These national paradigms all begin with "In the beginning was . . . ." After God had created men, men made organizations—but what did they make them of? Here are some of the paradigms I observed: In the beginning was . . .

the market	United States
the power	France
order	Germany
efficiency	Poland, Russia
consensus	Netherlands
equality	Nordic countries
systems	Britain
the family	China
Japan	Japan

The "market" paradigm dominates in economics, which has become an American science.[29] As North (1990) observes:

All theorizing in the social sciences builds, implicitly or explicitly, upon conceptions of human behavior. Some of the approaches rest on the expected-utility assumption in economic theory or the extension of that assumption into other social science disciplines, loosely termed rational choice theory. Other approaches raise some quite fundamental questions about the traditional economic approach. Although I know of very few economists who really believe that the behavioral assumptions of economics accurately reflect human behavior, they do (mostly) believe that such assumptions are useful for building models of market behavior in economics and, though less useful, are still the best game in town for studying politics and the other social sciences. (p. 17)

North is one of the rare economists to recognize that "rational choice theory" may not be so rational after all. As I argued in Chapter 1, what one considers rational or irrational is based on cultur-

ally constrained values choices. *Nationality constrains rationality.*

The paradigm difference is beautifully illustrated in a report in the newsletter of the European Group for Organizational Studies (EGOS) on a discussion in Paris between U.S. economist Williamson and two French social scientists, economist Favereau and sociologist Lazega ("Oliver Williamson in Paris," 1994). Williamson defended an "efficiency approach" to the study of organizations, even for the phenomena of power and authority. "I submit that there is less to power than meets the eye," he said. Favereau criticized transaction cost as being too thin a concept to be the basis of a general theory of organization, efficiency as being a weak incentive, and Williamson's notion of power as unilateral, whereas in France power is relational. Lazega also criticized Williamson's "limited conception of power." Williamson, he said, seemed to define power in a purely bilateral way, whereas "sociologists have long shown that power and the ability to put constraints on the behavior of others are also structural or systemic." The discussion had been announced as dealing with a supposed convergence between economics and sociology, but in fact it dealt with a divergence of implicit national paradigms, opposing Williamson's U.S. market to the French power. All the sources Williamson cited were American; all the sources Favereau and Lazega cited were French. But neither side seemed to be aware that the other spoke from a different context, or even that there is such a thing as a national context from which theories are written and criticized.[30]

The different national paradigms about organizations also limit the exportability of "agency theory," another popular theme in U.S. organizational analysis. *Agency* refers to the delegation of discretionary power by a principal to an agent, and since the 1980s the term has in particular been applied to the delegation by owners to managers. Agency theories are based on implicit assumptions about societal order, contractual relationships, and motivation. Such assumptions are bounded by national borders.[31]

Planning, Control, and Accounting

Planning represents an attempt to reduce uncertainty; control implies the exercise of power. Moreover, planning and control are complementary. It should be no surprise, then, that planning and control processes in organizations reflect basic cultural assumptions, and that they are related to the power distance and uncertainty avoidance norms of the dominant national culture. Planning and control systems are more than rational tools; they contain an element of ritual. It is extremely difficult to know how effective planning and control really are. In 1979, the dean of a well-reputed U.S. business school wrote: "Despite all the talk about planning it is still a primitive art. Very few organizations do as much as they claim to do, and few of those who do take planning seriously do it well" (Dill, 1979, p. 148). I doubt that much has changed since. The ritual elements in planning and control defy objective evaluation. There will always be believers and nonbelievers.

This implies that it would be prudent for researchers to be modest in identifying effective and ineffective planning and control systems in other cultures. Chapter 4 referred to the study of top management control in France, Germany, and Great Britain by Horovitz (1980). By the criteria set by the U.S. designers of planning and control systems, British managers did a better job of strategic planning than their German and French counterparts; the latter focused on details and short-term feedback. Yet the national economies of France and Germany did not do worse than those of the United States and Great Britain. The Canadian Henry Mintzberg (1993) has expressed strong skepticism about the effects of strategic planning. Rituals are effective for those who believe in them.

Planning and control systems impose norms on organizations, and it is no wonder that these reflect the more diffuse norms within people's mental programs. As argued above, the dimensions involved will be, in particular, power distance and uncertainty avoidance. Some suggested relationships are as follows:[32]

- Higher PDI supports "political" rather than "strategic" thinking.
- Higher PDI supports personal planning and control rather than impersonal systems. The higher in the hierarchy, the less formal the planning and control.
- Lower-PDI control systems place more trust in subordinates; in higher-PDI cultures such trust is lacking.
- Higher UAI makes it less likely that *strategic* planning activities are practiced, because these may put question marks to the certainties of today.
- Higher UAI supports a need for more detail in planning and more short-term feedback.
- Higher UAI implies leaving planning to specialists.
- Higher UAI implies a more limited view of relevant information.

This last point was illustrated in a study of information seeking by currency traders from more than 3,000 banks in 25 countries in 1993 (Zaheer & Zaheer, 1997). The dependent variable was the number of conversations with the electronic interbank network originating from the banks. The researchers dichotomized their countries into high and low UAI and hypothesized that banks in more uncertainty-avoiding countries would seek more information. In fact, the opposite was the case, and highly significantly so ($p < .0001$). In high-UAI countries new information from the network, which could potentially interfere with set procedures, was less welcome.[33]

An important cultural role in organizations is played by accounting systems and the people who administer them. In Chapter 1, culture was shown to be manifested in the form of symbols, heroes, rituals, and values. Accounting is said to be the language of business—this means that accounting is the handling of *symbols* that have meaning to the initiated in business only. Money is also a symbolic entity; its value and meaning are a matter of convention. Across national cultures, the meaning of money has been related to masculinity (Chapter 6); across occupational cultures, money means something else to accountants than it means, for example, to bankers.

Accountants are unlikely to become *heroes* in organizations themselves, but they have an important role in identifying and anointing heroes elsewhere in the organization, because they determine who are the good and bad guys. Their major device for this purpose is called *accountability:* holding someone personally responsible for results. Accounting systems in high-MAS societies are more likely than those in low-MAS societies to present results in such a way that a responsible manager is pictured as a hero or a bum.

Accounting systems in organizations can also be considered uncertainty-reducing *rituals,* fulfilling a cultural need for certainty, simplicity, and truth in a confusing world, regardless of whether this truth has any objective base. Gambling (1977), a British accountant who became a professor, has written that much of accounting information is after-the-fact justification of decisions that were made for nonlogical reasons in the first place. The main function of accounting information, according to Gambling, is to maintain morale in the face of uncertainty. The accountant "enables a distinctly demoralized modern industrial society to live with itself, by reassuring that its models and data can pass for 'truth' " (p. 150). This, however, will be more so in low-LTO Western countries than in East Asia (Chapter 7). According to a Canadian author: "Accountants typically construct reality in limited and one-sided ways. . . . the idea of objectivity in accounting is largely a myth" (Morgan, 1988, p. 477).

This explains the lack of consensus across different countries on what represents proper accounting methods. For the United States these are collected in the accountant's Holy Book, called the *GAAP Guide: Generally Accepted Accounting Principles*. Being "generally accepted" within a certain population is precisely what makes a ritual a ritual. It does not need any other justification. Once you have agreed on the ritual, a lot of problems become technical again: how to perform the ritual most effectively. Phenomenologically, accounting practice has a lot in common with religious practice (which also serves as an aid to uncertainty avoidance). Cleverley (1971) saw accountants as the "priests" of business. Sometimes we find explicit links between religious and accounting rules, such as in Islam, in the Koranic ban on calculating interest.

My own doctoral research, a field study in five Dutch business companies, dealt with the behavioral consequences of budgeting, and it unwittingly confirmed the ritual nature of budget accounting. In my dissertation, titled *The Game of Budget Control* (Hofstede, 1967), I do not refer to rituals or culture, but I found that budget accounting and control systems had more positive impacts on results if the systems were conceived of as "games." Games in all human societies are very specific forms of rituals, activities carried out for their own sake. Basically, my research showed that the proper ritual use of a system was a prime condition for its impact on results.[34] The technical aspects of a system—the things the professional literature worried most about—did not affect the results very much. The way the game was played gave the system its meaning in the minds of the actors, and this determined the impact. This was a cultural interpretation before *culture* had become a fashionable term in business.[35]

The symbols, heroes, and rituals in accounting rest on underlying *values* (Exhibit 1.4). The less an activity is determined by technical necessity, the more it is ruled by values and thus influenced by cultural differences. Accounting is a field in which the technical imperatives are weak. Historically based conventions play a more important role in it than do laws of nature. So it is logical for the rules of accounting *and* the ways they are used to vary along national cultural lines.

In large power distance countries, accounting systems will more frequently serve to justify the decisions of the top power holders: They are among the power holders' tools to present the desired image, and figures will be twisted to this end.

In strong uncertainty avoidance countries, accounting systems will contain more detailed rules as to how to handle different situations; in less strongly uncertainty-avoiding societies, more will be left to the discretion of the organization or even of the accountant. Accounting systems in high-UAI countries will also be more theoretically based—pretending to derive from consistent general economic principles. This is the case in Germany, where accounting has a scientific status. In France, the German system was introduced by the German occupants during World War II, and its scientific claims were so well received that it remained the French standard *système comptable* ever since. In low-UAI countries, systems are more pragmatic, ad hoc, and folkloristic. In the United States, tendencies to accept accounting traditions as established facts have resisted attempts to base them on general postulates. In Germany, annual reports to shareholders are supposed to use the same valuation of the company's assets as is used for fiscal purposes; in the Dutch, British, and U.S. systems, reports to the tax authorities are unrelated to reports to shareholders.

The system's stress on either short- or longer-term results is an expression of short- or long-term orientation, but a stress on short-term results can also be explained by individualism; for example, in an individualist environment like the United States, responsible managers may change employers at short notice. In individualist cultures the information in the accounting system will be taken more seriously and considered more indispensable than in collectivist ones. The latter, being "high context" according to Edward Hall (1976), possess many other and more subtle clues to the well-being of organizations and the performance of people, so they rely less on the explicit information produced by accountants. The accounting profession in such societies is therefore likely to carry lower status; the work of accountants is a ritual with little practical impact on decisions.

In more masculine societies such as the United States and Germany, accounting systems stress the achievement of purely financial targets more than they do in more feminine societies such as Sweden or the Netherlands.

Gray (1988) has postulated four dimensions of professional accounting that he suggests relate to national culture:

- Professionalism (professional judgment) versus statutory control (legal requirements)
- Uniformity versus flexibility
- Conservatism versus optimism (in evaluating accounts)
- Secrecy versus transparency

Gray (1988), as well as Perera and Mathews (1990), has hypothesized a number of relationships between these dimensions and the four IBM indexes. Salter and Niswander (1995) operationalized and tested Gray's hypotheses on data from 29 countries.[36] They found professionalism to be related negatively to uncertainty avoidance. Conservatism was positively related to UAI and negatively to MAS. Secrecy was positively related to

UAI and negatively to IDV. These relationships had all been predicted by Gray, but links with power distance that he had also predicted were not found. Uniformity, measured as consistency in measurement practices among clients of auditors in a country, was negatively related to UAI (counter to what was hypothesized) and positively related to MAS (not predicted). Salter and Niswander conclude: "It would appear that it is the desire for certainty, or conversely, the willingness to manipulate an uncertain future, which is the strongest cultural construct in determining the overall structure of the accounting profession, the nature of regulation, the nature of measurement, and the volume of information" (p. 392).[37]

Multinationals need standard accounting rules for consolidation purposes. Zarzeski (1996) compared 256 annual reports of companies in seven countries and found that the (negative) relationship between UAI and disclosure of information was stronger for local firms than for subsidiaries of multinationals, an evident effect of uniform rules in the latter.[38] Yet my research in IBM showed that tight international coordination did not prevent employees in different countries from holding quite different values. To the extent that the local interpretation of international accounting rules depends on values, the subsidiaries of multinationals will still deviate from what the head office expects.

Certified public accounting (auditing) firms have themselves become multinationals. Before the wave of cross-national mergers, Soeters and Schreuder (1988) compared professionals working in the Netherlands for local as well as for international (U.S.-owned) CPA firms, using my Values Survey Module 1982 (Appendix 4). The values scored by the Dutch in international firms were significantly different from those of the locals, and in the direction of the American values, for UAI (lower) and MAS (higher).[39] Soeters and Schreuder found evidence that this difference was due to self-selection rather than to on-the-job socialization. This means that after the subsequent mergers of the local firms with the international firms, these value differences should be surviving within the firms themselves—in the same way as they survived within IBM.

Arnold, Bernardi, and Neidermeyer (1998) have described an interesting research project involving professionals from these international firms (the "Big Six"). More than 200 auditors in eight countries supplied their subjective judgments about a test case.[40] They were asked to establish a "materiality cutoff level" for a client, that is, the level below which errors or differences in accounts can be ignored. The researchers expected auditors from higher-UAI countries to establish lower materiality cutoff levels (tolerate smaller errors), but they found exactly the opposite, and very significantly so. My interpretation of this finding is that these auditors protected their own credibility by establishing error tolerance levels that guaranteed they would make no mistakes. But the research project confirmed that merging professional firms from different countries does not eliminate differences in values and judgment.

Corporate Governance

There is a close historical link between capitalism and individualism. The stock exchange as invented in Britain translated Adam Smith's idea of the market as an invisible hand into corporate ownership. Pedersen and Thomsen (1997) listed the nature of the ownership of the 100 largest companies in each of 12 European countries.[41] Differences among these countries were vast. For example, in Britain 61% of the 100 largest companies had dispersed shareholders (no single owner holding more than 20%); in Austria and Italy no large companies at all had this ownership type. The percentages dispersed ownership were significantly correlated with IDV ($r = .65*$).

In the individualist value pattern, the relationship between the individual and the organization is *calculative* for both the owners and the employees; it is based on enlightened self-interest. In more collectivist societies the link between individuals and their organization is *moral* by tradition (Chapter 5). A hire-and-fire, but also a buy-and-sell, approach is ill perceived. Sometimes firing employees is even prohibited by law. If it is not, the costs of firing redundant employees, in terms of loss of public image and of goodwill with authorities, may exceed the benefits.

Differences in power distance also affect corporate governance. In high-PDI France, banking, the development of large companies, and foreign trade were strongly directed and controlled by the state according to the principle of mercantilism. Smaller businesses remained family owned.[42] In the study of the 100 largest companies in each of 12 European countries by Pedersen and Thomsen (1997), dominant ownership (one person, family, or company owned between 20% and 50%) was positively correlated with PDI ($r = .52*$), but surprisingly, one-person or one-family majority ownership (more than 50%) was negatively correlated with PDI ($r = -.62*$).[43]

A unique form of ownership, the cooperative, was found among 10% or more of the 100 largest corporations in Denmark, Finland, Norway, and Sweden, but also in Austria, and in 1% or less in Britain and Italy. In spite of the Austrian score, percentages were negatively correlated with MAS ($r = -.77**$). Cooperatives appeal to the need for cooperation in a feminine society.

In research for his Ph.D. dissertation at Tilburg University in the Netherlands, Radislav Semenov (2000), a Russian econometrist, compared the systems of economic governance of 17 Western countries and showed that culture scores explained their differences better than any of the economic variables suggested in the literature.[44] By a combination of power distance, uncertainty avoidance, and masculinity he was able to classify countries in terms of market, bank, or other control; concentration of ownership; mind-sets of politicians, directors, employees, and investors; formation and implementation of economic policy; and industrial relations. In a separate analysis he studied ownership of firms across 44 countries worldwide and found a significant relationship with uncertainty avoidance only. His study shows the importance of cultural considerations when researchers use one country's solutions as examples for others, as was frequently done in Eastern Europe in the 1990s.

Corporate governance is also related to corporate financial goals. It is naive to assume that such goals are culture-free. Weimer (1995) compared financial goals of German, Dutch, and U.S. business companies, using both questionnaires and interviews with executives. Although all stressed the making of profit, the Germans translated this into independence from banks, the Dutch translated it into book value, and the Americans related it to shareholder value (p. 336). This reflects the institutional differences among the countries (the strong role of banks in Germany) but also the prevailing ideologies (the shareholder as a symbol in the United States). These differences suggest relationships with UAI and IDV that may become visible if data from a broader range of countries become available. The finance function has been the last stronghold in business administration to escape cross-cultural analysis.

Motivation and Compensation

Motivation is a construct; it is an assumed force explaining behaviors. Culture enters the motivation picture in the behaviors themselves that differ and in the explanations for behaviors that differ as well, even where behaviors are the same. In explaining why she puts in extra effort on her job, an American may note the money she receives, a French person may mention her honor, a Chinese person may point to mutual obligations, and a Dane may mention collegiality. Different assumptions about motivation contributed to the limits of the validity of U.S.-based "agency theory" signaled earlier in this chapter.

The founding father of motivation theory is Sigmund Freud—but Freud is rarely quoted in the U.S. management literature on motivation. The classic motivation theorists in the U.S. management literature are still David McClelland, Abraham Maslow, Frederick Herzberg, and Victor Vroom.

Freud was Austrian, and there are good reasons in the culture profile of Austria in the IBM data why his theory would be conceived in Austria rather than elsewhere. According to Freud, we are impelled to act by unconscious forces within us, which he calls the *id.* Our conscious self-conception, the *ego,* tries to control the id, and an again unconscious inner pilot, the *superego,* criticizes the thoughts and acts of the ego. Feelings of guilt and anxiety develop when the ego is felt to be giving in to the id. Freud sees the superego as the product of early socialization, mainly of children by their parents. The Austrian culture is characterized by the combination of small power distance with strong uncertainty avoidance (Exhibit 4.2).[45] The low PDI means that there is no powerful superior who will take away one's uncertainties: One has to carry these oneself. Freud's superego is an inner uncertainty-absorbing device, an interiorized boss. High UAI indicates intolerance of deviance. Fairly low IDV implies an obligation to in-groups. Finally, a very high MAS score sheds some light on Freud's strong concern with sex (Chapter 6).

The U.S. culture profile differs from the Austrian by a much lower UAI score and a much higher IDV score. The strong individualism implies a calculative involvement of Americans in organizations. This explains the popularity in the United States of "expectancy" theories of motivation, which see people as pulled by the expectancy of outcomes, mostly consciously (Vroom, 1964), rather than as pushed by unconscious drives.

Exhibit 4.13 in Chapter 4 shows that the combination of UAI and MAS was the best predictor of "need for achievement" as a country-level motivator, as identified by McClelland (1961) in his content analysis of 1925 children's readers. The upper right-hand quadrant in Exhibit 6.17 (low UAI, high MAS) corresponds to the highest n_{Ach} as measured by McClelland. This quadrant includes the entire Anglo cluster plus some Asian countries: India, Philippines, Hong Kong, and (marginally) Singapore (interestingly, all these are former U.K. or U.S. colonies). The clustering of the Anglo countries suggests the cultural limitation of McClelland's achievement motivation concept. The societal norms for uncertainty avoidance and masculinity affect what will motivate people in different cultures. McClelland's achievement motive was based on one special set of societal norms, the one with which he was familiar.[46]

The combination of high IDV, low UAI, and high MAS in the United States also explains the popularity of Maslow's (1970) hierarchy of human needs. Maslow's supreme category, self-actualization, is a highly individualist motive. In research done in the mid-1960s among managers from 14 countries by Haire, Ghiselli, and Porter (1966), only the Americans ordered their needs almost exactly in the order of Maslow's hierarchy (security, social, esteem, autonomy, self-actualization; see the section on ethnocentrism in Chapter 1).

Along with Maslow's hierarchy, Herzberg's two-factor theory of motivation became popular (Herzberg, Mausner, & Snyderman, 1959). Herzberg claimed that in the work situation there are "motivators" with positive but no negative motivation potential and "hygienic factors" with negative but no positive motivation potential. The motivators are the "intrinsic" aspects of work—basically those related to Maslow's higher needs, esteem and self-actualization. The hygienic factors are the "extrinsic" aspects—basically those related to Maslow's lower needs, social and security. If Maslow's hierarchy is culturally constrained, so is Herzberg's theory.[47]

In my view, the implications for motivation of the UAI × MAS plot in Exhibit 6.17 are that the vertical, UAI axis opposes motivation by success to motivation by security—at the extremes, hope of success to fear of failure. The horizontal, MAS axis opposes ego needs to affiliation needs. Combining the two axes, we get four quadrants, each of which needs a different hierarchy to explain people's motives, rather than one universal hierarchy, as suggested by Maslow.

In quadrant 1 (United States, Great Britain, and their former dominions and colonies) motivation is based on personal, individual success, in the form of wealth, recognition, and "self-actualization." This is the classic McClelland-Maslow-Herzberg pattern.

In quadrant 2 (Japan, German-speaking countries, some Latin countries, and Greece) motivation is based on personal, individual security. This can be found in wealth and especially in hard work. Second-quadrant countries have grown fastest economically in the post-World War II period, contrary to McClelland's predictions.

In quadrant 3 (France, Spain, Portugal, former Yugoslavia, a number of Latin and Asian countries) motivation is based on security and relationships. Individual wealth is less important than mutual solidarity.

In quadrant 4 (Northern European countries plus the Netherlands) motivation is based on success and relationships. In this quadrant, success will be measured partly by the quality of the human relationships and of the living environment.

These four quadrants present a motivational world map that is a far cry from a universal order of needs. The implication of the different motiva-

tion patterns in different countries is that personnel policies aimed at motivating people will have different effects in different countries (their effects may also differ within the same country, for different classes of employees). This is perhaps nowhere as clear as in reactions to career opportunities. Careers imply trade-offs between uncertainty and security, between success and family life, and people's career behavior is therefore very much a reflection of their cultural values. The following quote is from a study of career attitudes among male middle managers in France, Britain, and Scandinavia:

> The French are slightly more sensitive to career tensions at all stages, possibly a reflection of working as middle managers in relatively structured and authoritarian organizations. Young British managers are particularly insensitive to their marriages, though this changes strongly in their mid-thirties, while the Scandinavians are more preoccupied than other nationalities with their wives during their twenties and early thirties. . . . While French managers believe more in a rigid separation of professional and private life—work should not in principle be allowed to interfere with family and leisure—the British executive perceives a fluid and much less clear boundary between the two domains. . . . Their time in private life is spent differently. The British are more passive and companionable, spending time relaxing, doing chores, and simply being together. The French are more active—playing sports, spending time with children, friends, or the extended family. . . . The French feel most "tied down" in their careers, whereas the British and particularly the Scandinavians feel "free." . . . The career strategy of the Frenchman is necessarily more defensive and risk-avoidant, while that of his British counterpart is more aggressive and risk-taking. (Bartolomé & Evans, 1979)

This quote illustrates not only the differences in uncertainty avoidance (which opposes Britain and Scandinavia on the one side to France on the other) but also the differences in masculinity (which oppose Britain to Scandinavia, with France in between).

In the 1980s, I was invited to speak at a seminar in Jakarta, Indonesia, about human resource development. Someone suggested I should address the problem of how to train Indonesian managers to replace "Theory X" with "Theory Y." These two theories are associated with the work of McGregor (1960; see Chapter 3), and they carry a strong humanistic missionary flavor characteristic of the 1950s, when his ideas were formulated.[48] The main thrust of Theory X is that the average human being has an inherent dislike of work and will avoid it if he or she can; therefore managers must coerce, punish, and control people to make them contribute to organizational objectives. The main thrust of Theory Y is that the expenditure of physical and mental effort in work is as natural as play or rest, and that under proper conditions, people will not only accept but even seek responsibility and exercise effort toward achieving organizational objectives. McGregor, evidently, defended Theory Y.

Before we apply this distinction to a culture other than the one with which the author was familiar, the United States of the first half of the 20th century, we should test what basic, unspoken cultural assumptions are present in both Theories X and Y. The assumptions are implicit in both:

1. Work is good for people. It is God's will that people should work.
2. People's capacities should be maximally utilized. It is God's will that people should use their capacities to the full.
3. There are "organizational objectives" that exist apart from people.
4. People in organizations behave as unattached individuals.

These assumptions reflect the value positions of an individualist, masculine society. None of them applies in Southeast Asian cultures. Southeast Asian assumptions, rather, would be as follows:

1. Work is a necessity but not a goal in itself.
2. People should find their rightful place, in peace and harmony with their environment.
3. Absolute objectives exist only with God. In the world, persons in authority positions represent God, so their objectives should be followed.
4. People behave as members of a family and/or group. Those who do not are rejected by society.

Because of these different culturally determined assumptions, McGregor's Theory X/Theory Y distinction has never been relevant in Southeast Asia. A distinction more in line with Southeast Asian cultures would not oppose mutually exclusive alternatives that disrupt the norm of harmony. The ideal model, rather, would be for opposites to complement each other, to fit harmoniously together. Let me call them Theory T and Theory T+, in which *T* stands for *tradition*.

Theory T could be as follows:

1. There is an order of inequality in this world in which everyone has his or her rightful place. High and low are protected by this order which is willed by God.

2. Children have to learn to fulfill their duties at the place where they belong by birth. They can improve their place by studying under a good teacher, working with a good patron, and/or marrying a good partner.
3. Tradition is a source of wisdom. Therefore, the average human being has an inherent dislike of change and will rightly avoid it if he or she can.

Without contradicting Theory T, Theory T+ would affirm the following:

1. In spite of the wisdom in traditions, the experience of change in life is natural, as natural as work, play, or rest.
2. Commitment to change is a function of the quality of leaders who lead the change, the rewards associated with the change, and the negative consequences of not changing.
3. The capacity to lead people to a new situation is widely, not narrowly, distributed among leaders in the population.
4. The learning capacities of the average family are more than sufficient for modernization.

Thus in my Jakarta lecture I argued that a Southeast Asian equivalent of human resource development should be based on something like Theories T and T+, and not on an irrelevant import like the Theory X/Y distinction. Foreign theories can no doubt serve as a source of inspiration, but they should be reconceptualized according to the best of the local traditions.

Compensation packages differ by country; employers and employees compare themselves primarily against others in the same national labor market. Schuler and Rogovsky (1998) used three data sets about national compensation practices for the employed population in general around 1990, together covering 24 countries.[49] They correlated the frequency of occurrence of various practices with my four IBM indexes. Some of the significant correlations found were as follows:[50]

- PDI was related negatively to workplace child care for managers, professional, and technical staff, and to nonmanagerial employee stock options and ownership.
- UAI was positively related to pay based on seniority and skill and negatively related to pay based on performance.
- IDV was positively related to pay for individual performance and to stock options and ownership for managers.
- MAS was positively related to payment of commission to nonmanagerial employees and negatively related to flexible benefits,

workplace child care for clerical and manual workers, and maternity leave.[51]

Pennings (1993) interviewed compensation officers and line executives from firms in France, the Netherlands, and the United States in the late 1980s about their companies' executive reward systems. Most French and Dutch firms paid fixed or nearly fixed compensation and based increases on subjective evaluation. Compensation in U.S. firms varied greatly from almost fixed to extremely variable and linked to accounting measures of performance. Beliefs about the relationship between pay and performance varied correspondingly. Such beliefs are difficult to test, as they become self-fulfilling prophecies.

Leadership and Empowerment

Chapter 3 showed that vertical relations in organizations reflect the common values of superiors *and subordinates* in a country. Leadership and subordinateship are inseparable. This is immediately clear in the political field: It is difficult to imagine that a Hitler would have been a successful leader in Great Britain, a Churchill in France, or a de Gaulle in Germany.

Ideas about leadership reflect the dominant culture of a country. Asking people to describe the qualities of a good leader is in fact another way of asking them to describe their culture. The leader is a culture hero, in the sense of a model for behavior (Chapter 1). In individualist countries leadership is often treated as an independent characteristic that a person could acquire, without reference to any corresponding subordinateship. It reminds me of the fairy tales in which "invisibility" is treated as a characteristic of the person who becomes invisible. In masculine cultures the leader is a masculine hero. The management literature in individualist, masculine cultures such as Australia, Britain, and the United States loves studies that describe desirable characteristics of leaders. They describe what the beholders like to be and to believe. Tolstoy (1865-69/1978) notes in *War and Peace:* "Men always lie when reporting deeds of battle.... in war nothing really happens exactly as we imagine and describe it" (p. 766). Tolstoy's skeptical view applies equally to organizational life. What really happens depends on leaders, on followers, and very much on the situation. Leadership is an attributed characteristic, often romantic; it is "an explanatory concept used to understand organizations as causal systems" (Meindl, Ehrlich, & Dukerich, 1985, p. 78).

Feminine cultures believe in modest leaders. A prestigious U.S. consulting firm was once asked to analyze decision making in a leading Dutch corporation. In its report, the firm criticized the corporation's decision-making style for being, among other things, "intuitive" and "consensus based." [52] The in-depth comparison of a U.S., a Dutch, and a French organization by d'Iribarne (see Chapter 3) showed that the consensus principle was precisely the essence of the success of the Dutch plant. The Dutch *polder* consensus model is supposed to be a keystone of the country's economy. Imposing a foreign leadership model (that is believed to be universal) in such a situation amounts to destruction of cultural capital.

A comparative content analysis of publications about chief executive officers (or their equivalents) in France, Germany, Japan, Sweden, and Taiwan showed considerable differences in the images presented (Jackofsky & Slocum, 1988). French CEOs were described as taking autocratic initiatives (high PDI); Germans as stressing the training and responsibilities of their managers and workers (low PDI, high UAI); Japanese as practicing patience and letting the organization run itself, aiming at long-term market share (high LTO); and Swedes as taking entrepreneurial risks and at the same time caring for their people's quality of working life (low UAI, low MAS). The one Taiwanese CEO in the sample stressed hard work and the family (low IDV).[53]

Another comparative study content analyzed more than 1,400 job advertisements for executives in eight European countries (Tollgerdt-Andersson, 1996).[54] The author classified the extent to which the ads stated required personal and social abilities, such as the ability to cooperate; this varied from 85% of cases in Sweden (and 80% in both Denmark and Norway) to 53% in Italy and 52% in Spain. I did a correlation and regression analysis on the percentages she published, against the four IBM indexes plus 1990 GNP/capita, and found low UAI ($r = -.86**$) to be the strongest related zero-order variable and low MAS to make a significant second-order contribution ($R = .95***, R^2 = .90$). Ability to cooperate is a soft criterion that was considered more valid in low-UAI, low-MAS cultures.

The first edition of *Culture's Consequences* showed a comparison among IBM technicians in France, Germany, and Great Britain on the appreciation of four leadership styles (Hofstede, 1980a, fig. 7.6). It measured to what extent those perceiving their boss as representing one of the four styles (Appendix 1, question A55) expressed satisfaction with this boss on 20 other questions. The French were most satisfied when they saw their boss as persuasive or paternalistic; the Germans, when they perceived him as participative or democratic (managing by majority vote). The British IBM technicians divided their sympathies over the persuasive-paternalistic and the consultative boss. The (more uncertainty-avoiding) French and German technicians preferred a boss with a theoretically pure, unambiguous style of resolving problems: through hierarchy in high-PDI France and through consensus in low-PDI Germany. The give-and-take intermediate "consultative" style, which demands a greater tolerance for uncertainty among subordinates, was appreciated only in Britain.

Similar differences among countries have been reported elsewhere. For example, close supervision was associated with more positive attitudes toward the boss among Peruvian workers, whereas the reverse was true for U.S. workers.[55] Both morale and productivity of Indian children were higher under authoritarian leadership, whereas the opposite had been found in the United States.[56] Indian assistants showed higher satisfaction and performance when working under "fraternal" foremen than under "assertive" or "nurturant" foremen (Kakar, 1971).[57] What represents appropriate leadership in one setting does not have to be appropriate for a differently programmed group of subordinates.

One of the oldest theorists of leadership in the world literature is Niccolò Machiavelli (1469-1527).[58] He described the most effective techniques for manipulation and remaining in power, including deceit, bribery, and murder; this has given him a bad reputation in the centuries afterward. Machiavelli wrote in the Italy of his day, and what he described was clearly a large power distance situation. We still find Italy on the higher-PDI side of Exhibit 4.1 (with all other Latin and Mediterranean countries), and we can assume from historical evidence that power distances in Italy in the 16th century were still considerably larger.

Leadership behaviors but also leadership theories that do not take collective expectations of subordinates into account are basically dysfunctional. The U.S. leadership style has been found to be dysfunctional in Greece and the Greek leadership style in the United States.[59] What in fact happens when foreign theories are taught abroad—and this I have personally witnessed—is that the theories are preached but not practiced. Wise local managers silently adapt the foreign ideas to fit the values of their subordinates. A country in which this has happened a lot is Japan.[60] Not-so-wise managers may try an unfitting approach once, find out it does not work, and fall back into their old routine.

Cultural limitations to leadership approaches have their consequences for the ways company policies function—for example, in the area of *grievance channels,* ways in which lower-level organization members can bring their complaints to those at the top of the organization. It is difficult to establish grievance channels in high-PDI environments; subordinates fear retaliation (for good reason), unrealistic and exaggerated grievances

may be aired, and the channels may be used for personal revenge against superiors who are not accessible otherwise.

The term *empowerment,* which became fashionable in the 1990s, applies, in fact, to all kinds of formal and informal means of sharing decision-making power and influence between leaders and subordinates: participative management, joint consultation, *Mitbestimmung,* industrial democracy (see Chapter 3), worker directors, worker self-management, shop floor consultation, codetermination. The feasibility of these various means relates to the value systems of the organization members—the subordinates at least as much as the leaders. The first cultural dimension involved, obviously, is power distance. Distributing influence comes more naturally to low- than to high-PDI cultures. At the ideological level the reverse may apply; Chapter 3 showed that the statement "Employees in industry should participate more in the decisions taken by management" in the IBM studies met with stronger endorsement in *high*-PDI cultures; an ideology can compensate for deficiencies of practice.

Mid-20th-century American theories of leadership such as McGregor's (1960) Theory Y versus Theory X, Likert's (1967) System 4, and Blake and Mouton's managerial grid (Blake, Mouton, Barnes, & Greiner, 1973) reflect small but not very small power distances (the United States ranked 16 from below out of 53 on PDI). They all advocate "participative management" in the sense of participation in the superior's decisions by subordinates *at the initiative of the superior.* In countries with still lower PDI values—such as Sweden, Norway, Germany, and Israel—models of management were developed that assumed the initiative was to be taken by the subordinates. In the United States this tends to be seen as infringing upon "management prerogatives," but in the lowest-PDI countries people do not think in these terms. One Scandinavian reportedly remarked to an American lecturer: "You are against participation for the very reason we are in favor of it—one doesn't know where it will stop. We think that is good." [61] On the other hand, U.S. theories of participative management are also unlikely to apply in countries much higher on the power distance scale. One study noted the embarrassment of a Greek subordinate when his expatriate U.S. boss asked his opinion on how much time a job should take: "He is the boss. Why doesn't he tell me?" (quoted in Triandis, 1973a).

The chances and opportunities for more informal or more formal empowerment are also affected by the country's level of uncertainty avoidance (Chapter 4). Thus both PDI and UAI should be taken into account, and the four quadrants of the PDI × UAI matrix (Exhibit 4.2) represent four different forms of distributing power. In quadrant 4 (Anglo countries, Scandinavia, Netherlands; PDI and UAI both low) the stress was on informal and spontaneous forms of participation on the shop floor. In quadrant 3 (German-speaking countries; PDI low, UAI higher) the stress was on formal, legally determined systems (*Mitbestimmung*). In quadrants 2 and 1 (high PDI) distributing power is basically a contradiction; it will meet with strong resistance from elites and sometimes even from underdogs or their representatives, such as labor unions. Where it is tried it has to be pushed by a powerful leader—by a "father type" such as an enlightened entrepreneur in the high-PDI, low-UAI countries (quadrant 1), or by political leadership using legislative tools in the high-PDI, high-UAI countries (quadrant 2).[62] Both mean imposed participation, which is, of course, a paradox. One way of making it function is to limit participation to certain spheres of life and to maintain tight control in others; this was the Chinese solution, in which participative structures in work organizations were combined with a strictly controlled hierarchy in ideological issues (Laaksonen, 1977).

If power redistribution is imposed, it may become self-destructive, because if it succeeds, continued imposition is no longer possible. The supreme paradox is that in high-PDI cultures unusually strong and enlightened leadership—that is, an unusually large power distance—is necessary to arrive at even a mild degree of power difference reduction. Only exceptional leaders with long lives in power succeed in this—and by their very success they may breed new dependence in their subordinates, which means that they failed after all. This helps to explain why societal norms like power distance levels are so persistent over the centuries.

Management Development and Organization Development

It should be evident from all that is written in this book and, in particular, in this chapter that there is no single formula for developing successful managers that can be used in different cultures. Not only is success defined differently in different cultures, but systems of initial education in schools and training on the job are also very different.

Developing managers across cultural barriers could thus be seen as an impossible task, but fortunately programs should not be judged exclusively on the basis of their cognitive content. They have other important functions that transcend their cognitive role. They bring people from different cultures and subcultures together, and by this act broaden their outlook. In many organizations, international management development programs

have become rites of passage that signal to the manager-participant as well as to his or her environment that from now on he or she belongs to the manager caste. Such programs provide socialization in the managerial subculture, either company specific or in general. They also provide a break with the job routine that stimulates reflection and reorientation.

Since the 1960s, the market for management training has offered programs using intensive interpersonal process analysis and/or feedback. These were developed in the United States (a pioneering institute was the National Training Laboratories in Bethel, Maine), and they have been known by many different names, including T-group training, sensitivity training, transactional analysis, and leadership profile analysis. Such programs have a strong cultural flavor. In cases where such programs were used with international participants, dysfunctional behaviors occurred that the trainers rarely understood. With Japanese, for example, the giving and receiving of personal feedback appeared virtually impossible and, when tried, resulted in ritualized behavior: The receiver of feedback felt that he must have insulted the sender in some way. Japanese participants in such programs concentrated on task rather than interpersonal process issues.[63] Most Germans, too, according to my observation, did not appreciate talking about process issues; they saw this as a wasteful deviation from the task.

The label *organization development* dates also from the 1960s. Organization development (OD) refers to programs in which managers and others try to resolve actual common problems. OD frequently also uses interpersonal process analysis and/or feedback. OD approaches always have a cultural flavor. They assume not too high PDI, low UAI, medium to high IDV, and low MAS;[64] the last of these makes OD somewhat countercultural in the United States. OD was never very successful in Latin countries (high PDI), which lacked the equality ethos needed for such programs. Latins believe less in the possibility of people's self-development. They will easily interpret interpersonal feedback competitively, unless it comes from a person seen as superior. Also, the training process creates insecurity that is often intolerable in view of the high UAI of Latin cultures. Furthermore, it has been claimed that Latin languages are ill suited for the discussion of processes in which action is more important than the abstract definition of problems. Latin organizations are not changed that way—they are usually changed only by crisis and revolution.[65] In any culture, organization development programs should be tailor-made to fit the local situation.[66] Tainio and Santalainen (1984) compared two OD programs in Finland, one U.S.-made and the other locally designed. In the U.S. program the effects were mainly noticeable in the behavior of individual managers. The Finnish program showed stronger and longer-lasting effects at the organizational level.

Performance Appraisal and Management by Objectives

Any organization in any culture depends on the performance of people. Monitoring the performance of subordinates is a theme in most management development programs, right from the lowest management level upward. Often there is a formal performance appraisal program that requires periodic written and/or oral evaluations of subordinates by their superiors. Exporting such programs across national borders once more calls for adaptation. In collectivist (low-IDV) countries, social harmony is an important ingredient for organizational functioning, even more crucial than formal performance, and a program that harms the former eventually damages the latter.[67] In such countries personal criticism may have to be given in an indirect way or through a trusted intermediary, such as an older relative. I remember a case in Pakistan in which the personnel department of a multinational produced all the paperwork of an internationally prescribed appraisal system to the satisfaction of its international head office—but the local managers carefully avoided the expected appraisal discussions.

In the United States, performance appraisal was further developed into management by objectives (MBO; Drucker, 1955, chap. 11). MBO may be the single most popular management technique. It is based on a cybernetic control-by-feedback philosophy; it is supposed to spread results orientation throughout the organization. MBO has been considerably more successful where results are objectively measurable than where they are a matter of subjective interpretation (Hofstede, 1994b, chap. 9). It has also been criticized as industrial engineering with a new name, applied to higher management levels and meeting the same resistance as industrial engineering did (Levinson, 1970). Of interest to us here is what has happened in the inevitable attempts to export MBO to other countries.

MBO reflects an American value position in that it presupposes all of the following:

- The subordinate is sufficiently independent to have a meaningful dialogue with the boss (not too high PDI).
- Both superior and subordinate are prepared to accept some ambiguity (low UAI).
- Both superior and subordinate see performance as an important criterion (high MAS).

Let us now take the case of Germany. This is also a below-average PDI country, so the dialogue element in MBO should present no problem. However, Germany scored considerably higher on UAI; consequently, the acceptance of ambiguity is weaker. The idea of replacing the arbitrary authority of the boss with the impersonal authority of mutually agreed-upon objectives, however, fits the low-PDI, high-UAI cultural cluster very well. The objectives become the subordinate's "superego." MBO in Germany has been strongly formalized and converted into "management by joint goal setting." [68]

The other case on which specific information is available is France. MBO was first introduced in France in the early 1960s, but it became extremely popular for a time after the 1968 students' revolt. People expected that this new technique would lead to the long-overdue democratizing of organizations. Instead of DPO (*direction par objectifs*), the French name for MBO became DPPO (*direction participative par objectifs*). Thus in France, too, societal developments affected the MBO system. Unfortunately, DPPO remained as much a vain slogan as did "*Liberté, égalité, fraternité*" (Freedom, equality, brotherhood) after the 1789 revolt.[69]

Organizational Cultures

The "Organizational Culture" Construct

This part of the chapter deals with differences of culture between organizations—and parts of organizations—within the same country or countries. In my terminology, *organizational* cultures are entirely distinct from *national* cultures; the two concepts are complementary. Organizational cultures (in Britain usually called *organization* cultures) distinguish organizations while holding their national environments constant; national cultures distinguish nations while holding organizational contexts constant, or at least as constant as possible. In line with the definition of culture presented in Chapter 1, organizational cultures are *the collective programming of the mind that distinguishes the members of one organization from another.* Nations and organizations represent two different levels of aggregation. The empirical base for this part of the chapter is not the IBM research but a separate study that compared 20 different organizational units in Denmark and the Netherlands in 1985 and 1986, which I designed and which was carried out under the label of IRIC, the Institute for Research on Intercultural Cooperation in the Netherlands, of which I was then the director. I will refer to it throughout this discussion as the IRIC study. I have described its methods in the latter part of Chapter 2.

Although the term *organizational culture* did not become common before 1980, the corresponding concept had surfaced in the organizational and management literature for at least half a century before. In the 1930s, U.S. management pioneer Chester Barnard (1938/1960) suggested "that every participant in an organization may be regarded as having a dual personality—an organization personality and an individual personality.... In referring to the aspects of purpose as cooperatively viewed, we are alluding to the *organization* personality of individuals" (p. 88). U.S. management professor E. Wight Bakke (1950) wrote: "A company or a union is a small society.... The systems through which people (and the materials and ideas with which they work) are bound together into a functioning whole may be classified as ... *bonds,* or devices, of organization" (p. 234). He then listed nine different bonds, including the functional specifications system, the status system, and the communication system, but also what he called "thoughtways." In his explanations, Bakke pointed to the roles of "reinforcements (folklore, symbols, slogans, etc.) for socially desirable behavior" (p. 235). He foreshadowed many elements of the later "culture" discussion.

In Britain, a book by Professor Elliot Jaques (1951) was titled *The Changing Culture of a Factory*—to my knowledge the first use of the word *culture* in the management literature. The book describes Jaques's long-term involvement with the Glacier Metal Company, London.[70]

> The culture of the factory is its customary and traditional way of thinking and of doing things, which is shared to a greater or lesser degree by all its members, and which new members must learn, and at least partially accept.... Culture is part of a second nature to those who have been with the firm for some time. (p. 251)

In the United States in the 1960s and 1970s, the concept of *organizational climate* became common (important sources are Litwin & Stringer, 1968; Schneider, 1975). The terms *climate* and *culture* were and are sometimes used interchangeably, but across the literature the following differences can be recognized:

- Climate derived from social psychology, culture from anthropology; this affects the methods by which they were and are studied.
- Climate is more closely linked with individual motivation and behavior than culture, which resides entirely at the organizational level.

- *Climate* has an evaluative connotation—there are wholesome and unhealthy climates—and thus partly overlaps with satisfaction; cultures can be different without one being objectively better than another.
- Climate can be seen as a subset of culture—for example, the "communication climate"—but not vice versa.[71]

The popularization of the term *organization(al) culture* and its equivalent *corporate culture* in the United States and elsewhere owes a lot to two books: *Corporate Cultures* by Deal and Kennedy (1982) and, even more, its companion volume, from the same McKinsey-Harvard Business School team, Peters and Waterman's (1982) *In Search of Excellence.*[72] Peters and Waterman's main thesis is that excellent companies are characterized by strong cultures and that shared values represent the core of such strong cultures:

> Without exception, the dominance and coherence of culture proved to be an essential quality of the excellent companies. Moreover, the stronger the culture and the more it was directed toward the marketplace, the less need was there for policy manuals, organization charts, or detailed procedures and rules. In these companies, people way down the line know what they are supposed to do in most situations because the handful of guiding values is crystal clear. (pp. 75-76)

Peters and Waterman list eight maxims, conditions for companies to become excellent, some of which I will come back to below.

These pioneering books were followed by an extensive literature on the topic, which has spread to other countries. In India, for example, Singh and Paul (1985) have written about "corporate soul," inspired by the "corporate culture" wave but using elements from Indian philosophical traditions; they refer to the "organizational psychounity." Organizations with "strong" cultures, in the sense of the quote above from Peters and Waterman, aroused positive feelings in some people and negative feelings in others. The culture of the IBM Corporation, one of Peters and Waterman's most excellent companies, had earlier been depicted with horror by the French social psychologist Max Pagès and his team, who studied IBM France; Pagès et al. (1979) called it *la nouvelle église* (the new church). Moreover, the universal desirability of having a "strong" culture, from an organizational point of view, was frequently questioned; such a culture could be a source of fatal rigidity.[73] Soeters (1986) has shown the similarity between the descriptions of Peters and Waterman's "excellent companies" and social movements for civil rights, women's liberation, religious conversion, and withdrawal from civilization. In the United States itself, postcards and other paraphernalia were seen bearing the slogan "I'd rather be dead than excellent." In a more dispassionate way, Lammers (1988) has shown that the "excellent companies" were simply the latest descendants of an entire genealogy within organizational sociology of ideal types of "organic organizations" described by the German sociologist Joseph Pieper in 1931, if not by others before, and reiterated in the sociological literature on both sides of the Atlantic.

Organizational or corporate culture is a *construct* (see Chapter 1). There is no consensus about its definition, but most authors will probably agree on the following aspects: Organizational cultures are (1) holistic, (2) historically influenced, (3) related to anthropological concepts, (4) socially constructed, (5) soft, and (6) relatively stable—that is, difficult to change. All of these characteristics of organizations had been recognized and described before; what was new about organizational culture was their integration into one construct. In an excellent encyclopedic article, Ouchi and Wilkins (1988) have shown that the "organizational culture" focus developed from and is still linked to all kinds of other currents in U.S. social science: "The study of organizational culture may be seen as a return to some of the most basic concerns about the nature of organizations and the appropriate methods for analysing them" (p. 223).

Among those writing about organizational cultures, some treat culture as something an organization *has,* whereas others treat it as something an organization *is* (Smircich, 1983). The former leads to an analytic approach and a concern with change. It predominates among management teachers and consultants. The latter supports a synthetic approach and a concern with understanding and is found almost exclusively among pure academics. The difference has exploded into an unholy paradigm war. The concern with change has produced some overly simplistic and mechanistic recipes; the concern with understanding, characteristic of "organizational symbolism," [74] has produced publications that tell us "more about the cultures of the researchers than [about those of] the researched" (Gregory, 1983, p. 359). Wisdom suggests that we look to "triangulation"—that is, pick the best from both paradigms while recognizing the strengths and limits of each.

A related unholy war has been fought between proponents of a qualitative approach versus a quantitative approach to the study of organizational cultures.[75] For both the "has" and the "is" paradigms much of the literature has consisted of qualitative case studies that "neglect appropriate validation procedures" (Saffold, 1988, p. 549), lacking objectivity and generalizability, plus pep

talks and "war stories." Again the need for triangulation is obvious; what is needed is a combination of a qualitative approach for depth and empathy with a quantitative approach for confirmation. This combined research strategy was used in the IRIC project, to be described below.

Differences Between
Organizational and National Cultures

Using the word *culture* in reference to both nations and organizations suggests that the two kinds of culture are identical phenomena. This is incorrect: A nation is not an organization, and the two types of culture are of different kinds.

> Organizations will not often, if ever, reach the depth and richness of socially shared understanding of the paradigmatic cultures studied by anthropologists. . . . Since the learning of organizational "culture" typically occurs in adulthood and since members of contemporary organizations rarely live in "total institutions" . . . and are thus exposed to alternative orientations, we assume that the social understandings in organizations, to the extent they exist, are neither as deep nor as immutable as the anthropological metaphor would suggest. (Wilkins & Ouchi, 1983, p. 479)

The difference between the two kinds of culture became visible in the different roles played in the IBM versus the IRIC research project by the manifestations of culture pictured in Exhibit 1.4: symbols, heroes, rituals, and values, of which the first three were subsumed under the name *practices.*

Among national cultures—comparing otherwise similar people—the IBM studies found considerable differences in values, in spite of similarities in practices among IBM employees in similar jobs but in different national subsidiaries. When people suggest that national cultures in the modern world are becoming the same, the evidence they cite is usually taken from the level of practices: People dress the same way, buy the same products, use the same fashionable words (symbols); see the same TV shows and motion pictures (heroes); and perform the same sports and leisure activities (rituals). These rather superficial manifestations of culture are sometimes mistaken for all there is; the deeper, underlying level of values, which moreover determines the meaning to people of their practices, is overlooked.

As will be shown below, the IRIC project found the relative weights of values versus practices at the organizational level to be exactly reversed with respect to the national level. Comparing otherwise similar people in different organizations

Exhibit 8.3.   The Balance of Values Versus Practices at the National, Occupational, and Organizational Levels

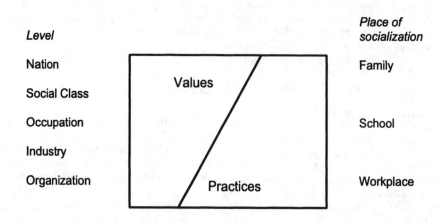

Level

Nation

Social Class

Occupation

Industry

Organization

Place of socialization

Family

School

Workplace

showed considerable differences in practices but much smaller differences in values.

Exhibit 8.3 illustrates that at the national level cultural differences reside mostly in values and less in practices (as long as we compare otherwise similar people). At the organizational level, cultural differences reside mostly in practices and less in values. An occupational culture level has been placed halfway between nation and organization, suggesting that entering an occupational field means the acquisition of both values and practices. In between the national and occupational culture levels one can put a social class culture level; in between the occupational and organizational culture levels, an industry level.

The differences in the values/practices balance pictured in Exhibit 8.3 can be explained by the different places of socialization (learning) for values and for practices; these are listed at the right side of the diagram. Values are acquired in one's early youth, mainly in the family and in the neighborhood, and later at school. By the age of 10, most of the child's basic values have been programmed into his or her mind. Organizational practices, on the other hand, are learned through socialization at the workplace, which most people enter as adults—that is, with the bulk of their values firmly in place. For the occupational values the place of socialization is the school or university, and the time is in between childhood and adulthood.

Exhibit 8.3 illustrates that national cultures and organizational cultures are phenomena of a different order. Using the same term, *cultures,* for both can be misleading. The conclusions from the diagram are at variance with the popular literature on "corporate cultures," which insists, following Pe-

ters and Waterman, that shared values represent the core of a corporate culture. On the basis of our research, *shared perceptions of daily practices* should be considered the core of an organization's culture.[76] In IRIC's organizational cultures study the employees' values differed more according to such criteria as their nationality, age, and education than according to their membership in the organization per se.

An explanation for the difference between Peters and Waterman's findings (and those of many other U.S. authors) and ours about the nature of organizational cultures is that the U.S. management literature rarely distinguishes between the values of founders and significant leaders and the values of the bulk of the organization's members; the latter are seldom studied at all. Descriptions of organizational cultures are often based only on the statements of corporate heroes. Our research has assessed to what extent leaders' messages have come across to members. The values of founders and key leaders undoubtedly shape organizational cultures, but the way these cultures affect ordinary members is through shared practices. Founders/leaders' values become members' practices.

This process of a transfer of the founders' values into the members' practices was described at the beginning of the 20th century by Max Weber.[77] In Weber's typology of social action, he distinguished (among other types) action toward a value (*wertrational*) from action dominated by habitual response (traditional). Our findings suggest that actions by ordinary organization members are more often traditional than *wertrational*.

If members' values depend primarily on criteria other than membership in the organization, the way these values enter the organization is through the hiring process: A company hires people of a certain nationality, age, education, gender, and so on.[78] Their subsequent socialization in the organization is a matter of learning the practices: symbols, heroes, and rituals. Personnel departments that preselect the people to be hired play a very important role in maintaining an organization's values (for better or for worse), a role of which personnel officers are not always conscious.

The IRIC Organizational Culture Research Project

The IRIC project sought to cover a wide range of different work organizations, allowing us to appreciate the ranges of culture differences that could be found in practice; this would then enable us to assess the relative weight of similarities and differences.[79] A crucial question was what represents "an organization" from a cultural point of view. One organization may include several culturally different departments, and these departments may consist of culturally different work groups. Determining what units are sufficiently homogeneous to be used for comparing cultures is both a theoretical and an empirical problem. We took a pragmatic approach and accepted as units of study both entire organizations and parts of organizations, following their management's judgment as to whether a unit was culturally homogeneous; afterward we could confirm or disconfirm this from the data collected. In a few cases the research results gave us reason to doubt a unit's cultural homogeneity, but it is unlikely that our overall conclusions have been substantially affected by this. In the end we got access to 20 units from 10 different organizations, 5 in Denmark and 5 in the Netherlands.[80] On the IBM dimensions these two countries belonged to the same cluster of low PDI, UAI, and MAS and high IDV.

The 20 units were from three broad kinds of organizations: (1) private companies manufacturing electronics, chemicals, or consumer goods (6 total divisions or production units, 3 head offices or marketing units, and 2 research and development units); (2) 5 units from private service companies (banking, transport, trade); and (3) 4 units from public institutions (telecommunications, police). Unit sizes varied in size from 60 to 2,500 persons. The sample of 20 units was small enough to allow the study of each unit in depth, qualitatively, as a separate case study. At the same time, it was large enough to permit statistical analysis of comparative quantitative data across all cases.

As described in Chapter 2, data were collected in three phases: interviews, paper-and-pencil survey, and company information gathering. Eighteen carefully trained Danish and Dutch inter-

viewers held in-depth interviews of 2-3 hours' duration each with nine informants per unit, a total of 180 interviews. Interviewers used a checklist based on a survey of the literature on the ways in which organizational cultures are supposed to manifest themselves, plus our own creative ideas. Manifestations of culture were classified into the four categories in Exhibit 1.4: symbols, heroes, rituals, and values.[81] The checklist contained questions such as the following:

- What terms are only used by insiders?
- What are famous words here? (to identify organizational symbols)
- What things are important here to get on?
- Are there, according to you, people who are of great importance to the organization? (to identify organizational heroes)
- What events are celebrated in the organization?
- What are some of the important rules—written and unwritten—that apply here?
- How are, according to you, important decisions made? (to identify organizational rituals)
- What do people especially like to see here?
- What are the greatest mistakes one can make here?
- What is the most negative (positive) image in the outside world about this organization that you can think of? (to identify organizational values)[82]

Interviewers were free to probe for more and other information if they felt it was there.

The interviews were used to create a qualitative, empathic description of the culture of each of the 20 cases. Extracts from 2 of the 20 unit gestalt descriptions made on the basis of the interviews are found in Appendix 7: The "TKB" case and the "DLM" case (the acronyms are invented).

The second phase of the research project was a paper-and-pencil survey containing 135 precoded questions, administered to a random sample from the unit consisting of about 25 managers, 25 college-level nonmanagers ("professionals"), and 25 non-college-level nonmanagers ("others"); a total of 1,295 usable questionnaires were collected, an average of 65 per unit.

The questionnaire was intended to collect information on the same four types of manifestations of culture as covered in the interview checklist: practices (symbols, heroes, and rituals) and values. Values items described what the respondent felt "should be"; practices items described what she or he felt "is." The distinction between the two was present not only in the conception of the researchers but also in the minds of the respon-

Exhibit 8.4 *F* Values for Analyses of Variance for Questions in the Organizational Culture Survey

	F Values for ANOVAs			
	Minimum	Maximum	Median	Limit[a]
10 questions on values across 10 countries[b]	3.2	46.7	8.0	3.1
10 questions on values across 20 organizations	1.6	6.4	4.0	2.5
18 questions on practices across 20 organizations	4.3	12.8	7.1	2.5

a. $p < .001$ significance limit.
b. From Exhibit 2.3.

dents. In a factor analysis of all 135 survey items for all 1,295 respondents, values items and practices items loaded consistently on different factors, with very little overlap. The questionnaire contained the following items:

- *Values.* This section consisted of 57 questions: 22 work goals, 28 general beliefs, and 7 other items that in the IBM studies had correlated with these. Most were taken from the IBM questionnaire (see Exhibit 5.11 and Appendix 1), some from Laurent (1983), and 5 new items were added on the basis of the interviews. As described in Chapter 2 for the cross-national study, work goals represented "values as the desired" (what people claimed to want for themselves) whereas general beliefs represented "values as the desirable" (what people included in their worldviews; the difference is explained in Chapter 1). The other questions included the desired and the actually perceived decision-making style of one's boss.

- *Practices: symbols and rituals.* This section consisted of 54 questions about perceptions of one's work situation. Of these, 15 were inspired by Reynolds (1986), who did a thorough scan of the anecdotal U.S. literature on corporate cultures for suggested dimensions of differences. The remaining 39 were based on the interviews. All questions were cast into a bipolar format under the general heading "Where I work . . ." and used 5-point scales; for example, 1 = *meeting times are kept very punctually* and 5 = *meeting times are only kept approximately.*

- *Practices: heroes.* This section included 7 questions about the "behavior of a typical member of the organization," using 5-point "semantic differential" scales; for example, 1 = *slow* and 5 = *fast.* Also included were 13 questions asked about reasons for promotion and dismissal, which were rated on 5-point scales of importance or frequency. All 20

questions in this section were inspired by the interviews.

- *Demographics.* In this section, 4 questions asked about the respondent's gender, age group, seniority with the employer, and education level. Finally, there was an open question asking the respondent for any additions or remarks.

For all 131 values and practices questions, without exception, unit mean scores differed significantly across the 20 organizational units. However, the 57 questions dealing with values tended to produce smaller differences between units than the 74 questions dealing with perceived practices. The range of the 20 unit mean scores for the group of values questions was from .32 to 2.09 points (mean .87); the range for the group of perceived-practices questions was from .68 to 3.22 points (mean 1.43).[83]

Ten values questions also used in the IBM study and subjected at that time to analyses of variance (ANOVAs) across countries and occupations (see Exhibit 2.3) were analyzed by similar ANOVAs across the 20 organizational units. Eighteen key practices questions (to be discussed below) were also subjected to ANOVAs.

The *F* values shown in Exhibit 8.4 are a measure of the variance explained by the criterion (country or organization). Again, all but one are significant at the .001 level. For the questions on values, country differences explained more variance than organization differences for any single question studied; for organizations, questions on practices had almost twice as much variance explained as questions on values.

The ANOVA results justified our research approach. Membership in an organization did explain a significant share of the variance in the answers by members for all 131 culture questions used in the survey. The (unpredicted) finding that values varied more across countries than across organizations, and that across organizations practices produced much wider ranges of answers than values, led to the distinction between national and organizational cultures pictured in Exhibit 8.3.[84] Other criteria included in all the ANOVAs reported were occupation level, gender, and age. Their effects did not differ systematically between the cross-national and the cross-organizational study, or between values and practices questions in the cross-organizational study.

Dimensions of Organizational Cultures

In the same way the cross-national study identified dimensions of national cultures, the cross-organizational study detected dimensions of organizational cultures. This called for a multivariate analysis. The data from the 131 survey items were condensed so as to explain the maximum share of their variance by the smallest possible number of meaningful factors. The answers on each question by 1,295 individual respondents were aggregated into mean scores for 20 organizational units. Each mean score was derived from a stratified sample of approximately equal shares of managers, professionals, and others.

The data formed a 131 × 20 ecological matrix: 131 variables, excluding the demographics, and 20 cases. We computed a 131 × 131 product-moment correlation matrix, correlating the 20 mean scores for each possible pair of questions. This showed that (1) values correlated with other values but rarely with practices (as we had already found in an earlier factor analysis of individual scores); (2) perceived symbols, rituals, and typical-member scores correlated among each other; and (3) reasons for promotion and dismissal correlated among each other but rarely with other items at all. We therefore decided to divide the questions, for analytic purposes, into three categories—57 values questions; 61 perceived symbols, rituals, and typical-member scores; and 13 reasons for promotion and dismissal—and to conduct separate factor analyses for these three categories.[85]

Practices questions. By far the clearest ecological factor structure emerged across the 20 organizational units for the 54 symbols and rituals questions in the "Where I work . . ." format plus the seven "typical member" questions.[86] Six very well interpretable factors could be extracted, together explaining 73% of the variance (see Exhibit 8.5).[87] The labels for the corresponding dimensions were partly based on interpretations by survey participants during the feedback discussions. These labels avoided as much as possible suggesting that one pole of the dimension was "good" and the other "bad."

Scores for each unit on each of the six dimensions were computed from the unit mean scores on

three key "Where I work . . ." items with high loadings (over .60) on the factor. We chose items that together represented the essence of the dimension, as we interpreted it, and that had enough face validity to convey this essence to the management and members of the units in the feedback sessions. In Exhibit 8.5 these key items are shown in boldface type. In an ecological factor analysis of only these 6 × 3 = 18 questions for the 20 units they accounted for 86% of the variance in mean scores between units.

Dimension P1, *process oriented versus results oriented,* opposed a concern with means to a concern with goals. The three key items show that in the process-oriented cultures people perceived themselves as avoiding risks and spending only limited effort in their jobs, and that they saw each day as pretty much the same. In the results-oriented cultures people perceived themselves as comfortable in unfamiliar situations and as putting in maximal effort, and they felt that each day brought new challenges.[88] A similar distinction is known from organization sociology. One of the best examples is Burns and Stalker's (1961) distinction between mechanistic and organic management systems. According to Burns and Stalker, mechanistic systems are among other things characterized by "the abstract nature of each individual task, which is pursued with techniques and purposes more or less distinct from those of the concern as a whole; i.e., the functionaries tend to pursue the technical improvement of means, rather than the accomplishment of the ends of the concern" (p. 120). Organic systems are characterized by "the 'realistic' nature of the individual task, which is seen as set by the total situation of the concern" (p. 121). Results orientation also corresponds with Peters and Waterman's (1982) first maxim: "A bias for action." [89] For this dimension it is difficult not to attach a "good" label to the results-oriented pole and a "bad" label to the other side. Nevertheless, there are operations for which a single-minded focus on the process is desirable. The most process-oriented unit among the 20 (score 00) was a production plant in a pharmaceutical firm. Drug manufacturing is an example of a risk-avoiding, routine-based environment in which it is doubtful whether one would want the culture to be results oriented. Departments with similar concerns exist in many other organizations. So even a results orientation is not always "good" and its opposite "bad."

Peters and Waterman's claim that "strong" cultures are more results oriented was supported by our data. We interpreted "strong" as "homogeneous" and operationalized it as the reverse of the mean standard deviation, across the individuals within a unit, of scores on the 18 key practices questions (3 per dimension). A low standard deviation means that different respondents from the

Exhibit 8.5   Results of Factor Analysis of Unit Mean Scores on 61 Practices Items Across 20 Organizational Units

Factor P1: Process oriented versus results oriented
.88   Employees are told when good job is done.
.88   Typical member fast.
.86   Comfortable in unfamiliar situations.
.85   Each day brings new challenges.
.78   Typical member initiating.
.75   Informal style of dealing with each other.
.73   Typical member warm.
.70   Try to be pioneers.
.70   Typical member direct.
.69   People put in maximal effort.
.67   Mistakes are tolerated.
.67   Typical member optimistic.
.63   Open to outsiders and newcomers (second loading).
.60   Managers help good people to advance (second loading).

Factor P2: Employee oriented versus job oriented
.84   Important decisions made by individuals.
.76   Organization only interested in work people do.
.69   Decisions centralized at top.
.68   Managers keep good people for own department.
.65   Changes imposed by management decree.
.64   Newcomers left to find own way.
.64   Management dislikes union members.
.62   No special ties with local community.
.60   Little concern for personal problems of employees.

Factor P3: Parochial versus professional
.87   People's private life is their own business.
.79   Job competence is only criterion in hiring people.
.73   Think three years ahead or more.
.63   Strongly aware of competition.
.62   Cooperation and trust between departments normal.

Factor P4: Open system versus closed system
.67   Only very special people fit in organization.
.67   Our department worst of organization.
.66   Management stingy with small things.
.64   Little attention to physical work environment.
.63   Organization and people closed and secretive.
.61   New employees need more than a year to feel at home.

Factor P5: Loose control versus tight control
.73   Everybody cost-conscious.
.73   Meeting times kept punctually.
.62   Typical member well-groomed.
.61   Always speak seriously of organization and job.

Factor P6: Normative versus pragmatic
.84   Pragmatic, not dogmatic in matters of ethics.
.68   Organization contributes little to society.
.63   Major emphasis on meeting customer needs.
.63   Results more important than procedures.
.63   Never talk about the history of the organization.

NOTE: All loadings over .60 are shown. Items with negative loadings are reworded negatively. Items in **boldface** were chosen as key indicators for the dimension. The six factors together explain 73% of variance.

same unit perceived their environment in much the same way, regardless of the content of the perceptions. Actual mean standard deviations varied from .87 to 1.08, and correlation between these mean standard deviations, as a measure of culture strength, and the unit's scores on "results orientation" was rho = -.71***.

Dimension P2, *employee oriented versus job oriented,* opposed a concern for people to a concern for getting the job done. The key items selected show that in the employee-oriented cultures people felt that their personal problems were taken into account, that the organization took a responsibility for employee welfare, and that important decisions were made by groups or committees. In the job-oriented units people experienced a strong pressure for getting the job done; they perceived the organization as interested only in the work employees did, not in their personal and family welfare; and they reported that important decisions were made by individuals.[90] This dimension corresponds to the two axes of Blake and Mouton's (1964) managerial grid. The fact that Blake and Mouton claimed employee orientation and job orientation to be two independent dimensions seems to conflict with our placing them at opposite poles of a single dimension. However, Blake and Mouton's grid applied to individuals, whereas our analysis was made at the level of social systems. It simply means that the units in our analysis tended to vary along the line 9,1–1,9 in Blake and Mouton's grid. Opinions about the desirability of a strong employee orientation differed among the leaders of the units in the study. In the feedback discussions, some top managers wanted their unit to become more employee oriented whereas others desired a move in the opposite direction.

Dimension P3, *parochial versus professional,* opposed units whose employees derived their identity largely from the organization to units in which people identified with their type of job. The key questions show that members of parochial cultures felt that the organization's norms covered their behavior at home as well as on the job; they felt that in hiring employees the company took their social and family backgrounds into account as much as their job competence; and they did not look far into the future (they probably assumed the organization would do this for them). On the other side, members of professional cultures considered their private lives their own business, they felt the organization hired on the basis of job competence only, and they did think far ahead.[91] Sociology has long known this distinction as "local" versus "cosmopolitan," the contrast between an internal and an external frame of reference (Merton, 1949/1968, pp. 447 ff.). The

parochial type of culture is often associated with Japanese companies.

Dimension P4, *open versus closed,* described the communication climate (Poole, 1985), a focus of attention for both human resources and public relations experts. The key items show that in the open system units members considered both the organization and its people open to newcomers and outsiders; they believed that almost anyone would fit into the organization and that new employees needed only a few days to feel at home. In the closed system units, the organization and its people were felt to be closed and secretive, even among insiders; members felt that only very special people would fit into the organization and that new employees needed more than a year to feel at home (in the most closed unit, one member of the top management team confessed that he still felt an outsider after 22 years).[92]

Dimension P5, *loose versus tight,* referred to the amount of internal structuring in the organization. According to the key questions, people in loosely controlled units felt that no one thought of cost, meeting times were only kept approximately, and jokes about the company and the job were frequent. People in tightly controlled units described their work environment as cost-conscious, meeting times were kept punctually, and jokes about the company and/or the job were rare. The data showed that a tight formal control system was associated, at least statistically, with strict unwritten codes in terms of dress and dignified behavior.[93] The tight-versus-loose distinction is well-known from the literature on management control (for example, see Hofstede, 1967, pp. 144 ff.).

Dimension P6, *normative versus pragmatic,* dealt with the amount of structuring in the unit's *external* contacts. It corresponds to the popular notion of "customer orientation." Pragmatic units were market driven; normative units perceived their task toward the outside world as the implementation of inviolable rules. The key items show that in the normative units the major emphasis was on correctly following organizational procedures, which were more important than results; in matters of business ethics and honesty, the unit's standards were felt to be high. In the pragmatic units there was a major emphasis on meeting the customer's needs, results were more important than correct procedures, and in matters of business ethics a pragmatic rather than a dogmatic attitude prevailed.[94] The pragmatic pole corresponds with Peters and Waterman's (1982) second maxim: "Staying close to the customer." Our empirical data showed "results orientation" and "customer orientation" to be two separate and independent dimensions. An organization can be results oriented but not customer oriented (example: one of the two police corps). The opposite combination can be found in service businesses: Trying to serve the customer does not automatically imply a results orientation.

Together, the six dimensions of perceived practices, P1 through P6, can be seen as a checklist for practical culture differences between organizations.

Values questions. Twenty-two work goals scores for each unit were standardized in the same way as had been done in the cross-national study (Chapter 2). For the remaining 35 values items no standardization was necessary and simple unit mean scores were computed. The 57 items × 20 units matrix was again factor analyzed. Three interpretable factors were retained (V1 through V3), together explaining 62% of the variance; see Exhibit 8.6.

V1, need for security, and V3, need for authority, resemble two dimensions from the cross-national study: uncertainty avoidance and power distance, respectively. We may be dealing with basically the same value complexes, but the individual items distributed themselves differently in the cross-organizational and in the cross-national case. V2, work centrality, was found in the cross-national case to be related to masculinity, but here again the items associated with the cross-organizational and the cross-national dimension were only very partially the same.[95]

All three factors were associated with the nationality of the unit: Danish or Dutch. In the cross-national study the Danish and Dutch IBM subsidiaries, on scales from 0 to 100, differed 30 points on UAI (the Netherlands more rigid), 20 points on PDI (Denmark more equal), 6 points on IDV (both quite individualist), and 2 points on MAS (both quite feminine). The relatively largest difference, therefore, was on the dimension of uncertainty avoidance, and this repeated itself as a difference on need for security in the cross-organizational study. However, in spite of the Danes' lower score on power distance in the cross-national study, the Danish units in the cross-organizational study scored higher than the Dutch on need for authority. On work centrality the Danish units all scored high, whereas the Dutch varied. Of course, the organizations in the two countries were not matched, so that the differences found contain the accidental effects of the particular samples of Danish and Dutch units studied.[96]

Questions about reasons for promotion and dismissal. These 13 items were factor analyzed separately. The 7 reasons for promotion were, in order of average endorsement across all 20 units, as follows: personality, performance, commitment to the organization, creativity, collegiality, diplomas, and seniority. The 6 reasons for dis-

missal were (in order of endorsement): stealing the equivalent of U.S.$500, stealing the equivalent of U.S.$50, alcohol during working hours, poor performance, conflict with the boss, and sex with a subordinate. These items, as mentioned above, did not correlate strongly with any other parts of the questionnaire, but only among themselves. In a factor analysis of the 13 item means for the 20 units there was a strong first factor (H1, *H* for *heroes*) opposing promotion for present merits (commitment, creativity, performance) to promotion for past merits (diplomas and seniority). A weaker second factor (H2) opposed dismissal for job-related misbehavior (stealing) to dismissal for off-the-job morals (sex).

Integrating the practices, values, and promotion/dismissal factors. The practices factors were the clearest and least ambiguous. This should be no surprise, because we have already seen that it was the practices questions that best discriminated between organizational units. In order to test the relationships among the three sets of factors (P1 through P6, V1 through V3, and H1 plus H2) we ran a second-order factor analysis of the factor scores for the 20 units on these 11 factors, plus the unit mean scores on five demographic indicators: gender, age, seniority, education, and nationality. The following three second-order clusters emerged:

1. P1 (process oriented) with V3 (larger need for authority), H2 (dismissal for off-the-job morals), and mean age, which looks like a "bureaucracy" cluster
2. P3 (professional) with V2 (strong work centrality) and higher mean education level, clearly a "professionalism" cluster
3. P4 (closed system) with V1 (stronger need for security), H1 (promotion on past merits), and Dutch rather than Danish nationality, which could be called a "conservation" cluster

The three other practice factors—P2 (employee versus job), P5 (loose versus tight), and P6 (normative versus pragmatic)—were not associated with other variables in the second-order analysis. The second-order analysis shows that adding the values and the promotion/dismissal factors did not upset the six-dimensional practices dimension structure; it only provided additional information about values, promotion/dismissal, and demographic aspects linked to some of the practices but not to others.

Validating the Practice Dimensions

The third phase of the research project used open-ended questionnaires followed by personal

Exhibit 8.6   Results of Factor Analysis of Unit Mean Scores on 57 Values Items Across 20 Organizational Units

---

Factor V1: Need for security
.92   Man dislikes work.
.91   Variety and adventure in work unimportant.
.89   Fringe benefits important.
.87   Main reason for hierarchical structure is knowing who has authority.
.87   When a man's career demands it, family should make sacrifices.
.86   Having little tension and stress at work important.
.83   Would not continue working if didn't need the money.
.83   The successful in life should help the unsuccessful.
.83   Pursuing own interest is not best contribution to society.
.76   Working in well-defined job situation important.
.75   Serving your country unimportant.
.75   When people have failed in life it's not their fault.
.74   Opportunity for advancement unimportant.
.74   Opportunities for training unimportant.
.73   Job you like is not more important than career.
.69   Being consulted by boss unimportant.
.66   Living in a desirable area unimportant.
.63   Employees afraid to disagree with superiors.
.63   Most people cannot be trusted.
.63   Desirable that management authority can be questioned (second loading).

Factor V2: Work centrality
.84   Work more important than leisure time.
.78   Competition between employees not harmful.
.65   Physical working conditions unimportant.
.65   Opportunities for helping others unimportant.
.64   No authority crisis in organizations.
.63   Does not prefer a consultative manager.
.62   Challenging tasks important.
.62   Prestigious company or organization important.
.61   Decisions by individuals better than group decisions.
.60   Working relationship with boss important.

Factor V3: Need for authority
.81   Most organizations better off if conflicts eliminated forever.
.70   Own manager autocratic or paternalistic.
.70   Undesirable that management authority can be questioned.
.65   Parents should stimulate children to be best in class.
.64   Employee who quietly does duty is asset to organization.
.62   Parents should not be satisfied when children become independent.
.61   Staying with one employer is best way for making career.
.61   Conflicts with opponents best resolved by compromise.

NOTE: All loadings over .60 are shown. Work goal item scores were first standardized across 22 items. Items with negative loadings are reworded negatively. The three factors together explain 62% of variance.

interviews with company officials in order to collect information about the unit as a whole. Examples are total employee strength, budget composition, key historical facts, and demographics of key managers. We called these the "structural" data. All were collected by me personally, as deciding on which questions would be relevant and could be asked called for a considerable amount of trial, error, judgment, and business experience; the questionnaire evolved during the initial interviews.

Organizational cultures will be partly predetermined by nationality, industry, task, and market, partly related to organizational variables such as structure and control systems, and partly unique products of idiosyncratic features such as the organization's history or the personality of its founder. Nationality, industry, task, and market of a unit are directly observable features. We found nationality (as well as the other demographics—education, age, seniority, and hierarchical level) primarily correlated with values, hardly with perceived practices.

For the organization's industry, task, and market, the scoring profiles of the 20 units on the six practice dimensions showed that dimensions P1 (process versus results), P3 (parochial versus professional), P5 (loose versus tight), and P6 (normative versus pragmatic) varied at least partly according to the type of work the organization did and the type of market in which it operated. In fact, these four dimensions reflected "industry cultures" common to all organizations within the same industry (see Exhibit 8.3).[97] The two remaining dimensions, P2 (employee versus job) and P4 (open versus closed), were independent of the industry and reflected the philosophy of founders and top leaders.

The structural data collection produced a large number of quantified data; 40 variables were retained as reasonably meaningful and comparable across units. Exhibit 8.7 lists their interpretable and significant correlations with the units' scores on the six practices dimensions.[98] Some of the variables were obviously intercorrelated: There was a clear cluster of variables related to the unit's size, such as annual budget, total invested capital, and number of employees. From this cluster the number of employees was the variable most strongly correlated with the culture dimensions. Size in terms of number of employees affected the correlations between culture and budget split (labor- versus material-intensive), so we controlled for it in the corresponding lines of Exhibit 8.7. None of the other correlations shown depended on size. Other intercorrelations among structural variables were of insufficient interest to be taken into account.

On dimension P1, process versus results orientation, manufacturing and office units tended to score on the process-oriented side and research and development and service units on the results-oriented side. Exhibit 8.7 shows a strong correlation between dimension P1 and the split between labor and material cost in the operating budget. Any operation can be characterized as labor-intensive, material-intensive, or capital-intensive, depending on which of the three categories of cost takes the largest share of its operating budget. Labor-intensive units, holding number of employees constant, scored as more results oriented, whereas material-intensive units, again holding number of employees constant, scored as more process oriented. If an operation is labor-intensive, people's efforts, by definition, play an important role in its results. This supports a results-oriented culture. The yield of material-intensive units depends more on technical processes, which stimulates a process-oriented culture.

The second-highest correlation of results orientation was with lower absenteeism. This is a nice

validation of the fact that, as one of the key questions formulated it, "people put in a maximal effort." There were three significant correlations between results orientation and aspects of the organization structure. Flatter organizations (larger span of control for the unit top manager) scored as more results oriented. This confirmed Peters and Waterman's (1982) seventh maxim: "Simple form, lean staff." Three simplified scales were used, based on the Aston studies of organizational structure (Pugh & Hickson, 1976), to measure centralization, specialization, and formalization. Both specialization and formalization were negatively correlated with results orientation: More specialized and more formalized units tended to be more process oriented. They were more like Burns and Stalker's (1961) mechanistic systems. The remaining correlations of results orientation were with having a top management team with a lower education level and one that has been promoted from the ranks: doers rather than figureheads. Finally, in results-oriented units, union membership among employees tended to be lower.

Scores on dimension P2 (employee versus job orientation) clearly reflected the philosophy of the unit's or company's founder(s) and top leaders as described and demonstrated during the interviews and feedback sessions. They also showed the possible scars left by past events: Units that had recently been in economic trouble, especially if this was accompanied through collective layoffs, tended to score as job oriented even if, according to our informants, the past had been different. As mentioned earlier, opinions about the desirability of a strong employee orientation differed among the unit leaders; in the feedback discussions some top managers wanted their units to become more employee oriented and some others desired the opposite.

The strongest correlations with dimension P2 in Exhibit 8.7 are with the way the unit is controlled by the organization to which it belongs. Where the top manager of the unit stated that his superiors evaluated him on profits and other financial performance measures, the members scored the unit culture to be more job oriented. Where the top manager of the unit felt his superiors evaluated him on performance against a budget, the opposite was the case: Members scored the unit culture to be more employee oriented. It seems that operating against external standards (profits in a market) breeds a less benevolent culture than operating against internal standards (a budget). Where the top manager stated he allowed controversial news to be published in the employee journal, members felt the unit to be more employee oriented, which validated the top manager's veracity. The remaining correlations of employee orientation were with the average seniority and age of employees (more senior em-

Exhibit 8.7   Product-Moment Correlation Coefficients Between Unit-Level Measures and Unit Scores on Six Dimensions of Practices Across 20 Organizational Units[a]

Structural Characteristic	P1	P2	P3	P4	P5	P6
Measures of size						
Annual budget			.61**			
Total invested capital		−.41*	.53**			
Number of employees			.60**			
Private (−) versus public (+)			−.39*			−.39*
Budget split in % (holding number of employees constant)						
Labor	.72***					
Materials	−.46*				.48*	
Measures of structure						
Span of control, top manager	.41*					
% supervisory personnel				−.39*		
Centralization score					.26[b]	
Specialization score	−.40*		.41*			.38*
Formalization score	−.40*			.43*		
Control system						
Top manager's boss focuses on profits		.61**				
Top manager's boss focuses on budgets		−.56**				
Controversial issues in employee journal		−.55**		−.39*		
Time budget of top manager						
% reading/writing memos					.66**	
% meetings/discussions			.51*			
Profile of top five managers						
At least one woman				−.38*		
Average education level	−.39*	−.42*	.58**		−.46*	
Average age			.46*			
Promoted from ranks	−.40*					
Profile of employees						
% women				−.78***	.45*	
% female managers				−.58**	.54**	
% absenteeism	−.60**				.39*	
Average seniority			.53**	−.39*		
Average age			.38*			
Average education men						−.47*
Average education women						−.41*
Recent growth in number						−.43*
Union membership	−.39*		−.59**			

a. Positive correlations indicate results orientation (P1), job orientation (P2), professional (P3), closed system (P4), tight control (P5), or pragmatic (P6).
b. Highest correlation with centralization score, not significant.
*p = .05; **p = .01; ***p = .001.

ployees scored as being in a more job-oriented culture), with the education level of the top management team (less-educated teams corresponded with a more job-oriented culture), and with the total invested capital (not with the invested capital per employee). Large organizations with heavy investment tended to be more employee oriented than job oriented.

On dimension P3 (parochial versus professional), units with a traditional technology tended to score as parochial and high-tech units as professional. The strongest correlations of this dimension in Exhibit 8.7 are with various measures of size: The larger organizations fostered the more professional cultures. Professional cultures also had smaller labor union membership, their managers had a higher average education level and age, and they scored higher on specialization. An interesting correlation is with the time budget of the unit top manager: In the units with a professional culture, the top managers claimed to spend a relatively large share of their time in meetings and person-to-person discussions. Finally, the privately owned units in our sample tended to score more professional than the public ones.

The philosophy of the organization's founder(s) and top leaders played a strong role in dimension P4 (open versus closed), just as it did for dimension P2 (employee versus job orientation). Communication climates in the units we studied seemed to have been formed historically without much outside rationale; some organizations had developed a tradition of being closed, others of remarkable openness. In the national context, however, open versus closed was the only one of the six practice dimensions significantly associated with nationality: An open organizational communication climate was more characteristic of Danish than of Dutch organizations. However, one Danish unit scored extremely closed, which corresponded to its external and internal image and to what respondents told us about its history.

The open/closed dimension in Exhibit 8.7 is responsible for the single strongest correlation in the matrix, $r = .78***$ between the percentage of women among employees and the openness of the communication climate. The percentage of women among managers and the presence of at least one woman in the top management team were also correlated with openness.[99] Other correlates of the open/closed dimension were formalization (associated with a more closed culture, a suitable validation of both measures), admitting controversial issues into the employee journal (associated with a more open culture, another validation), higher average seniority, and a higher percentage of supervisory personnel (both marginally associated with a more open culture, counter to what one might expect).

On dimension P5 (loose versus tight control), units delivering precision or risky products or services (such as pharmaceuticals or money transactions) tended to score as tight on control, whereas those with innovative or unpredictable activities tended to score as loose. The two municipal police corps scored on the loose control side (16 and 41 on the 0-100 scale): Police work is unpredictable, and police personnel have considerable discretion

in the way they want to carry out their task. The strongest correlation of the loose versus tight control dimension was with an item in the self-reported time budget of the unit top manager: Where the top manager claimed to spend a relatively large part of his time reading and writing reports and memos from inside the organization, we found tighter control. This makes perfect sense. We also found that material-intensive units had more tightly controlled cultures. As the results of such units often depend on small margins of material yields, this makes sense too.

Tight control in Exhibit 8.7 is also correlated with the percentages of female managers and of female employees, in this order. This is most likely a consequence of the type of activities for which women are hired. Tighter control is found in units with a lower education level among male and female employees and also among top managers. In units in which the number of employees had recently increased, control was felt to be looser; where the number of employees had been reduced, control was perceived as tighter. Employee layoffs are obviously associated with budget squeezes. Finally, absenteeism among employees was lower where control was perceived to be not so tight. Absenteeism is evidently one way to escape from the pressure of a tightly controlled system.

On dimension P6 (normative versus pragmatic), service units and those operating in competitive markets tended to score as pragmatic, whereas units involved in the implementation of laws and operating under a monopoly tended to score as normative. Exhibit 8.7 shows only two correlations with this dimension: Privately owned units in our sample were more pragmatic, public units were more normative (like the police corps), and there was a positive correlation between pragmatism and specialization, which we would not have predicted.

Conspicuously missing from Exhibit 8.7 are correlations with performance measures. We were unable to identify measures of performance applicable to so varied a set of organizational units; the ones we tried did not yield significant correlations. Also, as I will argue below, the relationship between culture and performance is contingent upon organizational strategy, so even from a theoretical point of view, across-the-board correlations between culture dimensions and performance should not be expected.[100]

Although the task and market environment clearly affected the scores on at least four of the practice dimensions, some individual units showed surprising exceptions: One production plant produced an unexpectedly strong results orientation even on the shop floor; TKB (Appendix 7) showed an amazingly loose control system in relation to its task. These surprises confirm that there was room for distinctive and creative elements in these unit's cultures. None of the correlations in Exhibit 8.7 was so strong as to preclude deviations by individual units from general patterns. In our interviews and during feedback discussions within the 20 participating units we found many idiosyncratic components of organizational cultures within the limits set by the task and the systems.

Organizational Subcultures

In order to be a meaningful subject for the study of its organizational culture, a unit should be reasonably homogeneous with regard to the cultural characteristics studied, sufficiently homogeneous for statements about the culture as a whole to be justified.[101] This means that there can even be different desirable study levels for different characteristics: Some aspects of a culture can apply corporationwide, whereas others will be specific to smaller units. Culture rifts within organizations can by themselves represent essential cultural information.[102]

In choosing the units for the IRIC study, we necessarily had to walk rather lightly over the issue of cultural homogeneity. The possibility of studying this aspect in more detail presented itself in 1988 when a Danish insurance company (3,400 employees) commissioned IRIC to compare its culture(s) with those found in the earlier project. The study was combined with a periodic measurement of employee attitudes, which meant that, unlike in the 20 units studied before, in this company all employees were included.[103] Initially, Danish IRIC collaborators held 24 open-ended interviews with a selection of informants from all levels and departments of the company. The survey questionnaire, designed after the interviews, included among its 120 questions the 18 (3 × 6) key questions about practices from IRIC's organizational culture study. Usable questionnaires were returned by 2,408 employees, a 71% response rate.

The total respondent population could be divided into 131 "organic" working groups. These were the smallest building blocks of the organization, whose members had regular face-to-face contact. For the sake of confidentiality, we agreed with the company that results for groups with fewer than 8 respondents would not be computed; in this case, groups were combined. The mean group size was 20; apart from one group of 54, all others were smaller than 35. Managers were not included in the groups they managed; rather, they were combined with colleagues at their level of the hierarchy. We took this step because otherwise the manager's answers in each group would have been drowned out by the answers of the much more numerous subordinates.

The 131 organic working groups were subject to a hierarchical cluster analysis on the basis of their 18 mean scores on the key culture questions.[104] In Exhibit 2.8 the same method was used to cluster the 53 countries and regions in the IBM set on the basis of their four national culture dimension scores. The analysis produces a *dendrogram* showing the proximity of the groups. As the full dendrogram was too unwieldy to be reproduced, its size has been reduced in Exhibit 8.8 to show only its main divisions (that is, its right-hand part), leaving out the smaller subdivisions. Exhibit 8.8 therefore does not show the clustering of working groups (*n* = 131) but the clustering of *clusters of* working groups (*n* = 30, comprising between 1 and 15 working groups each).

The dendrogram shows a first split between clusters 24-30 and the rest. The next split is between clusters 01-11 and 12-23. These three groups are the "superclusters" representing three markedly different subcultures in the company. Further splits were more difficult to interpret.

The three subcultures were as follows:

1. *Clusters 01-11, 49 working groups, 823 persons:* These working groups consisted of top management, nearly all other managers, central departments including personnel and data processing, and, from the product divisions, those involved in large, custommade insurances (for ships and industry). Most respondents in this subculture were highly educated. We called this the "professional" subculture.

2. *Clusters 12-23, 37 working groups, 614 persons:* These working groups consisted of the administrative departments and, from the product divisions, those involved in standard insurances (life, private risks, and business risks), except for the damage appraisers. Most respondents in this subculture were women. We called this the "administrative" subculture.

3. *Clusters 24-30, 45 working groups, 971 persons:* These working groups consisted of the personnel of the sales offices (this company sold its own products and did not operate through middlemen) and, from the different product divisions, all the damage appraisers. The analysis put salespersons and appraisers together although they belonged to quite different parts of the organization. What they had in common was being located away from the head office and having constant face-to-face contact with customers. We called this the "customer interface" subculture.

Exhibit 8.8. Simplified Dendrogram of Organizational Subcultures for a Danish Insurance Company

```
                                           re-scaled distance
                              8   10          15        20            25
 cluster    groups   persons  --------------------------------------------+
   01         9       254     -----+
   02         2        23     ------+
   03         7       102     --------------------+
   04         4        59     -----------+
   05         5        58     --+
   06         2        23     -----+                        +-------+
   07         7       119     --------------------+
   08         3        34     --+
   09         6       112     ----------+
   10         2        19     --------------------+
   11         2        20     --+                      +-----+
            _____
             49       823                                  |
   12         2        18     -----+
   13         1         8     -----------------+
   14         1        12     ---------+        +-----+
   15         1        11     -----------------+
   16         3        63     -----+
   17         6       103     -------------+     +------+
   18         2        21     --------------------+
   19         9       174     -------+
   20         4        71     ---------+      +---+
   21         2        22     --------------------+
   22         5        99     -----+
   23         1        12     ---------------+
            _____
             37       614
   24        15       341     --+
   25         1        31     -----------+
   26         6       127     -----------------+
   27         2        24     -------+         |
   28         7       151     ---------+       +-----------------+
   29        13       288     ---------------+
   30         1         9     ---------------+
            _____
             45       971
   
   total    131      2408
```

NOTE: The size of the original dendrogram has been reduced so that this exhibit shows only the right-hand part, cutting off at a rescaled distance of 8 points, thus combining the 131 working groups into 30 small clusters.

Exhibit 8.9 lists the mean scores on the six dimensions of organizational cultures for the three subcultures: professional, administrative, and customer interface. Each of the six scales stretches from 0 to 100 based on the extreme scores found among the 20 units of the earlier study.

On dimension 1 the customer interface subculture scored toward the results-oriented side, the administrative subculture scored toward the process-oriented side, and the professional subculture was in the middle. On dimension 2 all three subcultures scored employee oriented, but the customer interface subculture most and the professional subculture least. On dimension 3 all three scored parochial, but the professional subculture obviously least so. On dimension 4 all three scored quite open, but the customer inter-

Exhibit 8.9   Scores on Six Culture Dimensions for Three Subcultures Within a Danish Insurance Company

	Subculture		
	Professional	Administrative	Customer Interface
1. 0 = process oriented			
100 = results oriented	46	*34*	**59**
2. 0 = employee oriented			
100 = job oriented	**40**	33	*21*
3. 0 = parochial			
100 = professional	**34**	*21*	25
4. 0 = open system			
100 = closed system	*18*	19	**29**
5. 0 = loose control			
100 = tight control	**30**	19	*1*
6. 0 = normative			
100 = pragmatic	**67**	*54*	58

NOTE: Highest scores appear in **boldface**; lowest scores appear in *italics*. In the original sample survey across 20 organizational units, the .01 significance limit for differences in dimension scores between units lay at 5 points. In the insurance company survey, because of the much larger respondent populations, the .01 significance limit for differences in dimension scores lies at 1 point, so all differences in this exhibit are significant.

face culture surprisingly less open than the other two (salespeople keep their business secrets!). On dimension 5 all three subcultures scored very loose, the customer interface culture extremely so. Finally, on dimension 6 all three scored toward the pragmatic side, but it was the professional subculture (and not the customer interface subculture as one would expect) that was most pragmatic.

The mean absolute distance across the six dimensions between the professional and the administrative subculture was 10 points; between the administrative and the customer interface, 12 points; and between the professional and the customer interface, 15 points. The customer interface subculture represented a counterculture to the professional culture, which included higher management.[105]

Just before the survey was conducted, the company had gone through two cases of internal rebellion: from the salespersons and from the women. The sales rebellion had been a conflict about working conditions and compensation; a sales strike had only just been prevented. This problem can be understood as a product of the wide gap between the professional and customer interface subcultures. This rift on the culture map of the company proved quite dangerous. It is the customer interface people who bring in the business—without them, an insurance company cannot survive. However, the managers and professionals who made the key decisions in this

company belonged to a quite different subculture: a high-profile, glorified environment in which big money, business trends, and market power were daily concerns—far from the crowd who did the actual work and brought in the daily earnings.

The women's rebellion was about the lack of careers for women, and it had taken place after it became known that the share of female employees had passed 50%. This was a peaceful revolution: In Danish consensus style, a committee of female employees had been accepted as a discussion partner for the (entirely male) top management, and it had led to the issue of careers for women being covered in the attitude survey that was combined with the culture study. The rebellion can be understood as a result of the gap between the professional and the administrative subcultures. Management, which shared the professional subculture, held an image of the woman employee that placed all women in the administrative subculture: The women were seen as relatively uneducated employees in routine jobs, not upward mobile. The company's problem was that this image was no longer accurate, if it ever had been so. From the 1,700 women in the company, 700 now had higher education; many worked in professional roles, and even those in administrative roles were nearly as interested in careers as their male colleagues.[106] Interestingly, Denmark had one of the highest proportions of female employment in the world, but this did not prevent managers in this company from maintaining the stereotype of women's basically belonging to the administrative subculture.[107]

For an understanding of the culture of this insurance company, an understanding of the subculture split was essential. Unfortunately, those in management—caught in their professional culture—did not recognize the alarming aspects of the culture rifts. They took little action as a result of the survey. Soon afterward, the company started losing money; a few years later it changed ownership and top management.

The Usefulness of the Organizational Culture Construct

When trying to sell participation in the organizational culture research project to top managers of organizations, I claimed that "organizational culture represents the psychological assets of the organization, which predict its material assets in 5 years' time." This, of course, is a gratuitous slogan (who would ever be able to check its veracity?)—although in the above-mentioned case of the insurance company there was truth in it. In reality, as I see it now, the crucial element is not the organizational culture itself, but what (top) management does with it. I propose that four concepts (all of them "constructs" in the sense described in Chapter 1) have to be balanced, as pictured in Exhibit 8.10.[108]

The performance of an organization should be measured against its objectives, and top management's role is to translate objectives into strategy—even if by default all that emerges is a laissez-faire strategy. Strategies are carried out via the existing structure and control system, and their outcome is modified by the organization's culture; and all these four elements influence each other.

Our six-dimensional model of organizational practices did not support the notion that any position on a dimension was intrinsically "good" or "bad." Labeling positions on the dimension scales as more or less desirable is a matter of strategic choice, which will vary from one organization to another. For example, the popular stress on customer orientation (becoming more pragmatic on P6) is highly relevant for most organizations engaged in services and the manufacturing of custom-made quality products. It may be unnecessary or even dysfunctional, however, for the manufacturing side of organizations supplying standard products in a competitive price market or for units operating under government regulations.

This conclusion stands in flagrant contradiction to the "one best way" assumptions found in Peters and Waterman's (1982) eight maxims. What is good or bad depends in each case on where one wants the organization to go, and a cultural feature that means the organization is good at one thing inevitably implies that it is not so good at something else.

The link between strategy and culture in Exhibit 8.10 means that the two should fit;[109] and if they do not, one of the two should be adapted. Adapting the strategy is usually simpler and cheaper than trying to adapt the culture. Organizations are sometimes compared to animals. Suppose one's organization has a culture resembling an elephant: It is good at doing big, heavy jobs reliably. Suppose a new top manager comes in who aspires to a new strategy that will demand speed and flexibility. Who will change the elephant into an eagle?

Exhibit 8.7 shows several significant correlations between measures of structure and measures of culture. As structure is more deliberate than culture, I assume that in those cases the causality will have gone from structure to culture. The most effective way of changing organizational cultures is often through structural rearrangements, such as creating, closing, combining, or moving work groups, departments, or facilities. Organizational culture changes are not brought about by preaching but by changing the (rules of the) games played.

As far as the link between control and culture is concerned, culture represents an "organic" form of control of behavior, which from a management point of view may or may not be desirable, but it is a fact. Culturally imposed behaviors do not need to be enforced by organizational controls.[110] But when the intent is to change an organization's culture, again an effective means of doing this is to change control systems: who, what, where, at what level controls what, and in how much detail.

For the model in Exhibit 8.10 to be of use to management, a proper diagnosis should be made of the present state of the organization's culture and subcultures. This will very often demand the help of an outside consultant.[111] Top management should then evaluate the organization's cultural map in the light of possible strategies. What are its strengths and weaknesses? Can the strengths be better exploited and the weaknesses circumvented? Can the organization continue to live with its present culture? Deliberately changing an organization's culture is impossible without the active involvement of its top management; this is the one task that can never be delegated. The top manager(s) should personally believe in the feasibility of the change. Do its benefits outweigh its costs (which are always higher than expected)? Are the material resources and human skills available that will be needed for changing the culture? And if it has been decided that the culture should change, what steps will be taken to implement and monitor the changes, including periodic diagnoses to see how far the culture has moved? Does top

Exhibit 8.10. A Model for the Relationships Among Strategy, Structure, Control, and Culture

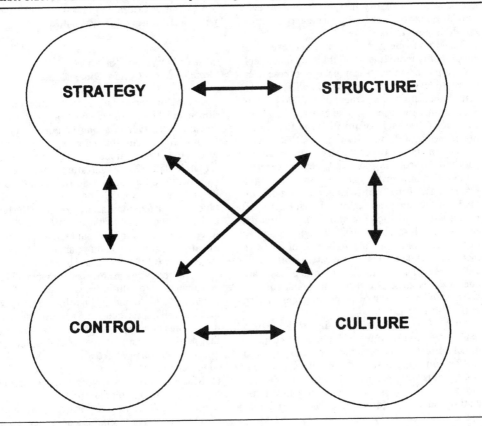

management realize its own crucial and lasting role in this process? Will top managers be given enough time by superiors, directors, or banks to take the process to its completion (and it always takes longer than one thinks)? Can a sufficient amount of support for the necessary changes be mobilized within the organization? Who will be the supporters and who the resisters? Can the supporters be activated and the resisters circumvented or put in positions where they can do no harm?

Given top management's commitment, organizational cultures are *somewhat* manageable.[112] However, those trying to manage an organization's culture(s) should take Morgan's (1986) warning to heart:

Our understanding of culture is usually much more fragmented and superficial than the reality. . . . Like organizational structure, culture is often viewed as a set of distinct variables, such as beliefs, stories, norms, and rituals, that somehow form a cultural whole. Such a view is unduly mechanistic, giving rise to the idea that culture can

be manipulated in an instrumental way. . . . Managers can influence the evolution of culture by being aware of the symbolic consequences of their actions and by attempting to foster desired values, but they can never control culture in the way that many management writers advocate. (p. 139)

One area where the link between strategy and organizational culture is crystal clear is that of mergers and takeovers. In Chapter 9, I will deal in more detail with international mergers and takeovers that involve national culture gaps, but mergers and takeovers within one national culture still have to cope with organizational culture clashes; they may be sources of major and often traumatic culture shocks that lead to a destruction of human capital and linger in employees' minds for the next 10 or 20 years. Such traumatic effects can be avoided or at least reduced through deliberate integration management,[113] but (too) few people in top management recognize and invest in this; they are usually too busy with and traumatized by the integration at their own level. Culture diagnosis of the partners prior to their integration can locate culture gaps, predict clashes, and serve as a basis for managing their integration (or even provide good arguments why a merger or takeover should be rejected).

Decisions to merge and to take or be taken over are probably more important than any other decisions top managements can make, yet these decisions are less founded on facts or unbiased information than almost any others. Premiums paid for acquisitions are based on wild guesses. In a comparison of 106 large acquisitions in the United States, Hayward and Hambrick (1997) have shown a relation between the size of the premiums paid and the acquiring company's chief executive officer's hubris level: "On average, we found losses in acquiring firms' shareholder wealth following an acquisition, and the greater the CEO hubris and acquisition premiums, the greater the shareholder losses" (p. 103). Dutch economist Schenk has concluded that only 15% of the large mergers and takeovers in the Western world in the 1990s created new value.[114] Part of the losses are due to the neglect of the organizational culture-clash problem and the corresponding destruction of the partners' psychological assets.

An implication of the model in Exhibit 8.10 is that studies trying to relate aspects of organizational culture to performance can be expected to yield results only if strategy, structure, and control systems are kept constant. Also, proving a relationship presumes that both "organizational culture" and "performance" can be reliably operationalized. Only a few studies meet these criteria. Gordon and DiTomaso (1992) compared 11 U.S. insurance companies that had participated in a common survey program. They operationalized "culture strength" in a way similar to what we did in the IRIC survey, as the inverse of the standard deviation of individual answers on survey questions, but only among managers. Culture strength in 1981 was significantly correlated with asset and premium growth rate between 1982 and 1987.[115] In a Ph.D. thesis, Koene (1996) measured the six practice dimensions plus aspects of perceived leadership and performance in 50 supermarkets of a Dutch chain. Shops differed primarily on the dimensions P2 (employee versus job oriented) and P4 (open versus closed), but the main determinant of performance was neither leadership nor culture but shop size. Christensen and Gordon (1999) used data from 77 U.S. firms from the files of Hay management consultants to test the relationship between organizational culture, as measured in the perception of practices by managers, and revenue growth. Dividing their companies into six industry types, they showed that relationships between culture and performance existed within industries but not across industries. Christensen and Gordon therefore also reject the "one best way" in organizational cultures and doubt the practice of hiring successful top executives from one industry to run a company in an entirely different industry.

How Universal Are the Six
Organizational Culture Dimensions?

The major outcome of the IRIC project is a six-dimensional model of organizational cultures, defined as perceived common practices: symbols, heroes, and rituals that carry specific meaning within the organizational unit. The source of the research data, 20 organizational units in two Northwestern European countries, is far too limited to claim universality for the model. Certain types of organizations, such as those in the health and welfare area, government offices, and armed forces, were missing from our set, and in other national environments additional practice dimensions that we never met could be relevant.

What I believe to be universal is that in other environments, too, differences among organizational cultures are partly quantifiable and can be meaningfully described using a limited number of dimensions of practices—perhaps five to seven—that partly overlap with the six described in this chapter. Information from some other sources supports this prediction. In India, Khandwalla (1985), in a study of managers across 75 organizations, using 5-point bipolar survey questions similar to our "Where I work . . ." questions, found a first factor closely resembling our process versus results orientation. A Swiss consultant, Cuno Pümpin (1984; see also Pümpin, Kobi, & Wüthrich, 1985), has described a seven-dimensional model, five dimensions of which are very similar to ours (results orientation, employee orientation, company orientation, cost orientation, and customer orientation), but the source of his model, other than common sense, is not clear from the published materials.[116] Several other measures of "organizational culture" are based on a one-best-way philosophy and/or a level-of-analysis fallacy signaled earlier. They use dimensions of perceptions of the culture by individuals (usually managers), not dimensions that contrasted organizations as such, and I will refer to them below in the subsection on the implications of the level of analysis. U.S. sociologists have regularly stressed the importance of studying organizations, and not just individuals, as the unit of analysis, but in the individualist academic tradition, this has been an uphill fight.[117]

The cultural limitations of the six-dimensional model imply that our questionnaire is not suitable for blanket replications. Interpreting the results is a matter of comparison. The formulas we used for computing the dimension scores were made for comparing an organization with the 20 units in the

IRIC study, but they are meaningless in other environments and at other times. New studies should choose their own units to compare and develop their own standards for comparison. They should at least repeat the first and second phases of our project—that is, start with interviews across the organizations to be studied in order to get a feel for the organizations' gestalts, and then compose their own questionnaire covering those issues that for these organizations describe the crucial differences in practices. Exhibits 8.5 and 8.6, which list the content of the questions we included, can serve as inspiration.

As long as quantitative studies of organizational cultures are thus part of a broader approach, they are both feasible and useful. In a world of hardware and bottom-line figures, the scores make organizational culture differences visible, and by becoming visible they move up on management's priority list. Since our study appeared, consultants have used this approach to create awareness of existing cultures in the design of strategy, to forecast and manage cultural problems in mergers and acquisitions, and to measure culture changes over time.

Individual Perceptions of
Organizational Cultures

Different individuals within the same unit do not necessarily give identical answers on questions about their perception of organizational practices.[118] In the IRIC project, we did not study this variance across individuals: Our concern was with the ecological phenomenon of organizational cultures. From a psychological point of view and also for methodological reasons, however, an individual-level analysis of the structure in the 1,295 answers is of interest. In Chapter 1, when discussing correlating data collected from individuals within societies, I stressed the differences among a global correlation among all individuals, a number of within-society correlations, and a between-society correlation, based on the mean scores of the variables for each society. My Hong Kong colleagues Kwok Leung and Michael Bond (1989) had shown a special interest in multivariate, multilevel analysis: N individuals divided over n "cultures." They have distinguished the following:

1. A *pancultural* analysis, pooling the data from all N individuals together, regardless of the culture they belong to
2. A *within-culture* analysis, limited to the individuals within each of the n cultures

3. An *ecological* analysis, performed on aggregate measures of the variables for each of the n cultures (usually the means)
4. An *individual* analysis, performed on the pooled data for the N individuals after elimination of the culture-level effects

At Bond's initiative, his associate Chung-Leung Luk performed the necessary data treatment for an individual analysis of the Danish-Dutch IRIC data.[119] He transformed the scores for the 1,295 individuals on the 61 practices questions and the 57 values questions by deducting from each score on each question the unit mean for that question. The $61 \times 1,295$ transformed practices matrix and the $57 \times 1,295$ transformed values matrix were separately factor analyzed.[120] In both cases six factors were retained for rotation, together explaining 27% of the variance in practices and 31% of the variance in values.[121] The factors were labeled as follows:[122]

- Practices factors
  IP1 Professionalism
  IP2 Distance from management
  IP3 Trust in colleagues
  IP4 Orderliness
  IP5 Hostility
  IP6 Integration

- Values factors
  IV1 Personal need for achievement
  IV2 Need for supportive environment
  IV3 Machismo
  IV4 Workaholism
  IV5 Alienation
  IV6 Authoritarianism

At the organizational level practices explained more variance than values (73% instead of 62%), whereas at the individual level they explained less (27% instead of 31%). A main conclusion from the IRIC study was that organizational cultures differ primarily in their practices, whereas organization membership per se does not account for much variance in values; whatever value differences were found between units could be accounted for by the hiring practices reflected in the demographics of their personnel. Education level, age, gender, and nationality were the main sources of value differences in the units.

The individual analysis presents the mirror image of this conclusion. This time we have forcibly eliminated differences in organizational cultures, and we look at the remaining variance *within* organizational units. Practices have a strong unit-level component, leaving less variance for differences in the perception of practices among individuals within units. Values, with a weaker unit-

Exhibit 8.11 Product-Moment Correlation Coefficients Between Individual Values Factor Scores and Individual Practices Factor Scores Across 1,295 Respondents

	IV1	IV2	IV3	IV4	IV5	IV6
IP1				.13***	−.36***	
IP2					.36***	
IP3		.11***	.09**		−.32***	.11***
IP4		.15***	.09**		−.19***	.14***
IP5		−.09**			.23***	−.09**
IP6	.13***	−.11***		.14***	−.28***	−.09**

NOTE: Only correlations beyond the .01 level are shown.
*p = .05; **p = .01; ***p = .001.

level component, reside to a larger extent in individuals.

So far individual values and individual perceptions of practices have been kept separate. A next step is to correlate them. For each of the 1,295 individuals, factor scores were computed on each of the 2 × 6 factors. This was done by adding the scores on the questions loading .35 or over for each factor (taking account of the signs in the factor analysis; questions loading on more than one factor were excluded). The correlations between the values and the practices factor scores are shown in Exhibit 8.11. As the products of an orthogonal analysis, the values scores among each other have close to zero correlations, as do the practices scores.

Of the 36 possible pairs in Exhibit 8.11, 19 are significantly correlated. The six strongest correlations are all with IV5, alienation. The value factor of alienation appears to affect the perceptions of all six practices clusters to a considerable extent. It is therefore less an enduring value than a state of mind, indicating a negative overall attitude about this job and this organization on the part of the employee. Alienated respondents score the organization as less professional (IP1), feel management to be more distant (IP2), trust colleagues less (IP3), see the organization as less orderly (IP4), feel more hostile (IP5), and perceive less integration between employees and organization (IP6).

The next-highest correlations between values and practices are between IP4 (orderliness) on the one hand and IV2 (need for supportive environment) as well as IV6 (authoritarianism). People with a greater need for a supportive environment and authoritarians will perceive more orderliness. IP6 (integration) is correlated with both IV4 (workaholism) and IV1 (personal need for achievement). Workaholics and achievers tend to feel more integrated in the organization. Finally,

IP1 (professionalism) correlates with IV4 (workaholism). Workaholics are more likely to perceive their work environment as professional. The other correlations in Exhibit 8.11 are lower and of marginal interest.

At the organizational level, values and practices were two clearly distinct kinds of phenomena, "values" being based (with only a few exceptions) on things desired and desirable in general, and "practices" being based entirely on descriptive perceptions of the actual work situation. In the individual analysis the values and the perceptions of practices are not so distinct. Perceptions are partly affected by values, and "values" partly reflect perceptions of the work situation.

Individual differences in values (plus perceptions of practices) can be explained by demographic criteria and differences in personality. We tested the influence of demographics by correlating nationality, gender, age, seniority with the organization, years of formal education, and hierarchical level with the individual values and practices factor scores. Not surprisingly, values produced more and stronger correlations with the demographics than did perceptions of practices. Values are more enduring characteristics of the person, whereas practices depend more on the situation. The strongest correlation ($r = -.32***$ across 1,295 individuals) was for IV2 (need for supportive environment) with low education (IV2 was also correlated with being nonmanager, female, and older). IV4 (workaholism) was correlated with higher education and being a manager; IV5 (alienation) with being younger, nonmanager, and less educated; IV6 (authoritarianism) with being less educated and female.

Some of the individual values and practices factor scores were also correlated with nationality (Danish or Dutch), but this should not be interpreted as an influence of the national cultures. Because the organizations studied in the two countries were not matched at all, these correlations did not apply to Danes in comparison to Dutch in general, only to those Danes and Dutch working in the units studied.

We could show the influence of differences in personality by relating individual differences in values and practices scores to personality types. Personality research, a core subject of psychology, made considerable progress in the 1990s. A consensus has been building that among the confusing variety of personality tests available, there is a common denominator of five dominant separate and useful dimensions of personality variation (the so-called Big Five):[123]

E: extraversion versus introversion
A: agreeableness versus ill-temperedness
C: conscientiousness versus undependability
N: neuroticism versus emotional stability
O: openness to experience versus rigidity

We wanted to test whether these five were also present in our findings, but for this purpose our 6 × 2 = 12 factor scores were still too many. In order to reduce their number, we performed a *second-order factor analysis* on the factor scores of our individuals for the six values factors IV1 through IV6 and the six practices factors IP1 through IP6. So we analyzed 12 variables (first-order factor scores) for 1,295 individuals.[124]

Six factors explained 69% of the total variance in the matrix. From the correlation pattern in Exhibit 8.11 it was predictable that most of the practices dimensions would collapse into one factor along with the values dimension (IV5) of alienation. Two other values dimensions, need for supportive environment (IV2) and workaholism (IV4), collapsed into one bipolar factor. The other three values dimensions, IV1, IV3, and IV6, survived as separate factors. Only one practice dimension, orderliness (IP4), remained as a separate factor.

Five of the six factors can be associated with one of the Big Five personality dimensions:

1. High IV5 (alienation) plus low IP1 (professionalism), high IP2 (distance from management), low IP3 (trust in colleagues), high IP5 (hostility), and low IP6 (integration); this factor shows conceptual overlap with personality dimension N (neuroticism as opposed to emotional stability). Some key adjectives for this personality factor, according to McCrae and John (1992, pp. 178-179), are *anxious* and *hostile*.
2. Low IV2 (need for supportive environment) plus high IV4 (workaholism) show conceptual overlap with personality dimension E (extraversion as opposed to introversion).

Key adjectives for this personality factor are *active* and *energetic*.

3. High IP4 (orderliness) shows conceptual overlap with personality dimension C (conscientiousness as opposed to undependability). Key adjectives are *efficient* and *organized*.
4. Low IV1 (personal need for achievement) shows conceptual overlap with O (openness to experience as opposed to rigidity). Key adjectives include *imaginative* and *original*.
5. Low IV3 (machismo) shows conceptual overlap with personality dimension A (agreeableness as opposed to ill-temperedness). Key adjectives include *altruist* and *modest*.
6. No personality factor was available for an association with high IV6 (authoritarianism). This may be a candidate for extending the Big Five into a Big Six; it is somewhat surprising that the Big Five do not include a corresponding factor.

Of course, the second-order factors do not fully overlap with the Big Five descriptions, but they get remarkably close. The similarities do support the conclusion that the differences in individual values and perceptions of practices within the same organizations are associated with differences in individual personalities.

Implications of the Level of Analysis: Gardens, Bouquets, and Flowers

The choice of the proper level of analysis, already stressed in Chapter 1, has played an important role in the present chapter. It has been shown that the same kind of data can be compared across countries, across organizational units, and across individuals, with very different results. Basically the comparison of countries belongs to political science or to anthropology, the comparison of organizations to sociology, and the comparison of individuals to psychology. If the students of our social environment remain locked within one of these disciplines, they will miss essential information available next door.

The cross-national study of the IBM data took what were supposed to be psychological data and aggregated them to the country level. At that level they melted into concepts like collectivism and individualism, which in turn caused a paradigm shift for cross-cultural psychology and proved relevant to a variety of other social science fields.

The database of the IRIC organizational culture study, analyzed at the level of organizational units, supported basic distinctions from organizational sociology (like Burns and Stalker's mechanistic versus organic systems, or Merton's local versus cosmopolitan orientation). The same database, analyzed at the level of individual variance around the organizational unit mean, supported the results of personality research in individual psychology (the Big Five).

Disciplinary parochialism and level myopia not only make the social sciences unproductive, they make them dull. It is exciting to explore more than one level of social reality. New generations of social scientists should not be fenced in at one level; they should feel free to transcend levels. Methodology textbooks can contribute to this. They should make the choice of the level of analysis a central theme. In the social science paradise there are flowers, bouquets, and gardens; a complete gardener can deal with all three.[125]

A fixation on the individual level has meant that most measures of "organizational culture" found in the literature are based on dimensions of perceptions of the culture by individuals (usually managers), not on dimensions contrasting organizations. In fact, they are based on pancultural analyses, in the terminology of Leung and Bond (1989), pooling the data from all individuals together regardless of the cultures they belong to; so they mix cross-organizational and cross-individual variance, but the latter tends to dominate. Xenikou and Furnham (1996, pp. 367 ff.) compared four such "organizational culture" instruments and distilled from them six common dimensions: (1) "openness to change in a cooperative culture," (2) "task-oriented organizational growth," (3) "the human factor in a bureaucratic culture," (4) "artifacts" (what I call symbols, heroes, and rituals), (5) "negativism and resistance to new ideas," and (6) positive social relations in the workplace." These dimensions show more overlap with the Big Five dimensions of personality than with the dimensions of organizational cultures (1 with **O,** 2 with **E,** 3 with **C,** 5 with **N,** 6 with **A**). They tell us more about the mind-sets of the managers describing the cultures than about the cultures themselves.

The same criticism applies to some of the studies trying to relate "organizational culture" to performance. Calori and Sarnin (1991) compared five French business companies through interviews and a sample survey. They developed dimensions of culture from a pancultural factor analysis, and from the correlation pattern of their questionnaire items they concluded that culture is linked to growth rather than to profits—but with data from just five French companies this is a daring generalization. Denison and Mishra (1995) have proposed that organizational effectiveness is based on four "cultural" traits: involvement, consistency, adaptability, and mission. They analyzed perceptions of these traits and their relation to subjective and objective measures of effective-

ness by CEOs from 764 U.S. companies, but again I believe this tells us more about the ideologies of these CEOs than about the functioning of their organizations.[126] As stated above, I basically object even to the theoretical assumption that one can relate organizational culture and performance at all without taking strategy into account; I see this as a naive "one best way" belief.

Occupational Cultures

In Exhibit 8.3 an occupational culture level is placed halfway between nation and organization, suggesting that entering an occupational field means the acquisition of both values and practices; the place of socialization is the school, apprenticeship, or university, and the time is between childhood and entering work. The place of occupational cultures in Exhibit 8.3 is supported by the results of ANOVAs like those in Exhibit 8.4: Occupation level was associated equally strongly with values and practices. I placed an industry culture level in between the occupational and organizational levels because an industry is characterized by distinct occupations and distinct organizations.

Dimension 3 from the organizational culture research project (parochial versus professional) suggested that in some organizational units employees derive their identity largely from the organization, whereas in other units they identify primarily with their type of job or occupation. This depends both on the nature of the job and on the culture of the organization. If occupational identities are strong, they may split the organization into different subcultures.[127] If an occupational identity is strong, one can speak of an occupational community: "A group of people who consider themselves to be engaged in the same sort of work; who identify (more or less positively) with their work; who share with one another a set of values, norms and perspectives that apply to, but extend beyond, work related matters; and whose social relationships merge the realms of work and leisure" (Van Maanen & Barley, 1984, p. 295). Occupational communities may themselves become organizations (like institutionalized professional associations), and they sometimes define career patterns.

Unlike for national and organizational cultures, I know of no broad cross-occupational study that allows us to identify dimensions of occupational cultures. Neither the five national culture (values) dimensions nor the six organizational culture (practices) dimensions will automatically apply to the occupational level.[128] From the five cross-national dimensions, only for power distance and masculinity/femininity did the index questions vary in the same way across occupations as they did across countries, so that these dimensions are applicable to occupational differences (see Chapters 3 and 6). Fonne and Myhre (1996) have illustrated this in a study of 60 members of Norwegian emergency medical service aircrews to whom they administered the cross-national Values Survey Module (Appendix 4). They found systematic value differences among pilots (highest PDI and MAS), doctors (lowest PDI and MAS), and paramedics (in between).

A classic field study related to industry and occupational cultures before the term was coined is William F. Whyte's *Human Relations in the Restaurant Industry* (1948). Whyte quoted a waiter who had immigrated from Europe:

> I worked in the old country, you know. I learned a lot of things over there. In that country, waiting is a profession, not like it is here. For one thing, we start at the bottom as an apprentice, and we learn from the ground up. . . . It was altogether different from the way it is here. This mass production stuff, I don't like it. Everybody is in a hurry. It is not a profession at all. It's more like a machine. (p. 96)

This story suggests that one dimension of occupational cultures should be "handling people versus handling things."

In one of the few books on occupational cultures, Raelin (1986) addresses the cultures of managers and professionals (such as accountants, lawyers, nurses, scientists)[129] in the U.S. context of the 1970s and 1980s. He discusses six potential culture-clash areas between the two: overspecialization, autonomy, supervision, formalization, real-world practice, and ethical responsibility. These suggest maybe five other potential dimensions of occupational cultures: specialist versus generalist, disciplined versus independent, structured versus unstructured, theoretical versus practical, and normative versus pragmatic.

From this literature and some guesswork, I would predict that in a systematic cross-occupational study the following dimensions of occupational cultures may well be found:

1. Handling people versus handling things (example: nurse versus engineer)
2. Specialist versus generalist or, from a different perspective, professional versus amateur (example: psychologist versus politician)
3. Disciplined versus independent (example: police officer versus shopkeeper)
4. Structured versus unstructured (example: systems analyst versus designer)
5. Theoretical versus practical (example: professor versus sales manager)

6. Normative versus pragmatic (example: judge versus advertising agent)

These dimensions will have stronger associations with practices than the national culture dimensions and stronger associations with values than the organizational culture dimensions. They may also be used for distinctions within professions; for example, medical specialists can be placed on the "handling people versus handling things" continuum, with probably pediatricians on the far "handling people" side (they often handle not only the child but the family as well) and surgeons and pathologists on the far "handling things" side.

Notes

1. See the comments by Goodstein (1981) and Hunt (1981), and my reply (Hofstede, 1981a). An amusing detail is that in my final version of the article I had made a number of changes at the request of the editor, but owing to an administrative error, my original, unchanged version got published.

2. See the extensive literature of the 1980s on Japanese management (e.g., Pascale & Athos, 1981) and the more recent literature on China (e.g., Shenkar & Von Glinow, 1994).

3. Montaigne, *Essais* II, XII, 34: "Quelle vérité que ces montagnes bornent, qui est mensonge au monde qui se tient au delà? [What kind of a truth is this that is bounded by a chain of mountains and is falsehood to the people living on the other side?]" (my translation).

4. This quote from Shaw comes from act IV of his 1903 play *Man and Superman.*

5. "There is nothing as practical as a good theory," is an observation attributed to Kurt Lewin.

6. For critiques of Porter's ethnocentrism, see Van den Bosch and Van Prooijen (1992), with an answer by Porter (1992), and Lowe (1996a, p. 131), who bases his comments on Redding's (1990) analysis of the Asian situation.

7. The term *social capital* was earlier used by Bourdieu (1980) for comparisons within France.

8. Laurent (1983) calls these models "mental maps."

9. In another of his studies with French, German, and British students, Stevens noticed a different meaning of time in the three groups. For the Germans, time was a source of pressure; they were constantly aware of its passing. For the French, time was a resource that should be controlled and utilized. For the British, time was a tool for orienting oneself.

10. Negandhi and Prasad (1971) compared 17 Indian organizations with 17 U.S. subsidiaries in India. The Indian organizations had more layers in the hierarchy (p. 60) but fewer formal control systems (p. 85).

11. Parsons (1951, pp. 182 ff.) developed a 2 × 2 classification of "principal types of social structure," in which he put China, Latin America, Germany, and the United States in the four cells. Parsons's dimension that corresponds to PDI is "universalistic" (low PDI) versus "particularistic" (high PDI); the dimension that corresponds to UAI is "achievement" (low UAI) versus "ascription" (high UAI). In Chapter 5, the universalistic/particularistic distinction was associated more with individualism, but for the four countries that Parsons considered, PDI and IDV cannot be separated. Chapter 4 showed the relationship between low UAI and achievement *motivation*.

12. Mintzberg (1983) recognized the role of values in the choice of coordinating mechanisms—for example, in determining levels of formalization—but he did not extend this to including national cultures in his typologies.

13. Mintzberg (1983) uses the term *machine* in a different sense than I do, following Stevens. Mintzberg's "machine bureaucracy" stresses the role of the technostructure—that is, the higher-educated specialists—but not the role of the highly trained workers who belong to the "operating core."

14. Examples are management by objectives for university professors and the use of PPBS (program planning budgeting system) by the federal government. The latter was introduced in the early 1960s by Secretary of Defense Robert McNamara, who came from the Ford Corporation; it is generally considered to have been a dramatic failure.

15. See Brossard and Maurice (1974) and Crozier and Friedberg (1977, p. 168).

16. The countries were AUL, BEL, CAN, CHL, FRA, GBR, GER, IND, IRA, ISR, JPN, NET, PAK, PER, PHI, SWE, SWI, TUR, and USA.

17. An example of ethnocentric use of U.S. instruments in leadership training was published by Osborn and Osborn (1986). They compared 875 U.S. and 206 Latin American managers trained by a U.S. training center on two personality tests. On the Myers-Briggs type indicator they found the Latins significantly more extroverted, sensing, thinking, and judging. On the FIRO-B, the Latins *wanted* less control and *expressed* more inclusion, control, and affection.

18. The countries were BEL, CAN, DEN, FRA, GBR, GER, GRE, NET, SPA, and USA.

19. A second part of Van Oudenhoven's (2001) study presented the same students with 20 statements indicating five different positions on each of the four IBM dimensions (such as "All decisions are made by the top of the organization" as the strongest PDI statement). They were asked to choose (a) which statement for each dimension applied most to local organizations they knew and (b) which they preferred. Van Oudenhoven correlated the IBM country scores with the answers of the 713 individuals. Using significance levels for 10 independent cases, only the correlations with IDV and MAS were confirmed. Perceived individualism correlated *negatively* with IDV ($r = -.69*$), and desired indi-

vidualism correlated positively ($r = .59*$). Perceived masculinity correlated significantly positively with MAS ($r = .68*$), and desired masculinity not at all. Why in one case the values (desired) dominate and in the other the perceptions is not clear to me; I would like to see these results replicated before I try to build a theory on them.

20. The content of this and the following subsections was popularized in two much-reprinted articles: Hofstede (1980b), the article to which I referred in the opening of this chapter, and Hofstede (1983b), which extended the database from 40 to 53 countries.

21. This quote is from a paper that Follett presented in 1925, as found in Metcalf and Urwick (1940, pp. 58-59).

22. A collection of 15 contributions by leading Europeans covered additional countries (Hofstede & Kassem, 1976). Researchers from Italy also focused on power, whereas those from Eastern Europe focused on efficiency and those from Northern Europe focused on change. The British and the Dutch were interested in a bit of all of these, but more than the others they were concerned with data collection, like their colleagues in the United States.

23. The stress on interests as the source of ideas is found throughout the works of Marx and Engels, but they focus almost exclusively on the modes of production. Merton (1949/1968, pp. 516 ff.) has shown how Marx's ideas were broadened by Scheler and Mannheim to include other institutional structures and group formations as existential bases of ideas.

24. Osigweh (1989a) has written about "the myth of universality in transnational organizational science."

25. I find Galtung's arguments for the existence of styles more convincing than his actual typology, which, like many typologies, is so vaguely defined it has little predictive value.

26. See Sampson (1977) and Hogan and Emler (1978).

27. The most-cited psychologists in the *Social Science Citation Index* are all Americans; the most-cited sociologists are nearly all Europeans, in spite of the fact that the *SSCI* is based mainly on U.S. journals.

28. My distinction of national paradigms can be found in Hofstede (1996a). Lammers (1990), in a review article on the sociology of organizations, has described three universally accepted dimensions: traditional versus modern, hierarchical versus democratic, and mechanical versus organic, with national varieties around this common core for GBR, GER, FRA, NET, and USA.

29. To some extent the same applies in organization theory. Thomas, Shenkar, and Clarke (1994) analyzed the contents of the *Journal of International Business Studies* (United States) during its 25 years of existence and found that the research reported in this "international" journal was developed in, and related to, the United States and countries culturally most similar to it (p. 684). Üsdiken and Pasadeos (1995) compared the content in 1990-91 of the leading journals *Administrative Science Quarterly* (United States) and *Organiza-*

tion Studies (Europe), and found a one-way flow of ideas from North America to Europe. As Hickson (1996) has observed, "Americans cite Americans and very little else" (p. 217).

30. The EGOS newsletter article provided summaries of the three discussants' arguments ("Oliver Williamson in Paris," 1994), but even the newsletter's editor did not show any awareness of the paradigm clash. A more extensive description of this deaf men's discussion is found in Hofstede (1996a).

31. Bird and Wiersema (1996) have shown this for the case of Japan versus the United States.

32. See Faucheux (1977) and Schneider (1989).

33. Zaheer and Zaheer (1997) also found that banks in more individualist countries sought less information, but this effect was not as strong ($p < .05$).

34. Many years later, Czarniawska-Joerges and Jacobsson (1989), in an article reporting on a study about budgeting in the Swedish public sector, called it "symbolic performance" and "a ritual of reason."

35. My 1967 dissertation made me an unconscious pioneer in the field later called *behavioral accounting.* Among other things, this field has produced several studies of the effects of budgets on people comparing Asian and Western countries: Singapore and Australia (Harrison, 1992, 1993; O'Connor, 1995), Japan and the United States (Chow, Kato, & Merchant, 1996; Ueno & Sekaran, 1992). Differences have generally been attributed to individualism/collectivism and power distance; similarities, to characteristics of the system.

36. These countries were ARG, AUL, BEL, BRA, CAN, CHL, COL, DEN, FIN, FRA, GBR, GER, HOK, ITA, JPN, KOR, MAL, MEX, NET, NOR, NZL, PHI, POR, SIN, SAF, SPA, SWE, TAI, and USA.

37. The demonstrated influence of national cultures on accounting systems has implications for accountants' professional ethics. The International Federation of Accountants in 1990 issued its *Guidelines on Ethics for Professional Accountants,* but Cohen, Pant, and Sharp (1992) have criticized this document because it does not take cultural differences into account.

38. The seven countries were FRA, GBR, GER, HOK, JPN, NOR, and USA.

39. Pratt, Mohrweis, and Beaulieu (1993) replicated Soeters and Schreuder's (1988) research approach with Australians and British working for local and U.S. CPA firms. The results for the British were similar to those found by Soeters and Schreuder, but for the Australians they were inconclusive.

40. The eight countries were DEN, FRA, GBR, IRE, ITA, NET, SPA, and SWE.

41. The countries were AUT, BEL, DEN, FIN, FRA, GBR, GER, ITA, NET, NOR, SPA, and SWE.

42. In 1977, Jacquemin and de Ghellinck found that half of the 200 largest corporations in France were still family controlled.

43. One-person or one-family ownership was positively correlated with 1990 GNP/capita ($r = .73**$). Foreign ownership was negatively correlated with GNP/capita ($r = -.72**$).

44. The countries were AUL, AUT, CAN, DEN, FIN, FRA, GBR, GER, IRE, ITA, NET, NOR, NZL, SPA, SWE, SWI, and USA.

45. It is likely that power distances all over Europe were higher in the days when Freud grew up (second half of the 19th century). However, even then Austrian power distances must have been relatively low, as culture patterns shift only slowly.

46. McClelland (1965) suggested that achievement motivation training would help Third World countries develop. He himself tried this in India. Interestingly, Exhibit 6.17 suggests that India (the Indian middle class) already shares American values facilitating achievement, so McClelland was preaching to the converted. Pareek (1968), on the basis of Indian development practice, proposed that next to achievement motivation his country needed "extension motivation" (concern for other people or the society as a whole) and a reduction of "dependence motivation." Extension motivation will be facilitated by low IDV and low MAS (relative to its wealth, India has a high IDV; see Exhibit 5.9). Dependence motivation relates to PDI, which is very high for India. All this suggests that achievement motivation training should not be seen as a psychological patent medicine against underdevelopment. Evaluations of achievement motivation training projects in Indonesia, Iran, Pakistan, and Poland did not produce conclusive results (Varga, 1977).

47. Herzberg's theory was disconfirmed for Dutch trainees (Hofstede, 1964) and in a wide variety of work settings in New Zealand (Hines, 1976).

48. This discussion is based on Hofstede (1988b).

49. The countries were ARG, AUL, AUT, BEL, BRA, DEN, FIN, FRA, GBR, GER, GRE, IRE, ISR, ITA, JPN, KOR, MEX, NET, NOR, POR, SPA, SWE, TUR, and USA.

50. Schuler and Rogovsky (1998) calculated rank correlations using Kendall's tau rather than Spearman's rho.

51. Schuler and Rogovsky's (1998) Table 2 indicates a positive correlation between MAS and maternity leave, but their text refers to a negative relationship; I have assumed that in the table the minus signs were lost.

52. For the full story, see the first edition of *Culture's Consequences* (Hofstede, 1980a, p. 381). Hartmann (1973) analyzed a comparable culturally biased review of German management by U.S. consulting firm Booz, Allen & Hamilton.

53. However, a comparison between more than 1,700 U.S. senior vice presidents and more than 400 British equivalents also showed considerable differences, both in career history and in attributed traits for executive success, in spite of the relative proximity of the two countries on the five dimensions (Norburn, 1987). Historical, educational, institutional, and economic differences between the countries and between the elite groups in these countries account for differences that the dimensions do not cover.

54. The countries were DEN, FRA, GBR, GER, ITA, NOR, SPA, and SWE.

55. See Williams, Whyte, and Green (1966).

56. See Meade's (1967) replication of Lippitt and White's (1958) experiments.

57. It is interesting that Kakar (1971) used a term based on a family relationship.

58. See Machiavelli's *The Ruler* (1517/1955).

59. See Triandis (1973b, p. 165).

60. The way Japan after World War II first accepted and then modified American organizational theories and finally started to export its own theories is clearly described from a Japanese point of view by Iwata (1982) and from a foreign point of view by Beechler and Pucik (1989).

61. See Jenkins (1973, p. 258); the lecturer was Frederick Herzberg.

62. Stohl (1993) interviewed 20 managers each from five European countries about their interpretation of "participation." The French nearly exclusively referred to formal participation; the British, Danes, Dutch, and Germans referred to both formal and informal forms.

63. See Cox and Cooper (1977).

64. See Jaeger (1986), Kreacic and Marsh (1986), and Pheysey (1993, p. 187).

65. This statement is inspired by Magalhaes (1984) and by discussions with Anne-Marie Bouvy and Giorgio Inzerilli.

66. Golembiewski (1993) has suggested ways in which OD practitioners may become more sensitive to cultural contexts.

67. For the case of Taiwan, this has been illustrated by Yiu and Saner (1984); for Pacific Rim countries in general, by Vance, McClaine, Boje, and Stage (1992).

68. In German, *Führung durch Zielvereinbarung*; see Ferguson (1973, p. 15).

69. In a French journal article, Franck (1973) wrote: "I think that the career of DPPO is terminated, or rather that it has never started, and it won't ever start as long as we continue in France our tendency to confound ideology and reality" (p. 8). The journal editor added: "French blue- and white-collar workers, lower-level and higher-level managers, and *patrons* all belong to the same cultural system that maintains dependency relations from level to level. Only the deviants really dislike this system. The hierarchical structure protects against anxiety; DPO, however, generates anxiety" (p. 14; my translations).

70. Glacier's chairman, Wilfred Brown, cooperated closely with Jaques and later became a prominent management author himself (see Brown, 1960).

71. This list is adapted from Hofstede (1998a, p. 486).

72. In the U.S. management literature, *corporate culture* in the singular had been casually used by Blake and Mouton (1964) as a synonym for climate. Harrison (1972) described what would later be called organizational cultures as "organization ideologies" and "the organization's character." *Corporate culture* figured in an article by Silverzweig and Allen (1976). The first article

referring explicitly to "organizational cultures," as far as I know, was written by Pettigrew (1979).

73. See, for example, the critiques of Wilkins and Ouchi (1983, p. 477), Schein (1985, p. 315), Weick (1985, p. 385), and Saffold (1988).

74. On organizational symbolism, see, for example, Pondy, Frost, Morgan, and Dandridge (1983); Frost, Moore, Louis, Lundberg, and Martin (1985); and Berg (1986).

75. This conflict has been described, for example, by Gherardi and Turner (1987) and Denison (1996).

76. What we called *practices* can also be labeled *conventions, customs, habits, mores, traditions,* or *usages*. As early as the 19th century, Edward B. Tylor (1871/1924) recognized them as part of culture: "Culture is that complex whole which includes knowledge, beliefs, art, morals, law, customs and any other capabilities and habits acquired by man as a member of society" (p. 33).

77. "When the organization of authority becomes permanent, the staff supporting the charismatic ruler becomes routinized" (Weber, in Gerth & Mills, 1948/1970, p. 297).

78. The study by Soeters and Schreuder (1988) across six certified public accounting firms operating in the Netherlands cited earlier in this chapter found evidence of self-selection of new employees according to the national values dominant in the firm (U.S. or Dutch), but not of socialization to the firm's values after entering.

79. The project discussed in this subsection is described in Hofstede, Neuijen, Ohayv, and Sanders (1990). More information can be found in Neuijen's (1992) Ph.D. dissertation.

80. The study originally tried to find sufficient units in the Netherlands only. As selling the project to managements turned out to be quite difficult (they had to allow outsiders in who would ask their employees tricky questions, and on top of this the organizations had to pay for participating), we gladly accepted an offer by a Danish consultant, Connector, to find a number of additional partners in Denmark.

81. We drew from an extensive literature about specific sources and manifestations of organizational cultures: the legacy of founders (Martin, Sitkin, & Boehm, 1985; Schein, 1983), myths (Westerlund & Sjöstrand, 1979), stories (Martin, Feldman, Hatch, & Sitkin, 1983; Wilkins, 1984), socialization processes (Pascale, 1985), and rites and ceremonials (Trice & Beyer, 1984). One of the most original suggestions we found was about the role of "communications to self": Some organizational texts are made to be read to oneself; "like mantras, they enhance" (Broms & Gahmberg, 1983).

82. The entire checklist is reproduced in Neuijen (1992, pp. 259 ff.).

83. Because most questions were scored on 5-point scales, the mean scores from two units could maximally differ 4.0 points. A difference-of-means test showed that in view of the size of the samples and the standard

deviations of the individual scores within these samples, a difference of means over .29 points was sufficient for significance at the .01 level in the most unfavorable case; in all other cases the limit was lower. Even the very lowest mean score range found, .32 points for one of the values questions, still indicates a significant difference from the highest to the lowest scoring unit on this question. All other ranges were significant beyond the .001 limit of .41 points.

84. A possible reason for the differences in explained variance between values and practices could be the processes by which the questions were chosen: Those about values were chosen for their potential to discriminate among countries; those about practices, for their supposed ability to discriminate among organizations. Our results could simply be artifacts of this selection process. However, in selecting we never deliberately associated "values" with "countries" only, or "practices" with "organizations." We discovered this association only after the fact. We added five new questions about values on the basis of interviews in the organizations, but these discriminated only marginally better among organizations than those taken from the cross-national questionnaire, with mean scores ranging across the 20 units from .81 to 1.09, with a mean of .97. So we believe the "artifact" explanation does not hold.

85. In Chapter 1, I explained why ecological factor analyses of flat matrices—that is, few cases in comparison to the number of variables, often fewer cases than variables—are statistically allowed. The stability of the factor structure for ecological matrices depends not on the number of aggregate cases, but on the number of independent individuals who contributed to each case. In our situation, it is based not on 20 units but on 1,295 respondents.

86. The method used throughout the project, as in the IBM studies, was principal-component factor analysis with orthogonal varimax rotation.

87. As ecological correlations tend to be stronger than individual correlations, one can expect to find high percentages of variance explained, and one should consider only variables with high loadings on a factor, say, more than .50 or .60.

88. Using the two cases in Appendix 7 as an illustration, on a scale from 0 to 100 in which 0 represents the most process-oriented unit and 100 the most results-oriented unit among the 20, TKB scored 2 (very process oriented, little concern for results), and DLM's passenger terminal scored 100—it was our most results-oriented unit.

89. Lammers (1986) has shown that Peters and Waterman's eight maxims for the "excellent corporation" correspond with the findings of a number of classic studies in organizational sociology on both sides of the Atlantic, including the work of Burns and Stalker (1961).

90. On a scale from 0 to 100, TKB scored 100 and DLM's passenger terminal 95—both of them extremely employee oriented.

91. DLM passenger terminal employees scored quite parochial (24); TKB employees scored about half-way (48).

92. On this dimension TKB again scored halfway (51) and DLM extremely open (9).

93. DLM scored extremely tight (96) and TKB scored again halfway (52)—but halfway is loose for a production unit, as comparison with other production units showed.

94. The DLM passenger terminal was the top-scoring unit on the "pragmatic" side (100), which shows that the president's message had come across. TKB scored 68, also on the pragmatic side; in the past, according to the interviews, it must have been more normative toward its customers, but the market changes had produced their effect.

95. See Chapter 6 and the reference to the related concepts of "job involvement" (Lodahl, 1964; Lodahl & Kejner, 1965) and "central life interest" (Dubin & Champoux, 1977; Dubin, Champoux, & Porter, 1975); however, these were considered properties of individuals, not of social systems.

96. In an attempt to focus on the organizational differences, we reran the factor analysis after shifting the scores of the Dutch units so that, on average, they equaled the Danish. Thus we artificially eliminated the country effects. We again found three factors, which could be labeled (1) work orientation (intrinsic versus extrinsic), (2) identification (with company versus with noncompany interests), and (3) ambition (concern with money and career versus family and cooperation, somewhat resembling the mas/fem dimension in the cross-national study). The first factor was strongly related to the unit population's mean education level (the higher educated had a more intrinsic work orientation) and the second to their age, seniority, and hierarchical level. Thus, even if we eliminated the nationality effect, value differences between organizational units depended primarily on demographics and only secondarily on membership in the organization as such.

97. Chatman and Jehn (1994) reported on a study across 15 firms in four different service industries in the United States, using answers by managers on how characteristic they considered each of 54 value statements for "my firm's culture." Industry explained more variance than firm in all respects except for perceived "outcome orientation." Outcome orientation resembles our P1, but Chatman and Jehn's finding is the opposite of ours. However, they used only managers as respondents and a set of dimensions designed at the individual, not the organizational, level. Their responding managers seem to have rated "outcome orientation" relative to other firms in their industry.

98. The analysis of the relationships between the structural data and the culture dimension scores was partly done by Koop Boer and Bernd Mintjes of the University of Groningen in the context of work on a master's thesis. Crossing 40 characteristics with six dimensions will obviously produce some correlations by pure chance: 2 or 3 at the .01 level and some 12 at the

.05 level. However, Figure 8.7 contains 15 correlations significant at the .01 level and beyond, and 28 at the .05 level, which is far more than chance could account for.

99. This correlation is affected by the binational composition of the research population: Denmark had a higher rate of women in the workforce than the Netherlands, and Danish units also tended to score more open. Within Denmark the correlation between percentage women employees and openness was also significant; within the Netherlands it stayed below the .05 significance level.

100. On the basis of a comparative study across 35 airline companies around the world, Rieger and Rieger (1989, p. 263) suggested that industries have an "ideal industry culture" and that organizations whose corporate cultures fit this ideal industry culture outperform those whose corporate cultures do not. But how is this ideal industry culture determined? Most likely, ideal culture is seen as the culture of the best-performing companies, which makes Rieger and Rieger's proposition tautological.

101. The discussion in this section is a summary of Hofstede (1998c).

102. Saffold (1988), Sackmann (1992), and Sinclair (1993) have all dealt with the phenomenon of cultural variety inside organizations.

103. The combination in one questionnaire with 2,590 respondents of an employee attitude survey and an organizational culture survey allowed us to study the relationships among attitudes, values, and perceptions of organizational practices at the individual level. A factor analysis of the total material showed that attitudes (how one feels about a situation) and values (what state of affairs one would prefer) are different constructs, not only in the minds of researchers but also in the minds of respondents. Most perceptions of practices at the individual level did not correlate with any of the other questions; they are a collective, not an individual, phenomenon (Hofstede, 1998a, p. 490). See, however, the subsection below on individual perceptions of organizational cultures, in which the individual variance is analyzed *after elimination of the collective variance*.

104. Ward's method of hierarchical cluster analysis was followed (Forst & Vogel, 1977).

105. This split into three subcultures fits amazingly well with a theoretical prediction by Jones (1983). Using a transaction cost approach, Jones distinguished three ideal-typical organizational cultures: production culture, bureaucratic culture, and professional culture. About countercultures in organizations, see Martin and Siehl (1983).

106. The (unpublished) results of the attitude survey provided strong proof of management's misconception. For example, the interviews had revealed that managers believed most women to experience conflicts between their work and their private and family lives. The survey, however, showed that whereas 21% of the women employees claimed to meet such conflicts, 30% of the men did. The women's explanation of this result was that if a woman took a job she had to have her family

problems resolved, whereas many men never consciously resolved these issues (see also Chapter 6).

107. There is an extensive literature on the gender side of organizations and organizational cultures; for example, see Gherardi (1995).

108. This is a more parsimonious diagram than the McKinsey consultants' "7-S" framework: structure, strategy, systems, shared values, skills, style, and staff (Peters & Waterman, 1982, p. 10).

109. Weick (1985) has stressed the similarities between the "culture" and "strategy" constructs; he has even argued that they may be substitutable for one another. But this would be true, I think, only for emergent strategies based on the default of management.

110. In 1986, before the completion of the IRIC research project, I guest edited a special issue of the *Journal of Management Studies*, assembling seven articles from different countries and disciplines on "organizational culture and control" (Hofstede, 1986b).

111. From a large study in Germany, Witte (1973, 1977) concluded that successful innovations in organizations required the joint action of two actors: a *Machtpromotor* (power holder) and a *Fachpromotor* (expert). He found that these should be two different persons; trying to combine the two roles compromised one of them. Witte's model probably applies best to countries like Germany, with small power distance (accessibility of power holders) and at least medium uncertainty avoidance (belief in experts).

112. I have summarized the main steps in managing (with) culture in a practical checklist in Table 8.2 in Hofstede (1991).

113. For an example from Australian public accounting firms, see Ashkanasy and Holmes (1995).

114. Schenk made this statement in an interview with journalist Robert Went in the Dutch weekly *De Groene Amsterdammer* (February 10, 1999).

115. Gordon and DiTomaso (1992) also found the value attached to "adaptability" to be associated with better performance.

116. In Belgium, De Cock, Bouwer, De Witte, and De Visch (1984) developed a questionnaire aimed at assessing "organizational climate and culture." However, the questionnaire uses an imposed factor structure based on climate studies from the 1970s; its dimensions do not resemble ours. In an article in a U.S. training journal, Wallach (1983) has described the Organizational Culture Index, which has three dimensions: bureaucratic, innovative, and supportive. Some aspects of these overlap with our practice dimensions, but the source of Wallach's operationalization is not clear.

117. For example, Glick (1985) has argued for distinguishing "organizational" from "psychological" climate.

118. Discussion in this subsection is based on Hofstede, Bond, and Luk (1993).

119. I have described the results of a *pancultural* factor analysis of the data from the large Danish insurance company that followed the original IRIC study in Hofstede (1998a). In this analysis the values questions

formed meaningful factors at the individual level, but the practices questions mostly did not load on any of the factors (see note 103).

120. The method employed was principal-component analysis with orthogonal varimax rotation.

121. Individual-level factor analyses explain a much smaller amount of variance than ecological factor analyses, and the loadings are considerably lower as well (the cutoff point for the ecological analyses was .60; for the individual ones, .35). This is to be expected, because ecological data contain less random error (it has been averaged out) and therefore ecological correlation coefficients, which are at the root of ecological factor analyses, are usually much higher than individual factor analyses.

122. For the items related to each factor, see Tables 1 and 2 in Hofstede et al. (1993).

123. Establishment of the Big Five is based on, among other contributions, fundamental research by McCrae and John (1992) and a broad review of the literature on personality measurement by Hogan (1992).

124. As a safety measure, we again eliminated any between-unit variance that might have reentered during the calculations by deducting from the value of each variable (in this case, first-order factor score) the unit mean for that variable. So for each of the 20 organizational units the unit mean on each variable was a guaranteed zero.

125. This paragraph is borrowed almost verbatim from G. Hofstede (1995, p. 216).

126. In an earlier study, Denison (1984) had related employee survey data and financial performance figures for 34 U.S. business firms from 25 different industries. He found a positive relationship between perceived participative decision-making practices and business success, but the direction of causality was not evident.

127. Bloor and Dawson (1994) describe the case of an Australian home-care service for the elderly, in which the geriatrics, physiotherapists, social workers, administrative staff, and paramedical aides all formed distinct subcultures.

128. Hofstede and Spangenberg (1987) showed that the same work goals questions formed different clusters when factor analyzed at the individual, organizational, and national levels, but also at the occupational level.

129. Raelin's (1986, pp. 8-9) full list mentions the following: accountants; airline pilots and controllers; architects, artists, and writers; clergy; doctors; engineers and computer scientists; foresters; lawyers; nurses; pharmacists; psychologists, counselors, and social workers; scientists (physical, mathematical, and life); teachers, librarians, and professors; and urban planners.

9

■

Intercultural Encounters

Summary of This Chapter

This chapter applies the framework laid out in this book to situations where cultures meet. It starts with general considerations about intercultural communication and cooperation, in particular the acculturative stress that such processes generate. Language and discourse play important roles that are often underestimated by monolingual authors. Acculturative stress causes culture shock, which is a very common phenomenon. It can lead to expatriate failure and early return, although common estimates of the frequency of such failures are grossly exaggerated. Acculturation and the effectiveness of expatriates can be improved through training in intercultural competence. Such training can raise individuals' awareness of their own cultural baggage and provide them with knowledge about other cultures, but it cannot develop intercultural skills—these can be acquired only on the spot.

The first area of intercultural encounters described is the interaction between majorities and minorities within countries and the acculturation (by assimilation or by integration) of migrants and refugees. This is followed by a discussion of problems of culture in international politics and in the functioning of international organizations. A separate subsection collects remarks about intercultural negotiations and the limited applicability of negotiation principles developed in Western countries. These relate again to processes of economic development; transfer of technology is always implicitly also transfer of culture. Worldwide attempts at development aid in the second half of the 20th century were often unsuccessful, and cultural processes on the sides of both donors and recipients played a major role in these failures.

The next part of the chapter deals with multinational business and with cross-border acquisitions, mergers, joint ventures, and alliances. It reviews literature on these topics from the 1980s and 1990s that tries to take culture (in terms of the dimensions described in this book) into account. A special subsection is devoted to international marketing and advertising, where initial expectations about globalization of markets have been crushed by stubborn and increasing cultural differences among consumers.

The final main section deals with intercultural encounters in schools, where intercultural skills may be learned but often are not, and in tourism, which provides unexpected opportunities for intercultural learning. The last part of that section addresses the desirability or undesirability of cultural relativism and looks ahead to a 21st-century world in which globalization does not imply cultural convergence.

Intercultural Communication and Cooperation

General Principles

Intercultural encounters are as old as humanity itself; they occurred as soon as two different tribes of humans met. Such meetings may have been peaceful and used for trade or hostile and a source of warfare, but the same basic processes of comparison, prejudice, and stereotyping that we find today must have taken place also 30,000 years ago.

Intercultural contact does *not* automatically breed mutual understanding. Rather, it confirms the groups involved in their own identities and prejudices. From the viewpoint of one group, members of another are not perceived as individuals but in a stereotyped fashion: All Chinese look alike; all Dutch are stingy. The concept of stereotypes was discussed in Chapter 1; stereotypes are at best half-truths, but they are unavoidable and should be taken into account. Unfounded stereotypes can affect people's perceptions of actual events: If a member of one's group attacks a member of another group, one may be convinced ("I saw it with my own eyes") that events happened the other way around. On the other hand, if groups seek constructive interaction, even unfounded stereotypes may be helpful in getting communication started.[1]

Intercultural encounters that forcibly expose individuals or groups to an alien cultural environment can be a source of heavy stress. Such "acculturative stress" affects, for example, members of traditional cultures subject to modernization.[2] Similar symptoms have been described for migrant workers and their families, and for "expatriates," the common term for employees working and living temporarily abroad; in the latter case, such symptoms are called *culture shock*.[3]

As illustrated over and over again in the preceding chapters, our mental software contains basic values. These are acquired early in our lives, and they become so natural as to be unconscious. The conscious part of our mental software consists mainly of the more superficial manifestations of culture: symbols, heroes, and rituals (Exhibit 1.4). The foreigner who makes an effort can learn some of the symbols and rituals of the new environment (words to use, how to greet, when to bring presents), but he or she is unlikely to acquire the underlying values; the foreigner will judge the new culture by the old values and find it lacking.[4] In a way, the visitor in a foreign culture returns to the mental state of an infant, in which he or she has to learn the simplest things over again. This leads to feelings of distress, of helplessness, and of hostility toward the new environment. Often the individual's physical functioning is affected. Expatriates and migrants have been found to have greater need for medical help shortly after their displacement than before or later.

The symptoms of culture shock include excessive preoccupation with the cleanliness of one's drinking water, food and surroundings; great concern over minor pains; excessive anger over delays and other minor frustrations; a fixed idea that people are taking advantage of or cheating one; reluctance to learn the language of the host country; a feeling of hopelessness; and a strong desire to associate with persons of one's own nationality. . . . Victims of culture shock also experience a decline in inventiveness, spontaneity, and flexibility to the extent that it interferes with their normal behavior. (Brislin & Pedersen, 1976, p. 13)

Lack of adaptation to alien cultural environments is not only a problem for individuals; it exposes organizations to communication breakdowns, loss of effectiveness, and sometimes complete failure.

The nature of adaptation problems depends on both the sending and the receiving culture. Members of host cultures receiving foreign visitors, sojourners, or migrants show psychological reactions that mirror those of the foreigners. They usually start with *curiosity*—the foreigner as a rare zoo animal. If the visitor stays and tries to function in the host culture, the second phase is *ethnocentrism*—evaluating the foreigner by the standards of the home culture and finding her or him lacking. The visitor will show bad manners, appear too rude or too polite, naive, dirty, and/or stupid. Ethnocentrism is to a population what egocentrism is to an individual: considering one's own little world the center of the universe. Some hosts never get past this ethnocentrism phase. If regularly exposed to foreign visitors, they may move into a third phase, *polycentrism*, the recognition that different kinds of people should be measured by different standards, and learn to understand the foreigners' behavior according to the foreigners' standards. This is a mild form of bi- or multiculturality.[5]

Chapter 4 showed that uncertainty-avoiding cultures will resist polycentrism more than will uncertainty-accepting cultures; high UAI is associated with *xenophobia*. However, individuals within a culture vary around the cultural average, so in intolerant cultures one may meet tolerant hosts, and vice versa. The tendency to apply different standards to different kinds of people may also turn into *xenophilia*—that is, the belief on the part of hosts that in the foreigner's culture everything is better. Some foreigners will be pleased to confirm this belief. There is a tendency among expatriates to idealize what they remember of home. Neither ethnocentrism nor xenophilia is a healthy basis for intercultural cooperation.

Chapter 5 distinguished collectivist from individualist societies. In the former—the majority in the world—people throughout their lives remain members of tight in-groups that provide them with protection in exchange for loyalty. In such societies, groups with different cultural backgrounds are out-groups, even more so than outgroups within the own culture. Integration across cultural dividing lines is more difficult in collectivist societies than in individualist societies. This is *the* major problem of many decolonized nations, such as those of Africa, where national borders were inherited from the colonial period and in no way respect ethnic and cultural dividing lines. Exhibit 5.7 plotted countries on both IDV and UAI; countries in its upper right-hand quadrant (collectivist, strong uncertainty avoidance) are most at risk for ethnic strife.

Establishing true integration among members of culturally different groups requires environments in which these people can meet and mix as equals. Sports clubs, universities, work organizations, and armies can assume this role. They allow trust and friendships to develop between culturally dissimilar persons, in which the culture gap gradually loses its threat.[6] Some ethnic cultures produce people with specific skills, such as restaurant owners, sailors, or traders, and these skills become the basis for their integration in a larger society.

Language and Discourse

Language plays a crucial role in intercultural interactions. In the Anglophone literature on intercultural encounters, the role of language tends to be underestimated; many of the authors are monolingual themselves, and it is almost impossible to grasp the importance of language if one has not struggled with learning one or more foreign languages. Having to express oneself in another language means having to adopt someone else's frame of reference. If one does not know the language of one's country of residence, one misses a lot of the subtleties of the culture and is forced to remain a relative outsider, caught in stereotypes. Language is a vehicle for our thoughts; Chapter 1 referred to the "Whorfian hypothesis," which stresses the capriciousness of this vehicle. Language is a major cause of cultural clashes.[7]

The skill of expressing oneself in more than one language is very unevenly distributed across countries. In Europe, small and wealthy countries do better than big and poorer ones. In a 1987 survey of the then 12 member countries of the European Union, tiny Luxembourg was the champion with a mean of 2.3 foreign languages spoken (that is, in addition to the local Letzebürgisch), followed by the Netherlands with 1.3 and both Denmark and Flanders (the Dutch-speaking region of Belgium) with 1.0.[8] At the low end came Britain and Italy, each with a mean of .3 foreign languages spoken, and Ireland with .2.

Paradoxically, having English, the world trade language (lingua franca), as one's mother tongue is a liability, not an asset, for truly communicating with other cultures. Throughout history, trade languages have played an important role in intercultural encounters. Contemporary examples, aside from the various derivations of English, are Bahasa (Malay) and Swahili. Trade languages are "pidgin" forms of natural languages, and the world trade language consist of pidgin forms of business English. Teachers of English as a second (or third, fourth, or fifth) language refer to "Englishes." [9] Discourse in trade languages limits communication to those issues for which these simplified languages have words; it misses the idiosyncrasies of local languages, which are the very essence of culture. Native speakers of English, especially when they are themselves monolingual, are tempted by the fallacious assumption that what foreign speakers can express in English words is all that the foreigners have on their minds.

Such a misperception occurred during an international management training program within IBM Europe, when at the end the trainers rated the participants' future career potential in the company. English was the course language. A longitudinal follow-up study of actual careers showed that the potential of native English-speaking participants had been systematically overrated and that of French or Italian speakers had been undervalued, with German speakers in between.[10]

This case is an example of the power of discourse. More in general, we use verbal clues to attach identities to members of our own and other groups, to express feelings of inclusion and exclusion, superiority and inferiority, tolerance and racism. These play a key role in intercultural encounters.[11] Clyne (1994, chap. 6) studied the discourse in English of Australian immigrants in their work situation. He used audio and video material of some 80 male and female speakers with some 20 native languages. Discourse patterns could be related to cultural value systems and communication problems to differences in PDI, UAI, and IDV.

A related subject is humor. What is considered funny is highly culture specific, and many jokes are untranslatable. Germans are often considered humorless by foreigners who don't recognize that senses of humor differ. Experienced travelers know that it is unwise to attempt to use jokes and irony abroad until one is absolutely sure of the other culture's conception of humor.

Culture Shock and Expatriate Failure

In their personal and family well-being, expatriates often (but not always) report an "acculturation curve," as shown in Exhibit 9.1.[12] In this diagram, feelings (positive or negative) are plotted on the vertical axis and time is plotted on the horizontal. Phase 1 is a (usually short) period of *euphoria:* the honeymoon, the excitement of traveling and of seeing new lands. Phase 2 is the period

Exhibit 9.1. The Acculturation Curve

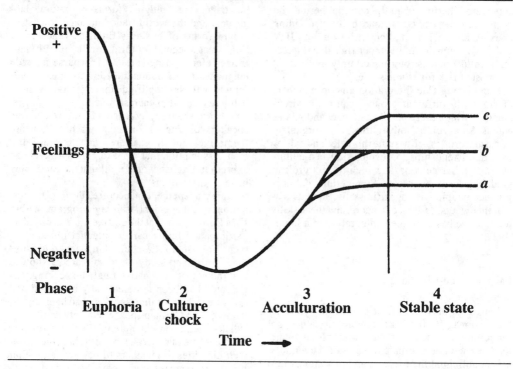

of *culture shock,* when real life starts in the new environment, as described above. Phase 3, *acculturation,* sets in when the visitor has slowly learned to function under the new conditions, has adopted some of the local practices, finds increased self-confidence, and becomes integrated into a new social network. Phase 4 is the *stable state* of mind eventually reached. It may remain negative compared to home (4a)—for example, if the visitor continues feeling an alien and discriminated against. It may be just as good as before (4b), in which case the visitor can be considered to be biculturally adapted, or it may even be better (4c). In the last case the visitor has "gone native"—he or she has become more Roman than the Romans.[13]

Culture shock and its corresponding physical and social symptoms may be so severe that an expatriate's assignment has to be terminated prematurely. Most international business companies have experiences of this kind with some of their expatriate employees. There have been cases of suicide among expatriate employees. Culture shock that affects an accompanying spouse seems to be the reason for early return more often than culture shock in the expatriate employee. The employee, after all, has the work environment, which offers a cultural continuity with home.[14]

Articles in the management literature have frequently cited high premature return rates for ex-

patriates, in particular managers and especially those from the United States. Harzing (1995) reviewed 31 mostly U.S. articles on the subject that appeared between 1960 and 1994 and found many statements like the following: "Empirical studies over a considerable period suggest that expatriate failure is a significant and persistent problem with rates ranging between 25 and 40 per cent in the developed countries and as high as 70 per cent in the case of developing countries" (p. 459). However, of the 31 articles that Harzing reviewed, only 4 described original research, and 3 of these covered single-country, single-nationality, or otherwise limited studies—basically studies that do not warrant generalization. The only multicountry, multinationality study was by Tung (1981, 1982). The other articles just quoted, and sometimes misquoted, other studies or did not mention their sources at all.

Tung's results concerning rates of premature recall of U.S., European, and Japanese expatriates are listed in Exhibit 9.2. They show that in the late 1970s, before intercultural training became very common, mean levels of premature recall of expatriates for Japanese and European companies were less than 10%; for U.S. companies the mean was somewhere in the lower teens, with exceptional companies reporting recall rates at the 20-40% level. This situation probably improved in the years afterward, if we assume that human re-

Exhibit 9.2 Percentages of European, Japanese, and U.S. Multinationals Reporting Certain Levels of Premature Recall of Expatriates

	Nationality of Company		
Level of Recall	European	Japanese	United States
<10%	97	86	24
11-19%	3	14	69
20-40%			7

SOURCE: Data from Tung (1982). Reproduced with permission.

sources managers worked on solving these problems. The message of dramatically high expatriate failure rates sounds good to intercultural consultants who are trying to sell expatriate training and to convince themselves and others of the importance of their work, but it is a myth.[15] A better sales argument for the trainers would be that premature return may be low, but it doesn't really measure the problem of expatriation: The damage caused by an incompetent or insensitive expatriate who stays is much larger.

Expatriates who successfully complete their acculturation process and then return home are likely to experience "reverse culture shock" when readjusting to their old cultural environment.[16] The reintegration of expatriates in many organizations is problematic;[17] one way organizations can avoid these problems is by giving every expatriate a sponsor in the home organization's senior management who will look after his or her career interests. Expatriates who have subsequently moved to *new* foreign assignments have reported that their culture-shock process started all over again. Evidently, culture shocks are environment specific—for every new culture there is a new shock.

The risk of expatriate failure, even if it is smaller than claimed by many, does call for careful selection of candidates. Often the technical demands of a job are so specific that little room is left for selection on other criteria. Even if there are candidates to choose from, the problem in selecting is that the number of variables that can affect success is so large.[18] Some are personal to the candidate (and his or her family members), whereas many others are situational to the expatriate job and the surrounding culture. Few persons in charge of selection are aware of the crucial variables in each case. Psychological tests are of little help; I know of no psychological test to date with any proven validity for predicting expatriate success, and any consultant's claim to possess such a test should be considered suspect. The ethics of psychological testing dictates that unless a relationship between test result and success criterion has been proven in a statistically sufficient number of cases, the test should not be used to reject

anybody. Such a relationship has simply never been shown.

Success in a previous expatriation is probably the only valid predictor of future success, although even here situational and cultural reasons may interfere. For example, extravert personalities who functioned well in an emotional (high-UAI) Latin culture may form a risk in a harmony-seeking Asian culture. Bicultural life experiences, such as having a parent or a spouse from a different culture or having lived abroad, are an asset.[19] Conditions predicting failure include a history of mental instability in the candidate or the candidate's spouse, as well as instability in their relationship. Expatriating a couple is no solution to their marital problems; outside their network of friends and relations, these problems can only increase. Extreme political views and/or xenophobic attitudes are also obvious warning signals.

At the same time, working as an expatriate can be very satisfying, more so than staying home, if the environment is not too poor and taxing, if the expatriate and his or her family bring sufficient interpersonal skills and intercultural interest, and if the expatriate manages to escape from expatriate ghetto life.[20]

Training in Intercultural Competence

The acquisition of intercultural communication abilities passes through three phases: awareness, knowledge, and skills.

Awareness is where it all starts: the recognition that one carries a particular mental software because of the way one was brought up, and that others who grew up in different environments carry different mental software for equally good reasons. A French social psychologist who spent time in the United States in the 1950s to learn about "sensitivity training" wrote about his cotrainers and trainees:

It became very clear to me that it was I, Max, but not my culture which was accepted. I was treated as just another American who had this exotic peculiarity of being a Frenchman, which was something like, say, a particular style of shirt. In general no curiosity existed about the intellectual world I was living in, the kinds of books I had written or read, the differences between what is being done in France or Europe and in the United States. (Pagès, 1971, p. 281)

And a British anthropologist wrote:

That which we know best is that of which we are least conscious. . . . the process of habit formation is a sinking of knowledge to less conscious and more archaic levels. (Bateson, 1967, p. 114)[21]

The awareness phase teaches participants to perceive people in their cultural context and to dig up the unconscious knowledge of their own mental programs.

New and additional *knowledge* should follow. If we are to interact with people in particular other cultures, there are things we have to know about these cultures. We should learn about their symbols, their heroes, and their rituals; although we may never share their values, we may at least get an intellectual grasp on where their values differ from ours.[22]

Skills, finally, are based on awareness and knowledge, plus practice. We have to learn to understand the symbols of the other culture, recognize their heroes, practice their rituals, and experience the satisfaction of getting along in the new environment.

Intercultural competence can be taught, but some students are more gifted than others. Persons with unduly inflated egos, low personal tolerance for uncertainty, histories of emotional instability, or known racist or extreme left- or right-wing political sympathies should be considered bad risks for training that, after all, assumes people's motivation and ability to gain some distance from their own cherished beliefs. Persons with some of the characteristics mentioned are probably unfit for expatriation anyway (see the previous section); if a family will be expatriated, it is wise to make sure that the spouse and children, too, have the necessary emotional stability and do not otherwise represent expatriation risks.

There are two types of intercultural competence courses: culture specific and culture general. *Culture-specific* courses focus on knowledge about the other culture; they are sometimes called "expatriate briefings." They inform the future expatriates, and preferably their spouses too, and sometimes their children, about the new country—its geography, some history, customs, hygiene, dos and don'ts, what to bring—in short, how to live. They do not spend much time on introspection into the expatriates' own culture. Such courses are extremely useful, but a suffi-

ciently motivated expatriate family can get this information from books and videos. In fact, the institutes offering this type of training usually maintain good book and video libraries for individual preparation.

An even better preparation for a specific assignment is, of course, learning the local language. There are many crash courses offered, but unless the learner is exceptionally gifted, learning any new language at business level will take at least a year full-time—a bit less if the course takes place in the foreign country and the learner is fully immersed. Most employers do not plan far enough ahead to allow their expatriates such a large amount of time for language learning, to their own detriment. If an expatriate gets this chance, it is very important that his or her spouse be involved as well. Women, on average, learn new languages faster than do men. They are also better at picking up nonverbal cultural cues.

Culture-general intercultural competence courses focus on awareness of and general knowledge about cultural differences. Awareness training reveals the learner's own mental software and where it may differ from that of others. Such training is not specific to any given country; the knowledge and skills taught apply in any foreign cultural environment. These courses deal less with how to live in another culture than with how to work: how to get a job done. In addition to the (future) expatriate, his or her spouse may attend the course, because an understanding spouse is a major asset during the culture-shock period.[23] Culture-general training is essential for those persons who in their work interact with a multitude of foreign cultures: These include superiors and staff in the home organization who deal with expatriates in different countries. Conditions for success include the commitment of top management, investment of a sufficient share of the trainees' time, and participation in the same type of program of a critical mass of company personnel.[24]

In the design of intercultural competence courses, *process* is as important as *content.* The learning process itself is culturally constrained, and trainers who are not aware of this communicate something other than what they are trying to teach. Writing from extensive experience in Hong Kong, Bond (1992) has warned about using Western procedures with Asian audiences.[25] The occupational culture of the emerging profession of intercultural trainers and consultants is built on the use of Western, mainly U.S., practices.[26]

Self-instruction is also possible. A classic instrument for this purpose is the "culture assimilator," a programmed learning tool consisting of about 100 short case descriptions, each depicting an intercultural encounter in which a person from the foreign culture behaves in a particular way. Usually, four explanations are offered for this behavior, one of which is the insider explanation given by informants from the foreign culture. The three others are naive choices by outsiders. The student picks one answer and receives a comment explaining why the answer chosen was correct (corresponding to the insiders' view) or incorrect (naive). Early culture assimilators were culture specific toward both the home and the host cultures.[27] They therefore were costly to make and had relatively limited distribution, but an evaluation study showed the long-term effects of their use to be quite positive.[28] Brislin, Cushner, Cherrie, and Yong (1986) composed the General Culture Assimilator, which incorporates the main common themes that were found in earlier specific instruments.[29]

Political Issues

Minorities, Migrants, and Refugees

Which groups are considered minorities in a country is a matter of definition. It depends on hard facts such as the distribution of the population, the economic situation of population groups, and the intensity of these groups' interrelations. It also depends on cultural values (especially uncertainty avoidance and collectivism) and cultural practices (languages, felt and attributed identities, interpretations of history), which affect the ideology of the majority and sometimes also of the minority, and the majority's and minority's levels of mutual prejudice and discrimination. Minority problems are always also, and often primarily, majority problems.[30]

Minorities in the world include a great variety of groups, from original populations overrun by immigrants (such as Native Americans and Australian Aborigines) to descendants of imported labor (American blacks and Mediterraneans in Northwestern Europe), to natives of former colonies (Indians and Pakistanis in Britain), to international nomads (Sinti and Roma people—"Gypsies"—in most of Europe and partly even overseas), to (descendants of) political, economic, or ethnic migrants or refugees. Their statuses vary widely, from underclass to entrepreneurial and/or academic elite.

In many countries the minority picture is highly volatile because of ongoing migration. The number of people in the second half of the 20th century who left their native countries and moved to completely different environments was larger than ever before in human history. The "Great Peoples' Migration" of the first centuries A.D. involved far smaller numbers. A main reason for the current level of migration is the availability of information about other parts of the world, which makes people flee from wars, political upheaval, and poverty toward presumed safety and better opportunities elsewhere. The effect in all cases is that persons and entire families are parachuted into cultural environments vastly different from the ones in which they were mentally programmed, often without any preparation. They have to learn new languages, but a much larger problem is that they have to function in new cultures.

Political ideologies about majority-minority relations vary strongly. Racists and ultrarightists want to close borders and expel present minorities—or worse. Civilized governments' policies aim somewhere between two poles on a continuum. One pole is *assimilation,* which means that minority citizens should become like everybody else and lose their distinctiveness as quickly as possible. The other pole is *integration,* which implies that minority citizens, although accepted as full members of the host society, are at the same time encouraged to retain links with their roots and their collective identity. Paradoxically, policies aiming at integration have led to better and faster adaptation of minorities than have policies enforcing assimilation. The choice of policy has an immediate impact on a country's educational system, for example, in the teaching of minority languages and in provisions for students with adaptation backlogs.[31] Chapter 6 showed in a comparison of 14 European host countries that host-country respondents in more masculine and poorer countries preferred assimilation, whereas those in feminine and wealthier countries favored integration.

Migrants and refugees are exposed to acculturative stress to an even larger extent than are temporary expatriates, while meeting less understanding for their culture shock. The level of acculturative stress increases with the cultural distance between home and host culture, as measured, for example, by the IBM indexes.[32] The following are poetic impressions from a Moroccan immigrant in the Netherlands who had to bridge a formidable cultural distance:

> Imagine: One day you get up, you look around but you can't believe your eyes. . . . Everything is upside down, inside as well as outside. . . . You try to put things back in their old place but alas—they are upside down forever. You take your time, you look again and then you have an idea: "I'll put myself upside down too, just like everything else, to be able to handle things." It doesn't work. . . . And the world doesn't understand why you stand right. (Bel Ghazi, 1982, p. 82; my translation)

Migrants and refugees often enter new countries as presumed temporary expatriates but end up staying. In nearly all cases, they move from more traditional, collectivist societies to more individualist societies. For their adaptation it is very important that they find support in communities of compatriots in their countries of migration, especially if they are single, but even when they come with their families, which anyway represent a much narrower group than they were accustomed to in their home countries. Maintaining migrant communities fits into an integration philosophy as described above. Unfortunately, host-country politicians, from their individualist value position, often fear the forming of migrant ghettos and try to disperse foreigners, falsely assuming that this will speed up their adaptation.

Migrants and refugees usually also experience differences in power distance. Host societies tend to be more egalitarian than the places the migrants have come from. Migrants experience this difference both negatively and positively—for instance, in lack of respect for elders but better accessibility of authorities and teachers, although they tend to distrust authorities at first.[33] Differences on mas/fem and uncertainty avoidance between migrants and hosts may go either way, and the adaptation problems in these cases are specific to the pairs of cultures involved.

First-generation migrant families experience standard dilemmas. At work, in shops and public offices, and usually also at school, they interact with locals, learn some local practices, and are confronted with local values. At home they try to maintain the practices, values, and relationship patterns of their countries of origin. They are marginal people between two worlds, and they alternate daily between one and the other.

The effect of this marginality is different for the different generations and genders. The immigrating adults are unlikely to trade their home-country values for those of the host country; at best, they make small adaptations.[34] The *father* tries to maintain his traditional authority in the home, but at work his status is often low: Migrants start in jobs nobody else wants. The family knows this, and he loses face toward his relatives. If he is unemployed, this makes him lose face even more. He frequently has problems with the local language, which makes him feel like a fool. Sometimes he is illiterate even in his own language. He has to call for the help of his children or of social workers in filling out forms and dealing with the authorities. He is often discriminated against by employers, police, other authorities, and neighbors. The *mother* in some migrant cultures is virtually a prisoner in the home, locked up when the father has gone to work. In these cases she has no contact with the host society, does not learn the language, and remains completely dependent on her husband and children. In other cases the mother has a job too. She may be the main bread-

winner for the family, a severe blow to the father's self-respect. She meets other men, and her husband may suspect her of unfaithfulness. The marriage sometimes breaks up. Yet there is no way back: Migrants who return home often find they do not fit in there anymore and migrate again, this time for good.

Members of the second generation, children born in or brought early to the new country, acquire conflicting mental programs from the family side and from the local school and community side. Their values reflect partly their parents' culture and partly their new country's, with wide variations among individuals, groups, and host countries.[35] The *sons* suffer most from their marginality. Some succeed miraculously well; benefiting from the better educational opportunities available, they enter skilled and professional occupations. Others, escaping parental authority at home, drop out of school and find collectivist protection in street gangs; they risk becoming a new underclass in the host society. The *daughters* often adapt better, although their parents worry more about them. At school they are exposed to equality between the genders, which is unknown in the societies from which they have come. Sometimes parents hurry them into the safety of arranged marriages with compatriots.[36]

Yet many of these problems are transitional; third-generation migrants are mostly absorbed into the host-country population, with host-country values. The are distinguishable only by their foreign family names and maybe by their specific religious and family traditions. This three-generation adaptation process has also operated in past generations; an increasing share of the populations of modern societies descends partly from foreign migrants.

Whether migrant groups are thus integrated or fail to adapt and turn into permanent minorities depends as much on the majority as on the migrants themselves. Agents of the host society who interact frequently with minorities, migrants, and refugees can do a lot to facilitate these groups' integration. Such agents include police officers, social workers, doctors, nurses, personnel officers, counter clerks in government offices, and teachers. Migrants coming from high-PDI, low-IDV cultures may distrust such authorities more than locals do, for cultural reasons.[37] Yet teachers, for example, can benefit from the respect their status earns them from the parents of their migrant students, but they will have to *invite* those parents (especially fathers) for discussion; the social distance perceived by the migrant parents is much larger than what most teachers are accustomed to. Unfortunately, in any host society a share of the locals—politicians, police, journalists, teachers, and neighbors—fall to ethnocentric and racist philosophies, compounding the felony of the migrants' lack of adaptation through primitive manifestations of uncertainty avoidance: "What is different is dangerous."

Particular expertise is demanded from mental health professionals who deal with migrants and refugees. Chapter 5 devoted a section to differences in ways of dealing with health and disability in collectivist and individualist societies. The high level of acculturative stress in migrants puts them at risk for mental health disorders, and methods of psychiatric treatment developed for host-country patients may not work with migrants, for cultural reasons.[38] In countries with large migrant populations, such as Australia, "transcultural" psychiatry and clinical psychology have become specializations.[39] One practical problem is that health insurance companies reimburse treatments on the basis of a classification system developed for Western (mainly U.S.) patients, and part of the immigrant patients' cases do not fit into the system's classifications.[40] A related specialization is the treatment of political refugees suffering from the aftereffects of war or torture.

Host-country citizens are not the only ones who can be blamed for racism and ethnocentrism; migrants themselves sometimes behave in racist and ethnocentric ways, toward other migrants and toward hosts. Living in an unfamiliar and often hostile environment, the migrants can be said to have a better excuse for such behavior. Some resort to religious fundamentalism, even though at home they were hardly religious at all. Fundamentalism is often found among marginal groups in society, and these migrants are the new marginals.

International Politics and International Organizations

Glen Fisher, a retired U.S. Foreign Service officer, has written a perceptive book titled *Mindsets* (1988) on the role of culture in international relations. In the introduction to a chapter titled "The Cultural Lens," he writes:

Working in international relations is a special endeavor because one has to deal with entirely new patterns of mindsets. To the extent that they can be identified and anticipated for particular groups or even nations, some of the mystery inherent in the conduct of "foreign" affairs will diminish. Thus the concern of this chapter: The role that culture and national experience play in producing predictable mindsets. (p. 41)[41]

Each of Chapters 3 through 7 has related a cultural values dimension to national politics, to political *processes* and/or political *issues*. The former are the ways the political game is played; the latter are the problems to which country politi-

cians attach priority and that they tend to defend on the international scene. These chapters showed that relationships between values and politics should always be seen against the backdrop of a country's national wealth or poverty (GNP/capita); the implication of values is moderated by the level of economic prosperity.

Differences in power distance and uncertainty avoidance (Chapters 3 and 4) affected primarily the political processes. Larger power distance implies political centralization, lack of cooperation between citizens and authorities, and more political violence. Stronger uncertainty avoidance implies more rules and laws, more government intervention in the economy, and perceived incompetence of citizens versus authorities; both larger power distance and stronger uncertainty avoidance imply more perceived corruption, after elimination of the effect of national wealth or poverty.

Individualism/collectivism and masculinity/femininity (Chapters 5 and 6) affect primarily the issues countries will defend. Individualism implies concern with human rights, political democracy, and market capitalism; collectivism implies concern with group interests. Masculinity implies a focus on economic growth and competition and a belief in technology; femininity implies a focus on supporting the needy in the country (welfare) and in the world (development cooperation) and on preservation of the global environment. Mas/fem relates to political processes in that in masculine cultures the political discourse is more adversarial, whereas feminine cultures are more consensus oriented.

Long- versus short-term orientation (Chapter 7) has not been explicitly linked to political processes or issues, but high LTO fits with pragmatism in politics; low LTO fits with a focus on principles, even ineffective ones, and vested rights.

The influences of values and of economic prosperity imply that a number of Western political axioms cannot be applied to non-Western countries and are not very helpful as global guidelines:

1. The solution of pressing global problems does not presuppose worldwide democracy. The rest of the world is not going "Western."[42] Authoritarian governments will continue to prevail in most of the world. Elections are not a universal solution to political problems. In poor, collectivist, high-PDI and strong-UAI cultures, elections may generate more problems than they resolve. One example is Algeria, where the first general elections in 1990 were won by fundamentalists committed to ending political freedoms, after which the military declared the results invalid and a wave of terrorism set in that lasted for 8 years and made tens of thousands of victims.[43] Another example is Russia, where the disappearance of communism and of the Soviet Union in 1991 left a power vacuum; institutions necessary to execute democratically made decisions were missing, and the local mafia established a kleptocracy.[44] Besides, even wealthy countries need not be democracies, as Singapore and Hong Kong have shown.

2. Free market capitalism cannot be universal; it presumes an individualist mentality that is missing in most of the world. Chapter 5 showed a statistical relationship between individualism and national wealth, but with the arrow of causality from wealth to individualism: Countries became more individualist after they increased in wealth, not wealthier by becoming more individualist. Free market capitalism suits countries that are already wealthy and is unlikely to turn poor countries into wealthy ones. The "Tiger" economies of East Asia that grew very fast in the mid-1960s to mid-1990s had a variety of economic systems with often strong involvement of government. An additional problem that economists seldom address is the ecological cost of economic development. The Western democracies' standard of living implies a degree of environmental pollution and depletion of resources that precludes extending this standard of living to the entire world population. Whoever seeks development for everybody should find a new way of handling our ecosystem: sustaining the rich countries' quality of life but drastically reducing its ecological cost. The concept of "economic growth" may in this respect already be obsolete; another measure for the quality and survival power of economic and ecological systems will have to be found.

3. Concepts of human rights cannot be universal. The Universal Declaration of Human Rights adopted in 1948 was based on individualist Western values, which were and are not shared by the political leaders or the populations of the collectivist majority of the world population.[45] Without losing the benefits of the present declaration, which, in an imperfect way, presents at least a norm that can be used to appeal against gross violations, the international community should revise the declaration to include, for example, the rights of groups and minorities.[46] On the basis of such a revised declaration, victims of political and religious fundamentalisms that deny rights to whomever is different can be protected; these rights should prevail over national sovereignty.

Military clashes have both superficial and deeper causes.

The great events of history are often due to secular changes in the growth of population and other fundamental economic causes, which, escaping by their gradual character the notice of contemporary

observers, are attributed to the follies of statesmen or the fanaticism of atheists. . . . the disruptive powers of national fecundity may have played a greater part in bursting the bonds of convention than either the power of ideas or the errors of autocracy. (Keynes, 1920, pp. 12-13)

A major reason for the peace among former foes in Europe in the beginning of the 21st century is that the populations have ceased to grow.

Huntington (1993) has predicted "the clash of civilizations" as the next phase in international politics, but what are civilizations? Some political clashes are a matter of conflicting values; others take place between parties sharing very similar values. The IBM database showed that respondents from the French- and Dutch-speaking regions of Belgium, involved in a perennial political struggle, held much the same values. The Serbs and Croats in the Yugoslav data, two ethnic groups that in the 1990s fought a civil war, also had rather similar scores, although the Serbs were more extreme. On the other hand, the German- and French-speaking Swiss, who usually live in peace together, produced quite different value profiles (see Chapter 2 and Appendix 5).

Like the Belgian and Serbo-Croat conflicts, the Catholic-Protestant strife in Northern Ireland, the Hutu-Tutsi civil war in Rwanda and Burundi, Africa, and many other clashes are based on presumed identities, rooted in history, that reside at the conscious level of practices (symbols, heroes, and rituals; see Chapter 1) but are fed by unconscious values shared by both opponent parties.[47] Exhibit 5.7 shows that most countries suffering ethnic strife combined strong uncertainty avoidance with collectivism. Ethnic conflicts are very difficult to understand, and therefore to predict, by outsiders unaware of the local values, identities, and histories; often the opponents belong to the same "civilization," in Huntington's terms.

Other international conflicts *do* reflect value differences. For example, Stewart (1991) has attributed the 1991 Arab/Persian Gulf War to mutual miscalculations, based on the U.S. side on a logic of respect for force and on the Iraqi side on a logic of status and pride; I translate this into high MAS, high IDV against high PDI, low IDV. The peaceful but painful separation of Czechoslovakia into Czechia and Slovakia in 1993 was also fed by differences in values; in a study using the Values Survey Module with groups of students, Slovak respondents scored higher on PDI and MAS and lower on UAI and IDV than their Czech colleagues.[48]

Public and nongovernmental organizations that span national boundaries depend for their functioning entirely on intercultural communication and cooperation. Most international organizations are not supposed to have home national cultures; key decision makers usually have to come from different countries. Examples are the United Nations and its subsidiaries, such as UNESCO and UNIDO, the European Union, the International Labour Office, and the World Council of Churches. Others have implicit home cultures related to their pasts—for example, religious organizations like the Roman Catholic Church (Italian) and the Mormon Church (American) and humanitarian organizations like the Red Cross (Swiss) and Amnesty International (British).

Confederations such as the United Nations and the European Union by definition should not have dominant national cultures. This is not a very great problem for the political parts of such organizations, in which people are supposed to act as representatives of their own countries and settle their differences through negotiation. It is, however, a considerable problem in these organizations' daily operations, where people are supposed to represent not their countries but the organizations as such. Organizations can function only if their members share some kind of culture—if together they can take certain things for granted. In the daily operations of the United Nations and the European Union, few things can be taken for granted. Personnel selection, nomination, and promotion procedures have to take account of arguments other than suitability for the job. Key persons may be transferred before they have learned their jobs; objectives are often unclear, and where they are clear, means-ends relations are nebulous. Such organizations can escape from ineffectiveness and waste only by developing strong organizational cultures at the level of shared practices (see Chapter 8). Good systems for performance evaluation are critical.[49] Differences in nationalities within these organizations again affect both the *process* and the *content* of the organizations' work: the way the organizations' bureaucracies function and the projects the organizations decide to undertake. As in the case of national politics, process is linked primarily with PDI and UAI, and content is linked primarily with IDV and MAS.

The European Union is to the present time by far the most advanced regional confederation (compared, for example, with NAFTA and ASEAN). At the time this is being written (2000), the European Union bridges 15 countries with quite different histories and cultural value profiles. Exhibit 9.3 shows the range of index scores among 14 EU countries (all except Luxembourg), both in IBM and in Hoppe's (1990) elite data, compared with the worldwide range across 53 countries and regions found in the IBM database. Missing in the European Union are only countries with very high PDI and MAS and countries with very low IDV and UAI. With this internal variety,

the European Union can be considered a laboratory for international cooperation in other parts of the world.

Different mind-sets among EU member countries with regard to the organization's processes led to the downfall of the Santer Commission (the EU cabinet) in 1999, after a report on corrupt practices by commission members had been leaked to the EU parliament by a Dutch (!) whistle-blowing internal auditor. The commissioners most blamed were former prominent politicians from France and Spain; political mores that would not have harmed their positions at home proved unacceptable in the international EU setting.[50] Compare France's and Spain's positions on UAI, PDI, and the Corruption Perception Index in Exhibit 3.19 with those of the other EU member states.

As of December 31, 1998, the number of cases against EU member states for failure to implement the European Communities' directives varied from 419 against France to 75 against Denmark. Across 14 countries these numbers were correlated with PDI ($r = .69**$), UAI ($r = .62**$), and MAS ($r = .47*$); a stepwise multiple correlation indicated independent contributions of PDI and MAS (multiple $R = .83***$). Member states with large power distances and masculine values were least inclined to obey the supranational directives.[51]

The European Union bridges two important historical rifts in Europe: the Latin versus Germanic rift, following the borderlines of the former Roman Empire, and the maritime versus continental rift, separating seafaring from inland countries. Another historical rift in Europe exists between the heirs of Rome and the heirs of Byzantium, following the splitting of the Roman Empire in 395 A.D. and the schism between the Roman and Byzantine Churches in 1054 A.D. Within the European Union only Greece inherited the Byzantine tradition. The Rome-Byzantium rift runs right through the Balkans and became visible during the Bosnia and Kosovo civil wars in former Yugoslavia in the 1990s.[52] In both wars, Byzantine Serbia played the aggressor role, and Byzantine Greece was the only EU country whose population sympathized with the Serbs. The Serbs' main supporter was Russia, the present center of Byzantine culture; Serbia, Greece, and Russia show similar value index profiles, with (very) high PDI and UAI and low IDV.[53]

Other Eastern European countries with a Byzantine inheritance are Albania, Bulgaria, Macedonia, Romania, Moldavia, Ukraine, and Belarus; they are the poorest members of the European family. Integrating them into a united Europe will take great effort; already Greece, although the wealthiest daughter of Byzantium, has a poor record in the implementation of EU poli-

Exhibit 9.3. Range of Scores for 14 European Union Member Countries in Two Studies, in Percentage of Range for Total World in 1970 IBM Study

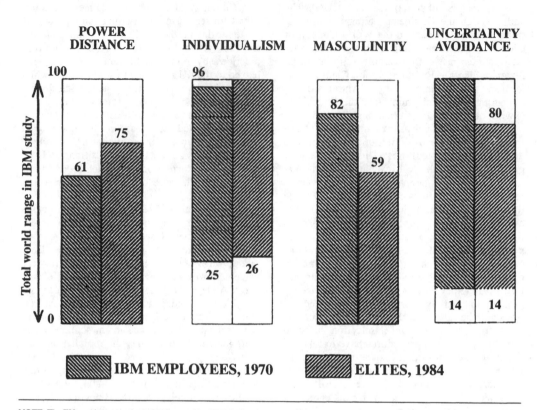

NOTE: The EU member countries in 2000 were Austria, Belgium, Denmark, Finland, France, Germany, Great Britain, Greece, Ireland, Italy, Luxembourg (no data), the Netherlands, Portugal, Spain, and Sweden.

cies. In 1946 a Hungarian philosopher explained the mind-set of Eastern European countries, which Western Europeans cannot understand, out of the daily fight for mere survival:

> One of the most characteristic features of the soul that has been tortured by fear and feelings of insecurity and major historical traumata and injuries is, that *it does not want to make a living out of its own existence* but it takes the position that it has a lot to *demand* from life, from history and from the others. In this state of mind the individual loses his sense of moral obligations and responsibilities towards the community. *He uses every moral rule to prove his own demands.* (Bibó, 1946/1986, p. 238)[54]

A very interesting part of European (re)integration takes place in border areas between countries. Until the late 19th century, when travel and communications became easier, geographic proximity was more relevant to many Europeans than nationality (which could shift through wars any-

way). People knew, visited, and married neighbors across state borders and learned enough of their neighbors' languages to trade and communicate. The 20th century turned borders into barriers and stimulated exchanges with other parts of the same state rather than with geographic neighbors. The establishment of the European Union has created new possibilities for cross-border regions that could become workshops for European integration, retying old bonds.[55]

A very visible form of intercultural cooperation throughout history has existed in times of war, when armed forces from different nations join in alliance against a common enemy. The United Nations and other supranational bodies have used and are using forces composed of battalions from different nations in peacekeeping actions. This is not necessarily a success formula; for example, the U.N. intervention in the Bosnian civil war in 1995 has been depicted, in a 1999 U.N. report, as a sheer disaster; the poorly coordinated "peacekeepers" were unable to prevent the slaughter of civilians virtually before their eyes. The North

Atlantic Treaty Organization depends entirely on intercultural cooperation. Research inside the armed forces has highlighted the importance of the cultural factor. Soeters (1997; Soeters & Recht, 1998) studied value orientations in military academies in 13 countries within and outside NATO.[56] This research showed not only that the values of student-officers reflect national patterns according to the IBM indexes, but that the academies had their own organizational cultures that could be positioned between bureaucratic and nonbureaucratic, and between occupational (professional) and institutional (parochial). These differences affect international cooperation among graduates of these academies.[57] In the 1960s and 1970s, some of the most innovative cross-cultural teaching materials originated from programs developed for U.S. military personnel who were to be stationed abroad. In the 2000s, cross-cultural training should become a key part of the training of all military personnel participating in international operations.[58]

One of the oldest forms of intercultural communication has existed in religions: within international religious organizations like the Roman Catholic Church, between pilgrims at international holy places like Mecca, between missionaries and the people they came to convert. Although such contacts have often been marked by ethnocentrism and intolerance, they have also been breeding places for intercultural understanding, the study of foreign languages, and the transfer of knowledge. Many missions practiced development cooperation before the term had been invented. Modern missions have started to use concepts from intercultural communication developed for the training of business expatriates and development cooperation workers.[59]

Intercultural Negotiations

Negotiations, whether in politics or in business and whether international or not, share some universal characteristics:[60]

- Two or more parties with (partly) conflicting interests
- A common need for agreement because of expected gain from such agreement
- An initially undefined outcome
- A means of communication between parties
- A control and decision-making structure on either side by which negotiators are linked to their superiors

Books have been published on the art of negotiation; it is a popular theme for training courses. Computer models of negotiations have been developed that use mathematical game theory to calculate optimal choices in negotiation situations.[61] However, these models are based on assumptions about the values and objectives of the negotiators, and these have been taken mainly from Western societies, in particular from the United States.

Negotiators in other countries behave according to their own national mental programs. Some studies have covered negotiation behavior within different cultures. Graham, Mintu, and Rodgers (1994) compared the results of a negotiation simulation with experienced businesspeople within each of 11 cultures, a total of 700 participants.[62] The task was a U.S.-designed buyer-seller game in which players negotiated for the prices of three commodities. Players from higher-IDV cultures made significantly higher individual profits ($r = .67*$). Players from higher-PDI cultures made significantly higher profit as buyers than they did as sellers ($r = .75*$). Players from higher-MAS cultures liked the game significantly more than did others ($r = .68*$). Lytle (1995) conducted another simulation with a total of 175 MBA students from Belgium, India, Thailand, and the United States; she chose her countries in order to reflect two levels of UAI and two levels of IDV. Cultural differences along these two dimensions significantly affected negotiators' stated goals and behavioral tactics, but not the benefits of the outcomes.

These simulations show that national culture affects negotiation behavior within countries but tell us little about *intercultural* negotiations; in the simulations everybody played according to the same (U.S.-made) rules, whereas in real-life intercultural situations every player plays according to his or her own culture's rules and is rarely aware of those of the others.

In international negotiations, the players may respect different rules as to the following:

- The nature of the control and decision-making structure on either side; the number of people involved and the distribution of decision-making power among them
- Reasons for trusting or distrusting the behavior of the other side (A certain amount of trust is an indispensable ingredient for successful negotiation.)
- Tolerance for ambiguity during the negotiation process
- Emotional needs of negotiators, such as ego enhancement or ego effacement

The descriptions of the dimensions of national culture in Chapters 3 through 7 suggest that these dimensions can affect negotiation processes in the following ways:

- Power distance affects the degree of centralization of the control and decision-making structure, and the importance of the status of the negotiators.

- Uncertainty avoidance affects the (in)tolerance of ambiguity and (dis)trust in opponents who show unfamiliar behaviors and the need for structure and ritual in the negotiation procedures.
- Collectivism affects the need for stable relationships between (opposing) negotiators. In a collectivist culture replacement of a person means that a new relationship will have to be built, which takes time. Mediators (go-betweens) have an important role in maintaining a viable pattern of relationships that allows negotiators to discuss problem content.
- Masculinity affects the need for ego-boosting behavior and the sympathy for the strong on the part of negotiators and their superiors, and the tendency to resolve conflicts by a show of force. Feminine cultures are more likely to resolve conflicts through compromise and to strive for consensus.
- Long-term orientation affects the perseverance with which desired ends are pursued, even at the cost of sacrifices.

A well-known U.S. approach to negotiation training derives from the Harvard Negotiation Project (Fisher & Ury, 1981), which has stated four principles for "coming to mutually acceptable agreements":

1. Separate the people from the problem.
2. Focus on interests, not positions.
3. Invent options for mutual gain.
4. Insist on using objective criteria.

All four of these principles contain hidden cultural assumptions:

1. Separating the people from the problem assumes an individualist value set. In collectivist cultures, where relationships prevail over tasks, this is an impossible demand. People are the first problem.
2. Focusing on interests, not positions assumes a not-too-large power distance. In high-PDI cultures negotiation positions are often linked to power issues, which are of primary importance; vital interests are sacrificed to the maintenance of power positions.
3. Inventing options for mutual gain assumes a tolerance for new solutions—that is, a not-too-large uncertainty avoidance. In high-UAI cultures, where "what is different is dangerous," some options are emotionally

unthinkable for reasons that seem mysterious to the other party.

4. Insisting on using objective criteria assumes that there is a shared objectivity between the parties. Cultural values, as I have argued in Chapter 1, include attributions of rationality. What is objective to one party is subjective from a cross-cultural point of view.

Thus all four of the Harvard principles for coming to mutually acceptable agreements reflect U.S. culture (high IDV, medium PDI, low UAI) and are not necessarily applicable to intercultural negotiations. The fact that intercultural negotiations demand different approaches has not always been obvious, especially to businesspeople. Adler and Graham (1989) conducted a negotiation simulation with more than 400 Canadian, Japanese, and U.S. businesspersons and found that the U.S. negotiators were the least adaptable; when negotiating internationally they did not change their behavior, they only felt less satisfied afterward.[63]

Effective intercultural negotiations demand insight into the range of cultural values to be expected among partners from other countries, in comparison with the negotiator's own culturally determined values. They also demand language and communication skills to guarantee that the messages sent to the other party or parties will be understood in the way they were meant by the sender, both cognitively and emotionally. They finally demand organization skills for planning and arranging meetings and facilities, involving mediators and interpreters, and handling external communications.

Experienced diplomats, from whatever country, usually acquire a professional savoir faire that enables them to negotiate successfully with other diplomats on issues on which they are empowered to decide themselves. This is part of their occupational culture, as defined in Chapter 8; it consists of common practices, commonly understood symbols, and learned rituals, rather than shared values. The problem is that in the negotiation of issues of real importance, diplomats are usually monitored by politicians, who have power but no diplomatic savoir faire. The politicians owe their present positions to strong convictions in harmony with the national values of their countries, and for this reason they have difficulty recognizing that others function according to different mental programs. Politicians often make statements intended for domestic use that diplomats then have to explain to foreign negotiation partners.

The amount of discretion left to diplomats is in itself a cultural characteristic that varies from one society and political system to another. Modern communication technology has contributed to limiting the discretion of diplomats; in past centuries, when communicating with home took weeks or months, diplomats had a more important personal contribution to make. This is why nowadays summit meetings are so important—they involve the people who do have the power to make decisions themselves. However, a trusted foreign minister or ambassador who has both the ear of the top leader *and* diplomatic sensitivity is a great asset to a country.

Permanent international organizations like the various U.N. agencies, the European Commission, and NATO have developed their own organizational cultures that affect the international negotiations taking place constantly within them.[64] Even more than in the case of the diplomats' occupational culture these organizational cultures reside at the more superficial level of practices, common symbols, and rituals, rather than of shared values. Exceptions are "missionary" international nongovernmental organizations, such as the International Red Cross, Amnesty International, and Greenpeace. Thus the behavior of international negotiators is influenced by culture at three levels: national, occupational, and organizational.

Business negotiations differ from political negotiations in that the actors are more often amateurs in the negotiation field. Specialists can prepare negotiations, but especially if one partner is from a large power distance culture, persons with appropriate power and status have to be brought in for the formal agreement. In the 1990s, international negotiations became a special topic in business education, so it appears hopeful that future generations of businesspersons will be better prepared.[65] Below, I will argue for the need for corporate diplomats in multinational organizations.

Economic Development, Nondevelopment, and Development Cooperation

The 19th century and the first half of the 20th century were the age of Europe; Europeans and their offspring overseas were the "lords of humankind," colonizing most of the outside world while wealth flowed from outside to inside.[66] World War II was the breaking point that completely changed the relationships between continents and between rich and poor countries. In the 30 years after the war, nearly all former colonies became independent. Freedom from want became recognized as a fundamental human right, and around 1950 programs of development aid were gradually started, financed by the rich countries and with the poor ones as receivers. The colonial jargon faded out: "Underdeveloped areas" were renamed "developing countries" (even if they did not develop) or the "Third World," and development "aid" became "assistance," and after that "development cooperation." Between 1950 and 2000 the equivalent of more than a trillion U.S. dollars in public money from the rich countries was spent on the development of the poor ones.

Chapter 6 showed that different rich countries spent different percentages of their gross national products on government-sponsored development cooperation (Exhibit 6.20). Norway, for example, in 1994 spent seven times as much per capita as the United States. The analysis in Chapter 6 suggested that development assistance money has been allocated according to the (psychological) needs of the donor countries rather than according to the material needs of the receivers. The percentage spent was strongly correlated with the rich countries' femininity scores.

Looking back at half a century of development assistance, most observers agree that the effectiveness of much of the spending has been dismal.[67] A number of countries did cross the line from poor to rich, especially in East Asia, but as Chapter 7 showed, this was due to their populations' own values and efforts, not to the amount of aid money received. In spite of the aid money flow, the income gap between rich and poor countries has not decreased. Development of poor countries is an uphill struggle because population growth may swallow any increase in resources. Cultural and religious traditions (in poor and in rich countries) that resist population control, aside from threatening regional and global peace, are development's worst enemies.[68] See also Chapter 6 about the influence of masculinity on fertility in poor and rich countries.

Nobody can develop a country but its own population. Development is in the minds, not in the goods. Foreign money and foreign experts are effective only to the extent they can be integrated into the local cognition.[69] Success stories in the development literature always stress the emancipation of the locals from foreign expertise.[70] The World Bank in 1992 launched a research program on "best practices" in Africa, of which the report in a number of case studies shows how quick results could be obtained when development programs built on indigenous institutions that had a strong hold on people's commitment, dedication, and sense of identity while at the same time implementing essential modernizations, such as strengthening the rule of law (Dia, 1996).

The dominant philosophy of development cooperation has too rarely recognized this need for local integration. Economic models have dictated policies.[71] Developing a country has for decades been considered primarily an economic and technical problem, a matter of transferring money and technology. Decisions about spending have been made by politicians advised by technocrats at both the giving and receiving ends. The existence of cultural mental programs on either side has received lip service at best, and the only mental programs used in development planning have been those of the donors. The very real fact of corruption, for example, has hardly ever been addressed in the literature.[72] Very little money has been spent on studying the mutual relationship between culture and technological change, although anthropologists like Mead (1955) and Foster (1962) had eloquently shown its crucial impact on results.

In his Ph.D. dissertation, discussed in Chapter 7, Read (1993) compared the economic histories of 114 countries since World War II and concluded that growth patterns have depended on the cultural context, using among other measures my five cultural indexes. Fast-growing nations belonged to one of five political/cultural clusters: "economic rebuilders" (e.g., West Germany and Japan), "uncertainty avoiders" (e.g., Greece and Portugal), "individualistic nations" (e.g., Ireland and Israel),[73] "open thrifty nations" (e.g., Hong Kong and Singapore), and "closed thrifty nations" (e.g., Malaysia and Thailand). Read concluded that "no one set of political policy prescriptions would appear appropriate for all nations" (p. 102).

Intercultural cooperation for economic development presupposes a two-way flow of know-how: technical know-how from the donor to the receiver and cultural know-how about the context in which the technical know-how should be applied from the receiver to the donor. A technical expert meets a cultural expert, and their mutual expertise is the basis for their mutual respect.

There is always a cultural gap between donor and receiving countries on the dimension of individualism/collectivism. Donor countries, by definition rich, are also culturally more individualist and receiving countries more collectivist. This implies that receivers will want the aid to benefit certain in-groups over others (a particularist way of thinking) whereas donors will want to serve certain *categories,* such as the urban poor or small farmers, regardless of in-group affiliation (a universalist way of thinking). Leaders in the receiving countries may, for example, want to repay their own villages or tribes for their sacrifices in providing the leaders with an education and enabling them to get to their present positions of power.

Usually there is also a gap on the dimension of power distance. Most donor countries score considerably lower on this dimension than the receivers, and the donors' representatives try to promote equality and democratic processes at the receiving end. Donors tend to be disturbed by the fact that they cannot get around powerful local lead-

ers, who want to use at least part of the aid to maintain or increase existing inequalities. These leaders rarely have any commitment to the kind of democracy the donors have in mind.

Development assistance projects carried out by engineers from rich countries often suffer from unrecognized differences in implicit assumptions about how organizations work. Take the story of a German engineering firm that was installing an irrigation system in an African country. Overcoming great technical difficulties, the engineers constructed an effective and easy-to-operate system. They provided all the necessary documentation for later use and repairs, translated into English and Swahili. Then they left. Four months later, the system broke down; it was never repaired. The local authority structure had not had an opportunity to adopt the project as its family property; it had no local "master."

There may or may not be gaps on mas/fem and on uncertainty avoidance, but in these cases they can be in either direction: The donor country could score higher or lower than the receiver. Such differences demand insight into the specifics of both cultures, with donor agents understanding the receiving culture *and their own,* and receiving end agents understanding the donor country culture and their own.[74]

Intercultural encounters in the context of development cooperation have an institutional and an interpersonal side. On the institutional level many receiving countries, but also many donor countries, lack the organizational framework to make cooperation a success. Usually the primitive institutional structures in the receiving countries are blamed. On the donor side, however, the situation is not always better. Many development agencies have grown out of their countries' foreign service, the main objective of which is the promotion of their countries' interests abroad. Diplomats lack both the skills and the organizational culture to act as successful entrepreneurs for development consulting activities. Development aid money often has political strings attached: It has to be spent in a way that satisfies the values of the donor country citizens and politicians, regardless of whether these values are shared by citizens and politicians at the receiving end. Projects funded by *international* agencies such as the World Bank do not have this constraint, but they have to satisfy the agency's objectives, which often also conflict with those of the receivers.

The institutional problem at the receiving end is the most serious for countries whose traditional institutional frameworks were destroyed during the periods of colonization and decolonization, especially in sub-Saharan Africa. Where no institutional traditions exist anymore, personal interests can prevail unchecked. Some politicians are out to enrich themselves without being controlled by traditional norms. Institutions cannot be created from scratch: They are living arrangements, rooted in values and history, that have to grow. The economic success of the countries of East Asia can also be explained from the fact that these countries all possessed centuries-old institutional frameworks that could be adapted to modern times.

Donor agents' perceptions of the receivers' needs may lead them to set the wrong priorities. In 1988 the development cooperation agencies of the four Nordic countries Denmark, Finland, Norway, and Sweden commissioned an evaluation of the "effectiveness of technical assistance personnel." The receiving countries involved were Kenya, Tanzania, and Zambia in East Africa, major receivers of aid from the Nordic countries. In 1987 these hosted some 900 Nordic expatriates at an annual cost of 1 million Swedish crowns apiece (a total annual cost of approximately U.S.$150 million). From these, 65% were implementers (carrying out projects themselves), 17% were controllers on behalf of the aid agencies, 11% were trainers of local personnel, and 7% were assistants in local institution building. According to the researchers, these ratios did not at all correspond to the real needs of the receiving countries. Human resources development in African countries had made rapid progress since independence, so in many areas there were sufficient supplies of qualified locals. Much of the work done by the foreign implementers could have been done by locals with the foreigners acting as trainers and consultants; this would also have produced a better multiplying effect of the know-how in the receiving country. It would have reduced the number of expatriates needed and changed the profile of skills required from them.[75]

A landmark study on "overseas effectiveness" was published by Hawes and Kealey (1979). The researchers questioned 250 expatriates working for the Canadian International Development Agency in six host countries, as well as 90 host-country counterparts. They distinguished three components of effectiveness:

1. Professional effectiveness, related to the performance of daily tasks, duties, and responsibilities on the job
2. Personal and family adjustment and satisfaction, related to the capacity for well-being while living abroad, as an individual and as a family unit
3. Intercultural interaction and training, related to involvement with the local culture and people, and with transfer of skills

Of these, the expatriates were found to be generally competent on components 1 and 2 but lacking on 3. Local counterparts stressed the transfer of job skills through intercultural interaction and training as the most crucial dimensions of expatriate success. Expatriates are often neither selected nor prepared for this side of their task. Expatriate-local relationships can be problematic. One Dutch couple taught 2 years at a university in Malawi without developing any relationships with Malawians.[76] A U.S. management researcher tried to do surveys in Tanzania but lost a year in frustration.[77] Expatriates who started their assignments as idealists returned with colonialist or racist views.[78]

Gifted young people from poor countries have often been sent abroad to study in North America, Australia/New Zealand, or a European country.[79] The contribution of this form of training to the improvement of management in the home country has generally been disappointing. The students get into a cultural quandary. They learn to adapt to the culture of the foreign country and to speak its language very well; some do brilliantly at their studies. But these accomplishments do not help them when they return home. In the first place, a lot of what they learn is context related: It is meaningful in the country of study, but meaningless in the less-developed home country. What is the use of stock market portfolio theories in a country where all businesses are owned by the ruling family? Second, they may have personal problems readapting to their native culture. For example, they may have unlearned the showing of deference to superiors, even incompetent ones, that the local (high-PDI) culture demands. Third, their "Western" orientation may be resented by others in their country; they may get involved in political strife and even be in physical danger from their enemies. For these reasons, a considerable percentage of these foreign students—and the most gifted—never return to their native countries; rather, they take up careers in the countries where they have studied. Still others do return home and move into local management, but they readjust their behavior to the local norms and don't do any better than their colleagues who did not receive an expensive foreign education. All in all, the payoff for poor countries of sending students abroad is often low.

Experienced managers and professionals from less-developed countries are also sent abroad for study, usually on shorter courses of up to a year. In these cases the payoff may be higher, not only because of the knowledge and skills they acquire but because of the contacts they establish. On the basis of their local work experience, they have a better chance of distilling from the course content whatever they can use. However, the selection of candidates is obviously based on their local relationships and may be more a matter of reward for loyalty than a choice based on competence. Courses serve more as a source of additional status and as paid vacations than as opportunities for learning (this, of course, sometimes applies in rich countries too).

Local management training institutes in poor countries meet with other problems. Although in this case the students are trained within the context of their own society, the subject matter taught is not necessarily relevant to that context. Many teachers in these institutes themselves studied abroad, and it is difficult for them as single persons to free themselves from the implicit ethnocentricity of the foreign theories they teach and the methods they learned to teach them with.[80] This ethnocentricity is hidden behind scientific verbiage, and even irrelevant theories may have high status value abroad. It takes considerable personal courage and independence of mind for a local teacher—or an expatriate Western teacher—to present more relevant alternatives and help the local scientific community to acquire sufficient self-confidence to support such alternatives.

Multinational Business

The Functioning of Multinational Business Organizations

If intercultural encounters are as old as humanity, multinational business is as old as organized states. Business professor Karl Moore and historian David Lewis have traced the origins of multinational business to the Assyrian trade with Anatolia around 1900 B.C., the Phoenician sea trade in the Mediterranean and beyond around 800 B.C., Greek exporting industries around 500 B.C., and Roman family corporations around 100 B.C. These authors have used their historical insights to denounce any claims that one particular type of capitalism is inevitably and forever superior to everything else (Moore & Lewis, 1999, p. 278).

The functioning of multinational business organizations hinges on intercultural communication and cooperation. Chapter 8 has related shared values to *national* cultures and shared practices to *organizational* (corporate) cultures. Weber, Shenkar, and Raveh (1996) compared 52 domestic and international mergers in the United States and concluded that "national culture differentials better predict stress, negative attitudes towards the merger, and actual cooperation, than corporate culture differentials do" (p. 1225). Multinationals abroad meet alien value patterns, but their

shared practices (symbols, heroes, and rituals) keep these organizations together. The basic values of a multinational business organization are determined by the nationality and personality of its founder(s) and later significant leaders. Multinationals with dominant home cultures have clearer sets of basic values and therefore are easier to run than are international organizations that lack such common frames of reference. In a multinational business organization the values and beliefs of the home culture are supposed to be taken for granted and serve as a frame of reference even for persons from other cultures who make careers in that organization. The Frenchman Jacques Maisonrouge, the first foreign top executive in IBM, expressed it as follows: "In order to succeed in this job, I have to be bicultural." [81] It is my impression that the failure rate of non-home-culture executives in multinational business organizations is much higher than that of home-culture executives, precisely because the former frequently do not succeed in becoming sufficiently bicultural. Obviously, a prolonged period of working in the home-culture environment is an asset in this respect.

This need for biculturality exists primarily for those non-home-culture members of multinational organizations who interact with the home office decision makers or their representatives abroad. Foreign subsidiaries of multinational organizations function internally more according to the value systems and beliefs of the host culture, even if they formally adopt home-culture ideas and policies. The value differences inside the IBM corporation on which the national culture indexes in this book are based prove this; d'Iribarne's (1989) analysis of the different functioning of three technically identically aluminum plants in France, the Netherlands, and the United States (Chapter 3) further confirms the point. Ordinary members of foreign national subsidiaries do not have to be bicultural; only those in "linking pin" roles between the national subsidiaries and the international superstructure need biculturality. This is necessary because these linking agents need a double trust relationship, both with their home-culture superiors and colleagues and with their host-culture subordinates.

Biculturality obviously implies bilingualism. There is a difference in coordination strategy between most U.S. and most non-U.S. multinational organizations. Most American multinationals put the burden of biculturality on the foreign nationals. It is the latter who are bi- or multilingual (most American executives in multinationals are monolingual). This goes together with the relatively short duration of the stays of American executives abroad; 2 to 5 years per foreign country is fairly typical. These executives often live in expatriate ghettos. The main tool of coordination consists of unified worldwide policies that can be maintained with a regularly changing composition of the international staff because they are highly formalized. Most non-American multinationals put the burden of biculturality on their own home-country nationals. They are almost always multilingual (with the possible exception of the British, although even these are usually more skilled in other languages than the Americans). The typical period of stay in another country tends to be longer, between 5 and 15 years or more, so that expatriate executives of non-American multinationals may "go native" in the host country; they mix more with the local population, place their children in local schools, and live less frequently in ghettos with others from their home countries. The main tool of coordination is these expatriate home-country nationals, rather than formal procedures.

Biculturality is extremely difficult to acquire after childhood, and the number of failures would be even larger were it not that what is necessary for the proper functioning of multinational organizations is only *task-related biculturality.* That is, only with regard to the tasks at hand do the linking persons have to be bicultural. With regard to other aspects of life—their tastes, hobbies, religious feelings, and private relations—they can afford to, and usually do, remain monocultural.

Perlmutter (1965) developed a typology of the multinational business corporation for which he distinguished three conceptions: ethnocentrism, polycentrism, and geocentrism. In *ethnocentrism,* the ways of working of the home culture are imposed abroad. In *polycentrism,* the maxim is "They know best," and operations abroad are left to the locals; the international links are mainly financial. *Geocentrism,* according to Perlmutter, is a kind of ideal end state in which all countries within the worldwide organization are equivalent and positions in the global organization can be reached by anyone, regardless of nationality, only on the basis of merit. Perlmutter identified different parts of different corporations as in different stages of ethno-, poly-, or geocentrism. His geocentrism idea was a typical complement to the convergence theory of national culture of the 1950s and 1960s. As our belief in convergence has disappeared, geocentrism looks less like a feasible or even desirable end state; it would put multinational business corporations in the difficult bind that international organizations are in: that of functioning without a common cultural reference frame. In fact, having a dominant national culture is an asset rather than a liability for the functioning of an organization, and such a culture should be fostered carefully.

The preceding chapters have offered many examples of the ways in which cultural values affect the practices and theories of organizations. Authors from individualist cultures tend to see multinationals primarily as places where individuals interact, less as places where cultures interact. Of course, cultural values play a role in the interactions of individuals.[82] More important, however, is their impact on corporate policies: Which policies should be immutable abroad, and which should be adapted to local circumstances? To what extent should local cultural habits be accepted, and to what extent should the foreign employer try to change them? What about performance standards, selection criteria, relationships with labor unions, compensation and benefits packages, protection against layoffs? [83]

Newman and Nollen (1996) have reported on a study of 176 work units in 18 foreign subsidiaries (Western and Asian) of one U.S. corporation in the computers and office products industry.[84] Units were involved in sales, service, and support and had a mean size of 55 employees, virtually all locals. The researchers used data from a regular employee attitude survey, from which they extracted perceptions of practices in five areas linked to my five dimensions of national cultures: employee participation (to be related to PDI), clarity about policies and direction (UAI), emphasis on individual contributions (IDV), use of merit-based rewards (MAS), and long-term problem solving and employment security (LTO). For dependent variables, they used the unit's return on assets (ROA) and return on sales (ROS), derived from the company's financial reporting system. For each dimension, they divided the countries into a high- and a low-scoring cluster and divided the work units from either cluster into high and low scorers on the corresponding attitude survey measure. For PDI, IDV, MAS, and LTO, the units with fitting practices performed better (in terms of ROA and/or ROS) than those with misfits. For example, on the mas/fem dimension units with high MAS plus merit-based rewards *and* units with low MAS without merit-based rewards *both* performed much better than high-MAS units without, and low-MAS units with, merit-based rewards. For UAI versus clarity the predicted effect was visible only in high-UAI countries. Newman and Nollen's ingenious project shows clearly that for best results a multinational's management practices should fit the local culture: Their research refutes the naive belief that "one size fits all."

There have been examples of multinationals successfully reforming local cultural traits. Laurent (1978; see Chapter 4) found that matrix organization did not suit the mental maps of French managers, but in the French subsidiary of one U.S. corporation where matrix organization had long been practiced, French managers who had learned to work with it had changed their mental maps on this point. In many Third World countries technologies are transferred from more economically advanced countries. In order to work at all, these technologies presuppose values that run counter to local traditions, such as a certain discretion of subordinates versus superiors (lower PDI) or of individuals versus in-groups (higher IDV). In this case the local culture has to be changed; this is a difficult task that should not be taken lightly and that calls for a conscious strategy based on insight into the local culture, in which acculturated locals should be involved.

Rosenzweig and Nohria (1994) studied the adaptation to local (U.S.) human resource management (HRM) practices in 249 U.S. subsidiaries of multinationals from eight foreign countries.[85] They measured the cultural distance between the parent country and the United States using a formula developed by Kogut and Singh (1988) based on the four IBM dimensions. Corporations from more culturally distant countries were somewhat less likely to follow local U.S. HRM practices ($p = .09$); they imposed their parent-country practices instead (Japan!). Parent-country HRM practices were more often maintained where the subsidiary employed more expatriates and communicated more frequently with the parent corporation (both $p = .01$). Local HRM practices were followed where employees were unionized ($p = .06$), where the subsidiary depended on local supplies ($p = .05$), and where the subsidiary had resulted from an acquisition ($p = .02$).

The handling of policy issues with regard to foreign subsidiaries is of course also an ethical issue. When values are formalized, they become ethics. Reeves-Ellington (1995) has described the introduction and implementation of a code of ethics by a middle-sized U.S. pharmaceutical corporation in its Africa/Asia region, based explicitly on the four IBM dimensions. The code reflects a deliberate choice for low PDI (in spite of local cultural trends in the region, no adaptation) and low UAI while striving for adaptation to a lower IDV and MAS.

The work situation is basically a very suitable laboratory for intercultural cooperation, as the problems are practical and results are visible to everybody. Yet managers, workers, and worker representatives are rarely in the front ranks for promoting intercultural understanding. Narrow economic interest viewpoints tend to prevail on all sides. A possible exception is the increasing use of expatriate manager training. Top executives chronically underestimate cultural factors in the case of mergers and acquisitions, as will be discussed below.

Experience has shown that differences in power distance are more manageable than differences in uncertainty avoidance. In particular, organizations headquartered in lower-PDI cultures usually adapt successfully in higher-PDI countries. Local managers in high-PDI subsidiaries use an authoritative style even if their international bosses behave in a more participative fashion.

Organizations headquartered in higher-PDI cultures have more problems functioning in lower-PDI cultures. Even between headquarters in medium-PDI United States and subsidiaries in countries with very low PDI, such as Denmark and Sweden, problems arise because U.S. top managers feel uncomfortable with what they experience as a lack of respect for basic managerial prerogatives.

Countries with high-PDI cultures have rarely produced large multinationals; multinational operations demand a higher level of trust than is normal in these countries, and they do not permit the centralization of authority, which managers at headquarters in these countries need in order to feel comfortable.

Differences in uncertainty avoidance represent a serious problem in the functioning of multinationals, whichever way they go. This is because if rules mean different things in different countries, it is difficult to keep the organization together. In low-UAI cultures like the United States and even more in Britain and, for example, Sweden, managers and nonmanagers alike feel definitely uncomfortable with systems of rigid rules, especially if it is evident that many of these rules are never followed. In high-UAI cultures like most of the Latin world, people feel equally uncomfortable without the structure of a system of rules, even if many of the rules are impractical and impracticable. At either pole of the uncertainty avoidance dimension, people's feelings are fed by deep psychological needs related to the control of aggression and to basic security in the face of the unknown (see Chapter 4).

In world business there is a growing tendency for tariff and technological advantages to wear off, which automatically shifts competition toward cultural advantages or disadvantages. On the four IBM dimensions any position of a country offers potential competitive advantages as well as disadvantages; these are summarized in Exhibit 9.4.[86] This exhibit serves to show that no country can be good at everything; cultural strengths imply cultural weaknesses. Chapter 8 arrived at a similar conclusion with regard to organizational cultures. This is a strong argument for making cultural considerations part of strategic planning and for locating activities in countries, regions, and organizational units that possess the cultural characteristics necessary for competing in these activities.

When an organization composes task forces of people from different national cultures or recruits staff for its international head office, two questions arise: Which nationals are likely to work well together, and which are likely to be good at

Exhibit 9.4 Competitive Advantages of Different Cultural Profiles in International Competition

Power distance small	*Power distance large*
Acceptance of responsibility	Discipline
Uncertainty avoidance weak	*Uncertainty avoidance strong*
Basic innovations	Precision
Collectivism	*Individualism*
Employee commitment	Management mobility
Femininity	*Masculinity*
Personal service	Mass production
Custom-made products	Efficiency
Agriculture	Heavy industry
Food	Chemistry
Biochemistry	Bulk chemistry
Short-term orientation	*Long-term orientation*
Fast adaptation	Development of new markets

what tasks? We should proceed with utmost modesty in using data about national cultures to predict the behavior of individuals, because values and talents vary widely within cultures, and different national cultures overlap in many respects (see Exhibit 1.7). Given this caution, a few propositions can still be made:

- If people are to work together in hierarchical relationships, differences in power distance are the most likely source of trouble (more so than differences on the other dimensions).[87]
- Among colleagues, differences in power distance and individualism/collectivism are especially problematic for the interaction process.[88]
- For ambiguous tasks (e.g., strategic planning), people from low-UAI cultures perform better than those from high-UAI cultures. If an ambiguous task is given to a group, the chairperson should preferably be chosen from a low-UAI culture.[89]
- For clearly defined and urgent tasks, people from high-UAI cultures are likely to perform better.
- Other factors being equal, people from low-UAI cultures can more easily acquire cross-cultural sensitivity than can those from high-UAI cultures.[90] However, personal factors play a crucial role: Persons who grew up or have lived abroad, who have parents from divergent nationalities, who have cross-national marriages, or who have studied foreign languages are more likely to be culturally sensitive regardless of their passports.
- Latin Europeans ("dependent individuals") do not function well in nonhierarchical peer groups with their own compatriots. Such groups easily engage in fights for leadership, or they concentrate on avoiding such fights; either comes at the expense of task performance. Latin Europeans function well in nonhierarchical *multicultural* groups in which their initial reactions are not reinforced.

Organizations moving to unfamiliar cultural environments are often unpleasantly surprised by adverse reactions on the part of the public or the authorities to what they do or want to do. Perhaps the effect of the collective values of a society is nowhere as clear as in such cases. These values have been institutionalized partly in the form of legislation (and in the way in which legislation is applied, which may differ considerably from what is actually written in the law); in labor union structures, programs, and power positions; and in the existence of organizations of stakeholders, such as consumers or environmentalists. The values are partly invisible to newcomers, but they become all too visible in press reactions, government decisions, and organized actions by uninvited interest groups.[91] Following are a few inferences that can be drawn from the value differences exposed in Chapters 3 through 6 with regard to the reactions of the local environment:

- Civic action groups are more likely to be formed in low-PDI, low-UAI cultures than elsewhere.
- Business corporations will have to be more concerned with informing the public in low-PDI, low-UAI cultures than elsewhere.[92]
- Public sympathy and legislation on behalf of economically and socially weak members of society are more likely in low MAS countries.

- Public sympathy and both government and private funding for aid to economically weak countries and in the case of disasters anywhere in the world will be stronger in affluent low-MAS than in affluent high-MAS countries.
- Public sympathy and legislation on behalf of environmental conservation and maintaining the quality of life are more likely in low-PDI, low-MAS countries.

Managing a multinational business corporation demands that one balance the four aspects pictured in Exhibit 8.10: culture, strategy, structure, and control. Culture, as argued, in this case means a combination of national and organizational culture components. Strategy is not necessarily deliberate—it may be "emergent," but at the corporation level it is reflected in the choice of product/market combinations and the choice of countries. Strategy is, of course, deeply affected by the strategists' cultural values.[93] Structure and control systems determine how this strategy is elaborated. For each business unit (carrying out one type of product/market business in one country), the structure and control systems determine which of the unit's inputs and outputs will be left to the unit's management and which will be coordinated from elsewhere in the corporation, from where, and how close or tight.[94]

The structure of a multinational, multibusiness corporation is based on choices between coordination along type-of-business lines or along geographic lines. The key question is whether business know-how or know-how about local conditions is most crucial for the success of the operation. The classic solution is a "matrix" structure. This means that every manager of a business unit has two bosses: one who coordinates the particular type of business across all countries and one who coordinates all business units in the particular country. For a time in the 1970s, matrix structures were very popular, but in practice they proved to be an imperfect answer to the coordination problem. They were costly, often meaning a doubling of the management ranks, and their functioning raised more problems than it resolved.

Actually, no single structural principle is likely to fit an entire corporation. External variety requires internal variety.[95] In some cases the business structure should dominate; in others, geographic coordination should have priority. This leads to patchwork structures that lack beauty and symmetry, but do follow the needs of markets and business unit cultures. The flexibility to use different degrees of and bases for coordination in different businesses and different parts of the world is more easily found in low-UAI than in high-UAI head offices. The diversity in structural solutions

advocated is one not only of place, but of time: Optimal solutions will very likely change over time, so that the periodic reshuffling that is a common plague in multinationals should be seen as functional.

The control systems that a multinational uses with its subsidiaries are obviously influenced by the culture of the parent country. Calori, Lubatkin, and Very (1994) have shown this to be the case for 75 foreign acquisitions in France and Great Britain. French corporations (high PDI and UAI) in Britain exercised more formal control, and U.S. corporations more informal control through teamwork. U.S. corporations in France used more procedures than did British corporations (lower UAI).

Control systems have also been related to the cultural distance between the parent and the subsidiary country. This has been interpreted as an "agency" problem—to what extent can locals be entrusted with the corporation's interest? Roth and O'Donnell (1996) have reported on a study of 100 subsidiaries in five countries of multinationals based in four countries, in two industries (scientific measuring instruments and medical instruments).[96] They used Kogut and Singh's (1988) measure of cultural distance based on the four IBM dimensions (see below). Cultural distances decreased the extent to which subsidiaries were given independent coordination tasks within the corporation. On the other hand, cultural distances increased the subsidiary top management's stated commitment to the parent corporation (my interpretation is that it was more often challenged) and the share of subsidiary top management's compensation based on *corporate* performance.[97]

Harzing (1999) studied the control of subsidiaries in multinationals through a questionnaire survey of 287 subsidiaries of 104 corporations from 9 home countries in 22 host countries.[98] She distinguished two dimensions of control systems: personal/cultural versus bureaucratic and direct versus indirect. The combination of these dimensions led to four control mechanisms: (1) personal centralized control (personal and direct), (2) bureaucratic formalized control (impersonal and direct), (3) output control (impersonal and indirect), and (4) control by socialization and networks (personal and indirect). Harzing also measured cultural distance using the Kogut and Singh (1988) formula based on the four IBM indexes. She found that larger cultural distances led to more personal centralized control, measured by the number of expatriates in the top five positions of the subsidiary and the likelihood of having a national of the parent company as the subsidiary's top manager. Larger cultural distances decreased the use of output control and bureaucratic formalized control (Harzing, 1999, p. 298). So the more culturally alien the subsidiary's location, the more a personalized style of subsidiary control was used.[99]

Harzing's study illustrates the extent to which multinationals are held together by people. The availability of suitable people is a major constraint to the strategy of multinationals. Two roles are particularly crucial:

1. *The country business unit manager:* This is the top person in a business unit in a country. As described earlier, he or she should be bicultural; in this case biculturality implies the ability to function in two cultures, the culture of the business unit and the corporate culture, which is affected by the corporation's home nationality.

2. *Corporate diplomats:* These are home-country or other nationals impregnated with the corporate culture, multilingual, from various occupational backgrounds, and experienced in living and functioning in various foreign cultures. They are the troubleshooters of multinational structures, as liaison persons in the various head offices or as temporary managers for new ventures.[100]

The availability of such people represents a major challenge for multinational human resources management. To ensure that the right people will be available when needed, organizations must practice timely recruiting of future managerial talent from different nationalities, arrange career moves through planned transfers in view of acculturation in the corporate ways, and provide cultural awareness training for business experts who will have to operate in foreign countries. This selection process is also affected by culture: Harzing (1999, p. 277) found, for example, that the percentage of female expatriates was perfectly negatively correlated with a country's Masculinity Index score.

International Acquisitions,
Mergers, and Joint Ventures

Classic ways of doing business abroad involved exporting to local agents or licensing local companies. In the latter decades of the 20th century, business corporations were expanding more and more through direct foreign investment. This implies a dramatic increase in intercultural interactions, involving not only national but organizational cultures.[101] Five modes of entry into foreign countries by business organizations can be distinguished: (1) the greenfield start, (2) the foreign acquisition, (3) the international merger, (4) the foreign joint venture, and (5) the strategic alliance with a foreign partner. The cultural implications of these modes differ considerably.

In the *greenfield start,* a corporation sets up a foreign subsidiary from scratch, usually sending over one expatriate or a small team to hire locals and gradually build up a local business. Greenfield starts are by their very nature slow, but their cultural risk is limited. The founders of the subsidiary are able to select employees who will fit the culture of the corporation. Greenfield starts have a high success rate. Many older multinationals have grown this way almost exclusively.

In the *foreign acquisition,* a local company is purchased wholesale by a foreign corporation. The local company's organizational culture and, of course, elements of its national culture are parachuted into the corporation. Foreign acquisitions are a fast way of expanding, but their cultural risks are considerable. To use an analogy from family life (such analogies are very popular for describing the relationships between parts of corporations), foreign acquisitions are to greenfield starts as the bringing up of a foster child, adopted in puberty, is to the bringing up of one's own child. One solution to the problems associated with integrating the new member is to keep it at arm's length—that is, not to integrate it but to treat it as a portfolio investment. Usually, however, this is not why the local company has been purchased. When integration is imperative, cultural clashes are often resolved through brute power: Key people are replaced by the corporation's own agents. In other cases, key people do not wait for this to happen and leave on their own account. Acquisitions often lead to a destruction of human capital, which is eventually a destruction of financial capital as well. Decisions about acquisitions tend to be made by executives eager to extend their power and seconded by financial experts who believe they have resolved the problem when they have established the proper purchase price. From a culture management point of view, this is when the problems start.

The *international merger* resembles the foreign acquisition, except that the partners are of roughly equal size or importance. The cultural risk is even larger than in the case of the foreign acquisition because cultural problems cannot be eliminated through a one-sided show of power. International mergers therefore have a very low success rate. Leyland-Innocenti, Chrysler UK, Imperial Typewriters, Vereinigte Flugzeugwerke-Fokker, Hoogovens-Hoesch, Citroen-Fiat, and Renault-Volvo are some of the more notorious failures.[102] There is little doubt that the list will continue to grow as long as management decisions about international ventures are based solely on power and financial considerations.

The oldest and most successful international mergers are probably Shell and Unilever, both British-Dutch. They show common characteristics: The smaller country held a majority of shares; *two* head offices were maintained—in spite of obvious inefficiencies—so as to avoid the impression that the corporation was run from one of the two countries only; there was strong and charismatic leadership during the integration phase; an external threat kept the partners together for survival; and governments stayed out of the game.

The *foreign joint venture* is the creation of a new business that pools resources from two or more founding parties. A foreign joint venture can be started greenfield, or the local partner may transfer part of its people collectively to the venture. In the latter case, the partner transfers part of its culture as well. Foreign joint ventures represent lower cultural risk than do foreign acquisitions and mergers, provided there is clear understanding about which partner supplies which resources, including which part of management. Joint ventures in which one partner provides the entire management have a higher success rate than do those in which management is shared between the partners. Sometimes foreign joint ventures will develop quite new and creative cultural characteristics, showing a synergy of elements from the founding partners. Foreign joint ventures are a limited-risk way of entering an unknown country and market. A foreign joint venture may be a temporary arrangement that ends with one of the partners buying the other out; but even when this happens, the venture has still served its purpose of starting the business abroad.

Foreign joint ventures were the dominant mode of entry for multinational business into mainland China after this huge market opened up in the late 1970s. In a remarkable show of herd instinct, foreign companies flocked into joint-venture agreements with Chinese partners, very few of which produced any returns for them. A typical example is Beijing Jeep, set up in 1979 as a joint venture of American Motors, later Chrysler Corporation; it got entangled in all kinds of miscommunications (Mann, 1989), and the U.S. partner lost large amounts of money. Yet in the 1990s the venture bounced back, and with a minority participation of Chrysler it eventually became a business success. Maybe the foreign partners wanted too much too soon; learning on both sides takes time—decades rather than years.[103] It is a common assumption that overseas Chinese investors, such as those from Hong Kong, Singapore, and Taiwan, do better in China than Western companies and are desirable intermediaries for business with the mainland.

The *strategic alliance with a foreign partner* represents the most prudent way of going international. Without setting up a new venture, the partners agree to collaborate on specific products and/or markets for mutual benefit. As the risks are limited to the project at hand, this is a safe way of getting to know each other; the alliance can be broken without endangering the survival of the partners. The acquaintance could develop into a merger, but in that case the partners will have much better insight into what the merger will mean, including some knowledge of each other's cultures, than they would have with a "cold" merger.

A number of publications in the 1980s and 1990s were devoted to the choice of modes of entry. In a study mentioned earlier in this chapter, Kogut and Singh (1988) analyzed 228 foreign entries into the United States by greenfield starts, acquisitions, and joint ventures.[104] They related entry mode to the parent country's UAI and to a measure of cultural distance based on all four IBM dimensions (PDI, UAI, IDV, and MAS).[105] Parent companies from uncertainty-avoiding countries chose more greenfield entries ($p < .05$) and more joint ventures ($p < .10$), so fewer acquisitions; culturally distant parent countries also chose more greenfield entries ($p < .01$) and more joint ventures ($p < .10$).[106]

Erramilli (1996) studied the ownership structure of 337 foreign subsidiaries of U.S. and European advertising agencies in the United States and Europe. Both home-country UAI and home-country PDI were highly significantly related to holding majority or full ownership of subsidiaries ($p < .001$), but the relationship with UAI was the stronger of the two.[107] This makes sense if we assume that full or majority ownership provides a sense of stability.

Grosse and Treviño (1996) analyzed the total level of direct investment in the United States from 23 foreign countries for the 12 years from 1980 through 1991. With other factors such as size controlled for, the investment from a foreign country was negatively related to both its geographic and its cultural distance from the United States.[108]

Using Kogut and Singh's measure of cultural distance, Li and Guisinger (1991) found that foreign entries into the United States from culturally distant countries were more likely to fail than were those from culturally close countries.[109] Acquisitions failed more often than greenfield entries. Interestingly, foreign-controlled firms as a group failed less often than U.S. domestic firms. In another study focusing on service industries based in Japan, the United States, and Western Europe, Li and Guisinger (1992) showed that levels of foreign investment were inversely related to the cultural distance between parent and host country. This applied to all three home countries/regions in the period 1976-80; for 1980-86 it was still true for Japanese parent corporations but no longer for U.S. and Western European corporations. This suggests a learning effect for operating in alien cultures.[110]

Barkema, Bell, and Pennings (1996) have reported on the survival rates of 225 foreign entries by companies from the Netherlands since 1966, by entry mode and by ownership of the venture (partly or wholly owned).[111] They used again the Kogut and Singh measure of cultural distance. They found survival rates to decrease with cultural distance, but more for joint ventures and acquisitions than for greenfield entries, and more for partly owned than for wholly owned subsidiaries, whatever the entry mode. Barkema et al. associated this with the need for "double-layered acculturation" in the riskier cases. They also showed the effect of learning, as the number of previous foreign entries into the same country or region decreased the risk. Barkema and Vermeulen (1997) tested the survival rates of 828 foreign entries of 25 Dutch multinationals in 72 countries between 1966 and 1994. In this case, differences in UAI decreased the survival rates of joint ventures ($p < .05$) and increased the likelihood of entry through wholly owned subsidiaries ($p < .10$). Barkema and Vermeulen also tested the effect of differences in long-term orientation, using Read's (1993) proxy for supplementing missing country scores (see Chapter 7), and found them to be even more strongly related to venture survival ($p < .01$) and entry through wholly owned subsidiaries ($p < .05$).

Differences in uncertainty avoidance can account for a finding by Forss, Rolander, and Kverneland (1982) that Swedish companies in Japan preferred joint ventures under Japanese management whereas Japanese companies in Sweden preferred wholly owned subsidiaries, also under Japanese management, and that both solutions were equally successful. Swedish culture tolerates much more uncertainty than does Japanese culture, so foreign managers at home and abroad are acceptable to the Swedes but hardly to the Japanese. Differences in cultural distance cannot play a role here, because the cultural distance is the same in both cases.

Tse, Pan, and Au (1997) analyzed some 3,000 foreign operations in China, divided into export, licensing, joint-venture, and wholly owned operations. They found a significant correlation ($p < .01$) between the parent country's PDI and equity-based entry, that is, entry by joint venture or wholly owned operation. Companies from high-PDI countries entering high-PDI China sought a position based on solid equity.

Luo (1999, p. 519) surveyed 96 foreign-based enterprises in China and found the cultural distance between the partners (according to the Kogut and Singh measure) to have a negative impact on the overall performance of the venture.[112]

Differences along the mas/fem dimension can be functional, as the operation of an organization demands both task performance and relations maintenance. The two British-Dutch multinationals Shell and Unilever, which have existed for more than half a century, combine two cultures similar on three dimensions but differing widely on mas/fem: Britain masculine, the Netherlands feminine. This can be seen as a happy marriage between complementary partners: "The English love to be admired, the Dutch like to admire" (Kuiper, 1983, p. 49).[113]

The integration of national markets in the European Union increases the number of cross-national ventures among member countries. EU countries, from Denmark to Portugal, differ primarily along the upper-left to lower-right diagonal in Exhibit 4.2, from small power distance, weak uncertainty avoidance to large power distance, strong uncertainty avoidance; but on this diagonal the differences among them are considerable and about as large as could be found anywhere in the world (Exhibit 9.3). Common membership in the European Union is therefore no insurance against cultural problems.

The conclusions from the previous studies were not confirmed by Morosini, Shane, and Singh (1998), who analyzed 35 foreign acquisitions in Italy by companies from the United States and from other European countries and 17 foreign acquisitions by Italian companies abroad. They used a different success criterion—the acquired companies' growth in sales in the 2 years following the acquisition—which they found to be *positively* related to their cultural distance with the acquiring parent country (using the Kogut and Singh formula, $p < .05$). Morosini et al. support this conclusion with interview results suggesting that precisely the variety led to synergy. They argue that cultural distance is not always a disadvantage. Country- and industry-specific factors can compensate for the problems caused by cultural distance.[114]

Hennart and Larimo (1998) have also reported results opposed to previous studies: Comparing Japanese and Finnish entries to the United States, they found that the lower-PDI, lower-UAI Finns used more wholly owned subsidiaries and the Japanese used more joint ventures.

The general conclusion from these studies is that cultural distance is an important variable in foreign entries, affecting both the choice of entry mode and the rate of success. Differences in UAI and secondarily in PDI play the leading part. Yet there are no simple and uniform rules that can be generalized across countries, industries, and points in time.

Whatever the combination of countries and whatever the mode of entry, the integration process has to be managed. It is highly desirable to let foreign (and domestic) acquisitions, mergers, ventures, and alliances be preceded by an analysis of both the national and the organizational cultures of the partners. If the decision is still to go ahead, this match analysis can be used as the basis for a cultural integration management plan. Such a plan should treat the integration as a management problem to be addressed explicitly; it should have the active support of the chief executive.[115] Cultural integration takes time, energy, and a lot of money unforeseen by the financial experts who design these ventures. The integration process should be monitored based on the views of members of both parties.

Integration problems may hide in unexpected places. An analysis of foreign acquisitions in Denmark found that clashes were often due to language:

> Even though most Danes are good at foreign languages, we . . . have examples of employees with seven to nine years of schooling who . . . were unable to communicate freely and advance beliefs on behalf of their colleagues because the foreign management fixed the agenda in their [the foreign] language, unaware that active participation and exchange of views in a discussion . . . needs a standard of English that is so high that it is mastered by only very few Danish employees. We also have examples of engineers who can easily communicate in German as long as they talk with German engineers about . . . the development of a product. But they have never learned how to discuss and argue in German in order to defend their interests when cooperation problems arise between a Danish and a German project group. (Gertsen & Søderberg, 1998, p. 193)

International Marketing, Advertising, and Consumer Behavior

Culture is present in the design and quality of many products, and in the presentation of many services.[116] An interesting example is the difference in passenger aircraft cockpit design between the two large actors on the world market, Airbus (European, primarily French-German) and Boeing (U.S.). Pilots familiar with both told Merritt (1995) that the Airbus has been designed to fly itself with minimum interference from the pilot, whereas the Boeing expects more discretion from and interaction with the pilot. The Airbus is the product of an uncertainty-avoiding design culture; the Boeing respects the low power distance pilot's supposed need to feel in command.

In 1983, Harvard University professor Theodore Levitt published an article titled "The Globalization of Markets" in which he predicted that technology and "modernity" would lead to a worldwide convergence of consumers' needs and desires. This he believed would enable global companies to develop standard brands with universal marketing and advertising programs. In the 1990s, more and more voices in the marketing literature expressed doubts about this convergence and referred to my culture indexes to explain persistent cultural differences.[117] Chapters 3-7 provided ample evidence of significant correlations of consumer survey data with the five indexes, mainly based on research by De Mooij (1998a, 1998b). Analyzing national consumer behavior data over time, De Mooij (2001) showed that contrary to Levitt's prediction, buying and consumption patterns in affluent countries in the 1980s and 1990s diverged as much as they converged. Affluence implies more opportunities to choose among products and services, and consumers' choices are affected by psychological and social influences:

> Consumption decisions can be driven by functional or social needs. Clothes satisfy a functional need, fashion satisfies a social need. Some personal care products serve functional needs, others serve social needs. A house serves a functional, a home a social need. Culture influences in what type of house people live, how they relate to their homes and how they tend to their homes. A car may satisfy a functional need, but the type of car for most people satisfies a social need. Social needs are culture-bound. (De Mooij, 1998b, pp. 58-59)

An example of the combination of functional and social needs cited by De Mooij (2001) is the development of the market for private cars across 15 European countries in the preceding decades. The number of cars per 1,000 inhabitants depended less and less on income: It was strongly correlated with GNP/capita in 1969 ($r = .93***$), but no longer in 1994 ($r = .42$, ns). This could be read as a sign of convergence. The share of these cars bought secondhand in 1970 was larger in wealthier countries ($r = .47*$ with GNP/capita), but in 1997 this correlation had disappeared ($r = .32$, ns), another sign of convergence. However, the preference for new cars over secondhand ones depended much more on UAI than on wealth ($r = .79***$ in 1970, $r = .80***$ in 1997); regardless of national wealth, uncertainty-avoiding cultures kept avoiding used cars, no convergence. And in 1997 for the first time a significant correlation emerged between preferring a new car and MAS ($r = .46*$, was $r = .22$, ns, in 1970).[118] Ownership of a second car in the family correlated with GNP/

capita in 1970 ($r = .58*$) but no longer in 1997 ($r = -.28$, *ns,* convergence), but the decisive index in 1997 had become MAS, $r = .62**$ in 1997 (was $r = .43$, *ns,* in 1970).[119] Owning a second car is a way for the family to assert itself, something that receives higher priority in masculine cultures.

From the cultural indexes, UAI and MAS resist convergence most: These two are independent of, and therefore unaffected by, wealth. Uncertainty avoidance stands for differences in the need for purity and expert knowledge; mas/fem "explains differences in the need for success as a component of status, resulting in a varying appeal of status products across countries. It also explains the roles of males and females in buying and in family decision making" (De Mooij, 1998b, p. 57). Such differences are often overlooked by globally oriented marketers who assume their own cultural choices on these dimensions to be universal.

The persistent influence of national culture on consumer behavior affects the validity of theories and practices in both marketing and advertising. Marketing theory mainly originated in the United States, and therefore it has been based on U.S.-centered assumptions about consumer motivation:[120]

The latter, combined with a universalistic attitude among American marketing management, has led to a marketing practice based on the principle that companies, products and brands should be differentiated from the competition and positioned as strong personalities. They should "stand out in a crowd of other brands" in order to be competitive. The metaphors used are "corporate identity" and "brand personality." This practice reflects the typical configuration of Individualism and Masculinity within US culture. . . . Academics worldwide have adopted the consumer behavior theories developed by their US colleagues, without realizing that these are not necessarily valid for other parts of the world. What motivates people to buy and use certain products is largely a matter of culture. Culture influences how people relate to each other in the buying process, whether decisions are made by individuals or groups, and what motivates someone to buy specific products. (De Mooij, 1998b, p. 56)

One important variable in consumer behavior is willingness to innovate. Lynn and Gelb (1996) measured national innovativeness in 16 European countries on the basis of a survey of more than 20,000 consumers in 1990 by Gallup International for Reader's Digest;[121] their index consisted of possession of a cordless telephone, a telephone answering machine, a home computer, a microwave, a compact disc player, and a video camera (these six formed one factor at the country level). The index was significantly correlated

with 1988 purchasing power parity (PPP, an alternative for GNP/capita, $r = .80***$), IDV ($r = .77***$), and UAI ($r = -.58**$). In a multiple regression, PPP and IDV made independent significant contributions; UAI did not. Steenkamp, Ter Hofstede, and Wedel (1999) measured consumer innovativeness using an attitude index, the Exploratory Acquisition of Products (EAP) scale, in a random mail survey of more than 3,000 consumers across 11 European countries.[122] At the individual level they found a significant negative relationship between EAP and Schwartz's individual "conservation" measure, which had been included in the survey. At the country level they used the Hoppe (1990) scores for the IBM indexes. They did not use correlations but regression coefficients, but these were significant at the .01** level for both IDV (positive) and UAI (negative). There was a weaker (.05* level) positive association between innovativeness and MAS. Without being conclusive, these two studies together suggest that high IDV and low UAI, at least, increase the market potential for certain innovative products.

The literature on advertising in the 1990s increasingly stressed the need for cultural differentiation and referred frequently to the IBM indexes. Several studies compared U.S. print and TV advertisements to similar ads in particular other countries.[123] Albers (1994) rated more than 1,800 business advertisements from 11 countries (1 from each of the 11 country clusters in the first edition of *Culture's Consequences*)[124] and four product categories on the use of 42 forms of "appeal." Every country had its own profile of appeals, significantly different from all others. In a correlation analysis with the four IBM indexes, Albers found PDI to be significantly positively correlated with the use of the appeals "ornamental," "status," and "dear" and marginally with "vain" ($p = .08$) and negatively with "wisdom" and "moral." UAI was significantly negatively related to "untamed," "magic," and "youth." IDV was significantly positively correlated with "family" (in a collectivist culture, family is too obvious to be used as an appeal). MAS was significantly positively correlated with "convenient" and marginally negatively correlated ($p = .10$) with "modest."

De Mooij (1998a, p. 261) collected and analyzed more than 3,400 television commercials from 11 countries.[125] She identified specific advertising styles for countries linked to cultural themes. Some of these could again be related to my culture indexes. Lonesome people are taboo in collectivist cultures (if nobody wants to join this person the product must be bad—in these cultures there are always several persons present in the picture). Discussions between mothers and daughters are shown in both high- and low-PDI cultures, but where PDI is high mothers advise daughters, and where it is low, daughters advise mothers. Similar conclusions have been presented by Alden, Hoyer, and Lee (1993), who compared humor in TV ads in Germany, South Korea, Thailand, and the United States. Although humor was used in all four countries (with some common elements), the two Asian countries featured more actors (low IDV) and more status differences between actors (high PDI). On the other hand, Cutler, Erdem, and Javalgi (1997) studied print ads from eight countries and found no relationship between the picturing of multiple persons and IDV;[126] they suggest this may be because these ads try to communicate to the *individual reader*. There was a marginal relationship between the use of personalized pronouns and IDV (*you* for the more individualist and *we* for the more collectivist cultures).[127]

The same global brand may appeal to different cultural themes in different countries. Uniform international advertising campaigns can have unpredicted local impacts. The nature and use of the product also play a role. Zhang and Gelb (1996) tested the appeal of an individualist and a collectivist advertisement on 80 students each in China and in the United States, for two products, cameras (socially visible) and toothbrushes (privately used). For the socially visible product, matching of the appeal to the culture (collectivist in China, individualist in the United States) had a very strong positive effect. For the privately used product, such matching had only a weak effect.[128]

Advertising, and television advertising in particular, is directed at the inner motivation of prospective buyers. At least some TV commercials can be seen as modern equivalents of the myths and fairy tales of previous generations, told and retold because they resonate with the software in people's minds; and, in spite of Levitt's prediction, these minds have not been and will not be globalized.

Cross-cultural marketing still offers many other areas for research. Weitzel (1999) asked panels of judges to classify packaging designs of five product categories (deodorant for women, mineral water, soup, cigarettes, and cigars) from seven countries on a number of design aspects.[129] Via factor analysis, she reduced the relevant dimensions of design aspects to five: expressiveness, context, symbolism, information, and brand identification.[130] Several country scores on these dimensions were significantly correlated with the IBM indexes, but the correlation patterns varied by product. For example, "expressiveness" of the package for deodorants was negatively correlated with MAS (more expressive packages in feminine countries); for mineral water, positively with UAI; and for cigars, positively with PDI.

Cross-cultural marketing research should not be confused with the earlier "lifestyles" research conducted by commercial agencies. Different agencies have sold different lifestyle typologies, distinguishing categories of consumers with similar values and assumed buying behaviors (for a review, see De Mooij, 1994, pp. 159 ff.). The lifestyles approach started with the VALS (Values and Life Styles) typology developed by the Stanford Research Institute in the United States in 1975 on the basis of the Maslow and Rokeach value classifications. In 1989, the VALS-2 was issued, which included nine types: fulfilleds, believers, actualizers, achievers, strivers, strugglers, experiencers, and makers. Chapter 1 has already signaled the limits of typologies: They are excellent for teaching and selling purposes but dubious in research, as new cases rarely fit ideal types. Also, the problem with a distinction of fundamental attitudes toward life is what one should include and what one should not: The choices made reflect the values of the researchers. The VALS-2 labels together carry a distinctive values flavor as to what (U.S.) people *should* live for. The practical usefulness of the lifestyle types in marketing is hard to prove; fashion and belief determine their use.

Market research agencies in other countries, Asian and European, have followed the trend, developing lifestyle typologies for their own national markets (De Mooij, 1994, pp. 165 ff.). A few have tried to cross national borders, offering "pancultural" lifestyles.[131] These have been based on the assumption that certain groups of consumers (such as young people) behave more like others in those groups in, say, Tokyo and New York than they do like people in other groups in their own countries. Eshghi and Sheth (1985) tested this assumption with consumption data for six products from four countries, split according to the lifestyle variable "traditional versus modern."[132] For all products, the country variable explained a much larger share of the consumption variance than the lifestyle variable. In view of the variety in national cultures, institutions, legislation, languages, and economic development among countries, there will be very few products for which an international lifestyle measure might be relevant, even within the European Union.[133] For the latter, Kale (1995) has proposed grouping countries for marketing purposes according to my indexes; he suggests three clusters characterized, respectively, by high MAS, high UAI, and low UAI/low MAS.

Further cultural differentiation, even in firms with globalized marketing approaches, is provided by the intermediate role of local sales forces, whose members translate (sometimes literally) the marketing message to local customers. For example, the degree of directness a salesperson can use is highly culturally dependent.[134] Ways of management and compensation of sales forces should be based on cultural values (theirs and the customers') and on characteristics of the industry.[135] Conceptions of business ethics for salespersons vary strongly from one culture to another; they are a direct operationalization of some of the values involved in the culture indexes.[136]

Even less than the markets for goods, markets for services support globalization. Services are by their very nature personalized toward the customer. International companies in the service field tend to leave considerable marketing discretion to local management.[137] Any traveler in a new country knows the insecurity involved in learning how to relate to personal service personnel. Lynn, Zinkhan, and Harris (1993) studied the phenomenon of tipping across 30 countries for 33 types of personal service professions, such as gas station attendants, hair stylists, taxi drivers, and waiters.[138] They found significant zero-order correlations between the number of tipped professions and UAI ($r = .42*$) as well as PDI ($r = .40*$); tipping clearly defines the mutual roles of client and service person (UAI) and stresses their inequality (PDI).[139]

Chances for globalization are relatively better for *industrial marketing,* the business-to-business area. Although industrial marketing is more culture sensitive than many newcomers to the international field realize, it is a scene where *international* purchasers and international salespersons meet. Technical standards are crucial, and participation in their establishment is a major industrial marketing instrument.[140] Negotiation processes become very important, and negotiation with foreign partners is an art that provides competitive advantages to those who master it better than others (see the discussion of intercultural negotiation above). It demands not only sensitive negotiators but also understanding head office staff to support them.

Schools, Tourism, and a Look Ahead

Intercultural Encounters in Schools

An American teacher at the foreign-language institute in Beijing exclaimed in class, "You lovely girls, I love you!" Her students, according to a Chinese observer, were terrified. An Italian professor teaching in the United States complained bitterly about the fact that students were asked to evaluate his course formally. He did not think that students should be the judges of the quality of a professor. An Indian lecturer at an African university saw a student arrive 6 weeks late

for the course, but had to admit the student because he was from the same village as the dean. Intercultural encounters in schools can lead to many perplexities.[141]

Most intercultural encounters in schools confront local teachers with foreign, migrant, or refugee students, or expatriate teachers, hired as foreign experts or sent as missionaries, with local students. Different cultural value patterns between teacher and student(s) are a regular source of problems. Chapters 3 through 7 discussed implications for education of the five dimensions of national cultures. They affect relationships between teachers and students, relationships among students, and relationships between teachers and their students' parents. The composition of the class also plays a role. Levy, Wubbels, Brekelmans, and Morganfield (1997) studied perceptions of teacher behavior among 550 U.S. high school students in 38 classes and found that perceived teacher dominance increased both with the share of foreign-culture students and with the number of different cultures in the same class.

As language is the vehicle of teaching, what was mentioned earlier about the role of language in intercultural encounters applies entirely to the teaching situation. The chances for successful cultural adaptation are better if the teacher is to teach in the students' language than if the student has to learn in the teacher's language, because the teacher has more power over the learning situation than any single student. The course language affects the learning process. A change of language implies much more than a transposition of words; ethnolinguistics shows that the role of language within the total set of cultural artifacts varies from country to country.[142]

At INSEAD, an international business school in France, I taught the same executive course in French to one group and in English to another; both groups were composed of people from several nationalities. Discussing a case study in French led to highly stimulating intellectual discussions but few practical conclusions. When the same case was discussed in English, it would not be long before someone asked "So what?" and the class tried to become pragmatic. Both groups used the same readings, partly from French authors translated into English, partly vice versa. Both groups liked the readings originally written in the class language best and condemned the translated ones as "unnecessarily verbose, with a rather meager message that could have been expressed in one or two pages." The comments of the French-language class on the readings translated from English were thus identical to the comments of the English-language class on the readings translated from French! What is felt to be a "message" in one language does not necessarily survive the translation process. Information is more than words: It is words within a cultural framework.[143]

Beyond differences in language, students and teachers in intercultural encounters run into differences in cognitive abilities. One British training manager stated, "Our African engineers do not think like engineers, they tend to tackle symptoms, rather than view the equipment as a system." But is there only one way for engineers to think? Fundamental studies by development psychologists have shown that the things we have learned are determined by the demands of the environment in which we grew up. A person will become good at doing the things that are important to him or her and that he or she has occasion to do often. Being from a generation that grew up before the introduction of pocket calculators in schools, I can do calculations by heart for which my children and grandchildren need a machine. Learning abilities, including the development of memory, are rooted in the total pattern of a society. In China the nature of the script (between 3,000 and 15,000 complex characters of up to 23 strokes each) develops children's abilities in pattern recognition and memorizing.

Intercultural problems arise also because expatriate teachers bring irrelevant materials with them. A Zairean friend, studying in Brussels, recalled how at primary school in Lubumbashi her teacher, a Belgian nun, made the children recite in their history lesson, *Nos ancêtres, les Gaulois* (our ancestors, the Gauls). A British lecturer repeated his organizational behavior course word for word during a visiting teaching assignment in China. Much of what students from poor countries learn at universities in rich countries is hardly relevant in their home-country situations. What is the interest for a future manager in an Indian company of mathematical modeling of the U.S. stock market? The know-how supposed to make a person succeed in an industrial country is not necessarily the same as the know-how needed to develop a poor country.

Finally, intercultural problems can be based on institutional differences in the societies from which the teachers and students have come, differences that generate different expectations as to the educational process and the roles of various parties in it. From what types of families are students and teachers recruited? Are educational systems elitist or anti-elitist? A visiting U.S. professor in a Latin American country may think he contributes to the economic development of the country, when in actual fact he only supports the continuation of elite privileges. What role do employers play in the educational system? In Switzerland and Germany, traineeships in industry or business are a respected alternative to a university education, allowing people to reach the highest positions, but this is not the case in France or

Greece. What roles do the state and/or religious bodies play? In some countries (France, Russia) the government prescribes the curriculum in great detail; in others, teachers are free to define their own. In countries where both private and public schools exist, the private sector may be for the elites (United States) or for the dropouts (Netherlands, Switzerland). Where does the money for the schools come from? How well are teachers paid and what is their social status? In China, teachers are traditionally highly respected, but poorly paid. In Britain, the status of teachers has traditionally been low; in Germany, high.

Intercultural Encounters in Tourism

Historically, tourism grew out of religious pilgrimages, and these are still a major reason for people to undertake long and stressful voyages (to Mecca, Santiago de Compostela, Lourdes). Sanctuaries on the island of Malta are supposed to have been a target for pilgrimages from Mediterranean countries some 5,000 years ago. Pilgrimages from Europe to Jerusalem between 1,300 and 1,600 A.D. were organized like Neckermann tours and used standard guidebooks comparable to the *Michelin Guide*.[144]

Modern tourism represents the most superficial form of intercultural encounter. Mass tourists spend 2 weeks in Morocco, Bali, or Cancún without finding out anything about the local culture at all.

Host-country personnel working for tourism will learn more about the culture of the tourists than vice versa; they discover the different behaviors of different tourist nationalities, albeit in a stereotyped fashion.[145] Their picture of how the tourists live at home will be highly distorted. What either side picks up from the other is only on the level of symbols (Exhibit 1.4): words, fashion articles, music.

The economic effects of mass tourism on the host countries may or may not be favorable. Traditional sources of income are often destroyed, and the revenues of tourism go to governments and foreign investors, so that local populations may suffer more than they benefit. The environmental effects can be disastrous. Tourism is, from many points of view, a mixed blessing.

Tourism can nevertheless be the starting point for more fundamental intercultural encounters. It breaks the isolation of cultural groups and creates an awareness that there exist other people who have other ways. The seed planted in some minds may ripen later. Some tourists start learning the language and history of a country they have visited and to which they want to return. Hosts start learning the tourists' languages to promote their businesses. Personal friendships develop between the most unlikely people in the most unlikely ways. From an intercultural encounter point of view, the possibilities of tourism probably outweigh the disadvantages.

The Influence of New Technology

Popular media often spread the belief that new communication technologies, such as e-mail, the Internet, and mobile telephones, will bring people around the world together in a "global village" where cultural differences will cease to matter. This belief in technology is in itself culturally determined; it is stronger in high-MAS, high-PDI societies (in Chapter 6 this was shown for biotechnology).

Unfortunately (or fortunately), the dominance of technology over culture is an illusion. Electronic communication will not eliminate cultural differences, just as faster and easier travel has not reduced cultural rifts. The software of the machines may be globalized, but the software of the minds that use the terminals is not.

Electronic communication enormously increases the amount of information accessible for its users, but it does not increase their capacity to absorb this information or change their preexisting values systems. Users have to select what information they recognize; this has always been the case, only the selection task has become much larger. We select our information according to our values. Like our parents, we read newspapers that we expect to give our preferred points of view, and, confronted with the new bulk of electronic information, we again pick whatever reinforces our preexisting ideas. Our relatively brief experience with the Internet so far has shown that people use it to do what they were doing anyway, only maybe more and faster.

Not only will cultural diversity among countries remain with us, but the new technologies may even increase differences between and within countries. Ethnic groups arrive at a new consciousness of their identity and ask for political recognition of this fact. Of course these ethnic differences have always been there—what has changed is the intensity of contact between groups, which has confirmed group members in their own identities. The spread of information on how people live elsewhere in the world has affected minorities, who compare their situation to the lives of others whom they suppose to be better off. Information about suffering and strife is also much more widespread than ever before. Pogroms, uprisings, and violent repression are not new inventions, but in the past relatively few people beyond those directly involved would know about them. Now they are visible on TV screens around the world.

The effects of the new technologies on users' physical and mental health are hardly known, but they may also disturb the global dream. Repetitive strain injuries, radiation effects, stress, and burnout all indicate that the new technologies may demand particular kinds of performance to which humans are ill adapted.

In summary, the new technologies will not by themselves reduce the need for intercultural understanding. When wisely used, they may be among the tools for intercultural learning. Research on the possibilities has only just started.[146]

Cultural Relativism, Convergence, and Divergence

Everybody looks at the world from behind the windows of a cultural home and everybody prefers to act as if people from other countries have something special about them (a national character) but home is normal. Unfortunately, there is no normal position in cultural matters. This is an uncomfortable message, as politically incorrect as Galileo Galilei's claim in the 17th century that the earth is not the center of the universe.

Cultural relativism is not a popular subject. I regularly participate in international discussion groups at scholarly meetings. Once one has been sensitized to it, it is impossible not to recognize the cultural influences on the interest areas and points of view taken by Scandinavians, French, Americans, Chinese, Japanese, Germans, British, Italians, or Dutch participants, not to mention the cultural influences on their ways of presenting their ideas. Yet I have noticed that drawing attention to the cultural component in our points of view is a risky strategy that polarizes the audience. Some think it highly enlightening, suddenly putting the entire discussion into perspective. Others, however, reject the notion of a cultural component rigorously, become upset, and feel threatened by it. "Possibly one of the many reasons why the culture concept has been resisted," Hall (1959/1965) wrote, "is that it throws doubt on many established beliefs. Fundamental beliefs . . . are shown to vary widely from one culture to the next. It is easier to avoid the idea of the culture concept than to face up to it" (p. 50). In addition, "the concepts of culture . . . touch upon such intimate matters that they are often brushed aside at the very point where people begin to comprehend their implications" (p. 165).

Yet I believe that the battle for the recognition of the cultural component in our ideas is worth fighting. More so now than one or two generations ago, most of us meet people with cultural backgrounds different from our own and are expected to work with them. If we maintain the naive assumption that because they look like us they also think like us, our joint efforts will not get very far. If we begin to realize that our own ideas are culturally limited, from that moment we need the others: We can never be self-sufficient again. Only others with different mental programs can help us find the limitations of our own. Once we have realized we are blind persons in front of the elephant, we start to welcome the exchange with other blind persons.

Some people wonder whether the advocated consciousness of the limits of one's own value system does not lead to moral laxity. Chapter 1 contains a call for "cultural relativism," the recognition that, as a famous French anthropologist expressed it, "one culture has no absolute criteria for judging the activities of another culture as 'low' or 'noble.' " But this is no call for dropping values altogether. As a matter of fact, this entire book shows that no human being can escape from using value standards all the time. Successful intercultural encounters presuppose that the partners believe in their own values. If not, they have become alienated persons, lacking a sense of identity. A sense of identity provides the feeling of security from which one can encounter other cultures with an open mind.

The principle of surviving in a multicultural world is that one does not need to think, feel, and act like someone else in order to agree with that person on practical issues and to cooperate. The IBM research to which Chapters 2 through 6 have been devoted has illustrated this. The value differences among employees in different countries working for this multinational have been shown to be considerable. Nevertheless, IBM-ers the world over cooperated in reasonable harmony toward practical goals. There is nothing unique about IBM in this respect; other people can and do cooperate across national borders. The fact that organizational cultures are relatively superficial and value-free phenomena, as was demonstrated in the IRIC research reported in Chapter 8, is precisely the reason international organizations can exist and be composed of different nationals, each with its own different national values.

People from cultures very dissimilar on the national culture dimensions of power distance, individualism, masculinity, uncertainty avoidance, and long-term orientation as described in the various chapters of this book can cooperate fruitfully. Yet people from some cultures will cooperate more easily with foreigners than others. The most problematic are nations and groups within nations that score very high on uncertainty avoidance, and thus feel that "what is different is dangerous." Also problematic is cooperation with nations and groups scoring very high on power distance, because such cooperation depends on the whims of single powerful persons. In a world kept together by intercultural cooperation, such cultural groups

will certainly not be forerunners. They may have to be left alone for some time until they discover they have no other choice but to join.

The evidence in Chapters 3 through 7 showed that there was no international convergence of cultural values over time, except toward increased individualism for countries having become richer. Value differences between nations described by authors centuries ago are still present today, in spite of continued close contacts. For the next few hundred years, countries will remain culturally very diverse.

You may consider me a pessimist, or someone who takes a static view of societies. I only try to be realistic. Mental programs do change, but slowly and not according to anyone's master plan. Changes take decades, if not centuries. If the inheritance of the Roman Empire still separates Belgium from the Netherlands, two countries in intimate contact for more than 2,000 years, we should not expect that anyone can change the minds of Serbs, Russians, or Albanians within a few years. In organizing our world, we had better take mental programs as given facts.

A popular business slogan is "Think globally, act locally." To me this phrase is both naive and arrogant. No one, as this book has amply proven, can think globally. We all think according to our own local software. What intercultural encounters are about is recognizing that we think differently but resolving our common problems anyway. The slogan should be "Think locally, act globally." [147]

Notes

1. Bond (1986, p. 273) demonstrated this for a group of U.S. exchange students in Hong Kong who were interacting with Hong Kong Chinese students. For an exhaustive review of the subject of intergroup relations across cultures, see Gudykunst and Bond (1997).

2. See Berry and Annis (1974a).

3. As far as I know, this term first appeared in an article by Oberg (1960), the title of which referred to "cultural shock." The classic source book on the subject is Furnham and Bochner (1986).

4. Gudykunst and Ting-Toomey (1988) have published an exhaustive text on interpersonal communication that uses my four-dimensional IBM model of cultural differences as its basic paradigm.

5. Perlmutter (1965) chose the terms *ethnocentric* and *polycentric* to describe two out of three phases in the development of a multinational business corporation (discussed later in this chapter).

6. Gudykunst, Chua, and Gray (1987) analyzed data from 158 foreign students in the United States about interactions with same-sex U.S. students. The amount of trust (need for uncertainty reduction pro-

cesses) in these relationships was strongly negatively affected by cultural distances in terms of all of my four IBM indexes, but cultural distance lost influence as relationships became more intimate, moving from acquaintance to friend to best friend. See also Gudykunst and Ting-Toomey (1988, p. 214).

7. See Lewis (1990, 1996).

8. See Hofstede (1991, p. 213). The survey included BEL (Dutch- and French-speaking regions), DEN, FRA, GBR, GER, GRE, IRE, ITA, Luxembourg, NET, POR, and SPA.

9. See Kachru (1988).

10. See Hofstede (1994b, chap. 15).

11. See Van Dijk, Ting-Toomey, Smitherman, and Troutman (1997).

12. Lysgaard described the acculturation curve in 1955, and it has been the subject of an extensive literature. See Torbiörn (1982, chap. 8), Furnham and Bochner (1986, pp. 130-136), Black and Mendenhall (1991), and Selmer (1999).

13. The length of the time scale in Exhibit 9.1 varies; it seems to adapt to the length of the expected expatriation period. People on short assignments of up to 3 months have reported phases of euphoria, culture shock, and acculturation within this period; people on long assignments of several years have reported culture-shock phases of a year or more before acculturation set in.

14. Zeitlin (1996) has suggested that the severity of culture shock is related to the cultural distance between home and host country; he produced a "cultural distance table" for 18 European countries plus the United States based on my IBM index values.

15. This myth is really extremely persistent. Not long ago, I reviewed a journal manuscript that once more referred to the 70% failure rate. In my review, I made the authors aware of the Harzing article. Much to my surprise, when the article was published, I found that the authors still referred to a 70% failure rate and justified it by citing Harzing (1995)!

16. See Sussman (1986).

17. See Tung (1997).

18. See Kealey (1996).

19. See Bell and Harrison (1996). However, the candidate should meet the other criteria as well. I know of at least one case in which a person with the right bicultural experience was a disaster in the new job for personality reasons.

20. Dunbar (1992) notes these conditions on the basis of a survey of 150 former expatriates of U.S. multinationals.

21. Bateson (1967) paid tribute for this insight to the British author and artist Samuel Butler (1835-1902).

22. Bhawuk and Triandis (1996) stress in particular an understanding of the difference between individualism and collectivism. This is the first dimension that U.S. authors, being embedded in the most individualist culture in the world, tend to write about, but their focus risks reducing cultural theory to just this one dimension and missing the other very important dimensions.

23. See Adler (1991). Adler has also produced a video series titled *A Portable Life* that includes interviews with spouses. Black and Gregersen (1991) found, based on a survey of some 260 U.S. expatriate wives, that those best adapted had initiated their predeparture training themselves, rather than receiving it through the company.

24. ITIM International is a worldwide network of trainers who provide culture-general cross-cultural training based on my research. The network's Internet address is http://www.itim.org. Banks and Waisfisz (1993) have published an article on ITIM International's principles of culture-general training.

25. For an overview of issues in the design of cross-cultural training and education programs, see Brislin and Horvath (1997).

26. This is evident from their professional association, SIETAR International (Dahlén, 1997; Hofstede, 1998d). SIETAR decentralized in the late 1990s.

27. See Fiedler, Mitchell, and Triandis (1970) and Foa and Foa (1974, pp. 320 ff., 333 ff.).

28. See Albert (1983).

29. See also Cushner and Brislin (1996). Elsewhere, the General Culture Assimilator was renamed the Cultural Sensitizer (Cushner & Landis, 1996). It has a strong U.S. cultural flavor. The differences it covers are almost exclusively those between the United States and Third World cultures; most of its scenarios deal with ind/col and power distance.

30. This paragraph is inspired in part by essays (based on U.S. conditions) by Saenger (1952) and Phinney (1996).

31. See Eldering and Kloprogge (1989).

32. See Bhagat (1985) and Bochner and Hesketh (1994).

33. Willems and Cottaar (1989) studied views about the majority culture among minorities in the Netherlands. Lack of respect was mentioned by Moluccans (from Eastern Indonesia), Chinese, and Turks.

34. Van den Berg and Bleichrodt (1996), inspired by the first edition of *Culture's Consequences* (Hofstede, 1980a, p. 143), compared interpersonal values between 577 immigrants in the Netherlands from six different countries or regions and 439 Dutch local citizens, using Gordon's (1976) Survey of Interpersonal Values (SIV) as described in Chapter 3. The immigrants had spent a mean of 8.7 years in the host country. Their SIV scores reflected clearly their home-country cultures. On three of the six SIV dimensions (support, recognition, and independence) there was a small shift, significantly correlated with length of residence, in the direction of the Dutch values; on the three others (conformity, benevolence, and leadership), there was none.

35. Hines (1973, 1974) found achievement motivation values of Greek immigrants in New Zealand and the United States to be carried over into the second generation. Shackleton and Ali (1990) gave the VSM 82 to ethnic Brits and second-generation British Pakistani and found the latter still scoring more like Pakistanis than like Brits in the IBM study; the Brits closely replicated

the British IBM scores. Georgas, Berry, Shaw, Christakopoulou, and Mylonas (1996) found that family values of Greeks in Canada, Germany, and the Netherlands depended more on age than on generation and host country, just as in Greece itself. Rosenthal and Feldman (1992) compared first- and second-generation Chinese in Australia and the United States and found an erosion of ethnic identification but no increase in individualism. Lalonde and Cameron (1993), however, found shifts toward mainstream values for students in Canada from four ethnic groups compared to their parents: blacks from the Caribbean, Chinese, Greeks, and Italians.

36. Many Muslim cultures are endogamous (that is, they allow marriage between first cousins; Todd, 1983), and girls are conveniently married to relatives back home.

37. Shaffer and O'Hara (1995) found this to be the case for immigrants in the United States versus immigration lawyers.

38. See Colijn (1995).

39. See, for example, Klimidis, Stuart, Minas, and Ata (1994).

40. Dr. Harry Minas of Melbourne, Australia, noted this problem in a personal communication.

41. Without being aware of my work, Fisher (1988) used a very similar approach to "culture." For example, he also used the computer analogy for the human mind.

42. See Huntington (1996).

43. Algeria was not in the IBM set, but it was certainly poor (1990 GNP/capita U.S.$2,060); I rate its culture as low IDV, high PDI, and high UAI.

44. Russia's 1997 GNP/capita was U.S.$2,740; it is rated as medium to low IDV and very high PDI and UAI (see Appendix 5).

45. A similar objection can be made to the U.N. Convention on the Rights of the Child, adopted in 1996 (see Murphy-Berman, Levesque, & Berman, 1996).

46. See Freeman (1995).

47. "Diversity enables mutual benefit; sameness causes war" (Maruyama, 1994, p. 57).

48. See Kolman, Hofstede, Noorderhaven, and Dienes (1999); see also Musil (1993) and Appendix 5.

49. See Hartwich (1996, 1998, 1999). Hartwich writes from his experience with international financial institutions: the World Bank, Inter-American Development Bank, Asian Development Bank, and African Development Bank.

50. A Dutch article warned against the threat of European influences for the integrity of Dutch public servants (Van Vugt, 1994).

51. This statement is based on information published in 1999 in *Eur-OP News,* the information bulletin of the European Communities' Publications Office (no. 4, p. 3). The numbers were as follows: FRA, 419; ITA, 329; GER, 293; SPA, 291; GRE, 241; BEL, 238; POR, 199; GBR, 174; AUT, 163; IRE, 146; Luxembourg, 115; NET, 114; SWE, 101; FIN, 81; and DEN, 75.

52. See Tomasic (1946) and Huntington (1993).

53. See the index scores in Appendix 5 as well as Hofstede (1993). In 1980, a Eurobarometer survey

asked representative samples of the population of the then 10 EU members to rate their trust in a number of other nations. Only the Greeks trusted the Russians more than they trusted the Americans. A total of 35% of the Greek respondents trusted the Russians, and 33% trusted the Americans. Across all 10 countries, the proportions were as follows: 20% for the Russians, 67% for the Americans (Inglehart & Rabier, 1982).

54. This excerpt is presented here as quoted in Varga (1993).

55. See, for example, Soeters (1993) about the political management of the Belgian/Dutch/German Maas-Rhine region and Barmeyer (1996) about small border-crossing enterprises in the French/German Lorraine-Saarland region.

56. The countries were BEL, CAN, DEN, FRA, GBR, GER, ITA, NET, NOR, SPA, USA, Belarus, and Hungary.

57. Soeters and Recht (1999) studied the values of 185 participants in the 6-month NATO Defense College course in Rome, at the beginning and at the end of the course, and found no convergence in cultural values. They suggest including explicit cross-cultural training in the program.

58. See Peterson and Bliese (1996).

59. See Bilis-Bastos (1998).

60. This section is based in part on Hofstede (1989b).

61. A prominent author on the mathematical modeling of negotiation is Raiffa (1982).

62. The 11 cultures were CAN (Anglophone), CAN (Francophone), CHI, FRA, GBR, GER, KOR, MEX, RUS, TAI, and USA.

63. Several U.S. publications of the 1980s have attempted to make U.S. businesspeople aware that they need to adapt their ways of negotiating when dealing with Japanese; see, for example, Moran (1985) and Stewart (1987).

64. See Kaufmann (1980, 1988).

65. For example, see Usunier (1996, chaps. 15-16) and Ghauri and Usunier (1996).

66. *The Lords of Humankind* is the title of a book by Kiernan (1969) about the British imperial age.

67. Examples include Paddock and Paddock (1973), May (1978), World Bank (1980), and Jankowicz (1994).

68. See Kapitza (1996).

69. See Smith (1987).

70. See Krause (1981) about self-help communities in Indonesia; Erdener (1991) about the village institutes in Turkey; Margulis, Motwani, and Kumar (1997) about the "tiffin carriers" in Mumbai, India, who perform a logistical miracle in distributing 200,000 hot lunches within 3 hours; and Henry and d'Iribarne (in d'Iribarne, Henry, Segal, Chevrier, & Globokar, 1998) about successful transitions to modern management in Mauritania, Cameroon, and Morocco.

71. Gudeman (1986) has argued that any society models its ways of livelihood; modeling is a basic human activity: "Humans are modelers: They translate

past activities into models for future action" (p. 44). Chapter 8 referred to the false assumption that Western models of management apply globally; the same assumption is made in economics. For a review of Gudeman's book, see Hofstede (1987).

72. Myrdal's (1968) profound study of the economic dilemmas of development in Asia did take cultural factors such as corruption into account. Porter's (1990) theory of "the competitive advantage of nations," discussed in Chapter 8, doesn't even mention corruption.

73. In Exhibit 5.1, Israel scored only moderately individualist (IDV 54), so that the label "individualistic nations" for this cluster is debatable.

74. Kedia and Bhagat (1988) have published a conceptual model of cross-national transfer of technology that hypothesizes the influence of differences between donor and receiver on each of the four IBM indexes.

75. See Forss, Carlsen, Frøyland, Sitari, and Vilby (1988). This project had originally been designed by the Institute for Research on Intercultural Cooperation in the Netherlands; IRIC had attempted to get development agencies *and* multinationals to join forces in a study about factors leading to the effectiveness of expatriates (Andersson & Hofstede, 1984). After the proposed public-private cooperation fell through, the Nordic development agencies went ahead on their own.

76. See Van Vlijmen-Van de Rhoer (1980).

77. See Fryxell (1992a) as well as the sarcastic rejoinder by Blunt (1992), who describes the presumed reactions of two imaginary Tanzanians, and a reply to Blunt from Fryxell (1992b).

78. See Brug (1981).

79. This paragraph and the two following are adapted from a report I wrote in 1983 for the International Labour Office in Geneva; most of this material was published in Hofstede (1984a).

80. Lynton and Pareek (1990), in a book originally published in 1967, insisted on the relevance of U.S.-style interpersonal training methods for the development of India and Indonesia, but I found little recognition in their work of the cultural and political environments in which their trainers, trainees, and institutions were embedded. They used the word *power* only in relationship to trainers' needs: "Of all their personal needs, the need for power may be the most salient and also the most treacherous for trainers" (p. 195). There is more to be said about power in the development processes of these countries. See also Chapter 3.

81. Maisonrouge made this remark during a presentation he gave at an IBM executive training session that I attended.

82. Elangovan (1995) relates the four IBM dimensions to managers' resolution of conflicts between subordinates.

83. Regarding compensation and benefits packages, see Hodgetts and Luthans (1993).

84. The foreign subsidiaries were in AUL, AUT, BEL, DEN, FRA, GBR, GER, HOK, ITA, JPN, MAL, NET, PHI, SIN, SPA, SWI, and TUR.

85. The countries were CAN, FRA, GBR, GER, JPN, NET, SWE, and SWI.

86. Support for the opposing positions of "food" (feminine) and "chemicals" (masculine) is found in a Ph.D. thesis by Meijaard (1998). Meijaard did an in-depth study of decision making in research and development in two multinationals in two industries (chemicals and food) in each of two countries (the Netherlands and the United States). His corporations were Akzo-Nobel (chemicals, Netherlands), Dow (chemicals, United States), H. J. Heinz (food, United States), and Unilever (food, Netherlands). All four have research facilities in both the Netherlands and the United States. Meijaard found R&D decision making to be determined more by industry than by country, and he characterizes attitudes in the food industry as relatively feminine and those in the chemical industry as relatively masculine. This would mean that the food industry better fits the culture of the Netherlands, and the chemical industry better fits the culture of the United States.

87. Merritt (1995) has illustrated this for the case of commercial airline crews.

88. This proposition is based on the findings in a Ph.D. dissertation by Noonan (1995), who held in-depth interviews with 23 U.S. and 17 non-U.S. managers and professionals about successful and unsuccessful interactions across cultures.

89. In my experience at INSEAD in the 1970s, discussion groups with British chairmen did better on average than those with chairmen of other nationalities.

90. See Edwards (1978, p. 36).

91. Even local organizations may be surprised by unfamiliar values in the environment if their managements have not followed the value shifts in their society due to the zeitgeist. For an example, see the case of the 1972 consumer boycott of the largest Dutch coffee-roasting firm because it refused to stop importing coffee from Angola, then still a Portuguese colony (Hofstede, 1994b, chap. 12).

92. This inference is inspired in part by a comparative study of corporate social reporting in France, Germany, and the Netherlands by Schreuder (1978).

93. Burgess (1995, p. 560), managing director of Andersen Consulting UK, related the way the strategic process takes place in companies to my five dimensions.

94. I elaborate on this point in Hofstede (1989c).

95. This is "Ashby's law of requisite variety" from systems theory.

96. The subsidiaries were in CAN, GBR, GER, JPN, and USA; they were subsidiaries of multinationals based in CAN, GER, JPN, and USA.

97. Cultural distances were positively related to the share of total compensation in the subsidiaries (at all levels) based on incentives. Neither Kogut and Singh (1988) nor I could find a plausible explanation for this.

98. The 9 home countries were FIN, FRA, GBR, GER, JPN, NET, SWE, SWI, and USA; the 22 host countries were ARG, AUT, BEL, BRA, DEN, FIN, FRA, GBR, GER, HOK, IRE, ITA, JPN, MEX, NET, NOR, SIN, SPA, SWE, SWI, USA, and VEN.

99. Compare Rosenzweig and Nohria's (1994) findings among foreign subsidiaries in the United States (see above) that cultural distance, the presence of expatriates, and the frequency of communication with the parent corporation were all associated with less adaptation to U.S. HRM practices.

100. See Saner, Yiu, and Søndergaard (2000).

101. Shane (1992a, 1994b) analyzed flows of income of U.S. companies from foreign licensing and foreign direct investments in 1977 and 1982. In both cases he found a relationship with the foreign country's PDI: Higher-PDI countries provided more income from licensing; lower-PDI countries, more income from direct investments. Shane interpreted this in terms of trust and the perception of transaction costs.

102. For case descriptions, see Grunberg (1981), Grange (1996), Olie (1996), and d'Iribarne (1998).

103. Luo (1999) has stressed the role of time-based experience in foreign-invested enterprises in China.

104. The period covered was 1981-85. Kogut and Singh's (1988) abstract refers to the analysis of 228 entries, but their Table 2 lists 506 entries from BEL, CAN, FRA, GBR, GER, ITA, JPN, MAL, NET, SAF, SWI, "Scandinavia," and "Other." I could find no information in the article regarding which 228 cases were used for the analysis.

105. Kogut and Singh's (1988) formula for cultural distance takes the mean of the squares of the differences in index scores for the parent country and the United States on the four dimensions PDI, UAI, IDV, and MAS, after having divided each of the squares by the variance of the index on the particular dimension.

106. Kogut and Singh (1988) repeated their analysis without the Japanese data to see whether the unique position of Japan could have influenced their results. Without Japan, entries into the United States by greenfield starts were still related to UAI ($p < .05$); entries by joint venture were still related to cultural distance ($p < .05$).

107. For these countries, UAI and PDI were correlated with $r = .98$!

108. Grosse and Trevino (1996), independent of Kogut and Singh (1988), have developed their own measure of cultural distance, which is simply the sum of the absolute values of the score differences on the indexes PDI, UAI, IDV, and MAS (no squaring, no dividing by the variance).

109. Li and Guisinger's (1991) study covered the period 1978-88.

110. Benito and Gripsrud (1992), analyzing the foreign direct investments of Norwegian manufacturing companies up to mid-1982, found no relationship between cultural distance and order of entry for that particular case.

111. Bell (1996) has further distinguished among minority joint ventures, 50/50 joint ventures, and majority joint ventures.

112. Pan (1996) analyzed data from more than 4,000 foreign joint ventures in China between 1979 and 1992 and found that culturally distant partners preferred a 50% equity share, whereas culturally more similar partners more often held minority participation. The latter demand a higher level of trust in the other partner.

113. Van Enter (1982) has also noted the complementarity of the two nationalities.

114. Chang and Rosenzweig (1998) followed the development of European and Japanese subsidiaries in the United States from 1975 to 1992 and concluded that industry effects were more important for foreign market entry than were region-of-origin (= country) effects.

115. Olie (1994) describes the integration process in three cases of German-Dutch mergers.

116. Discussion in this subsection leans heavily on ideas provided by Marieke de Mooij.

117. See, for example, Kale (1991); Milner, Fodness, and Speece (1993); Shoham and Albaum (1994); Dawar and Parker (1994); Dawar, Parker, and Price (1996); Roth (1995); and Nakata and Sivakumar (1996).

118. In a stepwise regression, adding MAS after UAI increased the share of variance explained, R^2 from .58 to .71.

119. A stepwise regression for 1970 showed the share of variance explained to be $R^2 = .34$ using only GNP/capita, .76 using GNP/capita plus MAS. In 1997, $R^2 = .38$ using only MAS, .67 for MAS plus PDI, .81 for MAS plus PDI plus IDV; GNP/capita did not play a role.

120. This criticism of international marketing according to U.S. values is repeated in a U.S. text on advertising by Anholt (2000).

121. The countries were AUT, BEL, DEN, FIN, FRA, GBR, GER, GRE, IRE, ITA, NET, NOR, POR, SPA, SWE, and SWI.

122. The countries were BEL, DEN, FRA, GBR, GER, GRE, IRE, ITA, NET, POR, and SPA.

123. Examples are Mexico (McCarty & Hattwick, 1992), Korea (Han & Shavitt, 1994), Japan (Javalgi, Cutler, & Malhotra, 1995), and France (Taylor, Hoy, & Haley, 1996).

124. See Hofstede (1980a, fig. 7.11). The countries selected were BRA, CHL, FIN, FRA, IND, ISR, JPN, MEX, SAF, TAI, and USA.

125. The countries were BEL, FRA, GBR, GER, ITA, JPN, NET, SAF, SPA, SWE, and USA.

126. The ads came from FRA, GBR, HOK+TAI (taken together), IND, JPN, KOR, TUR, and USA.

127. Cutler, Erdem, and Javalgi (1997) found a significance level of $p = .10$ in this case. De Mooij, recalculating on the basis of their published data, found $r = .62$, $p = .052$; separating Hong Kong and Taiwan, which increases the n to 9, produced $r = 62$, $p = .038$ (personal communication).

128. Some authors have suggested dividing countries into clusters for shared advertising campaigns. Sriram and Gopalakrishna (1991) have proposed six clusters based on a combination of economic indicators, culture indexes, and media usage data; Zandpour and Harich (1996), on a similar basis, have proposed four clusters. I still fear that such generalizations do insufficient justice to the variety in country cultures and products.

129. The countries were GBR, GER, JPN, NET, SPA, THA, and USA.

130. Seventeen design aspects across 35 (5 × 7) cases were reduced to these five.

131. See Chapter 7; this means lumping individuals from different cultures together in the same data set.

132. The products were automobiles, stereo equipment, deodorants, soft drinks, fruit juices, and alcoholic beverages; the countries were BRA, FRA, JPN, and USA.

133. Malhotra, Agarwal, and Baalbaki (1998) have argued that regional trading blocs such as the European Union, NAFTA, and ASEAN are useful for world trade, but they are not relevant categories for developing successful marketing strategies, whether from within or outside.

134. See Richins and Verhage (1987).

135. Usunier (1996, pp. 466-472) has operationalized cultural differences in approaches to sales force management with the help of my four IBM indexes.

136. See Dubinsky, Jolson, Kotabe, and Lim (1991) and Armstrong (1996).

137. For example, see Kassem (1989) and Kassem and Habib (1989).

138. The countries were ARG, AUL, AUT, BEL, BRA, CAN, COL, DEN, FIN, FRA, GBR, GER, GRE, HOK, IND, IRE, ISR, ITA, JPN, MEX, NET, NOR, NZL, POR, SPA, SWE, SWI, TUR, USA, and VEN.

139. In Lynn, Zinkhan, and Harris's (1993) calculations, Japan, where very few tips are given, was always an outlier. The authors related this to the "extreme emphasis the Japanese place on repaying debts and obligations" (p. 485). In a multiple regression across 29 countries, excluding Japan, significant contributions to the variance in the number of tipped professions were made by UAI and MAS rather than PDI, suggesting that tipping is also a form of assertiveness.

140. See Guillet de Monthoux (1984).

141. This subsection includes some material extracted from Hofstede (1986a).

142. See Riley (1988, pp. 25-27).

143. Saner and Yiu (1994) point to the cultural hurdles implicit in the Harvard case-style method for students (and teachers) outside the United States. They suggest different case designs and teacher roles for Southeast Asia, German-speaking countries, and Eastern Europe.

144. See Brefeld (1994).

145. Pizam and Sussmann (1995) have shown the different images of American, French, Italian, and Japanese tourists found among 123 British tour guides.

146. See Ulijn and Campbell (1999) and Ulijn and Kumar (2000).

147. *Lokales Denken, Globales Handeln* is the title of the 1997 German paperback version of my 1991 book *Cultures and Organizations: Software of the Mind.*

10

■

Using Culture Dimension Scores
in Theory and Research

Summary of This Chapter

In the 1980 edition of *Culture's Consequences,* I suggested six areas for continued research, and in the past 20 years all six have in fact been covered by others and/or myself. The professional literature presents applications of the four- or five-dimensional model of national cultures in a surprisingly wide range of academic disciplines and practical areas. The applications can be divided into reviews and criticisms, replications, extensions to new countries and regions, and paradigmatic uses.

This chapter addresses some common pitfalls in carrying out replications and extensions, about which the reader is cautioned. Of greater interest are the various paradigmatic applications of the model, for which Chapters 3 through 7 present many examples. Applications can be quantitative, using culture dimension index scores of countries as potential explanatory variables for various measured phenomena, along with other explanatory variables such as national wealth. Applications can also be qualitative; the model can serve to explain and to help us understand observed similarities and differences between matched phenomena in different countries. Quantitative use demands data for a sufficient number of countries, preferably 10 or more; qualitative use is possible for any comparison of 2 or more cases.

The model presented in this book does not represent a finished theory; all conclusions are falsifiable, and this volume is meant as a step in an ongoing exploration.

Applications of the Dimensional Model

The Fortunes of Continued Research in Six Areas

The penultimate section of the 1980 edition of *Culture's Consequences* was titled "Six Areas for Continued Research." It is reproduced here as it was, with a few shortcuts:

This book is, to a large extent, an exploration into new territory; specifically, the territory that lies between the various rather neatly defined disciplines of the sciences of man: anthropology, sociology, psychology, economics, political science, law, and medicine. I personally consider as the book's primary asset the development of a broad conceptual framework related to fundamental problems of human society, which allows qualitative analysis and quantitative measurement; in this way it is able to tie together a large number of studies by others, in the vast majority of cases hitherto unrelated. . . . Thus, it offers a beginning of synergy in a field where such synergy has been rare, in which individual studies are often like the proverbial needles in a haystack.

Most respectable research reports end with a call for more research, and in my case such a call is absolutely essential. This book has produced unfinished business, wrapped up because it should urgently be exposed to a wider readership. Below are listed the steps I feel must be taken next:

1. The concept of dimensions of national culture in general and the particular four dimensions, Power Distance, Uncertainty Avoidance, Individualism, and Masculinity, should be further underpinned, criticized, and complemented by reference to additional literature—in particular to literature of non-Anglo-Saxon origins—and by exposure to the comments of scholars and practitioners from a variety of national backgrounds.

2. The set of countries covered should be expanded from the present 40 to include others as well—the Socialist world, the smaller Third World countries. Eventually it should include all except the very small countries (the 1976 *World Bank Atlas* counts 125 countries with a population of over one million).

3. The time dimension should be expanded; both by historical analysis of meaningful indicators (such as those by Lynn and Hampson, see Chapter 4) and by repeat surveys. . . .

4. The analysis of differences in *national* cultures should be complemented with a further differentiation of regional, ethnic, occupational, and organizational subcultures. . . .

5. Most important, the *consequences for organizational, national, and international policy* of a better insight into dimensions of national culture should be elaborated. My theory of cultural differentiation is like a product of the research laboratory, which awaits the efforts of the development technicians to elaborate it into something of practical use. The present chapter is clearly incomplete. I count on the critical support of enlightened and creative practitioners to, for example, learn about how the new insights can contribute to turning cultural conflict in multicultural organizations into cultural synergy.

6. Beyond the consequences for policy—that is, for practice—the cultural relativism which my findings support calls for an effort at theory-building, especially in those countries in which theories of modern man, management, organization, and society must be imported wholesale from abroad. In the past 30 years there has been altogether too much reliance on American-made management and theories for countries in which neither the societal conditions nor the mental programming of the population were similar to those in the United States. There is a great lack of locally valid theories of management and organization in which the universally human, the globally imposed, and the culturally specific elements will be wisely recognized.

So far for the research ambitions in the 1980 editions, some progress has been made in all six areas; the dimensions have been further validated, as the present edition testifies; the number of countries covered has been expanded (Appendix 5); several repeat surveys have been conducted (although not in IBM); a major study has been devoted to organizational cultures (Chapter 8); policy makers, consultants, and trainers have used the message of the book in their projects; and a consciousness of the need for local, culturally fitting theories of management and organization has grown, especially in Asia.

Fields of Application

With the crucial support of Sage Publications and its president, Sara Miller McCune, the 1980 book reached a gratifyingly wide readership. According to the *Social Science Citation Index*, through the end of 1999 it had been cited in more than 1,800 articles in refereed journals from a large variety of disciplines.[1] The five journals providing the most citations were in cross-cultural and organizational psychology, organizational sociology, management, and communication.[2] In these disciplines the book has become more or less a classic (see the end of Chapter 2). At the 26th International Congress of Psychology in Montreal in August 1996, a symposium titled "The Consequences of *Culture's Consequences*" was held; it included contributions from five prominent cross-cultural psychologists.[3]

Psychologists have most often referred to individualism/collectivism, and more recently also to masculinity/femininity, but scholars from other disciplines have concentrated on other dimensions. Sociologists and management researchers have more often referred to power distance and uncertainty avoidance; long- versus short-term orientation, because of its association with economic growth, has appealed most to political economists.

Søndergaard (1994), analyzing the available citations of the 1980 volume up to 1988, classified them into four categories:

1. Mere mentioning, without further explanation (I call this "name-dropping" and consider it a bad habit of authors.)

2. Reviews and criticisms

3. Replications and extensions to other countries

4. Paradigmatic applications, relating the conceptual framework to empirical phenomena in various fields

The contribution of the citations to the state of the art in the comparative study of cultures increases from zero in category 1 to potentially dramatic in category 4.

Reviews and criticisms are most interesting when they come from unexpected areas or disciplines. Examples of these have been found in history, social anthropology, social geography, sociology of law, public administration, information technology, archives management, accounting and management control, marketing, laboratory management, total quality management, business ethics, engineering education, medical education, medical technology, and nuclear power regulation.[4]

Replications and Their Pitfalls

Replications are studies that administer questions used in the IBM research to new samples from two or more of the same countries.[5] Experience has shown that some questions have had to be reformulated when used with non-IBM populations. The Values Survey Module (VSM) was developed especially for replications; it went through a number of versions. The VSM, its history, and formulas for calculating the country indexes from it are described in Appendix 4.

Although replications appeal to many novice scholars, their results are often no more than marginally interesting, if only because they rarely cover sufficient numbers of cultures. Most replications compare only two or three samples, as the logistical problems of covering more are insurmountable for most master's or doctoral researchers. As Chapter 2 showed, the four IBM dimensions were based on statistical trends in a "population" of 40 countries. A trend found in a cloud of 40 dots cannot be falsified by just 2 or 3 of those dots. Reviewing 61 mostly smaller replications, Søndergaard (1994) showed that taken together these confirmed the dimensions, but that pure chance accounted for disconfirmation of particular dimensions in a minority of cases. Large-scale replications (more than 10 or 15 countries) have been few and far between; the ones available have been analyzed extensively in Chapters 2 through 7.

A problem for replications on few cultures is that the reliability of the measurement cannot be checked in the usual way. Thesis committees and journal reviewers often ask for proof of the reliability of the instruments used. Novice researchers, forgetting that they are comparing cultures, not individuals, then apply reliability calculations (such as Cronbach's alpha) on individual scores and find very low values. However, the reliability of a cross-country test can be tested only across countries.[6] This requires data from a sufficient number of countries—say, 10 or more—without which the reliability of the instrument can simply not be tested in the textbook way and has to be taken for granted based on the literature. Ph.D. candidates may have some trouble explaining this to thesis committee members who are not accustomed to ecological-level research.

The best proof of the reliability of the dimension scores is their validity in explaining outside phenomena according to some kind of theory or logic. An unreliable test (one in which the measures contain too much random noise and too little information) cannot produce valid results, so if validity is proven, reliability follows; I will come back to this below.

Trying to test the reliability of the dimensions across individual scores means committing a reverse ecological fallacy (see Chapter 1): Confusing cultures with individuals is the first pitfall of cross-cultural research, especially tempting to psychologists from individualist countries. As I have argued in Chapter 1, culture is no king-size personality; cultures are formed through the interactions of different personalities, both conflicting and complementary, which create a whole that is more than the sum of its parts.

The VSM is no personality test and should not be used as such. A trainer may administer a culture questionnaire to classroom participants for demonstration purposes, to show the kinds of issues involved.[7] However, he or she should not suggest, for example, that a personal Power Distance Index score or Individualism score predicts a person's effectiveness in another culture. There exist no valid formulas for computing dimension scores on the Values Survey Module for individuals. Also, I know of no personality tests that are valid for predicting expatriate success in a culture.[8]

Another pitfall for replications is the poor matching of samples. The scores on a question obtained for a group of respondents are affected by factors other than nationality—for example, depending on the question, by the respondents' education levels, genders, and ages; by the type of work organization; and by the point in time when the survey was conducted. Therefore, cross-national research should be done only on *matched samples*—that is, samples similar in all respects except nationality. These samples should, moreover, be of sufficient size—at least 20 and preferably 50 per country. It is meaningless to use the questionnaires for one single sample of respondents from one country and then compare the scores against those in this book, which are based on mutually matched IBM subsidiary populations. This would make sense only if it could be argued that the new sample is a match for the original IBM population in all important respects. Such a match is virtually impossible to make, if only because the IBM studies were done around 1970 and the point in time of the survey is one of the matching characteristics.

A third pitfall is the confusing of national cultures with other levels of culture. The dimensions were chosen so as to discriminate among national and maybe regional and ethnic cultures, but not for discriminating according to other (sub)cultural distinctions, such as gender, generation, social class, and organization.[9] (Power distance, exceptionally, is also relevant for social classes, occupation, and education levels; masculinity is relevant for distinguishing occupations.) One replication study used the Values Survey Module to discriminate between normal and orthopedically handicapped workers within the same factory in one country. The logic of this replication escapes me.

A fourth pitfall is ethnocentrism. The IBM dimensions were developed cross-culturally, but novice researchers often focus only on their own culture and judge the dimension scores from this culture's point of view and value system. They recognize only the issues considered relevant in their own society and ignore or consider taboo issues that may be relevant in other societies. In this way they miss precisely the culturally essential issues. For example, some replicating researchers have left out the mas/fem questions from the VSM because they judged these questions to be politically incorrect for themselves or for their respondents.

A fifth and rather naive pitfall is for researchers to formulate their own questions according to the way they understand the dimensions, somehow form indexes from these, and assume that these indexes are equivalent to the IBM indexes in this book. It is quite possible to formulate new questions that measure a dimension for a population, but their validity will have to be proven before one can draw any conclusions from responses; and in order to prove this validity it is necessary to use the new questions in at least some 15 countries along with the old questions and to show that the old and new scores are significantly correlated. The meaning of a question in a questionnaire study is not what the researcher thinks it should be, but what the respondents associate with it.

An example of a marginally acceptable, rather trivial replication is found in a doctoral dissertation by Ashkanani (1984), who surveyed small samples (20 and 21) of foreign graduate students in the United States from two countries/regions also represented in the IBM research: Iran and Arab countries. The two groups of foreign students can be considered matched samples. In both the IBM data and the student data, the two countries/regions had rather similar scores: For two dimensions the differences between Iran and the Arab countries were in the same direction as in the IBM study; for the other two, they were not. Given the small size of the samples, this result is not a surprise. In the same replication, Ashkanani also included scores from 33 U.S. graduate students. In this case the matching was less perfect (a foreign student is not in the same situation as a domestic student; also, the Americans were much older). Nevertheless, the differences in dimension scores between the Americans and the two groups of foreign students were in the predicted direction for all four dimensions.

Extensions to New Countries

Extensions of the research to countries and regions not in the IBM set can of course be very interesting. There is a demand for IBM-type index scores for additional countries. Studies extending the research to other countries should again be based on matched samples across these countries. Also, they should always include one or more of the countries in the IBM set, so that the new data can be anchored to the existing framework. The national culture index scores in this book, I want to emphasize again, describe only *differences* between countries: Their absolute value has no meaning. I have stressed the need for matched samples in the preceding paragraphs. As the new samples can never be matched with the original IBM samples, the new study should include at least one new sample from one IBM country for anchoring purposes, which means that the effect of the change of sample on the scores of the IBM country can be measured, and the scores for the new countries can be corrected for this effect. Finding matched samples across new and old countries is the main problem of extension research; few populations are as well-comparable internationally as the IBM population was in 1967-73.

Nanhekhan (1990) carried out a well-designed extension with the purpose of obtaining scores for Surinam, a former Dutch colony in South America not represented in the IBM research. She sought a company having similar operations in both Surinam and the Netherlands and surveyed employees in both. The Surinam sample was the smaller (about 25 employees), and Nanhekhan matched every Surinam respondent as well as possible with a respondent in the Netherlands, in all respects except nationality. She calculated the scores on the Values Survey Module for the two matched samples and then used the differences between the IBM index scores and the new scores for the Netherlands to adjust the Surinam scores to what they would have been for an IBM-type population. Nasierowski and Mikula (1998) used a similar approach to obtain scores for Poland; they used a carefully matched sample of Canadian respondents as their anchor to the original scores. The results of these studies are included in Appendix 5.

Using the
Dimensional Model as a Paradigm

The disadvantage of replication and extension studies is that they are caught in the straitjacket of my model and therefore unlikely to make basic new contributions. The IBM-based questionnaire is not necessarily the best instrument for detecting the essence of cultural differences in other populations. Researchers studying national and ethnic culture differences who can get access to a sufficient number of cultures—at least 10—may borrow (some of) the IBM questions, but they should primarily develop their own survey instruments aimed at the particular populations studied and based on empathy with the respondents' situation. Sample in-depth interviews and participant observation are ways of acquiring such empathy. The results of such surveys should be tested for underlying dimensions, and comparisons of the dimensional structures found, across overlapping countries, in different studies—including mine—will produce true synergy and advance the state of the art.[10] A prime example is the Chinese Value Survey study across 23 countries (Chapter 7), which added a new dimension to the four found in IBM.[11] However, studies of this kind demand considerable effort, expertise, network support, resources, and time.

More feasible for many aspiring researchers are projects exploring relationships among already existing data. My view is that there is no law that says Ph.D. researchers must collect their own raw data. Large amounts of measured information are already available in books and journals, on CD-ROM, and on the Internet. Relating the results of different and independent studies is "secondary research," and I consider it more important for the development of fundamental insights than most primary research. In this book Chapters 3 through 7 are full of references to such secondary research, relating country-level results of completely different studies to my national culture dimension scores (and implicitly to each other). At the same time, they are related to other variables, such as economic, geographic, and/or demographic indicators, testing cultural against alternative explanations so as to avoid a myopic focus on culture alone.

Typical examples of secondary research using the culture indexes are the comparisons with Schwartz's (1994) worldwide values surveys among students and elementary school teachers, Reitsma's (1995) analysis of the duration of decision making about major public works in six countries, the comparisons with the World Values Survey based on public opinion research in 43 societies worldwide (Inglehart, Basañez, & Moreno, 1998), and Kashima and Kashima's (1998) analysis of the relationship between culture and linguistic features of 39 languages. For a summary, see Appendix 6.

Interpretable and statistically significant relationships between the culture dimensions and data from completely different studies prove the validity of both. They implicitly also prove the reliability of the measures: An unreliable test cannot produce scores that relate meaningfully to outside data (see above and Chapter 2).

Paradigmatic users sometimes forget to choose among the dimensions; some believe their phenomena should be related to all of the dimensions, one by one. This is based on a misunderstanding. The strength of the model is precisely that it allows conceptual parsimony: It allows us to detect *which* dimension is responsible for a particular effect and which dimensions are not. Data from other sources are often significantly correlated with more than one of the IBM indexes. It all depends on which countries are included in the study; the set of countries determines the pattern of intercorrelations among the dimension scores. For example, if the set includes only European countries, PDI and UAI tend to be strongly intercorrelated and difficult to separate (Figure 4.2). Therefore, an outside variable significantly correlated with one of the indexes will often also correlate with one or more others. The analyses in Chapters 3 through 7 used stepwise multiple regressions on the four or five indexes to eliminate the spurious correlations.[12] Stepwise regression shows which indexes contribute independently to the relationship with the outside variable; only these should be included in the interpretation.

These examples are all quantitative; they use statistical methods to find explanatory variables for various measured phenomena, including culture dimension index scores of countries. Applications can also be qualitative; the model can serve to explain and to help us understand observed similarities and differences between matched phenomena in different countries. Quantitative use demands data for a large number of countries, preferable 10 or more; qualitative use is possible for any comparison of 2 or more cases, increasing the always-tenuous generalizability of case study results.[13]

Closing Remarks

In writing this book, and again in rewriting it after 20 years, I have felt a bit like Alice in Wonderland. One discovery followed another, and wherever I probed an area there was another behind it. This book is the result of exploratory research; it does not present a finished theory. Inspired by Karl Popper (1959), I have made an effort to formulate my conclusions in a tentative and falsifiable way—hoping for you, reader, to continue the exploration. By all means, check and correct my work, but even better, apply it and elaborate its lines of thought, making them serve the understanding of cultural differences and the improvement of intercultural communication and cooperation, which the world will increasingly and forever need.

Notes

1. These 1,800 are out of a total of 2,700 articles citing any of my publications.

2. As measured in the period 1989-93 (see Hofstede, 1996c, pp. 112-113). The five journals were the *Journal of Cross-Cultural Psychology, International Journal of Psychology, Journal of International Business Studies, International Journal of Intercultural Relations,* and *Organization Studies.* Together, these supplied 29% of 434 citations. In total, these citations were from 158 different refereed journals.

3. The symposium's convener was Peter B. Smith; other contributors were Michael Harris Bond, Mark F. Peterson, Shalom H. Schwartz, and Harry C. Triandis. I was the discussant. The proceedings have been published in Doré (1996).

4. Such reviews and criticisms in the field of history have included those of Leerssen (1988, 1989) and Stokvis (1997). Leerssen's comments were critical, but I took his criticism in a scientific historical journal as a compliment (see also Hofstede, 1989a). Examples of reviews and criticisms in other areas include the following: in social anthropology, Chapman (1997); in social geography, Steinbach (1991) and Berry, Conkling, and Ray (1993); in sociology of law, Hofstede (1988a) and Bruinsma (1995); in public administration, Kreacic and Marsh (1985); in information technology, Shore and Venkatachalam (1996); in archives management, Bearman (1992); in accounting and management control, Anthony (1988); in marketing, De Mooij (1994); in laboratory management, Ketchum (1993); in total quality management, Napier and Kroslid (1996); in business ethics, Vitell, Nwachukwu, and Barnes (1993); in engineering education, Mainwaring and Markowski (1991); in medical education, Klimidis, Minas, Stuart, and Hayes (1997); in medical technology, Beneken (1993); and in nuclear power regulation, Rochlin and Vonmeier (1994).

5. The discussion in this subsection is derived mainly from the appendix "Reading Mental Programs" in Hofstede (1991).

6. Test-retest reliability coefficients for the IBM questions are shown in Exhibit 2.4.

7. U.S. consultant Dr. John Bing of International Training Associates of Princeton (ITAP) developed a classroom exercise using 24 questions from the 1982 version of the VSM, 6 per dimension.

8. For factors predicting expatriate failure, see Chapter 9.

9. See Hofstede and Spangenberg (1987).

10. This is done, for example, in Smith and Schwartz (1997).

11. See Chinese Culture Connection (1987) and Hofstede and Bond (1988).

12. Generally, also including GNP/capita as an additional "index"—see Chapter 2.

13. Examples are management in the Indian subcontinent (Kanungo & Mendonca, 1994; Spink, 1996) and the growth of information technology in Australia and India (Plowman, 1999).

Appendix 1

Questions From the IBM Attitude Survey
Questionnaire Referred to in This Book

For the full questionnaire as standardized in 1971, see Hofstede, Kraut, and Simonetti (1976).

A Questions (used in all surveys, 1967-73 or 1968-73)

A1   Are you:
        1. Male (married)
        2. Male (unmarried)
        3. Female (married)
        4. Female (unmarried)

A2   How long have you been employed by this company?
        1. Less than one year
        2. One year or longer, but less than three years
        3. Three years or longer, but less than seven years
        4. Seven years or longer, but less than fifteen years
        5. Fifteen years or longer

A5-A18.   About your goals:
        People differ in what is important to them in a job. In this section, we have listed a number of factors which people might want in their work. We are asking you to indicate how important each of these is to you.

In completing the following section, try to think of those factors which would be important to you in an ideal job; disregard the extent to which they are contained in your present job.
PLEASE NOTE: Although you may consider many of the factors listed as important, you should use the rating "of utmost importance" only for those items which are of the *most* importance to you.
With regard to each item, you will be answering the general question:
"HOW IMPORTANT IS IT TO YOU TO . . ."
(Choose one answer for each line across)

How important is it to you to:

		of utmost importance to me	very important	of moder-ate impor-tance	of little importance	of very lit-tle or no importance
A5	Have challenging work to do—work from which you can get a personal sense of accomplishment?	1	2	3	4	5
A6	Live in an area desirable to you and your family?	1	2	3	4	5
A7	Have an opportunity for high earnings?	1	2	3	4	5

(Continued)

How important is it to you to:

		of utmost importance to me	very important	of moderate importance	of little importance	of very little or no importance
A8	Work with people who cooperate well with one another?	1	2	3	4	5
A9	Have training opportunities (to improve your skills or to learn new skills)?	1	2	3	4	5
A10	Have good fringe benefits?	1	2	3	4	5
A11	Get the recognition you deserve when you do a good job?	1	2	3	4	5
A12	Have good physical working conditions (good ventilation and lighting, adequate work space, etc.)?	1	2	3	4	5
A13	Have considerable freedom to adopt your own approach to the job?	1	2	3	4	5
A14	Have the security that you will be able to work for your company as long as you want to?	1	2	3	4	5
A15	Have an opportunity for advancement to higher level jobs?	1	2	3	4	5
A16	Have a good working relationship with your manager?	1	2	3	4	5
A17	Fully use your skills and abilities on the job?	1	2	3	4	5
A18	Have a job which leaves you sufficient time for your personal or family life?	1	2	3	4	5

A19-A32. About the satisfaction of your goals:

In the preceding questions, we asked you what you want in a job. Now, as compared to what you want, how satisfied are you at present with:

		very satisfied	satisfied	neither satisfied nor dissatisfied	dissatisfied	very dissatisfied
A19	The challenge of the work you do—the extent to which you can get a personal sense of accomplishment from it?	1	2	3	4	5
A20	The extent to which you live in an area desirable to you and your family?	1	2	3	4	5
A21	Your opportunity for high earnings in this company?	1	2	3	4	5
A22	The extent to which people you work with cooperate with one another?	1	2	3	4	5
A23	Your training opportunities (to improve your skills or learn new skills)?	1	2	3	4	5
A24	Your fringe benefits?	1	2	3	4	5

		very satisfied	satisfied	neither satisfied nor dissatisfied	dissatisfied	very dissatisfied
A25	The recognition you get when you do a good job?	1	2	3	4	5
A26	Your physical working conditions (ventilation, lighting, work space, etc.)?	1	2	3	4	5
A27	The freedom you have to adopt your own approach to the job?	1	2	3	4	5
A28	Your security that you will be able to work for this company as long as you want to?	1	2	3	4	5
A29	Your opportunity for advancement to higher level jobs?	1	2	3	4	5
A30	Your working relationship with your immediate manager?	1	2	3	4	5
A31	The extent to which you use your skills and abilities on your job?	1	2	3	4	5
A32	The extent to which your job leaves you sufficient time for your personal or family life?	1	2	3	4	5

A37   How often do you feel nervous or tense at work?

1. I always feel this way
2. Usually
3. Sometimes
4. Seldom
5. I never feel this way.

A43   How long do you think you will continue working for this company?

1. Two years at the most
2. From two to five years
3. More than five years (but I probably will leave before I retire)
4. Until I retire.

A48   If an employee did take a complaint to higher management, do you think he would suffer later on for doing this (such as getting a smaller salary increase, or getting the less desirable jobs in the department, etc.)?

1. Yes, the employee would definitely suffer later on for taking a complaint to higher management.
2. Yes, probably
3. No, probably not
4. No, the employee would definitely not suffer later on for taking a complaint to higher management.

A52   How often would you say your immediate manager is concerned about helping you get ahead?

1. Always
2. Usually
3. Sometimes
4. Seldom
5. Never

The descriptions below apply to four different types of managers. First, please read through these descriptions:

Manager 1	Usually makes his/her decisions promptly and communicates them to his/her subordinates clearly and firmly. Expects them to carry out the decisions loyally and without raising difficulties.
Manager 2	Usually makes his/her decisions promptly, but, before going ahead, tries to explain them fully to his/her subordinates. Gives them the reasons for the decisions and answers whatever questions they may have.
Manager 3	Usually consults with his/her subordinates before he/she reaches his/her decisions. Listens to their advice, considers it, and then announces his/her decision. He/she then expects all to work loyally to implement it whether or not it is in accordance with the advice they gave.
Manager 4 (version 1967-69)	Usually calls a meeting of his/her subordinates when there is an important decision to be made. Puts the problem before the group and invites discussion. Accepts the majority viewpoint as the decision.
(version 1970-73)	Usually calls a meeting of his/her subordinates when there is an important decision to be made. Puts the problem before the group and tries to obtain consensus. If he/she obtains consensus, he/she accepts this as the decision. If consensus is impossible, he/she usually makes the decision him/herself.

A54   Now for the above types of manager, please mark the one which you would prefer to work under.
1. Manager 1
2. Manager 2
3. Manager 3
4. Manager 4

A55   And, to which one of the above four types of managers would you say your own manager most closely corresponds?
1. Manager 1
2. Manager 2
3. Manager 3
4. Manager 4
5. He does not correspond closely to any of them.

A56   How many years of formal school education did you complete?
1. 10 years or less   6. 15 years
2. 11 years   7. 16 years
3. 12 years   8. 17 years
4. 13 years   9. More than 17 years
5. 14 years

A57   How old are you?
1. Under 20   5. 35-39
2. 20-24   6. 40-49
3. 25-29   7. 50-59
4. 30-34   8. 60 or over

A58   Considering everything, how would you rate your overall satisfaction in this company at the present time:

1. I am completely satisfied

2. Very satisfied

3. Satisfied

4. Neither satisfied nor dissatisfied

5. Dissatisfied

6. Very dissatisfied

7. I am completely dissatisfied

B Questions (used in all surveys, 1967-69 or 1968-69, but optional afterward)

B9   If you had a choice of promotion to either a managerial or a specialist position and these jobs were at the same salary level, which would appeal to you most? (You may already have been promoted in either direction, but just assume you could start again.)

1. I would have a strong preference for being a specialist

2. I would have some preference for being a specialist

3. It does not make any difference

4. I would have some preference for being a manager

5. I would have a strong preference for being a manager

B24   All in all, what is your personal feeling about working for a company which is primarily foreign-owned?

1. All in all, I prefer it this way

2. It makes no difference to me one way or the other

3. I would prefer that it was not this way

B25   Suppose you quit this company. Do you think you would be able to get another job in your line of work at about the same income?

1. Yes, definitely

2. Yes, probably

3. No, probably not

4. No, definitely not

B39   How often would you say your immediate manager insists that rules and procedures are followed?

1. Always

2. Usually

3. Sometimes

4. Seldom

5. Never

B44   How do you feel or think you would feel about working for a manager who is from a country other than your own?

1. In general, I would prefer to work for a manager of my own nationality

2. Nationality would make no difference to me

3. In general, I would prefer to work for a manager of a different nationality

How frequently, in your experience, do the following problems occur?

		very frequently	frequently	sometimes	seldom	very seldom
B46	Employees being afraid to express disagreement with their managers	1	2	3	4	5
B47	Being unclear on what your duties and responsibilities are	1	2	3	4	5
B49	People above you getting involved in details of your job which should be left to you	1	2	3	4	5
B51	Some groups of employees looking down upon other groups of employees	1	2	3	4	5

B52-B61. About general beliefs:

Our company has employees in many countries and we are interested whether the personal opinions of employees differ from country to country. Listed below are a number of statements. These statements are *not* about the company as such, but rather about general issues in industry. Please indicate the extent to which you personally agree or disagree with each of these statements (mark one for each line across).

Remember: We want *your own opinion* (even though it may be different from that of others in your country).

		strongly agree	agree	undecided	disagree	strongly disagree
B52	A corporation should have a major responsibility for the health and welfare of its employees and their immediate families	1	2	3	4	5
B53	Having interesting work to do is just as important to most people as having high earnings	1	2	3	4	5
B54	Competition among employees usually does more harm than good	1	2	3	4	5
B55	Employees lose respect for a manager who asks them for their advice before he makes a final decision	1	2	3	4	5
B56	Employees in industry should participate more in the decisions made by management	1	2	3	4	5
B57	Decisions made by individuals are usually of higher quality than decisions made by groups	1	2	3	4	5
B58	A corporation should do as much as it can to help solve society's problems (poverty, discrimination, pollution, etc.)	1	2	3	4	5
B59	Staying with one company for a long time is usually the best way to get ahead in business	1	2	3	4	5
B60	Company rules should not be broken— even when the employee thinks it is in the company's best interests	1	2	3	4	5
B61	Most employees in industry prefer to avoid responsibility, have little ambition, and want security above all	1	2	3	4	5

C Questions (discontinued in 1971 or before)[1]

C1-C8. About your goals:
How important is it to you to (Mark one for each line across):

		of utmost importance to me	very important	of moder- ate importance	of little importance	of very little or no importance
C1	Have the security that you will not be transferred to a less desirable job?	1	2	3	4	5
C2	Work in a department which is run effi- ciently?	1	2	3	4	5
C3	Have a job which allows you to make a real contribution to the success of your company?	1	2	3	4	5
C4	Work in a company which is regarded in your country as successful?	1	2	3	4	5
C5	Work in a company which stands in the forefront of modern technology?	1	2	3	4	5
C6	Work in a congenial and friendly atmo- sphere?	1	2	3	4	5
C7	Keep up-to-date with the technical de- velopments relating to your work?	1	2	3	4	5
C8	Have a job on which there is a great deal of day-to-day learning?	1	2	3	4	5

C9-C19. About general beliefs:
(Mark one for each line across)

		strongly agree	agree	undecided	disagree	strongly disagree
C9	A good manager gives his employees de- tailed and complete instructions as to the way they should do their jobs: He does not give them merely general directions and depends on them to work out the de- tails	1	2	3	4	5
C10	Most companies have a genuine interest in the welfare of their employees	1	2	3	4	5
C11	In general, the better managers in a com- pany are those who have been with the company the longest time	1	2	3	4	5
C12	There are few qualities in a man more admirable than dedication and loyalty to his company	1	2	3	4	5
C13	Most employees have an inherent dislike of work and will avoid it if they can	1	2	3	4	5
C14	Most employees want to make a real contribution to the success of their com- pany	1	2	3	4	5

		strongly agree	agree	undecided	disagree	strongly disagree
C15	For getting ahead in industry, knowing influential people is usually more important than ability	1	2	3	4	5
C16	By and large, companies change their policies and practices much too often	1	2	3	4	5
C17	A large corporation is generally a more desirable place to work than a small company	1	2	3	4	5
C18	Even if an employee may feel he deserves a salary increase, he should not ask his manager for it	1	2	3	4	5
C19	The private life of an employee is properly a matter of direct concern to his company	1	2	3	4	5

Note

1. Questions C1-C8 were used through 1971, C9 through 1970, C10-C14 through 1969, and C15-C19 through 1968.

Appendix 2

Country Scores on A, B, and C Questions
(except A5-A32 and C1-C8)

Exhibit A2.1 Country Scores on A Questions (Category 1 countries)

Country	Number of Resp.		A1	A2	A37	A43		A52	A54				A55	A56	A57	A58
	67-69	71-73				1-2	4		1-2	3A	3B	4B	1-2			
ARG	543	602	53	355	275	17	53	253	27	59	49	25	440	493	429	296
AUL	805	1,114	67	321	331	23	48	255	26	64	57	20	470	376	405	310
AUT	586	661	63	296	322	17	58	205	13	67	57	30	335	437	374	294
BEL	1,057	1,328	72	363	274	8	74	236	25	56	57	19	520	422	433	254
BRA	690	1,884	57	329	309	16	59	258	22	46	39	43	475	556	399	308
CAN	715	2,861	79	330	321	23	52	227	26	62	51	23	470	493	373	298
CHL	164		70	396	284	19	61	269	38	36		425	572	451	270	
COL	175	252	46	346	285	25	44	250	34	54	40	28	515	565	403	312
DEN	567	737	98	296	368	23	45	212	15	67	55	35	355	357	368	282
FIN	377	425	162	333	322	26	41	270	17	58	33	50	360	392	409	316
FRA	4,691	6,646	69	350	302	12	66	248	29	52	46	26	525	503	432	259
GBR	3,236	3,731	77	281	333	33	32	249	29	61	60	15	445	465	370	318
GER	3,477	7,907	52	344	314	19	53	225	15	61	49	40	445	398	427	302
GRE	111	127	133	336	263	11	57	231	14	60	70	18	465	614	434	296
HOK		88	88	240	334	38	22	272	34	60	46	22	615	628	301	300
IND	231		45	297	353	26	46	250	30	53		595	656	371	328	312
IRA	115	116	108	290	361	13	65	272	22		50	31	485	495	394	312
IRE	119	132	95	251	332	32	32	260	22	65	59	23	420	466	340	322
ISR	142	215	54	298	313	20	26	202	27	68	59	16	370	529	416	276
ITA	1,797		82	324	299	20	39	263	23	57		38	445	646	443	323
JPN	2,345	4,103	47	306	255	15	39	273	38	46	30	38	440	586	335	342
MEX	498	518	58	309	295	24	49	230	38	40	37	31	580	663	382	290
NET	593	1,204		346	323	16	55	235	18	59	49	34	435	518	340	300
NOR	360	459	81	340	348	31	43	245	15	62	60	31	370	437	427	285
NZL	173	240	66	295	334	26	37	231	24	69	61	18	450	461	361	311
PAK	37	70	40	287	380	6	67	275	30	59	49	21	555	544	359	298

476

PER	138	152	42	346	282	18	57	245	34	46	47	22	460	582	383	290
PHI	158	161	55	317	326	28	39	248	41	40	49	14	655	616	392	313
POR		243	79	285	288	10	68	269	19	53	41	43	475	306	399	311
SAF	349	518	65	271	317	25	41	237	33	53	46	23	475	458	357	297
SIN		58	88	284	363	42	28	311	43		32	27		455	327	354
SPA	600	1,202	50	291	300	14	65	250	25	57	51	23	530	542	384	303
SWE	1,128	1,304	79	342	350	37	25	266	19	58	46	37	360	366	410	255
SWI	951	1,160	64	285	308	31	36	209	20	61	55	29	430	573	382	264
TAI		71	50	248	296	20	31	237	42		38	23	535	648	383	293
THA		80	114	282	322	21	33	207	27		46	30	525	648	367	267
TUR	106	62	105	351	309	9	78	289	22	52	52	25	555	330	463	269
USA	3,967				331	15	60		29	65				495	423	
VEN	217	318	65	338	296	22	53	244	33	49	39	30	610	467	389	290
YUG		248	150	269	292				38	37			530	515	426	309
Total	31,218	40,997														
Mean of 40 countries			75	312	315	21	48	248	27	56	49	28	480	507	393	298

Zero-order product-moment correlation × 100 with

PDI			-05	08	-29	-13	24	42	63	-84	-49	-08	85	44	01	14
UAI			-07	36	-80	-81	65	-10	03	-41	-05	05	11	21	48	-24
IDV			07	10	23	11	-07	-28	-51	66	50	-03	-50	-41	16	-11
MAS			-43	-18	-29	-04	-06	-08	25	01	-05	-30	27	30	-31	40

NOTE: Scores are, where possible, the means of the 1967-69 and 1971-73 survey rounds and, for each survey round, of seven occupations; see Chapter 2. A1, A55 in tenths of %; A43, A54 in %; other questions in mean scores × 100. For country abbreviations, see Exhibit 2.1. Significance levels for the product-moment correlation coefficient for 40 cases: .05 level = .27; .01 level = .37; .001 level = .41.

Exhibit A2.2 Country Scores on B Questions (Category 1 countries)

Country	B9	B24	B25	B44	B46	B52	B53	B54	B55	B56	B57	B58	B59	B60	B61
ARG	368	178	192	154	285	143	182	288	409	258	374	176	319	289	360
AUL	332	204	189	175	329	183	175	312	397		337	196	330	311	335
AUT	307	197	193	170	364	219	192	274	417	280	345	196	328	281	317
BEL	306	200	207	173	265	171	196	252	401		347		294	295	311
BRA	318	186	173	176	271	181	179	283	424	246	389	193	318	282	351
CAN		203	178	176	324	193	173	322	410		352		328	336	363
CHL		171	185	161	314	158	176	320	423		389		296	272	356
COL	304	168	165	176	263	143	165	294	390	230	374	203	314	269	335
DEN	321	203	194	175	342	225	192	288	433		370		331	357	359
FIN	290	196	188	165	322	243	205	272	417	244	354	247	351	288	312
FRA	317	182	210	176	271	224	196	274	400	249	360	229	299	270	307
GBR	346	196	188	175	336	209	191	318	397	253	316	209	345	330	325
GER	324	196	193	183	333	170	201	264	425	248	367		338	302	325
GRE	323	157	171	169	248	135	159	301	415	242	336	178	255	241	323
HOK	344	167	165	182	298	146	160	322	387	253	348	233	277	330	348
IND		181	195	200	257	144	157	301	383		316		278	311	327
IRA				180	277	128	150	335	372	241	386	205	226	280	352
IRE	359	186	174	183	335	208	207	305	402		332	178	340	335	352
ISR	294	160	160	157	363	181	215	331	435	306	329	298	306	245	334
ITA	351	204	182	179	290	194	215	268	418		372		329	285	318
JPN	304	196	221		316	143	160	297	344	235	334	153	337	305	383
MEX	320	168	149	161	287	143	157	335	391	231	364	160	296	255	330
NET	303	199	204	177	328	171	193	237	423	228	356	188	347	339	334
NOR	321	191	203	146	317	262	228	308	421		370		336	265	308
NZL	341	195	182	170	358	211	181	341	403		324	196	334	304	351
PAK	284	172	194	196	308	122	177	303	406	232	359	200	232	239	345
PER	312	161	172	172	285	157	173	314	399	249	379	206	311	273	336

PHI	301	181	195	160	265	124	152	327	372	218	373	175	328	327	357
POR	284	163	204	176	258	222	186	231	440	203	390	181	286	235	308
SAF	334	175	194	172	321	174	173	334	395	261	329	216	306	330	336
SIN	340	176	136	200	266	174	178	310	380	226	352	215	286	350	350
SPA	296	191	203	152	296	205	203	248	423	241	393	238	328	266	333
SWE	332	203	186	176	329	277	202	298	416		375		352	314	362
SWI	312	202	161	170	333	224	192	263	423	280	342	189	327	293	345
TAI	322	205	182	148	300	143	153	296	355	225	343	202	257	308	349
THA	301	186	162	168	275	145	135	273	383	240	380	177	234	287	280
TUR		194	187	168	291	154	178	301	415	247	353	227	273	275	353
USA		174	197	192				329	415		322		314	307	380
VEN	265	152	173	178	264	153	162	299	402	251	373	195	310	280	331
YUG		131			299	160	172	313	365	241	359		306	280	326
Mean	317	185	182	172	304	179	181	297	403	245	357	203	308	294	338

Zero-order product-moment correlation coefficient × 100 with

PDI	-23	-48	-20	15	-87	-63	-63	05	-49	-65	34	-34	-48	-18	-07
UAI	-37	-44	02	-43	-35	-22	-05	-24	11	04	29	-12	-19	-80	-31
IDV	40	68	37	-02	58	62	60	-08	35	41	-44	16	61	41	06
MAS	12	-11	-01	20	-03	-37	-24	18	-30	-27	-41	-35	03	04	19

Same but controlling for acquiescence (IMP)

PDI	-17	-22	-05	25	-82	-48	-52	-05	-59	-63	11	-27	-39	00	-01
UAI	-34	-30	15	-42	-22	-05	13	-33	11	13	15	04	-08	-77	-38
IDV	38	44	25	-12	40	44	45	03	47	35	-19	03	55	26	18
MAS	12	-11	-01	20	-03	-42	-27	18	-30	-28	-47	-36	04	04	19

NOTE: Significance levels for the product-moment correlation coefficient: .05 level = .27; .01 level = .37; .001 level = .41. Scores for B46 exclude the answers of managers (see Chapter 3).

Exhibit A2.3 Country Scores on C Questions (32 Category 1 countries only)

Country	C9	C10	C11	C12	C13	C14	C15	C16	C17	C18	C19
ARG	334	305	298	272	384	220	319	301	256	396	355
AUL	345	297	350	321	387	228	321	340	308	379	381
AUT	363	317	372	326	398	238	288	317	248	360	269
BEL	346	311	348	251	366	225	298	308	264	349	351
BRA	290	329	356	286	385	212	345	317	263	338	358
CAN	353	272	370	325	392	218	322	348	299	392	381
CHL	336	300	290	238	395	222	369	334	247	342	364
COL	303	291	277	229	382	225	355	326	236	379	338
DEN	344	299	378	352	412	234	335	341	314	378	360
FIN	354	299	367	357	394	228	316	316	295	384	422
FRA	253	339	347	293	376	229	314	322	241	386	420
GBR	361	295	365	356	380	239	281	334	286	390	381
GER	331	315	363	318	378	236	293	326	249	372	245
GRE	264	324	345	298	362	200					
IND	282	261	349	249	367	215	287	296	283	358	319
IRE	374	301	344	321	390	230	327	343	297	403	389
ISR	312	301	347	316	397	197					
ITA	343	335	366			242					
JPN	369	257	361	286	389	224	326	294	280	377	355
MEX	313	286	287	237	380	237	375	331	238	353	347
NOR	348	274	357	327	409	226	362	340	342	349	392
NZL	366	265	346	325	402	218	334	344	294	371	388
PER	352	333	302	214	379	246	374	320	246	389	356
PHI	354	274	358	236	356	188	333	305	254	304	307
SAF	327	261	352	285	382	219	330	342	283	339	339
SPA	337	349	354	289	392	226					
SWE	339	310	374	251	418	225	325	351	314	360	390

SWI	370	293	370	332	405	228	312	341	298	371	282
TUR	296	304	372	290	378	199	320	340	316	381	370
USA	392	266	362	310	405	217	371	330	246	340	346
VEN	320	296	279	236	370	221	371	330	246	340	346
YUG	336										
Mean	335	299	345	291	387	223	328	327	277	367	354
Zero-order product-moment correlation coefficient × 100 with											
PDI	-47	04	-50	-78	-75	-27	38	-50	-61	-51	-08
UAI	-44	45	-44	-40	-43	-11	29	-52	-72	-06	-12
IDV	41	-14	70	73	44	24	-63	42	70	38	26
MAS	14	-21	-14	-06	-45	04	-25	-32	-41	05	-48
Same but controlling for acquiescence (IMP)											
PDI	-45	-09	-22	-66	-75	-40	-00	-56	-41	-38	07
UAI	-23	34	-59	-45	-32	22	16	-51	-71	04	-06
IDV	14	-10	45	50	25	-07	-32	52	51	17	15
MAS	20	-26	-09	02	-46	-04	-40	-32	-43	08	-47

NOTE: Country scores for C9-C14 are the means of seven occupations; for C15-C19, the means of five occupations. See Chapter 2. Significance levels for the product-moment correlation coefficient for 30 cases: .05 level = .31; .01 level = .43; .001 level = .47.

Exhibit A2.4 Scores on Selected A and B Questions for Category 2 Countries and Category 3 Regions

Countries	Number of Resp. 67-69	71-73	A37	A43 1-2	A54 3A	A55 1-2	B46	B60
COS	52	23	304	17	72	410	277	250
ECA	42	31	319	21	42	600	302	282
GUA	68	31	280	13	41	590	234	248
IDO	43	48	348	26	38	500	278	290
JAM	44	29	361	37	70	640	336	353
KOR		56	278	18	59	650	323	285
MAL	27	45	361	21	28	650	272	331
PAN	56	25	307	8	43	630	239	278
SAL	43	27	308	12	56	510	257	236
URU	86	46	293	11	59	560	283	238
Total Category 2	461	361						
Regions								
ARA	79	62	325	16	32	470	280	287
EAF		46	348	30	56	660	325	264
WAF		43	360	9	47	670	313	311
Total Category 3	79	151						
Rest								
BAH		8				Not Analyzed		
BOL		19						
DOM		20						
HOD		25						
NAT		16						
NIC		20						
TRI		22						
VIE		24						
Total Category 4		154						

NOTE: Scores are, where possible, the means of the 1967-69 and 1971-73 survey rounds. Scores are based on the available occupations and corrected for the occupation effects to match the occupation mix in the Category 1 scores; see Chapter 2. A43, A54 in %: A55 in tenths of %; other questions in mean scores × 100. Scores for A54 are based on 1967-69 data only; for countries only surveyed in 1971-73, fictitious 1967-69 A54 scores have been computed based on the regression of 1967-69 A54 scores and 1971-73 A54 scores across all countries surveyed twice. Scores for B46 exclude the answers of managers (see Chapter 3).

Appendix 3

**Standardized Country and Occupation Scores for Work Goal
(questions A5-18 and C1-C8)**

Exhibit A3.1 Standardized Work Goal Importance Scores for 40 Category 1 Countries and 14 Goals (A5-A18)

Country	IMP	SDG	A5	A6	A7	A8	A9	A10	A11	A12	A13	A14	A15	A16	A17	A18	INV	SOC
ARG	170	23	586	426	559	588	626	366	499	322	552	438	529	515	567	428	-15	-32
AUL	199	23	641	502	518	482	491	304	534	344	529	469	569	535	530	553	160	-53
AUT	201	36	629	317	578	523	585	363	517	373	584	452	574	492	553	462	21	-143
BEL	219	31	608	421	591	555	484	349	513	310	549	554	521	542	542	459	101	-21
BRA	164	17	602	466	474	614	658	349	508	353	466	356	566	532	572	486	-48	3
CAN	202	29	666	516	477	526	531	329	483	314	513	403	551	562	575	555	119	-12
CHL	171	17	552	440	505	601	604	455	384	441	460	608	431	484	561	474	-110	109
COL	162	31	610	454	532	566	640	435	502	389	490	414	530	502	634	299	-150	-71
DEN	195	31	579	562	452	606	543	328	436	372	608	488	432	565	534	497	94	170
FIN	233	31	624	470	477	571	584	370	365	383	560	513	485	566	521	511	53	120
FRA	213	24	602	452	523	563	587	310	489	322	558	513	506	543	527	505	83	34
GBR	207	28	624	492	563	494	499	278	525	321	555	471	588	520	536	533	156	-82
GER	203	28	611	336	607	496	525	444	500	336	576	572	548	510	504	436	69	-82
GRE	174	23	577	442	544	525	546	478	576	389	406	468	549	551	556	393	-60	-35
HOK	191	37	548	477	567	579	596	323	487	436	512	452	640	522	555	307	-99	-33
IND	191	25	616	345	468	510	561	377	562	404	507	509	580	576	558	427	-8	-31
IRA	180	30	582	450	501	599	584	411	480	326	521	482	609	551	548	356	-36	33
IRE	205	31	622	448	555	498	514	373	513	345	529	444	595	525	549	492	81	-89
ISR	182	29	629	373	471	559	584	442	483	313	548	455	557	580	563	444	15	15
ITA	197	31	628	470	528	528	546	390	639	367	561	290	509	520	526	498	103	-101
JPN	215	38	638	382	576	462	535	365	571	461	548	338	493	485	661	487	-18	-223
MEX	157	21	634	483	550	552	637	366	463	372	513	414	583	480	602	352	-81	-97
NET	190	24	573	617	445	585	505	481	437	318	561	449	464	561	498	505	118	181
NOR	212	25	586	603	492	554	544	395	385	382	516	512	388	617	528	499	75	209
NZL	209	33	604	474	511	520	507	283	525	424	565	363	565	550	540	572	117	-41
PAK	195	30	538	342	497	523	622	414	507	459	482	522	624	581	558	330	-145	2

PER	171	30	588	494	498	592	668	400	430	409	545	431	497	532	608	307	−135	40
PHI	170	21	603	468	544	491	571	381	438	424	488	517	630	506	580	361	−73	−71
POR	169	23	597	458	458	635	646	405	440	371	501	463	546	561	560	360	−94	96
SAF	194	25	641	443	549	491	547	329	504	337	513	477	576	566	573	456	60	−67
SIN	194	33	571	362	552	624	611	439	442	432	532	437	593	551	536	318	−122	12
SPA	184	30	579	437	475	583	612	225	485	426	537	505	518	526	567	524	2	38
SWE	192	24	595	613	427	572	506	397	443	346	479	578	456	605	516	467	85	223
SWI	216	32	670	346	530	533	553	473	473	339	595	407	513	484	552	534	71	−101
TAI	190	32	548	438	442	571	657	363	487	407	480	506	630	524	577	372	−133	27
THA	187	29	596	433	547	598	577	404	299	472	496	495	530	577	590	386	−120	82
TUR	177	30	591	403	469	585	557	432	546	357	516	547	532	536	581	349	−54	24
USA	197	22	688	552	553	534	475	382	493	267	492	454	575	499	521	516	164	−61
VEN	158	19	669	418	539	484	659	509	450	450	454	423	508	489	604	344	−154	−114
YUG	194	24	449	511	500	647	567	407	506	431	562	464	463	552	572	369	−92	147

Across 40 Category 1 countries

MEA	191	28	602	453	516	553	571	383	483	376	524	466	539	537	558	438	0	0
SDC	18	5	43	73	45	47	54	60	61	51	42	65	59	34	33	80	100	100

NOTE: Country scores are, where possible, the mean of two survey rounds and, for each round, of the standardized values for seven occupations. Total number of respondents in Category 1 = 65,378. All scores have been multiplied by 100. IMP, SDG = mean and standard deviation of raw scores across all 14 goals × 100. INV, SOC = factor scores × 100 (see Chapter 5). MEA, SDC = mean and standard deviation of standardized scores across countries × 100. For country abbreviations, see Exhibit 2.1.

485

Exhibit A3.2 Standardized Work Goal Importance Scores for Category 2 and Category 3 Countries/Regions and 14 Goals (A5-A18)

Country	IMP	SDG	A5	A6	A7	A8	A9	A10	A11	A12	A13	A14	A15	A16	A17	A18	INV	SOC
Category 2 countries																		
COS	164	30	533	378	462	644	604	474	516	446	507	565	463	569	533	305	-139	147
ECA	172	36	606	462	557	503	634	427	371	523	497	431	558	498	595	338	-167	-63
GUA	153	23	573	419	539	596	599	447	388	493	487	486	533	581	581	284	-178	67
IDO	186	28	479	551	552	490	598	452	393	445	502	450	608	542	600	339	-145	18
JAM	181	24	610	456	651	505	556	378	511	477	373	475	593	531	486	401	-45	-89
KOR	209	30	493	554	492	539	619	302	461	431	539	496	538	551	652	333	-129	56
MAL	175	27	566	307	502	581	559	379	548	448	527	530	578	574	569	337	-94	-2
PAN	152	26	579	407	512	564	642	413	435	437	475	557	498	529	602	349	-157	31
SAL	161	37	586	503	555	554	554	419	388	472	528	513	530	569	587	236	-122	51
URU	175	27	511	410	532	582	578	372	520	458	530	518	377	523	591	499	-57	59
Category 3 regions																		
ARA	184	34	566	425	527	544	576	340	516	414	504	464	584	570	574	397	-48	-14
EAF	198	31	606	428	503	557	605	370	451	451	447	419	540	632	591	402	-94	47
WAF	167	25	593	546	516	541	612	463	509	429	418	493	635	535	489	221	-120	19
Across 53 Category 1, 2, and 3 countries and regions																		
MEA	187	28	592	452	520	553	577	388	478	396	515	473	539	541	562	414	-28	6
SDC	19	5	46	72	45	45	49	58	62	58	46	62	60	34	37	88	102	92

NOTE: Country scores are, where possible, the mean of two survey rounds and, for each round, of the standardized values for seven occupations. All scores have been multiplied by 100. IMP, SDG = mean and standard deviation of raw scores across all 14 goals × 100. INV, SOC = factor scores × 100 (see Chapter 5). MEA, SDC = mean and standard deviation of standardized scores across countries × 100.

486

Exhibit A3.3 Standardized Work Goal Importance Scores for 19 Countries and 22 Goals (A5-A18 and C1-C8)

Country	MEG	SDG	A5	A6	A7	A8	A9	A10	A11	A12	A13	A14	A15	A16	A17	A18	C1	C2	C3	C4	C5	C6	C7	C8	ING	EGO
AUT	205	37	634	302	589	532	598	363	512	363	589	478	597	521	577	440	529	495	538	343	404	467	586	543	42	156
BEL	222	28	602	429	586	568	518	373	537	340	563	593	540	579	567	463	487	527	493	288	397	490	550	510	2	31
DEN	203	33	571	556	474	612	575	340	449	408	620	500	490	600	553	488	564	558	434	297	354	543	552	463	105	-106
FIN	235	36	596	473	495	595	591	371	389	398	564	547	505	615	547	507	570	535	453	292	349	555	593	461	120	-88
FRA	215	24	578	416	507	595	634	323	474	353	561	568	534	567	554	484	536	522	469	292	473	521	559	479	77	13
GBR	216	35	625	491	569	543	557	337	544	386	578	497	611	549	569	536	516	546	503	323	416	458	500	347	-4	95
GER	208	34	605	299	593	527	593	463	515	368	588	596	584	521	547	437	564	409	498	323	394	483	558	535	49	127
GRE	171	21	543	475	527	494	530	479	589	364	371	451	573	651	540	388	550	492	594	415	484	488	533	467	-256	-28
IRE	207	38	633	469	562	518	576	373	535	404	545	456	619	517	572	473	478	547	578	365	413	460	527	380	-55	113
ISR	191	33	618	393	440	589	597	422	528	392	576	484	550	594	591	466	543	580	515	375	429	488	535	295	-27	17
ITA	199	34	616	462	524	546	576	398	632	392	565	322	539	551	547	483	543	509	469	351	388	515	521	552	-8	36
NET	197	28	596	585	486	622	563	519	480	395	582	469	542	582	552	528	518	455	463	284	311	479	537	455	63	-45
NOR	215	36	572	561	506	561	577	437	420	427	532	514	456	613	554	501	558	551	457	306	292	533	549	521	68	-130
SAF	204	31	629	457	566	508	583	404	523	359	527	491	587	582	591	456	478	520	559	425	394	432	536	394	-96	97
SPA	191	25	492	490	479	575	629	280	491	436	531	569	520	549	573	538	440	573	500	285	392	545	613	498	117	-52
SWE	191	25	609	591	451	589	534	387	416	333	469	574	475	630	509	429	557	505	570	397	362	565	507	540	-121	-183
SWI	213	35	697	336	494	554	596	470	482	361	595	428	564	515	576	497	532	450	516	305	377	522	577	556	81	107
TUR	181	32	591	439	439	579	605	428	573	368	508	536	560	544	598	311	420	589	564	447	380	539	507	476	-150	-24
YUG	195	24	462	512	505	648	566	407	514	440	568	478	467	563	576	376	439	516	527	377	380	594	578	504	-7	-136
MEA	203	31	593	460	515	566	579	399	505	384	549	503	543	571	563	463	517	520	510	342	389	509	548	472	0	0
SDC	—	—	52	85	50	41	30	59	61	31	55	67	48	40	21	58	47	46	47	52	46	42	31	73	—	—

NOTE: Country scores are the mean of the standardized 1967-69 values for seven occupations. Total number of respondents = 18,052. All scores have been multiplied by 100. MEG, SDG = mean and standard deviation of raw scores across all 22 goals × 100. ING, EGO = factor scores × 100 (see Chapter 5). MEA, SDC = mean and standard deviation of standardized scores across countries × 100.

Exhibit A3.4 Standardized Work Goal Importance Scores for 38 Occupations and 22 Goals (A5-A18 and C1-C8)

Occupation	EDU	MEG	SDG	A5	A6	A7	A8	A9	A10	A11	A12	A13	A14	A15	A16	A17	A18	C1	C2	C3	C4	C5	C6	C7	C8
21	104	186	14	453	475	579	601	408	579	534	653	445	682	445	631	505	527	549	534	394	305	327	557	438	379
46	105	182	14	474	525	628	555	467	614	570	672	400	650	496	562	481	533	511	459	378	290	334	584	393	422
49	109	186	13	517	493	581	605	446	533	501	621	470	661	454	629	533	557	549	501	390	254	326	581	414	382
47	110	187	13	549	490	676	557	482	512	542	579	460	691	535	549	535	468	564	468	415	214	341	482	497	393
11	112	202	20	615	430	545	570	550	385	430	285	600	695	530	585	540	415	550	500	575	305	415	485	565	430
12	113	198	22	570	399	565	534	660	448	462	295	529	669	592	538	574	457	556	439	462	278	394	484	610	484
50	115	197	17	579	424	620	561	489	477	519	513	519	644	555	579	543	507	567	477	442	162	334	513	543	436
51	115	201	19	576	432	607	576	509	499	566	550	540	566	504	602	566	504	576	520	391	227	269	576	412	432
19	116	196	23	656	373	519	638	497	373	453	417	563	603	528	652	541	387	506	523	581	289	378	537	577	409
64	116	204	24	550	492	500	616	475	446	554	570	537	545	438	669	566	533	550	570	446	310	269	628	364	372
31	117	204	27	577	431	483	641	506	423	532	540	562	483	487	641	573	479	604	581	412	292	284	634	374	461
14	118	198	22	572	423	513	654	509	382	536	536	572	509	513	636	568	450	581	581	450	282	287	618	409	416
7	119	214	26	643	361	527	593	574	380	489	292	597	647	531	593	547	454	535	500	547	292	400	492	558	450
63	121	209	23	580	461	523	588	593	378	588	496	518	549	527	593	571	553	523	518	440	181	313	562	527	418
8	122	213	26	604	433	550	561	627	402	476	312	530	624	569	542	561	546	581	456	452	230	378	491	596	479
9	123	190	23	633	277	585	568	659	368	498	299	589	485	611	555	555	398	511	520	563	377	503	485	490	472
74	123	213	22	570	349	492	603	529	483	543	469	492	561	478	662	612	492	612	510	359	271	326	621	437	529
10	124	190	25	611	311	623	546	623	368	494	267	575	550	627	559	571	392	546	518	478	380	469	473	554	461
18	124	198	19	577	362	539	641	614	432	496	523	485	544	571	598	566	453	555	534	426	233	297	593	496	464
73	127	215	22	572	527	527	514	612	446	612	505	558	599	514	563	554	536	496	460	411	146	348	491	558	451
26	129	200	20	580	417	496	649	545	407	535	511	550	511	520	624	575	471	560	590	417	244	278	604	451	466
41	133	209	21	679	399	560	579	499	371	532	399	579	598	556	622	537	484	503	527	565	242	342	470	532	423
13	133	210	27	655	455	533	585	529	340	511	389	596	518	596	626	577	511	533	566	544	289	300	477	485	385
24	141	208	26	660	431	511	599	557	302	504	389	591	496	565	611	572	462	496	569	603	298	336	477	553	416
43	143	213	27	662	380	607	519	578	358	545	449	593	490	574	549	574	505	534	490	479	211	350	479	578	497
15	144	209	24	675	432	523	613	605	338	506	412	593	506	556	613	543	457	502	552	539	264	322	494	531	424
42	144	210	24	698	420	535	580	498	330	539	338	592	555	547	633	535	420	477	535	620	293	400	473	522	461

25	148	209	30	642	423	531	578	629	304	531	423	578	396	564	575	595	497	500	554	487	261	355	500	588	490
17	152	213	28	634	430	546	578	658	367	497	441	571	451	588	549	574	507	535	500	427	219	339	497	592	500
2	156	211	29	638	363	597	552	634	325	514	304	624	438	617	542	572	421	528	493	504	339	438	469	572	514
1	156	216	29	671	370	568	575	589	309	517	309	640	469	606	544	558	425	524	493	589	350	418	466	524	490
62	156	222	30	658	557	516	533	563	327	567	452	567	519	519	567	573	573	526	496	479	198	333	502	553	421
61	156	222	30	688	548	538	545	512	305	565	352	595	555	488	598	555	508	515	548	535	255	389	475	538	392
5	158	215	30	642	406	549	536	655	343	555	330	615	443	572	532	575	502	546	459	469	277	386	486	602	519
6	159	219	31	654	416	548	570	661	309	557	348	564	377	612	528	590	509	490	519	461	306	416	509	574	483
71	159	227	30	696	486	572	572	503	332	565	372	621	555	572	565	519	535	476	526	503	250	345	516	496	424
72	159	228	34	664	454	547	509	615	363	597	439	579	492	588	568	550	544	495	468	454	208	334	506	556	471
82	165	227	44	722	432	500	580	446	427	551	341	631	366	455	537	599	388	580	480	457	366	407	519	649	569
MEA	132	207	24	616	429	552	578	555	397	528	431	558	545	542	587	559	483	535	514	477	268	355	521	519	450
SDO	—	—	—	61	61	43	37	70	78	39	111	54	87	51	40	25	51	34	39	69	55	54	52	72	46

NOTE: For explanation of occupation numbers, see Figure 2.5. Occupation scores are based on unweighted total Europe or world data 1968-71; see Chapter 5. Total number of respondents = 48,895. All scores have been multiplied by 100. EDU = years of education × 10. MEG, SDG = mean and standard deviation of raw scores across all 22 goals × 100. MEA, SDO = mean and standard deviation of standardized scores across occupations × 100.

Appendix 4

Replicating the IBM-Style Cross-National Survey

Calculating Dimension Scores

The country scores on the initial four dimensions were based on a few specific questions in the IBM questionnaire (as reproduced in Appendix 1). Three questions were needed for computing the Power Distance Index (see Chapter 3):

$$PDI = 135 - (\% \text{ answer 3 in A54})$$
$$+ (\% \text{ answer 1 or 2 in A55})$$
$$- 25 \times (\text{mean score B46}).$$

Question B46 runs: "How frequently does the following problem occur: Employees being afraid to express disagreement with their managers?" In calculating PDI, for B46 only the answers by nonmanagers were used. Managers tended systematically to report fewer problems of this kind, but they were obviously not the ideal judges. From the seven occupational categories included in the country IBM samples, the two categories of managers were therefore excluded for this question.

Another three questions were needed for computing the Uncertainty Avoidance Index (see Chapter 4):

$$UAI = 300 - 40 \times (\text{mean score A37})$$
$$- (\% \text{ answer 1 or 2 in A43})$$
$$- 30 \times (\text{mean score B60}).$$

A set of 14 "work goals" questions, A5 through A18, were used for computing the Individualism Index and the Masculinity Index. The calculation was rather complicated: First, the raw mean scores per work goal per country had to be standardized across goals (horizontally). The process is described in Chapter 2, but the mathematics are resumed here. The formula used is as follows:

Standard score for goal G = $100 \times$ (mean score for 14 goals – raw score for goal G) divided by (standard deviation across 14 goals) + 500 (= constant).

For example, the raw mean score for Argentina for work goal A5 (challenge) was 1.50.[1] In Appendix 3, Exhibit A3.1, we read a value of 170 for IMP and of 23 for SDG, which means that the 14 work goal scores for Argentina (ARG) had a common mean of 1.70 and a common standard deviation of .23. The raw score for Argentina for A5 was therefore converted as follows:

Standard score A5 for Argentina =
$100 (1.70 - 1.50)/0.23 + 500 = 586.$

This is also what we find in Exhibit A3.1.

After standardization, the matrix of 14 standardized goals × 40 (Category 1) countries was factor analyzed (see the statistical section of Chapter 5). After orthogonal rotation this factor analysis produced two independent factors, INV and SOC. The factor analysis program gave factor scores on the INV and SOC axes for each of the 40 countries (last two columns of Exhibit A3.1, decimals omitted). These factor scores were converted into IDV and MAS scores through multiplying by 25 and –20, respectively (or by .25 and –.20 when we take into account that the decimals are omitted in Exhibit A3.1), and adding 50.

Later on, when new cases, not in the original set of 40, were added (such as Category 2 countries and Category 3 regions), the calculation became even more complex. The raw country work goal scores for the new cases were first standardized horizontally across goals, as before. After that, these standardized scores were standardized again but vertically, per goal across countries. The purpose of this second standardization was to position the score for each goal for each new country in the distribution of the same goal for the original 40 countries.

Again an example: In Appendix 3, Exhibit A3.1, for Costa Rica (COS), the first Category 2 country, the standardized score for A5 is listed as 533. We also read lower down in Exhibit A3.1 that for the 40 Category 1 countries the mean for A5 (MEA) was 602 and the standard deviation (SDC) was 43. Vertical standardization implies that the new standard score for A5 for Costa Rica becomes $(602 - 533)/43 = -1.60$ (or –160 if we omit the decimal). All the other scores for the new countries and regions were converted in a similar way.

Exhibit A4.1 Factor Score Coefficients for the Factor Analysis of 14 Work Goals in 40 Category 1 Countries

Work Goal	Factor Score for	
	INV	SOC
A5 Challenge	.12	.17
A6 Desirable area	.09	−.19
A7 Earnings	−.01	.22
A8 Cooperation	−.12	−.22
A9 Training	−.27	.00
A10 Benefits	−.14	−.03
A11 Recognition	.05	.18
A12 Physical conditions	−.22	.00
A13 Freedom	.14	.00
A14 Employment security	−.04	−.16
A15 Advancement	−.08	.17
A16 Manager	.04	−.22
A17 Use of skills	−.20	.13
A18 Personal time	.23	−.01

Then each of the converted scores was multiplied by a *factor score coefficient*, again produced by the 14 goals × 40 countries factor analysis program, and the products were summed for each country/region across the 14 goals, into an INV and SOC value. These were then converted into IDV and MAS scores in the same way as was done for the Category 1 countries. The factor score coefficients for IDV and MAS are listed in Exhibit A4.1.

Even before the appearance of the 1980 edition of *Culture's Consequences,* some people had asked permission to replicate the IBM-style research on other populations, and this led me to include in the book a "Values Survey Module recommended for future cross-cultural survey studies." [2] This "VSM 80" was a reduced and sometimes reworded version of the IBM questionnaire, with some new items added that dealt with issues not covered in IBM but that I judged from the book's analysis to be of potential interest.

The VSM 80 immediately raised a problem for the calculation of IDV and MAS. Their calculation as described above was so complex that it caused serious problems for replicators; also, the VSM 80 contained only 10 of the 14 work goal questions needed for the existing calculation method (in addition to 8 newly added goals). Shortly after the publication of the 1980 book I therefore developed simplified formulas for computing IDV and MAS. They were developed though a linear regression computation: finding the combination of the raw scores for the 10 remaining work goals that best predicted IDV and MAS for the 40 Category 1 countries. The formula for the Individualism Index was as follows:

$$IDV = -27 \times (\text{mean score A6})$$
$$+ 30 \times (\text{mean score A8})$$
$$+ 76 \times (\text{mean score A12})$$
$$- 43 \times (\text{mean score A18})$$
$$- 29 \ (= \text{constant}).$$

For the Masculinity Index, the formula was

$$MAS = -66 \times (\text{mean score A7})$$
$$+ 60 \times (\text{mean score A8})$$
$$+ 30 \times (\text{mean score A14})$$
$$- 39 \times (\text{mean score A15})$$
$$+ 76 \ (= \text{constant}).$$

So work goal A8 (cooperation) appears in both the IDV *and* the MAS formula. In total, only 7 of the 10 goals were needed to compute both IDV and MAS.

Across the 40 Category 1 countries, IDV values computed with the approximation formula correlated .96 with the exact IDV; the mean error of the approximated IDV scores above or below the exact scores was 5 points, and the maximum error observed was 16 points. For MAS, values computed with the approximation formula correlated .93 with the exact MAS; the mean error of the approximated MAS scores above or below the exact scores was 6 points, and the maximum error observed was 17 points.

Either formula uses four goals, two with positive and two with negative sign; this helps to cor-

Exhibit A4.2 PDI Scores as a Function of Education Level

This table lists the scores to be used for comparison with other samples if:

The Average Number of Years of Formal Education for the Surveyed Sample Is	and the PDI Score for the Surveyed Sample Is										
	00	10	20	30	40	50	60	70	80	90	100
10	−53	−42	−31	−20	−9	2	13	24	35	46	57
11	−43	−32	−21	−10	1	12	23	34	45	56	67
12	−33	−22	−11	0	11	22	33	44	55	66	77
13	−22	−11	0	11	22	33	44	55	66	77	88
14	−12	−1	10	21	32	43	54	65	76	87	98
15	−2	9	20	31	42	53	64	75	86	97	108
16	8	19	30	41	52	63	74	85	96	107	118

NOTE: The number of years of formal education is measured by the question "How many years of formal school education (or their equivalent) did you complete (starting with primary school)?" or an equivalent question such as A56 in Appendix 1.

rect the influence of acquiescence (see Chapter 2) without formally standardizing the scores; it can be seen as a quick-and-dirty way of standardizing.

Correcting Dimension Scores for Respondents' Education Levels

As part of a master's thesis, Bosland (1985c) measured the influence of respondents' education levels on the country scores. He computed correction tables to be applied when comparing samples with different education levels.

Respondents' scores on the four dimensions depend not only on their nationalities but equally on their occupations, genders, and ages (this is shown by the analysis of variance in Exhibit 2.4). After the country influence, the occupation influence was clearly the strongest; and what counted most for an occupation was the average number of years of formal education the occupation's incumbents would have completed (compare Exhibit 2.6).

Basing his work on the IBM database, Bosland (1985c) developed a table (see Exhibit A4.2) for correcting the PDI score of a sample as a function of its average number of years of formal education and of the PDI score obtained. For example, with an observed PDI score in the new sample of 60 and an average number of years of education of 14, the corrected PDI score will be 54.

For UAI, IDV, and MAS the correction process was easier: A single correction factor could be used regardless of the level of the score obtained (see Exhibit A4.3). For instance, a sample with an average education level of 15 years and observed levels of UAI of 100, IDV of 40, and MAS of 60 would get these adjusted values:

$$UAI = 100 - 9 = 91$$
$$IDV = 40 + 13 = 53$$
$$MAS = 60 - 5 = 55$$

New Versions of the Values Survey Module (VSM 81 and 82)

As described in Chapter 2, the initial research material consisted of an existing database made available by IBM. The values questions found to discriminate between countries had originally been chosen for IBM's internal purposes. They were never intended to form a complete and universal instrument for measuring national cultures. The Values Survey Module in the 1980 edition of *Culture's Consequences* tried to improve upon the IBM questionnaire by leaving out some questions and adding some new ones. It contained 27 content questions and 6 demographic items. Twenty IBM content questions were retained; 7 new items were taken from other sources or newly made up.

In 1981, the Institute for Research on Intercultural Cooperation (IRIC; of which I had been one of the founders in 1980) issued an extended experimental version of the VSM (VSM 81). On the basis of an analysis of results obtained with the 1980 and 1981 versions, a new and further-extended version was issued in 1982 (VSM 82).

The VSM 82 contained 47 content questions plus the 6 demographic questions. In all these versions of the VSM, 13 questions sufficed to calculate the four dimensions (3 each for PDI and UAI, 7 for IDV plus MAS). These were not necessarily the ideal items for measuring the essence of each dimension, but they were the best available, and their validity had been proven in the IBM case. If

Exhibit A4.3 Correction Factors for UAI, IDV, and MAS Scores as a Function of Education Level

This table lists the number of points by which the scores for the surveyed sample should be corrected for comparison with other samples if:

The Average Number of Years of Formal Education for the Surveyed Sample Is	For UAI	For IDV	For MAS
10	19	−20	27
11	13	−13	20
12	8	−7	14
13	2	0	7
14	−3	7	1
15	−9	13	−5
16	−14	20	−12

NOTE: The number of years of formal education is measured by the question "How many years of formal school education (or their equivalent) did you complete (starting with primary school)?" or an equivalent question such as A56 in Appendix 1.

one wanted to replace any of these questions with new and improved ones, the cross-cultural discriminatory power of these new items would first have to be proven. This is why other items were included in the VSM versions: 34 of them for the VSM 82. They were not needed for calculating the index scores, and their validity for cross-cultural use had not yet been proven, but they served an experimental purpose, and IRIC maintained a file on the answers collected by different users in different countries.

An initial analysis of replications using the VSM 81 and 82 appeared in Bosland's master's thesis, mentioned above. Its three parts describe (1) what happens if the VSM is used as a test of individual personality (showing, as was argued in Chapter 2, that the dimensions do not apply in this case), (2) comparative results of the replications, and (3) the stability of the dimension scores when applied to a new set of country samples (Bosland, 1985a, 1985b, 1985c). This stability was less than perfect—a good reason to continue to look for an improved instrument. Bosland did not suggest, however, how such an improved instrument should look; the available data were not sufficient for this purpose.

The Values Survey
Module 1994 (VSM 94)

Only in the 1990s had IRIC's VSM 82 files become large enough to issue an entirely new Values Survey Module, the VSM 94. Hoppe's (1990) replication for 18 mostly European countries (see Chapters 2 through 7) was very helpful, but it also had its restrictions. Hoppe's respondents were highly educated elites, so the effect of the difference in education level had to be corrected using the Bosland tables (see above, Exhibits A2.2 and

A2.3). Hoppe's countries were predominantly individualist and showed an unrepresentatively strong correlation between power distance and uncertainty avoidance (no large power distance, weak uncertainty avoidance cases). The latter two problems were resolved through the addition of data from other surveys for six non-European countries, although these were of course not perfectly matched with the Hoppe data. One request made of the new VSM version was that it should also be relevant to respondents without employers, such as entrepreneurs, students, and housewives. Therefore the questions about the behavior of the boss (A54 and A55) and about how long one wanted to stay with one's employer (A43) were replaced.

The VSM 94 contained 20 content questions plus the 6 demographic questions covering gender, age, years of formal education, type of occupation, nationality, and nationality at birth. Only 8 questions remained from the original 13 on which the IBM country scores were based. Four questions each were now needed to calculate each dimension score. The fifth dimension, long-term versus short-term orientation (see Chapter 7), was included for the first time. The VSM 94 questions are displayed in Exhibit A4.4.

The index formulas were as follows:

$$PDI = -35m(03) + 35m(06) + 25m(14) \\ -20m(17) - 20$$

$$UAI = 25m(13) + 20m(16) - 50m(18) \\ -15m(19) + 120$$

$$IDV = -50m(01) + 30m(02) + 20m(04) \\ -25m(08) + 130$$

$$MAS = 60m(05) - 20m(07) + 20m(15) \\ -70m(20) + 100$$

Exhibit A4.4 VSM 94 Questions

Please think of an ideal job—disregarding your present job, if you have one. In choosing an ideal job, how important would it be to you to . . . (please circle one answer in each line across):

> 1 = of utmost importance
> 2 = very important
> 3 = of moderate importance
> 4 = of little importance
> 5 = of very little or no importance

01.	have sufficient time left for your personal or family life	1	2	3	4	5
02.	have good physical working conditions (good ventilation and lighting, adequate work space, etc.)	1	2	3	4	5
03.	have a good working relationship with your direct superior	1	2	3	4	5
04.	have security of employment	1	2	3	4	5
05.	work with people who cooperate well with one another	1	2	3	4	5
06.	be consulted by your direct superior in his/her decisions	1	2	3	4	5
07.	have an opportunity for advancement to higher level jobs	1	2	3	4	5
08.	have an element of variety and adventure in the job	1	2	3	4	5

In your private life, how important is each of the following to you? (please circle one answer in each line across):

09.	Personal steadiness and stability	1	2	3	4	5
10.	Thrift	1	2	3	4	5
11.	Persistence (perseverance)	1	2	3	4	5
12.	Respect for tradition	1	2	3	4	5

13. How often do you feel nervous or tense at work?

    1. never

    2. seldom

    3. sometimes

    4. usually

    5. always

14. How frequently, in your experience, are subordinates afraid to express disagreement with their superiors?

    1. very seldom

    2. seldom

    3. sometimes

    4. frequently

    5. very frequently

How much do you agree or disagree with each of the following statements? (please circle one answer in each line across):

> 1 = strongly agree
> 2 = agree
> 3 = undecided
> 4 = disagree
> 5 = strongly disagree

15.	Most people can be trusted	1	2	3	4	5
16.	One can be a good manager without having precise answers to most questions that subordinates may raise about their work	1	2	3	4	5

(continued)

Exhibit A4.4 Continued

17.	An organization structure in which certain subordinates have two bosses should be avoided at all cost	1	2	3	4	5
18.	Competition between employees usually does more harm than good	1	2	3	4	5
19.	A company's or organization's rules should not be broken—not even when the employee thinks it is in the company's best interest	1	2	3	4	5
20.	When people have failed in life it is often their own fault	1	2	3	4	5

Some information about yourself (for statistical purposes):

21. Are you:
    1. male
    2. female

22. How old are you:
    1. Under 20
    2. 20-24
    3. 25-29
    4. 30-34
    5. 35-39
    6. 40-49
    7. 50-59
    8. 60 or over

23. How many years of formal school education (or their equivalent) did you complete (starting with primary school):
    1. 10 years or less
    2. 11 years
    3. 12 years
    4. 13 years
    5. 14 years
    6. 15 years
    7. 16 years
    8. 17 years
    9. 18 years or over

24. If you have or had a paid job, what kind of job is it?
    1. No paid job (including full-time students)
    2. Unskilled or semi-skilled manual worker
    3. Generally trained office worker or secretary
    4. Vocationally trained craftsperson, technician, informatician, nurse, artist, or equivalent
    5. Academically trained professional or equivalent (but no manager of people)
    6. Manager of one or more subordinates (nonmanagers)
    7. Manager of one or more managers

25. What is your nationality?

26. And what was your nationality at birth (if different)?

SOURCE: Copyright IRIC; reprinted by permission.

$$LTO = -20m(10) + 20m(12) + 40$$
(revised version 1999)[3]

In these formulas, m(03) is the mean score for question 03, and so on.

Differences Between the
VSM 94 and the VSM 82

Questions 9 through 12, referring to the LTO dimension, were new to the VSM 94. All other VSM 94 questions had appeared in the VSM 82 and mostly in earlier versions. For questions 13 and 14 the answer scales have been reversed, so that answer 5 has become 1, 4 has become 2, 2 has become 4, and 1 has become 5.

Questions A6, A7, A43, A54, and A55 from the IBM questionnaire (Appendix 1), which were part of the formulas for calculating the first four dimensions, did not return in the VSM 94. VSM 94 users who wanted to do longitudinal comparisons with the results of older studies were advised to add these five questions to the VSM 94 questions.

Reliability and
Validity of the VSM

See Chapter 10 for a more extensive explanation. The VSM is a test designed for comparing mean scores of matched samples of respondents across two or more *countries,* regions, or ethnic groups. It is not a personality test for comparing individuals within countries. The reliability of a cross-country test can be tested only across countries, but this presupposes data from at least some 15 countries. Cronbach alpha reliability coefficients across individuals are irrelevant.

However, the reliability of an instrument is implicitly tested through its proven validity. An unreliable test cannot produce valid results, so if validity is proven, reliability can be assumed. Validity is shown through significant correlations of test results with outside criteria related to the test scores by some kind of theory or logic. In this way the reliability of the VSM, even for smaller numbers of countries, can be proven indirectly.

At the time this is written (2000), the experience with the use of the VSM 94 is still limited. There have been both positive and negative signals about its validity. This should be seen as an ongoing research effort. Information about the state of the art of VSM research and about the latest available version can be obtained from IRIC, University of Tilburg, P.O. Box 90153, 5000 LE Tilburg, the Netherlands; e-mail iric@kub.nl. Applications for permission to use any version of the IBM questionnaire or the VSM should also be made at IRIC.

Notes

1. This information is not in the appendixes. If needed, the raw scores can be calculated back from Appendix 3, Exhibits A3.1, A3.2, and A3.3.

2. In the first edition of *Culture's Consequences* (Hofstede, 1980a), Appendix 1 contained the original IBM questions (as in the present edition) and Appendix 4 contained the first version of a Values Survey Module "recommended for future cross-cultural survey studies." In the 1984 abridged edition, the original IBM questions were not included and the Values Survey Module became Appendix 1 (Hofstede, 1984b).

3. Originally: $LTO = +45m(09) - 30m(10) - 35m(11) + 15m(12) + 67$. However, the first large-scale use of the new VSM in the EMS higher-income consumer survey 1997 (see Chapter 2) showed that question 9 and, to a lesser extent, question 11 provided erratic results. Only the country scores for questions 10 and 11 were mutually correlated in the predicted direction, and both correlated with the external criterion of marginal propensity to save (MPS: Read, 1993). So a new formula was developed that uses only questions 10 and 12.

Appendix 5

**Summary of Country Index Scores
(including additions)**

Exhibit A5.1 Index Scores and Ranks for Countries and Regions From the IBM Set

Country	Power Distance		Uncertainty Avoidance		Individualism/ Collectivism		Masculinity/ Femininity		Long-/Short-Term Orientation	
	Index	Rank	Index	Rank	Index	Rank	Index	Rank	Index	Rank
Argentina	49	35-36	86	10-15	46	22-23	56	20-21		
Australia	36	41	51	37	90	2	61	16	31	22-24
Austria	11	53	70	24-25	55	18	79	2	31[a]	22-24
Belgium	65	20	94	5-6	75	8	54	22	38[a]	18
Brazil	69	14	76	21-22	38	26-27	49	27	65	6
Canada	39	39	48	41-42	80	4-5	52	24	23	30
Chile	63	24-25	86	10-15	23	38	28	46		
Colombia	67	17	80	20	13	49	64	11-12		
Costa Rica	35	42-44	86	10-15	15	46	21	48-49		
Denmark	18	51	23	51	74	9	16	50	46[a]	10
Ecuador	78	8-9	67	28	8	52	63	13-14		
Finland	33	46	59	31-32	63	17	26	47	41[a]	14
France	68	15-16	86	10-15	71	10-11	43	35-36	39[a]	17
Germany	35	42-44	65	29	67	15	66	9-10	31	22-24
Great Britain	35	42-44	35	47-48	89	3	66	9-10	25	28-29
Greece	60	27-28	112	1	35	30	57	18-19		
Guatemala	95	2-3	101	3	6	53	37	43		
Hong Kong	68	15-16	29	49-50	25	37	57	18-19	96	2
Indonesia	78	8-9	48	41-42	14	47-48	46	30-31		
India	77	10-11	40	45	48	21	56	20-21	61	7
Iran	58	29-30	59	31-32	41	24	43	35-36		
Ireland	28	49	35	47-48	70	12	68	7-8	43[a]	13
Israel	13	52	81	19	54	19	47	29		
Italy	50	34	75	23	76	7	70	4-5	34[a]	19
Jamaica	45	37	13	52	39	25	68	7-8		
Japan	54	33	92	7	46	22-23	95	1	80	4
Korea (South)	60	27-28	85	16-17	18	43	39	41	75	5
Malaysia	104	1	36	46	26	36	50	25-26		
Mexico	81	5-6	82	18	30	32	69	6		
Netherlands	38	40	53	35	80	4-5	14	51	44	11-12
Norway	31	47-48	50	38	69	13	8	52	44[a]	11-12
New Zealand	22	50	49	39-40	79	6	58	17	30	25-26
Pakistan	55	32	70	24-25	14	47-48	50	25-26	0	34
Panama	95	2-3	86	10-15	11	51	44	34		
Peru	64	21-23	87	9	16	45	42	37-38		
Philippines	94	4	44	44	32	31	64	11-12	19	31-32
Portugal	63	24-25	104	2	27	33-35	31	45	30[a]	25-26
South Africa	49	35-36	49	39-40	65	16	63	13-14		
Salvador	66	18-19	94	5-6	19	42	40	40		
Singapore	74	13	8	53	20	39-41	48	28	48	9
Spain	57	31	86	10-15	51	20	42	37-38	19[a]	31-32
Sweden	31	47-48	29	49-50	71	10-11	5	53	33	20
Switzerland	34	45	58	33	68	14	70	4-5	40[a]	15-16
Taiwan	58	29-30	69	26	17	44	45	32-33	87	3
Thailand	64	21-23	64	30	20	39-41	34	44	56	8
Turkey	66	18-19	85	16-17	37	28	45	32-33		
Uruguay	61	26	100	4	36	29	38	42		
United States	40	38	46	43	91	1	62	15	29	27
Venezuela	81	5-6	76	21-22	12	50	73	3		
Yugoslavia	76	12	88	8	27	33-35	21	48-49		
Regions:										
Arab countries	80	7	68	27	38	26-27	53	23		
East Africa	64	21-23	52	36	27	33-35	41	39	25	28-29
West Africa	77	10-11	54	34	20	39-41	46	30-31	16	33

NOTE: 1 = highest rank. LTO ranks: 1 = China; 15-16 = Bangladesh; 21 = Poland; 34 = lowest.
a. Based on EMS consumer survey (see Exhibit 7.3).

Exhibit A5.2 Index Scores by Language Area for Multilingual Countries

Country and Part	Power Distance Index	Uncertainty Avoidance Index	Individualism Index	Masculinity Index	Long-Term Orientation Index
Belgium total[a]	65	94	75	54	
Dutch speakers[a]	61	97	78	43	
French speakers[a]	67	93	72	60	
Switzerland total[a]	34	58	68	70	
German speakers[a, c]	26	56	69	72	
French speakers[a]	70	70	64	58	
Yugoslavia total[a]	76	88	27	21	
Croatia (Zagreb)[b]	73	80	33	40	
Serbia (Beograd)[b]	86	92	25	43	
Slovenia (Ljubljana)[b]	71	88	27	19	
Canada total[a]	39	48	80	52	23
French speakers[d]	54	60	73	45	30
Australia total[a]	36	51	90	61	31
Aborigines[e]	80	128	89	22	−10

a. Based on IBM survey data.
b. Based on reanalysis of IBM survey data (Hofstede, 1993).
c. See also Kopper (1993).
d. Based on my interpretation of Rokeach Value Survey scores collected by McCarrey, Edwards, and Jones (1978); of work goal importance scores collected by Jain, Normand, and Kanungo (1979); IDV based on regression from data collected by Lambert and Klineberg (1967); and observations by Dr. Christoph Barmeyer (personal communication, 1999).
e. Based on observations of Dr. Ray Simonsen, Victoria University, Darwin (personal communication, 1998).

Exhibit A5.3 Index Score Estimates for Countries Not in the IBM Set

Country and Part	Power Distance Index	Uncertainty Avoidance Index	Individualism Index	Masculinity Index	Long-Term Orientation Index
Bangladesh	80	60	20	55	40
Bulgaria	70	85	30	40	
China	80	30	20	66	118
Czechia	57	74	58	57	13
Estonia	40	60	60	30	
Hungary	46	82	80	88	50
Luxembourg	40	70	60	50	
Malta	56	96	59	47	
Morocco	70	68	46	53	
Poland	68	93	60	64	32
Romania	90	90	30	42	
Russia	93	95	39	36	
Slovakia	104	51	52	110	38
Surinam	85	92	47	37	
Trinidad	47	55	16	58	
Vietnam	70	30	20	40	80

SOURCES: *Bangladesh:* LTO, see Chapter 7; other dimensions based on descriptive information. *Bulgaria:* based on observation and descriptive information. *China:* MAS, see Hofstede (1996b); LTO, see Chapter 7; other dimensions based on observation and an extensive literature (see Chapters 3, 4, 5, and 7). *Czechia:* Kruzela (1995), Thorpe and Pavlica (1996), and Kolman, Hofstede, Noorderhaven, and Dienes (1999). *Estonia:* MAS, Hofstede, Kolman, Nicolescu, and Pajumaa (1996); other dimensions, observation. *Hungary:* Varga (1986) and Kolman et al. (1999). *Luxembourg:* observation and clustering in European Union data. *Malta:* Hoppe (1990). *Morocco:* PDI and IDV from Helmreich and Merritt (1998); other dimensions, Arabic-speaking countries scores. *Poland:* Nasierowski and Mikula (1998) and Kolman et al. (1999). *Romania:* MAS, Hofstede et al. (1996); other dimensions, observation, and descriptive data. *Russia:* MAS, Hofstede et al. (1996); other dimensions, raw data from unpublished studies by Bollinger (1988) and Bradley (1998), observation and descriptive data. *Slovakia:* Kolman et al. (1999). *Surinam:* Nanhekhan (1990). *Trinidad:* Punnett, Singh, and Williams (1994). *Vietnam:* observation and descriptive information.

Appendix 6

Summary of Significant Correlations of
Country Index Scores With Data From Other Sources

Chapters 3 through 7 cited about 200 external (non-IBM) comparative studies in support of the cultural differences measured by my indexes. Those covering up to four countries were used for illustrative rather than statistical purposes. Those with five or more countries could be tested for statistically significant correlations with the indexes. A summary of these is presented in Exhibits A6.1 through A6.4. Unlike in the exhibits in Chapters 3 through 7, these four exhibits, with few exceptions, do not control for the influence of GNP/capita; they are limited to relationships with the culture dimensions per se. Also, these exhibits exclude straight replications using the various versions of the Values Survey Module.

Exhibit A6.1 assembles all significant correlations with data collected in 26 different surveys of representative samples of the population across between 5 and 27 countries. All five indexes are represented in the correlations, so that all five appear relevant.

Exhibit A6.2 lists significant correlations with the results of 46 different questionnaire studies of narrow samples, not representative of entire country populations but matched from country to country, such as samples of employees, students, mothers, or executives, across between 5 and 39 countries. Again all five indexes are represented.

Exhibit A6.3 groups the significant correlations with various indicators, from 56 different sources, measured at the country level. Again, all indexes are represented.

Exhibit A6.4 lists 12 studies that showed statistically significant associations with one or more of the four IBM indexes through means other than correlations.

Altogether, Exhibits A6.1 through A6.4 represent 140 sources of data external to IBM that statistically validate the IBM indexes—studies that only in rare cases had been related to each other in the past. For comparison: The first edition of *Culture's Consequences* noted 38 different sources. I described these as the "synergy harvest" of the IBM study (Hofstede, 1980a, p. 332) and predicted that the number of corroborative studies would keep growing, a prediction that has been borne out.

Each of Chapters 3 through 7 correlated an index with seven or eight country-level indicators (Exhibits 3.20, 4.22, 5.23, 6.24, and 7.8). Exhibit A6.5 summarizes the significant correlations found across the first four indexes. In the preceding chapters multiple regressions were computed of one index on the seven or eight indicators. For Exhibit A6.5 the multiple regression was done the other way around, for each of seven indicators on the four indexes. LTO was not included for lack of sufficient country data. LAT (geographic latitude) had an especially rich multiple regression pattern, but the only relationship that appeared for all countries, poor and wealthy alike, with the same sign was a negative correlation with MAS. Colder countries tended to be more feminine, and this trend was not affected by the countries' wealth. The correlation of latitude with UAI was positive across all countries and across the poor countries, but negative across the wealthy countries. Altogether, the stepwise regressions showed links with IDV nine times, with UAI five times, and with PDI and MAS each four times. Individualism, through its strong relationship with modernity, is the culture dimension most clearly associated with the state of the geographic-demographic-economic system as measured by these indicators.

Exhibit A6.6 shows the numbers of significant zero-, second-, and third-order relations between external variables and my culture indexes found in Exhibits A6.1 through A6.5. Significant higher-order relationships were found in only 20% of cases (71 out of 355)—not enough to suggest that one could simplify the picture

(Text continues on page 520)

Exhibit A6.1 Summary of Significant Correlations of Five Indexes With Survey Data; Representative Samples of Entire Populations

Survey and Scales	See Chap./ Exhibit	No. of Countries	Zero-Order Correlation With					Contributing to Multiple Regression
			PDI	UAI	IDV	MAS	LTO[a]	
Almond & Verba (1963)	4.15	5						
Citizen competence				−.96***		−.86*		−UAI
Reader's Digest (1970)	3.15	15						
Attitude toward younger people			−.65**	−.77**				−UAI, −IDV
Attitude toward older people			−.56*	−.56*				−PDI
Ornauer et al. (1976), year 2000	4.15	9						
Contribute yourself				−.64*				−UAI
Compromise not dangerous				−.90***	−.79**			−UAI
Take one day after another				−.73*				−UAI
Like living abroad				−.80**				−UAI
McGee (1977), free enterprise	6	6						
Preferred size of enterprise						.84*		+MAS
CCE (1978), retirement	6	9						
Salary over shorter working						.86**		+MAS
Hastings & Hastings (1981), human values								
Factor: worry money and health	4	13		.59*				+UAI
Factor: intellectual life	4	13					.56*	+LTO
Daily human relations	7	11					.83**	+LTO
Correct injustice	7	11					.64**	+LTO
Want more equality	7	11					.69**	+LTO
Stoetzel (1983), EVS		9						
Freedom over equality	3				.84**			+IDV
Polarization in politics	3		.71*					+PDI
Satisfaction with family	4			−.87**				−UAI
Home life balance	4			−.88**				−UAI, −MAS
Permissiveness Index	6					−.83**		−MAS
Eurobarometer (1990)	6	11						
Poor are unlucky						−.63*		−MAS
Poor are lazy						.52		+MAS
Harpaz (1990), MOW	6	7						
Security vs. physical conditions						.69*		+MAS
Autonomy vs. promotion			.68*					+PDI
Inglehart (1990), culture shift	3	17						
Want revolutionary action			.77**					+PDI
Frequently discuss politics			−.70**					−PDI
Gender gap in discussing								+MAS[b]

Survey and Scales	See Chap./ Exhibit	No. of Countries	PDI	UAI	IDV	MAS	LTO[a]	Contributing to Multiple Regression
			Zero-Order Correlation With					
Halman (1991), EVS	3	12						
Children should learn hard work			.76**					+PDI
Should learn independence			−.75***					−PDI
Work should be less important			.67**					+PDI
No children reason for divorce			.79***					+PDI
7 petty offenses justified (median)			.69**					+PDI
Owners should appoint managers			−.65*					−PDI
Couples cohabiting						−.52*		−MAS
Leung et al. (1990, 1992), students	5	4						
Conflict handling: threaten					.95*			+IDV
Same: accuse					.95*			+IDV
Same: falsely promise					.95*			+IDV
Same: ignore					.95*			+IDV
Same: comply			1.00*					+PDI
Dunlap et al. (1993), environment	6.21	20						
Protect rather than grow			−.42*					−PDI
Willing to pay for it			−.60**		.40*	−.48*		−PDI, −MAS
Veenhoven (1993), happiness	4							
1970-80 wealthy countries		15		−.61**				−UAI
1990 all countries		21		−.64**				−UAI
Dispersion of happiness		26		−.50*				−UAI
Eurobarometer (1994)	4.17	11						
Interest in politics			−.76**	−.76**	.55*			−UAI
Pro European government			.67*	.68*				−UAI
Lueschen et al. (1994), health care	5							
Satisfied with system		4			.93*			+IDV
Waiting times for doctors		5			−.86*			−IDV
Prefer cure over care		5	.85*					+PDI
Van Baren et al. (1995), biotechnology	5	12						
Correct answers on quiz				−.70**	.72**			+IDV
Biotechnology is a threat			−.52*			−.55*		−MAS, −PDI
Burkholder et al. (1996), gender	6							
Equal job opportunities		15	.74**		−.60**			+PDI
Same: wealthy countries		7				−.69*		−MAS
Gibson & Caldeira (1996), legal cultures	4	11						
Legal alienation				.88***				+UAI
No rule of law				.78**				+UAI

(Continued)

Exhibit A6.1 Continued

Survey and Scales	See Chap./ Exhibit	No. of Countries	Zero-Order Correlation With					Contributing to Multiple Regression
			PDI	UAI	IDV	MAS	LTO[a]	
Smulders et al. (1996), work environment	5	11						
Control over job					.81**			+IDV
Length of workweek					.80**			+IDV
Physical working conditions					.65*			+IDV
Eurobarometer (1997)	4.17	14						
Satisfied with democracy			−.68**	−.66**				−PDI
Opinion about institutions			−.51*	−.58*		−.72**		−MAS, −PDI
Send immigrants back				.58*		.54*		+UAI
Send unemployed back			.47*	.75**		.61**		+UAI, +MAS
Send illegal back				.71**		.67**		+UAI, +MAS
Integrate, not assimilate				−.64**	.48*	−.72**		−MAS
Inglehart (1997), dimensions	5.18	27						
Well-being vs. survival			−.72***	−.55**	.74***	−.39*	−.53*(11)	+IDV, −MAS, −PDI
Rational vs. traditional			−.56**		.49**			−PDI
Inglehart et al. (1998), WVS								
Freedom over equality	3	26	−.49**					−PDI
More technology good thing	3	26	.77***	.34*	−.64***			+PDI
Children should learn hard work	3	26	.69***					+PDI
Should learn obedience	3	26	.65***					+PDI
Should learn independence	3	26	−.66***					−PDI
Should learn unselfishness	5	26			.53**			+IDV
Should learn tolerance/ respect	5, 7	26			.46**		−.62*(12)	+IDV, −LTO
Should learn thrift	7	12					.70**	+LTO
How important: family	6	26				.50**		+MAS, +IDV
Same: friends, acquaintances	6	26	−.55**					−PDI, −MAS, +IDV
Same: religion	6	26						+MAS[b]
Same: leisure time	7	13					−.51*	−LTO[b]
% very happy	4.12	26	−.35*	−.55**	.48**			−UAI
% in good health	4.12	26	−.42*	−.75***	.49**			−UAI
Satisfied with life	4.12	26	−.63***	−.56**	.68***			+IDV, −PDI
Same: wealthy countries	4.12	19	−.52*	−.73***	.58**			−UAI
Satisfied with job	4.12	26	−.56**	−.53**	.59**			−IDV
Same: wealthy countries	4.12	19	−.53*	−.70***	.53*			−UAI
Satisfied with home life	4.12	26	−.49**	−.52**	.67***			+IDV, −MAS
Same: wealthy countries	4.12	19		−.71***	.67**	−.34*		−UAI
Other race not as neighbors	4.12	26	.51**					+PDI
Same: wealthy countries	4.12	19	.50*	.63**	−.44*			+UAI
Most people can be trusted	4.12	26	−.69***	−.72***	.62***			−UAI
Same: wealthy countries	4.12	19	−.63*	−.81***	.40*	−.46*		−UAI, −MAS
Trust own family	4.12	26	−.37*	−.51**				−UAI

Survey and Scales	See Chap./ Exhibit	No. of Countries	Zero-Order Correlation With					Contributing to Multiple Regression
			PDI	UAI	IDV	MAS	LTO[a]	
Child needs father and mother	4.12	24	.53**	.54**	−.59**			−IDV, +MAS
Same: wealthy countries	4.12	17		.78***	−.59**	.46*		+UAI
Women want home, not job	4.12	24	.68***	.47*	−.66***			+PDI, −IDV, +MAS
Same: wealthy countries	4.12	17	.55*	.70**	−.46*	.55*		+UAI, +MAS
Child suffers if mother works	7	12					.52*	+LTO
Parents need not earn love	6	26	.65***	.52**	−.57**	.54**		+PDI, +MAS
Marriage success: no in-laws	5, 7	26			.36*		−.60*(12)	−LTO, (+IDV)
Same: shared religion	5	26			−.37*			−IDV
Same: adequate income	5	26			−.35*			−IDV
Same: common interests	6, 7	26				.37*	−51*(12)	+MAS, (−LTO)
Will fight for country	4.12	26		−.45*		−.55**		−MAS, −UAI, −IDV
Proud to be nationality	4.12	26						−UAI[b]
Confidence in legal system	4.12	26		−.45*				−UAI
Confidence in the press	4.12	25	.66***		−.38*			+PDI
Confidence in trade unions	4.12	26				−.44*		−MAS
Confidence in the police	4.12	25	−.81***	−.66***	.68***			−PDI, +IDV
Same: wealthy countries	4.12	26	−.78***	−.90***	.47*			−UAI
Confidence in civil service	4.12	26		−.47**				−UAI, +PDI
Politically in center	6	26				.59**		+MAS
Politically left	6	26				−.36*		−MAS
Should be sexual freedom	6	25				.38*		+MAS
Clear guidelines good/evil	7	13						−LTO
Verweij (1998b), secularization	6	16						
Importance Christian rites						.72***		+MAS
Church attendance						.60**		+MAS
Confidence in the church						.59**		+MAS
Religiosity						.69**		+MAS
Orthodoxy						.73***		+MAS
Christian worldviews						.74***		+MAS
Williams et al. (1998), psychological traits	5	18						
"Individualistic" important					.41*			+IDV
De Mooij (2001), consumers		16						
"Marriage needs children"	5				−.72***			−IDV
Read newspaper 7 days/ week	3		−.69***					−PDI
Read newspaper yesterday	3, 4		−.66**	−.84***				−UAI
Confidence in the press	3		.55*					+PDI
Confidence in advertising	6					.53*		+MAS
Enjoy TV as 5 years ago	5				.72***			+IDV
Enjoy TV more than 5 years ago	5				−.83***			−IDV
See TV advertising as useful	5				.47*			+IDV
Own a computer	5				.63***			+IDV
Enjoy TV advertising	6					.55*		+MAS

(Continued)

Exhibit A6.1 Continued

Survey and Scales	See Chap./ Exhibit	No. of Countries	Zero-Order Correlation With					Contributing to Multiple Regression
			PDI	UAI	IDV	MAS	LTO[a]	
1997 Internet use	4	16		−.72***				−UAI
1997 teletext use	4			−.74***				−UAI
Own telephone answer machine	5			−.74***	.50*			+IDV
Read at least 1 book/year	4							−UAI
Read 12+ books/year	5				.72***			+IDV
Buy mostly fiction books	6					−.53*		−MAS
Women use lipstick	4			−.90***				−UAI
Use body lotions	4			−.84***				−UAI
Use deodorants	4			−.84***				−UAI
Use hair conditioner	4			−.83***				−UAI
Use facial moisturizing cream	4			−.75***				−UAI
Use face cleaner	4			−.73***				−UAI
Use mascara	4			−.64**				−UAI
Invests in stocks	4			−.64**				−UAI
Invests in gold and gems	4			.55*				+UAI
Do-it-yourself wallpapering	4			−.48*	.63**			+IDV, −UAI
Same: home painting	4			−.44*	.65**			+IDV, −UAI
Same: home carpentry	5				.50*	−.56**		−MAS, +IDV
Same: electric repairs	5				.50*			+IDV
Same: plumbing	5				.50*			+IDV
Live in detached house	5				.45*			+IDV
Live in apartment	5				−.56*			−IDV
Have private garden	5				.74***			+IDV
Own a caravan	5				.51*	−.57**		−MAS, +IDV
Home insurance	5				.64**			+IDV
Life insurance	5				.63**			+IDV
Partner involved in choice of car	6					−.63**		−MAS
Women are food shoppers	6					.68**		+MAS
Own filter coffeemakers	6					−.46*		−MAS
Makes own dress, knits	6					−.73***		−MAS
Owns cheap watch	6					−.51*		−MAS
Foreign good attractive	6					−.52*		−MAS
Doesn't know car engine power	6					.60**		−MAS
Pleasure flights business class	6					.59**		+MAS
Invest in mutual funds	7	15					−.66**	−LTO
Invest in real estate	7	15					.43	+LTO
Daily use of credit card	7	15					.54*	+LTO

NOTE: This table lists all studies publishing correlation coefficients (*r* and rho). For studies publishing only regression coefficients, see Exhibit A6.4. For straight replications, see Exhibits 4.10, 5.15, and 6.18.
a. For LTO, a deviant number of countries is added in parentheses.
b. Controlling for GNP/capita.

Exhibit A6.2 Summary of Significant Correlations of Five Indexes With Survey Data, Narrow Samples

Survey and Scales	See Chap./ Exhibit	No. of Countries	Zero-Order Correlation With					Contributing to Multiple Regression
			PDI	UAI	IDV	MAS	LTO[a]	
Morris (1956), ways to live	5	6						
Enjoyment vs. duty					.73*			+IDV
Haire et al. (1966), thinking								
Capacity leadership	3	19	.54**		−.49*			+PDI, −UAI, +MAS
Acquiescence in answers	5	14			−.71**			−IDV
Lambert & Klineberg (1967), children	5	11						
Ethnocentrism					−.89***			−IDV
Bass & Franke (1972)	5	6						
Openness vs. secrecy					.91**			+IDV
IMEDE (Hofstede, 1974b), Fiedler's LPC	4.14	16						
Mean LPC score				−.42*				−UAI, +PDI
IMEDE (Hofstede, 1976d), Gordon tests	3	14						
Conformity vs. variety					−.61***			−IDV
Decisive vs. practical-minded			.80***					+PDI
Gordon (1976), students SIV	3.14							
Conformity, men		17	.80***		−.76***	.44*		+PDI
Conformity, women		11	.82**		−.57*			+PDI
Independence, men		17	−.79***		.41*	−.54*		−PDI
Independence, women		11	−.90***		.60*			−PDI, −UAI
Support, men		17	−.70***		.68***			−PDI
Support, women		11	−.77**		.86**			+IDV
Benevolence, men		17		−.49*		−.59**		−MAS, +PDI
Recognition, men		17				.50*		+MAS
Laurent (1978), matrix	4.14	10						
Clarity of hierarchy			.61*	.78**				+UAI
Formalized management factor				.77**				+UAI
Bass & Burger (1979), IRGOM	5.19	12						
Hedonism vs. skill			−.66**		.76***			+IDV
Assertiveness vs. service						.84***		+MAS
Arbose (1980), executives	3	10						
Feel underpaid	3		.81**					+PDI
Career most satisfying	3		−.67*					−PDI
Career less good than before	3		.63*					+PDI
Not resign for unethical order	3		.67*					+PDI
Want to be CEO	6.19					.60*		+MAS
Would uproot family	6.19					.73*		+MAS

(Continued)

Exhibit A6.2 Continued

Survey and Scales	See Chap./ Exhibit	No. of Countries	Zero-Order Correlation With					Contributing to Multiple Regression
			PDI	UAI	IDV	MAS	LTO[a]	
Hastings & Hastings (1980), children	5	5						
Mothers want to live with children					−.84*			−IDV
Children aggressive reaction						.97**		+MAS
Ryback et al. (1980), aggression	6	6						
Allowed to express						.90*		+MAS
Kagitçibasi (1982), children	3	9						
Old-age security for men			.74*					+PDI
Same: women			.73*					+PDI
Ford (1985), Unilever	6	15						
% female managers						−.45*		−MAS
Pompe et al. (1986), entrepreneurs		9						
Working for family interest	3		.90***					+PDI
Self-confidence	5				.70*			+IDV
Bond/Chinese Culture Connection (1987), CVS	7	23						
Moral discipline			.55**		−.54**			+PDI
Integration			−.58**		.65***			+IDV
Human-heartedness						.67		+MAS
Edelmann et al. (1989)	4	5						
Duration of embarrassment				.98**				+UAI
Verbalization of emotions				.85*				+UAI
Buss (1989)/*Buss et al.* (1990), select partner	5	28						
Age difference with brides					−.75***			−IDV
Brides should be wealthy					−.70***			−IDV
Brides should be industrious					−.70***			−IDV
Brides should be chaste					−.57**			−IDV
Age difference with grooms					−.75***			−IDV
Grooms should be wealthy					−.73***			−IDV
Grooms should be industrious					−.50*			−IDV
Δ (grooms − brides), chastity				.49**		.39*		+UAI, +MAS
Same: industriousness						−.50***		−MAS
Williams & Best (1990a), gender	6							
Typicality of stereotypes		21				.52**		+MAS
Adjectives applied to one gender		21				−.56**		−MAS
Modernity of role conceptions		12			.54*			+IDV

Survey and Scales	See Chap./ Exhibit	No. of Countries	Zero-Order Correlation With					Contributing to Multiple Regression
			PDI	UAI	IDV	MAS	LTO[a]	
Lynn (1991), students	6							
Competitiveness index		31	.44**		−.41*			+PDI
Gender ratio of competitiveness		32				.44**		+MAS
Furnham (1993), 2 studies	3	12						
World is unjust place			.54*		−.60*			+MAS, +PDI[c]
Protestant work ethic			.80**					+PDI
Graham et al. (1994), negotiation	9	8						
Individual profits					.67*			+IDV
More profit as buyers			.75*					+PDI
Liked the game						.68*		+MAS
Scherer & Wallbott (1994), ISEAR		14						
Expression of anger: men	4			.54*				+UAI
Expression of guilt: men	4			.77**				+UAI
Same: women	4			.53*				+UAI
Expression of sadness: men	6					.51*		+MAS
Expression of joy: men	6					.50*		+MAS
Δ (women − men), guilt	5				.70**			+IDV
Same: joy	5				.63**			+IDV
Same: shame	5				.55*			+IDV
Same: anger	5				.53*			+IDV
Same: disgust	5				.50*			+IDV
Schwartz (1994), teachers	5.17	23						
Conservatism			−.45*		−.55**			−IDV, −UAI
Hierarchy					−.53**		.56*(14)	−IDV
Mastery						.53**		+MAS
Affective autonomy			−.46*		.45*		−.53*(14)	+IDV
Intellectual autonomy					.53**			+IDV
Egalitarian commitment					.49**			+IDV
Harmony				.45*				+UAI
Schwartz (1994), students	5	22						
Conservatism			.70***		−.66***			+PDI
Affective autonomy			−.83***		.85***			+IDV
Intellectual autonomy			−.49**		.48**			−PDI
Egalitarian commitment			−.47*		.45*			−PDI
Smith et al. (1994), event management	3	14						
Use own experience			−.78***					−PDI
Apply formal rules			.70**					+PDI
Involve subordinates			−.55*					−PDI
Wong & Birnbaum-More (1994), multinational banks	3	14						
Centralization (Aston)			.55**					+PDI
Attribution of achievement	4							
Yan & Gaier (1994): ability		5		−.91*				−UAI
Chandler et al. (1981): same		5		−.87*				−UAI

(Continued)

Exhibit A6.2 Continued

Survey and Scales	See Chap./ Exhibit	No. of Countries	Zero-Order Correlation With					Contributing to Multiple Regression
			PDI	UAI	IDV	MAS	LTO[a]	
Diener (1996)/*Diener et al.* (1995), students	4							
Subjective well-being		39			.62***			−UAI[b]
Levine et al. (1995), students								
Only marry if in love	5	11			.64*			+IDV
Make clean break	7	10					.76**	+LTO
Pavett & Morris (1995), managers	3	5						
Participativeness (Likert)			−1.00**					−PDI
Peterson et al. (1995), role conflict	3	21						
Role ambiguity and overload			.75***					+PDI
Best & Williams (1996), aging								
Which age is middle age: men	3	18	−.69**					−PDI
Same: women	3	18	−.73***					−PDI
Which age is old age: men	7	10					−.63*	−LTO
Same: women	7	10					−.62*	−LTO
Satisfied when old: men	7	10					.59*	+LTO
Same: women	7	10					.54	+LTO
"Father Figures" (1996)	5	10						
Business(wo)men live with parents					−.67*			−IDV
Gibbons et al. (1996), opposite sex	6	4						
Is fun					.98**			+IDV
Hofstede (1996b), Asian women								
Boyfriend needs personality	6	7				.94***		+MAS
Husband needs affection	7	8					.71*	+LTO
Responsibility is for men only	6	7				.96***		+MAS
Humility is also for men	7	8					.87***	+LTO
Sagie et al. (1996), motivation	4	5						
Avoid uncertain tasks			.90*	−.90*				+UAI
Schein et al. (1996), students	6	5						
Typical woman successful manager						−.92*		−MAS

Survey and Scales	See Chap./ Exhibit	No. of Countries	Zero-Order Correlation With					Contributing to Multiple Regression
			PDI	UAI	IDV	MAS	LTO[a]	
Smith et al. (1995, 1996), Trompenaars	5							
Individual vs. social		35	−.47**		.70***			+IDV
First MDS dimension		33			.70***			+IDV
Same without Eastern Europe		33	−.68***		.80***			+IDV
Second MDS dimension		33			−.74***			−IDV
Offermann & Hellmann (1997), subordinates	8	19						
Boss approachable			−.54**					−PDI
Boss builds teams			−.52*					−PDI
Boss delegates			−.44*					−PDI
Boss communicates			−.41*					−PDI
Boss controls				.61**				+UAI
Best & Williams (1998), gender	6	12						
Δ self-concepts men-women						−.67**		−MAS
Δ affective meaning self-concepts			.78***					+PDI
Williams et al. (1998), psychological importance	3	16						
5 PI/5 factors (median)			.63***		−.48*			+PDI
5 PI/ego states (median)			.45**					+PDI
NCES (1999), TIMSS	7							
Math performance: 4th grade		11					.58*	+LTO
Same: 8th grade		13					.72**	+LTO
Van Oudenhoven (2001), students	8	10						
Company bureaucratic			.66*	.63*				+PDI, +UAI
Company has individual work					.47			+IDV
Company has hostile ambience						.49		+MAS
De Mooij (2001), managers	3	16						
Involved in advertising			−.71***					−PDI
Involved in trade fairs			−.69***					−PDI
Involved in purchasing			−.66**					−PDI

NOTE: This table lists all studies publishing correlation coefficients (*r* and rho). For studies publishing only regression coefficients, see Exhibit A6.4. For straight replications, see Exhibits 3.13, 4.10, 5.15, 5.16. 6.18, and 7.3.
a. For LTO, a deviant number of countries is added in parentheses.
b. Controlling for GNP/capita.
c. Controlling for "just world" and GNP/capita.

Exhibit A6.3 Summary of Significant Correlations of Five Indexes With Country-Level Indicators

Survey and Scales	See Chap./ Exhibit	No. of Countries	Zero-Order Correlation With					Contributing to Multiple Regression
			PDI	UAI	IDV	MAS	LTO[a]	
McClelland (1961), readers	4.13							
1925 need for achievement		23	−.56***	−.60***	.42*			−UAI, +MAS
1925 need for affiliation	4, 7	23			.48**		−.85**(10)	−LTO (+IDV)
Moulin (1961)	3	14						
Nobel Prize index			−.50*	−.46*				−PDI
Cutright (1968)	5	12						
Occupational inheritance				.64*	−.71**			−IDV
Converse (1972), time use	5	6						
Self-started activities					1.00**			+IDV
Sectoral inequality	5							
Taylor & Hudson (1972)		32	.67***		−.71***			−IDV, +PDI
Cutright (1967)		33	.54***		−.60***	−.34*		−IDV, −MAS
Taylor & Hudson (1972)	5	39						
Press freedom	5	39	−.38**	−.40**	.51***			+IDV
U.N. (1973), traffic deaths	4.20	14						
1971 European data				.56*	−.62*	.51*		−IDV
ANWB (1975), speed limits	4.20	14						
1971 European data				.58*		.52*		+UAI
Lynn & Hampson (1975)	4.11	18						
Neuroticism				.73***	−.53*	.41*		+UAI
Extraversion			−.47*	−.44*				−PDI
Boulding et al. (1976)	6							
Segregation higher education		38		−.31*		.28*		−UAI
Same: wealthy countries only		18				.56***		+MAS
% professional women		34	−.41**		.46**			+IDV
Same: wealthy countries only		16		−.57*	.50*	−.64**		−MAS
Millendorfer (1976)	4	12						
National stress levels				.71***				+UAI
Aberbach & Putnam (1977)	4							
Law degrees for civil servants		5		.90*	−.90*			+UAI
de Bettignies & Evans (1977)	3.15	11						
Age of executives			.75**	.70**		.59*		+PDI
1979 identity card obligation	4	14		.85***				+UAI
Schmitter (1981), corporatism	5.20	15						
Organizational centralization					.57*			+IDV
Associational monopoly			.65**			.52*		+PDI, +MAS

Survey and Scales	See Chap./ Exhibit	No. of Countries	Zero-Order Correlation With					Contributing to Multiple Regression
			PDI	UAI	IDV	MAS	LTO[a]	
Jones et al. (1986), teenage fertility	6.23							
Weak uncertainty avoidance		11				.59*		+MAS
Strong uncertainty avoidance		11				−.49*		−MAS
Matsumoto (1989), facial expressions	5							
Correct perception happiness		15			.51*			+IDV
Correct perception sadness		15			−.50*			−IDV
Intensity ratings of anger		7			.67*			+IDV
Intensity ratings of fear		7			.79*			+IDV
Standard deviation ratings of fear		7			−.78*			−IDV
Nurses per doctor	4.19							
World Bank (1990)		50	−.32*	−.52***	.31*			−UAI
Gaspari & Millendorfer (1978)		15	−.54*	−.78***	.62**			−UAI
Sullivan (1991), gender gap	6							
Male-female equality		51	−.60***		.66***			+IDV
Same: wealthy countries		20				−.38*		−MAS
Humana (1992)	5.21							
Human rights respected		52	−.56***		.61***			+IDV
Same: wealthy countries only		25	−.48**		.73***			+IDV
Health % of budget		51	−.61***		.68***			+IDV
Same: wealthy countries only		24	−.41*		.56**		−.58*(10)	+IDV
Same: poor countries only		27				−.35*		−MAS
Education % of budget		52	−.48***	−.37***	.56***			+IDV
Same: wealthy countries only		25	−.63**	−.41*	.52**	−.39*	−.61*(11)	−PDI, −MAS
Military %, wealthy countries only		24	.37*				.53*(10)	+PDI
Read (1993), savings	7.3	23						
Marginal propensity to save							.58**	+LTO
Aviation accident rates	3.17							
Weener & Russell (1994)		33	.47**		−.62***			−IDV
Ramsden (1985)		18	.68***		−.69***			−IDV
Lester (1995)	5	26						
1980 divorce rates					.76***			+IDV
Lynn & Martin (1995)								
Norms for neuroticism test	4	25		.44*				+UAI
Norms for psychoticism	6	25				.36		+MAS
1985 alcoholism	4	22		.65***				+UAI
OECD & MIC (1995), literacy	6	7						
Rate own skills excellent						.71*		+MAS

(Continued)

Exhibit A6.3 Continued

Survey and Scales	See Chap./ Exhibit	No. of Countries	Zero-Order Correlation With					Contributing to Multiple Regression
			PDI	UAI	IDV	MAS	LTO[a]	
Reitsma (1995), public decision	4	6						
Duration infrastructure decisions			−.96*	−.97*				−UAI, −PDI
Income inequality								
UNDP (1996)	3.16	40	.42**					+PDI
Den Tex (1992)	3.16	12	.72**					+PDI
Kravis (1960)	3	8	.89**			.77*		+PDI
Kuznets (1963)	3	10	.86**	.80**	−.60*			+PDI
Bégué (1976)	3	12	.57*					+PDI
UNDP (1996)								
1983 official development aid	6.20	20				−.67**		−MAS
1994 official development aid	6.20	20		−.39*		−.78***		−MAS
Shift 1983-94	6.20	20			−.51*			−IDV, −UAI
% women in parliament	6.22	22	−.49*	−.56**		−.67***		−MAS, −PDI
% women in government	6.22	22	−.47*	−.62**		−.70***		−MAS, −UAI
Women as % of professionals	6	47	−.60***			−.44***		−PDI, −MAS
Schimmack (1996)	4	15						
Recognition of fear				−.49*				−UAI
Tollgerdt-Andersson (1996), job ads	8	8						
Require social abilities				−.86**				−UAI, −MAS
Harzing (1997), multinationals	3	22						
Response rates by subsidiary			−.61***					−PDI
Same by respondent nationality			−.67***					−PDI
Inglehart (1997)	4.16	23						
Participation in associations			−.52**	−.70***	.51**	−.47*		−UAI, −MAS
OECD (NRC Handelsblad, 1997), employment	4	17						
Average duration				.63**				+UAI
Pedersen & Thomsen (1997) governance	8	12						
Dispersed ownership					.65*			+IDV
Dominant ownership			.52*					+PDI
One-family ownership			−.62*					−PDI
Cooperative ownership						−.77**		−MAS
NRC Handelsblad (Jan. 22, 1997), recycling	3	15						
% of paper waste recycled			−.67**					−PDI
Frémy & Frémy (1998), Taylor & Hudson (1972)	4.21							
Catholics vs. Protestants		36	.63***	.77***	−.59***			+UAI, +MAS
Same: wealthy countries only		20	.59**	.75***	−.47*	.53**		+UAI, +MAS
Johnson et al. (1998)	4							
Economic Freedom Index (−)		53						None
Same: wealthy countries		26		−.66***				−UAI, +MAS, +PDI

Survey and Scales	See Chap./ Exhibit	No. of Countries	PDI	UAI	IDV	MAS	LTO[a]	Contributing to Multiple Regression
UNDP (1998)	6	17						
% of population in poverty						.57**		+MAS
% functional illiterates						.88***		+MAS
Kashima & Kashima (1998), languages								
First-person pronoun drop	5	60			−.75**			−IDV, +UAI
Multiple second-person pronouns	4	52		.43**				+UAI
Transparency International (1998)	3.19							
Corruption Perception Index		50	−.70***	−.38**	.71***			−PDI, −MAS, −UAI
Same: wealthy countries only		26	−.55***	−.78***	.47**	−.33*		−UAI, −PDI
Same: poor countries only		24				−.43*		−MAS
Levine & Norenzayan (1999)	5	23						
Walking speed in cities					.62**			+IDV
Working speed in post offices			−.57**					−PDI
Domestic political violence	3							
Van de Vliert et al. (1999)		50	.51***					+PDI
Schneider & Schneider (1971)		10	.93***	.70*				+PDI
Nesvold (1969)		37	.71***	.44**	−.52***			+PDI
Rummel (1963)		37	.39**					+PDI
De Mooij (2001), Euromonitor		16						
1996 sales of mineral water	4			.78***				+UAI
Fresh fruits	4			.66**				+UAI
Sugar	4			.46*				+UAI
Ice cream	4			−.76***				−UAI
Frozen foods	4			−.69***				−UAI
Confectionery	4			−.59**				−UAI
Savory snacks	4			−.57**				−UAI
Cereals	4			−.54*				−UAI
Tea	4			−.54*				−UAI
Milk	4			−.51*				−UAI
Fruit juices	4			−.48*				−UAI
Textile washing powders	4			.63**				+UAI
Daily newspapers	4			−.66**				−UAI
Main car bought new	4			.80***				+UAI
Have a dog	5				.62**			+IDV
Have a cat	5				.73***			+IDV
Pet food sales	5				.72***			+IDV
Rolls own cigarettes	6					−.69***		−MAS
Real jewelry	6					.66**		+MAS
De Mooij (2001), payment	4	15						
Agreed terms				.62**				+UAI
Actually observed terms				.68**				+UAI

NOTE: This table lists all studies publishing correlation coefficients (*r* and rho). For studies publishing only regression coefficients, see Exhibit A6.4.
a. For LTO, a deviant number of countries is added in parentheses.

Exhibit A6.4 Summary of Studies Showing Significant Relations With One or More Indexes, Other Than Through Correlation Coefficients

Study and Scales	See Chapter/ Exhibit	Number of Countries	Related Index(es)
Kaase & Marsh (1976), public	4	5	
Protest potential			+UAI
Repression potential			+UAI
Gudykunst (1989), students in U.S.		32	
Intergroup comparisons	4		−UAI
Ethnolinguistic vitality	4, 5		+UAI, +IDV, +MAS
Importance of gender, religion	5		−IDV
Group boundaries	6		+MAS
In-group identification	6		+MAS
Shane (1993), rates of innovation		33	
Trademarks granted per capita	4		−UAI
Patents granted per capita	5		−PDI, +IDV
Westbrook & Legge (1993)/*Westbrook et al.* (1993), disability	5	6	
Grief, shame, and pessimism			−IDV
Olah (1995), coping with stress	5	5	
Change environment			+IDV
Adapt to environment			−IDV
Shane et al. (1995), innovations		30	
Need support hierarchy	3		+PDI
Independence from rules	4		−UAI, +IDV
Cross-functional appeal	5		−IDV
Shane (1995), championing roles	4	68	
Transformational leader			−UAI
Organizational buffer			−UAI
Network facilitator			−UAI
Organizational maverick			−UAI
R. Bond & Smith (1996), conformity	5	14	
Meta-analysis of Asch studies			−IDV
Essau & Trommsdorff (1996), coping with stress	5	4	
Emotion focused			−IDV
Problem focused			+IDV
Shane & Venkataraman (1996), championing	4	28	
Renegade vs. rational style			−UAI, +IDV
Van Oudenhoven et al. (1998), conflict	6	5	
Problem solving toward superior			−PDI, −UAI
Problem solving toward colleague			−MAS
Wildeman et al. (1999), entrepreneurship	4	21	
Self-employment rate			+UAI

Exhibit A6.5 Summary of Significant Correlations of Seven Country-Level Indicators With the Four IBM Indexes, With Multiple and Stepwise Regressions

System-Level Indicator	Abbreviation	Zero-Order Correlation With				Squared Multiple Correlation R^2	Order in Stepwise Regression	
		PDI	UAI	IDV	MAS		First	Second
All 52 countries[a]								
Wealth	GNP	−.65***	−.25*	.85***		.73	.72 +IDV	
Past growth	EGP					.03		
Future growth	EGF					.03		
Latitude	LAT	−.68***		.79***		.78	.63 +IDV	.69 −MAS[b]
Population size	POP				.27*	.21	.08 +MAS	
Population growth	PGR	.55***		−.69***		.51	.48 −IDV	
Population density	PDN					.05		
IBM organization size[c]	ORS	−.30*		.72**		.63	.51 +IDV	.57 +PDI
28 poor countries[d]								
Wealth	GNP					.02		
Past growth	EGP					.13		
Future growth	EGF					.19		
Latitude	LAT	−.34*	.34*	.49**	−.39*	.60	.24 +IDV	.51 +UAI[e]
Population size	POP					.14		
Population growth	PGR				.34*	.28		
Population density	PDN		−.47**			.35	.22 −UAI	
IBM organization size[f]	ORS			.46*		.60	.21 +IDV	.34 +UAI
22 wealthy countries								
Wealth	GNP		−.55**	.66***		.47	.44 +IDV	
Past growth	EGP	.43*	.59**	−.61**		.48	.37 −IDV	
Future growth	EGF					.04		
Latitude	LAT		−.56**		−.58**	.50	.34 −MAS	.47 −UAI
Population size	POP	.54**			.40*	.50	.30 +PDI	
Population growth	PGR					.30		
Population density	PDN					.13		
IBM organization size	ORS			.49*		.44	.24 +IDV	.39 +PDI

NOTE: For definitions of indicators, see Exhibit 2.9.
a. Indicators for Nigeria used for West Africa; Zimbabwe for East Africa. Arabic-speaking region excluded.
b. Third order, .86 +UAI; fourth order, .78 −PDI.
c. 40 Category 1 countries only.
d. 1970 GNP/capita < $1,000.
e. Third order, .59 −MAS.
f. 18 Category 1 countries only.

Exhibit A6.6 Number of Significant Contributions to Multiple Regression With External Indicators, for Four IBM Indexes (from Exhibits A6.1-A6.5)

Order	PDI	UAI	IDV	MAS	Total
Zero	**86**	**90**	**105**	74	355
Second	13	14	9	**26**	62
Third	2	2	2	**3**	9
Total	101	106	116	103	426

NOTE: MAS appears significantly more frequently as a second- or third-order correlate than the three other indexes (chi-square = 14.4** with 3 degrees of freedom). LTO appeared 24 times.

substantially by subsuming any pair of indexes into one. Second, Exhibit A6.6 shows that MAS, especially, appeared more often as a significant higher-order correlate. IDV and PDI were both significantly correlated with wealth (GNP/capita: $r = .84$*** and $r = -.64$***, respectively), and for wealthier countries only, UAI was also correlated with wealth ($r = -.55$**); only MAS was entirely independent of wealth. As many external variables also have a wealth component, they will be related more easily to IDV, PDI, and UAI than to MAS. Exhibit A6.6 shows that whereas the four IBM indexes in total appeared with about equal frequency (between 101 and 116 times each), MAS came significantly more often in second or third place (29 times). This means that it takes a somewhat more sophisticated research approach to find the full implications of MAS differences than it takes to validate the other three indexes. I have previously drawn a similar conclusion from the data in the first edition of *Culture's Consequences;* at that time the total number of zero-order correlations found was only 65, against the present 355 (see Hofstede & Associates, 1998, tab. 1.4).

Appendix 7

Two Case Studies From the IRIC
Organizational Cultures Research Project

The TKB Case

TKB is a 60-year-old production unit in the chemical industry. Many of its employees are old-timers. Stories about the past abound. Workers tell about how heavy the jobs used to be, when loading and unloading were done by hand. They tell about heat and physical risk. TKB used to be seen as a rich employer. For several decades, the demand for its products exceeded the supply. Products were not sold, but distributed. Customers had to be nice and polite in order to be served. The money was made very easily. TKB's management style used to be paternalistic. The old general manager made his daily morning walk through the plant, shaking hands with everyone he met. This, people say, is the root of a tradition that still exists of shaking hands with one's colleagues in the morning. Rich and paternalistic, TKB has long been considered a benefactor, both to its employees in need and to the local community. Some of this has survived. Employees still feel TKB to be a desirable employer, with good pay, benefits, and job security. A job with TKB is still seen as a job for life. TKB is a company one would like one's children to join. Outside, TKB is a regular sponsor of local humanitarian and sports associations: "No appeal to TKB was ever made in vain."

The working atmosphere is good-natured, with a lot of freedom given to employees. The plant has been pictured as a club, a village, a family. Employees' 25th and 40th anniversaries with the company are given a great deal of attention, and the plant's Christmas parties are famous. These celebrations are rituals with a long history that people still value a lot. In TKB's culture—or, as people express it, in "the TKB way"—unwritten rules for social behavior are very important. One doesn't live in order to work, one works in order to live. What one does counts less than how one does it. One has to fit into the informal network, and this holds for all hierarchical levels. "Fitting" means avoiding conflicts and direct confrontations, covering other people's mistakes, loyalty, friendliness, modesty, and good-natured coopera-

tion. Nobody should be too conspicuous, in a positive or a negative sense. TKB-ers grumble, but never directly about other TKB-ers. Also, grumbling is reserved for one's own circle and is never done in front of superiors or outsiders. This concern for harmony and group solidarity fits well into the regional culture of the geographic area in which TKB is located. Newcomers are quickly accepted, as long as they adapt. The quality of their work counts less than their social adaptation. Anyone who disrupts the harmony is rejected, however good a worker he or she is. Disturbed relationships may take years to heal: "We prefer to let a work problem continue for another month, even if it costs a lot of money, above resolving it in an unfriendly manner." Company rules are never absolute. The most important rule, one interviewee said, is that rules are flexible. One may break a rule if one does it gently. It is not the rule-breaker who is at risk, but the one who makes an issue of it.

Leadership in TKB, in order to be effective, should be in harmony with the social behavior patterns. Managers should be accessible, fair, and good listeners. The present general manager is such a leader. He doesn't give himself airs. He has an easy contact with people of all levels and is felt to be "one of us." Careers in TKB are made primarily on the basis of social skills. One should not behave too conspicuously; one needn't be brilliant, but one does need good contacts; one should know one's way in the informal network, being invited rather than volunteering. One should belong to the tennis club. All in all, one should respect what someone called "the strict rules for being a nice person."

This romantic picture, however, has recently been disturbed by outside influences. First, market conditions have changed, and TKB finds itself in an unfamiliar competitive situation with other European suppliers. Costs had to be cut and human resources reduced. In the TKB tradition, this problem was resolved, without collective layoffs, through early retirement. However, the old-timers who had to leave prematurely were shocked that the company didn't need them anymore. Second, TKB has been severely attacked by environmentalists because of its pollution, a criticism that has received growing support in political circles. It is not impossible that the licenses necessary for TKB's operation will one day be withdrawn. TKB's management tries to counter this problem with an active lobby with the authorities, with a press campaign, and through organizing public visits to the company, but its success is by no means certain. Inside TKB, this threat is belittled. People are unable to imagine that one day there may be no more TKB. "Our management has always found a solution. There will be a solution now." In the meantime, attempts are made to increase TKB's competitiveness through quality improvement and product diversification. These also imply the introduction of new people from the outside. These new trends, however, clash with TKB's traditional culture.

The DLM Case

DLM is a European airline company that in the early 1980s went through a spectacular turnaround. Under the leadership of a new president the company switched from a product-and-technology to a market-and-service orientation. Before, planning and sales had been based on realizing a maximum number of flight hours with the most modern equipment available. Pilots, technicians, and disciplinarian managers were the company's heroes. Deteriorating results forced the reorganization. The president recognized that in the highly competitive air transport market, success depended on catering to the needs of current and potential customers. These needs should be best known by the employees with face-to-face customer contact. In the old situation these people had never been asked for their opinions; they were a disciplined set of uniformed soldiers, trained to follow the rules. Now they were considered to be "on the firing line," and the organization was restructured to support them rather than to order them around. Superiors became advisers; those on the firing line were granted a lot of discretion in dealing with customer problems on the spot and checking with superiors only after the fact—this implied acceptance of employees' judgment, with all risks that entailed.

One of the units participating in the study is DLM's passenger terminal at its main station. The interviews were conducted 3 years after the turnaround. The employees and managers are uniformed, disciplined, formal, and punctual. They seem to be the kind of people who like to work in a disciplined structure. People work shift hours, and periods of tremendous work pressure alternate with periods of relative inactivity. They show considerable acceptance of their new role. Talking about the company's history, they tend not to go back to before the reorganization; only some managers do. They are proud of the company; their identity is to a large extent derived from it, and social relationships outside the work situation are frequently with other DLM-ers. The president is often mentioned as a company hero. In spite of the discipline, relationships between colleagues tend to be good-natured, and there is a lot of mutual help. A colleague who meets with a crisis in his or her private life is supported by others and by the company. Managers of various levels are visible and accessible, although more managers than nonmanagers have trouble accepting the new role. New employees enter via a formal introduction and training program that includes simulated encounters with problem clients. This serves also as a screening device, to determine whether newcomers have the values and the skills necessary for this profession. Those who pass feel at home in the department quickly. The employees demonstrate a problem-solving attitude toward clients: They show considerable excitement about original ways to resolve customers' problems, in which some rules can be twisted to achieve desired results. Promotion is from the ranks and is felt to be on the basis of competence and collegiality.

It is not unlikely that this department, in particular, benefited from a certain "Hawthorne effect" because of the key role it had played in a successful turnaround. At the time of the interviews, the euphoria of the successful turnaround was probably at its highest tide. Observers from inside the company commented that people's values had not really changed but that the turnaround had transformed a discipline of obedience toward superiors into a discipline of service toward customers.

Appendix 8

The Author's Values

In Chapter 1, I stated that research into values cannot be value-free. In fact, few human activities can be value-free. This book reflects not only the values of IBM employees and IMEDE course participants but, between the lines, the values of its author. It will, I hope, be read by readers with a variety of different values. In this appendix I will try as best I can to be explicit about my own value system.

First, in terms of some of the measures used in this book, here is how I would rate various "work goals" (questions A5-A18 and C1-C8):

1. Of utmost importance to me: freedom (A13), personal time (A18)

2. Very important: challenge (A5), desirable area (A6), cooperation (A8)

3. Of moderate importance: earnings (A7), recognition (A11), physical conditions (A12), employment security (A14), manager (A16), position security (C1), efficient department (C2), contribute to "company" (C3), friendly atmosphere (C6), up-to-dateness (C7), and learning (C8)

4. Of little importance: training (A9), benefits (A10), advancement (A15), use of skills (A17)

5. Of very little or no importance: successful "company" (C4) and modern "company" (C5)

My "preferred manager" (question A54) is 3, the consultative boss.

Among the "general beliefs," I *strongly agree* with B58, "A corporation should do as much as it can to help solve society's problems (poverty, discrimination, pollution, etc.)." I *agree* with B52 ("A corporation should have a major responsibility for the health and welfare of its employees and their immediate families") and B56 ("Employees in industry should participate more in the decisions made by management").

I *disagree* with B59 ("Staying with one company for a long time is usually the best way to get ahead in business"), B61 ("Most employees in industry prefer to avoid responsibility, have little

ambition, and want security above all"), C9 ("A good manager gives his employees detailed and complete instructions, etc."), C10 ("Most companies have a genuine interest in the welfare of their employees"), C13 ("There are few qualities in a man more admirable than dedication and loyalty to his company"), C18 ("Even if an employee may feel he deserves a salary increase, he should not ask his manager for it"), and C19 ("The private life of an employee is properly a matter of direct concern to his company"). I *strongly disagree* with B55 ("Employees lose respect for a manager who asks them for their advice, etc."), B60 ("Company rules should not be broken, etc."), and C13 ("Most employees have an inherent dislike of work and will avoid it if they can"). I am undecided on the other "beliefs" (B53, B57, C11, C14, C15, C16, C17).

The origins of my value system, like everyone else's, are found in my national background, social class, family roots, education, and life experience. I was born in the Netherlands in 1928 and lived there until 1971. I was the youngest of three children of a high-ranking civil servant. Our family relationships were reasonably harmonious; my father had a modest but fixed income, so that we did not suffer from the 1930s economic crisis. There was enough of everything but not luxury; money was unimportant and rarely spoken of. What was important was knowledge and intellectual exercise, at which we were all quite good. I went to regular state schools and liked them. We lived through the German occupation (1940-45) without physical suffering but detesting the occupiers. I was too young at the time to understand the full scope of the ethical issues involved in Nazism, but I had seen my Jewish schoolmates being deported never to return. Only in the years after 1945 did I fully realize that for 5 years we had lived under a system in which everything I held for white was called black and vice versa; this made me more conscious of what were *my* values, and that it is sometimes necessary to take explicit positions. I completed a university education in the Netherlands and after that worked for half a year incognito as an industrial worker; thus I learned to some extent how an organization looks from below. I am a Protestant Christian but I do not claim absolute truth for my faith: I know too well how conditioned we all are by our cultural environment. I believe in the equality to God of all humankind, and my image of the ideal world is one without fear. I am married and we have four sons; as should be clear from my "work goals" scores described above, our family life is essential to me. It contains a certain tension between respecting each other's integrity and independence (including the children's) and at the same time maintaining close emotional links and liking to do things together. I hope our children will continue to go on well together without us. The distribution of gender roles in our family is rather classical; my wife has a university education and a broad intellectual interest, but so far has never built up any

continuous career of her own. She has carried the main burden of educational and household chores and followed the geographic moves dictated by my successive jobs.

Note

The text of this appendix is taken almost verbatim from the 1980 edition of *Culture's Consequences*. After 20 more years of life experience and world events, I might now choose different formulations here and there, but the important thing is that these were my values as I expressed them when the study was first conceived.

References

Years of first publication

Before 1960:	127 entries
1960-69:	157 entries
1970-79:	376 entries
1980-89:	334 entries
1990 or later:	543 entries

Aberbach, J. D., & Putnam, R. D. (1977). *Paths to the top: The origins and careers of political and administrative elites.* Ann Arbor: University of Michigan Press.

Aberle, D. F., Cohen, A. K., Davis, A. K., Levy, M. J., Jr., & Sutton, F. X. (1950). The functional prerequisites of a society. *Ethics, 60*(2), 100-111.

Abramson, P. R., & Pinkerton, S. D. (1995). *With pleasure: Thoughts on the nature of human sexuality.* New York: Oxford University Press.

Adebayo, A. (1988). The masculine side of Planned Parenthood: An explanatory analysis. *Journal of Comparative Family Studies, 19,* 55-67.

Adelman, I., & Morris, C. T. (1967). *Society, politics and economic development: A quantitative approach.* Baltimore: Johns Hopkins University Press.

Adizes, I. (1971). *Industrial democracy: Yugoslav style.* New York: Free Press.

Adler, N. J. (1984). Understanding the ways of understanding: Cross-cultural management methodology reviewed. *Advances in International Comparative Management, 1,* 31-67.

Adler, N. J. (1991). *International dimensions of organizational behavior.* Boston: Kent.

Adler, N. J., Campbell, N., & Laurent, A. (1989). In search of appropriate methodology: From outside the People's Republic of China looking in. *Journal of International Business Studies, 20,* 61-74.

Adler, N. J., & Graham, J. L. (1989). Cross-cultural interaction: The international comparison fallacy? *Journal of International Business Studies, 20,* 515-537.

Adorno, T. W., Frenkel-Brunswik, E., Levinson, D. J., & Sanford, R. N. (1950). *The authoritarian personality.* New York: Harper & Row.

Albers, N. D. (1994). *Relating Hofstede's dimensions of culture to international variations in print advertisements: A comparison of appeals.* Unpublished doctoral dissertation, University of Houston.

Albert, E. M. (1968). Value systems. In D. L. Sills (Ed.), *International encyclopedia of the social sciences* (Vol. 16). New York: Macmillan.

Albert, R. (1983). The intercultural sensitizer or culture assimilator: A cognitive approach. In D. Landis & R. W. Brislin (Eds.), *Handbook of intercultural training: Vol. 2. Issues in training methodology* (pp. 186-217). Elmsford, NY: Pergamon.

Alden, D. L., Hoyer, W. D., & Lee, C. (1993). Identifying global and culture-specific dimensions of humor in advertising: A multinational analysis. *Journal of Marketing, 57*(2), 64-75.

Alitto, G. S. (1986). *The last Confucian: Liang Shuming and the Chinese dilemma of modernity* (2nd ed.). Berkeley: University of California Press.

Allport, G. W. (1979). *The nature of prejudice.* Reading, MA: Addison-Wesley. (Original work published 1954)

Almond, G. A., & Verba, S. (1963). *The civic culture: Political attitudes and democracy in five nations.* Princeton, NJ: Princeton University Press.

Anderson, B. R. (1972). The idea of power in Javanese culture. In C. Holt (Ed.), *Culture and politics in Indonesia.* Ithaca, NY: Cornell University.

Andersson, L., & Hofstede, G. (1984). *The effectiveness of expatriates: Report on a feasibility study.*

Tilburg, Netherlands: Institute for Research on Intercultural Cooperation.

Anholt, S. (2000). *Another one bites the grass: Making sense of international advertising.* New York: John Wiley.

Anthony, R. N. (1988). *The management control function.* Boston: Harvard Business School Press.

ANWB. (1975). *ANWB handbook.* The Hague: Koninklijke Nederlandsche Toeristenbond ANWB.

Arbose, J. R. (1980). The changing life values of today's executive. *International Management, 35*(7), 12-19.

Argyle, M., Henderson, M., Bond, M., Iizuka, Y., & Contarello, A. (1986). Cross-cultural variations in relationship rules. *International Journal of Psychology, 21,* 287-315.

Argyris, C., & Schön, D. A. (1974). *Theory in practice: Increasing professional effectiveness.* San Francisco: Jossey-Bass.

Ariès, P. (1973). *L'enfant et la vie familiale sous l'Ancien Régime.* Paris: Seuil.

Aristotle. (1962). *The politics* (T. A. Sinclair, Trans.). Harmondsworth, Middlesex: Penguin.

Armstrong, R. W. (1996). The relationship between culture and perception of ethical problems in international marketing. *Journal of Business Ethics, 15,* 1199-1208.

Arnold, D. F., Sr., Bernardi, R. A., & Neidermeyer, P. E. (1998). *The effect of client integrity, culture, and litigation on European materiality estimates.* Unpublished manuscript, Union College, Schnectady, NY.

Aron, R. (1965). *Democratie et totalitarisme.* Paris: Gallimard.

Aron, R. (1967). *Main currents in sociological thought: Vol. 2. Durkheim, Pareto, Weber.* Harmondsworth, Middlesex: Pelican.

Aron, R. (1969). Two definitions of class. In A. Béteille (Ed.), *Social inequality: Selected readings.* Harmondsworth, Middlesex: Pelican.

Arrindell, W. A. (1998). Femininity and subjective well-being. In G. Hofstede & Associates, *Masculinity and femininity: The taboo dimension of national cultures* (pp. 44-54). Thousand Oaks, CA: Sage.

Arrindell, W. A., Hatzichristou, C., Wensink, J., Rosenberg, E., Van Twillert, B., Stedema, J., & Meijer, D. (1997). Dimensions of national culture as predictors of cross-national differences in subjective well-being. *Personality and Individual Differences, 23,* 37-53.

Asch, S. E. (1956). Studies of independence and conformity: A minority of one against a unanimous majority. *Psychological Monographs, 70*(9, Whole No. 416).

Ashkanani, M. G. A. (1984). *A cross-cultural perspective on work-related values.* Unpublished doctoral dissertation, U.S. International University.

Ashkanasy, N. M., & Holmes, S. (1995). Perceptions of organizational ideology following merger: A longitudinal study of merging accounting firms. *Accounting, Organizations and Society, 20,* 19-34.

Azumi, K. (1974). Japanese society: A sociological view. In A. E. Tiedemann (Ed.), *An introduction to Japanese civilization* (pp. 515-535). New York: Columbia University Press.

Baker, C. R. (1976). An investigation of differences in values: Accounting majors versus nonaccounting majors. *Accounting Review, 51,* 886-893.

Baker, H. D. R. (1979). *Chinese family and kinship.* London: Macmillan.

Bakke, E. W. (1950). *Bonds of organization: An appraisal of corporate human relations.* New York: Harper & Brothers.

Balandier, G. (1972). *Political anthropology.* Harmondsworth, Middlesex: Pelican.

Bales, R. F., & Couch, A. S. (1969). The value profile: A factor analytic study of value statements. *Sociological Inquiry, 39,* 3-17.

Bandura, A. (1986). *Social foundations of thought and action: A social cognitive theory.* Englewood Cliffs, NJ: Prentice Hall.

Bandyopadhyaya, J. (1978). Climate as an obstacle to development in the tropics. *International Social Science Journal, 30,* 339-352.

Bank, J., & Vinnicombe, S. (1995). Strategies for change: Women in management in the United Arab Emirates. In S. Vinnicombe & N. L. Colwill (Eds.), *The essence of women in management* (pp. 122-141). London: Prentice Hall.

Banks, P., & Waisfisz, B. (1993). Managing international teams: A practical approach to cultural problems. In H. Shaughnessy (Ed.), *Collaborative project management.* Chichester: John Wiley.

Bannock, G., Baxter, R. E., & Rees, R. (1972). *A dictionary of economics.* Harmondsworth, Middlesex: Penguin.

Barkema, H. G., Bell, J. H. J., & Pennings, M. (1996). Foreign entry, cultural barriers, and learning. *Strategic Management Journal, 17,* 151-166.

Barkema, H. G., & Vermeulen, F. (1997). What differences in the cultural backgrounds of partners are detrimental for international joint ventures? *Journal of International Business Studies, 28,* 845-864.

Barmeyer, C. I. (1996). *Interkulturelle Qualifikationen im deutsch-französischen Management kleiner und mittelständischer Unternehmen (mit Schwerpunkt Saarland/Lothringen).* St. Ingbert: Röhrig Universitätsverlag.

Barnard, C. I. (1960). *The functions of the executive.* Cambridge, MA: Harvard University Press. (Original work published 1938)

Barnouw, V. (1973). *Culture and personality.* Homewood, IL: Dorsey.

Barrett, G. V., & Franke, R. H. (1970). "Psychogenic" death: A reappraisal. *Science, 167,* 304-306.

Barrett, G. V., & Franke, R. H. (1971). *Psychological motivation and the economic growth of nations.* Rochester, NY: University of Rochester, Management Research Center.

Barry, H., Bacon, M. K., & Child, I. L. (1957). A cross-cultural survey of some sex differences in socialization. *Journal of Abnormal and Social Psychology, 55,* 327-332.

Barsoux, J. L., & Lawrence, P. (1990). *Management in France.* London: Cassell Educational.

Bartell, T. (1976). The human relations ideology: An analysis of the social origins of a belief system. *Human Relations, 29,* 737-749.

Bartol, K. M., & Butterfield, D. A. (1976). Sex effects in evaluating leaders. *Journal of Applied Psychology, 61,* 446-454.

Bartolomé, F., & Evans, P. A. L. (1979). Professional lives versus private lives: Shifting patterns in managerial commitment. *Organizational Dynamics, 7*(4), 2-29.

Bártová, E. (1976). Images of the woman and the family. In H. Ornauer, H. Wiberg, A. Sicinski, & J. Galtung (Eds.), *Images of the world in the year 2000: A comparative ten-nation study.* The Hague: Mouton.

Barzini, L. (1983). *The Europeans.* New York: Simon & Schuster.

Bass, B. M., & Burger, P. C. (1979). *Assessment of managers: An international comparison.* New York: Free Press.

Bass, B. M., & Franke, R. H. (1972). Societal influence on student perceptions of how to succeed in organizations. *Journal of Applied Psychology, 57,* 312-318.

Bateson, G. (1967). Style, grace and information in primitive art. In G. Bateson (Ed.), *Steps to an ecology of mind* (pp. 101-125). London: Paladin Granada.

Bateson, G. (1973). Morale and national character. In G. Bateson (Ed.), *Steps to an ecology of mind* (pp. 62-79). London: Paladin Granada. (Original work published 1942)

Bateson, M. C. (1994). *Peripheral visions: Learning along the way.* New York: HarperCollins.

Bearman, D. (1992). Diplomatics, Weberian bureaucracy, and the management of electronic records in Europe and America. *American Archivist, 55*(1), 168-181.

Beechler, S. L., & Pucik, V. (1989). The diffusion of American organizational theory in postwar Japan. In C. A. B. Osigweh, Yg. (Ed.), *Organizational science abroad: Constraints and perspectives* (pp. 119-134). New York: Plenum.

Beehr, T. A., & Bhagat, R. S. (1985). *Human stress and cognition in organizations: An integrated perspective.* New York: John Wiley.

Befu, H. (1971). *Japan: An anthropological introduction.* Tokyo: Charles E. Tuttle.

Bégué, J. (1976). Remarques sur une étude de l'OCDE concernant la répartition des revenus dans divers pays. *Economie et Statistique, 84,* 97-104.

Belden, T. G., & Belden, M. R. (1962). *The lengthening shadow: The life of Thomas J. Watson.* Boston: Little. Brown.

Bel Ghazi, H. (1982). *Over Twee Culturen: Uitbuiting en Opportunisme.* Rotterdam: Futile.

Bell, J. H. J. (1996). *Joint or single venturing? An eclectic approach to foreign entry mode choice.* Unpublished doctoral dissertation, Tilburg University.

Bell, M. P., & Harrison, D. A. (1996). Using intra-national diversity for international assignments: A model of bicultural competence and expatriate adjustment. *Human Resource Management Review, 6*(1), 47-74.

Bem, D. J. (1970). *Beliefs, attitudes, and human affairs.* Belmont, CA: Brooks/Cole.

Bem, S. L. (1974). The measurement of psychological androgyny. *Journal of Consulting and Clinical Psychology, 42,* 155-162.

Bem, S. L. (1975). Sex role adaptability: One consequence of psychological androgyny. *Journal of Personality and Social Psychology, 31,* 634-643.

Bendix, R. (1974). *Work and authority in industry: Ideologies of management in the course of industrialization.* Berkeley: University of California Press. (Original work published 1956)

Bendix, R., & Lipset, S. M. (Eds.). (1966). *Class, status and power: Social stratification in comparative perspective.* New York: Free Press.

Benedict, R. (1959). *Patterns of culture.* Boston: Houghton Mifflin. (Original work published 1934)

Benedict, R. (1974). *The chrysanthemum and the sword: Patterns of Japanese culture.* New York: New American Library. (Original work published 1946)

Beneken, J. E. W. (1993). The European scene of medical technology. *IEEE Engineering in Medicine and Biology, 12*(2), 44-48.

Benito, G. R. G., & Gripsrud, G. (1992). The expansion of foreign direct investments: Discrete rational location choices or a cultural learning process. *Journal of International Business Studies, 23,* 461-476.

Bennett, M. (1977a). Response characteristics of bilingual managers to organizational questionnaires. *Personnel Psychology, 30,* 29-36.

Bennett, M. (1977b). Testing management theories cross-culturally. *Journal of Applied Psychology, 62,* 578-581.

Berg, P. O. (Ed.). (1986). Organizational symbolism [Special issue]. *Organization Studies, 7,* 101-212.

Berger, B. (1971). *Societies in change: An introductory to comparative sociology.* New York: Basic Books.

Berger, P. L. (1990). *The sacred canopy: Elements of a sociological theory of religion.* Garden City, NY: Doubleday. (Original work published 1967)

Berger, P. L., & Luckmann, T. (1966). *The social construction of reality: A treatise in the sociology of knowledge.* Harmondsworth, Middlesex: Penguin.

Berry, B. J. L., Conkling, E. C., & Ray, D. M. (1993). *The global economy: Resource use, locational choice, and international trade.* Englewood Cliffs, NJ: Prentice Hall.

Berry, J. W. (1969). On cross-cultural comparability. *International Journal of Psychology, 4*, 119-128.

Berry, J. W. (1975). An ecological approach to cross-cultural psychology. *Nederlands Tijdschrift voor de Psychologie, 30*, 51-84.

Berry, J. W. (1976). *Human ecology and cognitive style: Comparative studies in cultural and psychological adaptation.* Beverly Hills, CA: Sage.

Berry, J. W. (1990). Imposed etics, emics, and derived etics: Their conceptual and operational status in cross-cultural psychology. In T. N. Headland, K. L. Pike, & M. Harris (Eds.), *Emics and etics: The insider/outsider debate* (pp. 84-99). Newbury Park, CA: Sage.

Berry, J. W., & Annis, R. C. (1974a). Acculturative stress: The role of ecology, culture, and differentiation. *Journal of Cross-Cultural Psychology, 5*, 382-406.

Berry, J. W., & Annis, R. C. (1974b). Ecology, culture and psychological differentiation. *International Journal of Psychology, 9*, 173-193.

Berry, J. W., Poortinga, Y. H., Segall, M. H., & Dasen, P. R. (1992). *Cross-cultural psychology: Research and applications.* New York: Cambridge University Press.

Berry, J. W., Segall, M. H., & Kagitçibasi, Ç. (Eds.). (1997). *Handbook of cross-cultural psychology: Vol. 3. Social behavior and applications.* Boston: Allyn & Bacon.

Berthoud, R. (1976). *The disadvantages of inequality: A study of deprivation.* London: Macdonald & Jane.

Besnard, P. (1976). Anti- ou ante-durkheimisme? *Revue Française de Sociologie, 17*, 313-341.

Best, D. L., & Williams, J. E. (1993). A cross-cultural viewpoint. In A. E. Beall & R. J. Sternberg (Eds.), *The psychology of gender.* New York: Guilford.

Best, D. L., & Williams, J. E. (1994). Masculinity/femininity in the self and ideal self descriptions of university students in fourteen countries. In A. M. Bouvy, F. J. R. Van de Vijver, P. Boski, & P. Schmitz (Eds.), *Journeys into cross-cultural psychology* (pp. 297-306). Lisse, Netherlands: Swets & Zeitlinger.

Best, D. L., & Williams, J. E. (1996). Anticipation of aging: A cross-cultural examination of young adults' views of growing old. In J. Pandey, D. Sinha, & D. P. S. Bhawuk (Eds.), *Asian contributions to cross-cultural psychology* (pp. 274-288). New Delhi: Sage.

Best, D. L., & Williams, J. E. (1998). Masculinity and femininity in the self and ideal self descriptions of university students in 14 countries. In G. Hofstede & Associates, *Masculinity and femininity: The taboo dimension of national cultures* (pp. 106-116). Thousand Oaks, CA: Sage.

Béteille, A. (1969). The decline of social inequality? In A. Béteille (Ed.), *Social inequality: Selected readings* (pp. 362-380). Harmondsworth, Middlesex: Penguin.

Béteille, A. (1977). *Inequality among men.* Oxford: Blackwell.

Bhagat, R. S. (1985). Acculturative stress in immigrants: A developmental perspective. In T. A. Beehr & R. S. Bhagat (Eds.), *Human stress and cognition in organizations: An integrated perspective.* New York: John Wiley.

Bhagat, R. S., Kedia, B. L., Crawford, S. E., & Kaplan, M. R. (1990). Cross-cultural issues in organizational psychology: Emergent trends and directions for research in the 1990s. In C. L. Cooper & I. Robertson (Eds.), *International review of industrial and organizational psychology* (pp. 55-99). New York: John Wiley.

Bhawuk, D. P. S., & Triandis, H. C. (1996). The role of culture theory in the study of culture and intercultural training. In D. Landis & R. S. Bhagat (Eds.), *Handbook of intercultural training* (2nd ed., pp. 17-34). Thousand Oaks, CA: Sage.

Bibby, G. (1965). *Four thousand years ago.* Harmondsworth, Middlesex: Penguin.

Bibó, I. (1986). The misery of the Eastern European small states. In I. Bibó, *Selected studies* (Vol. 2) [in Hungarian]. Budapest: Magvetô. (Original work published 1946)

Bidney, D. (1962). The concept of value in modern anthropology. In S. Tax (Ed.), *Anthropology today: Selections* (pp. 436-453). Chicago: University of Chicago Press.

Bierbrauer, G. (1994). Toward an understanding of legal culture: Variations in individualism and collectivism between Kurds, Lebanese, Germans. *Law and Society Review, 28*, 243-264.

Biggs, J. B. (1996). Approaches to learning of Asian students: A multiple paradox. In J. Pandey, D. Sinha, & D. P. S. Bhawuk (Eds.), *Asian contributions to cross-cultural psychology* (pp. 180-199). New Delhi: Sage.

Bigoness, W. J., & Blakely, G. L. (1996). A cross-national study of managerial values. *Journal of International Business Studies, 27*, 739-752.

Bilis-Bastos, K. F. (1998). *Inter-cultural conversion: An examination of cultural factors in 10-12 week international field educational placements.* Unpublished doctoral dissertation, Princeton Theological Seminary.

Bird, A., & Wiersema, M. F. (1996). Underlying assumptions of agency theory and implications for non-U.S. settings: The case of Japan. In P. A. Bamberger, M. Erez, & S. B. Bacharach (Eds.), *Research in the sociology of organizations: Vol. 14. Cross-cultural analysis of organizations* (pp. 149-180). Greenwich, CT: JAI.

Birnbaum, P. H., & Wong, G. Y. Y. (1985). Organizational structure of multinational banks in Hong Kong from a culture-free perspective. *Administrative Science Quarterly, 30*, 262-277.

Black, J. S., & Gregersen, H. B. (1991). The other half of the picture: Antecedents of spouse cross-cultural adjustment. *Journal of International Business Studies, 22,* 461-477.

Black, J. S., & Mendenhall, M. (1991). The U-curve adjustment hypothesis revisited: A review and theoretical framework. *Journal of International Business Studies, 22,* 225-247.

Blais, A. (1974). Power and causality. *Quality and Quantity, 8,* 45-64.

Blake, R. R., & Mouton, J. S. (1964). *The managerial grid.* Houston, TX: Gulf.

Blake, R. R., Mouton, J. S., Barnes, L. B., & Greiner, L. E. (1973). Breakthrough in organization development. In A. C. Bartlett & T. A. Kayser (Eds.), *Changing organizational behavior.* Englewood Cliffs, NJ: Prentice Hall.

Blanchflower, D. G., & Oswald, A. J. (1998). What makes an entrepreneur? *Journal of Labour Economics, 16*(1), 26-60.

Blau, P. M. (1960). Structural effects. *American Sociological Review, 25,* 178-193.

Bloom, B. S. (1964). *Stability and change in human characteristics.* New York: John Wiley.

Bloor, G., & Dawson, P. (1994). Understanding professional culture in organizational context. *Organization Studies, 15,* 275-295.

Blumberg, R. L., & Winch, R. F. (1972). Societal complexity and familial complexity: Evidence for the curvilinear hypothesis. *American Journal of Sociology, 77,* 898-920.

Blunt, P. (1992). East Africa strikes back: A rejoinder to "Inside East Africa, outside the research culture." *Organization Studies, 13,* 119-120.

Bochner, S. (1994). Cross-cultural differences in the self-concept: A test of Hofstede's individualism-collectivism distinction. *Journal of Cross-Cultural Psychology, 25,* 273-283.

Bochner, S., & Hesketh, B. (1994). Power distance, individualism-collectivism, and job related attitudes in a culturally diverse work group. *Journal of Cross-Cultural Psychology, 25,* 233-257.

Bocock, R. (1974). *Ritual in industrial society: A sociological analysis of ritualism in modern England.* London: George Allen & Unwin.

Boehnke, K., Scott, W. A., & Scott, R. (1996). Family climate as a determinant of academic performance: East Asian and Euro-American cultures compared. In J. Pandey, D. Sinha, & D. P. S. Bhawuk (Eds.), *Asian contributions to cross-cultural psychology* (pp. 119-137). New Delhi: Sage.

Bohannan, P. (1969). *Social anthropology.* London: Holt, Rinehart & Winston.

Bolton, R. (1994). Sex, science and social responsibility: Cross-cultural research on same-sex eroticism and sexual tolerance. *Cross-Cultural Research, 28,* 134-190.

Bond, M. H. (1983). How language variation affects intercultural differentiation of values by Hong Kong bilinguals. *Psychology, 2,* 57-66.

Bond, M. H. (1986). Mutual stereotypes and the facilitation of interaction across cultural lines. *International Journal of Intercultural Relations, 10,* 259-276.

Bond, M. H. (1988). Invitation to a wedding: Chinese values and economic growth. In D. Sinha & S. R. Kao (Eds.), *Social values and development: Asian perspectives* (pp. 197-209). New Delhi: Sage.

Bond, M. H. (1992). The process of enhancing cross-cultural competence in Hong-Kong organizations. *International Journal of Intercultural Relations, 16,* 395-412.

Bond, M. H., & Cheung, T. S. (1983). College students' spontaneous self-concept: The effect of culture among respondents in Hong Kong, Japan, and the United States. *Journal of Cross-Cultural Psychology, 14,* 153-171.

Bond, M. H., Leung, K., & Wan, K. C. (1982). How does cultural collectivism operate? The impact of task and maintenance contributions on reward distribution. *Journal of Cross-Cultural Psychology, 13,* 186-200.

Bond, M. H., & Smith, P. B. (1996). Cross-cultural social and organizational psychology. *Annual Review of Psychology, 47,* 205-235.

Bond, M. H., Wan, K. C., Leung, K., & Giacalone, R. A. (1985). How are responses to verbal insult related to cultural collectivism and power distance? *Journal of Cross-Cultural Psychology, 16,* 111-127.

Bond, M. H., & Wang, S. H. (1983). Aggressive behavior and the problem of maintaining order and harmony. In A. P. Goldstein & M. H. Segall (Eds.), *Global perspectives on aggression* (pp. 58-73). New York: Pergamon.

Bond, M. H., & Yang, K. S. (1982). Ethnic affirmation vs. cross-cultural accommodation: The variable impact of questionnaire language on Chinese bilinguals in Hong Kong. *Journal of Cross-Cultural Psychology, 13,* 169-185.

Bond, R., & Smith, P. B. (1996). Culture and conformity: A meta-analysis of studies using Asch's (1952, 1956) line judgment task. *Psychological Bulletin, 119,* 111-137.

Boring, E. G. (1968). Wundt, Wilhelm. In D. L. Sills (Ed.), *International encyclopedia of the social sciences* (Vol. 16, pp. 581-586). New York: Macmillan.

Boski, P., Van de Vijver, F. J. R., Hurme, H., & Miluska, J. (1999). Perception and evaluation of Polish cultural femininity in Poland, the United States, Finland, and the Netherlands. *Cross-Cultural Research, 33,* 131-161.

Bosland, N. (1985a). *The (ab)use of the Values Survey Module as a test of personality* (Working Paper 85-1). Tilburg, Netherlands: Institute for Research on Intercultural Cooperation.

Bosland, N. (1985b). *The cross-cultural equivalence of the power distance-, uncertainty avoidance-, individualism-, and masculinity measurement scales* (Working Paper 85-3). Tilburg, Netherlands: Institute for Research on Intercultural Cooperation.

Bosland, N. (1985c). *An evaluation of replication studies using the Values Survey Module* (Working Paper 85-2). Tilburg, Netherlands: Institute for Research on Intercultural Cooperation.

Bottomore, T. B. (1976). Equality or elites? In F. G. Castles, D. J. Murray, D. C. Potter, & C. J. Pollitt (Eds.), *Decisions, organizations and society: Selected readings* (pp. 405-422). Harmondsworth, Middlesex: Penguin.

Boulding, E., Nuss, S. A., Carson, D. L., & Greenstein, M. A. (1976). *Handbook of international data on women.* Beverly Hills, CA/New York: Sage/Halsted.

Boulding, K. E. (1978). *Ecodynamics: A new theory of societal evolution.* Beverly Hills, CA: Sage.

Boulding, K. E. (1985). *Human betterment.* Beverly Hills, CA: Sage.

Bourdieu, P. (1980). *Le sens pratique.* Paris: Éditions de Minuit.

Bourdieu, P., & Wacquant, L. J. D. (1992). *Réponses: pour une anthropologie réflexive.* Paris: Seuil.

Bovenkerk, F., & Brunt, L. (1976). *Binnenstebuiten en ondersteboven: De anthropologie van de industriële samenleving.* Assen, Netherlands: Van Gorcum.

Braudel, F. (1958). La longue durée. *Annales: Économies, Sociétés, Civilisations, 1958,* 725-753.

Brefeld, J. (1994). *A guidebook for the Jerusalem pilgrimage in the late Middle Ages: A case for computer-aided textual criticism.* Hilversum, Netherlands: Verloren.

Brislin, R. W. (1970). Back-translation for cross-cultural research. *Journal of Cross-Cultural Psychology, 1,* 185-216.

Brislin, R. W. (1993). *Understanding culture's influence on behavior.* Ft. Worth, TX: Harcourt Brace.

Brislin, R. W., Cushner, K., Cherrie, C., & Yong, M. (1986). *Intercultural interactions: A practical guide.* Beverly Hills, CA: Sage.

Brislin, R. W., & Horvath, A. M. (1997). Cross-cultural training and multicultural education. In J. W. Berry, M. H. Segall, & Ç. Kagitçibasi (Eds.), *Handbook of cross-cultural psychology: Vol. 3. Social behavior and applications* (pp. 327-369). Boston: Allyn & Bacon.

Brislin, R. W., & Pedersen, P. (1976). *Cross-cultural orientation programs.* New York: Gardner.

Brittan, A. (1977). *The privatised world.* London: Routledge & Kegan Paul.

Broms, H., & Gahmberg, H. (1983). Communication to self in organizations and cultures. *Administrative Science Quarterly, 28,* 482-495.

Brossard, M., & Maurice, M. (1974). Existe-t-il un modèle universel des structures d'organisation? *Sociologie du Travail, 4,* 402-426.

Broverman, I. K., Vogel, S. R., Broverman, D. M., Clarkson, F. E., & Rosenkrantz, P. S. (1972). Sex-role stereotypes: A current appraisal. *Journal of Social Issues, 28*(2), 59-78.

Brown, W. (1960). *Exploration in management.* London: Heinemann.

Brug, L. P. J. (1981). Hulp uit de hoogte: Ontwikkelingssamenwerking en cultureel conflict. *Intermediair, 17*(49), 25-29.

Bruins, J., Den Ouden, M., Depret, E., Extra, J., Gornik, M., Iannaccone, A., Kramarczyk, E., Melcher, W., Munoz, J., Ng, S. H., & Steller, B. (1993). On becoming a leader: Effects of gender and cultural differences on power distance reduction. *European Journal of Social Psychology, 23,* 411-426.

Bruinsma, J. F. (1995). *Kadi-rechtspraak in postmodern Nederland.* Inaugural address presented at Utrecht University.

Brunsson, N. (1985). *The irrational organization.* Chichester: John Wiley.

Bukkyo Dendo Kyokai. (1980). *The teaching of Buddha.* Tokyo: Author.

Burgess, K. (1995). Prospering in a global economy. *Journal of the Operational Research Society, 46,* 553-561.

Burkholder, R., Moore, D. W., & Saad, L. (1996). *Gender and society: Status and stereotypes.* Princeton, NJ: Gallup Organization.

Burns, T., & Stalker, G. M. (1961). *The management of innovation.* London: Tavistock.

Buruma, I. (1994). *The wages of guilt: Memories of war in Germany and Japan.* New York: Meridian.

Buss, D. M. (1989). Sex differences in human mate preferences: Evolutionary hypotheses tested in 37 cultures. *Behavioral and Brain Sciences, 12,* 1-49.

Buss, D. M. (1994). Mate preferences in 37 cultures. In W. J. Lonner & R. Malpass (Eds.), *Psychology and culture* (pp. 197-201). Needham Heights, MA: Allyn & Bacon.

Buss, D. M., et al. (1990). International preferences in selecting mates. *Journal of Cross-Cultural Psychology, 21,* 5-47.

Calori, R., Lubatkin, M., & Very, P. (1994). Control mechanisms in cross-border acquisitions: An international comparison. *Organization Studies, 15,* 361-379.

Calori, R., & Sarnin, P. (1991). Corporate culture and economic performance: A French study. *Organization Studies, 12,* 49-74.

Campbell, J. (1988). *Myths to live by.* New York: Bantam. (Original work published 1972)

Caplan, N., Choy, M. H., & Whitmore, J. K. (1992, February). Indochinese refugee families and academic achievement. *Scientific American,* pp. 18-24.

Caplan, N., & Nelson, S. D. (1973). On being useful: The nature and consequences of psychological research on social problems. *American Psychologist, 28,* 199-211.

Caplan, P. (1987). *The cultural construction of sexuality.* London: Tavistock.

Carr, S. C., Munro, D., & Bishop, G. D. (1996). Attitude assessment in non-Western countries: Critical modifications to Likert scaling. *Psychologia, 39,* 55-59.

Carroll, P. (1993). *Big blues: The unmaking of IBM*. New York: Crown.

Carver, C. S., Coleman, A. E., & Glass, D. C. (1976). The coronary-prone behavior and the suppression of fatigue on a treadmill test. *Journal of Personality and Social Psychology, 33*, 460-466.

Cascio, W. F. (1974). Functional specialization, culture and preference for participative management. *Personnel Psychology, 27*, 593-603.

Cattell, R. B. (1949). The dimensions of culture patterns by factorization of national characters. *Journal of Abnormal and Social Psychology, 44*, 443-469.

Cattell, R. B. (1953). A quantitative analysis of the changes in the culture pattern of Great Britain, 1837-1937, by P-technique. *Acta Psychologica, 9*, 99-121.

Cattell, R. B., Breul, H., & Hartman, H. P. (1952). An attempt at a more refined definition of the cultural dimensions of syntality in modern nations. *American Sociological Review, 17*, 408-421.

Cattell, R. B., & Gorsuch, R. L. (1965). The definition and measurement of national morale and morality. *Journal of Social Psychology, 67*, 77-96.

Cavalli-Sforza, L. L. (1987). Cultural evolution and genetics. In F. Vogel & K. Sperling (Eds.), *Human genetics* (pp. 24-33). Berlin: Springer-Verlag.

Cavalli-Sforza, L. L., & Cavalli-Sforza, F. (1995). *The great human diasporas: The history of diversity and evolution*. Reading, MA: Addison-Wesley.

Cavalli-Sforza, L. L., & Piazza, A. (1993). Human genomic diversity in Europe: A summary of recent research and prospects for the future. *European Journal of Human Genetics, 1*, 3-18.

Centers, R., & Bugenthal, D. E. (1966). Intrinsic and extrinsic job motivations among different segments of the working population. *Journal of Applied Psychology, 51*, 193-197.

Centre d'Etude des Revenus et des Coûts. (1976). La dispersion et les disparités de salaires en France au cours des vingt dernieres années. *Economie et Statistique, 80*, 83-89.

Chan, D. K. S., Gelfand, M. J., Triandis, H. C., & Tzeng, O. (1996). Tightness-looseness revisited: Some preliminary analyses in Japan and the United States. *International Journal of Psychology, 31*, 1-12.

Chandler, T. A., Shama, D. D., & Wolf, F. M. (1983). Gender differences in achievement and affiliation attributions: A five-nation study. *Journal of Cross-Cultural Psychology, 14*, 241-256.

Chandler, T. A., Shama, D. D., Wolf, F. M., & Planchard, S. K. (1981). Multiattributional causality: A five cross-national samples study. *Journal of Cross-Cultural Psychology, 12*, 207-221.

Chang, S. J., & Rosenzweig, P. M. (1998). Industry and regional patterns in sequential foreign market entry. *Journal of Management Studies, 35*, 797-822.

Chang, Y. N. (1976). Early Chinese management thought. *California Management Review, 19*(1), 71-76.

Chapman, M. (1997). Social anthropology, business studies, and cultural issues: Preface. *International Studies of Management and Organization, 26*(4), 3-29.

Chatman, J. A., & Jehn, K. A. (1994). Assessing the relationship between industry characteristics and organizational culture: How different can you be? *Academy of Management Journal, 37*, 522-553.

Chenery, H. B., & Strout, A. M. (1966). Foreign assistance and economic development. *American Economic Review, 56*(4), 679-733.

Cheng, C. (Ed.). (1996). *Masculinities in organizations*. London: Sage.

Chetwynd, J., & Hartnett, O. (1978). *The sex role system: Psychological and sociological perspectives*. London: Routledge & Kegan Paul.

Chew-Lim F. Y. (1997). *Evolution of organisational culture: A Singaporean experience*. Unpublished doctoral dissertation, University of Hong Kong, School of Business.

Chiasson, N., Dubé, L., & Blondin, J. P. (1996). Happiness: A look into the folk psychology of four cultural groups. *Journal of Cross-Cultural Psychology, 27*, 673-691.

Child, J., & Kieser, A. (1979). Organization and managerial roles in British and West-German companies: An examination of the culture-free thesis. In C. J. Lammers & D. J. Hickson (Eds.), *Organizations alike and unlike: International and inter-institutional studies in the sociology of organizations* (pp. 251-271). London: Routledge & Kegan Paul.

Chinese Culture Connection. (1987). Chinese values and the search for culture-free dimensions of culture. *Journal of Cross-Cultural Psychology, 18*, 143-174.

Chirot, D. (1994). *How societies change*. Thousand Oaks, CA: Pine Forge.

Chow, C. W., Kato, Y., & Merchant, K. A. (1996). The use of organizational controls and their effects on data manipulation and management myopia: A Japan vs US comparison. *Accounting, Organizations and Society, 21*, 175-192.

Christensen, E. W., & Gordon, G. G. (1999). An exploration of industry, culture and revenue growth. *Organization Studies, 20*, 397-422.

Clark, A. W., & McCabe, S. (1970). Leadership beliefs of Australian managers. *Journal of Applied Psychology, 55*, 1-6.

Cleverley, G. (1971). *Managers and magic*. Harmondsworth, Middlesex: Pelican.

Clyne, M. (1994). *Intercultural communication at work: Cultural values in discourse*. Cambridge: Cambridge University Press.

Cohen, A. (1974). *Two-dimensional man: An essay on the anthropology of power and symbolism in complex society*. London: Routledge & Kegan Paul.

Cohen, J. R., Pant, L. W., & Sharp, D. J. (1992). Cultural and socioeconomic constraints on international codes of ethics: Lessons from accounting. *Journal of Business Ethics, 11,* 687-700.

Cohen, P. (1973). *The gospel according to the Harvard Business School: The education of America's managerial elite.* Harmondsworth, Middlesex: Penguin.

Cole, M., Gay, J., Glick, J. A., & Sharp, D. W. (1971). *The cultural context of learning and thinking: An exploration in experimental anthropology.* London: Methuen.

Colijn, S. (1995). Het slechte(n) van een ivoren toren: psychotherapie en cultuurverschillen. *Systeemtherapie, 7*(3), 125-137.

Collett, P., & O'Shea, G. (1976). Pointing the way to a fictional place: A study of direction giving in Iran and England. *European Journal of Social Psychology, 6,* 447-458.

Collinson, D. L., & Hearn, J. (Eds.). (1996). *Men as managers, managers as men: Critical perspectives on men, masculinities and managements.* London: Sage.

Commission des Communautés Européennes (CCE). (1978). *Les attitudes de la population active à l'egard des perspectives de la retraite.* Brussels: European Economic Community.

Converse, P. (1972). Country differences in time use. In A. Szalai (Ed.), *The use of time.* The Hague: Mouton.

Cooper, C. L. (1982). [Review of the book *Culture's consequences*, by G. Hofstede]. *Journal of Occupational Behaviour, 3*(2), 123.

Cooper, R., & Cooper, N. (1982). *Culture shock! Thailand . . . , and how to survive it.* Singapore: Times Books International.

Coppock, R. (1977). Life among the environmentalists: An elaboration on Wildavsky's "Economics and environment/rationality and ritual." *Accounting, Organizations and Society, 2,* 125-129.

Cotta, A. (1976). An analysis of power processes in organizations. In G. Hofstede & M. S. Kassem (Eds.), *European contributions to organization theory* (pp. 174-192). Assen, Netherlands: Van Gorcum.

Cox, C. J., & Cooper, C. L. (1977). Developing organizational development skills in Japan and the United Kingdom: An experimental approach. *International Studies of Management and Organization, 6*(4), 72-83.

Craig, C. S., Douglas, S. P., & Grein, A. (1992). Patterns of convergence and divergence among industrialized nations: 1960-1988. *Journal of International Business Studies, 23,* 773-787.

Cronbach, L. J. (1970). *Essentials of psychological testing.* New York: Harper & Row.

Crowley, J. E., Levitin, T. E., & Quinn, R. P. (1973). Facts and fictions about the American working woman. In R. P. Quinn & T. W. Mangione (Eds.), *The 1969-1970 survey of working conditions.* Ann Arbor: University of Michigan, Institute for Social Research.

Crozier, M. (1964a). *The bureaucratic phenomenon.* Chicago: University of Chicago Press.

Crozier, M. (1964b, February). Le contexte sociologique des relations hiérarchiques. *Organisation Scientifique, 2,* 29-35.

Crozier, M. (1973). The problem of power. *Social Research, 40,* 211-228.

Crozier, M., & Friedberg, E. (1977). *L'acteur et le système: les contraintes de l'action collective.* Paris: Seuil.

Cushner, K., & Brislin, R. W. (1996). *Intercultural interactions: A practical guide* (2nd ed.). Thousand Oaks, CA: Sage.

Cushner, K., & Landis, D. (1996). The intercultural sensitizer. In D. Landis & R. S. Bhagat (Eds.), *Handbook of intercultural training* (2nd ed., pp. 185-202). Thousand Oaks, CA: Sage.

Cutler, B. D., Erdem, S., & Javalgi, G. (1997). Advertisers' relative reliance on collectivism-individualism appeals: A cross-cultural study. *Journal of International Consumer Marketing, 9*(3), 43-55.

Cutright, P. (1967). Inequality: A cross-national analysis. *American Sociological Review, 32,* 562-577.

Cutright, P. (1968). Occupational inheritance: A cross-national analysis. *American Journal of Sociology, 73,* 400-416.

Cyert, R. M., & March, J. G. (1963). *A behavioral theory of the firm.* Englewood Cliffs, NJ: Prentice Hall.

Czarniawska, B., & Wolff, R. (1986). How we decide and how we act: On the assumptions of Viking organization theory. In R. Wolff (Ed.), *Organizing industrial development* (p. 23). Berlin: Walter de Gruyter.

Czarniawska-Joerges, B., & Jacobsson, B. (1989). Budget in a cold climate. *Accounting, Organizations and Society, 14,* 29-39.

Dahl, R. A., & Tufte, R. (1974). *Size and democracy.* Stanford, CA: Stanford University Press.

Dahlén, T. (1997). *Among the interculturalists: An emergent profession and its packaging of knowledge.* Unpublished doctoral dissertation, University of Stockholm.

Dawar, N., & Parker, P. M. (1994). Marketing universals: Consumers' use of brand-name, price, physical appearance, and retailer reputation as signals of product quality. *Journal of Marketing, 58*(2), 81-95.

Dawar, N., Parker, P. M., & Price, L. J. (1996). A cross-cultural study of interpersonal information exchange. *Journal of International Business Studies, 27,* 497-516.

Deal, T. E., & Kennedy, A. A. (1982). *Corporate cultures: The rites and rituals of corporate life.* Reading, MA: Addison-Wesley.

Dean, D. G. (1961). Alienation: Its meaning and measurement. *American Sociological Review, 25,* 753-758.

de Bettignies, H. C., & Evans, P. L. (1977). The cultural dimension of top executives' careers: A comparative analysis. In T. D. Weinshall (Ed.), *Culture and* management. Harmondsworth, Middlesex: Penguin.

de Bettignies, L. A. (1976, November-December). Le choc de l'évenement ou l'inculpation d'un directeur d'usine. *Revue Française de Gestion*, pp. 118-125.

De Cock, G., Bouwer, R., De Witte, K., & De Visch, J. (1984). *Organisatieklimaat en-cultuur: theorie en praktische toepassing van de organisatieklimaatindex voor profit-organisaties (OKIPO) en de verkorte vorm (VOKIPO)*. Louvain, Belgium: Acco.

de Madariaga, S. (1928). Prefatory note, introduction and part 1. In S. De Madariaga, *Englishmen, Frenchmen, Spaniards: An essay in comparative psychology* (pp. vii-41). London: Humphrey Milford (Oxford University Press).

De Mooij, M. (1994). *Advertising worldwide: Concepts, theories and practice of international, multinational and global advertising*. Englewood Cliffs, NJ: Prentice Hall.

De Mooij, M. (1998a). *Global marketing and advertising: Understanding cultural paradoxes*. Thousand Oaks, CA: Sage.

De Mooij, M. (1998b). Masculinity/femininity and consumer behavior. In G. Hofstede & Associates, *Masculinity and femininity: The taboo dimension of national cultures* (pp. 55-73). Thousand Oaks, CA: Sage.

De Mooij, M. (2000). The future is predictable for international marketers: Converging incomes lead to diverging consumer behaviour. *International Marketing Review, 17*(3), 103-113.

De Mooij, M. (2001). *Convergence-divergence*. Unpublished doctoral dissertation, Universidad de Navarra.

Dempsey, P., & Dukes, W. F. (1966). Judging complex value stimuli: An examination and revision of Morris' paths of life. *Educational and Psychological Measurement, 26*, 871-882.

Denison, D. R. (1984). Bringing corporate culture to the bottom line. *Organizational Dynamics, 13*(2), 5-22.

Denison, D. R. (1996). What is the difference between organizational culture and organizational climate: A native's point-of-view on a decade of paradigm wars. *Academy of Management Review, 21*, 619-654.

Denison, D. R., & Mishra, A. K. (1995). Toward a theory of organizational culture and effectiveness. *Organization Science, 6*, 204-223.

Denmark, F. L., & Waters, J. A. (1977). Male and female in children's readers: A cross-cultural analysis. In Y. H. Poortinga (Ed.), *Basic problems in cross-cultural psychology*. Amsterdam: Swets & Zeitlinger.

Den Tex, N. (1992, November 19). Hoeveel arbeiders kost een directeur? [How many workers does a CEO cost?] *NRC Handelsblad*, p. 13.

Denzau, A. T:, & North, D. C. (1994). Shared mental models: Ideologies and institutions. *Kyklos: International Review for Social Sciences, 47*, 3-33.

Desplanques, G. (1973). A 35 ans, les instituteurs ont encore 41 ans à vivre, les manoeuvres 34 ans seulement. *Economie et Statistique, 49*, 3-19.

Deutscher, E. (1973). *What we say/what we do: Sentiments and acts*. Glenview, IL: Scott, Foresman.

De Vos, G. A., & Hippler, A. A. (1969). Cultural psychology: Comparative studies of human behavior. In G. Lindzey & E. Aronson (Eds.), *Handbook of social psychology* (Vol. 4). Reading, MA: Addison-Wesley.

Dhaouadi, M. (1990). Ibn Khaldûn: The founding father of Eastern sociology. *International Sociology, 5*, 319-335.

Dhawan, N., Roseman, I. J., Naidu, R. K., Thapa, K., & Rettek, S. I. (1995). Self-concepts across two cultures: India and the United States. *Journal of Cross-Cultural Psychology, 26*, 606-621.

Dia, M. (1996). *Africa's management in the 1990s and beyond: Reconciling indigenous and transplanted institutions*. Washington, DC: World Bank.

Diamond, M. (1993). Homosexuality and bisexuality in different populations. *Archives of Sexual Behavior, 22*, 291-310.

Dick, G. W. (1974). Authoritarian versus nonauthoritarian approaches to economic development. *Journal of Political Economy, 82*, 817-827.

Diderot, D. (1982). *Voyage en Hollande*. Paris: François Maspéro. (Original work published 1780)

Diener, E. (1996). Subjective well-being in cross-cultural perspective. In H. Grad, A. Blanco, & J. Georgas (Eds.), *Key issues in cross-cultural psychology* (pp. 319-330). Lisse: Swets & Zeitlinger.

Diener, E., & Diener, M. (1995). Cross-cultural correlates of life satisfaction and self-esteem. *Journal of Personality and Social Psychology, 68*, 653-663.

Diener, E., Diener, M., & Diener, C. (1995). Factors predicting the subjective well-being of nations. *Journal of Personality and Social Psychology, 69*, 851-864.

Dill, W. R. (1979). Issues and alternatives for industrial democracy. In G. Hofstede (Ed.), *Futures for work*. Leiden, Netherlands: Martinus Nijhoff.

Dinesen, I. (1942). *Winter's tales*. New York: Vintage.

Dinges, N. (1977). Interdisciplinary collaboration in cross-cultural social science research. *Topics in Culture Learning, 5*, 136-143.

Dion, K. K., & Dion, K. L. (1993). Individualistic and collectivistic perspectives on gender and the cultural context of love and intimacy. *Journal of Social Issues, 49*(3), 53-69.

d'Iribarne, P. (1989). *La logique de l'honneur: Gestion des entreprises et traditions nationales*. Paris: Seuil.

d'Iribarne, P. (1991). Culture et "effet sociétal." *Revue Française de Sociologie, 32*, 599-614.

d'Iribarne, P. (1994). The honor principle in the bureaucratic phenomenon. *Organization Studies, 15,* 81-97.

d'Iribarne, P. (1997). The usefulness of an ethnographic approach to the international comparison of organizations. *International Studies of Management and Organization, 26*(4), 30-47.

d'Iribarne, P. (1998). Comment s'accorder: Une rencontre franco-suédoise. In P. d'Iribarne, A. Henry, J. P. Segal, S. Chevrier, & T. Globokar (Eds.), *Cultures et mondialisation: gérer par-delà des frontières* (pp. 89-115). Paris: Seuil.

d'Iribarne, P., Henry, A., Segal, J. P., Chevrier, S., & Globokar, T. (Eds.). (1998). *Cultures et mondialisation: gérer par-delà des frontières.* Paris: Seuil.

Dogan, M. (1994). Use and misuse of statistics in comparative research: Limits to quantification in comparative politics. The gap between substance and method. In M. Dogan & A. Kazancigil (Eds.), *Comparing nations: Concepts, strategies, substance* (pp. 35-71). Oxford: Blackwell.

Dogan, M. (1998). The decline of traditional values in Western Europe: Religion, nationalism, authority. *International Journal of Comparative Sociology, 39*(1), 77-90.

Doi, T. (1971). *The anatomy of dependence: The key analysis of Japanese behavior.* Tokyo: Kodansha International.

Doré, F. Y. (Ed.). (1996). Abstracts of the XXVI International Congress of Psychology, Montreal, Canada, August 16-21 [Special issue]. *International Journal of Psychology, 31*(3-4).

Dorfman, P. W., & Howell, J. P. (1988). Dimensions of national culture and effective leadership patterns: Hofstede revisited. *Advances in International Comparative Management, 3,* 127-150.

Douglas, M. (1966). *Purity and danger: An analysis of the concepts of pollution and taboo.* London: Routledge & Kegan Paul.

Douglas, M. (1970, October 30). Environments at risk. *Times Literary Supplement,* pp. 1273-1275.

Douglas, M. (1973a). *Natural symbols: Explorations in cosmology.* Harmondsworth, Middlesex: Penguin.

Douglas, M. (1973b). *Rules and meanings: The anthropology of everyday knowledge. Selected readings.* Harmondsworth, Middlesex: Penguin.

Douglas, M. (1986). *How institutions think.* London: Routledge & Kegan Paul.

Douglas, M. (1996). *Thought styles.* London: Sage.

Douglas, M., & Wildavsky, A. (1982). *Risk and culture: An essay on the selection of technical and environmental dangers.* Berkeley: University of California Press.

Downey, H. K., Hellriegel, D., & Slocum, J. W. (1977). Individual characteristics as sources of perceived uncertainty variability. *Human Relations, 30,* 161-174.

Draguns, J. G. (1990). Culture and psychopathology: Specifying the nature of their relationship. In J. J.

Berman (Ed.), *Nebraska Symposium on Motivation: Vol. 37. Cross-cultural perspectives* (pp. 235-278). Lincoln: University of Nebraska Press.

Draguns, J. G. (1997). Abnormal behavior patterns across cultures: Implications for counseling and psychotherapy. *International Journal of Intercultural Relations, 21,* 213-248.

Drenth, P. J. D. (1985). Cross-cultural organizational psychology: Challenge and limitations. In P. Joynt & M. Warner (Eds.), *Managing in different cultures* (pp. 23-38). Oslo: Universitetsforlaget AS.

Drenth, P. J. D., & Groenendijk, B. (1984). Work and organizational psychology in cross-cultural perspective. In P. J. D. Drenth, J. Diederik, H. Thierry, P. J. Willems, & C. J. de Wolff (Eds.), *Handbook of work and organizational psychology* (pp. 1197-1229). Chichester: John Wiley.

Drever, J. (1952). *A dictionary of psychology.* Harmondsworth, Middlesex: Penguin.

Driver, H. E. (1973). Cross-cultural studies. In J. J. Honigmann (Ed.), *Handbook of social and cultural anthropology* (pp. 327-367). Chicago: Rand McNally.

Drucker, P. F. (1955). *The practice of management.* London: Mercury.

Dubin, R. (1956). Industrial workers' worlds: A study of the central life interests of industrial workers. *Social Problems, 3,* 131-142.

Dubin, R., & Champoux, J. E. (1977). Central life interests and job satisfaction. *Organizational Behavior and Human Performance, 18,* 366-377.

Dubin, R., Champoux, J. E., & Porter, L. W. (1975). Central life interests and organizational commitment of blue-collar and clerical workers. *Administrative Science Quarterly, 20,* 411-421.

Dubinsky, A. J., Jolson, M. A., Kotabe, M., & Lim, C. U. (1991). A cross-national investigation of industrial salespeople's ethical perceptions. *Journal of International Business Studies, 22,* 651-670.

Dudley, D. (1975). *Roman society.* Harmondsworth, Middlesex: Pelican.

Duijker, H. C. J., & Frijda, N. H. (1960). *National character and national stereotypes.* Amsterdam: North-Holland.

Dunbar, E. (1992). Adjustment and satisfaction of expatriate United States personnel. *International Journal of Intercultural Relations, 16,* 1-16.

Duncan, R. B. (1972). Characteristics of organizational environments and perceived environmental uncertainty. *Administrative Science Quarterly, 17,* 313-327.

Dunlap, R. E., Gallup, G. H., & Gallup, A. M. (1993). *Health of the planet.* Princeton, NJ: George H. Gallup International Institute.

Dunn, J. P., & Cobb, S. (1962). Frequency of peptic ulcer among executives, craftsmen and foremen. *Journal of Occupational Medicine, 4,* 343-348.

Dunphy, D., & Shi, J. (1989). A comparison of enterprise management in Japan and the People's Republic of China. In C. A. B. Osigweh, Yg. (Ed.),

Organizational science abroad: Constraints and perspectives (pp. 179-200). New York: Plenum.

Durkheim, E. (1930). *Le suicide: étude de sociologie.* Paris: Presses Universitaires de France. (Original work published 1897)

Durkheim, E. (1937). *Les règles de la méthode sociologique.* Paris: Presses Universitaires de France. (Original work published 1895)

Dwairy, M., & Van Sickle, T. D. (1996). Western psychotherapy in traditional Arabic societies. *Clinical Psychology Review, 16,* 231-249.

Earley, P. C. (1989). Social loafing and collectivism: A comparison of the United States and the People's Republic of China. *Administrative Science Quarterly, 34,* 565-581.

Earley, P. C. (1993). East meets West meets Mideast: Further explorations of collectivistic and individualistic work groups. *Academy of Management Journal, 36,* 319-348.

Earley, P. C. (1994). Self or group: Cultural effects of training on self-efficacy and performance. *Administrative Science Quarterly, 39,* 89-117.

Eckhardt, W. (1971). Conservatism, East and West. *Journal of Cross-Cultural Psychology, 2,* 109-128.

Edelmann, R. J., Asendorpf, J., Contarello, A., Zammuner, V., Georgas, J., & Villanueva, C. (1989). Self-reported expression of embarrassment in five European cultures. *Journal of Cross-Cultural Psychology, 20,* 357-371.

Edwards, L. (1978). Present shock, and how to avoid it. *Across the Board, 15,* 36-43.

Eibl-Eibesfeldt, I. (1976). *Der vorprogrammierte Mensch: Das Ererbte als bestimmender Faktor im menschlichen Verhalten.* Munich: Deutscher Taschenbuch Verlag.

Eibl-Eibesfeldt, I. (1988). *Der Mensch, das riskierte Wesen: Zur Naturgeschichte menschlicher Unvernunft.* Munich: Piper.

Eisenstadt, S. N. (1974). Cultural models and political systems. *European Journal of Political Research, 2,* 1-22.

Eisenstadt, S. N. (1981). Cultural traditions and political dynamics: The origins and modes of ideological politics. *British Journal of Sociology, 32*(2), 155-181.

Elangovan, A. R. (1995). Managerial conflict intervention in organizations: Traversing the cultural mosaic. *International Journal of Conflict Management, 6*(2), 124-146.

Eldering, L., & Kloprogge, J. (Eds.). (1989). *Different cultures, same school: Ethnic minority children in Europe.* Lisse, Netherlands: Swets & Zeitlinger.

Elias, N. (1980a). *Über den Prozess der Zivilisation: Soziogenetische und Psychogenetische Untersuchungen: Erster Band. Wandlungen des Vorhaltens in den Weltlichen Oberschichten des Abendlandes.* Frankfurt: Suhrkamp. (Original work published 1936)

Elias, N. (1980b). *Über den Prozess der Zivilisation: Soziogenetische und Psychogenetische Untersuchungen: Zweiter Band. Wandlungen der Gesellschaft; Entwurf zu einer Theorie der Zivilisation.* Frankfurt: Suhrkamp. (Original work published 1936)

Elias, N. (1987). The changing balance of power between the sexes: A process-sociological study: The example of the ancient Roman state. *Theory, Culture & Society, 4,* 287-316.

Ember, C. R. (1977). Cross-cultural cognitive studies. *Annual Review of Anthropology, 6,* 33-56.

Emerson, T. (1995, August 28). The rights of woman. *Newsweek,* pp. 20-26.

England, G. W., & Misumi, J. (1986). Work centrality in Japan and the United States. *Journal of Cross-Cultural Psychology, 17,* 399-416.

Erdener, C. B. (1991). Reconfiguring work-related values in a modernizing country: The village institutes of Turkey. *Advances in International Comparative Management, 6,* 57-79.

Erramilli, M. K. (1996). Nationality and subsidiary ownership patterns in multinational corporations. *Journal of International Business Studies, 27,* 225-248.

Escovar, L. A., & Escovar, P. L. (1985). Retrospective perception of parental child-bearing practices in three culturally different college groups. *International Journal of Intercultural Relations, 9,* 31-49.

Eshghi, A., & Sheth, J. N. (1985). The globalization of consumption patterns: An empirical investigation. In E. Kaynak (Ed.), *Global perspectives in marketing* (pp. 133-148). New York: Praeger.

Essau, C. A., & Trommsdorff, G. (1996). Coping with university-related problems: A cross-cultural comparison. *Journal of Cross-Cultural Psychology, 27,* 315-328.

Ester, P., Halman, L., & De Moor, R. (1993). *The individualizing society: Value change in Europe and North America.* Tilburg, Netherlands: Tilburg University Press.

Etzion, D., & Bailyn, L. (1994). Patterns of adjustment to the career family conflict of technically trained women in the United States and Israel. *Journal of Applied Social Psychology, 24,* 1520-1549.

Etzioni, A. (1975). *A comparative analysis of complex organizations: On power, involvement, and their correlates.* New York: Free Press.

Eurobarometer. (1980). *Public opinion in the European Community.* Brussels: European Commission.

Eurobarometer. (1990). *The perception of poverty in Europe.* Brussels: European Commission.

Eurobarometer. (1994). *Trends 1974-1994: Public opinion in the European Union.* Brussels: European Commission.

Eurobarometer. (1997). *Racism and xenophobia in Europe.* Brussels: European Commission.

Evan, W. M. (1977). Hierarchy, alienation, commitment, and organizational effectiveness. *Human Relations, 30,* 77-94.

Eyben, E. (1976). Musonius Rufus: ook vrouwen moeten filosofie studeren. *Hermeneus, Tijdschrift voor de Antieke Cultuur, 48*, 90-107.

Eysenck, H. J. (1953). Primary social attitudes: A comparison of attitude patterns in England, Germany, and Sweden. *Journal of Abnormal and Social Psychology, 48*, 563-568.

Eysenck, H. J. (1954). *The psychology of politics*. London: Routledge & Kegan Paul.

Eysenck, H. J. (1981, April 16). The four dimensions [Review of the book *Culture's consequences*, by G. Hofstede]. *New Society*.

Farberow, N. L. (Ed.). (1975). *Suicide in different cultures*. Baltimore: University Park Press.

Farmer, R. N., & Richman, B. M. (1965). *Comparative management and economic progress*. Homewood, IL: Irwin.

Father figures [Lifestyles special report]. (1996, September 12). *Far Eastern Economic Review*.

Faucheux, C. (1976). Cross-cultural research in experimental social psychology. *European Journal of Social Psychology, 6*, 269-339.

Faucheux, C. (1977). Strategy formulation as a cultural process. *International Studies of Management and Organization, 7*(2), 127-138.

Faucheux, C., Laurent, A., & Makridakis, S. (1976). Can we model the wild world or should we first tame it? In C. W. Churchman & R. O. Mason (Eds.), *World modeling: A dialogue* (pp. 109-115). New York: Elsevier North-Holland.

Fayol, H. (1970). *Administration industrielle et générale*. Paris: Dunod. (Original work published 1915)

Feather, N. T., & McKee, I. R. (1996). Global self-esteem and the fall of high achievers: Australian and Japanese comparisons. In J. Pandey, D. Sinha, & D. P. S. Bhawuk (Eds.), *Asian contributions to cross-cultural psychology* (pp. 200-213). New Delhi: Sage.

Feldman, A. S., & Moore, W. E. (1965). Are industrial societies becoming alike? In A. W. Gouldner & S. M. Miller (Eds.), *Applied psychology*. New York: Free Press.

Ferguson, I. R. G. (1973). *Management by objectives in Deutschland*. Frankfurt: Herder und Herder.

Fernandez, D. R., Carlson, D. S., Stepina, L. P., & Nicholson, J. D. (1997). Hofstede's country classification 25 years later. *Journal of Social Psychology, 137*, 43-54.

Festinger, L. (1957). *A theory of cognitive dissonance*. Evanston, IL: Row, Peterson.

Fiedler, F. E. (1967). *A theory of leadership effectiveness*. New York: McGraw-Hill.

Fiedler, F. E., & Chemers, M. M. (1974). *Leadership and effective management*. Glenview, IL: Scott, Foresman.

Fiedler, F. E., Mitchell, T., & Triandis, H. C. (1970). The culture assimilator: An approach to cross-cultural training. *Journal of Applied Psychology, 55*, 95-102.

Fioravanti, M., Gough, H. G., & Frere, L. J. (1981). English, French, and Italian adjective checklists: A social desirability analysis. *Journal of Cross-Cultural Psychology, 12*, 461-472.

Fishbein, M., & Ajzen, I. (1975). *Belief, attitude, intention, and behavior: An introduction to theory and research*. Reading, MA: Addison-Wesley.

Fisher, G. (1988). *Mindsets: The role of culture and perception in international relations*. Yarmouth, ME: Intercultural Press.

Fisher, R., & Ury, W. (1981). *Getting to yes: Negotiating agreement without giving in*. Harmondsworth, Middlesex: Penguin.

Fishman, J. A. (1974). A systematization of the Whorfian hypothesis. In J. W. Berry & P. R. Dasen (Eds.), *Culture and cognition*. London: Methuen.

Fiske, A. P. (1992). The 4 elementary forms of sociality: Framework for a unified theory of social relations. *Psychological Review, 99*, 689-723.

Fleishman, E. A., Harris, E. F., & Burtt, H. E. (1955). *Leadership and supervision in industry*. Columbus: Ohio State University, Bureau of Educational Research.

Foa, U. G., Anderson, B., Converse, J., Jr., Urbansky, W. A., Cawley, M. J., III, Muhlhausen, S. M., & Törnblom, K. Y. (1987). Gender-related sexual attitudes: Some cross-cultural similarities and differences. *Sex Roles, 16*, 511-519.

Foa, U. G., & Foa, E. B. (1974). *Societal structures of the mind*. Springfield, IL: Charles C Thomas.

Fonne, V. M., & Myhre, G. (1996). The effect of occupational cultures on coordination of emergency medical-service aircrews. *Aviation Space and Environmental Medicine, 67*, 525-529.

Ford, C. (1985). Women in management: The revolution that never happens. *Unilever Magazine, 56*(2), 14-18.

Form, W. (1979). Comparative industrial sociology and the convergence hypotheses. *Annual Review of Sociology, 5*, 1-25.

Forss, K., Carlsen, J., Frøyland, E., Sitari, T., & Vilby, K. (1988). *The effectiveness of technical assistance personnel*. Stockholm: Swedish International Development Agency.

Forss, K., Rolander, D., & Kverneland, A. (1982, December). *Some lessons from Swedish-Japanese business ventures*. Paper prepared for the 8th Annual Conference of the European International Business Association.

Forst, H. T., & Vogel, F. (1977). *Hierarchisch-agglomerative Klassifikation von Merkmalstraegern bzw. Merkmalen*. Kiel, Germany: Institut für Betriebswirtschaft.

Forster, E. M. (1936). *A passage to India*. London: Penguin. (Original work published 1924)

Foster, G. M. (1962). *Traditional cultures and the impact of technological change*. New York: Harper & Bros.

Foy, N. (1974). *The IBM world*. London: Eyre Methuen.

Franck, G. (1973). Epitaphe pour la D.P.O. *Le Management, 3,* 8-14.

Franke, R. H. (1997). Industrial democracy and convergence in economic performance: Comparative analysis of industrial nations in the 1970s and 1980s. *Research in the Sociology of Work, 6,* 95-108.

Franke, R. H., Hofstede, G., & Bond, M. H. (1991). Cultural roots of economic performance: A research note. *Strategic Management Journal, 12,* 165-173.

Freeman, M. (1995). Are there collective human rights? *Political Studies, 43,* 25-40.

Frémy, D., & Frémy, M. (1998). *QUID98: tout sur tout et un peu plus que tout.* Paris: Robert Laffont.

French, J. R. P., & Raven, R. (1959). The bases of social power. In D. Cartwright (Ed.), *Studies in social power* (pp. 150-167). Ann Arbor: University of Michigan, Institute for Social Research.

Frenkel-Brunswik, E. (1948). A study of prejudice in children. *Human Relations, 1,* 295-306.

Freud, S. (1963). *Sexuality and the psychology of love.* New York: Collier/Macmillan. (Original work published 1938)

Friday, R. A. (1989). Contrast in discussion behaviors of German and American managers. *International Journal of Intercultural Relations, 13,* 429-446.

Fridrich, H. K. (1965). *A comparative study of U.S. and German middle management attitudes.* Unpublished doctoral dissertation, Sloan School of Management.

Friedlander, F. (1965). Comparative work value systems. *Personnel Psychology, 18,* 1-20.

Friedman, M., & Rosenman, R. H. (1975). *Type A behavior and your heart.* Greenwich, CT: Fawcett.

Frijda, N., & Jahoda, G. (1969). On the scope and methods of cross-cultural research. In D. R. Price-Williams (Ed.), *Cross-cultural studies* (pp. 29-56). Harmondsworth, Middlesex: Penguin.

Fromm, E. (1965). *Escape from freedom.* New York: Avon.

Frost, P. J., Moore, L. F., Louis, M. R., Lundberg, C. C., & Martin, J. (Eds.). (1985). *Organizational culture.* Beverly Hills, CA: Sage.

Fryxell, G. E. (1992a). Inside story: Inside East Africa, outside the research culture. *Organization Studies, 13,* 111-117.

Fryxell, G. E. (1992b). Perils and pitfalls in cross-cultural evaluation: Thoughtful reflections on Blunt's rejoinder. *Organization Studies, 13,* 461-464.

Fukuyama, F. (1995). Social capital and the global economy. *Foreign Affairs, 74*(5), 89-103.

Furnham, A. (1993). Just world beliefs in 12 societies. *Journal of Social Psychology, 133,* 317-329.

Furnham, A., & Bochner, S. (1986). *Culture shock: Psychological reactions to unfamiliar environments.* London: Methuen.

Furnham, A., Bond, M. H., Heaven, P., Hilton, D., Lobel, T., Masters, J., Payne, M., Rajamanikam, R., Stacey, B., & Van Daalen, H. (1993). A comparison of Protestant work-ethic beliefs in 13 nations. *Journal of Social Psychology, 133,* 185-197.

Furnham, A., Kirkcaldy, B. D., & Lynn, R. (1996). Attitudinal correlates of national wealth. *Personality and Individual Differences, 21,* 345-353.

Furnham, A., & Ribchester, T. (1995). Tolerance of ambiguity: A review of the concept, its measurement and applications. *Current Psychology, 14*(3), 179-199.

Gallup, G. H. (1976). Human needs and satisfactions: A global survey. *Public Opinion Quarterly, 40,* 459-467.

Galtung, J. (1966). Rank and social integration: A multidimensional approach. In J. Berger, M. Zelditch, & B. Anderson (Eds.), *Sociological theories in progress* (pp. 145-198). Boston: Houghton Mifflin.

Galtung, J. (1981). Structure, culture and intellectual style: An essay comparing Saxonic, Teutonic, Gallic and Nipponic approaches. *Social Science Information, 20,* 817-856.

Gambling, T. (1977). Magic, accounting and morale. *Accounting, Organizations and Society, 2,* 141-151.

Gao, G., Ting-Toomey, S., & Gudykunst, W. B. (1996). Chinese communication processes. In M. H. Bond (Ed.), *The handbook of Chinese psychology* (pp. 280-293). Hong Kong: Oxford University Press.

Garfinkel, H. (1984). *Studies in ethnomethodology.* Cambridge: Polity.

Gaskov, V. M. (1985). *Sotsialnye problemi vzaimodeïstviya v mezhdunarodnich organizatsionnich sistemach* [The social problems of interaction in international business organizations]. Moscow: Mniipu (Irims).

Gaspari, C., & Millendorfer, J. (1978). *Konturen einer Wende: Strategien für die Zukunft.* Graz, Austria: Verlag Styria.

Gasse, Y. (1973). Contextual transposition in translating research instruments. *Meta* (Montreal), *18,* 295-307.

Gasse, Y. (1976). *Technological uniformity and cultural diversity in organizational structure.* Sherbrooke, Quebec: Faculté d'Administration, Université de Sherbrooke.

Geertz, C. (1968). *Islam observed: Religious development in Morocco and Indonesia.* Chicago: University of Chicago Press.

Geertz, C. (1973). *The interpretation of cultures: Selected essays.* New York: Basic Books.

Gelfand, M. J., Triandis, H. C., & Chan, D. K. S. (1996). Individualism versus collectivism or versus authoritarianism. *European Journal of Social Psychology, 26,* 397-410.

Georgas, J. (1989). Changing family values in Greece, from collectivist to individualist. *Journal of Cross-Cultural Psychology, 20,* 80-91.

Georgas, J. (1990). Intra-family acculturation of values in Greece. *Journal of Cross-Cultural Psychology, 21,* 378-398.

Georgas, J., Berry, J. W., Shaw, A., Christakopoulou, S., & Mylonas, K. (1996). Acculturation of Greek family values. *Journal of Cross-Cultural Psychology, 27,* 329-338.

George, K., & George, C. H. (1966). Roman Catholic sainthood and social status. In R. Bendix & S. M. Lipset (Eds.), *Class, status and power: Social stratification in comparative perspective.* New York: Free Press.

Gerritsen, M. (1995). Van rijksgrens naar dialectgrens: een onderzoek rondom de Nederlands-Duitse staatsgrens [From national to dialect boundary: A study on either side of the Dutch-German border]. In J. Cajot, L. Kremer, & H. Niebaum (Eds.), *Lingua Theodisca: Beiträge zur Sprach- und Literaturwissenschaft, Jan Goossens zum 65* (pp. 623-633). Münster, Germany: Lademacher & Geeraedts.

Gerth, H. H., & Mills, C. W. (1970). *From Max Weber: Essays in sociology.* London: Routledge & Kegan Paul. (Original work published 1948)

Gertsen, M. C., & Søderberg, A. M. (1998). Foreign acquisitions in Denmark: Cultural and communicative dimensions. In M. C. Gertsen, A. M. Søderberg, & J. E. Torp (Eds.), *Cultural dimensions of international mergers and acquisitions* (pp. 167-196). Berlin: Walter de Gruyter.

Ghauri, P., & Usunier, J. C. (Eds.). (1996). *International business negotiations.* Oxford: Pergamon.

Gherardi, S. (1995). *Gender, symbolism and organizational cultures.* London: Sage.

Gherardi, S., & Turner, B. (1987). *Real men don't collect soft data.* Trento, Italy: Università di Trento, Dipartimento di Politica Sociale.

Gibbons, F. X., Helweg-Larsen, M., & Gerrard, M. (1995). Prevalence estimates and adolescent risk behavior: Cross-cultural differences in social influence. *Journal of Applied Psychology, 80,* 107-121.

Gibbons, J. L., Richter, R. R., Wiley, D. C., & Stiles, D. A. (1996). Adolescents' opposite-sex ideal in 4 countries. *Journal of Social Psychology, 136,* 531-537.

Gibbons, J. L., Stiles, D. A., Schnellmann, J. de la G., & Morales-Hidalgo, I. (1990). Images of work, gender, and social commitment among Guatemalan adolescents. *Journal of Early Adolescence, 10*(1), 89-103.

Gibson, C. (1966). *Spain in America.* New York: HarperColophon.

Gibson, C. B. (1995). An investigation of gender differences in leadership across 4 countries. *Journal of International Business Studies, 26,* 255-279.

Gibson, J. L., & Caldeira, G. A. (1996). The legal cultures of Europe. *Law and Society Review, 30,* 55-85.

Glaser, W. A. (1971). Cross-national comparisons of the factory. *Journal of Comparative Administration, 3*(1), 83-117.

Glick, W. H. (1985). Conceptualizing and measuring organizational and psychological climate: Pitfalls in multilevel research. *Academy of Management Review, 10,* 601-616.

Globokar, T. (1989). Autres temps, autres lieux, ni père ni frère: Culture regional et autorité des contremaîtres dans une usine Yougoslave. *Annales des Mines, 16,* 78-86.

Godelier, M. (1978). Infrastructures, societies, and history. *Current Anthropology, 19,* 763-768.

Gohl, J. (1977). *Arbeit im Konflikt: Probleme der Humanisierungsdebatte.* Munich: Goldmann.

Goldman, J. G. D. (1994). Some methodological problems in planning, executing and validating a cross-national study of children's sexual cognition. *International Journal of Intercultural Relations, 18,* 1-27.

Goldmann, R. B. (1975). *Work values: Six Americans in a Swedish plant.* Unpublished manuscript.

Goldschmidt, W. (1966). *Comparative functionalism.* Berkeley: University of California Press.

Goldstein, H. (1987). *Multilevel models in educational and social research.* London: Charles Griffin.

Golembiewski, R. T. (1993). Organizational development in the Third World: Values, closeness of fit and culture-boundedness. *International Journal of Public Administration, 16,* 1667-1691.

Gonzalez, A. (1982). Sex roles of the traditional Mexican family: A comparison of Chicano and Anglo students' attitudes. *Journal of Cross-Cultural Psychology, 13,* 330-339.

Goodstein, L. D. (1981). Commentary: Do American theories apply abroad? *Organizational Dynamics, 10*(1), 49-54.

Goody, J. (1977). *The domestication of the savage mind.* Cambridge: Cambridge University Press.

Gordon, G. G., & DiTomaso, N. (1992). Predicting corporate performance from organizational culture. *Journal of Management Studies, 29,* 783-798.

Gordon, L. V. (1967). *Survey of Personal Values: Manual.* Chicago: Science Research Associates.

Gordon, L. V. (1975). *The measurement of interpersonal values.* Chicago: Science Research Associates.

Gordon, L. V. (1976). *Survey of Interpersonal Values: Revised manual.* Chicago: Science Research Associates.

Gorer, G. (1943). Themes in Japanese culture. *Transactions of the New York Academy of Sciences, 5,* 106-124.

Gorsuch, R. L. (1983). *Factor analysis.* Hillsdale, NJ: Lawrence Erlbaum.

Graham, J. L., Mintu, A. T., & Rodgers, W. (1994). Explorations of negotiation behaviors in 10 foreign cultures using a model developed in the United States. *Management Science, 40,* 72-95.

Grange, J. M. (1996). La fusion Renault-Volvo: un échec culturel. *Revue Française du Marketing, 2-3*(157-158), 77-87.

Granick, D. (1962). *The European executive.* Garden City, NY: Doubleday.

Graves, D. (1971, April). Vive la management difference. *Management Today*, pp. 81-83, 128.

Graves, D. (1972). The impact of culture upon managerial attitudes, beliefs and behaviour in England and France. *Journal of Management Studies, 9*, 40-56.

Gray, E. D. (1973). Masculine consciousness and the problem of limiting growth. In Committee on Merchant Marine and Fisheries of the House of Representatives (Ed.), *Growth and its implications for the future*. Washington, DC: Government Printing Office.

Gray, H. P. (1996). Culture and economic performance: Policy as an intervening variable. *Journal of Comparative Economics, 23*, 278-291.

Gray, S. J. (1988). Towards a theory of cultural influence on the development of accounting systems internationally. *Abacus, 24*(1), 1-15.

Gregg, P. M., & Banks, A. S. (1965). Dimensions of political systems: Factor analysis of a cross-polity survey. *American Political Science Review, 59*, 602-614.

Gregory, K. L. (1983). Native-view paradigms: Multiple cultures and culture conflicts in organizations. *Administrative Science Quarterly, 28*, 359-376.

Griswold, W. (1994). *Cultures and societies in a changing world*. Thousand Oaks, CA: Pine Forge.

Grosse, R. E., & Treviño, L. J. (1996). Foreign direct investment in the United States: An analysis by country of origin. *Journal of International Business Studies, 27*, 139-155.

Grunberg, L. (1981). *Failed multinational ventures: The political economy of international divestments*. Lexington, MA: Lexington.

Gudeman, S. (1986). *Economics as culture: Models and metaphors of livelihood*. London: Routledge & Kegan Paul.

Gudykunst, W. B. (1987). Cross-cultural comparisons. In C. R. Berger & S. H. Chaffee (Eds.), *Handbook of communication science* (pp. 847-889). Newbury Park, CA: Sage.

Gudykunst, W. B. (1989). Cultural variability in ethnolinguistic identity. In S. Ting-Toomey & F. Korzenny (Eds.), *Language, communication, and culture: Current directions* (pp. 222-243). Newbury Park, CA: Sage.

Gudykunst, W. B., & Bond, M. H. (1997). Intergroup relations across cultures. In J. W. Berry, M. H. Segall, & Ç. Kagitçibasi (Eds.), *Handbook of cross-cultural psychology: Vol. 3. Social behavior and applications* (pp. 119-161). Boston: Allyn & Bacon.

Gudykunst, W. B., Chua, E., & Gray, A. J. (1987). Cultural dissimilarities and uncertainty reduction processes. In M. L. McLaughlin (Ed.), *Communication yearbook 10* (pp. 448-471). Newbury Park, CA: Sage.

Gudykunst, W. B., Gao, G., Schmidt, K. L., Nishida, T., Bond, M. H., Leung, K., Wang, G., & Barraclough, R. A. (1992). The influence of individualism-collectivism, self-monitoring, and predicted-outcome value on communication in ingroup and outgroup relationships. *Journal of Cross-Cultural Psychology, 23*, 196-213.

Gudykunst, W. B., & Nishida, T. (1986). The influence of cultural variability on perceptions of communication behavior associated with relationship terms. *Human Communication Research, 13*, 147-166.

Gudykunst, W. B., & Ting-Toomey, S. (1988). *Culture and interpersonal communication*. Newbury Park, CA: Sage.

Gudykunst, W. B., Yang, S. M., & Nishida, T. (1987). Cultural differences in self-consciousness and self-monitoring. *Communication Research, 14*, 7-36.

Guilford, R. R. (1959). *Personality*. New York: McGraw-Hill.

Guillén, M. F. (1994). *Models of management: Work, authority, and organization in a comparative perspective*. Chicago: University of Chicago Press.

Guillet de Monthoux, P. (1984). *Marketing by obedience: Some notes on the normative paradigm for industrial marketing in Europe* (Discussion Paper 24). Lund, Sweden: University of Lund, Department of Business Administration.

Gurevich, A. (1995). *The origins of European individualism*. Oxford: Blackwell.

Guttman, L. (1968). A general normative technique for finding the smallest coordinate space for a configuration of points. *Psychometrika, 33*, 469-506.

Haas, M. (1969). Toward the study of biopolitics: A cross-sectional analysis of mortality rates. *Behavioral Science, 14*, 257-280.

Habib, S. (1995). Concepts fondamentaux et fragments de psychosociologie dans l'oeuvre d'Ibn-Khaldoun: Al-Muqaddima (1375-1377). *Les Cahiers Internationaux de Psychologie Sociale, 27*, 101-121.

Hagen, E. E. (1962). *On the theory of social change: How economic growth begins*. Homewood, IL: Dorsey.

Haire, M., Ghiselli, E. E., & Porter, L. W. (1966). *Managerial thinking: An international study*. New York: John Wiley.

Haley, K. H. D. (1988). *The British and the Dutch: Political and cultural relations through the ages*. London: George Philip.

Hall, E. T. (1965). *The silent language*. Greenwich, CT: Fawcett. (Original work published 1959)

Hall, E. T. (1976). *Beyond culture*. Garden City, NY: Anchor.

Hall, F. L. (1989). *Australians in a corporate culture: The national characteristics, are they intrinsic?* Unpublished doctoral dissertation, Macquarie University, Graduate School of Management.

Halman, L. (1991). *Waarden in de Westerse wereld: een internationale exploratie van de waarden in de Westerse samenleving*. Doctoral dissertation. Tilburg, Netherlands: Tilburg University Press.

Halman, L., & Petterson, T. (1996). The shifting sources of morality: From religion to post-materialism? In L. Halman & N. Nevitte (Eds.), *Political value change in Western democracies: Integration, values, identification, and participation* (pp. 261-284). Tilburg, Netherlands: Tilburg University Press.

Halman, L., & Vloet, A. (1994). *Measuring and comparing values in 16 countries of the Western world: Documentation of the European values study 1981-1990 in Europe and North America*. Tilburg, Netherlands: Work and Organization Research Centre.

Hamada, T. (1996). Unwrapping Euro-American masculinity in a Japanese multinational corporation. In C. Cheng (Ed.), *Masculinities in organizations* (pp. 160-176). Thousand Oaks, CA: Sage.

Hamilton, V. L., Blumenfeld, P. C., Akoh, H., & Miura, K. (1991). Group and gender in Japanese and American elementary classrooms. *Journal of Cross-Cultural Psychology, 22,* 317-346.

Hampden-Turner, C., & Trompenaars, F. (1997). Response to Geert Hofstede. *International Journal of Intercultural Relations, 21,* 149-159.

Han, S. P., & Shavitt, S. (1994). Persuasion and culture: Advertising appeals in individualistic and collectivistic societies. *Journal of Experimental Social Psychology, 30,* 326-350.

Haniff, G. M. (1976). Politics, development and social policy: A cross-national analysis. *European Journal of Political Research, 4,* 361-376.

Harbison, F. H., & Burgess, E. W. (1954). Modern management in Western Europe. *American Journal of Sociology, 60,* 15-23.

Harbison, F. H., & Myers, C. A. (1959). *Management in the industrial world: An international analysis.* New York: McGraw-Hill.

Harding, S., & Phillips, D. (with Fogarty, M.). (1986). *Contrasting values in Western Europe: Unity, diversity and change.* London: Macmillan.

Harpaz, I. (1990). The importance of work goals: An international perspective. *Journal of International Business Studies, 21,* 75-93.

Harris, M. (1977). *Cannibals and kings: The origins of cultures.* Glasgow: Fontana/Collins.

Harris, M. (1981). *America now: The anthropology of a changing culture.* New York: Simon & Schuster.

Harrison, G. L. (1992). The cross-cultural generalizability of the relation between participation, budget emphasis and job related attitudes. *Accounting, Organizations and Society, 17,* 1-15.

Harrison, G. L. (1993). Reliance on accounting performance measures in superior evaluative style: The influence of national culture and personality. *Accounting, Organizations and Society, 18,* 319-339.

Harrison, L. E. (1985). *Underdevelopment is a state of mind: The Latin American case.* Lanham, MD: Madison.

Harrison, R. (1972). Understanding your organization's character. *Harvard Business Review, 50*(3), 119-128.

Hartmann, H. (1973). Appraisal of "German management": Comments on a report by Booz, Allen & Hamilton. *International Studies of Management and Organization, 3*(1-2), 99-150.

Hartwich, D. (1996). Internationales Führungskräfte-Management: Erfahrungen in Internationalen Organisationen. In K. Macharzina & J. Wolf (Eds.), *Handbuch Internationales Führungskräfte-Management* (pp. 167-187). Stuttgart: Dr. Josef Raabe Verlags-GMBH.

Hartwich, D. (1998). Personnel management and organizational culture in European and international organizations. In C. Scholz & J. Zentes (Eds.), *Strategisches Euro-Management* (Vol. 2, pp. 268-290). Stuttgart: Schaffer-Poeschel Verlag.

Hartwich, D. (1999, February). *Managing multicultural staff: Experiences in international and European organisations.* Paper presented at the SIETAR Europe Conference, Trieste, Italy.

Harzing, A. W. K. (1995). The persistent myth of high expatriate failure rates. *International Journal of Human Resource Management, 6,* 457-474.

Harzing, A. W. K. (1997). Response rates in international mail surveys: Results of a 22-country study. *International Business Review, 6,* 641-665.

Harzing, A. W. K. (1999). *Managing the multinationals: An international study of control mechanisms.* Cheltenham, England: Edward Elgar.

Harzing, A. W. K., & Hofstede, G. (1996). Planned change in organizations: The influence of national culture. In P. A. Bamberger, M. Erez, & S. B. Bacharach (Eds.), *Research in the sociology of organizations: Vol. 14. Cross-cultural analysis of organizations* (pp. 297-340). Greenwich, CT: JAI.

Hastings, H. E., & Hastings, P. K. (1980). *Index to international public opinion 1979-1980.* Oxford: Clio.

Hastings, H. E., & Hastings, P. K. (1981). *Index to international public opinion 1980-1981.* Oxford: Clio.

Hatfield, E., & Rapson, R. L. (1995). *Love and sex: Cross-cultural perspectives.* Boston: Allyn & Bacon.

Hawes, F., & Kealey, D. J. (1979). *Canadians in development: An empirical study of adaptation and effectiveness on overseas assignment* (Technical report). Hull, Quebec: Canadian International Development Agency.

Hayward, M. L. A., & Hambrick, D. C. (1997). Explaining the premiums paid for large acquisitions: Evidence of CEO hubris. *Administrative Science Quarterly, 42,* 103-127.

Headland, T. N. (1990). Introduction: A discussion between Kenneth Pike and Marvin Harris on emics and etics. In T. N. Headland, K. L. Pike, & M. Harris (Eds.), *Emics and etics: The insider/outsider debate* (pp. 13-27). Newbury Park, CA: Sage.

Heberle, R. (1968). Tönnies, Ferdinand. In D. L. Sills (Ed.), *International encyclopedia of the social sciences* (Vol. 16, pp. 98-103). New York: Macmillan.

Heginbotham, S. J. (1975). *Cultures in conflict: The four faces of Indian bureaucracy*. New York: Columbia University Press.

Heidt, E. U. (1987). *Mass media, cultural tradition, and national identity: The case of Singapore and its television programmes*. Saarbrücken, Germany: Breitenbach.

Heller, F., Pusic, E., Strauss, G., & Wilpert, B. (1998). *Organizational participation: Myth and reality*. Oxford: Oxford University Press.

Helmreich, R. L., & Merritt, A. C. (1998). *Culture at work in aviation and medicine: National, organizational and professional influences*. Aldershot, England: Ashgate.

Hendrix, L. (1994). What is sexual inequality? On the definition and range of variation. *Cross-Cultural Research, 28,* 287-307.

Hennart, J. F., & Larimo, J. (1998). The impact of culture on the strategy of multinational enterprises: Does national origin affect ownership decisions? *Journal of International Business Studies, 29,* 515-538.

Henry, J. (1963). *Culture against man*. New York: Vintage.

Herbig, P. A., & Palumbo, F. (1994). The effect of culture on the adoption process: A comparison of Japanese and American behavior. *Technological Forecasting and Social Change, 46*(1), 71-101.

Herrick, J. S. (1973). Work motives of female executives. *Public Personnel Management, 2,* 380-387.

Herzberg, F., Mausner, B., Peterson, R., & Capwell, D. (1957). *Job attitudes: Review of research and opinion*. Pittsburgh, PA: Psychological Service of Pittsburgh.

Herzberg, F., Mausner, B., & Snyderman, B. B. (1959). *The motivation to work*. New York: John Wiley.

Hesiod. (1973). *Theogeny: Works and days*. Harmondsworth, Middlesex: Penguin.

Heuer, M., Cummings, J. L., & Hutubarat, W. (1999). Cultural stability or change among managers in Indonesia? *Journal of International Business Studies, 30,* 599-610.

Hicks, G. L., & Redding, S. G. (1983a). The story of the East Asian "economic miracle": I. Economic theory be damned! *Euro-Asia Business Review, 2*(3), 24-32.

Hicks, G. L., & Redding, S. G. (1983b). The story of the East Asian "economic miracle": II. The culture connection. *Euro-Asia Business Review, 2*(4), 18-22.

Hickson, D. J. (1996). The *ASQ* years then and now through the eyes of a Euro-Brit. *Administrative Science Quarterly, 41,* 217-228.

Hickson, D. J. (1998). A surprised academic: Learning from others while walking on thin ice. In A. G. Bedeian (Ed.), *Management laureates: A collection of autobiographical essays* (Vol. 5, pp. 93-128). Greenwich, CT: JAI.

Hickson, D. J., Hinings, C. R., Lee, C. A., Schneck, R. E., & Pennings, J. M. (1971). A strategic contingencies theory of intraorganizational power. *Administrative Science Quarterly, 16,* 216-229.

Hickson, D. J., Hinings, C. R., McMillan, C. J., & Schwitter, J. P. (1974). The culture-free context of organizational structure: A tri-national comparison. *Sociology, 8,* 59-80.

Hickson, D. J., McMillan, C. J., Azumi, K., & Horvath, D. (1979). Grounds for comparative organization theory: Quicksand or hard core? In C. J. Lammers & D. J. Hickson (Eds.), *Organizations alike and unlike: International and inter-institutional studies in the sociology of organizations* (pp. 25-41). London: Routledge & Kegan Paul.

Hickson, D. J., & Pugh, D. S. (1995). *Management worldwide: The impact of societal culture on organizations around the globe*. Harmondsworth, Middlesex: Penguin.

Hill, C., & Romm, C. T. (1996). The role of mothers as gift givers: A comparison across 3 cultures. *Advances in Consumer Research, 23,* 21-27.

Hines, G. H. (1973). The persistence of Greek achievement motivation across time and culture. *International Journal of Psychology, 8,* 285-288.

Hines, G. H. (1974). Achievement motivation levels of immigrants in New Zealand. *Journal of Cross-Cultural Psychology, 5,* 37-47.

Hines, G. H. (1976). Cultural influences on work motivation. In P. B. Warr (Ed.), *Personal goals and work design*. London: John Wiley.

Hines, T. (1987). Left brain/right brain mythology and implications for management and training. *Academy of Management Review, 12,* 600-606.

Hinings, C. R., Hickson, D. J., Pennings, J. M., & Schneck, R. E. (1974). Structural conditions of intra-organizational power. *Administrative Science Quarterly, 19,* 22-44.

Hippler, A. E. (1969). Fusion and frustration: Dimensions in the cross-cultural ethnopsychology of suicide. *American Anthropologist, 7,* 1074-1087.

Hjelholt, G. (1976). Europe is different: Boundary and identity as key concepts. In G. Hofstede & M. S. Kassem (Eds.), *European contributions to organization theory* (pp. 232-243). Assen, Netherlands: Van Gorcum.

Ho, D. Y. F. (1976). On the concept of face. *American Journal of Sociology, 18,* 867-884.

Ho, D. Y. F. (1978). The concept of man in Mao-Tse-Tung's thought. *Psychiatry, 41,* 391-402.

Ho, D. Y. F. (1979). Psychological implications of collectivism: With special reference to the Chinese case and Maoist dialectics. In L. Eckensberger, W. J. Lonner, & Y. H. Poortinga (Eds.), *Cross-cultural contributions to psychology* (pp. 143-150). Lisse, Netherlands: Swets & Zeitlinger.

Hobbes, T. (1973). *Leviathan or the matter, forme and power of a commonwealth ecclesiasticall and civil*. London: Dent, Everyman's Library. (Original work published 1651)

Hockett, C. F. (1954). Chinese versus English: An exploration of the Whorfian theses. In H. Hoijer (Ed.), *Language in culture* (pp. 106-123). Chicago: University of Chicago Press.

Hodgetts, R. M., & Luthans, F. (1993, March-April). U.S. multinationals' compensation strategies for local management: Cross-cultural implications. *Compensation and Benefits Review*, pp. 42-48.

Hoffman, R. C. (1987). Political versus rational sources of decision power among country clusters. *Journal of International Business Studies, 18*, 1-14.

Hofstede, G. (1964). Arbeidsmotieven van volontairs. *Mens en Onderneming, 18*, 373-391.

Hofstede, G. (1967). *The game of budget control*. Assen, Netherlands/London: Van Gorcum/Tavistock.

Hofstede, G. (1972). *A comparison of four instruments for measuring values* (Research Working Paper 1). Lausanne, Switzerland: IMEDE.

Hofstede, G. (1973). The importance of being Dutch: Nationaliteits- en beroepsverschillen in werkoriëntatie. In P. J. D. Drenth, P. J. Willems, & C. J. de Wolff (Eds.), *Arbeids- en organisatiepsychologie* (pp. 334-349). Deventer, Netherlands: Kluwer.

Hofstede, G. (1974a). *Experiences with England's Personal Values Questionnaire in an international business school* (Working Paper 74-3). Brussels: European Institute for Advanced Studies in Management.

Hofstede, G. (1974b). *Experiences with Fiedler's Least Preferred Co-Worker questionnaire in an international business school* (Working Paper 74-5). Brussels: European Institute for Advanced Studies in Management.

Hofstede, G. (1974c). *Experiences with Schutz's FIRO-B Questionnaire in an international business school* (Working Paper 74-22). Brussels: European Institute for Advanced Studies in Management.

Hofstede, G. (1975a). *Psephology in management or the art of using survey information* (Research Paper 147). Fontainebleau: INSEAD.

Hofstede, G. (1975b). *The stability of attitude survey questions: In particular those dealing with work goals* (Working Paper 75-45). Brussels: European Institute for Advanced Studies in Management.

Hofstede, G. (1976a). Alienation at the top. *Organizational Dynamics, 4*(3), 44-60.

Hofstede, G. (1976b). *The construct validity of attitude survey questions dealing with work goals* (Working Paper 76-8). Brussels: European Institute for Advanced Studies in Management.

Hofstede, G. (1976c). The importance of being Dutch: National and occupational differences in work goal importance. *International Studies of Management and Organization, 5*(4), 5-28.

Hofstede, G. (1976d). Nationality and espoused values of managers. *Journal of Applied Psychology, 61*, 148-155.

Hofstede, G. (1977a). *Cultural determinants of the avoidance of uncertainty in organizations* (Working Paper 77-18). Brussels: European Institute for Advanced Studies in Management.

Hofstede, G. (1977b). *Cultural determinants of the exercise of power in a hierarchy* (Working Paper 77-8). Brussels: European Institute for Advanced Studies in Management.

Hofstede, G. (1978). *Cultural determinants of individualism and masculinity in organizations* (Working Paper 78-4). Brussels: European Institute for Advanced Studies in Management.

Hofstede, G. (1980a). *Culture's consequences: International differences in work-related values*. Beverly Hills, CA: Sage.

Hofstede, G. (1980b). Motivation, leadership and organization: Do American theories apply abroad? *Organizational Dynamics, 9*(1), 42-63.

Hofstede, G. (1981a). Do American theories apply abroad? A reply to Goodstein and Hunt. *Organizational Dynamics, 10*(1), 63-68.

Hofstede, G. (1981b). Management control of public and not-for-profit activities. *Accounting, Organizations and Society, 6*, 193-211.

Hofstede, G. (1982). [Review of the books *Industrial democracy in Europe* and *European industrial relations*, by IDE International Research Group]. *European Journal of Operating Research, 11*(4), 198-200.

Hofstede, G. (1983a). *Cultural pitfalls for Dutch expatriates in Indonesia*. Deventer, Netherlands: Twijnstra Gudde International b.v.

Hofstede, G. (1983b). The cultural relativity of organizational practices and theories. *Journal of International Business Studies, 14*, 75-89.

Hofstede, G. (1983c). Dimensions of national cultures in fifty countries and three regions. In J. B. Deregowski, S. Dziurawiec, & R. C. Annis (Eds.), *Expiscations in cross-cultural psychology* (pp. 335-355). Lisse, Netherlands: Swets & Zeitlinger.

Hofstede, G. (1984a). Cultural dimensions in management and planning. *Asia Pacific Journal of Management, 1*(2), 81-99.

Hofstede, G. (1984b). *Culture's consequences: International differences in work-related values* (Abr. ed.). Beverly Hills, CA: Sage.

Hofstede, G. (1986a). Cultural differences in teaching and learning. *International Journal of Intercultural Relations, 10*, 301-320.

Hofstede, G. (Ed.). (1986b). Organizational culture and control [Special issue]. *Journal of Management Studies, 23*(3).

Hofstede, G. (1987). [Review of the book *Economics as culture*, by S. Gudeman]. *Organization Studies, 8*, 381-383.

Hofstede, G. (1988a). Maximumsnelheden, legitimatieplicht en retroactieve wetgeving: Wat is er met de Nederlandse cultuur aan de hand? In N. Roos (Ed.), *Eenheid en verscheidenheid van rechtsculturen en rechtssystemen* (pp. 19-25).

Maastricht, Netherlands: Maastricht University, Faculty of Law.

Hofstede, G. (1988b). McGregor in Southeast Asia? In D. Sinha & H. S. R. Kao (Eds.), *Social values and development: Asian perspectives* (pp. 304-314). New Delhi: Sage.

Hofstede, G. (1989a). Commentaar naar aanleiding van J. Th. Leerssen "Over nationale identiteit." *Theoretische Geschiedenis, 16,* 360-361.

Hofstede, G. (1989b). Cultural predictors of national negotiation styles. In F. Mautner-Markhof (Ed.), *Processes of international negotiations* (pp. 193-201). Boulder, CO: Westview.

Hofstede, G. (1989c). Organising for cultural diversity. *European Management Journal, 7,* 390-397.

Hofstede, G. (1991). *Cultures and organizations: Software of the mind.* London: McGraw-Hill.

Hofstede, G. (1993). *Images of Europe* (Valedictory address). Maastricht, Netherlands: Maastricht University, Faculty of Economics and Business Administration.

Hofstede, G. (1994a). The stress/satisfaction balance of occupations. In G. Hofstede (Ed.), *Uncommon sense about organizations: Cases, studies, and field observations* (pp. 51-66). Thousand Oaks, CA: Sage.

Hofstede, G. (Ed.). (1994b). *Uncommon sense about organizations: Cases, studies, and field observations.* Thousand Oaks, CA: Sage.

Hofstede, G. (1995). Multilevel research of human systems: Flowers, bouquets and gardens. *Human Systems Management, 14,* 207-217.

Hofstede, G. (1996a). An American in Paris: The influence of nationality on organization theories. *Organization Studies, 17,* 525-537.

Hofstede, G. (1996b). Gender stereotypes and partner preferences of Asian women in masculine and feminine cultures. *Journal of Cross-Cultural Psychology, 27,* 533-546.

Hofstede, G. (1996c). A hopscotch hike. In A. G. Bedeian (Ed.), *Management laureates: A collection of autobiographical essays* (Vol. 4, pp. 85-122). Greenwich, CT: JAI.

Hofstede, G. (1996d). Riding the waves of commerce: A test of Trompenaars' model of national culture differences. *International Journal of Intercultural Relations, 20,* 189-198.

Hofstede, G. (1997a). The Archimedes effect. In M. H. Bond (Ed.), *Working at the interface of cultures: Eighteen lives in social science* (pp. 47-61). London: Routledge.

Hofstede, G. (1997b). Riding the waves: A rejoinder. *International Journal of Intercultural Relations, 21,* 287-290.

Hofstede, G. (1998a). Attitudes, values and organizational culture: Disentangling the concepts. *Organization Studies, 19,* 477-492.

Hofstede, G. (1998b). *Entrepreneurship in Europe.* Maastricht, Netherlands: Studium Generale/House of Europe.

Hofstede, G. (1998c). Identifying organizational subcultures: An empirical approach. *Journal of Management Studies, 35,* 1-12.

Hofstede, G. (1998d). The internationalization of SIETAR International. In A. E. Fantini (Ed.), *Building bridges between continents: Keynote addresses from the SIETAR International XXIII Congress, Curaçao, Netherlands Antilles* (pp. 47-57). Putney, VT: SIETAR International.

Hofstede, G., & Associates. (1998). *Masculinity and femininity: The taboo dimension of national cultures.* Thousand Oaks, CA: Sage.

Hofstede, G., & Bond, M. H. (1984). Hofstede's culture dimensions: An independent validation using Rokeach's value survey. *Journal of Cross-Cultural Psychology, 15,* 417-433.

Hofstede, G., & Bond, M. H. (1988). The Confucius connection: From cultural roots to economic growth. *Organizational Dynamics, 16*(4), 4-21.

Hofstede, G., Bond, M. H., & Luk, C.-L. (1993). Individual perceptions of organizational cultures: A methodological treatise on levels of analysis. *Organization Studies, 14,* 483-503.

Hofstede, G., & Kassem, M. S. (Eds.). (1976). *European contributions to organization theory.* Assen, Netherlands: Van Gorcum.

Hofstede, G., Kolman, L., Nicolescu, O., & Pajumaa, I. (1996). Characteristics of the ideal job among students in eight countries. In H. Grad, A. Blanco, & J. Georgas (Eds.), *Key issues in cross-cultural psychology* (pp. 199-216). Lisse, Netherlands: Swets & Zeitlinger.

Hofstede, G., & Kranenburg, R. Y. (1974). Work goals of migrant workers. *Human Relations, 27,* 83-99.

Hofstede, G., Kraut, A. I., & Simonetti, S. H. (1976). *The development of a core attitude survey questionnaire for international use* (Working Paper 76-16). Brussels: European Institute for Advanced Studies in Management.

Hofstede, G., Neuijen, B., Ohayv, D. D., & Sanders, G. (1990). Measuring organizational cultures: A qualitative and quantitative study across twenty cases. *Administrative Science Quarterly, 35,* 286-316.

Hofstede, G., & Spangenberg, J. (1987). *Measuring individualism and collectivism at occupational and organizational levels.* In Ç. Kagitçibasi (Ed.), *Growth and progress in cross-cultural psychology* (pp. 113-122). Lisse, Netherlands: Swets & Zeitlinger.

Hofstede, G., & Van Hoesel, P. (1976). *Within-culture and between-culture component structures of work goals in a heterogeneous population* (Working Paper 76-26). Brussels: European Institute for Advanced Studies in Management.

Hofstede, G., & Vunderink, M. (1994). A case study in masculinity/femininity differences: American students in the Netherlands vs. local students. In A. M. Bouvy, F. J. R. Van de Vijver, P. Boski, & P. Schmitz (Eds.), *Journeys into cross-cultural psychology* (pp. 329-347). Lisse, Netherlands: Swets & Zeitlinger.

Hofstede, G. J. (1992). *Modesty in modelling: On the applicability of interactive planning systems, with a case study in pot plant cultivation.* Doctoral dissertation, Wageningen Agricultural University. Amsterdam: Thesis Publishers.

Hofstede, G. J. (1995). Open problems, formal problems. *Revue des Systèmes de Décision, 4*(2), 155-165.

Hogan, R. (1992). Personality and personality measurement. In M. D. Dunnette & L. M. Hough (Eds.), *Handbook of industrial and organizational psychology.* Palo Alto, CA: Consulting Psychologists Press.

Hogan, R. T., & Emler, N. P. (1978). The biases in contemporary social psychology. *Social Research, 45,* 478-534.

Hoijer, H. (1962). The relation of language to culture. In S. Tax (Ed.), *Anthropology today: Selections* (pp. 258-277). Chicago: University of Chicago Press.

Holmes, T. H., & Rahe, R. H. (1967). The social readjustment rating scale. *Journal of Psychosomatic Research, 11,* 213-218.

Homer. (1980). *The Odyssey* (E. V. Rieu, Trans.). Harmondsworth, Middlesex: Penguin.

Hoppe, M. H. (1990). *A comparative study of country elites: International differences in work-related values and learning and their implications for management training and development.* Unpublished doctoral dissertation, University of North Carolina at Chapel Hill.

Hoppe, M. H. (1993). The effects of national culture on the theory and practice of managing research-and-development professionals abroad. *Le Management, 23,* 313-325.

Hoppe, M. H. (1998). Validating the masculinity/femininity dimension on elites from nineteen countries. In G. Hofstede & Associates, *Masculinity and femininity: The taboo dimension of national cultures* (pp. 29-43). Thousand Oaks, CA: Sage.

Horovitz, J. H. (1980). *Top management control in Europe.* London: Macmillan.

Hox, J. J., & Kreft, I. G. G. (1994). Multilevel analysis methods. *Sociological Methods and Research, 22,* 283-299.

Hsu, F. L. K. (1971). Psychosocial homeostasis and jen: Conceptual tools for advancing psychological anthropology. *American Anthropologist, 73,* 23-44.

Hui, C. H., & Yee, C. (1994). The shortened individualism-collectivism scale: Its relationship to demographic and work-related variables. *Journal of Research in Personality, 28,* 409-424.

Huisman, D. (1985). Entrepreneurship: Economic and cultural influences on the entrepreneurial climate. *European Research, 13*(4), 10-17.

Huisman, D., & De Ridder, W. J. (1984). *Vernieuwend ondernemen.* The Hague: Stichting Maatschappij en Onderneming.

Humana, C. (1992). *World human rights guide* (3rd ed.). New York: Oxford University Press.

Hume, D. (1964). Of national characters. In T. H. Green & T. H. Grose (Eds.), *The philosophical works 3* (pp. 244-258). Aalen, Germany: Scientia Verlag. (Original work published 1742)

Hunt, J. W. (1981). Commentary: Do American theories apply abroad? *Organizational Dynamics, 10*(1), 55-62.

Huntington, S. P. (1993). The clash of civilizations? *Foreign Affairs, 72*(3), 22-49.

Huntington, S. P. (1996). The West unique, not universal. *Foreign Affairs, 75*(6), 28-46.

Husted, B. W. (1999). Wealth, culture, and corruption. *Journal of International Business Studies, 30,* 339-360.

Huth, H. (1980). *Eine Interkulturelle Vergleichsstudie an Mexicanischen und Deutschen Schülern zu Aspekten der Persönlichkeitsentwicklung und des Konzeptes der Psychologischen Differentiation.* Unpublished doctoral dissertation, Würzburg University.

Ibn Khaldûn. (1968). *Al-Muqaddima (Discours sur l'histoire universelle)* (Vol. 1). Paris: Sindbad. (Original work published 1377)

IDE International Research Group. (1981a). *Industrial democracy in Europe.* Oxford: Clarendon.

IDE International Research Group. (1981b). Industrial democracy in Europe: Differences and similarities across countries and hierarchies. *Organization Studies, 2,* 113-129.

Imamoglu, E. O., Küller, R., Imamoglu, V., & Küller, M. (1993). The social psychological worlds of Swedes and Turks in and around retirement. *Journal of Cross-Cultural Psychology, 24,* 26-41.

Ingersoll, V. H., & Adams, G. B. (1992). The child is "father" to the manager: Images of organizations in U.S. children's literature. *Organization Studies, 13,* 497-519.

Ingham, G. K. (1970). *Size of industrial organization and worker behavior.* Cambridge: Cambridge University Press.

Inglehart, R. (1990). *Culture shift in advanced industrial society.* Princeton, NJ: Princeton University Press.

Inglehart, R. (1997). *Modernization and postmodernization: Cultural, economic, and political change in 43 societies.* Princeton, NJ: Princeton University Press.

Inglehart, R., Basañez, M., & Moreno, A. (1998). *Human values and beliefs: A cross-cultural sourcebook.* Ann Arbor: University of Michigan Press.

Inglehart, R., & Rabier, J. R. (1982, August). *Trust between nationalities: Proximity, projection, historical experience and ease of communication.* Paper prepared for the 12th World Congress of the International Political Science Association, Rio de Janeiro.

Inkeles, A. (1960). Industrial man: The relation of status to experience, perception, and value. *American Journal of Sociology, 66,* 1-31.

Inkeles, A. (1966). The modernization of man. In M. Weiner (Ed.), *Modernization* (pp. 138-150). New York: Basic Books.

Inkeles, A. (1968). Society, social structure, and child socialization. In J. A. Clausen (Ed.), *Socialization and society* (pp. 74-129). Boston: Little, Brown.

Inkeles, A. (1969). Making men modern: On the causes and consequences of individual change in the developing countries. *American Journal of Sociology, 75,* 208-225.

Inkeles, A. (1977, September). *Continuity and change in the American national character.* Paper prepared for the annual meeting of the American Sociological Association, Chicago.

Inkeles, A. (1980). Modernization and family patterns: A test of convergence theory. *Conspectus of History, 1*(6), 31-63.

Inkeles, A. (1981). Convergence and divergence in industrial societies. In M. O. Attir, B. Holzner, & Z. Suda (Eds.), *Directions of change: Modernization theory, research, and realities* (pp. 3-38). Boulder, CO: Westview.

Inkeles, A. (1993). Industrialization, modernization and the quality of life. *International Journal of Comparative Sociology, 34*(1-2), 1-23.

Inkeles, A. (1997). *National character: A psycho-social perspective.* New Brunswick, NJ: Transaction.

Inkeles, A., & Levinson, D. J. (1969). National character: The study of modal personality and sociocultural systems. In G. Lindzey & E. Aronson (Eds.), *Handbook of social psychology* (Vol. 4, pp. 418-506). New York: McGraw-Hill. (Original work published 1954)

Inkeles, A., & Levinson, D. J. (1997). National character: The study of modal personality and sociocultural systems. In A. Inkeles, *National character: A psycho-social perspective.* New Brunswick, NJ: Transaction. (Original work published 1954)

Inkson, J. H. K., Schwitter, J. P., Pheysey, D. C., & Hickson, D. J. A. (1970). A comparison of organization structure and managerial roles: Ohio, U.S.A., and the Midlands, England. *Journal of Management Studies, 7,* 347-363.

INRA. (1993). *Europeans, science and technology: Public understanding and attitudes.* Brussels: Commission of the European Communities.

International Labour Office. (1976). *Yearbook of labour statistics.* Geneva: Author.

Inzerilli, G. (1989). *Societal culture and its impact on organizational behavior* (Management Report Series No. 51). Rotterdam: Erasmus University, Faculty of Business Administration.

Israël, L. (1995). *Cerveau droit cerveau gauche: cultures et civilisations.* Paris: Librairie Plon.

Iwata, R. (1982). *Japanese-style management: Its foundations and prospects.* Tokyo: Asian Productivity Organization.

Jackofsky, E. F., & Slocum, J. W. (1988). CEO roles across cultures. In D. C. Hambrick (Ed.), *The executive effect: Concepts and methods for studying top managers* (pp. 67-99). Greenwich, CT: JAI.

Jacobs, J. (1985). *Cities and the wealth of nations: Principles of economic life.* New York: Random House.

Jacobs, J. A. (1992). Women's entry into management: Trends in earnings, authority, and values among salaried managers. *Administrative Science Quarterly, 37,* 282-301.

Jacquemin, A., & de Ghellinck, E. (1977). *Familial control, size and performance in the largest French firms* (Working Paper 77-25). Brussels: European Institute for Advanced Studies in Management.

Jaeger, A. M. (1986). Organizational development and national culture: Where's the fit? *Academy of Management Review, 11,* 178-190.

Jain, H. C., Normand, J., & Kanungo, R. N. (1979). Job motivation of Canadian Anglophone and Francophone hospital employees. *Canadian Journal of Behavioural Science, 11,* 160-163.

Jankowicz, A. D. (1994). The new journey to Jerusalem: Mission and meaning in the managerial crusade to Eastern Europe. *Organization Studies, 15,* 479-507.

Jaques, E. (1951). *The changing culture of a factory.* London: Tavistock.

Javalgi, R. G., Cutler, B. D., & Malhotra, N. K. (1995). Print advertising at the component level: A cross-cultural comparison of the United States and Japan. *Journal of Business Research, 34*(2), 117-124.

Jenkins, C. D. (1971). Psychologic and social precursors of coronary disease. *New England Journal of Medicine, 284,* 244-255, 307-312.

Jenkins, D. (1973). *Blue and white collar democracy.* Garden City, NY: Doubleday.

Jick, T. D., & Mitz, L. F. (1985). Sex differences in work stress. *Academy of Management Review, 10,* 408-420.

Johnson, B. T., Holmes, K. R., & Kirkpatrick, M. (1998). *1998 index of economic freedom.* Washington, DC/New York: Heritage Foundation/Wall Street Journal.

Johnson, J. P., & Lenartowicz, T. (1998). Culture, freedom and economic growth: Do cultural values explain economic growth? *Journal of World Business, 33,* 332-356.

Jones, E. F., Forrest, J. D., Goldman, N., Henshaw, S., Lincoln, R., Rosoff, J. I., Westoff, C. F., & Wulf, D. (1986). *Teenage pregnancy in industrialized countries.* New Haven, CT: Yale University Press.

Jones, G. R. (1983). Transaction costs, property rights, and organizational culture: An exchange perspective. *Administrative Science Quarterly, 28,* 454-467.

Jordan, T. G. (1973). *The European culture area: A systematic geography*. New York: Harper & Row.

Joshi, M., & MacLean, M. (1997). Maternal expectations of child development in India, Japan, and England. *Journal of Cross-Cultural Psychology, 28*, 219-234.

Kaase, M., & Marsh, A. (1976, August). *The matrix of political action: Protest and participation in five nations*. Paper prepared for the 10th Congress of Political Science, Edinburgh.

Kachru, B. B. (1988). Teaching world Englishes. *ERIC/CLL* (Clearinghouse on Languages and Linguistics) *News Bulletin, 12*(1), 1, 3-4, 8.

Kagitçibasi, Ç. (1970). Social norms and authoritarianism: A Turkish-American comparison. *Journal of Personality and Social Psychology, 16*, 444-451.

Kagitçibasi, Ç. (1982). Old-age security value of children: Cross-national socioeconomic evidence. *Journal of Cross-Cultural Psychology, 13*, 29-42.

Kagitçibasi, Ç. (1996). *Family and human development across cultures: A view from the other side*. Mahwah, NJ: Lawrence Erlbaum.

Kagitçibasi, Ç. (1997). Individualism and collectivism. In J. W. Berry, M. H. Segall, & Ç. Kagitçibasi (Eds.), *Handbook of cross-cultural psychology: Vol. 3. Social behavior and applications* (pp. 1-44). Boston: Allyn & Bacon.

Kahn, H. (1979). *World economic development: 1979 and beyond*. London: Croom Helm.

Kahn, R. L., Wolfe, D. M., Quinn, R. P., Snoek, J. D., & Rosenthal, R. A. (1964). *Organizational stress: Studies in role conflict and role ambiguity*. New York: John Wiley.

Kakar, S. (1971). Authority patterns and subordinate behavior in Indian organizations. *Administrative Science Quarterly, 16*, 298-307.

Kale, S. H. (1991). Culture-specific marketing communications: An analytical approach. *International Marketing Review, 8*, 18-30.

Kale, S. H. (1995). Grouping Euroconsumers: A culture-based clustering approach. *Journal of International Marketing, 3*(3), 35-48.

Kalsbeek, J. W. H. (1976). *Mentale belasting*. Assen, Netherlands: Van Gorcum.

Kanter, R. M. (1977). *Men and women of the corporation*. New York: Basic Books.

Kanter, R. M. (1983). *The change masters: Innovation and entrepreneurship in the American corporation*. New York: Simon & Schuster.

Kanungo, R. N., & Mendonca, M. (1994). *Work motivation: Models for developing countries*. New Delhi: Sage.

Kapitza, S. (1996). The demographic dimension. In Forum Engelberg (Ed.), *Europe-Asia: Science and technology for their future. Science-economy-culture* (pp. 143-155). Zurich: Hochschulverlag.

Kashima, E. S., & Kashima, Y. (1998). Culture and language: The case of cultural dimensions and personal pronoun use. *Journal of Cross-Cultural Psychology, 29*, 461-486.

Kashima, Y., Yamaguchi, S., Kim, U., Choi, S.-C., Gelfand, M. J., & Yuki, M. (1995). Culture, gender, and self: A perspective from individualism-collectivism research. *Journal of Personality and Social Psychology, 69*, 925-937.

Kassem, M. S. (1989). Services marketing: The Arabian Gulf experience. *Journal of Services Marketing, 3*(3), 61-71.

Kassem, M. S., & Habib, G. M. (Eds.). (1989). *Strategic management of services in the Arab Gulf states*. Berlin: Walter de Gruyter.

Kata, K. (1975). On anxiety in the Scandinavian countries. In I. G. Sarason & C. D. Spielberger (Eds.), *Stress and anxiety 2* (pp. 275-302). Washington, DC: Hemisphere.

Katerberg, R., Smith, F. J., & Hoy, S. (1977). Language, time and person effects on attitude scale translations. *Journal of Applied Psychology, 62*, 385-391.

Kaufmann, J. (1980). *United Nations decision making*. Alphen a.d. Rijn, Netherlands: Sijthoff & Noordhoff.

Kaufmann, J. (1988). *Conference diplomacy: An introductory analysis*. Dordrecht, Netherlands: Martinus Nijhoff.

Kawasaki, I. (1969). *Japan unmasked*. Rutland, VT: Charles E. Tuttle.

Kealey, D. J. (1996). The challenge of international personnel selection. In D. Landis & R. S. Bhagat (Eds.), *Handbook of intercultural training* (pp. 81-105). Thousand Oaks, CA: Sage.

Kedia, B. L., & Bhagat, R. S. (1988). Cultural constraints on transfer of technology across nations: Implications for research in international and comparative management. *Academy of Management Review, 13*, 559-571.

Keesing, R. M. (1974). Theories of culture. *Annual Review of Anthropology, 3*, 79-97.

Kelen, B. (1983). *Confucius in life and legend*. Singapore: Graham Brash. (Original work published 1971)

Kelly, A. (1978). *Girls and science: An international study of sex differences in school science achievement*. Stockholm: Almqvist & Wiksell.

Kerr, C., Dunlop, J. T., Harbison, F. H., & Myers, C. A. (1960). *Industrialism and industrial man: The problems of labor and management in economic growth*. London: Heinemann.

Ketchum, S. M. (1993). Managing the multicultural laboratory: Part III. Putting the cross-cultural tools to work. *Clinical Laboratory Management Review, 7*(1), 20-33.

Keynes, J. M. (1920). *The economic consequences of the peace*. London: Macmillan.

Khandwalla, P. N. (1985). Pioneering innovative management: An Indian excellence. *Organization Studies, 6*, 161-183.

Kiernan, V. G. (1969). *The lords of humankind: European attitudes towards the outside world in the imperial age*. Harmondsworth, Middlesex: Pelican.

Kieser, A., & Kubicek, H. (1983). *Organisation*. Berlin: Walter de Gruyter.

Kim, K. I., Park, H., & Suzuki, N. (1990). Reward allocations in the United States, Japan, and Korea: A comparison of individualistic and collectivistic cultures. *Academy of Management Journal, 33,* 188-198.

Kim, U. (1995). Psychology, science, and culture: Cross-cultural analysis of national psychologies. *International Journal of Psychology, 30,* 663-679.

Kim, U., Triandis, H. C., Kagitçibasi, Ç., Choi, S.-C., & Yoon, G. (Eds.). (1994). *Individualism and collectivism: Theory, method, and applications.* Thousand Oaks, CA: Sage.

King, A. Y. C., & Bond, M. H. (1985). The Confucian paradigm of man: A sociological view. In W. Tseng & D. Wu (Eds.), *Chinese culture and mental health: An overview* (pp. 29-45). New York: Academic Press.

Kipnis, D. (1972). Does power corrupt? *Journal of Personality and Social Psychology, 24,* 33-41.

Kipnis, D., Castell, P. J., Gergen, M., & Mauch, D. (1976). Metamorphic effects of power. *Journal of Applied Psychology, 61,* 127-135.

Kirsch, T. (1985). Text and context: Buddhist sex roles/ culture of gender revisited. *American Ethnologist, 12,* 302-320.

Klein, K. J., Dansereau, F., & Hall, R. J. (1994). Level issues in theory development, data collection, and analysis. *Academy of Management Review, 19,* 195-229.

Klein, S. M., Kraut, A. I., & Wolfson, A. (1971). Employee reactions to attitude survey feedback: A study of the impact of structure and process. *Administrative Science Quarterly, 16,* 497-514.

Klimidis, S., Minas, I. H., Stuart, G. W., & Hayes, C. (1997). Cultural diversity in Australian medical education. *Medical Education, 31*(1), 56-68.

Klimidis, S., Stuart, G. W., Minas, I. H., & Ata, A. W. (1994). Immigrant status and gender effects on psychopathology and self-concept in adolescents: A test of the migration-morbidity hypothesis. *Comprehensive Psychiatry, 35,* 393-404.

Kluckhohn, C. (1951). The study of culture. In D. Lerner & H. D. Lasswell (Eds.), *The policy sciences* (pp. 86-101). Stanford, CA: Stanford University Press.

Kluckhohn, C. (1962). Universal categories of culture. In S. Tax (Ed.), *Anthropology today: Selections* (pp. 304-320). Chicago: University of Chicago Press. (Original work published 1952)

Kluckhohn, C. (1967). Values and value-orientations in the theory of action: An exploration in definition and classification. In T. Parsons & E. A. Shils (Eds.), *Toward a general theory of action* (pp. 388-433). Cambridge, MA: Harvard University Press. (Original work published 1951)

Kluckhohn, F. R. (1950). Dominant and substitute profiles of cultural orientation: Their significance for the analysis of social stratification. *Social Forces, 28,* 376-393.

Kluckhohn, F. R., & Strodtbeck, F. L. (1961). *Variations in value orientations.* Westport, CT: Greenwood.

Köbben, A. J. F. (1952). New ways of presenting an old idea: The statistical method in social anthropology. *Royal Anthropological Institute of Great Britain and Ireland Journal, 82,* 129-146.

Koene, B. A. S. (1996). *Organizational culture, leadership and performance in context: Trust and rationality in organizations.* Unpublished doctoral dissertation, Maastricht University.

Kogut, B., & Singh, H. (1988). The effect of national culture on the choice of entry mode. *Journal of International Business Studies, 19,* 411-432.

Kohn, M. L. (1969). *Class and conformity: A study in values.* Homewood, IL: Dorsey.

Kohn, M. L. (1971). Bureaucratic man: A portrait and an interpretation. *American Sociological Review, 36,* 461-474.

Kolman, L., Hofstede, G., Noorderhaven, N., & Dienes, E. (1999). Work-related values and cooperation in Europe. In *Konference PEF CZU, Agrární perspektivy VIII* [Proceedings of the Conference on Agrarian Perspectives] (pp. 884-890). Prague: PEF/CZU.

Komarovsky, M. (1976). *Dilemmas of masculinity: A study of college youth.* New York: Norton.

Kopper, E. (1993). Swiss and Germans: Similarities and differences in work-related values, attitudes, and behavior. *International Journal of Intercultural Relations, 17,* 167-184.

Koprowski, E. J. (1983). Cultural myths: Clues to effective management. *Organizational Dynamics, 12*(2), 39-51.

Kornhauser, A. (1965). *Mental health of the industrial worker: A Detroit study.* New York: John Wiley.

Krause, K. (1981). *Weisse Exporten nicht gefragt: Selbsthilfe in Indonesischen Dörfern: Protokolle.* Reinbek bei Hamburg, Germany: Rowohlt.

Kraut, A. I. (1975). Predicting turnover of employees from measured job attitudes. *Organizational Behavior and Human Performance, 13,* 233-243.

Kraut, A. I., & Ronen, S. (1975). Validity of job facet importance: A multinational, multicriteria study. *Journal of Applied Psychology, 60,* 671-677.

Kravis, I. B. (1960). International differences in the distribution of income. *Review of Economics and Statistics, 42,* 408-416.

Kreacic, V., & Marsh, P. (1985). Public enterprises in developing countries: Structure, performance and culture. *Public Enterprise, 5,* 379-391.

Kreacic, V., & Marsh, P. (1986). Organisation development and national culture in four countries. *Public Enterprise, 6,* 121-134.

Kroeber, A. L., & Parsons, T. (1958). The concepts of culture and of social system. *American Sociological Review, 23,* 582-583.

Kruzela, P. (1995). Some cultural aspects on Czech and Russian management. In B. Machová & S. Kubátová (Eds.), *Uniqueness in unity: The signifi-*

cance of cultural identity in European cooperation (pp. 222-235). Munich: SIETAR Europa.

Kuhn, T. S. (1970). *The structure of scientific revolutions* (2nd ed.). Chicago: University of Chicago Press.

Kuiper, L. (1983). *Anglo-Dutch cooperation: A marriage of true minds?* Unpublished master's thesis, Interuniversitaire Interfaculteit Bedrijfskunde.

Kumar, U., & Singh, K. K. (1976, July). *Interpersonal construct system of Indian manager: A determinant of organizational behaviour.* Paper presented at the International Congress of Applied Psychology, Paris.

Kunkel, J. H. (1970). *Society and economic growth: A behavioral perspective of social change.* New York: Oxford University Press.

Kuper, L. (Ed.). (1975). *Race, science and society.* Paris: UNESCO.

Kuznets, S. (1963). Distribution of income by size. *Economic Development and Cultural Change, 11*(2, part II), 1-80.

Kuznets, S. (1971). *Economic growth of nations: Total output and production structure.* Cambridge, MA: Belknap.

Kuznets, S. (1973). *Population, capital and growth: Selected essays.* London: Heinemann.

Laaksonen, O. J. (1977). The power structure of Chinese enterprises. *International Studies of Management and Organization, 7*(1), 71-90.

La Boétie, É. de. (1976). *Le discours de la servitude volontaire.* Paris: Payot. (Original work published 1548)

Lalonde, R. N., & Cameron, J. E. (1993). An intergroup perspective on immigrant acculturation with a focus on collective strategies. *International Journal of Psychology, 28*, 57-74.

Lambert, W. E., & Klineberg, O. (1967). *Children's views of foreign peoples: A cross-national study.* New York: Appleton-Century-Crofts.

Lammers, A. (1989). *Uncle Sam en Jan Salie: Hoe Nederland Amerika ontdekte.* Amsterdam: Balans.

Lammers, C. J. (1976). Towards the internationalization of the organization sciences. In G. Hofstede & M. S. Kassem (Eds.), *European contributions to organization theory* (pp. 25-42). Assen, Netherlands: Van Gorcum.

Lammers, C. J. (1981). Contributions of organizational sociology: Part II. Contributions to organizational theory and practice: A liberal view. *Organization Studies, 2*, 361-376.

Lammers, C. J. (1986). De excellente onderneming als organisatiemodel. *Harvard Holland Review, 8*, 18-25.

Lammers, C. J. (1988). Transience and persistence of ideal types in organization theory. *Research in the Sociology of Organizations, 6*, 203-224.

Lammers, C. J. (1990). Sociology of organizations around the globe: Similarities and differences between American, British, French, German and Dutch brands. *Organization Studies, 11*, 179-205.

Lammers, C. J., & Hickson, D. J. (1979a). A cross-national and cross-institutional typology of organizations. In C. J. Lammers & D. J. Hickson (Eds.), *Organizations alike and unlike: International and inter-institutional studies in the sociology of organizations* (pp. 420-434). London: Routledge & Kegan Paul.

Lammers, C. J., & Hickson, D. J. (Eds.). (1979b). *Organizations alike and unlike: International and inter-institutional studies in the sociology of organizations.* London: Routledge & Kegan Paul.

Lammers, C. J., & Hickson, D. J. (1979c). Towards a comparative sociology of organizations. In C. J. Lammers & D. J. Hickson (Eds.), *Organizations alike and unlike: International and inter-institutional studies in the sociology of organizations* (pp. 3-20). London: Routledge & Kegan Paul.

Langbein, L. I., & Lichtman, A. J. (1978). *Ecological inference.* Beverly Hills, CA: Sage.

Lasch, C. (1980). *The culture of narcissism: American life in an age of diminishing expectations.* New York: Warner.

Laszlo, E. (1973). A systems philosophy of human values. *Behavioral Science, 18*, 250-259.

Lau, L. Y., & Ranyard, R. (1999). Chinese and English speakers' linguistic expression of probability and probabilistic thinking. *Journal of Cross-Cultural Psychology, 30*, 411-421.

Laumann, E. O., Gagnon, J. H., Michael, R. T., & Michaels, S. (1994). *The social organization of sexuality.* Chicago: University of Chicago Press.

Laurent, A. (1978). *Matrix organizations and Latin cultures* (Working Paper 78-28). Brussels: European Institute for Advanced Studies in Management.

Laurent, A. (1983). The cultural diversity of Western conceptions of management. *International Studies of Management and Organization, 13*(1-2), 75-96.

Leakey, R., & Lewin, R. (1981). *People of the lake. Man: His origins, nature, and future.* Harmondsworth, Middlesex: Pelican.

Le Bras, H., & Todd, E. (1981). *L'invention de la France: Atlas anthropologique et politique.* Paris: Poche Pluriel.

Lederer, G. (1982). Trends in authoritarianism: A study of adolescents in West-Germany and the United States since 1945. *Journal of Cross-Cultural Psychology, 13*, 299-314.

Leerssen, J. T. (1988). Over nationale identiteit. *Theoretische Geschiedenis, 15*, 417-430.

Leerssen, J. T. (1989). Culturele verschillen en nationale ideologieën: een naschrift. *Theoretische Geschiedenis, 16*, 361-365.

Leff, N. H., & Sato, K. (1993). Homogeneous preferences and heterogeneous growth performance: International differences in saving and investment behavior. *Kyklos: International Review for Social Sciences, 46*, 203-223.

Lenski, G. E. (1966). *Power and privilege: A theory of social stratification.* New York: McGraw-Hill.

Lester, D. (1995). Individualism and divorce. *Psychological Reports, 76,* 258.

Leung, K. (1989). Cross-cultural differences: Individual-level versus culture-level analysis. *International Journal of Psychology, 24,* 703-719.

Leung, K., Au, Y. F., Fernández-Dols, J. M., & Iwawaki, S. (1992). Preference for methods of conflict processing in two collectivist cultures. *International Journal of Psychology, 27,* 195-209.

Leung, K., & Bond, M. H. (1984). The impact of cultural collectivism on reward allocation. *Journal of Personality and Social Psychology, 47,* 793-804.

Leung, K., & Bond, M. H. (1989). On the empirical identification of dimensions for cross-cultural comparisons. *Journal of Cross-Cultural Psychology, 20,* 133-151.

Leung, K., Bond, M. H., Carment, D. W., Krishnan, L., & Liebrand, W. B. G. (1990). Effects of cultural femininity on preference for methods of conflict processing: A cross-cultural study. *Journal of Experimental Social Psychology, 26,* 373-388.

Levi, L., & Andersson, L. (1974). *Population, environment and quality of life: A contribution to the World Population Conference.* Stockholm: Royal Ministry for Foreign Affairs.

Levine, R., Sato, S., Hashimoto, T., & Verma, J. (1995). Love and marriage in 11 cultures. *Journal of Cross-Cultural Psychology, 26,* 554-571.

Le Vine, R. A. (1973). *Culture, behavior and personality: An introduction to the comparative study of psychosocial adaptation.* Chicago: AVC.

Levine, R. V., & Norenzayan, A. (1999). The pace of life in 31 countries. *Journal of Cross-Cultural Psychology, 30,* 178-205.

Levinson, D. (1977). What have we learned from cross-cultural surveys? *American Behavioral Scientist, 20,* 757-792.

Levinson, H. (1964). *Emotional health in the world of work.* New York: Harper & Row.

Levinson, H. (1970). Management by whose objectives? *Harvard Business Review, 48*(4), 125-134.

Levinson, H. (1975). On executive suicide. *Harvard Business Review, 53*(4), 118-122.

Levinson, H., Price, C. R., Munden, K. J., Mandl, H. J., & Solley, C. M. (1962). *Men, management and mental health.* Cambridge, MA: Harvard University Press.

Lévi-Strauss, C. (1961). *Race et histoire* (suivi de L'oeuvre de Claude Lévi-Strauss, par Jean Poillon). Paris: Denoël.

Lévi-Strauss, C., & Éribon, D. (1988). *De près et de loin.* Paris: Odile Jacob.

Levitin, T. (1973). Values. In J. P. Robinson & P. R. Shaver (Eds.), *Measures of social psychological attitudes* (pp. 489-502). Ann Arbor: University of Michigan, Institute for Social Research, Survey Research Center.

Levitt, T. (1983). The globalization of markets. *Harvard Business Review, 61*(3), 92-102.

Levy, J., Wubbels, T., Brekelmans, M., & Morganfield, B. (1997). Language and cultural factors in students' perceptions of teacher communication style. *International Journal of Intercultural Relations, 21,* 29-56.

Lewin, K. (1952). *Field theory in social science: Selected theoretical papers.* London: Tavistock.

Lewis, O. (1961). *The children of Sanchez: Autobiography of a Mexican family.* New York: Vintage.

Lewis, R. D. (1990). Language and thought. *Cross-Culture Language, Thought and Communication, 2*(1), 6-8.

Lewis, R. D. (1996). *When cultures collide: Managing successfully across cultures.* London: Nicholas Brealy.

Li, J. T., & Guisinger, S. (1991). Comparative business failures of foreign-controlled firms in the United States. *Journal of International Business Studies, 22,* 209-224.

Li, J. T., & Guisinger, S. (1992). The globalization of service multinationals in the triad regions: Japan, Western Europe and North America. *Journal of International Business Studies, 23,* 675-696.

Likert, R. (1967). *The human organization.* New York: McGraw-Hill.

Likert, R. (1976). *New ways of managing conflict.* New York: McGraw-Hill.

Lincoln, J. R., & Zeitz, G. (1980). Organizational properties from aggregate data: Separating individual and structural effects. *American Sociological Review, 45,* 391-408.

Lindblom, C. E. (1959). The science of muddling through. *Public Administration Review, 19,* 78-88.

Lippitt, R., & White, R. K. (1958). An experimental study of leadership and group life. In E. E. Maccoby, T. M. Newcomb, & E. E. Hartley (Eds.), *Readings in social psychology.* New York: Holt, Rinehart & Winston.

Little, T. D., Oettingen, G., Stetsenko, A., & Baltes, P. B. (1995). Children's action: Control beliefs about school performance. How do American children compare with German and Russian children? *Journal of Personality and Social Psychology, 69,* 686-700.

Litwin, G. H., & Stringer, R. A. (1968). *Motivation and organizational climate.* Cambridge, MA: Harvard University, Graduate School of Business Administration, Division of Research.

Liu, I. M. (1986). Chinese cognition. In M. H. Bond (Ed.), *The psychology of the Chinese people* (pp. 73-105). Hong Kong: Oxford University Press.

Locke, R. R. (1996). *The collapse of the American management mystique.* Oxford: Oxford University Press.

Lodahl, T. M. (1964). Patterns of job attitudes in two assembly technologies. *Administrative Science Quarterly, 8,* 482-519.

Lodahl, T. M., & Kejner, M. (1965). The definition and measurement of job involvement. *Journal of Applied Psychology, 50,* 24-33.

Lomax, A., & Berkowitz, N. (1972). The evolutionary taxonomy of culture. *Science, 177*, 228-239.

Lonner, W. J., & Adamopoulos, J. (1997). Culture as antecedent to behavior. In J. W. Berry, Y. H. Poortinga, & J. Pandey (Eds.), *Handbook of cross-cultural psychology: Vol. 1. Theory and method* (pp. 43-83). Boston: Allyn & Bacon.

Lorenz, K. (1967). *On aggression.* London: Methuen.

Lowe, S. (1996a). Culture's consequences for management in Hong Kong. *Asia Pacific Business Review, 2*(3), 120-133.

Lowe, S. (1996b). Hermes revisited: A replication of Hofstede's study in Hong Kong and the UK. *Asia Pacific Business Review, 2*(3), 101-119.

Lowe, S. (1998). Culture and network institutions in Hong Kong: A hierarchy of perspectives. A response to Wilkinson: "Culture, institutions and business in East Asia." *Organization Studies, 19*, 321-343.

Lowe, S., & Oswick, C. (1996). Culture's invisible filters: Cross-cultural models in social psychology. In S. Gatley, R. Lessem, & Y. Altman (Eds.), *Comparative management: A transcultural odyssey* (pp. 90-116). London: McGraw-Hill.

Lowie, R. H. (1954). *Towards understanding Germany.* Chicago: University of Chicago Press.

Lueschen, G., Stevens, F., Vanderzee, J., Cockerham, W. C., Diederijks, J., Dhoutaud, A., Ferrando, M. G., Peeters, R., & Niemann, S. (1994). Health-care systems and the people: A five-nation study in the European Union. *International Sociology, 9*, 337-362.

Luhmann, N. (1975). *Macht.* Stuttgart: Ferdinand Enke.

Luhmann, N. (1976). The future cannot begin: Temporal structures in modern society. *Social Research, 43*, 130-152.

Luo, Y. (1999). Time-based experience and international expansion: The case of an emerging economy. *Journal of Management Studies, 36*, 505-534.

Lynn, M., & Gelb, B. D. (1996). Identifying innovative national markets for technical consumer goods. *International Marketing Review, 13*(6), 43-57.

Lynn, M., Zinkhan, G. M., & Harris, J. (1993). Consumer tipping: A cross-country study. *Journal of Consumer Research, 20*, 478-488.

Lynn, R. (1971). *Personality and national character.* Oxford: Pergamon.

Lynn, R. (1973). National differences in anxiety and the consumption of caffeine. *British Journal of Social and Clinical Psychology, 12*, 92-93.

Lynn, R. (1975). National differences in anxiety 1935-65. In I. G. Sarason & C. D. Spielberger (Eds.), *Stress and anxiety 2* (pp. 257-274). Washington, DC: Hemisphere.

Lynn, R. (1978). Ethnic and racial differences in intelligence: International comparisons. In R. Lynn (Ed.), *Human variation* (pp. 261-286). New York: Academic Press.

Lynn, R. (1981). Cross-cultural differences in neuroticism, extraversion and psychoticism. In R. Lynn (Ed.), *Dimensions of personality: Papers in honour of H. J. Eysenck* (pp. 263-286). Oxford: Pergamon.

Lynn, R. (1991). *The secret of the miracle economy: Different national attitudes to competitiveness and money.* London: Social Affairs Unit.

Lynn, R., & Hampson, S. L. (1975). National differences in extraversion and neuroticism. *British Journal of Social and Clinical Psychology, 14*, 223-240.

Lynn, R., & Hampson, S. L. (1977). Fluctuations in national levels of neuroticism and extraversion, 1935-1970. *British Journal of Social and Clinical Psychology, 16*, 131-137.

Lynn, R., & Martin, T. (1995). National differences for 37 nations in extroversion, neuroticism, psychoticism and economic, demographic and other correlates. *Personality and Individual Differences, 19*, 403-406.

Lynton, R. P., & Pareek, U. (1990). *Training for development.* New Delhi: Vistaar.

Lysgaard, S. (1955). Adjustment in a foreign society: Norwegian Fulbright grantees visiting the United States. *International Social Science Bulletin, 7*, 45-51.

Lytle, A. L. (1995). *The influence of culture in negotiation: A comparative intracultural study.* University Microfilms No. 95-21759.

Machiavelli, N. (1955). *The ruler.* Chicago: Gateway. (Original work published 1517)

Magalhaes, R. (1984). Organisation development in Latin countries: Fact or fiction. *Leadership and Organization Development Journal, 5*(5), 17-21.

Magee, B. (1975). *Popper.* Glasgow: Fontana/Collins.

Magli, I. (1984). Il quadro definitorio instituzionale di alcune "nuove" scienze dell'uomo: Antropologia culturale. In G. Varchetti (Ed.), *Scienze dell'uomo, cultura d'impresta e formazione* (pp. 31-33). Milan: Industrie Pirelli.

Mainwaring, D., & Markowski, K. (1991). Cultural factors in the structure and context of European engineering studies. *European Journal of Engineering Education, 16*, 299-307.

Malhotra, K., Agarwal, J., & Baalbaki, I. (1998). Heterogeneity of regional trading blocks and global marketing strategies: A multicultural perspective. *International Marketing Review, 15*, 476-506.

Maloney, P., Wilkof, J., & Dambrot, F. (1981). Androgyny across two cultures: United States and Israel. *Journal of Cross-Cultural Psychology, 12*, 95-102.

Mamman, A., & Saffu, K. (1998). Short-termism, control, quick-fix and bottom line. *Journal of Managerial Psychology, 13*, 291-308.

Mangione, T. W. (1973). Turnover: Some psychological and demographic correlates. In R. P. Quinn & T. W. Mangione (Eds.), *The 1969-1970 survey of work-*

ing conditions (pp. 335-372). Ann Arbor: University of Michigan, Institute for Social Research.

Mann, J. (1989). *Beijing Jeep: The short, unhappy romance of American business in China.* New York: Simon & Schuster.

Mant, A. (1979). *The rise and fall of the British manager.* London: Pan.

Marceau, J. (1977). *Class and status in France: Economic change and social immobility 1945-1975.* Oxford: Clarendon.

March, J. G., & Olsen, J. P. (1976). *Ambiguity and choice in organizations.* Bergen, Norway: Universitetsforlaget.

March, J. G., & Simon, H. A. (1958). *Organizations.* New York: John Wiley.

Margulis, S. T., Motwani, J., & Kumar, A. (1997). The tiffin carriers of Bombay, India: An organizational and logistical analysis. *International Journal of Commerce and Management, 7*(3-4), 120-140.

Marin, G., & Salazar, J. M. (1985). Determinants of hetero- and autostereotypes: Distance, level of contact, and socioeconomic development in seven nations. *Journal of Cross-Cultural Psychology, 16,* 403-422.

Marin, G., Triandis, H. C., Betancourt, H., & Kashima, Y. (1983). Ethnic affirmation versus social desirability: Explaining discrepancies in bilinguals' responses to a questionnaire. *Journal of Cross-Cultural Psychology, 14,* 173-186.

Markus, H. R., & Kitayama, S. (1991). Culture and the self: Implications for cognition, emotion, and motivation. *Psychological Review, 98,* 224-253.

Marsh, R. M. (1967). *Comparative sociology: A codification of cross-societal analysis.* New York: Harcourt Brace Jovanovich.

Marshall, B. K. (1977, Spring). Japanese business ideology and labour policy. *Columbia Journal of World Business, 12,* 22-29.

Martin, J., Feldman, M. S., Hatch, M. J., & Sitkin, S. B. (1983). The uniqueness paradox in organizational stories. *Administrative Science Quarterly, 28,* 438-453.

Martin, J., & Siehl, C. (1983). Organizational culture and counterculture: An uneasy symbiosis. *Organizational Dynamics, 12*(2), 52-64.

Martin, J., Sitkin, S. B., & Boehm, M. (1985). Founders and the elusiveness of a cultural legacy. In P. J. Frost, L. F. Moore, M. R. Louis, C. C. Lundberg, & J. Martin (Eds.), *Organizational culture* (pp. 99-124). Beverly Hills, CA: Sage.

Martin, W. F., & Lodge, G. C. (1975). Our society in 1985: Business may not like it. *Harvard Business Review, 53*(6), 143-152.

Martyn-Johns, T. A. (1977). Cultural conditioning of views of authority and its effect on the business decision-making process, with special reference to Java. In Y. H. Poortinga (Ed.), *Basic problems in cross-cultural psychology* (pp. 344-352). Amsterdam: Swets & Zeitlinger.

Maruyama, M. (1963). The second cybernetics: Deviation-amplifying mutual causal processes. *American Scientist, 51,* 164-179.

Maruyama, M. (1974). Paradigmatology and its application to cross-disciplinary, cross-professional and cross-cultural communication. *Dialectica, 28*(3-4), 135-176.

Maruyama, M. (1978). Symbiotization of cultural heterogeneity: Scientific, epistemological, and aesthetic bases. In M. Maruyama & A. M. Harkins (Eds.), *Cultures of future* (pp. 459-474). The Hague: Mouton.

Maruyama, M. (1994). *Mindscapes in management: Use of individual differences in multicultural management.* Aldershot, England: Dartmouth.

Maruyama, M. (1996). Bribing in historical context: The case of Japan. *Human Systems Management, 15,* 138-142.

Marx, K., & Engels, F. (1974). Manifest der Kommunistischen Partei. In K. Marx & F. Engels, *Werke* (Vol. 4). Berlin: Dietz. (Original work published 1848)

Maslow, A. H. (1970). *Motivation and personality.* New York: Harper & Row.

Masuda, M., & Holmes, T. H. (1967). The social readjustment rating scale: A cross-cultural study of Japanese and Americans. *Journal of Psychosomatic Research, 11,* 227-237.

Matsumoto, D. (1989). Cultural influences on the perception of emotion. *Journal of Cross-Cultural Psychology, 20,* 92-105.

Maurice, M. (1976). Theoretical and ideological aspects of the universalistic approach to the study of organizations. *International Studies of Management and Organization, 6*(3), 3-10.

Maurice, M., Sellier, F., & Silvestre, J. J. (1978). *Production de la hiérarchie dans l'entreprise: Comparaison France-Allemagne.* Aix-en-Provence: LEST.

Maurice, M., Sellier, F., & Silvestre, J. J. (1992). Analyse sociétale et cultures nationales: Réponse à Philippe d'Iribarne. *Revue Française de Sociologie, 33,* 75-86.

Maurice, M., Sorge, A., & Warner, M. (1980). Societal differences in organizing manufacturing units: A comparison of France, West Germany and Great Britain. *Organization Studies, 1,* 59-86.

May, B. (1978). *The Indonesian tragedy.* Singapore: Graham Brash.

Mayo, E. (1933). *The human problems of an industrial civilization.* New York: Macmillan.

McCarrey, M. W., Edwards, S., & Jones, R. (1978). Personal values of Canadian Anglophone and Francophone employees and ethnolinguistic group membership, sex, and position level. *Journal of Social Psychology, 104,* 175-184.

McCarty, J. A., & Hattwick, P. M. (1992). Cultural value orientations: A comparison of magazine advertisements from the United States and Mexico. *Advances in Consumer Research, 19,* 34-38.

McClelland, D. C. (1961). *The achieving society.* Princeton, NJ: Van Nostrand Reinhold.

McClelland, D. C. (1965). Wanted: A new self-image for women. In R. J. Lifton (Ed.), *The woman in America* (pp. 173-192). Boston: Houghton Mifflin.

McClelland, D. C. (1975). *Power: The inner experience.* New York: Irvington.

McClelland, D. C., & Burnham, D. H. (1976). Power is the great motivator. *Harvard Business Review, 54*(4), 100-110.

McClintock, C. G., & McNeel, S. P. (1966). Cross-cultural comparisons of interpersonal motives. *Sociometry, 29,* 406-427.

McCrae, R. R., & John, O. P. (1992). An introduction to the five-factor model and its applications. *Journal of Personality and Social Psychology, 60,* 175-215.

McEvedy, C., & Jones, R. (1978). *Atlas of world population history.* Harmondsworth, Middlesex: Penguin.

McGee, J. (1977). *The Europeans and free enterprise: Analysis of conference debate on public opinion poll* [Press release]. Brussels: Author.

McGrath, R. G., Macmillan, I. C., & Scheinberg, S. (1992). Elitists, risk-takers, and rugged individualists: An exploratory analysis of cultural differences between entrepreneurs and non-entrepreneurs. *Journal of Business Venturing, 7,* 115-135.

McGrath, R. G., Macmillan, I. C., Yang, E. A., & Tsai, W. (1992). Does culture endure, or is it malleable? Issues for entrepreneurial economic development. *Journal of Business Venturing, 7,* 441-458.

McGregor, D. (1960). *The human side of enterprise.* New York: McGraw-Hill.

McGregor, D. (1967). *The professional manager.* New York: McGraw-Hill.

Mead, M. (1951). *Soviet attitudes toward authority.* New York: McGraw-Hill.

Mead, M. (1955). *Cultural patterns and technical change.* New York: UNESCO/Mentor.

Mead, M. (1962a). *Male and female: A study of the sexes in a changing world.* Harmondsworth, Middlesex: Penguin. (Original work published 1950)

Mead, M. (1962b). National character. In S. Tax (Ed.), *Anthropology today: Selections* (pp. 396-421). Chicago: University of Chicago Press.

Meade, R. D. (1967). An experimental study of leadership in India. *Journal of Social Psychology, 72,* 35-43.

Meade, R. D., & Whittaker, J. D. (1967). A cross-cultural study of authoritarianism. *Journal of Social Psychology, 72,* 3-7.

Meadows, D. H., Meadows, D. L., Randers, J., & Behrens, W. W. (1972). *The limits to growth: A report for the Club of Rome's Project on the Predicament of Mankind.* London: Earth Island.

Meddin, J. (1975). Attitudes, values and related concepts: A system of classification. *Social Science Quarterly, 55,* 889-900.

Meijaard, J. (1998). *Decision-making in research and development: A comparative study of multinational companies in the Netherlands and the United States* [Doctoral dissertation. Erasmus University Rotterdam]. Amsterdam: Thesis Publishers.

Meindl, J. R., Ehrlich, S. B., & Dukerich, J. M. (1985). The romance of leadership. *Administrative Science Quarterly, 30,* 78-102.

Meltzer, L. (1963). Comparing relationships of individual and average variables to individual response. *American Sociological Review, 28,* 117-123.

Menzel, H. (1950). Comment on Robinson's "Ecological correlations and the behavior of individuals." *American Sociological Review, 15,* 674.

Merritt, A. C. (1995, October). *Some global cultural considerations.* Paper presented at the Royal Aeronautical Society conference "Commercial Pilot Selection and Training: The Next Ten Years," London.

Merritt, A. C. (2000). Culture in the cockpit: Do Hofstede's dimensions replicate? *Journal of Cross-Cultural Psychology, 31,* 283-301.

Merritt, A. C., & Helmreich, R. L. (1996). Human factors on the flight deck: The influence of national culture. *Journal of Cross-Cultural Psychology, 27,* 5-24.

Merton, R. K. (1968). *Social theory and social structure.* New York: Free Press. (Original work published 1949)

Metcalf, H. C., & Urwick, L. (Eds.). (1940). *Dynamic administration: The collected papers of Mary Parker Follett.* New York: Harper & Row.

Meyer, J. (1994). *Roze en blauwe wolken: een longitudinaal onderzoek naar seksetypering door ouders in de eerste levensjaren van hun kind.* The Hague: Ministry of Social Affairs and Employment.

Michaud, G. (Ed.). (1978). *Identités collectives et relations inter-culturelles.* Paris: Presses Universitaires de France.

Michels, R. (1911). *Vergleichende Liebeswissenschaft: Prolegomena, Gedanken und Untersuchungen.* Munich: Frauenverlag.

Michels, R. (1962). *Political parties: A sociological study of the oligarchical tendencies of modern democracy.* New York: Free Press. (Original work published 1915)

Milgram, S. (1974). *Obedience to authority: An experimental view.* London: Tavistock.

Millendorfer, J. (1976). *Mechanisms of socio-psychological development.* Vienna: Studiengruppe für Internationale Analysen.

Miller, E. J. (1976). The open-system approach to organizational analysis with specific reference to the work of A. K. Rice. In G. Hofstede & M. S. Kassem (Eds.), *European contributions to organization theory* (pp. 43-61). Assen, Netherlands: Van Gorcum.

Miller, G. A. (1956). The magical number seven, plus or minus two: Some limits on our capacity for processing information. *Psychological Review, 63,* 81-97.

Miller, S. M. (1960). Comparative social mobility. *Current Sociology, 9,* 1-89.

Mills, A. J. (1989). Gender, sexuality and organization theory. In J. Hearn, D. L. Sheppard, P. Tancred-Sheriff, & G. Burrell (Eds.), *The sexuality of organization* (pp. 29-44). London: Sage.

Milner, M., Fodness, D., & Speece, W. (1993). Hofstede's research on cross-cultural work-related values: Implications for consumer behavior. *European Advances in Consumer Research, 1,* 70-76.

Mintzberg, H. (1983). *Structure in fives: Designing effective organizations.* Englewood Cliffs, NJ: Prentice Hall.

Mintzberg, H. (1993). The pitfalls of strategic planning. *California Management Review, 36*(1), 32-47.

Misumi, J. (1985). *The behavioral science of leadership.* Ann Arbor: University of Michigan Press.

Montagu, A. (1997). *Man's most dangerous myth: The fallacy of race.* Walnut Creek, CA: AltaMira. (Original work published 1942)

Montesquieu (1989). *The spirit of the laws.* Cambridge: Cambridge University Press. (Original work published 1748)

Moore, B. (1966). *Social origins of dictatorship and democracy: Lord and peasant in the making of the modern world.* Harmondsworth, Middlesex: Penguin.

Moore, C. A. (1967). Editor's supplement: The enigmatic Japanese mind. In C. A. Moore (Ed.), *The Japanese mind: Essentials of Japanese philosophy and culture* (pp. 288-313). Tokyo: Charles E. Tuttle.

Moore, K., & Lewis, D. (1999). *Birth of the multinational: Two thousand years of ancient business history, from Ashur to Augustus.* Copenhagen: Copenhagen Business School Press.

Moran, R. T. (1985). *Getting your yen's worth: How to negotiate with Japan, Inc.* Houston, TX: Gulf.

More, T. (1965). *Utopia.* Harmondsworth, Middlesex: Penguin. (Original work published 1516)

Morgan, G. (1986). *Images of organization.* Beverly Hills, CA: Sage.

Morgan, G. (1988). Accounting as a reality construction: Towards a new epistemology for accounting practice. *Accounting, Organizations and Society, 13,* 477-485.

Morgenstern, O. (1975). Does GNP measure growth and welfare? *Business and Society Review, 15,* 23-31.

Morosini, P., Shane, S. A., & Singh, H. (1998). National cultural distance and cross-border acquisition. *Journal of International Business Studies, 29,* 137-158.

Morris, C. (1956). *Varieties of human value.* Chicago: University of Chicago Press.

Morris, C., & Jones, L. V. (1955). Value scales and dimensions. *Journal of Abnormal and Social Psychology, 51,* 523-535.

Morris, D. (1968). *The naked ape: A zoologist's study of the human animal.* New York: McGraw-Hill.

Morris, M. D. (1979). *Measuring the condition of the world's poor: The physical quality of life index.* New York: Pergamon.

Moulin, L. (1961). La nationalité des prix Nobel de science de 1901 à 1960. *Cahiers Internationaux de Sociologie, 31,* 145-163.

Mueller, F. (1994). Societal effect, organizational effect and globalization. *Organization Studies, 15,* 407-428.

Mulder, M. (1976). Reduction of power differences in practice: The power distance reduction theory and its applications. In G. Hofstede & M. S. Kassem (Eds.), *European contributions to organization theory* (pp. 79-94). Assen, Netherlands: Van Gorcum.

Mulder, M. (1977). *The daily power game.* Leiden, Netherlands: Martinus Nijhoff.

Mulder, M., Ritsema van Eck, J. R., & De Jong, R. D. (1971). An organization in crisis and non-crisis situations. *Human Relations, 24,* 19-41.

Mulder, N. (1978). *Mysticism and everyday life in contemporary Java: Cultural persistence and change.* Singapore: Singapore University Press.

Murdock, G. P. (1949). *Social structure.* New York: Free Press.

Murphy, R. J. L. (1979). Sex differences in examination performance: Do these reflect differences in ability or sex-role stereotypes? In O. Hartnett, G. Boden, & M. Fuller (Eds.), *Sex-role stereotyping* (pp. 159-167). London: Tavistock.

Murphy-Berman, V., Levesque, H. L., & Berman, J. J. (1996). UN convention on the rights of the child: A cross-cultural view. *American Psychologist, 51,* 1257-1261.

Musek, J. (1993). The universe of human values: A structural and developmental hierarchy. *Studia Psychologica, 35,* 321-326.

Musil, J. (1993). Czech and Slovak society. *Government and Opposition, 28,* 479-495.

Myrdal, G. (1968). *Asian drama: An enquiry into the poverty of nations.* New York: Pantheon.

Nakamaru, K. (1985). In Japan there's equal opportunity for men and women. *"Frankly Speaking": The Transpacific Forum of Japan Airlines, 28,* 4.

Nakane, C. (1973). *Japanese society.* Harmondsworth, Middlesex: Pelican.

Nakata, C., & Sivakumar, K. (1996). National culture and new product development: An integrative review. *Journal of Marketing, 60*(1), 61-72.

Nanhekhan, R. (1990). *Cultuurverschillen gemeten: aanknopingspunten voor wederzijds begrip tussen Nederlanders en Surinamers op de werkvloer.* Unpublished master's thesis, Free University, Amsterdam.

Napier, I., & Kroslid, D. (1996, December). *Review of the international TQM paradigm and its application to the work of Geert Hofstede.* Paper presented at the ANZAM '96 Conference, Wollongong, Australia.

Naroll, R. (1970). What have we learned from cross-cultural surveys? *American Anthropologist, 72,* 1227-1288.

Naroll, R. (1983). *The moral order: An introduction to the human situation.* Beverly Hills, CA: Sage.

Naroll, R., Michik, G. L., & Naroll, F. (1980). Holocultural research methods. In H. C. Triandis & J. W. Berry (Eds.), *Handbook of cross-cultural psychology: Vol. 2. Methodology* (pp. 479-521). Boston: Allyn & Bacon.

Nasierowski, W., & Mikula, B. (1998). Culture dimensions of Polish managers. *Organization Studies, 19,* 495-509.

National Center for Education Statistics (NCES). (1999). *Highlights from the Third International Mathematics and Science Study (TIMSS): Overview and key findings across grade levels.* Washington, DC: U.S. Department of Education, Office of Educational Research and Improvement.

Nauta, R. (1983). Distributive behaviour in a feminine culture. In J. B. Deregowski, S. Dziurawiec, & R. C. Annis (Eds.), *Expiscations in cross-cultural psychology* (pp. 371-380). Lisse, Netherlands: Swets & Zeitlinger.

Near, J. P., & Rechner, P. L. (1993). Cross-cultural variations in predictors of life satisfaction: An historical view of differences among West European countries. *Social Indicators Research, 29*(1), 109-121.

Negandhi, A. R., & Prasad, S. B. (1971). *Comparative management.* New York: Appleton-Century-Crofts.

Nesvold, B. A. (1969). Scalogram analysis of political violence. *Comparative Political Studies, 2,* 172-194.

Neuijen, B. (1992). *Diagnosing organizational cultures: Patterns of continuance and change.* Doctoral dissertation. Groningen: Wolters-Noordhoff.

Newman, K. L., & Nollen, S. D. (1996). Culture and congruence: The fit between management practices and national culture. *Journal of International Business Studies, 27,* 753-779.

Newson, J., Newson, E., Richardson, D., & Scaife, J. (1978). Perspectives in sex-role stereotyping. In J. Chetwynd & O. Hartnett (Eds.), *The sex role system* (pp. 28-49). London: Routledge & Kegan Paul.

Ng, S. H. (1977). Structural and nonstructural aspects of power distance reduction tendencies. *European Journal of Social Psychology, 7,* 317-345.

Ng, S. H. (1980). *The social psychology of power.* London: Academic Press.

Ng, S. H., Akhtar Hossain, A. B. M., Ball, P., Bond, M. H., Hayashi, K., Lim, S. P., O'Driscoll, M. P., Sinha, D., & Yang, K. S. (1982). Human values in 9 countries. In R. Rath, H. S. Asthana, D. Sinha, &

J. B. P. Sinha (Eds.), *Diversity and unity in cross-cultural psychology* (pp. 196-205). Lisse, Netherlands: Swets & Zeitlinger.

Noesjirwan, J. (1977). Contrasting cultural patterns of interpersonal closeness in doctors' waiting rooms in Sydney and Jakarta. *Journal of Cross-Cultural Psychology, 8,* 357-368.

Noonan, K. A. (1995). *Integration in the culturally differentiated organization.* Unpublished doctoral dissertation, University of Maryland.

Noorderhaven, N., & Tidjani, B. (1998). *The link between culture and governance: An explorative study with a special focus on Africa.* Tilburg, Netherlands: Tilburg University.

Norburn, D. (1987). Corporate leaders in Britain and America: A cross-national analysis. *Journal of International Business Studies, 18,* 15-32.

North, D. C. (1990). *Institutions, institutional change and economic performance.* Cambridge: Cambridge University Press.

Northrop, F. S. C. (1962). Cultural values. In S. Tax (Ed.), *Anthropology today: Selections* (pp. 422-435). Chicago: University of Chicago Press.

Oberg, K. (1960). Cultural shock: Adjustment to new cultural environments. *Practical Anthropology, 7,* 177-182.

O'Brien, R. M. (1979). The use of Pearson's *R* with ordinal data. *American Sociological Review, 44,* 851-857.

O'Connor, N. G. (1995). The influence of organizational culture on the usefulness of budget participation by Singaporean-Chinese managers. *Accounting, Organizations and Society, 20,* 383-403.

Oettingen, G. (1995). Cross-cultural perspectives on self-efficacy. In A. Bandura (Ed.), *Self-efficacy in changing societies* (pp. 149-176). New York: Cambridge University Press.

Offermann, L. R., & Hellmann, P. S. (1997). Culture's consequences for leadership behavior: National values in action. *Journal of Cross-Cultural Psychology, 28,* 342-351.

Oh, T. K. (1976). Japanese management: A critical review. *Academy of Management Review, 1,* 14-25.

Olah, A. (1995). Coping strategies among adolescents: A cross-cultural study. *Journal of Adolescence, 18,* 491-512.

Olie, R. L. (1994). Shades of culture and institutions in international mergers. *Organization Studies, 15,* 381-405.

Olie, R. L. (1996). *European transnational mergers.* Unpublished doctoral dissertation, Maastricht University.

Oliver Williamson in Paris or economics lesson? (1994, Summer). *EGOS [European Group for Organizational Studies] News,* pp. 1-3.

Organization for Economic Cooperation and Development (OECD). (1992). *Health systems facts and trends 1960-1991.* Paris: Author.

Organization for Economic Cooperation and Development (OECD) & Ministry of Industry of Canada

(MIC). (1995). *Literacy, economy and society: Results of the First International Adult Literacy Survey*. Paris: OECD.

Ornauer, H., Wiberg, H., Sicinski, A., & Galtung, J. (Eds.). (1976). *Images of the world in the year 2000: A comparative ten-nation study*. The Hague: Mouton.

Orpen, C. (1982). The effect of social support on reactions to role ambiguity and conflict: A study among white and black clerks in South Africa. *Journal of Cross-Cultural Psychology, 13*, 375-384.

Orwell, G. (1945). *Animal farm: A fairy story*. London: Secker & Warburg.

Osborn, T. N., & Osborn, D. B. (1986). *Leadership training in a Latin context: Issues and observations*. Greensboro, NC: Center for Creative Leadership.

Osgood, C. E., May, W. H., & Miron, M. S. (1975). *Cross-cultural universals of affective meaning*. Urbana: University of Illinois Press.

Osgood, C. E., Suci, G. J., & Tannenbaum, P. H. (1957). *The measurement of meaning*. Urbana: University of Illinois Press.

Osgood, C. E., Ware, E. E., & Morris, C. (1961). Analysis of the connotative meanings of a variety of human values as expressed by American college students. *Journal of Abnormal and Social Psychology, 62*, 62-73.

Osigweh, C. A. B., Yg. (1989a). The myth of universality in transnational organizational science. In C. A. B. Osigweh, Yg. (Ed.), *Organizational science abroad: Constraints and perspectives* (pp. 3-26). New York: Plenum.

Osigweh, C. A. B., Yg. (Ed.). (1989b). *Organizational science abroad: Constraints and perspectives*. New York: Plenum.

Otaki, M., Durrett, M. E., Richards, P., Nyquist, L., & Pennebaker, J. W. (1986). Maternal and infant behavior in Japan and America: A partial replication. *Journal of Cross-Cultural Psychology, 17*, 252-268.

Ouchi, W. G. (1980). Markets, bureaucracies, and clans. *Administrative Science Quarterly, 25*, 129-141.

Ouchi, W. G., & Wilkins, A. L. (1988). Organizational culture. In A. Westoby (Ed.), *Culture and power in educational organizations* (pp. 223-252). Milton Keynes, England: Open University Press.

Paddock, W., & Paddock, E. (1973). *We don't know how: An independent audit of what they call success in foreign assistance*. Ames: Iowa State University Press.

Pagès, M. (1971). Bethel culture, 1969: Impressions of an immigrant. *Journal of Applied Behavioral Science, 7*, 267-284.

Pagès, M., Bonetti, M., De Gaulejac, V., & Descendre, D. (1979). *L'emprise de l'organisation*. Paris: Presses Universitaires de France.

Pan, Y. (1996). Influences on foreign equity ownership level in joint ventures in China. *Journal of International Business Studies, 27*, 1-26.

Pareek, U. (1968). A motivational paradigm of development. *Journal of Social Issues, 24*(2), 115-122.

Pareto, V. (1976). Treatise on general sociology. In V. Pareto, *Sociological writings* (S. E. Finer, Ed.). Oxford: Blackwell. (Original work published 1916)

Parker, P. M. (1997). *National cultures of the world: A statistical reference*. Westport, CT: Greenwood.

Parkin, F. (1971). *Class inequality and political order: Social stratification in capitalist and communist societies*. St. Albans, England: Paladin.

Parsons, T. (1951). *The social system*. London: Routledge & Kegan Paul.

Parsons, T. (1977). *The evolution of societies*. Englewood Cliffs, NJ: Prentice Hall.

Parsons, T., & Shils, E. A. (1951). *Toward a general theory of action*. Cambridge, MA: Harvard University Press.

Pascale, R. (1985). The paradox of "corporate culture": Reconciling ourselves to socialization. *California Management Review, 27*(2), 26-41.

Pascale, R. T., & Athos, A. (1981). *The art of Japanese management: Applications for American executives*. New York: Simon & Schuster.

Patchen, M. (1965). *Some questionnaire measures of employee motivation and morale*. Ann Arbor: University of Michigan, Institute for Social Research, Survey Research Center.

Pavett, C., & Morris, T. (1995). Management styles within a multinational corporation: A five-country comparative study. *Human Relations, 48*, 1171-1191.

Payer, L. (1989). *Medicine and culture: Notions of health and sickness in Britain, the U.S., France and West Germany*. London: Victor Gollancz.

Peabody, D. (1985). *National characteristics*. Cambridge: Cambridge University Press.

Peabody, D. (1999). Nationality characteristics: Dimensions for comparison. In Y. T. Lee, C. R. McCauley, & J. G. Draguns (Eds.), *Personality and person perception across cultures* (pp. 65-84). Mahwah, NJ: Lawrence Erlbaum.

Pedersen, T., & Thomsen, S. (1997). European patterns of corporate ownership: A twelve-country study. *Journal of International Business Studies, 28*, 759-778.

Pelto, P. J. (1968, April). The differences between "tight" and "loose" societies. *TransAction*, pp. 37-40.

Pendle, G. (1976). *A history of Latin America*. Harmondsworth, Middlesex: Penguin.

Pennings, J. M. (1993). Executive reward systems: A cross-national comparison. *Journal of Management Studies, 30*, 261-280.

Pepitone, A. (1976). Toward a normative and comparative biocultural social psychology. *Journal of Personality and Social Psychology, 34*, 641-653.

Perera, M. H. B., & Mathews, M. R. (1990). The cultural relativity of accounting and international patterns of social accounting. *Advances in International Accounting, 3,* 215-251.

Perlmutter, H. V. (1965). L'entreprise internationale: trois conceptions. *Revue Economique et Sociale, Lausanne, 2,* 1-14.

Perrow, C. (1972). *Complex organizations: A critical essay.* Glenview, IL: Scott, Foresman.

Peters, T. J., & Waterman, R. H., Jr. (1982). *In search of excellence: Lessons from America's best-run companies.* New York: Harper & Row.

Peterson, M. F., & Bliese, P. D. (1996). The critical dimensions of cultural differences: Strategies for quickly learning coping skills in OOTW. In R. L. Phillips & M. R. Thurman (Eds.), *Future soldiers and the quality imperative: The Army 2010 Conference* (pp. 351-380). Washington, DC: Government Printing Office.

Peterson, M. F., & Smith, P. B. (1997). Does national culture or ambient temperature explain cross-national differences in role stress? No sweat! *Academy of Management Journal, 40,* 930-946.

Peterson, M. F., Smith, P. B., Akande, A., Ayestaran, S., Bochner, S., Callan, V., Cho, N. G., Jesuino, J. C., d'Amorim, M., Francois, P. H., Hofmann, K., Koopman, P. L., Leung, K., Lim, T. K., Mortazavi, S., Munene, J., Radford, M., Ropo, A., Savage, G., Setiadi, B., Sinha, T. N., Sorenson, R., & Viedge, C. (1995). Role-conflict, ambiguity, and overload: A 21-nation study. *Academy of Management Journal, 38,* 429-452.

Pettigrew, A. M. (1972, April). Managing under stress. *Management Today,* pp. 99-102.

Pettigrew, A. M. (1979). On studying organizational cultures. *Administrative Science Quarterly, 24,* 570-581.

Peyrefitte, A. (1976). *Le mal Français.* Paris: Plon.

Pheysey, D. C. (1993). *Organizational cultures: Types and transformations.* London: Routledge.

Philipsen, H., & Cassee, E. T. (1965). Verschillen in de wijze van leiding geven tussen drie typen organisaties. *Mens en Onderneming, 19,* 172-184.

Phillips, D. L., & Clancy, K. J. (1972). Some effects of "social desirability" in survey studies. *American Journal of Sociology, 77,* 921-940.

Phinney, J. S. (1996). When we talk about American ethnic groups, what do we mean? *Australian Psychologist, 51,* 918-927.

Pieper, J. (1931). *Grundformen sozialer Spielregeln.* Frankfurt: Verlag Josef Knecht.

Pirenne, H. (1939). *A history of Europe from the invasions to the XVI century.* London: George Allen & Unwin.

Pitts, J. R. (1968). Le Play, Frédéric. In D. L. Sills (Ed.), *International encyclopedia of the social sciences* (Vol. 9, pp. 84-90). New York: Macmillan.

Pitts, R. A., & Daniels, J. D. (1984). Aftermath of the matrix mania. *Columbia Journal of World Business, 19*(2), 48-54.

Pizam, A., & Sussmann, S. (1995). Does nationality affect tourist behavior? *Annals of Tourism Research, 22,* 901-917.

Plato. (1970). *The laws* (T. J. Saunders, Trans.). Harmondsworth, Middlesex: Penguin.

Plato. (1974). *The republic* (D. Lee, Trans.). Harmondsworth, Middlesex: Penguin.

Playford, J. (1976). The myth of pluralism. In F. G. Castles, D. J. Murray, D. C. Potter, & C. J. Pollitt (Eds.), *Decisions, organizations and society: Selected readings* (pp. 380-391). Harmondsworth, Middlesex: Penguin.

Plowman, T. S. (1999). The information superhighway: A comparative look at the growth of informational technology in Australia and India. *International Journal of Educational Telecommunications, 5*(2), 93-110.

Poirier, J. (1978). Aliénation culturelle et hétéroculture. In G. Michaud (Ed.), *Identités collectives et relations inter-culturelles.* Paris: Presses Universitaires de France.

Polley, R. B. (1989). Coalition, mediation, and scapegoating: General principles and cultural variation. *International Journal of Intercultural Relations, 13,* 165-181.

Pompe, J. H., Bruyn, M. H., & Koek, J. V. (1986). *Ondernemen in internationaal vergelijkend perspektief: starten, waarden, omgeving, problemen.* Groningen, Netherlands: Groningen University, Institute of Sociology.

Pondy, L. R., Frost, P. J., Morgan, G., & Dandridge, T. C. (Eds.). (1983). *Organizational symbolism.* Greenwich, CT: JAI.

Poole, M. S. (1985). Communication and organizational climates: Review, critique, and a new perspective. In R. D. McPhee & P. K. Tompkins (Eds.), *Organizational communication: Traditional themes and new direction* (pp. 79-108). Beverly Hills, CA: Sage.

Popper, K. (1959). *The logic of scientific discovery.* London: Hutchinson.

Population Crisis Committee. (1988). *Country rankings of the status of women: Poor, powerless and pregnant* (Briefing Paper 20). Washington, DC: Author.

Porter, M. E. (1990). The competitive advantage of nations. *Harvard Business Review, 68*(4), 73-93.

Porter, M. E. (1992). A note on culture and competitive advantage: Response to Van den Bosch and Van Prooijen. *European Management Journal, 10,* 178.

Powell, G., Posner, B. Z., & Schmidt, W. H. (1984). Sex effects on managerial value systems. *Human Relations, 37,* 909-921.

Powell, P. L., & Johnson, J. E. V. (1995). Gender and DSS design: The research implications. *Decision Support Systems, 14*(1), 27-58.

Pratt, J., Mohrweis, L. C., & Beaulieu, P. (1993). The interaction between national and organizational culture in accounting firms: An extension. *Accounting, Organizations and Society, 18,* 621-628.

Preiss, G. W. (1971). *Work goals of engineers: A comparative study between German and U.S. industry.* Unpublished master's thesis, Sloan School of Management.

Price, J. L., & Bluedorn, A. C. (1977). *Intent to leave as a measure of turnover.* Iowa City: University of Iowa, Department of Sociology.

Prins, R. (1990). *Sickness absence in Belgium, Germany (FR) and the Netherlands: A comparative study.* Unpublished doctoral dissertation, Maastricht University.

Prins, R., & De Graaf, A. (1986). Comparison of sickness absence in Belgian, German and Dutch firms. *British Journal of Industrial Medicine, 43,* 529-536.

Pryor, J. B., DeSouza, E. R., Fitness, J., Hutz, C., Kumpf, M., Lubbert, K., Pesonen, O., & Erber, M. W. (1997). Gender differences in the interpretation of social-sexual behavior: A cross-cultural perspective on sexual harassment. *Journal of Cross-Cultural Psychology, 28,* 509-534.

Przeworski, A., & Teune, M. (1970). *The logic of comparative social inquiry.* New York: John Wiley.

Pugh, D. S. (1976). The "Aston" approach to the study of organizations. In G. Hofstede & M. S. Kassem (Eds.), *European contributions to organization theory* (pp. 62-78). Assen, Netherlands: Van Gorcum.

Pugh, D. S., & Hickson, D. J. (1976). *Organizational structure in its context: The Aston Programme I.* London: Saxon House.

Pugh, D. S., & Hickson, D. J. (Eds.). (1993). *Great writers on organizations: The omnibus edition.* Aldershot, England: Dartmouth.

Pugh, D. S., & Hinings, C. R. (1976). *Organizational structure: Extensions and replications. The Aston Programme II.* London: Saxon House.

Pümpin, C. (1984). Unternehmenskultur, Unternehmensstrategie und Unternehmenserfolg. *GDI Impuls, Gottlieb Duttweiler Institut, 2,* 19-30.

Pümpin, C., Kobi, J. M., & Wüthrich, H. A. (1985). *La culture de l'entreprise: le profil stratégique qui conduit au succès.* Bern, Switzerland: Banque Populaire Suisse.

Punnett, B. J., Singh, J. B., & Williams, G. (1994). The relative influence of economic development and Anglo heritage on expressed values: Empirical evidence from a Caribbean country. *International Journal of Intercultural Relations, 18,* 99-115.

Putnam, R. D. (1973). The political attitudes of senior civil servants in Western Europe: A preliminary report. *British Journal of Political Science, 3,* 257-290.

Quinn, N. (1977). Anthropological studies on women's status. *Annual Review of Anthropology, 6,* 181-225.

Quinn, R. P. (1973). What workers want: General descriptive statistics and demographic correlates. In R. P. Quinn & T. W. Mangione (Eds.), *The 1969-1970 survey of working conditions* (pp. 203-262).

Ann Arbor: University of Michigan, Institute for Social Research.

Raelin, J. A. (1986). *The clash of cultures: Managers and professionals.* Boston: Harvard Business School Press.

Raiffa, H. (1982). *The art and science of negotiation: How to resolve conflicts and get the best out of bargaining.* Cambridge, MA: Belknap.

Ralston, D. A., Cunniff, M. K., & Gustafson, D. J. (1995). Cultural accommodation: The effect of language on the responses of bilingual Hong-Kong Chinese managers. *Journal of Cross-Cultural Psychology, 26,* 714-727.

Ralston, D. A., Gustafson, D. J., Cheung, F. M., & Terpstra, R. H. (1993). Differences in managerial values: A study of United States, Hong Kong and PRC managers. *Journal of International Business Studies, 24,* 249-275.

Ralston, D. A., Gustafson, D. J., Elsass, P. M., Cheung, F. M., & Terpstra, R. H. (1992). Eastern values: A comparison of managers in the United States, Hong Kong, and the People's Republic of China. *Journal of Applied Psychology, 77,* 664-671.

Ramsden, J. M. (1985, January 26). World airline safety audit. *Flight International,* pp. 29-34.

Randall, D. M. (1993). Cross-cultural research on organizational commitment: A review and application of Hofstede's Values Survey Module. *Journal of Business Research, 26*(1), 91-110.

Ravesloot, J. (1995). Courtship and sexuality in the youth phase. In M. DeBois-Reymond, R. Diekstra, K. Hurrelmann, & E. Peters (Eds.), *Childhood and youth in Germany and the Netherlands: Transitions and coping strategies of adolescents* (pp. 41-71). Berlin: Walter de Gruyter.

Ray, J. J. (1976). Do authoritarians hold authoritarian attitudes? *Human Relations, 29,* 307-325.

Read, R. (1993). *Politics and policies of national economic growth.* Unpublished doctoral dissertation, Stanford University.

Reader's Digest. (1970). *A survey of Europe today.* London: Author.

Redding, S. G. (1980a). Cognition as an aspect of culture and its reaction to management processes: An exploratory view of the Chinese case. *Journal of Management Studies, 17,* 127-148.

Redding, S. G. (1980b). Management education for Orientals. In B. Garratt & J. Stopford (Eds.), *Breaking down barriers* (pp. 193-214). Westmead, England: Gower.

Redding, S. G. (1990). *The spirit of Chinese capitalism.* Berlin: Walter de Gruyter.

Redding, S. G. (1994). Comparative management theory: Jungle, zoo or fossil bed? *Organization Studies, 15,* 323-359.

Redding, S. G., & Casey, T. W. (1976). *Managerial beliefs and behaviour in South-East Asia* (Working paper). Hong Kong: Hong Kong University, Centre of Asian Studies.

Redding, S. G., & Ng, M. (1982). The role of "face" in the organizational perceptions of Chinese managers. *Organization Studies, 3*, 201-219.

Redding, S. G., & Ogilvie, J. G. (1984, October). *Cultural aspects on cockpit communication in civilian aircraft.* Paper presented at the Conference on Human Factors in Managing Aviation Safety, Zurich.

Redding, S. G., & Richardson, S. (1986). Participative management and its varying relevance in Hong Kong and Singapore. *Asia Pacific Journal of Management, 3*(2), 76-98.

Redfield, M. P. (Ed.). (1962). *Human nature and the study of society: The papers of Robert Redfield.* Chicago: University of Chicago Press.

Rees, B., & Brewster, C. (1995). Supporting equality: Patriarchy at work in Europe. *Personnel Review, 24*(1), 19-40.

Reeves-Ellington, R. (1995). Organizing for global effectiveness: Ethnicity and organizations. *Human Organization, 54*, 249-262.

Reitsma, D. (1995). Major public works: Cultural differences and decision-making procedures. *Tijdschrift voor Economische en Sociale Geografie, 86*(2), 186-190.

Renier, G. J. (1931). *The English: Are they human?* London: William & Norgate.

Rescher, N. (1969). What is value change? A framework for research. In K. Baier & N. Rescher (Eds.), *Values and the future* (pp. 68-109). New York: Free Press.

Reynolds, P. D. (1986). Organizational culture as related to industry, position and performance: A preliminary report. *Journal of Management Studies, 23*, 333-345.

Richins, M. L., & Verhage, B. J. (1987). Assertiveness and aggression in marketplace exchanges, testing measure equivalence. *Journal of Cross-Cultural Psychology, 18*, 93-105.

Rieger, D. W., & Rieger, F. (1989). The influence of societal culture on corporate culture, business strategy, and performance in the international airline industry. In C. A. B. Osigweh, Yg. (Ed.), *Organizational science abroad: Constraints and perspectives* (pp. 229-265). New York: Plenum.

Riesman, D., Glazer, N., & Denney, R. (1953). *The lonely crowd: A study of the changing American character.* Garden City, NY: Doubleday.

Riley, P. (1988). The ethnography of autonomy. In A. Brookes & P. Greendy (Eds.), *Individualisation and autonomy in language learning* (pp. 12-34). London: Modern English Publications/British Council.

Ritti, R. R. (1964). Control of "halo" in factor analyses of a supervisory behavior inventory. *Personnel Psychology, 17*, 305-318.

Roberts, J. M., Arth, M. J., & Bush, R. R. (1959). Games in culture. *American Anthropologist, 61*, 597-605.

Roberts, K. H., & Boyacigiller, N. A. (1984). Cross-national organizational research: The grasp of the blind men. In B. M. Shaw & L. L. Cummings (Eds.), *Research in organizational behavior* (pp. 423-475). Greenwich, CT: JAI.

Robinson, J. P., Athanasiou, R., & Head, K. B. (1969). *Measures of occupational attitudes and occupational characteristics.* Ann Arbor: University of Michigan, Institute for Social Research, Survey Research Center.

Robinson, W. S. (1950). Ecological correlations and the behavior of individuals. *American Sociological Review, 15*, 351-357.

Roces, A., & Roces, G. (1985). *Culture shock: Philippines.* Singapore: Time Books International.

Rocher, G. (1974). *Talcott Parsons and American sociology.* London: Nelson.

Rochlin, G. I., & Vonmeier, A. (1994). Nuclear power operations: A cross-cultural perspective. *Annual Review of Energy and the Environment, 19*, 153-187.

Rodgers, W. (1969). *Think: A biography of the Watsons and IBM.* New York: New American Library.

Rokeach, M. (1972). *Beliefs, attitudes and values: A theory of organization and change.* San Francisco: Jossey-Bass.

Rokeach, M. (1973). *The nature of human values.* New York: Free Press.

Ronen, S., & Shenkar, O. (1985). Clustering countries on attitudinal dimensions: A review and synthesis. *Academy of Management Review, 10*, 435-454.

Roney, C. J. R., & Sorrentino, R. M. (1995). Self-evaluation motives and uncertainty orientation: Asking the who question. *Personality and Social Psychology Bulletin, 21*, 1319-1329.

Roper, M. (1994). *Masculinity and the British organization man since 1945.* Oxford: Oxford University Press.

Rorer, B. A., & Ziller, R. C. (1982). Iconic communication of values among American and Polish students. *Journal of Cross-Cultural Psychology, 13*, 352-361.

Rosenthal, D. A., & Feldman, S. S. (1992). The nature and stability of ethnic identity in Chinese youth: Effects of length of residence in two cultural contexts. *Journal of Cross-Cultural Psychology, 23*, 214-227.

Rosenzweig, P. M., & Nohria, N. (1994). Influences on human resource management practices in multinational corporations. *Journal of International Business Studies, 25*, 229-251.

Ross, M. W. (1983). Societal relationships and gender role in homosexuals: A cross-cultural comparison. *Journal of Sex Research, 19*, 273-288.

Ross, M. W. (1989). Gay youth in four cultures: A comparative study. *Journal of Homosexuality, 17*, 299-314.

Roth, K., & O'Donnell, S. (1996). Foreign subsidiary compensation strategy: An agency theory perspective. *Academy of Management Journal, 39*, 678-703.

Roth, M. S. (1995). The effects of culture and socioeconomics on the performance of global brand image strategies. *Journal of Marketing Research, 32,* 163-175.

Rotterstøl, N. (1975). Suicide in Norway. In N. L. Farberow (Ed.), *Suicide in different cultures.* Baltimore: University Park Press.

Rousseau, D. (1985). Issues of level in organizational research: Multi-level and cross-level perspectives. *Research in Organizational Behavior, 7,* 1-37.

Rousseau, J. J. (1972). *Du contrat social.* Oxford: Clarendon. (Original work published 1762)

Rubenowitz, S. (1968). Personnel management organization in some European societies. *Management International Review, 8*(4-5), 74-92.

Rubenowitz, S., Norrgren, F., & Tannenbaum, A. S. (1983). Some social psychological effects of direct and indirect participation in ten Swedish companies. *Organization Studies, 4,* 243-259.

Rubin, Z., & Peplau, L. (1973). Belief in a just world and reactions to another's lot: A study of participants in the national draft lottery. *Journal of Social Issues, 29,* 73-98.

Rudin, S. A. (1968). National motives predict psychogenic death 25 years later. *Science, 160,* 901-903.

Rummel, R. J. (1963). Dimensions of conflict behavior within and between nations. *General systems: Yearbook of the Society for General Systems Research, 8,* 1-50.

Rummel, R. J. (1972). *The dimensions of nations.* Beverly Hills, CA: Sage.

Runciman, W. G. (1969). The three dimensions of social inequality. In A. Béteille (Ed.), *Social inequality: Selected readings* (pp. 45-63). Harmondsworth, Middlesex: Penguin.

Russett, B. M. (1968). Delineating international regions. In J. D. Singer (Ed.), *Quantitative international politics: Insights and evidence.* New York: Free Press.

Ryback, D., Sanders, A. L., Lorentz, J., & Koestenblatt, M. (1980). Child-rearing practices reported by students in six cultures. *Journal of Psychology, 110,* 153-162.

Sackmann, S. A. (1992). Culture and subcultures: An analysis of organizational knowledge. *Administrative Science Quarterly, 37,* 140-161.

Sadler, P. J., & Hofstede, G. (1972). Leadership styles: Preferences and perceptions of employees of an international company in different countries. *Mens en Onderneming* (Leiden, Netherlands), *26,* 43-63.

Saenger, G. (1952). Minority personality and adjustment. *Transactions of the New York Academy of Sciences, 14,* 204-208.

Saffold, G. S. (1988). Culture traits, strength, and organizational performance: Moving beyond "strong" culture. *Academy of Management Review, 13,* 546-558.

Sagie, A., Elizur, D., & Yamauchi, H. (1996). The structure and strength of achievement motivation: A cross-cultural comparison. *Journal of Organizational Behavior, 17,* 431-444.

Salter, S. B., & Niswander, F. (1995). Cultural influence on the development of accounting systems internationally: A test of Gray's (1988) theory. *Journal of International Business Studies, 26,* 379-397.

Sampson, E. E. (1977). Psychology and the American ideal. *Journal of Personality and Social Psychology, 35,* 767-782.

Samsonowicz, H. (1970). Die Bedeutung des Grosshandels für die Entwicklung der polnischen Kultur bis zum Beginn des 16. Jahrhunderts. *Studia Historiae Economica, 5,* 92 ff.

Saner, R. (1989). Culture bias of Gestalt therapy: Made in U.S.A. *Gestalt Journal, 12*(2), 57-71.

Saner, R., & Yiu, L. S. (1994). European and Asian resistance to the use of the American case method in management training: Possible cultural and systemic incongruencies. *International Journal of Human Resource Management, 5,* 953-976.

Saner, R., Yiu, L. S., & Søndergaard, M. (2000). Business diplomacy management: A core competence for global companies. *Academy of Management Executive, 14*(1), 80-92.

Sarawathi, T. S., & Dutta, R. (1987). Cross-cultural research in developmental psychology: Retrospect and prospects in India. In Ç. Kagitçibasi (Ed.), *Growth and progress in cross-cultural psychology* (pp. 148-158). Berwyn, IL: Swets North America.

Sauvy, A. (1966). *Théorie générale de la population: Vol. 2. La vie des populations.* Paris: Presses Universitaires de France.

Sawyer, J. (1967). Dimensions of nations: Size, wealth and politics. *American Journal of Sociology, 72,* 145-172.

Sawyer, J., & Levine, R. A. (1966). Cultural dimensions: A factor analysis of the World Ethnographic Sample. *American Anthropologist, 68,* 708-731.

Sayles, L. R. (1963). *Individualism and big business.* New York: McGraw-Hill.

Scarr, S. (1996). Family policy dilemmas in contemporary nation-states: Are women benefited by "family-friendly" governments? In S. Gustavsson & L. Lewin (Eds.), *The future of the nation state* (pp. 107-129). Stockholm: Nerenius & Santérus.

Schachter, S., Nuttin, J., DeMonchaux, C., Maucorps, P. H., Osmer, D., Duijker, H. C. J., Rommetveit, R., & Israel, J. (1954). Cross-cultural experiments on threat and rejection: A study of the Organization for Comparative Social Research. *Human Relations, 7,* 403-439.

Schaefer, J. M. (1977). The growth of hologeistic studies 1889-1975. *Behavioral Science Research, 12,* 71-108.

Schama, S. (1987). *The embarrassment of riches: An interpretation of Dutch culture in the Golden Age.* New York: Alfred A. Knopf.

Schaufeli, W. B., & Van Dierendonck, D. (1995). A cautionary note about the cross-national and clinical validity of cutoff points for the Maslach Burnout Inventory. *Psychological Reports, 76,* 1083-1090.

Schaupp, D. L. (1973). *A cross-cultural study of a multinational company: Attitudes of satisfactions, needs and values affecting participative management.* Unpublished doctoral dissertation, University of Kentucky.

Schein, E. H. (1983). The role of the founder in creating organizational culture. *Organizational Dynamics, 12*(1), 13-28.

Schein, E. H. (1985). *Organizational culture and leadership: A dynamic view.* San Francisco: Jossey-Bass.

Schein, V. E., Mueller, R., Lituchy, T., & Liu, J. (1996). Think manager, think male: A global phenomenon. *Journal of Organizational Behavior, 17,* 33-41.

Scherer, K. R., & Wallbott, H. G. (1994). Evidence for universality and cultural variation of differential emotion response patterning. *Journal of Personality and Social Psychology, 66,* 310-328.

Scheuch, E. K. (1990). The development of comparative research: Towards causal explanations. In E. Oyen (Ed.), *Comparative methodology: Theory and practice in international social research* (pp. 19-37). London: Sage.

Schildhauer, J. (1985). *The Hansa: History and culture.* Leipzig, Germany: Edition Leipzig.

Schimmack, U. (1996). Cultural influences on the recognition of emotion by facial expressions: Individualistic or Caucasian cultures. *Journal of Cross-Cultural Psychology, 27,* 37-50.

Schludermann, S., & Schludermann, E. (1977). Achievement motivation: Cross-cultural and development issues. In Y. H. Poortinga (Ed.), *Basic problems in cross-cultural psychology* (pp. 149-159). Amsterdam: Swets & Zeitlinger.

Schmidt, S. M., & Yeh, R. S. (1992). The structure of leader influence: A cross-national comparison. *Journal of Cross-Cultural Psychology, 23,* 251-264.

Schmitter, P. C. (1981). Interest intermediation and regime governability in contemporary Western Europe and North America. In S. Berger (Ed.), *Organizing interests in Western Europe: Pluralism, corporatism and the transformation of politics.* Cambridge: Cambridge University Press.

Schneider, B. (1975). Organizational climates: An essay. *Personnel Psychology, 28,* 447-479.

Schneider, P. L., & Schneider, A. L. (1971). Social mobilization, political institutions, and political violence. *Comparative Political Studies, 4,* 69-90.

Schneider, S. C. (1989). Strategy formulation: The impact of national culture. *Organization Studies, 10,* 149-168.

Schneider, S. C., & De Meyer, A. (1991). Interpreting and responding to strategic issues. *Strategic Management Journal, 12,* 307-320.

Schonfeld, W. R. (1976). *Obedience and revolt: French behavior toward authority.* Beverly Hills, CA: Sage.

Schooler, C. (1998). History, social structure and individualism: A cross-cultural perspective on Japan.

International Journal of Comparative Sociology, 39(1), 32-51.

Schramm-Nielsen, I. (1989). *Relations de travail entre Danois et Français dans les Entreprises Privées.* Copenhagen: Integrated Modern Languages and Economics Centre.

Schreuder, H. (1978). *Facts and speculations on corporate social reporting in France, Germany and Holland* (Working Paper 78-42). Brussels: European Institute for Advanced Studies in Management.

Schubart, W. (1941). *Religion und eros.* Munich: Beck.

Schuler, R. S., & Rogovsky, N. (1998). Understanding compensation practice variation across firms: The impact of national culture. *Journal of International Business Studies, 29,* 159-177.

Schultz, P. W., & Zelezny, L. C. (1998). Values and proenvironmental behavior: A five-country survey. *Journal of Cross-Cultural Psychology, 29,* 540-558.

Schumacher, E. F. (1973). *Small is beautiful: A study of economics as if people mattered.* London: Sphere.

Schuman, H., & Presser, S. (1981). *Questions and answers in attitude surveys: Experiments on question form, wording, and context.* New York: Academic Press.

Schwartz, I. M. (1993). Affective reactions of American and Swedish women to their first premarital coitus: A cross-cultural comparison. *Journal of Sex Research, 30,* 18-26.

Schwartz, S. H. (1992). Universals in the content and structure of values: Theoretical advances and empirical tests in 20 countries. *Advances in Experimental Social Psychology, 25,* 1-65.

Schwartz, S. H. (1994). Beyond individualism/collectivism: New cultural dimensions of values. In U. Kim, H. C. Triandis, Ç. Kagitçibasi, S.-C. Choi, & G. Yoon (Eds.), *Individualism and collectivism: Theory, method, and applications* (pp. 85-119). Thousand Oaks, CA: Sage.

Schwartz, S. H., & Sagiv, L. (1995). Identifying culture-specifics in the content and structure of values. *Journal of Cross-Cultural Psychology, 26,* 92-116.

Seeman, M. (1977). Some real and imaginary consequences of social mobility: A French-American comparison. *American Journal of Sociology, 82,* 757-782.

Segall, M. H. (1996). [Review of the book *Individualism and collectivism,* by H. C. Triandis]. *Contemporary Psychology, 41,* 540-542.

Segall, M. H., Dasen, P. R., Berry, J. W., & Poortinga, Y. H. (1990). *Human behavior in global perspective: An introduction to cross-cultural psychology.* New York: Pergamon.

Sekaran, U., & Snodgrass, C. R. (1989). Organizational effectiveness and its attainment: A cultural perspective. In C. A. B. Osigweh, Yg. (Ed.), *Organizational science abroad: Constraints and perspectives* (pp. 269-292). New York: Plenum.

Selmer, J. (1999). Culture shock in China? Adjustment pattern of Western expatriate business managers. *International Business Review, 8,* 515-534.

Selye, H. (1974). *Stress without distress.* Philadelphia: J. B. Lippincott.

Semenov, R. (2000). *Cross-country differences in economic governance: Culture as a major explanatory factor.* Unpublished doctoral dissertation, Tilburg University.

Shackleton, V. J., & Ali, A. H. (1990). Work-related values of managers: A test of the Hofstede model. *Journal of Cross-Cultural Psychology, 21,* 109-118.

Shaffer, T. R., & O'Hara, B. S. (1995). The effects of country-of-origin on trust and ethical perceptions of legal services. *Service Industries Journal, 15*(2), 162-185.

Shane, S. A. (1992a). The effect of cultural differences in perceptions of transaction costs on national differences in the preference for licensing. *Management International Review, 32,* 295-311.

Shane, S. A. (1992b). Why do some societies invent more than others? *Journal of Business Venturing, 7,* 29-46.

Shane, S. A. (1993). Cultural influences on national rates of innovation. *Journal of Business Venturing, 8,* 59-73.

Shane, S. A. (1994a). Are champions different from non-champions? *Journal of Business Venturing, 9,* 397-421.

Shane, S. A. (1994b). The effect of national culture on the choice between licensing and direct foreign investment. *Strategic Management Journal, 15,* 627-642.

Shane, S. A. (1995). Uncertainty avoidance and the preference for innovation championing roles. *Journal of International Business Studies, 26,* 47-68.

Shane, S. A., & Venkataraman, S. (1996). Renegade and rational championing strategies. *Organization Studies, 17,* 751-771.

Shane, S. A., Venkataraman, S., & Macmillan, I. C. (1995). Cultural differences in innovation championing strategies. *Journal of Management, 21,* 931-952.

Shaver, P. R. (1973). Authoritarianism, dogmatism and related measures. In J. P. Robinson & P. R. Shaver (Eds.), *Measures of social psychological attitudes* (pp. 295-451). Ann Arbor: University of Michigan, Institute for Social Research.

Shenkar, O., & Von Glinow, M. A. (1994). Paradoxes of organizational theory and research: Using the case of China to illustrate national contingency. *Management Science, 40,* 56-71.

Shepard, J. M. (1971). *Automation and alienation: A study of office and factory workers.* Cambridge: MIT Press.

Shils, E. A. (1975). *Center and periphery: Essays in macrosociology.* Chicago: University of Chicago Press.

Shoham, A., & Albaum, G. (1994). The effects of transfer of marketing methods on export performance: An empirical examination. *International Business Review, 3,* 219-241.

Shore, B., & Venkatachalam, A. R. (1996). Role of national culture in the transfer of information technology. *Journal of Strategic Information Systems, 5*(1), 19-35.

Shorter, E. (1975). *The making of the modern family.* New York: Basic Books.

Silverzweig, S., & Allen, R. F. (1976). Changing the corporate culture. *Sloan Management Review, 17*(3), 33-49.

Simon, H. A. (1976). *Administrative behavior: A study of decision-making processes in administrative organization.* New York: Free Press. (Original work published 1945)

Sinclair, A. (1993). Approaches to organizational culture and ethics. *Journal of Business Ethics, 12,* 63-73.

Singelis, T. M., Triandis, H. C., Bhawuk, D. P. S., & Gelfand, M. J. (1995). Horizontal and vertical dimensions of individualism and collectivism: A theoretical and measurement refinement. *Cross-Cultural Research, 29,* 240-275.

Singh, J. P. (1990). Managerial culture and work-related values in India. *Organization Studies, 11,* 75-101.

Singh, N. K., & Paul, O. (1985). *Corporate soul: Dynamics of effective management.* Sahibabad, India: Vikas.

Sinha, J. B. P. (1992). Inner transformation of the Hindu identity. *Dynamische Psychiatrie, 25*(1-2), 50-59.

Sirota, D. (1970, January-February). Why managers do not use attitude survey results. *Personnel,* pp. 24-35.

Sirota, D., & Greenwood, J. M. (1971). Understand your overseas work force. *Harvard Business Review, 49*(3), 53-60.

Skocpol, T., & Somers, M. (1980). The uses of comparative history in macro-social inquiry. *Comparative Studies in Society and History, 22*(2), 174-197.

Slater, P. (1976). *The pursuit of loneliness: American culture at the breaking point.* Boston: Beacon.

Slocum, J. W., Topichak, P. M., & Kuhn, D. G. (1971). A cross-cultural study of need satisfaction and need importance for operative employees. *Personnel Psychology, 24,* 435-445.

Smelser, N. J. (1989). External influences on sociology. *International Sociology, 4,* 419-429.

Smircich, L. (1983). Concepts of culture and organizational analysis. *Administrative Science Quarterly, 28,* 339-358.

Smith, J. C. (1964). The theoretical constructs of Western contractual law. In F. S. C. Northrop & H. H. Livingston (Eds.), *Cross-cultural understanding: Epistemology in anthropology* (pp. 254-294). New York: Harper & Row.

Smith, P. (1987). Cross-cultural problems in management training for rural development. *Agricultural Administration and Extension, 24*(3), 149-164.

Smith, P. B. (1996). National cultures and the values of organizational employees: Time for another look. In P. Joynt & M. Warner (Eds.), *Managing across cultures: Issues and perspectives* (pp. 92-102). London: Thomson.

Smith, P. B., & Bond, M. H. (1993). *Social psychology across cultures: Analysis and perspectives.* New York: Harvester Wheatsheaf.

Smith, P. B., Dugan, S., & Trompenaars, F. (1996). National culture and the values of organizational employees: A dimensional analysis across 43 nations. *Journal of Cross-Cultural Psychology, 27,* 231-264.

Smith, P. B., & Peterson, M. F. (1988). *Leadership, organizations and culture.* London: Sage.

Smith, P. B., Peterson, M. F., Akande, D., Callan, V., Cho, N. G., Jesuino, J., d'Amorim, M. A., Koopman, P., Leung, K., Mortazawi, S., Munene, J., Radford, M., Ropo, A., Savage, G., & Viedge, C. (1994). Organizational event management in fourteen countries: A comparison with Hofstede's dimensions. In A. M. Bouvy, F. J. R. Van de Vijver, P. Boski, & P. Schmitz (Eds.), *Journeys into cross-cultural psychology* (pp. 364-373). Lisse, Netherlands: Swets & Zeitlinger.

Smith, P. B., Peterson, M. F., Misumi, J., & Bond, M. H. (1992). A cross-cultural test of the Japanese PM leadership theory. *Applied Psychology: An International Review/Psychologie Appliquée: Revue Internationale, 41*(1), 5-19.

Smith, P. B., Peterson, M. F., Schwartz, S., & Event Management Team Project. (2000). *Cultural values and making sense of work events: A 42-nation study.* Unpublished manuscript.

Smith, P. B., & Schwartz, S. H. (1997). Values. In J. W. Berry, M. H. Segall, & Ç. Kagitçibasi (Eds.), *Handbook of cross-cultural psychology: Vol. 3. Social behavior and applications* (pp. 77-118). Boston: Allyn & Bacon.

Smith, P. B., Trompenaars, F., & Dugan, S. (1995). The Rotter Locus of Control Scale in 43 countries: A test of cultural relativity. *International Journal of Psychology, 30,* 377-400.

Smulders, P. G. W., Kompier, M. A. J., & Paoli, P. (1996). The work environment in the 12 EU countries: Differences and similarities. *Human Relations, 49,* 1291-1313.

Soeters, J. L. (1986). Excellent companies as social movements. *Journal of Management Studies, 23,* 299-313.

Soeters, J. L. (1993). Managing Euregional networks. *Organization Studies, 14,* 639-656.

Soeters, J. L. (1996). Culture and conflict: An application of Hofstede's theory to the conflict in the former Yugoslavia. *Peace and Conflict: Journal of Peace Psychology, 2,* 233-244.

Soeters, J. L. (1997). Value orientations in military academies: A thirteen-country study. *Armed Forces and Society, 24,* 7-32.

Soeters, J. L., & Boer, P. C. (2000). Culture and flight safety in military aviation. *International Journal of Aviation Psychology, 10,* 111-133.

Soeters, J. L., & Recht, R. (1998). Culture and discipline in military academies: An international comparison. *Journal of Political and Military Sociology, 26,* 169-189.

Soeters, J. L., & Recht, R. (1999). *Convergence or divergence in the multinational classroom?* Unpublished manuscript.

Soeters, J. L., & Schreuder, H. (1988). The interaction between national and organizational cultures in accounting firms. *Accounting, Organizations and Society, 13,* 75-85.

Søndergaard, M. (1988). *A two-country case-study of two European management cultures.* Århus, Denmark: Århus School of Business, Department of Organization and Management.

Søndergaard, M. (1994). Hofstede's consequences: A study of reviews, citations and replications. *Organization Studies, 15,* 447-456.

Søndergaard, M. (1996). Scandinavian management: Ménage or manège? Findings from a comparative Danish-French study. In S. Jönsson (Ed.), *Perspectives of Scandinavian management* (pp. 97-125). Göteborg: BAS.

Sorge, A. (1983). [Review of the book *Culture's consequences,* by G. Hofstede]. *Administrative Science Quarterly, 28,* 625-629.

Spence, J. A., & Helmreich, R. L. (1983). Achievement-related motives and behavior. In J. T. Spence (Ed.), *Achievement and achievement motives.* San Francisco: W. H. Freeman.

Spencer-Oatey, H. (1997). Unequal relationships in high and low power distance societies: A comparative study of tutor-student role relations in Britain and China. *Journal of Cross-Cultural Psychology, 28,* 284-302.

Spicer, E. H. (1971). Persistent cultural systems: A comparative study of identity systems that can adapt to contrasting environments. *Science, 174,* 795-800.

Spink, P. (1996). [Review of the book *Work motivation,* by R. N. Kanungo & M. Mendonca]. *Human Relations, 49,* 501-522.

Srinivas, M. N. (1969). The caste system in India. In A. Béteille (Ed.), *Social inequality: Selected readings* (pp. 265-272). Harmondsworth, Middlesex: Penguin.

Sriram, V., & Gopalakrishna, P. (1991). Can advertising be standardized among similar countries? A cluster-based analysis. *International Journal of Advertising, 10,* 137-149.

Statham, A. (1987). The gender model revisited: Differences in the management styles of men and women. *Sex Roles, 16,* 409-429.

Stavig, G. R., & Barnett, L. D. (1977). Group size and societal conflict. *Human Relations, 30,* 761-765.

Steenkamp, J. B. E. M., Ter Hofstede, F., & Wedel, M. (1999). A cross-national investigation into the individual and national cultural antecedents of consumer innovativeness. *Journal of Marketing,* *63*(2), 55-69.

Steinbach, J. (1991). Stages of economic and social development in world countries. *Mitteilungen der Oesterreichischen Geographischen Gesellschaft,* *133,* 69-108.

Stevens, E. P. (1973). Marianismo: The other face of machismo in Latin America. In A. Pescatello (Ed.), *Female and male in Latin America.* Pittsburgh, PA: University of Pittsburgh Press.

Stevenson, H. W., & Lee, S. Y. (1996). The academic achievement of Chinese students. In M. H. Bond (Ed.), *The handbook of Chinese psychology* (pp. 124-142). Hong Kong: Oxford University Press.

Stewart, E. C. (1985). Culture and decision-making. In W. B. Gudykunst, L. P. Stewart, & S. Ting-Toomey (Eds.), *Communication, culture, and organizational processes* (pp. 177-211). Beverly Hills, CA: Sage.

Stewart, E. C. (1987). The Japanese culture of organizational communication. In L. Thayer (Ed.), *People, communication, organization* (pp. 136-182). Norwood, NJ: Ablex.

Stewart, E. C. (1991). *An intercultural interpretation of the Persian Gulf crisis.* Tokyo: Kanda University of International Studies, Intercultural Communication Institute.

Stiles, D. A., Gibbons, J. L., & Desilva, S. S. (1996). Girls' relational self in Sri-Lanka and the United States. *Journal of Genetic Psychology, 157,* 191-203.

Stiles, D. A., Gibbons, J. L., & Peters, E. (1993). Adolescents' views of work and leisure in the Netherlands and the United States. *Adolescence, 28,* 473-489.

Stinchcombe, A. L. (1965). Social structure and organizations. In J. G. March (Ed.), *Handbook of organizations.* Chicago: Rand McNally.

Stoetzel, J. (1983). *Les valeurs du temps présent: Une enquête Européenne.* Paris: Presses Universitaires de France.

Stogdill, R. M., & Coons, A. E. (1957). *Leader behavior: Its description and measurement* (Research Monograph No. 88). Columbus: Ohio State University, Bureau of Business Research.

Stohl, C. (1993). European managers' interpretations of participation: A semantic network analysis. *Human Communication Research, 20,* 97-117.

Stokvis, P. R. D. (1997). Nationale identiteit, beeldvorming, stereotypen en karakteristieken. *Theoretische Geschiedenis, 24,* 279-288.

Stroebe, W. (1976). Is social psychology really that complicated? A review of Martin Irle's *Lehrbuch der Sozialpsychologie. European Journal of Social Psychology, 6,* 509-511.

Sullivan, M. J. (1991). *Measuring global values: The ranking of 162 countries.* New York: Greenwood.

Sussmann, N. M. (1986). Re-entry research and training. *International Journal of Intercultural Relations, 10,* 235-254.

Sutton, C. D., & Moore, K. K. (1985). Executive women, 20 years later. *Harvard Business Review, 63*(5), 42-66.

Sutton-Smith, B., & Roberts, J. M. (1981). Play, games, and sports. In H. C. Triandis & A. Heron (Eds.), *Handbook of cross-cultural psychology: Vol. 4. Developmental psychology* (pp. 425-463). Boston: Allyn & Bacon.

Swanson, G. E. (1967). *Religion and regime: A sociological account of the reformation.* Ann Arbor: University of Michigan Press.

Tacitus, C. (1970). *The Agricola and the Germania* (H. Mattingly & S. A. Handford, Trans.). Harmondsworth, Middlesex: Penguin.

Taft, R. (1976). Cross-cultural psychology as a social science: Comments on Faucheux's paper. *European Journal of Social Psychology, 6,* 323-330.

Tainio, R., & Santalainen, T. (1984). Some evidence for the cultural relativity of organizational development programs. *Journal of Applied Behavioral Science, 20,* 93-111.

Takezawa, S. I. (1975). Changing workers' values and implications of policy in Japan. In L. E. Davis & A. B. Cherns (Eds.), *The quality of working life* (Vol. 1, pp. 327-346). New York: Free Press.

Tanaka-Matsumi, J., & Draguns, J. G. (1997). Culture and psychopathology. In J. W. Berry, M. H. Segall, & Ç. Kagitçibasi (Eds.), *Handbook of cross-cultural psychology: Vol. 3. Social behavior and applications* (pp. 449-491). Boston: Allyn & Bacon.

Tannen, D. (1992). *You just don't understand: Women and men in conversation.* London: Virago.

Tannenbaum, A. S. (1968). *Control in organizations.* New York: McGraw-Hill.

Tannenbaum, A. S., & Bachman, J. G. (1964). Structural versus individual effects. *American Journal of Sociology, 69,* 585-595.

Tannenbaum, A. S., Kavcic, B., Rosner, M., Vianello, M., & Wieser, G. (1974). *Hierarchy in organizations.* San Francisco: Jossey-Bass.

Tannenbaum, R., & Schmidt, W. H. (1958). How to choose a leadership pattern. *Harvard Business Review, 36*(4), 95-101.

Taormina, R. J., Messick, D. M., Iwawaki, S., & Wilke, H. (1988). Cross-cultural perspectives on foreign aid deservingness decisions. *Journal of Cross-Cultural Psychology, 19,* 387-412.

Tayeb, M. (1996). India: A non-tiger of Asia. *International Business Review, 5,* 425-445.

Taylor, C. L., & Hudson, M. C. (1972). *World handbook of political and social indicators.* New Haven, CT: Yale University Press.

Taylor, C. L., & Jodice, D. A. (1983). *World handbook of political and social indicators.* New Haven, CT: Yale University Press.

Taylor, F. W. (1903). *Shop management.* New York: American Society of Mechanical Engineers.

Taylor, R. E., Hoy, M. G., & Haley, E. (1996). How French advertising professionals develop creative strategy. *Journal of Advertising, 25*(1), 1-14.

Thiriez, H. (1995). *Jeux, cultures et stratégie*. Paris: Éditions d'Organisation.

Thoenig, J. C. (1982). Research management and management research: A discussion note. *Organization Studies, 3*, 269-275.

Thomas, A. S., Shenkar, O., & Clarke, L. (1994). The globalization of our mental maps: Evaluating the geographic scope of JIBS' coverage. *Journal of International Business Studies, 25*, 675-686.

Thorndike, E. L. (1939). On the fallacy of imputing the correlations found for groups to the individuals or smaller groups composing them. *American Journal of Psychology, 3*, 122-124.

Thorpe, R., & Pavlica, K. (1996). Management development: Contradictions and dilemmas arising from in-depth study of British and Czech managers. In P. Joynt & M. Warner (Eds.), *Managing across cultures: Issues and perspectives* (pp. 212-232). London: Thomson.

Tobacyk, J. J., & Pirttilä-Backman, A. M. (1992). Paranormal beliefs and their implications in university students from Finland and the United States. *Journal of Cross-Cultural Psychology, 23*, 59-71.

Tobin, J. J., Wu, D. Y. H., & Davidson, D. H. (1989). *Preschool in three cultures: Japan, China, and the United States*. New Haven, CT: Yale University Press.

Tocqueville, A. de. (1956). *Democracy in America*. New York: Mentor. (Original work published 1835)

Todd, E. (1983). *La troisième planète: Structures familiales et systèmes idéologiques*. Paris: Seuil.

Toer, P. A. (1982). *This earth of mankind*. Ringwood, Victoria, Australia: Penguin.

Toffler, A. (1971). *Future shock*. London: Pan.

Tollgerdt-Andersson, I. (1996). Attitudes, values and demands on leadership: A cultural comparison among some European countries. In P. Joynt & M. Warner (Eds.), *Managing across cultures: Issues and perspectives* (pp. 166-178). London: Thomson.

Tolstoy, L. N. (1978). *War and peace*. Harmondsworth, Middlesex: Penguin. (Original work published 1865-69)

Tomasic, D. (1946). The structure of Balkan society. *American Journal of Sociology, 52*, 132-140.

Tönnies, F. (1963). *Community and society*. New York: Harper & Row. (Original work published 1887)

Torbiörn, I. (1982). *Living abroad: Personal adjustment and personnel policy in the overseas setting*. Chichester: John Wiley.

Törnblom, K. Y., Jonsson, D., & Foa, U. G. (1985). Nationality, resource class, and preferences among three allocation rules: Sweden vs. USA. *International Journal of Intercultural Relations, 9*, 51-77.

Towler, R. (1984). *The need for certainty: A sociological study of conventional religion*. London: Routledge & Kegan Paul.

Transparency International. (1998). *Corruption Perception Index* [On-line]. Available Internet: http://www.gwdg.de/~uwvw/icr.htm

Triandis, H. C. (1971, August). *Some psychological dimensions of modernization*. Paper presented at the 17th Congress of Applied Psychology, Liege, Belgium.

Triandis, H. C. (with Vassiliou, V., Vassiliou, G., Tanaka, Y., & Shanmugam, A. V.). (1972). *The analysis of subjective culture*. New York: John Wiley.

Triandis, H. C. (1973a). Culture training, cognitive complexity and interpersonal attitudes. In D. S. Hoopes (Ed.), *Readings in intercultural communication* (pp. 55-68). Pittsburgh, PA: Regional Council for International Education.

Triandis, H. C. (1973b). Subjective culture and economic development. *International Journal of Psychology, 8*, 163-180.

Triandis, H. C. (1982). [Review of the book *Culture's consequences*, by G. Hofstede]. *Human Organization, 41*, 86-90.

Triandis, H. C. (1995). *Individualism and collectivism*. Boulder, CO: Westview.

Triandis, H. C., Kilty, K. M., Shanmugam, A. V., Tanaka, Y., & Vassiliou, V. (1972). Cognitive structures and the analysis of values. In H. C. Triandis (with V. Vassiliou, G. Vassiliou, Y. Tanaka, & A. V. Shanmugam), *The analysis of subjective culture*. New York: John Wiley.

Trice, H. M., & Beyer, J. M. (1984). Studying organizational cultures through rites and ceremonials. *Academy of Management Review, 9*, 653-669.

Trommsdorff, G. (1983). Value change in Japan. *International Journal of Intercultural Relations, 7*, 337-360.

Trompenaars, F. (1985). *The organization of meaning and the meaning of organization*. Unpublished doctoral dissertation, Wharton School.

Trompenaars, F. (1993). *Riding the waves of culture: Understanding cultural diversity in business*. London: Economist Books.

Tsai, H. Y. (1996). The concept of "mien tzu" (face) in East Asian societies: The case of Taiwanese and Japanese. In H. Grad, A. Blanco, & J. Georgas (Eds.), *Key issues in cross-cultural psychology* (pp. 309-315). Lisse, Netherlands: Swets & Zeitlinger.

Tse, D. K., Pan, Y., & Au, K. Y. (1997). How MNC's choose entry modes and form alliances: The China experience. *Journal of International Business Studies, 28*, 779-805.

Tu, W. M. (1991). A Confucian perspective on global consciousness and local awareness. *IHJ Bulletin, 11*(1), 1-9.

Tuchman, B. W. (1978). *A distant mirror: The calamitous 14th century*. Harmondsworth, Middlesex: Penguin.

Tugwell, F. (1972). *The "soft states" can't make it*. Santa Barbara, CA: Center for the Study of Democratic Institutions.

Tung, R. L. (1981, Spring). Selection and training of personnel for overseas assignments. *Columbia Journal of World Business, 15,* 68-78.

Tung, R. L. (1982). Comparative analysis of the selection and training procedures of U.S., European, and Japanese multinationals. *California Management Review, 25*(1), 57-71.

Tung, R. L. (1997). *A study of the expatriation/repatriation process.* (Internal report, Arthur Andersen, "Exploring International Assignees' Viewpoints")

Tylor, E. B. (1924). *Primitive culture.* Gloucester: Smith. (Original work published 1871)

Ueno, S., & Sekaran, U. (1992). The influence of culture on budget control practices in the USA and Japan: An empirical study. *Journal of International Business Studies, 23,* 659-674.

Ulijn, J. M., & Campbell, C. P. (1999). Technical innovations in communication: How to relate technology to business by a culturally reliable human interface. In C. T. Malkinson (Ed.), *Communication jazz: Improvising the new international communication culture* (pp. 109-119). New Orleans: IEEE.

Ulijn, J. M., & Kumar, R. (2000). Technical communication in a multicultural world: How to make it an asset in managing international businesses. Lessons from Europe and Asia for the 21st century. In P. J. Hager & H. J. Scheiber (Eds.), *Managing global communication in science and technology* (pp. 319-348). New York: John Wiley.

UNICEF. (1995). *The state of the world's children 1995.* New York: UNICEF/Oxford University Press.

United Nations. (1973). *U.N. demographic yearbook.* New York: United Nations, Statistical Office.

United Nations Development Program (UNDP). (1996). *Human development report 1996.* New York: Oxford University Press.

United Nations Development Program (UNDP). (1998). *Human development report 1998.* New York: Oxford University Press.

Üsdiken, B., & Pasadeos, Y. (1995). Organizational analysis in North America and Europe: A comparison of co-citation networks. *Organization Studies, 16,* 503-526.

Usunier, J. C. (1996). *Marketing across cultures.* London: Prentice Hall.

Usunier, J. C. (1998). *International and cross-cultural management research.* London: Sage.

Van Baren, F., Hofstede, G., & Van de Vijver, F. J. R. (1995). *Knowledge of and attitudes to biotechnology: The influence of national cultures. An application of DECOR.* Tilburg, Netherlands: Institute for Research on Intercultural Cooperation.

Vance, C. M., McClaine, S. R., Boje, D. M., & Stage, H. D. (1992). An examination of the transferability of traditional performance appraisal principles across cultural boundaries. *Management International Review, 32,* 313-326.

Van den Berg, R. H., & Bleichrodt, N. (1996). Personal values and acculturation. In H. Grad, A. Blanco, &

J. Georgas (Eds.), *Key issues in cross-cultural psychology.* Lisse, Netherlands: Swets & Zeitlinger.

Van den Bosch, F. A. J., & Van Prooijen, A. A. (1992). The competitive advantage of European nations: The impact of national culture, a missing element in Porter's analysis? *European Management Journal, 10,* 173-178.

Van de Vliert, E. (1998). Gender role gaps, competitiveness, and masculinity. In G. Hofstede & Associates, *Masculinity and femininity: The taboo dimension of national cultures* (pp. 117-129). Thousand Oaks, CA: Sage.

Van de Vliert, E., Schwartz, S. H., Huismans, S. E., Hofstede, G., & Daan, S. (1999). Temperature, cultural masculinity and domestic political violence: A cross-national study. *Journal of Cross-Cultural Psychology, 30,* 291-314.

Van de Vliert, E., & Van Yperen, N. W. (1996). Why cross-national differences in role overload? Don't overlook ambient temperature. *Academy of Management Journal, 39,* 986-1004.

Van Dijk, T. A. (1995). Discourse semantics and ideology. *Discourse and Society, 6,* 243-289.

Van Dijk, T. A., Ting-Toomey, S., Smitherman, G., & Troutman, D. (1997). Discourse, ethnicity, culture and racism. In T. A. Van Dijk (Ed.), *Discourse studies: A multidisciplinary introduction: Vol. 2. Discourse as social interaction* (pp. 144-180). Thousand Oaks, CA: Sage.

Van Enter, L. (1982). *The influence of the Dutch and English culture in Shell: Comparison and cooperation.* Unpublished master's thesis, London School of Economics.

Van Gunsteren, H. R. (1976). *The quest for control: A critique of the rational-central-rule approach in public affairs.* London: John Wiley.

Van Leeuwen, M. S. (1978). A cross-cultural examination of psychological differentiation in males and females. *International Journal of Psychology, 13,* 87-122.

Van Maanen, J., & Barley, S. R. (1984). Occupational communities: Culture and control in organizations. In B. M. Staw & L. L. Cummings (Eds.), *Research in organizational behavior 6* (pp. 287-365). Greenwich, CT: JAI.

Van Oudenhoven, J. P. (2001). Do organizations reflect national cultures? A ten nations study. *International Journal of Intercultural Relations, 25,* 89-107.

Van Oudenhoven, J. P., Mechelse, L., & de Dreu, C. K. W. (1998). Managerial conflict management in five European countries: The importance of power distance, uncertainty avoidance, and masculinity. *Applied Psychology: An International Review/ Psychologie Appliquée: Revue Internationale, 47,* 439-455.

Van Rossum, J. H. A. (1998). Why children play: American versus Dutch boys and girls. In G. Hofstede & Associates, *Masculinity and femininity: The taboo dimension of national cultures* (pp. 130-138). Thousand Oaks, CA: Sage.

Van Vlijmen-Van de Rhoer, M. L. (1980). Een blank isolement: Buitenlandse ontwikkelingswerkers in Afrika. *Sociologische Gids, 27,* 501-519.

Van Vugt, G. W. M. (1994). Europese integratie en de integriteit van het openbaar bestuur. *Openbaar Bestuur, 4*(11), 2-7.

Van Yperen, N. W., & Buunk, B. P. (1991). Equity theory and exchange and communal orientation from a cross-national perspective. *Journal of Social Psychology, 131,* 5-20.

Van Zessen, G. J., & Sandfort, T. (1991). *Seksualiteit in Nederland.* Amsterdam: Swets & Zeitlinger.

Varga, K. (1977). Who gains from achievement motivation training? *Vikalpa, 2,* 187-200.

Varga, K. (1986). *Az Emberi és Szervezeti Eröforrás Fejlesztése.* Budapest: Akadémiai Kiadó.

Varga, K. (1993, June). *"Either them, or us": National materialism in central Eastern Europe.* Paper presented at the Sixth Annual Conference on Conflict Management, Houthalen, Belgium.

Veenhoven, R. (1993). *Happiness in nations: Subjective appreciation of life in 56 nations, 1946-1992.* Rotterdam: Erasmus University, Department of Social Sciences.

Veiga, J. F., & Yanouzas, J. N. (1991). Differences between American and Greek managers in giving up control. *Organization Studies, 12,* 95-108.

Verhulst, F. C., Achenbach, T. M., Ferdinand, R. F., & Kasius, M. C. (1993). Epidemiological comparisons of American and Dutch adolescents' self-reports. *Journal of the American Academy of Child and Adolescent Psychiatry, 32,* 1135-1144.

Vertin, P. G. (1954). *Bedrijfsgeneeskundige aspecten van het ulcus pepticum.* Unpublished doctoral dissertation, Groningen University.

Verweij, J. (1998a). The importance of femininity in explaining cross-national differences in secularization. In G. Hofstede & Associates, *Masculinity and femininity: The taboo dimension of national cultures* (pp. 179-191). Thousand Oaks, CA: Sage.

Verweij, J. (1998b). *Secularisering tussen feit en fictie: een internationaal vergelijkend onderzoek naar determinanten van religieuze betrokkenheid.* Doctoral dissertation, Tilburg, Netherlands: Tilburg University Press.

Verweij, J., Ester, P., & Nauta, R. (1997). Secularization as an economic and cultural phenomenon: A cross-national analysis. *Journal for the Scientific Study of Religion, 36,* 309-324.

Vitell, S. J., Nwachukwu, S. L., & Barnes, J. H. (1993). The effects of culture on ethical decision-making: An application of Hofstede's typology. *Journal of Business Ethics, 12,* 753-760.

Vlassenko, E. (1977). Le point sur la dispersion des salaires dans les pays du Marché Commun. *Economie et Statistique, 93,* 64-72.

Vroom, C. W. (1981). *Indonesia and the West: An essay on cultural differences in organization and management.* Jakarta: Catholic University.

Vroom, V. H. (1964). *Work and motivation.* New York: John Wiley.

Vroom, V. H., & Yetton, P. W. (1973). *Leadership and decision-making.* Pittsburgh, PA: University of Pittsburgh Press.

Vunderink, M., & Hofstede, G. (1998). Femininity shock: American students in the Netherlands. In G. Hofstede & Associates, *Masculinity and femininity: The taboo dimension of national cultures* (pp. 139-151). Thousand Oaks, CA: Sage.

Wacoal Corporation, Corporate Communication Office. (1993). *Asian women now.* Tokyo: Author.

Wall, S. N., Frieze, I. H., Ferligoj, A., Jarosova, E., Pauknerova, D., Horvat, J., & Sarlija, N. (1999). Gender role and religion as predictors of attitude toward abortion in Croatia, Slovenia, the Czech Republic, and the United States. *Journal of Cross-Cultural Psychology, 30,* 443-465.

Wallace, A. F. C. (1970). *Culture and personality.* New York: Random House.

Wallach, E. J. (1983). Individuals and organizations: The cultural march. *Training and Development Journal, 37,* 29-36.

Walter, T. (1990). Why are most churchgoers women? In H. Rowdon (Ed.), *Vox angelica XX: Biblical and other essays from London Bible College.* London: Paternoster.

Warner, M. (Ed.). (1997). *Concise international encyclopedia of business and management.* London: Thomson.

Watts, A. (1979). *Tao: The watercourse way.* Harmondsworth, Middlesex: Pelican.

Webb, E. J., Campbell, D. T., Schwartz, R. D., & Sechrest, L. (1966). *Unobtrusive measures: Nonreactive research in the social sciences.* Chicago: Rand McNally.

Webber, R. A. (1969). *Culture and management: Text and readings in comparative management.* Homewood, IL: Irwin.

Weber, M. (1976). *The Protestant ethic and spirit of capitalism.* London: George Allen & Unwin. (Original work published 1930)

Weber, Y., Shenkar, O., & Raveh, A. (1996). National vs. corporate cultural fit in mergers and acquisitions: An exploratory study. *Management Science, 42,* 1215-1221.

Weener, E. F., & Russell, P. D. (1994). *Aviation safety overview: Regional perspectives.* Paper presented at the 22nd International Air Transport Association Technical Conference, Seattle, WA.

Weick, K. E. (1969). *The social psychology of organizing.* Reading, MA: Addison-Wesley.

Weick, K. E. (1985). The significance of corporate culture. In P. J. Frost, L. F. Moore, M. R. Louis, C. C. Lundberg, & J. Martin (Eds.), *Organizational culture* (pp. 381-389). Beverly Hills, CA: Sage.

Weimer, J. (1995). *Corporate financial goals: A multiple constituency approach to a comparative study of Dutch, US, and German firms*. Unpublished doctoral dissertation. Enschede, Netherlands: Twente University.

Weinreich, H. (1979). What sex is science? In O. Hartnett, G. Boden, & M. Fuller (Eds.), *Sex-role stereotyping* (pp. 168-181). London: Tavistock.

Weinshall, T. D. (Ed.). (1993). *Societal culture and management*. Berlin: Walter de Gruyter.

Weitzel, C. C. M. (1999). *Packaging design: Communicative value and culture*. Unpublished doctoral dissertation, Delft Technical University.

Welsh, D. H. B., Luthans, F., & Sommer, S. M. (1993). Managing Russian factory-workers: The impact of US-based behavioral and participative techniques. *Academy of Management Journal, 36*, 58-79.

Wertheim, W. F. (1956). *Indonesian society in transition: A study of social change*. The Hague: W. van Hoeve.

Westbrook, M. T., & Legge, V. (1993). Health practitioners' perceptions of family attitudes toward children with disabilities: A comparison of six communities in a multicultural society. *Rehabilitation Psychology, 38*(3), 177-185.

Westbrook, M. T., Legge, V., & Pennay, M. (1993). Men's reactions to becoming disabled: A comparison of six communities in a multicultural society. *Journal of Applied Rehabilitation Counseling, 24*(3), 35-41.

Westerlund, G., & Sjöstrand, S. E. (1979). *Organizational myths*. London: Harper & Row.

Westoff, C. F., Calot, G., & Foster, A. D. (1983). Teenage fertility in developed nations: 1971-1980. *Family Planning Perspectives, 15*(3), 105-111.

Whitley, R. D. (1990). Eastern Asian enterprise structures and the comparative analysis of forms of business organization. *Organization Studies, 11*, 47-74.

Whorf, B. L. (1956). *Language, thought, and reality*. Cambridge: MIT Press.

Whyte, W. F. (1948). *Human relations in the restaurant industry*. New York: McGraw-Hill.

Whyte, W. F. (1969). Culture and work. In R. A. Webber (Ed.), *Culture and management*. Homewood, IL: Irwin.

Whyte, W. H., Jr. (1956). *The organization man*. Garden City, NY: Doubleday.

Wildavsky, A. (1976). Economy and environment/rationality and ritual: A review essay. *Accounting, Organizations and Society, 1*, 117-129.

Wildeman, R. E., Hofstede, G., Noorderhaven, N. G., Thurik, A. R., Verhoeven, W. H. J., & Wennekers, A. R. M. (1999). *Culture's role in entrepreneurship: Self-employment out of dissatisfaction*. Rotterdam: Rotterdam Institute for Business Economic Studies.

Wilkins, A. L. (1984). The creation of company cultures: The role of stories and human resource systems. *Human Resource Management, 23*, 41-60.

Wilkins, A. L., & Ouchi, W. G. (1983). Efficient cultures: Exploring the relationship between culture and organizational performance. *Administrative Science Quarterly, 28*, 468-481.

Wilkinson, B. (1996). Culture, institutions and business in East Asia. *Organization Studies, 17*, 421-447.

Willems, W., & Cottaar, A. (1989). *Het beeld van Nederland: hoe zien Molukkers, Chinezen, woonwagenbewoners en Turken de Nederlanders en zichzelf?* Baarn, Netherlands: Ambo.

Williams, J. E., & Best, D. L. (1982). *Measuring sex stereotypes: A thirty-nation study*. Beverly Hills, CA: Sage.

Williams, J. E., & Best, D. L. (1990a). *Measuring sex stereotypes: A multination study* (Rev. ed.). Newbury Park, CA: Sage.

Williams, J. E., & Best, D. L. (1990b). *Sex and psyche: Gender and self-viewed cross-culturally*. Newbury Park, CA: Sage.

Williams, J. E., Satterwhite, R. C., & Saiz, J. L. (1998). *The importance of psychological traits: A cross-cultural study*. New York: Plenum.

Williams, L. K., Whyte, W. F., & Green, C. S. (1966). Do cultural differences affect workers' attitudes? *Industrial Relations, 5*, 105-117.

Williams, R. M. (1968). The concept of values. In D. L. Sills (Ed.), *International encyclopedia of the social sciences* (Vol. 16, pp. 283-287). New York: Macmillan.

Williamson, O. E. (1975). *Markets and hierarchies: Analysis and antitrust implications*. New York: Free Press.

Wilterdink, N. (1992). Images of national character in an international organization: Five European nations compared. *Netherlands' Journal of Social Sciences, 28*(1), 31-49.

Wirthlin Worldwide. (1996). *Asian values and commercial success* [On-line]. Available Internet: http://www.decima.com/publiens/report/wr9603.htm

Witkin, H. A. (1977). Theory in cross-cultural research: Its uses and risks. In Y. H. Poortinga (Ed.), *Basic problems in cross-cultural psychology* (pp. 83-91). Amsterdam: Swets & Zeitlinger.

Witkin, H. A., & Berry, J. W. (1975). Psychological differentiation in cross-cultural perspective. *Journal of Cross-Cultural Psychology, 6*, 4-87.

Witkin, H. A., & Goodenough, D. R. (1977). Field dependence and interpersonal behavior. *Psychological Bulletin, 84*, 661-689.

Witte, E. (1973). *Organisation für Innovationsentscheidungen: Das Promotoren-Modell*. Göttingen, Germany: Verlag Otto Schwarz.

Witte, E. (1977). Power and innovation: A two-center theory. *International Studies of Management and Organization, 7*(1), 47-70.

Wolfe, J. L. (1992). *What to do when he has a headache: How to rekindle your man's desire*. London: Thorsons.

Wong, G. Y. Y., & Birnbaum-More, P. H. (1994). Culture, context and structure: A test on Hong-Kong banks. *Organization Studies, 15*, 99-123.

World Bank. (1972). *World Bank atlas.* Washington, DC: Author.

World Bank. (1976). *World Bank atlas.* Washington, DC: Author.

World Bank. (1980). *World development report, 1980.* Washington, DC: International Bank for Reconstruction and Development.

World Bank. (1982). *World development report, 1982.* New York: Oxford University Press.

World Bank. (1984). *World development report, 1984.* New York: Oxford University Press.

World Bank. (1987). *World development report, 1987.* New York: Oxford University Press.

World Bank. (1989). *World development report, 1989.* New York: Oxford University Press.

World Bank. (1990). *World development report, 1990.* New York: Oxford University Press.

World Bank. (1992). *World development report, 1992.* New York: Oxford University Press.

World Bank. (1997). *World development report, 1997.* New York: Oxford University Press.

Worm, V. (1997). *Vikings and mandarins: Sino-Scandinavian business cooperation in cross-cultural settings.* Copenhagen: Handelshøjskolens Forlag.

Wright, P. (1974). The harassed decision maker: Time pressures, distractions, and the use of evidence. *Journal of Applied Psychology, 59*, 555-561.

Wrong, D. H. (1980). *Power: Its forms, bases and uses.* New York: HarperColophon.

Wu, T. Y. (1980). *Roots of Chinese culture.* Singapore: Federal Publications.

Wundt, W. (1911-1920). *Völkerpsychologie: eine Untersuchung der Entwicklungsgesetze von Sprachen, Mythus und Sitte.* Leipzig, Germany: Kröner.

Xenikou, A., & Furnham, A. (1996). A correlational and factor-analytic study of 4 questionnaire measures of organizational culture. *Human Relations, 49*, 349-371.

Yan, W. F., & Gaier, E. L. (1994). Causal attributions for college success and failure: An Asian-American comparison. *Journal of Cross-Cultural Psychology, 25*, 146-158.

Yang, K. S. (1988). Will societal modernization eventually eliminate cross-cultural psychological differences? In M. H. Bond (Ed.), *The cross-cultural challenge to social psychology* (pp. 67-85). Newbury Park, CA: Sage.

Yang, K. S., & Bond, M. H. (1980). Ethnic affirmations by Chinese bilinguals. *Journal of Cross-Cultural Psychology, 11*, 411-425.

Yates, J. F., & Lee, J. W. (1996). Chinese decision-making. In M. H. Bond (Ed.), *The handbook of Chinese psychology* (pp. 338-351). Hong Kong: Oxford University Press.

Yeh, R. S., & Lawrence, J. J. (1995). Individualism and Confucian dynamism: A note on Hofstede's cultural roots to economic growth. *Journal of International Business Studies, 26*, 655-669.

Yelsma, P., & Athappilly, K. (1988). Marital satisfaction and communication practices: Comparisons among Indian and American couples. *Journal of Comparative Family Studies, 19*, 37-54.

Yeung, I. Y. M., & Tung, R. L. (1996). *Achieving business success in Confucian societies: The importance of guanxi (connections).* New York: American Management Association.

Yiu, L. S., & Saner, R. (1984). Confucius say social harmony more important than performance. *Training and Development Journal, 38*, 28-29.

Yiu, L. S., & Saner, R. (1985). Value dimensions in American counseling: A Taiwanese-American comparison. *International Journal for the Advancement of Counseling, 8*, 137-146.

Zaheer, S., & Zaheer, A. (1997). Country effects on information seeking in global electronic networks. *Journal of International Business Studies, 28*, 77-100.

Zahn, E. (1984). *Das unbekannte Holland: Regenten, Rebellen und Reformatoren.* Berlin: Siedler Verlag.

Zaleznik, A., Kets de Vries, M. F. R., & Howard, J. (1977). Stress reactions in organizations: Syndromes, causes and consequences. *Behavioral Science, 22*, 151-162.

Zandpour, F., & Harich, K. R. (1996). Think and feel country clusters: A new approach to international advertising standardization. *International Journal of Advertising, 15*, 325-344.

Zarzeski, M. T. (1996). Spontaneous harmonization effects of culture and market forces on accounting disclosure practices. *Accounting Horizons, 10*(1), 18-37.

Zeitlin, L. R. (1996). How much woe when we go: A quantitative method for predicting culture shock. *International Journal of Stress Management, 3*(2), 85-98.

Zhang, Y., & Gelb, D. (1996). Matching advertising appeals to culture: The influence of products' use conditions. *Journal of Advertising, 25*(3), 29-46.

Zurcher, L. A., Meadow, A., & Zurcher, S. L. (1965). Value orientation, role conflict, and alienation from work: A cross-cultural study. *American Sociological Review, 30*, 539-548.

Name Index

Aberbach, J. D. 112, 173, 514
Aberle, D. F. 30
Abramson, P. R. 329, 349n105
Achenbach, T. M. 303
Ackermann, K. F. 203n25
Adamopoulos, J. 37n30
Adams, G. B. 277n65
Adebayo, A. 331
Adelman, I. 9, 27, 33, 117, 132, 277n79
Adizes, I. 110
Adler, N. J. 39n79, 370n2, 436, 455n23
Adorno, T. W. 93, 146, 161, 178
Agarwal, J. 459n133
Ajzen, I. 36n12
Akande, A. 556, 562
Akhtar Hossain, A.B.M. 554
Akoh, H. 276n56, 304
Albaum, G. 458n117
Albers, N. D. 449
Albert, E. M. 36n5
Albert, R. 455n28
Alden, D. L. 450
Ali, A. H. 455
Alitto, G. S. 354, 369, 371n34, 372n50
Allen, G, 303
Allen, R. F. 418n72
Allport, G. W. 74n10, 146, 154
Almond, G. A. 171, 172, 192, 194, 504
Anderson, B. 536, 537
Anderson, B. R. 139n47
Andersson, L. 208n113, 457n75
Anholt, S. 458n120
Annis, R. C. 305
Anthony, R. N. 466n4
Arbose, J. R. 106, 315, 337, 338
Argyle, M. 359
Argyris, C. 4
Ariès, P. 253, 345n28
Aristotle 81, 110
Armstrong, R. W. 459n136
Arnold Sr., D. F. 384
Aron, R. 81, 149n87, 204n33
Arrindell, W. A. 204n48, 296, 345n25

Arth, M. J. 178
Asch, S. E. 232
Asendorpf, J. 535
Ashby, W. R. 457n95
Ashkanani, M.G.A. 464
Ashkanasy, N. M. 420n113
Ata, A. W. 456n39
Athanasiou, R. 37n22
Athappilly, K. 230
Athos, A. 415n2
Au, K. Y. 447
Au, Y. F. 232
Averroes 243
Ayestaran, S. 556
Azumi, K. 166, 204n29

Baalbaki, I. 459n123
Babcock, M. D. 349n119
Bachman, J. G. 38n51
Bacon, M. K. 280
Bailyn, L. 315
Baker, C. R. 147
Baker, H.D.R. 25, 228
Bakke, E. W. 392
Balandier, G. 137n1
Bales, R. F. 8
Ball, P. 554
Baltes, P. B. 346n47
Bandura, A. 238
Bandyopadhyaya, J. 142n106
Bank, J. 310
Banks, A. S. 33, 110
Banks, P. 455n24
Bannock, G. 75n30
Barkema, H. G. 77n55, 447
Barley, S. R. 414
Barmeyer, C. I. 456n55, 501
Barnard, C. I. 392
Barnes, J. H. 466n4
Barnes, L. B. 389
Barnett, L. D. 142n108
Barnouw, V. 37n30, n42
Barraclough, R. A. 539

Subject Index

About the Author

Geert Hofstede (born 1928) graduated from Delft Technical University as a mechanical engineer and spent 10 years in Dutch industry in technical and management jobs. Studying part-time, he completed a doctorate in social psychology at Groningen University; his thesis was titled *The Game of Budget Control*. He subsequently joined IBM Europe, where he founded and managed the Personnel Research Department. His academic career started at IMD (Lausanne) and continued at INSEAD (Fontainebleau), the European Institute for Advanced Studies in Management (Brussels), IIASA (Laxenburg Castle, Austria), and Maastricht University, where he taught organizational anthropology and international management until he became Professor Emeritus in 1993. From 1980 to 1983 he returned to industry as Director of Human Resources of Fasson Europe at Leiden. He was the co-founder and first Director of the Institute for Research on Intercultural Cooperation (IRIC), now at Tilburg University, which he still serves as a Senior Fellow; he is also a Fellow of the CentER for Economic Research at Tilburg University. From 1993 to 2000 he was an Honorary Professor at the University of Hong Kong.

The classic *Culture's Consequences* (1980) is Geert Hofstede's best-known book. His popular text titled *Cultures and Organizations: Software of the Mind* (1991) has appeared in 16 languages, including Chinese, Korean, and Japanese. His articles have been published in the journals of different countries of Europe, Asia, and North America. He is among the top 100 most-cited authors in the *Social Science Citation Index,* and of these, one of few non-Americans. He has lectured in Dutch, English, French, and German at universities, training institutes, and in-company programs around the world, and has served as a consultant to national and international business and government organizations, including the World Bank, the Organization for Economic Cooperation and Development, the Asian Productivity Organization, and the Commission of the European Union.